CONTESTED
RETHINKING CANADIAN EXPERIENCE
SOCIOLOGY

SYLVIA M. HALE
St. Thomas University

Pearson Canada
Toronto

ISBN 978-0-13-246934-0

Vice-President, Editorial Director: Gary Bennett
Editor-in-Chief: Ky Pruesse
Senior Acquisitions Editor: Lisa Rahn
Marketing Manager: Arthur Gee
Senior Developmental Editor: Suzanne Schaan
Developmental Editor: Toni Chahley
Production Editor: Melissa Hajek
Copy Editor: Melissa Hajek
Proofreader: Dan Naccarato
Production Coordinator: Avinash Chandra
Composition: Aptara®, Inc.
Photo and Permissions Research: Amanda Campbell
Art Director: Julia Hall
Cover Design: Anthony Leung
Cover Image: Getty Images

1 2 3 4 5   14 13 12 11 10

Printed in Canada.

Twenty years ago when I first designed an introductory sociology text for Canadian students, I was inspired by the approach of the British text *The Problem of Sociology* (1983) authored by David Lee and Howard Newby. This text introduced sociology as a theoretical discipline concerned with exploring the roots of industrial capitalist society. Various societal institutions such as education, family, religion, bureaucracy, deviance, and so on, were covered as empirical tests of theory rather than described as elements of a social system. The main limitation of this text was that the presentation of major sociological theorists in chronological order meant that contemporary theory came last.

Contested Sociology recognizes that theoretical perspectives in sociology have not evolved as stages in a process in which new ideas are gradually replacing older ones. Rather they have developed in tandem as contested approaches to the analysis of contemporary issues. Systems theory, political economy, constructionist, and feminist perspectives reflect deep-rooted assumptions about which social processes are seminally important for understanding society. They focus on and elaborate different features of social life and their insights continue to drive social policy.

This text thus focuses on contested sociology, using the four major perspectives throughout as mental tools to make visible active social practices, and the underlying assumptions that drive them in contemporary social policies and struggles. Competing interest groups and the diverse attitudes and values that people bring to democratic debates are conceptualized in this text as integral to contemporary systems theory. The political-economy perspective focuses attention on the concentration of ownership of means of production in a profit-driven, global corporate capitalist system in which the Canadian economy is a small player. Interest-group theory has limited relevance to the understanding of how corporate capitalism shapes lived experience in Canada and elsewhere. Social constructionist theory has evolved far beyond its early beginnings in symbolic interactionism. It uses the conceptual and methodological tools of institutional ethnography to focus attention on the active practices through which people continually constitute, negotiate, sustain, and undermine the features of the social world that systems theory describes, and the active practices that accomplish the institutionalized power relations of corporate capitalism. Feminist theory has likewise evolved far beyond its early focus on women as an interest group distinct from men. It centres attention on relations of reproduction, the embodied lives of people as they struggle to raise children and to care for bodies of people throughout their lives from childhood to old age. These foundational social practices are still too readily marginalized in systems theory to the family institution, and ignored in political economy with its focus on global production and capitalist market forces.

Contested Sociology incorporates contemporary Canadian research that draws on each of the four major perspectives in all the chapters that focus on different substantive issues. It strives to challenge students to keep shifting perspectives to learn to see the guiding assumptions that underlie research questions and empirical evidence. Each chapter is designed to stand alone, although all presuppose familiarity with the overview of theory perspectives provided in Chapter Two. The goal is to provide a depth of understanding that prepares students well for advanced courses in sociology.

The goal of **sociology** is to understand the social world and our lives within it. As a discipline it develops the tools to explore critical questions: How does the social world work? How did it come to be this way and how is it changing? How are our individual lives—our biographies and our life chances—created and stunted by the social world that we ourselves, collectively, produce?

Sociology is the hub of all the social sciences. It forms the core discipline that underlies multiple specialized areas of study such as political science, economics, criminology, and Native studies. It forms the foundation of many professions, including social work, education, policing, journalism, urban planning, and political policy formation and analysis. The insights of sociology are also central to contemporary literature, arts, and drama.

The social world is not a tangible entity in the sense of a system that exists independently of the behaviours of the people who constitute it. People continually create and recreate the social world by the pressures or forces that we exert over each other and ourselves. Sociology is concerned with understanding the sources and the forms that these social forces take. During certain periods, as when countries go to war, or when the economy collapses, leaving hundreds of thousands of people adrift without jobs, these social forces may seem overwhelming, sweeping people along as helpless victims. Yet these are still human forces, pressures that people in groups bring to bear upon each other. Sometimes people resist, fighting back against such pressures and forcing changes. People continue to assert themselves, even within the most oppressive social institutions. Goffman (1961) describes how a patient, stripped of almost all autonomy in a large, closed ward of an asylum, still managed to assert himself against the system by urinating on the radiator—an ideal location for the act to produce maximum effect. People once harassed and criminalized for "deviant" sexual orientation embraced their label as "queer" and turned it into a mark of pride. Converging around slogans such as "We're here. We're queer. Get used to it," they and their supporters publicly celebrated their stigmatized identity in tumultuous Gay Pride marches. In Canada in 2005, they won the right to transform their partnerships into legally recognized marriage.

In a brilliant essay, C. Wright Mills (1959, Ch. 1) expresses the sense of ambivalence that people feel, given their positions as both victims and creators of **society**. Mills observes that people often feel as if they are in a series of traps in their personal lives. They feel that they cannot overcome their personal problems—and they are often correct. Individuals do not generally control the forces that affect their lives. These forces are socially located far beyond the immediate, personal settings in which people live, and it is difficult for people to see beyond their own private reality: their jobs, their neighbourhoods, their families. The more that threatening forces transcend their direct experience, the more trapped people feel. How do fishers of Newfoundland feel when cod stocks collapse and the fishery is closed? Or Alberta beef farmers when one case of mad cow disease is used to justify closure of the Unites States border to live cattle? Or residents of a small town when its major employer, a multinational corporation, closes local operations and moves to the United States? Or a huge corporation like General Motors slides into bankruptcy, dragging thousands of car dealerships with it? Or parents who see their children's lives bombarded by war toys, pornography, drugs, sex, the threat of AIDS? All these forces are more or less beyond the immediate control of the people who are affected by them. Personal successes and failures occur within definite social situations and reflect the effects of modern historical changes.

The information revolution in the media has increased people's awareness of world events. Anyone who reads newspapers or watches the news on television cannot help but be aware that we are living in the middle of upheaval everywhere: in the Middle East, Afghanistan, Africa, Latin America, Northern Ireland, and at home in Canada. International terrorism, in the form of bombings, skyjackings, and assassinations, has become a regular part of nightly news, especially since they happened so close to us in New York in 2001, Madrid in 2004, and London, England, in 2005. Suspicion, fear, and heightened security concerns overshadow all public events. Each time we catch an international flight, we are reminded that someone might want to blow it up. People fleeing from civil war, dictatorship, and persecution abroad seek refugee status in Canada almost daily. Still more come seeking to escape grinding poverty at home, only to be faced with Canada's own unemployment problems. Stories such as those of people gunned down on Toronto streets, and of scores of murdered sex-trade workers, are brought into our living rooms as we watch television.

While mass media increase our awareness of major events in the world, they do not necessarily increase our understanding of how and why they occur. When we struggle to make sense of what seems to be happening, we often draw on individual accounts, framing events in terms of individual motives and failings. People increasingly turn to the Internet to create and share weblogs or blogs in which to express their frustrations, and often strident opinions, about who and what should be blamed. It is easy to target greedy executives or incompetent workers for the collapse of corporations. People often blame parents for antisocial behaviour by youth, suggesting that the youths had been badly brought up and should have been disciplined more when they were younger. Others view the beggars panhandling on downtown streets, and lining up outside soup kitchens, as inadequate, lazy, or alcoholic individuals who could pull themselves up if they wanted to. It is easy to see riots as caused by a few troublemakers, outside agitators who should be put in prison, or to dismiss suicide bombers as mentally deranged individuals (Brym 2008, 37). But these individual explanations are inadequate to account for major shifts in patterns of behaviour affecting multiple communities.

In 2008 tens of thousands of Canadian workers suddenly lost their jobs due to global financial crises beyond their control.

AP Photo/Mike Derer

When we as individuals are faced with forces that we do not understand and cannot control, we often react by withdrawal. We retreat into our private lives, stop listening to the news, tell ourselves that the problems are not our responsibility, and try to forget them and get on with our own lives. When we cannot avoid the threats, we tend to react with fear, resentment, and hostility. Moral insensitivity can result from people's sense of being overwhelmed by historical changes that they do not understand and that may challenge cherished values. It is easier to demand that national borders be closed to refugees and alien immigrants than to cope in our immediate lives with the reality of transnational migrations prompted by global inequalities and war. Feelings of being overwhelmed by seemingly intractable problems of destitution in the midst of plenty may help to explain why so many residents petition city officials to clear their downtown streets of panhandlers, and demand that toilets and parks be locked so that homeless people cannot sleep in them. In some neighbourhoods people have resorted to covering hot air gratings with barbed wire to stop derelicts from huddling over them. People do not want shelters for the homeless, for young delinquents, or mentally retarded adults built in their neighbourhoods. Fear of unemployment, or the falling value of homes and savings—threatening their tenuous hold on a middle-class lifestyle—makes people easy prey for get-tough policies and glib political slogans that promise easy answers.

People need much more than information to overcome their sense of being trapped. We live in the age of the information revolution, with satellite printing of national newspapers, a multi-channel universe offering instantaneous around-the-world coverage of events on radio and television, in magazines, and a plethora of websites and blogs. Media flood us with information, but they do not ensure that we have the capacity to handle it, make sense of it, and distinguish the reliable information from that which is misleading. In some ways mass media actively work against our deeper understanding of issues, because they are designed to turn all information into entertainment to please mass audiences and particularly corporate advertisers, and to offend no one. They bring us horrendous news one minute, followed by sports scores and other trivia the next. We live increasingly in a world of hyper-reality in which what we see on television can seem more real than reality itself. Bystanders interviewed at scenes of terrorism or destruction frequently catch themselves saying it was like being in a movie. For C. Wright Mills, the special promise of sociology as a discipline is its capacity to process information. He uses the term the **sociological imagination** to describe "a quality of mind that will help [people] to use information and to develop reason in order to achieve lucid summations of what is going on in the world and of what may be happening within themselves" (Mills 1959, 5).

The basic assumption of sociology is that our life chances as individuals are understandable only within historically specific social situations. As Brym expresses it in his powerful essay on sociology as a vocation, "It's all about the Context" (2008, 81). No matter what the issue at hand, sociologists always raise the question "What was the social context in which that happened?"

One way to begin to grasp the fundamentally social context of life experiences is to explore comparisons among people in different situations. One's chances of getting a job, of getting rich, of dying from cancer, of being a Catholic or a Protestant or an atheist, of living in peace or going to war, are socially situated. Sociology as a discipline tries to grasp the nature of this relationship between individual biography and social–historical forces within society. Even the chances of getting caught up in a seeming natural disaster like Hurricane Katrina, which swamped much of the core of downtown New Orleans in September 2005, are socially structured by political decisions about whether or not to fund flood-control measures. Such decisions in turn reflect the vested interests of power-holders, and the social standing of people living in the communities known to be most vulnerable to flooding (Brym 2008, 53–75).

The way in which we tend to answer the question "Who are you?" in terms of our sex, age, profession, and ethnic background, situates us on a social map. Given information about people's occupations and incomes, we can predict a great deal about them: where they live, what kind of home and furnishings they have, what they read, what music they listen to, how they speak, how they vote, even whether they prefer sex with the light on or off (Berger 1963, 80–81).

This embeddedness of individual life chances within social structures becomes sharply visible for people living with special needs or disabilities (Dandaneau 2001, Ch. 5). They live their lives at the intersection of laws and administrative rules that determine who will qualify for available supports or income assistance, networks of competing interest groups that set priorities for budget allocations, and shifting definitions of "normal" that determine whether people like themselves will be accommodated within mainstream social institutions, with access to education and opportunities for meaningful work, or segregated out of sight in special facilities, or abandoned to cope as best as they can, or to die on the streets or in homeless shelters.

According to Mills (1959, 6–7), the sociological endeavour entails three broad categories of questions that focus on the structure of society, the patterns of social change, and the characteristics of the people who constitute the society. The first category includes such questions as:

What is the structure of this particular society? What are its major parts? How are these parts—education, church, polity, economy—interrelated? How does Canada differ from other societies and why?

All of us have immediate experience of how different elements of society affect each other. We know that the economy affects education, influencing decisions about whether to go to university or to take a job, and about what course of studies to follow. Religion affects voting patterns, the numbers of children people have, the chance that one will commit suicide. Work life affects family life, dictating the standard of living and also the time available for parenting.

As a total social system, Canada differs from other societies in multiple ways. It was founded as a predominantly white European settler society, with indigenous peoples pushed aside into reservations, and non-Europeans admitted only grudgingly and under unequal conditions. More recently, the makeup of Canadian society has become more visibly diverse, as patterns of global migration, policies promoting multiculturalism, and the Charter of Rights and Freedoms have loosened up the establishment.

This leads into the second major type of question emphasized by Mills: Where does our society stand in human history? How did it get to be this way and how is it changing now? How does any particular feature or episode of our society's history fit into the present situation? Sociology looks both backwards and forwards in an effort to understand contemporary society.

Successive generations of people can be thought of as cohorts, people born around the same time, who struggle with the dominant issues of their time. For people who were young adults in North America during the 1930s, the dominant issue was the Great Depression—a period when one-third of the labour force across North America were unemployed. This was followed by the turbulence and misery of the Second World War years, and then the post-war years of baby boomers who came of age in a period of rapid economic expansion. Young adults during the 1960s retroactively defined their cohort as the hippie generation, coalescing around struggles over civil rights, the Vietnam War, and feminism. They also lived under the cloud of the Cold War between East and West and the threat of nuclear war. Young adults in North America at the start of the twenty-first century, sometimes dubbed "the Millennials," find their lives shaped around new challenges. The dominant issues facing this age include international terrorism, globalization and competition over oil, global inequality, environmental degradation and global warming, and AIDS. This new millennium has opened with hard challenges facing humankind.

There are also powerful social changes closer to home. The lives and life chances of university students in the first

The vast majority of displaced people after Hurricane Katrina were poor and black.

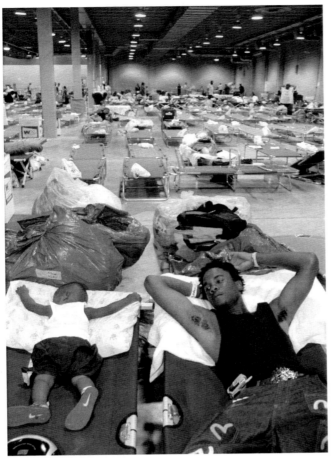

© TIM JOHNSON/Reuters/Corbis

decade of the twenty-first century differ in critical ways from the previous generation of students. Thirty years ago in Canada, higher education was considered a public good that society as a whole should pay for. In current political thinking, higher education is more often considered an individual consumer product that individual customers should pay for themselves (Reimer and Mueller 2006). The result is that students are often graduating with huge debts that will impact heavily on their future life choices. Students graduating in the 1970s could reasonably expect to find professional jobs that offered long-term security and pensions. Students graduating now are being advised to expect to change careers several times, and to think of themselves as entrepreneurs with flexible packages of skills to trade in an ever-changing global marketplace.

The third type of question is: What kinds of women and men make up our society? How are people selected and formed? How are we liberated and repressed? How are we made sensitive or blunted? What does the experience of years of unemployment do to young people who are out of work, and what does the constant fear of possible layoffs do

to people who are working? The 1960s were known for hippies, flower power, and campus radicalism, but students now seem more conservative and conformist than their earlier counterparts (Bibby 2009). We need to explore why these changes are happening. Young adults in Canada at the beginning of the new millennium grew up with the Charter of Rights and Freedoms, and with the Internet. As a cohort, they are more sensitized to issues of sexism, homophobia, and global inequalities, but at the same time are perhaps more cynical towards political involvement and more detached from each other and the larger community. Parents fear that the sensitivities of children are being blunted by violence on television, or excited in negative ways by war toys, pornography, and sexual predators on the Internet. The feminist movement in many ways radically altered the lives of women and men. Yet there are signs that young women do not identify with the movement. Does this mean that feminism was only a passing fad? Or does sensitivity to feminism only come with greater experience of the deeply gendered fissures that still run through the ruling institutions of society?

The student of sociology, Mills argues, has to be able to shift perspectives in imagination, to switch from looking at politics to looking at the family, the economy, and war, and to see their interconnections. It is not an easy discipline. The sociological imagination frequently makes the ordinary world look incredible. We commonly think of family relations, for example, as part of our uniquely private lives. It frequently comes as a shock to see how deeply these intimate relations are shaped by wider social forces. The basic message of sociology is that our society has not always been the way it is, nor is it inevitably this way, and it probably will not be so in the future. It can be different, and we need to understand how we can affect these changes through acting collectively. For this reason alone, the critical eye of sociology can often provoke opposition from powerful groups in contemporary society who benefit from the status quo and who do not want change or want it only in a particular direction.

An important distinction drawn in sociology is between **personal troubles** and **public issues** (Mills 1959, 8–10). Personal troubles stem from private matters that lie within an individual's character and immediate relations with friends and family. Public issues, by contrast, go beyond the personal, local setting to broader social forces that affect the life experiences of many people. An important part of learning to do sociology is learning to generalize from personal experience to broader social forces that this experience reflects. Consider unemployment. When only a few individuals are unemployed in a large city, it can reasonably be viewed as a private trouble, reflecting the particular problems of the unemployed individuals, and it can perhaps best be dealt with using an individual casework approach. But when 15 million people are unemployed out of a nation of 50 million, for example, unemployment is a public issue. It cannot be solved by helping individual cases. The structure of opportunities has collapsed.

Similarly, one or two homeless people living on park benches can perhaps be seen to reflect personal trouble. But when hundreds of thousands of people are out of work, or entire industries collapse, and one-fifth of children grow up in households that look to food banks to meet their basic needs, helping individuals will not solve the problem. Something in the structure of the economy, or of families, or of mental health services has broken down. We have to shift perspectives to see these problems as social issues, requiring changes in societal institutions.

Mills argues that the sociological imagination, the capacity to understand the relationships between elements of society and their impact on individual life chances, has become the central feature of modern society. It dominates how people think, how histories are written, the kinds of art we view and literature we read. Science and technology remain powerful forces in society, but they are no longer central to how people think, because they have failed us in important ways. In many respects, technology has conquered nature. We know how to get to the moon and beyond, how to grow food artificially, how to transmit thousands of conversations simultaneously on optical fibres, yet we are in a worse mess than ever. Technology has not solved our problems, but has become, instead, part of what traps us. Contemporary literature and art express the uneasiness people feel, but they cannot provide answers, except insofar as they may suggest new ways of seeing. It is the sociological imagination that seeks to explain social processes, the nature of our traps, and the underlying structural factors that give rise to them (Mills 1959, 14–15). Sociological explanations are more difficult and more elusive than explanations in the physical sciences because society is not a tangible, fixed entity ready for objective experimental research. The very sociological knowledge we generate is likely to alter the sets of relationships we are trying to study. In another sense, however, sociology may be easier and more rewarding than the physical sciences in that we ourselves are part of it, creators of the societies in which we live, able to understand social processes subjectively as participants in their production.

SOCIOLOGY AND THE SCIENTIFIC IDEAL

As a science, sociology is concerned fundamentally with the search for knowledge about society, but this search is both difficult and dangerous. It involves the study of people who,

as members of a society, generate their own sense of truth about the social world. Socially generated ideas can be grouped into two categories. First, they take the form of **common-sense understandings**, or assumptions about how things work, and why, based upon immediate experience. Secondly, they involve more coherent **ideologies**, or systems of values that justify certain kinds of actions or ways of life, sometimes to the detriment of the interests of other people. These ideologies strongly influence the way we see social reality. They tend to sensitize us in certain ways and to blind us in others.

Sociological analysis must typically confront and challenge ideologies. A critical problem is that sociologists may be as blinded by ideologies as other people, since they are themselves part of the society that they study, and they tend to accept the assumptions of people like themselves. Smith (1990, 40) has conceptualized ideology, not as specific beliefs, but as a biased form of *method* of inquiry about society, a method that entails in its effects a systematic means *not* to know and *not* to see the situations of others. Our thinking gets caught up in patterns of circular reasoning, or what Smith calls "ideological practices." As an example, children living on welfare appear to be failing in school because their mothers are stressed out and not coping well. Stressors in their mothers' environment are identified as poor housing and socially disorganized neighbourhoods. Mothers' failure to better cope with these environmental stressors then seems to explain their inadequate mothering. The solution appears to be stress-management classes and parenting classes (Swift 1995). The active social practices that continually reproduce poverty for one-fifth of Canada's children, and continually reproduce "mothers" as the site of primary responsibility for unequal educational outcomes, disappear from view.

Given that sociologists are predominantly well-educated, reasonably well-paid professionals, and until recently were predominantly male, it should come as no surprise that the values of such people tend to be represented in sociology to a greater extent than those of less privileged people. Poorly educated women living on welfare or people working in unskilled jobs, for example, do not tend to publish much in sociology journals. The scientific search for knowledge in sociology entails a major struggle to see past the taken-for-granted understandings and justifications of the professional middle-class world.

It is always easier to see through the ideologies of other groups than to see through one's own. The Nazi ideology of the superiority of the Aryan race has been discredited, but the ideology of capitalism and the work ethic are harder for most Canadians to see through. The ideology of "free market" and "free trade," for example, implicitly justifies price wars to crush small competitors; the ideology of profit justifies charging higher prices to poor people who often do not have access to alternative markets; it justifies laying off employees when the going gets tough and charging higher interest rates on money that poor people have to borrow. The ideology that effort and ability lead to success justifies labelling the unemployed as lazy or stupid. The Christian ideology that "man" was made in the image of God and given dominion over the beasts justifies human exploitation of everything on the planet. We cease to think about the lives of chickens in battery egg-production factories at the same time as we become enraged at the news of a pet dog being mistreated.

It is important to remember, however, that we are not merely blind victims of ideologies. We are also their creators and interpreters, and we can learn to analyze them, to challenge them, and to change them. The major problem with common-sense interpretations of the world, as with most ideologies, is not that they are totally wrong, but that they can be biased and partial. Common-sense knowledge is inevitably self-centred. It tends to focus narrowly on individual concerns rather than the diverse interests of other people in other situations. Common sense is incomplete, based on limited personal experience with only a hazy idea of what other people's lives are like. Ideology, too, has its limitations and can lead to intolerance. We often have a great deal invested in our beliefs, and it can be difficult to question and to change them, especially when change can have disturbing consequences. If we abandon the ideology that effort and ability lead to success, for example, it changes our responsibilities to the poor and the disadvantaged. We begin to feel uncomfortable about our own wealth and about the system that allows such discrepancies to exist.

Science, as a search for knowledge, attempts to provide explanations based upon impartial evidence. Impartiality is particularly difficult in the social sciences because people who are the subjects of research react to findings in a conscious way, and the theories themselves affect their behaviour. Even the physical sciences do not escape this social imprint because human society itself reacts with and alters the physical world. Socially learned values and ways of thinking also profoundly influence how research questions come to be asked.

In sociology, the problem of **objectivity** lies, in part, in the fact that sociologists cannot be impartial to what they study. Our own preconceptions and biases are hard to break. For example, part of the problem for prostitutes is that other people define them as a problem. There are alternative ways of looking at the subject. Perhaps the real problem is the sexual frustration of the men who seek out prostitutes, or the fact that soliciting is illegal, which makes the prostitutes prey to protection rackets and pimps. Perhaps the problem is the double standard, which leads to the arrest and prosecution of prostitutes while their customers go free. Perhaps there is no problem at all. Perhaps prostitution should just be seen as a service industry like any other and be left to operate freely as in the red-light district of Amsterdam. Alternatively, perhaps the real problem lies in the much bigger picture of worldwide sex trafficking in women from desperately poor countries, whose bodies are served up as toys for affluent male clients. How we come to think about an issue, and what we see as the immediate and underlying causes, powerfully impacts on what we want done about it. What is far harder to see are the social forces that structure what we think we know and how we know it.

Scientific Objectivity

Notwithstanding the values that researchers bring to their work, a measure of objectivity is possible in social science. At root, it is not researchers' values that matter so much as the research methods they use to collect their evidence. There are many different techniques, and although none are foolproof in completely avoiding bias, there are important principles of research that can reduce it.

The underlying philosophical assumption of all science is that it is relatively easy to find evidence to support an argument. Even stupid arguments can usually be backed up by some examples. It is important, therefore, to test an argument by deliberately searching for information and evidence that, if found, would show the argument to be wrong. Consider, for example, a researcher who is interested in studying divorce because she strongly disapproves of it and feels that it harms children. Such a researcher could still provide impartial evidence by deliberately allowing for the reverse data, the possibility that dissolution of an unhappy marriage is a good thing for the children involved. A minimum requirement for such a study would be comparative data from four types of families: those where the parents describe themselves as happily married; those where the parents describe their marriage as unhappy but say that they intend to stay together for the children; divorced families that describe themselves as happier since

Regina Leader-Post/Cam Cardow

the divorce; and divorced families that describe themselves as unhappy since the divorce. If data are gathered concerning children in all these sorts of families, the researcher allows for the possibility that children of divorced parents turn out to be happier and healthier than children living with parents in stressful, unhappy marriages. Useful research tests for the possibility that the researcher's starting assumptions might be wrong.

The critical element here is reasoned procedure, the disciplined, rigorous collection of evidence that deliberately tests for the opposite of the initial assumptions. Good research, of course, will attempt much more than this. Given that divorce, like marriage, does not always bring the same results, it is important to explain the conditions under which different outcomes are likely. Again, the ideal is that explanations will be tested, rather than assumed and supported with only selective examples.

In all scientific practice, regardless of the particular theories and methodologies adopted, three general principles are involved. The first is the need for systematic and public accumulation of experience and observations. It involves a search for evidence that incorporates a variety of people's experiences, not just those of one's own group. It is necessary to be clear about how the evidence was collected so that others can do similar research to check or challenge the results.

A second important principle of research is comparative investigation, incorporating data on people in different situations or different communities. A comparative focus is critically important in avoiding **ethnocentrism**, the tendency to assume that one's own group's way of doing things is more natural and proper than that of others. A sociological study of families, for example, might look at how family life is managed in other countries, other ethnic groups, or at other times in history. Through such comparative evidence, the study might explore the effects that different patterns seem to have on family members.

The third principle, and for philosophers of science the most important, is systematic doubt. Whatever the evidence looks like, it could be false, or misleading, or biased, or badly collected. Key factors may have been overlooked. Assumptions on which the research was based may turn out to be wrong. One may spend decades researching the effects of divorce upon children, only to conclude in the end that divorce is not the key issue at all; it is the poverty that so often accompanies divorce.

It can be very difficult to discover the "real" factors underlying a phenomenon. Some researchers spent three years studying the effects of illumination, rest pauses, and length of the working day on productivity of workers in a telephone assembly factory, only to conclude that these variables had next to nothing to do with productivity. The "real" factor was the attention that workers were

getting from the researchers, which made them feel important and valued instead of just one of a mass on the shop floor (Mayo [1933] 1960). Skeptical researchers later disputed this result. They argued that the "real" factors influencing productivity were the onset of the economic depression of the 1930s and the desperate need of two of the five women in the experimental group for money to support extended families when other relatives were unemployed (Carey 1967).

Facts can be elusive things. The ideal approach is to scrutinize the evidence, to question the theories and assumptions of any research, and to ask how the research was carried out and whether alternative strategies or additional data might have made the picture look different. Science is essentially a style of rigorous, systematic, critical thought, not a collection of facts to be memorized.

In sociological endeavour, controversy is critical. Given the biases and blind spots of researchers, the goal of systematic testing for the opposite of one's beliefs is often not attained. Researchers are often more concerned with supporting their theories than with testing them. Scientific journals are reluctant to publish articles that seem to show that starting assumptions were proven incorrect, as if it somehow meant that there must be something wrong with the research. For a long time, the assumption of differences between women and men was so strongly accepted that research that failed to substantiate behavioural differences between the sexes was simply discarded. Nicholson (1984, 4) estimates that for every published study showing differences between the sexes, six finding no difference remained unpublished. It is important that research that challenges established theories, whether those of the researcher or of larger groups, be conducted and be available to other researchers.

The problem of objectivity lies, in part, in the fact that sociologists are not impartial to what they study.

© Ilene MacDonald / Alamy

While it is essential that individual sociologists test their own data and theories, it is also important that the discipline encourage controversy among sociologists. When researchers disagree among themselves, it leads to a search for new evidence. New questions that might never have been thought of from one point of view can be brought forward by another researcher who started with different assumptions. Mutually incompatible assumptions provide the best challenge to each other. If your theory says that village life is happier and less isolating, and my theory is that city life is best and villages are stifling, our combined evidence is likely to be the best test of each other's assumptions. This is true of all science, not merely the social sciences. The philosopher Feyerabend (1970) has argued that whenever strong consensus emerges among a body of scientists that they have found the truth, the likely result will be dogmatism. More and more research will be done supporting the same assumptions, and it will be increasingly difficult for anyone to come up with alternative theories. Evidence that might well show the errors in the dominant theory is likely never to come to light because no one will be looking for it. In effect, controversy or lack of agreement over theories in sociology is not a problem, but an asset. It can even be argued that diversity in theoretical perspectives is a precondition for creative research (Hale 1992).

CONCLUSION

Current sociology is in no danger of sinking into dogmatic consensus. There is no one theoretical approach that dominates sociological research, but rather a number of schools of thought that begin from very different assumptions and are often very critical of each other's work. To be valuable for science, however, controversy should be organized, not just shouted opinions. Organized controversy entails checking the assumptions of different perspectives and challenging them with alternative evidence. Clarity of basic assumptions is essential.

This book sets out to present the controversies of sociology in an organized way. The theories of classical sociologists are presented in detail. We explore their basic assumptions, the logic behind them, and the consequences or predictions to which they give rise. These consequences are then tested by looking at relevant evidence, drawn mostly from contemporary Canadian research. Controversy among different theorists is used to clarify the strengths and the limitations of different theoretical assumptions by comparing the research results from studies based on different perspectives.

As students, I hope to encourage you to react to, not to accept, the text. Challenge arguments by examining their underlying assumptions, thinking up alternatives, and exploring counterevidence. The goal is to develop a capacity to shift perspectives and to question assumptions in a systematic way. Howard Boughey (1978, ix), in the introduction to his delightful little book, *The Insights of Sociology*, comments that the beginning scholar in the Sanskrit tradition must have the capacity to be aware of eight things simultaneously. This text attempts the lesser version of exploring four approaches to a problem. The basic philosophy of the text is that it is more important for you to develop the capacity for critical questioning than to amass facts.

SUGGESTED READING

Essays in Robert Brym's small book *Sociology as a Life or Death Issue* (2008) provide powerful insight into how to think sociologically. He explores questions such as: Why are some kinds of people in North American society far more likely to die violently than others? What are the social origins of hip-hop music and how is this genre of music changing? How was the "natural" disaster of Hurricane Katrina in New Orleans socially produced? And how can the study of sociology contribute to positive human freedom—to our capacity to act rationally as people in community?

Dandaneau's reflections as a sociologist on the life chances of his son, in Chapter 5 of *Taking it Big: Developing Sociological Consciousness in Postmodern Times* (2001) explores how one individual's life can be understood as embedded in and shaped by a nexus of societal institutions of politics, law, administration, education, and economics.

You might also search the Internet for summary reports and discussions of a sociological survey of Canadian youth conducted by Reginald Bibby, and published in summer 2009: *The Emerging Millennials: How Canada's Newest Generation is Responding to Change and Choice*. How closely do the responses of young adults surveyed by Bibby reflect how you think about issues? Why do you think they answered the questions as they did?

QUESTIONS

1. In the view of C.W. Mills, what are the social processes that might account for widespread evidence of cruel and insensitive behaviour?

2. What is the special promise of "the sociological imagination"?

3. How can we be both bombarded with information through a multi-channel universe and still not know what is going on?

4. According to Mills, what three fundamental questions are central to sociology?

5. What is the distinction between personal troubles and public issues? How might you explain this to the parents of a child brain damaged at birth by lack of oxygen?

6. Explain the idea that individual biography is embedded in social structures. Elaborate how you might explain this to fellow students worrying about student-loan debts.

7. Why is the science of sociology potentially much easier than natural sciences such as chemistry?

8. Why is the science of sociology potentially much more difficult than studying natural sciences?

9. List the three critical principles of scientific method in sociology.

10. In what ways can controversies in sociology be considered an advantage rather than a sign of confusion or ignorance?

WEB LINKS

Coping strategies for the scholarly tab
www.cbc.ca/news/background/personalfinance/studentdebt2.html
This is an archived report from June 11, 2007, by Joanna Pachner, on the growing debt facing university students in Canada. Subtopics include reports such as "A quick romp through the credit crunch," "Back-to-school tax breaks," "Student debt," and "Quick facts on student debt." This report not only provides statistics on student debt, but also allows the reader to analyze how the media pick up and report current issues.

Default: The Student Loan Documentary
www.youtube.com/watch?v=1463LHDLGvQ&feature=channel_page
This five-minute documentary shows the reality of getting an education.

Even though this is US-related, every Canadian student should see and discuss this video and what can be done about the escalating costs of education. Outstanding student-loan debt in the US has reached over $14 billion dollars.

Government of New Brunswick, Post-Secondary Education, Training and Labour
www.gnb.ca/0105/Index-e.asp
This site links New Brunswick students to the government departmental site that controls their post-secondary education. Sociology classes should discuss the "public face" of government discourse.

KEY TERMS

common-sense understandings

ethnocentrism

ideologies

objectivity

personal troubles

public issues

science

society

sociological imagination

sociology

REFERENCES

Berger, Peter L. 1963. *Invitation to Sociology: A Humanistic Perspective*. New York: Anchor Books.

Bibby, Reginald W. 2009. *The Emerging Millennials: How Canada's Newest Generation is Responding to Change and Choice*. Project Canada Books.

Boughey, Harold. 1978. *The Insights of Sociology: An Introduction*. Boston: Allyn and Bacon.

Brym, Robert. 2008. *Sociology as a Life or Death Issue*. Toronto: Pearson.

Carey, A. 1967. "The Hawthorne Studies: A Radical Critique." *American Sociological Review* 32: 403–416.

Dandaneau, Steven. 2001. *Taking it Big: Developing Sociological Consciousness in Postmodern Times*. Thousand Oaks, California: Pine Forge Press.

Feyerabend, P.K. 1970. "How to Be a Good Empiricist: A Plea for Tolerance in Matters Epistemological." In B.A. Brody, ed. *Readings in the Philosophy of Science*. Englewood Cliffs, New Jersey: Prentice Hall.

Goffman, Erving. 1961. *Asylums*. Harmondsworth, England: Penguin.

Hale, Sylvia M. 1992. "Facticity and Dogma in Introductory Sociology Texts: The Need for Alternative Methods." In William K. Carroll, Linda Christiansen-Ruffman, Raymond

F. Currie and Deborah Harrison, eds. *Fragile Truths: 25 Years of Sociology and Anthropology in Canada*. Ottawa, Ontario: Carleton University Press. 135–153.

Mayo, Elton. [1933] 1960. *The Human Problems of Industrial Civilization*. New York: Viking.

Mills, C. Wright. 1959. *The Sociological Imagination*. New York: Oxford University Press.

Nicholson, J. 1984. *Men and Women: How Different Are They?* Oxford: Oxford University Press.

Reimer, Marilee and Adele Mueller. 2006. "Accessing the Transition to Careers for Female Undergraduates in the Restructured University." *Canadian and International Education* 35 (1).

Smith, Dorothy E. 1990. *The Conceptual Practices of Power: A Feminist Sociology of Knowledge*. Toronto: University of Toronto Press.

Swift, Karen J. 1995. *Manufacturing "Bad Mothers": A Critical Perspective on Child Neglect*. Toronto: University of Toronto Press.

Thinking Theoretically

This chapter sets out four major perspectives that sociologists use to analyze social issues: functionalism, political economy, social constructionism, and feminism. Perspectives are broad ways of thinking about society that structure the kinds of questions that different sociologists find important and that guide research. The most useful way to think about perspectives is not whether they are right or wrong, but how useful they are for making sense of issues at hand. We will explore what assumptions sociologists make when they draw on different perspectives and the kinds of ideas and insights they provide.

You may well be wondering: *Why begin with theory? Why not begin with factual descriptions of broad features of Canadian society or personal experiences, and theorize later once we have some evidence?* The answer is that we have to draw on theories even to produce a description. Whenever we describe something, we have to decide what to pay attention to and what we can ignore, how we are going to organize and name features that seem important, and how to make connections between these features so that our description makes sense for others. Different theoretical perspectives give rise to such markedly different descriptions of aspects of society that even what constitutes a "fact" can be a matter of dispute. If I were to begin this text with a description of Canadian society, I would in effect be describing everything from my favourite perspective. After I had finished producing my description, the theory that would look like the best explanation for the evidence would be the one I had been using to organize the evidence.

For example, I could describe Canadian society in favourable terms as a peaceful liberal democracy, governed by the rule of laws that are framed within an overriding Charter of Rights and Freedoms. Ours is a relatively egalitarian and tolerant multi-ethnic society, in which people enjoy freedom of thought and expression and civil rights. Women and men have guaranteed equality rights under our Charter. Our economy is mostly based on a free-enterprise capitalist system that offers the large majority of citizens a very high standard of living, which is the envy of much of the world. Canada is one of the best, if not *the* best society in the world in which to live. There are minor problems, of course, including politically the separatist movement in Quebec, and the long-term problem of excessive poverty among Aboriginal or First Nations peoples within Canada. But these are problems that can be solved within our liberal democratic framework.

Alternatively, I could describe Canada in more negative terms as an unstable economy heavily dependent on the United States for our long-term economic survival. Our economy is based mostly on unsustainable resource extraction industries. Some industries, like the cod fishery in Newfoundland, have already collapsed, while other farming and mining enterprises are on the brink of failure. Everywhere, our environments are threatened by global warming, precipitated by the very industries on which we depend. Our privileged standard of living is extracted from misery of masses of exploited workers in other parts of the world. Our myth of equality is belied by the hundreds of thousands of Canadian-born children who live in dire poverty, and hundreds of thousands more whose life chances are stunted by racism and **sexism**.

I can also describe a Canadian society in which the immense concentration of mass media under the control of a few giant corporations renders illusory the myths of democratic values and freedom of thought. We live increasingly in a postmodern world in which we experience only pseudo, managed "freedoms." Our emotions are managed to the degree that a season without hockey interests many of us more than news of millions of people dying of starvation and disease elsewhere. Ours is a democracy in which most young people respond to evidence of massive corruption in high places only with cynical disinterest. Meanwhile, our supposedly affluent and privileged society is awash in antidepressants and illicit drugs. I could also describe a Canada in which men dominate all the important centres of power and influence in society, domestic violence remains one of our most pervasive and least prosecuted crimes, and the circulation of pornography is the most pervasive use of the Internet. Described this way, Canada appears more closely akin to George Orwell's classic *1984* than to a utopia.

Suddenly it does not seem so easy to describe "Canada." The goal of this text is to encourage you to explore the assumptions that give rise to these vastly differing descriptions of society that we come to know as Canada, and to search for and evaluate evidence for different viewpoints. Only as you develop the capacity to get behind any claims to describe "social reality," to recognize and make explicit the theoretical assumptions implicit in them, and to challenge them with alternative ways of looking and new forms of evidence, will you truly have the freedom to make reasoned decisions for yourself. Each chapter in this text is designed to make visible the interrelationship between description and theory by presenting competing theoretical perspectives in turn and exploring how they shape our understanding of what is going on.

SCIENCE AND PERSONAL CHOICE

All social sciences grapple with the tension between freedom and determinism, between individual human **agency** and constraining social **structure**. If science succeeds in explaining broad patterns of social behaviour, what does this imply about personal freedom and responsibility to choose how to behave? The box labelled "Choice and Constraints" below is designed to help you explore your personal sense of choice and agency—making decisions about your own future and working to achieve your personal goals, and some of the structural constraints that impact on your choices. Currently within Canada, roughly 30 percent of high school graduates go on to university, while 70 percent do not. Proportions of women and men who enter university is now roughly equal, although they are attracted to very different kinds of programs. Historically, what we see now is vastly different from a century ago when far fewer young men went to university, and almost no women. Exploring the complex mix of personal choices and structural constraints that underlie these patterns will give you a sense of what the agency/structure debate is about.

Sociologists generally agree that what we call "social structures" are best understood as produced by decisions and

Choice and Constraints

If sociologists can predict with some accuracy what kinds of people are more or less likely to enter university, what does that say about your choice in the matter?

You can "choose" to come to university, however difficult it might be, but how free are you to "choose" the conditions under which you do it? Can you choose how much money your parents will contribute, or the size of the student loan you can get, the cost of tuition, books, computer, room and board? How free are you to "choose" the grade point average at which you will be accepted or rejected? Alternatively, you can "choose" to drop out of university, but how far can you "choose" or even influence the consequences that would flow from this choice?—your future job chances, your future family income, your status in the neighbourhood?

You might insist that everyone in Canada has the chance to go to university if they are bright enough and work hard enough in school. But how much do you think your choice to continue in school might have been affected if you found yourself facing any of the following circumstances, either separately or in combination?

- there is pervasive hostility and violence in your school directed at people who look like you
- your friends and family members scoff at university as a waste of time and money relative to on-the-job technical training
- family life is so stressful that it leaves you feeling depressed and worthless, and unable to concentrate on school work

- your family is desperately short of money and young children are looking to you to support them now, not four years from now
- the fees double, and the student-loan program closes down
- university places are cut and university entrance grades are set 15 points higher than they are currently
- many people you know have achieved honours degrees but have since been unable to find work in their field

Try your hand at developing three lists:

- the factors that contribute to school life being experienced as enjoyable or as unpleasant or even a nightmare;
- the factors that contribute to university being comfortably affordable or extremely difficult;
- the likely financial consequences in your local area of a decision to leave school before grade twelve.

Which of these factors appear sufficiently important that they could change your decision to attend university or not?

Which of these factors can you change by your personal choice, perhaps with the help of your immediate family?

Which of these factors can local teachers or politicians change if they really want to?

Which of these factors are beyond the influence of local people?

From where would the most powerful support for change, and powerful opposition to change, likely come?

actions taken by people in the past. These structures include all the ways of organizing complex nation states like Canada—systems of government, law, administration, education, production, and so on. Few would argue that such structures emerged by themselves or have minds of their own, even though they might seem rigid and coercive at times. We also see these structures as maintained or altered by the decisions and actions of people in the present.

Having said this, we are still left with some big questions (Sharrock 1987, 126–127). We might agree that people make history, but in what ways is this true? We could say that the weight of history and social constraints are so great that people only have a marginal capacity to influence social structures or to make personal choices. The option of bowing to market forces or facing bankruptcy and ruin, for example, does not feel much like free choice. On the other hand, we could hold that people are capable of overcoming the limitations of the circumstances they find themselves in and reshaping those circumstances. But then we have to show how they are able to do this. Social organizations are human creations, but they are nonetheless capable of exacting conformity from vast numbers of people over long time spans and enormous geographic distances. The four major theoretical perspectives that are the focus of this text propose very different ways of thinking about how social structures dominate people and how people respond to, negotiate, change, and recreate social order in their everyday lives.

The remainder of this chapter is designed to give you basic conceptual tools for thinking like sociologists. It is divided into four sections that set out the basic assumptions behind each of four broad theoretical perspectives in sociology. Sociologists draw upon these assumptions to explore social life and to generate questions about what is going on, why social relations seem to be the way they are, and what might be useful strategies for effective social action. Each section concludes with a discussion of the concept of culture to illustrate the striking differences between perspectives. We begin with **functionalism**, the perspective that dominated North American sociology for many decades.

Functionalism: Society as a Social System

When sociologists use a functionalist perspective, they draw attention to the long-term familiar and predictable character of large-scale social organization, barring only catastrophic events. By far the best prediction of what life will be like next year in your town and region is that it will be much the same as last year. The central assumption is that social life can most usefully be understood by thinking in

very broad terms about society as a relatively self-contained and self-maintaining **system** of interrelated parts. This **social system** tends towards stability and balance over time through continual organizational adjustments between the parts. In other words, societies tend towards dynamic **equilibrium**. Sociologists are interested in how this overall structural equilibrium is maintained across generations, and they seek answers in the ways in which different parts of society are structured and functionally interrelated to meet the needs of the system as a whole. Parts, or the constituent organizations and **institutions** of society, are studied both for how they contribute to the system as a whole, and also how they are organized as subsystems in themselves, comprised of functioning parts.

To get a sense of how to analyze society using a functionalist perspective, think about how biologists study an animal's body. Biologists think of a body as a system, with all the body parts or organs carrying out distinct functions that work together to keep the body healthy, that is, in a state of dynamic equilibrium. They study particular organs, such as a heart, to determine what its primary function is, and how it is structured to perform this function. This can lead to ever more detailed research into the specialized structure of the heart muscle, electro-chemical impulses that maintain the precise heart rhythm, and the like. Medical researchers also probe further into what happens when a heart malfunctions, to identify structural problems and how they might be fixed. Biologists also study how specialized sets of organs are integrated into functioning subsystems of the body, like the circulatory system, the nervous system, the hormone system, and how these in turn impact upon and regulate each other.

Society as a Functioning System

It is a daunting task to identify all the functional requirements of a healthy society, although there is some agreement about important needs. All societies must work with the natural environment to physically sustain its members and to pattern heterosexual relations to produce and raise children. Societies need some orderly means of allocating critical functions among competent members and ensuring that such work is performed regularly. This in turn requires adequate systems of decision-making authority, communication, and administration. Societies also need some means to teach and motivate generations of members to participate in society in appropriate ways, and to effectively control disruptive forms of behaviour and emotions (Adapted from Aberle et al. 1950). Individual societies in turn can be analyzed as subsystems functioning within an increasingly interconnected global system of transnational economic, political, and legal institutions.

Aid workers in countries devastated by war or natural disasters give high priority to establishing a functioning system of law and governance.

THE CANADIAN PRESS/Tobi Cohen

Functionalist theory also draws attention to systemic dysfunctions, when the requirements of healthy social systems are not effectively being met. The state of civil war is a stark indication of the failure of political institutions within individual states; famine is an extreme measure of the failure of economic institutions; pervasive illiteracy is a measure of the failure of educational institutions, and so on. At the beginning of the twenty-first century the staggering number of civil wars raging in societies across the African subcontinent, parts of Southeast Asia, the Middle East, the former Soviet Union, and in Latin America testify to the fragility of many contemporary social systems, as do widespread famines, the rampant spread of AIDS, and the millions of refugees and displaced persons worldwide. Closer to home, the 1995 Quebec referendum on sovereignty where Quebeckers came within one percentage vote of opting out of Canada, and rumblings of Western alienation, remind us that Canadian political institutions are not functioning as well as they might. Many First Nations communities within Canada also show multiple signs of systemic dysfunction, with levels of poverty, family breakdown, substance abuse, suicides, and morbidity and mortality rates similar to those in the least-developed countries in the world.

Advisors to governments and to peacekeeping teams use functionalist analysis to guide the reconstruction of countries devastated by war or natural disasters. Typically, first priority is given to "humanitarian" needs for food, medicine, and clean drinking water. Then attention turns to providing law and order, governance, and all the complex organizations and institutions that sustain commerce, education, transportation, and so on. Directors know that if they fail to set priorities reasonably well, people may die from hunger, cold and disease, or the society may collapse into chaos.

Most sociological work in the functionalist tradition focuses on more manageable questions of how particular institutions within a society are structured and the functions they perform. Policy analysts in many professions draw upon the insights of functionalist theory to address social problems (Burnett 2004; Curran 2003). Families, collectively referred to as "the institution of the family," are generally considered the most basic organizing unit within any society. Families function to produce and nurture young people and to meet the intimate daily material and emotional needs of people. The broader education system, comprised of networks of schools, colleges, universities, school boards, textbook publishers, and the like, builds upon the specialized functions of the family by teaching young people the knowledge they will need to perform adult work, and reinforcing collective values and standards of behaviour of the society. The economic system, with its myriad of productive enterprises, produces and distributes material goods and services. Political institutions organize collective goals and legitimate power relations, and so on. The multiple organizations that form parts of each of these systems can in turn be studied as functioning systems in their own right.

Complexities in functionalist analysis result from several related factors. Firstly, any one organization or social arrangement always functions as part of a wider network of related organizations, and hence full analysis requires concern with external relations as well as internal operations. Quebec and First Nations communities function as distinct societies within Canada, while Canada functions as a small, prosperous nation state in global networks of transnational institutions. Secondly, social institutions are multifunctional. Too simplistic a definition of core functions can cloud understanding of what is happening. You might argue that the intended function of a school is to impart knowledge and skills, with success measured by formal examinations. But it would be a serious error to assume that preparation for examinations is all that schools do. Others may argue that teaching cultural and religious values and patriotic commitments are even more important than teaching technical skills. Schools also teach social skills. Severely learning-disabled children who cannot follow the academic curriculum may still have much to gain from being part of age-graded school classes. Distinctive functions may generate competing priorities and fierce struggles between subgroups over allocation of institutional resources.

Functionalists distinguish between **manifest functions** (or intended functions) of social institutions and **latent functions**—those that are less obvious and not directly intended, but which may still be important for society as a whole and for the people directly involved (Merton 1967, 73–138). Latent functions may explain the continuation of social organizations long after their intended function has become irrelevant or even devalued. A sanatorium set up for people with tuberculosis may continue after the epidemic has passed, as people struggle to find new uses for the centre because the jobs bring money into the community. Similarly, universities may be financed by governments primarily to promote a highly qualified workforce, but many students come for very different reasons. Increasing numbers of retired people register for university courses, long after they have ceased to be concerned with career advancement, because they enjoy the intellectual challenge and camaraderie of campus life. The manifest functions of sports may appear to be physical exercise and entertainment, but their importance may be eclipsed by the powerful latent function of promoting community spirit and nationalism (Merkel 2003). Many Canadian universities devote surprisingly large proportions of limited budgets to hockey teams and athletics scholarships for these reasons.

Latent functions, the unintended consequences of actions, are not necessarily positive for all members of society. Collective organizations may have some effects that are dysfunctional. The sociological theorist Robert Merton has argued that perhaps the most important contribution of functionalist theory is to reveal unintended and unwanted consequences of social organization. The expansion of formal education, for example, has as one of its consequences the enforced segregation of young people from adults and the adult world of work. It also prolongs the state of adolescence or "childhood" well beyond physical and sexual adulthood. Can you think of some potentially dysfunctional aspects of this arrangement? From the standpoint of people within these organizations, Giddens argues (1984, 293), unintended consequences most often result from restricted knowledge of all the wider and longer-term consequences of choices. Students who quit school early to take jobs may see the autonomy, the adult **status**, and the fun that come with earning money, without seeing how they are trapping themselves into a lifetime of dead-end, low-skilled work. On the other hand, people who commit themselves to years of higher education may not see the consequences of heavy debt loads, and delayed marriage and child-bearing years.

A further factor that complicates functionalist analysis is change. As we noted above, the functionalist perspective is primarily concerned with explaining how the social system is maintained in a state of equilibrium or balance. But this equilibrium is dynamic, not static. Any social organization that fails to change in response to changing external conditions risks becoming seriously dysfunctional. The functionalist perspective draws heavily upon biological sciences in identifying differentiation and specialization as fundamental processes involved in adaptive change of social systems. A classic example of functionalist analysis of systemic change is the gradual shift from family to school as the site of education. In less technologically advanced societies, families perform the major functions of nurturing children, educating them in the skills needed for adult life, and organizing economic production. However, as societies become more technologically advanced, the family is no longer adequate to meet all these system needs. The three primary functions of nurturing, educating, and producing become differentiated into different institutions. Families have become more specialized in performing the nurturing function, while schools specialize in education, and factories and businesses specialize in production. Similarly, in small organizations tasks may be relatively undifferentiated with a few individuals doing everything, but as the organization becomes larger and more complex, tasks are differentiated and divided among specialists.

In focusing attention on these adaptive changes in social systems, the functionalist perspective also points to important roots of dysfunction and conflict in failure to adapt to the needs of a changing environment. Conflict can be functional for a social system in promoting a willingness to change and thus overcoming rigidity in the system (Coser 1956).

Social Systems and Individual Members

A theoretical perspective that focuses on large-scale social systems must address the critical question of how to integrate individual people into the model without them appearing like mindless cogs in a machine, and also how such integration is smoothly perpetuated from one generation to another. The functionalist perspective conceptualizes this integration through the ideas of **role**, **socialization**, and **culture**.

Role   The concept of role focuses attention on typical and expected patterns of behaviour, particularly those regarded as appropriate and proper in specified situations (Biddle and Thomas 1966). The violation of these normatively valued expectations generate both surprise and disapproval. Institutions can be thought of as organized collections of interacting roles. An individual role can be thought of as the smallest unit of analysis for social institutions, the level at which actions of individual people are the central focus. No two individuals ever respond in exactly the same way in similar situations, but nonetheless it is rarely difficult to pick out common patterns. The idea of role draws attention to these patterns. Think about school teachers you have known. Each will be easily distinguished from the others, and each classroom experience different. Yet all teachers have certain behaviour patterns in common, certain expected and valued ways of behaving in classrooms that make them recognizably teachers, and not janitors or secretaries, or parents who may have helped out in school classes.

Roles and role expectations are relatively easy to see in formal organizations like schools and businesses. They are typically defined by jobs and job descriptions. In bureaucratic organizations the expectations, obligations, and minimum standards for performance are usually set out in great detail. In informal settings, normatively expected patterns of behaviour are less precise but evident nonetheless. The role expectations for schoolteachers are more closely bureaucratically defined than the role of mother of schoolchildren, but teachers can nonetheless articulate a set of normative expectations they have for mothers. People similarly know the limits of acceptable behaviour in settings like churches, restaurants, ball games, or family gatherings, even though they are not written down.

Functionalist theory regards these mutually recognized sets of expectations as centrally important in promoting stability in social interaction over time. Functionalist analysis commonly uses terms like **actor** and role-incumbent to shift the focus of attention from individual personalities to patterned expectations for behaviour. Different individuals can come and go as teachers, but the role of teacher remains constant as a predefined and recognizable feature of the school context.

The concepts of **role set** and **role strain** focus on how different role expectations interact and overlap. A role set usually refers to the sum of all other roles with which the incumbent of one specific role interacts. A school teacher, for example, interacts with pupils in class, with parents of these pupils, with other teachers, the school principal, members of the school board, and others, in the course of performing the teacher role. The notion of role set is also sometimes used to refer to the sum of all different roles that one individual performs. A teacher may also be a parent, a spouse, a child, a church member, city councillor, golf buddy, and so on.

The concept of role strain or **role conflict** refers to the tensions that can occur when the expectations and obligations associated with related roles clash. Different actors in a system of roles may have conflicting expectations of what a particular role entails. Teachers, for example, may find that parents want different things from them as teachers than does the school principal, and so have difficulty keeping both satisfied. Also, teachers may find themselves juggling competing obligations and expectations as parent, employee, and church member.

Socialization   This theoretical focus on shared normative expectations for appropriate and proper role behaviour gives rise to a series of questions. How do people come to recognize and adopt roles? How do people learn role expectations? How are role expectations transmitted over time as different people take up and leave roles? What motivates people to conform to social expectations?

A basic assumption within the functionalist perspective is that participation in social systems is for the most part voluntary. The large majority of individual members must want to conform to social expectations for any long-term stability or equilibrium to be possible. Even prisons rely heavily on the willingness of prisoners to conform to the rules in order to function. So the big question is: What motivates most individuals to participate willingly, competently, and consistently in social institutions, and to conform sufficiently well to the patterned expectations associated with multiple roles, to bring about the long-term stable functioning of social systems? The functionalist perspective sees lifelong processes of teaching and learning, termed "socialization," together with a shared system of meanings and values termed "culture," as the foundations of **social order**. What follows are some basic assumptions about how this socialization process works.

Children learn basic expectations for social behaviour primarily by watching and emulating the people around them. Parents are pivotally important as **role models**, but so are other care-givers, relatives, neighbours, teachers, and arguably also television characters. Favourite games for young children commonly include play-acting "mommy" or "daddy," and other familiar roles. Children and adults may imaginatively "take on the roles of **others**"—imagining what it might be like to do different jobs, or to be in different social situations. Later, this role-play is likely to be supplemented by more formal role-training or instruction in what is expected. Over a lifetime we take on many roles, first as youngest child and sibling, older sibling, school pupil, child-minder, parent, breadwinner, citizen, and the like. Functionalists think of the sum of all these roles as together making up our social selves. The social roles we play are not merely external patterns to which we conform; they become part of how we come to see ourselves, part of our identity.

A further important assumption underpinning **role theory** is that, for the most part, people want approval and acceptance. We appreciate receiving approval ourselves and reciprocally we tend to give approval to others who behave as we expect them to. Over time, we come to internalize the expectations around roles that we play, to feel that they are right and proper. This internalization process explains an important anomaly in functionalist theory. While the perspective conceptualizes society in very broad systemic terms, the actual behaviour of people is explained primarily by reference to the attitudes and values that people hold, and to the family backgrounds in which primary values are learned.

Controls over Individual Behaviour   The two concepts of role expectations and socialization account for how most individuals conform most of the time, and for societal reactions to lapses in conformity. Social controls at the level of individual behaviour can be thought of as circles of constraints, or **circles of social control** (Berger 1963, 68–70) (see Figure 1). These four circles comprise guilt, need for approval, economic sanctions, and finally force. Voluntary conformity is sustained by the innermost experience of guilt. Individuals internalize their role expectations and feel a sense of personal failure when they do not live up to them. Our desire for approval from people close to us acts as a secondary circle of constraint. If these intimate pressures are not sufficient to ensure reasonable conformity, then economic sanctions usually come into play. Non-conformists can expect to find that rewards and incentives which normally go along with approval will be withheld. In particular, they may find themselves unable to get or retain jobs. Finally, if economic sanctions fail to check deviance, more overt punishments may be administered. Children who break family rules may find themselves grounded and their allowance withheld. Adults who break societal laws may end up in prison. However, any social system, be it at the level of a family or a nation state, that must rely heavily upon punishments and force to exact conformity from members is inherently less stable than one whose members voluntarily conform.

Culture
The concept of culture is centrally important in the functionalist perspective, because it is understood as the central mechanism holding all the elements of social systems together. We will first describe it below as a concept within the functionalist theoretical model. Then we will return to it later to illustrate how it has been used as a tool within functionalist research to explore Canadian national and global relations.

In its broadest sense, the concept of culture refers to the overarching system of shared meanings, beliefs and values prevailing within a society, along with a shared material culture of scientific knowledge and technology. Shared beliefs and sentiments form the basis of moral order in society. The ritual practices that express these collective beliefs function to unite people together in a sense of community.

Culture is species-specific. All animals communicate with each other, but only humans communicate through

Figure 1   Circles of Social Control

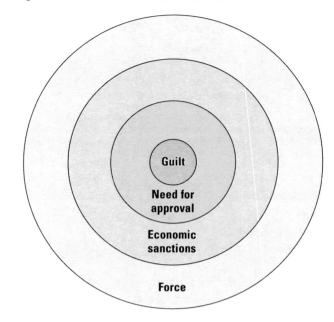

Source: Adapted from Berger 1963

abstract symbols, especially language. Language has critical survival value for humans, making possible advanced learning and complex systems of cooperation. Within the discipline of anthropology, which focuses on simpler societies, culture is commonly defined as "the whole way of life of a people," encompassing all that individuals would need to know to function as competent members of the society. In more complex societies, characterized by high levels of specialization and differentiation, shared culture is not so all-encompassing. Culture is viewed as a flexible system in which core values and meanings will be held in common by members of the society, but with much subcultural variation, reflecting distinctive social positions and experiences. This concept of subculture can be applied to distinctive communities within wider societies, such as villages, neighbourhoods, clubs, members of particular professions or work-groups, and so on.

A form of subculture that functionalist theory identifies as particularly significant is that associated with ethnic minorities, people with distinctive origins who may share distinctive languages, religious traditions, and the like. These differences may vary from minor aspects of personal life, like dress, food preferences, and family traditions, to broad patterns of private and public behaviour that set one group of people apart from others. The term assimilation refers to the process of change by which members of once highly distinctive subgroups come increasingly to adopt the cultural patterns of the wider social system.

Culture is transmitted across generations through socialization. The basic assumption here is that while members may not always live up to community values, they generally know what these values are and tend to use them to evaluate their own and others' behaviour. Through internalizing the generalized culture of their community, people are already oriented towards appropriate patterns of behaviour even before learning detailed expectations associated with particular roles. Culture is thus viewed as an essential mechanism serving to integrate roles within a society and to reduce friction between them. In complex societies, cultural values are widely codified into laws and religion and transmitted through media, literature, schools, religious organizations, symbols, customs, and traditions.

Shared language forms the core of any cultural system. Saussure (1964) defines language as essentially a system of signs, comprising the **signifier**, the words or images used, and the **signified**, the object to which it refers. He stresses, firstly, that the relationship between signifier and signified is essentially arbitrary. There is no inherent link between the sound "mother" and what this word refers to. Different languages use different sounds. Secondly, any word conveys meaning only in relation to an entire system of meaning or language, not in isolation. The word "mother," for example, can be defined only in relation to the associated words "child" and "father." Language is a system of grammar and symbols. Individual users must conform to this system in order to be understood.

Saussure argues further that language does not merely apply names to an already coherently known reality. Language actually organizes reality. As we apply names to chaotic sensory experiences we create some sense of meaningful order. People live in symbolic universes, experiencing the world as culturally constructed through language, and hence in some respects always unique to a given language system. For example, English words like "left," "right," and "centre" work to organize a cacophony of political views into a semblance of coherent orientations. Words like "adolescent," "teenager," and "retiree" are meaningful only within cultural systems that prolong "childhood" well beyond physical puberty, and that end productive employment well before physical senility or death. Such terms may have no direct translation and make no sense in other cultural systems. The Mi'qmac and Maliseet languages have no word for "boundary" (Bear-Nicholas 2004), reflecting the absence of a concept of ownership of land in pre-contact First Nations communities in the Maritimes. European meanings of terms for boundary and land ownership were not translatable into Aboriginal cultural systems, resulting in serious discrepancies in interpretations of the meaning of treaties.

Language usage also differs according to how well community members know each other and how similar their lifestyles are. In close-knit communities members can talk in condensed or restricted ways and be readily understood, while more elaborate and detailed forms of communication are required to get meanings across among strangers (Wuthnow et al. 1984, 103–104).

The study of language—or semiotics—provides a model for studying how people convey meanings through a host of other non-linguistic signs and gestures. Bodily gestures like facial expressions, hand signals, posture—such as slouched or upright—and spatial distance between bodies, convey culturally specific meanings like welcome or disapproval, acceptance or rejection, insolence or submission. Travellers to foreign cultures are commonly warned to learn the locally acceptable signs to avoid inadvertently offending people. Mannette (1992) suggests that subtle differences in culturally learned body language, reticence, clothing, demeanour, and tone of voice between Native defendants and non-Native jurors can convey dangerously flawed messages about probable guilt in criminal trials. Barthes (1971) analyzes a famous photograph of a black soldier saluting a French flag to clarify how the flag signifies France, the man's clothing signifies the armed forces, the salute signifies notions of duty, service, and obedience, and the man's dark skin signifies the history of French imperialism and the subjugation of people in the colonies. The photograph is unique, but the system of signs, or shared meanings by which the photograph communicates complex abstract messages to viewers, is highly structured. Advertisers routinely utilize these cultural associations between visual signs and abstract meanings to link their products to desirable states (Turner 1990, 21; Douglas 1979). The makers of Ski Yogurt show their product being eaten by people engaged in sailboarding, hanggliding, surfing, and skiing to create the image of yogurt as a lifestyle product associated with youth, vigour, and health. People also routinely use these shared symbol systems to convey impressions about themselves to others, including complex messages around sexual availability, religious orientation, community of origin, institutional membership, and the like.

Ritual practices are also inherent features of cultural systems that function to signify membership in a society and in various sub-communities, and simultaneously to strengthen integration. In Canada, we have national holidays, complete with military music, flag-waving, and fireworks, hockey nights showing national teams on television, and a host of other staged political events that signify and strengthen national unity. At the local and intimate level, everyday rituals like tidying, cleaning, and putting things in their place, and serving particular kinds of food on particular occasions, carry similar symbolic meanings, reinforcing among participants a sense of belonging and conforming to a shared moral order in the home and beyond (Douglas 1966, 1979; Wuthnow et al. 1984, 87).

Functionalist analysis of the integrative power of shared culture does not assume that all members of a given society will conform to the values, beliefs, and expected practices associated with a cultural system. What it does assume is that competent members will learn through socialization to recognize and understand these core elements, and will recognize non-conformity as deviant.

Culturally shared expectations for behaviour may not always function in positive ways for all members of a society. They may have latent dysfunctional consequences, especially when they fail to adapt to changing external conditions. Core values of individual competitiveness, and striving for consumer goods, if carried too far, can undermine other community values like compassion and sharing, and promote long-term environmental degradation and depletion of natural resources. Striving to maximize efficiency and time management can foster dysfunctional excesses like a workaholic mentality, regimentation, and diets surfeited in fast foods. These conflict with other cultural values, such as collegiality at work, family life, and community health. The functionalist view of societies as comprising systems of interrelated parts fosters awareness of how excesses in one subsystem can lead to dysfunctions in another and give rise to pressures to re-establish balance.

Systemic Conflict and Dysfunction

Functionalist theory focuses attention primarily on mechanisms that account for dynamic equilibrium in social systems. Weaknesses or inadequacies in the functioning of these basic mechanisms are used to account for conflict and disequilibrium or the breakdown of order. At the level of role performance, shared role expectations are assumed to promote stability. Hence, divergent role expectations promote instability. The emotional, nurturing expectations of family roles, for example, may clash with the instrumental expectations of work roles whenever the two role sets are inadequately separated. Processes of socialization are assumed to explain conformity to role expectations and cultural values. Hence, faulty socialization explains deviance. Children whose parents are bad role models are likely to learn bad practices. Violent parents breed violent children. Desire for approval promotes conformity. Hence, indifference to approval promotes deviance. Broken homes, or shallow emotional ties between children and parents, promote shallow concern for parental values. Consistency among many salient role models promotes conformity. Hence, inconsistency weakens it. Exposure to media violence or bad influences outside the home is likely to undermine other good influences. Hence, children who grow up in high-crime neighbourhoods are more likely to learn criminal attitudes and values than children in low-crime neighbourhoods.

These relationships are not viewed as deterministic, because there are multiple sources of socialization that may be inconsistent. The negative effects of dysfunctional families may be countered by more positive socialization from other sources, and vice versa. Nonetheless, family breakdown is considered a pivotal factor in social disorder.

Other kinds of social conflicts are assumed to stem from systemic maladjustments. Societal equilibrium is understood as dynamic and not static, because societies must continually change to respond to changing circumstances. Balance between functional subsystems of society promotes overall integration. Hence, imbalance is assumed to weaken societal integration. Rapid change in any one part of a social system is likely to generate conflicts with other subsystems. A common experience is for the economic subsystem to respond more rapidly to external pressures than the cultural subsystem, with such cultural lag generating high stress for individuals caught between discordant expectations. In such circumstances, conflict within the social system may be functional for pressuring more systemic adaptation to change and preventing excessive rigidity. Other systemic conflicts are generated by competing interests. Giddens (1984, 310–319) cites the examples of governments depending heavily on revenues from private business enterprise, and higher income earners paying more in taxes for publicly funded services like buses, schools, and health care while they themselves use cars and favour private schools and clinics. Government institutions play a critical role in the management of such competing interests.

Summary

We have now discussed all the core assumptions that underlie the functionalist perspective. Society is seen as a system of interrelated institutions that function together as a dynamic whole. The voluntary participation of individual members of society is sustained through the core mechanisms of role expectations and socialization. The overarching cultural system of shared meanings, beliefs, and values holds the entire social system together. Culture is internalized at the individual level through socialization, and it functions to integrate diverse roles at the institutional level and diverse institutions at the societal level.

The Functionalist Perspective on National Cultures in Global Society

This last section uses the concept of national cultures to illustrate the distinctive approach of functionalist analysis. We will refer back to this section later to show how strikingly different the descriptions and analyses of Canadian society are when viewed through other theoretical perspectives.

Canadian sociologists have long been interested in trying to characterize what is distinctively Canadian as against American national cultural values. This interest was promoted, Brym suggests (1989, Ch. 1), by the large numbers of American sociologists who filled positions in Canadian universities during the 1960s. American sociologists working within the functionalist perspective have tended to view the United States as a leading example of political and economic modernity. Typically, they explain this in terms of the distinctive culture that arose from the common experience of frontier settlement by rugged individualists, many of them Protestant nonconformists fleeing persecution in Europe. These experiences promoted a system of cultural values that emphasized individualism, free enterprise, private property, and rejection of religious authority, tempered by an abstract "civil religion" embodied in the Declaration of Independence, and presidential oaths of office (Bellah 1990).

Canadians, in contrast, seemed more conservative than Americans, with a greater tendency to respect authority and hierarchy, and to accept state control over the economy. The people who emigrated to the colonies of Upper Canada and Quebec were more likely to be Anglicans and Roman Catholic, or British Empire Loyalists who left America after the revolution of 1776. Analysts suggest that these relatively hierarchical churches inculcated cultural values of deep respect for authority (Clark 1968; Lipset 1976, 1985; Porter 1965, 1979). Lipset further concludes that English Canadians are generally more elitist and accepting of class divisions, less entrepreneurial or achievement oriented, less willing to take risks, more oriented to collective than individual interests, and more accepting of ethnic differences among people than are Americans (Brym 1989, 28). Horowitz further suggests (1985) that French Canada inherited a feudal political structure, and English Canada an aristocratic Tory political culture that conceptualizes society as a hierarchically ordered system rather than the liberal view of society as an agglomeration of individuals. These roots in different political cultures, Horowitz suggests, explains why a social-democratic party emerged in Canada but not in America.

Such sweeping generalizations about American and Canadian political cultures necessarily admit of many exceptions. But there is nonetheless a sense that it is meaningful to speak of different political cultures in the two countries. These differences are seen as reflected in far stronger support within the Canadian electorate for a federal medicare system, and for higher taxation to support a more generous social safety net. Cultural differences are reflected also in strikingly lower rates of violent crime in Canada. Different political cultures are also reflected in the Canadian federal government decision not to support the American-led initiative to invade Iraq in 2003 without the prior approval of the United Nations. Kalberg (2003, 17) similarly argues that the appeal to missionary idealism "to establish democracy in Iraq" and to "liberate the Iraqi people" resonates with American people still deeply influenced by the cultural legacies of ascetic fundamentalist Protestantism. German people, in contrast, reacted with almost universal skepticism, assuming that the "real motives" must be more secular national self-interest.

Cultural Integration in Multicultural Societies

The level of cultural integration in any society is seen as a particularly problematic issue from the functionalist perspective. A shared cultural system is assumed to be a central integrating mechanism in social systems. Hence, cultural diversity potentially threatens societal integration, risking division and conflict. Canada does not conform to this theoretical ideal of a cohesive community united through a single language and cultural system. Canada has two official languages—English and French, as well as some 60 or more First Nations languages and a host of heritage languages spoken in immigrant communities. These diverse languages reflect and reinforce a diversity of cultures. Relations between French and English Canada have been characterized as "two solitudes" with strong political movement within Quebec pressuring for separate sovereign status (Nesbitt-Larking 2001, 264–269). The 1995 Quebec referendum on sovereignty failed by a margin of less than 1 percent. Had it succeeded, the discussion of Canadian cultural institutions and societal integration in this text might well be very different.

Many immigrant communities continue to have close contacts and cultural ties with their communities of origin, facilitated by the Internet, satellite radio and television, and telephones, and they continue to retain their mother tongue and other elements of culture. Even within the dominant white English-speaking majority it is difficult to speak of a single unified cultural system. A more accurate characterization is that of fragmentation, with a diversity of "faith communities" including Christian, non-Christian, and atheistic, and a multiplicity of family forms and sexual practices. There is also an eclectic mixing of foods, clothing, musical and other artistic styles, borrowed from around the world. The global reach of mass media makes it impossible for Canadians to isolate themselves from these influences, even if they should wish to. The concept of **postmodernism** refers, in part, to this experience of cultural fragmentation and hybridization.

Globalization and National Culture

Two competing arguments have developed out of functionalist analysis concerning the future of national cultures, loosely referred to as neo-liberal and neo-conservative. The dominant neo-liberal argument is that globalization, the reality of global networks of communications and commerce, has already profoundly altered the nature of tradition and culture. Global systems of communications and global migration inevitably intrude on traditional cultures. In the face of this reality, Giddens argues (2000, 67) that a shift in cultural values towards rational, tolerant, and cosmopolitan acceptance of diverse autonomous subcultures becomes essential for wider societal and global integration. Giddens sees the main threat to stability or equilibrium in cosmopolitan societies not as diversity, but as fundamentalism in religious, family, or ethnic forms. He defines fundamentalism as "beleaguered tradition," characterized not by the content of beliefs, but by how they are defended or asserted—the non-reflexive insistence on conformity to a pre-existing set of practices. Traditions, he argues, still play an important role in giving social stability and continuity to social life. But they are becoming more cosmopolitan and accepting of diversity, and also more obviously commercialized and contrived for the tourist trade. He predicts further that nationalist sentiments will decline as citizens identify more with super-national systems of governance like the European Union and the North American Free Trade Agreement.

It is also widely predicted in functionalist analyses that modern cultural values will become increasingly defined in unifying secular and rational terms around values of political democracy and human rights, while potentially divisive expression of religious faiths will become privatized and separated from institutions of government (Berger 1967). In Canada, such adaptation has taken the form of The Canadian Charter of Rights and Freedoms. The Charter endorses official commitment to bilingualism in English and French at the federal level, an official policy of multiculturalism, and respect for Aboriginal treaty rights. All government-run institutions are officially secular, and religious

attendance within Canada has been dropping steadily over many decades (Bibby 1993; 2002).

Another line of theory developing from functionalist analysis, however, suggests that pressures of globalization may work to heighten commitment to nationalism and distinctive national cultures, rather than promoting cosmopolitan cultural values. One reason for this, Bernal suggests (2004) in his analysis of Eritrea's struggle for independence from Ethiopia, is the political recognition given to *nations* as subsystem units in the organization of global political and economic systems. It is specifically as nation states that small societies can claim a seat in the United Nations Organization, and claim eligibility for assistance from international agencies such as the World Bank and the International Monetary Fund (Bernal 2004, 14). The added international clout that national status would confer over merely provincial status is not lost on the people living in Quebec. It may also play a part in the insistence by political leaders of the Aboriginal peoples in Canada that their communities be recognized as *First Nations*, and that their signed treaties with Canada be recognized as having international status (Bear-Nicholas 2004). More generally, the spread of global consumer culture has proven compatible with heightened interest in the celebration of local cultures. Quebecois and Acadian nationalism both reflect these patterns, as do the revival of heritage and First Nations languages and cultures.

A stronger statement of this position, sometimes referred to as neo-conservatism, is that national sentiments, associated with a strong core of shared religious values, is essential for societal integration in the face of globalization. Strong national cultures function to promote the internalization of shared cultural values by the mass of citizens so as to promote social harmony and discourage antisocial, deviant behaviour. An essential function of political institutions—in conjunction with mass media, educational, and religious institutions—is thus the revitalization of a unifying national culture.

Canada and the United States have tended to take different positions between these two poles. Canadian political institutions have taken some steps to promote nationalism. The government-funded national radio and television networks, the Canadian Broadcasting Corporation (CBC), and the French-language equivalent, Société Radio-Canada (SRC), have an official mandate to promote Canadian national unity and to reflect bilingualism and multiculturalism. Cultural industries such as radio and television, newspapers and magazines, film and music, are explicitly protected from the free trade agreements that the Canadian government signed with the United States in 1989 and 1994 that otherwise grant American corporations the same rights as national corporations to pursue their business interests in

Canada. Federal regulations force Canadian broadcasters to include a minimum proportion of Canadian cultural content in their broadcasts. The ill-fated sponsorship program launched by the federal Liberal Party under Jean Chretien was intended to promote a federal presence at social and sporting events in Quebec after the 1995 referendum on separatism. However, these efforts have been largely perfunctory, with limited teeth or money invested in them.

In the United States, in contrast, there have been far stronger pressures to promote national unity and a swing towards fundamentalism in family and religious values. The widely predicted shift towards secularism and privatization of religious expression has not happened in contemporary American society (Berger 1999, Diamond 1998; Kintz and Lesage 1998). Nor does it hold for many Islamic societies (Esposito 2002).

The Political Economy or Marxist Perspective

The political economy perspective challenges us to think about society in very different ways from functionalist analysis, to ask different kinds of questions and to pay attention to different features of society. As you will see, this perspective gives rise to strikingly different descriptions of what matters most about Canadian society.

It is useful at the start to clarify the distinction between "conflict theory" as often described in North American sociology textbooks, and political economy theory, which has its roots in European sociology. Both fault functionalist analysis for failing to pay sufficient attention to issues of conflict, inequality, and power within social systems. Both approaches concur in emphasizing economic inequality and struggle over access to economic resources as critical features of society, and they concur also in giving more attention to power relations in the maintenance of social order. **Conflict theory** typically focuses attention on institutions within society that manage conflicts over resources, including competing political parties, trade unions, labour laws, social safety nets, and the like. **Political economy theory** pushes us to go beyond this analysis of conflict management to explore the structural features of capitalist economies that routinely produce and exacerbate the inequalities that generate the conflicts in the first place. Theoretically, what most distinguishes political economy theory from conflict theory is the exploration of structural problems or "contradictions" that are built in to the way contemporary capitalist economies function.

Karl Marx (1818–1882) is the acknowledged founder of political economy theory. Marx devoted his life's work to an analysis and critique of the social conditions he saw around him in nineteenth-century England, during the early period of industrialization. The suffering of factory workers and their families inspired him to write *Das Kapital* [Capital], a scathing critique of the economic system now known as **capitalism**. What Marx saw in industrializing Britain was not a society in equilibrium but a society riven by conflict, inequality, and turmoil. His powerful writings analyze what he saw as a long historical process through which an emerging elite of manufacturers and businessmen amassed wealth and power, particularly through colonial expansion, and came to dominate and displace the old aristocracy. Meanwhile at the bottom, masses of impoverished people, dislocated from the land, were flooding into cities to seek wage-work in the factories as their only means of survival. Marx wanted to understand how this economic order had emerged historically, how it worked, and how it might change.

Economy and Social Order

The first assumption of the political economy perspective is that the economy is the central defining feature of all societies. Political economy theory shares with functionalism the view of society as a system of interrelated institutions, but with the economy rather than culture or family as the central focus. How people collectively organize to exploit available natural resources and productive tools is the foundation that shapes all other features of society. As Marx expresses it, economy is the **base** and other societal institutions are the **superstructure**. This does not mean that the economy is all that matters. It means rather that we need to begin with the economy to fully understand the functioning of other societal institutions. For Canada and most other contemporary societies this is the global corporate capitalist economic system. Political economics analyzes political institutions, for example, from the standpoint of how they respond to and facilitate corporate profits, how they manage labour relations and defuse potential for revolt by economically disadvantaged classes of people. Legal institutions are studied for how they manage property relations, and how they function as arenas for struggle between employers and workers. Cultural institutions are analyzed for how prevailing beliefs and values reflect the interests of the dominant economic class and work to excuse and justify economic inequalities. Similar questions can be raised for all societal institutions—education, religion, family, and the like. These are qualitatively different kinds of questions from the functionalist view of meeting systemic societal needs.

Why is the economy considered so central? Marx reasoned that people must produce in order to live. People need food, shelter, and clothing in order to survive. Hence, they must organize themselves collectively to work with the aid of productive tools to transform available natural resources into products that meet their needs. The concept of economy refers to the **mode of production**—how people organize to turn resources into food—and the **relations of production**—specifically the kind of relations between people that arise through this organization.

Marx was centrally concerned with the organization of power over access to, control over, and exploitation of productive resources, and thus control over the wealth or surplus generated by human labour power. He argues that all history can be understood as the history of **class struggles**, the collective struggles of peoples subordinated within any particular system of production to overthrow that system and replace it with one that would be more productive and more widely inclusive.

Simple hunting-and-gathering economies, in which small groups of families cooperate to hunt wild animals and gather edible plants, were egalitarian in that everyone enjoyed similar access to available resources. Such economies, however, can only sustain small numbers of people at a low and uncertain standard of living. Settled agriculture, based on the domestication of cereals and beans, and herd animals for productive energy and transportation as well as for food, provided much greater scope for food production and thus sustained larger populations and more complex social organization (Diamond 1999). Inequalities emerged between elites who gained control over the productive resources of land and animals and managed the surplus produced, and the mass of people who worked the land. This feudal mode of production prevailed in Europe and much of Asia over many centuries.

The industrial revolution transformed productive potential by harnessing the mechanical energy from steam engines and later fossil fuels to drive machines. Machines made possible the mass production of goods because energy was no longer confined by the limitations of humans and animal energy. Increasing surplus production in turn promoted a population explosion, and the development of cities in which most people no longer depended on access to land for survival.

Marx saw emerging private ownership of the means of industrial production or "capital" as heralding profound changes in the organization of societies. Those who gain control over these productive resources, the capitalists, gain the capacity to generate and control enormous and potentially unlimited surplus production, while those lacking such resources have only their labour power to sell. They may be willing and ready to work, but without access to land or productive machinery they have no means to produce anything, and so must sell their capacity to work to those who control the means of production, in return for wages. Hence, Marx argues, two great classes of people emerge in capitalist societies—capitalists who own the means of production and wage-workers who do not.

In classical Marxist theory, the term **class** refers specifically to relationship to the means of production, not to income groups. Workers whose skills are scarce and in high demand by capitalists may command vastly superior incomes and standards of living than unskilled workers or those easily replaced. But when the crunch comes, they still depend on selling their labour power to capitalist employers. They still risk being laid off when corporations are downsizing.

Small business enterprises enjoy some measure of freedom from large capitalists, but they too operate under the shadow of bigger corporate capitalists. Their survival often depends directly on contracts with bigger corporations, or on the purchasing power of corporate employees' wages.

Contemporary Global Capitalism

The global character of contemporary capitalism is qualitatively different from what has gone before. With the breakdown of the Soviet-style communist economies of Eastern Europe and the gradual opening of China to a market economy, the capitalist economic form now dominates across the world. Increasingly capitalism is operating as a single global system, organized into transnational trading blocs. These economic networks are increasingly integrated into global corporations that own and manage multiple levels of the production process, linked together through computerized networks that crunch the vast inventory of information, and facilitate instantaneous communications around the globe. The global integration of national economies became starkly evident in 2008 when a crisis in the American financial system triggered massive worldwide recession.

To grasp the immensity of contemporary global corporate capitalist economic networks, it helps to focus on a few familiar consumer products and follow them through from production to purchase and consumption. Consider the blemish-free, look-alike tomatoes you may have brought home from your local supermarket (Barndt 2002). Chances are they began life in the thousands of acres of monocrop tomato greenhouses in Mexico. The seeds themselves come from transnational corporate-owned scientific plant breeding centres, where they are genetically modified to produce harder fruit with longer shelf life, often with an antifreeze gene inserted from Arctic flounder to produce fruit better able to withstand long transit times in refrigeration trucks and warehouses. Once germinated, the plants must be continually treated with chemical fertilizers, pesticides, and fungicides. Genetically identical plants are preferred to ensure that they all ripen with minimal variation in number of days and size of fruit to maximize efficient handling. When ready, workers have to pick them, sort them for ketchup, canning, or fresh fruit, pack them and douse them with ethylene gas to begin the ripening process. Then convoys of trucks drive them the 20-hour trip to the Mexican–American border where more workers inspect them, store them in corporate warehouses, and ready them for another fleet of truckers to drive them to corporate food outlets across North America. Finally, at the level of individual grocery stores, workers unpack them, display them for consumers, and check them through barcode scanners that record sales for inventory and reordering. The slice of tomato in your lunch connects you as an individual consumer with a vast network of workers, including scientists in research laboratories, chemical factories, Mexican farm labourers, truck drivers, and cashiers, and these workers in turn are connected to the bankers and finance workers that manage the flow of money that keeps this system in continual motion, the computer experts that manage the inventory, the corporations that build and manage the fleets of trucks, the warehouses, the grocery-store chains, and fast-food outlets.

If you have a cup of coffee with your tomato, this ties you in with another vast global corporate economic coffee-producing network that includes growers in coffee plantations in Central America and Africa, and the planters, pickers, packers, graders, and truckers that manage them, chemical workers who produce the styrofoam cups the coffee is served in, or the forestry-product workers that produce the paper cups and coffee filters, workers who grow and refine the sugar, farmers who supply the milk and cream, workers who produce and manage the supplies of clean drinking water that coffee is made with, and so on (Swift and Czerny 2003, Ch. 1). These integrated economic networks are so vast that it would be virtually a course in itself to analyze the entire trail in detail, and so far we have only looked at two food items. If you check the labels on your clothing, there is a high probability that you are wearing at least one piece of clothing that was made in China. With its vast labour force of ultra-cheap workers, China has become the leading country in the world for garment manufacture, from cheap Walmart versions to high-priced designer clothing. China's manufacturing economy has been growing at such a rate that economists widely predict that the economic output of the Chinese economy as a whole will rival that of the USA by the middle of the twenty-first century. During 2008–09, as the global economy lurched into severe recession under the impact of the crash of American financial institutions, China's economy was hit, but it still continued to grow. It was able to absorb some of the losses in international trade by shifting focus to its own vast markets. China now carries a large proportion of America's national debt.

This shift in manufacturing from comparatively high-waged developed economies to low-waged developing economies corresponded with structural transformations in Western European and North American labour markets from predominantly mass production and factory labour jobs to computers and electronics. Buzzwords for referring to the new economy include "the information economy," "the knowledge-driven economy," "entrepreneurial cities," "network economy," and the like (Fairclough 2003, 2). This restructuring of labour power in turn has profound implications for political and social relations. Relations between unionized labour and corporate bosses, and sources of profit or "surplus value" are also qualitatively different in "the new economy" where the dominant form of labour is professional and knowledge-based rather than manual. The income gap is growing between highly educated skilled labour and unskilled workers in developed societies.

Globally, while workers find themselves increasingly enmeshed in common networks of corporate power, they experience enormous inequalities in working conditions and material standards of living. Fluctuating coffee prices and cutthroat competition between small countries desperate to sell their primary export crop to corporate buyers may make the difference between coffee growers able to comfortably feed their families and send children to school, and near destitution. Workers in mass-production factories in China may be working on contract to middlemen suppliers for as little as 30 cents an hour, manufacturing clothes and shoes for which wealthy American consumers will pay hundreds of dollars. Migrant farm workers from Central America may be paid $1 an hour, compared with $7 minimum wages for part-time cashiers and shelf packers in Canadian grocery stores. At the top end of the salary scales, scientists and skilled workers may be earning more than $100 an hour, while chief executive officers who run large corporations can command annual incomes in salaries, stock options, and bonuses of millions of dollars annually.

Nation states in the developing world commonly lack the political clout to manage corporate investment capital or to challenge exploitative labour contracts. When corporate assets are measured against gross national products, roughly half of the top 100 economies in the world are corporations. These giant corporations are largely self-regulating economies that determine capital flows, allocation of resources, and labour across the globe. They have the power to shift investment capital and manufacturing contracts rapidly from one location to another to get the most profitable deals. Global financial markets are managed by transnational agencies like the International Monetary Fund (IMF), the World Bank, and the World Trade Organization (WTO). These developments are prompting new kinds of research into issues of how transnational institutions manage the flow of labour and international trade and investment. These new institutional forms conduct business in ways that are qualitatively different from treaties between nations. Nations no longer manage the global flow of capital, although they restrict the movement of labour (Hardt and Negri 2000, 3–10).

Environmental degradation on a global scale is another direct consequence of global capitalist production that few nation states or international regulating bodies have either the power or the will to curb. Monocrop agricultural production may be highly efficient, at least in the short term, for cheap mass production of agricultural goods, but with long-term costs such as loss of biodiversity, soil depletion, and chemical pollution. As newly developing countries strive to catch up to Western standards of living, and especially as China and the countries in the former Soviet Union embrace capitalist production, the demand for finite resources of raw materials and especially fossil fuels on world markets is accelerating, reflected in conflicts and wars fought between rival claimants for scarce resources. The ever-increasing rate of burning fossil fuels is contributing to dual phenomena of global warming and global pollution. The large majority of natural scientists the world over concur in their measurements of global warming at a pace that is melting polar ice caps, threatening to disrupt warm ocean currents that moderate northern climates, and has the potential to cause a catastrophic rise in sea-water levels sufficient to drown many coastal cities across the world. Political economists predict that such far-reaching geographic changes are likely to precipitate a collapse of our governing social institutions (Dandaneau 2001). Worst of all, scientists and business and political elites of all ideological stripes can see these processes occurring. They know in broad terms the economic practices that are producing them, but can see no economically viable way of stopping them. As Dandaneau expresses, it seems easier to destroy our planet than to change our mode of economic production.

Contradictions of Capitalism: The Paradox of Wealth and Poverty

The capitalist mode of production has proven vastly superior in generating wealth and mass consumption goods and services compared to any other way of organizing economic relations that has yet been tried. State-managed centralized industrialization under formerly communist regimes in China and the Soviet Union failed miserably in comparison, and were eventually abandoned in favour of "free market capitalism." Yet Marxist analysis of the underlying logic of industrial capitalism in nineteenth-century Europe led him to predict that, in the long run, the capitalist system would itself fail under the pressure of its own internal contradictions. Capitalist societies, he predicted, would be characterized by chronic instability and turmoil rather than equilibrium. They were destined eventually to be overthrown by a mass revolt of workers struggling against their exploitation.

Here we will sketch a brief outline of Marxist assumptions about how competition and profit motives work within the capitalist mode of production.

The first key assumption is that capitalist economies are oriented to production for profit through competition to sell products in the market. Capitalists invest in productive resources and hire labour power in order to convert raw materials into **commodities**—goods produced not for personal use, but for sale. Profits arise primarily through the gap between production costs, which include all the various raw materials, machinery, wages paid to workers, and the like, and the market value of the finished commodities.

The second assumption is that the most effective way to increase profits is to reduce labour costs by investing in labour-saving technology. Capitalists certainly strive to pay the lowest wages possible, until workers refuse to work for them, rebel, or in a closed system begin to starve. Capitalists can also strive to get the cheapest input resources possible, until no one will sell any to them. The third method of raising profits, however, is at least theoretically unrestricted—that of raising productivity through inventing labour-saving technology. Those capitalists who are first to invest in new labour-saving technology will be able to produce goods more cheaply than competitors in the market, undercut them, and so make large profits.

The third assumption follows from this. Capitalists will find themselves compelled to keep investing in the newest labour-saving, productivity-enhancing technology. It is this compulsion to keep investing and to strive unceasingly to invent new productive technologies that most explains the wealth-producing potential of capitalism. The system never stops advancing. Capitalists who become complacent will fall behind in the competition, find themselves unable to sell their more expensive products, and eventually face bankruptcy. Their employees will find themselves laid off.

This reasoning leads to a fourth assumption of the model, namely the tendency for capitalist corporations to expand in size and shrink in number. Corporations that invest successfully in labour-saving technology will make high profits and be able to invest in still better technology. They will also be in a position to buy out smaller and less efficient competitors. The global economy is now dominated by **multinational corporations** whose sales in billions of

The competitive compulsion of capitalist industries to keep on growing is threatening our global environment.

© Natural Visions / Alamy

dollars exceed the gross national products of many of the smaller nation states in which they do business. Yet no matter how large or powerful such corporations become they still cannot escape the competitive pressure to innovate further and cheapen or improve their products, or risk financial ruin. Not long ago General Motors (GM) commanded seemingly invincible dominance in the North American car markets. Yet by 2006, GM was losing market share to more fuel-efficient and lower-cost cars from Asia. By June of 2009, GM filed for bankruptcy, having lost a staggering $70 billion in two years. GM had a reported asset base of about $82 billion, but a debt of $172 billion.

Contradiction and Alienation in the Lives of Workers

What implications do these processes have for workers? Those who are employed within profitable capitalist enterprises at the cutting edge of new technology are likely to be among the more highly paid. The downside, however, is that labour-saving technology displaces workers so that high profitability can occur at the same time as competitive downsizing, rising structural unemployment, and increasing competition among workers for jobs. High unemployment in turn drives down wages as workers undercut each other to vie for limited employment options.

High unemployment predictably tends to generate crises of overproduction as purchasing power falls across the market. People may still want and need commodities but are unable to afford them. Capitalists can respond by dropping prices and thus cutting into their profit margins, cutting back production, or striving to produce cheaper goods with even less labour input. The result is recession. Eventually the economy tends to improve again as some technological breakthrough opens up new areas of production, stimulates capital investment and new employment opportunities, and thus a new period of prosperity. But in the long run the cycle will predictably repeat itself. The model predicts that capitalist economies can remain stable only by continually growing and expanding into new markets, and continually finding new sources of energy and raw materials to exploit. Even a slowdown in the rate of investment can create panic. This is the root of global environmental degradation.

The relentless cycle of competitive innovation and cost-cutting under threat of bankruptcy has serious implications for social relations between employers and employees. The model leads to the prediction that **alienation** will be widespread in capitalist societies. Alienation refers to the lived experience of structurally generated powerlessness in the face of economic forces largely beyond one's control. Work lacks meaning, relationships are shallow, and mutual obligations are limited to cash payment. Money seems to be valued over all else. The logic of capitalist relations implies that capitalists cannot afford to care too deeply about their employees or to feel obligated to them because it would impede their readiness to cut labour costs and downsize when necessary to remain competitive. Likewise, wage-workers would be unwise to commit themselves too much to their employers or their jobs when this is unlikely to be reciprocated in hard times. Caring deeply about the job one does makes little sense when products are only made for sale, and not for use and enjoyment by oneself or people one knows, and when profits from sales go only to employers, and especially if working faster and harder increases the likelihood of layoffs.

The model sketched out above is not by itself sufficient to make sweeping predictions for all circumstances. Rather, it works to highlight the contradictions inherent in capitalism and to guide research questions. Marx himself predicted that capitalist societies, characterized by sharp cleavages along class lines, would face an ever-present threat of revolt. Exploited masses, he reasoned, would always be ready to rise up and overthrow the entire capitalist system. This has clearly not yet happened, at least on the global scale that Marx once imagined. Many theorists take this as evidence that Marxist reasoning is itself flawed. Others argue that the Marxist assumptions about the inherent contradictions within capitalism are still valid, but that many factors have come into play that have so far managed to keep the system from spiralling utterly out of control. One such factor is that the predicted collapse of capitalism and the reasoning behind it are common knowledge to union leaders and business elites alike. This shared consciousness helps to stabilize the system by encouraging both sides to limit excesses of capitalist exploitation of labour, and to increase concern with legitimating capitalism as an economic system.

In any specific economic situation there are always multiple factors that influence how capitalist processes work. Here we can name just a few. The potential for innovative technology may generate new production and new demands for labour power, and so stave off crises of unemployment and overproduction. New markets may absorb excess production. Wars massively alter both the supply and the demand for certain kinds of resources and commodities. There may be local gluts and shortages of certain kinds of raw materials or labour power. Political interventions help to flatten out booms and slumps. Competing interests of locally owned businesses and those managed from headquarters outside the country or region also impact on regional capitalist economies. Research into the contemporary Canadian economy explores these processes, as we will see in later chapters.

In summary, we now have the core assumptions that underlie the political economy perspective. The organization of the economy, both in the short term and local situation and in the long term and global context, has a decisive impact on the social organization of communities and the life experiences of individual members. The capitalist economic system, by the inherent structure of how it works, generates social systems characterized by extremes of wealth and poverty at both local and global levels, and relations of power and dependence, chronic instability, alienation, and conflict.

Political Economy of Culture

This last section returns to the concept of culture to illustrate the kind of analysis generated by the political economy perspective and to contrast it with the functionalist perspective described earlier. Both perspectives share the view that culture—the prevailing system of beliefs and values—functions to promote societal integration. But they differ greatly in their understanding of how this integration works. Political economists view cultural traditions as growing out of material conditions and how people organize collectively to produce, distribute, and consume the goods and services that sustain

life. Aboriginal peoples of North America traditionally organized themselves cooperatively to live from the land through hunting, fishing, and gathering, making the technology they needed, and trading among the communities. This cooperative economic system fostered cultural values of sharing, reciprocity, and responsibility to others, and spiritual beliefs that see human beings as integrally one with the natural world. People knew that their economic survival depended on their involvement in such cooperative networks. These cultures are remembered in the stories of the people and the written records of European settlers and missionaries. Only vestiges of them survived three centuries of colonial wars with invading European traders and settlers from the early 1500s to the late 1800s (Bear-Nicholas 2004). Reservation economies have widely been reduced to dependence on welfare handouts from the Canadian federal government, fostering cultural systems that reflect fragmented identities, despair, boredom, alcoholism, and anger. Some of these communities are being drawn into the surrounding capitalist economy, establishing businesses on the reserves, and seeking off-reserve careers and wage-work. As discussed below, however, the cultural beliefs and values fostered by capitalism are so different that they threaten the very survival of Aboriginal cultures. First Nations communities across Canada are still struggling with the federal government to win land claims and treaty rights that might return their access to sufficient natural resources to make possible some restoration of communal economies.

The capitalist economic system is founded on private rather than communal ownership of productive resources. People exploit the natural world, extracting raw materials that can be manufactured into commodities for sale. The cultural values fostered by this economic system are those of domination over nature, competition, individual effort and achievement, personal consumption, and the amassing of personal wealth.

The classical Marxist theorist Antonio Gramsci developed the concept of **ideological hegemony** to explain how capitalist economic systems win consent and discourage revolt in the face of obvious inequality and instability. Ideological hegemony refers to a mode of ruling or hegemony that is based on ways of thinking that legitimate the economic order, and account for inequalities in morally justifiable ways. The capitalist system appears both reasonable and inevitable, while alternative economies, like Soviet- or Chinese-style communism, seem unworkable or worse. (Gramsci 1971; Giddens 1983, 20, 90; Nesbitt-Larking 2001, 86–88). Hence revolt seems wrong-headed, misguided, naive, and unreasonable.

Gramsci's theory reflects Marx's observation that the **dominant values** in a society are those of the dominant class. In feudal times the nobility were considered racially superior to common people, and their authority over lands delegated through the divine or God-ordained right of kings. Colonial rule was similarly justified through beliefs about racial, cultural, and technological superiority and the white man's burden to civilize more primitive peoples. The emerging class of capitalists challenged the hereditary rights of kings and nobles with new values of individual enterprise, effort, ability, and capacity to take risks, to innovate, and to succeed in a free competitive market. Those who failed to get ahead were viewed as lazy or of limited ability.

These hegemonic ideas or ways of thinking typically blame attitudes, values, and motivation, rather than economic conditions, as the cause of economic inequality. Wealthy societies generally and wealthy individuals are represented as naturally superior—either born with superior qualities or having superior cultural beliefs, values, and patterns of behaviour that result in their greater economic success. European colonizers saw themselves as bringing their more rational and superior civilization to more primitive peoples. Capitalists attribute their economic success to their superior cultural values—values of hard work, thrift, effort, ability, creativity, and the like. The poorest countries in the world appear to have clung too long to feudal communal values that stifle individual initiative, as do remaining communist countries. These countries have failed to make the adaptive cultural changes to promote scientific rationality and innovation, and individual entrepreneurial spirit that are required for capitalism to flourish. America represents the epitome of successful advanced capitalism. American cultural values are said to reward entrepreneurs, achievement, risk-taking, and Protestant individualism to a greater extent than Canadian culture, with its more communal Catholic culture (Lipset 1976, 1985; Porter 1965, 1979; Brym 1989, 28). Thus culture is said to explain why capitalism advanced more quickly and successfully in America than in Canada. Similarly, individual talents and work ethic are held to account for individual success while laziness and moral failure account for those who fall to the bottom.

Such explanations probably sound like common sense. Where they fail is that they totally ignore and obscure the entire workings of the exploitative, profit-driven capitalist economic system that we discussed above. That is what makes such ideas **ideological**. Ideologies are belief systems that function as *means not to know* and not to see what is actually going on. Hegemonic belief systems that account for structurally generated inequalities in terms of individual merit and cultural ethics, such as hard work, obscure the structural foundations of capitalism that generate the concentration of wealth, the compulsion to exploit cheap labour and raw materials on a global scale, and the investment cycles that generate chronic instability and structural unemployment that condemn masses of people to poverty.

From the political economy perspective there are more convincing structural explanations for Canada's poorer status relative to the USA. Canada has a "branch-plant" economy, dominated by corporations with their headquarters located outside the country. This means that Canadian managers have more limited opportunities for independent entrepreneurship than their American bosses. This is a reality that contributes greatly to the cultural differences observed by Lipset and others. What ruling ideas portray as natural and cultural superiority, political economy theory represents as the outcome of structural-generated advantages. Impoverished Third World countries face immensely greater structural disadvantages than does Canada.

Global Corporate Culture

The new world order of global corporate capitalism with almost instantaneous global communications is transforming cultures around the world. This does not necessarily mean the end of cultural diversity. Diversity may actually be good for business—opening new marketing opportunities. Advertisers support channels that appeal to specialized niche audiences because they can better target their message. Global media outlets typically modify content to appeal to local audiences, and local producers are generating more indigenous programming, in non-Western languages (Vivian and Maurin 2009, 296–298). However, much of this "new" programming still imitates cheap North American soaps, talk shows and "reality" shows. The dominant values promoted by corporate mass media around the world still project capitalism as the only viable and legitimate mode of economic organization. These values are framed in the moral language of free markets, and individual freedom and initiative (Fairclough 2003). Capitalists everywhere promote what Sklair (2002, 36) calls the "culture and ideology of consumerism." People are encouraged to identify the good life with commodities they can buy, these products pushed incessantly with advertising. What consumerism as ideology obscures from view is the appalling costs incurred in global plunder of natural resources, environmental degradation, pollution, global warming, and the exploitation of sweatshop labour by transnational corporations driven to squeeze costs and maximize shareholder profits (Klein 2000).

Images of popular culture and traditions around the world are routinely harnessed by advertisers to sell their brand-name products. The gap between advertising and culture is becoming increasingly blurred, Klein argues (Klein 2000, Ch. 3), as transnational corporations shift from sponsoring cultural events to actually buying artists and staging events, where the main point is to advertise brands. Television stations like MTV are 24-hour advertising channels, packed with giveaways, contests, awards ceremonies, and the like, featuring luxury products. Teenagers are hired to report back on "what's cool" so that these images can be built into advertising for such brand-name products as Nike sneakers and Hilfiger clothes. Truckloads of sneakers and sports clothes are dumped on playgrounds in black-American ghetto areas so that they can be seen "on the right people" to impress teenagers. Rebellious teenage countercultures are readily incorporated into product marketing images. Hip hop and gangsta rap that originated among disaffected American black youth rapidly became commodified for middle-class music buyers (Brym 2008). Radio stations won advertising back from television by featuring the incessant rotation of top-40 music hits (Vivian and Maurin 2009, 82). Teenagers around the world are incited to identify with the North American "teen image" and the consumer products that go with it. Younger and younger children are targeted as consumers, incited to pressure their parents to buy such products as the Big Mac with the latest Disney toy. Klein laments that there is almost no public space left in North America that is not saturated with advertising. Social networking sites like MySpace and Facebook are currently valued in the billions of dollars precisely because advertisers buy space. In 2009, a Russian businessman bought a 2-percent holding in Facebook for $20 million (*The Globe and Mail*, 27 May 2009, B1, 6). The estimated value of Google is about $22 billion. Top advertising agencies themselves are global corporations worth billions of dollars (Vivian and Maurin 2009, 189). They exercise tremendous veto power over media content. Any mass media channels, including Internet sites, that fail to attract advertisers will not survive.

The distinction between economic *base* and cultural superstructure that we discussed above is increasingly hard to draw in the contemporary knowledge-based economy. Knowledge and intellectual products are themselves becoming commodities for sale in global markets (Hardt and Negri 2000, 32). Management theories, for example, and the "social science" of business administration, are commodified—packaged as textbooks and courses for sale in global education markets. Corporate media giants sell culture to global audiences in the form of entertainment and news. These intellectual commodities affect us at very deep levels, influencing how we think about our self-identity and our relations with other people. They have the potential to profoundly influence spiritual awareness of what it means to be human.

Contemporary artistic culture in the era of corporate culture-for-profit is at risk of shifting from "creative" to "permissive" mode as corporations exploit copyright laws to stifle spin-off creative productions that draw from existing content (Lessig 2004). Historically, artists such as Walt Disney drew extensively from sources like the Brothers Grimm fairy tales and Buster Keaton's silent films like *Steamboat Bill* (Lessig 2004, 19), but no one can draw inspiration from Disney characters without first getting permission from the corporate juggernaut that owns Disney, and

paying hefty fees. Historically, creative productions passed into the public domain after 14 to 28 years, but the recent iteration of American copyright laws extended control for 95 years. Future artists cannot draw even short clips from old movies to create a new collage, even if the copyright owners, or their estates, cannot be found, without risking a multi-million-dollar lawsuit. One enterprising kid hacked into the DOS codes for Sony's Aibo dog, wrote a sub-program to make the dog dance to jazz, and posted it on the web for others to enjoy. Sony threatened him with a multi-million-dollar lawsuit for compromising their copyright (Lessig 2004, 154–156). Internet and digital file-sharing technology make available to everyone a potentially limitless archive of creative culture in all forms, but profit-driven copyright laws are stifling access to it.

In conclusion, the political economy perspective promotes a particular kind of research that strives to bring to light features of capitalist economic relations as the foundations of contemporary society—national, regional, and global. The perspective prompts research questions that would not arise from the functionalist perspective. Indeed, some political economists argue that the traditional functionalist perspective is itself a form of ruling ideology in that it functions to obscure deeply exploitative structures that underpin society, and thus helps to sustain them.

 # Social Constructionist Perspectives

Social constructionist perspectives begin from the core assumption that all social action is inherently meaningful. People reflect on situations and interactions and form subjective interpretations or understandings of what is going on. These subjective understandings guide how we respond. Unlike functionalist analysis, social constructionist analysis does not assume that shared meanings are given or fixed by preexisting cultural **norms**. Instead people are seen as continually working up a sense of shared meanings—negotiating, constructing, sustaining, or abandoning tentative definitions of situations as we interact with each other. Any sense we may have that social relations are orderly and meaningful, rather than chaotic and meaningless, depends on the work we do continually to actively sustain and communicate this shared sense of order and meaning. From this broad perspective, the work of doing sociology is itself meaning-constructing work. Any sense we have of "society" as an orderly social system is thus seen as a *result* of such meaning-construction work. Society is never simply "out there" to be studied in the way that biologists study organic systems. Rather, it comprises systems of shared meanings that we continually work up and shape through our reactions to them.

Essentially, what you are being asked to do here is explore how you and others you interact with make sense of social relations. We can ask this question at roughly three levels of complexity. First, we can explore what are the subjective meanings or definitions of situations that different individuals use to guide their responses to social situations. We know that how people see a situation affects how they respond. You are likely to feel and respond very differently if you think someone spilt coffee on you accidentally or if you think it was done deliberately. A second level of questioning is more difficult. How do individuals come up with definitions of situations? What kinds of reasoning processes or "sense-making practices" do individuals use in order to come up with their definition of the situation as accidental or deliberate? The third level of questioning is the most complex: How are authoritative definitions of social situations worked up? These are definitions of situations that large numbers of people in very different times and places are willing to accept as correct and use to guide their behaviour. Courts of law, for example, determine the conditions and limits of legal liability for injuries incurred from spilt coffee. The first level of questioning is associated with the approach of **symbolic interactionism**, the second with **ethnomethodology**, and the third with **institutional ethnography**. We will add some further distinctions to these three broad categories or groups below as we flesh them out in more detail.

Symbolic Interactionism

Symbolic interactionism explores the subjective meanings or "definitions of the situation" that guide how people respond to situations. The core research assumption of this approach is that people experience social interaction as meaningful. We respond to situations in terms of their subjective meanings for us rather than unthinking or instinctual responses to stimuli. This assumption is captured by the classic concept of "definition of the situation." If we differ in our definition of a situation then, predictably, our reactions will differ. This is because subjectively we are not responding to the same situation.

An example of this is a short story by Averchenko (Bonner 1994, 225) in which the "**facts**" are that one man hits another on the head with a brick after he was approached with a request to light a cigarette. As the man tells the story, he reacted with the brick because he saw the request for a light as a set-up for a robbery. His wife, however, saw what happened as a jealous reaction to attention that the other man was paying to her. The "victim" later describes himself as having been attacked by a lunatic. A newspaper account describes paramedics being called to pick up a drunken man who had fallen and cracked his head on a brick. The role of the sociologist as observer, Bonner

suggests, is not simply to add a fifth perspective to the story, but to facilitate the dialogue that makes possible a shared and mutual understanding of diverse interpretations of the stream of events. It is thus a critical and ethical endeavour. As sociologists we are not free to interpret the world whatever way we want, because we are constrained to continually test our assumptions against the resistance that others give when they talk back. Knowledge develops not by the "discovery" method in which we amass objective facts about an external reality, but by inquiry into the life-worlds and interpretive understandings that people bring to their social lives (Bonner 2001).

Symbolic interactionism draws attention to the symbolism that people use when giving accounts of events that shape our sense of what is happening and therefore what an appropriate response might be. Consider the debate that took place early in 2003 among government leaders around the world on whether to support the American-led proposal to use armed force to depose the government of Saddam Hussein in Iraq. The symbolism of "weapons of mass destruction" proved pivotal. Those who saw the situation as involving a brutal dictator who was amassing weapons of mass destruction in blatant defiance of United Nations sanctions, and with the intent of launching terrorist attacks against Israel and the United States, were predisposed to use force. Such a scenario was particularly convincing for those people already predisposed to view the world as a dangerous place and their communities as vulnerable to terrorism. Contrasting definitions of the situation, portraying Saddam Hussein as essentially contained and powerless, and the Americans as more concerned with controlling oil supplies than worried about weapons, militated against support for armed intervention. Intelligence reports of mobile weapons factories, backed by grainy video evidence of truck convoys, proved unconvincing.

The Rodney King trial in Los Angeles in 1992 gives another example of how people with different definitions of the situation at hand can interpret the same evidence in sharply different ways. The trial focused on a home video that masses of Americans who viewed it on television interpreted as showing racist white police officers beating a helpless black man. Jurors for the trial, however, interpreted the same video as consistent with the defence lawyer's account of Rodney King himself as behaving violently towards the police and so instigating the police response. The lawyer's account was consistent with other views widely held among jurors that associate black males in general with criminal behaviour and police as generally upholding law and order (Lewis 2001, 29). The Dziekanski inquiry in Canada in 2009 devoted weeks to listening to a litany of witnesses and experts debating what a nine-minute amateur video did or did not reveal about the circumstances in which police

Tasered Polish immigrant Robert Dziekanski before he died at the Vancouver airport on 14 November 2007. These examples draw attention to the symbolism embedded in descriptions that shape people's sense of what is happening and thereby what constitutes an appropriate response.

Labelling theory is a branch of symbolic interactionism that explores how public labelling generates a spiral of reactions. People respond to how they feel themselves judged and labelled by others, and in turn judge and respond to others in terms of how these others are socially labelled. Much of the research from this perspective has focused on micro-level interactions, exploring such issues as how judgments by parents and teachers influence the **self** concept and behaviour of children. Labelling theory is less concerned with the accuracy of the labels than with their impact, particularly in the possibility of self-fulfilling prophesies, as individuals feel pressured to conform to the public labels. Public labels tend to promote a spiral of action and reaction. People labelled as "deviant" may find themselves subject to ostracism and distrust and react to such treatment with anger and withdrawal, which reinforces the original deviant label. Stigmatized people may gravitate towards other similarly marginalized people, and so promote the sharing of deviant subcultural norms and behaviour. Favourable labelling, on the other hand, may prompt a positive spiral of action and reaction.

Internet sites like YouTube and MySpace have become the new public space in which reputations can be smirched or enhanced, but with the critically important difference that the social circle within which gossip circulates can rapidly expand to millions of viewers. An irate traveller in South Korea took a quick cellphone-camera image of a young woman who refused to clean up after her small dog pooped on the train. The image was posted on a popular blog, copied again onto an American blog, and then went global with 10 million viewers watching it in one month. The young woman was so widely shamed and embarrassed that she dropped out of university (Solove 2007, 1–2). In a similar incident, an American student sent a message to someone who listed Hinduism as an interest in his online profile, offering him money to write a five-page paper for her on the subject (Solove 2007, 76). He wrote a blog naming the student and his plan to write an essay with silly errors to punish her for plagiarism. The blog attracted attention and hundreds of comments, and soon became Internet-wide.

At the macro level entire groups and classes of people, and even entire societies, find themselves subject to the gaze of "others" who have the power to impose labels and to act upon them. Edward Said (1978) analyzes how the concept of "oriental" is largely a figment of Western colonial construction, but nonetheless extremely powerful in the political

representation of cultures and peoples geographically positioned to the south and east of Europe. Historically, research and writings produced by European colonizers dominated international scholarship and commanded more respect than non-Western research. As a result, scholars from Asia frequently find they need to travel to England to consult library sources on the history of their own societies. The characterization of Islamic societies by Western commentators and government leaders, often in painfully simplistic and derogatory ways, functions as a foil against which representatives of diverse Islamic societies struggle to redefine their nations in the global arena. People of Islamic cultural origin living in Western societies struggle similarly to portray a positive sense of themselves in the face of negative stereotypes. This was especially difficult in the strained political climate following the 11 September 2001 attack on New York, when the terms "Islamic" and "terrorist" were often juxtaposed in media summations of international conflict.

Lewis's studies of public opinion polls in the USA show how powerfully such generalized negative labelling works to influence electoral support for federal government policy initiatives on domestic and international issues. The term "welfare" refers to government income assistance for people without other financial resources, but the term carries a negative stigma that predisposes people to assume the worst on virtually any issue with which the term "welfare" is linked. Lewis reveals the extent of this stigma by asking students to estimate the average number of children that mothers receiving welfare have. Students wildly overestimated the correct average of less than two (Lewis 2001, 126). Students were also wildly inaccurate, although in predictable directions, in guessing the characteristics of foreign governments known to be allies or opponents of American foreign policy. Allies were assumed to be democracies and opponents dictatorships; allies were assumed to have exemplary human rights records and opponents bad records; opponents were assumed to endorse drug-trafficking while allies were clean, and so on (Lewis 2001, 130–134), These positive and negative associations were assumed with minimal reference to factual evidence, and they fostered easy support for aggressive government policies that targeted welfare recipients and stigmatized foreign governments.

The **dramaturgical model** is another branch of symbolic interactionism that explores how people actively present themselves to influence how others see them. Erving Goffman is particularly remembered for his use of drama and theatrical performance as a model for analyzing social interaction. Nowadays, people often post photos and video clips of themselves on social networking sites like Facebook to attract and impress their friends. Rather than viewing roles as predefined expectations, Goffman draws attention to how much freedom actors enjoy to negotiate their role performances. The bare outlines of role expectations may be culturally defined, but the details are not. Also, many social interactions involve informal encounters that do not take the form of predefined roles at all. Research in this tradition focuses on how people as actors in a social situation give and give off impressions through body language, how they strive to influence how others perceive them, how they take cues from each other, how they collude together to create scenes, how they use clothing and other props to manage images and to convey feelings like surprise, anger, hurt, pleasure, and so on. In multiple studies of informal interaction, Goffman illustrates the practices of secrecy, deference, and demeanour, team work, backstage collusions, and consensual performances before potentially critical audiences that characterize these encounters.

We live in an era where our primary means of appraising political leaders and candidates is through watching them on television. In politics it is widely claimed that having a television presence can make or break the electoral chances of candidates. An entire industry has grown up around *public relations* or "PR" with experts managing the television appearance of senior politicians and other public figures. Appearances by Canadian Prime Minister Stephen Harper and opposition leader Michael Ignatieff are carefully staged. A notable example of political theatre was former American president George W. Bush's Address to the Nation on 1 May 2003 to declare active fighting in Iraq. In the morning the president appeared in suit and tie, head bowed in prayer to lead the national day of prayer. In the evening he appeared wearing battle fatigues and carrying a helmet, on the deck of an aircraft carrier, with a backdrop of American flags, guns, fighter jets, and 5000 soldiers. The juxtaposition of religion and military power filled the newspapers the following day.

Such presentations require extensive backstage management and collusion by a team of workers. As in the theatre, this work has to remain hidden. Exposing the backstage carries the risk that one may undermine the credibility of the frontstage performance, Unlike the theatre, however, journalists and politicians from rival parties have vested interests in bringing about precisely such damaging exposure. Careers can be threatened by unguarded comments made "while the microphone is still running," or when an onlooker catches a gaffe on a cellphone camera and posts it on a blog site. Young people who post racy images of themselves on social networking websites are frequently mortified to learn that potential future employers often search the web for backstage information about job applicants.

Cassin (1979, 1980) draws on Goffman's notion of flawed performance to suggest a partial explanation for why women generally do not advance as rapidly as men in public

service. Men, she suggests, learn through conversation and socializing with senior managers how to present themselves as "ready for promotion." Her research shows how officials in junior government posts learned how to talk about the policy relevance of any work they were engaged in, without having to be prompted. In contrast, junior women were more likely to discuss technical details of their work, not connecting this to matters of policy unless specifically asked to do so. Women socialized less frequently with their all-male senior managers, and hence had less chance to learn how to talk the managerial talk in performance appraisals.

Ethnomethodology

Ethnomethodology begins from the same assumption as symbolic interactionism, namely that individuals respond to situations in terms of their subjective understanding of what seems to be going on. But it raises more complicated subsidiary questions: How do people generate subjective definitions of situations? How do people actively work at making interaction meaningful? How do we reason ourselves through routine everyday situations to achieve and maintain some sense of meaningful order?

The term "ethnomethodology" is derived from the Greek word for people, *ethno*, plus methods. It refers to the study of people's methods of reasoning, which they use to make sense of social situations. The perspective emerged in the 1960s as a response to nagging questions raised by functionalist and symbolic interactionist perspectives. The challenge that Psathas (1980) raises with respect to Goffman's work is that while he gives us wonderfully insightful descriptions of face-to-face interactions, he fails to show us, methodologically, how he comes up with his interpretations. Goffman imputes intentions to the actors he watches. He presumes to know what Actor A thinks about Actor B, and vice versa, but what Actors A and B are really thinking is not observable. Goffman does not stop the interaction in process to ask each actor to explicate in words precisely what each is thinking. Goffman must guess the thoughts and intentions of the actors from subtleties of the interaction.

In everyday interaction, when we discuss the motives that people might have for particular actions, we are effectively engaged in the work of producing a meaningful world, and producing our sense of being able to understand other people as acting in terms of motives (Bonner 2001, 273). This kind of "motive talk," Bonner argues, has distinctive rules or grammar. For it to be considered adequate, and not merely chatter, it must meaningfully connect the stream of events with reactions. Ethnomethodological research explores these reasoning processes. It studies how actors and observers in any social situation come to a collective under-

Women are nowhere equally represented in offices and roles in society where political, economic, and cultural power are wielded.

THE CANADIAN PRESS/Sean Kilpatrick

standing of what is going on, including how they draw inferences about the thoughts and intentions of others and orient themselves to these meanings.

Harold Garfinkel (1967) is recognized as the true founder of ethnomethodology. He studied the functionalist perspective as a graduate sociology student and began to question the explanatory value of the concept of learned role expectations in predicting behaviour in social situations. Something important seems to be missing from the explanation. How do people come to know, and to know in common, what "roles" are going on, and therefore which role expectations appropriately apply? Consider first the deceptively simple example Boughey (1978) gives of what he labels "cards night at a church." Commonplace expectations around the activity of card-playing might involve raucous laughter, back-slapping, competitive play, and the like, while expectations around church involve quiet, respectful behaviour. The question Boughey raises is: How do we decide which set of expectations to apply when the two activities merge—we are playing cards, but in a church? In Boughey's example much negotiating goes on among the participants. Men at one table engage in loud laughter but a woman at another table shushes them with the comment, "This is church, you know." The men retort, "Nah, but this is cards!" The central point Boughey is trying to get across here is that the participants cannot know in advance which set of predefined role expectations is going to govern the evening's interaction. Who is going to win this little battle for social control, and just how is it that their preferred definition comes to prevail? After the evening is over, functionalist analysis of role expectations can be fitted to the scene, but not before it happens. Boughey's further point is that people are not just playing their roles. They are actively negotiating them, sustaining or abandoning them as the evening wears on.

When people enter Internet discussion sites to post streams of comments and countercomments on current events that catch their attention, they are similarly involved in an interactive process of constructing meaning, testing whether others embellish or dismiss their views. Opinions can gradually become fixed and exaggerated through gossip, both on- and off-line, as individuals find others who support their view of events.

Boughey's example of card players in church is a simple one where only two options are presented. Many social situations potentially involve far more than two options, and the stakes are much higher. Consider the complexity of role relations referred to above in interaction between junior male and female employees and more senior management. Participants' sense of what is going on can shift from minute to minute. What begins as an informal, friendly conversation or having a beer together may shift suddenly into a mentoring session as a senior manager coaches juniors in how to present themselves properly and what is important to know. The conversation can simultaneously include a covert evaluation of a junior colleague's management potential, a set-up to glean information, and a chance to make an impression or to gain favours. Those who are less adept at reading and manipulating these complex role interactions are less likely to climb the corporate ladder.

In everyday interaction we are continually involved in making judgments about meaning that have far-reaching consequences for our lives. Susan Kreiger (1997, 196) describes her struggle to figure out the meaning behind how some students in a sociology class were responding to her. What did it mean when they seemed to avoid looking directly at her, or when they had trouble talking about the content of a text on lesbians? Was she a bad teacher, or was she feeling distant from the students, or did students simply find the material boring—or in retrospect, were they feeling afraid of her because they suspected she was a lesbian, or because they knew she had denied permission to a male graduate student to take her feminist research seminar the previous year and were punishing her? In her article she speaks of the nuances, the clues, the history of individually tiny signals that she believes add up to the invisible presence of homophobia that she senses without it being voiced.

Canadians have legal protection under the Human Rights Act, the Canadian Charter of Rights and Freedoms, and many union contracts, from discrimination on the basis of such characteristics as sex, race, religion, and disabilities, and more recently also sexual orientation. The central problem facing all the people involved in such cases is determining the *meaning* of the hurtful actions that have occurred. To gain legal redress the victims must prove beyond reasonable doubt that what they experienced as hurtful actions were instances of sexism, racism, or homophobia.

Defendants, however, invariably argue that their behaviour was not discriminatory but based on legitimate and reasoned grounds. Was Susan Kreiger wrongly denied a permanent teaching position because of homophobia, or because she rebuffed the sexual advances of a senior male colleague? Or was she legitimately passed over because her teaching or her scholarship were of poorer quality than another candidate, or because she was an abrasive, dysfunctional colleague? How do jurors decide?

Breaching experiments are a methodology widely used within ethnomethodological research. It involves deliberately violating common-sense expectations for behaviour in given situations, to expose patterns of common-sense reasoning, and how people respond when such reasoning is upset. The goal is to explore the common-sense knowledge that governs normal interaction, the tacit or seen-but-not-noticed rules of orderly relations that we competently use to negotiate our way through everyday activities. To do such research, sociologists must learn to suspend the **natural attitude**, to let go of the assumption that it is obvious what is going on, and to ask how is it that we, as competent members of our culture, know what is going on and what to do. Garfinkel devised the research method of breaching experimentsto make visible the tacit rules governing some everyday behaviour by deliberately disrupting them (1967, 41–49). Students in his classes were instructed to select some simple everyday interaction, like exchanging greetings or getting on a bus, to act briefly in a way that contravened some tacitly expected behaviour in that situation, and report on how other people reacted. Students were amazed at how upset and angry people became when these small episodes of social order were disrupted. Garfinkel suggests that people became angry because an unspoken but powerful moral obligation was being violated—the obligation people have to mutually sustain meaningful social interaction.

Garfinkel also set up an experiment where students received random yes or no answers to a series of questions they asked in what they thought was a social-work counselling session. Students readily made coherent sense out of these meaningless random answers. The experiment reveals how the students reasoned their way through this objectively meaningless exchange. They assumed without question that all conversation is intended to be meaningful, and they felt morally obligated to work at making the counsellor's comments make sense. Ethnomethodologists argue that this taken-for-granted work of making sense is the foundation of all social order.

Breaching experiments do not only happen in research laboratories. Giddens discusses how rebellious working-class boys in a school in England deliberately breached tacit rules of interaction to undermine the authority of their teachers. They conspired together to pretend not to hear or to understand anything their teacher said: "'Let's send him to Coventry when he comes,' 'Let's laugh at everything he says,' 'Let's pretend we can't understand and say, "How do you mean?" all the time.'"(Giddens 1984, 291, citing Willis 1981).

Lewis (2001, 185) uses trick survey questions in a similar way to Garfinkel's breaching experiment, to explore people's commonsense methods of reasoning in deciding how to vote in elections. One question asked American university students to identify whether Presidents Bush (Republican) or Clinton (Democrat) proposed a series of federal government policies. The vast majority relied on the informational shortcut of associating right-wing policies (pro-business, law-and-order agenda) with Republican and left-wing policies (pro-labour, social services agenda) with Democrats. Only between 3 to 5 percent of students correctly answered or guessed that the two presidents took the same stand on all issues—both supporting right-wing policies and neither supporting left-wing policies. A series of similar questions show how pervasively students rely on abstract **background understandings**, or what Schutz would call "**recipe knowledge**," to make sense of political affairs, and hence how readily they could be swayed by political slogans.

Conversation analysis or CA is a branch of ethnomethodology that focuses research attention on people's methods of regulating normal conversation. It enjoins researchers to suspend the natural attitude that it is obvious how people manage to talk, and to explore the tacit known-but-not-mentioned background understandings that make talk manageable. The central interest is with *how* talk is managed, not with linguistics or subject matter. The management of conversations both reflects and reinforces social inequality, with topics raised by subordinates less likely to be taken up by the next speaker, their turns more frequently interrupted, and their contributions more frequently qualified as questions (Isn't it? Don't you think?) than asserted as fact.

A central assumption of this perspective is that talk is *indexical*. An index in a book refers to subjects and information that are discussed elsewhere in the book but not in the index itself. Phrases used in a conversation similarly refer to background knowledge that participants are expected to have but that is not elaborated in the conversation under way. It follows then that the meaning of talk is not self-evident, but embedded in the background understandings that participants bring to it. Every conversation balances the risk that participants may not fully understand these unspoken referents and so not fully understand the talk, against the counter risk that an attempt to clarify every reference in every sentence of a talk would result in infinite regress.

Consider the following conversation between two people:

A: I have a child.

B: That's okay.

A: I also have a dog.

B: Oh, I'm sorry.

An outsider to this conversation might well find the exchange nonsensical, but to participants who know that A is a prospective tenant and B a prospective landlord it is readily understandable. We know that many landlords place restrictions on people to whom they rent premises, often prohibiting pets, and sometimes children. The two parties to this talk do not need to refer openly to this background knowledge because both assume that they both know it. If A does not know this background information, then the response "Oh I'm sorry" would make no sense and might prompt the question "What do you mean—you're sorry I have a dog?" There is also much more background knowledge that may be pertinent to the conversation. One participant may know that there are some municipalities in Canada that do not permit commercial landlords to discriminate against people with children or pets. Such information will colour how A's comments and B's responses are heard. The actors may also be expected to know that race is not a legally permissible ground for landlords in Canada to discriminate against prospective tenants so that reference to having a child will be heard differently from reference to being black. None of this background knowledge is explicitly mentioned in the brief exchange quoted above. What has been said is quite sufficient for both actors to know, and to know in common, that A will not be renting accommodation from B.

Conversation analysis at the macro societal level explores how the management of talk is centrally involved in political influence, particularly in the contexts of public debates, media interviews, and the like. The inherent indexicality of talk means that there will always be some vagueness with respect to what key terms in discussions actually refer to, and such vagueness is amplified when people talk in abstractions like "efficiency," "enterprise," or "left-wing" versus "right-wing." Vagueness allows for much leeway in interpreting and manipulating meanings. Conversation analysis tends to go into hyper-drive in mass media during election campaigns as professional commentators are hired to dissect stump speeches by candidates to pull every nuance of meaning from turns of phrase, and amateur bloggers hit their favourite websites to post their interpretations. Lewis (2001, 136) describes how questions used in public opinion polls are commonly so vague that people with widely differing views give affirmative answers. Pollsters and their corporate or government clients can then impose their own interpretation on the question when citing poll results to claim that respondents support a favoured policy alternative.

Institutional Ethnography

Institutional ethnography explores sense-making practices at the level of large-scale organizational settings where multiple participants are involved, and where most do not normally know each other, or ever interact directly (DeVault and McCoy 2002, 752). The central question is how are common understandings generated and sustained simultaneously in many different work sites that work to regulate and coordinate activities?

Within advanced industrial societies such as Canada, the meaning-construction work engaged in by people within formal organizations is particularly significant in generating shared meanings that guide behaviour over widely disparate work sites. This commonly involves the use of standardized forms and procedures to manage social interactions. People also draw upon the authority of professional training and status to claim expertise on which to legitimate and sustain authoritative definitions of situations. These professional ways of framing situations structure policies that become built into standardized procedures. Hence, the study of work practices by professionals in these organizational sites is central to the understanding of the social construction of power relations or *relations of ruling*.

Research in institutional ethnography typically begins with the experiences of an individual worker in a particular work site. The goal is to trace in meticulous detail the chains of activities that tie this work site to others. Typically, there are networks of **texts**, and particularly procedural manuals and standardized forms, files, and records that workers must complete at one work site and transmit to another. These are analyzed as critical mechanisms that generate common and authoritative definitions of situations for workers in multiple sites of activity. Research focuses on the indexical character of such texts, exploring how workers make sense of them, and how they condense the complex realities of people's lives into predefined categories. To do this categorizing, workers have to select, highlight, ignore, and discard masses of jumbled information about individual lives to produce what will be officially recognized as "knowledge" for practical purposes.

A key assumption of institutional ethnography is that these routine work practices, coordinated through networks of texts, are central to relations of ruling—that is, to the exercise of power and authority in contemporary society. Networks of standardized texts make it possible for officials at distant centres of power to exert detailed regulation over the activities of individual workers at a multitude of disparate local work sites. Managers within giant multinational corporations increasingly rely on electronic information networks to coordinate productive activities across the globe. Knowledge-workers, or professionals of all kinds, accomplish these power relations. They construct and disseminate most of the information on which others rely to make sense of what is going on in the world. In effect, they *produce* the culturally sanctioned appearance of social reality as most of us come to know and interpret it.

From this perspective, power and knowledge are inseparably connected (Foucault 1980). Knowledge-workers command authority based on their expertise to interpret "the facts of the matter," which then becomes the basis for administrators, corrections officers, social workers, and others to take action. The power wielded by experts works through persuasion rather than coercion. People who reject expert advice can readily be discredited as unreasonable. Political struggles of all kinds commonly involve struggles over meaning as subordinate groups challenge official ways of framing experience and try to propose alternatives. These struggles are variously referred to in literature as "reality-defining contests" (Loseke 1987, 235), "contestations over naming" (McKendy 1992, 60), or "the politics of interpretation" (Denzin 1992). One example is the struggle by the women's movement of the 1970s to reframe the issue of "family conflict" as "wife battery" to identify the underlying problem as one of male dominance rather than interpersonal frictions (Walker 1990a, 1990b). Successful shifts in representation mandate different courses of action. A "family conflict" frame promotes family counselling as the preferred solution while the "wife battery" frame promotes funding for transition houses for women and criminal prosecution for perpetrators. Environmentalists have similarly challenged the prevailing scientific representation of nuclear energy as clean, efficient, and safe (Clow 1993) in the hope of promoting different policy options around energy production and use.

Discourse analysis explores how people draw upon professional training to legitimate and sustain authoritative definitions of situations that work to determine policies, and to coordinate responses in multiple disparate sites of interaction. Professional discourses constitute part of the networks of power/knowledge through which relations of ruling work. Critical discourse analysis focuses research attention on how professionals frame issues and the relations of power embedded within these frames. Historical studies trace the links between shifts in scientific and professional discourses and shifts in cultural practices and state policies and legislation. Michel Foucault's work is famous for analyzing how shifts in knowledge claims within the disciplines of law, medicine, psychology, and psychiatry have impacted on the social labelling and treatment of behaviour associated with deviance, sexuality, child-rearing, schooling, and the like (1977; 1978). Other studies in the sociology of knowledge explore the influence of mass media in spreading particular representations or definitions of events, and how

different audiences draw upon these representations in making sense of their personal experiences.

This view of knowledge as socially constructed does not reduce material existence to interpretation, nor reduce fact to opinion, but it does assert that the lines between them are difficult to draw. The key distinction between facts and opinions is that facts are subject to verification by evidence, while opinions are not. However, while material evidence may be factual, the categories in terms of which we think about evidence, what we selectively notice or ignore, and how it becomes meaningful to us, are socially constructed, and what we believe about factual evidence strongly influences our opinions. A powerful illustration of this mixing of fact, categories of thought, and opinion, is evident in what people generally know and think about income-assistance policies, better known as welfare (Lewis (2001, 15). The question: "How large was the Canadian federal welfare budget in 2002?" appears to be a question for which there is a clear factual answer—"$ X-billion." But what is included and excluded from this amount—handouts to the poor, or salaries for the vast bureaucracy that administers welfare? And how large is this amount with respect to what? As an unqualified statement set by itself the amount may appear huge, but as a proportion of gross national product, or of all government expenditures, or in comparison with government assistance to industry, or to the military or civil servants' pensions, or comparable expenditures by governments in other developed countries, it appears much smaller. Stated as monthly income on which a welfare recipient must survive, compared with the cost of necessities like shelter, food, clothing, school supplies, bus fares, and the like, the amount appears minuscule.

What matters, Lewis argues, is not so much what we know as what we think we know, and *how* we know it. Facts never come to us devoid of interpretive framing, Pure factoids devoid of any context are the most ambiguous and misleading of all. Most of what we know about our society beyond immediate personal experience, and especially at the levels of national and international affairs, comes to us second hand through texts—in the forms of mass media reports on TV, radio, magazines, films, websites, and the like. We can think about such issues only through informational frames or representations that others have worked up.

Seen in this way, evidence of cultural differences between the USA and Canada, as reflected in opinion polls, can be traced to sharply differing informational climates rather than to fundamental differences at the level of personalities. Mass campaigns in corporate-owned media against welfare fraud and waste, and against incompetence and meddling of big government, are predictably reflected in subsequent opinion polls measuring widespread public support for welfare cuts and for private enterprise over big government running things. However, if questions are worded very differently, in terms of support for low-income people, and for a public medical insurance scheme, measured responses are highly favourable (Lewis 2001, Ch. 5). The responses are not self-contradictory, Lewis argues. Rather, the questions trigger very different indexical meanings and tap into different informational frames. As noted above, the government and corporate sponsors commissioning the polls have the power to select the interpretive schemes most conducive to their preferred policy options, should they choose to publicize results. Sharply differing public opinions in the USA and Canada in support or opposition to the armed invasion of Iraq in March 2003 also coincided with sharply differing informational framing of the issues in government and media representations.

In summary, the core assumption that underlies all the perspectives included under social constructionism is that social reality comprises meaningful interaction. People reflect on situations and interactions to form subjective interpretations of what is going on, and guide their responses accordingly. All social life, including relations of authority, power, and control, are constructed, negotiated, sustained, or demolished through meaning-making work. Hence, the central focus of social constructionist analysis is on these subjective meanings, how and why they emerge as they do.

Culture and Identity as Social Constructions

The analysis of culture from the social constructionist perspective is strikingly different from the functionalist and political economy approaches. Instead of trying to describe culture, social constructionism explores how people continually generate, negotiate, sustain, and challenge cultural meanings. Culture is thus an ongoing accomplishment, not some fixed body of beliefs and customs that can be described.

We live in an era of instantaneous and interactive communication where anyone with access to a computer with an Internet connection can post opinions, and all manner of creative productions, to share with others. People have always come together informally to make music, share poetry, and the like. Digital technology combined with the Internet now makes it possible for individuals to participate in what Lessig (2004) terms a creative commons. With relatively low-cost equipment, amateur bands playing in someone's garage can record their music and post it on the web. Sometimes, if they are talented and lucky, this can lead to more professional gigs. Visual artists can display their work without having to buy or compete for space in a gallery, people can post their home movies on YouTube and create links to other sites to invite audiences to view their work. Lessig's

vision is to promote a creative commons in which people are free to copy and use, or to "rip, mix and burn" (Lessig 2004, 203), anything they find on the Internet in a creative free-for-all, so long as what they create is not intended for commercial, profit-motivated use, and they in turn are willing to permit others to borrow from what they create and post on the web. Lessig himself has created a video lecture series that is available for anyone to download and use.

Social constructionist theory shares with postmodernism the view that all cultural meanings, and the sense of social identities that emerge from them, are essentially fluid and diverse. Attempts to describe or fix their characteristics freeze what is a dynamic process, giving at best only a short-term snapshot. In the postmodernist view of identity, individuals cannot be defined by such characteristics as nationality, race, religion, or even gender. This is both because we are all multi-faceted and because we continually re-think and redefine ourselves, depending on the contexts we find ourselves in and the experiences we have. Different facets of ourselves become salient or irrelevant in different situations, and in relation to different social and political struggles. We do not produce these self-images or narratives about ourselves out of nothing. We draw on cultural resources around us, resources that are becoming increasingly diverse and globalized with mass communications (Barker 1999, 3). The discourses of professionals and leaders in politics and business, and how these are represented in mass media, form important parts of the network of practices that sustain cultural meanings.

Barker recognizes the power of multinational corporations and media production conglomerates to spread capitalist consumer culture around the globe, but he stresses that people do not simply absorb these influences. They interact with them. They adapt and refashion some influences and reject or ignore others. Mass media productions do not convey identical meanings to people living in different social contexts. Neither is it only a top-down process of influence from people who dominate mass media to the rest of the world. Influence works both ways, with the result that people around the world are becoming more culturally homogenous in some respects, but simultaneously more diverse and hybrid in other respects. People's sense of themselves as being Muslim, Christian, or Jewish, for example, is continually being shaped by both local cultural influences and by global representations, and the contemporary politics of war and cultural imperialism.

The concept of *identity politics* draws attention to how people struggle to develop new ways of describing themselves, along with others who share these new representations (Barker 1999, Ch. 7). Examples of people actively working up new descriptions of themselves include generating a new self-consciousness around the idea of being a born-again Christian, a feminist, a First Nations person with clout under the Canadian Charter of Rights and Freedoms, or as a person with gay and lesbian sexual orientation seeking Charter recognition and respect. For people who feel marginalized within the dominant cultural discourse, these struggles over redefinition and re-presentation have profound political consequences, for they challenge the grounds of social inclusion and justice.

Professional discourses are particularly influential in creating cultural meanings in contemporary society, including sociological perspectives. People draw upon sociological research and explanations that they come across in magazines and other media to make sense of their own experiences. The research process itself can become circular as people who are being interviewed by social researchers and reporters draw upon their own knowledge of sociology and psychology to frame descriptions of themselves (Denzin 1992, Ch. 4). In Denzin's own studies, people he interviewed readily borrowed ideas from popular self-help psychology books, adopting such notions as "adult-children-of-alcoholics" to talk about themselves. When professors are called upon at short notice by media talk shows to comment on social events, they often do a quick search of online sites to see what other commentators have said as a shortcut to forming their own opinions. Young people who read Bibby's (2009) analysis of a survey of opinions and behaviour of young millennials, people who came of age in the first decade of this century, may well borrow ideas from it when talking about themselves, which then gives support to Bibby's analysis.

It is difficult to recognize and resist power or relations of ruling that take the form of professional expertise and advice because it seems like common sense. Resistance takes the form of reality-defining contests in which people struggle to establish competing interpretations of the way things are that support alternative policies for dealing with social problems. Within the social constructionist perspective, the study of power relations and the study of culture and counterculture overlap. Competing sociological perspectives are important tools in resistance movements. The study of sociology thus contributes both to the authoritative creation of culture and to its **deconstruction**.

Feminist Perspectives

The feminist perspective in sociology began to emerge as a distinctly recognized theoretical approach only in the 1970s, although it has roots in the long history of women's movements. Why the seventies? Universities across North America and Europe were expanding rapidly and opening their doors more widely to women, both as students and as junior faculty. Courses in gender studies expanded as numbers of women in universities expanded, reflecting the fact that female students are more interested in exploring gender issues. This observation opens up a series of further questions, including: Why were universities overwhelmingly male preserves prior to the 1970s? How and why did this change? and Why are men less interested in gender issues than women? The feminist perspective focuses attention on questions such as these, and in so doing, it profoundly challenges the adequacy of conventional sociological research and explanations.

Central Assumptions of the Feminist Perspective

A key assumption of feminism is that all features of social life need to be understood as gendered—not just the obvious area of family life, but everything—including the state, politics, the economy, criminal justice, education, universities, and the foundations of sociological discourse itself (Marshall 2000, 25). Gender is seen as a central organizing principle of social life. The Marxist perspective gives priority in explaining social structures to relations of production, or how people organize to produce material goods. Feminism gives priority to relations of *reproduction*, or how people organize to produce and nurture children, and more broadly to nurture and care for bodies throughout societies.

A second foundational assumption is that gender identities are best understood as social constructions, rather than the natural expression of biological differences. The concept of *gendering* refers to these social processes through which gender identities are accomplished—continually produced, reinforced, and struggled against in ongoing social structures and relationships (Marshall 2000, Ch. 5).

A third assumption of feminism is that gendering is hierarchical (Nakano Glenn 1997). Relations of reproduction are viewed as fundamental mechanisms through which inequalities of access to material resources, personal services, status, and power in society are organized. The work of reproductive labour, both in the narrow sense of bearing children and the broad sense of daily renewal of bodies, is pervasively feminized, privatized, and de-politicized, and located outside the organizational centres of social power (Acker 1997). Globally, women comprise about half the adult human population, yet they control only a tiny fraction of material resources. Culturally, those attributes associated with the feminine are pervasively less highly valued than those identified as masculine. It is still more complimentary to describe a girl as "acting like a boy" than to describe a boy as "behaving like a girl." Statistically, young women and men are now equally represented in Canadian universities, although concentrated in different disciplines. Yet this has not translated into gender equality in future careers and incomes earned. Women are nowhere equally represented in offices and roles in society where political, economic, and cultural power are wielded. The category of women whose career achievements in the public arena most closely resemble those of comparable men are women who remain single and childless, or a minority of elite women who are wealthy enough to hire nannies and housekeepers. Such partial equality is achieved at high personal cost.

The organizational practices that sustain and reinforce gender hierarchy are collectively referred to within feminist thought as *relations of patriarchy*. The feminist perspective encompasses both a positive and a normative project—a commitment to understand and make visible how gendering is accomplished, and a commitment to dismantle gender hierarchy.

A fourth assumption of the feminist perspective is that the production of knowledge is gendered. As a social process, the work of science is embedded in and reflects the historically specific contexts in which the struggle for knowledge occurs (Smith 1990). The profound shifts in sociology that have occurred since the 1970s as more women entered the academy indicates that what formerly passed as knowledge was not neutral but deeply gendered, reflecting male-centred interests and interpretive perspectives. Women scholars found that the prevailing concepts and explanations in sociology were inadequate to account for women's experiences. In the feminist jargon of the time, one could not just "add women and stir." Profound rethinking was needed.

More recently, feminist thought itself is being challenged from within as reflecting white, Western, professional, heterosexual women's experience, and not adequate to account for the situated experiences of more marginalized women. These challenges do not imply that scientific knowledge is impossible, but rather that all science is socially accomplished. The knowledge we derive from scientific work reflects the social organization of that work and needs to be interrogated as such.

The remainder of this section elaborates these basic assumptions of the feminist perspective and the experiences and reasoning behind them. The question raised above— why the feminist perspective emerged in the 1970s—still needs to be addressed. Part of the answer lies in economic changes. The 1970s was an era of relative prosperity for Europe and North America, with economic relations shifting increasingly from the mass-production factory system to information and service industries, expanding corporations, and expanding post-World War II welfare-state bureaucracies. This resulted in a high demand for women's labour as clerical and service workers. These new opportunities in turn encouraged women as well as men to seek higher education in unprecedented numbers. What remains to be

explained is why so many young women scholars were so dissatisfied with the existing functionalist, Marxist, and interpretive perspectives in sociology that they were driven to promote a paradigm shift in theory and methods. Karl Marx was driven to write his critique of capitalism by revulsion at the oppressive conditions of industrialization. What were these women struggling against in the 1970s and what were the experiences that they felt could not be accounted for by existing sociological explanations?

Feminism and Mainstream Sociology

A collection of life-histories of feminist sociologists (Laslett and Thorne 1997) throws some light on these questions. Women who studied sociology in the 1970s write of experiencing a sense of "bifurcated consciousness," in that the sociological explanations they were learning about did not fit with or account for their lived experiences (Laslett and Thorne 1997, 7). Women achieved access to higher education along with men but often under more difficult and highly gendered conditions. Women describe their emotional and physical exhaustion as they struggled with the relentless demands of managing relations of reproduction along with academic work. Laslett describes her own struggle with her children's illnesses, their sleeping problems, her own constantly interrupted sleep and interrupted studies, and her worries about childcare. Added to these worries were struggles to juggle the roles of graduate student, mother, wife, and hostess to her husband's colleagues, and a marriage that was beginning to unravel. The functionalist theory that prevailed in American sociology in the 1970s posited a structural separation of "public" work roles from "private" family roles. Women's lived experience did not fit with this model. Emerging feminist research identified women's work in the home, and how women absorb the emotional and material work of reproducing bodies, as the essential but unacknowledged underpinning for the abstracted public realm of men's work (Acker 1997). The supposedly "public" realm could not function if labour in the supposedly "private" realm were to be withdrawn. Their artificial separation in mainstream sociological theory needed to be rethought.

Feminist research promoted a methodology that begins not with an abstract model of social systems, but with the immediately experienced, concrete, material situation that individual women found themselves in. The research question then becomes: What are the organizational features and practices in the wider society that structure experience and sustain precisely this lived experience? This approach, which subsequently became known as institutional ethnography, was first used by women in sociology principally because there were so few resources for studying women's lives in the 1970s. The first women's studies or sociology of women courses offered in the seventies took the form of seminars in which graduate students and instructor together struggled to come up with questions, carry out their own research, and pool what they discovered. They could not begin with library research into existing theories because there was no body of academic sociological literature that could be studied. Seminar leaders struggled against the prevailing view that what they were doing was not scholarly and should not count for academic credit (Smith 1992a, 1992b). These seminars were the crucible in which much early **feminist theory** was formed.

The very absence of sociological literature on women fuelled questions about how and why previous sociological research had been so gender biased. This questioning leads back to the concrete material conditions of women's oppression. Historically, women have been systematically excluded from the creation of culture, along with other disprivileged people. Men almost exclusively occupied the leading positions in all the major professions such as medicine, psychology, law, sciences, theology, and all the disciplines pursued in the universities. When women began to enter universities and professions in large numbers, it was to find the dominant ideas, **paradigms**, methodologies, and standards for evaluating scholarship already entrenched. These concrete conditions of gendered inequality are embedded into all the professions, including the social sciences.

Feminist Disillusionment with Mainstream Sociology

Many of the feminist sociologists who contributed their life-histories to the collection by Laslett and Thorne describe themselves as initially attracted to Marxist sociology because of its focus on injustice and class struggle, and its commitment to radical social change. To students who came of age in the sixties and who were caught up in the American anti-Vietnam war movement, Marxist analysis of capitalism seemed to offer important insight. Feminist disillusionment with Marxism came from two sources, analytical and practical.

Analytically the central Marxist concept of *class*, rooted as it is in the abstract model of relations of production, excludes women (Acker 1997, 37; Nakano Glenn 1997, 81–82). Efforts to fit women's domestic work into Marxist categories has largely failed. A powerful example of this failure is provided by Nellie McClung (1972, 91–92) in her autobiography *In Times Like These*. A farmer with a 1000-acre farm would be classified within a Marxist framework as wealthy business class with substantial capital resources. The farmer's wife and children would be classified as sharing his status. Yet the males and females

within this family actually occupy very different class positions, measured by both property and inheritance laws of the time. When the male farm-owner died, his three sons between them inherited all the farm. His unmarried 40-year-old daughter, who had contributed farm and household labour all her adult life, got only $100 and one cow. His wife received merely "her keep with one of the boys." The three sons thus continued to have capital resources and could be classified as at least in the "small business" class. The daughter, however, had no productive resources of her own, and if her brothers did not wish to keep her, she would have to seek wage-work as a household servant. The widowed mother was left virtually destitute, beholden to her sons for "her keep." The feminist critique of Marxist class analysis is that it only works for men. Classifying this farmer's wife and his unmarried daughter as "wealthy business class" is ideological in that it obscures their actual dependent servant status. This would be true for all families where the business assets or career credentials are the property only of the man. But if this is true, then how should one classify "homemakers"?

A second source of disillusionment with Marxism came from practical political experience. Women who became active in left-wing politics in the seventies often encountered rejection from men on the left (Smith 1977; Smith and Malnarich 1983). They found their struggles on behalf of women's oppression characterized as divisive and misguided, and their concerns trivialized. Women were widely seen as politically backward for not supporting the union struggles of their working-class husbands and, at worst, as class enemies for their greater willingness to work for lower wages than men. What the Marxist activists did not comment on was the structurally gendered reality of the total economic dependence of homemaker-wives on their husband's wages to provide a home and security for their children and themselves. It is her husband's work and his wages, not hers. If he should choose to drink his money with his friends, or go on strike, or get fired or blacklisted for political agitation, her world comes crashing down, but it is still his business and not hers. Male activists, committed to the cause of class struggle, still largely failed to see women's oppression, and indeed sometimes actively contributed to the oppression in their personal lives.

Relations of Patriarchy

The multi-faceted character of women's oppression is illustrated in the account of the life of one woman living with an abusive husband, cited by Smith in her essay on the conflict between feminism and Marxism (1977, 40). Smith challenges her readers to figure out the nature of the trap that this woman, and thousands like her, found herself in. The trap has multiple dimensions, and all of them taken together constitute what feminists refer to as *relations of patriarchy*:

> [She] had endured a nightmare marriage for 30 years. Time and again she had tried to break out. She often went to her mother's but her husband had broken in there and taken her back. The police never did anything to stop him because it was a marital quarrel. Nobody else wanted to be involved. After all, she did have a roof over her head, didn't she? He always kept her short of money. She took a job once but had to work 12 hours to earn overtime to make her salary equal to a man's and that meant leaving the children alone in the evening. After six months of that she gave it up. Each time she and her children went back to her husband, he got her pregnant again. Each time they were treated worse because he knew they could not choose but take it. He used to taunt her with "Where can you go? What can you do?"

The challenge is to see how culture, socialization, the economy, class, schooling, childcare responsibilities, control over sexual relations, law, criminal justice, social services, welfare, and professional discourses are all interrelated in the lived experience of oppression that this woman endured. Culture and patterns of socialization are implicated in the assumptions people have about marriage and divorce, religious and moral obligations to sustain a stable two-parent home for children, differential responsibilities for parenting, and so on. These are revealed in the kinds of advice and support or rejection that women seeking to leave a relationship typically receive from various authority figures including religious leaders, social service workers, lawyers, and police, and also from relatives, friends, and neighbours. The economy is certainly implicated, with a gendered labour market in which women's average earnings are far below those of men. The large majority of children who depend financially upon a single-parent mother live below the federal poverty line. The public school system and curriculum are also implicated in gendered career training, guidance, and role-modelling for girls. Relations of reproduction are especially significant in this trap, with women expected to take the bulk of responsibility for childcare. For the woman in Smith's example, taking a job with the long hours required to support her children financially meant leaving them alone in the evenings. The combination of her husband's total control over sexual relations with her, and her lack of access to reliable birth control technology or to abortion, results in repeated pregnancies, and more children who depend on her care. The law, criminal justice, and the state are also heavily implicated. Smith's article was written in the late 1970s, when police routinely refused to intervene in domestic violence, and laws against rape did not apply to husband–wife relations. People in the women's movement fought long and hard to get state funding for transition houses—safe places for women and children fleeing abusive homes. But even now, almost three decades later, getting an effective restraining order against an angry, abusive spouse remains very difficult. Smith suggests further that should a marriage break down and the husband/father leave the relationship, the true nature of the trap for the wife/mother becomes fully visible, because she is still in it. Women who walk out on their children are sanctioned in very different ways from men who walk out. The feminist concept of *relations of patriarchy* tries to name and so to make visible this network of interrelated social processes.

Gender Bias in Mainstream Social Science

The challenge that the feminist perspective raises for mainstream sociological theory is how to account for the relative invisibility of these relations of **patriarchy**—their unnoticed or taken-for-granted character. We need to ask what it was about classical sociology that made women's oppression so difficult to see. McRobbie's (1991) feminist revisiting of Marxist cultural studies in England reveals just how marked was this failure to notice women and the specifically gendered character of oppression (Cohen 1955; Willis 1981; Hebdige 1979). The studies focused on working-class subcultures, but defined them entirely with reference to male behaviour, styles, and values. Girls, if they appear at all, are portrayed only in marginalized and stereotypical ways.

The problem is not merely that male researchers choose to study young men rather than young women, but that the terms of reference are so narrowly defined that entire dimensions of the boys' lives are left out, and their brutally patriarchal orientation to sexuality ignored. What we learn about

Skinhead boys bragged about hitting their girlfriends to keep them in line.

REUTERS/Ints Kalnins

is public behaviour of Teddy boys, mods, rockers, and motorcycle boys in the streets, and in relation to schools, work, and the criminal justice system. Girls are less free to be on the streets, less likely to be involved in violence, or to have sufficient disposable income to buy motorbikes, so they become invisible to researchers who focus only on the public world.

There is a structured absence of any attention to family and domestic life. We do not find out what happens when a "mod" boy goes home after a weekend on drugs. The lads may get by with each other on the streets but they do not eat, sleep, or make love there (McRobbie 1991, 19–20). There is little recognition of the extent to which the symbolic and temporary flight of teds, mods, and rockers from the "family trap" takes place at the expense of women, especially mothers and girlfriends. Marxist researchers like Cohen (1955), Corrigan (1979), Willis (1981), and Hebdige (1979) highlight and even celebrate the aggressive masculinity through which the lads kick against the oppressive structures of capitalism. They ignore how the language of these macho styles is unambiguously degrading to women. Studies recount how schoolboys scorn their teachers as "cunts," and voice their future goals as "f...ing as many women as I can" (McRobbie 1991, 21, citing Willis 1981). Skinhead boys brag about hitting their girlfriends to keep them in line, and take the welfare cheques intended to support the girlfriend and her baby. Yet male researchers seemed oblivious to these blatantly patriarchal aspects of the lower-class youth cultures they researched. In their writings they frequently reproduced the comments made about girls by the boys they studied as if they were simply factual statements. Fyvel, for example, refers in his study of Teddy boys to "dumb, passive teenage girls, crudely painted" (Fyvel 1963, cited in McRobbie 1991, 1). Willis similarly describes the unattached girls who hung around with the motorbike boys as follows: "What seemed to unite them was a common desire for an attachment to a male and a common inability to attract a man to a long-term relationship. They tended to be scruffier and less attractive than the attached girls" (Willis 1981, cited in McRobbie 1991, 1–2). Willis also dismisses them as "unforthcoming, unwilling to talk and they retreat, in giggles, into the background." McRobbie suggests that such comments more accurately display the researchers' biases and their unconscious adoption of the attitudes of the boys they are studying than any accurate description of the girls themselves.

Within these classical sociological perspectives, the roles of men and women in reproduction tended to be seen as "natural" or biologically determined, and thus not requiring sociological explanation. Such assumptions made the structural oppression of women difficult to see. Feminist theorizing challenged the taken-for-granted character of categories like "male" and "female," and "masculine" and "feminine," insisting that these are social constructions. These challenges to such fundamental notions of gender identity helped to foster **postmodernist** thought in sociology (Stacey 1997, 136; Marshall 2000, 68). Postmodernism refers to a contemporary approach within cultural studies and philosophy that focuses on uncertainty, impermanence, doubt, and the continual transformation and recombining of once-disparate categories. Feminist scholarship was influential in fostering these new schools of thought.

Sociology looks very different now from what it did in the 1970s. There is now a vast body of sociological research and literature on women. But some feminists remain concerned that the critical edge and politicizing potential of the feminist perspective is being lost (Marshall 2000, 24). Few male sociologists, either faculty or students, show much interest in courses focusing on women or gender issues (Connell 1997). Much mainstream research includes women as a category for sorting data but without critical feminist analysis. Marshall's survey of six Canadian introductory sociology texts (2000, 30–33) shows that gender as a category is rarely referenced outside chapters specifically on gender and family. Feminism as a body of theory gets short shrift.

Diversity in Feminist Thought

Feminist theory has not emerged all in one piece. It is not uncommon to find alternative and sometimes contradictory arguments within feminist literature. As noted above, feminist research in sociology began with a focus on women as *objects*, asking such basic questions as where are women in relation to the situation or issue being studied, how are they differently situated from men, and if they are not involved, why not (Lengermann and Niebrugge-Brantley 1990). This remains the major form in which feminist work has been incorporated into mainstream sociology.

Feminist research gradually shifted to the study of women as *subjects*, investigating how a shift in perspective from a typically male to female standpoint can radically alter our sense of what is going on. In an early study of union participation, male leaders criticized women as apathetic because they turned up irregularly for union meetings and mostly remained silent (Smith 1979, 16). From the standpoint of women, however, patriarchal union organization, not female apathy largely explained their limited involvement. Union meetings were routinely scheduled in late afternoon and evening time-slots—times when many women were otherwise occupied in picking up children from schools and daycare, giving them their dinner, and preparing them for bed. Women further complained that when they did speak up at union meetings their voices were not heard, and topics raised by them not followed up. Issues of particular interest to women, like maternity benefits, flexible hours, child-sick days, benefits for part-time workers, sexual harassment in the workplace, the wage gap between male and female workers, and the like, tended not to be taken seriously by male union members. They might be included in negotiations, but only to be traded off for percentaged wage increases which mostly benefited the already higher-paid male workers. What looks like apathy from one perspective looks like patriarchy from another.

Feminist standpoint sociology developed into the postmodern focus on multidimensional, shifting, and situated standpoints, with the recognition that women do not form a homogenous group. People experience themselves simultaneously in terms of gender, class, race, ethnicity, age, and sexual orientation. The relative salience of these dimensions of self varies with the situations and struggles people find themselves in (Marshall 2000, Ch. 2). Consider how vastly different the experience of being a mother of a pre-school-aged child is for women in the following situations: an undergraduate student, a teenage single parent with grade 9 education, the wife of a high-income professional breadwinner, a woman with a lesbian partner, a migrant woman working as a nanny in Toronto while her own children live in another country, a Native woman living on a reservation, a woman who herself holds a demanding executive position in a corporation. No one role description could meaningfully encompass all these experiences. Yet every situation is gendered, in the sense that the comparable experiences of women and men in equivalent situations would be markedly different.

SCHOOLS OF FEMINIST THOUGHT

Feminist theory varies with the assumptions that guide research and the kind of explanations that authors favour when trying to account for gender inequality. Five broad schools of feminist thought have been identified, although in practice there is much overlap (Jaggar and Rothenberg 1984; Tong 1989). **Liberal feminism** begins from the assumption that discrimination against women is the central mechanism perpetuating gender inequality—initially in the form of legal barriers to women's entry into higher education and the professions, and later in more subtle prejudices that work to reduce opportunities for women. **Marxist feminism** looks to the workings of capitalism to explain women's material subordination. It is in the interests of capitalists to divide workers along gender lines to facilitate the greater exploitation of women as cheap labour. Women's domestic labour is also exploited by capitalists as it cheapens the cost of reproducing and maintaining labour. **Socialist feminism** favours a more dual-systems theory approach, arguing that in addition to exploitation by capitalists, women as wives,

mothers, and daughters are exploited by men. The bodily support services that women typically provide for men in their homes serve to free up men's time for greater leisure and public-arena activities, and so gives men a major competitive edge as employees. **Radical feminism** locates the arena of gender inequality and struggle more squarely in male control over female sexuality and reproduction, particularly through the threat of sexual violence. **Cultural feminism** locates the struggle more in discourse, and internalization of cultural meanings that stereotype and often denigrate the female and the feminine.

To gain a feeling for the usefulness of these different explanatory approaches, you might try to apply each in turn to the situation described above of a woman who feels trapped in an abusive marriage. Different aspects of her situation are highlighted in turn, and all may play some role, although varying in importance for individual cases. Each approach has fostered political movements to struggle against these multiple dimensions of women's oppression.

As feminist theory has broadened to encompass recognition of the diversity of women's subjective positions, these theoretical distinctions are becoming less important. Theorists like Marshall (2000) advocate a rethinking of feminist frameworks to move towards a more fluid understanding of gendering as a process rather than the attribute of a person. The concept of *gendering* refers to a view of gender identities as emerging out of different material situations that men and women find themselves in as they take up particular practical struggles. The assumption here is that we do not first identify ourselves as female or male, and then take up gender issues. Rather, we first encounter gendered issues like struggles over reproductive labour, or sexual violence, and then identify ourselves as female or male in responding to these experiences. Gender identity is thus accomplished, not something fixed or given for either male or female individuals. All women or all men will not always feel themselves lined up on opposite sides of an issue. In some circumstances, being a woman and not a man may be the single most salient feature of one's identity. In others, being a black woman may be sufficiently different from being a white woman that racialized identity takes precedence.

Where feminist theory differs from abstract postmodernism, Marshall insists, is that there is a material base to gendered identity. This material base is not the fact of biological sex difference. It is the fact of gendered relations of reproduction, together with the myriad of gendered inequalities in access to and control over resources and services, status, recognition, sexual freedom, and the like. It is the gendered character of social structures, not biology, that continually reproduces gender as a salient feature of individual identity.

The Politics of Feminism and Backlash

Feminist theories create a language through which it has become possible to see women's oppression. This language itself has become contested and politicized, with both feminists and non-feminist critics and opponents struggling over the meaning and definition of "feminism." The hegemonic view of feminism in mass media, Vavrus maintains (2002, Ch. 1), is **postfeminist liberalism**, a view that works to depoliticize feminism by attributing all power differentials and under-representation of women in positions of status and influence to individual weaknesses, rather than to patriarchal societal structures. This hegemonic view accepts the right of women to work in formerly male-dominated jobs for higher salaries, and assumes that the "level playing field" between women and men has been largely achieved. Consequently, if women are manifestly not achieving equal status with men, it must be due to different average abilities and efforts and to different lifestyle choices. Postfeminist liberals readily point to evidence that gender equality has been achieved in completion of undergraduate degrees in Canada since 2000, although women and men tend to choose different programs. Women have long outnumbered men in most liberal arts and humanities undergraduate programs, while men dominate in physical sciences, computer science, mathematics, and engineering.

Postfeminist liberalism is not pro-patriarchy in the sense of favouring male dominance over women, but it is non-feminist. It suggests that problems based on sex and reproduction are largely resolved, and hence that feminism as a political movement is irrelevant or out of date. It represents feminist issues around relations of reproduction as matters of lifestyle choices, choices to prioritize having children and being with them over career ambitions. In this hegemonic representation, conflict between employment and home-making and child-rearing are best resolved by women prioritizing home-making roles while children are young, while men prioritize career and "breadwinning" roles. Assumed within this representation is the functionalist view of role conflict and incompatible role demands, best resolved by some level of gender-role segregation. Rather than seeing "the personal as political," postfeminist liberalism defines political struggles as private and personal matters. The structural features of gendered inequalities in all spheres of wealth, power, and influence in society are reduced to issues of personal abilities and lifestyle choices. The more extreme anti-feminist "backlash" position blames feminism itself for generating unnatural or unrealistic expectations among women. In this view, the women's movement foments competitiveness and hostility between women and men that feminism then denounces (Faludi, S. 1991; Vavrus 2002).

Theorizing Sexual Diversity

The assumption that gender identities are neither predefined nor fixed has opened space for more research into diverse and non-hegemonic forms of gendering, which Seidman (1996) loosely calls "queer theory"—focusing on gay, lesbian, bisexual, and transgendered identity formation, and the politics of struggles around which these identities emerge and coalesce. Queer theory challenges the binary categorization of gender into exclusively male or female, suggesting that this dualism is not natural, but rather the socially constructed effect of its continual reinforcement within all societal institutions. In so doing, queer theory challenges foundational cultural assumptions about social institutions like the family, and the organization of relations of reproduction. A Marxist focus traces the linkages between the shift from feudalism to individual wage-work and the emergence of the possibility of distinctive homosexual communities, first for males and later for females (Kinsmen 1987, Ch. 2; Frank 1987). The social constructionist approach, building on Foucault's (1978) seminal work traces how long historical shifts in conceptualization of sexual practices—as sinful activity, as specific "types" of people, as psychological or medical illness, or as lifestyle choice—are associated with profound shifts in institutionalized responses. The approach of institutional ethnography traces how such responses, particularly in schools, function to reinforce hegemonic heterosexuality, and simultaneously to construct the everyday lived experiences and gendered self-identities of people who live outside the hegemonic norm (Connell 1987; Khayatt 1992; Smith 1998). The postmodernist focus on identity politics explores how gendered subjectivities emerge and change in contexts of struggle around material concerns (Marshall 2000, Ch. 2).

The feminist perspective, in its diverse forms, challenges us fundamentally to let go of images and stereotypes of essential "maleness" or "femaleness." Feminist theory challenges the assumption that people can be meaningfully slotted into "male" or "female" categories, or that these categories constitute causes of subsequent behaviour. We are challenged further to resist thinking of "gender" as to do only with women, and to recognize that masculinity is as historically specific and socially constructed as femininity. Feminism posits gender identity, along with all other aspects of identity, as negotiated social processes, emerging from situated practical experiences, material interests, and struggles, and informed by available social and cultural resources. In this regard, feminism has a close affinity with postmodernism.

In summary, the feminist perspective places the social organization of relations of reproduction at the centre of sociological analysis. Reproduction is understood broadly to refer to the nurture and care of children and bodies generally. These relations are pervasively gendered and hierarchical, and systemically reinforced through all major societal institutions. They are also pervasively naturalized or biologized within mainstream (malestream) sociological perspectives, and thus rendered largely invisible or irrelevant to the discipline of sociology, or trivialized as obvious matters of private choice. Feminist theory struggles to make visible these gendered relations of ruling, with the wider political agenda of changing them.

Feminist Perspectives on Culture and Representation

Historically, women had only a limited presence in the creation of Western culture. The vast majority of famous composers, musicians, writers, painters, philosophers, theorists, mathematicians, and scientists throughout Western civilization have been men. Women's contributions to art have been noticed mostly in domestic niche activities like embroidery and quilt-making. Historical explanations for this apparent gender inequality in creative expression have commonly focused on the essence of womanhood itself, the essentially nature-based rootedness of women in family and repetitive cycles of pregnancy, breast-feeding, and care of children. Men, in contrast, appear as less constrained by nature, and thus freer to engage with the life of the mind, or culture.

This conception of culture as essentially a male creation is particularly pronounced in **psychoanalysis**, the influential school of analytical psychology founded by Sigmund Freud. Freud argues that the origins of culture are biologically rooted in male sexuality and founded on "the Law of the Father" (Freud 1905; Grosz 1990). The most basic primal drive for infants, Freud reasoned, is the urge to possess the mother who satisfies all basic physical needs and pleasures, and who is the first love object. But this primal sexual desire is taboo. It brings a boy in direct conflict with his father, arousing the profound anxiety that his more powerful father might retaliate and castrate him. Freud names this conflict *the Oedipus complex*. The Oedipus complex is resolved only by repression of incestuous sexual love into the unconscious, and the displacement of this powerful emotional energy into more acceptable motivations, recognized in the conscious mind as adult heterosexual love and the morals, values, and commitments of family and community life associated with it. The incest taboo is thus the origin of culture.

Girls, Freud reasoned, do not experience these powerful drives of emotional repression and displacement associated with the Oedipus complex, and hence do not contribute the same emotional forces to the creation of culture. Female infants also desire possession of the mother, but this cannot be realized. In Freud's view, this is not because of conflict with the father, but because girls lack a penis. Girls are biologically incapable of expressing powerful sexual drives in the same way as boys, and so are destined to become more passive. They can realize these primal drives only vicariously through pregnancy and giving birth to a male child. Girls overcome their biological castration to achieve true femininity as objects of male desire.

In psychoanalysis the distinction between male and female is the most basic of a series of binary or either/or distinctions that characterize Western culture—distinctions like presence/absence, active/passive, culture/nature, self/other, sacred/profane, public/private, and the like. In all these binary oppositions, the second or subordinate term is associated with female, and is defined through its relation to the primary male term. Woman is "not man," defined by what she lacks. Freud's theories have had a profound impact on studies of culture. The anthropologist Claude Levy-Strauss posits the Oedipus conflict as the principal universal feature of human culture, linked to the universal prohibition against incest, the principle of *exogamy* or rule that sexual relations and marriage ought to take place only outside the kinship group, resulting in the exchange of women across kin groups (Franklin et al. 1991, 9).

Feminist theories of culture struggle both within and against psychoanalytic theories to achieve a more positive understanding of women and women's contribution to cultural life. Jacques Lacan (Lacan 1972; Grosz 1990, 96–97; Barker 1999, 21) replaces the biological determinism in Freudian theory with a theory of language as the origins of culture. It is not the penis as biological fact that establishes male power over female, Lacan argues, but its cultural status as "phallus," as symbol of the social power that will accrue to male children but not to females. Our sense of ourselves as male or female is learned at the Oedipal stage as we first learn to talk. In our conscious mind we are aware only of the culturally acceptable ideas and emotions. All the emotions and drives that language fails to express are repressed into the unconscious mind, experienced only indirectly through metaphors or associations.

Feminist psychoanalysts like Mitchell (1975), Kristeva (1986) and Irigaray (1985) draw from Lacan's reformulation of Freud the insights that gendered identities, even deeply felt emotional experiences of femininity and motherhood, are best understood not as biological givens, but as socially constructed through language. Language pervasively separates infants into male and female, and imposes a gendered hierarchy in which mankind, man, male, masculine, he and his, prevails (Turner 1990, 28; Barker 1999, 88–94). They sketch a vision of a women-centred language that privileges not the phallus, but women's reproductive power—their capacity to give birth and to suckle infants. They acknowledge, however, that it is almost impossible to create such a transformative language without the prior transformation of social order. In the meantime feminists struggle to express alternative representations while using existing phallocentric language. As the feminist poet Audre Lorde expresses it, "the master's tools will never dismantle the master's house" (1984, 110–113).

An influential branch of feminist cultural critique has struggled to undermine the patriarchal bias in much of Western culture, by reversing the valuation of feminine and masculine. Mary O'Brien (1981) explores the theme that central religious images in Greek and Christian traditions are rooted in male envy of female reproductive powers. She cites the recurring theme of male gods who create offspring without female potency being involved, suggesting that such myths reflect efforts by men to compensate through culture for their alienation from birth and human continuity. The institution of marriage, with males defined as head of household and children named through their male lineage, can be seen as reflecting the same male drive to control reproduction vicariously through possession of a wife and her children. Nancy Chodorow (1978; 1989) offers another materialist interpretation of psychoanalysis, suggesting that girls are more passive because they do not need to break from their mother as boys do. They can identify directly with her as female, while boys are forced to break away from their mothers to identify with their fathers and other men. Girls may experience "penis envy" not as something they lack in a biological sense, but as a struggle for personal autonomy from mother and motherhood (Van Zoonen 1994, 23).

These feminist rereadings of psychoanalysis have been criticized in turn for assuming an *essentialist* version of gender identity—an identity that is fixed in infancy and thereafter unchanging (Van Zoonen 1994, 29–33; Barker 1999, 27–29). An alternative argument favoured in contemporary sociology is that people's sense of themselves as masculine or feminine emerges not solely or even primarily in early childhood experiences but throughout life, in response to historical and social situations that women and men find themselves in. Historically, the most direct explanation for male dominance over the creation of western culture is that powerful men have actively excluded women from access to the institutional structures that facilitate the creation of culture (Smith 1975). The most important of these institutions is education. Without access to higher education, most women have had limited opportunity to develop their intellectual potential. Professional positions associated with the creation of culture—positions in universities, the professions, law, politics, religion, art, and mass media—have been controlled almost exclusively by men. Only in the latter half of the twentieth century have women begun to enter these

positions in significant numbers. This reflects profound shifts in technology and social relations that women have been able to exploit to gain control over reproduction and potential for social and economic independence. Once women began to enter the citadels of cultural power, however, they encountered culturally entrenched frames of thinking and criteria for evaluation that reflected male experiences and preoccupations. Women were judged, and included or excluded, in terms of male standards of professional competence. Feminist scholarship has emerged slowly, and even now remains marginal in most professions. The challenge of the new millennium is to ensure that girls as well as boys gain access to computer technology, not just for social networking and word-processing (mea maxima culpa here), but knowledgeable access to the operating systems that enable electronic cultural creativity.

The shift in thinking about gendered culture from biological or essentialist explanations to an emphasis on social structures has prompted a critical focus on how agencies of socialization, especially schools, religious institutions, and mass media, represent and reinforce particular conceptions of femininity and masculinity. Feminist perspectives see cultural representations of male and female as highly politicized and saturated with power (Barker 1999, 22). Feminist research has challenged pervasive cultural portrayals of women in stereotyped roles as homemaker, wife-mother, secretary, and nurse, or shopping for household goods while authoritative male voice-overs give advice. Such research challenges also the anorexic models used to sell beauty products for women, and the dangerous pornographic representations of women's bodies as sex objects for male pleasure.

Postmodern feminist critics have challenged this research in turn for implicitly assuming that there is some "accurate" image of "real" women, in relation to which media representations can be shown to be distortions (Marshall 2000, Ch. 2). They also critique the assumption that there is a direct transfer from media messages or agents of socialization generally, to internalized identity. Audience members can and do reject messages, ignore or reinterpret them, depending on their own situations and struggles. This postmodernist approach views gender identity work as a continual process, in which women and men draw on available cultural images to work up a sense of personal identity. Practical material conditions, including opportunities for economic and social independence, profoundly influence how we come to think about ourselves.

Feminist consciousness-raising groups, growing out of the second-wave feminist movement of the 1970s, played an important role in encouraging women to explore alternative feminist cultural identities (Staggenborg 2001). Feminist cultural networks have in turn provided the organizational foundation for collective political action, focused around such issues as equal rights legislation, shelters for abused women, rape crisis centres, reproductive choice, and most recently the right of lesbian and gay couples to marry. Feminist networking sites continue to encourage the millennial generation of young people to reject essentialist definitions of femininity and masculinity and to be open to diverse possibilities.

CONCLUSION

Hopefully it is clear by now that there can be no one sociological description of Canadian society that precedes analysis. Different perspectives focus variously on integrating cultural systems, modes and relations of production, systems of knowledge production, or relations of reproduction. They highlight very different features of social experience, and alter the kinds of questions we think to ask about what we notice. The challenge of this course is to develop qualities of sociological imagination that will allow you to continually shift perspectives as you think about social life. The goal is to learn to recognize and articulate underlying assumptions, both explicit and implicit, in descriptions of social life that you read about, and that you produce for yourselves. This capacity gives you the freedom to decide for yourselves the usefulness of different perspective, alone and in combination. You will know why you are adopting one perspective rather than another, and more importantly, you will know what you are choosing not to pay attention to when you do this.

This theory chapter is pivotal for understanding the remaining chapters, which use these different theoretical perspectives as tools to explore many aspects of social life. A summary guide to key assumptions and concepts in each of the four perspectives is provided below to help you to grasp them and begin to apply them to new areas of social research.

Study Guide to the Core Assumptions of the Four Theoretical Perspectives

▣ FUNCTIONALISM

Society is conceptualized as a system comprising interrelated parts or institutions (e.g., family, polity, law, education). These parts function to meet the needs of the society. The system is characterized by **dynamic equilibrium**, meaning that it remains relatively stable and balanced over generations, although always absorbing and adapting to change.

Research Focus

Focus is on how institutions are structured, and the functions they perform; how stability is maintained over generations; how the system adapts to changes in external environment.

Examples of institutions include: *family*, which functions to care for children, meet emotional and nurturing needs of people; *education*, which functions to teach knowledge and skills for adult roles, and cultural values and standards of behaviour; *economy*, which functions to produce and distribute material goods and services; and *law*, which functions to maintain order and control deviance.

Each institution is also a system made up of smaller parts (e.g., a primary school comprises sets of *roles*—teacher, pupil, janitor, parents. Each role set performs functions for the school system as a whole. *Role expectations* are stable over time, but also adapt to changing social needs.

Variation in Functions

Manifest functions—intended functions (e.g., teach knowledge and skills)

Latent functions—unintended but important consequences (e.g., schools provide social space for children to meet, and to supervise teenagers)

Dysfunctions—unintended negative consequences for society (e.g., schools isolate young people from adults, label some children as "failures")

Core Processes Integrating Individuals into Social Systems

1. Roles: the smallest part of a social organization
    Roles comprise typical or expected patterns of behaviour. Individuals perform roles in the system (e.g., role of teacher, principal, pupil, parent, assistant).

    Role set comprises all the roles that one role incumbent interacts with, or sometimes all the roles that one individual plays. Role strain refers to conflicting expectations and other stresses inherent in a role.

2. Socialization: the process of learning role expectations and associated values
    Primary socialization occurs in infancy, particularly in the family.
    Secondary socialization occurs in public institutions (e.g., school, church, media).
    Internalization is the process of absorbing role expectations and values as part of oneself.

3. Culture: the flexible system of core values, meanings, and expectations of society that are transmitted across generations through socialization. These shared values integrate parts of society into a dynamic whole.
    Subcultures share most of the values of the majority of society, but differ in some elements, like religion, mother tongue, occupational values, and the like. Control over conflict and deviance:
    Conformity is usually voluntary. As socialized members of society we feel guilty when we violate learned values. We desire approval and acceptance by people close to us. When these informal controls fail, economic sanctions are imposed, with force and punishment as a last resort.

Conditions under which Social Order Breaks Down

1. faulty socialization, as when parents and significant others are poor role models, teaching bad values; family relations are strained or broken; or people learn deviant subcultural values in high-crime neighbourhoods

2. inconsistent role expectations and values, as when parental values clash with school or with media, resulting in confusion and limited internalization of values

3. social systems fail to adapt to external change

4. extreme ethnic diversity threatens integration

    Anomie—the collapse of community values

☒ POLITICAL ECONOMY

Society is a system comprising interrelated parts or institutions.

Social systems are characterized by relations of inequality, power, and dominance, in which conflict and struggle are endemic features.

The economy, defined by how a society organizes production and distribution, structures all features of society.

Capitalism, as the prevailing mode of production, is based on the private ownership of means of production or "capital" (land, tools, resources, money). It is viewed as an inherently inegalitarian and exploitative system.

Capitalism gives rise to two great classes of people: **Capitalists**, who own the means of production, and *wage-workers*, who sell their labour power to the capitalists for wages because they have no means to produce for themselves. The labour power of workers generates profits for capitalists.

How Capitalism Works

Capitalists compete to produce commodities to sell in market for profit. Profits arise primarily from the gap between wages paid to workers and the exchange value of commodities that workers produce.

How Profits May Be Increased

Longer workdays, lower wages, or higher prices have limited long-term impact. Labour-saving technology is most effective. Fewer workers produce more and better goods. Capitalists can beat competitors in market, raise profits and wages. In the long run competitors either catch up, or fail and go bankrupt. When competitors catch up, prices and profits drop and recession ensues. Capitalists *must* continually invest in technological development or risk bankruptcy.

Marxist Model of the Contradictions of Capitalism

1. Law of falling rate of profit. As all producers in market adopt new technologies, prices and profits fall while higher capital costs reduce returns on investment.
2. Law of polarization of classes. Capital becomes concentrated in ever-larger corporations as others fail to invest and go bankrupt.
3. Law of rising unemployment. Workers are continually being replaced by machines.
4. Crisis of overproduction. Unemployed workers cannot afford goods.
5. Law of increasing misery of masses. Wages drop as unemployment increases.
6. Cycles of booms and slumps.

Marxist predictions: Capitalism is inherently unstable. It simultaneously generates increasing extremes of wealth and poverty. History is the history of class struggles.

The superstructure of society ultimately reflects the organization of the economy.

Capital investment patterns determine structure of job market in society. Changing job markets structure individual life-chances and inequality. Politics manages decisions in interests of corporate capitalism. Religions pacify believers and reduce the likelihood of revolt. Schools mould children for the capitalist economy. Law protects the propertied classes from those who have no property. Family organizes consumption, sustains workers, nurtures next generation of workers. Mass media are owned and operated as capitalist corporations oriented to profits and capitalist values. Culture values reproduce the values and ideas of the dominant class.

Alienation—the lived experience of structurally generated powerlessness by workers who do not have access to means of production.

☒ SOCIAL CONSTRUCTIONIST PERSPECTIVES

Focus is on how people actively work up mutually meaningful interpretations of situations through routine, everyday practical activities, and in so doing produce what we collectively come to recognize as "social systems." Relations of power and ruling are understood as embedded in these routine practices for constructing meaning.

These approaches develop the following core assumptions:

- All social action is meaningful.
- People reflect on situations and interactions and respond according to their meaning.
- Shared meanings are not "given" or fixed. They are socially constructed.
- People actively work at negotiating, constructing, sustaining, or abandoning shared definitions of situations through ongoing social interaction.
- The sense of social interaction as orderly and meaningful rather than chaotic and meaningless depends on the work people continually do to actively sustain and communicate this shared sense of order and meaning.
- Any sense of society as an orderly social system is therefore the *result* of such meaning-construction work.

Social systems do not exist apart from such meaning construction.

- The meaning-construction work engaged in by people within formal organizations, and especially by people who speak with the authority of professional status, are particularly influential in coordinating shared meanings over widely disparate work sites.

- Hence the study of work practices in these organizational sites is central to the understanding of the social construction of power relations or *relations of ruling*.

Three Groupings Reflect Progression in Theoretical Questions

Group 1: Symbolic interaction, labelling, and dramaturgical model

Focus is on the subjective meanings that guide individual responses to situations.

- Individuals selectively notice and interpret their experiences.

- Public labels generate a spiral of action and reaction. People judge and react to others in terms of common labels. People react to labels they experience as imposed upon themselves by others, especially when these are negative or deviant.

- People strive to influence how they are seen by others through body language, talk, clothes, and the like.

Group 2: Ethnomethodology and conversation analysis

Focus is on the active practices by which people generate working definitions of situations.

- We interpret what others are thinking.

- We decide which roles or expectations are appropriate.

- We routinely check and modify our sense of what is happening.

- The methodology of breaching experiments reveals tacit behavioural rules by disrupting them and observing how people react.

- Conversation analysis studies the practices through which people organize everyday talk (e.g., exchange questions, greetings, take turns, check interpretations; expose the tacit unstated understandings on which interpretations depend, expose power relations embedded in management of talk, expose how people negotiate shared meanings to accomplish "working together").

Group 3: Institutional Ethnography and Discourse Analysis

Focus is on work practices in organizations that coordinate officially sanctioned and standardized definitions of situations across multiple work sites.

- networks of mundane regulations, standardized forms and procedures that regulate work of individuals in multiple work sites

- expose information-processing networks in large-scale organizations that produce officially recognized "knowledge" for practical purposes

- expose the power/knowledge relations or *relations of ruling* these mundane practices sustain

Discourse analysis focuses on how professionals construct interpretations and frame definitions of situations that count as "knowledge" for practical purposes of diagnosing problems and generating policies.

- explore how individuals in multiple work sites draw upon professional explanations to guide routine everyday behaviour

- expose how these professional discourses contribute to the power/knowledge relations that legitimate and guide *relations of ruling*

▣ FEMINIST PERSPECTIVE

Focus is on social life as gendered, or differently experienced by women and men.

Core Assumptions

1. **Relations of reproduction** are the central organizing feature of social life—that is, how people organize to produce children and nurture them to maturity, and also how people organize to nurture and care for bodies generally. These relations of reproduction underpin and support all other features of social life. They are profoundly gendered. "The personal is political"—the organization of relations of reproduction impact directly on all other aspects of social life.

2. Gender identities are social processes, not biological constructions. They are the outcome of struggle around profoundly gendered relations of reproduction, provision of care and access to power and resources. Essentialist dichotomies of male/female and masculine/feminine are themselves open to question as social constructions.

3. Gender processes are hierarchical. Men overwhelmingly control relations of power and authority within society. All features of social life associated with "masculine" are more highly valued and socially rewarded than "feminine."

4. The production of knowledge is gendered. Historically, women have been largely excluded from creation of Western culture. This marginalization of the standpoint of women has affected all knowledge. The conceptual frames and standards for judgment within all intellectual disciplines and pursuits (theology, philosophy, law, medicine, social sciences, humanities) have been developed by men.

Feminist Sociology Developed over Three Main Stages

1. Discover women as objects of study. Promote research that explores how women are differently situated relative to men in relation to any subject of sociology research.

2. View world through the subjective standpoint and experiences of women, promoting research into gendered understandings and meanings.

3. Challenge essentialist view of the standpoint of women as a singular position, promoting research into the differently situated experiences of women along dimensions of class, race, ethnicity, age, sexual orientation.

Diversity in Feminist Thought

Liberal feminism focuses on culture, attitudes, and values that integrate society. Views legal equality rights as central to women's equality.

Marxist feminism focuses on exploitation of women as cheap labour and views redistribution of resources as crucial for gender equity.

Socialist feminism focuses on the organization of both relations of reproduction and employment. Access to employment and redistribution of productive resources are important but insufficient, since reproductive work of childcare and raising children falls on mothers. Gender equity requires societal change at the level of family relations and employment.

Radical feminism focuses on male domination of women's sexual and reproductive power. Women's bodies are controlled through pregnancy and through threats of male violence at home and in the streets. Gender equity requires reproductive choice and criminal prosecution of sexual assault and sexual exploitation of women.

Cultural feminism focuses on cultural discourses and representations of women and men. Gender equity requires changes at the level of categories of language and cultural meanings.

SUGGESTED READING

Daniel Solove's book *The Future of Reputation: Gossip, Rumor, and Privacy on the Internet* (2007) draws extensively from functionalist and symbolic interactionist analyses to explore how communications on the Internet work to enforce conformity through public shaming.

Naomi Klein's very readable book *No Logo* (2000) explores the pervasive and powerful ways in which capitalist corporations shape youth culture through advertising and branding, and how they co-opt potentially rebellious countercultures into the value system of relentless consumption.

A study by Janet Rankin and Marie Campbell, *Managing to Nurse* (University of Toronto Press, 2006), uses

the approach of institutional ethnography to explore in pain-filled detail how the lives of nurses and patients in the wards are ruled by texts and statistics produced by clerks who track admissions and discharge. In particular, see Chapter 3 "Three in a Bed": Nurses and Technologies of Bed Utilization (45–64).

The series of essays by feminist sociologists in Lazlett and Thorne's edited collection *Feminist Sociology. Life Histories of a Movement* (1997) explores how feminist sociology grew out of the lived experiences of women who became university professors during the 1980s and '90s.

QUESTIONS

1. Which of the four ways of describing Canadian society best fits with how you tend to think about Canada? What does this suggest about blind spots in the common-sense view of society shared by you and your friends?

2. What central features of society are captured by the functionalist concept of *dynamic equilibrium*?

3. What three basic concepts in functionalism account for how individuals are integrated into social institutions? How are these concepts interrelated?

4. Explain Giddens' concept of *beleaguered tradition*. List some of the implications of this concept for how Canadians respond to immigration.

5. How does political economy theory distinguish between *base* and *superstructure*? What implications does this have for the family as an institution?

6. Explain how environmental degradation can be understood as a direct consequence of global capitalist production. How might the process be halted without undermining capitalism itself?

7. Explain Gramsci's concept of *ideological hegemony*. How is this relevant for the study of mass media culture?

8. Explore the relevance of labelling theory for understanding interaction between friends on social networking sites.

9. Explain the concept of *relations of ruling*. How does institutional ethnography try to explore these relations in organizations?

10. Explain the concept of ideological circles in social research or surveys of opinion. How might this be relevant for how you express yourself?

11. How are relations of reproduction implicated in culture?

12. Give four examples of social processes that contribute to *patriarchal relations*. How are these processes reflected in the experiences you have had?

13. Explain the concept of *postfeminist liberalism*. Explore how different schools of feminist thought challenge postfeminist liberalist thought.

WEB LINKS

Ethnologue: Languages of the World
www.ethnologue.com/nearly_extinct.asp
Endangered Languages gives an in-depth look at endangered and extinct languages. This critical look shows how the world is shifting and whole cultures of people disappearing. Endangered languages are listed on this site by country, and gives demographic information as contextual background. Hear endangered languages at the link: www.pbs.org/thelinguists/Endangered-Languages/Hear-Them-Spoken.html (from www.pbs.org/thelinguists/About-The-Film/)

National Geographic News
http://news.nationalgeographic.com/news/2007/09/070918-australia-video.html
Greg Anderson, director of Living Tongues Institute (LTI), David Harrison (LTI), and National Geographic Fellow Chris Rineer explore the Australian outback to talk with elders and record endangered languages. This 2007 video brings us some of that exploration. This site also links to related topics such as "Languages Racing to Extinction in Global Hotspots" and "'New World' Film Revives Extinct Native AmericanTongue"

POP!Tech
http://poptech.org/lldd/
Living languages digital dialogue: A global effort to address the intellectual impoverishment of language extinction: Through the partnership of the online subtitling platform dotSUB and National Geographic, ethnolinguist K. David Harrison presents the endangerment of the world's languages and culture. Through this platform, and in keeping with the theme "scarcity and abundance," Dr. K. David Harrison gives a fascinating presentation of his research on endangered and extinct languages and what that means to a global human knowledge base.

PBS
www.pbs.org/thelinguists/
The Linguists documents the explorations of Dr. Greg Anderson and Dr. David Harrison while searching for endangered languages, culture, and history. They report that, on average, one language disappears every two weeks. This is a tremendous loss to the human knowledge base. This link provides a trailer of the film as well as information on the researchers, endangered languages, the speakers, and a teacher's guide to endangered languages.

Forbes.com
www.forbes.com/2006/04/17/06ceo_ceo-compensation_land.html
Special Report: CEO Compensation (4.20.06): This link provides the statistics on the chief executives of America's 500 biggest companies. Information can be sorted by rank, name, company, total compensation, five-year compensation, shares owned, age, and efficiency. "CEO compensation," "Biggest CEO paychecks," "Best performing CEOs," "Worst performing CEOs," and "List highlights" are reported. Links are also provided for "Best bosses: Who earns their keep," "It's good to be king," "Six ways CEOs hide their pay," "Whole foods: Spinning CEO pay," and "Alcoa: Low performance, high CEO pay" are a few of the reports.

Top 10 salaries of Fortune 500 CEOs start with Richard Fairbank, Capital One, who reports a $448.58 million five-year compensation total. This site, of course, provides an excellent opportunity for political economy and Marxist discourse and content analysis.

Forbes.com
http://finapps.forbes.com/finapps/jsp/finance/compinfo/CIAtAGlancelw. jsp?passName=GM&passSymbol=GM&isOut=null&sedol=
Forbes provides in-depth information on the world of business. It is unparalleled in providing US financial content for the business world, and provides sociology students with an excellent opportunity to engage in content analysis. The top story at this link is: "Motors liquidation company: (NASDAQ other OTC: GM)" with links to "BMW: Out of the woods?," "Someone's feeling lucky on Opel," "GM to restructure," and "Stocks stumble."

The Financial Express
www.financialexpress.com
Financial Express provides online information and advice to the business community. The homepage subheadings are: news, markets, companies, economy, world news, and sports. The site provides archived and latest financial stories.

"Behind the Gates: Shin Won"
www.youtube.com/watch?v=XgQD9F_lgs8&eurl=http%3A%2F%2Fvideo%2Egoogle%2Eca%2Fvideosearch%3Fhl%3Den%26q%3DMade%2520in%2520Thailand%2520%252B%2520sweatshops%26um%3D1%26ie%3DUTF%2D8%26sa%3DN%26tab%3Dwv&feature=player_embedded

Labour activists and union leaders protest GAP's use of sweatshops. This seven-minute video shines light on the human rights abuses happening in the apparel industry, particularly in the Shin Won factory.

The American Presidency Project
www.presidency.ucsb.edu/ws/index.php?pid=68675
American President George W. Bush's "Address to the Nation" on May 1, 2003. This site provides links to public papers, State of the Union messages, inaugural addresses, radio addresses, fireside chats, press conferences, executive orders, proclamations, signing statements, press briefings, statements of administration policy, debates, convention speeches, party platforms, 2009 Transition, 2001 Transition, and an audio/video media archive. Other links are provided for the elections index and presidential libraries.

RetroBites: Gloria Steinem
www.youtube.com/watch?v=CSh8qlmyZZI
This short video shows Steinem in 1968. Moses Znaimer interviews Steinem about being a "groovy chick" and an" ex-Playboy bunny" who he thought had to be "stacked, absolutely stacked to be a Bunny girl."

"Gloria Steinem Speaks at Tulane"
www.youtube.com/watch?v=IBK0jY-ICMk
Steinem presents a lecture on the contributions women make and addresses the continuing inequality and challenges that women face. She focuses, however, on the hope of the current generation of young women of the twenty-first century. This 45-minute lecture took place through the academic and co-curricular programs of The Newcomb College Institute "to enhance the education of undergraduate women at Tulane University."

Riz Khan's One on One: Naomi Wolf
www.youtube.com/watch?v=bX2fsUq6mp8&feature=related
www.youtube.com/watch?v=DPycA_CzYdw&feature=channel
Wolf is interviewed by Riz Khan on her liberal and feminist views. Khan begins by asking, "Give us your definition of liberal feminism. How do you describe yourself?" Wolf states that she defines herself as a feminist very happily, but "I don't like the term liberal as a label . . . " "I don't see feminism as a women's issue anymore . . . " This is an interesting interview for any women's studies class.

Michael Messner, Pat Griffin, Mary Jo Kane—Third Wave Feminism in Sports
www.youtube.com/watch?v=luadmO7Cugc
Dr. Mary Jo Kane, professor at the University of Minnesota and director of Tucker Center for Research on Girls and Women in Sports, states, "As we enter into a new century, we are in what I call the best of times, and the worst of times with respect to media representation of female athletes. There has been both widespread acceptance and movement of women in sports that was unheard of 50 years ago, and at the same time there is an increasing backlash about their success and presence." This short five-minute video gives a brief look at the documentary *Playing Unfair*.

KEY TERMS

actor

agency

alienation

anomie

background understandings

base

breaching experiments

capitalism

capitalists

circles of social control

class

class struggles

commodities

conflict theory

conversation analysis

cultural feminism

culture

deconstruction

dominant values

dramaturgical model

dynamic equilibrium

dysfunctions

equilibrium

ethnomethodology

facts

feminist theory

functionalism

ideological

ideological hegemony

institutional ethnography

institutions

internalization

labelling theory

latent functions

liberal feminism

manifest functions

Marxist feminism

mode of production

multinational corporations

natural attitude

norms

others

paradigms

patriarchy

political economy theory

postfeminist liberalism

postmodernism

psychoanalysis

radical feminism

recipe knowledge

relations of production

relations of reproduction

role

role conflict

role models

role set

role strain

role theory

self

sexism

signified

signifier

social order

social system

socialist feminism

socialization

status

structure

subcultures

superstructure

symbolic interactionism

system

texts

REFERENCES

Aberle, D.F., A.K. Cohen, A.K. Davis, M.J. Levy Jr., and F.X. Sutton. 1950. "The Functional Prerequisites of a Society." *Ethics* 60 (Jan.): 100–111.

Acker, Joan. 1997. "My Life as a Feminist Sociologist; or, Getting the Man Out of My Head" in B. Laslett and B. Thorne, eds. *Feminist Sociology: Life Histories of a Movement.* New Brunswick, New Jersey: Rutgers University Press, 28–49.

Barker, C. 1999. *Television, Globalization and Cultural Identities.* Buckingham; Philadelphia: Open University Press.

Barndt, Deborah. 2002. *Tangled Roots: Women, Work, and Globalization on the Tomato Trail.* Aurora, Ontario: Garamond Press.

Barthes, Roland. 1971. "The Rhetoric of the Image." *Cultural Studies* 1.

Bear-Nicholas, Andrea. 2004. Comments on final manuscript: "Changing Your World: Investigating Empowerment." Native Studies Department, St. Thomas University, Fredericton, New Brunswick, Canada.

Bear-Nicholas, Andrea. 1994. "Colonialism and the Struggle for Liberation: The Experience of Maliseet Women." *University of New Brunswick Law Journal* 43: 223–239.

Bellah, Robert. 1990. "Civil Religion in America." In J.C. Alexander and S. Seidman, eds. *Culture and Society: Contemporary Debates.* Cambridge; New York: Cambridge University Press, 262–272.

Berg, Bruce. 2001. *Qualitative Research Methods for the Social Sciences.* 4th ed. Boston: Allyn and Bacon.

Berger, Peter. 1999. *The Desecularization of the World: Resurgent Religion and World Politics.* Washington: Ethics and Public Policy Center. Grand Rapids, Michigan: William B. Eerdmans.

Berger, Peter. 1967. *The Sacred Canopy: Elements of a Sociological Theory of Religion.* New York: Doubleday.

Berger, Peter L. 1963. *Invitation to Sociology: A Humanistic Perspective.* New York: Anchor Books.

Bernal, Victoria. 2004. "Eritrea Goes Global: Reflections on Nationalism in a Transnational Era." *Cultural Anthropology* 19 (1): 3–25.

Bibby, Reginald W. 2009. *The Emerging Millennials: How Canada's Newest Generation is Responding to Change and Choice.* Project Canada Books.

Bibby, Reginald W. 2002. *Restless Gods: The Renaissance of Religion in Canada.* Toronto: Stoddart.

Bibby, Reginald W. 1993. *Unknown Gods: The Ongoing Story of Religion in Canada.* Toronto: Stoddart.

Biddle, B.J., and E.J. Thomas, eds. 1966. *Role Theory: Concepts and Research.* New York: John Wiley and Sons.

Bonner, Kieran M. 2001. "Reflexivity and Interpretive Sociology: The Case of Analysis and the Problem of Nihilism." *Human Studies* 24: 267–292.

Bonner, Kieran. 1994. "Hermeneutics and Symbolic Interactionism: The Problem of Solipsism." *Human Studies* 17: 225–249.

Boughey, H. 1978. *The Insights of Sociology: An Introduction.* Boston: Allyn & Bacon.

Brym, Robert. 2008. *Sociology as a Life or Death Issue.* Toronto: Pearson.

Brym, Robert J., with Bonnie Fox. 1989. *From Culture to Power: The Sociology of English Canada.* Toronto: Oxford University Press.

Burnett, Jonathan. 2004. "Community, cohesion and the state." *Race and Class* 45 (3): 1–18.

Campbell, Marie, and Ann Manicom, eds. 1995. *Knowledge, Experience, and Ruling Relations: Studies in the Social Organization of Knowledge.* Toronto: University of Toronto Press.

Cassin, A.M. 1980. "The Routine Production of Inequality: Implications for Affirmative Action." Paper, Ontario Institute for Studies in Education.

Cassin, A.M. 1979. *Advancement Opportunities in the British Columbia Public Service British Columbia*. Economic Analysis and Research Bureau, Ministry of Industry and Small Business Development.

Chodorow, N. 1989. *Feminism and Psychoanalytic Theory*. Cambridge: Polity Press.

Chodorow, N. 1978. *The Reproduction of Motherhood*. Berkeley: University of California Press.

Clark, Samuel D. 1968. *The Developing Canadian Community* 2nd ed. Toronto: University of Toronto Press.

Clegg, S., and D. Dunkerley. 1980. *Organization, Class, and Control*. London: Routledge & Kegan Paul.

Clow, M., with S. Machum. 1993. *Stifling Debate: Canadian Newspapers and Nuclear Power*. Halifax: Fernwood.

Cohen, A.K. 1955. *Delinquent Boys: The Culture of the Gang*. New York: Free Press.

Connell, R.W. 1997. "Long and Winding Road." In Barbara Laslett and Barrie Thorne, eds. *Feminist Sociology: Life Histories of a Movement*. New Brunswick, New Jersey: Rutgers University Press, 151–164.

Connell, R.W. 1987. *Gender & Power*. Stanford, California: Stanford University Press.

Cooley, C.H. 1964. *Human Nature and the Social Order*. New York: Schocken.

Corrigan, P. 1979. *Schooling the Smash Street Kids*. London: Macmillan.

Coser, L.A. 1956. *The Functions of Social Conflict*. Glencoe, Illinois: Free Press.

Curran, Laura. 2003. "The Culture of Race, Class, and Poverty: The Emergence of a Cultural Discourse in Early Cold War Social Work (1946–1963)." *Journal of Sociology and Social Welfare* 30 (3): 15–37.

Dandaneau, Steven. 2001. *Taking it Big: Developing Sociological Consciousness in Postmodern Times*. Thousand Oaks, California: Pine Force Press.

De Saussure, F. [1916] 1964. *Course in General Linguistics*. New York: McGraw-Hill.

Denzin, N.K. 1992. *Symbolic Interactionism and Cultural Studies: The Politics of Interpretation*. Cambridge, Massachusetts: Blackwell.

DeVault, Marjorie L., and Lisa McCoy. 2002. "Institutional Ethnographies: Using Interviews to Investigate Ruling Relations." In Jaber E. Gubrium and James A. Holstein, eds. *Handbook of Interview Research Context and Method*. Thousand Oaks, California: Sage, 751–776.

Diamond, Jared. 1999. *Guns, Germs, and Steel: The Fates of Human Societies*. New York: Norton.

Diamond, Sara. 1998. *Not by Politics Alone: The Enduring Influence of the Christian Right*. New York; London: The Guildford Press.

Douglas, M. 1979. *World of Goods: Toward an Anthropology of Consumption*. London: Allen Lane.

Douglas, M. 1966. *Purity and Danger: An Analysis of the Concepts of Pollution and Taboo*. New York: Pantheon.

Esposito, John L. 2002. *Unholy War: Terror in the Name of Islam*. New York: Oxford University Press.

Fairclough, Norman. 2003. *Analyzing Discourse: Textual Analysis for Social Research*. New York: Routledge.

Fairclough, Norman. 2000. *New Language, New Labour*. London: Routledge.

Fairclough, Norman. 2000. "Discourse, Social Theory and Social Research: The Discourse of 'Welfare Reform.'" *Journal of Sociolinguistics* 4 (2).

Fairclough, Norman. 2000. "Global Capitalism and Critical Awareness of Language." *Language Awareness* 8 (2).

Faludi, S. 1991. *Backlash: The Undeclared War Against American Women*. New York: Doubleday Anchor Books.

Foucault, M. 1980. In C. Gordon, ed. *Power/Knowledge: Selected Interviews and Other Writings 1972–1977*. New York: Pantheon.

Foucault, M. 1978. *The History of Sexuality*. Vol. 1. New York: Vintage.

Foucault, M. 1977. *Discipline and Punish: The Birth of the Prison*. London: Allen Lane.

Frank, B. 1987. "Hegemonic Heterosexual Masculinity." *Studies in Political Economy* 24 (Autumn): 159–170.

Franklin, S., C. Lury, and J. Stacey, eds. 1991. *Off-Centre: Feminism and Cultural Studies*. Cultural Studies, Birmingham Series. London: HarperCollins Academic.

Freud, S. [1905] 1976. "Three Essays on the Theory of Sexuality." In J. Strachey, trans. and ed. *The Complete Psychological Works*. Vol. 7. New York: Norton.

Freud, S. 1905. "Three Essays on the Theory of Sexuality." *The Standard Edition of the Complete Psychological Works of Sigmund Freud*. Vol. 7. London: The Hogarth Press.

Fyvel, T.R. 1963. *The Insecure Offenders*. London: Chatto & Windus.

Garfinkel, Harold. 1967. *Studies in Ethnomethodology*. Englewood Cliffs, New Jersey: Prentice-Hall.

Giddens, Anthony. 2000. *Runaway World: How Globalization is Reshaping Our Lives*. New York: Routledge.

Giddens, Anthony. 1984. *The Constitution of Society: Outline of the Theory of Structuration*. Berkeley; Los Angeles: University of California Press.

Giddens, Anthony. 1983. "Four Theses on Ideology." *Canadian Journal of Political and Social Theory* 7.

Giddens, Anthony. 1979. *Central Problems in Social Theory*. London: Macmillan.

Goffman, Erving. 1963. *Stigma: Notes on the Management of Spoiled Identity*. Englewood Cliffs, New Jersey: Prentice-Hall.

Goffman, Erving. 1961a. *Asylums*. Harmondsworth, UK: Penguin.

Goffman, Erving. 1961b. "Role Distance." In *Encounters: Two Studies in the Sociology of Interaction*. New York: Bobbs-Merrill.

Goffman, Erving. 1959. *The Presentation of Self in Everyday Life*. Garden City, New Jersey: Doubleday.

Gramsci, Antonio. 1971. In Q. Hoare and G. Nowell-Smith, trans. and eds. *Selections from Prison Notebooks*. New York: International Publishers.

Grosz, E. 1990. *Jacques Lacan: A Feminist Introduction*. London: Routledge.

Hardt, Michael, and Antonio Negri. 2000. *Empire*. Cambridge, Massachusetts: Harvard University Press.

Hebdige, D. 1979. *Subculture: The Meaning of Style*. London: Methuen.

Horowitz, D.L. 1985. *Ethnic Groups in Conflict*. Berkeley: University of California Press.

Irigaray, L. 1985. C. Porter and C. Burke, trans. *This Sex Which is Not One*. Ithaca, New York: Cornell University Press.

Jaggar, A.M., and P.S. Rothenberg. 1984. *Feminist Frameworks: Alternative Theoretical Accounts of the Relations Between Women and Men*. 2nd ed. New York: McGraw-Hill.

Kalberg, Stephen. 2003. "The Influence of Political Culture upon Cross-Cultural Misperceptions and Foreign Policy. The United States and Germany." *German Politics and Society* 21 (3): 1–23

Khayatt, M.D. 1992. *Lesbian Teachers: An Invisible Presence*. Albany, New York: State University of New York.

Kinsmen, G. 1987. *The Regulation of Desire: Sexuality in Canada*. Montreal: Black Rose Books.

Kintz, Linda and Julia Lesage, eds. 1998. *Media, Culture, and the Religious Right*. Minnesota: University of Minnesota Press.

Klein, Naomi. 2000. *No Logo: Taking Aim At The Brand Bullies*. Toronto: Vintage Canada.

Kreiger, Susan. 1997. "Lesbian in Academe." In B. Laslett and B. Thorne, eds. *Feminist Sociology: Life Histories of a Movement*. New Brunswick, New Jersey: Rutgers University Press, 194–208.

Kristeva, J. 1986. T. Moi, ed. *The Kristeva Reader*. Oxford: Blackwell.

Lacan, J. 1972. "The Insistence of the Letter in the Unconscious." In R. DeGeorge and F. DeGeorge, eds. *The Structuralists: From Marx to Levi-Strauss*. Garden City, New York: Anchor Books, 287–324.

Laframboise, Celia, and Leigh West. 1987–88. "The Case of All-Male Clubs: Freedom to Associate or Licence to Discriminate?" *Canadian Journal of Women and Law* 2: 335–361.

Laslett, Barbara, and Barrie Thorne, eds. 1997. *Feminist Sociology: Life Histories of a Movement*. New Brunswick, New Jersey: Rutgers University Press.

Lengermann, P.M., and J. Niebrugge-Brantley. 1990. "Feminist Sociological Theory: The Near Future Prospects." In G. Ritzer, ed. *Frontiers of Social Theory: The New Synthesis*. New York: Columbia University Press, 316–344.

Lessig, Lawrence. 2004. *Free Culture: The Nature and Future of Creativity*. New York: Penguin Books.

Lewis, Justin. 2001. *Constructing Public Opinion: How Political Elites Do What They Like and Why We Seem to Go Along With It*. New York: Columbia University Press.

Lipset, Seymour M. 1985. "Canada and the United States: The Cultural Dimension." In C. Doran and J. Sigler, eds. *Canada and the United States*. Scarborough, Ontario: Prentice-Hall, 109–160.

Lipset, Seymour M. 1976. "Radicalism in North America: A Comparative View of the Party Systems in Canada and the United States." *Transactions of the Royal Society of Canada (Series IV)*. Vol. 14: 19–55.

Lorde, Audre. 1984. *Sister Outsider*. New York: Crossing Press.

Loseke, D.R. 1987. "The Construction of Social Problems: The Case of Wife Abuse." *Symbolic Interaction* 10 (2): 229–243.

Mannette, Joy A. 1992. "The Social Construction of Ethnic Containment: The Royal Commission on the Donald Marshall Jr. Prosecution." In Joy Mannette, ed. *Elusive Justice: Beyond the Marshall Inquiry*. Halifax: Fernwood Press.

Marshall, Barbara L. 2000. *Configuring Gender. Explorations in Theory and Politics*. Peterborough, Ontario: Broadview Press.

McClung, Nellie. 1972. *In Times Like These*. Toronto: University of Toronto Press.

McKendy, J. 1992. "Ideological Practices and the Management of Emotions: The Case of 'Wife Abusers.'" *Critical Sociology* 19 (2): 61–80.

McRobbie, Angela. 1991. *Feminism and Youth Culture*. London: Macmillan Education.

Mead, G.H. 1934. *Mind, Self, and Society*. Chicago: University of Chicago Press.

Merkel, U.D.O. 2003. "The Politics of Physical Culture and German Nationalism: Turnen versus English Sports and French Olympism." *German Politics & Society* 21 (2): 69–96.

Merton, Robert. 1967. *On Theoretical Sociology: Five Essays, Old and New*. New York: Free Press.

Miles, Robert, and Rudy Torres. 1996. "Does 'Race' Matter? Transatlantic Perspectives on Racism after 'Race Relations.'" In Vered Amit-Talai and Caroline Knowles, eds. *Resituating Identities: The Politics of Race, Ethnicity, and Culture*. Peterborough, Ontario: Broadview Press.

Mitchell, J. 1975. *Psychoanalysis and Feminism*. New York: Random House.

Nakano Glenn, Evelyn. 1997. "Looking Back in Anger? Re-membering My Sociological Career." In B. Lazlett and B. Thorne, eds. *Feminist Sociology: Life Histories of a Movement*. New Brunswick, New Jersey: Rutgers University Press, 73–102.

Nesbitt-Larking, Paul. 2001. *Politics, Society, and the Media: Canadian Perspectives*. Toronto: Broadview Press.

O'Brien, M. 1981. *The Politics of Reproduction*. London: Routledge & Kegan Paul.

Pizzey, E. 1975. *Scream Quietly or the Neighbours Will Hear*. London: Penguin Books.

Porter, John. 1979. *The Measure of Canadian Society: Education, Equality and Opportunity*. Toronto: Gage.

Porter, John. 1965. *The Vertical Mosaic: An Analysis of Social Class and Power in Canada*. Toronto: University of Toronto Press.

Psathas, G. 1980. "Early Goffman and the Analysis of Face-To-Face Interaction." In J. Ditton, ed. *Strategic Interaction: The View from Goffman*. London: Macmillan, 52–79.

Rushton, J.P. 1988. "Race differences in behaviour: A review and evolutionary analysis." *Personality and Individual Differences* 9 (6): 1035–1040.

Said, E. 1978. *Orientalism*. London: Penguin.

Seidman, Steven. 1996. *Queer Theory/Sociology*. Oxford: Basil Blackwell.

Seidman, Steven. 1994. *Contested Knowledge: Social Theory in the Postmodern Era*. Oxford; Cambridge, Massachusetts: Blackwell.

Sharrock, W.W. 1987. "Individual and Society." In R.J. Anderson, J.A. Hughes, and W.W. Sharrock, eds. *Classic Disputes in Sociology*. London: Allen & Unwin, 126–155.

Sklair, Leslie. 2002. *Globalization: Capitalism and its Alternatives*. Oxford: Oxford University Press.

Smith, Dorothy E. 1992a. "Sociology from Women's Experience: A Reaffirmation." *Sociological Theory* 10 (1): 88–98.

Smith, Dorothy E. 1992b. "Whistling Women: Reflections on Rage and Rationality." In W.K. Carroll (and others), ed. *Fragile Truths: 25 Years of Sociology in Canada*. Ottawa: Carleton University Press.

Smith, Dorothy E. 1990. *Texts, Facts, and Femininity: Exploring the Relations of Ruling*. New York: Routledge.

Smith, Dorothy E. 1979. "Using the Oppressor's Language." *Resources For Feminist Research*. Special Publication 5 (Spring).

Smith, Dorothy E. 1977. *Feminism and Marxism: A Place To Begin, A Way To Go*. Vancouver: New Star Books.

Smith, Dorothy E. 1975. "An Analysis of Ideological Structures and How Women Are Excluded: Considerations for Academic Women." *Canadian Review of Sociology and Anthropology* 12 (4): 353–369.

Smith, Dorothy E., and Gillies Malnarich. 1983. "Where Are The Women? A Critique of Socialist and Communist Political Organization." Paper presented at the Conference on Marxism: The Next Two Decades, University of Manitoba.

Smith, George W. 1998. "The Ideology of 'Fag': The School Experience of Gay Students." *The Sociological Quarterly* 39 (2): 309–335.

Solomos, J., and L. Back. 1994. "Conceptualizing Racisms: Social Theory, Politics and Research." *Sociology* 28 (1): 143–161.

Solove, Daniel J. 2007. *The Future of Reputation: Gossip, Rumor, and Privacy on the Internet*. New Haven; London: Yale University Press.

Stacey, Judith. 1997. "Disloyal to the Disciplines: A Feminist Trajectory in the Borderlands." In Barbara Laslett and Barrie Thorne, eds. *Feminist Sociology: Life Histories of a Movement*. New Brunswick, New Jersey: Rutgers University Press, 126–150.

Staggenborg, Suzanne. 2001. "Beyond Culture versus Politics. A Case Study of a Local Women's Movement." *Gender and Society* 15 (4): 507–530.

Swift, Jamie, and Michael Czerny S.J. 2003. *Getting Started on Social Analysis in Canada*. 4th ed. Toronto: Between the Lines.

Thorne, Barrie. 1997. "Brandeis as a Generative Institution: Critical Perspective, Marginality, and Feminism." In Barbara Laslett and Barrie Thorne, eds. *Feminist Sociology: Life Histories of a Movement*. New Brunswick, New Jersey: Rutgers University Press, 103–125.

Tong, R. 1989. *Feminist Thought: A Comprehensive Introduction*. Boulder, Colorado: Westview Press.

Turner, G. 1990. *British Cultural Studies: An Introduction*. Boston: Unwin Hyman.

Van Zoonen, Liesbet. 1994. *Feminist Media Studies*. London; Thousand Oaks, California: Sage.

Vavrus, Mary Douglas. 2002. *Political Women in Media Culture*. Albany: State University of New York.

Vivian, John, and Peter J. Maurin. 2009. *The Media of Mass Communication*. Toronto: Pearson.

Walker, G. 1990a. "The Conceptual Politics of Struggle: Wife Battering, the Women's Movement, and the State." *Studies in Political Economy* 33: 63–90.

Walker, G. 1990b. *Family Violence and the Women's Movement: The Conceptual Politics of Struggle*. Toronto: University of Toronto Press.

Weeks, P.A.D. 1988. "Musical Time as a Practical Accomplishment: A Change of Tempo." Paper presented to the Society for Phenomenology and the Human Sciences, Toronto.

Willis, P. 1981. *Learning to Labour: How Working Class Kids Get Working Class Jobs*. New York: Columbia University Press.

Wuthnow, R., J.D. Hunter, A. Bergesen, and E. Kurzweil. 1984. *Cultural Analysis: The Work of Peter L. Berger, Mary Douglas, Michel Foucault, and Jurgen Habermas*. London: Routledge & Kegan Paul.

A Critical Look at Methodologies

Sociologists use a variety of research techniques, adapting them for different kinds of research contexts and questions. An important distinction is often drawn between **quantitative methods** and **qualitative methods**. Quantitative methods, which include surveys and census data, try to generate statistical analysis of patterns and trends that apply to large numbers of people. Qualitative methods, which include observations and in-depth interviews, explore the subjective meanings that particular social settings have for members. While there is no fixed correspondence between theoretical perspective and methodology, certain combinations are more common than others. Theorists who favour functionalism, or systems theory, often emulate the physical sciences in stressing quantitative, objective data that can be analyzed using high-powered statistical techniques. Political economists draw heavily on statistical analysis of economic data to document exploitative class relations. Theorists who favour interpretive approaches often deride such approaches as "number crunching" that misses uniquely subjective features of social life. Feminist researchers have tended to side with qualitative approaches, seeking to give voice to the intensely personal and intimate experiences of women who often speak from the margins of society (Duelli Klein 1980; Kirby and McKenna 1989). However, these are not hard and fast divisions. Systems theory is also associated with the technique of participant observation in anthropology, in which researchers try to live as participants in another culture, learning from insiders how the complex web of social institutions comes together as a total cultural system. Many feminist researchers advocate methods to explore the systemic structures that generate women's experiences, which are not immediately visible to the people involved (G. Smith 1990). Yet other feminists have used surveys, census data, and statistical techniques to test generalizations about the situation of large numbers of women (Eichler 1985, 632–633; Allahar and Cote 1998; Lochhead and Scott 2000). The important question is not which method one might prefer, but which is more appropriate for the particular kinds of evidence one is trying to get. As you will see below, no method is foolproof.

Each has its particular strengths and utility, and its particular weaknesses and blind spots. The ideal, therefore, is to have a number of researchers coming at similar issues from different perspectives and starting points. Their studies then will not only complement each other and increase our overall understanding, but will reveal the limitations and blind spots of specific approaches.

The objective of this chapter is to help you to become intelligent readers of research. You should not just passively absorb "facts." It is important to become constructively critical of research findings by developing an awareness both of the strengths of good research and of the inevitable limitations of knowledge.

EXPERIMENTS

For researchers in the physical sciences, **experiments** are virtually the defining characteristic of the "scientific method." There is no better technique for testing precise causal relationships. The ideal experiment controls, or holds constant, everything that could possibly influence the phenomenon of interest, then allows one **variable** to change. If there is a change in the phenomenon, and the experiment was done properly, one knows that the manipulated variable, and only that one, caused the change. In the terminology of experimental research, the **independent variable** is the presumed cause. This is the one that is manipulated in the experiment to see the effect of its presence or absence. The **dependent variable** is the phenomenon that is thought to depend on or be influenced by the other variable.

One interesting sociological experiment began with the observation that students who habitually sat near the front of classrooms tended to get higher marks on average than students who habitually sat near the back (Dooley 1984, 20–23). Two plausible hypotheses were suggested. The phenomenon could be due to "self selection," that is, the more interested and able students chose to sit near the front. Alternatively, it could be that increased interaction and eye contact with the professor stimulated higher performance from students who sat at the front. An experiment was designed to test these theories. The professor let students choose where to sit on the first day of classes, then asked them to stay in that place for the next three weeks until he gave the first test. Then he randomly mixed everybody up, with some of the back-row people moving to the front, and some of the front-row people moving to the back. Three weeks later he tested the students again. The theory was that if self-selection causes the association, then making some of the better students sit at the back would make no difference to their test results. But if sitting at the front under the close eye of the professor was the real cause, then there should be noticeable changes in test results after students were moved. The results supported the self-selection **hypothesis**, showing that moving people randomly seemed to make little difference to the results. Good students choose to sit at the front while the weaker or less motivated students choose to sit at the back. It was interesting to note, however, that the level of participation, measured by their asking questions and getting involved in class discussions, did change as students were moved from back to front and vice versa. Closeness to the professor rather than personality characteristics of the students seemed to be the major factor in class discussion.

This study has all the elements of a true experiment. It includes a clear theory that either self-selection of where to sit, or proximity to professors, causes grades to be higher among students who sit near the front. In this experiment the dependent variable is grades. There are two independent variables—proximity to professor and self-selection. Two logical predictions are derived from this theory. If the theory of self-selection is correct, then moving the students will make no difference to their marks. If proximity to the professor is the correct theory, then moving students will make a clear difference. The researcher changes one variable—seat selection—and everything else is held constant. All students receive the same lectures and tests. The researcher observes what happens and decides which theory is correct on the basis of whether the results were as predicted.

Future researchers who wish to critique an experiment can first *replicate* or repeat it with different classes of students to see if the same pattern holds. You might try this experiment in your own sociology classes to see if you find comparable patterns. Researchers also need to closely examine the *measurement* of the dependent and independent variables to decide if there is a truly good fit between the original concepts and the measures used. If proximity to professor is a variable that works slowly, perhaps the three-week gap between first and second test is not sufficient to really judge its impact on grades. There may also be other hidden influences that were not entirely controlled in the experiment. For example, students may be reacting to the fact that they know what the professor is testing for.

A second experiment was designed to test the effect of different levels of severity in prosecution of domestic assault cases on likelihood of repeat offences (Sherman and Berk 1984; Sherman 1992). In this study the dependent variable was evidence of repeat offences, while the independent or proposed causal variable was reaction by police to domestic assault calls. In cooperation with the Minneapolis Police Department, the researchers arranged for 330 assault cases to be *randomly* assigned to one of three conditions: arrest and charge the offending spouse, order the offender out of the house for eight hours but not arrest, or merely give a verbal warning. Random assignment means that treatment of each case was determined by chance or luck of the draw. Neither police nor researchers could influence which offender would or would not be charged. This was to ensure that police did not bias the study by arresting the more unpleasant offenders. Cases where injuries were serious, or where a spouse insisted that an arrest be made, were exempted from the study. Researchers measured the effect of different treatments by examining police records of repeat offences and by telephone interviews with victims every two weeks for the next six months. The results showed large differences by treatment. Only 13 percent of those arrested assaulted their partner again over the six-month period compared with 26 percent of those who were separated from their partner but not arrested. This group differed little from those who were merely given a verbal warning. Researchers concluded that the "deterrence theory" was supported. Harsher punishment deters repeat deviance. This study was influential in changing police protocols in favour of mandatory arrests.

Replication of the study in six more cities, however, produced inconsistent results, with four of them showing long-term increases in domestic violence among those arrested. A detailed examination of cases suggested a new explanation. Offenders who were married and employed were less likely to offend if arrested, but those who were unmarried and unemployed were more likely to repeat offenses if arrested (Schutt 1996, 50; Sherman et al. 1992). Researchers proposed a new theory of social control. The shame resulting from a public arrest is a stronger deterrent when individuals have a "stake in conformity," or more to lose from deviant labelling. This fits the data, but has yet to be tested in a controlled experiment.

Critics of the original study suggest that measurement of the dependent variable is flawed (Dobash and Dobash 2000, 261). Both police records and victims' reports are well known to seriously underestimate the true extent of domestic violence. Perhaps the wives of employed men are also reluctant to face the shame of a second arrest, and victims may fear reprisals for talking with researchers. More than half the victims in the first study refused to carry out follow-up interviews (Schutt 1996, 48).

Experiments arguably work best in specially equipped settings like **small groups laboratories** in universities, designed so that researchers can control key variables that influence behaviour, such as seating arrangements, lighting, noise, whether subjects in the experiment can or cannot communicate with each other, the exact task that subjects engage in, and so on. Archibald (1978, Ch. 7) describes studies of coalitions and bargaining in competitive three-person games, and how all-male, all-female, and mixed-gender groups behave. The experiments suggest that in games with two women and one man, or with two men and one woman, the two members in the majority sex appear to compete for the member of the opposite sex. Each of the two men, for example, would try to get the woman on his side against the other man. All-female groups tended to be less egoistic than men, being more likely to form a three-way rather than a two-against-one coalition, dividing the outcomes equally.

Limitations of Social Experiments

The inherent limitation of experiments in such artificial and simplified contexts is that it is risky to generalize from them to predict how people will behave in more complex and longer-term social situations. It is commonly students from large undergraduate courses in sociology and psychology who are used as subjects for experimental research because they are readily available and easily persuaded to participate. We cannot assume that how students play games in a research laboratory will accurately reflect the behaviour of people in far more complex settings—for example, managers in business meetings. Archibald notes further that the competitive behaviour evident in these games may be culturally specific, reflecting how people have learned to behave in competitive capitalist societies rather than ones based on cooperative forms of economy.

When experiments are carried out in real-life settings, such as the classroom behaviour and the domestic violence arrest studies described above, researchers face major complications controlling the multiple and interconnected influences. Students can readily guess the seating-grades hypothesis and strategize to change the outcomes. Victims of domestic assault can exaggerate or cover up their experiences in anticipation that their abuser will be let off with a caution again or sent to prison, or they could refuse to say anything. Police officers can and did override their orders to randomize caution or arrest responses (Schutt 1996, 54).

Ethical Issues with Experiments

The evasive responses taken by police in the study of the effects of arrests on spousal abuse draws attention to serious ethical issues that arise in research involving people. Is it ethically acceptable for researchers to invoke the authority of the U.S. National Institute of Justice to force police officers to randomize whether they caution or arrest offenders, and to subject unsuspecting victims of domestic assault to such experimentation? The informed consent of police chiefs was gained prior to the study, but not the consent of individual officers who had to confront the families. Furthermore, the victims who call the police for help had no opportunity to refuse to participate in the experiment, or even to know that they were being experimented upon. This is notwithstanding the fact that how police respond to the domestic abuse call potentially opens victims to the risk of further assault. The counterargument in favour of doing this research is that the resulting data was critical for guiding future police protocols and perhaps protecting future victims. How do we balance the risk of harm to unwitting families caught up in the experiment with potential benefits from the knowledge gained?

Consider also the ethical issues involved in the experiment linking where students sit with test results. Suppose I want to test the hypothesis that proximity to me in my introductory sociology classes has a long-term influence on students' grades. Would it be ethically acceptable for me to force some of you to sit in the front or back rows for an entire semester against your own inclination, even if I have the power to make you conform? Remember that I am predicting that grades will be adversely affected by making people sit at the back.

The practical difficulties involved in manipulating people in social experiments, combined with serious ethical issues raised by such manipulation, has favoured the use of *quasi experiments* in sociology, rather than classical experiments. In quasi experiments, researchers rely on comparisons among naturally occurring settings where they do not try to randomize or otherwise control the people who are already involved. Research is weaker in that problems of self-selection and prior differences in kinds of people involved in different settings do impact on results, and other possible influences cannot be eliminated. On the other hand, the settings are more realistic and ethical concerns less pressing. Dobash and Dobash (2000) describe their study of two naturally occurring comparison groups of men prosecuted, found guilty, and placed on probation for domestic violence. One group of men was ordered by the presiding judge to participate in intensive court-mandated offender treatment programs while the comparison group comprised men sanctioned in other ways, including fines, traditional probation, and prison. Knowing that the two groups were not equivalent to start with, the researchers tried to measure and control for these differences by comparing the men individually on more than 30 theoretically relevant variables. They also measured the effects of treatment by in-depth interviews and postal questionnaires with both men and their women partners at intervention, three months following, and 12 months following. They concluded that the court-mandated programs did seem to reduce controlling and intimidating behaviour and improve quality of life for both men and women partners over the 12-month period. Results were also more positive for men in state-sanctioned marriages and for those who were employed than for those in the unmarried or unemployed categories. Researchers claim further that their in-depth interviews and follow-up questionnaires provide greater understanding of the subjective meanings and responses of the men and women involved, and hence the true causal processes at work, than does the exclusively experimental work of Sherman and Berk. We explore these methodological approaches below.

SURVEY RESEARCH

Questionnaires

Survey research is so commonly associated with sociology as to be virtually synonymous with the discipline in the minds of many people. Typically, surveys involve the use of **questionnaires** or structured interviews in which a series of questions is asked of large numbers of people. In theory, one could approach every person in a population when doing a survey, as when a census is taken. But in practice this is so expensive and time-consuming that usually only a sample of people is used. A **sample** comprises a small proportion of people carefully selected from a wider population. On a university campus with 30 000 students, for example, a researcher might interview a selected sample of 300 students (a 1-percent sample) to study aspects of student life. The goal is to use information gained from the sample to generalize to the wider population it represents.

It is very important that the sample be selected carefully so that it fairly represents the range of experience and characteristics in the population. The data garnered from a survey of 300 students in a local pub, for example, would not be representative of the student body as a whole since these students differ in important respects from others who rarely or never go to pubs and hence would not be included in the sample.

The ideal way to select a sample is through a random process. A *random sample* is one in which every member of a population has an equal chance of being selected, leaving no possibility that researchers can select their friends or particular types of people who might be easily available. To draw a random 1-percent sample of university students, we might get the registrar's list of students, close our eyes and stick a pin in the list to choose the first person for our sample, and then select every hundredth name thereafter, until we had the number of names we wanted for our survey. In practice, many surveys fall short of this ideal because randomized samples of people tend to be difficult to contact. While all students at one university are concentrated on one or two campuses, a random sample of the residents of Ontario would be spread over thousands of square miles and take years to contact them in person.

Sociologists have ways of stratifying or grouping members of such a huge population to make sampling more realistic while still being reasonably representative of the whole. A survey of the attitudes and experiences of New Brunswick parents regarding sexual health education at school and at home (Weaver et al. 2002) first selected a random sample of schools in the province, and then used the children to distribute 9533 surveys to their parents. A total of 4206 surveys were completed, with the bulk of non-returns reflecting parents who received multiple copies because they had two or more children in the schools. The same sampling frame was used to survey all middle school pupils (Byers et al. 2003), all high school pupils (Byers et al. 2003), and all teachers (Cohen et al. 2004) in the selected schools. The sample of parents was so large and so well randomized that the researchers were able to affirm, with a minimal risk of error, that fully 94 percent of parents in the province favoured the provision of sexual health education in schools. This survey was instrumental in the government's decision to introduce sexual health education into the school curriculum, notwithstanding vocal and organized opposition from a number of parents.

Smaller, low-budget, exploratory studies often settle for a partial and non-random sample of people who are easy to get. The caveat associated with such surveys is that, while

PEANUTS reprinted by permission of UFS, Inc.

their findings may be insightful, they cannot be assumed to describe accurately the wider population.

One important advantage that surveys have over experiments is that they permit **multivariate analysis**. As we have seen, experiments study the effect of change in one variable while all others remain the same. Surveys, in contrast, can gather information about a number of variables at the same time and explore how combinations of variables influence the issue of interest to the researcher. In a survey of students, for example, we might be interested in finding out why some maintain a high grade point average while others fail or barely scrape by. We have good reason to believe that no single variable can explain this. Multiple variables may be involved. We might want to not only find out about students' IQs, but also about how many classes they attend, how many hours a week they study, how often they visit a pub, how many hours of paid employment they have per week, the family responsibilities they carry, and so on. Do less intelligent students who study long hours do better or worse on average than highly intelligent students who spend more time socializing than studying? What difference does it make if we also take into account that some students come to university straight from school while others have not been in full-time education for years? With the aid of computers and statistical techniques it is possible to see how sets of variables interact in combination.

One example of large-scale survey research that I was involved in explored patterns of immigrant settlement and race relations in an English city (Richmond et al. 1973). It used a questionnaire with 172 questions, covering such topics as housing conditions and overcrowding, social and economic status, local slang and idioms, work experience, including discrimination in getting a job and possible prejudice experienced from fellow workers, satisfaction with the neighbourhood, interaction between residents of different ethnic origins, and continuing relations between immigrants and people in their country of origin. The survey also covered the topic of **acculturation**, the extent to which immigrants have adopted the culture—lifestyle, behaviour patterns, values, and attitudes—that prevails among local people.

Responses to a range of questions provided a wealth of material for understanding the life experiences of immigrants and their locally born neighbours, allowing researchers to explore a multitude of hypotheses concerning how variables might relate to each other. Do relations with neighbours improve with acculturation? Are immigrants measurably worse off than indigenous people with respect to housing? Does the level of cooperation or conflict with neighbours vary with ethnic groups, social class, or family size and structure? Does it vary in terms of whether immigrants keep their houses in good repair?

Since a complete **enumeration** of the 2633 households in the chosen area was used as the basis for the sample, one can be confident that the results are based on a representative cross-section of the community, free from the biased coverage that would occur if any volunteers or personal friends and contacts of the researchers had been used as sources of information. This particular study was carried out by a team of researchers who went door-to-door, called back many times, took great pains to encourage people to be interviewed because it was so important to learn how everyone felt, and arranged for foreign-language interviews whenever necessary. Virtually no other research technique could have provided the quality of information derived from this survey. Even living within the area as a member of the community would have been less effective, since friendship patterns and acquaintances are invariably limited and selective. Mailed questionnaires or forms that people are left to fill in themselves could not have achieved this very high level of coverage. This survey in Britain provided the blueprint for a number of similar surveys in Canadian cities at the York University Institute of Race Relations in Toronto, directed by Anthony Richmond.

Not all survey research is conducted like this. Such exhaustive surveys take a great deal of time, skill, and money. Under the broad term *survey*, there is a wide variety of techniques that can be used to ask people questions. At one extreme, tightly structured questionnaires can be mailed out for people to fill in themselves and post back to the research headquarters. Such an approach may be particularly valuable for collecting data on topics that are sensitive or embarrassing. People may feel more comfortable, for example, answering questions about their sexual behaviour, or suicidal thoughts and conflicts with parents, in an anonymous questionnaire than with an interviewer facing them. Mailed questionnaires are also quick, relatively cheap to administer, and can be mailed out simultaneously to very large numbers of people over wide geographic areas.

Limitations of Survey Research

A number of problems make self-administered questionnaires unsuitable for many kinds of research. Clearly, they cannot be used with illiterate subjects. They are also unsuitable for many less-educated people who, while able to read and write, may have difficulty understanding the language of the questionnaire and expressing themselves in writing. More generally, if the questions are the least bit vague or ambiguous, there is no way for the recipient to ask for clarification. Another common problem is inappropriate answer categories that do not fit the respondent's particular circumstances so that she or he is unable to answer accurately. Since recipients cannot explain to the researcher what the problem is, they are likely to answer randomly or pick an inappropriate response and leave it to the researcher to work out what they meant. In addition, the researcher has no way of knowing what people answering the questionnaire meant by their answers and can only assume that what they meant is what the researcher would have meant. There is much evidence that the wording of the questions themselves can determine, at least in part, the kind of answers given. Public opinion pollsters are notorious for asking vague questions that lend themselves to interpretations favoured by those who hire them to conduct the poll (Lewis 2001, 136).

Experiments designed to test how people respond to questionnaires suggest that people routinely try to read meanings into questions and construct appropriate answers, even when they cannot possibly know the answer. To oblige the researcher, subjects have been known to rank what, unbeknownst to them, were fictitious television programs. The resulting order is largely a product of the researcher's question, combined with vague associations that the wording raises in subjects' minds. It is entirely possible that other rank orders, such as ethnic preferences, may be equally artificial, with people creating a ranking to oblige the researcher, while actually having no particular preferences.

Other questions distort reality by imposing false answer categories or invalid combinations. Consider a question on the quality of relations between siblings that provides the following answer categories: 1) warm, cooperative, supportive relations; 2) helpful and cooperative much of the time; 3) strained, mildly competitive relations; 4) much competition and tension. The problem is that answer categories do not allow for the possibility that people may have very warm and supportive relations that are also very competitive, or tense relations that are not competitive. According to this question, competition is bad by definition, whatever the respondent might think.

Another problem with questionnaires is that the meaning of answers to questions is commonly context-dependent. For example, attitudes towards the desirability of large families depend heavily on whether one is thinking about family parties or education costs. The coded answer may be meaningless if interpreted out of context (Cicourel 1974). Similarly how one responds to a question on whether small towns are a good place to raise children will vary with the implicit frames of reference that different people use (Bonner 1997). Long-term residents may be positively valuing the closeness of their extended family members, while newcomers from the city may be positively evaluating their increased distance from interfering kin. Long-term members may be thinking of their commitment to their whole community, while short-term residents are evaluating their rational self-interests in easier parenting—shorter drives to get their children to and from varied activities than in a city. Objectively, the same questionnaire responses can represent very different underlying worldviews.

Responses to scales that try to measure strength of attitudes are also heavily influenced by different comparative reference groups that people may be thinking about when answering. If asked to indicate on a 10-point scale my level of support or opposition to Canada joining the USA in the 2003 war in Iraq, for example, I may well use how strongly my immediate friends seem to feel as a gauge for the strength of my own feelings. Similarly, how strongly I would rate my involvement in delinquent behaviour as a teenager will reflect how I compare myself to others around me, as well as how I actually did behave.

Distortions can also arise when researchers inadvertently build biased assumptions into a question. One question asked respondents to agree or disagree with the following statement: "If a married woman has to stay away from home for long periods of time in order to have a career, she had better give up the career" (Eichler 1988, 82–88). More working-class than middle-class respondents indicated agreement with this question, leading the researcher to conclude that working-class people hold more traditional views towards women's roles. Eichler, however, shows that this interpretation may reflect the biases of the researcher rather than the respondents. When a parallel question was added about whether married *men* had better give up their career, more working-class than middle-class people agreed with this as well. The two questions together suggest that what the responses of working-class people really show is a higher value placed on family life over careers generally for both women and men, while middle-class respondents were more inclined to value careers. The middle-class researcher had taken it for granted that a married man's career would have to take precedence over spending more time at home, and hence had not even thought to include the question.

In summary, surveys are only as useful as the quality of the questions asked. A critical reading of research must involve taking a hard look at the questions used to see whether the researcher's interpretation of the answers is warranted, or whether some other meaning could reasonably be applied. Reports that provide respondents' answers but omit the questions asked or the context in which questions were embedded are particularly suspect.

INTERVIEWS

Interviews as a methodology involve face-to-face discussion between researcher and people from whom the researcher hopes to learn information—these people are variously referred to as informants, subjects, respondents, or participants. As these terms suggest, interviews can vary widely.

At one extreme, interviews involve reading standardized questions to informants with a predefined set of response options designed to generate quantitative data for statistical analysis. Interviewers are commonly carefully trained to ensure that they do not bias responses by altering the tone or wording of the questions or revealing their own opinions on topics. Much research has gone into how the gender, race, and class characteristics of researcher vis-a-vis respondent may subtly influence responses, and how best to conduct an interview to minimize these effects.

At the other extreme, interviews seek qualitative in-depth life-story narratives focused around the research theme. Such interviews may last for several hours with neither researcher nor participant knowing beforehand all the issues that may be explored in the research conversation. Here there is no expectation of standardized responses. In a widely cited essay on feminist methods, Oakley (1981) flatly rejects the standard textbook advice for conducting detached, formal interviews as assuming a "masculine model of sociology and society" (Oakley 1981, 31). In her own research with women on their experience of childbirth, she describes her interviews as deeply personal encounters spread over some nine hours each. These interviews often involved intensely personal exchanges of information, advice, and feelings between herself and the women who participated or cooperated in the research.

Limitations of Interview Research

Interviews, no less than questionnaires, inherently raise problems of interpretation. Interviews have the advantage over questionnaires in clarifying meanings because the interviewer is there to correct ambiguities and misunderstandings. Response rates are commonly far higher. People may simply throw a questionnaire into the waste basket or never get around to answering it, but they will talk to someone standing in front of them, particularly if the researcher seems friendly and genuinely interested in listening to them. Researchers can also gather much additional, subtle information about confusion, disinterest, or worry by watching respondents' facial expressions, body language, and so on. This sensitivity is mutual, however, giving rise to concerns that respondents may tailor their answers to fit what they sense will please the researcher.

Interview responses are often not *authentic*, in the sense of conveying truly deep, inner feelings and convictions about an issue (Silverman 1993, Ch. 5). Respondents typically only have a few seconds to think up an answer to a question, and hence tend to respond by what immediately comes to mind. This is most likely to be a standard, culturally expected, common-sense response, or whatever they think will come across as an acceptable or meaningful answer.

They may also offer self-explanatory answers that will avoid prompting a series of "why do you think that?" type of follow-up questions.

The interview situation itself is also a social encounter in which respondents are necessarily presenting a public image of themselves to another person when being interviewed. Mothers of sick children discussing their encounters with medical practitioners routinely talked in ways that portrayed themselves as "morally adequate mothers." Part of such moral adequacy involved affirming that they thoroughly monitored their baby, and hence "knew" something was wrong before the doctor told them (Baruch 1981). In the same study researchers noted that mothers often recounted "moral atrocity stories" such as the callousness they noticed in doctors who would announce to them that their baby had a terrifying disability like cystic fibrosis and then not even give them time to ask questions. Videotaped recordings, however, showed that doctors routinely did wait for parents to ask questions, but parents were often experiencing too much shock to formulate any response. The discrepancies between the videotaped evidence and descriptions given by parents led the researchers to suggest that doctors tell parents about the diagnosis at one meeting and then arrange a later one for parents to ask questions.

The distortions that can occur between the meaning a person intends, and what their comments are interpreted to mean by a researcher, is evident in the reaction of one housewife to the race-relations survey discussed above. At first she did not want to be interviewed because she felt that if she raised even legitimate complaints about immigrants, researchers would automatically jump to the conclusion that she was racially prejudiced. She explained carefully that she did not dislike immigrants but hated the way that the immigrant men living in rooming houses on her street would whistle and shout sexual remarks when she walked past her, as if she were one of the local prostitutes. She was also disturbed and intimidated by the noise these men made as they crowded onto the steps outside their houses on warm summer evenings. In this neighbourhood it was common for landlords to rent a single room to eight to 10 men who had migrated from Pakistan without their families to find work in Britain. The female interviewer assured the woman that she could understand these feelings. But when the interviewer later discussed the conversation with a more senior male researcher, he responded bluntly that the woman obviously was prejudiced against immigrants and was merely rationalizing her responses. People would naturally be reluctant to express strongly racist views to a naive young white female interviewer, even when directly asked. Perhaps he was correct. But what if the woman meant what she said—that she was distressed not by their racial characteristics, but by the sexual taunts from crowds of frustrated

64   A Critical Look at Methodologies

single men? There was no way that researchers, out to prove English people are prejudiced, would believe her.

Ethical Issues in Interview Research

Important ethical issues arise in using interviews as a research tool. Codes of ethics for sociological research all emphasize the principle of informed consent. People being interviewed have a right to know in advance what the interview will be about and to refuse to be interviewed or to refuse to answer specific questions, and to terminate the interview at any time. Researchers also have an obligation to protect the confidentiality of informants. Beyond such standard advice, Oakley further reminds us that research can be an emotionally intense experience for participants who may be asked to relive powerful life situations like the birth of a child or being beaten by a partner. Research should not be undertaken lightly or carelessly. Hiller and DiLuzio (2004) describe how their research on internal migration within Canada became a catalyst for participants to rethink their entire migration experience, sometimes involving flight from family conflicts as well as unacknowledged feelings of loneliness and loss. Many spoke of how much they appreciated the opportunity presented by the interview to reflect on these experiences, but the interview could also be profoundly disturbing in opening old wounds and pain.

A group of women associated with the Canadian Research Institute for the Advancement of Women (CRIAW) got together in 1993 to draft a feminist code of ethics which makes explicit issues of power and privilege that arise in research, and explore how more egalitarian relations between research participants might be achieved (Muzychka and Poulin 1995).

Interview responses, when people only have a few seconds to think, commonly reflect culturally expected comments rather than inner feelings and convictions.

Shutterstock

PARTICIPANT OBSERVATION

Participant observation involves varying degrees of personal involvement in the everyday lives of the people being studied, sharing in their activities on a face-to-face level, observing, questioning, and learning how to participate in their life-worlds. This gives the researcher a uniquely valuable vantage point through which to develop a sympathetic understanding of social life from the perspectives of the people themselves. This is the preferred methodology of anthropology, since it is ideally suited to developing an understanding of the total culture of a people, especially those who live in small, isolated communities. In sociology, participant observation has been adapted to the study of distinctive subgroups such as work teams, churches, group homes, special-interest organizations, and the like.

The degree to which members of the subgroups are aware that they are being studied has varied from minimal to total disclosure. In his classic study of jazz musicians, Becker (1963) writes about his observations of the band in which he himself played, without openly adopting a separate role as "researcher." George Smith (1990) was an activist with the Toronto AIDS group whose political struggles he studied. Ammerman (1987) became a participating member of the Southside Gospel Church in Chicago. She informed the church elders that she was a sociologist interested in researching the religious community, but the vast majority of congregation members knew her simply as one of themselves. Rebekah Nathan (2005), an anthropology professor, enrolled as a freshman student to study student life. Students in research methods classes at my university have occasionally engaged in participant-observation studies of classroom interaction, testing the hypothesis that different seating arrangements—immovable seats in parallel rows, small-group tables, or large seminar rooms with seating in circles—alters the interaction between professor and students. Instructors knew about and consented to the research, but students enrolled in the classes were not informed. Student observers confirmed what professors have long suspected. Students who sit at the back with laptops open and eyes down are Twittering or text-messaging to each other, or watching YouTube videos, rather than paying attention to lectures.

In other cases researchers have openly represented themselves in the role of researcher, particularly in situations where they could not pass as a regular group member. Most Western anthropologists who wish to study non-industrialized and non-Western communities are obvious outsiders. Jean Briggs (1970) could not possibly pass as an Inuit when she studied a nomadic Inuit community. In fact, members of the community she lived with had to go out of their way to look after her. When Whyte conducted his classic study *Street Corner Society* (1943), the unemployed Italian men hanging out on the streets of Boston knew he was not one of them but were willing to have him participate in their daily activities. Warren (2003) sought the permission of the course instructors and students to sit in theatre classes and observe how students performed literature from diverse cultural backgrounds, and how, in the process, they performed "race." These researchers trade the risk that their presence will disrupt normal activities for the advantage that being known as a researcher gives them the freedom to ask questions and interview participants. Their common experience is that, as time passes, participants soon forget about the fact that they are being researched, and pre-established routines of behaviour re-emerge.

Participatory research offers unparalleled depth of insight, but lacks some of the systematic controls and potential for replication and checking that other research techniques permit. Researchers learn about the groups and activities they are studying through unique networks of personal experiences, friendships, and events. Another researcher, joining the group at another time, may have very different experiences. This raises the difficult question of whether one researcher is the more accurate, or whether the group culture itself may have changed over time. The famous anthropologist Margaret Mead has been accused of painting an overly harmonious picture of adolescent life in the Samoan community she studied, failing to see the teenage strife, delinquency, and illegitimacy that actually occurred (Mead 1928; Freeman 1983). The Samoans may have gone out of their way to hide this seamier side of community life. The quality of the final analysis in participant observation depends very heavily upon the personal resources and sensitivities of individual researchers. Warren (2003, 1–3) describes his excitement at his first tentative flash of insight into how "performing white superiority" gets done, while listening to a white researcher describing scenes in schools with predominantly white or black students. His elation was crushed when comments from a black woman in the audience brought the realization that something he was barely able to sense was obvious to her. His text is full of ethnographic descriptions of student performances through which he reads the active construction of racialization. Other observers of the same scenes, including students in the theatre classes, might well not notice these subtle nuances and patterns.

Ethical Issues in Participant Observation

Participant observation studies, like other forms of research, raise difficult ethical questions. Do sociologists have the right to conduct research on or in a group of people without their prior consent or knowledge? Would it be different if people know that the research is going on but do not understand exactly what it is that the researcher is looking for? Contemporary codes of ethics stress the importance of informed consent, but this does not solve the question of whose consent should be obtained. Practical and political considerations usually dictate that researchers get the permission of leaders or elders in a group or community. But it is hard to argue on moral grounds that such people can legitimately speak for everyone else. Should negative votes by a few participants have been sufficient to terminate Ammerman's study of Southside Church or Warren's study of theatre students? There are no easy answers to such questions, but sociologists have an obligation to raise them and deal with them as best we can. At the very least, researchers have an obligation not to carry out research in ways that might reasonably be expected to harm their subjects.

UNOBTRUSIVE MEASURES

Among the arsenal of social science research techniques are some that avoid risks of interaction biases between researcher and subjects by focusing on secondary analyses of records that are collected for other purposes and traces of events that have already happened. Some of these are described below.

Census Data and Official Records

Census data are immensely valuable for social science research. These comprehensive surveys of the entire population of a country, carried out every 10 years with government funding, and with the force of law to compel people to answer the questions, provides a wealth of information about the social, economic, and **demographic** characteristics of a people, on a scale that no other form of research can parallel. Many sociologists rely on census data as their primary source for studies of population change, hence making it a matter of considerable importance what kinds of questions are included in census forms. The omission of a simple question such as ethnic origin of parents, for example, would greatly hamper the study of migration, assimilation, and discrimination in the labour market. As noted above with respect to surveys, small changes in the wording of questions in census forms result in large changes in data collected. The 1961 Census in Canada included the question: "To what ethnic or cultural group did you or your ancestor (on the male side) belong on coming to this continent?" (Pryor et al. 1992). In 1981 the clause "on the male side" was deleted and the naming of multiple ancestries permitted, in recognition of feminist interests in descent through mothers. In 1986, the clause "on first coming to this continent" was dropped, in recognition of the fact that many "ethnic" groups, such as Aboriginal, French Canadian, American, Quebecois, Mexican, and the like, have not technically come from outside the continent of North America. Also, the pre-defined categories or mark-off boxes were altered to include "Black." A series of tests in 1986 experimented with how to include "Canadian" as an ethnic option in census forms. Responses varied from lows of 1 to 10 percent if "Canadian" was not explicitly mentioned, to highs of 30 to 53 percent when it was included as an example of ethnicity and listed as a separate mark box. The great variation in responses reveals the context-dependent character of peoples' ethnic self-identification. Shifting terminology in census forms also complicates any long-term analysis of trends in ethnic composition of the Canadian population.

Census data present problems for sociological analysis in other respects, in that the categories used to collect information may not be appropriate for research interests. The census, for example, records the total number of marriages for the period under consideration, but does not indicate whether a given marriage is a first or a subsequent one for the persons involved. It thus becomes impossible to determine how many **reconstituted families** may exist within a community. Similarly, the census records the number of single parents who have children living with them but does not record the number of men who have fathered children without a long-term attachment to the mother. Records of family income as units give no information on how much money the wife might actually have to call her own. Hence many interesting questions about family life cannot be answered using census data because the recording categories do not permit it (Eichler 1988, 21–23). Similar problems arise for sociological research that draws on records kept by other government and private agencies, such as crime statistics from the Department of Justice, poverty statistics from the Department of Health and Welfare, food-bank records of numbers of people registering for assistance, or international data collected by agencies such as Amnesty International.

It is important to remember that all such official reports are generated by staff within bureaucracies who want the information collected through particular forms to manage the practical activities of their organization (Smith 1999, 148–151). To understand what the statistics mean, one needs to look carefully at how and why they are collected. Research problems often arise because it is not always clear how particular experiences are coded into categories used for the statistics. Different record keepers may make these decisions quite differently. Suicide rates for a particular region of Switzerland, for example, jumped by 50 percent in one year when government bureaucrats replaced Catholic priests as keepers of the rates (Douglas 1967). Researchers who mistake the apparent increase in counted suicides as evidence of a real increase in the numbers of people choosing to kill themselves may be building up complex explanations for something that never happened. A change in whether police are encouraged to lay charges for any and all incidents of fighting among youth, or to calm the situation and leave, will drastically affect youth crime rates (Schissel 1997). How clerks interpret rules for classifying medical problems for purposes of workers' compensation claims will drastically affect rates of workplace-related illness (Doran 2002), and so on. No statistical data should be accepted at face value without questioning how they were generated and for what practical purposes.

Statistical Analysis

Statistical analysis in sociology has reached a high level of sophistication. With the aid of computers, it is possible to measure the relative impact of many variables upon each other. It is important to gain some understanding of statistics and how useful they can be for modelling social relations. But it is also important not to assume that just because evidence is presented in numerical form that it is somehow more scientific or rigorous or objectively true than any other form of presentation.

Statistical **correlations** do not prove **causality**. It may be possible to show that two variables are correlated, in that as one variable increases so does the other, without there being any direct causal relation between them. Bernard Shaw once pointed out a strong correlation between age of British men at death and the type of hat they wore. Men who wore top hats seemed to live much longer on average than men who wore cloth caps. Does this mean we should all start wearing top hats if we want to live longer? Of course not. The association reflects the fact that top hats were worn largely by upper-class men who had much better living conditions and healthier diets than the working-class men who generally wore cloth caps. Time ordering can also be tricky. There is a close relationship between the number of fire engines on the scene and size of fire but that does not mean that fire engines cause fires. There is also a relationship between age of women in marriage and number of children they bear. This could mean that delayed marriage causes fewer children through the biological mechanism of reduced fertility. However, the causal relation could be reversed. Reduced desire to have children causes people to delay marriage through the subjective mechanism of couples only wanting a legal marriage after deciding that they would like to have children (Uhlmann 2004, 82–83). In summary, statistics are a useful tool to show relationships between two or more measured variables but the causal processes that might account for such statistical evidence still need to be thought out. These processes include all the methodological practices that go into producing the measures.

Documentary and Textual Analysis

Techniques that focus on written documents provide opportunities for unobtrusive research into the social reality of the writers. Writing is an intentional form of communication of facts or records and impressions by the authors, often for specific audiences. Sociologists are frequently as interested in reading between the lines to explore the underlying assumptions of the authors as in reading the overt **text**. An early study by Thomas and Znaniecki, *The Polish Peasant in Europe and America* ([1919] 1971), used the letters and diaries written by Polish immigrants to America to piece together what life was like for these people. The inevitable limitation of such documents is that one cannot be certain that what the immigrants wrote was, or was intended to be, an accurate description of their experience. Immigrants may feel under pressure not to worry family members left behind, to make their accounts more rosy than their experiences really were, and to leave out references to activities of which relatives might disapprove. In the same way, letters that students write home may not be accurate accounts of what they have actually been doing at university. But what they do provide is evidence of the frames that the authors themselves bring to bear on their social reality as they try to make their experiences accountable to others. It is frequently this aspect, as much as factual data, which interests sociologists.

The technique of **content analysis** aids the study of written materials. In such analysis the content of samples of written materials, such as newspapers, letters, or website documents, is counted into predefined categories determined by the theoretical hypothesis. Depending on the research focus, this may involve counting the number of times particular topics are raised within a given time frame, the number of column inches devoted to these topics, the number of positive or negative adjectives used to convey approval or disapproval of the topic, and so on. The same technique can readily be modified to count numbers of minutes devoted to certain topics on television. Chomsky (1988) used this technique to powerful effect to show how US mass media ignored violence perpetrated by dictators favourable to the USA while giving extensive coverage to similar violence by communist regimes. Hackett (1989) similarly counts minutes of coverage to illustrate the bias in Canadian television coverage of foreign news, vastly favouring news of the USA and Western Europe over the rest of the world.

Textual analysis, also called **discourse analysis**, involves a more sophisticated study of the form, as distinct from the content of particular pieces of writing, to reveal in detail how meaning is constructed within a text. Early work by Dorothy Smith (1974, 258–259) draws attention to how the factual property of statements is not intrinsic to them, but is conveyed by the social organization of the text itself.

When a statement is prefaced by the words "in fact," or bluntly stated without qualification, as in "X is conservative," then the statement comes across as unarguably factual. Yet if the same statement is prefaced by qualifiers like "I think," "I believe," or "she said that X is conservative," it conveys the sense that the statement is an opinion that can be subject to questioning and interpretation. Official accounts of events convey the aura of facticity through depersonalized language as if it were aggregate knowledge from no particular place or person. Bystander accounts, in contrast, are presented in the "I saw" or "it seemed to me" form, conveying more limited, opinionated knowledge.

Another powerful tool for framing different versions of reality, Smith argues, is the location of "brackets" or cut-off points that mark the beginning and end of an account of an event. For example, when brackets are placed at one time frame, a confrontation between police and street people may appear as an instance of people throwing rocks at police who then have to defend themselves. But if the brackets are widened to include events several days or weeks earlier, then the same event may appear as police harassment of people who eventually fight back.

Contemporary discourse analysis pays precise attention to nuanced details of language through which meanings are conveyed, including buzzwords, cross-references, active or passive verb tenses, modalities such as "will" and "should" versus "might" and "could," and the like, so that readers and listeners are drawn into accepting or absorbing the preferred interpretation (Fairclough 2003). In one of his many analyses, Fairclough (2002, 133) sets out a detailed list of key concepts found in the language of free-enterprise capitalism, and then applies it to documents produced by the World Bank and by then British prime minister Tony Blair to show how they represent elements of a narrow kind of neo-liberal policy as if they were inevitable, irreversible features of evolutionary economic change occurring without human agency, thus leaving "adjustment" as the only rational option.

Conversation Analysis

Conversation analysis has developed out of ethnomethodology, focusing on the intimate ways in which people accomplish a shared sense of order and meaning in conversation. The basic assumption is that conversations are structurally organized so that no order is accidental or irrelevant. A question structures any response as an answer, or as an evasion that needs some explanation. A greeting structures any response as a returned greeting, or as some level of rejection that again needs explanation. Relations of equality or hierarchy are signalled by whose topics are picked up or dropped, who interrupts whom and whether signals of wanting to say something are acknowledged or ignored. Hesitations, qualifications, repetitions, and the like signal nuances of meaning. Tone of voice also contributes significantly to the implications of what is said (Opie 1992). These basic forms of interaction are regarded by ethnomethodologists as the foundations of social order. Orderly talk is required before any other level of meaningful interaction can take place. Techniques of conversation analysis are now part of the regular tools used by journalists and political analysts to comment on speeches by political leaders. Van Dijk (1993, Ch. 3) uses this technique to interrogate political speeches for implicit racism, particularly highlighting qualifications as in "We do this, but they..." forms of speech. Internet chat rooms and websites provide new sources of publicly available written conversations for research using combinations of conversation and textual analyses.

The ethical issues that arise in using already published materials as sources of data are less pressing than those that intrude into private thoughts and experiences. Mostly they concern the need to recognize that the materials being studied were produced for other purposes. We cannot be certain that what analysts find in materials was recognized by those who first produced them. A graduate student interested in discussions of childbirth experiences posted on the Internet felt it was ethically necessary to contact the writers first through posted email addresses to ask permission. Those who did not reply or whose email addresses no longer functioned were omitted from her sample, even though this meant losing three-quarters of the potential sample (Nuernberger 2004).

INSTITUTIONAL ETHNOGRAPHY— PUTTING IT ALL TOGETHER

Institutional ethnography is fundamentally a research methodology that begins with individual experience as an entry point for studying routine organizational practices that produce these experiences. Institutional ethnography as a theoretical perspective and methodological approach requires the simultaneous use of different techniques— observation, interviews, analysis of standardized questionnaires, textual analysis, and conversation analysis—to explore how individual behaviour in one situation is tied into networks of control and power outside that immediate setting. So far we have been describing specific techniques in isolation, but often researchers use them in combination to get a more rounded understanding of their topic.

We will trace how these research techniques work together using the example of Ng's 1986 study *The Politics of Community Services*. The setting is a service agency in Toronto devoted to helping immigrant women find employment. Ng begins her study with **participant observation**, volunteering as a counsellor who could work with Chinese immigrants.

Taking up this role enabled her to experience the counsellor role for herself, and to know first-hand what she had to learn to get the job done. She was also positioned to *observe* closely how fellow counsellors were doing their work, and how they were visibly interacting with each other and with clients. She immediately encountered the **standardized questionnaire** used by counsellors to interview each new client. Ng learned what information was needed to translate Chinese qualifications and past work experiences and force-fit them into the detailed categories on the employability assessment form. Techniques of conversation analysis alerted her quickly to power relations controlling the counsellor–client interaction. These were not ordinary conversations with standard turn-taking and signalling of topic shifts. Rather, counsellors routinely cut clients off in mid-sentence, and abruptly shifted topics. Doing the job made it clear that the standardized questionnaire almost totally controlled the conversation, dictating the order of topics and the precise details needed. Discussion of topics that did not fit the form were summarily cut off. Conversation analysis also alerted Ng to the unequal power relations between counsellors and potential employers who regularly telephoned the agency looking for cheap labour. Ng could hear the conciliatory and pleading tones used by counsellors when talking with employers, followed by mumbling and sometimes smothered rage after the phone was put down. She could also hear the bullying tones used to pressure clients to take available jobs whether they wanted them or not. Ng also learned rapidly that the standardized forms were essential to produce the weekly and monthly *statistical analyses* required by the government as a condition of funding. Standardized forms enabled counsellors to calculate precisely the number of clients served, their ethnic backgrounds and employment experiences, and the number of job placements made. Until these required statistics were calculated and provided to the satisfaction of the government liaison officer no one got paid, office rental fees went into arrears, and even the coffee supplies were not replenished. She could also observe counsellors locking new clients out of the office for several days until the paperwork was finished. *In-depth interviews* with counsellors enabled Ng to put the whole picture together. She could explore with them what the agency used to be like when it was staffed by volunteers trying to help immigrant women in their struggle to adjust to the city, care for their families, and access jobs, and how drastically the agency changed once it received government funding and became incorporated. She could piece together how accountability to the government for funding required both the use of standardized forms and the generation of statistics demonstrating the placement of prescribed numbers of clients from approved ethnic backgrounds into employment. Keeping these numbers up in turn explained why counsellors resorted to bullying clients to take job openings and supplicating employers who were sometimes openly racist. Ng experienced, watched, and heard about the frustration and despondency that counsellors felt. By the end of her study she could pinpoint precisely how *relations of ruling* worked in a chain of command through government funding regulations, accountability rules, statistical records, standardized forms, restricted interaction between counsellors and immigrant women, and pressure on these women as "clients" to fill undesirable job openings. The study made visible how counsellors were themselves an integral part of the chain, their roles transformed from advocates on behalf of immigrant women to de facto government employees servicing the cheap labour-force requirements of local employers.

The exact methodologies associated with institutional ethnographies vary with each setting. What they share in common is a commitment to begin with the actual lived experience of individuals in their routine, everyday lives, and to work outwards to discover how those experiences are actually put together through people's ongoing coordinated activities (Smith 2006, 1). Such research entails a combination of finely detailed observation of how workers carry out some routine activity, close attention to workplace conversations through which workers communicate with each other their sense of what they are doing, close attention to standardized texts (paper or electronic) that regulate how this routine activity is to be carried out and recorded, what happens to that text after the worker has finished with it, and in-depth interviews to draw on workers' expert knowledge of how and why they do things the way they do. All of these methodologies are focused on the specific question of how routine work gets done and the relations that rule them.

Ethical Issues in Qualitative Research

The ethics of doing institutional ethnographies are complex. The research involves two levels of data collection—the particular setting, and the wider relations of ruling or chains of command that organize work within that setting. Gaining access to a research site can be tricky in that those who have the authority to give permission may be directly implicated in the research results without having control over how the research itself gets done (Campbell and Gregor 2002, 61–69). Issues of confidentiality may arise around the materials that employees work with. Protecting the privacy of clients, disclosure of organizational information, disruptions to the efficient use of employees' time, and the like, can all raise concerns. Methodologically it is also impossible to know the boundaries of the project in advance, or exactly who needs to be interviewed or what texts or discourses need to be examined. University research ethics committees tend to be suspicious of research proposals that do not spell out such details in advance. There is also the question of who will use the knowledge gained into

organizational practices and whose interests might be enhanced or damaged by such knowledge.

The issue of ethical procedures for qualitative research and ethnographies in particular remains hotly debated (Van den Hoonaard 2002). The *Tri-Council Policy on Ethics Involving Human Subjects*, which came into force in Canada in 2000, covers Medical, Natural Sciences and Engineering, and Social Sciences and Humanities research councils in Canada. As a condition of being eligible to receive any research funding, every Canadian university is required to establish ethics-review committees to review all research, whether funded or not, to ensure that it meets the Tri-Council policy guidelines. At the heart of the debate is whether the biomedical research model is appropriate for sociological research. Medical researchers are required to give detailed information to subjects about exactly what procedures will be involved and all known or suspected risks, and to tell subjects that they can drop out of the research at any time. Signed consent forms are designed to ensure such full disclosure and to ensure that subjects have willingly consented to participate. Van den Hoonaard voices concerns of many social science researchers that these formal standards are not appropriate for the kinds of research they do and that they can actually be non-ethical if applied too rigidly. Research that begins from clear hypotheses and uses experiments and standardized questionnaires to gather data may fit quite closely with the medical model. Much qualitative and ethnographic research that relies on observation and fieldwork begins with a broad focus of interest. Specific research questions emerge and change over time through intensive observation and interviewing (Van den Hoonaard 2001, 23; O'Neill 2000). Research ethics committees that require hypotheses and procedures to be defined in advance have made it extremely difficult for qualitative research to gain approval.

A second major focus of concern is signed consent forms. On the positive side, they ensure that the researcher has indeed properly informed participants of their rights and the nature of the research. But in practice consent forms may function more to protect the legal interests of the funding councils, universities, and researchers than to protect subjects. In many areas of research that involve sensitive issues and social problems, people who are willing to participate in the research are fearful that signing their names to consent forms threatens their anonymity. It is now commonplace for researchers to ask for signed consent forms to be returned with "anonymous" standardized questionnaires. Since social science researchers do not enjoy legal protection from court orders forcing them to divulge sources of information, signed consent forms could potentially get informants into trouble. In one case a doctoral student at Washington University was pressured to surrender field data on a radical animal-rights group, raising the real possibility that he might have to go to prison to protect his informants (Comarow 1993, A44, cited in Van den Hoonaard 2001, 26). Less dramatically, signed consent forms compromise the anonymity of surveys. As individuals fill out private and perhaps embarrassing information, they know that they cannot conceal their identities from researchers. A compromise approach is for researchers to sign a letter that they give to participants outlining their research interests, identifying research sponsors, providing contact addresses and a clear statement of how the identity of participants and the confidentiality of information learned will be protected. Taped interviews can then begin with a question whether the informant freely consents to be interviewed, to which the informant can answer "Yes" without otherwise identifying himself or herself.

Yet another area of debate concerns what should happen to data once the research has been completed. Current guidelines suggest that all data be securely protected, and destroyed within one year. This protects data from being used for purposes other than those disclosed to informants when they consent to participate, but at the same time it prevents scholars from using the data for legitimate secondary analysis and future comparative research.

Research ethics for Carroll and for contributors to his collection, *Critical Strategies for Social Research* (2004), goes beyond Tri-Council concerns with informed consent, and disclosure of risk, to focus attention on the underlying power/knowledge relations in which all social research is necessarily embedded. From Carroll's perspective, standard social science research involves ethically questionable social relations—relations of power that reduce "informants" to objects used by researchers to collect data that the researcher wants. Morally responsible research ethics, in contrast, entails that the researcher ask in whose interests this research is being conducted, and whose interests will be served by the knowledge generated? For Carroll, critical research is research that will empower subordinated and marginalized people to gain the knowledge that they can use to understand the social processes that structure their lives, and to act effectively to change their situation. Linda Tuhiwai Smith (2004) suggests 25 indigenous research projects that are explicitly designed to help generate the kinds of knowledge that Aboriginal people need to promote their cultural survival, self-determination, healing from the wounds of colonialism, and their struggles for social justice. Critical research methods, Carroll argues, should involve cooperating with subordinated people so that they themselves learn the methodological tools and skills they need to be able to conduct their own research.

Research generates knowledge that is legally defined under copyright law as belonging to the collector of that knowledge, unless by prior agreement copyright has been legally signed over by the researcher to the informants. This law has profound implications for indigenous peoples. Over many years, biomedical researchers have used indigenous informants to gain knowledge of traditional plants and medicines. Researchers have subsequently patented the information to profit themselves and the pharmaceutical companies funding the research. From the perspective of indigenous peoples, their knowledge has effectively been stolen from them to profit others. Another example of the theft of indigenous knowledge involves the collection of 80 tapes containing 5000 pages of traditional stories recorded from Aboriginal informants over many years. Initially the researcher had agreed to turn over copyright to the First Nations bands that contributed the stories. However, when it became clear how valuable the publication of these stories could be, the researcher claimed that legally all the stories belonged to him as their collector (Bear-Nicholas 2006). The case was still before the courts some 10 years later, in 2006, with First Nations lawyers arguing that the cultural knowledge belongs to the indigenous peoples and the researcher arguing that the collected stories constitute his private intellectual property.

Researchers are always enjoined not to cause harm to their subjects, yet this principle too is not always straightforward. People live in society not as isolated individuals, but as members of complex and often hierarchically ordered groups and communities. Knowledge about the social organization of these groups may simultaneously support the interests of one sector while compromising the interests of another. This recognition greatly complicates the issue of informed consent. Is it sufficient, for example, that an individual member of a First Nations band agrees to tell a researcher about tribal medical knowledge or to recount tribal stories, or should the consent of band council officials be sought first, or even a plebiscite of all band members? Bear-Nicholas (2006) recounts the example of government-funded research conducted under the auspices of a university department that interviewed First Nations people about their memories of land-use practices from the past. Respondents were offered inducements of $100 to participate in the research. It turned out later that this research on land use might be used by the government in a court case involving Aboriginal wood-cutting rights. The band feared that individuals may have taken the money and even fabricated memories of land use that would be used as evidence in court.

First Nations communities in New Brunswick, as elsewhere, have been actively involved in working out research ethics protocols that must be followed in all future research involving First Nations people. Of central concern in these protocols are issues of collaborative research, research designed to develop knowledge useful to First Nations peoples, and the vesting of that intellectual property with First Nations and not with external researchers.

CONCLUSION

In conclusion, research raises important ethical issues for which there are no easy answers. It is important to be mindful of the human dignity of the people we study, and at the same time not to exaggerate the very small potential for harm or risk to people from sociological research. The vast majority of people who participate in research enjoy the experience. As Hiller and DiLuzio (2004) note, the people they interviewed often expressed their deep appreciation at the opportunity to share their migration experiences with others and were fascinated to learn whether their experiences were similar to those of others. Pecora (2002) points out that in contemporary Western culture, people compete in the thousands for a chance to appear on "reality" TV shows and discuss their private lives in the media. Many thousands more display their personal lives on webpages that celebrate intimacy as public performance, while millions visit the webpages to look. In the postmodern fantasy world of mass media, Pecora suggests "television is now doing the kind of social psychological research our universities no longer permit" (Pecora 2002, 356).

SUGGESTED READING

The study by R. Emerson and Russell P. Dobash, "Evaluating Criminal Justice Interventions for Domestic Violence" (2000), provides both a detailed critique of a standard experimental design and an excellent example of the strengths of a quasi experiment using already existing groups of domestic-violence offenders.

Any of the research reports by Byers et al. (2003), Cohen et al. (2004), and Weaver et al. (2002), listed in the references, offer valuable examples of how effective well-designed random-sample surveys can be for assessing public opinion about a controversial topic like introducing sexual health education into school curriculum.

A short, accessible account by Timothy Diamond, "Where Did You Get the Fur Coat, Fern?", in the edited collection by Dorothy Smith (2006), *Institutional Ethnography as Practice* (pages 45–63), conveys the emotional depth of his research into nursing home care, using the methodology of participant observation. This same chapter provides an excellent example of in-depth interviewing. It is written up as a question-and-answer conversation during which Dorothy Smith interviews Timothy Diamond about his research experiences. It also models institutional ethnography, showing how Diamond came to understand the ruling relations that governed the lives of residents and care-givers in the institution of the private, for-profit, nursing home. Diamond published this study as *Making Grey Gold* (University of Chicago Press, 1992).

Norman Fairclough has published a large number of books and research articles in which he uses the technique of critical discourse analysis to analyze political texts. He displays in meticulous detail how these texts work to legitimate the narrow political objectives of neo-liberal economics. A number of these articles are part of the "creative commons." They can be found on the Internet by searching for "Norman Fairclough" and can be downloaded for free.

QUESTIONS

1. How do experiments work to explore a possible link between two variables with changes in one of them causing changes in the other? List some of the reasons why it is so difficult to carry out valid experiments that involve people.

2. What exactly is meant by a random sample? Outline some techniques that survey researchers use to get a random sample.

3. List some of the reasons why it is not reasonable for researchers to simply assume that whatever someone says during an interview represents "authentic" inner feelings and convictions.

4. List some of the issues involved for researchers in deciding whether or not to disclose that they are doing research to the people they are studying.

5. What features of Canadian census data make it simultaneously immensely valuable for sociological research and immensely frustrating and problematic for studying historical trends?

6. Explain the distinction between the techniques of content analysis and discourse analysis in the study of written texts.

7. List the key features of research using the technique of conversation analysis. How does this focus differ from the interests of researchers who use interviews?

8. What do institutional ethnographers see as the essential starting point for their research?

9. Explain some of the reasons why researchers who use a qualitative approach in sociology feel constrained by efforts to establish a formal ethical code of conduct governing sociological research.

10. Explain some of the reasons why the critical Marxist researcher William Carroll finds the focus on formal codes of research ethics insufficient as a guide to ethical research.

WEB LINKS

Government of Canada: Statistics Canada
www12.statcan.ca/census-recensement/2006/rt-td/eth-eng.cfm
This Government of Canada site provides statistical and census information for ethnic origin and visible minorities. Links are provided for the following topic headings: data products, analysis series, reference materials, and geography. The site also links to information for the 2006 Census, 2001 Census, 1996 Census, and even 2011 Census materials.

Interagency Advisory Panel on Research Ethics
www.pre.ethics.gc.ca/english/tutorial
This site allows the user to log in and take the TCPS tutorial. The tutorial is designed to educate researchers about the goals of the policy and how to interpret and implement its guidelines. The tutorial covera a number of topics, includes a summary of key points, and demonstrates their application of key principles to four case studies.

pdxjustice Media Productions
www.pdxjustice.org/node/1#Chomsky15Mar1989B
"pdxjustice Media Productions is an independent producer of video and audio programming for community radio, public access cable television, and free-on-demand streaming via the Internet." The organization brings to the public urgent and critical social justice problems by way of access to some of the most critical speakers of our day, such as Naomi Klein, *The Rise of Disaster Capitalism*; Kevin Phillips, *Bad Money*; Rashid Khalidi, *40 Years of Occupation*; Nena Baker, *The Body Toxic*; Antonia Juhasz, *The Tyranny of Oil*; P. Sainath, *Globalizing Inequality*; and Noam Chomsky, *Manufacturing Consent*.

KEY TERMS

acculturation

causality

census

content analysis

conversation analysis

correlations

demographic

dependent variable

discourse analysis

enumeration

experiments

hypothesis

independent variable

multivariate analysis

participant observation

qualitative methods

quantitative methods

questionnaires

reconstituted families

sample

small groups laboratories

standardized questionnaire

survey research

text

textual analysis

variable

REFERENCES

Allahar, Anton L., and James E. Cote. 1998. *Richer and Poorer: The Structure of Inequality in Canada*. Toronto: Lorimer.

Ammerman, N. 1987. *Bible Believers: Fundamentalists in the Modern World*. New Brunswick, New Jersey: Rutgers.

Archibald, W.P. 1978. *Social Psychology as Political Economy*. Toronto: McGraw-Hill Ryerson.

Baruch, G. 1981. "Moral Tales: Parents' Stories of Encounters with the Health Profession." *Sociology of Health and Illness* 3 (3): 275–296.

Bear-Nicholas, Andrea. 2006. Conference on Research and Research Ethics in First Nations Communities: Developing Research Ethics Protocols that Work. St. Thomas University, Fredericton, New Brunswick, Canada, 23 February 2006.

Becker, H.S. 1963. *The Outsiders: Studies in the Sociology of Deviance*. New York: Free Press.

Bonner, Kieran. 1997. *A Great Place to Raise Kids: Interpretation, Science, and the Urban–Rural Debate*. Montreal and Kingston: McGill-Queen's University Press.

Briggs, J.L. 1973. *Never in Anger: Portrait of an Eskimo Family*. Cambridge, Massachusetts: Harvard University Press.

Byers, E. Sandra, Heather A. Sears, Susan D. Voyer, Jennifer L. Thurlow, Jacqueline N. Cohen, and Angela D. Weaver (Psychology UNB). 2003. "An Adolescent Perspective on Sexual Health Education at School and at Home: I. High School Students." *The Canadian Journal of Human Sexuality* 12 (1): 1–17.

Byers, E. Sandra, Heather A. Sears, Susan D. Voyer, Jennifer L. Thurnow, Jacqueline N. Cohen, and Angela D. Weaver. 2003. "An Adolescent Perspective on Sexual Health Education at School and at Home: II. Middle School Students." *The Canadian Journal of Human Sexuality* 12 (1): 19–33.

Campbell, Marie, and Frances Gregor. 2002. *Mapping Social Relations: A Primer in Doing Institutional Ethnography*. Aurora, Ontario: Garamond Press.

Carroll, William K., ed. 2004. *Critical Strategies for Social Research*. Toronto: Canadian Scholars' Press.

Chomsky, N. 1988. *Manufacturing Consent: The Political Economy of the Mass Media*. New York: Pantheon.

Cicourel, A.V. 1974. *Theory and Method in a Study of Argentine Fertility*. New York: Wiley.

Cohen, Jacqueline N., E. Sandra Byers, Heather A. Sears, and Angela D. Weaver (Psychology UNB). 2004. "Sexual Health Education: Attitudes, Knowledge, and Comfort of Teachers in New Brunswick Schools." *The Canadian Journal of Human Sexuality* 13 (1): 1–15.

Comarow, M. 1993. "Are Sociologists above the Law?" *The Chronicle of Higher Education*, 15 December, A44.

Dobash, R. Emerson, and Russell P. Dobash. 2000. "Evaluating Criminal Justice Interventions for Domestic Violence." *Crime and Delinquency* 46 (2): 252–270.

Dooley, D. 1984. *Social Research Methods*. Englewood Cliffs, New Jersey: Prentice Hall.

Doran, C. 2002. "Medico-legal Expertise and Industrial Disease Compensation." In Gayle MacDonald, ed. *Social Context and Social Location in the Sociology of Law*. Peterborough, Ontario: Broadview Press.

Douglas, J. 1967. *The Social Meaning of Suicide*. Princeton: Princeton University Press.

Duelli Klein, R. 1980. "How To Do What We Want To Do: Thoughts about Feminist Methodology." In G. Bowles and R. Duelli Klein, eds. *Theories of Women's Studies*. Berkeley: University of California Press.

Eichler, M. 1988. *Families in Canada Today: Recent Changes and Their Policy Consequences*. 2nd ed. Toronto: Gage.

Eichler, M. 1985. "And the Work Never Ends: Feminist Contributions." *Canadian Review of Sociology and Anthropology* 22 (5): 619–644.

Fairclough, Norman. 2003. *Analysing Discourse: Textual Analysis for Social Research*. London: Routledge.

Fairclough, Norman. 2002. "Critical Discourse Analysis as a Method in Social Scientific Research." In Michael Meyer and Ruth Wodak, eds. *Methods of Critical Discourse Analysis*. London: Sage, 121–138.

Freeman, D. 1983. *Margaret Mead and Samoa: The Making and Unmaking of an Anthropological Myth*. Cambridge, Massachusetts: Harvard University Press.

Hackett, Robert. 1989. "Coups, Earthquakes, and Hostages? Foreign News on Canadian TV." *Canadian Journal of Political Science* 22: 800–824.

Hiller, Harry H., and Linda DiLuzio. 2004. "The Interviewee and the Research Interview: Analyzing a Neglected Dimension in Research." *Canadian Review of Sociology and Anthropology* 41 (1): 1–26.

Kirby, S., and K. McKenna. 1989. *Experience, Research, Social Change: Methods from the Margins*. Toronto: Garamond.

Lewis, Justin. 2001. *Constructing Public Opinion: How Political Elites Do What They Like and Why We Seem To Go Along With It*. New York: Columbia University Press.

Lochhead, Clarence, and Katherine Scott. 2000. *The Dynamics of Women's Poverty in Canada*. Status of Women Canada.

Mead, M. 1928. *Coming of Age in Samoa: A Psychological Study of Primitive Youth for Western Civilization*. New York: Blue Ribbon Books.

Muzychka, Martha, and Carmen Poulin, with Barbara Cottrell, Baukje Miedema, and Barbara Roberts. 1995. *Feminist Research Ethics: A Process*. Canadian Research Institute for the Advancement of Women (CRIAW).

Nathan, Rebekah. 2005. *My Freshman Year: What a Professor Learned by Becoming a Student*. Ithaca & London: Cornell University Press.

Ng, Roxana. 1995. "Multiculturalism as Ideology" In Marie Campbell and Ann Manicom, eds. *Knowledge, Experience, and Ruling Relations: Studies in the Social Organization of Knowledge*. Toronto: University of Toronto Press, 35–48.

Ng, Roxana. 1986. *The Politics of Community Services: Immigrant Women, Class, and the State*. Toronto: Garamond.

Nuernberger, Kim. 2004. "Negotiations in Narrative: Exploring the Discursive Constructions of Childbirth in Internet-Based Birth Stories." Paper presented at Canadian Sociology and Anthropology Association meetings, University of Winnipeg, 3 June.

Oakley, Ann. 1981. "Interviewing Women: A Contradiction in Terms." In Helen Roberts, ed. *Doing Feminist Research*. London and New York: Routledge, 30–61.

O'Neill, P. 2000. "Good intentions and awkward outcomes: Ethical gatekeeping in fiend research." Paper presented at the 17th Qualitative Analysis Conference, Fredericton, New Brunswick, 18–21 May.

Opie, A. 1992. "Qualitative Research, Appropriation of the 'Other' and Empowerment." *Feminist Review* 40 (Spring): 52–69.

Pecora, Vincent P. 2002. "The Culture of Surveillance." *Qualitative Sociology* 25 (3): 345–358.

Pryor, Edward T., Gustave J. Goldman, Michael J. Sheridan, and Pamela M. White. 1992. "Measuring ethnicity in 'Canadian':

an evolving indigenous category?" *Ethnic and Racial Studies* 15 (2): 214–235.

Richmond, A.H., M. Lyon, S. Hale, and R. King. 1973. *Migration and Race Relations in an English City*. London: Oxford University Press.

Schissel, Bernard. 1997. *Blaming Children: Youth Crime, Moral Panics, and the Politics of Hate*. Halifax: Fernwood.

Schutt, Russell K. 1996. *Investigating the Social World: The Process and Practice of Research*. Thousand Oaks, California: Pine Force Press.

Sherman, Lawrence W. 1992. *Policing Domestic Violence: Experiments and Dilemmas*. New York: Free Press.

Sherman, Lawrence W., and Douglas A. Smith, with Hanell D. Schmidt and Dennis P. Rogan. 1992. "Crime, Punishment, and Stake in Conformity." *American Sociological Review* 23: 117–144.

Sherman, Lawrence W., and Richard A. Berk. 1984. "The Specific Deterrent Effects of Arrest for Domestic Assault." *American Sociological Review* 49: 261–272.

Silverman, David. 1993. *Interpreting Qualitative Data: Methods for Analysing Talk, Text and Interaction*. London: Sage.

Smith, Dorothy E. 2006. *Institutional Ethnography as Practice*. Toronto: Rowman & Littlefield Publishers.

Smith, Dorothy E. 1999. *Writing the Social: Critique, Theory and Investigations*. Toronto: University of Toronto Press.

Smith, Dorothy E. 1974. "The Social Construction of Documentary Reality." *Sociological Inquiry* 44 (4): 257–268.

Smith, George. 1990. "Political Activist as Ethnographer." *Social Problems* 37 (4): 629–648.

Smith, Linda Tuhiwai. 2004. "Twenty-five indigenous projects." In William K. Carroll, ed. *Critical Strategies for Social Research*. Toronto: Canadian Scholars' Press, 75–90.

Thomas, W.I., and F. Znaniecki. [1919] 1971. *The Polish Peasant in Europe and America*. New York: Octagon Books.

Uhlmann, Allon J. 2004. "The sociology of subjectivity, and the subjectivity of sociologists: A critique of the sociology of gender in the Australian family." *The British Journal of Sociology* 55 (1): 79–97.

Van den Hoonaard, Will. 2004. "Giving Voice to the Spectrum: Is there a Way Out of the Ethics-review Mazeway?" Canadian Sociology and Anthropology Association meetings, Winnipeg, 4 June.

Van den Hoonaard, Will. 2002. *Walking the Tightrope: Ethical Issues for Qualitative Researchers*. Toronto: University of Toronto Press.

Van den Hoonaard, Will. 2001. "Is Research-Ethics Review a Moral Panic?" *The Canadian Review of Sociology and Anthropology*. 38 (1): 19–36.

Van Dijk, Teun A. 1993. *Elite Discourse and Racism*. London: Sage.

Warren, John T. 2003. *Performing Purity: Whiteness, Pedagogy, and the Reconstitution of Power*. New York: Peter Laing.

Weaver, Angela D., E. Sandra Byers, Heather A. Sears, Jacqueline N. Cohen, and Hilary E.S. Randall (Psychology UNB). 2002. "Sexual Health Education at School and at Home: Attitudes and Experiences of New Brunswick Parents." *The Canadian Journal of Human Sexuality* 11 (1): 19–31.

Whyte, W.F. 1943. *Street Corner Society*. Chicago: University of Chicago Press.

The Microsociology of Everyday Life

by Peter A.D. Weeks

In his review essay entitled "On the Microfoundations of Macrosociology," Randall Collins (1981) offers the following definitions for two extremes of sociological concern. **Microsociology** comprises "the detailed analysis of what people do, say, and think in the actual flow of momentary experience." **Macrosociology** comprises "the analysis of largescale and longterm social processes, often treated as selfsubsistent entities such as 'state,' 'culture,' and 'society.'" Collins also draws attention to the recent upsurge in **radical microsociology**, which refers to the study of everyday life in secondbysecond detail. It entails the use of audio and video recordings to permit the close analysis of conversations and nonverbal interaction. Collins argues that these new techniques in microsociology are helping to develop a view of how larger social patterns are constructed out of micromaterials.

Collins advocates a **microtranslation strategy**, which shows how macrosocial structures can be understood as patterns of repetitive microinteractions. He argues that, strictly speaking, there is no such thing as a state, an economy, a culture, a social class. There are only collections of individual people acting in certain kinds of microsituations. Terms such as *state* or *class* are a kind of shorthand. They are abstractions and summaries of different microbehaviours in time and space. The causal mechanisms or active agents in any sociological explanation of macrosocial patterns must be microsituational. Microsituations make up the empirical basis of all other sociological constructions. Researchers never leave their own microsituations. They compile summaries of microsituations by using a series of coding and translating procedures from which they produce macroanalytical constructs (Collins 1981, 988–989).

This chapter presents an overview of diverse approaches to the microsociology of everyday life, with the main emphasis on ethnomethodology. This markedly different approach seeks to show how the very notion of structures or social classes used in explanations by traditional sociology can be studied as ongoing accomplishments of the people involved, rather than as external entities that direct the interaction.

Macrosciology attempts to explain social behaviour in terms of larger social structures, arrangements, or organizations. For example, functionalism represents what Tom Wilson has termed a "normative paradigm" in which the observed orderly patterns of behaviour, feeling, and thinking are analyzed as resulting from individuals' conformity to norms and role expectations resulting from their socialization in the context of the socializing agencies of the family, education, and so forth. Thus, behaviour is seen as tied to the social systems in which individuals are enmeshed. These social systems are comprised of various positions, or statuses, organized in relation to each other. Each status carries with it cultural norms that specify the ways in which individuals are expected to behave as they play the roles attached to a position. A person's behaviourgoing to work, handing in a term paper, standing in line at a bankis considered explained when it has been presented in accord with the norms associated with a particular role. People learn and accept their roles in a social system through the process of socialization.

In principle, according to the functionalists, every situation comprises roles with predefined expectations that people need to know in order to participate. These expectations include exactly what one has a right to ask of other people, how to judge their performance, who is permitted to play what roles, and whether or not it is appropriate to express emotions towards others in the situation.

But, if we think about it, some very awkward questions come up. As you recall, the functionalists themselves recognize that any particular individual has a number of statuses or positions at the same time. For example, you may be not only a student in this situation but also a female, of a certain ethnicity, a sister, a tenant, president of a club, etc. At this particular moment, especially if you meet someone, just how do you decide which role of social identity is relevant? We might think of the case in which a female student is in a male professor's office where there is an expectation that the categories of female, Protestant, and perhaps being relatively young are supposed to be irrelevant to the business-at-hand, that is, solving an academic problem or whatever. But, this presupposes that the two parties can agree on *which of many possible types* of situations is happening at the moment. They do not announce themselves with neon lights! Think also of when these same individuals meet in a pub. Further, this might be complicated by the situation where a number of students are on a pub crawl in which they may be writing autographs on one another's T-shirts, and the female student jokingly asks that professor to add his signature. While the previous situation was more straightforward, the latter is less routine, requiring a greater amount of interpretation by the parties involved. So while the functionalists may invoke norms and roles to explain behaviour, the interpretive perspective claims that they fail to account for how people construct their understandings or definitions of the situation—that is, how they *apply* them at any one moment. Think of people performing music. There may be the notes on the paper in front of them, but at any one moment, which ones are to apply? How do they know where they are at? Thus, we move from a "normative" to an "interpretive" paradigm, as we shall see.

One more example should make this clear. Work roles are particularly welldefined because work situations typically entail interaction between a number of specialized roles, oriented to the achievement of specified broader functions. Talcott Parsons's (1951, 454–479) analysis of professionalclient interaction, particularly that between medical doctor and patient, in many respects set the standard for such research. In the process of training, a physician learns not only the technical knowledge of medicine, but also a set of attitudes and rules that governs professional interaction with others in related roles as patients, colleagues, nurses, and staff. Above all, doctors must learn to be neutral and objective and to avoid emotional attachment to patients (an example of the "pattern variable" of "affectivity vs. neutrality").

Certain guidelines establish the limits of any relationship between doctor and patient. Parsons argues that such guidelines or norms are functional, because they facilitate the physician's penetration into the personal affairs of the patient, which is essential for effective treatment, while protecting the patient from exploitation. When people are sick, they are particularly vulnerable to emotional, sexual, and financial manipulation. They must expose private parts of their bodies and divulge information that is potentially damaging. The rules governing the practice of medicine protect the patient from exploitation and also protect the doctor from excessive or inappropriate demands from the sick person.

The doctor–patient relation shows how interaction between two people in the privacy of an office is structured in precise detail by the predefined norms of behaviour for persons playing the roles. Each person enters the setting with clear and mutually shared expectations as to how each is supposed to behave vis-à-vis the other. Deviations will be subject to sanctions, including the threat of formal reprimand for professional misconduct. These predefined rules for behaviour can be directly explained as necessary for the smooth and adequate functioning of the health-care system.

It is too simplistic to try to account for smooth interaction in terms of learned role expectations. A great deal of work—improvising, joking, interpreting, second-guessing, and manipulating—must go on for any particular performance to be carried off. What we need to study in any given situation, therefore, is precisely how people collectively accomplish the work of creating and sustaining a

Microsociology studies the work people do—the improvising, joking, interpreting, second-guessing, and manipulating—to collectively accomplish their shared definition of a situation, such as "doctor–patient" interaction.

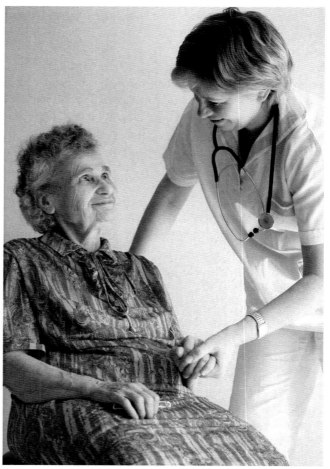

Shutterstock

particular definition of the situation, so that they perceive each other to be playing a specific role rather than some other possible one.

Returning to the doctor–patient relation, Emerson's research (1970) on gynaecological examinations illustrates in detail the work that goes into it. In Parsons's account, described above, the rules seem non-problematic; the doctor should be emotionally detached, altruistic, and committed to viewing illness in an objective way. Emerson, however, asks how such abstract rules are *actually practised*. She argues that maintenance of the definition of the situation of a gynaecological examination requires much effort and skill on the part of the doctor and nurse to guide the patient through this precarious scene. In theory, doctors should be able to conduct gynaecological checkups in the same matter-of-fact manner that they would carry out for an examination of the ear. But in the actual microsituation, this is not possible.

Emerson argues that the situation involves several role definitions simultaneously, which each have to be managed if the encounter is to work. From a purely medical perspective, the woman is merely a gynaecological specimen. But she is also a woman who is striving to retain her personal dignity while having her sexual parts penetrated by metal instruments. If her emotional stress is not attended to, she may become so physically tense that it will be impossible to conduct the examination without causing considerable pain. If pain is added to humiliation, the "specimen" may get up and leave the office. If we observe carefully, we find that meanings in this situation are created anew at every moment. Thus, Parsons and other functionalists do not account for just how this happens. What are the detailed practices of which such "neutrality" consists? We might, as a start, think of the medical or clinical language that is used to refer to body parts rather than the slangish "boobs," etc. and various practices such as having the patient undress behind a screen. Such aspects need to be investigated if we are to give an adequate explanation of how the doctor-patient relation is accomplished and, indeed, what happens when deviance, such as sexual assault, occurs.

The interpretive paradigm thus questions the macrosociological assumption that explanation of social life is to be found in abstract structures that operate and manipulate us "behind our backs." According to them, functionalists run the risk of **reifying** society when they conceive of social rules as existing outside and above ongoing human activity and what people themselves do. People appear as "cultural dopes," programmed to play their roles as if they were puppets, with social structures pulling the strings or operating "behind people's backs." Functionalists describe what people do in a given situation, but not the actual mechanisms that produce and maintain the collective sense of what is going on. It is through continual processes of mutually negotiating the sense of what is happening now, and what will happen next, that people produce the patterns that functionalists subsequently observe as a particular role.

INTERPRETIVE PERSPECTIVES AND THEIR MAJOR PRINCIPLES

Interpretive theory shifts the focus of explanation from macrostructures to microinteractions. This approach developed primarily out of dissatisfaction with functionalism, particularly with the image of people as programmed puppets obedient to predetermined role expectations. Further, it employs the basic assumption that it is people's interactions which are directly observable while the structures such as institutions, the economy, the social-class system, etc. are abstractions that we invent, which are not. Even the simple question of where a university department is or what it is seems deceptively simple until we think of it a little more deeply. Is it a physical location? If so, is someone still a member of that department when he/she leaves the office or region of the university? Further, we can ask whether it is the social structures that are "real" as with Durkheim's "social facts" that are "external and constraining" on us, or is society ultimately people interacting in concrete, observable situations? Are we to take a holistic or top-down approach or a bottom-up or even grassroots or atomistic approach to explaining social life? This is the essence of what has been termed recently as the "macro–micro debate."

At this point, let us take a brief survey of some major types of interpretive perspectives. Rather than attempting a rigorous exposition of the histories of the development of them, the objective here is to present their basic principles and some of the more suggestive concepts that you can apply to situations you observe. Remember that we are shifting our focus from "structures" to ongoing social "processes."

Symbolic Interactionism

Perhaps the earliest interpretive perspective developed in the United States in the early twentieth century was symbolic interactionism, founded by George Herbert Mead and further developed by Herbert Blumer of the University of Chicago. Symbolic interactionists hold that the social world is constructed by individuals interacting through the use of shared symbols.

They place great emphasis on the ways in which individuals are taught by significant others (individuals important to them) to share symbols and the ways symbols lead to common patterns of action. They also see the learned symbols of the self—that is, self-images—as very important in determining what individuals do (Douglas 1980, 16).

Sociology operates on the principle that human beings are **symbol** users—with symbols being observable objects or events such as sounds that refer to objects or concepts other than themselves. Human beings are, to a great extent, liberated from instinctual and biological programming, relying instead on their symbol-using powers to live in the world. But any one symbol may mean many different things, and thus we have the problem of how people can communicate at all. For example, raising one's arm 45 degrees from the vertical could be a salute, hailing a taxi, a threat, or pointing to something in the sky! So, how do humans come up with shared meanings? Mead's answer is that it is language that contains the required sets of meanings on which people draw. It is through language that we not only learn the meanings typically attached to specific symbols by others in our society, but also construct a sense of "self" in relation to others. Mead has characterized social interaction as a "conversation of gestures." Gestures are treated as symbolic actions that have to be interpreted. For example, when A raises his arm, B may fill in with an imaginative projecting into the future—that A is about to strike him! This involves another central concept in symbolic interactionism—that of "taking the role of the other." To interpret a given gesture or word, one needs to put oneself in the position of the other person. Social interaction and the social order we observe thus fundamentally depend on sets of shared meanings and moment-to-moment interpretations in concrete situations.

Herbert Blumer conceives of social organization as fundamentally people actively fitting their actions together. As he states:

> A society consists of individuals interacting with one another. The activities of the members occur predominantly in response to one another or in relation to one another (Blumer 1969, 7).

Symbolic interaction is ignored by the functionalists we have studied, yet Blumer takes it to be of central importance in its own right. It is not just the result of social structures being "external and constraining" upon us, but we as actors in society are regarded as making significant interpretations and choices in what we do. We include another strategic quotation from Blumer, which will lead us to consider another central concept of symbolic interactionism, namely that of the "self":

> Put simply, human beings in interacting with one another have *to take account of what each other is doing or is about to do*; they are forced to direct their own conduct or handle their situations in terms of what they take into account. Thus, the activities of others enter

as positive factors in the formation of their own conduct; in the face of the actions of others one may abandon an intention or purpose, revise, check or suspend it, intensify it, or replace it . . . *One has to fit one's own line of activity in some manner to the actions of others. The actions of others have to be taken into account* and cannot be regarded as merely an arena for the expression of what is disposed to do or sets out to do (Blumer 1969, 8, italics added).

But this presupposes the ability of human beings to monitor *themselves as well as others*. Earlier on, Mead developed a concept of self that, in part, involved a two-way distinction: that between an "I" as the source or creator of actions—the *subject*, as in ordinary sentences such as "I play guitar," and as *object*, that is, what others see and what you as the subject also sees in being proud of *yourself* or ashamed of yourself. What symbolic interactionists emphasize is that we not only observe others and adjust our actions accordingly, but we are also monitoring ourselves in terms of imagining how others may be perceiving us—what Cooley termed the "looking-glass self." Besides, we are imaginatively *anticipating how others might react*. That this may not work that smoothly is reflected in the well-known Robert Burns poem, which reads:

> O wad some Pow'r the giftie gie us
>
> To see oursels as others see us!
>
> It wad frae mony a blunder free us,
>
> And foolish notion. (Robert Burns, *To a Louse*)

Thus, the interaction even between two individuals (let's call them A and B) already is more complicated than we may have thought and involves, at the very least:

a. A observes B's gestures and words and interprets what they might mean, in terms of B's intentions and what he/she might do next. After all, we cannot "read" minds directly, can we?

b. B does the same with A's gestures,

c. A observes his/her own gestures and words and imagines how B is reacting now and might react in the upcoming moments, and

d. B does the same.

We could think of this as "internal conversation"—imaginatively rehearsing what you are going to say to or do with the other person. This is the time—partly for some comic relief—to think in terms of the Peanuts cartoon with each second-guessing what the other is thinking and might do. It is evident that, in the course of even the most ordinary interaction, actions are based on a massive amount of interpretation (hence, the name of these perspectives as "interpretive"). Individuals or "actors" are seen as active creators of meaning, figuring out what is going on and making significant decisions. Thus, they are far from the functionalists' view of them as mere "cultural dopes" or passive role-players!

We come to the final part of this section with Blumer's critique of what he calls "variable analysis." This is the attempt to apply a positivistic or "natural-science" model to social events, in terms of relating one "social fact" (in Durkheim's terms) to at least one other "social fact." Take the familiar example of the influence of birth-control campaigns on fertility rates. As Blumer states:

> In my judgment, the crucial limit to the successful application of variable analysis to human group life is set by the process of interpretation or definition that goes on in human groups. This process, which I believe to be the core of human action, gives a character to human group life that seems to be at variance with the logical premises of variable analysis (Blumer 1978, 71).

While we might at first think of a birth control program as a unitary variable (such as the number of people visiting birth control clinics, the time period of the program), Blumer insists that we need to consider the program in terms of how it enters into the lives of the people. It will have a very different effect depending on just what it means to the people involved. Here is an instance of the phrase used often by symbolic interactionists and well worth remembering—that is, to take into account "the point of view of the actor." We, as social scientists, are not to determine what something *really* means, but we must reconstruct what it means to a typical actor in that situation. Recall the point that any given gesture or object may mean many different things, and how we react to it depends on what it means for us. It is not just a simple stimulus to which we have been conditioned to respond in a fixed way. Think of the case of a brown coil of something in a dark shed. If we think it is a dangerous, poisonous snake, we get out of there fast! However, if we think it is a coil of rope, we shall be much calmer, of course, and perhaps use it in our next yard project. Getting back to Blumer's example, think for a moment of just what might influence the meaning that the birth control program has for the people involved. Here are some that Blumer has suggested: their level of literacy, the clarity of the printed information, the manner and extent of its distribution, and the social position of the directors of the program (Blumer 1978, 97). Perhaps you could offer other ideas. Thus, the effects of one social arrangement on another have to be viewed as being mediated by the meanings of the people involved.

To conclude this section, let us summarize the major principles of symbolic interactionism:

a. Social life including "social structures" have to be conceived as the outcomes of social interaction.

b. People act towards things on the basis of the meaning that the things have for them. Thus, we as sociologists have to take into account the point of view of the actor, that is, those very meanings. We should not impose our meanings upon them.

c. Interaction and role-taking: By reading and interpreting the gestures of others, humans communicate and interact. They can read each other, anticipate each other's responses and *adjust to each other*. Without this, interaction could not occur. In turn, patterns of social organization could not exist.

d. This presupposes that people have a sense of self and are engaged in what Giddens calls "reflexive self-monitoring."

e. In most situations, communication and cooperation are possible because of the shared meanings, prevalent among members of the society, which have been acquired through language.

Finally, even though we may regard the economy, the political system, the language, etc. as socially constructed, it is not to deny that they are real and are experienced as critical limitations and resources in our everyday lives. As W.I. Thomas once said: "Situations defined as real are real in their consequences." It is not simply individual fantasy or fiction! Basically, their model of society is one of a kind of *negotiated consensus*, and their emphasis is on *process in interaction* rather than on social structures that are external and condition what we do.

Now we turn to a derivative of this approach, labelling theory, which was developed in connection with the study of deviance. We shall give just a brief sketch here before proceeding to the dramaturgical approach of Erving Goffman.

Labelling Theory

Labelling refers to the process by which deviant behaviour and deviant people are categorized as such by the rest of society. Think of this quotation from *Outsiders*, a landmark book by Howard S. Becker in the 1960s:

> *Social groups create deviance by making the rules whose infraction constitutes deviance*, and by applying those rules to particular people and labelling them outsiders. From this point of view, deviance is *not* a quality of the act the person commits, but rather a consequence of the application by others of rules and sanctions to an 'offender'. The deviance is one to whom the label has been successfully applied; deviant behaviour is behaviour that people so label (Becker 1963, 9, italics in original).

Consistent with the principles of symbolic interactionism, Becker's position is that deviance is not inherent in the act but essentially depends on *interpretation* by others of what a person does. Deviant acts, then, are a matter of social definition. But as we see in the quotation, there are two levels in this:

1. the rules themselves—whether informal, as in our moral standards, or else formal in terms of being framed in laws. Becker is concerned with how these rules are created and discusses what he calls "moral entrepreneurs" who actively campaign to have given rules or laws legislated or repealed. We can think these days of the attempts by various groups and politicians to decriminalize the possession of marijuana, in the historical context where other "moral entrepreneurs" successfully pushed to make it illegal in the first place.

2. the application of those rules to particular individuals. This can refer to whether an individual's actions are perceived as deviant or even whether that person in general is essentially deviant and thus morally inferior, not to be trusted, etc.

The basic point is that how people are treated depends on whether they are *perceived* as deviant rather than whether they really have broken rules or are deviant personalities, in terms of being delinquent, mentally ill, gay or lesbian, etc. After all, as Becker points out, there may be "secret deviants" whose rule-breaking or illegal acts may not have been caught or who, like gays and lesbians, have kept "in the closet." There may be public occasions on which such a label is attached, as in a court trial or psychiatric examination. Labelling theorists are very much concerned with the consequences of such labelling for self-concepts and the resulting behaviour. Thus, rather than being concerned, as are functionalists or Marxists, with the social-structural causes or correlates of deviant behaviour (assuming that it can be measured in some non-problematic way), labelling theorists focus on how deviance is perceived in the first place in immediate situations and how definitions of behaviour or types of persons are negotiated through concrete interaction.

Goffman and the Dramaturgical Approach

Erving Goffman develops some of the ideas of symbolic interactionism in a distinctive direction by comparing everyday interaction to theatre. Probably his best known early work is in his book entitled *The Presentation of Self in Everyday Life* (1959). In a number of his works, he explores the often taken-for-granted patterns in social interaction in various public places and other settings—what he later calls "the interaction order." For our purposes, I have selected a few of these concepts and ideas that hopefully will be insightful and interesting to apply to your own observations,

and hence am devoting more space to this than the preceding varieties of interpretive perspectives.

First, in employing dramaturgical analogies, Goffman argues that in interaction, people in one another's immediate physical presence are continually communicating—whether or not they are actually speaking. Each person consciously or unconsciously communicates the set of social categories that he/she desires the other person to believe that he/she has. So consider what a person communicates by their appearance, clothing, gestures, demeanour in entering a room, etc. before he/she has even spoken a word. Even the setting itself may convey various messages. Consider the uses of these aspects in advertisements, which use photographs that are manipulated versions of everyday scenes. It is in the interest of individuals to control and predict the activities of others, and therefore, any one of them tries to impress on others that he/she is a certain type of person. Goffman aptly calls this "impression management," which is accomplished through "sign activity" of which he distinguishes two types. The first is the verbal, the words, which the person can easily control, but the verbal is tested against the less controllable aspects, such as expressions, bodily appearance, and body language, which people take to be more telling of their genuine motives. For example, it may be easy to say that you enjoy your host's pickled cabbage, but your gestures, such as grimaces, squirming, and not asking for seconds, may give you away!

Consistent with the analogy to the theatre, we can think of people playing various roles. Goffman's concept of "dramatic realization" highlights the fact that people not only carry out the technical aspects of their role expectations but also the ceremonial. It is not enough simply to do the job, but also one needs to look the part. For example, it is not enough for a waitress to serve the customer by noting the details of their order and arranging with the kitchen to come up with it, but she has to also appear to be attentive though not too obtrusive in regards to the wishes of the customer and not just slouch back and read the newspapers when all the orders have been taken. These days, in some financial institutions, it is reported that there is a return to formal dress, such as men's suits, to create a sense of professionalism and trustworthiness. For Goffman, these roles are treated as "performances," as if on stage. In a sense, we are trying to generate ideal versions of these roles ("idealization") with the less admirable or inconsistent ones being kept hidden. For example, the messy aspects of preparation are accomplished at another time and place unseen by the "audience" for whom the "performance" is intended. The musical or theatrical performance on stage is the result of numerous rehearsals which the public does not witness. Your student paper as presented to the instructor is a relatively polished version—a final draft—in which all the searchings, puzzlement, research, errors, and their correction (now with the benefit of spell checks) are no longer accessible to that particular audience. Goffman is thus emphasizing the creation of appearances and idealized selves (i.e., "impression management"), the sense of self for which accidents or incongruities could be shattering, thus causing embarrassment. Recall the cliché that first impressions are important, although they may falter at any moment, such as when one's dignity is compromised by slipping on a banana peel! We can think of many other examples, such as the authority of President Clinton being compromised by his sexual relations (however one defines them!) with Monica Lewinsky.

This brings us to the next distinction that Goffman creates—that between "front regions" and "back regions" in our society. "Regions" in this context are conceived of as spaces with physical barriers to perception (Goffman 1959, 106). The front region, like the stage, is the place where the performance is given, while the back region, like backstage, is where the pressures to perform a given role are relaxed (and unseen to an audience) and where performances are prepared. The preparatory work for a performance is hidden from the general public, such as in the case of funeral parlours where the work of preparing the corpse is hidden. Automobile garages are not as well hidden, where the repair of vehicles goes on. Think of other back regions in various buildings, such as sub-basements where janitors have their lockers and often pin-ups, or bathrooms and bedrooms in houses where private activity, such as bodily functions including sex, goes on. Also, public washrooms for men are segregated from those for women, and within them booths with lockable doors are provided. We could, in the current context, extend this to luggage at airports where the private interiors are invaded for security reasons, or the case of underwear with the shifting boundaries between what is meant to be seen and what is not. It has been argued elsewhere that voyeurism is an eroticizing of what is considered to be private. Consider also the effects on privacy of recent technology such as videocameras for surveillance purposes, or cell phones for private conversations in public places such as restaurants or trains.

On the changes of behaviour and role expectations as one moves from one region to another, here is Goffman's quotation from the novelist George Orwell (of *1984* fame), where a waiter goes into a hotel dining room and then back to the kitchen:

> It is an instructive sight to see a waiter going into a hotel dining-room. As he passes the door a sudden change comes over him. The set of his shoulders alters; all the dirt and hurry and irritation have dropped off in an instant. He glides over the carpet, with a solemn priest-like air. I remember our assistant

maître d'hôtel, a fiery Italian, pausing at the dining-room door to address his apprentice who had broken a bottle of wine. Shaking his fist above his head he yelled (luckily the door was more or less soundproof),

> "*Tu me fais*—Do you call yourself a waiter, you young bastard? You're not fit to scrub floors in the brothel your mother came from. *Maquereau!*"

> Words failing him he turned to the door; and as he opened it he delivered a final insult in the same manner as Squire Western in *Tom Jones*.

> Then he entered the dining-room and sailed across it dish in hand, graceful as a swan. Ten seconds later he was bowing reverently to a customer. And you could not help thinking, as you saw him bow and smile, with that benign smile of the trained waiter, that the customer was put to shame by having such an aristocrat to serve him (quoted in Goffman 1959, 121–122).

This example illustrates a feature of interaction often ignored by sociologists, that is, the variation of behaviour by *space*. Think of the police employing assumptions of what type of people are expected to be in certain locations in the city and when to be on the alert for suspicious persons (Goffman 1971, Ch. 6).

Goffman's somewhat later work on *Behavior in Public Places* highlights the point that social activity systematically varies not only by space but also by *time*. In this study, he begins with these distinctions:

a. Gathering:

any set of two or more individuals whose members include all and only those who are at the moment in one another's immediate presence (Goffman 1963, 16).

b. Situation:

the full spatial environment anywhere within which an entering person becomes a member of the gathering that is (or then does become) present. Situations begin when mutual monitoring occurs, and lapse when the second-last person has left (18).

c. Social Occasion:

This is a wider social affair, undertaking, or event, bounded in regard to place and time and typically facilitated by fixed equipment; a social occasion provides the structuring social context in which many situations and their gatherings are likely to form, dissolve, and re-form (for example, a social party, a workday at the office, a picnic, or a night at the opera) (18).

Thus, the "gatherings" refer to the groups of people involved, while the "situation" refers to the physical setting in which the gathering takes place. But the important point is that it is the "occasion" that provides the context. Thus, to take an example familiar to university students, the "situation" may be a classroom one has entered on a Friday morning around 10:20 in which the "occasion" as collectively defined may be one of informal chatter and perhaps the leisurely taking out of notebooks and pens and taking off jackets, etc. with the decibel level quite high perhaps. But then, when the professor enters close to 10:30, all becomes, at least ideally, quiet and we now have a different "occasion" within the same "situation" or setting, namely that of the lecture or class session. Both students and professors are expected to be there in that space at that particular time for a designated duration. Later writers such as Foucault and Giddens take up this point in terms of the architecture and time-management in the school system as facilitating discipline and control of the students. Thus, Goffman alerts us to the dimensions of both time and space in everyday interaction.

Note that each "occasion" has its distinctive sets of norms and role expectations. As Goffman states:

> Each class of such occasions possesses a distinctive ethos, a spirit, an emotional structure, that must be properly created, sustained, and laid to rest, the participant finding that he is obligated to become caught up in the occasion, whatever his personal feelings (19).

Thus, when we enter a church service or a school class late, we are expected to drop the expectations of what we might have been expected to do or get away with in the hall or washroom to the distinctive set of norms and "situated roles" in that particular setting. Sometimes, this is not so straightforward as when there may be "duelling occasions" as when the people in the same setting have different definitions of what the occasion is and therefore what is acceptable. Take a bar scene where a musical group is performing. What is an acceptable level of bar noise? Some people may be talking and joking with one another loudly, taking for granted that this is a place primarily for talking and drinking, while the musicians may expect some level of listening or that the noise level be kept down enough so that they can hear one another and be heard by those who are interested.

This brings us to Goffman's concept of "situational proprieties" and their violation as "situational improprieties" about which he has this to say:

> To engage in situational impropriety . . . is to draw improperly on what one owes the social occasion (194).

Situational proprieties, then, give body to the joint social life sustained by the gathering, and transform the gathering itself from a mere aggregate of persons present into something akin to a little social group, a social reality in its own right (196).

Simply stated, these are norms that apply to specific settings, public ones but not necessarily so, more precisely "occasions", and this is what he alerts us to. Under certain circumstances that will not be elaborated here, "situational improprieties," or acting inappropriately according to the norms of a given situation, can be viewed as symptoms of mental illness. Some of these norms Goffman considers in terms of appropriate *involvements*. He makes a distinction between what he calls "main involvement" and "side involvement," which he defines in this way:

> A main involvement is one that absorbs the major part of an individual's attention and interest, visibly forming the principal current determinant of his actions.

> A side involvement is an activity that an individual can carry on in an abstracted fashion without threatening or confusing simultaneous maintenance of the main involvement (Goffman 1963, 43).

Examples of the latter include humming while working or knitting while listening (with this having been traditionally more acceptable for women). These days, it becomes questionable as to whether this could include listening to iPods or text-messaging while attending a school or university class. We also encounter this issue with the use of cellphones in restaurants or concerts and even in automobiles (where the question of safety arises). Also, we can think of musical performances where, in the case of the classical music concert, usually in a special concert hall, the audience is expected to be quiet and show little bodily movement during a piece only to applaud at the end thereof, while at a bar with a jazz group on stage, a certain level of conversational buzz is acceptable and even the sounds of the cash register and the mixing of cocktails. Of course, we can ponder what is an acceptable level of bar noise. Prohibitions against certain involvements are made explicit as, for example, not smoking in many places.

Further, as Goffman observes, there are norms about the very *objects of involvement*. Self-directed acts such as picking one's teeth, dozing off, scratching (and masturbation as an extreme) are definitely forbidden. Also, being "away," letting one's mind wander, and looking "out of it" are discouraged. It seems that a norm is to appear to be engaged in some way with the setting, to be "with it." Some minimal main involvement is required to avoid the appearance of being utterly disengaged. This is why waiting rooms and passenger airlines are supplied with magazines and newspapers, and even why these are brought into restaurants or dining rooms for people who are eating alone. Goffman cites an interesting quotation from a book entitled *Subways Are for Sleeping*:

> One idiosyncrasy that he . . . has discovered but cannot account for is the attitude of station policemen toward book readers. After seven-thirty in the evening, in order to read a book in Grand Central or Penn Station, a person either has to wear horn-rimmed glasses or look exceptionally prosperous. Anyone else is apt to come under surveillance. On the other hand, newspaper readers never seem to attract attention and even the seediest vagrant can sit in Grand Central all night without being molested if he continues to read a paper (quoted in Goffman 1963, 59).

In fact, newspapers can serve as what Goffman calls "involvement shields" behind which one can afford to be vacant or daydreaming.

A final note on this aspect is his concept of "civil inattention," which highlights another familiar feature of interaction in public places. When people are in one another's immediate physical presence but not engaged in "focused interaction" such as a conversation, there is a possible range from one extreme of openly staring at another person to the opposite of ignoring them totally—the "nonperson treatment" of servants, for example, as if they are not there at all. But in most situations, "civil inattention" is considered proper, an in-between alternative where people give minimal acknowledgement of one another's presence but where they respectfully go on with their own activities. This is how Goffman describes it:

> One gives to another enough visual notice to demonstrate that one appreciates that the other is present (and that one admits openly to having seen him), while at the next moment withdrawing one's attention from him so as to express that he does not constitute a target of special curiosity or design (Goffman 1963, 84).

This is such a delicate adjustment that there are many infractions of it. For example, to avoid being caught looking too much may be facilitated by wearing dark glasses. This can also be severely tested when someone of very divergent social status or physical appearance is present, such as various handicapped persons. It is also seen in the case of many typical males when confronted by young females in revealing clothing or, as I recall, being in a swimming pool in southern Spain chatting with a topless young woman while avoiding staring at her breasts. An amusing example occurs in the movie *Tootsie*, where Dustin Hoffman plays the character of a man who impersonates females in order to get work and observably tries hard to play it cool in a dressing

room with half-naked women. Think also of people passing by one another on the street where one usually avoids eye contact, although one might occasionally go so far as to say hi. We shall end this discussion with an amusing account of the problem of where to look that Goffman quotes from a writer:

> The act of waiting for an elevator brings out the suspicious streak in people. You arrive before the closed landing door and push a button. Another person comes along and after a glance of mutual appraisal, you both look quickly away and continue to wait, thinking the while uncharitable thoughts of one another. The new arrival suspecting you of not having pushed the button and you wondering if the new arrival is going to be a mistrusting old meanie and go give the button a second shove . . . an unspoken tension which is broken by one or the other of you walking over and doing just that. To stare the other in the eye seems forward and usually the eye doesn't warrant it. Shoes are convenient articles for scrutiny— your own or those of the other personal—although if overdone, this may give the impression of incipient shoe fetishism.

> It continues even inside the elevator . . . especially in the crowded and claustrophobic boxes of the modern high buildings. Any mutual exchanges of glances on the part of the occupants would add almost a touch of lewdness to such already over-cozy sardine formation. Some people gaze instead at the back of the operator's neck, others stare trance-like up at those little lights which flash the floors, as if safety of the trip were dependent upon such deep concentration (quoted in Goffman 1963, 137–138).

In one of his later articles, Goffman develops the argument that there is a distinctive "interaction order" with its own processes and structures that are independent of the larger social structure. We are to study these in their own right and not merely treat them as effects of larger patterns such as social class, gender, or power structures. An amusing example is in a Herman cartoon where a king with his crown on comes into a restaurant, whereupon the waitress says something to the effect of "I don't care who you are, but everyone takes his hat off in this restaurant!" Processes in the interaction are relatively circumscribed in space and time. For example, when people are in one another's immediate physical presence, there is impression management going on, the figuring out of the intentions and purposes of others' actions and even attempts to conceal these, and all of this has a ritualistic character (Goffman 1983, 3). In addition, individuals are faced with "personal-territory contingencies" such as being vulnerable to physical assault, sexual molestation, robbery, etc. We can think of these in familiar settings as factories, airports, hospitals, or public thoroughfares. As he notes, social rituals or situational norms, as we referred to them earlier, are only loosely coupled with social structures and are interactional in character. Examples are the priority of being served (as in lineups), who goes through a door first, who has a right to interrupt another in talk, or the distinctive turn-taking organization in courts and classrooms in contrast with informal conversation. The norm of first-come, first-served blocks the influence of wider differences of social class, age, and gender, and people are expected to maintain discipline in the line in order to maintain the precedence of service (Goffman 1983, 15). Although this is only a fragment of Goffman's discussion, we have a further example of a continuing controversy in sociology—that of the "macro–micro debate."

Before moving into ethnomethodology, here are a couple of final thoughts about Goffman's work. First, Goffman's writings make it sound as if social interaction is highly scripted. But my studies of jazz improvisation raise the point that even these everyday activities involve *improvisation* in their moment-to-moment unfolding. The participants cannot predict precisely what is going to happen next or how others will react. Even if we are following scripts, timing is critical! Yet, despite all this improvisation, typical and recognizable patterns emerge after all. Further, in his analyses of the interactional order, Goffman often employs concepts such as "impression management," "presentation of self" for "audiences," "role distance," and so forth, which he claims describes what is really going on in those scenes even though the participants themselves might not realize it. More recently, Rod Watson argues that to present all actions as, say, forms of play acting, espionage, etc. is to give "ironic accounts" of them—that is, to downplay them (Watson 1991, 10). We need to ask: Is this how the people we are studying actually see these activities and situations? Is he being consistent with the principles of the interpretive perspectives, especially symbolic interactionism as we discussed at the beginning of this chapter? Is he taking or being true to the point of view of the actor? It seems that he is *imposing* his concepts from an analytical stance on what the people are doing. Is this not reminiscent of what we found with the macrosociological perspectives along the lines of, Don't listen to those people as they do not know what they are really doing, while we as social scientists do. Remember Merton's claim that one of the best contributions sociologists can make is to discover the latent functions behind social arrangements, or the Marxist claim that they can determine the true class interests of people who, due to ideology, lack class consciousness or a true understanding of them. It reminds me of a *New Yorker* cartoon where the man says to his wife as they are coming out of a theatre something to the effect that he enjoyed the show but they tell him he was "manipulated"!

Seen from the interpretive perspective, functionalists make the mistake of reifying society when they fail to link their macroscopic concepts of functioning systems to the detailed examination of mundane interaction. They treat social rules as if they existed as factual entities outside of human activity. Interpretive theorists stress that norms do not exist in isolation, to be unambiguously applied when the proper situation presents itself. Instead, norms are produced and reproduced through actual behaviour in particular settings. We are constantly engaged in processes of interpretation, defining and redefining the situation in which we find ourselves. We must constantly ask ourselves questions. Who am I to them? What are we doing together? In effect, we are actively engaged in the construction of reality.

Ethnomethodology

Interpretive perspectives in general explore how the variety of expectations concerning social behaviour are actively negotiated by participants. Ethnomethodology pushes the questioning still further by examining the participants' practical reasoning in making sense of their activities in the situations in which they occur. Recall the functionalists' point that any person inhabits a number of social positions at the same time, and thus has a number of role expectations that may clash at times (role conflict). But they do not tell us just which of these many possible identities (for example, being a student, female, of a given ethnic group, president of a club, a resident, or a musician) is relevant at a given moment. How do participants come to decide collectively that it is this role and not some other possible role that is being played at this particular time? Also, which of the number of possible contexts is relevant to understand what they are doing or talking about? We might be in a faculty member's office, but that may not be relevant at the time when we are chatting about last night's hockey game!

Ethnomethodology focuses on how members of a given society or community use their common-sense knowledge and their **background understandings** to make sense to themselves, and to one another, of their activities, the situation they are in, and the wider social structure in which any particular activity is embedded.

The study of research methods in social science explores how social scientists use their practical research activities to arrive at their conclusions about what is going on. This process often involves asking the participants themselves what they think is happening and accepting the explanations offered. Ethnomethodology seeks to understand ordinary participants' methods for deciding what is happening.

The term *ethnomethodology* is derived from the Greek work *ethnos*, referring to people or members of a society, and *methodology*, referring to the methods of reasoning that people use to make sense of the social world around them. Harold Garfinkel (1967, vii) offers the following definition:

> Ethnomethodological studies analyse everyday activities as members' methods for making those same activities visibly rational and reportable for all practical purposes, i.e., "accountable" as organizations of commonplace everyday activities.

Ethnomethodologists ask this sort of question: What precisely do members do in detail that makes their activities "accountable," that is, observable or socially recognizable for what people take them to be? In other words, how do people organize their social activities in such a way that others can make sense out of them? Thus, practical reasoning or sense-making can be seen in at least two ways:

1. interpreting the actions of others and situations, and
2. producing one's own activities, thus embodying or making observable one's understandings in what one does.

These are actually very complex processes, and we need a great deal of background understandings about our society or our community to accomplish them successfully. Most of them seem to us to be common-sense behaviours that we do not give a second thought to. But then, we do need to view this in the context of being a stranger to this culture or the situation when we travel to other parts of the world. It is not just a matter of learning the other language but also the innumerable background understandings that one learns mainly through trial and error.

Let us take a deceptively simple example of a queue or service lineup. What are members' methods of producing a queue? How do people recognize or signal to each other that they are in a queue and are not just standing around? Perhaps people have simply been socialized to expect queues in certain places, and so they invoke common-sense understandings to recognize them. The notion of queue-forming is certainly more established in some cultures than others. Many a hapless British tourist in Canada has found this out after queuing expectantly to board a bus or train, only to be swept aside as the local people surge forward in a mass. However, even when the common-sense notion of queuing is shared, it is by no means obvious when and where queues do or do not exist. In crowded airports or shops, or in front of busy service counters, for example, people may be spread out sideways as well as in front of and behind each other. Yet this may constitute a queue in that members are collectively aware of the ordering, of who is in front of whom, even when they are arranged in a bunch. Finally, taking up the argument of the preceding paragraph, before we join the queue, we have to *interpret* what is going on, then when we are in it and gradually getting up to the front of it, we are also incorporating our understandings about lineups in our very behaviour, so that we are, in effect, *producing* or reproducing that socially recognizable formation.

Ethnomethodologists study exactly how we organize the details of what we are doing to create and sustain our collective understanding that this is the distinctive kind of social order we call a queue. This does not mean that people always follow the rules of queuing when there is a lineup. But it does mean that failure to conform, as when someone pushes to the front, is recognizable by the people involved as a violation, and hence as requiring some explanation or **accountability**. Once people have formed the notion that what is going on is queuing, then just about any behaviour that seems consistent with this is likely to be considered accounted for. You assume, for example, that a man standing behind another in a lineup is himself queuing up. He might actually be lost, or spying on people, or even just standing around waiting to find out what other people are standing around for. But you are unlikely to question his motives, unless you are watching some kind of mystery thriller. However, any behaviour that does not conform to the behaviour of queuing immediately threatens our notion of what is going on, and so requires some account. We tend to search for or to demand some valid excuse that will confirm for us that, yes, this is a queue, but that person is not in it because of some particular reason. Once too many people seem not to be keeping in the proper order, our notion that this is a queue is likely to fall apart.

Ethnomethodologists focus on what they term **practical reasoning**, or the methods by which ordinary people, in their everyday affairs, mutually create and sustain their common-sense notions of what is going on. It is people's capacity to do this that makes it possible for sociologists to talk about the notion of social structures. Again, we are removed from the macrosociological perspectives we dealt with earlier. Recall that Durkheim enjoined us to "treat social facts as things," that is, givens "out there" such as social class and education. But Garfinkel points out that this leaves out the fundamental question of how they are even produced and made recognizable in the first place. He therefore urges us to adopt a modification of Durkheim's aphorism to read: "Treat social facts as *ongoing accomplishments*" (Garfinkel 1967, vii).

In summary, ethnomethodology inquires into the methods whereby we, as members of a society or community, organize our activities so that we, as well as sociologists, come to recognize the patterns that we think of as **social structures**. By suspending what phenomenologist

Children actively reproduce the social organization of queuing as they establish and negotiate their places in the line.

Purestock/Getty Images

Alfred Schutz termed "the natural attitude" or our ordinary common-sense, pragmatic view of looking at the world, in order to view ordinary social activities such as talking or queuing as if they were "anthropologically strange" or problematic, we can begin to explore the many taken-for-granted practices and rules for practical reasoning through which our world becomes socially constructed. Let us look first at Garfinkel's "breaching experiments" in order to explore these basic ingredients of everyday social order.

Background Understandings and Indexicality

Garfinkel developed his now-famous technique of breaching experiments to explore how people create social order in everyday interaction. The ways in which order is produced are exposed by finding out what would disrupt given social scenes. Experimenters begin with the stable features of the scene and ask what can be done to make trouble. Garfinkel suggests that

> the operations that one would have to perform in order to produce and sustain anomic features of perceived environments and disorganized interaction should tell us something about how social structures are ordinarily and routinely being maintained (Garfinkel 1963, 187).

There are a number of these experiments, such as insisting on paying more than the stated price for an item at a checkout counter or bargaining over the price, which is not usually done in this part of the world. Another was having his students return to their homes and act as if they were merely boarders, that is, polite strangers rather than members of their families. The results were disturbing indeed, and it is not recommended that you try this (see Garfinkel 1967). One procedure for disrupting and thus exposing the practical reasoning that underlies social order is to demand

that the meaning of common-sense remarks be explained. In the two examples given below (from Garfinkel 1967, 42–43), (S) refers to the subject trying to have a normal conversation and (E) refers to the experimenter or ethnomethodologist requesting that the subject explain his or her commonplace remarks.

S: Hi, Ray. How is your girlfriend feeling?
E: What do you mean, "How is she feeling?" Do you mean physical or mental?
S: I mean how is she feeling? What's the matter with you? (He looked peeved.)
E: Nothing. Just explain a little clearer what you mean.
S: Skip it. How are your med school applications coming?
E: What do you mean, "How are they?"
S: You know what I mean.
E: I really don't.
S: What's the matter with you? Are you sick?

. . .

On Friday night my husband and I were watching television. My husband remarked that he was tired. I asked, "How are you tired? Physically, mentally, or just bored?"

S: I don't know, I guess physically mainly.
E: You mean that your muscles ache or your bones?
S: I guess so. Don't be so technical.
(After more watching.)
S: All these old movies have the same kind of old iron bedstead in them.
E: What do you mean? Do you mean all old movies, or some of them, or just the ones you have seen?
S: What's the matter with you? You know what I mean.
E: I wish you would be more specific.
S: You know what I mean! Drop dead!

In both cases the subjects clearly expected that the experimenters would rely upon common background understandings to make sense of their **utterances**. Garfinkel suggests that such expectations are essential features of all spoken interaction. When the experimenters did not use their background understandings, the subjects almost immediately expressed anger and indignation. As Garfinkel expresses it, people feel they are morally entitled to have their talk treated as intelligible, and they react with swift and powerful sanctions when it is not.

Another set of experiments explores the **indexical** or context-dependent character of conversations. When we talk, we invariably include only brief references to, or indications of, the context and subject matter. We expect other participants to fill in the rest—the background understandings that make talk possible. Garfinkel illustrated this by asking his students to take a scrap of a conversation in which they had participated, and note in the left-hand column what had actually been said and in the right-hand column what they and their partners understood they were talking about. One such analysis is given in Figure 1.

It is quickly apparent from the fragment of conversation in Figure 1 that there were many matters that the partners understood but did not mention. These were the background understandings that both partners required in order to carry on a meaningful exchange. For example, the statement, "Dana succeeded in putting a penny in the parking meter," would hardly be intelligible without the background knowledge that Dana was a young child. Otherwise, we might surmise that Dana was a severely handicapped adult. Similarly, the reference to Dana being "picked up" only makes sense when we have the background understanding that Dana, as a young child, is too short to reach most parking meter slots. In another context, the reference to "being picked up" might have a totally different meaning, like getting into a vehicle that has stopped, going out on a date, or accepting an offer to go off somewhere, possibly for a sexual encounter!

Words and actions are always indexical and thus context-dependent. Words in ordinary conversations for practical purposes can only briefly refer to the many background understandings that participants in the conversation must invoke in order to understand what is being said. If every participant in every conversation insisted on having all elements of that conversation explicated, talk would be impossible. Thus, what the parties are referring to, such as in the above fragment of conversation, are not said in so many words but are merely "glossed."

The mix of background understandings required to carry on conversations is the stuff of which many cartoons and jokes are made. What strikes us as funny is the invoking of meanings and contexts other than the one that we know should be applied. One example is the image of two Martians standing at a stop sign, wondering how long they have to wait before it says "go." The cartoon reminds us that, in order to be effective, the deceptively simple device of a stop sign requires complex background understandings from people. Where does one stop when one sees a stop sign? At the point where the sign stands? On the road next to it? On the side of the road directly in front of it? Does one stop indefinitely? If not, when does one start again? Does the sign apply only to cars, or to pedestrians and cyclists as well? Does the sign mean the equivalent of "arrêt" in Quebec, or does it stand only as a symbol of Anglophone imperialism that can be ignored by all Francophones? Clearly if a sign had to explicate all possible background understandings, it would be useless. Signs, by definition, stand as indicators for background knowledge that all competent members of a community are expected to have. One final point: It is not just that a sign like that requires interpretation, but also that ethnomethodology is interested in members' practices in *doing that very interpretation*.

The recognition that ordinary interaction is indexical, its meaning dependent upon context and upon background understandings supplied by participants, means that no social event can ever be totally unambiguous. The full meaning of

Figure 1   The Indexical Nature of Conversation

Husband:	Dana succeeded in putting a penny in a parking meter today without being picked up.	This afternoon as I was bringing Dana, our four-year-old son, home from the nursery school, he succeeded in reaching high enough to put a penny in a parking meter when we parked in a meter parking zone, whereas before he has always had to be picked up to reach that high.
Wife:	Did you take him to the record store?	Since he put a penny in a meter that means that you stopped while he was with you. I know that you stopped at the record store either on the way to get him or on the way back. Was it on the way back, so that he was with you or did you stop there on the way to get him and somewhere else on the way back?
Husband:	No, to the shoe repair shop.	No, I stopped at the record store on the way to get him and stopped at the shoe repair shop on the way home when he was with me.
Wife:	What for?	I know of one reason why you might have stopped at the shoe repair shop. Why did you in fact?
Husband:	I got some new shoelaces for my shoes.	As you will remember I broke a shoelace on one of my brown Oxfords the other day so I stopped to get some new laces.
Wife:	Your loafers need new heels badly.	Something else you could have gotten that I was thinking of. You could have taken in your black loafers which need heels badly. You'd better get them taken care of pretty soon.

Source: Garfinkel (1967)

any interaction cannot be stated in an objective, factual account, devoid of subjective interpretation. It does not follow, however, that all meaning is therefore subjective, and we can interpret interaction any way we see fit. On the contrary, ethnomethodology starts with the observation that most social actions and communications have an orderly character. Members of a community are routinely competent at selecting precisely those aspects of the relevant context required to make sense of the interaction. In the jargon of ethnomethodology, it is **members' competences** that make order possible. If someone says to you, "Mary is out to lunch," you generally know which Mary this refers to, and whether the intended meaning is that she has gone elsewhere to eat lunch or is showing signs of mental incompetence. You may both grin at the statement to show that you know the alternative meanings, but you nonetheless know, and know in common, what the intended meaning is. Similarly, when one person asks another whom they know well "How was it last night?", we might find this very vague. The pronoun "it" could refer to an indefinite range of things or events. How imprecise! How unsuitable for an academic essay! But the question is usually clear enough for all practical purposes, because the parties fill it in with background understandings. No problem!

Indexicality has important implications for research methods in sociology, especially for survey research in which questionnaires are commonly used. Researchers gamble when they assume that respondents all invoke the same context and the same background understandings in answering questions as the researchers intended. Respondents take a similar gamble when they assume the researchers will invoke the appropriate background understanding to know what they meant by their answers.

In a study of race relations in England, researchers designed a series of questions to measure cultural attitudes of racial prejudice held by white English residents towards non-white immigrants (Richmond et al. 1973). One of the respondents refused to answer any questions because she feared that anything she said would be interpreted as prejudice. Later she explained that neighbouring houses were crammed full of single immigrant men from the Caribbean and Asia, who often sat out on the front steps in the evenings. These man habitually whistled at and propositioned her when she walked by. She resented their sexism, not their racial difference, but her complaints were nonetheless coded into the survey as racial prejudice.

Now we move on to another feature of practical reasoning in everyday life, which again we take for granted.

The Documentary Method of Interpretation

The search for patterns in the vague flux of everyday interaction is a critical component of members' methods of making sense of what is going on around them. Garfinkel refers to this process of imposing patterns as the **documentary method of interpretation**. Although this method was developed in the scholarly contexts of archaeology and history, Garfinkel is claiming that this is another feature of our practical everyday reasoning, that is, looking for underlying patterns in the midst of the details of what we observe. Hence we habitually search for such a pattern in any new situation. We know that activities and conversations are indexical. We know that the surface appearance cannot be more than a sign of broader background knowledge to which it refers and which we are expected to know and use in order to make sense of what we are experiencing. In our ordinary reasoning, therefore, we treat actual appearances not as all there is to know, but as signalling some presupposed underlying pattern. Once this pattern is deduced, at least tentatively, it provides clues to the interpretation of other details of the surface appearance. These details appear as instances of the supposed pattern. This reasoning process is thus circular, continually moving between surface appearances and hypothesized underlying pattern. Each becomes defined and redefined in terms of the other. In the jargon of ethnomethodology, the relation between appearances and underlying pattern is **reflexive**, or mutually determining.

Figure 2 gives a simple example of this reflexive process. When we notice such an element in a book, we almost automatically assume it is not some random doodling that is on the page by accident. We assume it is a picture, and a picture of something. One possibility is that the pattern underlying the specific lines of the drawing might be a duck. With this in mind, we interpret the protuberances on the left as the bill and the small indentation on the right of the figure as irrelevant. But if we adopt the idea that the pattern is a rabbit, then the same features are interpreted differently. The features on the left are ears, and the small indentation on the right now has relevance as the rabbit's mouth. The same surface appearances can thus be seen as instances of totally different features once a new underlying pattern comes to mind (Heritage 1984, 86–87).

Figure 2   The Reflexive Nature of Perception

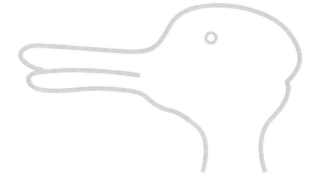

Source: Adapted from Heritage, (1984, 87).

One interpretive scheme that may be invoked to account for a series of actions that otherwise appear as out of order is the act of labelling a particular person as deviant, as we referred to earlier in this chapter. Once someone is so labelled, the risk is that, by the same documentary reasoning processes, all other details of that person's life tend to become reinterpreted as instances of the new underlying pattern of deviance. Actions previously accounted for as within the normal range, or as mild aberrations that might result from stress or from too much alcohol, come to be seen as the result of the person's essentially deviant character. Past actions are reinterpreted *retrospectively* to fit the new pattern of accounting, so as to confirm that this person was deviant all along. As Garfinkel states:

> [T]he former identity stands as accidental; the new identity is the "basic reality". What he is now is what, "after all", he was all along (Garfinkel 1956, 421–422).

At the same time, these accounts have a *prospective* character in that they shape how the person's future actions will be interpreted. The deviant label provides such an all-encompassing accounting scheme that it is very difficult to break.

Rosenhan (1973) reported the experience of some researchers who faked hallucinations to gain admission to a mental hospital. It took a significant length of time for their "normality" to be recognized. They behaved normally from the time of their admission to the hospital onwards, but everyone around them, including patients, nurses, and doctors, interpreted whatever they did as what deviants do. Their protestations that they were normal, and that they had merely faked hallucinations to get into the hospital, were not believed. The fact that they took notes was not seen as a research activity but as a symptom of a deviant mental state. The researchers were eventually discharged as schizophrenics "in remission" rather than as people who were "normal all along."

The underlying reasoning processes examined in all of these studies are similar. Hospital personnel, defence lawyers, and police officers all drew on their sense of an underlying pattern of typical deviant behaviour in order to interpret details of surface appearances. And we need to emphasize that Garfinkel takes this to be a practice common to our everyday practical reasoning. We are often trying to figure out, from bits and pieces of evidence, what really happened or, when we meet a new person, trying to ascertain from the various words used as well as appearance and actions, what kind of a person this is. Can they be trusted, for example?

Practical Reasoning in Organizations

The sense-making practices of officials and members of organizations are basic elements in the accomplishment of a fac-tual reality on which orderly, everyday administration depends. Zimmerman (1974) conducted a pioneering study of caseworkers in a public-assistance agency to explore how they decided matters of fact about applicants for assistance. Caseworkers were required to be skeptical of applicants' stories concerning eligibility and to treat such stories as merely claims that had to be evaluated against relevant documentary evidence. Caseworkers were under pressure to decide such matters quickly since they had heavy caseloads and were expected to dispose of each case within a 30-day period.

What interested Zimmerman was how certain kinds of records or pieces of paper seemed to be accepted immediately as factual, without further investigation, while other pieces of paper were rejected. When one caseworker recounted an incident where an applicant for old-age assistance had told the caseworker that she had lost her citizenship papers stating her age, but had copied her birth date on a piece of paper for the use of the agency, all the caseworkers laughed. Yet no caseworkers laughed when they were handed citizenship papers, birth certificates, bank statements, medical records, and the like, as proof of claims. For practical purposes, any paper that was signed by someone in an official position, and bore the letterhead of an organization, was treated as an objective, impersonal, and unquestionable statement of fact, while anything stated by a person was merely a claim. Caseworkers refused even to consider the possibility that official papers might themselves be open to doubt or in need of any investigation. To do so would be to risk calling their entire view of an ordered world into question.

Zimmerman points out that the papers the caseworkers treated as factual were put together by the same kind of reasoning that they themselves used to produce documents attesting that a particular applicant was eligible for assistance. Caseworkers accomplished their own **social construction of reality** by using selected bits of previously constructed reality.

Much of the surface appearance of social reality comes to us not through direct experience but through documents. These documents, which may be written or on tape or film, are produced by professionals and people in positions of authority within organizations. Ethnomethodological research explores how the manner in which such documents are constructed influences the practical reasoning processes of their audiences.

A study of the news media (Jalbert 1999) draws attention to the normally loaded categories in which various parties to a conflict are presented, and particularly to the subtle use of grammatical devices that create the underlying patterns that audiences use in interpreting details of the events. For example, the actions of one party to a conflict may be expressed in the active grammatical voice while the actions of the other party are expressed in the passive voice. The effect is to convey the impression that responsibility for the conflict rests with the former.

The sense that a particular news report is impartial, and therefore a credible factual account, is similarly created by subtle structuring devices. For example, a typical underlying notion is that there are always at least two parties to a conflict. Reporters may incorporate quotations from two parties to a debate and thus trigger the interpretive response that they have covered the issue. The possibility that there may be many more sides to the issue, or that the two parties quoted may be merely variants of the same side while the opposing side is unrepresented, disappears from view (Tuchman 1972). The problem is that we, as consumers of the news, see only the final report. We generally know nothing about the various practices, unquestioned assumptions, stereotypes, organizational pressures, and so forth, which influenced the story's production (Smith 1990, 66).

Another form of practical reasoning studied by ethnomethodologists concerns what they term **reality disjunctures**—the occasions in which people hold different interpretations of "the facts" and challenge those held by others. In these cases, they claim or believe that the others' versions are faulty, and this can go both ways. Situations like these occur all the time in courts with the varying stories of what happened in an accident, for example, or in medical settings where the patient and the psychiatrist may disagree on what the problem is. So the question becomes: How do people resolve these disagreements as a practical matter? How is it that they manage to sustain the conviction that they are living the same world? This is what E.C. Cuff aptly describes as the "problems of versions" (Cuff 1993).

Pollner proposes that, in some situations, members employ the terms "the ironicizing of experience"—that is, citing that experience as a symptom of a pathological state. Thus, hallucinations are dismissed as something that a person experiences, but which *in fact* is not there. Similarly, to be paranoid is to suspect a conspiracy against oneself that again, in fact, is not occurring at all. Thus, we may say that this person is just seeing things! But this does presuppose that some of us are in a position to determine what is *really* going on. How are we to know this, or can we unmistakably know it?

However, in most cases, we are not doubting the others' mental competence, but rather invoke another line of reasoning—that is, that there are *exceptional problems with observations*, as in traffic courts. The idea is that there might have been a barrier to their perception which, if it were not there, the person would have indeed seen things as we have "correctly" seen them. Take these examples:

Puzzle: How could a defendant claim that he did not exceed 68 miles an hour and an officer claim that he did?

Solution: The defendant had a faulty speedometer.

Puzzle: How could a defendant claim that the vehicle in front of him and not his camper held up traffic and an officer claim that it was the camper?

Solution: The camper blocked the officer's vision.

Puzzle: How could a defendant claim that drag racing did not occur at a specified time and place when an officer claims that it did?

Solution: The officer was actually referring to a different time. (Hester & Eglin 1992, 214)

In this way, their belief in a common world is sustained without implying that anyone is insane—despite the different versions of the same events. Peter Eglin argues that one of the devices for resolving such "reality disjunctures" is to invoke an "appearances/reality dichotomy"—the idea that what is seen may be only the *appearance* of things, while beneath the surface *reality* may be perceived if the observer uses the proper methods. An implication of this line of reasoning is that reality will appear different depending on your viewpoint (Eglin 1979, 370). Returning to our traffic-court example, it is typically suggested that barriers to perception, such as a large truck in front of someone, might have prevented an otherwise competent person from seeing a change in the traffic light, etc.

Thus, we can relate these examples to Garfinkel's reworking of Durkheim's aphorism and conceive of them in terms of "fact as an ongoing accomplishment."

The Social Construction of Gender

Ethnomethodology has also made important contributions to feminist studies. The state of being either male or female is generally taken for granted as a biological fact, although we recognize that the associated attributes of masculinity and femininity may, in varying degrees, be socially constructed. Garfinkel's (1967, Ch. 5) pioneering work in this field is based on extensive interviews with a **transsexual** who was born a boy but chose to be a girl.[1] Garfinkel met her when she was 19 years old and had entered the hospital for a sex-change operation. He refers to her as Agnes. Agnes was born and raised a boy and had the normal sexual characteristics of a boy until puberty. At this point she developed the secondary sexual characteristics of a female: female body shape, ample breasts, and an absence

_____

[1]Note that the term "transsexual" needs to be distinguished from "transvestite." The former refers to a more or less permanent sex change, while the latter is simply dressing in clothes typical of the opposite sex. Think of the lead character in the movie *Tootsie*, who does it just to get more work in acting.

of facial hair. Agnes insisted that she had been a girl all along, and that her male genitalia were simply the result of some biomedical abnormality. She successfully persuaded surgeons to amputate them and to surgically construct a vagina. Some years later, Agnes confided to Garfinkel that she had developed a female body shape at puberty by taking estrogen, which she had obtained by forging her mother's prescription. At the time when he carried out his initial interviews with Agnes, he did not know this.

What interested Garfinkel was how Agnes was accepted by her friends, including her boyfriend, as female, despite her abnormal physical state and her early upbringing as a boy. What he learned from Agnes was how she had deliberately controlled all the surface appearances of her interactions with others to be consistent with the underlying interpretive pattern of a typical female. In a sense, Agnes performed a lifelong breaching experiment, in which she constantly negated what would otherwise be the taken-for-granted assumption that she was a male. In learning how she had done this, Garfinkel could explore how our typical understanding of what it is to be an adolescent female in North American society is socially constructed.

A major problem for Agnes as a young adult was her childhood. She was well aware that boys and girls are typically raised in very different ways in North American

Why is it that parents often encourage children raised as girls to wear frilly dresses but not children raised as boys?

© Jed Share/Kaoru Share/Blend Images/Corbis

society. They are dressed differently, given different toys, encouraged to get involved in very different activities, and expected to learn different skills. Upbringing plays a major role in explaining why adolescent boys and girls think and talk about different things. In order to be accepted by her teenage friends as having been a typical female all along, Agnes had to cover up most of her childhood and invent an appropriate biography. Garfinkel (1967, 148) quotes Agnes as saying:

> "Can you imagine all the blank years I have to fill in? Sixteen or seventeen years of my life that I have to make up for. I have to be careful of the things that I say, just natural things that could slip out. . . . I just never say anything at all about my past that in any way would make a person ask what my past life was like. I say general things. I don't say anything that could be misconstrued." Agnes said that with men she was able to pass as an interesting conversationalist by encouraging her male partners to talk about themselves. Women partners, she said, explained the general and indefinite character of her biographical remarks, which she delivered in a friendly manner, by a combination of her niceness and modesty. "They probably figure that I just don't like to talk about myself."

In her everyday behaviour as an adolescent female mixing with other students at college, Agnes had to monitor every aspect of her activities and her conversations. As Garfinkel expresses it, Agnes, along with other transsexuals, had to earn her right to live in her chosen sexual status, and she lived under the constant fear that disclosure would ruin this. She developed an acutely uncommon-sense awareness of social relations and how they are structured to display sexual status as natural patterns of behaviour that are part of the routinized seen but unnoticed backgrounds of everyday affairs (Garfinkel 1967, 118). These patterns are so familiar to us and so unconsciously part of our everyday behaviour that most of us would find it very difficult to articulate in detail what it is that we notice as typically female or male behaviour. Yet people who choose to adopt a sexual identity different from the one with which they were born and brought up need to develop an acute awareness of these patterns and how to conform to them.

Agnes was so anxious to pass as a normal female that she became painfully concerned with conforming to all the surface features consistent with being typically female. She felt she had to achieve convincingly feminine dress, makeup, and grooming. She had to manage appropriately feminine comportment—talking, sitting, and walking like a typical woman, and so on. Talking like a woman requires knowing a wide range of issues from the perspective of a typical woman rather than from that of a typical man. Agnes became a "secret apprentice," picking up this detailed knowledge of women's experience through conversations with roommates and other girlfriends, learning how to talk about boyfriends, dates, clothes, and other topics typical of teenage girls. She dared not risk doing or saying anything that might trigger in an onlooker the thought that she was behaving like a boy, because any detailed questioning might disclose her secret transsexual identity.

Agnes carefully avoided any activities that might expose her anomalous genitalia, and at the same time she developed a set of excuses for not participating that would sound justifiable or reasonable to others. She refused, on the grounds of modesty, to undress anywhere where she might be seen by others, and she refused, on the excuse of not being in the mood, to go swimming if there were no private dressing rooms available. She told Garfinkel that she even avoided driving a car lest she have an accident where her secret might be discovered.

In summary, Agnes felt she was always on display in that she had to demonstrate in every detail of her surface appearance that she was as she appeared to be, naturally female. Most of us assume that other people will automatically recognize our appropriate sex. We do not expect to have to prove it or demonstrate it, and we would probably get angry very quickly if anyone challenged us or demanded such proof. In a sense, we have a moral right to have our appropriate sex identity recognized, just as we have a moral right to expect others to understand common-sense remarks in ordinary conversations. Transsexuals cannot automatically claim that right to be recognized; they have to actively earn their sex identity. In accomplishing this, they make visible all the details of everyday behaviour that create and sustain for us our identities as one sex or the other.

Thus, we have, by invoking a "deviant case" or "perspective by incongruity," discovered that:

1. From the standpoint of an adult member of our society, the perceived environment of "normally sexed persons" is populated by two sexes and only two sexes, "male" and "female"

. . . .

4. The members of the normal population . . . are essentially, originally, in the first place, always have been, and always will be, once and for all, in the final analysis, either "male" or "female" (Garfinkel 1967, 122).

We should note that these assumptions have since been questioned by researchers exploring gay, lesbian, transgendered, and bisexual gender identities. Thus, we have an additional example of ethnomethodology's insistence of taking social facts not as givens but as ongoing accomplishments of members' methods. What have been taken, in effect, as Durkheimian "social facts" need to be questioned.

Conversation Analysis

Conversation analysis is a branch of ethnomethodology that focuses on the detailed features of talk and their role in creating and sustaining our sense of social order. We need to point out that "conversation" in this context refers to more than what we usually think of as casual chatting. A more accurate term is "talk-in-interaction" which covers a range of speech exchange from the casual to the more structured varieties, such as courtroom dialogue, classroom interaction, television interviews, or exchanges between doctors and patients. Conventional macrosociology tends to ignore talk altogether, or to treat it as a passive medium through which major social structural variables relate to one another. We need to remember that much of our social life, including the major political decisions, are conducted through talk of various kinds.

Conversation analysis explores in minute detail how talk itself is structured. Typically this involves analyzing tape recordings of conversations. Specialized **transcripts** are made, which are designed to capture hearable details of talk, such as intonation, pauses, the stretching of vowels, and the overlapping of turns, all of which may be significant for making the talk comprehensible. Video recordings are now used to study the non-verbal aspects of talk as well. The use of videotape recordings makes possible repeated and detailed examination and reinterpretation of data while eliminating any risk of distortion arising from the limitations of respondents' memories (Heritage 1984, 238). Tape recordings also avoid the problem, which plagues conventional sociology, that data are coded into preset categories in ways unknown to the researcher.

Conversation analysis focuses on members' methods of producing recognizable forms of talk and understandable utterances. In other words, it analyzes how people get their meaning across to others in conversations and how they continually recognize and repair the instances when the meaning has not been completely clear. Transcripts of conversations, interviews, court hearings, lessons, and the like, are analyzed to discover the very general features of how talk is structured. Researchers look for the context-free features of these speech-exchange systems. These are features or structures that are common to all conversation, regardless of topic or situation and the age, sex, social class, or ethnicity of the participants. In a sense, these universal features can be viewed as the machinery through which people communicate verbally for all sorts of purposes.

Listening to recordings and/or poring over transcripts makes it clearly evident that people in everyday life organize their conversations in incredible detail. One critical aspect of this is the organization of **turn-taking**. Generally, in a conversation, one party talks at a time, and the transitions between speakers' turns usually occur with little or no gap or overlap. This is despite the fact that the order in which the participants speak and the length of the conversation as a whole are not preprogrammed. Even where there are violations of these features, such as when two people start to talk at the same time, systematic repair mechanisms come quickly into play to restore order.

This turn-taking machinery is worked out by the participants in the immediate ongoing setting of the talk. Such organization depends on the participants listening carefully to one another so as to figure out just the right moment to start speaking without interrupting. Despite the fact that the alternations of talk are improvised *moment by moment*, people are able to produce a recognizable order in their talk that can be detected by close listening and analysis (Sacks, Schegloff, and Jefferson 1974). Similar machinery of talk governs the familiar activities of opening up conversations and bringing them to a close. The interpretive practices and improvised manoeuvres involved give a structure to conversations that goes far beyond simply starting to speak or instantly shutting up.

A further common aspect of the machinery of talk is that utterances occur in pairs. Questions, for example, are expected to be followed immediately with answers, summonses are followed with acknowledgements, and greetings with return greetings. These are **adjacency pairs**—a first pair-part of one type is expected to be followed immediately by a second pair-part of the same type. Hence, the moment that one participant in a conversation says a first pair-part, by asking a question or offering a greeting, the situation of the talk has changed, because the people involved know that they are accountable for coming up with appropriate responses. If they do not do so, their failure will be immediately noticeable and will require some explanation. For example, when A greets B, A's greeting has a prospective character in the sense that it changes how B's next utterance will be heard. If B returns the greeting, then it acts as an acknowledgement that A and B are mutually involved in the interaction. But if B fails to respond, B's silence will be "hearable" as a silence and will require some explanation. It is not the same situation as silence if A's greeting had not occurred. The silence is out of order and A, together with other listeners, will need to think about whether B's silence is intelligible as, for example, an insult or a failure to hear A's greeting (Heritage 1984, 106–109).

Conversation and Gender Conversation analysis can be used as a resource to explore differences in how females and males employ the various conversational practices such as those outlined above. A number of feminist and other scholars aim to show how events like interruptions, lapses in the flow of conversation, attentiveness or the absence of it are related to the problems of power and dominance in social life. It is argued that this differential or asymmetrical use of these resources (such as who interrupts whom) may show how gender inequality is displayed and reproduced in the very details of male–female interaction. For example, Zimmerman and West (1975) recorded two-party conversations in coffee shops and other public places around a university campus—collecting equal numbers of male-male, female-female, and male-female interactions for the sake of comparison. These were overheard and then cleared with the parties afterward. What they found was that in *same-sex* conversations, **overlaps and interruptions** were symmetrically distributed, but in *cross-sex* conversations, virtually all the interruptions and overlaps were by *male speakers* (Zimmerman and West 1975, 115). Another point of comparison is that of "**minimal responses**." Ordinarily, immediate responses such as "uh hmm," "uh huh," and "yeah" display active hearership—displaying continuing interest and co-participation in topic development. But when the response is minimal and delayed, this may indicate a point in the conversation that the parties find problematic. As Zimmerman and West state:

> [R]etarding the response may function to signal a lack of understanding or even disinterest in and inattention to the current talk. The silence that follows a delayed minimal response reflects, we believe, the other speaker's uncertainty as to her partner's orientation to the current state of the conversation (Zimmerman and West 1975, 123).

This point is picked up and explored by Pamela Fishman, who analyzed conversations between men and women in their homes. She states:

> In a sense, every remark or turn should be seen as an attempt to interact. It may be an attempt to open or close a conversation. It may be a bid to continue interaction: to respond to what went before and elicit a further remark from one's interlocutor. *For an attempt to succeed, the other party must be willing to do further interactional work. That other person has the power to turn an attempt into a conversation or stop it dead* (Fishman 1978, 399, italics added).

Her research showed that it is the women who did most of the "support work" while the men "dragged their feet"—displaying their lack of interest in what the women were talking about. As Fishman sums it up:

The women worked harder than men in interaction because they had less certainty of success. They did much of the necessary work of interaction, starting conversations and then working to maintain them (Fishman 1978, 404).

But can we be certain that it is indeed *gender* at work here? Are we imposing a macrosociological variable onto these observed interactions (Schegloff 1987, 215)? They may be conflating gender with *status*—with males often having higher status than females, as is prevalent in our society. A strategic case study is one by Candace West involving video recordings of encounters between male and female patients and their doctors. She asks: "What happens, though, when the conventional stratification of the sexes is reversed, e.g., when a doctor is a 'lady'?" (West 1984, 89). A major representative of this, Talcott Parsons, holds that a key to the therapeutic practice of medicine is the *essential asymmetry of the physician–patient relationship*, in which it is the physician who is charged with the legal responsibility for restoring the patient back to health (West 1984, 94). However, as we have emphasized in this chapter, the *emphasis on social roles* is not sufficient to explain behaviour in immediate, practical situations. Candace West reminds us that:

> Whatever the scripts that may exist for the physician–patient encounter, they must always be negotiated on the basis of the situational exigencies of social life (West 1984, 95).

Here, she finds that although the male physicians interrupted patients far more than the reverse and that the interactions between female doctors and female patients are almost symmetrical, when it comes to encounters *between female physicians and male patients*, it is the *male patients that do most of the interrupting* (p. 97). What West concludes tentatively is this:

> What is warranted, for the findings reported here, is the suggestion that gender can have primacy over status where women physicians are concerned. These data indicate that gender can amount to a "master" status . . . even where other power relations are involved (West 1984, 102).

Thus, conversation analysis gives another set of tools for exploring gender and gender inequalities as ongoingly accomplished through the details of everyday observable practices and interaction among women and men.

"Institutional Talk" or Talk at Work
More recently, the techniques of conversation analysis have similarly been applied to other settings such as courtrooms, classrooms, media including television news interviews, doctor–patient interviews, calls to emergency and police

centres, and numerous others. These have been referred to as "institutional talk" or "talk at work." These studies give a new perspective on the microsociological bases of control over information, biases in decision-making, and the exercise of power.

For example, studies of formal talk during classroom lessons (McHoul 1978; Heap 1979) give us intimate details of how children organize their turn-taking in round-robin reading. We see how teachers strategically time their interruptions or utterances like "uh-h?" to signal to a child that the previous word was not quite right and that some error repair is needed. The student who has made the mistake displays **interactional competence** when she or he takes up this hint and inserts the proper word in the proper sequence in the subsequent reading (Weeks 1985). Similarly, other studies (Mehan 1979; McHoul 1990; Weeks 1994) look at **typical sequences** in lessons starting with the teacher's question, then the student's response followed by the teacher's comment or evaluation. Often, however, negative evaluations are avoided in favour of asking that student or other students questions that encourage them to suggest alternative answers. The unequal opportunities to employ turn-taking moves that we considered earlier is evidenced in the teacher's extended turns and the familiar practice of students' raising their hands to bid for the next turn for which the teacher chooses the specific student. After reading such studies, we gain a sense of precisely how teachers do their work of teaching, and how children do their work.

Finally, I shall refer to Peter Eglin's recent article on a setting most familiar to you, in which he asks: "Just what is it about the operations of universities that makes them universities?" (Eglin 2009, 40). While this might strike you as belabouring the obvious, we are returning to the discussion at the beginning of this section of the chapter, as reflected in his statement:

> The goal is to describe and analyze the embodied methods of practical reasoning and action by means of which parties engaged in the life of the university render their activities *accountable*—that is, observable and reportable—as *university-specific* activities (Eglin 2009, 40, italics in original).

To this end, he takes an extract from a transcript which covers the beginning part of a university class:

P: [Professor passes out sheets]

P: [background noise—random chatter] [professor adjusts the podium] I uh (.2) for (.2) Wednesday [random chatter stops] I've decided to pass around uh (.5) question sheet for the discussion uh just to give you a little more . . . guidance for the Sudan discussion on Wednesday = and = I'll say a few words about that uh once those sheets are around uh while they're going around (.5) uh the essays I should be able to have them back for Wednesday that's my goal anyways I still have a few to grade um so hopefully I'll be able to get through them by Wednesday? And then uh have them available to you to pick up during the discussion class [class continues for 90 minutes uninterrupted]. (Eglin 2009, 44)

We can say that this is observably a class given by the professor to students, but at the beginning of it where the lecture proper has not yet started. As long-accustomed members in this setting, we readily recognize that the sheets here are handouts and we can repair the indexical expression "Wednesday" which, though it refers to an indefinite range of possible Wednesdays, it is taken here to refer to the next class in a series that is typically held on Mondays, Wednesdays, and Fridays. Note that as soon as the person identifiable as the professor mentions it, the random chatter among the students suddenly stops. In this setting, then, "I uh (.2) for (.2) for Wednesday" is hearable as an announcement that the class is beginning—rather than merely as a reference to dates. It is thus observable as being within a familiar set of institutional arrangement of class schedules, etc. Unlike other sociological approaches, ethnomethodology/conversation analysis generates rigorous studies of just how lessons are "ongoingly accomplished."

This mode of inquiry can be fruitfully applied to current **media**, whether the mass media of radio and television or CMC (computer-mediated communication) over the Internet. First, we can draw on studies of news interviews as further examples of "institutional talk," as characterized by "the special character of speech exchange systems to which the participants can be found to orient themselves" (Hutchby 2006, 25). Although we may take it for granted, we should note that the activity of talking is a key component of most programs in the media. If we take news interviews on radio or television as a specific example, we find that they consist of a chain of question-and-answer sequences in which the interviewers ask the questions while the interviewees (politicians, experts, etc.), ideally at least, answer the questions (Hutchby 2006, 122). A key question is just how the interviewers maintain *a stance of neutrality* while, on occasion, challenging politicians or other figures in the news. In turn, we may ask how these people go along with, evade, or challenge the questions put to them by the interviewers. Another aspect to explore is the ways in which this talk is designed to be received by the overhearing audience (in contrast with ordinary conversation) rather than the interviewer himself/herself (see also Heritage 1985). For example, unlike ordinary conversation, interviewers generally refrain from "mm" or "oh yes" types of acknowledgements as talk is being produced for an audience. One more feature of such talk is "formulations," which Garfinkel and Sacks (1970, 351) originally defined as "conversationalists' practices of saying in so many words

what they are doing." In this context, they can be viewed as "gists" or summaries of the talk-so-far, which provide a means of packaging or repackaging the central point in the interviewee's turn for the overhearing audience. But it could be a stronger or more contentious version that challenges the interviewee. This provides him/her the opportunity to agree, disagree, or otherwise react to that formulation (Hutchby 2006, 129–133).

Finally, observe the detailed practices of just how these interviews are neatly *brought to an end* in order to meet the network schedule. Steven Clayman has studied how an essentially spontaneous and improvised encounter is made to end at a specified time to fit the standardized program schedule (Clayman 1989, 660). While the functionalists and many of us might take temporality for granted as necessary to coordinate specialized activities in complex modern societies, that is, as a sort of Durkheimian "social fact," Clayman chooses to examine how the temporal aspect of social activities is constituted through members' detailed practices. Recall also Goffman's treatment of temporality in terms of "occasions" being bounded in both space and time, but not revealing to us how the participants actually *accomplish* these temporal transitions. Turning again to news interviews, Clayman argues that, unlike ordinary conversation, they are subject to two restrictions: first, turn types are restricted to questions and answers by interviewers and interviewees respectively, and second, the overall length of the encounter is fixed in advance (Clayman 1989, 669). Watch carefully the "pre-closing moves" by the interviewer consisting of "thanks" addressed to the interviewees and also "closing prefaces," which may take the form of announcing that termination is impending, and also a formulation of what has been said and its significance. In an earlier turn, there could be what Clayman calls "closing projections," such as "Just one last thing," or "Do you have a final quick comment?" (Clayman 1989, 672–673). Thus, through the use of transcripts from recordings of these programs, this approach can recover the detailed practices through which these familiar forms of media programs are ongoingly accomplished.

Finally, we turn briefly to conversation as related to **technology**. Nowadays, there are numerous ways in which conversational practices interface with technological devices, ranging from the telephone to the Internet. These function as a means by which individuals and groups can create a sense of co-presence even though they are separated from one another in *space* and also, in many cases, in *time*. For example, it has been argued that the telephone facilitates "intimacy at a distance" (even to the extent of phone sex!). Consider media expert Marshall McLuhan's apt statement that on the telephone, "the sender is sent" (McLuhan and McLuhan 1988, 153). But, we have to ask: What aspects of a person are sent by the respective media?

Clearly, the Internet involves sending the sender in an especially discarnate or disembodied manner (even more so than on the telephone)—merely via written words (Levinson 1999, 56). As a consequence, regarding CMC (computer-mediated communication), there is much concern about interaction and relationships via e-mail, newsgroups, and SNS (social networking sites) such as Facebook, in terms of whether these are genuine communities or merely "pseudo-communities." Much of this writing invokes an essentialist "deficit model," which claims that, compared with the alleged richness of "face-to-face" communication (so well described by Goffman), CMC interactions are deficient because of the lack of visual cues and even tones of voice. It is argued that this allows for fraud, false identities, and second-rate relationships (including the hazards of online dating!). This is well expressed in the *New Yorker* cartoon, reproduced many times, with two dogs in front of a computer screen with one saying to the other: "On the Internet, nobody knows you're a dog"!

The concern for ethnomethodology is not the intrinsic nature of the technology as such, but rather people's *detailed observable practices in using it*. This is part of ethnomethodology's interest in "human–machine interaction." How do they modify their management of talk as described earlier when interacting through these new media? We find that, despite the limitations mentioned above, they develop a sense of real communities and authentic relationships after all. Just how do they do this? For example, one obvious device in e-mails is to employ "emoticons" such as ":-)", which express emotions, humour, or irony not otherwise conveyed in bare text. Ian Hutchby introduces the useful concept of "affordances," which basically refers to the potentials resulting from any given technology—only some of which are actually adopted by the users. In other words, these are the possibilities for and limitations to social action (Hutchby 2001, 26). Thus, the uses by different groups may differ considerably from those envisioned by the creators of the technology. Conversation analysis researchers, with their detailed examination of transcripts of such talk, can provide a rigorous insight into these issues.

Ethnomethodological Studies of Work

Recent developments in ethnomethodology are moving beyond the analysis of conversations to explore the intimate details of practical reasoning that make possible the joint activities of people at work. The kinds of work processes studied range from improvised jazz performances (Sudnow 1978) to discoveries in astrophysics (Garfinkel, Lynch, and Livingston 1981) and research in a biological sciences laboratory (Lynch 1985).

These studies are in contrast with the conventional sociology of occupations that tends to tell us a great deal about the occupation in question and the lives of the workers. What we do not learn is exactly how people do what they are doing or the taken-for-granted practical reasoning and background understandings on which it is based (Heritage 1984, 293–299). Ethnomethodology explores **"the missing what."**

An excellent example of the contrast between conventional and ethnomethodological studies of work is Becker's (1951) study of professional musicians (in the symbolic interactionist tradition) and Sudnow's (1978, 1979) ethnomethodological studies of jazz improvisation. Becker focuses on musicians' work as a service occupation in which the players have personal contact with members of their audience who exert pressure on how they do their work, particularly on the musical selections they are asked to play. Becker's specific interests are:

1. the conceptions that musicians have of themselves and of the non-musicians for whom they work and the conflict they feel to be inherent in this relation;

2. the basic consensus underlying the reactions of both commercial and jazz musicians to this conflict; and

3. the feelings of isolation musicians have from the larger society and the way they segregate themselves from audience and community (Becker 1951, 249).

His analysis is based on 18 months of interviews and participant observation as a jazz pianist. He describes how musicians think of themselves as artists who possess a mysterious gift that sets them apart from outsiders, whom they regard as "squares." The musicians feel that the audience, who are mostly squares, have no right to dictate what they should play. But since the audience is the major source of their income, they are faced with the dilemma of whether to "go commercial," which implies abandoning the creative principle but making a good living, or to stay with what they consider good jazz but make a precarious living. Commercial musicians look down on the audience, but they choose to sacrifice self-respect and the respect of their peers in order to enjoy the advantages of steady work and higher income (Becker 1951, 254).

In the actual playing situation, the musicians segregate themselves from the audience as much as possible by playing on a platform and positioning the piano to act as a physical barrier that reduces direct interaction with, and therefore undesirable influence from, the audience. Becker concludes that generally musicians are hostile towards audiences and that they tend to associate mostly among themselves.

This study is in many ways a fascinating account of the lives of musicians, but a crucial aspect has been ignored.

We learn about the musicians' roles, their relations with the audience, their career choices, and their distinctive subculture, but we learn nothing about their actual musical activities, despite the fact that Becker was a participant musician. We do not learn even the most elementary information, such as how all the members of the band manage to start playing at the same time, let alone stay together despite the lack of a conductor. Garfinkel sums up the problems with Becker's study thus:

> We learn from Becker . . . that there are jazz musicians, where they work, whom they work with, what they earn, how they get their jobs, what the audience size and composition is . . . but . . . nowhere in the article can it be read and no interrogation of the article can supply that it is just in those places, with just those persons . . . at just those times, under the circumstances at hand, these parties must in and of their local work *make music together*. The curiosity of the reportage . . . is that Becker's article *omits entirely . . . and exactly what the parties are doing* that makes what they are doing for each other recognizable, just so, just what, just this that is going on, namely, their making music! (Garfinkel 1976, 36, italics added)

In contrast, Sudnow (1978) raises the question of how jazz musicians actually manage to play. His study focuses on the stages he went through learning to play jazz piano. He also discusses the frantic character of playing with other people when they set the pace at which his hands had to move. Sudnow argues that aspects of tempo and rhythm are integral parts of any social interaction. We have to pay attention to how people notice changes in tempo and how these are accomplished (Sudnow 1979, 117). Thus, even though Becker's study falls within the first interpretive perspective we looked at, namely symbolic interactionism, we find a significant difference of approaches. While the former describes the relationships involved, the musicians' descriptions of their work (including their distinctive language or "argot"), the latter goes even deeper to examine the practical reasoning (members' methods) of making sense of one another's activities from moment to moment. For example, we can inquire into just how jazz musicians manage synchrony (that is, keeping together) throughout the performance of a tune. It is definitely not enough to have music sheets in front of them, for the specific place in the tune at any given moment depends on what they have collectively accomplished so far. A standard practice is to set a tempo (what I call a "temporal context") by either counting in at the beginning or having the drummer set the beat. During the performance, the musicians need to listen to one another and monitor their own playing in that context. Also, various practices of "musical saves" when errors or the unexpected happens are part of the skills developed

by these musicians—playing on the fact that the audience is likely not nearly so familiar with the tune or at least musical conventions as they are. The discovery of their detailed practices, or "the missing what," requires an ethnomethodological type of inquiry that involves an insider's perspective (see Weeks 2009). Finally, we should remember that playing music together applies to any genre, including pop music, and not just jazz (see Schutz 1964 for a general perspective on this).

Ethnomethodological studies of professional scientists at work explore the practical everyday reasoning through which scientists collectively arrive at the belief that they have made a discovery. Garfinkel, Lynch, and Livingston (1981) begin with the question: "What does the optically discovered pulsar consist of as the 'night's work'?" Fortuitously, a tape recording of the astronomers' shop talk was available, as well as their notebooks recording the observations they made on an oscilloscope in the observatory. From this, Garfinkel and company pursued their interest in this discovery *as a real-time production*, just as it was unfolding over time, in the context with their previous sightings on that series of nights with that specific set of equipment. They were interested not only in the scientists' "embodied practices" (using the equipment, making the readings, etc.) but also their "practical reasoning" (making sense of the readings on the oscilloscope). Recall our earlier discussion of the "retrospective–prospective" character of accounts—in terms of how the meanings of words and actions change over time. It is important to note that a discovery is only accountable as such in the course of a *series* of observations. In addition, there is the basic problem that, since we cannot observe these pulsating stars directly but have to rely on scientific instruments, how can we know that there really is that kind of star out there? How do they establish that they have indeed made such a discovery? What does this discovery consist of in its detail for all practical purposes?

Another prominent study of this type was conducted by Michael Lynch (1985) of the laboratory research into the regenerative processes in the brain. In addition to making close observations of scientists' "embodied practices" of reading electronic microscope plates and "executing" rats in order to make slices of their brains for examination, Lynch employed ethnographic field notes and audio recordings of their shop talk. Again, conventional sociological and historical accounts of science are far removed from the detailed and practical (and often messy!) laboratory tasks done on a day-to-day basis at the bench. But in order to understand even the shop talk, let alone the other activities, the researcher in ethnomethodology requires a fair understanding of the specialized field under study. Lynch had to become very informed about neurological science in order to decipher what was going on, just as one would need to know quite a bit about music in order to understand what musicians are talking about. You will recall the earlier discussion of "indexicality" where much of what the parties are talking about are just assumed and thus not said in so many words. We need the particular background understandings in order to be minimally competent participants.

A pervasive and annoying problem for scientists is what is called "artifacts"—that is, displays that are the result of errors, equipment faults, inadequate preparation, etc.—rather than the natural occurrences or objects under study. But then, similar to the pulsar situation, just how do the scientists decide whether they have discovered a new object or process, or just messed up? Relatively straightforward would be a "staining artifact," which is visible as an opaque dark patch on a micrograph with no depth of details under magnification—in other words, a blob. "Knife marks" are linear streaks that are clearly different from the appearance of cells on the plate. Other types of possible artifacts may be far more tricky. Thus, ethnomethodologists are again interested in the "practical reasoning" that distinguishes artifacts from discoveries.

Recent Studies

Talk can be analyzed as forms of action—such as commitments or evasion of responsibility, promises, commands—that are done through words. A striking example is the more recent analysis by Lynch and Bogen (1996) of testimony given in the Iran–Contra hearings by Lieutenant-Colonel Oliver North who, in his Marines uniform bedecked with medals, was the object of what became "Olliemania"—in which a covert agent and admitted liar came to be dubbed "the hero America needs!" The Iran–Contra affair began in 1985 when members of the White House National Security Council (NSC), including President Reagan's National Security Advisers, collaborated with a set of international arms salesmen, mercenaries, and Israeli and Iranian officials to arrange a series of covert sales of US weapons to Iran. Oliver North was a key coordinator of these operations. In 1986, the NSC began diverting some of the profits from the Iranian arms sales to aid the Contras seeking to overthrow the Marxist Sandinista government in Nicaragua, despite Congress's prohibition of such sales. Despite the destruction of many documents relevant to these operations, the Iran–Contra affair became a scandal leading to the televised Congressional investigation that could well have brought down the presidency. But by the time the committee issued its final report in November 1987, the case had become so inconclusive that it failed to do so.

This very inconclusiveness was built into the records and testimony that made up the evidence. Even the writing of the original documents, as well as their shredding, was designed to protect the Iran–Contra participants from a later anticipated official investigation such as that which in

fact occurred. Oliver North and his colleagues openly admitted that these covert operations, including the securing and hiding of caches of funds, fabricating false accounts, and shredding documents, were aimed at what they called "plausible deniability." As Lynch and Bogen explain:

> "Plausible deniability" refers to a collection of techniques through which parties to an event anticipate the possible historical significance of that event . . . Plausibly deniable records and recording practices are designed to facilitate denials and to provide alternative rationales for activities and events that may later come under hostile scrutiny (Lynch and Bogen 1996, 63).

An important objective was to protect President Reagan such that he could plausibly or credibly deny any direct involvement in these operations or even any knowledge of them. In this light, we gain a very different idea of the process of writing history from the conventional or common-sense one. While we might ordinarily think that it involves searching for documents as evidence for objective, reliable accounts of what really happened, here we find that the documents themselves and their occasional destruction are meant to alter that very historical record!

We shall mention just a couple of aspects of this extensive study, with reference to Oliver North's testimony—the puzzle as to whether he was still lying as he had admitted doing so in the past, and the strategic use of claims not to remember various incidents. First, were Oliver North and his colleagues now coming clean, or were they continuing to mislead and withhold evidence? Here is North's rationale for lying previously and claiming now to be telling the truth:

> North: No, Mister Nields, the reason for shredding documents, and the reason the Government of the United States gave me a shredder . . . again I want to go back to the whole intent of the covert operation. Part of . . . a covert operation is to offer plausible deniability of the association of the government of the United States with the activity, part of it is to deceive our adversaries. Part of it is to ensure that those people who are at great peril, carrying out those activities, are not further endangered. All are good and sufficient reasons to destroy documents. And that's why the government buys shredders by the tens and dozens . . . I came here to tell you the truth. To tell you and this committee, and the American people, the truth, and I'm trying to do that Mister Nields (quoted in Lynch and Bogen 1996, 22)

For many Americans, his being forthright in his admissions enhanced his current credibility. Here he is claiming that he lied in the past with good intentions—to protect these covert operations which, if revealed, would damage national security and play into the hands of America's

Oliver North successfully managed his testimony during the Iran–Contra hearings to appear as a truthful witness who admitted to lying.

© Wally McNamee/CORBIS

enemies. Covert activities are, in effect, themselves a lie, albeit in the national interest. But how do we know he is not *still lying*? Here is another problem of "practical reasoning" in this context. So the paradox looks like this:

1. Lying is justified to prevent our adversaries from knowing our secrets.

2. Our adversaries have access to this very testimony.

3. I am not lying now. *And I really mean it, honest!* (Lynch and Bogen 1996, 43)

Second, we come to the issue of memory and its implications for responsibility for the activities in question. Throughout the hearings, the testimony was framed as remembered, recalled, or recollected matters of fact. Oliver North's testimony made repeated use of the following phrases:

"I don't recall,"

"I can't recall a specific date,"

"I guess" and "I don't remember,"

"I don't have a specific recall of that at this time point,"

"I don't think so, I mean you may refresh my memory" (Lynch and Bogen 1996, 180).

Ordinarily, we might hear these phrases as statements about the internal operations of memory in the mind of the individual, but as you will no doubt notice, they are employed in a highly strategic manner. The problem is that it is difficult to decide whether "I don't recall" is being used evasively or not. Jeff Coulter has pointed out the *difference between forgetting and not remembering.* To say you forgot something is to imply that there was indeed something to be forgotten in the first place. But to say "I don't remember" or "I don't recall" does not necessarily mean there was any event or object to be remembered (Lynch and Bogen 1996, 183). Even so, that might not always be an easy out, as one could be held *responsible for remembering,* that there is no excuse not to—as, for example, if the person clearly was a direct participant and was there at that particular time (Lynch and Bogen 1996, 200). One more complication was that Oliver North shredded a large number of documents and professed not to recall which ones, or whether they had been destroyed because of their value as possible evidence. Here is our final piece of testimony in which he starts off with an apt pun:

Nields:	Sir, do you remember the question?
North:	My memory has been shredded. If you would be so kind as to repeat the question.
Nields:	You've testified that you shredded documents shortly after you heard from Director Casey that Furmark had said monies had been used from the Iranian arms sales for the benefit of the Contras.
North:	That is correct.
Nields:	My question to you is—did you or did you not shred documents that reflected Presidential approval of the diversion?
North:	I have absolutely no recollection of destroying any document which gave me an indication that the President had seen the document or that the President had specifically approved. I assumed that the three transactions which I supervised or managed or coordinated—whatever words you're comfortable with, and I can accept all three—were approved by the president. I never recall seeing a single document which gave me a clear indication that the President had specifically approved this action. (quoted in Lynch & Bogen 1996, 221)

Thus, "plausible deniability" in the context of the claim that the president did not know about the diversion of funds from Iran arms sales to the Contras is supported.

To conclude, the Iran–Contra study involves a close examination of the talk involved in the Congressional investigation employing some of the methods of conversation analysis, but the interest here is not in the typical *forms of talk* generated (such as the turn-taking structure), but just how talk is *used to accomplish various actions*—adjudicating on responsibility, generating a historical record of these events, and so forth. Thus, we have a very different approach to the process of writing history from the conventional one of gathering facts!

A final point is that this type of analysis is well suited to the study of *courtroom* procedures in general, where, among other things, the types of questions influence or even constrain the kinds of answers or testimony that results.

In summary, ethnomethodology focuses on the ways in which we, in our everyday lives, use our common-sense knowledge and background understandings to make sense to ourselves and to each other what is going on around us. Our sense of reality, including all the familiar features of our society, is created through such practical everyday reasoning. The central contribution of ethnomethodology is its focus on the methods or practices by which people actively create a sense of what is happening in intimate, everyday interactions, and how they actively construct their own actions in order to make what they are doing sensible to others. These sense-making processes form the basis of all social life.

CONCLUSION

The critical value of microsociology is that it provides a means of discovering how social relations are produced through the everyday activities of individual people. Macrostructures can be conceived as consisting of collections of individual people acting in certain kinds of micro-situations. What gets done is accomplished by *people*, not by abstract systems. These interpretive perspectives provide a corrective to the tendency to reify social structures, that is, like Durkheim, to treat them as social facts that are given or just out there to be discovered by the appropriate scientific methods. As Blumer pointed out, we need to take into account how people in concrete situations interpret them in order to understand why they act as they do.

We started our survey of interpretive perspectives with symbolic interactionism, which has as its central argument that people act on the *meanings* that words, gestures, actions, or situations have for them. These are conceived as *symbols* which, though directly observable, require interpretation. On that basis, social science is said to be essentially different from the natural sciences in that their inquiries must take these various meanings into account. The unitary descriptions of variables of Durkheimian or positivist sciences just do not fit this social reality.

Labelling and related social constructionist approaches lead one to question the active practices that researchers use to produce the evidence that they subsequently analyze. For example, before we take data such as crime rates or suicide rates as "facts," we need to consider the chain of judgments (involving, of course, interpretations) from the state of what gets reported in the first place all the way to sentences in court or coroners' inquiries (see Douglas 1967). In

addition, these theorists are concerned not just with the "labels" as such, but also the real-life consequences for those who are labelled.

Goffman is highly celebrated for his brilliant insights into the "interaction order," especially concerning people's behaviour when in one another's immediate physical presence—now a strategic basis of contrast with the ever-growing computer-mediated communication in cyberspace. He has drawn on observations and many literary sources, although, in contrast with ethnomethodology and conversation analysis, very rarely on the basis of recordings and transcripts. Some scholars wonder if he is imposing his concepts on the people he describes in claiming them to be engaged in "impression management," presenting themselves in strategic ways, and the like. Does his analysis relate to people's experiences? It is worth thinking about.

In contrast, ethnomethodology and conversation analysis demand a rigorous reference to fine-grained observations of what people say and do. Their claims need to be based on the details of what is observable—ideally using recordings and specialized transcripts derived from them, as we have seen. Their emphasis is on "members' methods" for making their activities observable for what they are.

However, it has often been argued that these microsociological approaches fail to address the larger issues of power, inequality, and conflict—what could be described as the burning problems in our troubled world. On the contrary, interpretive methods can bring to light the detailed observable *social processes* through which these occur—for example, seeing power *in action*. These fill in "the missing what" only glossed by the standard macrosociological perspectives.

We are thus thrown back into what has been called "**the macro–micro debate**." How do we link everyday interaction or even what Goffman called "the interaction order" to what seem to be massively real macrostructures—systems of inequality, power, technology, globalization—which appear to be large forces shaping our very experiences? Do we need a different perspective to analyze them?

SUGGESTED READING

Symbolic Interaction

For a classic statement of the principles of symbolic interactionism, Chapter 1 of Herbert Blumer's book on the subject (1969) is a convenient reference. In another article entitled "Sociological Analysis and the Variable" (1978), Blumer criticizes conventional macrosociology, which tends to analyze the effects of one variable (an independent variable) on another (or dependent variable), such as the effects of a media campaign on people's subsequent behaviour. Taking the example of measuring the effectiveness of a birth-control campaign on reducing fertility, Blumer insists that we need to recognize that people will respond depending on what a number of aspects of this campaign mean to them. It is not merely a simple relation between cause and effect.

The symbolic interactionist approach has led to many interesting ethnographies involving close observations of people's activities in a great variety of settings. In the early days of "the Chicago School" headed at that time by Robert Park, a former newspaperman, students were encouraged to explore various Chicago neighbourhoods first-hand. In this line, a classic is Nels Anderson's *The hobo; the sociology of the homeless man* (1923) and later William Foote Whyte's *Street Corner Society: The Social Structure of an Italian Slum* (1981), where he tells of how he became accepted by the local people and traced their activities and connections. In a later study, Robert Prus observed the daily work of sex-trade workers and their networks in *Hookers, Rounders, and Desk Clerks: The Social Organization of the Hotel Community* (1980). We should note that Gary Alan Fine did numerous ethnographies in a variety of settings, ranging from *Kitchens: The Culture of Restaurant Work* (1996) to *Authors of the Storm: Meteorologists and the Culture of Prediction* (2007). For current work of this type, check out the journals *Symbolic Interaction* and *Journal of Contemporary Ethnography*.

Labelling Theory

In *Outsiders* (1963, revised in 1973), Howard Becker lays out a classic formulation of labelling theory and also includes his work on jazz musicians and marijuana use. Also, John Lofland expands on this, giving many examples in *Deviance and Identity* (1969). Ned Polsky makes first-hand observations of pool hustlers and writes on pornography in *Hustlers, Beats, and Others* (1967). In that vein, there is a recent study of sex workers based on interviews with 60 of them, with the objective of presenting their own analysis of, and resistance to, the common stereotypical interpretations of their lives—Leslie Ann Jeffrey's and Gayle MacDonald's *Sex Workers in the Maritimes Talk Back* (2006). Social constructionist perspectives on deviance in various settings are contained in a convenient reader edited by Lori Beaman, entitled *New Perspectives on Deviance: The Construction of Deviance in Everyday Life* (2000).

Goffman

The dramaturgical perspective is set most usefully in *The Presentation of Self in Everyday Life* (1959), *Behavior in Public Places* (1963), and *Interaction Ritual* (1967). A convenient overview is Greg Smith's *Erving Goffman* (2006).

Ethnomethodology/Conversation Analysis

A clear explanation of ethnomethodology and how to apply it is set out in Alain Coulon's *Ethnomethodology* (1995) and David Francis's and Stephen Hester's *An Invitation to Ethnomethodology: Language, Society, and Interaction* (2004). Wes Sharrock and Bob Anderson contribute a thoughtful but brief overview in *The Ethnomethodologists* (1986).

Recommended as further introductions to conversation analysis are George Psathas's *Conversation Analysis: The Study of Talk-in-Interaction* (1995) and Paul ten Have's *Doing Conversation Analysis: A Practical Guide* (1998).

Applications of conversational analysis include J. Maxwell Atkinson's and Paul Drew's *Order in Court: The Organization of Verbal Interaction in Judicial Settings* (1979), Steven Clayman and John Heritage's *The News Interview: Journalists and Public Figures on the Air* (2002), and the more familiar setting of classrooms in Peter Eglin's "What Do We Do Wednesday? On Beginning the Class as University-Specific Work: A Preliminary Study" (2009). Also, applications to talk in a variety of other settings are contained in the collection edited by Paul Drew and John Heritage, *Talk at Work: Interaction in Institutional Settings* (1992), ranging from psychiatry, news interviews, diagnoses, court proceedings, and rape trials. Applications to current media include Ian Hutchby's *Conversation and Technology: From the Telephone to the Internet* (2001) and *Media Talk: Conversation Analysis and the Study of Broadcasting* (2006).

QUESTIONS

1. What are the common principles of the interpretive perspectives reviewed here?

2. In what ways do the approaches of symbolic interactionism and ethnomethodology question the conventional social sciences? What do they claim to be the differences between the natural sciences and the social sciences? In other words, what is distinctive about the subject matter of the social sciences?

3. What are the key differences among symbolic interactionism, labelling theory, Goffman's dramaturgical model, and ethnomethodology?

4. What are some of the norms that need to be observed when people are in one another's immediate physical presence?

5. Contrast a macrosociological perspective to an interpretive one in terms of how they would analyze a specific social activity or organization.

6. Outline the essential ideas of ethnomethodology in terms of the following:
   a. "social facts" as ongoing accomplishments of members' methods,
   b. indexicality and "background understandings", and
   c. documentary method of interpretation
   Give examples.

7. What are the essential concepts and approaches of conversation analysis to talk-in-interaction? Give examples.

8. Taking classroom interaction as an example, explain how an ethnomethodogical/conversation analysis study would differ from functionalist and Marxist approaches to education.

WEB LINKS

The Iran–Contra Affair: 20 Years On
www.gwu.edu/~nsarchiv/NSAEBB/NSAEBB210/index.htm
This website is hosted by The National Security Archive at George Washington University. This link provides analysis and scanned copies of documents such as "George H.W. Bush Diary," "U.S. Policy Toward Iran, TOP SECRET," and CIA memorandum "Lunch with Ollie North."

"Reagan Tapes Iran Testimony," February 17, 1990
www.murraywaas.net/id35.html
This is a link from the website of author and journalist Murray Waas. Waas has written for the *Los Angeles Times, The Boston Globe, The New Republic,*

ABC News and other prominent newspapers. He was also a 1993 Pulitzer Prize finalist for reporting on US foreign policies. His writings are often critical of US policy and involvement in global wars, writing repeatedly about US involvement in the Middle East. This site provides access to many of his newspaper articles. Waas can also be followed on Twitter at http://twitter.com/murraywaas

KEY TERMS

accountability

adjacency pairs

background understandings

documentary method of interpretation

indexicality

interactional competence

macro–micro debate

macrosociology

media

members' competences

microsociology

microtranslation strategy

minimal responses

the missing what

overlaps and interruptions

practical reasoning

radical microsociology

reality disjunctures

reflexive

reification

social construction of reality

social structures

symbol

symbolic interaction

technology

transcripts

transsexual

turn-taking

typical sequences

utterances

REFERENCES

Becker, Howard S. 1951. "The Professional Dance Musician and His Audience." *American Journal of Sociology* 57: 136–144.

Becker, Howard S. 1963. *Outsiders*. New York: Free Press.

Blumer, Herbert. 1969. *Symbolic Interactionism: Perspective and Method*. Englewood Cliffs, New Jersey: Prentice-Hall.

Blumer, Herbert. 1978. "Sociological Analysis and the Variable." In Jerome G. Manis and Bernard N. Meltzer, eds. *Symbolic Interaction: A Reader in Social Psychology*. 3rd ed. Boston: Allyn and Bacon.

Clayman, Steven E. 1989. "The Production of Punctuality: Social Interaction, Temporal Organization, and Social Structure." *American Journal of Sociology* 95 (3): 659–691.

Clayman, Steven E. 1988. "Displaying Neutrality in Television News Interviews." *Social Problems* 35: 474–492.

Collins, Randall. 1981. "On the Microfoundations of Macro sociology." *American Journal of Sociology* 86: 984–1014.

Cuff, E.C. 1993. *Problems of Versions in Everyday Situations*. Boston: International Institute for Ethnomethodology and Conversation Analysis/University Press of America.

Douglas, Jack. 1967. *The Social Meanings of Suicide*. Princeton: Princeton University Press.

Douglas, Jack D. et al. 1980. *Introduction to the Sociologies of Everyday Life*. Boston: Allyn and Bacon.

Eglin, Peter. 1979. "Resolving Reality Disjunctures on Telegraph Avenue: A Study of Practical Reasoning." *Canadian Journal of Sociology* 4: 359–377. (Later reanalyzed in Dorothy Smith. 1990. "The Active Text: A Textual Analysis of the Social Relations of Public Textual Discourse." In *Texts, Facts, and Femininity: Exploring the Relations of Ruling*. London & New York: Routledge.)

Eglin, Peter (2009). "What Do We Do Wednesday? On Beginning the Class as University-Specific Work: A Preliminary Study." *Canadian Review of Sociology* 46 (1): 39–57.

Emerson, J. 1970. "Behavior in Private Places: Sustaining Definitions of Reality in Gynecological Examinations." In H. Dreitzel, ed. *Recent Sociology, No. 2: Patterns of Communicative Behavior*. New York: Macmillan.

Fishman, P. 1978. "Interaction: The Work Women Do." *Social Problems* 25: 397–406.

Garfinkel, Harold. 1976. "Manual for Studies of Naturally Organized Activities." Unpublished manuscript. Department of Sociology, University of California.

Garfinkel, Harold. 1967. *Studies in Ethnomethodology*. Englewood Cliffs, New Jersey: Prentice-Hall.

Garfinkel, Harold. 1963. "A Conception of, and Experiments with, 'Trust' as a Condition of Stable Concerted Actions." In O. J. Harvey, ed. *Motivation and Social Interaction*, New York: Ronald Press: 187–238.

Garfinkel, Harold. 1956. "Conditions of Successful Degradation Ceremonies." *American Journal of Sociology* 61: 420–424.

Garfinkel, Harold, Michael Lynch, and Eric Livingston. 1981. "The Work of a Discovering Science Construed with Materials from the Optically Discovered Pulsar." *Philosophy of the Social Sciences* 11: 131–158.

Garfinkel, Harold, and Harvey Sacks. 1970. "On Formal Structure of Practical Actions." In John C. McKinney and Edward Tiryakian, eds. *Theoretical Sociology: Perspectives & Developments*. New York: Appleton-Century-Crofts, 337–366.

Goffman, Erving. 1983. "The Interaction Order." *American Sociological Review* 48: 1–17.

Goffman, Erving. 1971. *Relations in Public: Microstudies of the Public Order*. New York: Harper.

Goffman, Erving. 1963. *Behavior in Public Places*. New York: Free Press.

Goffman, Erving. 1959. *The Presentation of Self in Everyday Life*. New York: Doubleday.

Heap, James L. 1979. "Classroom Talk: A Criticism of McHoul." Occasional Paper of the Project on the Social Organization of Reading Activities, Department of Sociology in Education, Ontario Institute for Studies in Education, Toronto, Canada.

Heritage, John. 1985. "Analyzing News Interviews: Aspects of the Production of Talk for an Overhearing Audience." In Teun A. van Dijk, ed. *Handbook of Discourse Analysis*. San Diego, California: Academic Press, 95–117.

Heritage, John. 1984. *Garfinkel and Ethnomethodology*. Cambridge, UK: Polity Press.

Hester, Stephen, and Peter Eglin. 1992. A *Sociology of Crime*. London & New York: Routledge.

Hutchby, Ian. 2006. *Media Talk: Conversation Analysis and the Study of Broadcasting*. Maidenhead, UK & New York: Open University Press.

Hutchby, Ian. 2001. *Conversation and Technology: From the Telephone to the Internet*. Cambridge, UK: Polity Press.

Jalbert, Paul. 1999. "Critique and Analysis in Media Studies: Media Criticism as Practical Action." In Paul L. Jalbert, ed. *Media Studies: Ethnomethodological Approaches*. Lanham, Maryland: University Press of America.

Levinson, Paul. 1999. *Digital McLuhan: A Guide to the Information Millennium*. New York: Routledge.

Lynch, Michael. 1985. *Art and Artifact in Laboratory Science: A Study of Shop Work and Shop Talk in a Research Laboratory*. Boston: Routledge & Kegan Paul.

Lynch, Michael, and David Bogen. 1996. *The Spectacle of History: Speech, Text, and Memory at the Iran–Contra Hearings*. Durham, North Carolina: Duke University Press.

McHoul, A.W. 1990. "The Organization of Repair in Classroom Talk." *Language and Society* 19: 349–377.

McHoul, Alexander. 1978. "The Organization of Turns at Formal Talk in the Classrooms." *Language and Society* 7: 183–213.

McLuhan, Marshall, and Eric McLuhan. 1988. *Laws of Media: The New Science*. Toronto: University of Toronto Press.

Mehan, Hugh. 1979. *Learning Lessons: Social Organization in the Classroom*. Cambridge, Massachusetts: Harvard University Press.

Parsons, Talcott. 1951. *The Social System*. Glencoe, Illinois: Free Press.

Richmond, A.H., M. Lyon, S. Hale, and R. King. 1973. *Migration and Race Relations in an English City*. London: Oxford University Press.

Rosenhan, D. L. 1973. "Being Sane in Insane Places." *Science* 179 (January): 250–258.

Sacks, Harvey, Emanuel Schegloff, and Gail Jefferson. 1974. "A Simplest Systematics for the Organization of Turn-Taking for Conversation." *Language* 50: 696–735.

Schegloff, Emanuel. 1987. "Between Micro and Macro: Contexts and Other Connections." In Jeffrey Alexander, ed. *The Micro–Macro Link*. California: University of California Press, 207–234. (Includes a critique of Zimmerman & West.)

Schutz, Alfred. 1964. "Making Music Together: A Study in Social Relationship." In Arvid Brodessen, ed. *Collected Papers, Studies in Social Theory (Schutz)*, vol. 2. The Hague: Martinus Nijhoff, 159–178.

Smith, Dorothy E. 1990. "The Social Organization of Textual Reality." In *The Conceptual Practices of Power: A Feminist Sociology of Knowledge*. Toronto: University of Toronto Press, 60–80.

Sudnow, David. 1979. *Talk's Body: A Meditation Between Two Keyboards*. New York: Alfred A. Knopf; Harmondsworth, UK: Penguin.

Sudnow, David. 1978. *Ways of the Hand: The Organization of Improvised Conduct*. Cambridge, Massachusetts: Harvard University Press.

Tuchman, Gaye. 1972. "Objectivity as Strategic Ritual: An Examination of Newsmen's Notions of Objectivity." *American Journal of Sociology* 77 (4): 660–678.

Watson, Rodney. 1991. "The Understanding of Language Use in Everyday Life: Is There a Common Ground?" In Graham Watson and Robert M. Seiler, eds. *Text in Context: Contributions to Ethnomethodology*. Beverly Hills: Sage, 1–19.

Weeks, Peter A.D. 2009. "Towards an Ethnomethodological Study of Jazz Improvisation." Submitted to *Journal of Contemporary Ethnography*.

Weeks, Peter A.D. 1994. "The Quest for Reasonableness and Reasoning in a Mathematics Lesson." Occasional paper, Department of Sociology, University of Manchester.

Weeks, Peter A.D. 1985. "Error-Correction Techniques and Sequences in Instructional Settings: Toward a Comparative Framework." *Human Studies* 8: 195–233.

West, Candace. 1984. "When the Doctor is a 'Lady': Power, Status and Gender in Physician–Patient Encounters." *Symbolic Interaction* 7 (1): 87–106.

Zimmerman, Don H. 1974. "Fact as a Practical Accomplishment." In Roy Turner, ed. *Ethnomethodology: Selected Readings*. Harmondsworth, UK: Penguin Education, 128–143.

Zimmerman, Don H., and Candace West. 1975. "Sex Roles, Interruptions and Silences in Conversations." In Barrie Thorne and Nancy Henley, eds. *Language and Sex: Difference and Dominance*. Rowley, Massachusetts: Newbury House Publishers, 105–129.

Gender Relations: Competing Perspectives

Gender relations are moving to the centre of cultural, social, and political struggles in the 1990s. Much of the taken-for-granted character of relations between women and men—and also between men and men, and women and women—have been challenged by feminist theory, the active politics of the women's movement, emerging struggles around gay and lesbian sexual orientation, and men's liberation movements.

Contraception changed the character of intimate sexual relations, increasing the possibilities for sexual expression outside of procreation. But a host of new problems and questions have emerged alongside sexual liberation. The reduced risk of pregnancy has changed the moral debate around adolescent sexual activity, but the potential for "liberation" has also increased the potential for coercive and exploitative relationships as girls in particular find themselves under increased pressure to be sexually active and available. Medical concerns have arisen around the spread of virulent forms of sexually transmitted diseases, particularly the epidemic of Acquired Immune Deficiency Syndrome (AIDS). Other concerns have focused around the commercialization of sexuality in advertising, pornography, and prostitution, and associated struggles around public definitions of morality, censorship, and freedom of speech. The 1980s were also marked by heightened awareness of the sometimes exploitative and violent character of sexual relations, reflected in the proliferation of accounts of battery within the home, sexual abuse of children, sexual assault and date rape, sexual harassment, and violent attacks against gay men, and also increasing anger and frustration directed against campaigns focusing on these issues.

Sexual politics have brought to light new patterns of power, interest, and conflict. Within the economy, struggles have focused on employment equity policies, affirmative action, and non-discrimination on the basis of gender and sexual orientation. These, in turn, are associated with a questioning of the appropriateness of traditional division of domestic responsibilities, child care, and breadwinning within families. Patterns of change have been neither unidirectional nor uncontested. Alongside the politics of feminism and gay liberation are the politics of religious fundamentalism and the "New Right" concerned with the reinforcement of traditional family and sexual values.

These arenas of confrontation reflect profound confusion over the appropriateness of emerging patterns of sexuality and gender relations. The goal of this chapter is to explore this contested terrain of gender relations through four major theoretical perspectives within current sociology—functionalism, political economy, social constructionism, and feminism—comparing and contrasting the different explanatory frameworks.

The study of gender relations is particularly useful for giving a sense of how the focus of sociological analysis differs from approaches of biology and psychology. The sex dichotomy of male and female is commonly viewed as an immutable biological state, but contemporary analyses in sociology have challenged this assumption as ideological rather than factual, developing a different conceptualization of sex differences and gender relations as socially constructed rather than given. We begin this discussion with a brief overview of biological theories of gender as the background against which specifically sociological theories have developed.

BIOLOGY OR SOCIAL LEARNING: THE FOUNDATIONS OF GENDER

Functionalist theory in sociology stays closest to the biological view of sex differences, but with an important qualification. Functionalism begins with the assumption that there is a biological basis to the specialization of functions for males and females in society, but it sees this specialization as structured by socialization. In functionalist writing the terms **sex** and **sex roles** are typically used to refer to differences in male and female bodies and reproductive capacities that are presumed to be universal. The terms **gender** and **gender roles** refer to socially acquired behavioural differences that vary across cultures and historical periods. In practice, as we will see below, much controversy surrounds this distinction.

Functionalist theory argues that the long dependency of human infants, necessitating many years of adult care, is the biological root of gender relations (Goode 1982). The reproductive strategy of having few offspring and caring intensively for them is held to predispose long-pairing relationships in family settings, since the nurturing female depends on her male partner for support and protection. These biological imperatives are also seen as dictating fundamental differences in the roles of adult males and females. Females are seen as physically handicapped by long pregnancy and breastfeeding, and are homebound with dependent infants and young children. Hence, they are more tied to the domestic arena. This was especially so in the era before widespread use of contraception when women could expect to be either pregnant or breastfeeding for most of their adult lives. Males, in contrast, are freer to move away from the home, and since they are also physically stronger, they are best suited biologically to perform the roles of hunter and protector. With industrialization, the importance of physical strength declined, but males are still freer to work away from home every day as principal breadwinners while females are seen as biologically better suited to remain at home as principal caregivers for small children. These roles can certainly overlap, with fathers giving some time to child care and mothers some time to work outside the home, especially when children are older, but the basic predispositions and principal responsibilities remain. In some feminist writings, particularly those of Shulamith Firestone, liberation for women is seen as ultimately requiring a technological revolution that would free women from the biological imperatives of pregnancy.

The thesis of social Darwinism elaborates on the biological roots of behaviour, maintaining that many of the differences in average behaviour between men and women emerged through a long evolutionary process that selectively developed traits conducive to survival. While males and females produce both testosterone and estrogens, the higher average levels of the hormone testosterone in males compared to females is seen as predisposing males to greater aggressiveness, a trait that enhances their survival as hunters. Aggressiveness would not have the same adaptive value for females who do not participate in the hunt. Conversely, higher average levels of estrogens in females may predispose them to the more passive, nurturing behaviour necessary in caring for infants. Some theorists argue further that the relative sexual promiscuity of males reflects the biological evolution of traits that increase the survival of the male's gene stock (Dawkins 1976). Promiscuity has little reproductive value for females since they can bear only a limited number of offspring. Conversely, females

have a strong need to form pairing relationships to support themselves during pregnancy and the care of infants. Lionel Tiger (1969) argues further that males selectively evolved the traits of teamwork and male bonding as adaptive to their survival as hunters, and this predisposition now gives males an advantage over women in business and politics, or other similar activities in the public arena that involve teamwork. The argument has been expanded to assert that patriarchy or domination by males over females in society is biologically determined, since males have a competitive edge over females in all assertive public leadership roles (Goldberg 1973).

Studies of differences in male and female behaviour among animals is widely cited as supporting evidence for the biological roots of human behaviour. A common example is Harlow's studies of infant rhesus monkeys who had been separated from their mothers. The males appeared to be naturally more aggressive, to engage in more rough-and-tumble play, and to initiate more games (Harlow 1962; 1965).

Current work in the field of **sociobiology**, the study of the biological bases of social behaviour, goes beyond speculative evolutionary arguments to explore differences in brain functioning of males and females. These include studies that suggest that girls on average are predisposed to be better than boys at verbal skills and the recognition of interrelated patterns. Boys are generally better than girls in thinking that involves linear logic and mathematical skills. The gender-inversion theory of homosexuality suggests that the hormones and brain patterning of homosexuals may be congenitally those of the opposite biological sex. This theory is held to account for the tendency of gay men to display "effeminate" characteristics, and for their concentration in careers in the arts. Lesbians are seen as congenitally predisposed towards masculine characteristics.

The Limitations of Biological Explanations

Much of the early sociobiological theories concerning evolutionary traits cannot be tested scientifically against evidence. They are based on imaginative speculation, not biological research. Elaine Morgan, in her book *The Descent of Women* (1972), offers a critique that is partly serious and partly a parody of what she sees as essentially "male-centred" theories of evolution. She speculates that evolutionary functions can be thought up for all kinds of traits that distinguish women from men, with female traits generally having greater survival value for the species. Take, for example, the evidence that baldness is common among men but rare among women. Morgan speculates that during the prehistoric period when our human ancestors lived in shallow coastal waters, it would have been very important for the survival of infants that their mothers had long hair. Naked apes are slippery when wet and the infants of bald mothers would be more likely to drown. Baldness in males would have no evolutionary consequences. Similarly, it might have been advantageous for females to develop fat on their buttocks since they would have had to sit on sharp rocks at the water's edge to breastfeed their young.

The main value of Morgan's work lies not in these proposals as such, but how they illustrate the speculative character and the male bias of more widely accepted versions of evolutionary functions. Whatever the appeal of certain arguments about evolutionary traits, their usefulness in understanding the contemporary social behaviour of men or women is minimal. The conditions under which male hunting packs had any survival value have long gone. So, at least within Western societies, have conditions under which women could expect to be pregnant and suckling infants throughout their adult lives. As Connell puts it, evolutionary theories are about 2 million years out of date (1987, 72).

Other aspects of sociobiology have been supported by evidence from studies of animal behaviour, but there are several serious problems with extrapolating from animals to humans. In the first place, the animals chosen are often selected to make the point in question. Rhesus monkeys, for example, are known to be a particularly aggressive primate species. Male baboons are much more docile and might be cited to support very different conclusions about innate male behaviour with respect to aggression. Analogies drawn between animal and human behaviour leave out what is most characteristic of the human species—the capacity for language, intellect, imagination, and learning. These attributes play such an overwhelmingly important part in the social behaviour of people that comparisons with primates in which such attributes are minimal or nonexistent can have little explanatory value.

Efforts to link biological differences between males and females to differences in behaviour have generally been inconclusive. A common argument is that boys and men are generally more aggressive than girls and women because they have more of the hormone testosterone. But other evidence reverses this cause-and-effect relationship, suggesting that social context and emotions of aggression and anger produce fluctuations in testosterone levels. Rather than the body determining behaviour, social relationships are seen as producing characteristics of the body.

The argument advanced by Goldberg (1973) that patriarchy is inevitable because males enjoy an aggressive advantage over women in competition is seriously flawed in other ways. It assumes that there is open competition between women and men, and that women lose. The historical experience of women in most societies, however, is that they have never been given the opportunity to compete on

equal terms with men for positions of power in society. The institutional arrangements that feminists refer to as "patriarchy" are precisely those that block opportunities for women to compete. Biological evidence of small average differences between women and men in hormones, body size, or mathematical abilities, even if taken at face value, are not adequate to explain why so few women are found in positions of major political authority and economic power in most contemporary societies. The extensive overlapping of characteristics and abilities among women and men would support the prediction of far greater social equality than is actually found.

In general, theories that try to account for gender differences by reference to biological factors tend to be both too weak and too strong. On the one hand, the connections established between biology and human behaviour are generally very weak. On the other hand, theories that rely on biological explanations assume a uniformity within the categories of male and female that cannot account for tremendous variation in gender behaviour. This variation is evident among people with homosexual orientations as well as heterosexual. The images of "butch-femme" women and effeminate men implied by the gender-inversion theory of homosexuality at best applies to only a small minority of people who would identify themselves as homosexuals. To account for such variation we need to shift focus from biology to social learning as the basis of gender relations.

Psychoanalysis

Psychoanalysis, as a branch of psychiatry, lies midway between biological and social explanations for gender relations. In the classic theory first proposed by Sigmund Freud (1856–1939), the biological fact that boys possess a penis, while girls "only" have a clitoris, is seen as a central determinant of different temperament and personality of adult males and females (Freud [1905] 1976). Freud suggests that during the phallic stage of development, beginning around three to four years of age, a boy experiences strong urges to compete with his father sexually for possession of his mother. He learns to repress this drive, and later to displace it onto other women, out of fear that his father might retaliate and castrate him. Infant girls, in contrast, experience a sense of mutilation and sexual powerlessness at not having a penis, which accounts for their relative passivity.

Freud's work has been widely criticized for its deterministic, ahistorical, and male-biased assumptions. Contemporary rereading of Freud's thesis suggests that what Freud interpreted as universal features of human sexuality are better understood as the historically specific characteristics of sexuality developed within late nineteenth- and early twentieth-century patriarchal bourgeois families—the family background of most of the patients that Freud treated for neurosis in his Vienna clinic. Mechanisms of repression and displacement of sexual drives, which are central to Freudian theory, have been reconceptualized as deep psychological responses to power relations within families dominated by an all-powerful husband–father figure. Feminist rereading of stories told by female patients suggests that these are not merely childhood fantasies, as Freud surmised, but accounts of incest. The neurosis displayed by these patients seems more likely to reflect the trauma of sexual abuse than displaced penis envy. Feminist psychoanalysis has generated further theoretical interest in the potential effects on gender-identity formation in families where a powerful father figure is absent (Chodorow 1978). The theoretical insights of psychoanalysis have also been incorporated into theories of homosexuality, drawing on the Freudian notion that children have inherently bisexual instincts and drives that are moulded and channelled into socially acceptable heterosexual forms through early childhood experiences within the nuclear family. The mechanisms of psychological repression and displacement are seen as controlling bisexual drives but never fully erasing them.

In general these rereadings of Freud's work retain the insights concerning the importance of the unconscious mind, and mechanisms of repression and displacement, but with a significant change in underlying assumptions. The explanatory focus has shifted away from notions of innate biological drives and towards a greater emphasis on the role of historically changeable family forms and patterns of culture in the development of adult gender identity. This shift in focus has facilitated the incorporation of aspects of psychoanalytic theory into contemporary sociological perspectives on gender relations.

Functionalist Theory of Gender Roles

Functionalist theory of gender relations incorporates a decisive shift to focus on social environment and social learning, an approach often referred to as *socialization theory*. Infants are assumed to have sex but not gender. Gender roles do not depend upon innate biological or psychological drives. They are learned through the processes of **gender-role socialization**. The basic idea of functionalism is that people in society can be thought of as occupying social positions to which a set of expectations are assigned. These expectations or norms define which actions are appropriate to given positions. Individuals acquire and internalize norms and these guide behaviour, much like actors in a play conform to a script. Becoming a man or a woman means taking on a general role ascribed to one's sex, such that in almost all social

contexts there are two distinctive sets of roles corresponding to different social expectations of males and females. Individuals are inserted into social relations through learning the role behaviour appropriate to their sex. Functionalist theory is centrally interested in the people and institutions responsible for this learning—the "agents of socialization"—including parents, family, teachers, peers, religious leaders, mass media, and the like. Research focuses on the scripts—the gender patterns and stereotypes that are taught, the different treatment of boys and girls, and the ways in which models of femininity and masculinity are conveyed to children. Deviance from acceptable gender behaviour is understood in terms of faulty socialization, especially in early childhood experience. This approach has the advantage over sociobiology of offering an explanation for both the variation and the consistency in patterns of male and female behaviour within a given culture. It also offers a policy for reforming gender relations through changing expectations and challenging stereotyped attitudes.

Variations among Cultures

Margaret Mead's (1935) classic study of three New Guinea tribes—the Arapesh, the Mundugamore, and the Tschambuli—emphasized the malleability of human gender-role behaviour and the importance of socialization over biology. She described marked differences in the specific behaviours ascribed to males and females in the three cultures. Among the Arapesh, both males and females were socialized to be gentle, nurturing, responsive, cooperative, and willing to subordinate themselves to the needs of others. Both men and women participated actively in childbirth. They were both said to "bear the child," and it was believed that only through the continual caring and participation of the father could the child grow in the mother's womb or continue into healthy adulthood. According to Mead, authority and aggression were repugnant to both Arapesh men and women. Arapesh men did not provoke fights, and rape was unknown. In contrast, among the Mundugamore, both men and women were expected to be aggressive rather than nurturing. The people practised headhunting, and emotions of hostility, hatred, and suspicion permeated their relationships. Even their families were organized on the basis of the theory of natural hostility among members of the same sex. Fathers and daughters formed one rival group against mothers and sons. Within the third culture, the Tschambuli, women were expected to be more dominant, impersonal, and managing than men, while men were expected to be less responsible and more emotionally dependent than women, in effect the opposite of feminine and masculine expected in Western societies. Later studies have modified Mead's findings, suggesting that she overstated the cultural differences, but her general thesis remains that the gender-role behaviour of women and men are powerfully influenced by upbringing and cultural expectations.

Functionalist theory assumes that individuals come to internalize the gender-role behaviour patterns appropriate for their biological sex through socialization. Primary socialization occurs within the family. It is principally here that infants acquire language and gender identity, and learn the basic norms and appropriate attitudes and values of their sex. Secondary socialization involves learning and teaching in the public arenas of school, church, work, and mass media. The two spheres of socialization are directly connected during childhood since parents commonly select the daycares, churches, and schools that their children attend, and monitor their friendships and the mass media to which they are exposed. Socialization continues in some degree throughout adult life as individuals enter new roles and form new associations, but the influence of parents in early childhood learning is considered decisive in gender identity formation. We know from studies of young children that they learn to accurately define their own gender and that of others from a very early age (Mackie 1991, 79).

Behavioural Traits within a Culture

Primary socialization into gender roles in Western cultures begins from the moment of birth as infants are assigned an identity as male or female on the basis of genitals. Sex-typing may begin even before birth, as parents speculate that an active fetus is most likely to be male and a quiet one female. From the first day of life parents tend to see, and to respond to, boy and girl babies differently. Girls are more often described as little, beautiful, cute, weak, and delicate, whereas boys are described as firmer, larger, more alert, stronger, and hardier. This occurs despite objective evidence that male and female babies are on average of equal size and activity level, and female neonates are generally more robust than males.

The behavioural traits identified as specifically male or female are actively promoted and reinforced by parents. For example, a study of the content of rooms that parents provide for children (Rheingold and Cook 1975; Greenglass 1992, 208) showed that boys' rooms tended to have vehicles of all kinds, building blocks, toy tools, sports equipment, machines, and military toys. Girls' rooms most often had dolls, dollhouses, stuffed animals, and domestic toys of all kinds for playing house.

Activities and interests encouraged by parents commonly emphasize the same gender-typing. Domestic chores are commonly allocated to boys and girls differently. Boys tend to be encouraged more than girls to be independent, for example by being allowed to cross streets alone at a younger age, to play away from home for long periods without first telling parents where they would be, and using sharp scissors without adult supervision. There is no objective evidence that boys are any more advanced than girls at such skills. If anything, boys tend to be more impulsive and less mature (Hoffman 1977; Greenglass 1992, 210). Parents also see female toddlers as needing more help, encourage them to ask for more help, and restrict and supervise them more. As a result, boys and girls develop different kinds of competence and coping skills. As adults, men strive for success and take risks to attain it, while women are socialized not to take risks and to perceive risks as threatening failure. Early in life they learn not to have high expectations for themselves, and so as adults they tend to be less self-confident, less assertive, and more timid than men. They tend to rely more on others than do boys, have a greater need for social approval, and are more likely to break down or cry under stress. All these traits are seen as detrimental to women who try to function in adult work roles that require leadership or management skills (Hale 1987, 491;

BACK BENCH

© Graham Harrop

Hennig and Jardim 1981; Fenn 1980; Larwood and Wood 1977). On the positive side, girls are encouraged to be more nurturing, to display emotions, to be open to others, to be skilled listeners, and to be more empathetic than boys, traits that prepare them well for adult roles as caregivers.

There is much evidence to suggest that gender-typing is more rigidly enforced for boys than for girls. Boys are under greater pressure not to be "sissies" than are girls not to be "tomboys," and boys are subject to much more physical and non-physical punishment, as well as more praise, in pressuring them to behave in a "masculine" way. Fathers are also more likely to emphasize gender-typing in their interaction with children than are mothers (Greenglass 1992, 209; Lynn 1974; Mackie 1991, 109–110). Fathers worry when boys seem unaggressive and unwilling to defend themselves, while they do not worry about unaggressive girls. David and Brannon (1976, 12) summarize the traditional requirements of the masculine gender role as: (1) no sissy stuff—with a stigma on all stereotypically feminine characteristics; (2) the big wheel—the need to be looked up to and to have symbols of success and status, especially as a breadwinner looked up to by his wife, if no one else; (3) the sturdy oak—portraying a manly air of toughness, confidence, and self-reliance; and (4) "Give 'em Hell"—the aura of aggression, violence, and daring. The most important of all is no sissy stuff—not behaving like girls. Boys are socialized to suppress emotions that suggest vulnerability, and especially not to cry. The involvement of boys in sports is widely cited as critical in the development of appropriate masculinity. Male athletes commonly report feeling pressured, even bullied, into participation in sports by their fathers (Messner 1992). Teamwork, competition, winning at any cost, and aggression are important aspects of organized sports for boys. There is no comparable pressure on girls to become involved in sports, and if they do, the aspects of having fun tend to be stressed over competition and winning.

Problems in Family Socialization

From the perspective of socialization theory, failure to exhibit appropriate adult gender-role behaviour can be accounted for primarily by faulty upbringing, especially within the family. A central cause for concern in studies addressing the notion of a "masculinity crisis" is the gender confusion that boys may experience when appropriate male role models are absent from their families (Brittan 1989, 25–26). Young boys may scarcely see their father when he is working away from home all day or working very long hours. High levels of unemployment may mean that fathers are home for longer periods, but inability to hold a steady job undermines a father's ability to provide an appropriate male role model for his sons. The erosion of the father's

authority and status within the home may be further exacerbated if the wife-mother is employed. Of particular concern within research on socialization is the growing numbers of single-parent, female-headed households. In functionalist theory this deviation from the traditional nuclear family form is seen as likely to result in deviant psychological development, especially for boys. The fear is that fatherless boys may find it difficult to achieve proper gender identity, and may act out their resulting insecurities and anxieties in negative ways, through delinquency, violence, and hostility towards women. Chodorow (1978) and Dinnerstein (1976) link psychoanalysis and functionalism in their theory that the masculinity crisis may be generated by the extreme differentiation and specialization in gender roles in Western societies, which leave mothers almost totally responsible for childcare. Boys, they suggest, are engulfed in the overflowing influence of women, the combination of maternal care and discipline that translates into

Gender traits are often promoted by parents who encourage boys to play with vehicles, tools, machines, and sports and war toys.

Shutterstock

power over boys. They suggest that boys resent and try to escape from women's power, rather than struggling to repress Oedipal conflicts with respect to an all-powerful father figure. The key problem is not a too-powerful father, but a weak or absent father, or a too-powerful mother.

The challenge of raising sons to be appropriately masculine is a difficult one for feminist mothers. Van Gelder and Carmichael (1975) studied the attitudes of mothers, including those in leadership positions in feminist organizations. As many as one-third of these mothers worried that they might unwittingly be responsible for their sons "unnecessarily" becoming homosexual. None of them worried that a liberated or feminist upbringing would turn girls into lesbians, but they feared that it might turn boys into homosexuals. They gave serious thought to non-sexist child-rearing for their girls, but not for their boys. Among their peers, boys who fail to display appropriately masculine behaviour, who are unathletic or bookish, or who enjoy "effeminate" activities like dance, knitting, or even cooking, are likely to be taunted by such gibes as "What are you, a fag?" Such homophobic taunting seems to function as a powerful technique for enforcing conformity to stereotypically masculine gender-role behaviour (Fine 1992, 138; Lehne 1976).

Those concerned with promoting the advancement of women in prestigious and better-paid careers in business and management see the prevailing pattern of socialization for girls as a critical limiting factor. Studies of women in management roles suggest that competitive team sports, particularly football, are important in socializing boys into skills of leadership and teamwork, and notions of planning, tactics, strategies, and playing to win (Hennig and Jardim 1981; Fenn 1980; Larwood and Wood 1977). Girls who have no comparable socialization experience are severely handicapped as adults if they try to enter roles in politics, business, and management, where skills of leadership and teamwork are very important. Liberal feminists, working within the functionalist perspective, have focused attention on restrictive stereotypes of adult roles for women, especially in mass media and school textbooks. They stress the importance of non-traditional role models for girls in changing the distribution of gender roles for women and men.

The Limitations of Socialization Theory

Socialization theory offers major advantages over biological explanations for gender relations in that it provides a workable explanation for broad differences between cultures, and places at the centre of analysis the specifically human characteristics of social learning. It is, however, open to criticism as an overly simplistic form of explanation that ignores much of the complexity of gender relations.

The model relies on an implicit notion of normal male and female gender-role behaviour, and implies that there is consensus among agents of socialization as to what these norms are. Critics argue that neither assumption fits the evidence. There seems to be too much variation in how women and men behave. If we were to use what we know about normative expectations to predict actual behaviour of males and females in specific situations, we would be wrong more often than correct. A study conducted in rural India tried to predict women's responses to new employment opportunities on the basis of prevailing norms for women's behaviour that emphasized domesticity and strict seclusion within the home (Hale 1988). All the predictions failed. Cultural norms did predict what women thought other people thought, but not at all what the women had internalized as standards for themselves. This discrepancy, between the prevailing culture and what women actually wanted to do, calls into question the meaning of "culture" as the accepted set of norms, attitudes, and values of the people. It suggests that the culture of rural India reflects more how men want women to behave than the internalized values of women themselves.

There is also extensive evidence of inconsistencies, conflict, and contradictions between different agents of socialization that belies the notion of normative standards. They may teach conflicting messages about gender-role expectations to children. What parents teach may differ from school teachers, and both may differ from mass media or peers, or religious teachings. Consistency among all socialization agents in a given community may be the exception rather than the rule. Moreover, individual agents are themselves often inconsistent in what they teach. Studies of families suggest that contradictory pressures and demands are routinely placed on children (Connell 1987, 192–193). Mass media similarly offer contradictory messages about appropriate gender-role behaviour. The notion of distinctive patterns of socialization for boys and girls also seems to have been overdrawn. The body of research on parent–child interaction with babies and preschoolers that was reviewed by Maccoby and Jacklin (1974) failed to find clear-cut differences in either the amount or kind of parental talk or nurturing behaviour towards sons and daughters.

The unquestioned assumption within functionalist theory that there are distinctive male and female gender roles has promoted extensive research into differences in upbringing and behaviour of boys and girls. However, for every published study that confirms expected differences, several more are discarded as flawed because no significant differences were found. Connell suggests that were it not for the powerful influence of gender-role theory on research, we would be focusing on sex similarity studies rather than sex differences (1987, 170).

Critics also challenge the assumption that deviation from normative standards for gender-role behaviour can be accounted for in terms of faulty socialization (Brittan 1989, 23–24). The bookish and unathletic boys, the male ballet dancers, the women with leadership and management skills, cannot all be explained away by reference to malfunctioning socialization. The assumption that children mechanically internalize standards that they are taught ignores both choice and resistance in human behaviour. Children may reject what they are taught, or they may choose to mix gender traits in ways that conflict partially or perhaps fundamentally with how they were brought up. The theory that homosexuality is the result of faulty parental role modelling loads unnecessary guilt onto parents, without any evidence of specific parenting practices being linked to the sexual orientation of children. It also denies any agency to individuals who come to identify themselves as homosexual.

There is, furthermore, a strongly conservative ideology embedded in the assumptions that specific feminine and masculine gender identities are necessary for psychological health, and that boys who lack immediate male role models will be disturbed and deviant in their own self-identity. Such assumptions imply that there is only one way to be psychologically healthy and all other patterns are sick.

There seems to be something seriously wrong with the theory. It seems that normative standards do exist for male and female behaviour. Most of us know what they are and can list them when asked. Yet the majority of people we know do not seem to have internalized them in the way that the functionalist theory of socialization predicts. The normative pattern of the nuclear family with male breadwinner and female homemaker is not the prevailing form of gender-role behaviour. Connell suggests that what we begin to see here is that what is "normative" is not a definition of normality, but a definition of what holders of social power wish to have accepted (1987, 51–52). Yet this analysis of power is precisely what is missing from functionalist theory.

We do not speak of "race roles" or "class roles" because in such relations power differentials are obvious. But the assumption that gender roles reflect natural differences between women and men functions to obscure the dimension of power in the structuring of gender relations. Socialization theory implicitly assumes that all problems of inequality in relations between women and men can be accounted for by upbringing, with the corollary that if society were to alter the prevailing role models all such inequities could be eliminated. Critics reject such arguments as simplistic at best, and at worst as ideological distortions that legitimate inequality. Critics argue that the pervasive inequalities in occupational status, income, and political influence between women and men cannot be reduced simply to learned psychological predispositions; all the difficulties encountered by the token few women in management positions cannot be meaningfully attributed to lack of experience on football teams. Nor can the prevalence of pornography, violence against women within families, or rape be accounted for simply by boys' resentfulness at the authority of mothers during their infancy. Such explanations ignore the vested interests in the maintenance of relations of domination, and the active strategies and power dynamics that shore them up (Connell 1987, Ch. 9; Brittan 1989).

Once we come to see gender-role stereotypes as embedded in power relations, we are led to question the interests that structure and maintain them. Socialization theory describes how males and females are supposedly trained to fit the mould of acceptable masculine and feminine behaviour, but it does not address the question of why the moulds have the characteristics that they do. Why are boys raised to be aggressive and competitive? Why are girls not also raised like this? Such questions point to issues of social and economic structures that are not addressed within socialization theory itself. The force of such criticism is not that socialization has no influence on adult behaviour or gender relations, but that it is too limited and too individualistic in focus to account for complex structural patterns of gender-based inequality in society. A different kind of analysis seems to be needed to explain the structural patterns of gendered inequality.

The Political Economy of Gender Relations

Political economy theory focuses on patterns of economic organization and their importance in shaping all other social relationships, including gender. The contemporary Canadian economy is part of a global system of advanced corporate capitalism. This means that it is characterized by private enterprise, which is dominated by giant corporations that compete on world markets to sell commodities for profit, with smaller sectors of small-business people and primary producers in farming, fishing, and forestry. The majority of people in Canada's labour force do not work for themselves, but find careers in corporations or state bureaucracies. An individual's social class is defined in terms of their relationship to the system of production, whether they own or control capital, and their situation with respect to the labour market.

A central argument within political economy theory is that the attitudes and values that people hold are shaped by their immediate practical experiences in the daily processes of survival or earning a living. Attitudes and values are thus effects rather than principal causes of behaviour. Analysis of gender relations, and the different attitudes, values, and behaviour of women and men, is embedded in the understanding of class relations within capitalism.

The Influence of Gender on Class Situation

Friedrich Engels, a long-time collaborator with Karl Marx, suggests in his classic essay on the rise of private property, the family, and the state ([1884] 1978) that in the earliest hunting-and-gathering economies, authority and descent within kinship systems were probably organized around women as the only known parent. Men most likely played a secondary role within extended matriarchal households. However, Engels argues, this probably changed dramatically with the introduction of more advanced means of production, such as domesticated animals and cultivated land. As men gained control over these means of production they would have been able to break the authority of women and organize descent and inheritance through the male rather than the female line. Men would have been in a position to control and enslave women because women and their children would be economically dependent upon them. Women's work was still essential, but socially subordinate. They worked for their husbands. Engels refers to this point in history as the world historical defeat of the female sex, and the first example of class relations. The solution to the subordination of women to men, in Engels' view, would be to draw women into the labour force, and to abolish the bourgeois pattern in which men control the family wealth. Communism—the communal ownership of all means of production—promised ultimate equality for all members of society.

Prior to industrialization, most economic production took place in households, with no clear division between domestic and productive work, or between family production and consumption. With the rise of industrial capitalism this pattern changed dramatically. Production shifted into centralized factories, and households became units of consumption. Increasingly, men went out of the home to work for wages, while women remained within the home, taking principal responsibility for child care and domestic work. This shifting pattern of economic production is widely seen as decisively important in structuring gender relations. It liberated many people from the confines of the old households and made possible new forms of independence and sexual expression, but it simultaneously trapped others in a narrow private realm.

Women's involvement in the paid labour force has varied greatly with the economic situation of their families and shifting labour demands. But such involvement has not provided a basis for economic independence for women, with the exception of a minority in professional careers. With the development of industrial capitalism, women from the wealthier capitalist and upper middle classes were expected to remain within the home devoting themselves to domestic duties, the management of servants, and the care and moral upbringing of children. For women from the poorer classes, however, some means of supplementing family income was essential. Men's wages were commonly so low that it was impossible for a family to survive on them. While the cult of gentile domesticity for women, and notions of childhood as the age of innocence, prevailed as ideals among the upper classes, working-class women and children were more likely to experience the drudgery of working appallingly long hours under bad conditions and for very low incomes (Synnott 1992, 196–197).

Historical records of women's employment in Canada are sparse and unreliable (Wilson 1986, Ch. 5). There were generally no records kept of women's unpaid farm labour in the pre-industrial rural economy. In the cities, until the beginning of the twentieth century, the two major occupations open to working-class women were domestic service or labour in their own homes for the developing textile and clothing industries. Under the "putting out" system, women and children sewed in their homes or in small shops for a middle man who sold the completed goods to a manufacturer. Women could supplement the family income through such work, but could not achieve any financial or social independence. Women who worked in domestic service had no privacy and were under the constant control of their employers. By the end of the nineteenth century, textile and garment factories were expanding in Canada, while demand for domestic servants was declining with the introduction of electricity and home appliances. Accounts suggest that women gladly traded the isolation and controls of domestic service for factory work, but conditions of work and levels of pay remained abysmal. A Royal Commission on the Textile Industry, published in 1938, described women and young girls working 75 to 80 hours a week in conditions thick with dust, heat, fumes, and gases, and for weekly wages of 50 cents to three dollars, often cut on the pretext of "flawed work" (Wilson 1986, 86–87). Such wages were insufficient to live on, even as a single person.

There is scattered evidence of women's involvement in unions and strikes in the nineteenth century, but efforts to improve working conditions for women were isolated and of short duration (Prentice et al., 1988). Women were concentrated in unskilled jobs, or scattered in small workshops or in domestic service, which made it very difficult for them to organize collectively. Most reformers of the day, together with trade unionists, employers, and fellow labourers, saw women's labour-force participation as undesirable at best. Government policies to regulate women's employment focused on morality and the importance of segregating women from men in the factories. Working conditions and wages were ignored. Employment for women was described as temporary and secondary, and their incomes merely supplemental to the man as the main family breadwinner. The cheap labour of women and children was generally seen as unfair competition that dragged down men's average wages. A few voices were raised in favour of the argument that equal pay for women and men would eliminate this problem (Prentice et al., 1988, 137). But most unions focused their efforts on attaining "**family wages**" for male employees so that women would not have to work. The plight of women who had no male protector was overlooked.

Women from the lower middle classes who had access to some education had a somewhat wider range of employment options. Many found work as nurses and teachers, but at the turn of the century these were not the kind of professions we think of today. Nursing schools were connected to hospitals and provided a constant source of unpaid labour. In the early 1900s, for example, the entire nursing staff of Toronto General Hospital were unpaid nurses in training. This meant there were limited jobs for graduate nurses— they mostly did home nursing, with sporadic employment and very low pay (Wilson 1986, 84). Women teachers were paid half of a male teacher's salary, on the excuse that they were temporary workers who would soon quit their jobs. In many jurisdictions this was ensured by legislation that prohibited hiring married women as teachers. The assumption was that women ought to be supported by husbands. The plight of women who had to support themselves was not addressed.

Current patterns of employment for women in Canada emerged during the period of prosperity following the Second World War. The growth of corporate capitalism and the associated expansion of bureaucracies and government administration increased demand for labour in offices, sales, and service. Women were available to meet these demands. While the number and range of jobs available to women increased, however, the organization of the dual labour force has changed little. By the mid-1980s, approximately two-thirds of single women and half of married women with children were employed. But women remain concentrated within a much more limited range of jobs than do men. In 1983, 60 percent of all women worked in three occupational categories—clerical, service, and sales, all of them relatively low paid. A further 15 percent worked in medicine and health, and teaching. Only a tiny minority of women worked as executives or in positions of decision-making power within corporations. The 1982 figures show

that average salaries of women employed full-time equalled about 64 percent of average salaries for men. Professional women fared the best but they are far from typical. Women working in factory and service jobs earned only 54 to 56 percent of men's wages. Moreover, a quarter of all women are employed only part-time so that their actual incomes are very low. Most of those working part-time are married. Half of all married women are not employed at all: they are full-time homemakers.

What these figures mean is that notwithstanding all the changes in labour-force participation, the majority of women remain dependent on a man's wages to maintain a decent standard of living. They either are not employed at all, work part-time, or work in jobs where they do not earn sufficient income to support themselves and one child. Legislation requiring that women and men receive the same pay for the same job has little effect in a system where most women are employed in jobs that men rarely do. The lives of women who have to support themselves continue to be very difficult, particularly when they have children. Single mothers are often considered a welfare problem. Unless they are part of the small minority of women who have professional careers, the kind of jobs they can expect to get will provide an income little better than welfare if they have to deduct childcare, medical and dental expenses, and pay for clothes and transportation to get to work. Government policies focus on trying to force absent fathers to pay maintenance. The question of whether women with children ought to be dependent on men is rarely raised. It is taken for granted.

The institutionalized organization of women as secondary members of the paid labour force assumes that all women are tied to men, and that they are financially dependent upon men. These structures and their justification in social values constitute what is termed **heterosexism** in lesbian politics. For a woman to declare herself publicly a lesbian means to accept that she will not be tied to a man, and will therefore have to support herself for the rest of her life. It means learning to cope in a society that is not materially organized to incorporate women alone (Bunch 1975). The gendered character of class relations has a special immediacy for lesbians, Bunch argues, because its impact is inescapable. Lesbians need to develop political consciousness as a matter of survival, not merely idealism. Women who are tied to men by material interests may be committed in principle to fighting discrimination against women in the job market, but tend to back away when it is their man's job prospects that are threatened by feminist hiring practices. Women who have experienced marital breakdown may experience the force of heterosexism with similar intensity, although it is easier for ex-wives to shift blame onto individual men rather than onto the institutionalized structures of heterosexism.

Lesbians need to develop political consciousness as a matter of survival, not merely idealism.

© Danny Ogilvie

The rise of capitalism in Europe is closely associated with the historical emergence of homosexual men as a distinct social category (Kinsman 1987b, Ch. 2). Kinsman argues that capitalism afforded these men avenues for personal freedom that were not available to lesbians. By separating work from household, capitalist relations created social space in which young men could earn their own discretionary income and live autonomously. This made it possible for men who engaged in same-gender sex to congregate, and to develop networks that provided places where they could meet for sex and where they could develop a distinctive identity and self-awareness. By the early eighteenth century, such networks of gay men were clearly established in London and Paris. Opportunities for young women to achieve financial autonomy from the household were much more restricted. Kinsman estimates that it was only towards the end of the nineteenth century that equivalent lesbian networks began to emerge.

The Influence of Class on Gender Relations

A central idea in Marxist thought is that it is not consciousness that determines existence, but rather existence that determines consciousness. The notion of existence refers to experience of the daily struggle to survive, while consciousness refers to how people come to understand the social world around them and the attitudes and values they have towards it. Marx also argued that the dominant ideas in any society, those that receive public backing and support by agents of socialization, are the ideas of the dominant class.

Prevailing gender stereotypes can be linked directly to how different classes of women and men experience the struggle for economic survival. The idealized version of masculinity described in functionalist theory incorporates many of the values pressured into executives within the corporate capitalist system, where competitiveness, aggression, and hard-nosed unemotional decision-making are considered good business practice. Ruthless executives who are capable of firing 50 men at a shot and imposing their will on subordinates are widely admired (David and Brannon 1976, 27). Young executives are expected to prove themselves by fitting into the corporate image and working long hours, including evenings and weekends. Men who break the stereotype by balking at decisions that hurt others, not being highly competitive, and especially by avoiding working overtime to give more of themselves to family and children, risk jeopardizing their careers and their family's economic future. Currently only a very small proportion of all corporate executives are women, but the same pressures apply to them. Many find it extremely difficult to meet these demands and to cope with the pressures of running a home and raising a family (Maynard and Brouse 1988).

Working-class factory jobs carry different pressures. They commonly entail endless days of physically demanding work, often under conditions of dirt, fumes, noise, and demanding mindless obedience to machine-paced tasks. Typically, factory workforces have been segregated along gender lines, with textiles and light assembly work overwhelmingly female and heavy industry overwhelmingly male. Gray (1987) suggests that male blue-collar workers typically develop shop-floor cultures that value toughness, swearing, and rough behaviour, and exaggerated maleness that gives their work status as "man's work." The alienation generated by such work, and by the emotional coldness of competitive capitalism, has been cited as an important factor in domestic violence, as men displace repressed emotions and anger onto weaker targets in the home (Luxton 1980, Ch. 6). The wretched conditions endured by women in nineteenth-century textile factories, however, were not cited as precipitating abusive behaviour by women.

The application of political economy theory to women's behaviour draws attention to how particular conceptions of "femininity" are organized into work requirements in many of the jobs that are typically considered "women's work" (Connell 1987, 103; Hochschild 1983). Receptionists, secretaries, flight attendants, and others in similar jobs are pressured to smile at those they serve, to speak in honeyed tones, to be sexually attractive, and to put up with sexual overtures at work, in order to sell the company product or to keep offices running smoothly. Women in part-time, low-paid, and insecure jobs tend to acquire histories and attitudes that reflect this experience; these can readily be attributed back onto them as justification for their economic position. Women, not jobs, become associated with high labour turnover and low ambition (Wilson 1986, 122–123).

The occupation that is most stereotypically defined as women's work is homemaking. Approximately half of all married women in Canada are full-time homemakers, and most of the others assume principal responsibility for it in addition to their paid jobs. As work, it involves multiple services for family members including the standard tasks of cooking, cleaning, and shopping, the less visible "expressive" work of emotional support and tension management, and the physical, emotional, and tutorial care of children. It is performed in relative isolation in private homes. A Statistics Canada report, published in April of 1994, estimated that the dollar value of unpaid housework would amount to $319 billion annually if all services rendered had to be purchased on the open market. But this does not alter the fact that women who do housework full-time are defined as outside the labour force and ineligible even for minimal Canada pension benefits. From the perspective of political economy theory, the defining characteristic of housework is that it is unpaid, and those who do such work are dependent on the income-earning labour of others. It is outside the capitalist market system, notwithstanding its importance in maintaining and reproducing the labour force. Many of the traits defined as typically feminine—putting the needs of others first, being emotional rather than task-oriented or rational, being followers rather than leaders, deferring to men in important decisions, and the like—can be seen as appropriate responses to the lifetime experience of being financially dependent and powerless.

In summary, what functionalist theory interprets as appropriate gender-role behaviour for males and females in different social classes, political economy theory interprets as the structural demands placed on male and female workers by corporate capitalism. It makes good economic sense that boys in school concentrate on training for jobs while girls in school concentrate on getting married. Girls who look around them are likely to see very few women earning incomes that make them financially independent of a male wage. Only girls who make top marks in school can reasonably aspire to professional careers with large salaries. The "cult of femininity" among working-class girls—their preoccupation with makeup, clothes, and getting a boyfriend—is not based on a romanticized view of love and marriage so much as fear of being a "maiden-aunt" struggling to get by in a low-paying job and dependent on the generosity and pity of their parents (McRobbie 1991). Efforts by teachers toward a new kind of socialization that discourages gender stereotyping and promotes feminist consciousness-raising have little impact in the face of what girls and their parents see as the realistic options open to them (Gaskell 1988, 166; Gaskell, McLaren, and Novogrodsky 1989).

The Limitations of Political Economy Theory

Political economy theory describes the gendered character of class relations and draws attention to its importance in structuring gender relations. But the framework does not adequately account for how or why this gendered class structure exists. Why is it that male workers earn substantially higher average incomes than female workers, even when obvious factors linked to labour productivity, such as level of education, years on the job, and working full- or part-time, are controlled? Why are women ghettoized in such a limited range of jobs? How did the economy come to be organized so that women rather than men assume principal responsibility for unpaid, domestic work?

The classic explanation offered within political economy theory for such patterns takes a functionalist form. The dual labour market exists because it is functional for the capitalist system. Business people need the cheap labour of women to increase profits. They also need the reserve army of women who can be hired and fired easily in order to ride out fluctuations in the market. Capitalism needs the unpaid domestic labour done by women to maintain current workers and reproduce the next generation of workers. But there are a number of logical and practical flaws with such arguments. Relations of subordination of women to men long predate the rise of capitalism. Capitalism was shaped by and also took advantage of pre-existing patriarchal relations, but did not produce them. Women's labour may have been essential to the pre-industrial patterns of production organized around large family households. But this did not afford them equal status with men. Legally and politically, women had few rights. Household authority rested squarely with men. The rise of capitalism made life generally easier for women by reducing domestic drudgery and providing at least some opportunities for financial independence.

The argument that capitalism needs and therefore per-petuates the status of women as secondary, marginal, and cheap workers contradicts the logic of a profit-driven econ-omy. In principle, if women in general are a cheap labour pool, and if they are as productive as men, then it would make good business sense to hire *only* women. If women are discriminated against by other, irrational employers, then their labour would be cheap. It makes good business sense to hire the people that others discriminate against to re-duce one's own labour costs. Either way, demand for women's labour should rise, which would increase their wage-bargaining power, and the differential price of male and female labour should decrease (Wilson 1986, 114). This generally does not happen, suggesting that the roots of the dual labour market do not rest solely in the play of business interests in the market.

Marxist analysis, with its focus on class and wage labour, provides a powerful explanation of the development of class society, and the reproduction of class domination, but its categories are fundamentally gender-blind. The the-ory does not address the question of why particular people fill particular jobs, or specifically why women are systemat-ically subordinated in the labour market relative to men (Hartmann 1984). What remains to be analyzed is why and how women are available to be exploited as cheap labour by capitalists, and the complicity of trade unions and male co-workers in these practices.

Political economy theory similarly fails to treat as prob-lematic the division of labour that places principal respon-sibility for homemaking on women. Marx himself regarded how men and women organize to reproduce children within families as natural or biologically determined, and hence as not warranting the kind of critical analysis that he directed to how people organize to produce commodities. Current feminist theory challenges this naturalness as ideology that obscures complex relations of power between men and women. Engels argued that patriarchal family relations arose when men gained control of means of production ([1884] 1978). But the theory fails to explain how and why it was men and not women who took such control, particu-larly when women supposedly held power in the communal, matriarchal households, and commonly did much of the work of cultivation and caring for domesticated animals. The theory presupposes male dominance in the process of trying to explain it.

Political economy theory suggests that the alienating conditions of work under capitalism and the aggressive, competitive behaviour that the system promotes, may be important in generating the frustrations and aggression that are manifest in domestic violence. But it is a large intellec-tual jump to assert that class oppression and alienation pro-duce rapists, gay bashers, and child molesters (Brittan 1989,

69). The incidence of wife battering may well increase with unemployment, but it is not confined to such conditions. The predispositions that facilitate wife battering or attacks on gays and lesbians exist prior to the unemployment or to the job frustration, constructing particular categories of people, and marking them as acceptable targets.

The prevalence of sexual harassment against women in the workplace, and similar patterns of hostility and violence directed against gay men and lesbians, also cannot readily be accounted for within the framework of political economy theory. Discrimination in employment on the grounds of sexual orientation has been explicitly declared illegal under the Human Rights Code of Ontario since 1986, yet lesbian teachers still fear to identify themselves, under the very real expectation of harassment (Khayatt 1990). One school board voted to drop all reference to non-discrimination clauses in their hiring policy rather than acknowledge that they might possibly hire lesbians as teachers. Gay men sim-ilarly face discrimination and harassment in employment. It is very difficult to be openly gay and hold an executive po-sition. If they cannot be fired directly for sexual orientation, other excuses are likely to be used (Kinsman 1987b, Ch. 8).

In summary, while political economy theory seems to offer important insights into the organization of gender re-lations, there is much that remains outside its focus. Sexual politics have brought to light patterns of power, interests, and conflicts that cannot readily be understood in terms of conventional class analysis. Gender inequality is clearly linked to class inequality, but cannot be simply subsumed under it. We need an expanded theoretical framework to understand the interrelationship between patriarchal and capitalist relations.

Sex and Gender as Social Constructions

The social constructionist perspective challenges much of what we generally take for granted as factual characteristics of people and society. All aspects of social life are regarded as processes that people accomplish rather than entities that can be described. Sex and gender are no exception. In our common-sense thinking, we tend to view a person's sex as given, as a biological fact of life. Someone is either a male or a female; males display the gender characteristics of masculinity and females display femininity. Social construc-tionist theory pressures us to set these common-sense as-sumptions aside. It continually translates nouns into verbs, entities into practices. Instead of taking the two sex cate-gories male and female as obvious, it asks "How do people do categorizing work such that they end up with two unam-biguous groupings?"

Similarly, rather than treating male or female as nouns, constructionists ask "How are maleness and femaleness accomplished? How do people, in their practical, everyday interactions, accomplish themselves as male or female?" The study of what we customarily think of as gender attributes of masculinity and femininity also shifts the focus from describing characteristics to describing what people do to accomplish for themselves and for others the sense of being masculine or being feminine. How do we come to know, and know in common, what is recognizably being masculine or being feminine, and how do we accomplish such categorizing work for practical purposes?

Terminology becomes confusing at this point. Earlier we defined *sex* as biological attributes and *gender* as associated behavioural expectations that are socially learned. But this distinction no longer works. Some theorists use the term *gender* exclusively to convey the meaning that everything is socially accomplished, including what we usually think of as biologically determined. But this tends to obscure what aspect of common-sense thinking is being challenged at any particular point. We will use the term *sex* when the discussion focuses specifically on challenges to what are commonly thought of as biological states or attributes. However, this usage is not followed with any consistency in the literature being cited.

Sex as Social Construction

We opened this chapter with a discussion of biological theories about the foundations of male and female roles in society, where at least the notion that there are males and females could be taken as a given, and that it is obvious which category an individual fits into. Probably most of you read this section without the thought even crossing your mind that there might be anything problematic about it. However, the ethnomethodological study by Kessler and McKenna (1978) makes precisely such obviousness problematic. Ethnomethodology involves the study of members' methods of making sense of what seems to be going on. This includes how people draw on background understandings and practical reasoning in a continual process of formulating and reformulating accounts of what is happening that seem to make sense for the purposes at hand. Kessler and McKenna applied this approach to the question of how people, in their everyday reasoning, come to decide whether someone is male or female. They first tried a simple experiment with stick drawings to see what features a sample of 950 people would use to label the figure as male or female, and how many features had to change before people changed their label. What they found was that once people had categorized the sex of the figure, almost any surface features could be changed without affecting the label. Once

people labelled a particular figure male, for example, the addition of a series of typically female characteristics, including breasts, narrow waist, broad hips, long hair, low muscle mass, and absence of facial hair, were not sufficient to prompt people to change their labels.

Common sense suggests that we see surface features and then form a decision about a person's sex, but in practice reasoning seems to work the other way around. People decide what sex someone is, and then interpret surface features to be consistent with that categorization. For example, suppose we were told that person X has a female gender identity, prefers male sex partners, wears skirts and dresses, has some facial hair, and has feminine interests. Would this be sufficient to determine conclusively whether the person is male or female? The answer is no. We need to have attributed the category male or female to the person *before* we could evaluate the information. If we were told that this person is a female, we would see all the information as consistent with a typical woman who perhaps has a cosmetic problem with facial hair. However, if we were told that this person is a male, we would see the same information as consistent with a male transvestite, perhaps with a different kind of hormone imbalance.

Kessler and McKenna's experiments with stick drawings indicated that the presence of a penis was often decisive in people's reasoning. If the stick figure had a penis, it was generally labelled male no matter what other features were added, even a vagina. This reasoning that gender attribution is genital attribution, and specifically that having a penis determines maleness, was put into medical practice in 1984 when conjoined twins were surgically separated at the pelvis in a Toronto hospital. The twin boys had only one penis between them. From the moment of separation, the twin without the penis was called a girl, her testicle was removed, and a "vagina" constructed from a piece of colon. "She" was thereafter shown in pictures with a ribbon or barrettes in her hair and wearing a dress. In terms of this practical reasoning, being female does not seem to have any positive status. It is defined by the lack of a penis, notwithstanding that the child had male chromosomes and a testicle, and lacked any female genitalia or reproductive capabilities.

The irony in everyday life is that classification of people by sex is almost always made without seeing a person's genitals. The surface features that people so readily discounted when looking at stick figures are all we have to go on. This leaves open the question of how do we accomplish gender attribution. You might try an experiment for yourselves. Instead of assuming you know what sex someone is, put this in doubt. Go to a shopping mall, particularly during a winter noon hour when high-school students tend to congregate there. Now suppose you are told that at least one teenager is a transvestite, claiming a sex category incongruent with genitals. Concentrate on how you do the work of categorizing the teenagers by sex, and trying to find the anomalies. How often are you not quite certain? How would you test your conclusions—knowing that transvestites would angrily deny your insinuation that they might be other than they appear, and that non-transvestites would be equally angry if you made such a suggestion to them?

A famous description of cross-sex passing is Garfinkel's study of Agnes (1967, Ch. 5). Agnes was apparently born and raised as a male, but decided at puberty that she wished to be female. So she forged her mother's prescriptions for estrogen to promote growth of breasts, copied all the behaviour patterns that she thought were "typically feminine," and was successful in getting all her acquaintances, including her boyfriend, to think of her as female. As a young adult she underwent a sex-change operation to have her penis converted into a vagina.

Kessler and McKenna suggest that transsexuals and transvestites can manage to "pass" relatively easily in our society because we so readily assume that individuals have to be either one sex or the other, and that they are what they appear to be. The Olympic Games is one context in which concerns have been raised that men might try to pass as women in order to gain an unfair advantage. It was even considered possible that some countries might be so set on winning medals that they would surgically alter male athletes to look like females. In the early 1960s a chromosome test was developed, using cells from an athlete's mouth. Evidence of a Y chromosome is taken as proof that an athlete is not female and cannot compete as a woman. One woman who competed in the 1964 Olympic Games, winning several medals, was banned in 1967 when Y chromosomes were detected in her cells. However, she continued to live, in her own and in others' eyes, as a female.

Three or More Sexes? Opening up Options

The above discussion has been based on the assumption that there are only two sex categories and they are mutually exclusive, however tricky it might be in practice to slot everybody exclusively into one of them. But why be so certain that there can be only two? We have some evidence that people in other societies have not taken it for granted that sex is dichotomous, or determined solely by presence or absence of male genitals. Prior to colonization, some North American Indian tribes, including the Zuni, the Navajo, and the Mojave, accepted and revered individuals who were thought of as having a third sex that incorporated aspects of both male and female (Midnight Sun 1988; Roscoe 1988). In anthropological literature this third sex is often referred

to as the **berdache**. The term cannot be translated into contemporary Western notions such as "homosexual." The berdache were thought of in very different ways. They had culturally defined, multidimensional social roles, and were accorded status and prestige in terms of their religious, economic, kinship, and political roles, not the single dimension of sexual orientation. Among the Mojave, such third-sex individuals often attained high prestige as shamans, or as the partners of shamans or chiefs. Biologically female berdache who adopted the male sex observed the menstruation taboos of their female partners rather than of themselves, and at social gatherings they sat with the men. Biologically male berdache would feign pregnancy and stillbirth, and scratch their legs to draw blood to imitate menstruation. The sexual partners of these individuals retained the gender identity associated with their own biological sex.

Enforcing Two Sexes: Closing Options

If it is possible in principle to categorize people in terms of three or perhaps more sexes, and far from straightforward to categorize them exclusively into either male or female, then how is it that we take for granted the rigid categorization of male or female? How do we accomplish and sustain the social construction of our world as made up of two distinct sexes, despite the failure of human reality on almost any count to be strictly dimorphic (Connell 1987, 75)? Connell's answer is that this definitely does not come naturally. It has to be worked at. Sustained effort to exaggerate differences between people categorized as male and female is needed precisely because biological logic cannot sustain the gender categories (Connell 1987, 83). Similarities far outweigh differences. Children have their sex categorization vehemently imposed upon them long before this has any relevance for purposes of sexual reproduction. Obsessive efforts go into the sex-typing of clothes and adornment, and the production of body images that exaggerate muscular physique for males and physical slimness and beauty for females. Frank (1992, 275–276) describes how teenaged boys actively worked on their bodies to produce desired effects, especially through involvement in sports and weight training. Until relatively recently in Western societies, girls were actively discouraged from involvement in muscle-building programs. When women did become involved in intensive sports training, the magnitude of supposed biological differences in the strength, endurance, and speed of male and female athletes dwindled to a fraction of its former size. Women who currently participate in Olympic sports can beat all but a small minority of men. They routinely shatter world records set by men at the turn of the century.

In summary, in social constructionist theory, bodies are not "givens." We are not simply born with our bodies. They are sites of action that men and women work on by a multitude of practices including sports, training, diet, and clothing. Surgical intervention is an extreme form of action on a continuum that has included such instruments of torture as whalebone corsets, spike-heeled shoes, and other forms of clothing that restrict, twist, and shape bodies into the moulds considered naturally male or naturally female.

Gender as Social Construction

Members' methods for establishing the categorization of individuals into male and female are directly implicated in members' methods for accomplishing the recognition of masculinity and femininity as distinctive behavioural patterns. Much social science literature in the functionalist tradition is preoccupied with identifying sex-based differences in behaviour. Typically, such work begins with sex dimorphism as given, describes sets of traits associated with the two categories, conceptualizes these as typically male and typically female normative patterns, and defines these as the cultural norms for the group or groups with which the individuals are identified.

From the perspective of social constructionist theory, there are serious problems with this approach. The research process appears to be circular in two respects. Firstly, behavioural traits are commonly used in practical reasoning to decide the sex category in which to place the individuals being studied. Secondly, the methods used to discover typical traits actively work to create the realities of masculinity and femininity that such research is intended to describe. Psychological scales designed to measure masculinity and femininity, such as those developed by Bem (1974), provide valuable illustrations of such circularity. Social constructionist analysis focuses not on the accuracy of such scales for describing reality, but on the detailed methods used by scientists to produce the scales themselves (Connell 1987, 171–174; Eichler 1980, 62). A common approach is to develop long lists of adjectives describing behavioural traits, and then ask a large sample of people to classify each adjective as more typical for a male or more typical for a female. Bem used a checklist of 400 adjectives. The final scale includes only those adjectives that are consistently identified by judges as typical for one sex with a high level of statistical accuracy. Further trials are used to eliminate adjectives or "items" that seem inconsistent with the others on the scale, in how people respond to them. Finally, when used to measure the supposed masculinity or femininity of particular people, responses to all items are added together and averaged, since any one item alone might be unreliable as a measure of the underlying gender trait.

The systematic deconstruction of these scales reveals the practices that produce the "reality" of gender traits that they supposedly describe. In the first stage, the selection of adjectives deemed to constitute gender-specific traits depends heavily on the view of the panel of judges. Typically, these comprise undergraduate psychology students. Eichler suggests that what poor, black women from American inner cities might recognize as "typical for a male" or "typical for a female" are likely to be very different from what psychology students pick out. But their opinions are not normally asked. Hypothetically, a wide enough variety of judges might result in no consistent list of gender-linked adjectives.

The next step in scale formation accomplishes the construction of masculine and feminine as opposing categories. The vast majority of adjectives were seen by judges as commonly applying to both males and females, from which we might reasonably conclude that there is no gender dimorphism. But all these adjectives are eliminated. The scale devised by Bem, for example, includes only 40 of the original 400 adjectives, 20 for the masculinity measure and 20 for femininity. These practices construct gender traits as residual terms. Gender is what is left over when all the characteristics that men and women share are eliminated. "Masculine" thus necessarily constitutes what "femininity" is not, and vice versa. Final confirmation of sex-linked "gender" traits is achieved when researchers routinely discard as faulty those studies that do not find expected gender dimorphism.

These scales carry the aura of scientific objectivity backed by precise statistical data, which gives them considerable influence. Individual men and women who do not score higher or lower on the appropriate masculinity or femininity scale, may appear in the eyes of themselves and others to be gender deviants. But such apparent deviance or conformity to supposed gender traits are entirely an artifact of the scale's construction. The core of the constructionist critique of such measures is that they are inherently flawed because the underlying conceptualization of gender is false. Gender is not an essence or entity that can be abstracted and measured, but rather an ongoing accomplishment in social interaction. With this shift in focus, the central research question becomes how do people accomplish gender. What are the practices that individuals use to accomplish themselves as recognizably, accountably masculine or feminine for practical purposes in particular social situations?

Accomplishing Masculinity

Conversations with 14 young men about what it means to be a man revealed a high level of anxiety and doubt (Frank 1992). Most were not at all sure of their own masculinity, and went to considerable lengths to try to assert it, to themselves as much as to others. The boys talked of the strategies they adopted to accomplish themselves as recognizably, accountably masculine in everyday interaction. Most of them worked on their bodies, trying to build up muscle. Frank describes them as "using their bodies like suits of armour that they carry with them for protection" (1992, 275–276). Those who could usually did some sports, or otherwise they made a point of hanging around with bigger boys who did. They generally avoided friendships with girls lest they compromise their appearance of being masculine, but at the same time they tried to get a girlfriend to establish themselves as heterosexual. They were well aware that there was no clear way to establish themselves conclusively as heterosexual, and felt continually under pressure to display their claims to "proper" masculinity. Typically, they engaged in "dirty talk" about girls and exaggerated heterosexist posturing with other boys. Another study of boys on Little League baseball teams revealed that they constantly taunted each other with comments like "You're a faggot," "What a queer," and "Kiss my ass" (Fine 1992). Most of the boys had only the vaguest notion of gay sexual behaviour and had never met anyone they knew to be gay. The taunts were mostly directed at boys who did not display the bodywork, sports, and sex talk associated with masculinity claims. The main intent of such taunts, Fine suggests, is to reinforce the generally shaky sense of what proper masculinity should look like. The most insecure boys used such taunting the most to assert to themselves and to other boys their own accomplished masculinity.

Many of the boys who talked to Frank (1992) spoke of the gap they sensed between their public facade of exaggerated masculinity claims and the private practices and fantasies that they kept to themselves, or shared with only close confidants. Some were heterosexual in both practice

and fantasies, while others had homosexual fantasies; others engaged in homosexual practices while maintaining a surface of heterosexuality. For those boys who do recognize homosexual desires in themselves, the exaggerated heterosexist taunting can be painful and even frightening (G. Smith 1992). The term *heterosexism* generally refers to the practices and the patterns of discourse, or ways of thinking and talking, that enforce heterosexual masculinity as "normal" and all other forms of sexual desire as aberrant. Heterosexism organizes the relations within which homophobic attitudes emerge as hostile personal attitudes toward gays, often by people who have never met any. Such an attitude set often coexists with a rigid demarcation of male versus female tasks and activities, and a view of girls and women as inferior to boys and men (Fine 1992; Lehne 1976). Racism, or rigid notions about racial distinctions and relative superiority and inferiority of such groupings, is also a common corollary of homophobia.

Accomplishing Femininity

For young women, the practical accomplishment of themselves as recognizably feminine is complicated by the particularly amorphous and contradictory character of the concept. Scientific models of femininity in gender-trait scales generally portray it in passive or indirect forms as less aggressive and assertive, and less associated with initiative or risk-taking than masculinity. The women's movement has openly challenged traditional models of appropriate roles for women, to the point that being considered feminine is not necessarily complimentary. Smith (1990) suggests that the fashion industry may play a pivotal role in organizing ways of thinking and talking about femininity, supported by an array of mass media that includes women's magazines, television, advertising, retail displays of cosmetics and fashion, and romantic novels. The ubiquitous presence of the media makes it possible for total strangers to strike up conversations about fashions and the fashion industry's conception of femininity, and understand each other. They are likely also to understand how the fashion industry codes particular clothing styles and body shapes to convey certain messages about femininity. Preoccupation with clothes and cosmetics arguably plays a similar part in accomplishing femininity for young women as sports do for young men. But the relationship does not appear to be one of straightforwardly copying fashion images. We have some evidence of how girls actively manipulate fashion images and even consciously choose to get fat to create oppositional versions of femininity (Orbach 1979; Findlay 1975, 59). A group of working-class girls in Britain saw fashion and cosmetics as a way of asserting their independence from school and their superiority over middle-class girls who wore

Participation on sports teams is one way that young men work at accomplishing masculinity.

The Toronto Star/P. Gower

"horrible" school uniforms (McRobbie 1978). Conversely, working-class girls on the Yonge Street strip in Toronto flaunted the standard fashion by cross-dressing in black leather (Smith 1990). The problem is that the meanings attached to such behaviour are continually in flux. It is also unclear whether women follow fashions or fashions follow women. The fashion industry is fine-tuned to pick up cues about innovations in clothing and to reproduce them in new styles, in an endless effort to keep women as fashion consumers. No sooner do teenagers take to ripping holes in their jeans and patching them with coloured rags than the fashion industry produces jeans with holes and patches already made.

In summary, the view of masculinity and femininity that emerges from constructionist theory is very different from the traditional functionalist approach of socialization theory. There is no predefined set of cultural norms that individuals internalize and express in behaviour. Rather, the notions of what being a male and being a female might mean are actively constituted by the participants in ongoing interaction. Any subsequent description of behaviour as conforming to subcultural norms is an after-the-fact accounting. In effect, ethnographers in the functionalist tradition create the reality of norms in the process of observing, categorizing, and assigning normative labels to the behaviour they describe. This is a circular process in that whatever people do becomes what the cultural norms are. This descriptive labelling of patterns as cultural norms, however, misses the processes involved in their constitution.

Currently, we lack a body of research that explores in intimate ways how young men and women accomplish what it means to be a man or a woman. Frank's study is limited to a small number of boys, and we do not have information on their class backgrounds or social situation. Strategies adopted by other groups of boys may differ widely from the pattern of bodywork, sports, and girlfriend that these boys describe. We also have very little understanding of the strategies by which girls accomplish being female, with or without the contradictory image of being feminine and fashion-conscious.

Sexuality as Social Construction

In common-sense accounting, sexuality is a biological fact of life. The experience of erotic desires, the intensity of attendant emotions, and the preoccupation with attracting members of the opposite sex, are thought to reflect the surge of sex hormones at the onset of puberty. But conflicting and contradictory accounts of what has been understood to be natural sexuality in different historical periods and societies cannot be easily reconciled with the notion of biological

determination. During the Victorian era in Europe and North America, the official view of what constituted natural sexuality defined people as procreators rather than erotic beings (Katz 1990). Prevailing notions of true love, true womanhood, and true manhood stressed purity and freedom from sexuality. In the medical discourse of the Victorian era, erotic impulses and desires to masturbate, especially when displayed by women, were defined as physiological disorders of such seriousness as to warrant surgical intervention to cure them. In 1906 a gynaecological surgeon estimated that some 150 000 American women had undergone an ovariotomy—removal of the ovaries—to control female personality disorders (Carby 1982, 222). The last recorded clitoridectomy—removal of a woman's clitoris—was performed in the United States in 1948 on a five-year-old child as a cure for masturbation.

Such views stand in stark contrast to those prevailing in contemporary North America where the absence of erotic desire is considered abnormal. Far from being a diseased state, eroticism is heralded. Advertisers routinely exploit it to sell commodities, striving to identify their products with sex appeal. Media idols and pop stars who can incite erotic passions in mass audiences stand to reap huge profits.

Social constructionist theory does not address the issue of which version of sexuality is "natural," or which version might best describe subcultural views of appropriate sexuality. It raises questions about how prevailing notions of sexuality come to be constituted in particular historical periods, and especially the role of experts in the construction of common-sense reasoning. The objective is to deconstruct discourses about sexuality, to reveal how they sustain the appearance of truth. Discourses are the prevailing ways of thinking and talking about an issue such as sexuality. Expert discourses within medicine and the social sciences have a powerful impact on common-sense reasoning. They appear to have scientific credibility as factual descriptions of the way things are. People draw on them in constructing accounts of their own experiences, both for themselves and for others. Discourses do not provide descriptions of normal or typical behaviour, but rather conceptualizations that serve to "normalize" and legitimate certain behaviour patterns and to subordinate others. Relations of power are embedded in the authoritative interpretations of experts. When these interpretations gain ascendancy, they mandate courses of action to bring people in conformity with them. As noted above, Victorian medical discourse about sexuality justified actions that would now be considered grievous bodily mutilation. Successful normalization sustains the uniformity that functionalist research can describe as "norms" for the society or the subgroups being studied.

The work of Michel Foucault on *The History of Sexuality* (1978) is a formative study in this field. Foucault traces broad historical shifts in discourses around sexuality, linking them to changing economic relations, and the state's increasing concern to control the behaviour of the emergent working-class masses who flooded the cities in the late nineteenth century. With the rise of capitalism, families changed from centres of production to privatized units of consumption. Individuals worked for wages outside the home, creating the possibility for young men, and occasionally young women, to become financially independent. They had more opportunities than ever before to live alone and to experiment with sex for pleasure, outside of procreation. New forms of authority emerged to control this freedom.

Foucault argues that experts within medicine and the social sciences took over the traditional authority of churches and family elders in the management of sexuality. A virtual obsession with sexuality emerged in these disciplines behind the mask of Victorian prudery and repression, with sex increasingly proposed as the cause of anything and everything. This, in turn, justified extensive inquisition into it. Sex was conceptualized as a taboo topic, a powerful psychic force that was hidden from people or repressed into their unconscious. Hence experts were justified in extracting hidden sexual drives and preoccupations through forced confession. Confession, in turn, came to be treated as therapy, required for diagnosis and "normalization."

Within medical discourse, erotic heterosexual desire became defined as normal with all other forms of sexuality as illnesses or perversions that should be subject to treatment. Categories of sexual "types" proliferated in medical and psychiatric discourses: types of women included the indifferent or obsessive mother, the frigid wife, or the nervous and neurotic woman; types of men included the impotent, the perverse, and the sadistic husband; children were categorized as the masturbating child, or the precocious and already-exhausted child. In 1869, the term *homosexual* was introduced as a category within the discourses of psychology, psychiatry, medicine, and law. Formerly sodomy was considered just a form of non-procreative sexual practice proscribed by the church. It became transformed in medical discourse from an activity to a particular type of person. Such persons thereby became subject to the power and control of experts in the professions.

These professional discourses were not simply objective or detached scientific theorizing. They mandated courses of action that subjected people to intensive surveillance and control, justified by the powerful ideology of scientific rationality. Foucault maintains that the goal behind the professional fixation on sex was to attain deeper power and control over the body. Norms of sexual development were defined from childhood to old age, with all possible deviations described and labelled as forms of illness to be treated. Children were conceptualized as latent sexual beings who must be continually controlled and repressed through perpetual surveillance, discipline, precautions, and punishments.

Educators, doctors, school administrators, and parents were all implicated in this discourse. Parents were used to spread new notions of sexuality, and then for monitoring it under the guidance of experts. Masturbation by children was constituted as a secret and forced into hiding as a form of abnormality. Then it became possible to justify compelling children to admit to practising it so that they could be subjected to correction and treatment. This, in turn, multiplied the power exerted by experts in medicine, law, and education. Foucault suggests that this fixation on childhood sexuality and its repression, monitored by segregation and surveillance in the family, created the very environment that would promote incest. The family thus became constituted as the focus of still more intensive monitoring, confession, and therapy. Donzelot (1979) documents two centuries of government intervention in families justified through the discourses of medical and social work experts. The status of women's work as homemakers was improved, but at the same time that work was subordinated to directives from experts as to how it should be performed (Ehrenreich and English 1979).

The practice of confession is embedded in relations of power. The person who confesses is seen as ignorant of his own psychic processes, or at best as having only incomplete knowledge. It is the listener—the priest, doctor, psychologist, social worker, or educator—who is seen as having the knowledge to interpret what is said, and to treat the person with the aim of normalizing their behaviour. Techniques of knowledge and strategies for power are thus tightly interrelated.

People who engaged in forms of same-gender sex were subjected to a combination of legal punishments and forced therapy that amounted to psychological and social terrorism (Kinsman 1987a, 106). They were portrayed as types of people who threatened social order. Military elites saw intense friendships between men as undermining discipline; gay men were hounded from government jobs as potential national security risks. It was not until 1969 that homosexual acts conducted in private between consenting adults aged 21 and over became decriminalized in Canada, two years after a similar legal amendment was passed in Britain. Since then the struggle over policing has centred on the definition of *private*. Any living spaces within the armed forces, gay bath houses, even closed toilet cubicles, could be declared "public" areas for purposes of policing. Even a photograph could constitute evidence of public sex, in that a third person, the photographer, must have been present.

During the four years after homosexual acts were decriminalized in Britain, the conviction rate for homosexual offences increased by 160 percent (Kinsman 1987b, 143).

Power and Resistance

Power is always an ongoing accomplishment, never absolute or attained once and for all. For Foucault, any exercise of power inevitably generates resistance because people never can be reduced to the socialized, normative role-players envisioned in functionalist theory.

The power of scientific expertise is no exception. But it is unique in that it is generally not experienced as force imposed from above, but rather as normal, rational activity generated in ordinary, everyday interaction. Parents and educators turn to experts to learn how to do a better job of parenting and teaching children. Psychologists and social workers study their disciplines in order to help people overcome their problems and feel "normal." Resistance seems irrational. It is difficult even to be sure what one is rebelling against when the mechanisms of power—confession, exposure, and therapy—are themselves often presented as rebellion against Victorian prudery and repression.

Nonetheless, people do resist the force of scientific rationality. The medical and scientific discourses that defined homosexual activity in terms of aberrant personality types also provided a focus for self-identity, and for resistance to forced therapy and to the deviantizing practices of policing. People involved in same-gender sex adopted the label *homosexual* as a basis for claiming a distinct identity and therefore grounds for some recognition, and human rights protection (Foucault 1978, 101; Kinsman 1987a, 111). Demands for "gay liberation" challenged the assumed naturalness of heterosexuality. Gay networks slowly transformed into ghetto communities in cities such as Toronto and Montreal, organized around gay commerce and markets. They fostered the emergence of distinctive cultural values and claims to respectability as a quasi-ethnic group, with a new stratum of "experts" who act as spokespersons for the "gay community" (Kinsman 1987b, Ch. 10). Lesbians have not emerged to the same extent as gay men, in part reflecting their more limited access to economic resources.

The rise of gay culture and attendant claims to quasi-ethnic status have brought important gains in the form of greater public acceptance, but not without costs. Pressures to establish respectability by emphasizing masculinity or macho-style gay behaviour marginalizes those who do not fit the ascendant gay-cultural definitions. The political dilemma is that in accepting the categorizing of homosexuality as a personality type, people who engage in same-gender sex adopt the hegemonic heterosexual discourse that defines them as a deviant minority. On the other hand, in deconstructing the category to challenge the notion of "types of people" they undermine the basis for political activism in naming their own sexual experiences and resisting oppression. Activists argue that the deconstruction of the category "homosexual" must await the deconstruction of the category "heterosexual."

The Limitations of Social Constructionism

The social constructionist perspective avoids the deterministic implications of the functionalist theory of socialization into gender roles, and also simplified versions of economic relations determining gender. The conceptualization of sex and gender relations as ongoing accomplishments allows for enormous variation in their expression and for rapid, dynamic change. Discourse analysis holds up for inspection whatever is taken to be factual statements about human nature as socially constructed and subject to negotiation.

The main criticism launched against this perspective is that it does not go far enough in its own investigation of the dynamics of power that structure discourse. The central feature of sexuality and gender relations is inequality—the privileging of a particular expression of male sexuality and the generalized dominance of males over females. Social constructionist analysis exposes the power of such myths to structure the practices that constitute gender relations. But such analysis does not by itself explain why it is male sexuality, and a particular form of masculinity, that becomes privileged in this discourse. We have to look outside the discourse itself to explore the relations of male domination that the talk reflects. Male sexuality, gender inequality, and the privileging of male sexuality in discourse is not itself the effect of discourse, although this is a potent mechanism through which such patterns are maintained. What needs further investigation is the institutionalized and systemic character of gender inequality. This is the central focus of feminist theories of gender relations.

Feminist Theories of Gender Relations

When feminist theory is viewed in its broadest sense as an approach that asks questions about women in society and makes their presence visible in the theory and practices of sociology, then everything discussed in this chapter can be classified under the rubric of *feminist*. The sociology of gender relations, including the study of masculinity and men's roles, had its origins in the feminist movement.

In this section, however, we will go beyond the inclusion of women as a topic, to concentrate on the second stage in development of feminist theory that seeks to explore the social world from the standpoint of women. In particular, we will explore the thesis specific to feminist theory, namely that the social world can be meaningfully understood as organized in terms of **patriarchy**. The patriarchy thesis asserts that there is a systematic and institutionalized complex of relations and practices that organize and perpetuate the subordination of women to men. This pattern cannot be reduced to the voluntary behaviour or attitudes of individuals. It is systemic to how social relations are organized.

There is much diversity within feminist thought. The liberal, Marxist, socialist, and radical feminist perspectives approach the study of women's subordination in different ways and are associated with different political strategies for transforming patriarchal structures. These labels, however, are not precise and they tend to be used inconsistently in feminist literature. As conceptual divisions, they are useful for ordering the overview of feminist literature on gender relations, but as we will see, the approaches overlap considerably in practice.

Liberal Feminism: The Struggle for Equal Opportunity

Liberal feminist thought focuses on the issue of equal rights for women and men in the public arena, with a special emphasis on legal reforms. Historically, it was a long and bitter struggle to win recognition for any independent legal status and political rights for women. Prior to 1929, women in Canada were not fully recognized as "persons" under the British North America Act. Even thereafter, the inclusion of women under "persons" was only selectively applied by the courts. With few exceptions, Canadian women were systematically and universally disenfranchised. It was 1918 before women were granted the right to vote in federal elections. Most of the provinces extended the franchise to women over the six-year period from 1916 to 1922, but Quebec did not do so until 1940.

For the majority of women, the most important legislation defining their status was probably the marriage contract. In British and Canadian marital law until the latter half of the nineteenth century, married women were subsumed under the legal personhood of their husband. They were barred from owning or disposing of property in their own names. Their husband's authorization in writing was required before they signed any legal contracts. All children born to a married woman were the legal heirs of her husband. If the marriage broke down for whatever reason, and the woman separated from her husband, he retained absolute legal custody of any children (Smart 1984).

Piecemeal changes in these laws were won only very slowly, and often in forms that made it difficult for the majority of women to benefit. In the 1890s, married women gained the right to own and dispose of their own property. For women from wealthier families who inherited property, this was a significant change. It meant that they did not automatically relinquish control of it to their husband on marriage. But few women had any means to earn money or amass property in their own name. Any property that the husband brought with him into the marriage belonged legally only to him. So also did all the property that the couple amassed during the marriage. In the infamous Murdoch case, in 1975, the Supreme Court of Canada decided that a wife who had worked alongside her husband to run the family ranch for more than twenty years had done "just about what the ordinary rancher's wife does" and had "no right to a share in it" upon dissolution of her 25-year marriage to an abusive husband (Bissett-Johnson 1988). Only in the 1980s were marital property laws in Canada amended to state that the work of homemakers in nurturing the family entitled them to an equal share in family property.

Changes in legislation governing divorce and custody of children came equally slowly. By the late 1880s in Canada, mothers were granted the right to petition for a custody order, but to be successful they had to prove their exemplary character. Desire to leave a marriage was in itself evidence of being a bad mother, unless extreme abuse could be demonstrated. Also, any suggestion of adultery on the mother's part was considered sufficient to disqualify her, although no such strictures were applied to adulterous fathers (Backhouse 1991, Ch. 7).

A feminist review of Canadian legal history provides ample evidence of institutionalized patriarchy, but by the 1980s most of the obvious examples of discriminatory laws had been repealed. The enactment of the Canadian Charter of Rights and Freedoms in 1981 seemed to epitomize the triumph of liberal feminism. It enshrines absolute legal equality for male and female persons, together with endorsement of affirmative action to ameliorate social inequalities. Section 15 of the Charter states:

1. Every individual is equal before and under the law and has the right to equal protection and equal benefit of the law, without discrimination and, in particular, without discrimination based on race, national or ethnic origin, colour, religion, sex, age, or mental or physical disability.

2. Subsection (1) does not preclude any law, program or activity that has as its object the amelioration of conditions of disadvantaged individuals or groups including those that are disadvantaged because of race, national or ethnic origin, colour, religion, sex, age, or mental or physical disability.

Section 28 of the Charter further states:

> Notwithstanding anything in this Charter, the rights and freedoms referred to in it are guaranteed equally to male and female persons.

The aftermath of the Charter, as with many of the legal reforms that preceded it, has been disappointment and disillusionment with the power of law to radically change gender inequalities. In practice, the rights of women are always subject to interpretation and to counterclaims from other interests. Gender bias still appears to be pervasive within the Canadian justice system (Brockman and Chunn 1993). In addition, hard-won rights are not necessarily permanent. The National Action Committee on the Status of Women (NAC) came out strongly against the proposed Charlottetown Accord in 1992 that would have amended the Canadian Constitution. Among other serious reservations, NAC specifically feared that the Canada Clause included in this Accord would have permitted Section 28 of the Charter to be overridden in the interests of language and culture. Native women would also have had their Charter protection removed under the new proposals for Aboriginal self-government.

The central problem for liberal feminist analysis is that guarantees of legal equality have not been sufficient to overcome pervasive economic and social inequalities between women and men. Women vote, but they are not voted for as often as men. Women are entitled to an equal share in marital property and have the right to sue for divorce and custody of children equally with men, but this does not solve the financial problems facing women who are single parents. As we have seen, women typically earn incomes almost 40 percent below the average incomes for men. Commonly, divorced women find they cannot afford the mortgage payments on the half of a house they might receive. Broad estimates suggest that divorce typically results in a 73 percent decline in the living standards for women with young children in the first year after divorce, and a 43 percent rise in men's incomes in the same period (Eichler 1988, 249). The strict application of gender neutrality in custody disputes can also readily result in fathers looking like the better parent; they are more likely to have a stable job, a higher income, and to remarry, and so to have a new wife to act as caregiver for the children (Boyd 1993, 172–175). True gender equality in society seems to be much more complex than legal equality.

Marxist Feminism: Challenging Exploitation in the Economy

Marxist feminist thought focuses particularly on the exploitative character of capitalist relations and the super-exploitation of women as cheap, part-time, and temporary labour power. This perspective tries to redress the gender blindness of traditional Marxist theory, and the inadequacy of mainstream or "malestream" attempts to add women as a topic without rethinking the theoretical frameworks. Hartmann laments that "the 'marriage' of marxism and feminism has been like the marriage of husband and wife depicted in English common law: marxism and feminism are one, and that one is marxism" (Hartmann 1984, 172).

Feminist research into the history of women's labour-force participation has documented the systematic practices by male-dominated unions and by employers that have contributed to the subordination of women workers. Male workers had good reason to fear that the availability of women as cheap labour would undermine their own ability to command high wages. They responded by restricting the access of women to apprenticeships, and by promoting protective legislation to limit the hours that women and children could work (White 1980, 12–18; Hartmann 1984, 182). Such legislation did help women who had little bargaining power to protect themselves, but it simultaneously made them less attractive to employers relative to men. Historically, it was also common practice for male-dominated unions to bargain for lower wages and lower increases for women workers within their own ranks. The justification was that men needed a family wage, whereas women should be supported by men.

By the 1970s, such practices had largely disappeared in Canada. The Canadian Labour Congress (CLC) endorsed principles of equal opportunity for women, equal pay for work of equal value, paid maternity leave without loss of seniority or benefits, and affirmative action policies for women (White 1980, 65–73). By the mid-1980s, the CLC also endorsed free choice on abortion. The problems, however, remain. A relatively small proportion of employed women are union members, provision for maternity and parenting responsibility are very limited, and there are wide discrepancies in the average pay of women and men.

Women are typically employed in sectors of the labour market that have always been hard to unionize, namely services, retail trades, and finance, especially banks, and they are isolated and fragmented in a myriad of small offices. From such locations it is extremely difficult even to communicate with fellow workers, let alone to organize collectively. Where women have tried to unionize they have often met ferocious resistance from employers fearful of losing their pool of cheap labour. Banks have a particularly notorious reputation for breaking unions. In 1980 there were 7600 bank branches in Canada and only 65 were unionized. Unions that had formed had frequently been broken by intimidation and penalties, including the proliferation of expensive and long-drawn-out grievances, contracts that were worse than agreements in non-unionized branches, and the transfer of union members to other branches (Warskett 1988). Contract clauses of particular interest to women, such as maternity leave and flexible hours, are very hard to win even by established unions, because employers often cut back on pay raises when improved benefits are demanded. Few union members, women included, want to accept such conditions.

The gender-segregated character of the labour force makes it possible for large discrepancies in average pay for women and men to continue despite tough equal pay legislation. Discrimination is hard to demonstrate when there are no comparison groups of identically situated men to measure against women. Female-dominated professions like nursing, kindergarten teaching, and secretarial work thus continue to be among the lowest paid relative to the levels of education and job skills required. To counter the problem of job segregation, feminists have fought for legislation to guarantee "equal pay for work of equal value." Such legislation is now law in the Canadian federal government and the Ontario provincial government. In principle, jobs are compared on a points system that quantifies such characteristics as skill level, experience, responsibilities, hazards, and the like. In practice, such schemes are very difficult to operationalize because so much subjective judgment goes into assessments (Armstrong and Armstrong 1992). The private sector has so far largely resisted such evaluations. The prevailing cry is that any enforcement of such policies would bankrupt employers (Breckenridge 1985). The cheap labour of women seems to be a requirement for capitalists to be competitive.

Marxist feminist analysis of patriarchy has served to highlight many of the practices that constitute the subordination of women within the labour force. But like liberal feminism, the strategies for transforming these practices are still far from achieving the goal of substantive equality for women and men. The systemic nature of patriarchal relations goes deeper than a reorganization of opportunities within the labour force can resolve.

Socialist Feminism: The Double System of Social Production

Socialist feminism explores the complex ways in which **relations of reproduction** within the family are interlinked with relations of production within the economy. Relations of reproduction refers to how people organize to produce children and raise them to maturity. Relations of production refers to how people organize to produce goods. The core argument is that transformation of relations in both fields of human practices are needed to substantially alleviate the subordination of women. Patriarchy, in other words, is multifaceted and not confined to the public arena.

The organization of reproduction within the home forms part of the explanation for women's disadvantaged position within the wage-labour market. Studies suggest that even when women are employed full-time in paid jobs they still do the bulk of domestic, childcare, and people-servicing work at home (Armstrong and Armstrong 1990, 72–74). In effect, men take advantage of the labour power of women so that they can return to their jobs relaxed and refreshed while women return exhausted from their double day. Legislation to prevent discrimination against women employees does nothing to resolve the built-in discriminatory practices that assume that "normal" employees are not responsible for childcare. Hence when particular employees—usually female—ask for childcare leave or flexible working hours, it sounds like an appeal for special treatment (Mackinnon 1989, 219). Similarly, potential employees who have a combination of undesirable traits, such as being older, lacking in current work experience, having large gaps in their employment careers, and who seem likely to quit the job after a few years, are less likely to be selected than applicants with few or none of these negative traits. Strictly gender-neutral hiring practices will do nothing to resolve the fact that typically it is women rather than men who manifest all of these negative traits. These patterns are rooted in the domestic division of labour, and their transformation would require systemic changes that are much more complex than law reform. Eisenstein (1984) argues that the women's movement has precipitated a crisis in liberal thought precisely because the principles of individual freedom and equality do not work when applied to women and men.

The elimination of systemic disadvantages that women face in employment would entail a reorganization both of domestic labour and paid employment so as to make childbirth and caring for children inconsequential for education and career opportunities of women and men. Some of the changes in the social relations of childcare that feminists have proposed include provision of extended parenting leave for both mothers and fathers with full incomes and guaranteed job security, child-sick-leave days, flexible working hours, universally accessible, quality daycare facilities, and guaranteed income support for children and homemakers. But such proposals are contrary to the traditional discourses of mothering that idealize full-time caring for children in the home. They have been strongly resisted by the powerful "New Right" or moral conservative movement as undermining a man's responsibility to support mothers and children, and hence threatening family life and social order itself (Eichler 1985). In a sense, the New Right is correct. Socialist feminist theory exposes the extent to which traditional patterns of organizing domestic relations work to perpetuate a social order in which the majority of women are socially marginalized in private homes and economically dependent. This patriarchal social order is precisely what is being challenged.

Radical Feminism: The Struggle Against Exploitative Sexuality

Radical feminist theory carries the exploration of domestic relations more deeply than socialist feminist concerns with division of labour, to highlight the sphere of private and intimate relations between women and men. The core argument is that the root of patriarchy lies in sexuality—specifically in the systemic institutionalization and legitimation of male sexual dominance. In a multiplicity of ways, laws and social practices can be shown as organized to protect and defend male ownership, control, and use of female sexuality and reproductive power. Sexual oppression of women parallels and perhaps even surpasses in importance the exploitation of women's labour power, with women's economic dependence being a critical strategy used by men to secure women's sexual subordination (O'Brien 1981).

Historically, the marriage contract did not merely give the husband effective control over material property. It defined wives explicitly as the sexual property of their husband. Until as recently as the 1980s, rape in marriage was a legal impossibility in British and Canadian law. A husband had the legal right to the sexual services of his wife as and when he chose. But there was no reciprocal responsibility on the husband's part to meet his wife's sexual needs (Smart 1984, 94–95). A wife's refusal to have sexual intercourse constituted grounds for divorce as an act of cruelty, but a husband's refusal to have intercourse with his wife constituted only "natural disinclination" and not cruelty. Not until 1966 did the Courts of Appeal in Britain begin to apply the principle of sexual frustration equally to wives in considering divorce. Adultery was always considered a more serious offence for a wife than a husband.

Historically also, both the authority of the Catholic Church and British common law recognized the right of a husband to beat his wife for her moral betterment, or in effect to enforce his right to her obedience. This is the origin of "the rule of thumb" that refers to the convention that such beatings were proper so long as the stick used was no thicker than a man's thumb. Fathers had the same acknowledged right to thrash children into obedience. Wives have never been accorded the religious or legal right to beat their husbands, no matter what their behaviour. Canadian law no longer condones the thrashing of wives and children, but domestic violence is still endemic in many families. It was the early 1970s, thanks in large measure to the women's movement, that wife battery received public attention. It is exceptionally difficult to measure the incidence with any accuracy, but the physical evidence of battered women in transition houses, and the results of many surveys, suggest that some 10 percent of women have been beaten at least once by their male partner. An important effect, and arguably the main intent behind wife battery, is the woman's subservience to the man's will.

The crime of rape is regarded in feminist jurisprudence as the most extreme expression of male power to subordinate and exploit women as sexual objects for their use. Historically, it was not regarded as a crime against women at all, but a violation of a man's property right over his chaste wife or virginal daughter. Theoretically, the sexual violation of women who had transgressed the norms of chastity was unimportant, because such women had no value to lose (Clark and Lewis 1977, Ch. 7). Subsequently, under the impact of more liberal sexual mores and the women's movement, legislation was changed to focus on a woman's right to consent to sexual intercourse. This shift in thinking, however, did not significantly alter courtroom practices. The onus of proof was placed on women to demonstrate to the court that she did not consent to intercourse. Judges and jurors were predisposed to believe that any woman who was not a chaste wife or virgin probably did consent to have sex, or that the alleged rapist could reasonably have assumed that she was consenting, and hence that he was not guilty. In 1983 in Canada, the crime of rape was redefined as "sexual assault" shifting the focus from penetration by a penis to unwanted sexual touching. The new law removes the legal exemption against a victim's husband being charged with rape, and also incorporates sexual assaults against males (DeKeseredy and Hinch 1991, 62–65). The term *rape*, however, is still widely used and defended as a stronger and descriptively more accurate term to describe most of the offences.

Radical feminist studies of courtroom practices suggest that while the laws may have changed, the old notions that a virgin or chaste married woman is valuable, whereas other women are "open territory," still prevail in the minds of police, jurors, and judges. A woman's sexual history remains critical in a defendant's claim that he had an honest-if-mistaken belief that the woman consented to sexual intercourse with him because she had consented with other men in the past. Feminists denounce such arguments as ludicrous, and contend that sexual history has no bearing on the critical question of whether the woman might be lying about having consented to sex with the man on trial. Arguably, it is women with chaste reputations rather than sexually active women who would be more likely to misrepresent consensual sex as rape (Boyle and Rowley 1987). But this is not typically how judges and jurors reason. Many studies suggest that in rape trials the woman's character is on trial more than the defendant's. The publicity surrounding such trials helps to constitute the discourse around acceptable feminine behaviour. Women who do not abide by the rules can expect little protection from courts if they are sexually violated. In principle, prostitutes are entitled to the same legal protection from sexual assault as other women, but in practice they have little hope of winning their case.

Prostitution is condemned within radical feminist theory as a trade in women's bodies that expresses and reinforces their status as objects for male use. A double standard has always prevailed in the laws that govern its management and prosecution to target the women who sell their sex, not their male customers. Historically, the major concern behind vigilance and control over prostitutes was fear that they would spread diseases to young men—particularly to soldiers (Bland 1985). Few worried that soldiers might spread diseases to women. Efforts by feminist groups in the nineteenth century to protect women from false entrapment and forced vaginal inspections under the Contagious Diseases Act only seemed to strengthen patriarchal relations, providing justification for increased custodial control over women (Walkowitz 1983, 423–424).

Current legislation in Canada makes prostitution semi-legal. It is not illegal to sell sex, but it is illegal to solicit customers in a public place, to communicate for the purposes of prostitution, to create a public nuisance, or to keep a bawdy house. The net result of such legislation is to give police broad powers to arrest and prosecute women while customers are left alone. These laws significantly increase the risks to women from sometimes deranged or violent male customers. To avoid a charge of soliciting in a public place, the women must get into a customer's car before negotiating a deal or being able to check him out. Similarly, to avoid a charge of keeping a bawdy house, the woman must go to a customer's room rather than bringing different customers back to the same room in which the woman might arrange some protection for herself. Even having a boyfriend is risky because he can be charged with living on the avails of her work. The semi-legal status of prostitution means that the women who do this work have no legal recourse for crimes committed against them (Scott 1987).

In radical feminist theory, pornography ranks alongside prostitution as trade in women's bodies, a multibillion-dollar industry that sells women as sexual objects for men. The extreme position is that any erotica can be seen as problematic in that by packaging women as objects it serves to normalize and naturalize sexism (Mackinnon 1989, Ch. 11; Dworkin 1980). It is morally easier to rape an object than a person, and easier to see women who complain as unnaturally frigid, manipulative, or lying. Others, however, see no problem with nonexploitative erotica depicting sex between consenting adults, and argue against any policing of sexuality for pleasure (Valverde 1987).

There is greater consensus among feminists on the evils of that segment of hard-core pornography that depicts the violent penetration, bondage, and dismemberment of women's bodies as a sexual release for men. But there remains a sharp division of opinion about strategies for dealing with it. Activists such as Mackinnon and Dworkin argue strongly in favour of censorship and prosecution on the grounds that it constitutes hate literature. But many others argue against censorship on practical grounds. Violent pornography is a symptom, not a cause, of sexism, and in a deeply sexist society censorship rarely works as feminist advocates intend. On the one hand, illicit materials only increase in value. They do not disappear. On the other hand, experience indicates that censors often ban materials that women themselves want, such as information on contraceptives and sex education. The main targets of censorship by Canada Customs have been bookstores that carry lesbian and gay erotica. Ironically, even Dworkin's book opposing violent pornography has been banned because it discusses violent sex (*Globe and Mail*, 12 Feb. 1994, D1, D5).

Men's Liberation or Antisexism

Feminist analysis of gender relations as patriarchy raises difficult questions for the relationship of men generally to the women's movement. Responses within the men's movement have varied from active hostility and backlash against feminism (Faludi 1991) to challenges to hegemonic forms of masculinity, and to attempts to deal with issues of male privilege and power in relations with women. From the feminist perspective, any approach to men's liberation that does not directly address this power imbalance constitutes antifeminism. Much of the literature on **men's liberation** has focused on the oppressive character of male socialization. Men are invited to learn how to become more nurturing and emotionally expressive, and more involved with children. The problem with this focus is that it rarely incorporates an analysis of sexism as political action (Lyttleton 1990). In its extreme form, oppression disappears altogether; it is men who are oppressed while women are conceptualized as having the power of motherhood, or the power to engulf and humiliate men behind the scenes. Men's liberation becomes part of the discourse of sexism that challenges women's struggle towards social equality. From the feminist perspective, an antisexist men's movement has to begin with the recognition of power and incorporate the intention to counteract it. The power of hegemonic heterosexist masculinity to marginalize and subordinate other expressions of masculinity is part of this antisexist struggle.

Limitations of Feminist Theory

Taking the standpoint of women has illuminated aspects of the social world that were invisible to mainstream social theories. The concept of patriarchy has proven a powerful analytical tool in challenging the taken-for-grantedness of gender relations and turning the spotlight on practices of gender inequality. The problem with this spotlight approach, however, is that many of the subtleties and inconsistencies of social life disappear from view.

Feminist theorizing is prone to categoricalism, the tendency to view social relations in terms of two internally undifferentiated categories of male and female, related by power and conflicts of interest. This singular view of a woman's standpoint is being challenged by women from many different minority group backgrounds as itself an oppressive form of theorizing that reflects white, middle-class, heterosexist bias. Women of colour have argued that systemic racism—the inequalities organized along lines of racial and ethnic differences—has as profound an impact as gender inequalities upon their lives and those of their family members (Kline 1989). They cannot simply align themselves politically with women and against men. Other women cite classism and the social organization of poverty as more central to their lives than gender. Women who never excelled in school find little to interest them in the preoccupation of academic feminists with gender equality in professional careers. Lesbian women describe their sense of oppression and ostracism as they struggle against the heterosexism within the mainstream feminist movement (Bunch 1975; Kinsman 1991, 93). A typical response within feminist analysis has been to try to incorporate diversity by adding categories to the theory of gender. But as the "isms" proliferate, the analytical utility of division into categories itself comes into question. A more dynamic analysis of practical politics seems needed.

An implicit functionalism underlies much feminist theorizing, particularly radical feminism. Analysis tends to be framed in terms of how the social system is organized for a purpose, and that purpose is male control of women's sexuality. The function of elements within the system is understood through the contribution they make to the maintenance of this pattern. The conceptualization of the state as a patriarchal system organized to protect and defend male dominance is an extreme statement of this

position (Mackinnon 1989). This approach, however, has all the limitations and the rigidities of systems theory. It posits a level of systematization and singularity of purpose that do not reflect experience. It is by no means evident that state repression is directed principally at women. When the state is repressive, young men are much more likely to be the targets than are women (Connell 1987, 128). In Canadian prisons, for example, men outnumber women by a ratio of more than nine to one. Although it may be true that women are more likely to be attacked by men than men are to be attacked by women, it is also true that other males are far more likely to be targets of male violence than are women. The notion of patriarchy offers little to the understanding of men's experience of other men (Frank 1992, 297).

The relationship between state institutions and the women's movement is full of inconsistencies. Universal franchise, affirmative action policies in employment, and Charter protection are only some examples of state support for cherished goals of the women's movement, and these coexist with policies to reduce child support or daycare programs. The legal system is similarly full of inconsistencies and contradictory practices. Like the state, it is more usefully understood as the site of multiple practices and struggles than as the unified and purposive agent of sexist policy (Smart 1989, Ch. 1). Women's experiences within nuclear families are similarly so diverse and multifaceted that they cannot be captured solely by the notion of family as a patriarchal institution.

The active agency of women themselves is curiously understated in some feminist writings. They are sometimes portrayed as the passive victims of male aggression and dominance than as actively constructing their own lives. This has been especially true with respect to the analysis of sexuality. Some of the women who work as prostitutes describe their ambivalent relationship to feminism, rejecting the patronizing image of themselves as victims (Scott 1987; Kinsman 1986). Underneath the radical feminist critique of prostitution and pornography they suggest is a puritanical conception of female passionlessness and male sexual control.

These disagreements seem to stem less from the intent of feminist analysis than the effect of an overly simplistic conceptualization of power. While power is recognized in feminist theory, the practical politics of choice, doubt, strategy, planning, error, and transformation are often not adequately developed (Connell 1987, 61). The current trend in feminist sociology within Canada is towards a merging of social constructionist and feminist analysis that seeks to retain the insights into gender inequality that the concept of patriarchy provides, while avoiding the rigidities of systems theory analysis.

SUGGESTED READING

Elaine Morgan's book *The Descent of Women* (1972) gives a very entertaining and insightful critique of sociobiological explanations of gender differences and human evolution. She speculates on a woman-centred sociobiology and in the process reveals the biases inherent in much of this literature. Esther Greenglass's article on "Socialization of Girls and Boys" (1992) provides many illustrations of how mothers and fathers interact differently with sons and daughters and how these experiences may be linked to distinctive gender traits.

Susannah Wilson's book *Women, The Family and the Economy* (1986), especially Part 3 on women's work, gives a powerful historical analysis of how women have been exploited in the Canadian labour force, and what the impact is on other aspects of women's lives. Meg Luxton's study of the lives of women in the small mining town of Flin Flon, *More than a Labour of Love* (1980), is a deeply moving account of the impact of virtual lifelong economic dependency on relationships between husbands and wives in the town.

Harold Garfinkel's study of Agnes in *Studies in Ethnomethodology* (1967, Ch. 5) is an unusual and fascinating account of the social construction of an alternative gender. Agnes describes how she accomplished "being normally and naturally a female all along" for years before her sex-change operation.

Jonathan Katz's article "The Invention of Heterosexuality" (1990) pushes us to recognize how what we currently assume to be "natural" heterosexual desires and feelings are quite recent inventions that reflect specific historical and cultural conditions. Gary Kinsman's article "Men Loving Men: The Challenge of Gay Liberation" (1987a) pushes us to recognize and to question heterosexist assumptions concerning what is "normal." Didi Khayatt's study of "Legalized Invisibility: The Effect of Bill 7 on Lesbian Teachers" (1990) reveals how vulnerable and secretive are the lives of lesbian teachers, notwithstanding legislation that formally prohibits discrimination on the basis of sexual orientation.

Heidi Hartmann's article on "The Unhappy Marriage of Marxism and Feminism" (1984) provides a detailed historical account of the organized discrimination practised by male workers against women co-workers. Catharine A. Mackinnon's text *Toward a Feminist Theory of the State* (1989) offers a series of essays from a stridently radical feminist perspective that document the power and the violence associated with patriarchy.

QUESTIONS

1. Distinguish between sex role and gender role. What is problematic about this distinction?
2. What key observation is used to support the theory of biological determinism in role behaviour?
3. In functionalist theory, what key process is held to account both for variation and for stability in gender-role behaviour?
4. How do sociobiology and functionalism differentially explain the apparent predisposition for females to do domestic work?
5. In feminist psychoanalysis, what single factor is seen as explaining the ambivalence and hostility of many men towards women?
6. What problem challenges the prediction that gender equality would follow women's entry into the paid labour force?
7. Contrast functionalist and Marxist explanations for evidence that girls appear less motivated than boys to do advanced school work.
8. What is the goal of ethnomethodological analysis with respect to gender?
9. List three mechanisms by which Eichler feels the Bem scale produces a distorted view of gender behaviour.
10. List two ways in which Foucault sees the "knowledge" of experts as a power mechanism.

KEY TERMS

berdache

family wages

gender

gender roles

gender-role socialization

heterosexism

men's liberation

patriarchy

relations of reproduction

sex

sex roles

sociobiology

REFERENCES

Armstrong, P., and H. Armstrong. 1992. "Lessons from Pay Equity." In *Feminism in Action*. Ed. M.P. Connelly and P. Armstrong. Toronto: Canadian Scholars Press, 295–316.

Armstrong, P., and H. Armstrong. 1990. *Theorizing Women's Work*. Toronto: Garamond.

Backhouse, C. 1991. *Petticoats and Prejudice: Women and Law in Nineteenth-Century Canada*. Toronto: Women's Press.

Bem, S.L. 1974. "The Measurement of Psychological Androgyny." *Journal of Consulting and Clinical Psychology* 42 (2): 155–162.

Bissett-Johnson, A. 1988. "Murdoch Case." In *The Canadian Encyclopedia*. 2nd ed. Vol. 3. Edmonton: Hurtig, 1405.

Bland, L. 1985. "In the Name of Protection: The Policing of Women in the First World War." In *Women-In-Law: Explorations in Law, Family, and Sexuality*. Ed. J. Brophy and C. Smart. London: Routledge & Kegan Paul, 23–49.

Boyd, S.B. 1993. "Investigating Gender Bias in Canadian Child Custody Law: Reflections on Questions and Methods." In *Investigating Gender Bias: Law, Courts, and the Legal Profession*. Ed. J. Brockman and D. Chunn. Toronto: Thompson Educational, 169–190.

Boyle, C. and S.W. Rowley. 1987. "Sexual Assault and Family Violence: Reflections on Bias." In *Equality and Judicial Neutrality*. Eds. S. Martin and K. Mahoney. Toronto: Carswell, 312–326.

Breckenridge, J. 1985. "Equal Pay's Unequal Effect." *Report on Business Magazine* (Dec.).

Brittan, A. 1989. *Masculinity and Power*. Oxford: Basil Blackwell.

Brockman, J., and D. Chunn. 1993. *Investigating Gender Bias: Law, Courts, and the Legal Profession*. Toronto: Thompson Educational.

Bunch, C. 1975. "Not for Lesbians Only." *Quest* 11 (2): 245–248.

Carby, H.V. 1982. "White Woman Listen! Black Feminism and the Boundaries of Sisterhood." In *The Empire Strikes Back: Race and Racism in 70s Britain*. Centre for Contemporary Cultural Studies. London: Hutchinson, 212–235.

Chodorow, N. 1978. *The Reproduction of Mothering: Psychoanalysis and the Sociology of Gender*. Berkeley: University of California Press.

Clark, L.M.G., and D.L. Lewis. 1977. *Rape: The Price of Coercive Sexuality*. Toronto: Women's Press.

Connell, R.W. 1987. *Gender and Power: Society, the Person and Sexual Politics*. Palo Alto, California: Stanford University Press.

David, D.S., and R. Brannon, eds. 1976. *The Forty-Nine Percent Majority: The Male Sex Role*. New York: Random House.

Dawkins, R. 1976. *The Selfish Gene*. London: Oxford University Press.

DeKeseredy, W.S., and R. Hinch. 1991. *Woman Abuse: Sociological Perspectives*. Toronto: Thompson Educational.

Dinnerstein, D. 1976. *The Mermaid and the Minotaur: Sexual Arrangements and Human Malaise*. New York: Harper & Row.

Donzelot, J. 1979. *The Policing of Families*. New York: Pantheon.

Dworkin, A. 1980. "Pornography: A Hatred Without Bounds." *New Directions for Women* (Nov.–Dec.): 20.

Ehrenreich, B., and D. English. 1979. *For Her Own Good: 150 Years of Experts' Advice to Women*. Garden City, New York: Anchor Books.

Eichler, M. 1988. *Families in Canada Today: Recent Changes and Their Policy Consequences*. 2nd ed. Toronto: Gage.

Eichler, M. 1985. "The Pro-Family Movement: Are They For or Against Families?" *Feminist Perspectives Series*. Ottawa: Canadian Research Institute for the Advancement of Women.

Eichler, M. 1980. *The Double Standard: A Feminist Critique of Feminist Social Science*. London: Croom Helm.

Eisenstein, Z.R. 1984. *Feminism and Sexual Equality: Crisis in Liberal America*. New York: Monthly Review Press.

Engels, F. [1884] 1978. "The Origins of the Family, Private Property, and the State." In *The Marx-Engels Reader*. 2nd ed. Ed. R.C. Tucker. New York: W.W. Norton, 734–759.

Faludi, S. 1991. *Backlash: The Undeclared War Against American Women*. New York: Doubleday Anchor Books.

Fenn, M. 1980. *In the Spotlight: Women Executives in a Changing Environment*. Englewood Cliffs, New Jersey: Prentice-Hall.

Findlay, B. 1975. "Shrink! Shrank! Shriek!" In *Women Look at Psychiatry*. Ed. D.E. Smith and S.J. David. Vancouver: Press Gang.

Fine, G.A. 1992. "The Dirty Play of Little Boys." In *Men's Lives*. 2nd ed. Ed. M.S. Kimmel and M.A. Messner. New York: Macmillan, 135–143.

Foucault, M. 1978. *The History of Sexuality*. Vol. 1. New York: Vintage.

Frank, B. 1992. "Hegemonic Heterosexual Masculinity: Sports, Looks and a Woman, That's What Every Guy Needs to be Masculine." Paper presented at 26th Annual Meeting of Atlantic Association of Sociologists and Anthropologists. Session on Violence and Social Control in the Home, Workplace, Community and Institutions. ISER Conference Paper #3, ISER, Memorial University of Newfoundland.

Freud, S. [1905] 1976. "Three Essays on the Theory of Sexuality." In *The Complete Psychological Works*. Trans. and ed. J. Strachey. Vol. 7. New York: Norton.

Freud, S. 1905. *The Standard Edition of the Complete Psychological Works of Sigmund Freud*. Vol. 7. *The Three Essays on the Theory of Sexuality*. London: The Hogarth Press.

Garfinkel, H. 1967. *Studies in Ethnomethodology*. Englewood Cliffs, New Jersey: Prentice-Hall.

Gaskell, J. 1988. "The Reproduction of Family Life: Perspectives of Male and Female Adolescents." In *Gender and Society: Creating a Canadian Women's Sociology*. Ed. A.T. McLaren. Toronto: Copp Clark Pitman, 146–168.

Gaskell, J., A. McLaren, and M. Novogrodsky. 1989. *Claiming an Education: Feminism and Canadian Schools*. Toronto: Our Schools/Our Selves Education Foundation.

Goldberg, S. 1973. *The Inevitability of Patriarchy*. New York: William Morrow.

Goode, W.J. 1982. *The Family*. 2nd ed. Englewood Cliffs, New Jersey: Prentice-Hall.

Gray, S. 1987. "Sharing the Shop Floor." In *Women and Men: Interdisciplinary Readings on Gender*. Ed. G. Hofmann Nemiroff. Toronto: Fitzhenry & Whiteside, 377–402.

Greenglass, E. 1992. "Socialization of Girls and Boys: How Gender Roles Are Acquired." In *Sociology for Canadians: A Reader*. 2nd ed. Ed. A. Himelfarb and C.J. Richardson. Toronto: McGraw-Hill Ryerson, 203–212.

Hale, S.M. 1988. "Male Culture and Purdah for Women: The Social Construction of What Women Think Women Think." *Canadian Review of Sociology and Anthropology* 25 (2): 276–298.

Hale, S.M. 1987. "The Documentary Construction of Female Mismanagement." *Canadian Review of Sociology and Anthropology* 24 (4): 489–513.

Harlow, H.F. 1965. "Sexual Behavior in the Rhesus Monkey." In *Sex and Behavior*. Ed. F.A. Beach. New York: Wiley.

Harlow, H.F. 1962. "The Heterosexual Affectional System in Monkeys." *American Psychologist* 17: 1–9.

Hartmann, H.I. 1984. "The Unhappy Marriage of Marxism and Feminism: Towards a More Progressive Union." In *Feminist Frameworks: Alternative Theoretical Accounts of the Relations Between Women and Men*. 2nd ed. Ed. A.M. Jaggar and P.S. Rothenberg. New York: McGraw-Hill, 171–189.

Hennig, M., and A. Jardim. 1981. *The Managerial Woman*. New York: Anchor Books.

Hochschild, A. 1983. *The Managed Heart*. Berkeley: University of California Press.

Hoffman, L.W. 1977. "Changes in Family Roles, Socialization and Sex Differences." *American Psychologist* 32: 644–667.

Katz, J.N. 1990. "The Invention of Heterosexuality." *Socialist Review* 1: 7–34.

Kessler, S.J., and W. McKenna. 1978. *Gender: An Ethnomethodological Approach*. Chicago: University of Chicago Press.

Khayatt, M.D. 1990. "Legalized Invisibility: The Effect of Bill 7 on Lesbian Teachers." *Women's Studies International Forum* 13 (3): 185–193.

Kinsman, G. 1991. "'Homosexuality' Historically Reconsidered Challenges Heterosexual Hegemony." *The Journal of Historical Sociology* 4 (2): 91–111.

Kinsman, G. 1987a. "Men Loving Men: The Challenge of Gay Liberation." In *Beyond Patriarchy: Essays by Men on Pleasure, Power and Change*. Ed. M. Kaufman. Toronto: Oxford University Press, 103–119.

Kinsman, G. 1987b. *The Regulation of Desire: Sexuality in Canada*. Montreal: Black Rose Books.

Kinsman, G. 1986. "Whores Fight Back: Valerie Scott of CORP on Empowering Prostitutes." *Rites* (May): 8–9, 19.

Kline, M. 1989. "Women's Oppression and Racism: A Critique of the 'Feminist Standpoint.'" In *Race, Class, Gender: Bonds and Barriers*. Ed. J. Vorst et al. Toronto: Between the Lines (for the Society for Socialist Studies, Winnipeg).

Larwood, L., and M.M. Wood. 1977. *Women in Management*. Lexington, Massachusetts: Lexington Books.

Lehne, G.K. 1976. "Homophobia Among Men." In *The Forty-Nine Percent Majority: The Male Sex Role*. Ed. D.S. David and R. Brannon. New York: Random House, 66–92.

Luxton, M. 1980. *More than a Labour of Love: Three Generations of Women's Work in the Home*. Toronto: Women's Press.

Lynn, D.B. 1974. *The Father: His Role in Child Development*. Monterey, California: Wadsworth.

Lyttleton, N. 1990. "Men's Liberation, Men Against Sexism and Major Dividing Lines." In *Women and Men*. Ed. G. Hofmann Nemiroff. Toronto: Fitzhenry & Whiteside, 472–477.

Maccoby, E., and C.N. Jacklin. 1974. *The Psychology of Sex Differences*. Palo Alto, California: Stanford University Press.

Mackie, M. 1991. *Gender Relations in Canada: Further Explorations*. Toronto: Butterworths.

Mackinnon, C.A. 1989. *Toward a Feminist Theory of the State*. Cambridge, Massachusetts: Harvard University Press.

Maynard, R., with C. Brouse. 1988. "Thanks, But No Thanks." *Report on Business Magazine* (Feb.): 26–34.

McRobbie, A. 1991. *Feminism and Youth Culture*. Houndsmills, UK: MacMillan Education.

McRobbie, A. 1978. "Working Class Girls and the Culture of Femininity." In *Women Take Issue: Aspects of Women's Subordination*. London: Hutchinson, 96–108.

Mead, M. 1935. *Sex and Temperament in Three Primitive Societies*. New York: William Morrow.

Messner, M. 1992. "Boyhood, Organized Sports, and the Construction of Masculinities." In *Men's Lives*. 2nd ed. Ed. M.S. Kimmel and M.A. Messner. New York: Macmillan, 161–173.

Midnight Sun. 1988. "Sex/Gender Systems in Native North America." In *Living the Spirit: A Gay American Indian Anthology*. Ed. W. Roscoe and comp. Gay American Indians. New York: St. Martin's Press, 32–47.

Morgan, E. 1972. *The Descent of Woman*. New York: Stein & Day.

O'Brien, M. 1981. *The Politics of Reproduction*. London: Routledge & Kegan Paul.

Orbach, S. 1979. *Fat Is a Feminist Issue: A Self-Help Guide for Compulsive Eaters*. New York: Berkley Books.

Prentice, A., et al. 1988. *Canadian Women: A History*. Toronto: Harcourt Brace Jovanovich.

Rheingold, H., and K. Cook. 1975. "The Content of Boys' and Girls' Rooms as an Index of Parent Behavior." *Child Development* 46: 459–463.

Roscoe, W. 1988. "The Zuni Man–Woman." *Outlook* 1 (2): 56–67.

Scott, V. 1987. "C-49: A New Wave of Oppression." In *Good Girls/Bad Girls:Sex Trade Workers and Feminists Face to Face*. Ed. L. Bell. Toronto: Women's Press, 100–103.

Smart, C. 1989. *Feminism and the Power of Law*. London: Routledge.

Smart, C. 1984. *The Ties That Bind: Law, Marriage and the Reproduction of Patriarchal Relations*. London: Routledge & Kegan Paul.

Smith, D.E. 1990. "Femininity as Discourse." In *Texts, Facts, and Femininity: Exploring the Relations of Ruling*. Ed. D.E. Smith. New York: Routledge, 159–208.

Smith, G.W. 1992. "The Ideology of 'Fag': Barriers to Education for Gay Students." Ontario Institute for Studies in Education. Mimeographed.

Synnott, A. 1992. "Little Angels, Little Devils: A Sociology of Children." In *Sociology for Canadians: A Reader*. 2nd ed. Ed. A. Himelfarb and C.J. Richardson. Toronto: McGraw-Hill Ryerson, 191–202.

Tiger, L. 1969. *Men in Groups*. New York: Random House.

Valverde, M. 1987. "Too Much Heat, Not Enough Light." In *Good Girls/Bad Girls:Sex Trade Workers and Feminists Face to Face*. Ed. L. Bell. Toronto: Women's Press, 27–32.

Van Gelder, L., and C. Carmichael. 1975. "But What About Our Sons?" *Ms* 4: 52–56.

Walkowitz, J.R. 1983. "Male Vice and Female Virtue: Feminism and the Politics of Prostitution in Nineteenth-Century Britain." In *Powers of Desire: The Politics of Sexuality*. Ed. A. Snitow, C. Stansell, and S. Thompson. New York: Monthly Review Press, 419–438.

Warskett, R. 1988. "Bank Worker Unionization and the Law." *Studies in Political Economy* 25 (Spring): 41–73.

White, J. 1980. *Women and Unions*. Ottawa: Supply and Services Canada (for the Canadian Advisory Council on the Status of Women).

Wilson, S.J. 1986. *Women, the Family and the Economy*. 2nd ed. Toronto: McGraw-Hill Ryerson.

Loss of Community?
The Rural–Urban Debate

The question mark in the title of this chapter is significant. It is a signal that what you will find here is not a collection of factual knowledge. Rather, you will confront conflicting evidence and interpretations concerning the nature of rural and urban communities, both now and in the past. This on-going debate surrounding patterns of social change calls into question many fundamental assumptions about the nature of human communities.

The methodology of social science is a critical issue in this chapter. The first section traces the processes of formulating a theory, spelling out its basic assumptions, testing them against evidence, and framing conclusions about whether the original theory worked and how it might be modified or replaced by alternative theories that seem better able to account for the evidence at hand.

The classical loss of community thesis originated in the conservative worldview that prevailed in late nineteenth and early twentieth centuries in Europe. The assumptions implicit in this pessimistic worldview were spelled out in a theory concerning the characteristics of community life and how they were being threatened by forces of industrialization and urbanization. This theory has empirical consequences, and it is these consequences that can be compared with evidence collected through research. In principle, evidence that conflicts with the expected consequences challenges the assumptions on which the initial theory was based and so prompts its revision. In practice, however, this linear progress is complicated by the development of competing theories that search for very different kinds of evidence. What is particularly problematic is that theories can easily generate blind spots and distortions in the amassing of evidence. As a result, new research may generate more and more evidence that seems to lend overwhelming support for the prevailing theory. Competing theories face a major battle in reinterpreting what is perceived as existing "knowledge."

LOSS OF COMMUNITY THESIS

The loss of community thesis is rooted in the belief that, from the nineteenth century onwards, communities in Europe underwent profound changes with the development of industrialized, urban centres. The thesis includes a nostalgia for the past and for a vision of a more humane form of **community** characterized by harmonious, integrated, and stable relationships, and collective sentiments of loyalty and belonging. In contrast, the present social world is seen as characterized by growing individualism, with concomitant disharmony, disintegration, instability, disloyalty, and lack of sense of belonging. In effect, the thesis constitutes a basic critique of **industrialization** and urban life.

Gemeinschaft and Gesellschaft: Community and Association

The German theorist Ferdinand Tönnies was the first major exponent of the loss of community thesis, which was set out in his study entitled *Gemeinschaft und Gesellschaft* (1887). The term **gemeinschaft** can loosely be translated into English as *community* and **gesellschaft** as *association*. Tönnies argues that the pattern of social life that emerged with industrialization differed profoundly from what went before. Pre-industrial society is characterized by what Tönnies refers to as "natural will." Relations among people are governed by natural ties of kinship and long-established friendship, by familiarity and liking, and by age-old habit and customary ways of doing things. Industrial society, in contrast, is characterized by "rational will." Relations among people are governed by careful deliberation and evaluation of means and ends, or the advantages that people expect to gain from others. Tönnies viewed the gemeinschaft community as akin to the natural community of a living organism. It involves an underlying consensus based on kinship, on residence in a common locality, and on friendship. Relations exist for their own sake and cannot be arbitrarily terminated. Social position or status in such a community is clearly defined by birth, based on who one's parents and ancestors were, and on one's sex and age. Personal achievements, education, property, and the like, matter little compared with status ascribed by birth. Moreover, most people remain within the same status group, as peasants or nobles, throughout life. People are also geographically immobile, staying in or close by the same locality.

These stable communities are generally homogenous. People are descended from the same racial stock, and they share the same ethnic identity, religion, language, and way of life, all enforced by the central institutions of church and family. These institutions in turn derive their strength from the people's unquestioned acceptance of them as natural. Core values within this culture are the sanctity of kinship ties, solidarity as a community, and attachment to the locality. People share a sentimental attachment to conventions handed down through generations of ancestors. Their community operates through dense networks of interaction among people who are highly interrelated through marriage, who know each other well, and who know that they hold cherished values in common.

The gesellschaft pattern of relations differs so greatly from this traditional form as scarcely to warrant the term "community." Tönnies refers to this form as an association of people based on principles of contract and exchange. He views such society as merely a mechanical aggregate rather than a living organism, an artificial society that is transitory and superficial, and emerges out of competitive struggles among individuals who do not feel themselves bound together by either kinship or religion. People are geographically mobile and, hence, tend to be heterogenous with respect to racial and ethnic origins and religious beliefs. Relations among individuals are impersonal, based on rational calculation of advantage. In such calculations the spirit of neighbourly love and the virtues and morality of community life are lost. People tend to collect in large-scale agglomerations rather than in small local groups.

Tönnies' vision of gesellschaft—the collapse of community life into an association of individuals motivated by calculated self-interest—was intended as a critique of the order of society underlying industrialization. The fundamental values of capitalism, and the rational pursuit of profit and individual advantage generate dehumanized and artificial relations.

George Simmel, a German theorist who was a contemporary of Tönnies, modified Tönnies' ideas to apply more specifically to rural versus urban settings. Simmel identified gemeinschaft patterns with rural communities and gesellschaft with urban. He proposed further that a unidirectional process of change was occurring from rural to urban type. Urban life appeared essentially rational, with only weak emotional attachments. Diverse occupations and interests further weakened local controls. Simmel feared that this weakening of communal solidarity in urban areas would lead to the collapse of a stable social order. Rural community life appeared to be superior to urban lifestyles.

The overwhelming impression that comes through these theories of urbanism is a sense of loss and regress, rather than positive change for the better. The term "loss of community" expresses dissatisfaction with the quality of contemporary urban life and a desire to return to a more humane society where individuals were integrated into stable and harmonious communities of family, neighbours, and friends. The past may well not have been as rosy as this idealized image of integrated community life, but the feeling of loss cannot be dismissed as merely misguided nostalgia, for what they articulate is a deep criticism of the present.

The Chicago School

A number of sociologists working together at the University of Chicago in the late 1920s and 1930s developed a broad body of theory and research into urban life that became known as **The Chicago School** of urban sociology. Louis Wirth, Robert Redfield, Robert Park, and Ernest Burgess are important individual theorists in this group. They researched stages in the development of the city of Chicago in the industrial heartland of America. Successive waves of immigrants with diverse racial, ethnic, and linguistic backgrounds, arrived from many parts of the world, attracted by expanding opportunities for jobs and commerce. The city thus provided an inexhaustible natural laboratory for the study of urban life. Park and others developed the *concentric zone theory* of urban development (Park 1932, 1952; Park et al. 1925, 1967). Typically, impoverished newcomers settled first in densely populated inner city areas where older, slum housing was cheap. Over time, they gradually moved outwards to find somewhat better accommodations while new immigrants took their places in the city centre. Longer-term residents in the new zone were in turn moving yet further outwards to more spacious suburbs.

One of these Chicago theorists, Louis Wirth, in his essay "Urbanism as a Way of Life" (1938), set out a formal theory in which he suggests that the characteristics of the city *as a city* explain the patterns of culture identified by Tönnies, Simmel, and others. Wirth identified three critical variables as causal determinants of the gesellschaft type of community: size, density, and heterogeneity.

The large size of urban centres inevitably gives rise to differentiation between people. It becomes impossible to know and to interact with everyone over a wide variety of concerns. Hence, interactions inevitably become limited and specialized, and therefore superficial, transitory, and anonymous. The result, suggests Wirth, is the experience of individual loneliness within the urban crowd.

The second key variable is *density*. People are concentrated in a limited space where they experience overcrowding and pollution. Like rats artificially crowded together in laboratories, people are forced into a competitive struggle for space. Laboratory rats, housed in a spacious cage, live peacefully together. But as more and more animals are crowded into the same space, their behaviour changes. They become increasingly aggressive and more likely to inflict injuries on one another (see studies by Hall 1966, Ch. 1; Calhoun 1963; Michelson 1970, 6–7). Wirth reasoned that overcrowding in cities would generate similar antisocial behaviour among people.

The third variable is *heterogeneity*. People with different racial and ethnic backgrounds and different occupations and statuses are mixed together. In the face of such heterogeneity, people have divided allegiances and hence cannot form a secure sense of belonging, either to their locality or to the people around them.

Notice the subtle but important shift in basic assumptions made by Tönnies and Wirth. For Tönnies, the industrial capitalist values of rational, calculated self-interest both led to the breakup of community life and promoted the impetus to gather in cities that offered economic advantages. In the Chicago School model developed by Wirth, it is the gathering in cities, and the passive variables of size, density, and heterogeneity, that leads to the loss of community values and their eventual replacement by superficial individualism. The critical challenge to capitalism disappears. It is simply urbanism that is seen as causing the changes in community life.

The Chicago School model draws on the same basic assumptions as the functionalist or systems theory perspective. Functionalism emphasizes shared culture and moral consensus as the foundations of social order. **Culture** comprises the complex mix of language, history, symbol systems, values, attitudes, and behavioural expectations. Broad cultural values, along with patterned expectations for behaviour in specific roles, are internalized through early socialization within families, and reinforced by the institutions of church and school. The central social controls that reinforce conformity are internalized sense of guilt, and desire for acceptance and approval. These moral bases for order and control are weak or absent in the urban agglomeration. *Heterogeneity* of social backgrounds means that urban residents lack a common core of culture and moral consensus. Individuals cannot assume that other people have internalized the same behavioural expectations and values. Distrust and fear in interpersonal relations are the likely result of this unpredictability. Moreover, *large size*, and the resulting prevalence of limited and specialized interaction among strangers,

Figure 1 Circles of Social Control

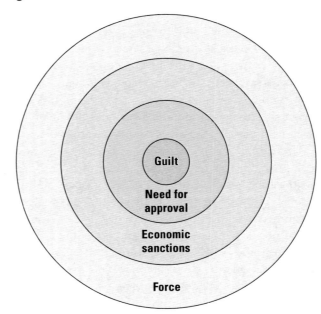

Source: Adapted from Berger (1963), *An Invitation to Sociology,* Doubleday 1963.

weakens traditional sanctions on behaviour. People have less concern with social approval and acceptance from strangers. The other variable, *high density*, increases frustrations and competition and so promotes aggression and crime. In terms of Berger's model of circles of social control (see Figure 1), the intimate controls of guilt and need for social approval cannot be expected to work in this context. With these sanctions weakened, control increasingly has to take the form of force—the option of last resort.

In summary, Wirth's Chicago School model of rural and urban communities predicts that where population settlement is small in size, of low density, and relatively homogenous, as in rural areas, one can expect the sense of community to be strong and characterized by intimate cooperation, and a clear sense of security and personal identity. In contrast, in large cities such as Toronto and Montreal, and more so in metropolises such as Chicago and New York, relationships will be superficial and competitive, with limited sense of belonging to a cohesive and satisfying community. In effect, one can expect to find a rural-to-urban continuum with the sense of community being strongest in the smallest settlements and steadily weaker as the size of the city, overcrowding, and diversity of inhabitants increase.

It is important to keep in mind that while arguments may sound plausible, they are not necessarily correct. They need to be tested in a systematic way against evidence, and this includes looking for cases that might contradict the predictions and so reveal weaknesses in the assumptions. Evidence also has to be scrutinized for the biases and distortion that preconceived notions can impose. The most useful and productive way to test a theory is to compare it with an alternative theory that begins from different assumptions and makes different predictions.

MARXIST THEORY: COMMUNITY AND ECONOMY

An important alternative theory to the Chicago School model is the political economy perspective, which draws heavily on the work of Karl Marx. It starts from different assumptions and makes different predictions about the changing quality of rural and urban community life. This theory finds the same evidence of dehumanization—loss of community and dissatisfaction among people in contemporary urban, industrial society—but explains this evidence in terms of different causes. Marx saw nothing inherently bad about the shift from rural to urban living. On the contrary, he saw city life as liberating people from mind-numbing subservience to land and endlessly repetitive traditional patterns of life (Marx and Engels [1845] 1965, 38; Marx and Engels [1947] 1970, 39–95; Bonner 1998, 166–170). In the cities people were free to think and work independently, and to develop more fully their creative and productive potential.

If city life were experienced as alienating, Marx reasoned, it was not due to factors like size, density, and heterogeneity, but to the dehumanizing effects of capitalism. Capitalism is a system of private control over productive resources that exploits human labour power for private profit. Conditions of poverty, unemployment, and insecurity generated by capitalist organization of production are identified by Marx as fundamental causes of dehumanization in urban society. This theory does not predict that people living in small towns or rural areas will be any more or less happy than people in urban areas. It predicts rather that people who have economic security, and who control their own means of production, will develop satisfying social relations with others, while this sense of community will collapse when fundamental economic security is undermined. To the extent that villages are comprised of farmers or small producers who have both security and independence, such communities are likely to be contented and cohesive. But economically insecure rural poor are predicted to be as likely as the urban poor to experience a breakdown in sense of community.

Political economy theory is closer to the original ideas of Tönnies than is the Chicago School model. It implies an indictment not of cities as such, but of the values of rational, calculated self-interest that pervade industrial capitalist society at all levels. The classical theorist Max Weber argued that this capitalist culture of rationalism would spread pervasively from cities to rural areas, obliterating any cultural distinctions between them. He noted that farmers across the great wheat-producing states in America have always had more in common with urban capitalists than with the traditional agriculturalists of Europe. In essence they were entrepreneurs, wedded to the values of competitive economic individualism, rather than to the folk communities of European villagers (Weber 1946, 364). Weber thus concurred with Marx in predicting that there would be minimal difference between the quality of community life in urban and rural areas.

In the following review of research in rural and urban sociology in Canada, we explore first the contribution of traditional theory to the analysis of pre-capitalist rural life in Quebec, followed by comparative studies of contemporary rural and urban communities. With respect to each broad area, we draw attention to evidence that seems to contradict the basic assumptions of the Chicago School model. Similar research contexts are re-examined from the perspective of political economy theory to test the extent to which it can account for these apparent contradictions. Later in the chapter, we explore the contribution of the social constructionist perspective and the closely related work of feminist urban geography.

FOLK SOCIETY: A TEST OF THE CHICAGO SCHOOL THESIS

Robert Redfield (1947), another contributor to the Chicago School, elaborated an **ideal-type model** of **folk society** to contrast with urban society, drawing on the work of Tönnies, Simmel, and Wirth. An ideal-type model is designed as a tool for research to highlight typical features of the kind of society or social institution being studied. Any particular case may not have all the features listed in the model, but the broad characteristics should be visible. Redfield was particularly interested in the folk communities typical of relatively isolated rural areas. In his model he highlighted five key features: (1) folk communities are organized around family and kinship ties; (2) they involve intimate face-to-face relations; (3) they have minimal specialization or division of labour; (4) people are united by a strong sense of local identity, loyalties, and obligations; and (5) the members support a deep commitment to shared cultural values and ways of behaviour.

The model of an urban society incorporates the opposite of these key features, namely: (1) weak family ties; (2) superficial relations between strangers; (3) a high degree of specialization of occupations; (4) limited cohesion; and (5) readiness to adopt new and changing values and ways of behaving. Redfield suggests that the typical differences between a hamlet, a village, a trading centre, and a city can be described in terms of a systematic and linear process of change from folk to urban characteristics.

Redfield (1930) found strong support for his thesis that rural communities are more cohesive than urban centres in his pioneering study of life in Mexico in the 1930s. He describes the small village of Tepoztlan as a homogeneous, smoothly functioning, well-integrated, contented, stable, and harmonious community. He compared it favourably with a neighbouring town, which he characterized as heterogeneous and faction-ridden.

This powerful support for his folk society model was not to go unchallenged, however. A study of the same village by Oscar Lewis (1949), conducted less than 20 years later, shattered the harmonious image, and with it, some of the credibility of Redfield's thesis. Lewis argues that Redfield biased his research by focusing only on cooperative and unifying factors. He charges Redfield with glossing over evidence of violence, cruelty, disease, suffering, poverty, economic and social maladjustment, and political schisms. Redfield later attempted to defend himself by arguing that Lewis had imposed his own value judgments on his research. Lewis wanted to find support for the Marxist argument that the low material standard of living in Tepoztlan gave rise to social maladjustment. Hence, he went out of his way to look for evidence of suffering and stress in the community, and then overemphasized the problems that he found. Whatever the validity of this response by Redfield, Lewis's work did challenge the image of the village as an ideal-type gemeinschaft community.

Quebec Folk Society

In Canadian research, studies of the folk society of rural Quebec offer powerful and convincing descriptions of life that accord closely with the gemeinschaft image. But these studies, too, have been subject to the criticism that researchers found just what they were looking for, rather than what was actually there. A widely cited study of French-Canadian folk society is one by Horace Miner (1939) on the parish of St Denis. Robert Redfield wrote the introduction to the book, and he leaves no doubt that he views St Denis as the epitome of a folk society: "Habitants live in terms of common understandings which are rooted in tradition . . . Fundamental views of life are shared by everyone, and these views find consistent expression in the beliefs, institutions, rituals, and manners of the people" (Redfield 1964, 58). Sanctions have a strongly sacred character in St Denis. The way of life of the people is endorsed by the priest, but followed because of deeply felt convictions of the people themselves rather than due to any pressure from outside authority. The family system is also strong, pervasive, and certain in its effects. Almost all aspects of life—work, getting married, finding a career, politics—are largely determined by position in a family. There is minimal social disorganization.

Redfield and Miner acknowledge that St Denis was part of a modern urbanized world, not an isolated peasant community, but argue that this connection is weak. People do have connections with the city, and even relatives who live there, but their exposure to alien influences is mediated by the Catholic Church, which "has stood between the changing world and the habitant, preventing admission of elements which she [the church] condemns and interpreting admitted elements in accordance with the faith, and with the local culture" (Redfield 1964, 60). When local ways are threatened, the church minimizes the influence of outside forces and so helps to preserve the folk character of the community.

The only threat to this way of life has come from the structural problem of land pressure (Miner 1964, 66), a consequence of traditionally large families, indivisible small farms, and limited supply of land. Farmers needed money to educate sons for alternative city jobs or to buy farms for them. The result, suggests Miner, was the gradual erosion of independent subsistence farming as a way of life. Farmers slowly became more dependent on the outside economy. The only other solution to the land pressure problems would have been to cut the birth rate, but Miner argues that this was strongly opposed by the Catholic Church, which has always played a vital role in the rural parish. Birth rates declined rapidly in urban areas during the interwar years, but not in the villages, suggesting to Miner that the old culture of religion and **familism**—or life centring on the family—was not disrupted.

Hubert Guindon (1964) and Marcel Rioux (1964) similarly defend the appropriateness of the folk society model as applied to rural Quebec until well into the twentieth century. They cite evidence of strong family ties, low geographic and social mobility, the central importance of inherited land, and the powerful moral leadership of the clergy in perpetuating the folk character of communities such as St Denis. Rioux characterizes rural Quebec as made up of small communities, with few outside contacts, and with people bound together by organic ties of family, culture, and church. It is this folk cultural identity, Rioux suggests, that underlies contemporary Quebec nationalism and the sense of French-Canadian identity. Although Quebec has an urban population, Rioux argues that the province can still be characterized as essentially a rural folk culture.

Challenging the Folk Culture Model

It is Philippe Garigue (1964) who challenges the validity of this folk society thesis in the context of rural Quebec, notwithstanding the wealth of data in its support. Garigue, like Oscar Lewis, argues that the model has led researchers to overemphasize evidence that supports it, and to minimize the relevance of empirical data not related to the definition. He suggests that the concept of *folk society* is not valid in French-Canadian history nor is it appropriate for contemporary rural Quebec. Historically, he argues, there never were the equivalent of close-knit, self-contained, traditionalist, organic communities in rural Quebec. The land was colonized by a process of ribbon development out from small towns that acted as colonial trading posts. Individual farms were established in parallel rows, first fronting a river and then on an interior road build for the purpose.

This pattern of settlement worked against the development of close-knit communities, suggests Garigue. Farmers were fiercely individualistic. They built houses in the middle of their own individual plots about three miles away from neighbours in either direction. Only much later did communities or villages begin to emerge, once a church was built in the district. The church provided an initial gathering place around which other buildings were established. Old people tended to move near the church when they retired, and the locality slowly began to function as a service centre for the district. Only at this stage could a village be said to exist. But the development of such a village centre did not substantially alter the private family individualism of independent farmers. In 1663, Louis XIV of France tried, for administrative convenience, to force settlers or habitants to build houses in village groups rather than on their own land (Falardeau 1964, 20). But such edicts were strongly resisted. Farm families refused to move. People maintained social relationships with the families living on neighbouring plots, but had no desire to form village communities. Parishes were not formed until long after colonial settlement, and they constituted only huge administrative areas. Throughout most of Quebec's history, they could not be equated with rural communities.

Tenancies were frequently bought and sold (Garigue 1964, 126). This too challenges the notion of cohesive, long-settled folk communities. In addition, one researcher found that entire families had moved away from parishes to seek their fortune elsewhere. Nobody seemed to find this unusual or regrettable (Gérin 1964, 36).

The structural constraints of large families, indivisible farms, and limited land meant that the majority of children in any large family could not settle near home. They had to seek a livelihood elsewhere. Thus, there was considerable geographic mobility within families, contradicting the folk society model, despite the near truism that there was low mobility among the people who stayed behind. Usually only the youngest son would inherit the family farm when the parents were too old to farm it themselves. Older sons left. Only the lucky ones among them got farms in neighbouring parishes. This accounts for the observation that rural families in the 1950s were not usually centred in one commu-

nity, but were spread all over the province of Quebec and beyond (Garigue 1964, 134).

Garigue challenges even the notion of an all-embracing church with a subservient flock of parishioners. He cites evidence of widespread accounts of laypersons who refused to obey their priests, or even the bishop, over such matters as building a church and paying dues (Garigue 1964, 129–30). Thus, in multiple ways, Garigue argues that rural settlement in Quebec does not conform to the folk society model. The concept, he suggests, is a myth, an ideology imposed on the data by the researchers. The intensely individualistic, independent farmers that Garigue found have more in common with the image of nuclear family individualism, characteristic of urban life, than with the Chicago School caricature of people embedded within an organic folk society.

The Myth of Quebec Motherhood

Another strong challenge to the notion of folk culture in Quebec comes from an unlikely source, a re-evaluation of fertility data. Marie Lavigne (1986) questions the image of the fertile French-Canadian mother, dominated by the Catholic clergy and local political elites advocating a large French-speaking population. Québécois women have been portrayed as fertile mothers, responding not only to Catholic admonitions to have as many children as possible but also to nationalistic propaganda exhorting "the revenge of the cradle." Lavigne questions how we can reconcile this image with the history of the women's movement in Quebec from the nineteenth century onwards. Her answer is that this fertile mother image is largely a myth, applying at best to about one-fifth of all Quebec women from the 1850s onwards, when her data began. Folk culture values, admonitions from the clergy, lack of access to modern contraceptives, and their illegality prior to 1968 notwithstanding, the birth rate in Quebec fell steadily every decade between 1850 and 1961.

As Table 1 shows, of the women born during the years 1887, 1903, and 1913, at least 25 percent never became

Table 1 Birth Cohorts of Women by Marital Status and Number of Children, Quebec

0	10.8	13.7	11.9
1–2	15.8	21.2	25.2
3–5	21.9	22.8	27.4
6–9	19.7	16.3	14.7
10 or more	17.7	11.0	6.5
Unmarried women	14.1	15.0	14.3
Total	100	100	100

Source: Lavigne (1986). Calculations based on Henripin (1968)

mothers. Most of these childless women remained unmarried, and only a small minority of them became nuns. A further 15 to 25 percent of women made only a minimal contribution to fertility rates by having one or two children. At the other extreme, the ideal, typically large family of 10 or more children was produced by less than one-fifth of the 1887 **cohort**. This ratio dropped to about one in 15 women by 1913. The percentage of women having six or more children also dropped from almost 40 percent to just over 20 percent in the same period. This sharp drop indicates that many girls whose mothers had large numbers of children did not see this model of motherhood as the one they wanted to copy.

Clearly large numbers of women did practice contraception, regardless of the church's teachings on the subject. Interviews in 1950 with elderly women who had their families at the turn of the century indicated that they had not been particularly influenced by church doctrine, despite outward conformity, They practised contraception and still went to church. Lavigne argues from these data that we have to revise our view of the influence of religion on family life in Quebec. It appears to have been considerably shallower than the folk culture model would lead us to believe. We only have to compare these data with Redfield's commentary at the beginning of the study of St Denis—with his references to the sacred character of sanctions, the deeply felt convictions of the people, and the family system as "strong, pervasive, and certain in its effects"—to realize how significant a challenge Lavigne's work presents to taken-for-granted theories.

We still need to ask where the image of fertile French-Canadian women comes from if the majority of women did not conform to it. Lavigne points out that the collective memory that all Québécois ancestors had large families derives from the fact that most people remember the same minority of women. For example, if hypothetically 10 women have one child each and one woman has 10 children, half of the resulting children in the second generation will have grown up in a large family, even though 91 percent of families did not conform to this pattern.

From Lavigne's article we learn that strong convictions, even when they appear well substantiated by evidence, may still give a false overall picture. The folk society concept of large families, inherited land, and overarching religious control by the Catholic Church is not wholly false, in that it does apply to a proportion of people. The problem is that it may not fit more than half the members of the community. The majority of women and men made decisions about their family size that conflicted with the teachings of the church. It cannot even be assumed that women with large families were mindlessly following church edicts. Lavigne suggests that economic factors, like the usefulness of child labour on farms and in the textile mills or the disadvantages of large families once schooling became compulsory, played a role in decisions about family size. Women make rational choices in historical-economic circumstances, Lavigne suggests, rather than conforming unquestioningly to cultural norms. It would seem, then, that the folk culture model obscures more than it reveals about life in rural Quebec.

Contemporary Rural Communities: Challenging the Chicago School Model

The Chicago School model predicts that village communities, characterized by small size, low density, and homogeneity should be socially cohesive, with residents sharing attachment to locality and to a core of shared cultural values. Studies of villages draw heavily on this model (Strathern 1982; Rapport 1993). However, not all studies support this rosy image. Samuel Clark's controversial study of four villages in the Miramichi and Bathurst areas of New Brunswick conducted during 1972–73, describes social life as anything but well-integrated and cohesive. The impression is one of people shut in on themselves, having little contact with the outside world or with their immediate neighbours (Clark 1978, Ch. 3). "No one ever visits," said one respondent. "Television ruined that," said another. "People visit less now, got no reason to visit . . . I'm not one for visiting." Many residents complained about the lack of social activity in their area, yet they gave no indication of intending to do anything about it. "There's not much social life here. People don't try to get together," was a typical response.

Two sets of ties did have some meaning—kinship and church. Almost everyone in the communities was either a relative or a neighbour of a relative of someone else in the community, and few new people moved in. Yet Clark found that kinship obligations appeared shallow and rarely extended beyond the immediate family circle. In Catholic communities virtually everyone went to mass, while in Protestant areas church attendance tended to be associated with higher status. But in either case church did not form the focus of much active social life.

Apart from what limited social life developed around kinship and church, the communities had few organized social activities. A few residents said they belonged to clubs or bought a newspaper, but most did not. Clark concludes that what was generally obtained was "what might be described as a state of anomie." **Anomie** is a state of social breakdown, characterized by weak bonds between people, a limited sense of meaningful relations, and the lack of any strong commitment to shared norms and regulations guiding inter-actions. Most residents expressed little sense of social obliga-tion to their local community, and many gave vent to their grievances, discouragement, and, at times, despair. The dom-inant attitude was a fatalistic acceptance of things as they were.

The two other communities in the study, located on the outskirts of large towns, showed similarly impoverished social life. There was evidence of a good deal of animosity and little visiting among neighbours. One person described her neighbours as "a God-damned bad crowd—from way back in the woods where they never see no people, only bear and fox. Maybe is good people. We can't tell" (Clark 1978, 92). Insecurity and fear of crime were widely felt in these communities. Interviewing was actually cut short because "the field-workers had reason to fear for their physi-cal safety had they attempted any extensive interviewing in the more congested parts of the inner area" (Clark 1978, 73). People were suspicious that interviewers on the project might be government agents, checking on them with the intention of cutting off their welfare payments.

Clark's study is not alone in finding that small size, low density, and homogeneity do not ensure close community ties. The image of idyllic rustic communities may be part of our collective cultural mythology, but it is not part of the contemporary reality of village and small-town life. A 1983 study of towns and villages in Canada cites public opinion polls that record preferences for farm and small community living, and nostalgia for the peace and friendliness and sim-plicity of life in the countryside for city-weary, ecology-conscious, and independent urbanites. But the study itself found little evidence to support these images (Hodge and Qadeer 1983, 131). The study suggests that, while individ-ual towns and villages differ widely from each other, pat-terns of daily life show minimal differences between rural and metropolitan centres.

The study further showed that small communities are not necessarily safer places than big cities. The per capita incidence of crimes of violence may actually be higher in small towns than in cities. To the outside world, small towns and villages may present a face of serenity, but internally they are communities with a fair degree of individualism and social division (Hodge and Qadeer 1983, 143). Smallness results in high visibility, and hence familiarity between resi-dents, but this does not necessarily lead to sociability and friendliness. Often small towns harbour a hard core of poverty that is combined with a general indifference towards the poor. Prejudice is also often present. Racial and ethnic minorities may be tolerated, but they are often made to feel unwelcome.

These negative accounts of social disorganization in rural communities should not be taken to imply that all, or even most, rural communities are characterized by social anomie. Towns and villages vary widely, and many residents experience a satisfying community life. The critical point here is that smallness, low-density living, and homogeneity by themselves do not guarantee integrated community spirit. To explain such patterns we need more complex theories than the Chicago School model provides.

 # Political Economy Analysis of Small Communities

Researchers who begin from the perspective of political economy offer new insights into the economic determi-nants of loss of community and why such loss seems more in evidence in some contexts than in others. They focus not on the demographic characteristics of different localities, but on the surrounding economy and the destructive impact of economic insecurity, poverty, and exploitation. Political economy theory predicts that, regardless of size or location, the communities that will show the most evidence of social disorganization and demoralization will be areas of rela-tively severe poverty, or more importantly, where people are losing their basic sense of economic security and control over their life situation.

The study of villages in the Miramichi region of New Brunswick in the early 1970s gives ample evidence of pro-longed economic decline, which is consistent with the con-ditions of social anomie found by researchers. Clark suggests that the poor quality of farmland, with the exception of iso-lated pockets of fertile soil near rivers, could support only a **subsistence** level of living. In other words, the farms might provide sufficient food, fuel, and building materials to meet the basic necessities of life for a family, but they provided little surplus produce that could be marketed. Most farmers depended on supplementing their farm income with part-time work as woodsmen, fishers, or labourers. Some farms became more prosperous as the opening of nearby urban markets promoted commercial farming, but success was not possible for all, and many were ruined by debt (Clark 1978).

A collection of articles on primary producers in the Atlantic region (Burrill and McKay 1978) documents the extensive destruction of the rural Maritime economy to the state of near catastrophe for many communities. Between 1941 and 1981, for example, the number of farms in New Brunswick dropped from 26 000 to 4000, as highly mechanized corporate capitalist farming took over the po-tato industry. What happened to the 22 000 displaced farm-ers and their families? Where did they go? Many of the young people with options migrated from the region, going to Alberta and Toronto. Many more people, who lacked the financial and educational resources to move long distances, drifted into the outskirts of smaller towns in the Miramichi area, forming the settlements described in Clark's study. They survived as best they could on intermittent, low-wage work and welfare. Thousands of families lived below the poverty line in the substandard housing that still dots the area. Small fishing communities in the Atlantic region fared little better as factory freezer trawlers threatened the survival of the small inshore fishery, and the centralization of fish-packing plants caused many of the smaller, local plants to close. Families that once survived on wage-work at the packing plants fell back onto welfare.

Clark himself tends to blame impoverishment, minimal levels of education, and lack of experience of industrial work for the apparent inability of many Miramichi residents to move in search of better opportunities. A few of the more enterprising people did get out, he suggests, but the remainder are trapped by cheap housing, unemployment insurance or welfare payments, and the absence of any social or educational skills that might equip them to survive in a city such as Toronto.

William Dunn, a sociologist who worked directly with Clark on the study, and who is himself a native of this area, disagrees strongly with Clark's historical-cultural perspective. While supporting the quotations, and the sense of anomie that the people expressed, Dunn argues strongly for a more critical neo-Marxist analysis of the findings. In particular, he stresses the high levels of poverty and welfare that researchers found in three of the four villages studied. He comments "that the very poor should lack interest in literature is not surprising. When one struggles day by day to survive, there is not time for literature, or any other interests that middle-class folk take for granted" (*Miramichi Leader*, 9 March 1988, 5). People on welfare, people who have lost their means of independent subsistence, do not tend to give generously to the local United Way. Nor do they generally show much interest in the arts. They cannot. They are victims of the system. From this perspective, the "social anomie" described by Clark has little to do with the culture of the people, or with "a few bad apples," says Dunn. Powerlessness, dependency, and loss of hope for the future breed anger, frustration, and sometimes violence. The underlying factor is fear. It was precisely such feelings that led residents in one community to threaten researchers for fear that they might be collecting evidence that could be used to cut welfare cheques, the only source of meagre economic security for many local families in the early 1970s. These people had already lost their dignity as independent farmers, farm workers, and fishers. They probably could not take much more.

The Marxist theorist James Sacouman (1980, 1981) similarly rejects Clark's notion that poverty might be accounted for by an inadequate rural culture, arguing instead that the uneven development of farming, fishing, and forestry in the Maritimes was the result of organized capitalist policies. This process he terms the **semiproletarianization** of the domestic mode of production. What he means by this is that people who once worked for themselves as small farmers, woodlot owners, or small fishers, or some combination of these activities, have been pushed into a situation where they have to take part-time wage-work to survive. The jobs made available to them are seasonal, insecure, and at the bottom of the wage scale, so that it is impossible to survive on wages alone. The fact that people in the region could provide for themselves, at least in part, through subsistence farming has meant that employers in big corporations have been able to exploit them, paying below **subsistence wages** or extremely low prices for the raw materials. Merchants also benefited from unequal exchange: they bought products from rural producers at low prices and sold supplies at high prices. The result was that merchants always came out on top, and the rural population was unable to accumulate any wealth.

The political economy thesis similarly predicts a high level of anomie in many First Nations communities, despite the structural advantages of small size, low density, and cultural homogeneity. Native reserves in Canada are commonly so lacking in an economic base that they cannot provide a standard of living above welfare for the residents. Welfare dependency, loss of dignity, and the absence of hope for the future manifest themselves in exceptionally high rates of alcoholism, suicide, and domestic violence (Muise 2003; Anderson and Lawrence 2003; Baskin 2003).

A sense of powerlessness, of being pawns in a game played by impersonal government agents, seems to characterize residents of the remote Innu village of Davis Inlet in northern Labrador. The village made headlines in Canadian newspapers in the 1990s for the high numbers of adults addicted to alcohol and young children addicted to sniffing gasoline. In a failed Canadian experiment, the federal government allocated $150 million dollars to build a new village on the mainland, but these new houses were extensively vandalized even before people moved into them. Substance abuse appears as pervasive as ever (Moore 2003). We explore further below the long history of colonialism that helped to generate these conditions.

Conclusion: Functionalist Model or Marxist Model of Rural Community Life?

The evidence presented here does not consistently support the functionalist, Chicago School model of a folk society.

The key variables of small size, low density, and homogeneity clearly do not suffice to ensure that villages will be cohesive and integrated. Rural-to-urban settings do not form a simple continuum from folk communities to urban agglomerations. The evidence does support the Marxist model that high levels of economic stress and insecurity do undermine community relations, even in small, homogenous settlements.

The next section examines the predictive utility of these models for understanding social life in urban areas.

URBAN COMMUNITIES: THE MYTH AND THE REALITY OF ANOMIE

The focus of this section is on testing Wirth's model of urbanism as a way of life, with respect to different residential zones. If many rural communities do not fit the folk image, can it be argued that the metropolitan environment characterized by large size, high-density living, and heterogeneity, necessarily results in a loss of community? The thesis predicts that local neighbourhoods would decline in significance in urban centres. Nuclear families would be mobile and hence isolated, detached from stronger allegiance to kinship ties beyond those of husband, wife, and dependent children. Social disorganization would increase with the demise of traditional bases of social solidarity. Political economy theory, in contrast, predicts that symptoms of social disorganization will be concentrated in zones characterized by poverty and high levels of unemployment. Demographic features of high-density living and ethnic diversity are expected to be largely irrelevant, once levels of poverty are taken into account. The following review of research begins with the more outward zone of the suburbs, and moves inwards through a lower-middle-class borough, a working-class area, and finally the inner city.

Ecological Zones and Urban Community Life

Early Chicago School theorists developed a model of cities as made up of distinctive zones or *ecological areas*, typically with factories and cheap housing for low-paid workers and immigrants in the inner-city core near the railroads, surrounded by circles of progressively better housing further out (Driedger 2003). By the mid-twentieth century, however, this pattern was clearly beginning to change. Manufacturing and assembly work has been moving increasingly to developing countries where wages are cheaper, being replaced in the centres of capitalism by the post-industrial economy of high-technology, information and financial services, and mass consumption. This economic transition has fostered very different kinds of urban

infrastructure (Stevenson 2003). High-rise office buildings, often owned by giant transnational corporations, began to replace factories, giving rise to the now familiar city skylines marked by skyscrapers. Abandoned factories and slum housing are being replaced with centres for recreation and tourism for high-income consumers. Cities now compete in global markets to offer "world-class" environments for "festival marketplaces" and simulated local attractions, complete with museums, centres for expressive arts and cultural activities, upscale hotels, restaurants and shopping boutiques, and the like (Driedger 2003, 99–100). Upscale high-rise apartments and condominiums joined the mix. Middle-class families, attracted by the recreational and cultural amenities, began to buy up and renovate formerly working-class housing in city centres. Low-income families who formerly inhabited these areas are finding themselves increasingly excluded, their homes bulldozed or priced and taxed beyond reach. The poor have not disappeared from the inner cities, but they are crammed into devastated areas and subsidized slum-clearance housing, out of sight of the tourists (Driedger 2003, 97). Our survey of community life in different urban zones must be qualified by recognition that these zones are often areas in transition.

Suburbs Suburbs are characterized by relatively more spacious homes and lower density than housing in city centres, and tend also to have economically and ethnically more homogeneous populations. Wirth's model would predict that suburbs would likely be characterized by relatively greater social integration and sense of shared community life. Descriptive studies of life in the suburbs, however, suggest a closer fit to the gesellschaft model. Relations among neighbours tend to be superficial, transitory, and limited to a narrow range of interests, rather than forming thick or multi-faceted loyalties. While residents may espouse ideals of family togetherness and close community life, these are hard to achieve.

Research by Dyck (2002) found that both parents in most suburban families needed to earn incomes to be able to afford the high property values, and commonly they both faced long daily commutes to and from work. Individual families also tended to be highly mobile in and out of new suburban housing. Hence, neighbours are mostly strangers. People walk a fine line, Dyck suggests, between desiring to protect their family privacy from prying neighbours and desiring to avoid total domestic isolation (Dyck 2002, 106). Ideal neighbours are "friendly" but not "friends," pleasant but not intruding into one's private family life.

These relations are not necessarily experienced as anomic or unsatisfying. Dyck's study focuses on how the involvement of children in organized sports provides a mechanism for their parents to associate with their neighbours, in what Dyck describes as compartmentalized but nonetheless enjoyable relations. Involvement of parents is voluntary and can range from superficial to dedicated. At a minimum, parents are expected to provide transportation for their children to and from practices and games, and to support their children's efforts by showing up to watch them at least some of the time. Amateur sports organizations also depend heavily on some parents becoming more actively involved in fund-raising and coaching. As parents stand around waiting for their children, they come to know each other at least by sight and to share in common their children's sporting interests. One weekend bus trip to a track meet mixed together the children and 20 adults who barely knew each other before the trip. This experience can be viewed very differently, depending on whether it is compared with the gemeinschaft or the gesellschaft model. Dyck describes it as "a remarkably enjoyable and memorable experience" (116) that gives a limited and fleeting, but nonetheless meaningful sense of community. But it can equally well be described as pleasant, but nonetheless compartmentalized, limited, and fleeting. In all likelihood fellow travellers on the bus trip will not end up crossing the boundary from "friendly" to "family friends." Also, as children grow up, change schools, get bored with athletics and drift away from the club, their parents will likely not interact again.

Other studies present similarly mixed impressions of suburban life as comprising thinly connected and partial communities, but on the other hand offering opportunities for multiple, personally chosen "networks of interpersonal ties that provide sociability, support, information, a sense of belonging and social identity" (Wellman 2001, 18). The days have gone, Wellman argues, when people visited by walking from door to door, limiting their social relations to a few blocks from home. Now people drive or fly from place to place and use the telephone to talk with each other. Entertaining takes place in people's homes more often than local pubs. Cell phones and wireless electronic messaging systems mean that person-to-person communication can occur almost anywhere, anytime. Family members can talk to each other even if they are all doing different things in different places. Community is liberated from location. Individual family members can each develop their own personal social networks and interact across multiple separate networks simultaneously. What appears to be isolation and disconnection from traditional viewpoints can be experienced as socially rich and meaningful networks. Ironically, Wellman notes, the "wired" individuals tended to know more of their neighbours than the non-wired, able to name 25 of them on average, compared with eight for the non-wired.

The suburban experience can thus be argued both ways. From the classical functionalist perspective suburban life is much closer to shallow association than to close-knit community. From the political economy perspective, the relative economic stability enjoyed by families that can afford to live in suburbs, their access to telephones and computers, cars and air travel, and their ability to enrol themselves and their children in exclusive clubs, means they can afford a quality social life without necessarily knowing any of their immediate neighbours.

Research on high-density residential areas closer to the city centres offers a clearer test of the theory that city life predisposes residents to gesellschaft-style agglomerations of individuals with limited ties to neighbours or neighbourhood. Described below are studies of middle-class areas, working-class areas, and lastly the inner-city slum-housing zones.

Middle-Class Boroughs   Research in the Metropolitan Toronto borough of East York did not bear out the predictions of the Chicago School model (Wellman 1978; Shulman 1976). The major difference between the borough and the suburbs described above is that borough residents are more long-settled. A study of a small sample of young, Native-born, Anglophone lower-middle-class couples found a high level of social integration. Geographic closeness between generations was quite high. People valued being near to other family members and wanted frequent interaction with them. Three-quarters of the sample visited kin in the metropolitan area at least once a week. The minority whose parents lived farther away saw them less frequently. Couples expressed a sense of obligation to keep in contact with other family members. They regularly initiated contacts and participated in common ritual activities such as birthdays and anniversaries. Almost one-third saw their parents more than any other persons. The telephone was also a common means of contact.

The studies in East York note that mutual aid was very important between young couples and their parents. Almost half the young couples had lived with one set of parents during the early years of marriage, before they could afford a place of their own. Common forms of aid included young people caring for sick parents, and grandparents babysitting their grandchildren. Parents also gave financial aid in crises, while young adults helped their parents with house repairs and with other needs of older people. The prediction that urban life would result in the breakdown of kinship ties was not substantiated in East York.

The related prediction that high mobility would result in social isolation was similarly not supported by the data from studies in Fredericton and Montreal (McGahan 1982, 239–241). Geographic mobility did not reduce the size of the **kin universe**. The average number of kin contacted did not differ between the mobile and non-mobile urbanites. The non-mobile people had more face-to-face contacts, while the others used letters and telephones to keep in touch with relatives. There was no difference between them in the importance that they accorded to the kinship bond. The death of central connecting relatives was more important than mobility in terminating kin ties.

French-Canadian families provide a particularly valuable test of the thesis that family ties decline with urban residence, given the strength of the image of large, traditional rural families. One would expect city families to present a very different picture from rural ones. McGahan's data from urban Montreal, however, totally contradict the prediction that nuclear family isolation would be evident in urban areas. People in the Montreal sample were able to name, on average, 215 relatives. Women were generally able to name more relatives than could men, and wives could often name more of their husbands' relatives than the husbands themselves knew (Garigue 1956). Women had much greater knowledge of the affairs of the kin group and interacted with the group more frequently. Contact with both parents and siblings was sustained regardless of geographic location. In the French-Canadian community in St. Boniface, Manitoba, mobility also did not disrupt kinship bonds (Piddington 1965). Instead, migrant kin tended to cluster together, and chain migration was common. Intermarriage among distant kin was not uncommon.

Working-Class Zones   Studies of residents in stable working-class zones in large cities show a similar pattern of close identification with neighbourhood and kin. McGahan (1982) cites the example of a study conducted in the 1970s in Toronto's Cabbagetown, a locality then inhabited predominantly by Anglo-Saxon, blue-collar, semiskilled and unskilled workers with below-average incomes (Lorimer and Phillips 1971). Family roles were very traditional and were segregated along age and sex lines, but family ties were strong, with mutual support and obligations. Circles of close friends commonly included kin, often parents and adult children. The impression given by the research is that these working-class residents derived much satisfaction from living in Cabbagetown, and had a strong sense of community cohesion and identity with the neighbourhood. This was evidenced in their ability to come together in organized opposition to the city's urban renewal plans that threatened to disrupt their narrow residential streets.

This sense of cohesive community life closely matches the findings of similar studies. A famous one by Young and Wilmott (1957) focuses on the working-class area of Bethnal Green in East London. In the heart of one of the largest cities in the world, the authors found not an anonymous gesellschaft but a stable, homogenous, and very close-knit community. On a shopping trip, for example, one of their respondents met 63 people she knew, 38 of whom were

relatives. Herbert Gans (1962) found a similar pattern in the Italian neighbourhood in Boston. Gans calls his study "The Urban Villagers" to emphasize the similarities he found between urban neighbourhood life and images of rural folk society. Social life in Greenwich Village in the heart of New York is similarly described as living up to its name in sustaining a village-like atmosphere of interactive pleasantness and familiarity on the sidewalks, as residents habitually walked to do their errands (Jacobs 1961). Local shopkeepers functioned as "public characters" (Jacobs 1961, 68) who would keep spare keys for their neighbours, watch out for their neighbours' children, and warn parents if they were getting out of hand.

In summary, these studies of long-settled middle- and working-class boroughs in the heart of large cities clearly contradict Wirth's thesis that cohesive community life is not possible in high-density residential areas. Two of the three predictors—size and density—are shown to fail, although the third predictor of heterogeneity might still be useful. Over the past decades in many cities in Canada and the United States, the cohesiveness of these old working-class communities has been disrupted by the influx of middle-class renovators looking for the convenience of downtown residence. This process, which is known as **gentrification**, is examined in much greater detail below. In the context of Cabbagetown in the 1970s, McGahan describes relations between long-term residents and renovators as "cautious but edgy," with a mutual recognition that they are quite different types of people. Newcomers tend to be less noisy and "troublesome" than some working-class residents, but on the other hand these newcomers cause more annoyance by making a fuss about such things as the congestion created by neighbours parking on the street (McGahan 1982, 273).

Inner-City Slums   The strongest predictions of urban anomie and blight in the Chicago School thesis are directed at the inner city, seen as the locality with the highest density and the most mobile and heterogeneous populations. The rival political economy perspective makes a similar prediction, based on high rates of unemployment and poverty. The term "**inner city**" refers to the central areas of older properties within large cities. These may encompass a wide variety of neighbourhoods, including the commercial core of office blocks, newly gentrified areas, stable working-class areas, slums, and "skid row." The focus here will be on urban slums.

Town planners commonly assume that social deterioration goes along with physical deterioration, and that urban slums are dangerous areas to be avoided. Yet even here researchers have found evidence of integrated community life based on loyalties to ethnic groups and to territory. One famous study was conducted in the mid-1960s in the Addams area in Chicago. This area comprised roughly a square kilometre and had a population of 20 000 people, including Italians, blacks, Mexicans, and Puerto Ricans (Suttles 1968). Even in this area of high density, heterogeneity, and poverty, an underlying social order existed with territoriality and ethnicity providing bases for association and integration. A certain mutual trust and predictability developed among the various groups, subdivided by ethnicity, territory, age, and sex. Sectoral conflicts emerged from time to time, but residents were also able to cooperate against a common enemy from outside the neighbourhood. Street life was critical for forming personal acquaintances. People got to know each other as they lounged on street corners or met informally in local businesses and corner stores. In effect, the mainstream view of slums as anomic was not supported by the residents themselves. For most it was a viable community with which they could identify. Residents in subsidized housing in two inner-city apartment blocks in England knew that their area was stigmatized by outsiders as an aggressive, dangerous, crime-ridden neighbourhood (Foster 1995, 568), yet insiders came to think of it as "quite a family estate" where neighbours looked out for each other.

A study of men on skid row reflects the same discovery that, behind the appearance of destitution and personal disorganization, there was nonetheless a recognizable and, in some measure, supportive social organization (Harper 1979). When Harper spent two weeks living and travelling with a man who habitually lived on skid row, he found that the man had a network of lifelong friends, and that together they had their own complex system of stratification and moral obligations. African American street vendors who scratched out a living on the sidewalks of Greenwich

An upscale bohemian residential district of Manhattan where Duneier studied the men who make a living selling magazines on the sidewalk.

© Atlantide Phototravel/Corbis

Village selling used books, or magazines retrieved from the garbage, developed community networks of friendship and support both among themselves and with their customers (Duneier 1999). Many of the regulars thought of themselves and were generally regarded as "public characters" whose regular presence and watchful eyes on the street promoted a sense of security and community.

The Limits of "Community": Exclusion and Anomie

A note of caution here is that, just as Redfield and Miner found what they were looking for in describing harmonious village relations, so other researchers may be overemphasizing the sense of social organization in the slums, to the exclusion of tensions and hostilities. The fact that people manage to develop meaningful relationships and sense of home-place under difficult conditions does not mean that the sense of community is always experienced.

The zones for which there is most consistent evidence of urban anomie and social disorganization are areas to which people have been relocated after forced slum clearance programs, especially so where this rehousing takes the form of high-density high-rise apartment blocks. Conceived by architects and urban planners as experiments in constructive social engineering, they have largely been experienced as massive social failures. Such areas are pervasively described as characterized by graffiti, broken elevators, wasted parklands, and smashed windows (Stevenson 2003, 87; Jencks 1984, 9). Such repeated vandalism, often causing millions of dollars' worth of damage, is interpreted by Jencks and others as expressions of resistance by the powerless to the oppressive power and values of the dominant developers who pushed them into these living quarters.

The failure of developers to recognize or to value the importance of local community networks plays an important role in the social anomie that has so often followed slum clearance projects. It may be that professional planners, used to suburban lifestyles, with non-localized social networks based on cars, telephones, and electronic communications, have a learned incapacity to see the support networks that enable impoverished people to survive in urban slums. Forced relocation destroys these survival networks, moving isolated and impoverished people in among strangers. Public housing projects offer few advantages over the slums they replace. They are still overcrowded, the noise level intense, and services and facilities not maintained. The stigma of public housing creates a negative stereotype that residents feel deeply. Tenants may have improved accommodation, but they mostly viewed it unfavourably (McGahan 1982, 278–282), complaining of swearing, drinking, fighting, noisy and destructive people, and limited social controls, particularly over children. Controls are typically imposed from outside the area, by police and social workers. Thus, suggests McGahan (1982, 281), in the public housing projects "extensive solidarity is inhibited by mutual distrust, inability to co-operate, and subordination to external authorities." Residents lack control over their total life situation.

Aboriginal people living in inner-city Winnipeg, many of them displaced from marginalized reserves by poverty and loss of status, conveyed a pervasive sense of being disconnected, disjointed, and fragmented at the community level. They spoke of keeping to themselves to such a degree that few had even met fellow Aboriginals living in the same area. A typical comment was, "For all these years I've been in here, I've never bothered nobody. Nobody bothers me, I don't bother nobody" (Silver 2006, 53). This is notwithstanding the fact that Winnipeg has the highest concentration of urban Aboriginals in all Canada. Barely any of those interviewed by Silver and his colleagues had had any contact with the local Neighbourhood Association, most believing they would be rejected there and stereotyped as unemployed, drunken Indians (Silver 2006, 44).

In summary, the best we can conclude from these accounts is that results are mixed. Evidence of integrative community relations, local loyalties, and kinship ties, even in densely populated, mobile, and heterogenous urban environments, challenge the classical functionalist thesis linking urban life to loss of community. Political economy theory accounts for some of the contradictory evidence in that people who are experiencing serious economic stress, whether in rural or urban communities, find it difficult to sustain cohesive social relations. Yet the study of the Addams area of Chicago shows again that poverty does not preclude cohesive community life any more than wealth ensures it. The failure of these multiple field studies to find consistent evidence of either gemeinschaft-style folk communities in rural areas or gesellschaft-style shallow associations in urban areas has prompted efforts to move away from simplistic models and to rethink theories about community life.

 # Interpretive Perspectives: Rethinking the Concept of Community

Interpretive perspectives in sociology challenge the implicit determinism in both the functionalist and political economy approaches to analyzing community life. Structural characteristics of relative size, density, and heterogeneity, and relative economic well-being of residents, may be associated with different patterns of community life. But the subjective meanings that these characteristics hold for people can differ widely, reflecting diverse life-worlds.

Efforts to rethink the concept of "community" in light of the failure of traditional theories has prompted what Amit terms "a cacophony of definitions, descriptions, and claims" about community that have proven of limited analytical usefulness (Amit 2002, 1). In his influential text *The Symbolic Construction of Community* (1985), Cohen suggests that "community" carries mostly symbolic rather than descriptive meaning, conveying a sense of cultural boundaries or of similarity and difference. "Community" signifies some boundary between people who share something in common compared with others who are dissimilar on some key characteristics. The idea of cultural or "imagined" community has been widely adopted to refer to religious, ethnic, and nationalist sentiments that link together large numbers of people spread over wide geographic areas who do not know each other and never meet face-to-face (Anderson 1983, 1991; Winland 1993; Driedger 2003). Driedger lists a series of studies of what he terms "classic clusters or communities": of the Chinese in Vancouver (Anderson 1991); Chinese across Canada (Li 1998); blacks in Nova Scotia (Henry 1973); Jews in Montreal (Shaffir 1974); Portuguese in Toronto (Anderson 1974); blacks in Toronto (James 1990); French in Calgary (Stebbins 1994); and others.

The problem with this concept of imagined community, Cohen argues, is that usage of the term "community" has become so vague and imprecise as to be virtually meaningless. In his epilogue (2002) to Amit's edited collection, he strongly repudiates the ideas he set out in his 1985 text, even though the book was so successful. What concerns him is that the term "community" is being applied to virtually any set of people. It "has become a way of designating that *something* is shared among a group of people at a time when we no longer assume that *anything* is necessarily shared" (2002, 169; emphasis in original). In everyday talk, he suggests, "community" implies more a moral idea than a description of reality. It reduces to a collectivity, like the collectivity of parents who share in common the experience of adopting children from overseas (Howell 2002), or of having children involved in athletics (Dyck 2002), or people who know each other only through visiting the same electronic chat room (Wellman 2001). Sometimes it carries no meaning at all, as in "the community of nations" or "fragile plant community" (Cohen 2002, 168). Reference to ethnic communities may sound superficially more meaningful, but when used in sweeping generalizations, as if to imply that everyone in Toronto who has an Irish ancestry belongs to the "Irish community," it has no analytical value. The concept is not attached to any theory of how a sense of belonging to such an imagined community could be realized.

What seems to be needed is a more subtle and nuanced understanding of what researchers mean by community, and what people mean when they speak about or think of themselves as members of "communities."

Other authors argue that we cannot simply assume that face-to-face communication between people who live in close geographic proximity to each other is necessarily any more authentic or meaningful to participants than communication through electronic means (Thurlow et al. 2004). In discussing "community," they argue, we need to distinguish normative or moral prescriptions about what communities ought to be from empirical descriptions of how people experience them in their everyday lives. Communities are ultimately less about numbers or place than activities and feelings (Thurlow et al. 2004, 111). In this sense, both online and offline communities can be experienced as social networks capable of supporting strong ties between people. Multiple-user sites like LambdaMOO and Second Life invite thousands of people to come together to create new international social worlds. To find out how meaningful they are, one has to join them and participate. A study of an online bulletin board for the Queer Sisters organization in Hong Kong suggests that such boards help to promote offline community by posting information, managing group activities, and facilitating discussion of issues (Nip 2004). Such boards can also function as places to chat with like-minded people, keep in touch, and even express passions and offer apologies, and other difficult emotions that people find hard to say in face-to-face encounters. Nip concurs with Wellman in finding no evidence that online communications competed with or detracted from offline communication.

Symbolic Interaction: Community as Life-World

Symbolic interactionist research reminds us that it is not possible to give one objective, neutral description of a town or a neighbourhood because the subjective meanings that people bring to a sense of place differ widely with their differing life situations and experiences. Residents of a small prairie town responded with disbelief to social science research data that showed no difference between city and small-town locations on such measures as crime and incidence of domestic violence. "Does this mean we are all stupid?" they asked (Bonner 1999, 87). Their lived experiences as former urban residents who had moved to live in a small town belied the implied sameness. Surveys showed that fully 80 percent of small-town residents concurred that small towns are a better place to raise children, and similar numbers of city residents agreed with them (Bonner 1999, 3). What parents of young children experienced was a greater sense of visibility and familiarity among small-town

neighbours, which encouraged them to feel more secure when their children were out by themselves. They felt that other residents knew their children and would watch out for them, and importantly, would inform them if the children were getting into trouble. Parents also found it much easier to get their children to local activities. The combination of familiarity, convenience, and visibility in small towns significantly reduced their anxiety as parents and freed up their time, making small towns a better place than the city to raise children.

Residents with different life-worlds experienced the same small towns in markedly different ways. Adults without children, or whose children had grown up and left, experienced the same residential areas as constraining and boring, with city life looking more inviting. Markedly different again were the subjective life-worlds of "hometowners," people who had grown up with their parents and grandparents in these small towns and rural areas, rather than moving into them from cities. Hometowners drew on very different symbolic meanings to talk about their love for the place, reflecting images more closely tied to the classic sense of folk communities. They emphasised the importance of extended kinship ties, of having multiple family members living nearby, and a shared sense of unlimited obligations for care for their children, and the elderly.

The irony that was not immediately visible to newcomers who praised small-town life was that the measures they applied when judging small towns as better places to raise children reflected the displaced values of urban dwellers focused on private consumption needs and pragmatic self-interest, rather than the folk society values of community obligation. As they purchased property in the small towns they used real-estate values like saleability, amenities, quality of housing, and services (Ramp 2001, 353; Bonner 2002, 6–7). Their privatized and instrumental orientation to small-town life threatened the very sense of community that attracted them. Can any place be that great, Bonner asks, if we have a purely instrumental orientation towards it (1999, 140)? What values are we teaching our children when we talk about place in such terms? The risk Bonner sees is that the values of objective social science measurement that permit comparative statistical evaluation of different living spaces both reflect and promote the same values of real-estate consumerism. Such "objective" science risks undermining the alternative hometowner's folk society or gemeinschaft worldview precisely as it tries to define and describe it (Bonner 1998, 183; 1999 Ch. 8).

The physical infrastructure of place also invokes different subjective meanings and attachments for people who have lived different lives in relation to that space. Old streets and buildings carry special memory traces for long-term residents of inner-city spaces who remember them as once established working-class neighbourhoods. Residents of economically deprived neighbourhoods in six European cities described their sense of place mostly through memories of how they came to be in that locality, where they would hang out and play as children, the small shops where neighbours would meet and exchange gossip, and local pubs where they could go for a laugh (Corcoran 2002). For them a sense of place is "experienced rather than rationally examined or economically valued" (Corcoran 2002, 51). These same streets held no intrinsic value for transient newcomers seeking cheap housing in deindustrialized areas of town, or for the families of professionals drawn to newly gentrified apartment and condominium complexes. Newcomers, often immigrants, refugees, and asylum-seekers, tended to hang out in different spaces and to favour their own ethnic shops. Some of the long-established shopkeepers harboured deep resentment against newcomers, not simply because their small shops, already hit by supermarkets, were losing trade, but because they themselves were losing their centrality as public characters in the neighbourhood (Corcoran 2002, 57–58; Wells and Watson 2005). The new "gentry" also related to space in markedly different ways from old-timers, tending to segregate themselves behind locked gates, to shop outside the locality, and to come and go in cars, rather than spending time chatting on the sidewalks. They push up housing prices beyond the reach of the children of old-timers, and so contribute to the breakup of local extended families and the deterioration in the lives of aging parents left behind (Corcoran 2002, 61).

City planners and developers tend to bring subjective meanings to urban space that are more closely akin to the ideas of the "gentry" than the old-timers. The irony is that they risk homogenizing space and thus destroying the very sense of specialness of place and urban-village community life that initially attracts professional families to the newly

Community life in cities is actively accomplished by neighbours.

© Mark Richards/Photo Edit

gentrified properties. Dublin and Toronto are cities with vastly different histories and infrastructures, yet city plans look and sound the same, with the same discourse of "investing" in (rather than subsidizing) culture, to attract tourists, and a creative class of highly educated, bright, and mobile residents (Dowler 2004, 25). "Heritage" becomes an exercise in branding. The international financiers that invest in downtown development and gentrification and "spectacularization" are themselves cosmopolitans who share the values of consumer capitalism and the globalized economy (Bonner 2002, 3). They expect the same services and lifestyles in cities across the globe. In this mindset, "place" becomes merely interchangeable "space." How these financiers and planners conceptualize "community" and "place" matters in that they wield great influence over future city space, both to design new places and to shape how old places come to be seen as mere space to be bulldozed out of the way.

Social Constructionism: Accomplishing "Community"

The social constructionist perspective shifts the focus of inquiry to active practices of people as they engage in doing things that bring into being and sustain their sense of community, or alternatively behaving in ways that undermine those relations to generate what sociologists call anomie. Here we return briefly to the debate around how best to conceptualize "community" and rethink the ideas as active practices.

If community implies "boundary" or similarity among insiders and difference from outsiders, as Cohen suggests, then the issue to be explored is how people sustain this sense of boundary. What differences count as sufficiently or strategically "different" to be foregrounded in exclusion of others? What differences can be ignored or viewed as inconsequential, and backgrounded to permit belonging?

If community is not bounded by location, as studies of transnational religious and ethnic communities imply, then how do people sustain emotional relations across geographic space? How does location work in sustaining a sense of "us" and "not us," even when people do not live in the locations with which they feel some identification? How are boundaries located and negotiated in social relations, and how is this similar to and yet different from immediate physical location?

If communities are imagined, how do people realize this in everyday relations? How do they sustain emotions of loyalty, belonging, similarity, and identity in imagined social relations? Further, if individuals inhabit multiple, competing, and partial networks of relations, as Wellman's studies of computer-mediated networks imply, then how do people pull these together into a coherent sense of body and social space? How are boundaries, and sense of inclusion and exclusion, negotiated and realized in practice?

Further, the questions can also be asked in reverse: If community is actively organized, realized, and brought into being by what people do, then how is the loss of community actively produced? If community is understood as a deeply rooted feature of social life, then loss or anomie is not merely absence of community. It implies active destruction, brought about by dis-organizing and unsettling practices. These are practices of excluding, differencing, discounting, and ignoring, through which marginalized people come to experience themselves as not belonging.

Community Boundaries as Social Relations From the perspective of social constructionist theory, locating community or home-place is not simply a matter of locating some administrative borough or village with predefined boundaries. It is a matter of how people who live there organize everyday patterns of interaction and how they move to and from home. In her study of a rural area northeast of Winnipeg, Sprenger (2002) notes four administratively distinct localities on the local map: an Ojibway First Nation reserve; the Pine Falls Bush Camp owned by a forestry company; a Francophone village; and a mill and company townsite. They each have long histories as separate settlements. They are also culturally and linguistically distinct, with English, French, and Ojibway commonly spoken. Other smaller rural populations with distinct local names are dotted about the map, and include many family farms, churches, pubs, a liquor store, and what is locally recognized to be a brothel. At the intersection of two highways that cross the area is a Mohawk filling station and restaurant called Clark's Corner. The locality covers several hundred square kilometres. Sprenger tracks the routine everyday interactions of people from all these localities as they come and go through Clark's Corner restaurant. The constant banter across the tables indicates that the diverse residents recognize and interact with each other as locals, sharing the in-group experiences that permit the truncated or "indexical" speech patterns of people who know they do not have to explain the local jokes and references. Routine markers of community continually dissolved as fair-skinned men wore Native jackets, and Anglophone waitresses answered Ojibway customers in French.

One February night a dance or community social was sponsored by a Catholic women's church group as a fundraiser for a family whose house burned down. Truckers drove in from the bush camp some 200 kilometres away. Young people came from the nearby Native reserve, others hitchhiked in from town; forest-workers and mill-workers mixed with Métis and Francophones. In the parking lot,

RCMP and band constables broke up skirmishes between students from rival English, French, and Ojibway high schools. Police even participated in selling illegal hash oil, which became part of the fundraiser. For all these people, Sprenger suggests, this is "home-place." Community is defined by who attends, who is welcomed, who is turned away, who talks, dances, or drinks together, and who fights with one another.

Sustaining Cultural Communities Beyond Spatial Location Cultural or imagined communities, as understood in the social constructionist perspective, are not located through predefined cultural attributes or characteristics that people can be objectively seen as having in common. Community is the outcome of active practices through which people organize social relations around particular similarities so as to generate and sustain a mutually recognized and experienced sense of belonging and membership. The focus of interest is thus on the practices that produce community, and not the characteristics of the members. There is no assumption that all people sharing particular similarities will think of themselves or be seen as members of a common community. The life-story narratives of two men of Caribbean background living in England (Olwig 2002) shows that one thinks of his English village as home-place while the other considers "backhome" as the Caribbean. They share a common Caribbean ancestor, but experienced very different relations with immediate workmates and neighbours in England, and different non-local family ties. Olwig concludes that there is no such thing as "a Caribbean diaspora" into which migrants fit. Rather, individuals continually construct for themselves networks of interpersonal relations through which a sense of belonging or not belonging emerges.

Communities can also be understood as continually coming into being in the face of changing personal situation and social contexts. Elderly people in an ex-mining town come together in social clubs for the active elderly. As they talk together, they define what they sense they have in common and the boundaries that distinguish them from others. They are working-class, unlike the posh residents of surrounding suburbs. They are old-timers with long roots in the locality, unlike younger people who move away in search of work. And they are able to live independently and are not incontinent or confused, unlike the senile people in nursing homes (Dawson 2002). Within these boundaries they sustain a viable community life, sustaining membership by covering for each other's slow physical and mental decline as long as possible.

Cultural or imaginary communities are not necessarily bounded by location. Nor are they necessarily all-embracing, as the folk society model would suggest. People can negotiate membership in multiple and partial communities whose boundaries shift with context and activities. A study of Norwegian adopters of transnational children (Howell 2002) explores how many of these parents worked up a sense of community together. Before they met they had in common the emotionally harrowing experiences of struggling unsuccessfully to become pregnant, registering for adoption, being evaluated, and several subsequent years of waiting before a potential adoptive child became available. The transnational adoption agency first brought a number of these couples together for information sessions on adoption, and organized groups to travel together to a designated orphanage where they commonly waited several weeks to actually receive their children. The sharing of these emotionally intense experiences provided the basis for building a sense of community. Many of the couples valued these relations enough to keep in contact and to travel long distances for regular reunions. The adoption agency also organized regular reunions of parents who had used their agency, and published magazines with updated pictures of the children. Parents constructed a sense of extended family ties from the fact of having travelled together or having children from the same orphanage. Parents often described these reunions as "for the children" but Howell notes that they also served important functions for the parents themselves. In this specific context parents foregrounded the biological fact of transnational adoption as what they all shared in common. Space and location also worked as important signifiers of sameness for parents of children from the same orphanage, or same region.

Parents also negotiated another community for their children among family members and neighbours, in which social kinship was foregrounded and biological differences backgrounded as insignificant. All the parents worked at "kinning" their children as soon as they arrived home in Norway. This involved taking them to the location of their ancestral family roots in rural Norway—ideally the family farm or fjord to which they could trace ancestors. They took numerous photographs of children with extended kin in these locations, and commonly dressed the children in national costume and distinctively local styles of dress. Significantly, Howell notes that immigrants, who make up 20 percent of the population of Oslo, almost never gained sufficient acceptance from Native Norwegians to make this transition into local costume (2002, 93). When the first-ever immigrant woman was appointed to lead the preparatory committee for Norwegian National Day in 1999, she faced vocal hostility and was explicitly denied the right to wear a local costume. The same difference of origin that was foregrounded to exclude immigrants was backgrounded for transnational adopted children to include them as Norwegian through the kinship of their parents. A third

potential community for transnational adoptees could be ethnic solidarity with fellow immigrants from the same origin country. Howell finds, however, that almost none of the adoptees pursue this, even though they often find themselves mistaken for immigrants by others. The largest majority actively distance themselves from immigrants, and also from other adopted young people. What they foreground is their kinship ties with the extended family of their adoptive parents.

In summary, membership in cultural communities cannot be read from spatial location, or from physical characteristics like skin colour or origin. The boundaries of sameness and difference, and belonging and exclusion, are continually negotiated and sustained in different contexts of interaction. People's sense of belonging to a community of parents of transnational adoptive children is only one of a number of social networks to which these parents feel they belong. It is fully compatible with a sense of belonging to the local communities of ancestral village and residential neighbourhood, and an electronic community of adoptees.

Demolishing Community: Active Practices of Social Dis-Location

When community life is understood as actively being organized, realized, and brought into being by what people do, it implies the converse understanding of *loss* of community life as also actively produced. The sense of community life as being lost does not reflect a structural feature of the community or the neighbourhood itself. Rather, it emerges as the outcome of active practices that continually break up relationships, undermine local organizations, and selectively exclude people from localities where they once felt a sense of belonging, or where they seek to be included. In the next section we will focus on active practices of community dis-location as they are experienced with respect to the colonized, the poor, the homeless, and unwelcomed newcomers.

Colonialism and the Settler City

The settler cities of Canada were all founded through varying degrees of violence as European settlers ignored the prior claims of indigenous peoples and drove them out of the way.

The discourse of pioneers taming the "empty" wilderness obscures the presence of complex systems of overlapping rights that guided how different peoples used the lands for hunting, fishing, gathering food, seasonal migrations to follow herds of caribou, bison, and deer, seasonal settlements as winter and summer camps, and sacred places to bury their dead. Sometimes, as in the case of the Maliseet people along the St. John River in New Brunswick (Martin 2002, 232–233, citing A. Bear-Nicholas), this dispossession occurred through settlers blatantly taking over land that officials at the time knew had not been conquered by, ceded to, or purchased by the colonial government in Britain. Sometimes it occurred through the settlers' ignorance or lack of understanding of indigenous conceptions of use rights rather than "ownership" over land. Within the prevailing European view of land, it was, and mostly still is, the presence of buildings, fences, and boundary markers that signify valid possession. Without such markers, land appeared as *terra nullis*—land devoid of people—rather than *terra populi*—land occupied by settled communities (Blomley 2004, 92). Native peoples appeared as transients, not settled in one place, and hence having no enforceable legal claim to the place compared to Europeans who cleared the land, fenced it off, and constructed permanent buildings and roads.

European settlers enclosed ever-expanding territories for cities and towns, farms and ranches, industrial development, and resource-extraction enterprises, reserving only bounded tracts of land for indigenous peoples to call their own. The active practices that continue to undermine and disorganize communities on these reservations are well known. Canadian government agents exercise sweeping powers under the Indian Act to "manage" governance, law enforcement, and economic relations within them, in ways that are foreign to indigenous practices. Most reserves were established historically in areas least desired by European settlers—areas with limited access to economic resources for viable community development. It is also difficult to calculate the enormity of the destabilizing impact on generations of parenting practices and kinship networks within Aboriginal communities of the Canadian government policy of educating Native children in residential schools. On some reserves it meant that there were no people present between the ages of six and 16. Young people raised in institutions lack the experiences of kinning and parenting that most of us take for granted. As families fell apart under these strains, ravaged by experiences of powerlessness and despair, poverty, anger, and alcoholism, social workers from the 1960s onwards removed many children from reserves to find foster homes and adoptive parents in non-Aboriginal families. Aboriginal peoples continue to struggle to build satisfying communities in the face of these formidable challenges.

Colonial dispossession continues to be actively contested through Aboriginal land claims being pursued in Canadian courts. These include a specific claim, filed by two First Nations Bands in 2001, to Native ownership of 4.2 hectares of land on which the British Columbia Legislature now sits (Blomley 2004, 107–108), and claims to lands occupied by Simon Fraser University in Burnaby (Blomley 2004, 135). These court challenges remain profoundly unsettling processes within the settler cities, as continuing reminders that historic injuries still resonate in

ongoing tensions between descendants of settlers and Aboriginal peoples. The confrontation at Ipperwash in 1995, when Native protester Dudley George was killed by a police bullet, was one of many such struggles. The Chippewan community to which George belonged have been struggling for 50 years to get back their village lands expropriated by the Canadian military during the Second World War (Bressette 2003). The original agreement was that the land would be returned after the war, but this never happened, as the military continued to use it as a cadet training facility.

The colonial dispossession of Aboriginals from urban lands is now largely complete, Blomley argues, but not their displacement from the cities. Recent Statistics Canada data (2003) estimate that half of all Aboriginal people in Canada now live in urban areas, one quarter of them in 10 urban areas, mostly in Prairie cities. Overwhelmingly Aboriginals are concentrated in the inner-city cores of crumbling properties, cheap rooming houses, and shelters. Here, along with others among the urban poor, they experience continuing quasi-colonial practices of dispossession and dislocation that are explored below.

Colonizing the Inner City: "Gentrification" and the Politics of Property

The politics of gentrification, Blomley argues (2004), are inherently colonial. The way developers typically talk when referring to the inner-city zones slated for bulldozers parallels closely the discourse of earlier European colonizers. They promise to "clean up" the area and tame the urban wilderness. From the viewpoint of developers, the poor people who inhabit cheap hotels and shelters look like transients, without commitment or roots in the area, unlike property owners who appear settled. Hence, even areas that are densely populated with poor people look "empty." Poor people are described as congregating in the zone only because services like community kitchens and shelters are provided there. Hence, the poor, along with the services they use, can readily be moved out.

Practices of mapping, almost always done by groups with authority, help in this process of emptying and re-allocating space. Landscaping, suggests Blomley, is a way of thinking about land that highlights particular claims while obscuring others. Maps produced by European settlers superimposed boundaries and grids onto space, dividing regions into plots that could be sold. The presence of indigenous peoples disappeared. Developers' maps similarly rezone space in ways that make current uses invisible. In the Vancouver area of Downtown Eastside, Blomley tracks the multiple interests and use rights of hotel residents, shelter residents, and coalitions of homeless who inhabit the streets. None of these interests were represented in developers' maps. What locals saw as a park for community use near the waterfront, developers saw as "just weeds, rock and junk" (Blomley 2004, 47). New zoning regulations passed by city council to encourage owners to enhance the value of their properties and attract upscale tourists resulted in large-scale evictions of poor people. One such resident, who became an icon in the local resistance movement, had lived in the same hotel room for 30 years. As a non-owner, his claims to residency, like thousands of others', are invisible.

Excluding the Homeless Bodies

Urban renewal in the interests of creating attractive public space for upscale recreation and consumption necessarily involves displacement of the most economically marginal. People who are homeless, who literally inhabit the public street, are routinely excluded from the definition of legitimate "public" as interpreted by city developers. They are constituted as a problem for the public rather than a part of the public (Kawash 1998). City parks that are intended to be attractive to tourists must be made off-limits to the homeless.

The homeless person occupies embodied space, but has no place in which to be. In Kawash's harrowing description of embodied homelessness, a city map for a homeless person consists of sleeping places, warm places, eating places, safe places, panhandling places, and especially toilet places. The corollary, excluding the homeless, involves systematically excluding from the city map the places where the homeless can be. Padlocking parks at night protect the legitimate public users from homeless bodies who might otherwise congregate there to sleep. Public toilets are routinely locked at night, when legitimate tourists are tucked into their hotels and restaurants. City bylaws prohibit sleeping on park benches or sitting on sidewalks, or panhandling anywhere that might be annoying to more affluent tourists. In a vicious circle homeless people who cannot find accessible public toilets eliminate bodily wastes in public places, evoking the very disgust that legitimates their being excluded from public places. The homeless are especially unwelcome in "festival centres"—the gentrified city centres commonly built precisely on the sites of abandoned factories and slums that homeless people formerly inhabited. When special festivals of global significance are planned, such as the Olympic Games in Vancouver, homeless people are often herded up and dumped outside the city, with the warning that if they return they risk arrest and imprisonment for vagrancy. Kawash ends her article with the warning that the violence of the expulsion and containment of the homeless in ever smaller city spaces threatens to undermine the very public security that such containment is intended to protect.

The National Film Board of Canada's 1998 film *East Side Showdown* (Director Robin Benger, Producer Peter Starr) powerfully dramatizes the ongoing class struggle between homeless residents and people trying to gentrify the Toronto neighbourhood of Dundas and Sherbourne. On one side are close to a hundred people who live in large shelters in the area and many more near-homeless who live in overcrowded, cheap rooming houses. Many of these have lived in the area all their lives. They are supported by local church leaders and anti-poverty activists agitating to gain access to boarded-up industrial properties that could provide shelter. Lined up on the other side are better-off residents who have invested heavily to fix up downtown homes, and to open a bed-and-breakfast business catering to upscale tourists. They are increasingly desperate to clear the streets of people they sometimes refer to as scum. Supporting them are the police, and developers with plans to convert abandoned industrial sites into upscale condominiums and offices. The destitute are driven a few blocks further east where their embodied and unwelcomed presence seems likely to precipitate another round of struggle.

The Un/settlement of an Urban Slum Community

The history of the black community of Africville on the Bedford Basin on the outskirts of Halifax is a long and checkered story of settlement, struggle, encroachment, exclusion, and eventually forced expulsion in a slum clearance project in 1964 (Clairmont and Magill [1974] 1999; Nelson 2002). The community traces its beginnings to William Brown and William Arnold, who purchased about 13 acres of land from white merchants in 1840 and established a church, elementary school, post office, and a few stores. Black families had been moving into the areas over the previous 30 years as it offered some means of livelihood from fishing and wage-work in the city. They were mostly descendants of slaves and freed slaves who migrated from America after the War of 1812. Like indigenous peoples before them, they were allocated spaces to settle in "small lots of rocky soil and scrubby forest" (Clairmont and Macgill 1999, 28) inadequate for people to survive off the land. By 1851 there were an estimated 54 blacks living in the Africville area. Their numbers had expanded to about 400 by 1964.

Active practices by city politicians and surrounding businesses for the over 120 years of Africville's existence produced its characteristics as a marginalized slum. Despite the fact that it was within the city limits, the city flatly refused to provide even basic services like water lines, sewage, and garbage collection, and denied police and fire protection. Roads into the area were unpaved and

The once close-knit urban black community of Africville was demolished and is now commemorated only with a plaque in the park that replaced it.

C.M.H.C./Library and Archives Canada/PA-170736

© Nova Scotia Museum

unplowed. Meanwhile the community became encircled with a host of businesses and activities that no other neighbourhood wanted, including night-soil deposit pits in 1858, followed by a bone mill, two slaughter houses, a leather tanning plant, a tar factory, the Rockhead prison, a hospital for infectious diseases, and an open city dump. By the early 1950s the overflowing dump was moved directly onto Africville land, 350 feet from the nearest house (Clairmont and Magill 1999, 109; Nelson 2002, 214–219). The area then readily became referred to as "the slum by the dump."

When the city decided in the 1960s that it wanted the land for industrial redevelopment, the practices that produced the area as a slum were obscured from public consciousness by the discourse of good intentions, and "putting the community out of its misery" (Nelson 2002, 222). Bulldozing the properties could be characterized as compassionate relocation. Nelson describes the violence done to the community in the process of this "benevolent" relocation. As with most slum-clearance projects, families were relocated as standard nuclear family units, without recognition that children might be cared for through alternative extended family networks and communities of support. Families that had more children than the norm for new housing projects had to divide up their children. In some cases single mothers were required to marry the fathers of their children to qualify for new housing (Nelson 2002, 225). Extended community support networks were broken up.

Economically, many families found themselves living in better housing but otherwise financially worse off than they were in Africville. After generations of intermarriage

and handing down of houses within families, many inhabitants lacked clear title to properties and so did not qualify for homeowner compensation. Many found themselves paying rent for the first time. The assortment of illicit and semi-legal practices that provided income in Africville were lost, as was access to fishing for food.

The importance of what was lost can be measured in part by the tenacity with which these displaced residents and their descendants have clung to the memories of the Africville community more than 40 years after their relocation. Oral testimonies of former residents, recorded at the North Branch Public Library, September 1986, speak of communal bonds of religion and mutual self-help, and of their well-kept gardens, their homecrafts, their music, and their memories of ministers, deacons, teachers, and elders (Clairmont and Magill 1999, 296). Annual reunions continue to take place on what is now the 25-acre Seaview Memorial Park. However, anything that might remind visitors to the park of the history of the area has been purged, with the exception of a small plaque. There are plans to build a swimming pool in the area where the city formerly refused to supply drinking water and sewer pipes. Nelson ends her article with the question: Why was it that the Africville community was subjected to forced relocation in the interests of industrial redevelopment, when no such development ever occurred? Why was it so important to the white community of Halifax to remove a black community?

Community Life After Slum Clearance Africville residents managed to sustain a sense of collective community identity after their relocation, focused around demands for compensation that are still before the Nova Scotia courts. As individual families, however, most found they could not sustain the sense of kinship intimacy and independence that they enjoyed in Africville (Clairmont and Magill 1999, 232–233). The more general experience of people who are rehoused is that the quality of community life that emerges in slum-relocation zones is socially impoverished and unsatisfying, typically associated with high rates of vandalism, crime, and family breakdown. Economically disadvantaged people are uprooted and bundled together into subsidized housing complexes, under the patriarchal authority of government agencies. The relocation that turns them into "grateful" recipients of welfare housing brings with it a powerlessness that promotes the social collapse that is subsequently attri-buted to the character of the recipients themselves.

Some tentative insight into practices that contribute to this sense of powerlessness comes from personal discussions with single-parent women who lived in subsidized housing projects. Among other experiences, these women described city housing officers giving them certain semi-legal privileges, such as paying them to do small jobs without having to declare the money as income. Once they accepted such a perk they were under obligation to the official, and also subject to the threat that disclosure could mean losing their accommodation. Several women felt trapped in a vicious circle of compliance, including providing sex, because they had accepted such favours. Also, women who were not certain of their rights as tenants were easily intimidated and would not risk openly trying to assert control over their lives in the housing project, for fear of being evicted on some technicality. Teenaged children also face pressure to prove themselves as members of local gangs, or to face reprisals. Such comments suggest there may be systematic practices that sustain the powerlessness of residents in housing projects as ongoing accomplishments, but we need more detailed research to explore them.

Unwelcomed Newcomers: Subtle Practices of Exclusion

The borough of East York, as described above by Wellman (1978) and Shulman (1976), was a tightly cohesive urban folk community in the 1970s, held together by class and ethnic homogeneity and extended networks of kin and friends. Over the next 30 years, the composition of the borough changed with the significant influx of immigrants into the Greater Toronto Area. Before 1960 most immigrants came from Britain and Europe, but since then the majority came from parts of Africa, Asia, and the Middle East. By 2000, Toronto became home to some 200 000 Muslims, and many of them settled in East York (Isin and Siemiatycki 2002).

Negotiating the boundaries of sameness and difference, belonging and exclusion, in a changing residential area raises challenges for both long-term residents and newcomers. It is important to recognize that people living in the same city zone tend to have much in common, with the exception of areas undergoing rapid re-development, as described above. Family incomes tend to be similar, influenced by ability to pay going rents and real-estate values in a particular zone. People also seek proximity to, or easy transportation to, places of employment. Position in family life cycle also tends to be similar. People with young children tend to gravitate towards suburban housing close to schools and playgrounds, while the young and single are drawn to apartments in areas with appealing night life, and older people seek low-maintenance housing in quiet areas close to the services they need, and so on. The salience of differences that reflect origin, language, religion, and physical characteristics of skin colour are negotiated in relation to these similarities.

People who are recent immigrants, and especially those experiencing language barriers, also value the social support of living close to others with whom they share language, religion, and other customs in common (Simich 2003). These concerns tend to reduce with time, Bannerji argues (2000, 159), unless external pressures push people to turn inwards. As newcomers begin to spread across the city, they find it attractive to settle in places where they know someone already, or which have places of worship and shops that sell the kinds of food they like. Real-estate agents often assist in directing them to such zones. Through such mechanisms of choice and attraction, it is common to find zones in every large city where there are relatively high concentrations of people with particular ethnic minority characteristics. They share similarities with, as well as differences

Women's work is often crucial for the continuation of family farming as a way of life.

© Caro/Alamy

from, other residents, and these are reflected in negotiations over the use of space.

Groups of Muslims who settled in East York found themselves embroiled in stormy negotiations with the municipal council in 1995 over space for a place of worship and an associated meeting place for social activities (Isin and Siemiatycki 2002). New bylaws, passed just as they were negotiating for a new mosque, restricted the number of tax-exempt religious buildings in the area and increased requirements for on-site parking for new constructions, while exempting existing churches. Muslim newcomers denounced the bylaws as discrimination, while long-term residents praised them as a means to protect the tax base and control excessive parking. The eventual compromise was approval of a smaller mosque with no social hall. People involved in lobbying for the new mosque came to feel that zoning technicalities reflected deeper interests in restricting the presence of Muslims in the neighbourhood. They felt themselves in, but not fully included within the borough.

ETHNIC FOLK COMMUNITY AS POLITICAL IDEOLOGY

The Chicago School thesis presents the folk society model as the ideal form of community, with people closely knit together by bonds of shared cultural values and lifestyles, with low social and geographic mobility helping to foster long-term ties of friendship and kinship. What is missing from this view are the active practices of inclusion and exclusion that promote and sustain such ethnic homogeneity and cohesion. Nostalgia for Africville should not obscure the experiences of poverty and exclusion from white settler society that pushed black-skinned people into this marginalized settlement. The pride and resilience of Aboriginal peoples also should not obscure the colonial practices that established the reservations and that continue to support political structures governing First Nations communities that many members find oppressive.

Missing also from the image of "ethnic homogeneity" is recognition of relations of power and inequality that internally divide folk communities. When people cohere for protection and support around mini-nationalities of ethnic difference and visible-minority status, this has important consequences for internal community structure and politics (Bannerji 2000). Elites within these communities develop vested interests in promoting cultural conformity and stifling dissent, to bolster their own political power base as spokespersons for their community. Those who question traditional practices appear disloyal and even subversive. Bannerji views nostalgia for tradition and community as modern formulations that invent a mythic and rigid picture of tradition to sustain current political interests.

 # Feminist Theory: Gendered Community Space

The feminist perspective, and particularly feminist urban geography, led the way in social constructionist analysis of community life. Feminist research drew attention to the close interrelationship between spheres of activity traditionally thought of as separate—the spheres of private and public, domestic and productive work, family life and employment. In exploring these relations, feminist researchers developed innovative ways of seeing how community life was sustained through women's work. This section explores the gendered character of community life, and women's active practices that work to sustain community networks and social life in rural and urban areas.

Rural Life as Gendered Accomplishment

Community life is gendered. Typically, women and men are differently situated in community networks, reflecting their different responsibilities for homemaking, childcare, and breadwinning. In "folk" communities, both rural and urban, women's work has proven essential to maintaining the ongoing character of tradition.

Accounts of change in rural areas from a political eco-nomy perspective document the widespread shift from small family farms to large-scale, mechanized corporate agribusiness, with rural communities devastated as thousands of farm families sell out and move away, rural schools close, and small businesses go bankrupt. What these accounts largely obscure are the active strategies and choices worked out by the families involved. Machum's study of women's work in potato farming in New Brunswick (1992) describes two very different survival strategies that hinged directly on the value that women placed on "the family farm" as a way of life. A shift in focus from *what* women do to *why* they do it was prompted by one of Machum's respondents exclaiming, "Why are we doing this? Are we crazy?" (1992, 92). Love of farming as a way of life motivated this woman and many like her to do a tremendous range of income-generating and income-conserving work to support the farm—planting several acres of vegetables, canning and freezing a year's supply of food, producing eggs, milk, and butter, participating in other farm work and often also holding a paid job to cover family consumption costs, and otherwise minimizing expenditures on household goods. These families actively resisted mechanizing their farms to hold on to these ideals, against persistent pressure from government and agribusiness.

When women withdrew this intensive level of unpaid farm labour, the entire character of farming and rural life began to change. Farms often closed down or shifted towards capital-intensive industrial production. Women increasingly sought off-farm careers. Their goal for their children was often not to continue the farm, but to "go where the money is." The preservation or demise of the rural way of life is thus neither automatic nor inevitable. It is the outcome of active strategizing in which women's commitment is centrally important.

Accomplishing "Kinship" in Urban Folk Communities

The active practices through which women worked to sustain social relations with kin and neighbours similarly proved crucial in sustaining the folk community character of boroughs of East York and Montreal, and in East London, described above. The studies document how wives typically telephoned their parents more frequently than did their husbands, and organized most of the social events that brought people together. The extensive networks of kin and friends, sometimes estimated at upwards of 200 people, do not happen by biological accident. They have to be worked at. This is especially true when families are mobile and kin spread out geographically across provinces and cities where meeting would not occur by chance. Older family members tend to be particularly important in forming the centre of networks of kin. Early studies only provide glimpses of the work involved in maintaining these networks—writing letters, making regular telephone calls, keeping track of birthdays, actively organizing get-togethers, and doing the extensive amount of food preparation associated with celebrating special events like Thanksgiving and Christmas. Bella (1992) describes how staging the magnificent family feasts and family gift exchanges around Christmas became both a moral imperative and a test of homemaking skills for wives in Western Europe from the Victorian era onwards. Women's magazines and department stores like Eaton's and The Bay focused extensive advertising and promotions to persuade women to outdo themselves year after year in performing these kinship rituals. Wellman (1992; 2001, 25) refers to women as historically "the kin-keepers of western society" providing the extensive emotional and domestic support required to sustain kin networks. These community-building patterns may well have changed as mothers are more likely to be in full-time employment outside the home.

Wellmann (1992) further suggests that community relations have become more focused around private and domestic venues rather than local pubs and clubs in walking distance from home, now that most families have cars and telephones. The result, he suggests (1992), is that men more often spend their leisure time at home, and rely more on the informal social ties between couples that their wives develop. Women help to maintain many of their husbands' friendships through providing entertainment at home. Women also do much of the work of sustaining community networks through minding each others' children and organizing sleepovers and social activities among their children's friends.

Accomplishing Suburbia

Work in feminist urban geography during the 1980s uncovered the extensive practices through which women restructured the privatized realm of suburbia into social networks that supported home-based income-earning activities compatible with childcare (Mackenzie 1986b, 92–93).

Contacts among friends and neighbours were redesigned as working networks, sources of contact, advice and assistance, and referral systems, linking child-minders with mothers needing the service, and knitters and dress-makers with their clientele, tutors with students, and the like. Women also organized mutual aid networks to develop facilities such as drop-in centres and playgrounds to support their "domestic-community work." Research into the working lives and the "hidden economy" of women's work highlights how different the experience of suburban living can be for men and women. People who leave the suburbs during the day to work elsewhere may develop few ties within the suburbs, while people who are trying to transform them into work centres may find them teaming with networks of support services and clientele (Mackenzie 1986a). In developing their networks, women have had to struggle with the implicit gender-role biases built into the organization of public transit. Urban planners of the 1950s envisioned suburbs as places where women would remain at home while men commuted to and from work in the city centres. The hub-and-spokes design of most transit systems serving suburbs proved very inconvenient for women whose home-based income-earning activities often require lateral movements from one suburban district to another at irregular hours (Michelson 1988, 89).

Organizing Community Economy

Women's work in organizing a domestic-community economy took on special significance in the community of Nelson in the British Columbia interior during the 1980s (Mackenzie 1987b). The resource-extraction economy of Nelson underwent severe economic recession with massive cutbacks in mining, smelting, and forestry, and concomitant loss of jobs in industry as plants either closed down or "rationalized" their operations. Secure, highly paid, unionized jobs for men disappeared. Once-marginal economic activities, largely done by women, expanded to fill the gap. Mackenzie describes how women's community networks broadened to form the West Kootenay Women's Association, to provide support and resources for small enterprises. The local Doukhobour community revived its farming and food processing cooperatives, largely inactive since the 1940s. They joined forces with the politically active feminist movement and back-to-the-landers attracted to a self-sufficient rural lifestyle. Together they organized a variety of alternative employment, including woodworking, home renovation, machinery maintenance, food processing cooperatives, artisans' cooperatives, home childcare services, and related nursery education classes. They used the recently deserted university buildings to develop a Summer School of the Arts and to promote tourism and the sale of artwork.

The outcome, suggests Mackenzie, was a radical transformation of a formerly gender-segregated, resource-based male-working-force town. Women gained prominence in community activities as the informal economy was transformed into the public economy, and in the process, kept the community of Nelson going when the formal economy pulled out (Mackenzie 1987a, 248–249).

Gendered Inequality in Community Life

Women, as primarily responsible for homemaking and childcare, are differently located from men in residential communities. They are also differently vulnerable to practices described in the previous section that disorganize and unsettle community life. Colonial laws and practices that established reservations for indigenous people in Canada undermined the status of women in these communities by defining Native status and right of residence exclusively through the male line. Aboriginal women held rights to residency and housing only through their fathers and husbands. Those who married non-status men lost their status as Native and thus their right to live within the reservation. Over the years this has resulted in large numbers of women and their descendants who still consider themselves Native, but who have no community or land base—in a sense, no home (Lawrence and Anderson 2003, 12). Bill C-31, passed by the Canadian federal government in 1985, eventually revoked this rule so that Status-Indian women can now retain their status on marrying out, but this does not automatically confer a right to band membership or to residence or housing on reservations.

The "right" to live on reservations has also commonly meant living in communities ravaged by poverty, powerless-

ness, anger, alcoholism, and despair. Women have borne the brunt of this misery, expressed in levels of family violence and sexual abuse far in excess of non-Native communities (Muise 2003, 35). For these combinations of reasons—loss of tribal status, lack of housing and employment, and violence—women of Aboriginal heritage have migrated into the cities in higher numbers than men.

Aboriginal people in the cities are even more marginalized. In the prairie cities of Winnipeg, Regina, and Saskatoon, 60 percent of Aboriginal households live below the poverty line, rising to 80 to 90 percent of women-headed households (Razack 2002, 133). Ninety percent of Aboriginal children in Regina drop out of high school before graduating. The population of impoverished and homeless people who inhabit the streets of inner-city slums are thus both racialized and gendered, as well as classed. Under these wretched conditions large numbers of Aboriginal women turn to the sex trade. Here they face harassment by police, often at the behest of middle-class property owners seeking to gentrify their streets and clear the neighbourhood of "scum." Forceful displacement and harassment combine to drive these women into concealed spaces where they are even more vulnerable to violence, a violence that is largely unwitnessed and unpoliced (Blomley 2004, 151; Razack 2002, Ch. 5). Frightening numbers of women from such inner-city streets have disappeared or been murdered, with few arrests. As both Razack and Blomley observe, these women continue to be victimized by colonial practices of dispossession and patriarchal power.

Patriarchy in Ethnic Folk Communities

Nostalgia for close-knit, community life based on ties of kinship and shared culture, which is evident both in Tönnies' image of gemeinschaft and in the Chicago School model of folk society, obscures the often oppressive and patriarchal character of these communities. Immigrants are more likely to turn inwards into homogenous ethnic sub-communities when they feel unwelcome in the wider host society, as when outsiders voice disparaging remarks about their skin colour or cultural habits, when other children reject their children as playmates, when neighbours object to having a mosque or other minority cultural symbols built nearby, when potential employers reject their non-Canadian qualifications, and the like (Bannerji 2000).

Practices that encourage people to cohere around ethnic folk communities also make it difficult for people to challenge or change oppressive practices within these communities. Political elites that emerge to speak on behalf of ethnic minorities in multicultural politics typically develop vested interests in sustaining the image of a united cultural front. The combination of such external and internal pressures can promote an exaggerated and rigid identification with tradition that has little to do with nostalgia.

Women in such enclave communities typically bear the brunt of such traditionalism, pressured to conform to pre-modern family roles as nurturing and self-sacrificing wives and mothers within the patriarchal family mould, and to dress and behave in ways that symbolize the culture to the outside world. Feminist calls for change can be readily discredited as violating the authenticity of the community itself (Bannerji 2000, 164–167). In a bitter irony, exposure to ethnocentric views in the Canadian host society that disparage non-white cultures as pre-modern and primitive contribute to entrenching such traditions as self-defining features of ethnic folk communities.

Matriarchal family patterns and egalitarian political structures were widespread among pre-contact Aboriginal communities in Canada, but this has not protected them from the imposition of "invented" traditions that reflect the Indian Act's patriarchal character, and that subject women to the authority of male elites in the name of preserving community values. Martin-Hill (2003, 114–115) describes the re-victimization of Aboriginal women by newly established male "elders" who use their authority to scold women in public for supposed violations of "tradition" such as not wearing skirts or not observing elaborate rituals around menstruation. Maracle (2003, 77) similarly laments the rigid enforcement of gender stereotypes by elders who exclude women from learning to drum or learning the teachings, seeing these practices as reflecting the patriarchal values of the colonizers, rather than authentic tradition.

The active agency of women and the support networks that they establish are nonetheless centrally important in sustaining community life. Aboriginal women draw on traditions to build a positive spiritual sense of themselves as Aboriginal peoples, even as they challenge patriarchal practices (Blaney 2003, 167). It is predominantly the women in non-status Mi'qmac communities in Newfoundland who form networks through which to share what they know of tradition and medicines to bring healing to often traumatized families (Muise 2003). Urban Aboriginal women have led the way in developing Native Friendship Centres (Maracle 2003, 72–73). First they opened their homes to shelter homeless newcomers to the urban centres. Then they organized small gathering places for tea and talk, and eventually established permanent centres. These spontaneous leaders in urban community building, Maracle argues, were mostly women, leaving the men who held formal authority running to catch up.

The experience of community is thus highly gendered and politicized. From the perspective of feminist theory, the concept of community is ideological, in the sense that it implies a unity that obscures deep divisions along the lines of gendered class relations and inequalities in political power.

CONCLUSION

The study of rural and urban sociology has a long history, but many questions remain unanswered, and the developing approaches of social constructionism and feminism indicate that there are still many more questions yet to be formulated. The folk-urban thesis popularized by Chicago School theorists has not stood the test of comparative research. Rural communities are not uniformly or even generally characterized by the close-knit, integrated social life envisioned in the notion of folk society. Neither do urban neighbourhoods fit the image of shallow and detached associations between strangers. The predictions of political economy theory that link community integration with economic security have a better fit with evidence. But such explanations fail to take account of the tenacity with which people fight to hold viable communities together in the face of economic hardship. The practical activities of people involved in creating and sustaining community integration are now being more extensively explored, particularly under the impetus of feminist research. But as this research has expanded, the concept of community itself is being challenged for obscuring too much. Community cannot be defined independently of the practices that continually draw people together into a sense of belonging, and simultaneously undermine these fragile social connections.

A valuable lesson to be learned from the classical loss of community debate is the importance of subjecting evidence to a critical evaluation. The folk-urban model sounds convincing. It fits the preconceptions that most of us have about simple rural life, where people care about each other, and about anonymous crowds in the city, where self-interest prevails. But however convincing this argument sounds, when the assumptions are systematically tested against the evidence and they do not hold up, it is essential to adopt the same critical approach to all other theories in sociology, and indeed in all other fields of study.

SUGGESTED READING

Mitchell Duneier's ethnography *Sidewalk* (1999) explores the community of marginal poor black men who make their living selling salvaged magazines on the sidewalk of Greenwich Village, an upscale residential area of Manhattan in New York City famous for its artists and celebrity residents. These men who live off the sidewalk are not part of the close-knit community described by Jane Jacobs as a place where shopkeepers would keep spare keys for neighbours, and let her know if her kids were getting out of hand on the street (Ibid., 7, citing Jane Jacobs 1961, *The Death and Life of Great American Cities*). Nonetheless, the ethnography explores how they accomplish for themselves a meaningful and complex social world.

Kieran Bonner's study *A Great Place to Raise Kids* (2002) accomplishes both an ethnography of small-town life in rural Saskatchewan and a symbolic interactionist critique of mainstream sociological research that tries to impose "objective" descriptions on the diverse and contradictory subjective meanings that attachment to place has for those who live there.

Nicholas Blomley begins his critical study *Unsettling the City* (2004) with the observation that the pristine, quiet, English countryside, with its open fields and manor houses, conceals a bloody and violent past when peasants were forcibly driven from the land. His study of Canadian cities reveals a similarly violent past of colonial dispossession, and ongoing class warfare as corporate developers reshape city centres, oblivious to the lives of long-term residents.

The collection of articles edited by Sherene Razack, *Race, Space, and the Law. Unmapping a White Settler Society* (2002), explore ruling relations that structure life experiences in marginalized communities. These include Razack's powerful account of the lives of Aboriginal women in inner-city space: "Gendered Racial Violence and Spatialized Justice: The Murder of Pamela George" (121–156) and Jennifer Nelson's account of the inner-city black community of Africville in Halifax: "The Space of Africville. Creating, Regulating, and Remembering the Urban 'Slum'" (211–232).

QUESTIONS

1. How does the debate around "loss of community" reflect the values scientific inquiry described in the section on scientific objectivity at the end of Chapter 1? Cite evidence that challenges the objectivity of historical studies of Quebec folk society.

2. Clarify the differences between Tönnies' model of loss of community in urban industrial society and that put forward by Chicago School theorists such as Louis Wirth. How are these subtle differences relevant for designing research on urban communities?

3. How do theorists who favour a political economy perspective challenge the more functionalist analysis of problems evident in some New Brunswick rural communities in the 1970s?

4. How do studies of middle-class and working-class urban neighbourhoods in the 1970s challenge Louis Wirth's model of urban community life?

5. Explain the concept of "imagined community." How does this concept work to link the experiences of parents supporting their children's hockey games and teens visiting Internet chat rooms?

6. Explain how Bonner uses the approach of symbolic interaction to explore "life worlds" in small towns. How does he suggest that migrants from cities to small towns misunderstand and perhaps even threaten the character of small-town community life even as they praise it?

7. How does social constructionist analysis alter how we think about community boundaries? Give examples of boundaries as social construction.

8. Explain Blomley's view that some forms of colonization are still ongoing in modern Canadian cities. What processes are involved?

9. Explain the concept of folk community as political ideology. How might this be relevant for understanding ethnic enclaves in Canadian cities?

10. List five ways in which work done by women can be understood as accomplishing suburbia?

WEB LINKS

Youtube.com
www.youtube.com/watch?v=3eDkAG3R0h8
Video of John Mellencamp singing "Small Town." Students see how the image and memory of small town is constructed nostalgically.

TED Ideas Worth Spreading
www.ted.com/talks/majora_carter_s_tale_of_urban_renewal.html
Majora Carter's *Tale of Urban Renewal*. Carter tells us of the "poverty injustice" for those of particular race and class. Health, education,

environment, and work challenges face the people who live in the South Bronx because of what she calls "flawed urban policy." Carter honestly tells of violence and desperation for those living in the ghetto.

Ontario Coalition Against Poverty
http://update.ocap.ca/housing?page=5

Relief and Resistance: A Poor People's History of East Downtown. This link shows photos, videos, and news coverage of the March Against Poverty. Videos posted to YouTube include speeches given by the protesters in Queens Park, interviews, and media reports on the state of housing in Ontario.

Documentary Educational Resources
www.der.org/films/being-innu.html

Being Innu. This link provides a short summary and five-minute preview of the documentary *Being Innu.* Topics include aging, agriculture, Americana, animals, archeology, and art, to urban, village, water, women's studies, and youth. The site's archives boasts as being "one of the most historically important resources of ethnographic film in the world today."

The Assembly of First Nations
www.afn.ca

In both English and French, this Assembly of First Nations' website provides the story of First Nations through policy, press releases, and media

advisories, upcoming events, current issues, programs, employment opportunities, and links to other provincial territorial organizations.

Where are the Children? Healing the Legacy of the Residential Schools
www.wherearethechildren.ca/en/remembering2.html

This website allows us to explore the Canadian government's attempt at assimilation and the history of ethnocide and genocide. Because of the honesty of the site, we can share in the stories and photos of a traumatic time for First Nations people.

The Native Women's Association of Canada
www.nwac-hq.org/en/documents/nwac.billc-31.jun2007.pdf

Aboriginal Women and Bill C-31: An Issue Paper. Prepared for the 2007 National Aboriginal Women's Summit, the Native Women's Association of Canada presents a response and recommendations to the legislated inequalities present in Bill C-31.

Canadian Immigrant magazine
http://thecanadianimmigrant.com

This online magazine is Canada's first national magazine by and for Canadian immigrants. It provides links to immigrant stories, careers, housing, health, education, news stories, and settling in Canada.

KEY TERMS

anomie

Chicago School (The)

cohort

community

culture

familism

folk society

gemeinschaft

gentrification

gesellschaft

ideal-type model

industrialization

inner city

kin universe

semiproletarianization

subsistence

subsistence wages

suburbs

REFERENCES

Amit, Vered, ed. 2002. *Realizing Community. Concepts, Social Relationships and Sentiments.* London; New York: Routledge.

Amit, Vered. 2002. "Reconceptualizing Community." In V. Amit, ed. *Realizing Community: Concepts, Social Relationships and Sentiments.* London; New York: Routledge, 1–20.

Anderson, Benedict. [1983] 1991. *Imagined Communities: Reflections on the Origin and Spread of Nationalism.* London; New York: Verso.

Anderson, G. 1974. *Networks of Contact: The Portuguese and Toronto.* Waterloo, Ontario: Wilfrid Laurier University Press.

Anderson, K. 1991. *Vancouver's Chinatown: Racial Discourses in Canada 1875–1980.* Montreal; Kingston: McGill–Queen's University Press.

Anderson, Kim, and Bonita Lawrence, eds. 2003. *Strong Women Stories, Native Vision and Community Survival.* Toronto: Sumach Press.

Bannerji, Himani. 2000. *The Dark Side of the Nation: Essays on Multiculturalism, Nationalism and Gender.* Toronto: Canadian Scholars Press.

Baskin, C. 2003. "From Victims to Leaders: Activism Against Violence Towards Women." In K. Anderson and B. Lawrence, eds. *Strong Women Stories, Native Vision and Community Survival.* Toronto: Sumach Press, 213–227.

Bear-Nicholas, A. 1994. "Colonialism and the Struggle for Liberation: The Experience of Maliseet Women." *University of New Brunswick Law Journal* 43: 223–239.

Bear-Nicholas, A. "St. John River Society and the Dispossession of the Maliseet People." Unpublished. St. Thomas University Dept. of Native Studies.

Bella, Leslie. 1992. *The Christmas Imperative: Leisure, Family, And Women's Work.* Halifax: Fernwood.

Blaney, Fay. 2003. "Aboriginal Women's Action Network." In K. Anderson and B. Lawrence, eds. *Strong Women Stories, Native Vision and Community Survival*. Toronto: Sumach Press, 156–170.

Blomley, Nicholas. 2004. *Unsettling the City: Urban Land and the Politics of Property*. New York; London: Routledge.

Bonner, Kieran. 2002. "Understanding Placemaking: Economics, Politics and Everyday Life in the Culture of Cities." *Canadian Journal of Urban Research* 11 (1): 1–16.

Bonner, Kieran. 1999. *A Great Place to Raise Kids: Interpretation, Science, and the Urban-Rural Debate*. Montreal; Kingston: McGill–Queen's University Press.

Bonner, Kieran. 1998. "Reflexivity, Sociology, and the Rural-Urban Distinction in Marx, Tönnies, and Weber." *The Canadian Review of Sociology and Anthropology* 35 (2): 165–189.

Bressette, Shelly E. 2003. "The truth about us: Living in the aftermath of the Ipperwash crisis. In K. Anderson and B. Lawrence, eds. *Strong Women Stories, Native Vision and Community Survival*. Toronto: Sumach Press, 228–241.

Burrill, G., and I. McKay, eds. 1978. *People, Resources, and Power: Critical Perspectives on Underdevelopment and Primary Industries in the Atlantic Region*. Fredericton: Acadiensis Press.

Calhoun, J.B. 1963. "Population Density and Social Pathology." In L. Duhl, ed. *The Urban Condition*. New York: Basic Books, 33–43.

Clairmont, D.H., and D.W. Magill. [1974] 1999. *Africville: The life and death of a Canadian black community*. 3rd ed. Toronto: Canadian Scholars Press.

Clark, S.D. 1978. *The New Urban Poor*. Toronto: McGraw-Hill Ryerson.

Cohen, Anthony P. 2002. "Epilogue." In V. Amit, ed. *Realizing Community: Concepts, Social Relationships and Sentiments*. London; New York: Routledge, 165–170.

Cohen, Anthony P. 1985. *The Symbolic Construction of Community*. London; New York: Tavistock Publications.

Corcoran, Mary P. 2002. "Place Attachment and Community Sentiment in Marginalised Neighbourhoods: A European Case Study." *Canadian Journal of Urban Research* 11 (1): 47–67.

Dawson, A. 2002. "The mining community and the ageing body: Towards a phenomenology of community?" In V. Amit, ed. *Realizing Community: Concepts, Social Relationships and Sentiments*. London; New York: Routledge 21–37.

Dowler, Kevin. 2004. "Planning the Culture of Cities: Cultural Policy in Dublin and Toronto." *Canadian Journal of Irish Studies* 30 (2): 21–29.

Driedger, Leo. 2003. "Changing Boundaries: Sorting Space, Class, Ethnicity and Race in Ontario." *The Canadian Review of Sociology and Anthropology* 40 (5): 593–621.

Duneier, Mitchell. 1999. *Sidewalk*. New York: Farrar, Straus and Giroux.

Dyck, Noel. 2002. "'Have you been to Hayward Field?' Children's sport and the construction of community in suburban Canada." In V. Amit, ed. *Realizing Community: Concepts, Social Relationships and Sentiments*. London; New York: Routledge, 105–123.

Falardeau, J.C. 1964. "The Seventeenth-Century Parish in French Canada." In M. Rioux and Y. Martin, eds. *French-Canadian Society*. Vol. 1. Toronto: McClelland & Stewart, 19–32.

Foster, Janet. 1995. "Informal Social Control and Community Crime Prevention." *British Journal of Criminology* 35 (4): 563–583.

Gans, H. 1962. *The Urban Villagers*. Glencoe, Illinois: Free Press.

Garigue, Philippe. 1964. "Change and Continuity in Rural French Canada." In M. Rioux and Y. Martin, eds. *French-Canadian Society*. Vol. 1. Toronto: McClelland & Stewart, 123–137.

Garigue, Philippe. 1956. "French-Canadian Kinship and Urban Life." *American Anthropologist* 58: 1090–1101.

Gérin, L. 1964. "The French-Canadian Family: Its Strengths and Weaknesses." In M. Rioux and Y. Martin, eds. *French-Canadian Society*. Vol. 1. Toronto: McClelland & Stewart, 32–57.

Guindon, Herbert. 1964. "The Social Evolution of Quebec Reconsidered." In M. Rioux and Y. Martin, eds. *French-Canadian Society*. Vol. 1. Toronto: McClelland & Stewart, 137–161.

Hall, E.T. 1966. *The Hidden Dimension*. Garden City, New York: Doubleday.

Harper, D. 1979. "Life on the Road." In J. Wagner, ed. *Images of Information*. Beverly Hills: Sage, 25–42.

Henry, F. 1973. *Forgotten Canadians: The Blacks of Nova Scotia*. Toronto: Longman Canada.

Hodge, G., and M.A. Qadeer. 1983. *Towns and Villages in Canada. The Importance of Being Unimportant*. Toronto: Butterworths.

Howell, Signe. 2002. "Community beyond place: Adoptive families in Norway." In V. Amit, ed. *Realizing Community: Concepts, Social Relationships and Sentiments*. London; New York: Routledge, 84–104.

Isin, Engin F., and Myer Siemiatycki. 2002. "Making Spaces for Mosques: Struggles for Urban Citizenship in Diasporic Toronto." In S. Razack, ed. *Race, Space, and the Law: Unmapping a White Settler Society*. Toronto: Between the Lines, 185–209.

Jacobs, Jane. 1961. *The Death and Life of Great American Cities*. New York: Vintage.

James, C.E. 1990. *Making it: Black Youth, Racism and Career Aspirations in a Big City*. Oakville, Ontario: Mosaic Press.

Jencks, C. 1984. *The Language of Postmodern Architecture*. London: Academy Editions.

Kawash, Samira. 1998. "The Homeless Body." *Public Culture* 10 (2): 319–339.

Lavigne, Marie. 1986. "Feminist Reflections on the Fertility of Women in Quebec." In R. Hamilton and M. Barrett, eds. *The Politics of Diversity: Feminism, Marxism, and Nationalism*. Montreal: Book Centre, 303–321.

Lawrence, Bonita, and Kim Anderson. 2003. "Introduction: For the Betterment of our Nations." In K. Anderson and B. Lawrence, eds. *Strong Women Stories, Native Vision and Community Survival*. Toronto: Sumach Press, 11–22.

Lewis, Oscar. 1949. *Life in a Mexican Village: Tepoztlan Restudied*. Urbana, Illinois: University of Illinois Press.

Li, Peter. 1998. *The Chinese in Canada*. 2nd ed. Toronto: Oxford University Press.

Lorimer, J., and M. Phillips. 1971. *Working People: Life in a Downtown City Neighbourhood*. Toronto: James Lewis and Samuel.

Machum, S. 1992. "The Impact of Agribusiness on Women's Work in the Household, On-the-farm and Off-the-farm: A New Brunswick Case Study." Master's thesis. Department of Sociology and Social Anthropology, Dalhousie University.

Mackenzie, Suzanne. 1987a. "Neglected Spaces in Peripheral Places: Homeworkers and the Creation of a New Economic Centre." *Cahiers de géographie du Québec* 31 (83) (Sept.): 247–260.

Mackenzie, Suzanne. 1987b. "The Politics of Restructuring: Gender and Economy in De-Industrialized Areas." Paper presented to the Canadian Association of Geographers, Hamilton, Ontario.

Mackenzie, Suzanne. 1986a. "Feminist Geography." *The Canadian Geographer* 30 (3): 268–270.

Mackenzie, Suzanne. 1986b. "Women's Response to Economic Restructuring: Changing Gender Changing Space." In R. Hamilton and M. Barrett, eds. *The Politics of Diversity: Feminism, Marxism, and Nationalism*. Montreal: Book Centre, 81–100.

Maracle, Sylvia. 2003. "The Eagle Has Landed: Native Women, Leadership and Community Development." In K. Anderson and B. Lawrence, eds. *Strong Women Stories, Native Vision and Community Survival*. Toronto: Sumach Press, 70–80.

Martin, M. 2002. "The Crown Owns All the Land? The Mi'gmaq of Listuguj Resist." In G. MacDonald, ed. *Social Context & Social Location in the Sociology of Law*. Peterborough, Ontario: Broadview Press, 229–246.

Martin-Hill, Dawn. 2003. "She No Speaks and other Colonial Constructs of 'The Traditional Woman.'" In K. Anderson and B. Lawrence, eds. *Strong Women Stories, Native Vision and Community Survival*. Toronto: Sumach Press, 106–120.

Marx, Karl, and Friedrich Engels. [1847] 1970. *The German Ideology*. New York: International Publishers.

Marx, Karl, and Friedrich Engels. [1845] 1965. *Manifesto of the Communist Party*. Peking: Foreign Languages Press.

Mawani, Renisa. 2002. "In between and Out of Place. Mixed-race Identity, Liquor, and the Law in British Columbia, 1850–1913." In S. Razack, ed. *Race, Space, and the Law: Unmapping a White Settler Society*. Toronto: Between the Lines, 47–69.

McGahan, P. 1982. *Urban Sociology in Canada*. Toronto: Butterworths.

Michelson, W. 1988. "Divergent Convergence: The Daily Routines of Employed Spouses as a Public Affairs Agenda." In C. Andrew and B.M. Milroy, eds. *Life Spaces: Gender, Household, Employment*. Vancouver: University of British Columbia Press, 81–102.

Michelson, W. 1970. *Man and His Urban Environment: A Sociological Approach*. Reading, Massachusetts: Addison-Wesley.

Miner, Horace. 1964. "Changes in Rural French-Canadian Culture." In M. Rioux and Y. Martin, eds. *French-Canadian Society*. Vol. 1. Toronto: McClelland & Stewart, 63–75.

Miner, Horace. 1939. *St. Denis: A French-Canadian Parish*. Chicago: University of Chicago Press.

Moore, Dene. 2003. "Chief of Labrador Innu asks for help in treating gas-sniffing children." *Canadian Press*, Oct. 27.

Muise, Gertie Mai. 2003. "Where the Spirits Live: Women Rebuilding a Non-status Mi'kmaq Community." In K. Anderson and B. Lawrence, eds. *Strong Women Stories, Native Vision and Community Survival*. Toronto: Sumach Press, 25–36.

Nelson, Jennifer J. 2002. "The Space of Africville: Creating, Regulating, and Remembering the Urban 'Slum.'" In S. Razack, ed. *Race, Space, and the Law: Unmapping a White Settler Society*. Toronto: Between the Lines, 211–232.

Nip, Joyce Y.M. 2004. "The Relationship Between Online and Offline Communities: The Case of the Queer Sisters." *Media, Culture & Society* 26 (3): 409–428.

Olwig, Karen F. 2002. "The ethnographic field revisited: Towards a study of common and not so common fields of belonging." In V. Amit, ed. *Realizing Community: Concepts, Social Relationships and Sentiments*. London; New York: Routledge, 124–145.

Park, Robert E. [1932] 1952. *Human Communities: The City and Human Ecology, Volume 2; The Collected Papers of Robert Ezra Park*. Glencoe, Illinois: The Free Press.

Park, Robert E., Ernest W. Burgess, and Roderick D. McKenzie, eds. [1925] 1967. *The City*. Chicago: Chicago University Press.

Piddington, R. 1965. "The Kinship Network Among French-Canadians." *International Journal of Comparative Sociology* 6: 145–165.

Ramp, William. 2001. "Book Reviews: Kieran Bonner, A Great Place to Raise Kids: Interpretation, Science and the Urban–Rural Debate." *Canadian Review of Sociology and Anthropology* 38 (1): 349–355.

Rapport, Nigel. 1993. *Diverse World-Views in an English Village*. Edinburgh: University of Edinburgh Press.

Razack, Sherene H. 2002. "Gendered Racial Violence and Spatialized Justice: The Murder of Pamela George." In S. Razack, ed. *Race, Space, and the Law: Unmapping a White Settler Society*. Toronto: Between the Lines, 121–156.

Redfield, R. 1964. "French-Canadian Culture in St-Denis." In M. Rioux and Y. Martin, eds. *French-Canadian Society*. Vol. 1. Toronto: McClelland & Stewart, 57–62.

Redfield, R. 1947. "The Folk Society." *American Journal of Sociology* 52 (Jan.): 293–303.

Redfield, R. 1930. *Tepoztlan, a Mexican Village: A Study of Folk Life*. Chicago: University of Chicago Press.

Rioux, Marcel. 1964. "Remarks on the Socio-Cultural Development of French Canada." In M. Rioux and Y. Martin, eds. *French-Canadian Society*. Vol. 1. Toronto: McClelland & Stewart.

Sacouman, R.J. 1981. "The 'Peripheral' Maritimes and Canada-wide Marxist Political Economy." *Studies in Political Economy* 6 (Autumn): 135–150.

Sacouman, R.J. 1980. "The Semi-proletarianization of the Domestic Mode of Production and the Underdevelopment of Rural Areas in Maritime Canada." Unpublished paper.

Shaffir, W. 1974. *Life in a Religious Community: The Lubavitcher Chassidim in Montreal*. Toronto: Holt, Rinehart and Winston.

Shulman, N. 1976. "Role Differentiation in Urban Networks." *Sociological Focus* 9: 149–158.

Silver, Jim. 2006. *In Their Own Voices: Building Urban Aboriginal Communities*. Halifax: Fernwood.

Simich, Laura. 2003. "Negotiating Boundaries of Refugee Resettlement: A Study of Settlement Patterns and Social Support." *The Canadian Review of Sociology and Anthropology* 40 (5): 575–592.

Simmel, George. 1950. "The Metropolis and Mental Life." In *The Sociology of George Simmel*. Glencoe, Illinois: Free Press, 409–424.

Sprenger, Audrey. 2002. "Communities are Social: Locating Homeplace in the Sociology of Law." In G. MacDonald, ed.

Social Context and Social Location in the Sociology of Law. Peterborough, Ontario: Broadview Press, 209–228.

Statistics Canada 2003. "Aboriginal Peoples of Canada: A Demographic Profile."

Stebbins, R.A. 1994. *The Franco-Calgarians: French Language, Leisure, and Linguistic Life-Style in an Anglophone City.* Toronto: University of Toronto Press.

Stevenson, Deborah. 2003. *Cities and Urban Culture.* Philadelphia: Open University Press.

Strathern, Marilyn. 1982. "The Village as an Idea: Constructs of Village-ness in Elmdon, Essex." In A.P. Cohen, ed. *Belonging, Identity and Social Organization in British Rural Cultures.* Manchester: University Press, 247–277.

Suttles, G.D. 1968. *The Social Order of the Slum.* Chicago: University of Chicago Press.

Thurlow, Crispin, Laura Lengel and Alice Tomic. 2004. *Computer Mediated Communication: Social Interaction and the Internet.* London; Thousand Oaks; New Delhi: Sage.

Tönnies, Ferdinand. [1887] 1957. *Community and Society.* New York: Harper and Row.

Weber, Max. 1946. "Capitalism And Rural Society in Germany." In Hans Gerth and C.W. Mills, eds. *From Max Weber: Essays in Sociology.* New York: Oxford University Press, 363–385.

Webster, C.W., and John Hood. 2001. "Surveillance in the community: Community development through the use of closed-circuit television." In L. Keeble and B.D. Loader, eds. *Community Informatics: Shaping Computer-Mediated Social Relations.* London; New York: Routledge, 220–239.

Wellman, Barry. 2001. "Physical place and cyberplace: The rise of networked individualism." In L. Keeble and B.D. Loader, eds. *Community Informatics: Shaping Computer-Mediated Social Relations.* London; New York: Routledge, 17–42.

Wellman, Barry. 1992. "Which types of ties and networks give what kinds of social support?" *Advances in Group Processes.* Vol. 9: 207–235.

Wellman, Barry. 1978. "The Community Question: The Intimate Networks of East Yorkers." University of Toronto Centre for Urban and Community Studies and Department of Sociology.

Wells, Karen, and Sophie Watson. 2005. "A Politics of Resentment: Shopkeepers in a London Neighbourhood." *Ethnic and Racial Studies* 28 (2): 261–277.

Winland, D.N. 1993. "The Quest for Mennonite Peoplehood: Ethno-religious Identity and the Dilemma of Definitions." *Canadian Review of Sociology and Anthropology* 30 (1): 110–138.

Wirth, L. 1938. "Urbanism as a Way of Life." *American Journal of Sociology* 44 (1): 1–24.

Young, M. and P. Wilmott. 1957. *Family and Kinship in East London.* London: Routledge & Kegan Paul.

Cohesion and Morality: A Critical Look at Durkheim

Sociological theory in the eighteenth and nineteenth centuries was powerfully influenced by belief in progress and evolution of social and biological forms from simpler to more advanced states. Where Tönnies expressed nostalgia for an idealized past when communities were simpler and more cohesive, other theorists embraced an idealized future in which societies were becoming progressively more dynamic and heterogenous. They viewed the industrial and political revolutions occurring in Europe and North America not as a threat to social order, but as the emergence of a new and potentially better order based on science and reason. This new order promised to liberate individuals from the constraints of superstition and feudalism. The central question that concerned them was how individuals, freed from traditional constraints, could nonetheless cohere into a greater whole called society.

THE EMERGENCE OF THE SCIENTIFIC STUDY OF SOCIETY

Early theorists of society struggled to account for the spectacular advance of science and the Industrial Revolution in European societies. Prevailing theories of progress conceptualized societies as developing through a series of stages, with non-industrial societies viewed as being at earlier stages of development than Western European cities. Comparative studies of supposedly more primitive societies promised to yield insights into the origins and course of development of technologically advanced societies. Such theories gathered momentum under the impact of colonialism. Following the European conquest of Africa and Asia, and the Americas, the colonizers and missionaries began to study these subjugated societies. They tended to take for granted the superiority of European societies and the more "primitive" or "uncivilized" status of the peoples they conquered.

Auguste Comte and Positive Society

Auguste Comte (1798–1857) developed one of the earliest and most famous theories of societal progress. Comte wrote during the restoration of Bourbon monarchy in France, following the turbulent period of the French Revolution and the defeat of Napoleon in 1815. Comte sought to understand the basis of the new order in which the old powers of absolute monarchy, military, and church had been swept away. Comte argued that changes at the level of society reflect fundamental changes in prevailing ways of thinking and reasoning. He proposed a law of three stages in which the emergence of distinct types of knowledge and belief is associated with distinct forms of organization of society and social institutions.

The **theological stage** is a form of society dominated by primitive religious thought. People seek to explain events and phenomena in terms of supernatural forces such as gods or spirits. Such a society is based on intuition, sentiment, and feelings. It is ruled by priests and by military personnel, and its moral structure is centred around blood ties.

The **metaphysical stage** of society is associated with a limited development of critical thought. It is marked by a transition to belief in a single deity and some kind of unified reality. People try to explain phenomena in terms of abstract forces rather than irrational spirits. Such forms of thought foster a concept of society as unified around a centralized state.

The third stage is **positive society** based on scientific **empiricism**. Science seeks to explain phenomena through factual knowledge derived from observation, experiment, comparison, and prediction. It rejects religious explanations as unobservable and untestable. Scientists rather than priests become the intellectual and spiritual leaders of emerging rational, industrial society.

Changes in patterns of thought are thus mirrored in changing social structures. In military states progress is based on conquest and plunder, but in industrial states wealth is generated by the rational, scientific organization of work. Comte reasoned that war would have little place in industrial societies since plunder was no longer the basis of wealth. Comte saw scientific reasoning as the decisive feature of societal progress. The application of science to the large-scale organization of labour in factories fosters the unparalleled development of wealth and resources in Western European societies.

What was needed to complete the transition to a positive society was a science of society itself—*sociology*. Sociology, Comte reasoned, would complete the study of **natural laws**, which had begun with the physical world. The scientific study of the laws of society promised to provide a factual basis on which to reorganize society in more rational ways. Comte is one of the first philosophers to advocate the study of society in essentially the same way as the physical sciences, using methods of controlled observation and experiment to search for law-like or invariant relations between observable social phenomena. Such methods would have vast practical applications for engineering controlled social change.

Problems with Comte   The direct influence of Comte's ideas on modern sociology is small. Comte's theory of intellectual and social progress through theological, metaphysical, and positive stages lacks any clear statement of the mechanisms that might drive such changes, or why either the prevailing forms of thought or forms of societal organization should develop in the directions he proposed. Comte also failed to develop clear ideas on how to link observed empirical regularities with unobservable "laws" that he proposed as explanations. The main value of his thought in the history of sociology lies in his insistence that all questions about change and variation in human nature and social organization can in principle be settled by scientific investigation. In this sense he is the father of the discipline of sociology.

Herbert Spencer and Social Evolution

The British philosopher Herbert Spencer (1820–1903) was strongly influenced by Comte's classification of stages in the development of societies and his scientific approach to the study of social organization. Spencer's goal was to develop a grand theory of **evolution** that would explain the mechanisms underlying social progress. These evolutionary mechanisms, he reasoned, were essentially the same for the physical, biological, and social phenomena (Keat and Urry 1982, 80). All matter, he argued, tends to move from a state of relatively disorganized flux towards increasing order and stability. In the course of this movement, simple forms and

structures give rise to more complex ones by means of two simultaneous processes: differentiation and integration. **Differentiation** refers to the breakdown of simple, unspecialized structures into many separate specialized parts. **Integration** means the development of a specialized **function** that preserves unity among the differentiated parts. Societies evolve towards even greater institutional complexity based on greater specialization of tasks or division of labour. This complexity is integrated through the development of some central coordinating agency, such as the modern state.

Spencer saw competitive struggle as the fundamental mechanism governing evolutionary change in both organic and social systems. Competition encourages more complex and specialized forms to emerge out of simpler ones. Organisms that develop the flexibility to adapt to a specialized niche or develop specialized ways of obtaining food or other scarce resources gain a competitive edge. Competitive struggle between social groups similarly promotes flexible adaptation that gives rise to differentiation and specialization, and in turn the need for centralized regulation and integration. Groups that cannot make the necessary adaptations will be eliminated in favour of those that can. It was Spencer, not Darwin, who first coined the phrase "survival of the fittest" to describe this process.

For adaptations to be successful in promoting the survival of social systems, Spencer reasoned, they must meet three critical conditions or functions. There must be a *sustaining system*, which comprises economic arrangements, such as agricultural and industrial production, that provide a means of livelihood for members of society; a *distribution system*, which allocates products and services between members; and a *regulation system*, which manages and coordinates these separate activities. More advanced societies are those with more flexible systems of regulation, namely those based on voluntary rather than forced compliance.

Spencer's ideas had enormous impact on the society of his time. Leading industrialists such as the Carnegies and the Rockefellers welcomed him when he travelled through the United States in 1882. His model of competitive advantage meshed perfectly with their view of themselves as the fittest competitors to survive in economic markets. Competitive struggle in economic markets maximizes economic progress by favouring the most flexible and adaptive competitors while the weaker ones fail.

Problems with Spencer   Spencer's view of societies as all evolving at different rates on a single evolutionary path from essentially the same "primitive" origins to more "advanced" states has been widely challenged. Critics argue that different societies have developed in very different ways, and there is no reason to assume that all will converge into one societal form. Moreover, some of the societies that Spencer viewed as primitive may have regressed into that state due to the impact of western colonial conquest rather than as a result of inherently weak adaptive mechanisms. Spencer's main contribution to the development of sociology is seen in his conception of society as a functioning system comparable to biological organisms. Spencer pioneered the comparative study of whole societies as functioning systems that develop and change through processes of differentiation and specialization, giving rise to social forms with specialized functions. His ideas had a major influence on the development of structural functionalist theory.

DURKHEIM'S THEORY OF MORALITY AND COHESION

Emile Durkheim (1858–1917) shared with Comte and Spencer a concern with the comparative evolution of societal forms and a commitment to a positivist or natural-science methodology that seeks to identify cause-and-effect relations shaping social behaviour (Keat and Urry 1982, 81–82). He rejected the idea that deities or metaphysical forces could explain the observable social world. At the same time, however, he stressed the importance of internal mental states or consciousness of individuals, as well as their moral beliefs and values and their motives for actions, in structuring social order. Durkheim's influence upon the subsequent development of sociology far exceeds that of Comte and Spencer.

Emile Durkheim (1858–1917), a pioneer in the scientific study of society.

Library of Congress

Details of Durkheim's personal life give valuable insights into his sociology. He lived through the horror of civil war, and the misery of being a displaced person and a member of a minority group that faced systemic discrimination. These experiences prompted his central interest in studying the moral foundations of social cohesion and order. Durkheim was born a Jew in the Rhineland province of Alsace, a territory fought over by France and Prussia during the nineteenth century. His family moved to France during a period when anti-Semitism was widespread.

France at that time was just emerging from a long period of political instability that had begun with the French Revolution of 1789, followed by the Napoleonic Wars, the restoration of the Bourbon monarchy, further revolutions in 1830 and 1848, and the coup d'état of Napoleon's nephew Louis Napoleon, whose government suffered a crushing military defeat by Prussia in 1870. In the chaos that followed, workers in Paris staged a revolt and briefly established an independent local government in Paris between March and May 1871, known as the Paris Commune. Marx praised the Commune as a true proletarian or workers' uprising. Government troops, however, brutally crushed the Commune with mass executions. Eventually, a more stable Third Republic emerged, which was to last until the German invasion of 1940. The young Durkheim strongly supported the Third Republic and the promise of stability that it brought. He saw himself as a socialist but, unlike Marx, he rejected revolutionary class politics in favour of a more administrative form of socialism.

As a Jew in mostly Catholic France, Durkheim experienced anti-Semitism first-hand. He became involved politically in the Dreyfus case in 1894. Alfred Dreyfus, an Alsatian Jew like Durkheim, was a French army officer. He was falsely accused of selling information to the Germans and was convicted on the basis of minimal evidence. After a counterintelligence review concluded he was innocent, it was a full two years before his case was reopened and he was pardoned. All France took sides in what came to be seen as a blatant case of **anti-Semitism**.

Durkheim himself was an atheist, but he understood the intense commitment of Jews to their community and the power of Judaism as a social force. In his social thought, Durkheim insisted that religious tolerance and respect for individual differences were essential moral foundations for social cohesion in a modern multiracial, and multiethnic society.

These themes of emotional commitment to community and recognition of the religious character of such commitment, combined with recognizing the importance of respect for individual rights and tolerance for diversity, are central to Durkheim's sociological writings. Each of his major works addresses the question of the origins and nature of **morality** as the expression of the relationship between individuals and society. In his first major work, *The Division of Labour in Society* ([1893] 1964), Durkheim develops his theory of how societies evolve from relatively simple, undifferentiated, small-scale communities to complex and heterogeneous industrial societies, based on new forms of social cohesion. His most significant contributions to contemporary sociology are his pioneering work in the application of scientific methods to the study of society, his focus on macrosocietal structures as the basis for understanding individual happiness, his explication of the foundations of social order in industrial society, and his seminal concept of *anomie* or moral breakdown. These contributions are examined in detail below.

The Scientific Study of Morality

Durkheim insists that social forces form a distinct level of reality from individual psychology. He argues that scientific methods should be used to study **social facts** as if they were things ([1893] 1964, 14). Durkheim does not claim that social facts can be observed like physical objects, but rather that they share the characteristics of things in two respects: they are *external* to individuals, and they exercise *constraints* over individual behaviour. When people feel external constraints on their behaviour, they are experiencing the presence of social facts. Wishful thinking by individuals will not make such constraints disappear.

In the preface to *The Division of Labour in Society* ([1893] 1964, 32), Durkheim defines his goal as using scientific methods to explore the regularities or "laws" that explain moral life. He argues that the conditions under which people live in society give rise to moral rules, and these rules change when society changes. Moral rules in complex industrial societies are necessarily different from those in simpler societies. Moral order, for Durkheim, refers to two central features of society. The first is *integration*, or the achievement of a sense of **solidarity** and cohesiveness with others. The second is **regulation**, which involves restraint on the pursuit of self-interest, including self-restraint or **altruism**.

Durkheim's main argument in *The Division of Labour in Society* is that there are two fundamentally different kinds of solidarity and therefore of morality. First, there is **mechanical solidarity**, which is based on sameness and shared conditions. This idea is captured in the saying that "birds of a feather flock together." People feel closer to others with whom they share very similar backgrounds and experiences than with those who seem very different. The other form of solidarity is **organic solidarity**. This is based on recognition of differences that complement and complete us and that are experienced in exchange and mutual dependence. Durkheim gives the example of the bonding between a woman and a man in marriage, where their differences and resulting dependence unites them. Durkheim argues that organic solidarity based on complementary differences is ultimately stronger than the simpler mechanical solidarity based on sameness.

Law and Morality

We can study moral order through how members of the society regulate each other's behaviour. Durkheim argues that members of any community will view behaviour that threatens the solidarity of their community as immoral, and will sanction it. Law constitutes the codified morality of a society. Hence the study of law provides an objective basis for the scientific study of the underlying moral life of the society.

Different kinds of solidarity are reflected in different kinds of law. *Mechanical solidarity* based on sameness promotes penal or **repressive law**. Such law is concerned with the punishment of offenders who have transgressed the shared values of the community. Durkheim uses the French words **conscience collective** to refer to this sense of collective moral awareness and mutual obligation, defining it as "the totality of beliefs and sentiments common to the average citizens of the same society" (Durkheim [1893] 1964, 79). There is some disagreement over whether conscience collective should be translated into English as "collective conscience"—referring to people's sense of what is right or wrong—or as "collective consciousness"—referring to people's sense of involvement in a community. The French term implies both meanings. Many sociologists who write about Durkheim's work prefer to use the French form to alert readers that the term has this dual meaning.

Durkheim emphasizes that the totality of beliefs and sentiments associated with the conscience collective forms a system that has its own life and exists independently of individual members of society. Any one member encounters these beliefs and sentiments as social facts, as constraints upon behaviour above and beyond individual whims or feelings. Repressive laws control behaviour that violates the collective conscience of the community of people. The societal function of punishment is not primarily to take revenge against the perpetrator of crime, but to publicly reaffirm collective values and thus to strengthen the collective conscience itself.

Organic solidarity, based on differences and mutual dependence, is reflected in **restitutive law** or contract law, including commercial, contractual, constitutional, and administrative regulations. Restitutive law is less concerned with punishment than with the return of things as they were, or with re-establishing reciprocal obligations between members of a society. Contracts presuppose a division of labour among people who have specialized functions and who therefore depend upon each other to perform these functions in dependable ways.

Durkheim uses these two models—mechanical solidarity with its repressive laws, and organic solidarity with its restitutive laws—to describe the evolution of society from simple agricultural to complex industrial patterns.

Societies Based on Mechanical Solidarity

People who live in simpler, preindustrial societies lead very similar lives, with little specialization or division of labour beyond that associated with age and sex. The result, Durkheim reasoned, is that people feel bound to each other mostly by a sense of sameness and shared beliefs and sentiments. The stronger the uniformity of beliefs and practices in such communities, the stronger the social solidarity— hence the intensity with which these beliefs and practices are defended against diversity.

For Durkheim, any strong convictions that are shared by members of a community will inspire reverence, and thus take on a religious character. Violation of strongly-shared convictions will be viewed as sin, and laws upholding them will be essentially repressive. Repressive or penal law is thus, at root, religious law. Religion is critically important and tends to regulate all details of social life. Nonconformity constitutes a threat precisely because uniformity of beliefs is the basis of solidarity. If such beliefs were allowed to weaken through tolerance for nonconformity, then the very cohesion of the community itself would be threatened.

Transition in Forms of Society   Mechanical solidarity based on sameness can be very powerful in relatively isolated and homogeneous communities, but it cannot retain its hold over individual consciousness in the face of rapid social change, or in the context of heterogeneous, multiethnic, and multi-religious societies such as the France of Durkheim's time. The erosion of mechanical solidarity as a unifying force is the inevitable result of the cultural, demographic, and economic changes that occur with industrialization. Communication expands over vaster areas, linking formerly isolated and distinct communities. Populations expand, so that people are forced to diversify their economies in order to survive. Division of labour promotes cooperation among diverse and distinct groups of people. These changes profoundly affect the moral basis of social order. The conscience collective of beliefs and sentiments shared among diverse peoples must necessarily become more abstract and detached from locality. As Durkheim expresses it, "the gods take leave of space." The god of humanity is necessarily less concrete than the god of an individual clan. Division of labour

makes possible individual emancipation from group culture. As people develop specialized functions, they have different life experiences and so develop different perspectives on life. Once people experience diversity and freedom of thought, Durkheim reasons, they experience liberties as increasingly more necessary and inevitable. There can be no turning back.

Societies Based on Organic Solidarity   Organic solidarity is a form of social cohesion that grows out of division of labour and interdependence. As people become more specialized, they also become more dependent upon each other. A homesteading family engaged in subsistence farming, for example, may survive with little or no help from similar homesteaders, but specialized workers in a factory cannot survive without a host of other specialized workers supplying their other basic needs. Members of a society characterized by advanced division of labour are united by mutual obligations and not merely by sentiments of sameness. Cooperation is essential. It cannot be neglected.

One of the theories of urbanism suggests that increasing size, density, and heterogeneity in populations inevitably weakens social cohesion. Durkheim rejects this view, arguing instead that homogeneous societies, made up of relatively undifferentiated family groupings, are actually more fragile. The parts, or family groupings, that make up such societies can break away from each other and remain relatively independent in their small villages or kin communities. This is impossible in societies characterized by advanced division of labour. Heterogeneous, urban societies may foster a far greater degree of individualism, but these individuals are also far more interdependent. Specialized parts need each other and cannot break away. Diversity gives rise to ties of mutual obligation and cooperation that grow progressively stronger as specialization increases.

In heterogenous societies, repressive or religious law declines in importance as the core of common beliefs and sentiments declines. Restitutive or contract law expands in its place to regulate division of labour, defining the rules of justice that guide individual contracts. Respect for the individual and for individual rights constitutes the fundamental ground of justice, or what Durkheim calls the "**precontractual basis of contract**." Such respect is not merely good, it is essential for social order and cohesion in modern society. The religion of **humanism**, or moral individualism, replaces the religious dogma of simpler societies. Its moral core is not selfish self-interest, but reciprocal obligations and mutual respect. Even purely economic contracts presuppose a precontractual basis of moral standards that underlies and regulates the agreements between people and determines standards of justice.

Problems with Durkheim Critics challenge Durkheim's model of a unilinear process of change from mechanical to organic solidarity as seriously oversimplified. Division of labour and contractual obligations occur within and between non-specialized, simpler societies, and likewise, mechanical solidarity is evident in industrial societies, manifest in strong identification with religious and ethnic groups. Repressive, penal law has by no means disappeared in modern societies. Authoritarian regimes abound in the twenty-first century, demanding conformity to dominant religious and political doctrines.

In defense of Durkheim, the transition from mechanical to organic solidarity is better understood as involving a relative shift in the importance of shared culture over interdependence of labour, rather than an absolute shift from one form of solidarity to another. As a member of the Jewish community in France, Durkheim was well aware of the continuing strength of religious and ethnic affiliations, and he probably did not intend his formulation to be interpreted in absolute terms. Specialization and differentiation exist in non-industrialized societies, but not to the same extent as in industrial societies.

The criticism, that repressive religious law has not disappeared, is harder to deal with. Division of labour has the potential for sustaining organic solidarity based on mutual obligation and duty, with humanism as the supreme religion. Yet this state is far from being realized. The struggle to establish a universal commitment to human rights is one of the most pressing international moral issues of our time. Respect for basic human rights is an important requirement for political stability in our interdependent world community, but it has not yet been achieved. Like the Marxist vision of a socialist utopia, Durkheim's vision of a cohesive, cooperative world community has nowhere been realized.

Anomic Division of Labour

Durkheim's concept of **anomie** remains a lasting contribution to sociological understanding of the moral ills of contemporary industrial society. Anomie is a complex concept, referring to a relative absence or confusion of values and to a corresponding lack of clear regulations or norms for behaviour. In a state of anomie, people feel lost and disorganized, unsure of how to behave or what to believe in, so that their lives come to feel meaningless or purposeless.

Durkheim's analysis of **anomic division of labour** anticipates contemporary writing on the meaninglessness of much industrial work and the breakdown of moral order in the face of injustice and inequality. Conflicts are not a necessary result of industrialized society, and they cannot be resolved by a retreat to the mechanical solidarity of nationalism or religion. Moral uniformity cannot be forced in the face of functional diversity. The key problem, Durkheim argued, is lack of just regulation. Parts of the social order are insufficiently coordinated, leaving individual workers with a sense of isolation and meaninglessness. The **laissez-faire economic system**, with its powerful inducements to selfish behaviour, hurts people. Workers feel separated and alone, without a sense of how their work is important for others.

Unjust or forced division of labour, Durkheim argues, is a major cause of anomie. People experience division of labour as just when they can choose their occupations freely to best fit their natural talents. People lose this sense of natural cooperation when they are forced against their will into unjust contracts. The conditions for just contracts are violated by inherited wealth and poverty. There cannot be rich and poor at birth, says Durkheim, without there being unjust contracts (Durkheim [1893] 1964, 384).

Fractionalized work is a further cause of anomie. Such work occurs when bosses try to deskill and cheapen their workforce by breaking jobs down into small, repetitive components.

It is difficult for people to feel they are contributing to an organic community of interdependent workers when their own contribution is so obviously unimportant and they themselves so easily replaced. Work becomes meaningless when jobs are reduced to monotonous routines determined by a machine. Cooperative division of labour is very different from such forced **fragmentation**. Durkheim insists that ensuring justice in the treatment of workers is a moral imperative in industrial society. It is not enough that there be rules governing contracts; the rules must be just.

The analyses of Durkheim and Marx are largely in agreement thus far. Where they diverge is on the question of whether just and egalitarian regulation of work can be achieved within a profit-driven capitalist economic order, and the role of class conflict in achieving justice for workers. Durkheim describes factors that give rise to "abnormal forms" of division of labour. Marx exposes the origins of these abnormal forms in the exploitative structures of capitalism, and calls on workers to unite to overthrow their chains. The Marxist thesis is that justice is impossible within a profit-motivated system where a small class of people controls the means of production upon which others depend. From this perspective, capitalism itself creates the lack of regulation, the **egoism**, and the immorality in collective life that Durkheim identifies as abnormal. *Alienation* rather than anomie is the central concept in Marxist theory.

The remainder of this chapter focuses on Durkheim's seminal study *Suicide* ([1897] 1951).

SUICIDE: A SCIENTIFIC STUDY OF HAPPINESS AND SOCIAL COHESION

Durkheim designed his study of suicide as a scientific test of his central theory that individual happiness depends upon two central conditions of the moral order of society: integration and regulation. When the moral order of a society is disturbed or undermined, he reasoned, the level of unhappiness among members of that society will rise. The challenge Durkheim faced was to find some objective scientific method that draws on observable, empirical evidence or "social facts" to study such essentially intangible and subjective states as social integration and unhappiness. Durkheim's brilliantly innovative proposal was to use data on suicide rates to measure the level of unhappiness within a society. He defines suicide as "intentional self-death by any action known to have that effect" (Durkheim [1897] 1951, 44)—a definition that focuses on intent to die rather than on the outcome of action.

The act of committing suicide is a private individual act, but suicide *rates* are social facts. The suicide rate is the actual number of people per 100 000 population recorded as having intentionally killed themselves. It is a statistic that is regularly published by government agencies. Suicide, thankfully, occurs relatively rarely, and it is almost impossible to observe directly. When statistics are kept for large populations and over long periods of time, however, it becomes possible to study patterns and to compare differences in rates among societies and smaller communities within them. For Durkheim, therefore, officially recorded suicide rates provide objective facts that can stand as **indicators** of the general level of happiness of members of different communities.

Durkheim was not trying to predict suicide by any one individual but rather to predict the conditions that increase the general level of unhappiness in a society, and thus the proportion of people unhappy enough to consider killing themselves. He carefully examines bio-medical factors such as mental illnesses, but concludes that such illnesses tend to occur randomly across populations and do not account for differences in rates of suicide between social groups. Durkheim's theory is that specific kinds of social conditions generate increasing unhappiness and higher suicide rates.

Durkheim's Model of Social Order and Suicide Rates

Durkheim theorized that two central features of social order influenced levels of happiness: integration and regulation. Integration refers to people's sense of closeness and bonding between themselves and others, while regulation refers to

people's sense of stability and clarity in normative expectations. Abnormal states of either integration or regulation in society, he reasoned, whether too weak or too excessive, would threaten the general level of happiness of members. Logically, his model predicts four abnormal states, each associated with a particular form or type of suicide.

1. Integration: Social bonds give happiness

Weak Integration: **Egoism**	Excessive Integration: **Altruism**
Paired comparisons: Protestant–Catholic	Army: Officers, enlisted men vs. conscripts
Married–Single	Religious martyrs, suicide bombers
Children–Childless	
Widowed with children–Widowed without children	Inuit: old leave group when food scarce
Rural–Urban	Japan, Korea: honour suicides
Ethnic minority–Majority	
Educated–Uneducated	

2. Regulation: Normative order gives happiness

Weak Regulation: **Anomie**	Excessive Regulation: **Fatalism**
Sudden wealth: boom, lottery win	Slaves Older childless married women
Sudden poverty, loss of social position	Very young husbands Women in extreme patriarchal society (China, Japan, India)
Divorce	

Weak integration is associated with **egoistic suicide**, when people lack a sense of strong bonds linking them with others. Weak regulation fosters **anomic suicide**, when people lack a sense of their place in society and what is expected of them. At the other extreme, excessive integration fosters **altruistic suicide**, when people submerge their individuality into the group and sacrifice themselves for the group. Lastly, excessive regulation fosters **fatalistic suicide**, when people's lives are entirely regimented by group norms.

To test the model using scientific methods, Durkheim needed observable measures of each of his four key types of societal conditions. While his measures were crude by contemporary standards he does provide an impressive array of evidence to support his model.

To test the proposed association between weak integration and *egoistic* suicide, Durkheim used a series of comparisons based on religious affiliation and marital status as indicators of relative weakness or strength of social bonds. Protestants, he reasoned, emphasized free inquiry by individuals while Catholics have a ready-made faith and relative certainty of beliefs. Thus Protestant communities on average would have weaker social cohesion than Catholics. Durkheim predicted that Protestants would have higher suicide rates than Catholics. Official suicide rates kept for Protestant and Catholic administrative areas in Europe over many decades confirmed this prediction. In Protestant areas the recorded suicide rates were significantly higher than in Catholic areas.

Secondly, he reasoned that single and childless people have weaker social bonds relative to married people with children, and hence predictably would have higher rates of suicide. Almost all the comparative data on rates of suicide confirmed these predictions. Single men committed suicide more often than married men, childless married men more than husbands with children, and childless widowers more than widowers with children. Similarly, Durkheim reasoned that urban areas are less cohesive than rural because people are less likely to know each other. Again his prediction was supported: urban communities did have higher rates of suicide than rural ones. Durkheim further reasoned that highly educated people would experience lower social cohesion than less educated people because education promotes critical thinking and hence reduced acceptance of traditional norms and practices.

A particularly significant comparison is between Jews and Gentiles. Jews are predominantly urban dwellers and are highly educated, both factors associated with higher suicide rates in general. As a persecuted religious minority, however, they tend to be intensely cohesive. Durkheim hypothesizes that the internal cohesion would counteract the divisive forces of urbanism and education. The data confirm his prediction that Jews have lower suicide rates than non-Jews, lower even than Catholics.

There is only one statistic that goes against Durkheim's predictions. Women had higher suicide rates when married than when never married, although the rates were lower when they had children than when they were without children. Durkheim concludes that marriage benefits men more than women. Men, he suggests, need restraints more than women, an argument developed further below in the discussion of anomic suicide. In general, however, the recorded suicide rates were strongly consistent with Durkheim's theoretical prediction that, under conditions where bonds of social cohesion are relatively weak, suicide rates are relatively high.

Durkheim's second broad theoretical prediction is that rates of *anomic* suicide will be higher under social conditions when people experience a sense of loss of meaningful regulations ordering their lives. When people have a clear sense of their position in life, have meaningful goals and realistic expectations as to what they should be and should become, then they are contented and happy. But when these constraints are vague, and the limits unclear, people tend to become dissatisfied with their lot, unhappy, and frustrated. Durkheim predicts that the suicide rate, reflecting the proportion of people too unhappy to live, will increase as social regulation declines.

The main data with which he tests this prediction are periods of economic boom or bust compared with periods of relative stability. One might expect that people may become depressed during periods of economic collapse, but Durkheim shows that boom times are similarly associated with higher suicide rates. When people suddenly become rich, he reasoned, the regulations that shaped their former lives may lose all meaning, and their lives lose direction. Most people expect to work hard all their lives to provide and care for themselves and their family members, but if they suddenly win a fortune, then much of the point of working or doing anything may be lost. Regulations are lacking. Goals appear without limit and consequently without value or meaning. Under such conditions of anomie, Durkheim reasoned, suicide rates go up. Sudden poverty may also plunge people into despair, not simply because of privation, but because all the standards and expectations of their former position in life no longer apply.

Similar feelings of anomie may follow divorce, when the regulations and sexual constraints of marriage are suddenly lifted. The relationship holds at the aggregate level of societies as a whole, and not only at the individual level. Durkheim reasoned that during periods when the institution of marriage itself is weakened by rising divorce rates, the marriage tie would offer weaker protection from social disorganization (Besnard 2000b, 134). Durkheim's evidence confirmed that communities with high divorce rates also have high suicide rates, again with men suffering more than women. As noted above, Durkheim reasoned that men need the constraints of marriage more than women, because general social controls on men's sexual freedom are so much weaker than for women. Divorced men are more prone to go on drunken sprees, consort with many different women, and then fall into despair and suicide. The explanation is only guesswork on Durkheim's part, as he had no direct data on motives, but the gender difference in suicide rates by marital status in western societies has stood the test of time. Divorced people have a four to five times higher rate of suicide than do married people, with divorced men being significantly more vulnerable than women.

Excessive Integration and Regulation Durkheim theorized that excessive levels of integration or regulation also disrupt social balance, giving rise to *altruistic* and *fatalistic* suicide respectively. *Altruistic suicide* occurs when social bonds are so strong that people submerge their individuality into the group and become willing to sacrifice themselves for the honour or well-being of the group. Durkheim identifies suicides by military officers or samurai in traditional Japan as altruistic suicides. Samurai would rather die by falling upon their own swords than dishonour the emperor. During the Second World War, Japanese kamikaze pilots flew their planes directly into their target, knowing that they would die, but willing to do so for the success of their country in war. During times of famine, old or sick Inuit people would sacrifice themselves by walking away from their camp to die so that others could travel more swiftly in search of food.

Durkheim suggests that excessive integration, and thus altruistic suicide, is comparatively rare in modern society because individualism is valued more intensely than religion or group commitment. Only in the army did he find evidence of excessive integration and high rates of altruistic suicide. Groups with stronger commitment to the army had higher suicide rates—army personnel more than civilians, volunteers more than conscripts, officers more than privates, and re-enlisted men more than newcomers. If suicide rates were merely due to the hard life of the army, Durkheim reasoned, one would have expected all these rates to be reversed. Volunteers, officers, and re-enlisted men are more committed to their group and more willing to die for their unit and their country. More recent examples of altruistic suicide have included members of the Irish Republican Army imprisoned by the British government, who starved themselves to death to assert their status as "prisoners of conscience" rather than "common criminals." In contemporary conflicts in the Middle East, altruistic suicide has sadly become commonplace, with scores of people willing to offer their lives as suicide bombers to attack targets they identify as enemies of Islam.

The state of excessive regulation in society, Durkheim theorized, would lead to an increase in *fatalism*, a despair arising when society offers minimal room for individuality. Durkheim found few conditions of excessive regulation in his data from European societies, but suggests that higher suicide rates among very young husbands and older childless married women might fit this category because their lives are so tightly constrained. We argue below that excessively patriarchal societies show higher rates of fatalistic suicide among women.

Methodological Challenges to Durkheim's Study

Over a hundred years after it was first published in 1897, Durkheim's study of suicide rates is still famous as a classic application of scientific methods to social issues. Durkheim hoped his analysis would revolutionize social science approaches to the phenomenon of suicide, but this recognition was not to come for another 60 years (Besnard 2000a, 97–105). Early critics reasoned that notwithstanding obvious social patterning, suicidal behaviour had to be understood primarily in psychological terms. Durkheim guessed that his four types of suicide were associated with psychological states such as loneliness, meaninglessness, submission, and despair, but he had no evidence to support such claims. Contemporary research into suicide motivation typically relies on analysis of suicide notes, or interviews and surveys with individuals who attempt but do not complete suicidal acts. However, in defence of Durkheim's methodology, statistical patterns differ markedly between attempts and completed suicides and may well reflect different psychological states (Lester 1997a, Ch. 1).

Other critics note that Durkheim lacked modern statistical techniques, and reanalyses of his original data have raised questions about some of Durkheim's findings. His famous generalization that Protestants have higher suicide rates than Catholics has become the focus of particularly sharp debate. In Durkheim's data, being "Protestant" was highly correlated with living in urban areas and being involved in business or entrepreneurial capitalism (Tomasi 2000, 15; Pickering 2000b, 66). Since all these states are associated with heightened individualism, it was not possible for Durkheim to separate their individual effects. Others challenge the circular way in which Durkheim reasoned from data to theory (Gane 2000), finding statistical patterns and then working up his theory to fit them. While such observations are interesting they do not test the accuracy of the theory.

A more serious methodological problem that arises with respect to all forms of aggregate data is the risk of **"ecological fallacy"**—the fallacy of arguing from grouped data to individual behaviour. In his discussion of anomic suicide, Durkheim shows that economic booms are associated with increased suicide rates. However, it is not possible to argue directly from such data that individuals who suddenly become wealthy are more prone to commit suicide. It might be impoverished individuals who feel left out of the rising wealth they see around them that push up the suicide rates. Durkheim did have some individual-level cause-of-death data to support his generalizations (Besnard 2000a, 119), but it remains difficult to determine whether suicide data reflect the tip of an iceberg of widespread unhappiness, or islands of misery in a wider sea of relative contentment with life.

A final area of methodological concern focuses on the questionable quality of national statistics on suicide rates themselves (Varty 2000). It is never easy to distinguish true suicides from homicides or accidental deaths, and coroners with differing religious convictions or institutional pressures to disguise problematic rates may well sway the classification of cases. Durkheim concluded that the data were good enough for his purposes, but as we discuss further below, social constructionist analysis casts some doubt on whether theories about motives for suicide can ever be clearly separated from classification of deaths (Douglas 1967).

Theoretical Challenges to Durkheim's Analysis

Durkheim's theoretical focus on structural factors at the societal level as causal explanations for suicide rates has been repeatedly challenged by theorists who find individual-level psychological explanations such as stress and personal sense of loneliness more appropriate (Halbwachs [1930] 1978; Travis 1990). Others argue that macro-level societal structures may impact on local relations and these in turn impact on individuals (Berkman et al. 2000).

Durkheim's four-part model of weak and excessive integration and regulation, giving rise to four different types of suicide, has been widely challenged. Durkheim himself could find only weak support for his model of excessive social constraints. As evidence of fatalism, he offers only the high suicide rates among young husbands and elderly childless wives. Similarly for altruism he cites only the high suicide rates within the armed forces. Other critics argue further that the distinction between anomie and egoism is weak, and might usefully be collapsed into a single category with "low integration" as the decisive societal condition explaining all suicides (Pope 1976).

More recent research, however, is coming out in favour of Durkheim's more complex four-part model (Davies and Neal 2000). Fatalism resulting from excessive regulation did not show up strongly in Durkheim's Eurocentric data, but it has proven useful to account for higher suicide rates among women in the strongly traditionalistic and closed rural societies of China, Japan, and India. Role expectations were so rigidly defined that people had no means to escape their excessively regulated lives. Evidence that suicide rates *fell* in Japan as the society became more individualistic cannot be explained by egoism (Davies and Neal 2000, 45). The concept of altruism also best accounts for obligatory suicides practised among the more privileged strata, particularly military elites in these hierarchical, collectivist societies.

In summary, Durkheim's *Suicide* is acclaimed as a masterpiece of sociological investigation, notwithstanding its flaws. It has inspired a host of later studies that explore the multiple questions it raises. His study shows irrefutably that suicide is socially patterned, a patterning that purely biomedical and psychological explanations cannot account for. His theoretical model remains dominant in suicide research, and his four types are widely accepted and applied (Lester 1997a, 133). The remainder of this chapter explores how contemporary theoretical perspectives in sociology have absorbed and responded to Durkheim's approach.

Suicide Rates—Statistics Canada

Sociological theories that address suicide rates must try to account for the following patterns: Canada as a whole enjoys exceptional advantages of political and economic stability, yet has suicide rates that approximate the global average. Within Canada, suicide rates are higher among young adults than older people, markedly higher among men of all ages than among women, and especially high for young men compared to young women. Rates among Inuit and First Nations peoples of all ages are some six times higher than Canadian averages, ranking among the highest of any community in the world.

In detail, international statistics cited by Lester (2003, 1157–1158) rank Canada thirty-fourth out of 69 countries with an overall suicide rate of 12.7 per 100 000, similar to the USA but higher than Britain at 8.1, and lower than France, Germany, and Sweden with rates between 17 to 20 per 100 000. Canada ranks far lower than countries recently separated from the former Soviet Bloc and the Russian federation with a rate of 26.5 per 100 000. The Canadian average, however, glosses over marked variation in rates by gender and race. Canada, along with other European societies, has a long established pattern of significantly higher rates for males than females. Among the age group 15 to 24, for example, suicide rates for men were 24.7 per 100 000 compared with 4.9 for women (Lester 2003, 1159–1160). Expressed another way, in Canada, young men are five times more likely to die from suicide than young women.

When suicide rates are separated out for First Nations communities within Canada there are striking differences. Between 1979 and 1991, the rates for the total population of Canada fluctuated between 13 and 15 per 100 000. For First Nations peoples, the rates fluctuated between a low of 28 and a high of 45 per 100 000—a rate that exceeds any nation state included in the World Health Organization list. Suicide rates for Aboriginal youth cited by Tester and McNicoll (2004) far exceed those for non-Aboriginal Canadians. In the age range 10 to 19, Aboriginal males approach 60 per 100 000 compared with 10 for non-Aboriginal males. In the most vulnerable age range, 20 to 29, the comparative rates are 108 and 30. For young females the rates are lower, but the gap between Aboriginal and non-Aboriginal remains striking. For the age range 10 to 15, the rates are 21 per 100 000 for Aboriginal females and 2.5 for non-Aboriginal females. In the most vulnerable 20-to-29 age cohort, the rates are 28 and 6 respectively. Tester and McNicoll note further that not only are suicide rates among Aboriginal peoples of Canada several orders of magnitude higher than for other Canadians, these rates are continuing to rise. Rates in Nunavut Territory were recorded as 48.7 per 100 000 in 1985–87. By 1988–90 the rate was 66.7. Then it rose again to 75.1 by 1991–93 and 85.5 by 1994–96. Similar dramatic increases are recorded for Inuit communities in Alaska, Greenland, Arctic Quebec, and Labrador. The remainder of this chapter explores how the four main theoretical perspectives in contemporary sociology draw upon and develop Durkheim's ideas.

Functionalist Perspectives on Suicide

The functionalist perspective draws extensively on Durkheim's model, linking higher suicide rates to periods of rapid social change that lead to social disorganization and weakened integration and regulation. The social upheaval in former Soviet bloc countries, as they shifted from communism to free market capitalism in the 1990s, explains the higher-than-average national suicide rates in these countries. In Canada, the rapid social and economic changes associated with the Quiet Revolution within Quebec in the 1970s was associated with a very rapid rise in suicide rates (Boyer et al. 1998; Sakinofsky 1998, 43). Quebec shifted from being ninth out of 10 Canadian provinces for male suicide rates in 1950 to first by 1990, and from being seventh to third for female rates. The strains of modernization and secularization, associated with a radical change in values and a steep decline in church attendance, are seen as responsible for widespread anomie. The numbers of people getting legally married declined while divorce rates rose sharply, factors noted by Durkheim as indicators of weakened social integration and regulation. Patterns in Quebec are consistent with national statistics from 53 modern nations (Lester 1997a, 126). Lester argues that these data strongly support Durkheim's theory that both weak integration and excessive integration are associated with higher-than-average suicide rates. Societies that are moderate on measures such as marriage rates and religious freedom have the lowest comparative suicide rates, while societies scoring high on both or low on both had higher suicide rates. The Quiet Revolution in Quebec seems to have shifted the society from moderate to low levels of social integration, with increasing suicide rates as the result.

Most functionalist research focuses on integration at the level of families and local communities. Surveys that measure suicidal thoughts and attempts typically show that family problems are important predictors of suicidal thoughts and behaviour. Adolescents most at risk of suicidal thoughts are those with a history of family disruption, a sense of not feeling loved within the family (Wild et al. 2004), having parents who are divorced or who have died, parents who have drug and alcohol problems, family violence, and especially when combined with experience of sexual abuse (Graham et al. 2004; Rossow and Lauritzen 2001; Lester 1997a, Ch. 5). Victims of bullying and marginalization at school are also more prone to suicidal thoughts, although the correlation is less strong (Baldry and Winkel 2003). Other plausible relationships between patterns of psychological or physical punishment by parents and suicidal thoughts as possibly the expression of aggression turned inwards show inconclusive results.

Studies using cause-of-death statistics confirm Durkheim's finding that marriage and children offer protection from completed suicide, and particularly so for men. Higher divorce rates continue to put men more at risk of suicide than women, but there have been some changes since Durkheim's time, with single men at less risk of suicide than formerly. Surveys that try to measure strength of social integration or bonds typically ask questions about number of close friends and relatives, membership in religious and voluntary associations, and frequency, intensity, and extent of social supports. These measures are closely associated with measures of personal sense of well-being and positive coping strategies, and overall mental and physical health (Berkman et al. 2000).

Measures of religious affiliation have had mixed results. In modern society, commitment to spiritual values of any kind seems more important than distinctions between Protestant or Catholic (Garroutte et al. 2003). Conformity to prevailing cultural values, rather than what the values are, seems to protect adolescents from suicidal thoughts (Lam et al. 2004). Among adolescents in Hong Kong, for example, girls and boys were less at risk of suicidal thoughts when they accepted sex-typical role expectations. Commitment to values of self-direction and independence reduced the risk for boys but was irrelevant for girls, while conversely endorsement of values of obedience and respect for elders reduced risk for girls but was irrelevant for boys.

Rural and Urban Differences

Durkheim felt safe in assuming that rural communities were relatively cohesive and had lower suicide rates compared to urban areas experiencing social dislocation because of the rapid influx of migrants seeking factory work. Current research, however, suggests that rural life is losing its protective character. Suicide rates in rural areas in many parts of the world have been rising rapidly, in some places exceeding rates for urban areas. A study in England and Wales recorded a tenfold increase in suicides for rural males and a fourfold increase for rural females between 1981 and 1998 (Middleton et al. 2003). Similar patterns have been reported in Australia (Bourke 2003; Dudley et al. 1997; Cantor et al. 1995), Japan (Otsu et al. 2004; Charlton 1995), and Sweden (Ferrada-Noli 1997). Explanations for the rise in suicide rates in rural areas are varied. The study in England and Wales found no association between changes in suicide rates and changes in measures of socio-economic status or unemployment rates. In contrast, Bourke's Australian study did find heightened rates of unemployment, low education levels, and a dearth of social and youth services. She also describes rigid cultural expectations for young men and women in rural Australian society, centred around exaggerated masculine images of hard-drinking, football-playing men who accept violence, and images of passive women focused on domestic duties. Those who do not fit in, she suggests, feel shamed and marginalized. Any admission of feeling depressed is further stigmatized as weakness, thus discouraging troubled youth from seeking the help of professional mental health-care workers.

Expanding agribusiness practices in Canada and other countries are also destabilizing rural communities. Corporate farming requires both heavy capital investments and fewer workers. The results are widespread bankruptcies, economic stress, and declining communities as young people move away in search of alternative work, while working lives for those who remain are more akin to urban factory work than traditional family farms. A Canadian study further suggests that exposure to pesticides in forestry and agriculture might be a contributing factor in rising rates of mental illness and suicide (Green 1991). Rural gentrification is simultaneously taking place in rural areas close to large urban population centres, as wealthy urban families buy up rural homes and estates that local residents cannot afford. They may also help to spread urban individualistic consumer values in rural areas. While explanations vary, the emerging consensus remains that rural communities no longer seem to offer the protection they once did from risk of suicide.

Functionalist Analysis of Aboriginal Suicide Rates

Functionalist analysis of the exceptionally high suicide rates among indigenous peoples in Canada and abroad focus attention on the destruction of Aboriginal cultures and associated social dislocation and family breakdown. Indigenous peoples the world over have suffered the social trauma of forced and rapid social and economic change. Societies that subsisted for centuries by means of communal hunting and gathering have been forced to abandon their traditional

lifestyles as they are pushed from traditional homelands by western colonizers. Simplistic assumptions that Aboriginal people would adapt easily to sedentary life, often on reservations, and to the demands of formal education required to find employment in modern industrial economies have proven false (Sinclair 1998; Kirmayer et al. 1996, 1998a, 1998b; Balikci 1970). Successive colonial governments in Canada deliberately suppressed the cultures of First Nations peoples by policies that outlawed what colonizers saw as primitive and barbaric religious rituals and practices. Governments further ordered that First Nations children be removed from their parents and sent to residential schools across Canada, where they were instructed only in English or French, and taught only the Christian religion. The expectation was that children would quickly assimilate the now dominant Western culture. However, all too often they absorbed the attitudes of their colonial teachers who saw Native traditions as primitive and inferior to Western culture. Children resisted the alien and sometimes racist Western culture, but after ten years of such schooling they returned to their own communities largely ignorant of their own cultural traditions and unable to speak their native languages.

Functionalist theory posits family as the primary agent of socialization into community and culture. The experience of being raised in residential schools left many of these young adults ill-equipped to raise their own families, thus contributing to widespread family breakdown within First Nations communities. Mental health surveys show strong correlations between high rates of family breakdown and high rates of suicidal thoughts and attempts among Native and Inuit peoples. Measures of family breakdown include having parents with drinking and/or drug problems, having parents separated or dead, having relatives with psychiatric problems or who have themselves attempted or committed suicide, family violence, and sexual abuse (Tester and McNicoll 2004, 2632). A study of Inuit families by Jean Briggs (1985; 1995) suggests that many Inuit parents lack adequate parenting skills. Parents, she argues, vacillate between intense attachment, bonding, and nurturing relations with children, and the need to treat children in controlling, aggressive, and even rejecting ways, both to protect themselves from the loss of their children and to push the children into independence. Inuit children in return experience great difficulties when they have to leave home to go to high schools. In effect, Briggs suggests, traditional Inuit family culture has failed to adapt to modern demands.

Functionalist analysis promotes a range of policies or interventions to reduce these suicide-risk factors, including school and community programs to foster positive Aboriginal identities and cultural heritage, and to bring elders and youth together. The government also pays for mental-health professionals to work in the indigenous communities to provide counselling and parenting skills workshops (Report of the Advisory Group on Suicide Prevention 2003). Available evidence suggests, however, that these programs are having little success in reducing suicide rates (Leenaars and Lester 2004).

THE POLITICAL ECONOMY PERSPECTIVE ON SUICIDE

While functionalist theories build on Durkheim's analysis of the breakdown of moral order in society, Marxist or political economy analyses explore the economic forces that cause such moral breakdown. This analysis focuses attention on values of competition and pursuit of profits over community obligations and loyalties that pervade capitalist economies. These pressures foster the egoism that Durkheim associates with weakened social integration. Capitalists cannot afford to be too committed to their workers. Workers displaced by technological advances are expected to uproot and move to wherever employment options are better, regardless of family ties. Crass consumerism promoted by advertising teaches individuals to value themselves and others by their possessions. These values, combined with ever-growing income gaps between the poor and the wealthy, foster the anomie of meaningless striving for empty goals that Durkheim associates with loss of regulation.

Both Durkheimian and Marxist perspectives incorporate a sense of fatalism, although understood in very different ways. Durkheim's model points to despair that arises when people feel their lives totally controlled by inflexible cultural rules from which they cannot break free. Political economy theory notes that despair also arises when people experience their lives as ruled by impersonal market forces that seem to work like some inexorable machine, grinding the "inefficient," the "unproductive," and the "obsolete" in its path. Unprofitable enterprises close down no matter how dependent communities may be on the lost jobs. Undercapitalized farms go bankrupt no matter how strongly farm families may love their way of life. People find themselves unemployable when technological developments render their skills and talents obsolete. Individuals, entire communities, and even nation states across the globe feel powerless to influence these market forces within which their lives are embedded. Marxist analysis suggests that only the collective consciousness of workers uniting in their struggle to overthrow the capitalist system might foster the moral force of self-sacrifice for the communal good that Durkheim associates with altruistic suicide.

Research into the effects of capitalist relations on suicide rates is complicated by the pervasiveness of the global capitalist system. There are no societies remaining outside the system that can function as comparison groups. A further complication is that evidence of an association between economic booms or slumps and suicide rates does not tell us which individuals become more suicide prone. We do not know whether it is the newly rich in economic boom times who lose a sense of meaning in their lives, or the poor people who are left behind in the sea of rising prosperity. Likewise, rising suicide rates when economies contract might reflect the despair of the newly poor, or the anguish of the guilt-ridden rich living in a sea of poverty who find their lives meaningless. We need data at the level of individuals to explore such questions. However, when researchers do collect data at the individual level, they tend to analyze the results in terms of individual misfortune or failings and lose sight of the structural forces that shape these data. This is easy to do when, on an aggregate level, economic conditions look good.

A study of variation in suicide rates and economic inequalities among Canadian provinces between 1969 and 1971, and between 1979 and 1981, shows just how tricky such analysis can be. Provinces with relatively higher male suicide rates were those with more rapidly expanding job opportunities for males. Yet ironically, these provinces simultaneously had higher male unemployment rates (Sakinofsky and Roberts 1987; Sakinofsky 1998, 41). So many new workers migrated into these provinces in search of work that they outstripped the positions available. Women also started looking for work in far higher numbers, resulting in a sharp rise in both employment and unemployment rates for women in the relatively higher-suicide provinces. The authors conclude that the misery of unemployment was intensified by living in the midst of communities experiencing unprecedented prosperity. Higher suicide rates during the era of the Quiet Revolution in Quebec may reflect the same crushing impact of rising expectations followed by failure. Other studies suggest that there is a time lag of some nine months between becoming unemployed and experiencing suicidal thoughts, and that people may slowly become adjusted to it after two years (Sakinofsky 1998, 42).

A similarly complicated mix of prosperity and poverty seems to underlie the rising suicide rates in rural England studied by Middleton et al. (2003). The index of social deprivation that they developed, using measures like unemployment rates, overcrowded living conditions, households that are renting rather than owning, and the like, was not statistically associated with suicide rates. But the practice of wealthy city families buying up rural property may have obscured the reality of widespread rural poverty. Studies of rising suicide rates in rural Australian communities do suggest that increasing poverty, relative to larger towns, was a significant factor (Bourke 2003; Cantor et al. 1995). Rural unemployment rates were particularly high among young people, especially males in the 15-to-24 age range. People in these small towns were reluctant to discuss suicides, although most knew someone who had done it. When they talked, they used terms like "waste," "shame" and "poor mental health" that carried the implication of personal failure. Suicides are committed by sick individuals who fail to contribute productively to their society. The pervasive sense of shame inhibited people who were experiencing suicidal thoughts and feelings from seeking professional help, thus exacerbating the problem. Whatever conclusions we draw from these complex data, there is little doubt that unemployment is an extremely stressful experience for workers and their families. Unemployment is associated with high levels of anxiety, depression, fear, loneliness, insomnia, headaches, and stomach problems (Horwitz 1984). The global economic crisis in 2008–09 is very likely to be associated with spikes in suicide rates across the world.

Suicide and Alienation in Aboriginal Communities

Marxist analysis of suicide rates among Aboriginal peoples focuses attention on the colonial destruction of indigenous economies. Few Canadian studies have explicitly employed a Marxist framework to address suicide rates, but all reports document the extremes of poverty and unemployment that characterize most Aboriginal reservation communities in Canada. It is important to recognize that Marxist theoretical analysis involves more than a simplistic assertion that poverty leads to misery and suicide. The concept of alienation refers explicitly to the loss of human relationships, justice, and meaning in work. Giving Aboriginal people larger welfare cheques does not resolve alienation at this deeper level. Some reservations in Canada have benefited from lucrative oil revenues but measures of social breakdown, including suicide rates, remain high. Welfare payments do not provide any sense of meaningful participation in interdependent networks of human production. The discovery of oil on the Hobbema reserves near Edmonton in the 1950s resulted in large royalty payments to individual band members, with trust funds payable to underage members on their eighteenth birthday once as high as $100 000. Children dropped out of school, seeing no point in education or employment. Gambling, drugs, and gangs flourished. Now the energy resources are mostly gone and the reserves sunk back into poverty and anomie.

Marxist analysis suggests that the functionalist-inspired policies to promote Aboriginal cultural revival are likely to fail for the same reasons. Marxist theory views culture as emerging from practical lived experience. Culture cannot float free from economic realities. Indigenous hunting and gathering economies fostered a communal and egalitarian spirituality that values the intimate connection between humanity and the natural world. A reservation economy based on welfare payments or individual wage-work cannot sustain these cultural values. Nothing short of a total reorganization of indigenous economies, ideally along communal lines and based on sustainable economic resources, seems likely to achieve a lasting solution.

Suicide Rates as Social Constructions

The social constructionist approach to the study of suicide has shifted the research focus to the professional practices used to gather evidence, categorize it, and interpret it to produce our understanding of suicide rates and the risk factors associated with suicidal behaviour. This approach reminds us that knowledge inherently involves potential relations of power and control. What we know about suicidal behaviour and, more importantly, what we think we know and *how* we know it, are not simply matters of academic debate. Statistics and reports about suicide rates have immediate practical relevance for government policies, and the practices of social services workers rely on such studies and reports to decide how best to intervene in peoples' lives to reduce the incidence of suicidal behaviour.

Durkheim's classic study, like many others inspired by it, relied on cause-of-death statistics kept by government agencies to test his theory of how weak and excessive integration and regulation influence suicidal behaviour. Constructionist analysis suggests that the patterns that Durkheim found in these statistics are not necessarily accurate as descriptions of causes of death. Rather, they reflect the decision-making practices of innumerable coroners working in different jurisdictions (Douglas 1967). Douglas suggests that when coroners decide how to classify cause of death in ambiguous cases, they routinely rely on many of the very same common-sense theoretical assumptions that Durkheim himself was looking for.

It may seem simple and unambiguous enough at first glance to make decisions about how someone died. But consider some of the following situations. A man dies when his car crashes at high speed into a tree, or dies from carbon-monoxide poisoning when his car engine is running in a closed garage; a women dies from an overdose of sleeping pills, or is found dead in her room with the doors and windows stuffed shut and the gas coming from an unlit heater. A coroner who assigns the label *suicide* to such cases, in effect, assigns responsibility for the death to the individual who has died. But how does one make such decisions? Was the car crash just an accident, or did the man intentionally drive full speed into a stationary object in the realistic expectation that this would end it all, while still permitting the family to claim his life insurance? Did the woman intentionally take an overdose of pills in order to die, or did she simply wake up in the night confused and half drugged and take some more pills without being conscious of what she was doing? Or again, did she intend only to take a non-lethal dose as a cry for attention or help? Did the old woman intend to gas herself, or had she simply stuffed the cracks to keep out the cold and became a victim when the gas fire did not ignite properly or blew out? Suicide, by definition, means intentional self-death, but did these people intend to die? We cannot know for certain because we cannot ask the dead.

The label *suicide* imputes motives after the fact, and coroners can only do this by guesswork, by looking for suicide notes, or by asking witnesses or close family members, and then deciding whether it was likely this person intended to die. This line of reasoning leads to other questions. How many witnesses were consulted with respect to assumed motives? One might get different answers from an estranged wife or from a Catholic priest. Suicide rates are the outcome of decisions such as these. Their "factual" character is much more problematic than the neat tables in Statistics Canada reports would have us believe.

Douglas challenges all the patterns that Durkheim claims to have found. As a first step, Douglas shows that huge changes in suicide rates occurred when the method of counting changed. In Prussia in 1868, for example, Catholic priests kept the records of suicides. The rate jumped 50 percent in one year when the methods were reformed and civilian officials began keeping the rates. Similar jumps occurred in the official statistics in Austria, Hungary, and Italy when recording methods changed. Douglas concludes that changes of between 10 and 50 percent can be attributed to methods of collection alone. Durkheim's tests of his theories of suicide causation often rely on smaller differences than these. Hence, the possibility arises that the patterns Durkheim describes might reflect more how different coroners did their work than how different social factors influenced suicidal behaviour.

Douglas further suggests that all the reasons hypothesized by Durkheim as causes of low social cohesion, and hence higher suicide rates, are the same reasons that influence coroners to make their decisions one way rather than the other. During the period in which Durkheim did his study, suicide was considered a mortal sin for Catholics and was sufficient grounds for denying them a Christian burial. One can realistically expect that when Catholic priests kept the rates, they would go to great lengths to give the benefit of the doubt to the deceased and list the death as accidental, and that Catholic family members would do likewise. Protestant record keepers and witnesses would not be under such pressure. Douglas shows that Catholic cantons in Switzerland recorded fewer suicides than did Protestant cantons, but more accidents. Douglas concludes that different rates may reflect different concealment and not real differences in the propensity of Catholics and Protestants to kill themselves.

Similarly, Douglas suggests that all the conditions of higher social integration listed by Durkheim are associated with a higher propensity, and ability, to cover up a suicide. When a person is married and has children, these family members are likely to want to influence a coroner to see the death as accidental, while a divorced person living alone has no one to speak for him or her. Members of a small rural community might be more likely to close ranks and cover up damning evidence of a suicide in their midst than neighbours in a loosely integrated city area. Durkheim was correct in claiming that the number of deaths officially classified as suicides is lower among Catholics, married people, and villagers, but differences in rates may be solely an artifact of how coroners were influenced to make their decisions. Smith (1983) goes further than Douglas in demonstrating the essential circularity of theory and data in studies of suicide. She cites cases showing that witnesses and family members, as well as coroners, rely upon theories about motives for committing suicide when they produce accounts of what happened.

Consider the man who crashes his car into a tree. People generally believe that a married man with children is unlikely to commit suicide, but that a divorced man who keeps to himself might well be miserable and potentially suicidal. Thus, if the victim were a married man, friends might well comment, when questioned by a coroner, that he was a happy man, a bit reckless with the car perhaps, and so assure themselves and the coroner that it was an accident. If the victim were divorced, friends would be much more likely to comment that they had always feared that he would do something terrible to himself, poor man, how miserable he must have been, and thus convince themselves and the coroner that his death was probably a suicide. All that is needed for people to become convinced of the truth of their speculation is for like-minded people to reinforce their interpretation. People tend retrospectively to pick out the incidents that support their emerging theory, and they downplay evidence to the contrary. Experts who analyze such accounts for features of suicidal behaviour are likely to discover in them the theories that people use when they put their accounts together.

In defence of Durkheim's study, Durkheim was aware that available statistics were shaky but judged them good enough for his purpose. More recent studies routinely do check for obvious shifts and inconsistencies in how officials compile statistics. Douglas himself was more interested in researching how coroners do their work than testing the validity of official statistics. While he speculates that coroners and witnesses might engage in systematic bias and cover-up in reporting suicides, he does not offer evidence that this actually happens.

Ideological Practices in Research on Aboriginal Suicide Rates

Constructionist analysis focuses attention on how evidence is structured by the methods people use to gather it, and the standpoint or interpretive frame that guides what people pay attention to. Most of what we know about suicide rates among Canadian Aboriginal peoples is gathered under the direction of federal and provincial government agencies, and structured to be useful to the various professionals—social workers, mental-health workers, and teachers—employed by the governments to work with Aboriginal communities. How these professionals understand the causes of suicide influences what researchers pay attention to, the kinds of evidence highlighted or ignored, the connections found within the evidence, and by extension, the policies recommended to address the extremely high suicide rates found within Aboriginal communities. Constructionist analysis prompts us to think about this diverse body of research as forms of discourse, or ways of talking about experiences, rather than as sets of factual knowledge. To get a sense of how significant this shift in perspective can be, we look at Tester and McNicoll's (2004) critique of research on high suicide rates among the Inuit of northern Canada.

The methodology most frequently used by sociologists is quantitative survey research that asks large samples of people about socio-psychological risk factors associated with suicidal attempts and feelings (Kirmayer et al. 1996, 1998a, 1998b). Family problems are strongly associated with suicide attempts. High-risk factors include having been adopted, having parents who are separated or dead, having alcoholic or drug-addicted parents, experience of being sexually abused, especially by close relatives, and having friends or relatives who have attempted or committed suicide. Individual factors associated with suicidal behaviour include drug and alcohol abuse, self-perception of poor health, and having a personal mental-health problem in the previous year. Qualitative case-study research complements survey data in exploring in greater depth the maladaptive parenting strategies that contribute to family disorganization. Briggs (1995) draws attention to what she sees as bonding problems between Inuit parents and children. These are manifest in contradictory practices like intense attachment to and overprotection of children, combined with aggressive and rejecting behaviour as parents try to compensate by pushing adolescents out of the home. A high

death rate in Inuit communities from epidemics of smallpox, measles, and influenza contributes to such dysfunctional child-rearing practices, as do memories of residential schools, and the necessity of adolescents leaving isolated communities to attend high school.

Extensive mental-health diagnostic research within Aboriginal communities has also unearthed evidence of widespread diagnosable mental illness, including high levels of anxiety neurosis, psychosis, and schizophrenia (Sampath 1976; Travis 1990). Possible causes include the effects of extreme isolation and genetic inbreeding in small communities, particularly among very isolated northern communities. Yet other research focuses on cultural factors associated with social disorganization at the community level (Balikci 1970; Kral 1998; Kirmayer et al. 1996, 1998a, 1998b). On the one hand, the loss of traditional religious and social values is associated with a loss of identity and low self-esteem at the individual level. On the other hand, traditional cultural patterns that were once appropriate for life in small-scale, nomadic hunter-gatherer communities are identified as dysfunctional for adaptation to modern industrial societies.

This extensive and diverse body of research guides comprehensive intervention strategies by social workers, health professionals, law-enforcement officers, and teachers (Royal Commission on Aboriginal Peoples 1995). Family social workers use survey data on high-risk factors to help identify individuals at risk of committing suicide, and to intervene in pathological family units. When felt necessary, children can be removed from dysfunctional families and placed in foster homes or hostels. Case-study research by Briggs guides professionals in implementing parenting-skills classes, counselling services, and programs for early intervention in problem families. Evidence of extensive mental illness has been used to pressure the Canadian government to commit high levels of funding to increase the numbers of mental-health professionals in these communities. Policing has expanded in an effort to stem the tide of drug trafficking and curb alcoholism. Educational programs have been developed for schools that attempt to resocialize children to help them bridge the immense gap between traditional Inuit culture and the culture of modern Western societies. These programs typically incorporate traditional stories, arts and crafts, and where possible, courses in Native languages, with the goal of fostering a positive self-identity among children. At the same time schools promote exposure to television, computers, and the Internet, which teach the norms and values more appropriate for modern Western industrial society.

Intensive suicide-prevention programs along these lines have been widely instituted in Inuit and other Aboriginal communities over the last 20 years. New studies repeat the calls on the Canadian government to expand these programs still further and to ensure that all professionals work together to integrate their services. Yet, despite this mountain of research and well-intentioned professional commitment to bring suicide rates down, the results have been dismal. Suicide rates continue to rise, and evidence from program-evaluation research indicates that suicide levels in communities with comprehensive prevention programs are no lower than in communities without them (Leenaars and Lester 2004; Breton et al. 1998).

Research from the Inuit Standpoint: Colonial Rule

Research from the Inuit standpoint reverses the direction of the gaze. Rather than focusing on problems within their communities, the gaze turns outwards to focus on the practices that colonial governments have imposed on them. Consider how you and members of your own family might feel if you endured the following experiences. Imagine that everyone you know is rounded up, without any consultation or explanation, and confined to a small settlement far from where you once lived. Strangers take over the lands you once lived on and flood them for hydro development, so you cannot ever go back. Meanwhile, all your family members lose whatever means of livelihood they once had. Now you live on welfare. In your new settlement area you experience a litany of acts of great cruelty. Your family dogs are shot dead by police, meaning that you lose both your pets and your primary means of transportation (dog sleds), and you also lose any hope of hunting for food. Your new settlement area is constantly monitored and controlled by foreign police, your community affairs administered by foreign agents, your religious beliefs and practices are criminalized, and your traditions openly denigrated by these foreign agents, who refer to your family members as stupid, ignorant, and primitive. In effect, everyone you know is confined to an open prison. Then the greatest act of cruelty of all. Every child between the ages of six and 16, in every family you know, is forcibly removed from home and placed in prisons a thousand miles away. Parents and children have no means to communicate with each other for the 10 years that children are confined. When your children are finally released you barely recognize each other, and you cannot talk easily because you no longer speak a common language. You can find nothing to do. Young people can marry and have children of their own, but you know that these children in turn will be taken away by foreign government agents when they reach six years of age. Would it be surprising if you and people you loved became suicidal under such conditions, or that you turned to alcohol and drugs to deaden your sense of helplessness and shame? All these conditions and worse have been experienced by indigenous peoples in Canada.

Within this reversed gaze, the evidence of suicidal behaviour amassed by colonial researchers takes on new meanings. The multitude of "risk factors" identified in survey research as causes of suicide appear as merely spurious. Alcoholism, addictions, suicides, psychoses, and family dysfunctions all become visible as symptoms of the same underlying experience of colonization. These symptoms are endlessly reinforced in vicious cycles that cannot be broken so long as the underlying condition of colonization remains. People who feel helpless, either to provide for themselves or to protect or even hold on to their own children, are likely to exhibit the pathologies found in these studies. Elders too traumatized and ashamed to talk about their experiences with young people cannot make strong leaders.

The conditions of overt colonial oppression described above have thankfully retreated, but their legacy remains. White social workers may do the best they know how to intervene in at-risk families to try to protect another generation of children from harm. But from the standpoint of the colonized, these social workers retain their awful powers to take children away. One of the greatest fears of families on welfare is the power of social workers to remove children from parents who are considered failures. White police officers, along with Native colleagues, may do their best to stem the scourge of drug trafficking and alcohol. But they represent the same law-enforcement officers who, in earlier times, forced families to move, shot the dogs, enforced child removals, and legalized the pillage of traditional lands by foreign corporations. White teachers may do their utmost to teach the skills needed to adjust to Western society. But in the gaze of the colonized these represent the same authority figures who crushed already traumatized children in residential schools.

Mainstream sociologists may also do their best to research the conditions underlying suicide rates as objectively as possible, but their theoretical discourse for the most part continues to blame the colonized for their own victimization (Tester and McNicoll 2004). The discourse of "social disorganization" faults traditional cultures for failure to adapt to change, or failure to adjust to the demands of modernization. But the discourse omits the horrific details about what changed, and how changes were brought about, and by whom such changes were enforced. The discourse of "loosely integrated societies" borrows from Durkheim's theories but ignores the outside controls and forces that produce and perpetuate such weak integration in aboriginal communities. The discourse of "risk factors" incorporates moral judgments about blame. Mothers whose own lives are filled with misery are blamed for the fetal alcohol syndrome that renders their children exceptionally hard to care for. The hopeful discourse of "narratives" that encourages elders to talk and to recreate lost traditional cultures ignores the history of colonialism that undermines their capacity to talk. The discourse of "social isolation" ignores the systemic marginalization and racism that perpetuates this isolation. The discourse of "mental-health professionals" ignores the long history of shame and distrust of whites, and the continuing politics of power that trigger the symptoms of psychosis that psychiatrists diagnose as illness.

From the standpoint of the colonized, solutions to the problem of escalating suicide rates lie not in ameliorative programs traditionally proposed, but in the end of colonialism itself. This entails the settlement of land claims, the return of sufficient resources for economic self-sufficiency as communities, and compensation for exploited resources on traditional lands. It also requires structures that return political autonomy to communities, and ensure political power for First Nations communities in the heart of colonial Canadian government. It further requires an end to the ongoing colonizing practices within the centres of Canadian cities, manifest in the continuing displacement of First Nations peoples.

In summary, this shift in standpoint from the gaze of the colonizers to the gaze of the colonized does not invalidate the evidence gathered by survey research, mental-health studies, case studies, and cultural studies described above. But it does profoundly alter how we understand this evidence, the causal connections we infer among facets of evidence, and the conclusions we draw. The shift in standpoint also affects the direction of future research, focusing attention on the legal structures and institutional practices that perpetuate the colonial experience. Objectivity in social science research thus depends less on the methods we use to gather evidence than on the deliberate adoption of different standpoints. Aboriginal researchers have called explicitly for more "decolonizing methodologies" (Smith 1999) that take as their starting point the issues and questions crucial to indigenous peoples around the world.

 # Feminist Theory: Suicide as Gendered Practice

Suicide is clearly gendered behaviour. Rates for committed suicides and for attempted suicides differ markedly for women and men. But they differ in opposite directions. In Canada, as in most Western societies, men kill themselves far more often than women, but women attempt suicide far more often than men. Theoretical explanations differ markedly, depending on which statistic is given primacy.

Firstly, with respect to completed suicide rates, official statistics across Western societies from Durkheim's time to the present show that suicide rates for men are significantly higher than for women. Statistics Canada Health Reports for 2004 (Volume 15.2) cite the male suicide rate as 21.8 per 100 000 compared with 5.4 for women—a ratio of 4:1. Among Canadian youth in the age range 15 to 24, the ratio is as high as 5.2:1. Comparable World Health Organization data report suicide rates for the United States as 17.1 per 100 000 for males and 4.0 for females; for the United Kingdom, 11.8 for males and 3.3 for females; and for France, 26.1 for males and 9.4 for females (www.who.int/mental_health/prevention/suicide). These gaps are so consistent and so large that suicide is widely described as "a masculine behaviour" (Neuringer and Lettieri 1982, 14–15).

On the other hand, reported suicide *attempts* have consistently shown higher rates for women. Statistics Canada Health Reports (Volume 15.2) show the hospitalization rate for females as 108 per 100 000 and 70 for males. For the most vulnerable age group, 15 to 19, the comparative rates were 221 for females to 87 for males, a ratio of over 2.5:1. Since the number of attempts is several times greater than the number of completed suicides, the combined figures suggest that women may have a higher overall rate of suicidal behaviour.

Feminist research generally gives more weight to the high frequency of attempted over completed suicides, suggesting that the combined numbers for completed and attempted suicides give a more valid measure of suicidal behaviour generally. Counted in this way, it is women who are more depressed and suicidal than men, by a ratio of 2.5:1, notwithstanding their lower death rates. This view is supported by separate medical evidence that shows twice as many women as men in Canada diagnosed with depressive illnesses and prescribed antidepressant medication (Stoppard and McMullen 2003, 1; McMullen 2003, 18).

The explanations offered for higher rates of depression among women parallel those described above with respect to Inuit suicide rates. A straightforward explanation is physiology—depressed people are thought to have lower brain-serotonin levels, a condition that can be remedied with drugs. But physiology alone will not account for the wide variation in rates of depressive illness across communities. Changes in brain chemistry may themselves be triggered by socio-psychological factors that promote feelings of depression. Sociological explanations focus attention on contradictory cultural pressures and demands placed on women in contemporary Western societies. Women are pushed to fulfill the roles of youthful sexual idols, wives and mothers, and career women, often simultaneously. Women readily absorb cultural values that admire autonomous individuals with freedom, responsibility, and achievement, and then blame themselves for failing to live up to the image (McMullen 2003, 32). Mothers of young children often find themselves juggling the multiple demands and stresses of paid job, caring for husband, caring for children, and running a home, managing on limited sleep and without time to care for themselves. They may pressure husbands to help, but the majority do not (Hochschild 1989). Alternatively, women may find themselves outside the social loop, isolated and undervalued as full-time homemakers, dependent on husband or welfare for the survival of themselves and their children. Such dependence makes these women especially vulnerable to domestic violence. Should anything go wrong in this complex family balancing act, blame tends to fall more on wives than husbands. Gendered economic inequalities are reflected in the feminization of poverty. Women in the labour force are concentrated in a much narrower range of occupations than men, and typically earn less money. Patriarchal social structures result in women having unequal access to positions of power and influence in most sectors of society. Women may feel much anger about their situation but may be culturally inhibited from outwardly expressing it. Anger turned inwards may promote both depression and suicidal feelings (Jack 2003). Feminist theory thus has little difficulty accounting for higher rates of depression among women.

Suicide Rates among Men

When the focus shifts from suicidal attempts to committed suicides, men are clearly the primary victims in Western societies. In Canada, the ratio is between 4 and 5 male deaths to 1 female death from suicide in all age cohorts from 15 to 75 and older. Men are less frequently diagnosed with depression than women. Yet they seem to be less protected from falling into the depth of despair that leads to suicide.

The classic explanation posed for the higher rates of completed suicides for men invokes a mixture of biology and socialization (Lester 1997a, Ch. 12). The argument suggests that males are naturally more aggressive, especially young men with high testosterone levels. Males are also socialized to be more physically violent than females, and to externalize their anger. Males who kill themselves are more likely to use violent means like guns and knives. Women are more likely to use passive means like drug overdoses, or cutting their wrists—means that are less likely to result in quick death. This line of reasoning further implies that women may be more suicidal than men but less effective at carrying out the act.

An alternative argument is that suicide attempts in general may be a distinctively different form of behaviour from completed suicides, and reflect different motives. Attempts may be more a cry for help or attention, rather than a failed attempt to kill oneself. However, this may be true also for some of the committed suicides. There is no way to be sure. There is some evidence to suggest that men and women may have different motives for killing themselves—based on a small study of 264 suicide notes in Australia, of which 198 were left by men. Notes left by women suggested a theme of wanting to die or wanting to escape. Notes left by men more often expressed anger towards others and a desire to make them suffer, especially with respect to thwarted love affairs (Lester et al. 2004).

Research into social conditions that may differentially protect women and men from committing suicide continues to draw heavily on Durkheim's classic theory of levels of societal integration and regulation. Durkheim reasoned that strong social bonds between people, and especially the bonds of marriage and family, offered the best protection from egoistic suicide. He predicted that married people would have lower suicide rates than never married or divorced and widowed people. The presence of children, he predicted, would strengthen this protection. These predictions worked in all cases for men. But there was one significant exception for women. Married women without children were *not* protected more than unmarried women. The presence of children offered protection, but not the state of marriage itself.

To account for this anomaly, Durkheim reasoned that men needed the constraints of marriage more than women. Single and divorced men, without the constraints of marriage, were likely to engage in sexually loose behaviour with many different women, be unable to find any satisfaction or regulation in their lives, and fall into despair. Women, in contrast, are more strongly constrained by societal norms—perhaps even overly constrained. The state of marriage thus did not offer significantly more protection from loss of regulation.

Durkheim's theory is difficult to test with government statistics because data on suicides by marital status rarely indicate whether or not the victims had children. Suicide rates are lower for married than single women, as they are for men, but married women are also far more likely to have children than single women. An interesting test situation that Besnard exploits for research occurred in France between 1973 and 1975 (Besnard 2000b). A combination of legal and social changes resulted in a sharp increase in divorce rates and a decline in rate of first marriages. Besnard reasons that during this period the state of marriage as a social institution was weakened. If Durkheim's theory is correct, a weakening of the marital institution would lower the protection against suicide that marriage affords men, relative to single men. Conversely, the weakening of the institution of marriage would improve the situation for married women because of the greater option of getting out. Besnard found the data consistent with these predictions, thus supporting Durkheim's theory. Strong marital institutions protect men, he argues, but may produce an excess of restraint for women, hence slightly increasing the risk of fatalistic suicide.

Marital Institutions and Suicide Rates Cross-Culturally

Comparative evidence from non-European societies provides opportunities to test these generalizations further. The evidence Durkheim used to develop his model was confined to European states, but national statistics are now available virtually worldwide. Comparative data challenge the assumption that suicide rates for men are universally higher than for women. Lester (1997b) found that death rates from suicide continue to be significantly higher for men than women across all Western societies. However male/female ratios are more even in Asian nations. In the special case of China, suicide rates are higher for women. These data contradict the argument noted above that biological characteristics like testosterone levels make men innately more violent and prone to suicide than women. They also contradict the argument that women are innately less capable of killing themselves than men. However, they support Durkheim's argument that an excess of regulation in collectivist societies like Japan and China increases the risk of fatalistic suicide.

A case study of suicide in rural China (Meng 2002) offers a particularly vivid illustration of fatalistic suicide. The article recounts a harrowing story of the life and death by suicide of a woman who challenged cultural norms by marrying for love against the wishes of her parents and mother-in-law. She then faced rejection and unrelenting harassment from her in-laws who branded her a troublemaker. Her husband sided with his parents, beating her for showing disrespect to his mother. Her efforts to get away failed since she would have had to abandon her children. Only after her death did she gain some revenge. Her suicide publicly shamed her in-laws, and her natal family demanded extensive compensation and an elaborate funeral. Behind this one story is a backdrop of rigid controls over women's lives, enforced by powerful vested interests.

One of the implications of this international evidence is that suicide rates are likely to differ for ethnic minorities living in the West. The Statistics Canada Health Reports (Volume 15.2) on committed suicides shows lower rates for immigrants overall than for the Canadian-born. The Report's authors suggest that these differences may reflect the greater social integration of immigrant communities, especially in large cities like Toronto, Montreal, and Vancouver. The gap between suicide rates for women and men is smaller than among the Canadian-born—a ratio of 2.7 men for 1 woman among immigrants compared with 4 to 1 for Canadian-born. Immigrant males thus have significantly lower rates of suicide than Canadian-born males, while the pattern for immigrant and Canadian-born women is closer.

An important qualification in the interpretation of these data is the distinction drawn above between completed suicides and suicide attempts or self-harm. The Statistics Canada report on hospitalization for suicide attempts does not show this breakdown. However, a study in Britain (Bhardwaj 2001) reports that among Asian females in the age range 15 to 35, incidents of suicide and self-harm combined are two to three times higher than for white, African, and Caribbean female counterparts. Self-harm is defined as overdosing on drugs, slashing or burning themselves, and eating disorders. Bhardwaj describes women in these communities as subject to increasingly rigid social controls. They are held responsible for maintaining community and family honour. Any deviation from rigidly defined family and marital roles is severely punished. Speaking out about domestic violence is defined as bringing public shame on a family, and itself heavily sanctioned, as is any attempt by women to leave their family. When a woman feels she has no control over anything else, Bhardwaj suggests, the last remaining site for control is her own body. Refusing to eat, slashing herself, burning herself, and swallowing pills offer small acts of defiance. Women talked about the sense of temporary release they felt from self-harm, and also their hope that such acts might draw attention from family members and bring about some positive changes in their lives.

The code of silence imposed on women by the wider community, however, makes any intervention or treatment difficult. Culturally sensitive mental-health staff are important but not sufficient. A critical problem is that social workers and family physicians within the Asian communities commonly see themselves as "self-appointed community caretakers." They are known to side with their community rather than with individual female clients, and report confidences back to family members. Women who expose their problems risk further revenge and punishment.

From the standpoint of the host society looking into minority communities, it is easy to locate the source of the problem in traditional Asian cultures that clash with the more progressive or liberal Western culture of the host society. But when we gaze outwards from the standpoint of minority communities, other pressures come into view. Bhardwaj views the increasingly rigid practices of conformity and closure within Asian immigrant communities in Britain as themselves a form of reaction to racist and exclusionary practices in white British society. In Canada, Bannerji (2000) similarly sees the inward-looking closure of Asian communities as a response to practices that "minoritize" non-white immigrants. National politics are in turn located in the wider framework of global struggles, particularly since the September 11, 2001, bombings of the World Trade Center in New York, and the Pentagon. In Canada, and globally, claims to distinctive culture and religion are powerful levers for exerting political influence. The enhanced status of male elites as spokespersons for their communities with host-society officials in turn depends upon maintaining strong internal cohesion, a central component of which is control over women's behaviour as symbols of minority cultural integrity.

CONCLUSION

Durkheim's analysis of the social foundations of suicidal behaviour has stood the test of 100 years of further research, notwithstanding flaws in data collection and statistics. His theoretical model of weak and excessive integration and regulation leading to four distinctive kinds of suicide—egoistic, anomic, altruistic, and fatalistic—are still widely applied. His emphasis on the structural foundations of individual motivation is closer to Marxist thought than much contemporary research on individual risk factors. For Durkheim, as for Marx, modernization as such is not the cause of rising suicide rates, but rather how modernization is instituted. In Marxist analysis, egoism and anomie are symptoms of selfish individualism and cutthroat competition at the heart of capitalist economic relations. These values are in turn reflected in the individualistic focus on much contemporary research into risk factors. The other side of Durkheim's theoretical model, which focuses on conditions of excessive integration and regulation, and their reflection in altruistic and fatalistic suicides, becomes more significant when we move beyond a Eurocentric focus. The rise in altruistic suicide bombers in the Middle East, and fatalistic suicides among Aboriginal peoples and women in some Asian societies, can be seen as rooted in global practices of colonialism and racism.

SUGGESTED READING

Tester and McNicoll's article "Isumagijaksaq: mindful of the state: social constructions of Inuit suicide" (2004) presents an in-depth description of the history of an Inuit community and relations with white colonizing society. It provides a powerful critique of well-meaning but ideological practices of social workers and authority figures struggling to reduce the high suicide rates in the community.

Meng's essay "Rebellion and revenge: the meaning of suicide of women in rural China" (2002) presents a very personal account of her interview with a woman in rural China and her subsequent analysis of why this woman later committed suicide. It is one of the very few studies that brings meaning to Durkheim's concept of fatalistic suicide.

Dorothy Smith's essay "No One Commits Suicide: Textual Analysis of Ideological Practices" (1983) provides a unique analysis of several texts to show how authors organize their description of accounts of depressive illness and suicide to support or "intend" a particular understanding of that behaviour, and how a small shift in emphasis brings into focus a very different understanding of the relationships and pressures involved. These include a discussion of accounts of Virginia Woolf's suicide, by her husband and her nephew, and of a young mother alternately described as psychotic, or as struggling to cope under very difficult circumstances.

QUESTIONS

1. Why did Durkheim consider the development of human rights to be essential for stability in modern society?

2. Explain Durkheim's argument that social cohesion in modern industrialized societies is based on a different moral order than in simpler societies. How does Durkheim suggest that we can study this scientifically?

3. Explain Durkheim's concept of *anomie*. List the factors that Durkheim saw as leading to *anomic* division of labour.

4. How does Durkheim's study of societal integration and regulation and suicide rates reflect the values of scientific inquiry? Cite evidence from the social constructionist perspective that challenges the objectivity of suicide rates that Durkheim used.

5. Explain Durkheim's concept of *egoistic* suicide. What evidence did he give to support this argument?

6. How does the functionalist perspective in modern sociology draw upon Durkheim's model of the social roots of suicide? What policy implications does this have for working to reduce suicide rates in Canadian Aboriginal communities?

7. How does social constructionist analysis challenge the factual character of Statistics Canada data on suicide rates? How might the true factual character of these statistics be improved?

8. How does social constructionist analysis challenge mainstream sociological survey research on risk factors for individual suicide as ideological? What implications does this have for social work on reserves?

9. How does feminist research help to make sense of very different rates of suicide and suicide attempts by men and women in Canada? What implications might this have for social work with young men?

10. How does feminist research draw on Durkheim's concept of "fatalism"? What implications might this have for social work within ethnic folk communities in Canada?

KEY TERMS

altruism

altruistic suicide

anomic division of labour

anomic suicide

anomie

anti-Semitism

conscience collective

differentiation

ecological fallacy

egoism

egoistic suicide

empiricism

evolution

fatalistic suicide

fragmentation

function

humanism

indicators

integration

laissez-faire economic system

mechanical solidarity

metaphysical stage

morality

natural laws

organic solidarity

positive society

precontractual basis of contract

regulation

repressive law

restitutive law

social facts

solidarity

theological stage

WEB LINKS

Living with Suicide: Shared Experiences and Voices of Loss
www.pbs.org/weblab/living
This PBS site is dedicated to those who have experienced loss through suicide. Stories are strong and provide insight into life-changing and earth-shaking experiences. Subheadings include "Hushed Tones: An Introduction," "Shared Voices: Read Others' Experiences," "Your Voice: Contribute Your Story," and "Conversations: Comments and Open Discussion."

Welcome to LisaLing.com: Trying to Do Good Female Suicide Bombers
www.lisaling.com/fembomb
Journalist Lisa Ling reports on the growing number of girls and women who "use their bodies to deliver an attack." The site also provides a discussion forum, photos, and video. The site links to "Issues," "Poems," and a "Be Inspired" section, which includes stories from people such as: Rachel Lloyd, founder of GEMS; Zainab Salbi, founder of Women for Women International; and Dr. Sanduik Ruit, Himalayan Cataract Foundation.

They Committed Suicide Because of Bullying
www.metacafe.com/watch/461754/
they_committed_suicide_because_of_bullying/
This is a video remembering young children who committed suicide because of the devastating effects of bullying. The site also provides links to other stories on bullying such as: "How can social communities prevent cyber bullying?"; "Oprah Winfrey: Bullying and Suicide"; "Bullying Story"; and "PSST, World Intro, Stop Bullying and School Violence."

PBS Frontline World: Sri Lanka—Living with Terror, May 2002
www.pbs.org/frontlineworld/stories/srilanka/
This is a PBS documentary produced by reporter Joe Rubin on his 34 days in Sri Lanka. A "Reporter's Diary" and a 16-minute video explain the terror of his trip. This site also provides links to a map, Sri Lanka's background, and other stories of human rights abuses and suicide bombings such as: "The Making of a Suicide Bomber"; "A Lonely Warrior for Human Rights"; "Fighting Terror with Paint Brushes"; and "From Anil's Ghost, by Michael Ondaatje."

PBS Frontline World: Seeds of Suicide—India's Desperate Farmers
www.pbs.org/frontlineworld/rough/2005/07/seeds_of_suicid.html#
"Suicide by pesticide: It's an epidemic in India, where farmers try to keep up with the latest pest-resistant seeds only to find themselves trapped in a vicious cycle of pesticides that don't work, drought and debt." Chad Heeter shares the desperation and distress of Indian farmers who are at the mercy of "globalization, trade policies and technology." "Seven farmers a day were merely killing themselves." This short video shows grief and misery when farmers drink pesticides, and suicide visits a family.

REFERENCES

Atkinson, J. 1978. *Discovering Suicide*. London: Macmillan.

Baldry, A.C., and F.W. Winkel. 2003. "Direct and vicarious victimization at school and at home as risk factors for suicidal cognition among Italian adolescents." *Journal of Adolescence* 26 (6): 703–716.

Balikci, A. 1970. *The Netsilik Eskimo*. Garden City, New York: The Natural History Press.

Bannerji, Himani. 2000. *The Dark Side of the Nation: Essays on Multiculturalism, Nationalism and Gender*. Toronto: Canadian Scholars Press.

Berkman, L.F., T. Glass, I. Brisette, T.E. Seeman. 2000. "From Social Integration to Health: Durkheim in the New Millennium." *Social Science and Medicine* 51 (6): 843–857.

Besnard, P. 2000a. "The Fortunes of Durkheim's Suicide." In W.S.F. Pickering and G. Walford, eds. *Durkheim's Suicide: A Century of Research and Debate*. London; New York: Routledge, 97–125.

Besnard, P. 2000b. "Marriage and Suicide: Testing the Durkheimian Theory of Marital Regulation a Century Later." In W.S.F. Pickering and G. Walford, eds. *Durkheim's Suicide: A Century of Research and Debate*. London; New York: Routledge, 133–155.

Bhardwaj, Anita. 2001. "Growing up Young, Asian, and Female in Britain: A Report on Self-harm and Suicide." *Feminist Review* 68 (Summer): 52–67.

Bourke, Lisa. 2003. "Toward understanding youth suicide in an Australian rural community." *Social Science and Medicine* 57 (12): 2355–2365.

Boyer, R., G. Légaré, D. St-Laurent, and M. Préville. 1998. "Epidemiology of Suicide, Parasuicide, and Suicidal Ideation in Quebec." In A.A. Leenaars, S. Wenckstern, I. Sakinofsky, R.J. Dyck, M.J. Kral, and R.C. Bland, eds. *Suicides in Canada*. Toronto: University of Toronto Press, 67–84.

Breault, K.D., and A.J. Kposowa. 2000. "Social Integration and Marital Status: A Multivariate Individual-level study of 30,157 Suicides." In W.S.F. Pickering and G. Walford, eds. *Durkheim's Suicide: A Century of Research and Debate*. London; New York: Routledge, 156–179.

Breton, J.J., R. Boyer, H. Bilodeau, S. Raymond, N. Joubert, and M.A. Nantel. 1998. *Review of Evaluation Research on Suicide Intervention and Prevention Programs for Young People in Canada: Theoretical Context and Results*. Montreal: Government Documents.

Briggs, Jean. 1995. "Vicissitudes of attachment: Nurturance and dependence in Canadian Inuit family relationships, old and new. *Arctic Medical Research* 54 (Supplement 1): 24–32.

Briggs, Jean. 1985. "Socialization, family conflicts and responses to culture change among Canadian Inuit." *Arctic Medical Research* 40: 40–52.

Burr, J. 2002. "Cultural stereotypes of women from South Asian communities: Mental health care professionals' explanations for patterns of suicide and depression." *Social Science & Medicine* 55: 835–845.

Cantor, C.H., P.J. Slater, and J.M. Najman. 1995. "Socioeconomic Indices and Suicide Rates in Queensland." *Australian Journal of Public Health* 19: 417–420.

Charlton, J. 1995. "Trends and Patterns in Suicide in England and Wales." *International Journal of Epidemiology of Suicide* 24: 45–52.

Cheung, F.M. 1996. "Gender Role Development." In S. Lau, ed. *Growing Up the Chinese Way*. Hong Kong: The Chinese University Press.

Cormier, H., and G. Klerman. 1985. "Unemployment and Male Labour Force Participation as Determinants of Changing Suicide Rates of Males and Females in Quebec." *Social Psychiatry* 20: 109–114.

Davies, C., and M. Neal. 2000. "Durkheim's Altruistic and Fatalistic Suicide." In W.S.F. Pickering and G. Walford, eds. *Durkheim's Suicide: A Century of Research and Debate*. London; New York: Routledge, 36–52.

Davies, C., M. Neal, J. Varty, G. Walford, R.A. Jones, and W. Ramp. 2000. "Teaching Durkheim's Suicide: A Symposium." In W.S.F. Pickering and G. Walford, eds. *Durkheim's Suicide: A Century of Research and Debate*. London; New York: Routledge, 180–200.

Dooley, D., R. Catalano, K. Rook, and S. Serxner. 1989. "Economic Stress and Suicide: Multilevel Analyses. Part 2: Cross-level Analyses of Economic Stress and Suicidal Ideation." *Suicide and Life Threatening Behaviour* 19 (4): 337–351.

Douglas, J. 1967. *The Social Meaning of Suicide*. Princeton, New Jersey: Princeton University Press.

Dudley, M.J., N. Kelk, T. Florio, J. Howard, B. Waters, C. Haski, and M. Alcock. 1997. "Suicide among young rural Australians 1964–1993: A comparison with metropolitan trends." *Social Psychiatry and Psychotic Epidemiology* 32: 251–260.

Durkheim, Emile. [1897] 1951. *Suicide*. New York: Free Press.

Durkheim, Emile. [1893] 1964. *The Division of Labour in Society*. London: Collier-Macmillan.

Eckersley, R., and K. Dear. 2002. "Cultural Correlates of Suicide." *Social Science & Medicine* 55 (11): 1891–1904.

Ferrada-Noli, M. 1997. "Social Psychological vs Socio-economic Hypothesis on the Epidemiology of Suicide." *Psychological Reports* 81: 307–316.

Fullager, Simone. 2003. "Wasted Lives: Social Dynamics of Shame and Youth Suicide." *Journal of Sociology* 39 (3): 291–307.

Gane, M. 2000. "The Deconstruction of Social Action: The 'Reversal' of Durkheimian Methodology from *The Rules* to *Suicide*." In W.S.F. Pickering and G. Walford, eds. *Durkheim's Suicide: A Century of Research and Debate*. London; New York: Routledge, 22–35.

Garroutte, E.M., J. Goldberg, J. Beals, R. Herrell, and S.M. Manson. 2003. "Spirituality and attempted suicide among American Indians." *Social Science and Medicine* 56 (7): 1571–1579.

Gove, W. 1979. "Sex differences in the epidemiology of mental disorder." in E.S. Gomberg and V. Franks, eds. *Gender and Disordered Behavior*. New York: Brunner/Mazel.

Graham, M., H.P. Bergen, A.S. Richardson, L. Roeger, and S. Allison. 2004. "Sexual Abuse and Suicidality: Gender Differences in a Large Community Sample of Adolescents." *Child Abuse and Neglect* 28 (5): 547–563.

Green, L. 1991. "A cohort mortality study of forestry workers exposed to phenoxy acid herbicides." *British Journal of Industrial Medicine* 48: 234–238.

Halbwachs, Maurice. [1930] 1978. *The Causes of Suicide*. London; Henley: Routledge & Kegan Paul.

Hochschild, Arlie. 1989. *The Second Shift* New York: Avon.

Horwitz, A.V. 1984. "The Economy and Social Pathology." *Annual Review of Sociology* 10: 95–119.

Jack, D.C. 2003. "The Anger of Hope and the Anger of Despair." In S.J. Stoppard and L.M. McMullen, eds. *Situating Sadness: Women and Depression in Social Context*. New York; London: New York University Press, 62–87.

Jackson, P.R., and P.B. Warr. 1984. "Unemployment and Psycholgoical Ill-health: The Moderating Role of Duration and Age." *Psychological Medicine* 14: 605–614.

Johnson, B.D. 1965. "Durkheim's One Cause of Suicide." *American Sociological Review* 30: 875–886.

Katt, M., P. Kinch, M. Boone, and B. Minore. 1998. "Coping with Northern Aboriginal Youths' Suicides." In A.A. Leenaars, S. Wenckstern, I. Sakinofsky, R.J. Dyck, M.J. Kral, and R.C. Bland, eds. *Suicides in Canada*. Toronto: University of Toronto Press, 212–226.

Keat, Russell, and John Urry. 1982. *Social Theory as Science*. 2nd ed. London: Routledge.

Killias, M., J. van Kesteren, and M. Rindlisbacher. "Guns, violent crime, and suicide in 21 countries." *Canadian Journal of Criminology* 43 (4): 429–448.

Kirmayer, L.J., L.J. Boothroyd, and S. Hodgins. 1998a. "Suicide in the Northwest Territories: A descriptive review." *Chronic Diseases in Canada* 19 (4): 152–156.

Kirmayer, L.J., C. Fletcher, and L.J. Boothroyd. 1998b. "Suicide among the Inuit of Canada." In A.A. Leenaars, S. Wenckstern, I. Sakinofsky, R.J. Dyck, M.J. Kral, and R.C. Bland, eds. *Suicide in Canada*. Toronto: University of Toronto Press, 179–188.

Kirmayer, L.J., M. Malus, and L.J. Boothroyd. 1996. "Suicide attempts among Inuit youth: A community survey of prevalence and risk factors." *Acta Psychiatrica Scandinavica* 94: 8–17.

Kral, M.J. 1998. "Suicide and the Internalization of Culture: Three Questions." *Transcultural Psychiatry* 35 (2): 221–233.

Krull, C., and F. Trovato. 1994. "The Quiet Revolution and the Sex Differential in Quebec's Suicide Rates: 1931–1986." *Social Forces* 72 (4): 1121–1147.

Kunce, Mitch, and A.L. Anderson. 2002. "The Impact of Socioeconomic Factors on State Suicide Rates: A Methodological Note." *Urban Studies* 39 (1): 155–162.

Lam, T.H., S.M. Stewart, P.S.F. Yip, G.M. Leung, L.M. Ho, S.Y. Ho, and P.W.H. Lee. 2004. "Suicidality and Cultural Values among Hong Kong Adolescents." *Social Science & Medicine* 58 (3): 487–498.

Leenaars, Antoon A., and David Lester. 2004. "The Impact of Suicide Prevention Centres on the Suicide Rate in the Canadian Provinces." *Crisis: Journal of Crisis Intervention and Suicide Prevention* 25 (2): 65–68.

Leenaars, A.A., S. Wenckstern, I. Sakinofsky, R.J. Dyck, M.J. Kral, and R.C. Bland, eds. 1998. *Suicides in Canada*. Toronto: University of Toronto Press.

Lester, David. 2003. "Adolescent Suicide from an International Perspective." *American Behavioral Scientist* 46 (9): 1157–1170.

Lester, David. 1997a. *Making Sense of Suicide: An in-depth look at why people kill themselves*. Philadelphia: The Charles Press.

Lester, David. 1997b. "Suicide in International Perspective." *Suicide and Life Threatening Behavior* 27: 104–111.

Lester, D., and A.A. Leenaars. 1998. "Suicide in Canada and the United States: A Societal Comparison." In A.A. Leenaars, S. Wenckstern, I. Sakinofsky, R.J. Dyck, M.J. Kral, and R.C. Bland, eds. *Suicides in Canada*. Toronto: University of Toronto Press, 108–121.

Lester, D., P. Wood, C. Williams, and J. Haines. 2004. "Motives for Suicide: A Study of Australian Suicide Notes." *Crisis: Journal of Crisis Intervention and Suicide Prevention* 25 (1): 33–34.

Maltsberger, John T. "Letter Across the Pacific: The Conscience of Martyrs." *Crisis: Journal of Crisis Intervention and Suicide Prevention*. 25 (2): 88–90.

McMullen, Linda M. 2003. "'Depressed' Women's Constructions of the Deficient Self." In S.J. Stoppard and L.M. McMullen, eds. *Situating Sadness. Women and Depression in Social Context*. New York; London: New York University Press, 17–38.

Meng, L. 2002. "Rebellion and revenge: The meaning of suicide of women in rural China." *International Journal of Social Welfare* 11: 300–309.

Middleton, N., D. Gunnell, S. Frankel, W. Whitley, and D. Dorling. 2003. "Urban-rural differences in suicide trends in young adults: England and Wales 1981–1998." *Social Science and Medicine* 57 (7): 1183–1194.

Morgan, Jenny, and Keith Hawton. 2004. "Self-reported Suicidal Behavior in Juvenile Offenders in Custody: Prevalence and Associated Factors." *Crisis: Journal of Crisis Intervention and Suicide Prevention* 25 (1): 8–11.

Neuringer C., and D.J. Lettieri. 1982. *Suicidal Women. Their Thinking and Feeling Patterns*. New York: Gardiner.

Nolan, P.D. 2003. "Questioning Textbook Truth: Suicide Rates and the Hawthorne Effect." *American Sociologist* 34 (3): 102–111.

Otsu, A., S. Araki, R. Sakai, K. Yokoyama, A.S. Voorees. 2004. "Effects of urbanization, economic development, and migration of workers on suicide mortality in Japan." *Social Science and Medicine* 58 (6): 1137–1146.

Pickering, W.S.F., and G. Walford. 2000a. "Introduction." In W.S.F. Pickering and G. Walford, eds. *Durkheim's Suicide: A Century of Research and Debate*. London; New York: Routledge, 1–10.

Pickering, W.S.F. 2000b. "Reading the conclusion: *Suicide*, morality and religion." In W.S.F. Pickering and G. Walford, eds. *Durkheim's Suicide: A Century of Research and Debate*. London; New York: Routledge, 66–80.

Platt, S.D. 1986. "Parasuicide and unemployment." *British Journal of Psychiatry* 149: 401–405.

Platt, S.D. 1984. "Unemployment and suicidal behavior." *Social Science and Medicine* 19: 93–115.

Pope, W. 1976. *Durkheim's Suicide: A Classic Analyzed*. Chicago: University of Chicago Press.

Ramp, W. 2000. "The Moral Discourse of Durkheim's *Suicide*." In W.S.F. Pickering and G. Walford, eds. *Durkheim's Suicide: A Century of Research and Debate*. London; New York: Routledge, 81–96.

Report of the Advisory Group on Suicide Prevention. 2003. *Acting on What We Know: Preventing Youth Suicide in First Nations*. Government documents.

Roberts, R., Y.R. Chen, and C. Roberts. 1997. "Ethnocultural Differences in Prevalence of Adolescent Suicidal Behaviors." *Suicide and Life Threatening Behaviour* 27: 104–111.

Rossow, I. and G. Lauritzen. 2001. "Shattered Childhood: A Key Issue in Suicidal Behaviour among Drug Addicts?" *Addiction* 96 (2): 227–240.

Royal Commission on Aboriginal Peoples. 1995. *Choosing Life: Special Report on Suicide among Aboriginal People*. Canada Communication Group, Minister of Supply and Services.

Sakinofsky, Isaac. 1998. "The Epidemiology of Suicide in Canada." In A.A. Leenaars, S. Wenckstern, I. Sakinofsky, R.J. Dyck, M.J. Kral, and R.C. Bland, eds. *Suicides in Canada*. Toronto: University of Toronto Press, 37–66.

Sakinofsky, I., and R. Roberts. 1987. "The Ecology of Suicide in the Provinces of Canada: 1969–71 to 1979–81." in B. Cooper, ed. *The Epidemiology of Psychiatric Disorders*. Baltimore: John Hopkins University Press, 27–42.

Sinclair, C.M. 1998. "Suicide in First Nations People." In A.A. Leenaars, S. Wenckstern, I. Sakinofsky, R.J. Dyck, M.J. Kral, and R.C. Bland, eds. *Suicides in Canada*. Toronto: University of Toronto Press, 165–178.

Smith, Dorothy, E. 1983. "No One Commits Suicide: Textual Analysis of Ideological Practices." *Human Studies* 6: 309–359.

Smith, Linda Tuhiwai. 1999. *Decolonizing Methodologies* London: Zed Books.

Stack, S. 2001. "Occupation and Suicide." *Social Science Quarterly* 82 (2): 384–396.

Stack, S. 1982. "Suicide: A Decade Review of the Sociological Literature." *Deviant Behaviour: An Interdisciplinary Journal* 4: 41–66.

Statistics Canada Health Reports. Volume 15 (2), 2004.

Stillman, D. 1980. "The Devastating Effect of Plant Closures." In M. Green and R. Massie, eds. *The Big Business Reader*. New York: Pilgrim Press, 72–88.

Stoner, K.L. 2004. "Militant Heroines and the Consecration of the Patriarchal State: The Glorification of Loyalty, Combat, and National Suicide in the Making of Cuban National Identity." *Cuban Studies* 34: 71–96.

Stoppard, Janet M., and Linda M. McMullen, eds. 2003. *Situating Sadness: Women and Depression in Social Context*. New York; London: New York University Press.

Taylor, S. 1988. *Durkheim and the Study of Suicide*. London: Longman.

Tester, Frank J., and P. McNicoll. 2004. "Isumagijaksaq: mindful of the state: social constructions of Inuit suicide." *Social Sciences and Medicine* 58 (12): 2625–2636.

Tomasi, L. 2000. "Emile Durkheim's Contribution to the Sociological Explanation of Suicide." In W.S.F. Pickering and G. Walford, eds. *Durkheim's Suicide: A Century of Research and Debate*. London; New York: Routledge, 11–21.

Travis, Robert. 1990. "Halbwachs and Durkheim: A Test of Two Theories of Suicide." *British Journal of Sociology* 41 (2): 225–243.

Trovato, F. 1998. "Immigrant Suicide in Canada." In A.A. Leenaars, S. Wenckstern, I. Sakinofsky, R.J. Dyck, M.J. Kral, and R.C. Bland, eds. *Suicides in Canada*. Toronto: University of Toronto Press, 85–107.

Varty, J. 2000. "Suicide, Statistics and Sociology: Assessing Douglas' Critique of Durkheim." In W.S.F. Pickering and G. Walford, eds. *Durkheim's Suicide: A Century of Research and Debate*. London; New York: Routledge, 53–65.

Warr, P.B., and P.R. Jackson. 1987. "Adapting to the unemployed role: A longitudinal investigation." *Social Science and Medicine* 25: 1219–1224.

Wild, Lauren G., A.J. Flisher, and C. Lombard. 2004. "Suicidal ideation and attempts in adolescents: Associations with depression and six domains of self-esteem." *Journal of Adolescence* 27 (6): 611–624.

Functionalist Perspectives: Law and Social Order

The functionalist perspective views systems of law and criminal justice as central institutions that function to maintain social order and manage deviant behaviour that threatens this order. In this view, law states the moral rules and agreed codes of conduct of society. Crime is defined as behaviour that violates the moral rules of society, and the criminal justice system functions to deter and punish crime, to reform offenders or to remove them from mainstream society.

Functionalism draws extensively on Durkheim's classical theoretical work, and particularly his concept of the *conscience collective*, or common conscience, the body of shared norms, beliefs, and sentiments that form the foundations of social cohesion. Durkheim studies law to explore the moral basis of social cohesion, and how the moral order changes as societies evolve. In his seminal study, *The Division of Labour in Society*, Durkheim traces the increasing importance of contract over penal law, as European societies changed from relatively homogeneous communities to highly differentiated industrial societies. He argues that the moral foundations of industrial society, reflected in contract law, are respect for justice and for individual human rights.

This next section examines historical changes in Canadian law to explore the moral or normative order of Canadian society.

Early Canadian Law and Societal Values

The laws that settlers established in Canada were modelled initially on British and French common law. This body of law has evolved over time, with a major shift occurring in 1982, with the patriation of the Constitution and the promulgation of the Canadian Charter of Rights and Freedoms.

The history of laws governing immigration to Canada from the nineteenth century to the present are briefly highlighted below because they are particularly insightful in revealing shifts in normative values from those of white settler society to contemporary multiculturalism. These laws explicitly defined the kinds of people who were welcomed into Canada in various periods and those who were not.

Nineteenth-century laws make it very clear that cultural homogeneity was far more strongly and centrally valued than individual justice or human rights. People from Britain and France were favoured, while people from China, Japan, and other parts of Asia were opposed. Section 38(c) of the Immigration Act of 1910 states clearly the concern of the time that newcomers share the customs and normative values that prevailed in societies of Britain and France, or be sufficiently similar that they could be expected to assimilate quickly into mainstream culture. Others were to be systematically excluded. Specifically to be denied entry were "any *nationality* or *race* of immigrants . . . *deemed unsuitable* having regard to the climatic, industrial, social, educational, labour [conditions] . . . or because such immigrants are deemed *undesirable* owing to their peculiar customs, habits, modes of life, methods of holding property and because of their probable inability to become readily assimilated or to assume the duties and responsibilities of Canadian citizenship within a reasonable time after their entry" (Jakubowski 1999, 104; emphasis in original). Chinese males were welcomed as labourers for mines and railroads, but a head tax and other restrictions blocked them from bringing wives and families. Continuous passage laws were designed to curtail immigrants from Asia. A "gentleman's agreement" with Japan permitted trade but minimized immigration. Jewish refugees from Nazi Germany were denied entry in 1939. All these actions, which now look blatantly discriminatory, conformed to the laws of the time. They were publically defended by political leaders as appropriate to ensure cultural cohesion and social order within the Dominion. The Indian Act of 1876, reflecting earlier provincial laws, was similarly designed to foster the rapid assimilation of indigenous peoples to Canadian European culture, or to pressure them onto separate reservations. Few people among mainstream white Canadians of the time saw reason to protest any of these laws.

The values of cultural conformity and Victorian morality that underlay restrictive immigration laws were further reflected in legislation designed to manage those immigrants who were approved. Middle-class women who organized the recruitment of women from Britain for domestic service explicitly wanted young, virtuous "girls" who would be future mothers of the nation (Arat-Koc 1999, 129–132). People who conformed to values of middle-class decorum were sought. Not just anyone from Britain would do. Recruiters feared that lower-class women would bring vices such as sexual license, drinking, and gambling with them. Recruiters arranged for migrant women to be closely supervised to guard against sexual misconduct. Laws empowered Canadian authorities to deport anyone deemed "unsuitable," with the definition of "unsuitable" left sufficiently vague as to give maximum leeway to law enforcers. Further laws required that migrant women sign contracts before they left Britain to commit themselves to working for one year in a domestic service placement assigned to them—in effect binding them to indentured labour. These contracts had to be signed again immediately on arrival in Canada to ensure they were legally binding within Canadian provinces.

A host of other morality laws governing pornography, prostitution, and homosexuality, dating back to before Confederation, were enforced with punitive religious justification in the name of ensuring social order. The same class of elite women who sponsored and chaperoned the new "mothers of the nation" had campaigned for the temperance movement, succeeding briefly in banning the manufacture, importation, and sale of alcohol.

The Charter of Rights and Freedoms, promulgated in 1982, followed the pattern Durkheim predicted in stressing individual human rights rather than cultural assimilation. Multicultural policies enacted in the 1970s, and in the subsequent Canadian Multiculturalism Act of 1987, reinforced this shift in legal practice. The Charter formalized important principles to which all current and future laws must comply. The equality guarantees in Section 15(1) of the Charter means that any law that can be shown to be discriminatory is null and void. As a specific exception to this rule, Section 25 asserts that nothing in the Charter shall be construed as infringing or denying Aboriginal treaty rights, or other rights that they have acquired over the years. Section 27 of the Charter further defines Canada as officially bilingual and multicultural, with people having the right to preserve and enhance their multicultural heritage.

The Charter also provides that every individual within Canada has the right to life, liberty, and security of the person, the right not to be arbitrarily detained or imprisoned, the right to a fair trial, and to be presumed innocent until proven guilty, among other protections. Respect for justice and individual human rights, rather than cultural conformity, is now officially recognized in law as the foundation of social cohesion. The official symbol of law is a blindfolded maiden, untouched and uncorrupted, and blind to differences of race and social status, carrying the scales of justice (Comack 1999, 21). The judiciary that administers law is formally separate from the legislature that makes law. The practice of law is also bound by the principle of precedent, intended to ensure that the law treats every case in legally comparable ways.

Individual Rights or Social Cohesion? A Clash of Concerns

From the functionalist perspective, the major question surrounding the Charter is how to reconcile the need for cultural consensus to ensure social cohesion and order with the divisive potential inherent in respect for individual diversity and rights. Political leaders in the province of Quebec refused to endorse the Charter of Rights and Freedoms in 1982 because of their concerns that the Charter provided insufficient protection for the distinctive francophone culture of Quebec. Virtually all references to Durkheim's theoretical writings in sociological studies on law focus on his concept of *conscience collective* and mechanical solidarity based on shared culture. His model of organic solidarity between specialized and interdependent people, based on respect for individual diversity and human rights, is generally ignored. Many Charter challenges that have come before the Supreme Court have pitted guarantees of individual rights against the restriction in the opening clause that such rights and freedoms are subject to "reasonable limits" that can be "justified in a free and democratic society."

Laws that govern immigration, or the types of people welcomed or discouraged from entering Canada, have changed markedly since the early 1960s to eliminate any explicit reference to racial and cultural characteristics. Laws like those once enacted against Chinese and other Asian workers are now unconstitutional. What the functionalist perspective sensitizes us to, however, is how the practical implementation of immigration law is still slanted in favour of immigrants who share mainstream Western cultural backgrounds, notwithstanding the far larger numbers of non-Western and non-white immigrants. The points system, with its emphasis on fluency in English or French and higher educational qualifications that fit exactly with Canadian models, the discretionary powers given to administrators, and the physical location of the maximum number of visa offices, all work to favour cultural conformity

(Jakubowski 1999). Laws that create a special status of "guest workers" for "underqualified" domestic workers, continue to make it very difficult for women from the Caribbean to obtain landed immigrant status (Arat-Koc 1999). People who are rejected as immigrants have little opportunity to challenge their exclusion.

The foundational Charter principle of individual human rights is itself being challenged in the climate of heightened fear of terrorism after the attacks on the World Trade Center in New York and the Pentagon on September 11, 2001. Canadian governments in the past have claimed that suspension of human rights is justifiable in exceptional circumstances in the interests of protecting the security and order of the society as a whole. In October 1970, the Trudeau government called on the War Measures Act, first passed in 1914, to suspend civil liberties in response to the kidnapping of two politicians by the terrorist *Front de Libération du Québec* (FLQ). One of the two hostages was murdered. During the three months in which the War Measures Act was in force some 450 people were detained in Quebec, most of whom were eventually freed without being charged with any criminal offence. It remains contentious whether these measures were justified. Some believe they were useful in controlling terrorism in Quebec, while others argue that terrorism was averted by the growth of a democratic separatist movement in the 1970s, leading to the election of the *Parti Québécois* government in 1976 (Smith 1988, 1558). The War Measures Act itself was not nullified by the Charter of Rights, although it has not been used since 1970.

In principle, the Charter guarantees the right of *habeas corpus*—the right not to be arbitrarily detained or imprisoned, the right to a prompt trial with legal representation, and to be presumed innocent until proven guilty. But since the September 11 attacks, the Canadian government has suspended these rights for at least five individuals suspected of possible involvement in planning terrorist activities, in the higher interest of protecting society as a whole. Security certificates issued by the Solicitor General hold these individuals in long-term detention although they have not been explicitly charged or convicted of any offence. The government lacks sufficient evidence to convict them in open court, but claims sufficient covert information to fear that they might conspire to commit acts of terrorism if released. Almost a decade after the September 11 attacks, no Charter challenge had been launched in their defence.

In the United States, far greater numbers of people are being held as security risks under similar exceptional legislation. Rights of habeas corpus have been totally denied to several thousand people detained on suspicion that they might be aiding or planning terrorist activities. It has also become common practice for refugees admitted to the USA to be detained in prison for months, and in some cases for years, pending administrative investigation of their cases (Detention Watch Network News Issues 14–18, 2000–01). These individuals are presumed to be a potential threat to social order and security until they can prove themselves to be harmless. President Obama campaigned on the promise that he would close the prison at Guantanamo Bay, enforce the prohibition against torture, and shift prosecution of suspected terrorists from military to civilian courts. Months into his term in office, however, these promises have proven difficult to implement.

In Canada, small numbers of refugees take sanctuary in church basements for months, and sometimes years, at a time to avoid deportation while pleading for reviews of their cases. The argument that lax immigration or refugee laws threaten the security of Canada as a whole is hard to counter. However, it is also clear that concern to protect the security of Canada from possible terrorist activity has compromised Charter principles in exceptional cases, and members of ethnic minority groups are the people most affected. Individuals have been picked up, interrogated, deported, and tortured in the name of possibly extracting information on potential terrorism.

Law and Moral Order

An important assumption within the functionalist perspective is that commitment to a shared cultural system of normative beliefs, values, and sentiments is a necessary foundation for social order. This does not mean that cultural beliefs can never change. Current standards of sexual behaviour have clearly changed significantly from Victorian standards of the nineteenth century. What functionalism does assume is that some recognized and widely respected normative system is necessary. The legal system functions to specify the boundaries of acceptable behaviour. As soon as the Charter of Rights and Freedoms was promulgated, challenges were raised as to how much personal freedom individuals could or would be granted to transgress mainstream norms before they would be subject to "reasonable limits prescribed by law."

In the influential Butler decision on pornography in 1992, the Supreme Court came down strongly on the side of community standards rather than individual freedom (Johnson 1999). The Butler case began in 1987 when Winnipeg police seized the entire inventory of a pornographic video store owned by Donald Butler, and charged him with 250 violations of Section 163(8) of the Criminal Code concerning possession of obscene materials. Butler appealed to the Supreme Court on the grounds that this law contravened his rights under Section 2 of the Charter guaranteeing "freedom of thought, belief, opinion, and expression." The court upheld the reasoning that community standards of tolerance for obscenity should legitimately limit public access to obscene material in the interest of the proper functioning of society. The Court did not explicitly define these community standards, but argued that they should properly be determined by jurors for individual cases, with due sensitivity to local community standards. Following this decision, Butler's case went back to trial and he was convicted on most of the original charges. Subsequently, customs officers responsible for controlling the flow of pornographic materials across Canadian borders seized quantities of material destined for bookstores catering to gay and lesbian customers, as well as pornography that uses children. Customs officers judged homosexual erotica as potentially more threatening to Canadian values than traditional erotica destined for heterosexual males.

Crime Rates and Weakening Civil Order

The functionalist perspective views some level of crime as normal. Any behaviour that transgresses legally defined boundaries of acceptable behaviour constitutes crime. The concept of **deviance** encompasses a broader range of nonconformist behaviours that transgress normative expectations of society without necessarily breaking specific laws. The criminal justice system punishes law-breakers and, in so doing, functions to clarify and uphold the legally permissible limits of behaviour for the majority of conforming members of society.

What counts from the functionalist perspective is not the fact that some crime occurs, but the rate of criminal behaviour in the population, and particularly the high crime rates among certain sectors of the population. Increases in rates of criminal behaviour are viewed as symptoms of a weakening of community life. Most functionalist research into criminal behaviour focuses on conditions of failed socialization where community standards and values are not adequately transmitted, efforts to identify types of people most prone to commit crimes, and techniques of deterrence. Various theories within this broad perspective include anomie, differential opportunity, differential association, and deviant subculture.

THE ANOMIE THEORY OF CRIME

The concept of anomie, as developed by Durkheim, refers to a relative absence or confusion of values and a corresponding lack of clear regulations or norms for behaviour. People feel lost and unsure of what to believe in or how to behave. Robert Merton (1968) systematized this concept into a general model, the **anomie theory of crime**, sometimes referred to as *strain theory*, to classify types of deviant behaviour and

Table 1 Merton's Typology of Modes of Adaptation (1968, 194)

Mode of Adaptation	Culturally Valued Goals	Socially Approved Means
Conformist	accept	accept
Innovator	accept	reject
Ritualist	reject	accept
Retreatist	reject	reject
Rebel	replace	replace

conditions in which high rates might be expected. Merton argues that deviance is a symptom of dissociation between culturally valued goals and socially approved means to achieve them. Strains develop because not everyone has the means needed to attain goals they have learned to value. Merton's model defines the five logically possible ways to respond to this situation (see Table 1). **Conformists** accept both culturally valued goals and socially acceptable means to achieve them. Such people must constitute a majority of the population in any given society for that society to be stable or orderly. **Innovators** accept cultural goals such as material success but use illicit means such as theft, prostitution, or drug trafficking to achieve them. Merton suggests that this category accounts for the relatively high crime rates found among lower-class people. **Ritualists** give up on culturally valued goals, no longer even trying to attain them. They ritualistically obey the rules and conform to outward behaviour patterns but have no motivation to succeed. **Retreatists** reject both goals and means, withdrawing into various forms of apathy. Merton suggests that homeless people, dropouts, skid-row alcoholics, and drug addicts fit into this category. Drugs provide a retreat for those who have failed in society. Finally, **rebels** are people who generate new goals and means. One example would be political activists who reject the values of money, individualism, and competition associated with capitalist consumer culture and favour alternative forms of social organization like communes.

Merton's typology is valuable for drawing attention to unequal opportunities and the strains generated by inequality. It accounts for the high rates of crime among poor people and disadvantaged minority groups in terms of the greater obstacles they face in achieving the success goals of the dominant culture.

Control theory, developed by Travis Hirschi (1969), focuses attention on the first category in Merton's model. Hirschi predicts that conformity to mainstream behavioural norms is most likely when individuals build strong attachments to conventional others, and are committed to and frequently involved in conventional activities through family, school, and church. A rise in rates of deviance are caused by erosion of ties to family and church, and reduced involvement in community activities.

The **differential opportunity theory** of delinquency developed by Cloward and Ohlin (1960) complements Merton's model by suggesting that access to criminal opportunities may explain why some nonconformists become deviant innovators while others remain ritualists or retreatists. Deviant careers are fostered in contexts where getting away with crime is relatively easy, or illicit means are readily accessible.

Subcultural theories of crime modify Merton's approach by questioning his assumption that there is only one set of cultural norms in complex societies such as Canada. Subculture theories focus attention on distinctive subcultural socialization through which people learn unusual behaviour patterns. These people appear to engage in deviant behaviour from the perspective of mainstream society, but are normal conformists rather than innovators or rebels. The only difference is that they are conforming to unusual subcultural values learned from their neighbourhood or peer groups. To use Merton's terminology, they have learned both deviant goals and means. Sutherland and Cressey (1960) proposed the theory of **differential association** to account for the behaviour of professional thieves and children from neighbourhoods where crime rates are high. Business people, Sutherland suggests, may learn attitudes of contempt for legal regulations that restrict sharp business practices like misleading advertising, infringing patents, unfair labour practices, and the like ([1949] 1961). Hence, they engage in such activities without feeling like deviants. Recent high-profile criminal cases that have involved business executives convicted of fraud, including Canadian newspaper tycoon Conrad Black, claim their supposed "crimes" were consistent with normal business practices.

More commonly, differential association theory is used to account for high rates of deviance among youths who "hang out with the wrong crowd" (Peace et al. 2000, 4–5). Associations vary in frequency, duration, priority, and intensity, influencing the likelihood that individuals will internalize particular group values. As individuals begin to become publicly associated with deviant subgroups, the vicious cycle of reaction and counteraction described by labelling theory begins to happen. Others who disapprove of their deviant friends and activities begin to avoid them, driving them further to the margins of society.

Merton first applied his model to cultural strains associated with unequal means to achieve individual economic success, but as a generic model it can be applied to any culturally desirable goals that are not easily achieved. In contemporary society, for example, achieving fame and celebrity may parallel economic achievement as a goal, generating new forms of deviant adaptation to structural constraints (Parnaby and Sacco 2004). *Conformity* involves achieving public recognition in the media, celebrity status in the entertainment industry, winning the lottery, and the like. But few of us can hope to win such fame legitimately. *Innovators* seek notoriety through attention-grabbing acts of vandalism or deviance that the media then channel into millions of homes; *ritualists* scale down the "celebrity" goals to a mundane level like waving at a television camera during public events or putting risqué pictures on a personal website and imagining others looking at them; *retreatists* give up on both goals and means, developing social phobias against appearing in any situation where others may look at them; *rebels* challenge the legitimacy of the cultural and economic structures that push celebrity status and consumer goods by defacing advertisements and exposing global systems of exploitation that underlie mass consumer society.

Gang Subculture: Rebels, Innovators, or Retreatists?

Subcultural theories of deviance have often been applied in studies of youth gangs found in many large urban centres in North America, and particularly those associated with lower-class and ethnic minority neighbourhoods (Cohen 1955; Thrasher 1963; Miller 1958; Totten 2000). Descriptions of gang cultures often read like studies of exotic tribes with their own internal social organization, moral codes, and sanctions. Typically, gang culture grants prestige to those who rebel, get into trouble, outsmart others, take risks, and are tough and autonomous. Violation of legal norms for its own sake is a respected part of the culture. In the eyes of gang members, fighting, vandalism, sexual conquests, joy-riding in stolen cars, heavy use of alcohol, illicit drugs, and smoking represent conformity to gang expectations rather than rebellion. Hirschi's concept of control theory can be readily applied as gang members commonly show limited respect for or involvement in mainstream institutions like school or religion. They associate primarily among themselves. In Willis's classic study of working-class boys in school in Britain (1981), the "lads" openly ridiculed school work, challenged the authority of teachers, and kept their involvement in class-work to the minimum.

Alternative views of gang behaviour, however, question the usefulness of explanations in terms of subcultural conformity to account for what motivates gang members. Claimed gang values are not just different from prevailing societal values; they are an exaggerated reversal of them. This complicates the application of Merton's typology because it is unclear whether gang members are truly conforming to an alternative cultural system, or rebels wishing to replace the dominant cultural system, or merely retreatists whose exaggerated talk covers fear of failure. Greenberg (1981) notes that interest in gang membership among lower-class boys drops off sharply as they reach school-leaving age and begin to find jobs and earn money. Much delinquent behaviour among juveniles, he suggests, reflects status frustration. As teenagers, they want brand-name clothes, cigarettes, cars, and motorbikes, and access to pubs and other adult entertainment. But as underage "children" in school they have few opportunities to earn money. With adult status and a job, gang values lose their appeal. Willis's "lads" similarly do not include all working-class boys in school, but rather those who are not succeeding by school standards. They have little hope of achieving more than factory jobs, even if they do conform to school norms.

For Totten also, experiences of frustration and failure seem to account better for gang behaviour than conformity to subcultural norms. Interviews with boys in gangs around Ottawa revealed very traditional views of what makes an "ideal man"—someone who is the family breadwinner, with a good job, material possessions, and a devoted homemaker-wife who defers to him (2000, 76). But few of the adult men in their lives had achieved these ideals. The more common experience was chronic unemployment, and even the humiliation of dependence on employed wives. The boys sometimes spoke of their own raging anger and frustration that they did not have jobs while girls they knew had money to pay for dates. This anger was often expressed in violence against their girlfriends, much as they describe seeing their mothers beaten up by their fathers.

Theories that focus on *family breakdown* and *inadequate socialization* as the root causes of deviant behaviour complement this analysis of status frustration because such experiences so commonly occur together. A subsequent study of young offenders convicted of murder and manslaughter (Kelly and Totten 2002) reveals how deeply most of them were harmed by difficult, impoverished lives. Overwhelmingly, they come from families unable to cope—mired in addictions, alcoholism, and mental illness, and neglectful of their children (Kelly and Totten 2002, 8). *Social disorganization* theory suggests that periods of rapid social change, associated with accelerated urbanization, immigration, and technological advances, increase the likelihood of communities and families breaking down (Peace et al. 2000, 7). Proportions of youth at risk of becoming deviant rise as the inevitable result.

Anomie theory, along with these complementary theories of family breakdown, inadequate socialization, and social disorganization, forms a syndrome of experience that helps to account for the exceptionally high crime rates among Aboriginal peoples (Gill 2002, 178–179). Gill cites 1999 data from the Elizabeth Fry society, estimating that Aboriginal people nationwide were nine times more likely to go to prison than non-Aboriginal Canadians. Aboriginal people represent 2 percent of the adult population of Canada, but accounted for 11 percent of admissions to federal prisons at the beginning of the 1990s and fully 17 percent by 1998 (Statistics Canada 1991, 1, cited in Gill 2002, 179). Proportional incarceration rates for Aboriginal youth are, if anything, worse. Functionalist theory traces the roots of these troubles to the breakdown of cultural norms and family life within Aboriginal communities. Primary socialization into traditional native cultural values were undermined in many communities as children between the ages of six to 16 were removed from reservations to be educated in residential schools. Misery and loneliness, and vulnerability to physical and sometimes sexual abuses, marred these schools as centres for secondary socialization. Young adults graduating from these schools were frequently ill-equipped psychologically to establish functional families of their own, resulting in trans-generational family breakdown (Braun 2002; Cote and Schissel 2002). Chronic poverty, alcoholism, child abuse, and conflict with the law are pervasive features of life on reservations and among Aboriginal peoples living in urban areas. The gradual resocialization of people into traditional Aboriginal cultures, both in native communities and among Aboriginal people in prisons, is widely described as a critical process helping to change these patterns to bring about emotional healing and family stability, which in turn are reflected in reduced incidence of antisocial behaviour (Anderson and Lawrence 2003).

In summary, the varied theories outlined above offer complementary rather than competing explanations for deviant behaviour. What they all have in common is the concept of **anomie**—a confusion of values and lack of clear regulations or norms for behaviour. The theories highlight different aspects of the same underlying experience of family breakdown and loss of community, of people who lack strong ties to institutions of family, school, or religion, who reject others and feel rejected in turn. Young people, and particularly young men, find themselves adrift, rejecting and often inverting the values and expectations of the dominant society that they feel unable to live up to, but without any satisfying alternative.

Gender Socialization and Crime

Traditional research in criminology largely avoided the question of gender differences by focusing only on males. As Adelberg and Currie (1987) expressed it, women are "too few to count" in criminology. Overall, only about 12 percent of all criminal code violations are attributed to women, and these tend to be less serious offences. Women make up fewer than 10 percent of inmates in Canada's prisons. Only with respect to the one offence of prostitution do convictions of women outnumber men. Theorists who have tried to account for these gender differences have generally found anomie theory difficult to apply to women (Leonard 1982; Morris 1987). Anomie theories that focus on family breakdown, deviant neighbourhood subcultures, and frustrated economic success goals would not predict such differences. After all, girls and boys grow up in the same families and neighbourhoods. Women also typically face greater barriers to economic achievement than men, and are more likely to live in poverty. Yet women as a whole are responsible for only about one-fifth of all property offences, and these are mostly for petty theft like shoplifting rather than large heists. Even in extremely anomic circumstances of divorced, single parenthood, crime rates among women remain far below averages for men.

Differential socialization of girls and boys is still the dominant explanation for lower crime rates among girls, along with implicit notions that girls may naturally be less aggressive than boys. Role theorists point out that, even though girls and boys grow up together, they are socialized differently and have different success goals. Girls tend to be protected and supervised more at home and encouraged to seek help in difficult situations, rather than to fight. They are given dolls to play with and expected to help with housework and care of younger children. They grow up to see being a wife and mother as their primary adult role, with economic success secondary. Wife-mothers are expected to defer to husband-fathers within the family. Boys, in contrast, are socialized to be tough and independent, to participate in physical contact sports, to fight back when hit, and to take risks. They are also freer to move around the neighbourhood without adults chaperoning them. They grow up to see getting a job and earning money as their primary role, with nurturing and caregiving roles as secondary. Such differences predispose boys to get into more trouble than girls and to be more physically violent. As adults they are more centrally affected by status frustrations that focus on money and power, and hence more prone to crime.

These theories predict that as the socialization of girls and boys becomes more similar their crime rates would tend to converge. Differential opportunity theory similarly predicts that as the women's liberation movement increased women's opportunities to commit crimes, more girls would get into trouble (Adler 1975; Faith and Jiwani 2002). Hypothetically, the converse might also happen. If boys are brought up to be more nurturing and home-centred, and see their fathers sharing more of the nurturing and child-care responsibilities within the family, crime rates for boys and young men should decline.

Currently, there is more evidence to show rising crime rates and greater violence among girls than declining rates for boys. Official statistics for youth crimes in Canada during the 1990s suggest that convictions for violent offences rose 127 percent for girls during the decade, while rates for boys rose only 67 percent (Bell 2002, 132–135). Bell notes, however, that much of this change can be accounted for by changes in policing practices, and a greater tendency to lay charges for common assaults than in the past. Percentages also vary wildly depending on the base year from which they are counted. A rise from one homicide to two, for example, can be described as an impressive 100 percent increase. Gender differences in actual rates of assault and robbery convictions remain large, with 90 percent of violent crimes still attributed to men.

A study of six adolescent girls who have been convicted of assaulting their peers supports the theory that such violence is a learned response to family environments in which conflict is "frequent, vehement, and ugly," with physical punishment designed to hurt and degrade (Artz 1998, cited in Bell 2002, 140). Artz argues further that these homes are strongly hierarchical and male-dominated. Girls learn early that men are more important and powerful than women, and that power resides in physical force. All the girls convicted of assaulting other girls had themselves been victimized. In effect they come from the same kind of families as the boys in Totten's study of male gangs, described above. Boys learn to dominate by physical force, while girls learn to expect such abuse from boyfriends and to defer to them, and fight girls who threaten to win the attention of boys. A survey of 1500 high-school students (Artz and Riecken 1994) found that girls who hit others were far more likely than non-violent girls to have experienced sexual and physical assault. Growing up in homes marred by violence is a common feature in multiple studies of women serving time in prison (Bell 2002, 143). The 2009 case of a woman charged, along with her boyfriend, with abduction and murder of eight-year-old Victoria Stafford closely fits this profile of seriously dysfunctional upbringing.

POLICING AND COMMUNITY CONTROLS

Punishment and incarceration are common responses to criminal behaviour. In principle, punishment functions to make offenders pay for harm to others and to deter future potential deviants from copying such behaviour. Punishment also serves to remind people of the legally defined boundaries of acceptable behaviour, and thus to reinforce conformity among the general population. Punitive law enforcement, however, risks exacerbating the causes of deviance identified in functionalist analysis. Imprisonment may worsen deviance by bringing younger or first-time offenders into close and extended association with more hardened criminals, thus increasing the likelihood of deviant socialization. Criminal convictions carry strong negative labels that further contribute to the social marginalization that fosters deviant behaviour (Dick et al. 2004). Punishment also does little to improve the conditions of community breakdown that are the foundational cause of anomie.

These concerns have led sociologists to propose more community-based strategies for reducing crime rates and for dealing with offenders. The core of proposals that the sociologist Giddens (1998, 87–88) gave to the British government of Tony Blair is that police and the government need to work together with citizens to improve community standards, and to support all institutions involved in socialization of young people. He recommended sponsoring parenting programs at the community level to teach effective parenting skills, especially targeted at parents of children at risk. Previous conservative British Prime Minister Margaret Thatcher even suggested the possibility that parents be held legally responsible, and subject to heavy fines for crimes committed by their underage children. Giddens and others further propose policies to keep families intact wherever possible, to promote mediation to resolve disputes between parents over children, and to insist on joint and continuing parenting responsibilities after divorce. In addition, police have experimented with curfews for children under 10 years of age to prevent them from being on the streets between 9 p.m. and 6 a.m. while not under the supervision of a "responsible adult" (James and James 2001, 220–223). Police were also given increased powers to stop children outside school during school hours and return them to school (James and James 2001, 217). In Canada in 2004, some municipalities proposed curfews after 11 p.m. for juveniles under age 16, to cut down on vandalism. While the proposal met with much popular support, opponents warned that it might violate the age-discrimination proscription in the Charter of Rights and Freedoms. The more general principle underlying all these proposals is that parents need to be pressured to assume greater responsibility for supervising their children's behaviour and teaching more respect for societal values.

Schools and education also feature centrally in Giddens' recommendations for strengthening community values and preventing crime among youth (James and James 2001, 215–219; Giddens 1998, 125). Schools are enjoined to teach the values of self-discipline and control, reinforced by increased supervision and monitoring of children's behaviour while in school. School councils were instituted to involve children directly in arbitrating student complaints and managing disruptive behaviour. Frequent standardized testing and the ranking of schools and teachers are designed to increase discipline as well as standards. The British government also sponsored programs that place increased pressure on parents to give children more help with their homework, with a view to increasing the effective involvement of parents and local communities in the education of their children (James and James 2001, 217).

Community policing programs provide a third avenue designed to strengthen community involvement in the management and reduction of crime. These range from informal "neighbourhood watch" programs and street patrols by officers to state-sponsored joint programs between citizens and police (Klinenberg 2001). In Chicago, where police have organized monthly citizens' meetings in every neighbourhood since 1995, some 6000 citizens participate monthly and over a quarter of a million participated at least once during the first four years. A staff of roughly 50 workers regularly visit churches and schools in the neighbourhoods to encourage citizens to attend the meetings. Attendees are further encouraged to go to court when neighbourhood "thugs" are on trial, to show that they care about crime prevention, and to participate in neighbourhood watch programs and informal monitoring of delinquent activities in the local streets. The city government supports these police-citizen meetings by expediting responses to all complaints voiced through the meetings, from graffiti to broken street lights. Klinenberg suggests that community policing is providing avenues for previously isolated citizens to become involved in community life. Greater involvement promises to strengthen commitment to shared normative consensus.

A variety of community-based *restorative justice* programs are also being developed to manage the sentencing and sanctioning of offenders as an alternative to the prison system. These include approaches like peer courts or juvenile conferencing for first-time offenders, community sentencing circles, and the involvement of victims and family members in deciding appropriate punishment and community service work through which offenders can make reparation to individuals and communities for the harms they have caused (White 2002; Dick et al. 2004). Programs specifically for Aboriginal inmates try to draw them into a greater awareness of their cultural and religious heritage and build a sense of belonging to their ancestral communities. After years of struggle to gain recognition for Aboriginal spirituality as a religion within the definition used by the Canadian criminal justice system (Waldram 1997), many Canadian prisons now offer special services, including pipe ceremonies, healing circles, sweat lodge, and other sacred ceremonies, with community elders as religious leaders and counsellors. Evaluation studies suggest these programs have had significant success, notably with men formerly segregated in prisons as dangerous offenders (Braun 2002).

Manifest and Latent Functions: The Unintended Consequences of Crime Control

An important assumption within the functionalist perspective is that all social institutions are interconnected in an overall system. Changes in one arena of activity have implications for multiple other sites of action that are not easily foreseen or controlled. The **manifest functions** or intents of a new policy may be to strengthen social order and community values, and so protect citizens from crime. However the **latent functions** of the policy may include disrupting balance in other areas of society, which generate new problems or dysfunctions for social order. Labelling theory, described above, points to a classic example of dysfunctional consequences of well-intentioned policies. Imprisonment and punishment deter offenders, but incarceration promotes deviant socialization and negative labelling, which increase the risk of recidivism. The primary deviance that prompted the initial punishment may be relatively minor, compared with the long-term consequences of **secondary deviance**, especially for juveniles (Dick et al. 2004).

Recognition of these negative consequences promoted many of the community-based programs described above. Critics warn, however, that these programs may also have unintended consequences that serve to reinforce rather than replace dominant forms of processing offenders through prisons (White 2002). When implemented as cheap and marginal programs appropriate only for trivial and first-time offences, they reinforce the view that hard-line criminal justice and prison terms are appropriate for all others. They also reinforce the view of crime as individual failure rather than a symptom of problems at community level. Dick et al. similarly warn that more research is needed into the latent consequences of peer courts for juvenile offenders. We still do not know how effective they are in avoiding negative labelling or shaming, or how to strike a balance between too strict and too lenient punishment, or how readily juveniles internalize the idea that they have been treated fairly or unfairly by peers (2004, 1454–1456). James and James (2001) warn that parent-education programs, school councils, and standardized monitoring of school performance introduced in Britain may work to reduce children's agency and human rights rather than enhancing participatory democracy.

Articles in the July 2004 volume of *American Behavioral Scientist* provide a litany of other examples of unintended policy consequences. Aggressive policing of illicit drugs raises their street value and thus profitability for organized crime, and so increases drug trafficking. All interventions in problem gambling functioned to make problem gambling worse (Russell and Preston 2004). Displaying losses to discourage players promotes "chasing behaviour"—a desperate urge to win back lost money; slowing the rate of play promotes longer playing time; mandatory closing periods promote frenzied binge gambling, and so on. Medicaid funding intended to provide long-term nursing-home care for the poor is rapidly exhausted as wealthier families develop asset-transfer schemes so as to qualify for the aid (Wegner and Yuan 2004). Heightened airline security after the September 11, 2001,

terrorist attacks served mostly to heighten public awareness of the impossibility of total security and hence increased insecurity (Russell and Preston 2004). Gun-free zones, intended to increase safety around schools, daycares, and hospitals in the USA, function to attract criminals who feel safer in such zones (Roots 2004). These authors all warn sociologists of the need to study the unintended consequences of policies they promote. Roots carries the functionalist notion of system equilibrium to its logical extreme by arguing that even well-meaning policies necessarily disturb the natural system equilibrium. All laws intended to block certain behaviours encourage counteractions to get around them, and hence stimulate their own violation (Roots 2004, 1386).

Few researchers are as pessimistic as Roots in dismissing virtually all policy intervention as doomed to failure. But there is copious evidence that many decades of criminal justice intervention have failed to rid societies of crime, or even to stabilize crime rates. The number of violent crimes has declined somewhat in recent years, a fact usually attributed to an aging population. But overall incarceration rates are rising, drug abuse is rising exponentially notwithstanding decades of "war on drugs," child pornography and gambling are spreading exponentially through the Internet, organized crime has become global in size, prostitution rings operate globally through sex-tourism, and fear of crime remains pervasive (Reiman 2001, Ch. 1). Reiman concludes that "nothing succeeds like failure," in that the solution most favoured by political leaders amounts to expanding the very criminal justice system that has failed in the past.

From the functionalist perspective, the main conclusion drawn is that maintaining systemic equilibrium is very difficult. This is particularly so during periods of rapid social change, both within individual societies and in the surrounding global environment. The task facing leaders working within existing institutions of socialization and criminal justice is to achieve a reasonable balance between individual autonomy and social control. Some of the critics cited above, however, argue that what we need is new ways of thinking about crime that offer the potential for very different and hopefully more effective modes of social response. Alternative sociological perspectives explore these ideas more closely.

Political Economy Perspective: Law and Criminal Justice under Capitalism

The political economy or Marxist perspective places the structures of capitalism at the centre of analysis of crime, rather than socialization of individuals into the moral order of society. The needs of the capitalist economic system are seen as driving changes in all other institutions of society, including law. Law functions to facilitate the accumulation of profits and to legitimate the resulting concentration of wealth (Comack 1999, 36–44; Quinney 1975; Chambliss 1975). Accumulation of wealth requires laws to enforce contracts and to safeguard property ownership and profits. Legitimacy of that wealth requires laws to manage relations between capital (employers) and labour (employees) in ways that reduce the potential for class conflict. In effect, Quinney argues, law functions at every stage, from enactment to enforcement, to protect and enhance the interests of the propertied ruling class.

As Durkheim recognized, restitutive or contract law increased exponentially with the rise of industrialization and capitalism in Europe. Currently within Canada an estimated 80 percent of all law is concerned with boundaries of property, transaction, and contract (MacDonald 2002, 26).

Law reduces the risk of class conflict by giving a semblance of legitimacy or justice to contractual relations between capital and labour. Law protects the personal property and well-being of workers, so that they too develop a stake in the system. Marxist theorists are quick to point out that this does not mean that law is designed to *resolve* the basic contradiction between property owners and wage labourers; rather law is a *symptom-solving* mechanism (Chambliss 1986; Comack 1999, 41). The official version of law as dispensing blind justice promises equal treatment to all individuals under law, regardless of poverty or wealth. Detractors comment that this amounts merely to prohibiting rich and poor equally from sleeping under bridges or panhandling on public transit. Defenders argue, however, that if legitimation is to work, equality under the law cannot be merely a sham (Comack 1999, 43; Thompson 1975). To maintain its appearance as fair, and therefore to function effectively in providing the social stability that capitalism needs, law must truly dispense justice at least some of the time. Hence law can function sometimes in the interests of workers against employers, and citizens against corporate capital.

Reiman (2001, 1–9) argues the extreme position that the capitalist system *needs* to criminalize the poor—the lumpenproletariat of the underemployed, jobless, and **marginal workers**. Criminalization facilitates the control of this class of people most likely to support insurrection against the inegalitarian economic system. It justifies the state's use of police, courts, and prisons to manage this population. The maintenance of a stable, visible class of criminals who are portrayed as pathological individuals further functions to win support of the mass of useful workers for institutionalized suppression, and diverts attention from the systemic contradictions of capitalism. The negative labelling of ex-convicts can be seen as useful from this viewpoint.

Not all Marxist theorists agree with the extreme argument of Quinney and Reiman that law is an instrument directly controlled by capitalists. What they do generally agree on is that law enforces social order in inherently exploitative, inegalitarian, and conflict-ridden capitalist societies. Capitalists do not always win struggles to control laws, but they do have a commanding advantage. Law upholds a moral order that endorses property ownership, competitive individualism, and consumerism.

Alienation, rather than anomie, is the central concept through which antisocial behaviour is understood. Alienation refers to a syndrome or interrelated pattern of lived experiences shared in varying degrees by people across different class-sectors of society. These experiences include being powerless to secure one's own future in economies dominated by corporate giants and volatile job markets, feeling trapped in a cycle of meaningless jobs rewarded with shoddy consumer goods, estranged from one's own sense of self-respect in a culture that values only wealth and glamour. Above all, alienation refers to **isolation** from others in a moral order that promotes competitive individualism. Even those who succeed in this capitalist system, capitalists themselves, experience alienation. They too are isolated from meaningful social relations with others, trapped as they are in relentless competitive struggle for profits.

Law for the Propertied Class: Legalizing Colonization

We begin this analysis with the origins of capitalism itself as an economic system in the conversion of feudal estates to private property during the seventeenth and eighteenth centuries in England. The rolling farmlands of southern England may look the picture of tranquil gentility, but two centuries ago these lands were scarred with the blood and horror of what Marx terms "reckless terrorism" (Blomley 2004, xvii, citing Marx [1867] 1976, 713–733). Rural peasant families who had lived on and worked the lands for many generations were ruthlessly dispossessed and evicted by nobility who wanted to privatize the lands for commercial crops. In some particularly horrendous instances, **peasants** who refused to move were burned alive in their homes as villages were torched (Clegg and Dunkerley 1980, 48). Landless and destitute, these ex-peasants were forced to move into the cities to seek wage-work in factories that expanded rapidly with the invention of steam engines.

It is particularly significant that these mass evictions took place under the rule of law. The nobility were recognized in law as the rightful property owners of the former feudal estates, and had the legal right to evict peasants as they chose. A series of legal decisions emphasized the absolute property rights vested in the big estate owners over the coincident use-rights of villagers established over centuries of practice (Thompson 1975). Thompson describes one such law, called *The Black Act*, passed in 1723. It imposed the death sentence for any peasant caught with a blackened face, a disguise widely used by peasants while hunting on privatized lands. The death sentence was also imposed for such acts as poaching, hurting cattle, cutting trees, and burning haystacks or barns on the estates. The wording of the laws appears neutral and impartial, merely protecting property held by one individual against damage or theft by another. But what such terminology obscured was class warfare. The laws created two classes of people—those who owned the means of production, and those who did not.

A similar body of laws legalized the colonization of Canada by merchant companies and settlers from Britain and France. Under the doctrine of *terra nullis*, lands that were not developed for agricultural or commercial use and not inhabited by Christians were legally deemed to be uninhabited (Razack 2002, 2–3; Blomley 2004, 3; Martin 2002, 229). Such lands were therefore deemed to be legally available for settlement by European settlers. *Terra populi*, in contrast, were lands to which merchant companies or individuals had legally documented private ownership, registered by the state. The discipline of cartography mapped and named "space" in ways that meant it could be legally divided up, bounded, and sold in plots. These laws made it possible for Europeans to think of themselves as "pioneers," the first people to tame and settle the wilderness—as if colonization never happened. The presence of indigenous peoples and their ancestral practices that recognized multiple use-rights to lands were rendered invisible. Western law, argues Blomley, was thus an instrument of civilization and of empire, facilitating the violent dispossession of indigenous peoples and simultaneously legitimating and depoliticizing their colonization. Cities across Canada were routinely settled by force of law. Maps laid out boundaries for new towns and parcelled out plots for sale. Indigenous residents were deemed to have no legal ownership or rights to residence, and were driven outside the town boundaries (Blomley 2004, 107; Razack 2002, 128–136). Constructed legally as "wards of the state," indigenous peoples were "given" reservations, held in trust for them by the state. Police brutality and settler violence were routinely practised to enforce their spatial containment and their exclusion from city boundaries.

More recently, the development of hydroelectric projects in northern Canada was carried out with essentially the same view of land as "empty space," or more specifically as crown-owned land, with few individuals having clear property rights (Martin 2002). The Canadian legal system has found it almost impossible to determine appropriate compensation for Natives who lost their means of subsistence as lands on which they hunted were flooded, and migration paths for big game disrupted. Commercially the lands have no value. Individual Natives have no clear property rights based on formal purchase agreements. Yet these lands provided for the subsistence needs of entire communities. Depending on the standpoint taken, financial compensation should be minimal or should be sufficient to sustain entire communities for generations. Typically, compensation claims drag through the courts for years. Twenty-five years after their lands were flooded in 1977 by the Manitoba Hydro project, the Cree had still not received compensation (Gill 2002, 172). Meanwhile, Manitoba Hydro had become the fourth largest electrical utility in Canada with net revenues well over $1 billion annually.

A similar struggle continues over the federal government's appropriation of Native reservation lands at Ipperwash in 1942 for a wartime military base, and later for a training base (Bressette 2003). Displaced people crowded onto a neighbouring reserve, impoverishing both groups. An interim settlement of $2.2 million, intended as compensation for the wartime takeover of land, was finally agreed upon almost 40 years later. Half this amount was held in trust for future generations, leaving only $1000 per capita for the displaced people who qualified legally as status Indians. Local people are still struggling to get the land back. During one such confrontation in September 1995, Anthony "Dudley" George died from a police bullet.

Colonizing the Inner City

The central assertion of Blomley's study of the politics of property is that colonization is an ongoing process in cities across Canada, not something that happened a century or more ago.

Ipperwash confrontation over land claims during which Dudley George died.

(CP PHOTO) 1995 (Str-Moe Doiron)

His study of conflicts over property rights in downtown east-side Vancouver draws close parallels between the legalized dispossession of indigenous peoples and the contemporary eviction of low-income residents from districts undergoing gentrification or corporate development. As with indigenous peoples, the multiple users of contested sites become invisible in law against the legally legitimated rights of property owners.

Community policing meetings become sites for class struggle between the rights of middle-class property owners to unimpeded enjoyment of their newly gentrified homes and small bed-and-breakfast businesses, pitted against the rights of residents of nearby homeless shelters and rooming houses, prostitutes, and other users of space. Typically, police side with property-owning residents' associations against the poor, regardless of who are the newcomers and who the long-term residents, and regardless also of their relative numbers. Police routinely pressure homeless people and shelter residents to keep moving until they are forced out of targeted streets. Bylaws are enacted to prohibit loitering or sleeping on park benches, and to lock public parks and toilets in the evenings so that homeless residents cannot stay in them. These laws function to preserve these "public" spaces for propertied residents (Kawash 1998).

In some instances, people have been denied the right to be within city limits at all. Saskatoon police stand accused in the 1990s of routinely arresting Aboriginal men who appeared drunk on the streets, and dumping them miles outside town, forcing them to walk home. Sometimes this was done on winter nights with temperatures approaching −30°C. The frozen body of 17-year-old Neil Stonechild was found outside of town in late November 1990. Credible witnesses swear that on the night when he disappeared they saw him handcuffed and screaming in the back of a police cruiser (*Globe and Mail*, 28 October 2004, A1). The bodies of three Aboriginal men were found frozen in similar circumstances. A fourth man testified that he too had been dumped by police outside of town on a freezing night, but managed to survive. The public inquiry held in 2004 found that police at the time made minimal effort to investigate these allegations, and indeed actively threatened and intimidated witnesses who tried to speak out.

In law, Blomley argues, it is the propertyless who appear as "transient," and whose claims to use rights appear unfounded. Rights to private ownership of property trump all other rights of residency and community rights to use and enjoy the space. Similarly, a rooming-house owner seeking to renovate property to attract upscale customers can use the force of law to evict tenants from his property, even if those tenants have lived in the same room for 30 years (Blomley 2004, Ch. 1). There is nothing inevitable or obvious about such property rights, Blomley insists. They are a

particular way of seeing moral relationships, and a way of not seeing other possible forms of communal claims to entitlement. Rights in property are not absolute. Homeowners, for example, do not have unencumbered rights to make as much noise as they wish, to rent rooms to any number of tenants, to chop down all the trees, to leave garbage in the front yard, to cover the roof with advertising signs, and so on. These legal restrictions, however, are designed primarily to protect the property values of the neighbourhood. There are no laws that protect the space-usage rights of the homeless from their propertied neighbours.

Social activists and long-term homeless residents of downtown east-side Vancouver joined forces in 1995 in an attempt to reclaim "community" usage rights to an abandoned department store, based on its years as public space for shopping and entertainment in the neighbourhood (Blomley 2004, 39–46). Squatters moved into the building, urging the government to turn it into low-income public housing. The city, however, sided with developers who proposed to demolish the building and build upscale condominiums. Police were called in to evict the squatters on grounds of "public safety." In a related struggle, local activists argued that a public park and beach area in Vancouver extensively used by homeless people was threatened by the plans of corporate developers to build a casino complex for tourists (Blomley 2004, 46–50). From the perspective of law, however, the park appeared merely as derelict space, to which none of the regular users had proprietary rights. Within the maps produced by developers, the contested community space was merely empty space. The area was effectively *terra nullis*—devoid of prior property owners whose interests needed to be considered in development plans.

Even when individuals do have some legal title to property this does not necessarily protect them from legal expropriation of land for other purposes supported by the state. This is especially so for slum-clearance projects when the properties in question are of low taxable or real-estate value and proposed developments are of greater economic value. The expropriation and subsequent obliteration of the black settlement area known as Africville by the city of Halifax in the 1960s was all carried out legally. This is notwithstanding the fact that the site of the settlement was legally purchased by the settlement's founders in 1840. Shabby properties, not serviced by either piped water or sewage, were classified as slums and hence legally of little value for purposes of financial compensation. Many current residents were unable to produce legal documentation of home ownership, because homes had often been shared and handed down among extended family members. Hence residents had the legal status only of squatters—not entitled to any financial compensation when their homes were expropriated beyond small gifts of $500 from a benevolent city (Nelson 2002, 216). For Nelson, it was "precisely the legality of the process" that appeared so strikingly violent (2002, 223). Every avenue through which former residents might pursue legal redress and compensation were closed to them. The final irony for Nelson is that after the settlement was destroyed, the proposed commercial development never materialized. The area was turned into a public park. When two prior residents subsequently set up a tent in the park in an effort to pressure the city for better compensation, the city passed bylaws to lock the only park toilet, and to ban sleeping in public parks overnight. The presence of campers was thus declared illegal, and they were evicted.

Treaty Rights and Legal Practice

Aboriginal peoples have a special legal status within Canada that is recognized in the Charter of Rights and Freedoms. Section 35 of the Charter states: "The existing aboriginal and treaty rights of the aboriginal peoples of Canada are hereby recognized and affirmed." Section 25 further affirms that nothing in the Charter shall be construed in any way that detracts from treaty or other rights that pertain to Aboriginal peoples. In the ensuing two decades since the Charter was proclaimed, land claims and other treaty issues have been continually going through the courts. While there have been some successes, particularly in negotiating the implications that individual treaties have for subsistence and commercial access of Natives to natural resources, few major issues have been resolved.

Major problems result from the poor fit between the formal structure and functioning of the Canadian legal system and the structures needed to establish the meaning of treaties (Martin 2002; Monture-Angus 1999; Anderson and Lawrence 2003). A significant assertion by Aboriginal peoples themselves is that treaties pertain to international law, signed between First Nations and the British colonial government, subsequently replaced by the Canadian federal government. Hence, treaties have different legal status from other Canadian laws. Even the jurisdiction of Canadian colonial courts to decide treaty issues has been challenged. The interpretation of treaties is made more complex by language barriers, and particularly by the very different ways in which agreements are understood and remembered in the oral traditions of First Nations communities at the time and the formal, legal and written language in which treaties are preserved by colonial governments. It is not always clear that individuals whose names appear as signatories to treaties had the legal status or moral right to represent the First Nations communities at the time. The land claims of First Nations communities that did not enter into treaties, and hence never formally ceded lands to colonial authori-

ties, are also in dispute. These claims drag interminably through the courts. The Indian Act that establishes the legal definition of an Indian is itself a colonial document that is hotly contested. First Nations communities argue that they, and not a colonial government document, should define who their members are. Nonetheless, the distinction between status and non-status Indian remains centrally important in claims relating to treaty rights.

Even when these problems are set aside, it is questionable whether prevailing legal methods of reasoning are appropriate for deliberations on treaty rights. The rule of law in capitalist societies asserts both that everyone is subject to the law, and secondly that the law treats everyone as legal equals. What is presumed in this official version of law is the norm of a legal person as "able-bodied, autonomous, rational, educated, monied, competitive and essentially self-interested" (Comack 1999, 23, citing Naffine 1990, 52). Marxist theory views this notion of autonomous individuals, detached from community, as itself a product of capitalist relations of production. This means that legal reasoning routinely functions in ways that make it very difficult for communities to pressure their rights specifically as communities, rather than as individuals. Residents of Africville were treated in law as legal individuals within family units as spouses and dependent children. Whatever claims they may have had as a community, wanting to retain their residential and extended kinship networks in a new location, were not heard in court. Lawyers and judges trained in prevailing methods of legal reasoning are ill-equipped to consider claims that pertain to communities rather than individuals.

Aboriginal treaty rights pertain essentially to communities, compounding all the problems noted above in pressuring claims through Canadian courts. Everything that was done to indigenous peoples over three centuries of colonial wars was done through legal statutes. Now the onus rests entirely on First Nations peoples themselves to establish, interpret, and enforce treaty rights and land claims. Monture-Angus, herself holding advanced degrees in law, concludes that the legal system, by the very way that it functions, cannot bring about transformative change—and indeed is not designed to do so. Each small success at the Supreme Court level, won at enormous cost in money and energy, only seems to generate more court cases. In a supposedly landmark decision in the *Delgamuukw* case in 1997, the Supreme Court of Canada modified evidentiary rules to accommodate oral histories on an equal footing with written historical documents in determining historical facts. The result, however, was merely that the case returned to court for retrial. This case, which concerned Aboriginal title of hereditary chiefs, had already taken 374 days at trial and 141 days taking evidence out of court (Monture-Angus 1999, 81).

Another landmark Supreme Court ruling in 1999 determined that Donald Marshall, a Mi'qmac, had the right, under a 1761 treaty, to fish for eels without a licence and out of season. By 2004, the same treaty was back in court with the New Brunswick government contesting a lower-court interpretation that this reasoning implied a right to cut and sell timber from crown land (*The Daily Gleaner*, 23 September 2004, A2). The Supreme Court ruled earlier that treaty rights need to be interpreted to fit contemporary situations rather than being frozen in the pre-industrial context in which they were first concluded. However, the difficult legal issue remains of how standard reasoning for contract law can be applied to treaties more than 200 years old. In yet another case, agreement was reached on restricted fishing rights for the Mi'qmac in Quebec. But this too collapsed into violent confrontations with police over whether their agreed 72 hours of fishing were to be on three consecutive days or six half-days (Martin 2002, 236). As Monture-Angus observes, every legal success seems to lead only to another legal challenge.

Property Laws and Class Struggle

In summary, property laws, by their very existence, support the interests of the propertied classes against those who do not own property. These laws are structured to recognize as legal rights those that are based on the commercial purchase of real-estate as a commodity. The moral order that is sustained by property laws is that of individual competitive rights to purchase real estate.

Property laws appear neutral and objective, but from the beginnings of the capitalist system to the present, they embody class war. Other forms of spatialized rights to use and inhabit space are not visible within the justice system. Occasionally the rights of people without commercial property are sustained in law. Treaty rights are interpreted as rights to restricted subsistence and commercial access to Crown resources. Shelters for the homeless and subsidized housing for the poor do sometimes win rights to space, along with limited rights for renters against arbitrary powers of owners. But these exceptions are visible within the capitalist system only as "special favours" or gifts. Indigenous peoples and others who assert rights to inhabit space that are not based on purchased property appear as nuisances, disturbing the more legitimate rights of purchasers of real estate to the unimpeded enjoyment of their property. Protection of plants and animals in the way of commercial exploitation of primary resources is similarly a nuisance that is occasionally accommodated but rarely highly valued. Any gains that non-propertied "**outsiders**" make are won at high price in terms of time, efforts and money, and negative labelling. They have not achieved transformative visions of the validity of multiple and shared use rights to space that falls outside the capitalist model. At worst, small gains by outsiders may function to legitimate the fairness of the justice system, and thus reinforce the class structures that it represents.

The Political Economy of Crime and Criminology

A central assumption of political economy theory is that the capitalist system is criminogenic. *Alienation* in its varied forms is endemic in a social system that generates great inequalities in wealth and poverty and promotes a moral order that privileges the values of competitive individualism and ownership of consumer goods as the primary measure of self-worth.

There is significant overlap between functionalist and political economy theories in analysis of how poverty contributes to criminal behaviour. Both approaches make visible the crimes of desperation as people steal food and necessities that they cannot afford to purchase. Both approaches also see the crimes of frustration generated by the gap between socially valued goals and access to legitimate means to achieve them. Advertising incites impoverished people to want expensive consumer goods that they cannot afford, leaving them open to the lure of "innovative" criminal means to satisfy their desires. Desperation and relative deprivation combine to account for higher rates of petty crime among poor people, particularly break-and-enter and theft. Political economy theory differs from functionalism in placing this awareness in the context of a capitalist system that functions continually to reproduce an economically insecure class of underemployed and unwanted workers, and to exacerbate the gap between rich and poor.

Both functionalism and political economy theory see the desperation and deprivation underlying high crime rates among Aboriginal peoples. But while functionalism stresses anomie, the loss of community values and religion, family breakdown, and personal misery, political economy theory highlights the long and continuing history of colonialism. The systematic and brutal separation of Natives from means of production in lands and resources, and their marginalization on colonial postage-stamp reservations must bear much of the responsibility for the ensuing collapse of Aboriginal communities. Economic marginalization was made immeasurably worse by the colonial politics of the Indian Act that vested political power to manage reservation governance and resources in the hands of the Indian Affairs bureaucrats rather than First Nations themselves (Dyck 1992). The forced placement of children in residential schools is but one example of the state-enforced **powerlessness** of First Nations peoples.

The approach known as *left realism* combines a sensitivity to social injustice as the root of crime, with a recognition that crimes committed out of desperation or deprivation nonetheless do threaten the well-being of community life. All too commonly the victims of these crimes come from the same deprived communities as the victimizers. Predatory crimes of burglary, theft, and mugging, and violence of all kinds, occur far more commonly in poor neighbourhoods than in better-off areas. Left realists argue that punitive law-and-order approaches to crime control do little to deter antisocial behaviour among people already punished by deprived social lives. *Restorative justice* and peacemaking approaches that strive to bring perpetrators and victims together as members of the same communities offer more hope of reducing destructive behaviour at the neighbourhood level (Morris 2000). Where left realism differs most from mainstream functionalist approaches is in the kinds of structural changes advocated at the societal level to reduce crime rates. Functionalists stress socialization, family responsibility, parenting classes, and stronger ties to school and religion as solutions to individual pathology. Left realists insist that lasting reduction in crime rates requires a reduction in economic injustices that incite people to crime. Few theorists on the left see a total transformation from capitalist to communal economies as a realistic or even a desirable option. But policies that promote progressive taxation, a strong social safety net, investment in social housing, and commitment to job protection and full employment would help. For First Nations communities, an economic resource base sufficient to establish communal self-sufficiency and political autonomy are essential (Boldt 1993).

Drug Wars as Class Wars

Drug use as a social problem is most visible in inner cities among the poor, the destitute, and marginalized people. In a vicious interaction between cause and effect, people are most likely to seek a drug-induced euphoria when their current lives are miserable and they see no hope for the future. In black and chicano ghettoes in American cities in particular, there are no decent jobs, no health care, poor education, and infant mortality rates approaching Third World levels (Ransom 1991, 6). In such contexts drug use is rampant. Drug addiction generates a desperate need for money to buy more drugs, promoting predatory criminal behaviour like burglary, theft, and drug trafficking. These people create the most nuisance for law-abiding society, especially for their lower-class neighbours. Of all the people involved in the drug trade, these are the most likely to end up in prison (Siegel and McCormick 2003, 378). Individual pathology is the mainstream functionalist explanation. These people tend to come from impoverished families, with parents who also have criminal records; they do poorly in school and end up as young adults with little hope of succeeding in compet-

itive job markets. They sink into a life of crime and chronic drug use, with frequent periods in prison (Saner, MacCoun and Reuter 1995, 362–373). Recreational drug users among better-off people who can afford to pay for their drugs without resorting to crime may be far larger in number, but they do not attract the attention of either police or neighbours.

Largely invisible to this scenario are the organized business networks where the real profits are made. Profits are staggering. The markup from coca leaf purchase price to street value for cocaine is about 75 times, with $4 worth of leaves fetching $300 as finished cocaine (Siegel and McCormick 2003, 385). It is the illegality of the product that sustains both these incredible profits and the street crimes needed to pay for them. From this perspective, the criminal-justice solution to drug trafficking is itself a major contributor to the problem. Efforts to control the manufacture of drugs at the source and their trading by international cartels have proven futile. Even the much-hyped capture in 1993 of the billionaire Colombian drug lord Pablo Escobar, whose Medellin drug empire once controlled 80 percent of all cocaine imported into North America, barely created a dent in the flow of drugs. Competitive cartels across Latin America and elsewhere immediately filled the gap (Siegel and McCormick 2003, 384). Efforts to rein in drug traffickers within Canada and the USA have proven equally futile for the same reasons. The demand is insatiable and the profits immense. Occasional major drug busts only help the trade by temporarily removing some competitors and raising drug prices.

Given the obvious failure of the criminal justice system to stem the drug trade the question arises why does the "war on drugs" continue? The moral argument that controlling drugs works to protect vulnerable populations from dangerous substances has been widely discredited. Marijuana has proven relatively harmless and non-addictive, but it is still illegal in Canada. Other illegal drugs have not been shown to be markedly more addictive than legal ones like alcohol and nicotine (Reiman 2001, 37–38; Alexander 1990). The death rate among users of cigarettes is, if anything, higher than death rates among cocaine users. Risks of HIV-AIDS infections arise from sharing dirty needles, not from drug use as such. Reports of drug-crazed behaviour are largely exaggerated. The main danger and nuisance arises from crimes committed to get drugs rather than from crazed behaviour while on them. Cocaine derivatives are reputed to be widely used as recreational drugs of choice among middle-class people. But middle-class people are largely ignored by the criminal justice system.

It is in relation to "victimless" crimes like illicit drug use that the instrumentalist Marxist argument is most convincing—that the criminal justice system functions in capitalist societies primarily to control the economically marginal populations. While efforts to stamp out drug use and drug trafficking have largely been futile, the criminalization of drugs works very well in providing legitimation for regular surveillance and control over poor people. Opium laws were first introduced in Canada in 1908 primarily to control the Chinese migrant-worker population in cities like Vancouver. The Chinese were left alone when their labour was needed during the height of railroad construction, but by the 1900s they were unwanted, and their cheap labour posed a competitive threat to other workers. Laws were passed to restrict their immigration and settlement, and white workers turned against them. A particularly bad riot in 1907 that targeted Chinese workers caused extensive property damage. It was during the investigation of this damage that officials discovered opium dens. They used this information against the Chinese. The Opium Narcotic Act of 1908 and the wider Opium and Drug Act of 1911 gave police expanded powers of search and seizure that were directed against Asian minorities (Siegel and McCormick 2003, 374; Comack 1985).

Currently, drug laws legitimate mass surveillance, directed overwhelmingly at lower-class people who are marginalized from the capitalist system. The policy of zero tolerance for drugs, initiated in the early 1990s in the USA, provides a rationale for extensive police powers to suspend civil liberties, enter homes and vehicles, and search occupants. Blacks are the prime targets of such searches. As of the early 1990s an estimated one-quarter of all young black males in New York City had criminal records for drug-related offences. Whites make up 30 percent of arrests for sale and possession of drugs but less than 10 percent of all commitments to state prison for drug-related crime. Blacks make up 10 percent of the population of New York State but 50 percent of prison inmates (Cockburn and Cohen 1991). In many US states, individuals with a criminal record are prohibited from voting in elections, thus marginalizing them even further.

In Canada, the Charter of Rights in principle protects people from arbitrary search and seizure. If police happen to find drugs in a private home or vehicle that they had no prior warrant to search, the find may not be accepted as evidence in court. Police need a search warrant, signed by a judge, to enter private homes. However, these are relatively easy to get when drug use is commonplace among targeted populations, and the powers they confer are extensive. In one case in Halifax in 2001, police had a warrant to search a dance hall on a tip that a bottle of ecstasy pills was hidden there. They proceeded to strip search everyone present (Siegel and McCormick 2003, 246). In principle, citizens do not have to submit to being searched if they have not been arrested, but a police spokesperson suggested that anyone refusing to be searched under such circumstances likely would be placed under arrest.

The international "war on drugs" can similarly be analyzed as a war on the powerless and impoverished peasant farmers in South American countries such as Peru, Bolivia, and Colombia. Wracked by debt and collapsing commodity prices since the 1980s, and unable to compete with multinational agribusiness corporations who have taken over prime agricultural lands, peasants on marginal hill farms have turned to growing coca as the one crop for which they can get a good price (Ransom 1991; Rance 1991). Americans have responded by spraying crops with harmful defoliants, and also by providing military funding to cooperating Latin American governments. These interventions were futile from the perspective of drug control, Rance suggests, but effective politically in facilitating extensive American government intervention in the internal politics of Latin American countries. The main beneficiaries have been military governments, bankrolled on the promise of repressing coca farming among peasants, and simultaneously repressing potential communist uprisings among peasants. American multinational corporations find it safe to do business in these cooperating countries. In 1989 the American government sent 20 000 troops into Panama to arrest General Noriega on drug-trafficking charges. A puppet ruler, beholden to the USA, replaced him. Accusations surfaced at the time that the American Central Intelligence Agency (CIA) had itself been heavily involved in drug trafficking as a means to fund the Contra rebels in their bid to overthrow the elected socialist government in Nicaragua (Ransom 1991).

Meanwhile, the immense profits made from international drug trafficking have to be disguised. Canadian banks are required to report any suspiciously large deposits, but privacy laws protect deposits in banks in Switzerland, Luxembourg, the Bahamas, and the Cayman and Virgin Islands. Profits are routinely laundered through investments in legitimate businesses and real estate, and international arms deals. Political economists criticize the blinkered focus on traditional criminology on individuals who end up in prison, and drug offences at street level. The workings of vast international networks of drug-related business, and the complicity of governments in these networks, cannot be understood in terms of pathological individual socialization.

The Other Drug War: Promoting Drugs for the Healthy

While the war to reduce the trafficking and use of illicit drugs appears to be having limited success, beyond the criminalization of pusher and users, a different kind of drug war is being waged much more successfully by pharmaceutical companies to promote drug sales and drug use. A collection of papers presented at a 1999 Health Policy Conference (Barer et al. 2000) document the mass marketing to healthy people of supposedly medicinal drugs with minor therapeutic value for a few people. Prominent in the list is the promotion of cholesterol-lowering drugs. A close inspection of research data suggests only mild evidence of a link between cholesterol and heart disease in young and middle-aged men only, and no association in women or the elderly. Cited research also shows no documented improvement in morbidity or mortality from either cholesterol testing, or lowering it with drug treatment. Yet by the early 1990s, an estimated 30 percent of Americans and 20–25 percent of Canadians were being prescribed these drugs on medical advice that lowering cholesterol might reduce their risk of dying from heart attack or stroke. Pharmaceutical companies are making astronomical profits from inducing between a quarter to a third of North American adults to consume these drugs daily for the rest of their lives. Mass-marketing strategies that include direct-to-consumer advertising on American television aim to saturate the market of adults with drug plans or sufficient disposable income to afford them. A similar saturation marketing strategy seeks to persuade healthy middle-aged adults, on dubious evidence, that taking an aspirin a day will help their heart.

Papers presented at the conference further note that pharmaceutical companies are able to exert extensive control over trials to test the efficacy of drugs. A typical strategy is to include very large samples of doctors who each contribute only a small number of patients, and hence do not see the overall picture. Data collection, interpretation, analysis, and publication are all controlled by the corporation. Negative data, such as that found by physician Nancy Olivieri in her trial of the heart drug deferiprone in 1997, can easily be overlooked or discounted as sloppy research, and not shared with other researchers.

Corporate Crime as Conformist Behaviour

The two central assertions in the political economy perspective—that capitalist systems are criminogenic, and that the criminal justice system is an instrument of class control—make their strongest case in relation to corporate crime. Classic anomie-related theories of individual pathology do not apply at this level. In terms of Merton's typology, the people involved in corporate crime are conformists. They suffer no gap between desirable goals and legitimate means to achieve them, no background of frustration, deprivation, low self-esteem, or negative labelling. They have not been socialized into deviant subcultures. They are, for the most part, good, moral people, good parents and upstanding citizens (Bakan 2004, 50). They conform directly to the prevailing normative values of capitalist society—autonomous, rational, competitive individualism oriented to economic

achievement. Business corporations are the defining feature of any capitalist society. The argument that Bakan forcefully makes, both in his book and film called *The Corporation* (2004), is that business corporations are criminogenic in their most basic structure. Corporations are legal entities, run by managers in the interests of millions of shareholders. Managers are required by law to put the interest of making money for shareholders above all others, or they can be sued. Social responsibility is acceptable *only* in so far as it is demonstrably of benefit to corporate standing and profitability. This is the logic of a tax on carbon emissions, or cap-and-trade system. Corporations can only be induced to cut their output of climate-warming carbon dioxide when they can save money or make profits from doing so. Corporations seek to commercialize every aspect of life, particularly schools and entertainment centres, with the goal of winning customers and enhancing product sales. Even a catastrophe like the September 11, 2001, terrorist attack was immediately translated into an opportunity by commodities brokers to secure profits for their clients in gold markets that would be affected by the crisis (Bakan 2004, 111).

The kinds of crimes that corporate executives are charged with are defined primarily, if not exclusively, in terms of breaching fiduciary duty to maximize returns to shareholders. Recent high-profile cases have concerned business executives treating as personal income profits from business activities that should legitimately have gone to shareholders. This was the main charge against Conrad Black and his partner David Radler in 2007. Another high-profile corporate crime involved conspiring to misrepresent the realistic value of corporate assets on stock markets so that investors pay significantly more for the stock than it turns out to be worth. The charge against Enron executives was that they developed an accounting system that represented anticipated future profits as if they had already been realized, and then disguised real losses until the corporation went bankrupt in 2001. A more serious charge against Bernard Madoff in 2008 was that he used money from new investors to pay the apparently fabulous returns to previous investors, thus encouraging yet more investors to invest a total of $65 billion into his company that actually had no assets at all.

The damage caused by these definably criminal practices was dwarfed in 2007 by the perfectly legal corporate practices that gave rise to the sub-prime mortgage crisis that crippled the entire global financial system. Banks and investment companies, mostly in the US, offered millions of mortgages worth trillions of dollars at super-cheap opening rates of interest and no down payments to people with limited incomes, driving up house prices in the process. The lenders then bundled these risky mortgages into securities, supposedly backed by mortgage assets that could be sold to investors. Other companies sold insurance to cover possible default on these potentially risky investments. Over roughly a five-year period between 2002 and 2007, all the companies made astronomical profits in the multiple trillions of dollars, and their executives made huge bonuses. The process began to unravel by 2008 as between a quarter to a half of sub-prime mortgage holders defaulted on their payments as real interest costs came due. As their repossessed homes flooded the markets, their inflated value dropped far below outstanding mortgages, ruining investors who put up the original mortgage monies. Insured investors claimed for their losses, only to find that insurance companies did not have sufficient assets to cover the claims. Giant multinational banks, investment houses, and insurance companies effectively went bankrupt, taking millions of shareholders down with them across the globe, including foreign governments and corporate pension funds. None of these practices was technically criminal, because there was no effective legal regulation of finance capital either at the national or global level. Executives whose business practices had bankrupted their corporations still claimed entitlement to giant bonuses, taking their cuts from taxpayer-funded bailout packages. Only after the crash have global political leaders begun to talk seriously about establishing international rules to regulate global finance capital.

The Non-Regulation of Corporate "Crime"

The non-regulation of harmful business practices has long been a pervasive feature of law in capitalist societies. Since the 1980s, governments in North America have progressively favoured policies of deregulation. Transnational corporations, many of them economically more powerful than the nation states in which they do business, have been left largely free to govern themselves. A century of struggle to develop laws protecting the interests of employees and customers, and the environment, have been systematically repealed, under pressure from the World Trade Organization to liberalize international trade. Laws and regulatory agencies governing corporate crime have become more lenient, or been abolished altogether (Snider 1999; 2002). In 1997, the Canadian government closed down its research laboratories responsible for testing the safety of food and drugs. This was at a time when escalating numbers of companies were being caught putting untested and harmful products on the market. The budget for Environment Canada was cut by 30 percent in 1993–94, and the environment demoted from a senior to a junior ministry in 1997, despite a litany of environmental disasters. Fines for unlawful pollution declined by two-thirds in Ontario between 1995 and

1997. Annual workplace deaths in Canada are four times higher than the homicide rate, yet agencies charged with protecting the health and safety of employees have been weakened. A particularly tragic example of weak protection of workers' health and safety is the Westray mine in Nova Scotia. A series of inspection reports between 1991 and 1992 warned of safety violations and hazardous working conditions at the mine, but no charges were laid (Siegel and McCormick 2003, 350). On May 19, 1992, a methane gas explosion ignited coal dust in the mine, killing 26 miners. Criminal charges were laid alleging 52 violations of the Occupational Health and Safety Act, and two underground managers were charged with manslaughter and criminal negligence. Later, however, all charges were dropped as too vague. A long list of other corporate crimes causing injury and death can be added to the Westray saga, for which there has been minimal retribution or punishment (Snider 1999, 186–196). Snider estimates that the average amount stolen annually by bank robbers is less than 4 percent of the total stolen by corporate fraud. Typical fraud includes selling mislabelled products, tampering with evidence of harmful working conditions, conspiracy to restrict trade, false advertising, falsifying records, insider trading, hot deals and fast stock flips by mutual-fund operators, and the like. Fraudulent auditing that made companies appear financially sound and attractive to investors lay beneath the recent collapse of Enron and WorldCom, in which many thousands of families lost their life savings.

Snider's central point is that such pervasive corporate misconduct falls largely outside the criminal justice system. Nation states, she argues, have virtually given up the struggle to control corporate criminals through law. Without independent regulatory agencies to check on corporate behaviour, corporate crime effectively disappears from public view. High publicity to a handful of cases, like Martha Stewart going to prison in 2004 for lying to investigators, gives the impression of justice being served, obscuring the reality of minimal investigation of corporate practices. The application of terms like "fraud," "crime," and "criminal" to these corporate practices are really misnomers because they are rarely criminalized. They are viewed more as sharp business practices that are occasionally taken to excess, rather than crimes that should be prosecuted. Corporations are legally required to maximize profits for investors and they tend to be faulted only when they fail.

The criminogenic character of contemporary corporate capitalism is revealed as much in currently legitimate practices as in the semi-legal grey areas listed above. The race to the bottom to find the cheapest sweatshop labour for assembly work; ecological damage in the race to maximize the cheapest resource inputs; gambling trillions of dollars daily on currency exchanges regardless of impact on economies; contracts to exchange weapons for oil in countries facing civil war; lobbying to defeat legislation that might control fuel efficiency and pollution; using patent laws to prohibit development of alternative vehicle designs that threaten profits of gasoline-based models; saturation advertising and restrictive contracts to sell junk food and pop to school children; and the list goes on. Many corporate employees who do this work protect their own self-esteem by an alienated consciousness, living morally compartmentalized lives (Bakan 2004, 54–55). Bakan, himself a law professor, argues that legal regulation of corporations is possible. But capitalist governments lack the political will to pass or enforce the legislation.

Political economy theory advocates a shift in the sociological definition of crime itself from "breaking the law" to social harm. When laws can be shown to be implicated in class wars, blind obedience to law is not always morally defensible. Similarly, when legal corporate practices can be shown to cause more widespread social harm than much of what is now classified as criminal behaviour, the question of what kinds of acts deserve penal sanctions is revealed as strongly politicized. Economically marginalized lower-class people are vastly over-represented in prisons in part because they are targeted by the criminal justice system, while the social harms committed by better-off people who work in the heart of the corporate capitalist system are ignored.

Social Constructionist Perspective: Struggles over Meaning

The social constructionist perspective shifts the focus of inquiry from the behaviour of criminals to the study of the criminal justice system itself as the site of struggles over meaning. It highlights the active practices of people who work within criminal justice agencies that together produce a working understanding of normalcy, deviance, and criminality for the practical purposes of social control.

Marked historical shifts in how discipline and punishment have been meted out in European societies reflect fundamental changes in the nature of social order (Foucault 1977; Ramp 2000). In the eighteenth century it was customary to hold public executions, as highly dramatized rituals designed to instill fear in onlookers. For the crime of treason against the king, a criminal might be hung, drawn, and quartered, and the body parts thrown to dogs. By the twentieth century in Europe, however, executions and other punishments were hidden from view behind prison walls. Foucault argues that these changes reflect the transition from the rule of king and nobility over subjects to a democratic order based on self-sovereign citizens. In the former, kings ruled by fear,

controlling their subjects by power over death. Violent and public punishments are still common in contemporary societies governed by military dictatorships. In democracies, in contrast, states exercise power over life rather than death. Citizens are controlled through a variety of techniques designed to produce "normalized" and productive populations. In nineteenth-century Europe penitentiaries, along with orphanages, work-houses, convents, and mental hospitals, were designed to correct abnormal behaviour. Surveillance and treatment administered by experts in social and physical sciences began to take precedence over raw punishment. Social science disciplines, as bodies of scientific knowledge, were increasingly used to discipline unruly bodies, especially the bodies of women, children, and marginalized populations. The "psy" professions—psychoanalysis, psychology, and psychiatry—became increasingly influential in many branches of social work, medicine, therapy, probation, and education.

The central impetus for the rise of new forms of social control, Foucault argues, was class war. Social order of nineteenth-century Europe was profoundly shaken by the chaos and violence of the French Revolution of 1789, during which the feudal nobility were attacked by masses of destitute workers who were flooding into the cities. From then onwards, disciplining the lower classes in the cities became a central concern of the emerging capitalist states of Europe. Landless ex-peasants, freed from the controls of the feudal estates, had to be moulded into docile factory workers. Donzelot, a student of Foucault, explores how the notion of "juvenile delinquent" was invented around that time as part of a set of state practices for "policing families" (1979). Unruly juveniles, together with their mothers, were brought before justices and notables in special courts where they were subject to the "psy" professions. Routinely, juveniles and their mothers were sentenced to continual surveillance or "probation," with the threat of more punitive sanctions if they resisted. Conviction for some crime was not a requirement for these juvenile courts, only unruly behaviour or lack of respect for authority figures. Freudian psychoanalysis became an important conceptual tool in policing families. Freud reasoned that boys whose incestuous sexual fantasies were not adequately repressed by a strong father figure would fail to develop normal cultural controls for impulsive, egocentric behaviour. Agents of the state were thus justified in imposing patriarchal controls within the family through the practices of social work, therapy, and probation. Psychoanalytic theory is sufficiently vague, Donzelot suggests, that it justifies limitless therapy and surveillance, since parents could never know for certain whether they were parenting well, or being overly lax or overly controlling with their children. Either extreme leaves their children "at risk," with no clearly correct middle ground.

Foucault predicted that the importance of law and courts would decline relative to the "psy" professions, but others suggest that the legal system has retained its power by incorporating these professions into itself. Judges draw on professional expertise in court but retain their power to pass judgment and determine treatment (Smart 1989b). We will see examples below of cases in which lawyers for the defence and the prosecution have called upon the "expert" testimony of psychologists to bolster their arguments, but they still must convince a judge or jury.

Criminology as Ideology

Marx defined theories as *ideological* to the extent that they obscure structural causes of social problems, while blaming victims as the cause of their own disadvantage. Social constructionist analysis explores the active practices by which ideological work gets done, particularly in professions like criminology. They trace how prevailing explanations for problems are constructed and managed within professions, and how they work to legitimate certain kinds of state policies while discrediting others.

During the 1960s, mainstream criminology stressed theories of delinquent personalities, linked to inadequate socialization and poor family upbringing as the primary explanations for crime. The preferred methodology of the time was longitudinal studies designed to profile and predict the life patterns of "chronic offenders." Then, for a brief period, more radical ideas held sway, including labelling theory, critical discourse analysis, Marxist class analysis, cultural Marxism and radical feminism. All of these approaches were sharply critical of the focus on pathological individual psychology, shifting attention instead to inegalitarian and criminogenic social structures, and the role of the prison system itself in generating recidivism.

Yet when we look at mainstream criminology textbooks at the beginning of the twenty-first century, especially those published in the USA, the dominant theories and methodology have reverted back to those prevalent in the 1960s—favouring longitudinal surveys that focus on "risk factors," and that prioritize early family life and inadequate mothering (Doran 2000). The only major shift Doran notes is an expanded focus from lower-class youth to youth in general as "at risk." Critical theories have been largely silenced or co-opted into socialization theory—included in mainstream texts as of historical interest for students, but not important for training future practitioners in the criminal justice system. The feminist emphasis on patriarchal victimization of women has been reduced to including women as objects in survey research.

The current resurgence of this faulty-parenting thesis, together with heavy emphasis on individual responsibility,

seems to coincide with a marked decline in welfare state policies within corporate capitalist states in Europe and North America. Governments are withdrawing money from social services while increasing budgets for police and prisons. This shift from welfare state to penal state suggests that Foucault may have underestimated the continuing power of the state to punish (Wacquant 2001). The growth of the penal state and the unrestrained growth of big corporations appear to be occurring in tandem.

Potential resistance to a repressive economic order has been incorporated and silenced, Doran suggests (2000), within what he terms "new games of power sharing," including community policing and sentencing circles. Even the potentially critical Marxist approach of left realism has largely abandoned demands for transformative structural change, pressuring the more accommodating option of restorative justice at the community level. A few Aboriginal leaders continue to pressure for more radical structural change, demanding compensation for the destructive effects of residential schools, and pressuring land claims as the only real solution to anomie within reservation societies (Monture-Angus 1999). Even as she voices these demands, however, Monture-Angus herself largely despairs of using law as a tool for transformative change. A legal system that reduces everything to individual responsibility cannot hear the struggles of colonized communities, or those of women crushed by patriarchal violence. Aboriginal mothers are still blamed as individuals for fetal alcohol syndrome (FAS) that ravages First Nations children, without recognition of the crushing structural factors that underlie these symptoms of despair.

How did this happen? Doran asks. What are the practices or *relations of ruling* within the criminal justice system in capitalist societies that silences social criticism, and shifts the blame back onto individual families? How is the academic discipline of criminology complicit in this process? How do governments within democratic societies persuade citizens to accept increasingly repressive policing? The following section explores the mundane practices that co-opt resistance into mechanisms of control.

Ruling Practices: Creating Fear

Fear of crime is a strong motivating force for citizens to push for more repressive policing, and these fears seem to be increasing regularly in communities across Western Europe and North America, especially in the USA (Altheide 2002; Schissel 1997). Objectively, Altheide argues, citizens are safer and more secure and living longer lives than previous generations, but that is not how most people say they feel. The social constructionist perspective analyzes levels of fear within communities as the outcome of active practices by opinion leaders that frame social meanings. Mass media of all forms, police and other formal agents of social control, politicians, businesses that sell security systems, and even social scientists, are linked in fear-generating networks that create and sustain a climate of panic in which citizens don't merely tolerate, but actively demand aggressive policing and ubiquitous electronic surveillance systems. Television and the information-entertainment (infotainment) industry lie at the heart of the network, serving up an almost daily diet of shocking criminal violence, with an approach dubbed "if it bleeds it leads." Altheide (2002, 21) cites 1998 data showing that the national murder rate in the USA had fallen 20 percent since 1990, but coverage of murders in network newscasts was up 600 percent in the same period. Multiple studies cite similar evidence of media preoccupation with stories of violent crimes committed by youths even though most youth crimes are non-violent (Faith and Jiwani 2002, 83–90). Feature stories of "killer girls" and violent girl gangs distort the reality that less than 1 percent of crimes by girls involve violence. Levels of fear, Altheide suggests, are self-perpetuating, as fearful people tend to stay home and watch more television, and become more fearful as they consume more infotainment. Mobile people with limited interpersonal connections with neighbours are particularly open to such influences. In this climate of fear people increasingly welcome all kinds of public surveillance, taking comfort in the electronic assurance that "you are being watched" (Pecora 2002, 347).

This does not mean that all fear is unrealistic or crime waves illusory, but rather that fear of crime can spiral way out of proportion to actual events. Given the right circumstances, media images of pervasive crime can trigger criminal behaviour itself, in a mutually reinforcing spiral (Sacco 2003). Extortion rackets associated with Italian immigrants in New York at the beginning of the nineteenth century received dramatic coverage in newspapers, embellished with images of mysterious and foreign criminal conspiracies and secret societies, dubbed the "black hand crime wave." Such coverage in turn promoted a climate of fear in which petty criminals found it easy to frighten potential victims to hand over money by even hinting in extortion notes that they might be part of the "black hand" gang. More crime fuelled yet wilder newspaper coverage of black-hand extortion rackets that fuelled more fear, especially among new immigrants, and more victims ready to hand over money to extortionists while being too fearful to report them to police or to testify in court. The spiral burned out after some 20 years, Sacco suggests, as immigration rates dropped, and prohibition against the legal sale of alcohol offered more lucrative criminal opportunities.

Crime reporters get most of their material from institutional sources within the justice system, and particularly from the police. The result is that media coverage of crime tends to be framed from the law-and-order perspective. The pervasive message is that police work is difficult and dangerous and requires more and more resources to be effective. Getting "soft on crime" is not a rational option. Politicians use infotainment as a backdrop for popularizing tough policies that pinpoint anti-social or deviant individuals as the cause of social malaise, while businesses use it to sell a plethora of home security systems. Self-sustaining and mutually beneficial networks of motivations sustain the climate of fear.

Family life is at the core of the fear message, with fear *for* children and fear *of* children as recurring themes. Training in fear for the safety of children begins early in life, as parents, teachers, and social workers are warned to street-proof children to avoid all strangers, especially men, to reduce the risk of abduction and sexual assault. On October 22, 2004, a new computer game for children was released in Canada, designed explicitly to train children to distrust and avoid any adult they do not know. The CBC announcer noted that hundreds of children disappear annually. During the 1990s, local authorities in Britain placed signs in public washrooms warning parents to "Watch Your Child" because it only takes a minute for a child to be grabbed. In schools across Canada in 2004, children practised "code red" drills to lock classroom doors and hide under desks in preparation for possible armed intruders (*Globe and Mail*, 18 October 2004, A8). Spokespersons for the Ontario school board acknowledge that there has been no recent increase in school violence, and that children are more at risk of being struck by lightning than being shot in school, but counter that children watch television and are well aware of the threat of terrorism and school attacks. A group of seniors putting on a puppet show for elementary school children in Fredericton in 2004 were warned in advance that school policy prohibits any interaction between the children and outside visitors, since visitors have not had police checks. Similar policies control who is permitted to work with children in church Sunday schools. All such practices are strongly defended as rational risk management.

The discourse of "stranger danger" in popular culture focuses on risk avoidance as the constant responsibility of adults in charge of children. Media coverage and official statistics on missing children convey the impression that the hundreds of thousands of children who go missing annually are abducted and violated by strangers (Best 1987, 1989). The evidence indicates that almost all of these cases are not newsworthy—they involve children who were quickly found to have been with friends, or were snatched by parents involved in custody disputes, or teenagers who run away from home. The small fraction of cases that truly involve abduction by strangers, however, attract infotainment attention.

These cases then come to typify for citizens what happens when children go missing. These practices produce what functionalist analysis describes as typical cultural attitudes. Foucault further suggests that the constancy of media and professional interest in sexual abuse of children may be a significant factor inciting sexual interest in and abuse of children, especially inside families (Foucault 1978). Incest becomes a more thinkable or normalized option as individuals hear more about it.

A parallel discourse incites fear *of* children as often uncontrollable and prone to violent criminal behaviour (Schissel 1997; 2002). Crime-and-fear stories are featured in the media alongside images of girls and boys who are armed, on drugs, antisocial, and dangerous. Schissel cites extensive data showing that conviction and incarceration rates for youth in Canada more than doubled after 1985, following the passing of the *Young Offenders Act* in 1984. The statistics reflect not a sudden explosion in criminal and violent behaviour, but a redirection into courts of petty offences that would formerly have been dealt with at the informal level of schools and neighbourhoods. The promotion of "zero tolerance" policies for violence encourages teachers and others to report schoolyard bullying and scuffles to police (Faith and Jiwani 2002, 89). Under new legislation, teachers themselves would risk an assault charge should they try to physically restrain an angry child. The resulting surge in "crime" rates is readily associated in infotainment with cases of newsworthy violence. Exceptional cases such as the murder of 14-year-old Reena Virk in Victoria, BC, in 1997, following a severe beating by teenaged girls (Bell 2002, 129), and the murder of two-year-old James Bulger in England in 1993 by two 10-year-old boys (Siegel and McCormick 2003, 293), combined with evidence of soaring conviction rates, feed into a climate of fear. Masses of citizens lobby politicians to demand aggressive policing so that their families can feel safe. The prevailing functionalist explanation for such violence in terms of abusive, dysfunctional homes (Siegel and McCormick 2003, 293) supports a wider discourse of moral and spiritual degeneration of youth.

Ruling Discourses, Theorizing Crime and Fear

Mainstream sociological and criminological theories of criminal behaviour are more likely to promote fears than to allay them. Anomie theories that focus on family and community breakdown frighten people who are themselves geographically mobile and disconnected from stable neighbourhood ties. Longitudinal studies use surveys to track cohorts of children through their school years, asking a series of questions about individual circumstances and behaviours that can be correlated with future deviance and criminal records. Such surveys are designed to pick out classic predictive factors like broken homes, single mothers, mothers on welfare, drug and alcohol use/abuse in homes, and abuse of physical discipline. Survey data then provide the scientific basis for identifying "youth at risk" of criminogenic behaviour, and in turn legitimate state intervention in families at risk.

Networks of social workers, psychologists, teachers, probation officers, child-protection workers, and others, are employed in current practices of policing families. Together they are engaged in the ideological work of "manufacturing 'bad' mothers" (Swift 1995). Both survey research design and social work practices function to turn the spotlight on parenting, or more specifically failed mothering, as the cause of criminogenic youth. The structured economic and social circumstances under which mothers do their work get factored out of the picture. When "poverty" is statistically controlled, it is the mothers who fail to manage, rather than the miserable conditions they endure, that appear as the central predictor of children who fail. Since there is no viable alternative to mothers caring for children, especially when marriages break up, mothers must be "policed to care" (Swift 1995, 113–115). The cycle theory of neglect blames poor mothering in one generation for poor mothering in the next, legitimating long-term state intervention at the level of families. Aboriginal families in Canada are statistically the most at risk of state intervention, with their children three times more likely to be taken into state care than non-Native children. From the perspective of Aboriginal communities, child-welfare legislation functions as insidious continuing colonization, separating yet another generation of youth from their Aboriginal cultures (Swift 1995, 128–130). Other visible minorities in Canadian society, including gay

Panhandlers and squeegee kids come across as aggressive and threatening to nervous pedestrians.

CP PHOTO/Toronto Sun-Fred Thornhill

and lesbian parents, are drawn into this same network of intensive surveillance under threat of the legalized removal of their children (Wachholz 2002). Shocking media coverage of neglected and abused children, and neglecting and abusive parents, readily legitimate these policing practices in the views of other citizens.

Critical Marxist theories point to high levels of structural unemployment and welfare rates set far below the levels that parents need to provide shelter, food, and clothing for their children as the root of much family breakdown. But this critical discourse is largely silenced by more strongly articulated claims that there are jobs available for those who wish to work (Doherty 2000). Since "normal" people have jobs, unemployed people appear abnormal, lazy, or otherwise deficient. Low welfare rates are easily legitimated for normal citizens through discourses of deficit reduction, and fears that welfare handouts encourage dependency and laziness and undermine the will to find work. Hopelessness, drug and alcohol abuse, and petty crime form a vicious cycle that feeds into popular images of the poor as irresponsible and guilty.

In a social climate already charged with fear, Marxist-inspired analysis of criminal behaviour in terms of anger and desperation arising from poverty and relative deprivation function to promote fear of the poor as dangerous. Panhandlers and squeegee kids come across as aggressive and threatening to nervous pedestrians and drivers in their locked-down vehicles. A few encounters with people begging for change and youths armed with damp sponges prompt editorials and complaints to politicians from business people and tourists demanding legislation to clear such people from the streets (Schissel 2002, 124). The enactment of the *Safe Streets Act* in Ontario (January 2000) outlawed soliciting persons who are in vehicles or standing in queues to use bank machines, telephones, toilets, or transit. Soliciting includes trying to clean car windows for money (Moon 2002, 73–74; Hermer and Moser 2002).

A currently popular explanation for crime in America is that crime is rational economic behaviour governed by cost-benefit estimates. This view implies that most people will commit theft and fraud if they figure the risks of getting caught are small and the expected punishment light relative to the potential for high profits from crime (Zedner 2003, 29). Cost-benefit analysis views crime as expected, normative, rational everyday behaviour—a far cry from Durkheim's classic definition of crime as the violation of community values. Again, a vicious spiral of causality may be happening. As people are trained from childhood to expect others to steal from them, they are less likely to feel guilty and deviant when they themselves consider stealing

from others. The growing dominance of economic analysis of crime, Zedner suggests, is driving the shift to a security-conscious society. Property owners expect to have to install security systems in their homes and offices, to drive in locked cars, and often also to carry weapons. Such defensive practices are not proportional to risk—the highest proportion of concealed weapons permits are issued for upscale, low-crime neighbourhoods while most break-ins happen in poor areas (Altheide 2002, 1). Police spokespersons routinely lecture seniors' groups on the advisability of security systems, although objectively seniors as a group are least often victimized by crime.

Security alarms and locked cars function as daily reminders that people should be fearful of others. Trusting strangers is not rational behaviour. The argument that copycat vandalism will quickly escalate if even one house in a street is left with a broken window further criminalizes trivial delinquencies, inciting other residents to demand swift, punitive responses. As people grow more distrusting, social solidarity is further undermined, in yet another vicious spiral of interacting cause and effect. As more people are charged with offenses, crime rates rise, proving that more prisons are needed. The end result is that the very failure of the criminal justice system to reduce crime rates works to legitimate a penal state and to focus attention on antisocial individuals rather than economic structures (Reiman 2001).

In the aftermath of the September 11, 2001, terrorist attacks (9/11) in New York and Washington, the US government has issued almost permanent yellow and orange alerts warning citizens of the ever-present threat of another terrorist attack. As the state signals constant threats to national security, individuals respond by seeking greater private protection even as they demand heightened state regulations (Zedner 2003). Private security guards now outnumber state police in the USA, employed to patrol commercial buildings, shopping malls, and public transit. Closed-circuit television systems (CCTV) trawl continually for suspects. Youths, the poor and homeless, and members of marginalized ethnic minorities often find themselves excluded from supposedly public places like shopping malls as private guards evict them for loitering on private mall property. Heightened security promises reduced risk but at the price of eroding civil liberties, especially the liberties of marginalized groups. Under the Homeland Security Act of 2002, the US government has the right to investigate every aspect of citizens' lives—including their e-mails, Internet websites visited, and credit card records, without requiring any prior evidence of criminal activity. In Canada, all but 18 of the 2544 applications by the Canadian Security Intelligence Service

(CSIS) for intelligence-gathering warrants were approved between 1993 and 2003 (*Globe and Mail*, 15 November 2004, A6). These warrants grant agents similarly invasive powers to search for information on suspected terrorists or foreign spies.

The paradox is that more security generates more insecurity as citizens are continually reminded of risk. Heightened airline security only serves to expose the practical impossibility of achieving total security (Russell and Preston 2004). Media frequently carry exposés by reporters and others who manage to get forbidden items through checking systems, leaving passengers feeling less secure than before the scanners and armed guards were visibly in place. What is happening, suggests Zedner, is a significant shift in the nature of policing from "criminal justice," which deals with people who have actually committed offences, to a "security state" that polices suspect populations profiled in advance as at risk of having criminal intent.

Community policing and neighbourhood watch programs feed directly into the climate of fear, encouraging citizens to spy on their neighbours and report anything suspicious or unusual to the police. "Reality TV" programs like *Crime Stoppers* and *America's Most Wanted* encourage individuals to regard spying on their neighbours and "snitching" on them to authorities as the right thing to do (Pecora 2002, 347). People who rarely interact with their neighbours in any social events come together to monitor others whom they distrust (Klinenberg 2001). Anyone who looks different, who does not fit the profile of "normal" attracts greater surveillance. The goal of neighbourhood security inevitably presumes that there are people who are unfit to belong in the area and who ought to be excluded. Distrust, suspicion, and fear, Klinenberg suggests, are fast becoming central features of neighbourhood culture and local politics.

In summary, these prevailing discourses about crime show considerable variety at a surface level, focusing attention on family and community breakdown, poor parenting, unemployment and poverty, anger and desperation, rational greed, and desire to get consumer goods without working for them. Yet they all feed into the same underlying cultural theme of fear. This underlying or "deep structure" cross-cuts class divisions to create a sense of consensus that all "reasonable" citizens share (Doran 2002b; Hall 1974). This fear may be experienced differently by citizens at different social class levels. The better off have good reason to fear that their luxury homes, cars, and other possessions are coveted by others who do not have them, while the poor have even greater reason to fear that the anger and despair associated with poverty and broken families will explode into violence mostly in their own neighbourhoods. Liberals may blame

environment while traditionalists blame moral breakdown, and others privately blame racialized minorities and immigrants, but all can agree on the need for stronger policing. Deeper questions about the criminogenic character of globalized corporate capitalist society rarely enter this public debate on crime, fear, terror, good-and-evil, and policing (Doran 2002b, 165). Still more rarely is the reasonableness of fear itself opened to question.

Research on living in a high-crime subsidized housing estate in Britain reminds us to be cautious in interpreting "evidence" of fear of crime. Survey data did not fit with how people talked about their lived experience of life on the estate. While most people had indicated in response to an abstract survey question that they were fearful at the thought of muggings, break-ins, and the like, this did not mean that they were fearful in their everyday lives (Foster 1995). People knew that many residents in the two large apartment blocks where they lived had criminal records, and knew that some were actively involved in illicit activities. But nonetheless most people felt secure because they were familiar with their neighbours, and people kept an eye out for each other and constrained troublemakers. As one local police officer put it, "a lot of them are sailing very close to the wind but they don't shit on their own doorstep. They have their own code" (Foster 1995, 571). Most people, including local police, felt that informal controls such as neighbours, or the well-known local beat police officer speaking to family members, worked better to keep deviance under control than formal arrests. During a period when inexperienced new officers and the local authority staff tried more heavy-handed threats, the common response was not to tell the police anything (Doran 2002b, 579).

Policing Practices: Deviantizing Work

Police on street patrols and citizens who work with them in community policing and neighbourhood watch programs are engaged in practices of constituting normalcy, deviance, and criminality in the interests of maintaining security and order within the community. Police are mandated to apprehend people who violate laws, and to act pre-emptively to prevent crimes from being committed. Citizens are encouraged to call police whenever they notice suspicious activities in their neighbourhood. Foster's study of a subsidized housing estate in Britain, described above (1995), suggests that community policing works best as a backup to informal sanctions rather than as a heavy-handed presence. Neighbours spoke directly to troublemakers or their parents, with the threat of calling in formal sanctions if all else failed. These sanctions worked across racial boundaries by white residents approaching

Bengali neighbours they knew to ask them to speak to troublesome Bengali youth, and vice versa.

Social constructionist analysis explores the routine everyday reasoning methods that police and citizens on watch use to decide what looks sufficiently "suspicious for this time and place" to take action. Deviance and crime are not simply "there" to be noticed by vigilant citizens; they are actively constituted through the ways in which police and their citizen assistants notice and categorize the flow of street life. Such decisions are also inherently associated with class war, constituting who is considered acceptable and who should be excluded from the neighbourhood. Enforcing the new *Safe Streets Act*, for example, requires multiple judgments: What constitutes "an aggressive manner" of begging or merely offering a window-washing service? When are pedestrians "a captive audience" with respect to where begging is prohibited? Similarly with respect to policing prostitution, what constitutes "soliciting for the purposes of prostitution" or merely standing around, or responding to an invitation? What constitutes "loitering with intent" to commit a crime, or merely sitting on a bench? With respect to youth on the streets, what constitutes criminal vandalism or merely excusable pranks? In shopping malls, what distinguishes a normal shopper from a vagrant or potential thief who should be ushered out?

The routine reasoning methods used in making these decisions produce statistics on arrest profiles, with their class-race-age-gender characteristics (James 2002). Young Native and black males dressed in cheap clothing attract the greatest attention, while conservatively dressed, neat-looking, older white women and men pass unnoticed. Since 9/11, people of Arab and Muslim appearance also attract disproportionate suspicion. Only in the rare cases when victims caught in the net of a suspicious gaze successfully challenge their labelling do people pause to consider their reasoning. In the fall of 2004, newspapers carried stories of a Canadian of Arab appearance being imprisoned and intensely interrogated for two weeks under suspicion of terrorist activity. His suspicious behaviour apparently consisted of photographing Toronto's landmark CN Tower from a city bus. Two black males made the news when judges agreed they had been wrongly arrested and roughed up by police, in one case for "suspiciously" driving an expensive car, and another for merely looking vaguely like another suspect. These two are typical of a very long list of aggressive encounters between police and racialized citizens (James 1998, 2002; Comack 1999, 54–55). In each case police spokespersons expressed not remorse but incredulity at the stupidity of judges for not understanding the realities of how police work on the streets gets done. Police frequently allude to the inherent usefulness of racial profiling in their work even as they deny that racial profiling occurs.

The Power of Law: Defining "Truth"

Courts of law are accorded special authority to define truth through practices of legal reasoning, rules of inference, adversarial debate, and final judgment beyond reasonable doubt (Smart 1989a, Ch. 1). It is a criminal offence in law to challenge the conclusions of a judge or jury, except on grounds of technical procedures that are themselves determined by a higher-court judge. No other profession is accorded a similar level of deference.

Social constructionist analysis focuses attention on the routine reasoning practices used by lawyers, judges, and jurors in determining the "truth" of cases that come to court. Lawyers are trained to select specific evidence that has legal relevance for a case at hand, filtering out and disqualifying much lived experience that participants themselves may consider relevant. Lawyers for the prosecution present the particulars of a case in a form that intends the conclusion that the police have indeed apprehended the guilty persons. Lawyers for the defence must respond to these particulars to try to construct them into an alternative account that suggests the defendant might be innocent (Smith 1990, Ch. 4). Smith points out that when judges and jurors share similar notions about typical criminals as do the police, members of stigmatized minorities have greater than average difficulty in sustaining an alternative account of their behaviour. Native and black defendants in Canada rarely face people like themselves on juries (Aylward 1999). People living on the street are even less likely to face any juror who has experienced everyday life the way they do. Poor people may also be unable to afford experienced lawyers, while drug lords can hire a battery of them.

Courts of law are accorded special authority to define truth through practices of legal reasoning.

CP PHOTO/Jonathan Hayward

These routine practices involved in "making a case" become visible mostly in the rare cases when judgments are overturned. In one intensely analyzed case, Donald Marshall, a Mi'qmac man, was found to have been wrongly convicted of murder after spending 11 years in prison. A public inquiry into the case in 1988 heard evidence that the police may have bullied witnesses into perjuring themselves in the original trial to secure the conviction, and covered up subsequent evidence pointing to an alternative culprit (Mannette 1992). More importantly, Mannette argues, the general climate of fear and hostility towards Natives in Sydney, Nova Scotia, at the time made it easy both for teenage witnesses and for jurors to convince themselves that the police account was correct, and extremely difficult for the 17-year-old Mi'qmac defendant to present himself as innocent.

Investigations into other cases of wrongful conviction show that the Marshall case cannot be understood simply as an aberrant example of racism. Comparable accounts of bullied testimony and failure to disclose subsequent evidence surfaced in 1992 when the murder conviction of David Milgaard was overturned, after he had served 20 years in prison. Individual police officers associated with these cases commented on the routineness of the procedures used, their own certainty that they had apprehended a guilty person, and the necessity of working up evidence and witnesses to convince a jury. In 1994, Milgaard's mother, Joyce Milgaard, helped to found an association of lawyers and other experts dedicated to the reinvestigation of murder convictions where plausible challenges to the original construction of evidence can be worked up. During the fall of 2004, as a decision on the Stephen Truscott case was being made, there were more than 40 other plausible wrongful conviction cases under investigation.

"NOT MAKING THE CASE"

The routine reasoning practices that sustain certain cases as credible also work to constitute other cases as not credible, or not founded. Legal reasoning that presumes a defendant innocent until proven guilty can make many cases difficult to process because they hinge on the relative believability of different people involved.

In Canada, investigation and judgment on cases of alleged discrimination are the exclusive responsibility of provincial and federal human rights commissions, subject to the overriding authority of the Charter. In principle, human rights legislation is designed to protect and to provide redress for people from all forms of unjustified discrimination, including but not limited to grounds of race, gender, sexual orientation, religion, national or ethnic origin, colour, marital and family status, and disability. In

practice, the system is plagued by such a litany of problems that it has been challenged as discriminatory in itself, and possibly in violation of Charter rights to equality of treatment (Aylward 1999, 165–174). Aylward cites evidence that the vast majority of human rights complaints are rejected at the investigation state—with discrimination on the basis of race rejected more than any other grounds (Aylward 1999, 166).

Overt discrimination, as when an employer bluntly states that he will not hire Indians, is easy to recognize, but the vast majority of cases involve covert and subtle unfairness. Human rights investigators begin with the assumption that equality of treatment is the norm. It is the responsibility of a complainant to prove beyond reasonable doubt that alleged distressing experiences were explicitly caused by discrimination on the basis of some specified ground like race. Defendants routinely raise counter-claims, arguing that the alleged discrimination was either imaginary, or legitimately due to poor work experience, poor quality schooling, or other failings compared with the preferred applicant, or to disagreeable personality, or a host of other negative characteristics. This leaves the complainant with the burden of proving that none of these other excuses apply. MacKinnon concludes that the one time a person of colour alleges discrimination is the one time that race will be deemed irrelevant (MacKinnon 1987, 65). *Critical race litigation* seeks to raise the consciousness of lawyers and jurors on how the lived experiences of racialized minorities are routinely disqualified in courts, and to promote alternative legal analysis.

The large majority of allegations of sexual assault are also dropped before they even reach a courtroom (Du Mont 2003). The legal presumption that a defendant is innocent until proven guilty places the burden on the complainant to prove that the sex was not consensual. In multiple ways the experiences of rape victims are disqualified in court, with the social status of the complainant as a central determining factor in believability. Du Mont concludes from her survey of hospital, police, and prosecution records, as well as extensive reviews of other studies, that women who are poor, have low education, are unemployed, and/or have a higher risk of sexual assault are significantly less likely to have their cases result in a charge. Judges generally tended to view sexual assault cases as less serious than physical assault cases and to minimize the impact of injury and harm to victims (Du Mont 2003, 315). Du Mont's data is consistent with earlier research by Clark and Lewis (1977) showing that women who work in the sex trade, along with women on welfare, and black and Native women, are comparatively the least likely to be believed, while professional women are most likely to have their cases viewed as founded. Du Mont concludes that while the law on sexual assault was substantially changed in 1983, judicial discretion at all stages, from deciding to lay charges to achieving convictions and sentencing still reflect long-standing "rape myths" that blame the victim.

Institutional Ethnography: Disqualification as Organizational Practice

Studies of administrative rules governing eligibility for workers' compensation or legal aid reveal how *relations of ruling* work at the level of routine everyday practices in state agencies. Historically, compensation for injured workers has long been a focus of class struggle, with workers blaming unsafe working conditions while employers blamed worker negligence (Doran 2002a). The rules changed in Canada in the early twentieth century to introduce the principle of no-fault liability for compensation for workplace injury. Doran traces how professional medico-legal discourse works to disqualify workers' lived experience of workplace-aggravated illness and death. Experts use statistics to calculate the proportion of any given illness that might be attributable to the workplace, ignoring how workers experience their own illnesses and their conditions of work.

Court social workers have authority to decide who is eligible for legal aid for domestic disputes involving divorce, custody, and domestic violence (Beaman 2002). They have discretion to decide such issues as whether there is sufficient evidence of domestic abuse to warrant a shift from custody mediation to a court case, whether a woman has sufficient access to disputed family assets to pay her own lawyer, whether she is sufficiently recovered from mental illness to get back to work and earn money for a lawyer, and the like. Beaman argues that women's lived experiences are routinely disqualified from the decision-making process. Their stories of threats, emotional abuse, depression, domestic assets being totally withheld from them or sold for less than the mortgage, and the like, are routinely filtered out of legal relevance, as court workers deem them insufficient grounds to qualify them for legal aid. Without access to legal aid, such stories never reach the courts. Court workers in turn are closely monitored to ensure that priority spending of scarce legal-aid monies goes to criminal cases.

It is through such mundane reasoning practices at the levels of routine policing of streets, routine sorting of evidence to determine whether or not cases will proceed to court, or be heard as "reasonable" by jurors, human rights commissioners, medical experts, court social workers, or employees at multiple locations within networks of formal administration that construct what we come to know as social justice and its gendered, ethnic, raced, and classed character.

 ## THE FEMINIST PERSPECTIVE: GENDERED LAW

The feminist perspective explores how institutions of law and criminal justice work to disadvantage women, notwithstanding the formal commitment of contemporary legal systems to principles of objectivity, gender neutrality, and equality under the Charter.

Law underpins the structure of family life—the institution that functionalist theory views as the foundation of society. Law defines who can or cannot be legally married, the legal age of consent to marriage, the responsibilities that spouses assume on marriage, property and inheritance rights, terms of divorce, custody of children, adoption, surrogacy, the rights and responsibilities that parents who are not married have towards their children, and the like. Family law has been the site of feminist struggles in Canada dating back over two centuries. The legal status of marriage as a binding contract becomes particularly evident at the point of divorce, where one or both parties consider breaking the contract. Hence, laws governing divorce are the main focus of the following section.

Historically, Canadian family law, rooted in British common law, reinforced a normative male-headed, patriarchal family form (Smart 1984; McBean 1987). Legally, a wife was subsumed under the civil status of her husband, meaning that only a husband could enter into a legally binding contract. All marital property belonged exclusively to the husband, including any that a wife might have brought into the marriage and any money that she might subsequently earn. Children were defined in law as belonging only to the father. On separation or divorce, for whatever reason, the children were legally bound to remain with their father, regardless of age. The explicit intent of these laws was to reinforce the marital union by making it punitively difficult for a wife-mother to leave.

These laws slowly began to change between the 1880s and 1920s under pressure of the argument that a morally sinful unmarried mother had more rights in law than respectable married women. However, these changes were slow, niggardly, and interpreted by judges in ways designed to minimize threats to the marital union. Property rights were changed to permit a married woman to retain property that she herself inherited or brought into the marriage, but gave her no right to any share in marital property. Mortgages and tenancies remained exclusively in the husband's name. A wife who could prove that she had been wilfully deserted by her husband was given the right to sue him for maintenance and custody of children. However, this right was subject to the stringent conditions that she be a morally deserving and deserted wife and mother. "Morally deserving" was interpreted in law to mean that she maintain strict sexual abstinence. Any evidence to suggest that she had sex with another man was sufficient grounds for her ex-husband to stop paying maintenance and to have the children removed. This rule applied regardless of whether the husband was sexually involved with other women.

The right to seek a divorce was also slowly extended to women under the stringent condition that a wife prove herself the victim of adultery, desertion, or cruelty. As late as the 1960s, some judges were still interpreting "cruelty" in sexist ways (Smart 1984, 94), arguing that a wife could not fault her husband for the "natural disinclination" to have sex with her, but she herself would be guilty of cruelty if she refused to fulfil her marital duty to have sex with her husband. Only if a wife were truly blameless and deserving in the eyes of a judge did she have a right to maintenance after marital breakdown. If she were guilty of breaking up her children's home by leaving their father without good cause, or by committing adultery, she could be deemed a bad wife and mother and lose both maintenance and any right to appeal for custody of her children. Legal decisions controlling custody of children gradually shifted towards the "tender years doctrine" reasoning that infants needed to be with their mothers, until age seven, when legal guardianship of their father resumed.

Gender Equality, the Charter, and Family Law

Major shifts in family law towards the principle of gender equality in marriage eventually came about in North America and Western Europe under the impact of second-wave feminist struggles. They were endorsed in Canada in 1985 with the passage into law of the gender equality rights provision of the Canadian Charter. While they are a marked improvement over earlier laws, feminist research highlights the gendered inequalities still inherent in family law. These continuing inequalities are rooted in the substantially very different social and economic situations of wives and husbands that are obscured by the formal application of legal equality rules.

Marital property laws changed significantly in Canada in the 1980s, following political outrage that erupted after the 1975 Supreme Court decision on the Murdoch case. The Murdochs divorced after 25 years of marriage, during which they both developed the family ranch. Mrs. Murdoch had regularly worked the ranch by herself for five to eight months of most years while her husband had employment elsewhere. Yet upon divorce, the Supreme Court determined that legally the ranch and the house upon it belonged solely to her husband because the original down payment and mortgage were in his name only. Her quarter-century of unpaid labour on the ranch counted for nothing (Machum 2002, 136–137; Atcheson et al. 1984, 26). Machum notes further that Canadian tax laws from 1969 excluded wages to a farmer's wife as a business-expense deduction, although wages to a farmer's children and other hired hands were deductible. A farmer's wife was also explicitly not eligible for unemployment insurance or a Canada Pension.

Changes were made to family property laws after 1980 to explicitly recognize for the first time that domestic work and childcare should count equally with financial contributions in creating an interest in family property on marriage breakdown, including family businesses (Keet 1990). While laws governing division of marital property vary somewhat by province, the family home is recognized across Canada as belonging equally to both spouses, regardless of who paid for it.

The principle of formal legal equality between women and men is now entrenched in the Charter of Rights, Sections 15(1) and 28. Earlier family laws that overtly subordinated wives to husbands are now unconstitutional. Substantial equality, however, has not been achieved in the actual lived experiences of women and men going through divorce. Critical feminist legal theory challenges the concept of formal equality as ideological in that it obscures the unequal social and financial realities facing women and men that commonly result in very unequal outcomes from supposedly equal treatment in law (Razack 1991; Koggel 1994; Jhappan 1998; L'Heureux-Dubé 1997; Liu 2000). So long as wives generally take more time out from employment for pregnancy, childbirth, and early childhood care, take primary responsibility for domestic work and child-rearing, and when employed earn significantly lower incomes on average than their husbands, they do not face divorce on an equal financial footing (Cheal 1999, Ch. 4). Wives who have been full-time homemakers for any length of time during a marriage may be left with half a house but no means to continue mortgage payments. Maintenance awards based on the principle that divorcing adults should become self-supporting within a reasonable time typically result in women having a substantially lower standard of living after divorce while men typically are financially better off (Steel 1987; Richardson 1996, Ch. 9).

Judges have considerable discretion in setting property and maintenance awards, weighing such factors as the likelihood that the ex-wife can become financially self-supporting, the ex-husband's financial situation and possible responsibilities towards a second family, how childcare is being shared, and the like. Judges also consider the viability of any commercial enterprise owned by an ex-spouse. It is not in the interest of the court or the partners to bankrupt a business by dividing assets. Concern for the viability of a farm commonly results in judicial decisions that give an ex-farm-wife no share in farm assets for many years, until the primary farmer retires or sells the farm (Keet 1990). Determining the interest that one spouse may have in career opportunities of the other can be very complex. In one case a wife had worked for years to support her husband and child while the husband studied dentistry. The marriage broke up as he graduated, a period when she had a low-wage job and no prospects while he had great earning potential but no assets (McCallum 1994). She had put her career development on hold to support him and their child, but on divorce the professional credentials and their income-earning potential were exclusively his. Critical feminist litigation struggles to make visible the structurally gendered inequality that underlies these stories that are obscured by objective, gender-blind application of equality.

Aboriginal Women's Rights The Indian Act of 1876 imposed patriarchal family relations onto Aboriginal peoples. Under Section 12(1)(b) of this Act, only Native males could pass on their status as Native to their spouse and offspring, and with it, the right to live on reservations. Native women who married non-Native men lost their status and had to leave their reserves. Property and housing on reserves was held only by men. This rule was justified initially by the argument that it would prevent white men from gaining possession of Native lands and property through their Native wives—an argument that itself presumed that husbands normally controlled the property of their wives. The Act was modified only in 1985 with the passing into law of Bill C-31, which enabled women who lost their status through marriage to regain it, along with the children of these marriages. The descendants of men who had lost status by becoming enfranchised were also included.

Hailed by feminists as a major victory on behalf of Native women, the changes still leave important inequalities between Native women and men (Monture-Angus 1999). Men who marry a non-status woman continue to pass on status to their children and grandchildren. Women who marry out pass their status only to their children; both their sons and daughters lose status if they themselves marry a non-status person. Over time, Monture-Angus suggests, the law that removes status from the great-grandchildren of men and the grandchildren of women who marry non-status persons means that the absolute number of status Natives is likely to decline. Other forms of discrimination against status-Native women under the Indian Act remain unchanged. Certificates of possession, the system of property ownership on reserves, are normally only in the name of the male partner in a marriage. The Supreme Court determined that matrimonial property laws do not apply on

reservations, so that on divorce, Native women often find themselves with no property and no place to live. Monture-Angus concludes that while some 104 000 persons won the right to call themselves status Natives as a result of the 1985 Act, there has been little real change in the status of women on reserves.

Custody as Unequal Equality Rights

Following the Charter, the federal Divorce Law of 1985 replaced the old terminology of husband/wife and father/mother with the gender-neutral terms "spouse" and "parent" to be consistent with equality rights. The new law also substituted "best interests of the child" for earlier doctrines of paternal guardianship or maternal tender-years. Joint custody was declared the legally preferred option following divorce. This incorporated both the long-argued feminist position that fathers and mothers should be equally responsible for the care of children, and psychology research highlighting the value to children of close contact with fathers. Fathers' rights groups also challenged the prevalence of children remaining with mothers while fathers paid support as a violation of men's equality rights. The "friendly parent rule" incorporated into the Divorce Law enjoins judges to take into account the readiness of one parent to facilitate children's access to their other parent in deciding where best a child should live.

Critical feminist litigation has struggled to make visible the gendered inequalities that are obscured by the application of formal-legal equality rules to custody disputes. Custody of children is decided mostly by parents themselves without going to court, with children remaining with their mothers in the large majority of cases (Brophy 1989; McBean 1987; Graycar 1989). It is in the 10 to 15 percent of cases where custody is disputed that court-mandated divorce mediators or judges are called upon to balance equality rights of parents and best interests of children, in a context where parents themselves may be fighting and using children as pawns to get at each other (Sandberg 1989). Gendered inequalities rooted in family structures carry over into these disputes.

The gender-neutral term "parenting" obscures vastly different expectations for level of primary childcare from mothers and fathers, when the model of male breadwinner and female homemaker is considered normative (Boyd 1987, 1989a, 1989b; Fineman 1989a, 1989b). The principle of joint legal custody does not necessarily or even usually entail equal co-parenting at the level of daily care of children. Mothers may find themselves doing the bulk of all childcare while having their parenting decisions vetoed by their ex-husbands (Gordon 1989). Traditionalist judges have also been known to conclude that it is more in children's best interests that they live with their father and a homemaker stepmother than with a biological mother who is employed full time, especially in demanding careers (Graycar 1989). Many judges have further concluded that it may not be in children's best interests to live with an overtly homosexual parent, and hence awarded disputed custody to the "normal" parent (Arnup 1994; Boyd 1997; McCarthy and Radbord 1998; Wachholz 2002).

The presumption that divorce mediation is a cheaper and less adversarial route than courts for settling property and custody disputes may be valid for the majority of families. However, it obscures inequalities of power experienced by financially dependent spouses victimized by years of emotional and physical abuse, who may be ignorant even of how much money or property their spouse might have, and be terrified of appearing to be an "unfriendly parent" and losing their children if they fight too hard. Such lived inequalities in power may render people unable to represent their own interests or to negotiate their legally recognized rights in mediation (Girdner 1989; Bottomley 1985). A history of violence in the family can be obscured in custody and access decisions both because some victims are afraid to speak up, and because some judges deem violence irrelevant if it was directed at the partner rather than the children (Rosnes 1997). Even when custody is awarded primarily to one parent, the principle of preserving a child's access to both parents sets up a situation where a vindictive noncustodial parent can repeatedly use the courts, in the name of Charter equality rights, to harass and control the lives of the ex-spouse and children until the last child reaches legal adulthood (Gordon 1989; Graycar 1989; Delorey 1989; Holtrust et al. 1989). Such power relations can be established even when the parents were never married.

Neilson (2003) criticizes amendments to the 1985 Divorce Act, introduced in Bill C-22 in 2003, for not sufficiently protecting the post-divorce interests of children from families where there was violence between parents. The bill usefully replaces concepts of parental "rights" with "responsibilities," and removes the presumption that shared parenting and maximum contact is always best for families where there has been violence. However, she argues that legislation needs to go further to explicitly direct lawyers to fully document evidence of abuse and violence when parenting decisions are being made, to mandate reviews of mediation agreements in family violence cases, to formally recognize domination and control as forms of abuse, and to shift the onus of proof onto the abusive parents to demonstrate that contact will be safe and beneficial for both children and the victimized parent. Without such changes, she argues, victimized parents still face the daunting double onus of both proving that assault occurred and proving that

children will be harmed by further contact. This may be all but impossible if they are denied legal aid.

These cases show how difficult it is to fairly apply the principle of legal equality rights in family law when power relations between spouses are manifestly unequal. In critical feminist litigation, even the use of the gender-neutral term "spouse" is ideological in that it obscures the lived reality that the large majority of dependent, subordinated, and abused spouses are women, and the economic and socially dominant spouses are men.

Policing Domestic Violence

Violent homes breed more violence. Children who witness violent conflicts between their parents are emotionally harmed even when they themselves are not directly targeted (Neilson 2003, 13–14; Jaffe et al. 1990). Girls charged with assaulting their peers are very likely to have grown up in homes characterized by exaggerated patriarchal dominance enforced by frequent physical violence (Artz 1998; Artz and Riecken 1994; Bell 2002). Boys who beat up their girlfriends have commonly seen their fathers use force to control women (Totten 2000). Children who kill have commonly grown up in worlds where violence is the normative way to handle conflict (Kelly and Totten 2002). Women and men in prison for crimes involving violence pervasively describe childhoods marred by physical and sexual assaults (Comack 1996; McKendy 1997). Homicides in Canada, and especially homicides committed by women, far more often involve family members than strangers. Yet domestic violence cases are among the most difficult arenas of policing work.

Historically, wife-beating was viewed as a private matter, a legitimate means for men to discipline unruly wives (Smart 1992; Clark 1992). Until laws changed in the 1980s, police routinely ignored or delayed responding to such calls hoping the fight would die down without intervention, or they quickly tried to calm the situation and leave. Arrests were likely only where use of weapons indicated an imminent threat of grievous bodily harm or murder.

Feminists have struggled to change these police protocols, calling for mandatory arrests for domestic assaults, the same as if they occurred between individuals on public streets (Walker 1990; 1992). Domestic fights, however, are particularly complex. The partner who calls the police, typically a woman, commonly continues to live with the accused spouse and may well face worse retaliation. Economically dependent women, especially those with children, may see few options for themselves beyond a short stay in a transition house. They will still be tied to their abusive partner through children and economic dependence. They may also still love their partner and call the police only to control the immediate situation of a drunken rage. Police who respond to domestic disturbances risk becoming targets of rage from both perpetrator and complainant.

Domestic conflict is often mutual. Survey research using the Conflict Tactics Scale cites self-report data suggesting that males and females are almost equally responsible for starting mild and serious physical and emotional attacks on partners (Straus and Gelles 1986; Straus 1993). Gay and lesbian partnerships are no exception. Feminists note that statistics on domestic homicide, and on serious injuries requiring hospitalization, overwhelmingly involve female victims and male perpetrators (Kurz 1993; DeKeseredy 2000; Comack et al. 2002). Many females who admit to fighting their partner say they are responding to long-term abuse and threats. Females are also far more likely to be trapped in abusive relationships because of economic dependence and a sense that they ought to hold the family together for their children. They also face the realistic fear of retaliation against themselves and their children if they try to leave (Bowker 1993). Women who return to abusive relations have been found legally culpable in their own injuries (Hughes 1993). When police do not take domestic assaults seriously and courts give minimal sentences, women in seriously abusive partnerships may legitimately feel they have no place to turn.

Critical feminist litigation has struggled to make visible in courts the devastating psychological impact of long-term emotional and physical abuse on female partners as a mitigating factor in cases where women kill their partner (L'Heureux-Dubé 1997). In the landmark Lavallée case in 1990, the Supreme Court of Canada recognized battered wife syndrome as a legitimate defence of necessity in homicide. The defence recognizes that some female partners may become so humiliated, emotionally crushed, isolated, and threatened by the long-term abusive and controlling behaviour of a male partner that killing him becomes a reasonable act of self-defence. Such defence, however, is usually subject to rigorous challenge in court (Liu 2000; Boyle and Rowley 1989; Crocker 1985). Some judges have rejected the defence of battered woman syndrome for women who did not act in sufficiently submissive, dependent ways, and who fought back aggressively when a partner was beating them. These judges require the same self-defence rules that apply to men who kill during fights with other men. A "reasonable man" is expected to walk away from a fight rather than return to the scene of conflict, and to use no more than "sufficient" force to defend himself in a fight. Similar reasoning suggests that a once-battered wife who returns to the partnership is complicit in the violence. Also, since she was not killed during a previous beating, it seems unreasonable that she would need to kill her partner in self-defence during a second beating. Trials often hang on

competing expert testimonies from psychologists for the Crown and the defence on why a battered woman would not simply leave the relationship (Bowker 1993).

Aboriginal women living on reserves are far more likely than non-Aboriginal women to suffer long-term and extreme physical abuse from their male partners. They are also less likely to receive help from police (Dell 2002), or to have anywhere else to go except the streets when they leave their partner. Monture-Angus (1999) describes violence towards women on reserves as an inseparable fact of life—a systemic and lifelong experience that is not individual, but part of a lived experience of colonialism suffered by entire communities of people. She describes her own experience of child sexual abuse, rape, and a battering partnership as nothing unusual. Countless other Aboriginal women, many of them in prison, share stories of multifaceted violence—beginning with child abuse, rape, regular sexual abuse, witnessing of a murder, watching their mothers repeatedly beaten, and beatings at the hands of staff and other children in juvenile detention centres (Comack 1996). Women who flee the violence on the reserves commonly find themselves little better off in the cities, where they face repeated violence from men while working in the sex trade.

Monture-Angus and others see the alcoholic rages and violence of Aboriginal men as rooted in the humiliation, emotional destruction, and sexual and physical violence that men themselves endured throughout a long history of broken homes, abusive residential schools, and juvenile detention centres, economic hopelessness, and absence of coherent cultural identity—all symptoms of several hundred years of colonialism (Cote and Schissel 2002). Ethnographic research by Wilson and Pence (2006) makes visible how legal discourse and case-management practices that focus on individual responsibility for domestic violence on Aboriginal reserves pervasively fail to understand or address the lived experience of Aboriginal women, and function to undermine rather than support the "sacred circle" of community life that offers healing and protection to women.

Policing Sexual Assault

Historically, women were legally the property of their fathers and husbands. Men could sue for damages if their daughter or wife was raped. Little damage was considered done if the woman raped was either not a virgin daughter or not a chaste wife. Rape within marriage was legally impossible—marriage itself entailed a woman's agreement to have sex whenever and however her husband wished it. Feminist struggles over the years slowly challenged these assumptions to focus on the harm done to individual women themselves.

Rape trials (renamed "sexual assault" in Canada in 1983) remain a hotly contested arena of struggle in law. Often the question on trial is not whether sex occurred, but whether or not it was consensual. The goal of critical feminist litigation is to show how legal processes in rape trials work to disqualify women's experience of their own sexuality (Smart 1989a, Ch. 2). The "seduction scenario" that underlies most rape trials holds that males always want sex while women are often out of touch with their real sexual feelings and need to be pressured. When pressure is seen as part of normal sex, rape can be understood as merely "undue" pressure—a bit over the line but not a serious crime, unless there is evidence of bodily injury. Huge differences in estimates of the prevalence of date-rape on college campuses largely reflect such distinctions. It is quite possible for a woman to say she was raped and for a man to say they had consensual sex, with neither of them intentionally lying (Koss and Cook 1993; MacKinnon 1989, Ch. 9). Jurors who are themselves familiar with the cultural scenario of seduction may have a hard time distinguishing normal sex from rape when a criminal conviction hangs on their judgment.

In rape trials, as in all other criminal trials, the defendant has a right to be presumed innocent until proven guilty. Past sexual behaviour is explicitly *not* relevant to the immediate question of whether the accused committed rape in the particular instance before the court. The complainant must prove to the court beyond reasonable doubt that she did not consent to sex, and the defence lawyer's job is to discredit her testimony in whatever way possible. Evidence concerning the woman's lifestyle and past sexual behaviour are directly relevant to challenging her claim of non-consent in court. Hence, in many rape trials it is the complainant's behaviour rather than the defendant's that is on trial.

Rape trials are widely described as resembling pornographic scenarios as lawyers for the defence push the complainant, as their primary witness, to give more and more details of the seduction process and the body parts involved to convey the impression for jurors that the complainant was on some level a willing participant (Smart 1989a, Ch. 2). In the simplistic, binary logic of legal reasoning, Smart suggests, any evidence that a woman consented to some intimacy with a man—by going out with him, drinking with him, inviting him home, listening to music, kissing—implies that she consented to sexual intercourse, and therefore that what happened was not rape. Also in legal logic, if she cannot prove she did not consent, it means that he is innocent and so she must have lied. This in turn feeds the view that women generally are prone to make up stories about rape to get men into trouble.

Feminist lawyers struggled for years to challenge these presumptions that discouraged all but the toughest of women from going to court. Significant changes in Canadian law were legislated in 1983 to address some of these problems, but with uneven results (Kelly 1997). Studies have repeatedly shown that sexual assaults are significantly less likely to be reported to the police, to have the report result in charges, and to have the charges result in a conviction, compared with other physical assaults. A study of Toronto police reports from the 1970s, before revisions to sexual assault laws (Clark and Lewis 1977), showed that the large majority of rape cases reported to police never came to trial. While reports made by professional women were all deemed "founded," only about half of those made by working-class women and students were accepted, a quarter of those made by housewives, and only a fifth of those by separated and divorced women. Only about 4 percent of impoverished women on welfare had their reports treated as "founded." Complainants who had been hitchhiking or drinking, or who had met their alleged assailant in a bar, were turned away. Lawyers could undermine a complainant's credibility in court simply by asking a question like "Are you on the pill?" even if the judge said she did not have to answer.

A follow-up study of women seeking help from an urban sexual assault treatment centre in Ontario in 1994, a decade after the revisions, suggests little has changed in legal practice (Du Mont 2003). Of 284 women who sought help, 187 (66 percent) reported the sexual assault to the police. Of these 87 (47 percent) resulted in police laying charges, and 31 (17 percent) resulted in a conviction, or about 11 percent of all women who came to the treatment centre. Even the 31 cases that resulted in convictions are problematic. All of them involved physical force, such as being pushed to the floor, choked, punched, slapped, grabbed, burned, and/or bitten, and in 10 cases, or one-third, the assailant carried a weapon. Yet only one case was prosecuted as a serious, level-three charge of sexual assault. Du Mont notes that sexual assaults by a current or previous partner were three times more likely to be under-charged than assault by a stranger. Assaults against a sexually active woman or a woman of "poor reputation" were the least likely to result in convictions (Du Mont 2003, 312).

The 1983 legislation replaced the term "rape" with "sexual assault," reasoning that assault carries no implication of consent by a victim. The prohibition against sexual assault charges being laid by a spouse was also removed. In accordance with Charter equality rights, gender-neutral terminology is used so that both alleged assailants and alleged victims can be either female or male. Anal and oral penetration are included along with vaginal penetration in the definition of sexual assault.

Other key legal changes affect how sexual assault trials proceed. First, the doctrine of "recent complaint" was repealed to permit adult victims of childhood assault to press charges. Formerly it was presumed that a true victim of rape would complain immediately after the violation happened, and hence complaints about behaviour that supposedly occurred years earlier were probably vindictive lies. Defence lawyers responded by calling on the expert testimony of psychologists to debate theories of repressed or recovered memories, and to suggest that feminist therapists might generate false beliefs in the minds of emotionally troubled clients.

A second change in legislation prohibited judges from counselling jurors not to convict a defendant on the word of a primary witness without corroboration. Formerly, judges could warn jurors not to convict unless medical evidence like torn clothing and bruises or semen were present. Now jurors decide such issues themselves, although defence lawyers can still argue that the absence of sufficient corroborating evidence invalidates a case.

The third and most contentious change involved restrictions on the use of past sexual history of the complainant. Formerly, defence lawyers routinely tried to discredit a complainant in the eyes of jurors by implying she was sexually promiscuous and hence a "consenting type" of woman. The 1983 legislation required the defence to give notice to a judge that they wished to ask about past sexual activity of the complainant, and provide evidence of its relevance before such questions could be asked in front of jurors. The qualifier was that defence lawyers could compel the complainant to answer such questions, whereas formerly a judge could permit her not to answer. Defence lawyers responded by launching a Supreme Court challenge that any restrictions on their ability to probe into the sexual history of a complainant interfered with their clients' right to a fair trial and were therefore unconstitutional. Feminist lawyers countered that a woman's sexual behaviour logically has no relevance to a sexual assault trial (Boyle and Rowley 1989). The issue at trial is whether or not a woman is lying when she claims she did not consent to sexual intercourse with the defendant. Who is more likely to lie about consenting to sex—an openly sexually active woman or a former virgin or chaste wife with a reputation to protect? Why is it logical to assume that a woman who has several sexual partners probably said yes to the defendant, while a woman without another sexual partner would repel him? If a defendant can prove that a woman had just had sexual intercourse with another man at the scene, is it logical that she would promptly want sex again with the defendant? Even if a woman has had sexual inter-

course with the defendant in the past, can she never say no in the future? The validity of defence claims that the complainant's past sexual history is relevant at all depends on the cultural acceptance of the virile-male/grudging-woman seduction scenario described above. From the perspective of women's experience of their own sexuality, argue Boyle and Rowley, none of these arguments make sense.

In 1992, the Supreme Court partially upheld defence lawyers' right to probe sexual history, recasting restrictions in terms of "scope of permissible inquiry" (Kelly 1997). Defence lawyers countered with new techniques designed to undermine a complainant's credibility by presenting her as emotionally unstable and therefore prone to false memories and distorted understanding of sexual experiences, vulnerable to suggestions from therapists, and the like. A central strategy is to demand access to any and all possible records on the complainant's past. These include medical records from family doctors, gynaecologists, hospitals, any physician who prescribed medication, files from social workers, child protection services, therapists, school counsellors, other school records, and personal letters. Any complainant who was a victim of abuse as a child, or who has had contact with child protection services, or who sought any kind of counselling, or whose family needed welfare, is vulnerable to such blanket searches. Refusal to divulge or to hand over any records can become grounds for dismissing the case. Lawyers for the defence can also try to generate records by asking that the complainant be assessed by a psychologist or gynaecologist of the defence counsel's choosing.

In summary, anyone who lays a charge of sexual assault, the vast majority being women, can expect to be cross-examined in court on all aspects of their emotional, psychological, behavioural, and sexual histories, with information being presented in ways designed to discredit them. Virtually nothing will remain private.

Policing Child Sexual Abuse

Allegations of child sexual abuse are particularly hard to prosecute because primary witnesses are minors whose testimony may not stand up to the rigours of courtroom challenge.

Historically, public panics around issues of child abuse focused on the sale of children into prostitution, sons in aristocratic families abusing servants, abuse by fathers and stepfathers, and perverted strangers (Smart 1989a, Ch. 3). By 1908 in England, incest with a daughter, granddaughter, sister, or mother was officially declared a crime, although prosecutions were rare. The most common response was not to prosecute the adult male suspect, but to remove the children into foster care. Victims of incest were viewed as morally damaged and possibly unfit to mix with other innocent children. The central concern, Smart suggests, was not to protect children but to protect families. By as late as the 1970s, it was typical to blame the "problem" on cramped living quarters, the lack of separate bedrooms for children, or frigid wives who drove frustrated male partners to look elsewhere. More recently in Canada the focus has included sexual abuse of children by priests and teachers in residential schools, and by other adults having unsupervised contact with children.

Since 1983 in Canada, the removal of time constraints on laying charges has made it easier for adults to lay charges against offending parents and other adults for abuse that happened during childhood. This avoids the problems involved in cross-examining minors in court, but the lapsed time exacerbates problems of faulty memory and limited corroborating evidence. Conviction is still very difficult if the defendant flatly denies the charges and the complainant cannot cite supporting evidence that others knew about what was happening at the time. In 1994, for the first time in Canada, an adult daughter successfully sued both her parents—her stepfather for sexual abuse, and her mother for failing to protect her from that abuse (Grace and Vella 1994). The heavy financial damages awarded against the mother in this case effectively deemed the mother equally if not more responsible for the sexual abuse than the stepfather. Feminist critics voice concerns that the decision did not take into full account the mother's circumstances as an abused, financially dependent woman herself, who feared that Children's Aid workers would take her child from her if she said anything, and who had no lawyer to defend her. When these conditions are ignored, mothers take the blame for whatever goes wrong.

Policing the Sex Trade

Prostitution is the one and only offence for which women are convicted more frequently than men. For all other criminal convictions in Canada, men outnumber women by ratios of 8 or 10 to 1, but for sex-trade convictions women outnumber men by 6 to 4. The anomaly behind this statistic is that selling sex is not and never has been illegal in Canada. Consenting adults can legally buy and sell sex for money. It is the practices that facilitate the sex trade that are criminalized—appearing to be a vagrant or loitering on the streets in a disorderly way, soliciting customers, having a house that is openly used for purposes of trading sex, inciting individuals to work in the trade, and living off the money that these individuals make.

The prosecution of people under sex-trade laws is gendered, classed, and raced. Women are prosecuted more harshly than men, especially streetwalkers, who are considered the bottom of the sex-trade hierarchy, and visible-minority women. Sellers, not customers, are assumed to cause all the problems. Male customers are rarely bothered by police. Pimps who organize much of the trade and live off the earnings of sex-trade workers are rarely prosecuted. Women who work in higher-class massage parlours, escort services, and as call girls servicing wealthier clientele are also rarely bothered (Fedec 2002, 262). It is the women who walk the streets looking for customers, and especially the Aboriginal and other non-white women among them, who are most frequently prosecuted. They also bear more than their share of the pervasive violence suffered by sex-trade workers.

Normal Men, Deviant Women   The classic cultural assumptions of sexually virile males and reticent women that underlie the seduction scenario in rape trials also underlie the social controls placed on prostitution. Male sexual needs are represented as naturally strong and easily aroused. Any man who has no steady sexual partner, or married men whose wife permits sex only grudgingly, are naturally expected to look for sex elsewhere. Hence, the reasoning goes, the customers of prostitutes are "normal" and unproblematic males (McIntosh 1978). The question of why there are still so many men who want to purchase sex in the sexually liberated context of contemporary Western societies is rarely raised or considered of any interest. However, women who parade the streets looking for paying customers for sex are represented as deviant, sinful women who corrupt the morals of those around them, threaten families, and spread diseases, and hence need to be strictly and harshly controlled.

In pre-Confederation Canada vagrancy laws were used to control women (Shaver 1994; Larsen 2000). Any woman found loitering in a public place without a legitimate reason could be arrested. The law only applied to women. After Confederation, laws changed to criminalize men who procured girls into prostitution and lived off their earnings, but convictions were rare. Policing focused primarily on women selling sex on the streets as causing a nuisance for other residents.

The sexual **double standards** through which prostitution was judged became particularly blatant during the First World War years in England. The "Defence of the Realm Act," passed in 1914, dealt with the state's concern to protect soldiers from "infesting, preying, haunting harpies" who hung around the army camps, infecting soldiers with venereal diseases (Bland 1985). The new Act banned women in towns where soldiers were stationed from being in taverns or on the streets between 7 p.m. and 8 a.m., with penalties of up to two months in prison. Another law made it a criminal offence for any woman, prostitute or not, to have sexual intercourse with a soldier if she was infected with a venereal disease. This gave police the right to arrest any woman found near army bases and hold them for up to a week pending a medical examination. Feminists dubbed this forced inspection "rape by steel speculum" (Walkowitz 1982). Some nineteenth-century feminists struggled against these double standards, trying to shift the focus towards the protection of girls and women trapped into prostitution. But the social stigma against prostitution was such that most of the women active in the women's movements themselves feared being associated with them.

The contemporary women's movement in Canada remains divided on how to think about prostitution (Shaver 1994). The dominant view is that women who engage in prostitution are young, poor, troubled individuals who are running from abusive homes and often addicted to drugs, and who sink into prostitution as a means of survival. Prostitution degrades all women, not just those working in the trade, because it reinforces the patriarchal view of women as objects for male use. From this perspective, rescuing women from the sex trade makes more sense than defending their legal rights. The alternative liberal view is that the sex trade is best understood as work that women can choose to enter, which offers better-than-average pay for women's work, particularly in the higher-status massage parlours and call-girl end of the trade (Jeffrey and MacDonald 2006). Even well-educated women with other career options may be drawn to work as strippers or in peep shows because it feels exotic, wild, and rebellious (Mestemacher and Roberti 2004; Razack 1998) Arguably, the sex trade is not intrinsically more degrading work than what many other women do who trade sex for entertainment, or the work of athletes who also trade their bodies for money (Shaver 1994). From this perspective, legalizing the sex trade makes sense as a necessary basis for controlling working conditions and protecting women from violence. Its semi-legal status, which justifies constant police harassment, makes it almost impossible for women to organize collectively to protect themselves.

Gendered Policing of Gender-Neutral Laws

Equality Rights provisions in the Canadian Charter prompted significant changes in the laws governing prostitution to make them explicitly gender neutral. Vagrancy laws that made it illegal just to be standing around on the streets were replaced by regulations that criminalize all public communication for the purposes of prostitution, applying to sex-trade workers and customers alike. The definition of "public" includes automobiles and prohibits any attempt to stop automobiles or to impede pedestrians (Larsen 2000, 64). It also applies to any place open to public view, even if the actual conversations cannot be heard by other people.

Changes in terminology did not radically change policing practices. The view that streetwalkers rather than their customers generated the "nuisance" remained largely unchanged. Shaver (1994) cites data suggesting that 90 percent of arrests continued to be of sex-trade workers rather than customers or pimps, and women rather than gay male prostitutes. An important practical reason for this bias is that it is far easier for the police to get convictions for streetwalkers. They are easy to arrest, and rarely beat charges. They look like part of the criminal underclass to both judges and jurors, and can often be charged with additional offences like drug possession and theft (Fedec 2002, 261–262). In contrast, male customers charged with procuring offences look like law-abiding men. Courts commonly stay the charges or find them not guilty. Pimps, the men who organize the trade and live off the avails of prostitution, are similarly difficult to convict. To win a case, police need all the prostitutes working under a pimp to appear in court and testify against him. Few prostitutes are willing to do this, through a mixture of loyalty, dependency, and realistic fear of repercussions.

Women who work in massage parlours and as call girls are also less likely to be bothered by police. They are less visible and less of a nuisance at street level. This is also the sector of the trade in which pimps are concentrated because profits are easy. Fedec (2002, 260) cites one massage-parlour worker who paid $30 a day to the parlour, plus $10 for each client. She also kept only about 30 percent of the money she raised from calls while working in the phone-sex industry.

Detailed studies of the impact of the 1985 law on policing in Vancouver and Toronto confirm that the focus remains overwhelmingly on street nuisance and on women sex-trade workers (Larsen 2000, 57–60). The Vice Squad in Vancouver responded initially with large-scale sweeps in all the streets where prostitutes habitually worked, and prosecutors began to restrict the areas in which women could be seen, as a condition of probation. The long-term result was to concentrate more of the sex trade in the downtown eastside region, but with no reduction in numbers of women on the streets. In Toronto, police had some initial success in reducing the trade by arresting customers, but this drove more workers into massage parlours and escort services, under the control of pimps. As police began to focus on these venues, the numbers in the streets increased again. The police practice of constantly pushing prostitutes from one area to another only spread the nuisance. Charter challenges also weakened somewhat the powers given to police to criminalize people for merely talking to each other on the street.

Larsen concludes that the 1985 law was largely ineffective in reducing street prostitution.

Violence in the Sex Trade   The most disturbing effect of the new law, according to people who work for the rights of prostitutes, is a marked increase in the levels of violence experienced by street prostitutes (Larsen 2000, 59). The extreme definition of "public communication" for the purpose of prostitution criminalizes talking in a parked car where others can see, even if they cannot hear, the exchange. As a result, prostitutes are pressured to jump into moving cars before they can check what the potential customer is like. Repeated police sweeps in residential areas have also driven workers into poorly lit back lanes and more deserted industrial areas where they are in greater danger. Larsen cites a claim by a spokesperson for prostitutes' rights that while only one prostitute was murdered in Vancouver between 1978 and 1985, fully 40 were murdered between 1986 and 1992 (Larsen 2000, 59).

The combination of public apathy towards the plight of sex-trade workers and ineffective policing of violence against prostitutes further increases the propensity for violence. People who witness a prostitute being attacked routinely ignore it rather than coming to her aid (Fedec 2002, 254, 264). Men who are widely known to have beaten up a number of prostitutes are left free to victimize more girls. Such police inaction, Fedec suggests, sends a message that prostitutes are disposable objects that men can attack without repercussions. Increasingly, Razack argues (2002, 142), there are geographic spaces within Canadian cities where violence is permissible. These are the marginal zones—the spaces into which streetwalkers are pushed, along with the homeless and the vagrant.

The pervasiveness of violence in the lives of sex-trade workers on the streets challenges liberal assumption that street prostitution is merely a job that some women choose. Such a view may hold for white women attracted to the thrill of the sex trade, who can choose to enter and to leave the marginal zones. It holds also for male customers who can engage in temporary slumming with impunity. What distinguishes them from the poor and racialized streetwalkers, Razack argues, is precisely their ability to enter temporarily and to leave with their respectability intact. Destitute and racialized women do not have the option of leaving. Colonizing practices that drove Aboriginal people from the settler cities continue to marginalize and exclude them. Aboriginal women, deprived of property and often of status rights on reservations by the Indian Act, and often fleeing violence, disproportionately end up in urban slums. An estimated 60 percent of urban Aboriginal households, and 80 to 90 percent of women-headed households, live below the poverty line (Razack 2002, 133). Prostitution offers survival, much as it does for other racialized migrant women fleeing destitution in Third World countries. Homeless white women, trapped in these marginal zones by histories of abuse and addictions, find themselves similarly racialized. These women's bodies are presumed to be sexually available. It is not an option they select, but a predefined category they must continually struggle against.

The pervasive violence enacted against the bodies of streetwalkers further challenges the cultural assumption that male customers who buy their bodies are simply average men seeking outlets for normal sexual urges. Violence is not an anomaly in the lives of streetwalkers, Razack insists, but a central feature. Violence functions to establish and confirm the dominance of white male colonizers, expressing their sense of entitlement to buy and to use the bodies of subjugated women. It is that unquestioned sense of entitlement that most horrifies Razack in her review of court records of the murder of Pamela George in 1995 by two young white males from Regina University. The young men felt comfortable bragging with their friends about beating up an "Indian hooker." In this case, as in others, being a hooker is treated in law as tacit consent to beatings, if not to murder (Hughes 1993).

The climate of indifference of the public and police towards this endemic violence has made it possible for large numbers of women in Canada to go missing and presumed murdered with police barely bothering to look for them. Aboriginal women are disproportionately among the murdered. An Amnesty International report released October 2004 (Jacobs 2004) lists 32 Aboriginal women missing from reserves in northern BC and presumed murdered on the notorious Highway 16. The body parts of 22 women were found on a pig farm near Vancouver in 2003. The farm owner, Robert Pickton, was convicted of murdering six of these women. A police task force set up after this discovery is investigating the disappearance of 60 women from Vancouver over the last decade, 16 of them status Natives. The overall number of missing Aboriginal women in Canada over the last 50 years may be as high as 500. Status Native women aged 25 to 44 are five times more likely to die from violence than any other women in Canada of the same age. Official statistics do not separately categorize non-status Native women and mixed-race women.

Child Prostitution

The legal age of consent to sexual intercourse is 16 when both sexual partners are under 18, and otherwise 18 years of age. Sex between adults and children under 18 is legally defined as a crime of sexual assault. This is routinely ignored for runaway teenagers who end up on the streets as prostitutes. Young women, and girls as young as 11 to 13 years of age, are in high demand in the sex trade because they are physically attractive, more forbidden and therefore more exciting, and because they are believed less likely to carry venereal diseases (Fedec 2002, 258). The growth in the international sex-tourism industry offers the bodies of children from impoverished developing countries for sex with wealthy Westerners able to afford the trips. Local governments tacitly encourage the trade because it brings in coveted foreign currency. Canada has had a law against child sex tourism since 1997, but as of mid-2009 only three people had been convicted. Benjamin Perrin, a UBC law professor, counts 156 Canadians who have faced charges abroad for engaging in child sex abuse, but none have been charged in Canada (www.ctv.ca, "Trial of a Sex Tourist", 7 March 2009).

Pornography

Pornography feeds into the sex-trade industry. MacKinnon (1989, Ch. 11) identifies pornography as the theory and rape as the practice of male power and domination over women. Pornography offers women's bodies as objects for male use. Feminist analysis of pornography, like prostitution, vacillates between viewing it as sexual freedom for women and sexual exploitation (Smart 1989a, Ch. 6). Feminists who oppose censorship of pornography point to the multiple ways it has been used against women's interests, to ban books on contraception and sex education, to challenge artistic representation of nude bodies, and to oppose sexual liberation. Feminists who call for censorship generally have violent, sadistic images in mind, but government bureaucrats who work on provincial boards of censors are rarely feminists (King 1985; Diamond 1985). Censor Boards have commonly found explicit sex and lesbian erotica more threatening to community standards than explicit violence. Concern with the exploitation of women who make pornography assumes a view of women as passive victims, rather than active agents who can make their own choices about involvement in the lucrative pornographic film industry.

Other feminists who favour criminalizing pornography counter that the extreme violence against women portrayed in hard-core pornography constitutes a hate crime. It endangers all women because it promotes the treatment of women's bodies as objects to be abused, and feeds the myth that women enjoy being raped. Radical feminists suggest that women who have been sexually assaulted by men who habitually watch hard-core pornography should be able to sue the industry for harm done to them (MacKinnon 1989, Ch. 11). Women who have fled battering relationships commonly report stories of male partners acting out violent and degrading scenes from pornographic videos (Busby 1994; MacKinnon 1987, 163–196) but such stories rarely carry sufficient evidence of direct causal connection to constitute proof in a court of law.

Feminist lawyers who sought intervener status with the Supreme Court of Canada in the 1992 Butler case, discussed above, walked a fine line between these two positions. The case hinged on whether possession and sale of pornography in Canada was protected under Section 2 of the Charter guaranteeing "freedom of thought, belief, opinion, and expression." Feminist lawyers argued that depictions of erotica and explicit sex should be protected, but that hard-core pornographic materials that degrade, humiliate, and subordinate women contravene the equality rights provision of the Charter and hence should not be protected (Busby 1994). The Supreme Court upheld the constitutionality of laws controlling pornography as a reasonable limit on freedom of expression, but not for the reasons advanced by feminist lawyers. The Court's reasoning stressed violation of community standards rather than women's equality rights. After the decision, police and censor boards continued to focus on materials depicting homosexual erotica rather than sexual violence.

There is far broader consensus favouring the criminalization of child pornography—materials depicting the rape of pre-pubescent children and infants—but enforcing workable laws to control such materials is far from easy. Child pornography is a global and multi-billion-dollar business. It is pervasively available over the Internet, where it is extremely hard to police. Profits from Internet pornography are so high that the industry is credited with largely sustaining the "free" global Internet. The debate that is emerging is whether a society's interest in controlling "offensive" materials such as child pornography is sufficient to justify granting police and other agents of social control extensive powers to monitor private Internet use by citizens. As the technology for such monitoring advances, the arena of struggle around protection of citizens' right to privacy over the state's right to control objectionable practices will inevitably expand.

CONCLUSION

Feminist debates around the role of law in policing prostitution and pornography draw from the competing insights of different theoretical perspectives. The functionalist perspective of liberal and cultural feminism focuses attention on prevailing values of autonomous individualism and hedonistic mass consumption that legitimate buying sex for personal pleasure. Brand-name advertising industries and mass entertainment that sexualize the clothing and appearance of women, and of younger and younger children, help to make all aspects of the sex trade seem normative rather than deviant. The implicitly racist and colonial values of white settler society normalize the use of racialized minority bodies in marginalized city zones in ways that would be felt as more obviously deviant if performed in white middle-class communities. Marxist feminism focuses on the lure of profits, and gross inequalities in wealth and poverty at global and local levels that drive the sex-trade industry. Desperation and poverty ensure no shortage of women and boys who turn to the sex trades. Social constructionism explores struggles over meaning, highlighting the entertainment-for-advertising industry that sexualizes almost everything to titillate consumers to buy commodities. Policing practices and social controls at all levels of society work to deviantize prostitutes but not their customers, and to disqualify the lived realities of endemic violence as consensual trade. Socialist feminism highlights how supposedly gender-neutral laws operate in the highly gendered social contexts of domestic responsibilities, domestic violence, and family breakdown, and inegalitarian job markets that all interact to fuel prostitution. Radical feminism challenges the double standards that paint sexually active men as normal but sexually active women as sluts. The virile-male/grudging-female seduction scenario works to normalize a predatory male sexuality that fuels the sex-trade industry. Patriarchal laws that structure tenuous rights to property and status on reservations, combined with domestic lives tortured by violence, drive disproportionate numbers of Aboriginal women into the marginal zones of street prostitution. When these marginalized women are assaulted, they have no lawyers to defend them. When they go missing, police do not search for them.

The sociology of law covers a vast terrain that can only be skimmed in this chapter. The theme that unifies this chapter is Durkheim's original insight that the study of law provides a basis for objective, scientific study of the moral order of social life. Through functionalist analysis of law we traced the gradual shift in Canadian moral code from cultural homogeneity under colonial British rule to a more open multicultural society in which diversity, equality, and individual rights are legally protected, although criminal justice practices are still tempered by racial and ethnic bias. Anomie theory traces the roots of deviance or violation of the moral order in family breakdown, with law enforcement functioning to reinforce community control.

Analysis of law through the lens of political economy makes it clear that the dominant values of Canadian society are those that favour advanced corporate capital. Laws are designed to protect private propertied interests, and to safeguard the pursuit of profits and shareholder value. This legal protection commonly holds even when corporate interests are measured against significant social harms. Courts have intervened to punish actions by executives that defraud investors of profits, but direct regulation of corporate profit-seeking activities remains minimal.

Criminal law functions to manage and diffuse potential for class conflict and revolt in the face of increasing extremes of wealth and poverty.

Social constructionist analysis reveals how ruling relations work within the justice system itself and through administrative regulations. Legal discourse functions to legitimate policing and surveillance required to reinforce moral codes that favour capitalism and to manage the destabilizing impacts of anomie and alienation. Courts assert the power to define truth with respect to alleged violations of legal codes.

The feminist perspective highlights how the rule of law functions in subtle but pervasive ways to define gender equality rights in ways that still sustain a patriarchal moral code with respect to family structures and functioning and double standards of sexual codes of conduct. Criminal law functions to protect morally deserving women while offering limited protection for women who transgress moral codes.

SUGGESTED READING

Totten's study of male youth gang members in the Ottawa region, *Guys, Gangs, and Girlfriend Abuse* (2000), includes graphic descriptive accounts of the cultural values that these adolescent boys cite to justify aggressive behaviour

towards their girlfriends. Totten debates the extent to which the gang subculture represents a "deviant" minority culture or an exaggerated expression of mainstream values around manhood that the boys feel unable to emulate. Kelly and

Totten's research, *When Children Kill* (2002), further explores the anomic family backgrounds of children convicted of crimes of extreme violence. Sandra Bell's article "Girls in Trouble" (2002) is one of the few that focuses closely on deviant behaviour by girls. She addresses the question of whether girls are becoming more like boys in acting out violent deviant behaviour.

Klinenberg's article "Bowling Alone, Policing Together" (2001) explores how middle-class residents who interact with others in only limited ways use the institution of community policing to enforce narrowly-defined cultural homogeneity on newcomers.

The books by Blomley, *Unsettling the City* (2004), and Razack, *Race, Space and the Law* (2002), offer a range of chapters and articles that explore how laws governing property and real-estate transactions work to legalize ongoing colonialism in Canadian cities. Joel Bakan's book *The Corporation: The Pathological Pursuit of Profit and Power* (2004) explores how rules of legal incorporation work to produce the criminogenic character of business corporations. He includes interviews with corporate executives who talk about how conflicted they feel in violating their own personal moral codes to carry out their corporate responsibilities. This book complements the National Film Board film *The Corporation*.

David Altheide's book *Creating Fear: News and the Construction of Crisis* (2002) gives many examples of how the infotainment industry, with its insatiable appetite for lurid crime stories, encourages audiences to be fearful for their personal safety and to assume levels of crime that far exceed reality. These fears in turn contribute to a political agenda favouring heightened punishment and prisons.

Essays by Chris "Nob" Doran, "'Growing Up Under Suspicion'" (2000) and "'Making Sense' of Moral Panics" (2002), explore the administrative regulations and practices that function to individualize and manage class conflict, even while the formal discourse of rules and regulations make no mention of class relations.

Sandra Wachholz's essay "Confronting the Construct of Child Neglect as Maternal Failure" (2002) similarly explores how both media and mainstream criminal justice discourse encourages people to blame family background, or specifically mothers, for deviant behaviour, and legitimate heavy-handed legal surveillance of impoverished and marginalized families, while discounting the injustice of the conditions under which they live.

Elizabeth Comack's book *Women in Trouble* (1996) describes the lived experiences of 24 young, uneducated, and unemployed Aboriginal women in prison in Canada. Her analysis begins with women's own accounts of their lives and how they came to break the law—driving a car repeatedly without a licence, writing bad cheques, being with the wrong crowd when violence and theft erupts, and the like. Comack argues persuasively that these women are not "other." They are no different from the rest of us "law-abiding" citizens. They are women struggling to cope in difficult life circumstances where they have few if any options that do not involve breaking the law. While this study is now more than a decade old, these life stories remain powerful testimonies to the powerlessness and abuse that pervade the lives of Aboriginal women "in trouble" with the law.

Lesley Jeffrey and Gayle MacDonald's study *Sex Workers in the Maritimes Talk Back* (2006) provides wonderfully detailed stories of the lived experiences and values of women in the Maritimes who work in the sex trade. Chapter 1 "It's the Money, Honey" includes candid stories of the financial rewards of this line of work, which compares very favourably with low-paid service-sector work otherwise available to these women. These women also talk back powerfully against mainstream moral codes that condemn their way of earning a living while ignoring pervasive double standards and inequalities that perpetuate the trade.

Katharine Kelly's article "You Must Be Crazy If You Think You Were Raped" (1997) gives a history of feminist struggles to transform rape trials that left women feeling that they were being raped again in court, only to find that defence lawyers shifted tactics to challenge their mental health.

QUESTIONS

1. How does functionalist theory use law to investigate Durkheim's notion of a shift from mechanical solidarity to organic solidarity as Canada became a more advanced industrial society? What is the evidence for legal limits to the shift away from cultural homogeneity?

2. How does Merton's *anomie* theory of crime help to account for gang behaviour by Canadian youth? How do *differential opportunity* theory and *subculture* theory complement Merton's model of deviance?

3. How does the policy of community policing address the roots of social deviance, as identified by anomie theory? What are some of the problems or dysfunctions associated with community policing?

4. Explain how law worked historically in Canada to legalize the transfer of lands from indigenous to immigrating European people. Explain Blomley's argument that Canadian law still functions to legalize some forms of colonialism in Canadian cities.

5. Explain the argument within political economy theory that laws criminalizing drug use function to manage class conflict. How does this argument differ from the functionalist view of the manifest function of laws that control drugs? How is the law implicated in supporting the questionable trafficking in drugs by pharmaceutical companies?

6. How does the law function to legalize and legitimate corporate capitalist practices that result in social harms, or violations of Canadian moral codes?

7. Explain the argument in social constructionist analysis that mainstream or functionalist perspectives on criminology are *ideological*. How does this argument reflect Dorothy Smith's critique of ideological practices in social science research, as defined in chapter one of this text?

8. Explain how policing practices work to define behaviours that do or do not constitute violations of the criminal code for practical purposes of law enforcement.

9. Explain Doran's analysis of how administrative regulations function to manage conflicting class interests in favour of corporate capitalist interests.

10. Give four examples of how specifically gender-neutral laws framed to protect equality rights of women and men in Canada still function in ways that support patriarchal family structures.

11. Explain the argument within feminist theory that laws designed to protect individuals from sexual assault function to support moral codes that accept a sexual double standard for Canadian women and men.

12. Explain the feminist argument that legislation to manage the sex trade enforces a moral code of sexual double standards for Canadian women and men. How does this legislation function to legalize forms of racialized colonialism in Canadian cities?

WEB LINKS

Jonestown: The Life and Death of People's Temple
http://video.google.com/videoplay?docid=1984081816666746895
This link provides access to the one-and-a-half-hour documentary of the tragic events of the Jonestown massacre. This site also links to several news stories and short videos such as *Mass Suicide at People's Temple: Jonestown Death Tape, Jonestown: Paradise Lost,* and *Jim Jones and the Jonestown Tragedy.*

Waco: A New Revelation (1999) (Part 1 of 2)
http://video.google.ca/videoplay?docid=5510108493532885562&hl=en

Waco: A New Revelation (1999) (Part 2 of 2)
http://video.google.ca/videoplay?docid=2962656895645965329&ei=
ptZvSq7ULoHCqgKl2Zn8Cg&q=Waco+-
+A+New+Revelation+(1999)+(Part+2+of+2&hl=en)
Dr. Frederick Whitehurst, a former FBI agent who reviewed results of the tragedy at the Branch Davidian ranch in Waco, Texas, believes that the public was never told the full truth about what happened. This two-hour documentary explores the events at the compound. The FBI and CIA challenge the claim that the deaths in the compound were suicides.

rajshri.com
www.rajshri.com/home.aspx?lgid=274&catid=-1
This site provides free Indian movies, TV shows, trailers, movie songs, music videos, documentaries, and short films for both adults and children. The famous Indian movie *Mahabharat* is available at www.rajshri.com/

searchresults.aspx?seval=Mahabharat. English translations of the children's series of *Mahabharat—Tales of Ekalavya, Stories of Draupadi, Tales of Karna,* and others run approximately a half hour. This link also provides access to the adult television version of *Mahabharat* with English subtitles. The equally famous stories of Ramayana are also found at rajshri.com at www.rajshri.com/searchresults.aspx?seval=Ramayana. Indian children's stories such as *Maharishi Valmiki* and *Ramayana* are available with English subtitles.

Indian documentaries
www.rajshri.com/landing.aspx?lgid=274&catid=263
This link provides access to documentaries such as *Reality Behind Religion, Khalse Da Hola (Darshan Yatra Sri Anandpur Sahib)—Punjabi, In Search of Spirituality, Indus Valley to Indira Gandhi,* and *I Am God.*

Bill Moyers on Faith & Reason
www.pbs.org/moyers/faithandreason/perspectives3.html
This PBS website explores through podcasts, videos, and text such issues as perspectives on gender and religion, perspectives on myths and sacred texts, and faith and reason. Understanding that movies such as *The Da Vinci Code* and *The Passion of the Christ* inform us in particular ways, Moyers interviews some of the brilliant thinkers of our day such as Salman Rushdie, David Grossman, Jeanette Winterson, Margaret Atwood, Mary Gordon, and Richard Rodriguez. Viewers are also invited to join the discussion board.

KEY TERMS

alienation

anomie

anomie theory of crime

conformists

deviance

differential association theory

differential opportunity theory

double standards

innovators

isolation

latent functions

manifest functions

marginal workers

outsiders

peasants

powerlessness

rebels

retreatists

ritualists

secondary deviance

subcultural theories of deviance

REFERENCES

Adelberg, Ellen, and Claudia Currie, eds. 1987. *Too Few To Count: Canadian Women in Conflict with the Law*. Vancouver: Press Gang Publishers.

Adler, Freda. 1975. *Sisters in Crime: The Rise of the New Female Criminal*. New York: McGraw-Hill.

Alexander, B.K. 1990. *Peaceful Measures: Canada's Way Out of the "War on Drugs"*. Toronto: University of Toronto Press.

Altheide, David L. 2002. *Creating Fear: News and the Construction of Crisis*. New York: Aldine De Gruyter.

Anderson, Kim, and Bonita Lawrence, eds. 2003. *Strong Women Stories, Native Vision and Community Survival*. Toronto: Sumach Press.

Arat-Koc, Sedef. 1999. "'Good Enough to Work but not Good Enough to Stay': Foreign Domestic Workers and the Law." In E. Comack, ed. *Locating Law: Race/Class/Gender Connections*. Halifax: Fernwood, 125–159.

Arnup, K. 1994. "Mothers Just Like Others: Lesbians, Divorce, and Child Custody in Canada." *Canadian Journal of Women and the Law* 3 (1): 18–32.

Artz, Sibylle. 1998. *Sex, Power and the Violent School Girl*. Toronto: Trifolium Books.

Artz, Sibylle, and T. Riecken. 1994. "The Survey of Student Life." In *A Study of Violence Among Adolescent Female Students in a Suburban School District*. Victoria: British Columbia Ministry of Education, Education Research Unit.

Atcheson, M.E., M. Eberts, B. Symes, with J. Stoddart. 1984. *Women and legal action: Precedents, resources, and strategies for the future*. Ottawa: Canadian Advisory Council on the Status of Women.

Aylward, Carol. 1999. "How to Engage in Critical Race Litigation" in C. Aylward, ed. *Canadian Critical Race Theory: Racism and the Law*. Halifax: Fernwood, 134–173.

Bakan, Joel. 2004. *The Corporation: The Pathological Pursuit of Profit and Power*. Toronto: Viking Canada.

Barer, M.L., K.M. McGrail, K. Cardiff, L. Wood, and C.J. Green, eds. 2000. *Tales from Other Drug Wars*. University of British Columbia Centre for Health Services and Policy Research. Papers from 12th Annual Health Policy Conference, 1999.

Beaman, Lori. 2002. "Legal Discourse and Domestic Legal Aid: The Problem of Fitting In." In G. MacDonald, ed. *Social Context & Social Location in the Sociology of Law*. Peterborough, Ontario: Broadview Press, 69–89.

Bell, Sandra. 2002. "Girls in Trouble." In B. Schissel and C. Brooks, eds. *Marginality and Condemnation: An Introduction to Critical Criminology*. Halifax: Fernwood, 129–156.

Bernhard, Bo J., and Frederick W. Preston. 2004. "On the Shoulders of Merton: Potentially Sobering Consequences of Problem Gambling Policy." *American Behavioral Scientist* 47 (11): 1395–1405.

Best, Joel. 1989. *Images of Deviance*. New York: Aldine De Gruyter.

Best, Joel. 1987. "Rhetoric in Claims-Making: Constructing the Missing Children Problem." *Social Problems* 34 (2): 101–121.

Bland, Lucy. 1985. "In the Name of Protection: The Policing of Women in the First World War." In J. Brophy and C. Smart, eds. *Women-In-Law: Explorations in Law, Family, and Sexuality*. London: Routledge & Kegan Paul, 23–49.

Blomley, Nicholas. 2004. *Unsettling the City: Urban Land and the Politics of Property*. New York; London: Routledge.

Boldt, M. 1993. *Surviving as Indians: The Challenge of Self-Government*. Toronto: University of Toronto Press.

Bottomley, Ann. 1985. "What is Happening in Family Law? A Feminist Critique of Conciliation." In J. Brophy and C. Smart, eds. *Women-In-Law: Explorations in Law, Family, and Sexuality*. London: Routledge & Kegan Paul, 162–187.

Bowker, Lee. 1993. "A Battered Woman's Problems are Social, not Psychological." In R. Gelles and D. Loseke, eds. *Current Controversies on Family Violence*. Newbury Park, California: Sage, 154–165.

Boyd, Susan. 1997. "Lesbian (and Gay) Custody Claims: What Difference Does Difference Make?" *Canadian Journal of Women and the Law* 15: 131–152.

Boyd, Susan. 1989a. "Child Custody, Ideologies, and Employment." *Canadian Journal of Women and the Law* 3: 111–134.

Boyd, Susan. 1989b. "From Gender Specificity to Gender Neutrality: Ideologies in Canadian Child Custody Law." In C. Smart and S. Sevenhuijsen, eds. *Child Custody and the Politics of Gender*. London; New York: Routledge & Kegan Paul, 126–157.

Boyd, Susan. 1987. "Child Custody and Working Mothers." In S. Martin and K. Mahoney, eds. *Equality and Judicial Neutrality*. Toronto: Carswell, 168–183.

Boyle, Christine, and Susannah W. Rowley. 1989 "Sexual Assault and Family Violence: Reflections on Bias." In S. Martin and K. Mahoney, eds. *Equality and Judicial Neutrality*. Toronto: Carswell, 312–326.

Braun, Connie. 2002. "Seeking Alternatives to Segregation for Aboriginal Prisoners." In B. Schissel and C. Brooks, eds. *Marginality & Condemnation: An Introduction to Critical Criminology*. Halifax: Fernwood, 355–380.

Bressette, Shelly E. 2003. "The truth about us: Living in the aftermath of the Ipperwash crisis." In K. Anderson and B. Lawrence, eds. *Strong Women Stories, Native Vision and Community Survival.* Toronto: Sumach Press, 228–241.

Brooks, Carolyn. 2002. "New Directions in Critical Criminology." In B. Schissel and C. Brooks, eds. *Marginality & Condemnation: An Introduction to Critical Criminology.* Halifax: Fernwood Publishing, 29–53.

Brophy, Julia. 1992. Case comments for "New Families, Judicial Decision-Making, and Children's Welfare." *Canadian Journal of Women and the Law* 5: 484–497.

Brophy, Julia. 1989. "Custody Law, Child Care, and Inequality in Britain." In C. Smart and S. Sevenhuijsen, eds. *Child Custody and the Politics of Gender.* London; New York: Routledge & Kegan Paul, 217–244.

Busby, Karen. 1999. "'Not a victim until a conviction is entered': Sexual violence prosecutions and legal 'truth'." In E. Comack, ed. *Locating Law: Race/Class/Gender Connections.* Halifax: Fernwood, 260–288.

Busby, Karen. 1994. "LEAF and Pornography: Litigation on Equality and Sexual Representations." *Canadian Journal of Law and Society* 9 (1): 167–192.

Chambliss, William. 1986."On Lawmaking." In S. Brickey and E. Comack, eds. *The Social Basis of Law.* 1st ed. Toronto: Garamond Press.

Chambliss, William. 1975. "Toward a Political Economy of Crime." *Theory and Society* 2 (2): 149–170.

Cheal, David. 1999. *New Poverty: Families in Postmodern Society.* Westport, Connecticut: Praeger.

Chunn, Dorothy E. 1999. "Feminism, Law, and 'the Family': Assessing the Reform Legacy." In E. Comack, ed. *Locating Law: Race/Class/Gender Connections.* Halifax: Fernwood, 236–259.

Clark, Anna. 1992. "Humanity or Justice? Wifebeating and the Law in the Eighteenth and Nineteenth Centuries." In C. Smart, ed. *Regulating Womanhood: Historical Essays on Marriage, Motherhood and Sexuality.* London; New York: Routledge, Ch. 9.

Clark, L.M.G., and D.L. Lewis. 1977. *Rape: The Price of Coercive Sexuality.* Toronto: Women's Press.

Clegg, S., and D. Dunkerley. 1980. *Organization, Class, and Control.* London: Routledge & Kegan Paul.

Cloward, Richard A., and Lloyd E. Ohlin. 1960. *Delinquency and Opportunity: A Theory of Delinquent Gangs.* Chicago: Free Press.

Cockburn, A., and A. Cohen. 1991. "Explosive Mix." *New Internationalist* (Oct.): 14–15.

Cohen, A.K. 1955. *Delinquent Boys: The Culture of the Gang.* New York: Free Press.

Comack, Elizabeth. 1999. "Theoretical Excursions." In E. Comack, ed. *Locating Law: Race/Class/Gender Connections.* Halifax: Fernwood, 19–68.

Comack, Elizabeth. 1996. *Women in Trouble: Connecting Women's Law Violations to Their Histories of Abuse.* Halifax: Fernwood.

Comack, Elizabeth A. 1985. "The Origins of Canadian Drug Legislation: Labelling versus Class Analysis." In T. Fleming, ed. *The New Criminologies in Canada.* Toronto: Oxford, 65–86.

Comack, Elizabeth, Vanessa Chopyk, and Linda Wood. 2002. "Aren't Women Violent Too? The Gendered Nature of Violence." In B. Schissel and C. Brooks, eds. *Marginality & Condemnation: An Introduction to Critical Criminology.* Halifax: Fernwood, 235–252.

Cote, Helen, and Wendy Schissel, with Nino Mikana Ike Ka-Pimoset (Woman Who Walks Two Roads). 2002. "Damaged Children and Broken Spirits: A Residential School Survivor's Story." In B. Schissel and C. Brooks, eds. *Marginality & Condemnation: An Introduction to Critical Criminology.* Halifax: Fernwood, 175–192.

Crocker, Phyllis L. 1985. "The Meaning of Equality for Battered Women who Kill Men in Self-defence." *Harvard Women's Law Journal* 18: 121–153.

DeKeseredy, Walter. 2000. *Women, Crime and the Canadian Criminal Justice System.* Cincinnati: Anderson Publishing.

Dell, Colleen A. 2002. "The Criminalization of Aboriginal Women: Commentary by a Community Activist." In W. Chan and K. Mirchandani, eds. *Crimes of Colour.* Peterborough, Ontario: Broadview Press, 127–138.

Delorey, Anne Marie. 1989. "Joint Legal Custody: A Reversion to Patriarchal Power." *Canadian Journal of Women and the Law* 3 (1): 33–44.

Diamond, Sara. 1985. "Pornography: Image and Reality." In V. Burstyn, ed. *Women Against Censorship.* Vancouver: Douglas & McIntyre, 40–57.

Dick, Andrew J., Dan J. Pence, Randall M. Jones, and H. Reed Geertsen. 2004. "The Need For Theory in Assessing Peer Courts." *American Behavioral Scientist* 47 (11): 1448–1461.

Doherty, Jason. 2000. "The Social Construction of Welfare Recipients as 'Lazy'." In L. Beaman, ed. *New Perspectives on Deviance: The Construction of Deviance in Everyday Life.* Scarborough, Ontario: Prentice-Hall, 150–162.

Donzelot, Jacques. 1979. *The Policing of Families.* New York: Pantheon.

Doran, Chris "Nob". 2002a. "Medico-legal Expertise and Industrial Disease Compensation: Discipline, Surveillance and Disqualification in the Era of the 'Social'." In G. MacDonald, ed. *Social Context & Social Location in the Sociology of Law.* Peterborough, Ontario: Broadview Press, 159–180.

Doran, Chris "Nob". 2002b. "'Making Sense' of Moral Panics: Excavating the Cultural Foundations of the 'Young, Black Mugger'." In W. Chan and K. Mirchandani, eds. *Crimes of Colour: Racialization and the Criminal Justice System in Canada.* Peterborough, Ontario: Broadview Press, 157–176.

Doran, Chris "Nob". 2000. "'Growing Up' Under Suspicion: The Problematization of 'Youth' in Recent Criminologies." In L. Beaman, ed. *New Perspectives on Deviance: The Construction of Deviance in Everyday Life.* Scarborough, Ontario: Prentice-Hall, 192–207.

Du Mont, Janice. 2003. "Charging and Sentencing in Sexual Assault Cases: An Exploratory Examination." *Canadian Journal of Women and the Law* 15: 305–341.

Dyck, Noel. 1992. "Negotiating the Indian Problem." In D. Miller, ed. *The First Ones: Readings in Indian/Native Studies.* Saskatoon: Saskatchewn Indian Federated College Press, 132–140.

Faith, Karlene, and Yasmin Jiwani. 2002. "The Social Construction of 'Dangerous' Girls and Women." In B. Schissel and C. Brooks, eds. *Marginality & Condemnation: An Introduction to Critical Criminology*. Halifax: Fernwood, 83–108.

Fedec, Kari. 2002. "Women and Children in Canada's Sex Trade: The Discriminatory Policing of the Marginalized." In B. Schissel and C. Brooks, eds. *Marginality & Condemnation: An Introduction to Critical Criminology*. Halifax: Fernwood, 253–267.

Fineman, M. 1989a. "The Politics of Custody and Gender: Child Advocacy and the Transformation of Custody Decision-Making in the USA." In C. Smart and S. Sevenhuijsen, eds. *Child Custody and the Politics of Gender*. London; New York: Routledge & Kegan Paul, 27–51.

Fineman, M. 1989b. "Custody Determination at Divorce: The Limits of Social Science Research and the Fallacy of the Liberal Ideology of Equality." *Canadian Journal of Women and the Law* 3 (1): 88–110.

Foster, Janet. 1995. "Informal Social Control and Community Crime Prevention." *British Journal of Criminology* 35 (4): 563–583.

Foucault, Michel. 1978. *The History of Sexuality*. London: Allen Lane.

Foucault, Michel. 1977. *Discipline and Punish*. London: Allen Lane.

Gavigan, Shelley A.M. 1999. "Poverty Law, Theory, and Practice: The Place of Class and Gender in Access to Justice." In E. Comack, ed. *Locating Law: Race/Class/Gender Connections*. Halifax: Fernwood, 208–230.

Giddens, A. 1998. *The Third Way: The Renewal of Social Democracy*. Cambridge, UK: Polity Press

Gill, Sheila D. 2002. "The Unspeakability of Racism: Mapping Law's Complicity in Manitoba's Racialized Spaces. In S. Razack, ed. *Race, Space, and the Law: Unmapping a White Settler Society*. Toronto: Between the Lines, 157–184.

Girdner, Linda K. 1989. "Custody Mediation in the United States: Empowerment or Social Control?" *Canadian Journal of Women and the Law* 3: 134–154.

Gordon, Jane. 1989. "Multiple Meanings of Equality: A Case Study in Custody Litigation." *Canadian Journal of Women and the Law* 3: 256–268.

Grace, Elizabeth K.P., and Susan M. Vella. 1994. "Vesting Mothers with Power They Do Not Have: The Non-offending Parent in Civil Sexual Assault Cases: J. (L.A.) V.J. (H) and J. (J)." *Canadian Journal of Women and the Law* 7: 185–195.

Graycar, R. 1989. "Equal Rights v. Fathers' Rights: The Child Custody Debate in Australia." In C. Smart and S. Sevenhuijsen, eds. *Child Custody and the Politics of Gender*. London; New York: Routledge & Kegan Paul, 158–189.

Green, L.C., and Olive P. Dickason. 1989. *The Law of Nations and the New World*. Edmonton: University of Alberta Press.

Greenberg, D.F. 1981. "Delinquency and the Age Structure of Society." In D.F. Greenberg, ed. *Crime and Capitalism: Readings in Marxist Criminology*. Palo Alto, California: Mayfield, 118–139.

Hall, S. 1974. "Deviance, Politics and the Media." In P. Rock and M. McIntosh, eds. *Deviance and Social Control*. London: Tavistock, 261–305.

Hermer, Joe, and Janet Moser, eds. 2002. *Disorderly People: Law and the Politics of Exclusion in Ontario*. Halifax: Fernwood.

Hirschi, Travis. 1969. *Causes of Delinquency*. Los Angeles: University of California Press.

Holtrust, N., S. Sevenhuijsen, and A. Verbraken. 1989. "Rights for Fathers and the State: Recent Developments in Custody Politics in the Netherlands." In C. Smart and S. Sevenhuijsen, eds. *Child Custody and the Politics of Gender*. London; New York: Routledge & Kegan Paul, 51–77.

Hughes, Patricia. 1993. "How Many Times a Victim?: L. (A) v. Saskatchewan (Crimes Compensation Board) and Pigeau v. Cromwell, P.C.J." *Canadian Journal of Women and the Law* 6: 502–512.

Jacobs, B. 2004. "Stolen Sisters: A Human Rights Response to Discrimination and Violence Against Indigenous Women in Canada." *Amnesty International Report*, 4 October 2004.

Jaffe, Peter, David Wolfe, and Susan Wilson. 1990. *Children of Battered Women*. London: Sage.

Jakubowski, Lisa Marie. 1999. "'Managing' Canadian Immigration: Racism, Ethnic Selectivity, and the Law." In E. Comack, ed. *Locating Law: Race/Class/Gender Connections*. Halifax: Fernwood, 98–124.

James, Carl E. 2002. "'Armed and Dangerous': Racializing Suspects, Suspecting Race." In B. Schissel and C. Brooks, eds. *Marginality & Condemnation: An Introduction to Critical Criminology*. Halifax: Fernwood, 289–308.

James, Adrian L., and Allison James. 2001. "Tightening the net: Children, community, and control." *British Journal of Sociology* 52 (2): 211–228.

Jeffrey, Lesley, and Gayle MacDonald. 2006. *Sex Workers in the Maritimes Talk Back*. Vancouver: University of British Columbia Press.

Jhappan, Radha. 1998. "The Equality Pit or the Rehabilitation of Justice." *Canadian Journal of Women and the Law* 10: 61–107.

Johnson, Kirsten. 1999. "Obscenity, Gender, and the Law." In E. Comack, ed. *Locating Law: Race/Class/Gender Connections*. Halifax: Fernwood, 289–316.

Johnson, Rebecca. 2002. "The Persuasive Cartographer: Sexual Assault and Legal Discourse in R. v. Ewanchuk." In G. MacDonald, ed. *Social Context & Social Location in the Sociology of Law*. Peterborough, Ontario: Broadview Press, 247–272.

Kawash, Samira. 1998. "The Homeless Body." *Public Culture* 10 (2): 319–339.

Keet, Jean E. 1990. "The Law Reform Process, Matrimonial Property, and Farm Women: A Case Study of Saskatchewan, 1980–1986." *Canadian Journal of Women and the Law* 4 (1): 166–189.

Kelly, Katharine D. 1997. "'You Must Be Crazy if You Think You Were Raped': Reflections on the Use of Complainants' Personal and Therapy Records in Sexual Assault Trials." *Canadian Journal of Women and the Law* 9: 178–195.

Kelly, Katharine D., and Mark Totten. 2002. *When Children Kill: A Social-Psychological Study of Youth Homicide*. Peterborough, Ontario: Broadview Press.

King, Lynn. 1985. "Censorship and Law Reform: Will Changing the Laws Mean a Change for the Better?" In V. Burstyn, ed. *Women Against Censorship*. Vancouver: Douglas & McIntyre, 79–90.

Klinenberg, Eric. 2001. "Bowling Alone, Policing Together." *Social Justice* 28 (3): 75–80.

Koggel, Christine M. 1994. "A feminist view of equality and its implications for affirmative action." *Canadian Journal of Law and Jurisprudence* 7 (1): 43–60.

Koss, Mary, and Sarah Cook. 1993. "Facing the Facts: Date and Acquaintance Rape." In R. Gelles and D. Loseke, eds. *Controversies in Sociology*. Newbury Park, California: Sage Publications.

Kurz, Demie. 1993. "Physical Assaults by Husbands: A Major Social Problem." In R. Gelles and D. Loseke, eds. *Current Controversies in Family Violence*. Newbury Park, California: Sage, 88–103.

L'Heureux-Dubé, Claire. 1997. "Making Equality Work in Family Law." *Canadian Journal of Family Law* 14: 103–127.

Larsen, Nick. 2000. "Prostitution: Deviant Activity or Legitimate Occupation?" In L. Beaman, ed. *New Perspectives on Deviance: The Construction of Deviance in Everyday Life*. Scarborough, Ontario: Prentice-Hall, 50–66.

Leonard, E.B. 1982. *Women, Crime, and Society: A Critique of Theoretical Criminology*. New York: Longman.

Liu, Mimi. 2000. "'A Prophet With Honour': An Examination of the Gender Equality Jurisprudence of Madam Justice Claire L'Heureux-Dubé of the Supreme Court of Canada." *Queen's Law Journal* 25: 417–478.

MacDonald, Gayle. 2002. "Critical Theory and the Sociology of Law: Contradiction and Currency." In G. McDonald, ed. *Social Context & Social Location in the Sociology of Law*. Peterborough, Ontario: Broadview Press, 23–46.

Machum, Susan T. 2002. "The Farmer Takes a Wife and the Wife Takes the Farm: Marriage and Farming." In G. MacDonald, ed. *Social Context & Social Location in the Sociology of Law*. Peterborough, Ontario: Broadview Press, 133–158.

MacKinnon, Catharine A. 1989. *Toward a Feminist Theory of the State*. Cambridge, Massachusetts: Harvard University Press.

MacKinnon, Catharine A. 1987. *Feminism Unmodified: Discourses on Life and Law*. Boston: Harvard University Press.

Mannette, Joy A. 1992. "The Social Construction of Ethnic Containment: The Royal Commission on the Donald Marshall Jr. Prosecution." In J. Mannette, ed. *Elusive Justice: Beyond the Marshall Inquiry*. Halifax: Fernwood, 63–77.

Martin, Melinda. 2002. "The Crown Owns All the Land? The Mi'gmaq of Listuguj Resist." In G. MacDonald, ed. *Social Context & Social Location in the Sociology of Law*. Peterborough, Ontario: Broadview Press, 229–246.

Marx, Karl. [1867] 1976. *Capital: A Critique of Political Economy*. Vol. 1. Harmondsworth, UK: Penguin Books.

McBean, Jean. 1987. "The Myth of Maternal Preference in Child Custody Cases." In S. Martin and K.E. Mahoney, eds. *Equality and Judicial Neutrality*. Toronto: Carswell, 1184–1192.

McCallum, Margaret E. 1994. "Caratun v. Caratun: It seems that we are not all realists yet." *Canadian Journal of Women and the Law* 7: 197–208.

McCarthy, M., and J.L. Radbord. 1998. "Family Law for Same Sex Couples: Chart(er)ing The Course." *Canadian Journal of Family Law* 14: 103–127.

McIntosh, Mary. 1978. "Who Needs Prostitutes? The Ideology of Male Sexual Needs." In C. Smart and B. Smart, eds. Women, Sexuality and Social Control. London: Routledge & Kegan Paul, 53–64.

McKendy, John. 1997. "The Class Politics of Domestic Violence." *Journal of Sociology and Social Welfare* 24 (3): 135–155.

Merton, Robert. 1968. *Social Theory and Social Structure*. New York: Free Press.

Mestemacher, Rebecca, and Jonathan Roberti. 2004. "Qualitative analysis of vocational choice: A collective case study of strippers." *Deviant Behavior* 25: 43–65.

Miller, W.B. 1958. "Lower Class Culture as a Generating Milieu of Gang Delinquency." *Journal of Social Issues* 14 (2): 5–19.

Monture-Angus, Patricia. 1999. "Standing against Canadian Law: Naming Omissions of Race, Culture, and Gender." In E. Comack, ed. *Locating Law: Race/Class/Gender Connections*. Halifax: Fernwood, 76–97.

Moon, Richard. 2002. "Keeping the Streets Safe from Free Expression." In J. Hermer and J. Moser, eds. *Disorderly People: Law and the Politics of Exclusion in Ontario*. Halifax: Fernwood, 65–78.

Morris, A. 1987. *Women, Crime and Criminal Justice*. Oxford: Basil Blackwell.

Morris, Ruth. 2000. *Stories of Transformative Justice*. Toronto: Canadian Scholars' Press.

Mossman, Mary Jane. 1986. "Feminism and Legal Method: The Difference It Makes." *Australian Journal of Law and Society* 3: 30–52.

Naffine, Ngaire. 1990. *The Law and the Sexes: Explorations in Feminist Jurisprudence*. Sydney: Allen and Unwin.

Neilson, Linda C. 2003. "Putting Revisions to the Divorce Act Through a Family Violence Research Filter: The Good, The Bad and the Ugly." *Canadian Journal of Family Law* 20: 11–56.

Nelson, Jennifer J. 2002. "The Space of Africville. Creating, Regulating, and Remembering the Urban 'Slum'." In S. Razack, ed. *Race, Space, and the Law: Unmapping a White Settler Society*. Toronto: Between the Lines, 211–232.

Parnaby, Patrick, and Vincent Sacco. 2004. "Fame and strain: The contributions of Mertonian deviance theory to an understanding of the relationship between celebrity and deviant behavior." *Deviant Behavior* 25 (1): 1–26.

Peace, K.A., L.G. Beaman, and K. Sneddon. 2000. "Theoretical Approches in the Study of Deviance." In L. Beaman, ed. *New Perspectives on Deviance: The Construction of Deviance in Everyday Life*. Scarborough, Ontario: Prentice-Hall, 2–17.

Pecora, Vincent P. 2002. "The Culture of Surveillance." *Qualitative Sociology* 25 (3): 345–358.

Quinney, R. 1975. "Crime Control in Capitalist Society: A Critical Philosophy of Legal Order." In I. Taylor, P. Walton, and J. Young, eds. *Critical Criminology*. London: Routledge & Kegan Paul, 181–202.

Ramp, William. 2000. "Moral Spectacles: Norm and Transgression in the News Media." In L. Beaman, ed. *New Perspectives on Deviance: The Construction of Deviance in Everyday Life*. Scarborough, Ontario: Prentice-Hall, 18–49.

Ransom, D. 1991. "The Needle and the Damage Done." *New Internationalist* (Oct.): 4–7.

Rance, S. 1991. "Growing the Stuff." *New Internationalist* (Oct.): 10–13.

Razack, Sherene. 2002. "Gendered Racial Violence and Spatialized Justice: The Murder of Pamela George." In S. Razack, ed. *Race, Space, and the Law: Unmapping a White Settler Society.* Toronto: Between the Lines, 121–156.

Razack, Sherene. 1998. "Race, Space, and Prostitution: The Making of the Bourgeois Subject." *Canadian Journal of Women and the Law* 10: 276–338.

Razack, Sherene. 1991. *Canadian Feminism and the Law: The Women's Legal Education and Action Fund and the Pursuit of Equality.* Toronto: Second Story Press

Reiman, Jeffrey. 2001. *The Rich Get Richer and the Poor Get Prison: Ideology, Class, and Criminal Justice.* 6th ed. Boston: Allyn and Bacon.

Richardson, C. James. 1996. *Family Life: Patterns and Perspectives.* Toronto: McGraw-Hill Ryerson.

Roots, Roger I. 2004. "When Laws Backfire: Unintended Consequences of Public Policy." *American Behavioral Scientist* 47 (11): 1376–1394.

Rosnes, Melanie. 1997. "The Invisibility of Male Violence in Canadian Child Custody and Access Decision-Making." *Canadian Journal of Family Law* 14: 31–60

Russell, Perry A., and Frederick W. Preston. 2004. "Airline Security After the Event. Unintended Consequences and Illusions." *American Behavioral Scientist* 47 (11): 1419–1427.

Sacco, Vincent F. 2003. "Black hand outrage: a constructionist analysis of an urban crime wave." *Deviant Behavior* 24: 53–77.

Sandberg, Kirstin. 1989. "Best Interests and Justice." In C. Smart and S. Sevenhuijsen, eds. *Child Custody and the Politics of Gender.* London; New York: Routledge & Kegan Paul, 100–125.

Saner, Hilary, Robert MacCoun, and Peter Reuter. 1995. "On the Ubiquity of Drug Selling among Youthful Offenders in Washington, DC, 1985–1991: Age, Period, or Cohort Effect?" *Journal of Quantitative Criminology* 11: 362–373.

Schissel, Bernard. 2002. "Youth Crime, Youth Justice, and the Politics of Marginalization." In B. Schissel and C. Brooks, eds. *Marginality and Condemnation: An Introduction to Critical Criminology.* Halifax: Fernwood, 109–128.

Schissel, Bernard. 1997. *Youth Crime, Moral Panics, and the Politics of Hate.* Halifax: Fernwood.

Shaver, Frances M. 1994. "The Regulation of Prostitution: Avoiding the Morality Traps." *Canadian Journal of Law and Society* 9 (1): 123–145.

Siegel, Larry J., and Chris McCormick. 2003. *Criminology in Canada: Theories, Patterns, and Typologies.* Scarborough, Ontario: Nelson Thomson.

Smart, Carol. 1992. "Disruptive Bodies and Unruly Sex: The Regulation of Reproduction and Sexuality in the Nineteenth Century." In C. Smart, ed. *Regulating Womanhood: Historical Essays on Marriage, Motherhood and Sexuality.* London; New York: Routledge, 7–32.

Smart, Carol. 1989a. *Feminism and the Power of Law.* London; New York: Routledge.

Smart, Carol. 1989b. "Power and the Politics of Child Custody." In C. Smart and S. Sevenhuijsen, eds. *Child Custody and the Politics of Gender.* London; New York: Routledge & Kegan Paul, 1–26.

Smart, Carol. 1984. *The Ties That Bind: Law, Marriage and the Reproduction of Patriarchal Relations.* London: Routledge & Kegan Paul.

Smith, Denis. 1988. "October Crisis." In M. Hurtig, ed. *The Canadian Encyclopedia.* Edmonton: Hurtig Publishers, 1558.

Smith, Dorothy E. 1990. *The Conceptual Practices of Power: A Feminist Sociology of Knowledge.* Toronto: University of Toronto Press.

Snider, Laureen. 2002. "'But They're Not Real Criminals': Downsizing Corporate Crime." In B. Schissel and C. Brooks, eds. *Marginality & Condemnation: An Introduction to Critical Criminology.* Halifax: Fernwood, 215–234.

Snider, Laureen. 1999. "Relocating Law: Making Corporate Crime Disappear." In E. Comack, ed. *Locating Law: Race/Class/Gender Connections.* Halifax: Fernwood, 183–207.

Steel, Freda M. 1987. "Alimony and Maintenance Orders." In S. Martin and K.E. Mahoney, eds. *Equality and Judicial Neutrality.* Toronto: Carswell, 155–167.

Straus, Murray A. 1993. "Physical Assaults by Wives: A Major Social Problem." In R. Gelles and D. Loseke, eds. *Current Controversies on Family Violence.* Newbury Park, California: Sage, Ch. 4.

Straus, Murray A. and R.J. Gelles. 1986. "Societal Change and Change in Family Violence from 1975 to 1985 as Revealed by Two National Surveys." *Journal of Marriage and the Family* 48: 465–479.

Sutherland, E.H. [1949] 1961. *White Collar Crime.* New York: Dryden.

Sutherland, E.H., and D. Cressey. 1960. *Principles of Criminology.* Philadelphia: Lippincott.

Swift, K. 1995. *Manufacturing "Bad Mothers": A Critical Perspective on Child Neglect.* Toronto: University of Toronto Press.

Thompson, E.P. 1975. *Whigs and Hunters: The Origin of the Black Act.* London: Allen Lane.

Thrasher, F.M. 1963. *The Gang: A Study of 1,313 Gangs in Chicago.* Chicago: University of Chicago Press.

Totten, Mark. 2000. *Guys, Gangs and Girlfriend Abuse.* Peterborough, Ontario: Broadview Press.

Wachholz, S. 2002. "Confronting the Construct of Child Neglect as Maternal Failure: In Search of Peacemaking Alternatives." In G. MacDonald, ed. *Social Context and Social Location in the Sociology of Law.* Peterborough, Ontario: Broadview Press, 181–208.

Wacquant, Loïc. 2001. "The Advent of the Penal State is Not a Destiny." *Social Justice* 28 (3): 81–87.

Waldram, James B. 1997. *The Way of the Pipe. Aboriginal Spirituality and Symbolic Healing in Canadian Prisons.* Peterborough, Ontario: Broadview Press.

Walker, Gillian A. 1992. "The Conceptual Politics of Struggle: Wife Battering, the Women's Movement and the State." *Studies in Political Economy* 33: 66–90.

Walker, Gillian A. 1990. *Family Violence and the Women's Movement. The Conceptual Politics of Struggle.* Toronto: University of Toronto Press.

Walkowitz, Judith. 1982. "Male Vice and Feminist Virtue: Feminism and the Politics of Prostitution in Nineteenth-century Britain." *History Workshop Journal* 1: 79–93.

Wegner, Eldon L., and Sarah C.W. Yuan. 2004. "Legal Welfare Fraud Among Middle-Class Families." *American Behavioral Scientist* 47 (11): 1406–1417.

White, Rob. 2002. "Restorative Justice and Social Inequality." In B. Schissel and C. Brooks, eds. *Marginality & Condemnation: An Introduction to Critical Criminology*. Halifax: Fernwood Publishing, 381–396.

Willis, Paul. 1981. *Learning to Labour: How Working Class Kids Get Working Class Jobs*. New York: Columbia University Press.

Zedner, Lucia. 2003. "Too Much Security?" *International Journal of the Sociology of Law* 31: 155–184.

Durkheim's Legacy and the Sociology of Religion

Durkheim's last major work, *The Elementary Forms of Religious Life* ([1915] 1976), still represents a milestone in the sociology of religion. In this study he ties the analysis of religion intimately to his conception of the nature of social cohesion and, in effect, to the foundations of society itself. His first premise is that religion has been universally present in all known societies. Hence, it cannot be accounted for as merely illusion or superstition. Illusion would long ago have been displaced by the advances of science.

Durkheim further reasoned from a comparative study of major religions that the notion of "divine revelation" cannot account for the universality of religion as a social institution. Religions do not share any common doctrine about divinity.

Some religions have as their central doctrine a belief in a single god, while others believe in a multiplicity of gods and goddesses. Yet other religions have no concept of a god. Buddhism is a religion, but its basic concept of enlightenment is non-theistic. In many tribal religions there are no gods, only **totem** animals, plants, or rocks that constitute cult objects.

So what central characteristics do all religions have in common? Firstly, argues Durkheim, they all comprise sets of beliefs that are shared—held by all adherents. Secondly, they all have certain rituals that all believers collectively perform. Further, all religious thought draws some distinction between the **sacred** and the **profane** or worldly. The distinction is absolute and is manifest in ritual prescriptions and prohibitions surrounding the sacred realm. From these characteristics Durkheim derives his fundamental definition of **religion**: "Religion is a unified system of belief and practices, relative to sacred things, which unite into a single moral community called a church, all those who adhere to them" (Durkheim [1915] 1976, 10).

All religions have a "church," in the sense of an organization that performs rituals and ceremonies on a regular basis for a particular group of worshippers (Giddens 1971, 107).

What does this sacred realm refer to? What is it in people's normal, everyday experience that is so powerful that it could give rise to the sacred? For Durkheim, the one reality that has all the characteristics people attribute to the divine is society itself. Society is a force far greater than any individual. It brought us to life and it can kill us. It has tremendous power over us. Everyone depends on it. Our sense of ourselves and the concepts and language through which we think and communicate come to us through society. The community, omnipresent and omnipotent, comprises an anonymous, impersonal force to which all belong. *God* is the symbolic expression of the intensity of our feeling of community with others. It is this human community that arouses in us the sense of the divine, and which has moral authority over us. The duality of the human person and the *soul* is, like religion, found everywhere, and so cannot be illusory. For Durkheim, the concept of soul symbolizes the force of the group within the self, the duality of human nature as both individual and social.

We derive a tremendous sense of emotional energy from belonging to a group. It gives us courage beyond any level that we could muster alone. It makes us capable of heroism and sacrifice and gives us confidence to achieve things we could not otherwise reach. Such energy can also become fanatical, powerful, and potentially dangerous (Collins 1982, 39–41). These intangible but very real forces are part of what religion expresses.

Durkheim's major work, *The Elementary Forms of Religious Life* focuses on the most primitive form of religion—totemism among the Aboriginal hunting and gathering societies of Australia. His central argument is that the conceptual structure of Aboriginal religion can be understood as mirroring the structure of their clan communities. The communities have no wealth and no hierarchy, and the different clans that make up the tribe are equal. Each clan has a sacred totem that gives the clan its name and is the centre of its special rituals and beliefs. The totem is the emblem of the clan and has sacred force because it transcends the individual in representing the group. The sacred force is not intrinsic to the animal or plant selected as a totem any more than a Christian cross is sacred. The sacredness resides in its nature as a symbol. Just as all clans within the hunting and gathering society are equal, so all the totems of the different clans are religiously equal. Durkheim describes the seasonal rituals that draw the clans together. These deeply sacred ceremonies, in which all the different totems are honoured, symbolize and strengthen the bonds between people, unifying them during the long seasons when they must separate into small wandering groups in search of food.

Durkheim was aware that as social life becomes more diversified the shared values of mechanical solidarity can no longer form a central unifying force. In societies character-ized by advanced division of labour, religion must take a very different form. As a Jew in anti-Semitic France of his day, Durkheim knew first-hand how deeply divisive reli-gious intolerance could be. He argued that the core values of organic solidarity must be respect for individuality and human rights. People develop a sense of belonging to highly differentiated societies not through sameness with others, but through awareness of mutual interdependence and moral obligation. This develops despite, or in fact because of, the tremendous diversity of lifestyles and values in the world community. For Durkheim, the religion that best expressed such core values was humanism, a religion in which tolerance for diversity is a basic premise (Neyer 1960). This was a utopian vision which Durkheim hoped might eventually be achieved.

Durkheim's anthropological data with respect to Aboriginal social structures and religious practices were somewhat limited, and a number of his specific descriptive claims have been criticized, but his overall conception of the nature of religious experience and its grounding in the everyday experience of communal life still stands as a semi-nal argument in the sociology of religion.

Contemporary Functionalist Theory of Religion

Durkheim's analysis remains central to the study of religion from the functionalist perspective. This perspective assumes that any social institution that persists through time does so because it meets important needs for the social system of which it is a part. A phenomenon such as religion, which is found in all known societies, must therefore serve some indispensable function for the maintenance of society. That function is social integration.

Religious beliefs are centrally important features of cul-ture, the system of shared beliefs, values, and attitudes learned through socialization. Since human survival is not biologically programmed, Berger argues, humans are compelled to create culture in order to learn how to live in the world. Religion legitimates this cultural order; it pro-vides a sacred canopy (Berger 1967, 15; Dawson 1998a, 16–20). Through myths, rites, and doctrines, religious prac-tices make sacred the social order, commonly linking it to a sense of a larger divine purpose, and imbuing it with moral authority, meaning, and stability. Myths of common origins link individuals in quasi-kinship relations to each other and to the original members of their community, stretching back conceptually to the beginnings of time and forwards to an indefinite future. Daily and weekly prayers and seasonal rituals and feasts both organize and give meaning to the pas-sage of time (Seul 1999, 560–561). As Seul expresses it, the central function of religion is to stabilize individual and group identity. It defines relations to self and to others, to the non-human world, the universe, and to God, or to that which one considers ultimately real or true. It is broader than any other cultural institution. It promotes stability of the social order in offering a timeless sense of an orderly and meaningful universe, especially in the face of ethnic pluralism and social disruption.

Religious stories and texts are repositories of commu-nity memory. As they are taught to successive generations through oral and written traditions, they promote a group sense of identity and of special place and purpose in the uni-verse. Seul views religious identity as stronger than ethnic or national identity because it carries a sense of place in eternity and because it addresses the fullest range of human needs (Seul 1999).

The sacred canopy works for both faithful and non-believers, although at different levels. Believers may under-stand religious values as divinely inspired, as the expression of divine will to guide human life. Non-believers may understand religion as the reflection and projection onto an abstract plane of our deepest human values. The outcome is similar—a shared reverence and respect for the core collec-tive conscience and consciousness of human community.

In practical everyday terms, religion performs tension-management functions, helping to hold communities together in the face of disappointment, suffering, illness, and death (Yinger 1957, 7–12). At the individual level, all human desires for power, love, knowledge, and consolation find expression in religious beliefs. Rites such as communion reinforce the bonds of kinship between us. *Representative rites*, the dramas and myths that repeat the actions of our an-cestors, perpetuate tradition and reinforce a sense of belong-ing to the past and to the future of our community. Above all, religion helps people to grapple with death. The hope of salvation eases suffering. Funeral rites draw us together, reaffirming the value of the life lived, and the continuity of family and moral community despite bereavement.

Functionalist theory also draws upon Durkheim's notion of stages in societal evolution with a corresponding evolution of more complex forms of religion. Different types of societies have different types of gods, reflecting their own unique structures. The very simple, non-hierarchical patterns of totemic religion can promote cohesion in Aboriginal societies, but more complex and abstract systems of beliefs and rituals are required in societies that are more highly differentiated.

In agricultural communities, which are larger than hunting and gathering societies and have some accumulated wealth, the nature of religious belief is different (Collins 1982, 48–50). In particular, Collins argues, the role of kinship ties and inheritance and thus the position of women is more important, and this is reflected in fertility rites and the worship of goddesses. As societies become more hierarchically organized, the gods are likely to be thought of as arranged in a hierarchy as well. Finally, in literate, cosmopolitan civilizations, the concept of God as a single, transcendent reality emerges. This type of religion aims to be universal. It reflects a rationalized, literate society with sufficient political power that it can foster the idea of a universal state.

The Challenge of Religious and Ethnic Diversity

If one accepts the argument that religion performs such important functions for the social system and individual members, then the issues raised by Durkheim become critical. What happens to faith in modern societies where it is increasingly accepted that social structures are not divinely ordained but constructed by people, and designed, studied, and criticized by various branches of the social sciences? What happens to religious faith when societies become highly diversified and multiple faiths vie for attention within the same social system? There are three broad patterns of response to these challenges, which can loosely be described as secularism, religious individualism, and revivalism.

Secularism   The secularization thesis put forward by many theorists suggests that religion would lose its hold over people in the modern, industrial world. The social sciences would gradually replace religion in legitimating the social order, while religion would play a more marginal role as a matter of private, individual choice (Dawson 1998a, 20). Various forms of *civil religions* (Bellah 1967) have been proposed as taking over the integrative functions once performed by religion, with nationalism perhaps the most important. Secular leaders work to promote a sense of shared citizenship and common destiny to integrate people across class and racial and ethnic diversity. Nationalist

rhetoric helps to sanctify the state as collective entity, and to mobilize support for common goals. Symbolism in the form of anthems, flags, and ceremonies, functions to foster a sense of identity across diverse citizens. Sports, at local and international levels, also draw people together in a sense of community, spurred on by nationwide media coverage. Intermediate-level organizations such as voluntary ethnic associations may also serve as substitute civil religions. Neeman and Rubin's (1996) study of the minority Rumanian ethnic association in Israel describes how it functioned to redefine Rumanian identity in positive terms as immigrants who have contributed to building Israeli society. In public ceremonies the leaders modified Jewish religious symbolism to appeal to a sense of shared Jewish identity while omitting specifically religious referents that would marginalize the largely non-religious membership. Such "civil religious" institutions are generally seen as compensating in part for the decline in shared commitment to religion in complex societies. But they generally do not function to the same depth as religious beliefs in legitimating core societal values.

The secularization thesis is supported by evidence of a pronounced and continuing decline in church attendance in all Western societies. Bibby (1993, 12–58) reports survey data showing that active church attendance in Canada has dropped in every decade since the Second World War, with the partial exception only of numerically marginal evangelical Protestant churches and new-age cults. A common life-cycle pattern is for young adults to leave their church, with some returning in later life when they are raising their own children. But statistically, for every two who leave, only one returns. The evangelical or conservative Protestant churches seemed to be holding their own in the 1990s, but mostly by "winning the switching competition" rather than attracting those with no prior church affiliation (Bibby 1993, 44–45). Bibby's surveys of *Teen Trends* (1992; 2000) indicate that the attendance of teenagers in churches had dropped by the 1990s to the lowest level since the war, and even those attending displayed limited commitment. Bibby's latest survey (2000) suggests a slight reversal of the trend within Canada, with more churches noting an increase in their numbers since the previous year.

The central problem with this secularization thesis, however, is that there is too much evidence that contradicts it. Notwithstanding the decline in church attendance, the broader prediction that the mass of people in industrialized societies would embrace secularism and rationalism and reject religion has not happened. In the United States, a country with one of the highest levels of education, science, and technology in the world, religion has not only not disappeared, it has gained in strength and has become a powerful influence in politics (Collins 1982, Ch. 2). There are religious groups of many kinds, including fundamentalist sects that take the Bible as literally true, and evangelical programs on radio and television. Oriental religions have made a greater influx into Western societies than at any previous time, with Hindu gurus, Buddhist monks, and followers of Krishna appearing in large numbers (Collins 1982, 31). Cults, or movements of radically individualistic religious seekers, have proliferated in North America. By 1999, the Federal Bureau of Investigation in the USA identified more than 1500 cults predicting that the advent of the second millennium in the year 2000 would herald catastrophic upheavals analogous to those prophesied in the Book of Revelations in the Bible. There has also been rising numbers of people drawn to fundamentalist and evangelical sects, groups that have broken away from mainstream churches to found highly solitary and doctrinally homogeneous and strict movements. Religion is clearly not a spent force in modern Western societies, although the forms that it takes differ from the past.

Religious Individualism

A journalist's commentary with the provocative title "Give them Jesus, but hold the theology" (Nolen, *Globe and Mail*, 2 January 1999, A1) reported that "Jesus is a hot-selling item in popular culture," his image selling on T-shirts, tote bags, and gowns in trendy shops. Books about Jesus were top sellers for Random House, along with Buddhism, Jungian philosophy, Judaism, and Sufism. The same article reported that the number of students majoring in Religious Studies at Queen's University rose from 40 to 90 between 1994 and 1999.

Survey results support the argument that most North Americans view religion as a matter of individual choice (Roof and Gesch 1995). Gallup polls conducted in the USA report that 81 percent of respondents agreed that "one should arrive at his or her own religious beliefs independent of a church or synagogue," and 78 percent agreed that "one can be a good Christian or Jew without attending a church or synagogue" (Roof and Gesch 1995, 63). The authors see two distinctive styles in these responses: the "religious" style oriented to institutional membership, prescribed rituals, and dogma; and the "spiritual" style oriented to unofficial, experiential, and individualistic beliefs. The style of detached spiritualism, they suggest, more closely mirrors prevailing secular values of achievement, equality, and competitive individualism.

A study of three cohorts of practicing Catholics supports this generalization of a marked shift in religious orientation from institutional to individual conceptions of faith (Williams 1996). Those raised during the 1930s and 1940s—the years of the Great Depression—tended to see the institution of the church as mediating between themselves and God. They emphasized adherence to the catechism, and to formal teachings and rituals. The baby boomers raised during the 1950s and 1960s, an era of greater prosperity and upward mobility, as well as some revolutionary changes proposed by the Second Vatican Council, expressed more ambivalence towards the authority of the church. The post-Vatican II cohort, raised in the 1970s and 1980s, were the most individualistic. They spoke of faith as a personal spiritual journey, and an intimate relationship with God. Of the three cohorts they were the least likely to be concerned with church teachings or with participation in sacraments.

Functionalist analysis of the simultaneous decline in attendance of traditional religious institutions and the rise of cults draws on Durkheim's insight that the transition from homogenous to heterogeneous societies characterized by global communications, ethnic diversity, and advanced division of labour, would lead inexorably to the emancipation of the individual from the group.

Lee (1995, 381) describes Unitarian Universalism, an extreme variant of liberal Protestantism, as the institutional form of religion that most closely epitomizes Durkheim's "cult of the individual." Individuals seeking personal answers to the ultimate questions of life are seen as the only spiritual authority, not church dogma or scripture. The church or "Fellowship" has no official creed, but promotes the principles of justice and equality, freedom of belief and acceptance of difference. A rational humanist and atheistic orientation dominated the movement by the 1960s with services resembling academic gatherings. In the decades that followed, however, the movement was transformed by the influence of a variety of cult-like movements, including Zen, new age, Aboriginal spirituality, and neo-paganist goddess spirituality and feminist witchcraft. What drew these strange bedfellows together, Lee argues, was that both humanism and spiritualism vest the individual with authority in matters of belief, and ground mystical belief in direct experience. Dawson (1998a) similarly argues that the decline of centralized religious authority, and increasing religious tolerance, pluralism, and privatization, were essential for cults to arise. Cults, in Dawson's view, are in many ways compatible with the social sciences and cultural pluralism. Their foci on personal well-being, on mind-body healing, on change through collective spiritual effort, on images of God as accessible, and experiential cosmic energy, environmental consciousness, and holistic views of the world that overcome dualisms of mind/body, human/animal, nature/culture, are essentially modernist in orientation. Many of their practices have direct relevance in fields of health, justice, and peace.

The downside of commitment to radical individualism and openness to diversity of ideas is relatively weak integration or solidarity among members. Lee notes that Unitarian

Universalists on average have the second-highest incomes of any American religious group but rank lowest in financial giving to their churches (Lee 1995, 392). Three-quarters of members described their attendance as only moderate (25 percent) or low to nil (49 percent), and only 5 percent of children raised in the church continued as adult members. Durkheim's hypothesis that individualism and diversity are incompatible with mechanical solidarity seems to be supported by the Unitarian Universalist experience.

Lee suggests that cults similarly face problems of low commitment, with membership tending to be temporary and occasional (Lee 1995). Dawson disagrees, arguing that cults can attract a tightly knit core of devotees who maintain in-group solidarity by segregating themselves from the wider society, particularly those closest to a charismatic leader. Membership in such exclusionist cults can function to give a sense of family, community, identity, and belonging for members.

Religious Revivalism Religious individualism and secularism taken together account for only a very small proportion of religious practices in modern pluralistic societies. Fundamentalist and evangelical movements attract far greater numbers of adherents, despite, or perhaps *because of*, their anti-modernist orientation. The roots of fundamentalism, Ammerman contends (1987), lie in the social changes of the mid-nineteenth century, reflecting a reaction against industrialism and secularism. Fundamentalists claim to be preservers of the old Protestant faith of the Puritan founding fathers of America. When they were unable to halt the drift towards liberalism in mainstream denominational churches, they broke away to found independent, non-denominational churches of their own. The central tenet of all fundamentalist religious orientation is scriptural literalism. For Christian fundamentalists, the Bible as written is viewed as the only and the absolute religious authority. The Bible is understood as the revealed word of God, and not the product of human imagination. Fundamentalists are also millennialist, drawn to the biblical prophecies of the second coming of Christ, particularly as expressed in the Book of Revelation. From their perspective modern industrial societies appear as evil, and turned away from God. Parallels can readily be drawn between evidence of pervasive family breakdown, sexual depravity, addictions, deviance, violence, and wars, and biblical descriptions of the reign of the Antichrist expected to precede Christ's triumphant return. Millennialism is thus inherently political, representing a profound criticism of society and the state. Fundamentalism emerged as a central political force in the United States in the 1970s, surprising the social scientists of the time who expected secularism and individualism to prevail. Adherents of fundamentalist churches are

characterized by highly disciplined lives, eschewing alcohol, swearing, or dancing, and placing heavy emphasis on traditional gender roles and family values. Members of the church that Ammerman studied displayed an intense sense of belonging, with over half of them attending church functions more than twice a week and many four or more times weekly. Church and fellow church members were the centre of their social lives.

Millennialism is primarily but not exclusively a Protestant phenomenon. Luebbers (2001) describes a similar fundamentalist apocalyptic movement within Catholicism. Here too adherents see themselves as preserving the true Catholic Church against crises of modernism that threaten its foundations. Their central criticism of society is what they see as increasing "protestantization," meaning separation of the state and other societal institutions from religion. A particular source of righteous anger for all fundamentalists is the removal of religious education from public schools.

The appeal of fundamentalist Christianity, Ammerman suggests, is primarily to suburban middle- and lower-middle-class people (1987, 8). Suburbia is where tradition meets modernity, where small-town religion meets the modern city. The incomes, occupation, and education levels of people Ammerman interviewed were typical of the American middle class. Surprisingly also, only 17 percent of the women were full-time housewives, and almost half worked full time outside their home. In short, with the exception of their religious beliefs, they appear as typical mainstream Americans.

Fundamentalist or "conservative" Protestant churches have also had a strong appeal among some immigrants to North America, particularly those from Chinese (Yang 1998) and Korean (Chong 1998) origins. Both authors suggest that a central factor in this appeal is the affinity between traditional Confucian values of filial piety and moral discipline and conservative Protestant moral standards. Yang carefully rejects common explanations for the conversion of Chinese immigrants to Christianity. These are not "rice-bowl" Christians looking for social services and handouts. Most of the Chinese members were middle-class suburban residents with professional occupations. If assimilation was their main goal, mainstream churches would have been a better choice, or no church at all. Similarly there are many other secular ethnic-Chinese associations they could belong to without requiring religious conversion. The pull, Yang argues, lies precisely in the moral conservatism and the doctrinal fundamentalism that neither liberal Protestant churches nor secular associations could provide. Chinese people have suffered through three generations of social and political turmoil—forced modernization, Western imperialism, Japanese aggression, civil war between Nationalists and Communists, the Cultural Revolution, and years as refugees. Some had moved so many times during their lives that "Heavenly Home" in the Lord was the only permanent address they could give. Their own Chinese cultural traditions had been smashed, leaving them open to and highly responsive to the promise of certainty, of absolute beliefs and strict moral standards found in the fundamentalist church. Yang estimates that fully 32 percent of all Chinese-Americans are members of fundamentalist Christian churches, compared with less than 1 percent of people in mainland China.

Chong's study of second-generation Korean Americans shows that they too are drawn to fundamentalist Korean-Christian churches. They identify close parallels between Confucian ethics of submission to parental authority, chastity, purity, devotion, self-control, and perseverance, and conservative Protestantism (1998, 277–278). Appeal to traditions of secular Confucianism lacks the authority that appeal to God commands in the moral education of their own children. They also find a strongly cohesive sense of community and support for their Korean identity in the fundamentalist church.

Religion and Conflict

Functionalist analysis of religion leads to an ominous prediction. Religion is seen as a core institution that grounds both individual and group identity, and sustains societal integration, inspiring loyalty and commitment to a society's central values. It follows, therefore, that the presence of more than one religious tradition within the same society will foster divergent identities and divided loyalties and commitments, which heighten the risk of disunity and conflict within the social system.

Religion is not the only institution that supports social cohesion. Nationalism, with the symbolism of anthems, flags, and ceremonies, helps to foster a sense of identity across diverse citizens. Sports, at local and international levels, also draw people together in a sense of community. Such institutions arguably function to compensate for the decline in shared commitment to religion in complex societies, but neither encompasses core values to the depth of religion.

Dawson reasons that the personalized spirituality of the "me" generation neither sustains nor threatens social integration. Individuals attracted to such practices are not readily mobilized for collective action. Cults, however, are a different matter because they do inspire intense group loyalties that separate adherents from the wider society. Violent confrontations have erupted from time to time between some cults and mainstream American society. Dawson cites the mass murder-suicide of the People's Temple of Jim Jones in 1978, the military attack on the Branch Davidian compound at Waco, Texas, in 1993, and the cult suicides of the Solar Temple in 1994 and Heaven's Gate in 1997. Dawson's analysis suggests that both cults and mainstream society share the blame for these tragedies. On the one hand there is widespread prejudice against some cults, fuelled by ill-informed media propaganda portraying cult members as brainwashed zombies and fanatics engaged in ritualistic torture. Such prejudice has prompted governments to use force against cults. In response, intense beliefs of cult members promote interpretations of such attacks as foreshadowing biblical apocalypse, in the face of which violent counteractions and mass suicides appear rational.

Bad as such confrontations have been, cults in general present little threat to the integration of the overall social system. Dawson (1998a, Ch. 5) estimates that out of some three thousand new religious movements in the USA, with 10 million members, only a handful have caused any disruption to social order. Most cults are localized and attract only small numbers of adherents around a charismatic figure. Their members seek only the right to practice their faith in private.

A potentially far more serious threat to societal cohesion is the presence of different major religions, commanding the adherence of significant proportions of the population, with the wider support of millions of people worldwide. Examples of societies torn by violent conflict between members of different religious groups include Northern Ireland, which has suffered through more than 30 years of war between Catholics and Protestants, and India, which was born in blood in 1947 when the old colonial empire split violently into predominantly Muslim Pakistan and predominantly Hindu India. In 2001, the state of Gujarat was again torn by violence between Hindu and Muslim communities, leaving hundreds dead. Yugoslavia also broke up in the late 1990s along religious lines into Catholic, Orthodox, and Muslim enclaves. Jewish and Muslim communities within Israel itself and wider Palestine have been mired in half a century of conflict.

Examples like these lend support to the argument that "ethnic cleansing" into separate homogeneous religious communities is necessary to ensure societal cohesion. Yet there are far more extensive counter-examples of communities in which there has long been peaceful co-existence between Catholics and Protestants, Hindus and Muslims, Jews and Christians. Religious diversity does not automatically undermine societal cohesion. Hence, we need to explore the conditions under which religious diversity is more or less likely to be associated with conflict.

This is the question addressed by Jonathan Fox (1999b) in his survey of 105 ethno-religious minorities in states around the world. Fox argues that religious institutions show two opposite tendencies: to promote quietism and acceptance of the status quo, and to become mobilized for organized protest against the status quo. Circumstances outside the religious institutions themselves determine which possibility becomes paramount.

Catholicism at different times has supported violent crusades, and quiet submission to state authority, as has Judaism. Black churches in the USA long supported quietism, encouraging slaves to accept their situation on earth in return for the promise of eternal grace to follow death. But black churches were also centrally involved in mobilizing congregants in civil rights protests in the late 1960s. The Baha'i faith is theologically pacifist and committed to non-violence, but it is descended from a messianic movement that was once associated with terrorism in nineteenth-century Iran. Pacifism, Fox suggests, grew out of defeat. Native religions in North America have similarly embraced the warrior values of the Sun Dance rituals and the pacifism of the Ghost Dance (Burridge 1969), and supported mobilization for political protests in recent years.

Fox notes further that the theologies of most long-established religions are sufficiently diverse and complex that they lend themselves to contradictory interpretations. Single myths, like the expectation of a triumphant return of a spiritual leader to bring justice on earth, have been interpreted to justify messianic revolts as well as indefinite quiet waiting (Burridge 1969, 123).

Fox's survey of minority religious communities suggests that religious institutions tend to inhibit protest movements, but they become positively correlated with mobilization for protest and rebellion when political discrimination and grievances over autonomy are high, and especially when religious institutions themselves are threatened. Under such circumstances, the more advanced the level of organization of religious institutions, the more likely that religion will form the basis for organized political action. Religious organization can vary from merely meeting in private homes, or a few houses of worship, to a full ecclesiastical network with paid staff and international connections.

Religious institutions facilitate mobilization in many ways. They offer convenient places to meet, and they are safer in the sense of being less likely to be targeted by an opposing group or the government. Under repressive governments they may be the only legal place for large groups to meet. They also have access to communication media—vital to any oppositional movement. They can provide legitimacy to a movement, and their role in providing social services within a community strengthens their base for influence.

Seul concurs that religious beliefs in and of themselves do not cause social conflicts. Most communal conflicts are over rights and recognition, not propagation of faith (1999, 564). However, he argues, religion does provide the basis for positive social identity that provides the fault line along which intergroup identity and resource competition occurs. The reason is that religion provides symbolic and moral grounds for legitimation of group action, as well as institutional resources for mobilization. Religion is a key cultural marker, Seul argues, because it is often experienced as closer to one's core identity and sense of group belonging than other potential focal points like race, birthplace, nation, or ancestry. In Yugoslavia, he suggests, religion was the only cultural marker that could reliably distinguish Bosnian Muslims from their Serb and Croat counterparts.

Seul notes further that once group conflict emerges around incompatible interests or uneven access to resources, the conflict itself works to intensify group identities, making the divisions more intractable (Seul 1999, 558 and 566). Moreover, religion can serve as a primary marker dividing groups in conflict whether the religious group identities are lightly or firmly held, and even when many members do not adhere to religious tenets at all. Bosnian Muslims, he argues, are highly secularized, yet their leaders could still champion the homogenization of a Muslim ethno-religious identity clearly identified with Islam. Seul concludes that it is always possible for latent religious affiliations to become the basis for group cohesion in times of social stress, even in highly secularized societies such as the former Yugoslavia.

In conclusion, divergent religious identities can and do become the focus for group identification and mobilization in situations of social conflict that can tear societies apart. This may happen even though the roots of the conflicts commonly lie outside the tenets or doctrines of religion.

Political Economy of Religion

The political economy perspective focuses analysis on the material conditions of existence, economic inequality, and relations of class, power, and domination in society. Political economy overlaps with the functionalist perspective in seeing how religions function to legitimate social order, and compensate for suffering, but it focuses more directly on how religions legitimate conditions of inequality, exploitation, and oppression. In particular, political economy theory explores how dominant economic class relations are reinforced through their control over cultural institutions such as organized religion. It is through such control, Marx predicted, that the prevailing ideas in any society come to be those favoured by the dominant economic class.

Marx himself addressed the issue of religion only in a fragmentary way. Much of what now stands as the political economy of religion was developed by later theorists who extrapolated on Marxist thought. Marx characterized religion as a powerful form of ideology that legitimates and strengthens class domination by inculcating among subordinate people an acceptance of subordination. In the Marxist critique of functionalist theory, religion functions as an "opiate of the masses." Religions that stress acceptance of suffering, with reward in the life after death, drug people into passivity and submission. As we shall see below, **puritanism**, which prevailed in nineteenth-century England during the period when Marx was writing, was a particularly notorious target for such criticism. It was an ethic that justified the wealth and power of capitalists as somehow ordained by God or merited on the basis of holy grace, while poor people were enjoined to endure suffering or hardship as trials that would prove their worthiness for ultimate salvation in the life beyond death.

Early Marxist writings did not entirely discount the radical potential of religion. However distorted its particular message might be, Marx recognized that "religious distress is at the same time real distress and the protest against real distress" (Baum 1979, 30). The problem for Marx was that religion was all too often a powerful force that prevented people from recognizing their real situation and rebelling against it.

Engels ([1884] 1978), a close confederate of Marx, explicitly recognized the affinity between the ideas underlying communism and Christianity, particularly as reflected in early Christian communities. Christianity appeared as a religion of slaves and emancipated slaves, of poor people deprived of all rights. Like **socialism**, it promised forthcoming salvation from bondage and misery. The major difference between them was that Christianity did not want to accomplish the transformation in this world but beyond it, in heaven, in eternal life after death. Engels accounts for this difference by reference to the historical condition of slaves and the absence of a strong working-class structure that would have made the socialist revolution possible at the time when Christianity first took hold. It expressed people's practical experience of powerlessness to alter their material conditions on earth. Christianity subsequently became the dominant religion of the Roman Empire, and its promise of salvation after death was tied to a message of passivity and submission to earthly rulers. Traditional Christian notions of God as "Lord" and "Master" who demanded total obedience was again a realistic expression of people's experience of feudalism. Relations of economic production in Europe would have to change markedly before alternative conceptions of God could take root in the minds of the mass of people. The individualistic spirituality of the "me" generation would also have to await the development of capitalist society, which broke feudal bonds and obligations and made possible the emergence of individual wage earners and consumers.

Max Weber's Contribution

Much of Max Weber's work was acknowledged to be a conversation with the ghost of Marx, an effort both to elaborate Marx's ideas and to go beyond them. Weber's contribution was to undertake a historical, comparative study of world religions and of the varied forms of religious expression among different social classes within Western industrial societies. Weber documents how closely religious expression reflects diverse life experiences. The road to salvation varies markedly with social position (Weber [1922] 1964, Ch. 6 and 7). People who do different kinds of work and who occupy different places within a society, whether as peasants, warriors, intellectuals, or business people, have very different religious tendencies, even with the same overarching religious tradition such as Christianity.

Peasants have a secure relation to the land but experience the vagaries of weather and unpredictable natural forces. They have little interest in rationalized theology and are more inclined towards magic. The ethic of warriors, on the other hand, is not compatible with a kind-hearted divinity. Concepts of an otherworldly god with systematic ethical demands have very little or no appeal. Warriors are drawn towards an image of a god of power and towards a religion that allows them to view their adversaries as morally depraved. The Old Testament god Yahweh, for example, is essentially a god bent upon war, revenge, and punishment.

The New Testament religion of Jesus is, in contrast, the religion of a subordinate people under the Roman Empire. Here the salvation ethic rather than justification of war is paramount. The self-esteem and honour of disprivileged people rest on a promise for the future and on their significance in the eyes of a divine authority who has values different from those of the world. For such people, breakaway sects and cults of heroes and saints have special appeal.

The Distinctive Religion of the Capitalist Class

Weber's most famous study in the sociology of religion, *The Protestant Ethic and the Spirit of Capitalism* ([1904] 1930), explores in depth the ethic of the business class in Europe. Weber observed that members of the business class in Europe were disproportionately adherents of a puritanical Calvinist form of Protestantism, even though the dominant religion of Europe at that time was Catholicism. The religious dogma of **Calvinism** advocated a sober, frugal style of living, and prohibited alcohol, dancing, and luxuries. It also stressed a disciplined obligation to work as a means to serve God. The Calvinist conception of God was of a harsh, all-knowing, all-powerful being, incomprehensible to humans. From the assumption that God knew in advance who would be damned, and who saved, came the doctrine of **predestination**. There could be no salvation through the church or magical sacraments or human actions, only through grace. Such beliefs generated intense psychological feelings of insecurity and concern with finding indications of whether one might be among the damned or the blessed. Success in economic activities came to be seen as pre-eminently a sign of God's grace, while poverty or failure was a measure of lack of moral fervour and of damnation.

Such ideas, Weber argues, provided unique encouragement to capitalism. Work was a duty, and amassing wealth a sign of grace, but self-indulgence or spending such wealth on idle consumption was a sign of damnation. Hence, the only moral option was to invest wealth in expanding business. The Catholic Church of the period forbade usury, or lending money with interest, as profiting from the distress of others, but Calvinism supported it as morally proper business behaviour.

Weber does not address the issue of whether Calvinist religion promoted capitalism or capitalism promoted Calvinism. Rather, he speaks of an *elective affinity* between the two. By elective affinity, Weber means the mutual attraction between the business lifestyle and the **Protestant ethic**, the tendency for this kind of ethic to promote behaviour and values conducive to good business practices, and the propensity for people who spend their lives in business to be attracted to this kind of moral teaching. Business people were drawn to, and stimulated by, the ethic of work as a duty and economic success as a sign of grace. This ethic provided a moral justification for wealth. Poverty, on the other hand, was a sign of moral depravity, and to help the poor would be akin to helping the devil. Such dogma justified harsh and punitive treatment of destitute people to force them to become more industrious and self-sufficient.

"Where in heaven's name does he get these bizarre 'left wing' notions? 'The meek shall inherit the earth,' indeed!"

© Punch/Rothco

The old Calvinist faith equating wealth with God's grace, and poverty with damnation, may not strike us as credible today. But these ideas have contemporary parallels in moralistic interpretations of poverty. In his recent study of religious charities in Canada, Burman (1996, 69–83) found the pervasive attitude that people in need of charity are spiritually and humanly flawed, with service providers viewing themselves as having a duty to correct, to discipline, and to help the poor overcome their shortcomings. Those who came for food without willingly accepting the sermons about thrift and the work ethic were widely disparaged.

Puritanism and the Working Class Calvinist doctrines held little appeal outside the business class. It was **Methodism** that spread the puritan message to the working classes in Europe. Puritanism as a general philosophy advocated scrupulous moral behaviour and extreme strictness in adherence to details of religious practice. Many forms of spontaneous enjoyment and leisure, including parties, dancing, and especially sex, were seen as sinful and were either banned or very strictly controlled. Methodist tracts stressed the sinfulness of youth, the threat of eternal damnation, and the state of humans as blind, fallen, helpless sinners, but for divine grace. These doctrines translated into an extremely harsh edict of repression and inhibition: "A more appalling system of religious terrorism, one more fitted to unhinge a tottering intellect and to darken and embitter a sensitive nature, has seldom existed" (Thompson 1963, 410, quoting Lecky 1891).

The Marxist historian E.P. Thompson (1963, Ch. 11) leaves no doubt that the puritanical doctrines embodied in Methodism fit the Marxist vision of religion as imposing on the masses the values of the dominant capitalist class. The religious discipline of Methodism was very effective in controlling the industrial working class. The major problem for employers during the early stages of industrialization was the immense resistance of workers to the unnatural and hateful restraints of machine-paced work. What was needed, from the employers' viewpoint, was education not only in methodical habits, but also in punctilious attention to instructions, fulfillment of contracts on time, and the sinfulness of embezzling materials. Mere wage payment could never secure "zealous service." An inner compulsion was needed, and this is what Methodism provided.

The question still to be answered is how the repressive doctrines of Methodism came to appeal to wide sections of the working class. Thompson (1963, 391) argues that Methodism spread among the poor because it stressed spiritual egalitarianism and religion of the heart rather than the intellect. The simplest and least educated might attain grace through sincere repentance and forgiveness of sin. This forgiveness, however, was always conditional and provisory, lasting only so long as the penitent went and sinned no more. Perpetual service to the church itself and methodical discipline in all aspects of life were demanded. In return, membership within the Methodist church provided a kind of community for people uprooted by the Industrial Revolution. The church offered much mutual aid, some recognition for sobriety, chastity, and piety, all values that contributed to family stability. It also provided an emotional opiate, not unlike the real opiates that were widely consumed during this period. Methodism offered religious consolation to people oppressed by war and the wretched conditions of industrial working-class life.

Fundamentalist churches in America continue to provide sanctuaries of solace and hope for racialized black people. Obama (2008) describes his own church, the Trinity United Church of Christ in Chicago, as a vibrant community whose pastor, Rev. Wright, preached a gospel message that focused on care for the sick, ministry to the needy, daycare services, scholarships, prison ministries, and outreach services for those suffering from HIV/AIDS. It is a community that cherishes stories of survival and freedom for oppressed people and, above all, offers "the audacity of hope." Church services vibrate with participants shouting, clapping, crying, screaming, and carrying the message of redemption and love to the rafters.

The Social Gospel in Canada

While Puritanical doctrines promoted quietism among the working masses, the institutional organization of Methodism provided a base for political mobilization. The chapels and the bible camps provided separate meeting places for workers and gave them experience in oratory and leadership. The institution of weekly penny collections for the chapel was the forerunner of union dues, providing a financial base for class action. The very success of Methodist theology in incorporating the poor contained the seeds of a more radical spiritual message, promoting an egalitarian, social justice fringe that embraced socialist doctrines of collective social responsibility. Socialist-Methodist leaders such as J.S. Woodsworth conducted extensive research into the appalling conditions of the poor in Winnipeg at the beginning of the twentieth century. What he saw convinced him that the churches could not hope to minister to the spiritual needs of the working classes without also caring for the physical conditions of their lives.

The **Social Gospel movement**, which flourished in Canada in the period between 1880 and 1920, stressed the links between Christianity and socialism (Allen 1975). The meaning of sin and salvation was translated in social rather than individual terms, so that social justice became central to the Christian message. Under the leadership of radical ministers from Methodist, Anglican, and Presbyterian churches, adherents of the Social Gospel promoted trade unions and lobbied for the Lord's Day Observance Act to grant Sundays off for workers. By 1913, the church union became the Social Services Council of Canada, which was active in the provision of schools, libraries, savings banks, nurseries, and clubrooms for the working classes.

By the 1920s, however, the Social Gospel movement was in decline. Orthodox sectors of the churches withdrew their support, especially after the Russian Revolution and the Winnipeg General Strike. They feared growing labour power and strikes. Methodists as a whole grew richer and tended to place more stress on individualism and entrepreneurship than collective responsibility. Within the establishment churches the Social Gospel movement retreated to a radical fringe role. The spirit of the movement found more direct political expression of the Prairies in the formation of the Co-operative Commonwealth Federation (CCF) led by Woodsworth and Tommy Douglas, a Baptist minister turned political reformer. The CCF later became the New Democratic Party.

Churches in America that minister to predominantly black members still continue to function as centres for political protest and social activism. Reverend Wright, pastor of the Trinity United Church of Christ that Barack Obama attended in Chicago, gained notoriety for his fiery speeches condemning endemic racism at home and brutal militarism abroad. "God damn America for killing innocent people," he raged after the 9/11 terrorist attack. "America's chickens have come home to roost!" Obama (2008) distanced himself from the incendiary rhetoric, but also defended the pastor, noting that leaders of churches serving black congregations across America share a similar rage at the failure of American society to live up to the moral code entrenched in the United States Constitution. Wright's error, Obama declared, is not in his rage against racism, but in seeing American society as static and unable to change.

Religion and Class Conflict: Establishment Churches and the Radical Fringe

The history of Methodism in Canada reflects the inherently contradictory relations between religious institutions and class conflict. On the one hand mainstream Puritan doctrines clearly supported dominant class interests, but these doctrines were open to reinterpretation to support the political aspirations and protests of the subordinate working class. The Catholic Church has similarly been the centre of class struggle and conflicting scriptural interpretations, with a radical fringe that supported **liberation theology** and subversive workers' movements, but for the most part associated with dominant colonial rulers.

The scriptural interpretation of Genesis that gave rise to the "Hamitic hypothesis" in Rwanda is clearly traceable to the political interests of Belgian colonial rulers seeking to promote a buffer group between themselves and the Hutu majority (Masire 2000). According to this hypothesis, the numerically dominant Bantu tribespeople, the Hutu, were descendants of Noah's younger son Ham, cursed by his father to be a "servant of servants . . . unto his brethren" (Genesis 9:25), while Tutsi were descendants of the favoured son Shem. This interpretation, widely propounded by Belgian missionaries in Rwandan churches and church-run schools, legitimated the colonial government's favouring of Tutsi as local administrators, subordinating the Hutu. The bitter resentment generated by such a racist interpretation of scriptures played a role in provoking and legitimating the genocidal slaughtering of some 800 000 people within about 100 days, the victims mostly ethnic Tutsi, along with many moderate Hutu. In June 2001, two Benedictine nuns from the Hutu majority were convicted in Belgian court of war crimes for assisting the Hutu militia in a mass killing.

In Canada the Catholic and Protestant churches also served the interests of colonial rulers, legitimating the cultural destruction of Native communities and their assimilation through church-run schools. The Catholic and United churches of the twenty-first century in Canada have little difficulty in accommodating Native spirituality, or in seeing the Native vision of a Great Creator as compatible with the Christian message of a universal loving God. Yet a century ago Native spirituality was denounced as primitive and pagan, and its adherents seen as "lost souls" doomed to eternal damnation unless the church saved them.

In Latin America the institutional Catholic Church has become integrally implicated in class conflict, with priests sometimes finding themselves on opposite sides in violent civil wars. Marchak's (1999) study of the church in Argentina describes how the Catholic Church, as the state religion, is aligned with the wealthy landowning and capitalist class. It functions openly to legitimate a succession of military governments, institutionalized by the Vatican's authorization of separate diocese for military chaplains (Marchak 1999, 253). A strong affinity was forged between conservative Catholic values and the military, founded on shared commitment to the preservation of order. This support remained strong right through the period of state terrorism during the 1970s and '80s, when some 30 000 citizens disappeared and thousands more were tortured in state-run concentration camps throughout the country. The central moral legitimation for this terror was the need for social cohesion after years of guerrilla war. The establishment church was oriented to the moral concerns of stability, order, discipline, community, authority, and obedience. Marchak argues that it was the support of the majority of the Argentinean people for such values that made a military government acceptable and state terrorism possible.

Back in the 1960s, and especially under the influence of the Second Vatican Council of 1968, this tight institutional linkage between the church, the landowning oligarchy, and the military had come under pressure from a small radical movement of priests inspired by doctrines of liberation theology. This doctrine interprets concepts of salvation, sin, and conversion in social rather than individual terms, inspired by the social covenant of the Old Testament between God and the people of Israel in which God fulfills the promise to deliver the Israelites from bondage as a people. God is conceptualized as one who takes the side of the oppressed, the excluded, and the slaves, inspiring ministry committed to promoting change for social justice (Betto 1993; Baum 1979; 1981).

In Argentina as elsewhere, the priests inspired by liberation theology helped to support workers' movements and trade union struggles for better wages and conditions of work. During his first term in office in 1946, the populist leader Juan Peron frequently cited papal encyclicals and the social reform aspects of liberation theology to legitimate his government. But by the early '70s it was his centralized state, combining the military and elites within hierarchical, highly bureaucratized unions, which was being challenged. Peron authorized the persecution of these dissidents, ushering in the period of violent state terrorism known as "the dirty war." The liberation theology movement was always marginalized within the main body of the church. By 1975 it was silenced by the Catholic hierarchy in Rome, and the priests attacked as subversive communists. Sixteen priests in all were murdered, including their most outspoken leader, Padre Mugica, while others were imprisoned and tortured.

Parallels to Argentina's "dirty war" can be found in other countries in Latin America. Guatemala is just emerging from a brutal civil war lasting from 1960 to the peace accord of 1996. In June 2001, a tribunal found a priest and three military men guilty of the 1998 slaying of an activist Roman Catholic bishop. Bishop Gerardi was bludgeoned to death at his Guatemala City seminary two days after he presented a report blaming the military for most of the killings and disappearances of that country's civil war (*Globe and Mail*, 9 June 2001, A15).

Across Latin America the workers' movements and liberation theology were associated with communist subversion, denounced by the Vatican as promoting atheistic Marxism. Within communist Poland, however, similar workers' movements were openly supported by the Vatican and the institutionalized Catholic Church as working to undermine communism.

In America the "Christian right," comprising networks of conservative Protestant churches, have long formed a solid voting block for the Republican Party. In 1996 they formed an estimated 7 percent of the population, but

24 percent of registered voters, and 60 percent of these voted Republican (Diamond 1998). The Christian Right political platform favoured strong law-and-order policies, supported expanding police and military financing, stressed obedience to authority as a central value, favoured school prayers, corporal discipline of children, and traditional "family values," including favouring tax advantages for stay-at-home mothers. They opposed sex education in schools, opposed gay rights, and strongly opposed abortion rights. Historically they supported McCarthy's anti-communist campaigns and attacks on liberal clergy. They denounced communism and Antichrist, as threatening the spread of Christian evangelism globally, and as threatening free-enterprise capitalist business interests. Former American president George W. Bush identified himself strongly with the Christian Right (Singer 2004). Religious leaders like Pat Robertson and Billy Graham campaigned hard for him, exhorting Christians to consider Bush the candidate that God endorsed.

Revivalist meetings in the USA are typically so large that they need to be held in a sports arena.

© Julian Calder/CORBIS

The Christian Right established a huge media empire in America to promote its conservative message. Pat Robertson's Christian Broadcasting Network (CBN) opened in 1961, and by 1997 had 257 television stations. Robertson's Family Channel cable reached into an estimated 59 million households, with weekly audiences of 2 million people. By 1994, sales of books from Christian bookstores were valued at $70.5 million. And Contemporary Christian Music (CCM) comprised about 10 percent of the entire American music industry, valued at more than $1 billion. The Christian media empire cross-promotes its products by radio, television, books, and evangelical magazines and newspapers.

Conclusion

In conclusion, religion is centrally concerned with issues of power and with the moral basis of people's obligations to society (Burridge 1969, 4–7). The earlier functionalist argument suggests both that religion makes sacred the social order, and that it forms a critical base for personal identification with a social group. Religious doctrines provide orientations through which to justify, to accept, and more rarely to challenge the principles of order. New religions or new interpretations of doctrine emerge, Burridge suggests, during periods of social unrest when these principles are called into question. In societies that are inegalitarian, where members are differentially situated in relations of power and authority, access to, and control over critical material resources, and stratified along race, ethnic, and gender lines, religious doctrines cannot avoid concern with power. Pacifism or an inward-looking focus on spiritual individualism in a context of an inegalitarian social order necessarily condones and supports that inequality. Doctrines of spiritual equality and social justice challenge that order.

Social Constructionist Perspective on Religious Experience

Social constructionist analysis focuses on religious experience as ongoing accomplishment rather than as existing institution. Religion is conceptualized as continually brought into being and sustained as meaningful experience through the discourses and the active practices of adherents. From this perspective, the descriptive generalizations of both functionalist and political economy perspectives are rephrased as questions of process. Beginning from Durkheim's struggle to establish a definition of religion, one can ask:

How do people negotiate and sustain for themselves and for others the sense that what they are doing constitutes "religion" and not something else? How do people accomplish and sustain a sense that they share a certain religious identity as a community of believers? How do people accomplish a sense of the sacredness of activities over the merely "mundane"? How do people negotiate and sustain for themselves and for others a sense of well-being through religious activity in the face of disappointment, suffering, illness, and death? How do people reinforce and sustain for each other a sense of the salience of specifically "religious" identity over other possible cultural markers, and how does such salience become politicized as a focus for community action? How do people accomplish shifts in interpretation of religious meanings from support for the status quo to support for protest and rebellion?

In short, social constructionist analysis requires that we stand outside the taken-for-granted character of established religious institutions to explore how it is that their sacredness emerges. To date, such research has tended to focus more on newer and more marginal forms of religious expression rather than mainstream churches. This section draws extensively on studies of Aboriginal spirituality and fundamentalist Christian sects and cults.

Recognizing "Religion" as Practical Accomplishment

Aboriginal peoples have had to struggle for everything that adherents of mainstream religions within Canada have been able to take for granted. They have struggled to win recognition of their practices as "religion," to have their sacredness understood, and to bring a new sense of religious identity into being. Historically, Aboriginal spiritual practices were not seen by European colonizers as religious observances, but rather as primitive and even barbaric practices that presented obstacles to spiritual salvation. Successive amendments to the Indian Act outlawed important aspects of potlatch ceremonies and spirit dancing. Christian missions were authorized to remove Aboriginal children from their communities and educate them in residential schools where only Christianity was recognized as religion. Aboriginal communities were commonly pushed aside as Euro-Canadian settlements and industrialization expanded, and their people relocated to reserves or to urban areas. Much of the knowledge of Aboriginal spiritual traditions was lost.

It was in this social context of cultural anomie, traumatized communities, and wounded people that Aboriginal spiritual leaders in the 1970s began their work of recreating positive and meaningful Aboriginal spiritual identity. In this recreation process, they have had to draw upon fragmented memories of elders, somehow preserved and transmitted despite the disruptive forces of colonization, and the truncated ceremonies held in secret and in isolated communities where colonization came late. These oral cultures have no sacred texts preserved in libraries that could be studied. Neither was there ever a single pan-Aboriginal culture to use as a model. In Canada alone there are over 11 different Aboriginal language families, encompassing over 300 distinctive languages.

The reclaiming of Aboriginal spirituality therefore involves complex processes of borrowing, adaptation, interpretation, reconstitution, and creation. In this process the scholarly discourses of social sciences have functioned both as resources and as impediments. On the positive side, ethnographic studies of Aboriginal cultures by anthropologists provide descriptions of lost traditions. On the negative side, classical functionalist conceptions of "tradition" and "religion" posits them as relatively invariant systems of thought and action specific to particular social systems. From this viewpoint, evidence of change, borrowing, and adaptation, and of the recent post-colonial origins of certain supposedly sacred myths, prompt challenges that they are inauthentic, made up by the storytellers, or not really native. Such challenges have invoked intense and angry debate involving scholars and Aboriginal peoples who feel that their professional competence and/or their religious identities are under attack (Parkhill 1997; Paper 1993; Clifton 1990). The social constructionist perspective, in contrast, views all traditions not as entities but as ongoing accomplishments. References to historical origins are themselves social constructions, certain agreed ways of evaluating social practices.

The struggle for recognition of Aboriginal spirituality as religion became politicized in the early 1980s when a few Aboriginal inmates began to pressure Corrections Services Canada for permission to hold a pipe ceremony and a sweat-lodge ceremony inside a prison (Waldram 1997, 11). Canadian law guarantees all prisoners the right to practice their faith. The problem was that Aboriginal ceremonies were not regarded as religious. The warden of Kent prison in BC argued that a permit would be needed for an eagle feather under wildlife protection regulations, the pipe was a potential weapon, the medicine bundle was suspicious and would have to stay with the warden, the sweat lodge was a security risk, and the burning of sweetgrass and sage would not be permitted in the cells. It took the combined efforts of a pending Charter challenge, a 34-day spiritual fast by prisoners that attracted media attention, and a talking circle organized by a Métis psychologist, before the warden could be convinced that Aboriginal practices did constitute a religion. It still took another seven months before the first ever sweat-lodge ceremony was held in a Canadian prison.

Through the harmony of sacred earthen and wooden pipe and human breath, purifying smoke rises as prayer to the Creator.

Meanwhile the ringleaders at the Kent Institution were branded as troublemakers, separated, and transferred to other prisons. Rather than quietening them, however, they spread the protest movement to other prisons.

As part of their struggle to have the pipe ceremony recognized as religious, elders felt obliged to call on the professional services of an ethnographer to claim that the pipe-smoking ritual was pan-Indian and more than 2000 years old (Paper 1993, 369). Eventually, by 1988, six years after the Charter of Rights and Freedoms came into force in Canada, the Solicitor General's Office officially recognized the pipe ceremony and the sweat lodge as forms of religious practice, with constitutional protection. Elders were deemed spiritual advisors analogous to Christian chaplains.

Struggles for recognition still continue. The practice of Aboriginal spirituality within prisons is hampered by pressures to conform to Euro-Canadian standards, which expect religious ceremonies to take one hour on Sunday mornings, and maybe an evening prayer meeting in one specific room in prison. Such expectations do not encompass Aboriginal ceremonies that require participation in natural outdoor surroundings, the preparation of food and sweat lodges, and periods of fasting that last from a few hours to four days (Waldram 1997, 17). Elders also complain of having their sacred pipes and medicine bundles violated by prison searches, and of sweat-lodge ceremonies being interrupted by prison drills. It was 1996 before policy guidelines recommended that involvement in Aboriginal ceremonies and healing programs in prisons should count equally with participation in mainstream programs for parole hearings.

Negotiating "Authentic" Religious Identities

Debates over what constitutes "authentic" religious tradition are not unique to Aboriginal spirituality. Mennonite leaders and scholars adopted a functionalist perspective when they tried to define "What is a Mennonite" for their bicentenary celebrations in Ontario (Winland 1993). They succeeded only in generating divisive arguments around competing interpretations, highlighting the reality that there is not, and never was, a clear Anabaptist heritage (Waldram 1997, 118–119). Historical research revealed a plurality of Mennonite origins, continuous migration, and multiple instances of conflict and schism over issues of faith and culture. Privileging any one example as definitive risked alienating adherents to all the other options. In ways directly analogous to the Aboriginal experience, the demand for authenticity did not fit with the dynamic character of lived cultural experience. Mennonite unity, Winland suggests, depends on vagueness and flexibility in definitions. Mennonite doctrines and practices became broadly stretched to encompass lifestyle changes from isolated village communities to diversified and urbanized professionals. The core ideal of "community" was transformed from a bounded geographic social entity to a symbolic or virtual community of believers scattered across North America and beyond.

Winland's research revealed that how individuals expressed their sense of their own Mennonite identity varied with the context in which they found themselves and the form in which questions are asked. When the concern was with evangelizing and recruiting new members, they tended to focus on Anabaptist doctrines, but when the context of discussion was their everyday lives, they were more likely to describe their Mennonite identity with reference to German or Russian ethnic roots, their heritage language, and their kin and friendship networks. Non-believers often still identified themselves as Mennonites on the basis of such social ties. Vietnamese refugees or "boat people" lived the contradiction between doctrine and ethnicity. Many became converts after Mennonites helped them to enter Canada. But while accepted as believers they felt marginalized by the ethnic clannishness of congregation members.

Negotiating Sacred Meanings

Religious symbols and rituals are not automatically experienced as sacred. They must be continually reinforced among a community of believers. Aboriginal spiritual leaders had to teach the symbolic meanings of traditional objects and practices to people who had little if any direct knowledge of the spirituality of their ancestors, and who commonly experienced their communities as deeply traumatized by anger, alcoholism, and violence. The people Waldram describes had spent much of their lives in and out of prison, and were surrounded by white society and prison authorities who saw nothing of religious value in the feathers, pipes, herbs, and bundles that spiritual elders brought with them.

Elders began by telling stories, revealing the symbolism behind the objects and gestures to Aboriginals and to others who showed interest, and repeating the meanings as they used them in ceremonies. The sacredness of the pipe, with its earthen bowl and wooden stem and the feathers that adorn it, lies in its symbolic representation of the unity of earth and living things, and the purification of the smoke, brought into harmony through human breath. Sweetgrass, woven into three strands, represents the unity between mind, body, and spirit, while the rising smoke purifies the body and joins with the sun and the wind to carry one's prayers to the Creator. The sweat lodge represents the womb of mother earth, and the rocks and the steam the coming of life and the creative force of the universe. Together they bring the hope of renewal and rebirth—the chance to cleanse body and mind of anger and failure, to welcome the coolness of air when the door opens—four times, in each direction of the universe, the hope to begin again. In the sacred fasts, and the intense exhilaration of spirit dancing, to experience the power to overcome hunger, thirst, exhaustion, and pain, to give sacrifice to the Creator, and to find strength for the life ahead.

The sense of their sacredness was created slowly from teaching the symbolic meanings and especially from teaching their connection with Aboriginal ancestry. While these ceremonies are open to all who seek them, they carry the very special symbolism for peoples of Aboriginal descent in that they honour the religions of their ancestors, stretching back to times long before colonialism shattered their communities and their cultures, enfolding them in the spirituality of their grandmothers and grandfathers, the ancient ones who went before them. In honouring their ancestors they also give honour and respect to each other. This more positive valuing of self, Waldram suggests, was centrally important in the life-changing experiences for prison inmates who participated in Aboriginal ceremonies. For many this was the first time their ethnic identity had been positively valued.

The situation of fundamentalist Christians could hardly seem more different from that of Aboriginal spiritual leaders. No Canadian officials would challenge the status of the Bible as sacred text in the same way that Aboriginal medicine bundles have been challenged. Yet research into fundamentalist Christian congregations in North America makes vividly evident how issues of relevance, meaning, and interpretation are continually negotiated as matters of everyday practical lives. Fundamentalists assert as a matter of basic doctrine their certainty that the Bible, specifically the King James Version, is the literal word of God, not human imagination (Ammerman 1987, 51). It is considered totally correct, including in matters of geography, history, and science. These claims are widely contested and need to be continually defended in relations with non-members.

Within the community of believers, the sacredness and the literalness of the Bible can be taken as given, but the meanings that can be read into specific verses, and how particular verses get to be selectively applied to specific concerns, is highly flexible and personalized. These meanings and their applications are continually negotiated. Verses can have different meanings and relevances for different individuals, and for the same individual in different situations. A preacher is expected to cite biblical verses to demonstrate that everything he says are God's words, which congregants are encouraged to read in their personal Bibles as he preaches. But his active interpretation of which phrases to apply to which issues is considered a highly creative and admired skill. Individual church members are also expected to regularly display for each other through verbal witnessing how a line of scripture they may have read earlier in the week can be seen as insightful for something that happened to them (Ammerman 1987, Ch. 4). Such witnessing actively displays how a variety of meanings can be read into any biblical verse, especially when cited out of context. Witnessing does not merely display knowledge of the Bible. It actively constructs and sustains for fellow believers their faith that the Bible is indeed relevant for their lives.

The work of interpreting and sustaining symbolic meanings is essentially social, generated through fellowship with others who share similar worldviews (Ammerman 107; Berger 1967, 21–22). Weekly prayer meetings provide a context in which individuals learn how others translate events in their lives into biblical language, and apply verses to support their interpretations and actions. Members routinely draw on hindsight to discern patterns and purposes not visible to them at the time, but that can be interpreted in retrospect to confirm that God's plan worked for them in the past, and thus can be relied upon in the present. Much "ideological work" is required to make beliefs fit circumstances.

Sustaining Religious Identities

Aboriginal spiritual leaders, or elders, working in prisons emphasized to Waldram that fostering a sense of positive Aboriginal cultural identity was the first step in a spiritual path. Individuals did not normally become involved in Aboriginal ceremonies because they expected spiritual healing to come out of them. They were usually curious initially to learn more about Aboriginal cultures, to show solidarity with other Aboriginal "brothers," and to work out their own often negative feelings about their Aboriginal ancestry (Waldram 1997, Ch. 4). Elders started by offering educational workshops and presentations to inmates about Aboriginal traditions. Then they would teach the meaning of various ceremonies by explaining them as they were performed. As they gradually got individuals interested enough to come to meetings regularly. they offered extensive individual counselling to develop deeper understanding of spiritual meanings. The sense of belonging to the group comes first, they suggested, and then an intensive process of working together and supporting each other to develop a more positive sense of their Aboriginal heritage and to overcome the embarrassment and shame that many had experienced. Only then could spiritual growth begin.

Analogous processes of developing a positive identity and sense of belonging sustain spiritual growth as fundamentalist Christians. Gathering in small groups for weekly prayer meetings is especially powerful at strengthening identification with fundamentalism, Searl suggests (1994), in that the activity of prayers combine nurturing support to members with continual reinforcement of symbolic meanings. The Jesus story is personalized for participants multiple times over, week after week, as each in turn links the selected text to some event in their lives. These exercises demonstrate repeatedly how to see Jesus as present in their daily lives, thus validating their faith and beliefs. Participants also share their concerns, worries about health, employment, housing, family problems, and beyond, and weave them into prayers that they commit to say for each other throughout the week. At the next meeting, each of the concerns for which prayers have been offered is discussed again. Each member knows that some 20 other people are remembering them in individual prayers throughout the week. These prayer and Bible-study groups affirm each member's identity as a fundamentalist Christian, and insulate them from the ridicule they often face from non-believers.

Spiritual Healing as Transformation in Symbolic Meanings

The institution of religion is commonly associated in functionalist analysis with tension-management, functioning to hold communities together in the face of disappointments, suffering, illness, and death. How does this come about? How do people create and sustain for themselves and others a sense of well-being through "having faith" or "being religious"? For Aboriginal elders, it was the intensely social processes of learning and sharing new symbolic meanings that empowered sacred ceremonies to bring healing to the traumatized lives of inmates (Waldram 1997, 74–80). Symbolic healing involves processes of interpretation, negotiation, and manipulation of cultural meanings so as to radically transform how people understood their own suffering, and therefore how it might be changed. They translated symptoms of alcoholism, drug abuse, violence, suicides, and despair within Aboriginal communities from evidence of personal failures to evidence of colonialism and

oppression. The healing power of this spiritual redefinition of experience works at both the community and the individual level. An Aboriginal inmate described the rage he carried towards his father as he remembered him savagely beating his mother during alcoholic binges, and raping his sisters. Most of the families around him suffered similarly as parents, and children in turn sank into alcoholism and violence. Immersion in Aboriginal spirituality brought a sense of forgiveness—both for his father and himself, as the past gained new symbolic meaning as an expression of the deadness and evil his people carried inside (Waldram 1997, 47). This transformation in understanding opened up the hope of achieving a new sense of peace and pride in their Aboriginal identity and therefore in each other. Healing, the elders argued, involved a lifelong process of integrating individuals into a religious community, and mutually supporting each other in accepting the symbolic meanings. This acceptance in turn depended heavily on the personal examples of the elders themselves, many of whom had overcome histories of rage, violence, addictions, and prison to transform their lives.

In ways closely analogous to Aboriginal spirituality, fundamentalist Christians continually reinforce ways of talking about suffering in biblical terms. Church members repeatedly encourage each other to offer personal testimonies about misfortunes in ways that link them to God's plan, either as punishment for sin, as the devil's work in testing the faithful, or as God's way of using their suffering as living proof for others of how trusting in the Lord inspired them to triumph over it (Ammerman 1987, Ch. 4). Such witnessing wins high status and recognition from listeners, who offer comfort through ritualized praying aloud for the afflicted. Silent members are even urged to offer such testimonials lest God send them something worse to worry about.

In the Chinese fundamentalist church the preacher drew direct links between their experiences of suffering, both through the tumultuous Chinese history and in their everyday lives, with the suffering of Christ (Yang 1998). Members knew what it was like to be ridiculed by the media, their colleagues, and even their family members for their fundamentalist beliefs—their biblical literalism, avoidance of alcohol, dancing, and the like. The preacher cited the verse from John 16:33: "You will have trouble in this world" as the basis for his sermon on suffering, reminding congregants how Jesus suffered and died for his church and how his disciples were persecuted and hated by their contemporaries. He concluded by challenging his listeners: "Are you willing to suffer for the Lord? . . . Those who suffer for the Lord will be blessed by the Lord."

When conceptualized in such terms, suffering leads to salvation. A number of new converts spoke of how comforting they found these stories of suffering, sin, and salvation, especially those weighed down with feelings of guilt and shame about their former lives. It was precisely through their shame and redemption that they could see themselves as transformed into powerful witnesses to others of God's healing love.

Storytelling as Ideological Work

Storytelling is common to all these accounts of spiritual healing. Singleton (2001) identifies storytelling as the central process through which people create and sustain religious culture. When people tell a story they necessarily order events in a particular way, draw connections, attribute causality, and bring closure to experience. Understood in this way, language does not merely describe external events, it brings experience into being by making it meaningful. Stories about faith healing told by Pentecostal believers are designed to rebut the arguments of skeptics and support their view that "what really happened" was miraculous. Typically they tell of cases where expert medical healers declared themselves powerless to treat the illness, but friends and relatives prayed and the patient somehow recovered, to the astonishment of doctors. The physical healing is also presented as not merely arbitrary but purposive, helping to further God's work of winning doubters to faith in the Lord.

The way such stories are told varies with the audience. When witnessed before receptive church audiences they are offered as demonstrable proof of the existence of God. They work to sustain the practice of praying for miraculous healing while also creating for the congregation the reality of the healing powers of prayer. Singleton concludes that praying for miraculous healing is a key religious ritual in Pentecostal and Charismatic churches, and storytelling is an essential part of the ritual. Narratives create an interpretive order for events that ascribe religious causality and counter skepticism.

Symbolic Repair Work When Prophecies Fail

Inevitably prayers are not always answered in ways that supplicants wish. Sick people die, evil seems to prevail over good, and prophecies fail. The forms in which stories are told must accommodate and interpret these realities in ways that sustain the faith. One of the strategies is to bracket or close off events under discussion so that they are relatively unaffected by future outcomes. Singleton gives the example of a faith-healing story where a relative miraculously recovered from cancer and was able to travel widely afterwards and to witness to her church on the power of prayer. When she later died of cancer, despite more prayers, the storyteller

comments: "I think God wanted to take her" (Singleton 2001, 134). Through the telling of the story, it is God who takes her, and not the cancer, and the conviction that she was healed earlier remains unchallenged. Hindsight can also be used to demonstrate that prayers were answered, although in ways that the supplicant did not understand at the time. Someone fails to get a job after intensive praying, but later something better turns up, or the job turns out to have had negative features that God knowingly shielded them from (Ammerman 1987, 60). Faith in God and in the power of prayer is not shaken.

Prophecies that fail can be similarly renegotiated through strategies that retroactively guide a better understanding of God's plan. Many cult members and fundamentalist Christians took very seriously the Y2K prediction that computers would massively fail as the last two digits of the date changed from 99 to 00 with the coming of the second millennium (Tapia 2002). Some likened it to prophecies in the Book of Revelations that catastrophe and social chaos would presage the rule of the Antichrist before the second coming of Christ and the final battle between Evil and Good. Computers and satellite technology was likened to the biblical Tower of Babel that God destroyed as a punishment for man's pride. In January 2000, after nothing untoward happened, the people who believed the prophecies handled the dissonance in a variety of ways. Some argued that the year 2000 was not yet over so things might yet happen, that there had been some problems, that people had been inspired to come together and to make good lifestyle changes to become less dependent on technology, which was what God had wanted, and that the prayers of the faithful had been answered by God in postponing the punishment of the world. Again, faith in God's plan and in biblical literalism was not challenged.

Cults that have predicted the landing of flying saucers present an extreme example of the power of unfalsifiable belief, but their strategies for reconciling false prophecies with evidence are similar (Tumminia 1998). The original prophecies had been misinterpreted by the media; a flying saucer did land but it was spirited away by the US military and its occupants killed; or that space beings had been trying to communicate to the prophetess about murderous experiences thousands of years earlier when they had previously visited earth, urging her and her followers to prepare themselves better before the space visitors dare come again.

Politicizing Religious Beliefs

The Y2K experience reminds us that religious prophecy does not occur in a vacuum. People accomplish religious practices and symbolic meanings as part of much broader social and cultural relations, and with varying access to material and symbolic resources. The links drawn between computer failure and the Book of Revelation may be peculiar to certain fundamentalist Christians, but the fears around technological dependence and the awesome power it gives to those who control it are far more widespread. Millennialism also speaks to a profound criticism of the evils of contemporary society. The form that such criticism takes may be different but the concerns resonate far beyond fundamentalist congregations.

Fundamentalist Christians find their vision of the good society places them at odds with what they see as the chaos and sinfulness of the world around them. Their claims to authentic spirituality have frequently become politicized, as around the issue of teaching creationism alongside evolutionism in school science programs. The appeal of creationism, even to those who do not accept it as dogma, is that it places the special relationship between humanity and God above science-driven materialism. Fundamentalists have found strong allies among those favouring a strong law-and-order, and family-values political agenda. The influence of the religious right in American politics is much wider than their numbers of committed adherents would suggest.

Aboriginal spirituality is also inherently political, both in the critique of the historical and contemporary status of Aboriginal peoples as First Nations within Canada, and the critique of the exploitative relationship that mainstream Christian culture has with the natural world. The Mi'qmac people of Nova Scotia drew on religious symbolism in 1989 to challenge proposals for a gravel pit on Kelly Mountain, arguing that the plan would desecrate a sacred site for their religion, a cave associated with their mythical hero Glooscap (Hornborg 1994). In this conflict, claims and counterclaims to spiritual authenticity were highly politicized. Each claim implicitly articulated different conceptions of the "good" society, and hence was inherently about relations of power, even when these were not spelled out. The mining corporation maintained that it primarily wanted to help local people by providing 100 new jobs. It never acknowledged the legitimacy of the claims made about the cave, giving only economic reasons for withdrawing its proposal. The Aboriginal community as a whole, along with environmentalists, claimed authentic spirituality in defending Kelly Mountain against corrupt, materialistic corporate white culture. Hornborg suggests that the Mi'qmac people generally showed little interest in the cave itself, either before or after the confrontation. Its primary importance was as symbol of a different spiritual relationship to the mountain.

Claims to spiritual authenticity were subject to continual and often acrimonious negotiation, not only between Mi'qmac and white society, but also between many levels of the Mi'qmac community itself. The traditional Grand Council claimed a greater authenticity to speak for Mi'qmac spirituality than elected band chiefs whom they characterized as corrupt. The band council in turn was split, with those who adopted traditional spirituality claiming greater authenticity than corrupt Catholics. Among the traditionalists, the Mi'qmac Warriors claimed greater authenticity than corrupt "pacifists." Each level down attacked the next level up as illegitimate, selling out in return for resources. The Kelly Mountain confrontation gave a welcome opportunity for the Mi'qmac to cohere around a common external target.

The struggle to create and sustain religious institutions always takes place within a wider societal context that affords markedly uneven access to resources. The Canadian Charter of Rights and Freedoms enshrines the principles of religious freedom in a multicultural Canada, and gives explicit legal recognition to the status and treaty rights of Aboriginal peoples. This significantly alters the dynamics of confrontations such as that over Kelly Mountain. The official policy of multiculturalism in Canada also alters the dynamics of struggles by immigrants to create religious institutions that reflect traditions from their homelands.

Mass Media and Transnational Religious Politics

Religious television programs have come to play an increasing role in the representation of faith traditions, especially for ethnic minority traditions. Gillespie (2000) describes the enormous impact, in India and Britain, of the four-year-long serialization of sacred Hindu epics Mahabharata and Ramayana on Indian state television between 1988 and 1992. In India alone these "sacred soaps" attracted estimated audiences of between 80 and 100 million viewers, with tens of millions more in the Hindu diasporas throughout the world. Hindu viewers in Britain spoke of the close connection they felt with relatives in India as they imagined them watching the same series. Many felt it as a devotional act, ritually purifying themselves prior to watching each episode. They were also a highly critical audience, rejecting the more secularized British version as an offensive misunderstanding of the moral teachings inherent in the epic dramas. The Hindi-language version, with subtitles, was used by British families to teach both language and religious traditions to their children.

The dramas also carried powerful political messages, heightening religious consciousness and specifically Hindu nationalism, which could be exploited by Hindu nationalist political parties to mobilize anti-Muslim sentiments (Gillespie 2000, 171). One instance of this was the rioting that erupted in Ayodhia as Hindus vowed to replace a mosque with a Hindu temple on the supposed site of the birthplace of the God Rama. Hundreds of people, mostly Muslims, died in communal violence in January 1992, and Hindu/Muslim conflicts were heightened around the world.

Gillespie (2000, 172) describes how politicians in India used television to "reinvent tradition," appropriating the imagery and narratives of moral breakdown and impending social chaos in the Mahabharata to fit contemporary political struggles. In Britain also, the epic discourse of the fragility of social order, threats to moral order, and the importance of religious duty or dharma, inspired young people already angered by experiences of poverty and class and racial inequalities.

Building Religious Experience in the Diaspora

Immigrant community institutions are constructed in a global context of transnational relations and networks, and transnational conflicts. The experiences of Asian Buddhist religious communities in Toronto reflect just how great a difference such factors can make (McLellan 1999). Wealthy business-class immigrants from Hong Kong and Taiwan had the money and connections needed to establish more than 20 temples in Toronto alone, serviced by large numbers of ordained clergy. They also drew on international networks for professional advice and experience in coping with interfaith activities, and expressions of hostility and discrimination from neighbours. Cambodian refugees had none of these resources. They arrived in Canada severely traumatized by the brutality of the Khmer Rouge regime of 1975–79 followed by years in refugee camps. Fear pervades even their relations with fellow ethnic Cambodians as both victims and torturers of the Khmer Rouge regime find themselves living in close proximity, and even in the same apartment building in Toronto (McLellan 2001, lecture comments). They struggle to create some sense of Buddhist traditions in Toronto without any professional leadership, with limited education, low incomes, limited meeting spaces, no monks or nuns to give any professional leadership, deep-rooted fear of government agents, and no supportive networks to help in dealing with hostile neighbours who oppose renovations and parking spaces around their meeting areas (1999, 143). Religious and ethnic divisions limit even the support they receive from other Buddhist communities in the city.

Deep political fractions on a world scale impact on the immigrant religious communities in Canada. In cosmopolitan cities like Vancouver, Toronto, and Montreal, East Asian Muslim, Hindu, and Sikh religious communities struggle to coexist in the full knowledge of religious and sectarian violence between their communities of origin, as do the synagogues and mosques of peoples from the Middle East. The circumstances under which these peoples draw on religious symbolism to sustain and change individual and group identities as hyphenated Canadians is deeply politicized. Even the ostensibly simple and personal choice of a Muslim woman wearing or not wearing a headscarf has different and politically charged spiritual meaning after the September 11, 2001, terrorist attacks in New York and Washington. However old the roots of religious practices and symbolism may be in the historical past, their interpretation is always ongoing, involving the practical accomplishment of a spiritually meaningful life in the context of a fractured and violent world.

 # Feminist Perspectives: Religion as Gendered Politics

Feminist analysis focuses on how religious beliefs, practices, and institutional structures shape and are shaped by gender politics. The feminist struggle for gender equality engages with religion both as obstacle and as resource. As a central institution legitimating social order, religion is directly implicated in supporting **patriarchy**—patterns of social organization of gender and relations of reproduction in families that are often inegalitarian, exploitative, and oppressive. Religious discourses also constitute a resource on which women and men draw in giving meaning to their relations, and in forming conceptions of a "good" and "moral" society. As such, religion can mobilize people to challenge as well as to sacralize and accept established social order.

Religion and Patriarchy

Early feminist analysis of religion focused on women as objects in relation to religious beliefs and practices. Feminists were often stridently critical of mainstream religions as patriarchal institutions that have functioned for centuries to excuse and to actively promote the subordination of women to men, to confine women in narrowly prescribed "proper" roles, and to exact religiously sanctioned punishment on women who transgressed these roles.

Feminist critics of Judeo-Christian traditions find no shortage of historical and scriptural evidence (Daly 1973; Ruether 1975; Kolbenschlag 1979). Kolbenschlag documents how the Genesis story has readily been understood as ordaining women's proper subordination to men. Adam was created first and God speaks directly only to him. Adam has creative potency, with Eve created from his rib. Eve knows God's word only through her husband, and she is deceived by the serpent. Man is thus divinely sanctioned as family head and spiritual leader. Paul's letter to the Ephesians (5:22–24) states this bluntly: "Wives, submit yourself unto your own husbands . . . therefore as the church is subject unto Christ, so let the wives be to their own husbands in everything." According to Paul's letter to Timothy (1 Timothy 2:11–14), women's submission and silence in church is also divinely ordered: "Let the woman learn in silence with all subjection . . . I suffer not a woman to teach, nor to usurp authority over the man, but to be in silence. For Adam was first formed, then Eve. And Adam was not deceived, but the woman being deceived was in the transgression." Paul's views have roots in Greco-Roman philosophy, in which woman is conceptualized as "nature," her essential role being to carry and suckle the young, while man rises above nature to achieve culture, rationality, and thus civilization (Kolbenschlag 1979, 183). Theologians like Saint Augustine, Saint Thomas Aquinas, Barth, Bonhoeffer, John Knox, and Luther are all cited as insisting that women must be subordinate to their husbands, and silent in church (Daly 1973, 5; Kolbenschlag 1979, 183). Eve is the evil temptress, the devil's gateway. The other powerful biblical image for women is the virgin mother, a state unattainable by any real women. Hence, to be a normal woman is to be a failure (Ruether 1975, 18–19).

The vision of God as male, as radically "other" than female, is what most angers Kolbenschlag, who sees it as mutilating the female spirit. Not made in the image of God, women cannot represent Christ as a priest in the Roman Catholic Church (Kolbenschlag 1979, 184). Daly vents her anger more fiercely, declaring that for women to remain in such a church is like blacks becoming members of the Ku Klux Klan (Daly lecture at St. Thomas University, 1984). Feminist critics trace what they see as institutionalized **misogyny** or woman-hating in the Christian Church, dating back to the fourth century canon law, which declared women unclean and unfit for church office. It reached its peak in the fifteenth to seventeenth centuries when the Christian Church gave its authority to the slaughter of hundreds of thousands of women as witches, depicted as carnal temptresses in consort with the devil (Jong 1981, 69). The women most at risk from witch hunts were those who transgressed the prescribed roles of virgin daughter or submissive wife and mother (Larner 1984, 84).

The two other world religions that have roots in the Old Testament, Judaism and Islam, share similar patriarchal traditions. Under orthodox Judaic religious tradition women have no significant role in synagogue or the world of study. Women are not permitted to study or to participate in the interpretation of religious laws, collectively known as the Talmud. During religious services, women sit separately from men, behind a screen. Women cannot become rabbis.

They are not called to read the Torah, they are not permitted to say public prayers for the dead, or to pray at the Temple Wall in Jerusalem. They are not counted among the quorum needed for prayer (Kaufman 1991, 59–64). Even separated women's prayer groups are regarded with suspicion. Religious laws define man as leader and family head. Verses from the Torah's book of Exodus list a wife as property, and give a man the right to sell his daughters into bonded servitude (Goldstein 1998, 37). Divorce laws give men the initiative. A man may leave his wife and remarry without a divorce contract, while if he refuses to give a divorce contract to his wife, she cannot remarry (Kaufman 1991, 134–135).

Orthodox Islamic religious tradition is also strongly patriarchal. Muslim theology is based on two sets of sacred texts—the Qur'an, which is viewed as the actual word of God, recorded by Muhammed in the early seventh century, and the *hadiths*, reports of Muhammed's personal traditions and lifestyle that were collected after his death, and used to guide behaviour. All interpretive authority and all positions of structural privilege in mosques are vested in an all-male clergy (Read and Bartkowski 2000, 398–399). Under Qur'anic religious laws men are managers of the affairs of women. Women are enjoined to be obedient to their husbands, and to meet all his sexual desires. At the same time, her seductiveness is seen as a threat to social order, and is strictly controlled. The Qur'an dictates that respectable women "cast down their eyes, guard their private parts, and to reveal not their adornments . . . save to their husbands" (Moghissi 1999, 22). Her adultery is punishable by public stoning. Conversely, a man may have up to four wives, and hire as many temporary wives as he can afford (Moghissi 1999, 23). Divorce is a male prerogative. A man may divorce a wife without her consent, or even her knowledge. He retains custody of children and is deemed to have the power of life or death over them.

Women in Contemporary Religious Institutions

Contemporary religious institutions in Western societies no longer conform to these extremist positions, although most are still far from preaching or practising full gender equity. The presence of women in leadership positions within religious institutions provides some measure of the impact of women's movements. Beginning in the mid-1800s, many Christian denominations changed their rules to formally permit the ordination of women as clergy. Data from the United States show that by 1890 about 7 percent of denominations gave full clergy rights to women, this rising to about half by the 1990s (Chaves 1997, 18). A survey of Canadian churches in 1987 revealed that only 29 out of

80 denominations ordained women to the full ministry (McAteer 1989). The United Church of Canada led the way with 15.4 percent of all ministers being women, and half of all its theology students. The Reverend Lois Wilson was elected as the first woman moderator in 1980. The Anglican Church of Canada approved the ordination of women in 1975, but the mother church in England held out until 1994, amid divisive debate and court challenges, with many thousands of priests threatening to defect to the Catholic Church in protest over the issue. The official position of the Catholic Church remains that women cannot be called to the priesthood. The American Jewish Reform synagogues began to ordain women to the rabbinate in 1972 (Hunt 1999, 105). Rabbi Laura Geller (1995, 243) recalls that in June 1973 she was one of only two female students in the Hebrew Union College in New York and there was only one female rabbi in the USA. By June 1993 there were 219 female students and 52 ordained women rabbis. In Canada, however, Rabbi Elyse Goldstein, writing in 1998, describes herself as "one of the only female rabbis in Canada" (1998, 179). Progress is slow.

A change in the rules does not necessarily translate into a change in practices. Chaves notes that there was no surge in actual recruitment of women as clergy until the 1970s, in response to the second-wave feminist movement. By 1970 only 7 percent of clergy in the United States were women, this rising to 10 percent by 1990 (Chaves 1997, 1). Data by Anderson and Clarke (1990, 23) for Canada suggest that females made up less than 1 percent of Canadian clergy by 1981, perhaps reflecting the prominence of Roman Catholicism.

In many denominations, the rules permitting the ordination of women changed far earlier than their practices. The main explanation, Chaves argues, is that rule-change performs a largely symbolic function, responding to external rather than internal pressures (1997, 5). Individual churches and interdenominational networks often went along with rule changes in response to political pressures but without any real commitment to act on them. Chaves demonstrates further that there were no marked differences in broad progressive spirit or lay-member support for gender equity between denominations that changed rules early or late. Resistance was the norm across them all. Nor was there any marked difference in the numbers of women actually doing pastoral work, regardless of rules permitting or forbidding their formal ordination (Chaves 1997, Ch. 2). In the 1990s the Seventh Day Adventists continued to deny women full clergy status, yet dozens of women were working as clergy, some as sole pastors. Similarly, in the Roman Catholic Church some 300 priestless parishes were being "pastored" by women, who were functioning as priests in almost every sense, including presiding at worship and dis-

tributing communion (Chaves 1997, 24). Most of them served in small rural parishes, in effect the same low-status congregations as those most likely to have female ministers in denominations that formally grant clergy status. Chaves suggests that market forces best explain the apparent similarity in practice in both "conservative" and "liberal" churches. Congregations unable to hire male ministers, because of a clergy shortage or lack of money, turn to women, regardless of formal rules. Shortage of male clergy directly affects the numbers of women called to serve, but not whether the rules change.

The strongest correlations Chaves finds with rule change are decentralization and autonomous women's missions. When a woman comes along who happens to be an exceptional preacher, and who wants to be ordained, it is far easier for individual congregations in decentralized denominations like the Disciples of Christ to change their rules to fit her case than it is when the governing body of a centralized denomination like Presbyterians has to be persuaded (Chaves 1997, 139–140). Further, while the large majority of denominations developed Women's Mission Societies, those that permitted women more autonomy to manage funds and make decisions changed rules to ordain women faster than those that subordinated the missions under supervision of male elites. In the former, women gained greater experience of leadership, and access to resources through which to lobby congregations for rule change.

Chaves concludes that the denominations most resistant to formally ordaining women as clergy are those that hold the Bible to be the absolute word of God, or hold that the Sacrament of Eucharist actually transforms bread and wine into the body and blood of Christ (Chaves 1997, Ch. 5). Neither position logically or historically requires opposition to women's ordination, he argues. The Bible is ambiguous on the matter of gender and preaching. The passages in Paul's letters, cited above, can be read as ordering that women submit and be silent, but other passages can be read as stressing that gender and nationality have no relevance in Christ's followers (Galatians 3:28 and Acts 2:16–18). Denominations that oppose women's ordination find the first references definitive and the other verses secondary, while those that accept women's ordination reverse the priority. Equality is definitive, while other verses refer to the local problem that struggling churches in Corinth need not put up with ignorant women who boss their husbands and disrupt church services. Belief in biblical inerrancy is compatible with either reading. Belief in sacramentalism is likewise compatible in practice with women serving as the "icon" of Christ. The priests representing Christ in the Eucharist do not have to be "male" any more than they must be "married-Hebrew-bearded-fishermen" like the disciple Peter (Haring 1999, 118). The core of the resistance to ordination of women, Chaves argues, is neither logic nor history, but a moral opposition to liberal individualism or modernism that secular demands for gender equity have come to symbolize. It speaks to religion as based on an alternative divine moral order that cannot be judged by relativist secular values.

As the meaning of women's ordination shifted from divine calling to a gender equity issue, resistance increased (Chaves 1997, 125–126). In 1980, Pope John Paul II reaffirmed the edict banning altar girls. In 2000, he cited the divinely ordered distinctions between maleness and femaleness as grounds for the Vatican's principled opposition to the United Nations Convention to Eliminate Discrimination against Women (Manning, *Globe and Mail*, 5 June 2000, A13). The Vatican also opposed a UNICEF campaign to distribute emergency contraception to teenage girls in war zones, citing the inviolability of the procreative role of women and the sanctity of the essence of life.

The argument that opposition to women's ordination reflects a broader opposition to modernization and to liberal-individualistic values of advanced capitalist societies, rather than opposition to gender equity as such, resonates with other critics. Kaufman (1991, 7–9) argues that opposition to modernism was a primary motivation for newly orthodox Jewish women to return to orthodoxy. For them, secular modern culture promoted the "cult of individualism," selfishness, moral relativism, and male irresponsibility for family. Sexual liberation all too often felt like sexual exploitation of women by men. They were drawn to what they saw as the moral certainty and community focus of Orthodox Judaism. A recurrent explanation for the rise of Islamic fundamentalism across the world is that it reflects a symbolic rejection of decadent Western culture and colonialism (Moghissi 1999, 16–17). A return to the practice of veiling for women expressed the cultural anxiety and rage that Muslims felt towards colonizers who sexualized and exploited "Oriental" women, and inferiorized subjugated cultures. The argument for an "Islamic feminism" holds that it is an act of defiance against the social corruption of Western market economies and consumerism, offering an indigenous and non-Westoxicated model of liberated women (Moghissi 1999, 41). Changes in gender relations triggered by the spread of capitalism and feminism are seen as threatening a more holy social order.

Careers in the Clergy: Challenging Gender Hierarchy

Counting numbers, like listing denominations that have changed their rules to permit female ordination, gives only a partial picture of women's continuing struggle for acceptance within religious institutions. Surveys have shown that the majority of ordained women in the United Church found themselves confined to administrative posts, or to churches with small and shrinking congregations, as members switched to male-led churches (McAteer 1989). In the Episcopal Church, as numbers of women entering the clergy surged during the 1970s, the occupational structure changed (Nesbitt 1997, 115–123, 161; May 1999, 90). A proliferation of part-time, low-paid and non-stipendiary positions developed, including directors of education, youth-group workers, and service work for hospices. Women became heavily overrepresented in these positions. While valuable in themselves, such roles marginalize women, and do not give them the experience needed for denominational influence or authority. Surveys of seminary graduates revealed that large numbers of women had left the ministry, feeling that they had no career in the church (May 1999, 93). Many also reported experiencing harassment and discrimination from colleagues and laypeople. Ebaugh similarly records the disappointment of many Catholic nuns who were encouraged by the openness of the Second Vatican Council of 1965 to work with priests in parish ministry. Many withdrew from the work during the 1980s "disillusioned by the powerlessness, subjugation, and frustration of dealing with male cleric superiors" (Ebaugh 1993, 144). The same pattern of institutional marginalization occurred in Reform Judaism. Geller reports that after 20 years and 200 women rabbis, no woman had achieved leadership roles in 1000-person congregations, the traditional measure of career success (1995, 246). One explanation is that women seek more balance between career and family lives than men, limiting their hours of work in the "greedy profession" of ministry. But for Geller this does not account for the "stunning and depressing" difference in men's and women's career paths. Salary discrepancies get wider above entry-level ranks, with no women serving in midsized congregations earning even close to the median salary.

Nesbitt holds out little hope for women gaining authority in religious institutions beyond token levels (Nesbitt 1997, 164). She suggests that the possibility of ordination may itself have served to weaken the women's movement within the churches. A few ambitious individuals can be co-opted by the illusion of access to leadership and then constrained to conform to the male-dominated institution. The general consensus is that the structures of male control within religious institutions remain largely unchallenged.

Feminizing Religious Institutions: The Difference Women Make

Nesbitt's suggestion, which is taken up by others (May 1999; Hunt 1999) is that women's greatest contributions to religious institutions has not been inside the formal leadership hierarchy but outside it. Ironically, the very exclusion of women from the Roman Catholic priesthood has encouraged nuns to seek alternative forms of ministry that are less hierarchical and more ecumenical than the mainstream church. Writing in 1999, Hunt estimates that more than 26 000, or 10 percent of Roman Catholic parishes in the USA, had no resident priest, and in 82 percent of these sisters served as ministers. Without the formal authority of the priesthood, Hunt suggests, these sisters ran their parishes as "disciples of equals," encouraging collaborative leadership among the laity, and promoting a strong commitment to gender equity. For years many have quietly offered the Eucharist without benefit of ordained priests. As Catholic women no longer covet ordination as their central goal, they are no longer easily controlled by the church hierarchy (Haring 1999). Nesbitt suggests that such practices may have far more significant implications for radical change than is happening in other churches that ordain women and then co-opt and marginalize them (1997, 165).

Women as ministers and as theological scholars have fostered a feminist revisioning of religious texts and a reinvention of religious rituals oriented to women's lives. Women scholars revised church history to emphasize how actively women were involved as preachers in the first two centuries after Christ, challenging the Catholic Church's claim that women had never served in these roles (May 1999, 91; Hunt 1999, 104). Women reinterpreted Paul's letters to highlight his support for gender equity among Christ's followers, and his close working relationship with Priscilla as co-evangelist (Anderson and Clarke 1990, 39). Jesus can readily be represented as a feminist with a close following of women who were disciples in all but recognition. The outspoken Catholic feminist and former nun Joanna Manning riled against the Pope's patriarchal biblical interpretations in her provocative book *Is the Pope Catholic?* (1999). In it she argues that such teachings violate the more fundamental Christian message that "in God there is no male or female."

Catholic nuns have been active in creating rituals designed to explore "the feminine aspect of the divine" and to ritually empower women (Neitz 1995, 291). One such spiritual program known as *Limina* recovers the goddess symbolism in the liturgical cycle, and the triple-spiral symbol for the Holy Trinity in the Celtic Catholic Church. This symbolism is woven into ritual dances to celebrate life passages of women through menarche, pregnancy, childbirth, and menopause. Limina organizers had to struggle with opposition from conservative Catholic groups, finding themselves denigrated as "witches" and "put through hell" for weeks before a Limina celebration in the Newman Centre in Chicago (Neitz 1995, 292–293).

Ebaugh (1993) reminds us that nuns have long functioned as powerfully liberating role models for Catholic girls, as university-educated professionals and as top administrators of schools, hospitals, orphanages, and charitable institutions in earlier times when girls were expected to accept the wife-mother role or be denigrated as "old maids" (1993, 133–148). With the liberalization following the Second Vatican Council, nuns left cloisters and religious habits to experiment with styles of living in the community, styles of dress, self-choice of careers, timing of prayers, and patterns of self-government. When the more conservative church hierarchy tried to rein them in, many refused to return to the old ways, choosing to leave the church to found lay orders. Others acquiesced to Rome in formal statements but interpreted them in radical ways. The camaraderie and social support found in the convents also formed a model for the women's movement. Frustration with dealing with male cleric superiors in the parishes fostered social activism and feminist commitments to stand with the powerless and to transform oppressive structures. Ebaugh concludes that nuns have become central figures in feminist movements in North America.

Jewish feminist scholars have similarly revisioned the Torah, the first six books of the Old Testament. Goldstein emphasizes that the first chapter of Genesis reveals that man and woman were created simultaneously from the earth, signalling their fundamental equality. The Adam and Eve story comes in the second chapter, leaving as an open question what happened to the first woman (Goldstein 1998, 21, 44–58). Goldstein also highlights the accounts of powerful foremothers in the Exodus story (69–82) and the story in Numbers 27 of the five daughters of Zelophehad (83–88), who successfully challenged the male system of inheritance. As a rabbi, Goldstein urges Jewish women to reject the layers of sexism and male commentary that cover the original text so as to find the valued personhood of women in Torah (Goldstein 1998, 30). Feminist scholars have also promoted a gender-inclusive revision of Jewish religious law, seeing law as designed to be community-building and spiritually nurturing rather than a body of harsh strictures from an authoritarian God (Gordon 1995).

Female rabbis in the Reform synagogues, like their Christian counterparts, have fostered a wide variety of religious rituals specifically to celebrate women's lives. The *bat mitzvah* or coming-of-age ceremony for daughters parallels the *bar mitzvah* for boys. The 14 days of ritual impurity during and after menstruation and the required ritual bath in the *mikveh* before sexual relations can resume have been reinterpreted as a covenantal ceremony for women (Goldstein 1998, 104–114). Women rabbis have further transformed Judaism by creating covenant ceremonies for daughters, and ceremonies and rituals for healing from loss, miscarriage, abortion, infertility, adult survivors of incest, children leaving home, and menopause (Geller 1995, 246). Geller concludes that laypeople experience female rabbis in more closely personal and socially equal ways than they do male rabbis.

Islamic feminists likewise have reinterpreted and contextualized the *hadiths* or reports of the Prophet Muhammed's personal traditions and lifestyle to argue that they do not dictate the religious laws controlling women's lives, and moreover that veiling long preceded Islam and so cannot be a symbol of commitment to Islam (Read and Bartkowski 2000, 399–400). Feminists argue that women can be "unveiled, autonomous, independent, economically successful, educated, and articulate women" and still be devout Muslims (Moghissi 1999, 139).

Negotiated Meanings: Hearing Women's Voices

The interpretive perspective focuses on women as subjects, or active agents who negotiate religious meanings. Religious discourses are thought of as resources on which people draw in negotiating personally meaningful gendered-religious-ethnic-class identities. Feminism and fundamentalism represent strongly opposing religious discourses to which Western women in particular are exposed. Much feminist research focuses on the question of how or why so many women are drawn to fundamentalist denominations that stand in stark contrast to feminism. How do these women reconcile the two discourses and negotiate for themselves beliefs and practices that support their own agency and self-identification as religious women within the boundaries of fundamentalist church doctrine?

Researchers have noted many parallels between fundamentalist Protestantism, charismatic Catholicism, new Orthodox Judaism, and Islamic fundamentalism. At the heart of each of these traditions is a vision of family life that Stacey refers to as *patriarchal profamilism*, a vision in which the male is spiritual head and leader of the family (Stacey 1987; Kaufman 1991, 10). Women are enjoined to submit to the authority of their husbands and to devote their lives centrally to nurturing husband and children within the home. This contradicts the feminist vision of gender equity, rejection of stereotyped gender roles for women and men, and encouragement of women to break from the confines of private family life to seek careers and influence in the public arena.

It is important not to assume that women who belong to the same religious denomination all think alike. Beaman's research (2001) on Mormon women distinguishes three broad categories: self-identified "Molly Mormons" who are happy as stay-at-home moms; "moderates" who

struggle with male authority but who accept it so long as men use it responsibly; and Mormon "feminists" who are bitter about the limits on women's responsibilities and roles. Those women who most supported the fundamentalist Protestant vision of family life endorsed distinct gender roles as natural and God-given. They spoke of themselves as finding fulfillment in traditional female roles of wife and mother, and a sense of security and stability in ceding to their husbands the leadership role in the family. Yet while they rejected some features of feminism they nonetheless drew on other aspects of feminist discourse to speak of their ideals for family life. They emphasized that distinct gender roles and even submission to male authority could be compatible with equality and teamwork between wife and husband. As mothers they expected to be consulted in family decisions and felt that they wielded considerable influence in family decisions. Some argued that the role of mother was so centrally important that giving leadership roles to men in family and church only balanced men's otherwise subordinate position. Most importantly, women argued that their membership in the fundamentalist church gave them institutional authority to make demands on men as fathers to give central importance to their family responsibilities as nurturers and caregivers as well as providers. In effect, these fundamentalist women adapted feminist rhetoric to their personal situation, modifying male gender roles to be more feminine.

Commitment to traditional female roles also did not preclude paid employment. Ammerman records that the proportion of fundamentalist women with paid employment parallels the national average, except that they were more likely to have part-time jobs. One woman commented that she felt certain that God wanted her family to buy a particular house, and hence certain that God approved of her seeking paid employment to help meet the mortgage.

A study of men identified with the evangelical Protestant movement The Promise Keepers (Everton 2001) argues similarly that commitment to biblical literalism and inerrancy, and to male leadership as divinely ordained, is compatible with equality in marriage. Adherents embrace traditional gender roles, but call on men to interpret "leadership" in terms of service. Husbands are enjoined by Paul (Ephesians 5:25) to love their wives even as Christ loved the church and gave himself for it. Men are called upon to treat their wives as equal partners in marriage, to contribute equally to the care of children, and to encourage their wives to pursue their vocational dreams.

A study of 150 newly Orthodox Jewish women echoed the sentiments of the fundamentalist Protestant women described above (Kaufman 1991). As new converts to Orthodoxy these women spoke of their profound distrust and disillusionment with feminism. The secular culture they left behind was remembered as one that devalued women and feminine values, focusing on work and equal pay to the neglect of family. Sexual liberation felt more like sexual exploitation, leaving women with no grounds to say no to men's advances, while supporting men's irresponsibility and unwillingness to make lasting commitments. In contrast, they spoke of feeling strongly valued as mothers and wives within the Orthodox community. Their sex-segregated public lives gave them a sense of community with other women, greatly strengthened by sharing the demanding rituals of orthodoxy. All the routines of life, dressing, covering their hair, buying and preparing kosher food, keeping the Sabbaths, were daily reminders of faith, the rituals sacralizing these formerly mundane activities. The exacting rules of ritual impurity and required sexual abstinence for 14 days during and after menstruation was widely experienced as liberating, even "feminist" in giving women control over their own sexuality. It gives them the right to say no with the institutional weight of 5000 years of religious tradition to support them. The monthly cleansing ritual gave deep spiritual meaning to recurring cycles in women's lives. For these newly Orthodox women, the restrictions that Jewish feminists challenged were reconstructed as blessings that enriched their lives. They claimed that orthodoxy enhanced their status as women, and gave them greater claims on men as husbands and fathers within patriarchal religious structures. The paradox noted by Kaufman (1991, 1) is that these Orthodox women expressed the feminist potential in reactionary stances and the reactionary potential in radical feminist positions. The term "post-feminist" seemed more appropriate than "anti-feminist" to express these contradictory features.

Islamic fundamentalist women also challenged the Western interpretation of wearing the veil as necessarily a sign of women's subordination (Read and Bartkowski 2000). This study of veiled and non-veiled Muslim women living in Texas showed how women actively negotiated their gender, religious, and ethnic identities through the symbolism of veiling. Muslim women living in the USA are exposed to a variety of discourses about gender both inside Muslim circles and beyond, providing cultural resources on which to draw in negotiating their bodily practices. Women who chose not to wear the veil emphasized Islamic feminist discourse linking the veil to pre-Islamic practices, practices designed not to symbolize devotion to Allah, but to control and oppress women. For these women, veiling reinforced invidious gender distinctions that worked to women's collective disadvantage. They objected to Muslim women being ordered to hide their bodies because Muslim men were unwilling to control or manage their own sexuality. They also objected to veiling as a highly politicized practice intended to segregate Middle Easterners from supposedly

decadent Westerners. At its best, veiling is only a voluntary cultural practice. Devotion to Allah can be signalled more meaningfully through prayers and service, and commitment to the five pillars of Islam.

Women who chose to wear the veil, however, interpreted its meanings in very different ways. Veiling for them did signal religious commitment, and a sense of being recognizably Muslim to others in public places, and so more connected with the broader community of Muslim women. They emphasized their right to a distinctive ethnic identity rather than a politicized opposition to Westernization. The veil also gave a sense of "freedom within protected space," rendering them less vulnerable to explosive male sex drive, and so freer to move in the public arena. They felt that when they were veiled, men treated them more respectfully, focusing on their intellect rather than their bodily appearance. These veiled women felt able to reconcile their traditional practices with certain features of feminist discourse as they understood them—freedom, respect, and avoidance of a focus on women as bodies.

Gillespie (2000) describes a similar mixing of patriarchal religious tradition and feminist discourse in the voices of Hindu women in London who watched the television dramatization of the religious epic Mahabharata. These women readily identified feminist themes in the story of Lord Krishna's protection of Draupadi. Draupadi's husband, who has a weakness for gambling, loses her in a bet with his cousin. As she rages against this violation, and the failure of her in-laws to protect her, the winner attempts to humiliate her by tearing off her sari in public. Lord Krishna intervenes, giving her a sari of infinite length so that she cannot be shamed. Krishna then incites Draupadi's in-laws into war with their cousins in the name of female honour and chastity as the highest moral values. In a society where women have no right to choose a spouse, or to divorce, or to remarry on the death of their spouse, and who owe total loyalty and obedience to in-laws, Draupadi's spirited defence of herself, and Lord Krishna's protection, carry powerful messages about the status of a wife and daughter-in-law, and the respect due to her. The Hindu women were disgusted by a Western film portrayal of the Draupadi story that they felt misrepresented the nuances of female empowerment and distorted the meaning of the rage displayed by Draupadi.

The theme that these disparate women's voices have in common—fundamentalist Protestant, Orthodox Jewish, veiled Muslim, and devout Hindu—is the merging of elements of feminist discourse with patriarchal religious tradition. The last question explored below is the extent to which such merging at the level of discourse co-opts and undermines the deeper feminist politics of women's equality and empowerment.

Depoliticized Feminism: Violent Contradictions

The subtext of fundamentalist women's discourse is that women can find fulfillment and social status in traditional wife and mother roles. If women accept submission to their husbands rather than competing with them, they will be rewarded with status and respect, and will establish their right to responsible nurturing and support. Muslim women, who practice modesty through veiling their bodies, will win respect from men and be free from sexual advances and harassment.

What happens when this is not the case? In the dark underbelly of patriarchal familism is domestic violence and emotional abuse. Fundamentalist Protestant women are no less likely to experience domestic violence than secular women. However, they are more likely to remain in the situations (Nason-Clark 1997, 7, 14). They are subject to the same pressures as other women, such as fear of reprisal or worse violence if they try to leave, and lack of financial resources to support children without a male breadwinner. In addition, they face the full weight of religious prescription sacralizing their role in maintaining the family. Church teachings stress the importance of an intact Christian family and the mother's primary spiritual responsibility to ensure this; belief in the hierarchical model of family life as God's design for marital harmony; a model of forgiveness that emphasizes "seventy times seven"; and the glorification of suffering as part of the process towards spiritual maturity. All these teachings are reinforced by the belief that their faith separates them from the godless secular society around them, and that God works miracles to bring sinners to repentance (Nason-Clark 1997, 56). Fundamentalist women may confide in other church women or in their pastor, but are discouraged by their own beliefs and by their clergy from seeking help from secular sources such as transition-house counsellors (Nason-Clark 1995, 121–122; 1997, 83–108). Religious discourse characterizes those not "born again" as sinners who undermine Christian family values. Fundamentalist religion does not condone male violence or male dominance behaviour in the home. But the principles of male leadership and female submission do lend justification to those husbands who are abusing their power. Pastors who advised abused women generally conceptualized family violence as reflecting lack of spiritual growth and the solution as a family issue, with reconciliation as the goal. Women who chose to remain in abusive marriages often saw themselves as suffering servants of Christ.

Orthodox Judaism condemns wife abuse as a violation of scripture, and defines it as grounds for divorce, or at least compensation, but Orthodox religious law still makes it very difficult for women to seek divorce (Graetz 1995). Contemporary rabbinic courts in Israel deny divorces to between 8000 and 10 000 women per year. Rabbinic courts, Graetz argues, can tell husbands what to do but they do not follow up on it. Rabbis are unwilling to change or interpret traditional law in ways that would undermine men's rights over their wives. Like Protestant clergy they are caught between pro-family rhetoric and the reality of abused women.

Veiled Muslim women, even when their entire bodies are hidden beneath black drapes, are not immune to being raped. When this crime happens, women living under Shari'a or Islamic religious law have virtually no recourse. Women are held morally responsible for comporting themselves in ways that will not excite male sexual drive, so they largely take the blame for inappropriate sexual behaviour. To be seen in public improperly veiled, like leaving some hair visible, is punishable by public lashing. For a woman to successfully charge a man with forcing her to have sex against her will, she must have four male witnesses, all of impeccable character, to support her claim. Failing this, she herself is likely to be jailed for admitting that she has had unlawful sex. Adultery is punishable by the woman being stoned to death (Moghissi 1999, Ch. 6). The blood money payable to the family of a man who is killed is twice that for a woman. A husband is justified in killing a wife whom he judges to have besmirched "family honour."

The feminist reading of the Draupadi story by Hindu women comes up against the same essential limitation. The epic can be read as giving divine support to the status and respect owed to women as wives and daughters-in-law, but it does not thereby empower them to break out of the patriarchal order that holds women into arranged marriage and submission to in-laws.

Moghissi is fiercely critical of what she terms postmodernist Western scholarship for condoning such violence against women through its stand of principled cultural relativism. On the surface religious fundamentalism and scholarly postmodernism seem diametrically opposed, but in practice, Moghissi argues, they support each other (Moghissi 1999, Ch. 4). Fundamentalists believe in absolute truth of religious principles as revealed to Muhammed in the seventh century. Postmodernists deny the possibility of absolute or objective truth, and honour difference, and the authenticity of other voices, especially of submerged non-Western voices. Hence they silence Western feminist opposition to violence perpetrated against women in the name of Islamic religious law. The portrayal of rigid controls imposed on women's bodies by fundamentalist Islamic law as an authentic response by submerged cultures to Western imperialism only serves to reinforce the treatment of women as objects.

Moghissi asserts a critical difference between Islamic and other forms of religious fundamentalism—Islam has become the state religion in many countries of the Middle East and Asia. Obedience to religious laws is not a matter of choice, as it is for Muslim minorities in North America, or for Orthodox Jews even in Israel, or for fundamentalist Christians in the West. In Islamic states, religious laws are imposed on women with the full force of state judiciaries. Moghissi challenged the assumed authenticity of "Muslim feminist" voices (Moghissi 1999, 75) who speak of "liberation within protected space" of the veil or the harem. In a context where women are savagely punished and criticized for violating dress and behavioural codes, verbal compliance is a form of self-protection. As anthropologists have shown, women living in harems often create meaningful, coherent, and understandable lives, but they are still living in prison. Women who stay in abusive marriages may see themselves as suffering servants of Christ, but they are still being abused. Muslim women living in Texas do not face punishment from the state for being unveiled any more than fundamentalist Protestant women face prison terms for drinking and dancing in public venues. But they may well face ostracism and other forms of punishment within the segregated worlds of family and church. Thoughts and preferences are not freely expressed under such social constraints.

In summary, the way these fundamentalist and orthodox women describe their lives suggests that feminist discourse and gender politics have significantly influenced religious discourse and practices, even in denominations that officially oppose core feminist commitments. But the challenge of feminist analysis still stands that these religious institutions and practices support a patriarchal social order.

CONCLUSION

This chapter has explored the implications of Durkheim's definition of religions as systems of beliefs and practices relative to the sacred core of social life that draws adherents together into bonds of moral community. It explores also the implication religious thought is never static. As societies evolve and change, so will systems of religion.

Functionalist analysis focuses research on how religion legitimates moral order. In contemporary individualistic and competitive capitalist society, overtly secular civil religions such as nationalism and individual spiritualism have emerged alongside conservative religious communities that reaffirm elements of enduring value from an older moral order.

Political economy theory focuses research on how religious thought and practices reflect and express conflict in societies riven by class and ethnic conflict. It reminds us that all religious thought is centrally concerned with issues of power and with the moral basis of people's obligations to society. Research inspired by Max Weber explores the elective affinity between religion and social class, the distinctive systems of religious thought that emerge among and are attractive to people in very different occupational class positions. Class-based religions work in contradictory ways. Mainstream religions typically legitimate the status quo of power and privilege, while religious thought among the subordinated and oppressed alternatively draw people together to endure difficult lives and to seek hope and salvation in the promise of a better future, yet carry within them the seeds of critique and rebellion.

Social constructionist analysis reminds us that religious systems of thought and practice are never static or given, but continually brought into being and sustained by ongoing repetition, renewal, borrowing, adaptation, interpretation, reconstitution, and creation.

Feminist research explores how mainstream religions have functioned to legitimate and sacralize patriarchal moral order and make that order meaningful for women and men, and how feminist thought fosters alternative religious expression that challenges that moral order.

SUGGESTED READING

Nancy Gibbs, in her article "The Pursuit of Teen Girl Purity" (*Time* 172, 28 July 2008, 36–39), discusses the growing popularity of purity balls. Fathers in tuxedos and young daughters in formal gowns attend this annual event, where they make promises to each other—she to practice abstinence and he to protect her purity and virtue. This is a photo essay with photos by Marvi Lacar. For more of Marvi Lacar's purity ball photos, go to www.time.com/time/photogallery and see her photo essay, "The Purity Ball."

Using church attendance, religious salience, private religiosity, and family religiosity as measures of religious involvement, Amy Burdette and Terrence D. Hill ("Religious Involvement and Transition into Adolescent Sexual Activities," *Sociology of Religion* 70, Spring 2009) found that an association could be shown between the religious involvement of teens and a delayed transition into sexual activity. This association was most pronounced on measures of religious salience, an interesting finding because, as Burdette and Hill pointed out, salience is the one measure that is controlled by teens themselves.

Carl Raschke ("Evangelicals in the Public Square," *Social Science and Modern Society* 46, March/April 2009, 147–154) acknowledges the current rise of evangelism and its corresponding influence on American politics. He argues that, after 60 years of lost influence, it returned with the Ronald Reagan administration and continued on through both Bush presidencies. However, he suggests that it is a new evangelism based on consumerism. He predicts that evangelical Christianity is "now poised for a disastrous fall" because, he says, today's evangelicals have lost their "moral and historical bearings."

Studies in Religion 37: 3–4, 2008: This volume contains a debate between Thiessen and Dawson on one side and Bibby on the other. The 2 articles are: Thiessen, Joel, and Lorne L. Dawson, "Is there a renaissance of religion in Canada? A critical look at Bibby and beyond," 389–415, and Bibby, Reginald W., "The perils of pioneer-ing and prophecy: A response to Thiessen and Dawson," 417–425.

Reginald Bibby has written extensively on religion in Canada. He has based his books and articles on data that he has been collecting every five years since 1975. In his most recent survey he noted a slight increase in attendance at a number of mainline churches and concluded that "organized religion might be showing some signs of new life." In their article, Thiessen and Dawson question Bibby's methods and interpretation of the data and express doubt that there is a "renaissance of religion" in Canada. In his response, Bibby wrote: "My so-called renaissance thesis is just that—a thesis in need of testing. I haven't adopted it; I have posed it" (421).

Barack Obama's defence of his long-time pastor Rev. Wright in his campaign speech "A More Perfect Union" (Presidential campaign speech, 18 March 2008) gives powerful insights into the role of black churches in sustaining a sense of community and "the audacity of hope" in marginalized people in America. Rev. Wright's speeches, which are easily found on the Internet, give voice to the rage and potential for political revolt among black congregations.

Sara Diamond's book *Not by Politics Alone: The Enduring Influence of the Christian Right* (1998) explores the power and extent of fundamentalist Christian media networks in North America.

QUESTIONS

1. How does Durkheim relate primitive religious ceremonies among Australian Aboriginals to Judaic religion in his own time? In what ways are they similar, despite obvious differences?

2. Explain Berger's concept of a "sacred canopy." How is this concept relevant for non-believers? How is this relevant for understanding what some theorists call "civic religions"?

3. How does functionalist theory account for the appeal of fundamentalist Protestant churches for Asian immigrants who have not been brought up as Christians? What functions does religion perform for immigrant communities? How does this differ from its functions for Canada as a whole?

4. Why did Karl Marx call religion "the opiate of the masses"? How does political activism in American churches with mostly black members both support and challenge Marx's view of religion?

5. What did Max Weber mean by the elective affinity between capitalism and the Protestant ethic? How does he explain the attraction of Calvinism to the business class?

6. Explain how Marxist theorists see a link between communism and Christianity. How is this helpful in understanding liberation theology in Latin America, or the Social Gospel movement in Canada?

7. Explain the concept of religion as practical accomplishment in social constructionist theory. How does this concept help to explain the work of Aboriginal elders in prisons, and leaders of women's prayer groups in a fundamentalist church?

8. How does the practice of witnessing work to sustain faith in fundamentalist Christian communities?

9. What evidence does Beaman give to support her argument that one cannot assume that all women who attend the same church think the same way? How is this helpful in understanding how devout Muslim women choose whether or not to wear the veil or hijab?

10. A number of researchers have concluded that there has been little change in the male hierarchical structure of many religious institutions, even those that ordain women. Discuss women's resistance, both from within and from without their churches, synagogues, and religious communities.

WEB LINKS

Stock Exchanges Worldwide
www.tdd.lt/slnews/Stock_Exchanges/Stock.Exchanges.htm
The growing interest in trading commodities and buying/selling stocks is evident from the increase in number of stock exchanges. This site provides a list of the world's major stock exchanges within Africa, Asia, Europe, Middle East, North America, and South America.

Canadian Council of Chief Executives
www.ceocouncil.ca
The CCCE is an umbrella organization that connects many of Canada's largest transnational corporations such as Bombardier Inc., Canadian banks and lending institutions, Federal Express Canada, General Electric Canada, Giant Tiger Stores, IBM, and oil companies. Thomas d'Aquino, chief executive and president says "We engage in an active program of public policy research, consultation, and advocacy. Building a stronger Canada economically and socially is our national mandate. Helping to make Canada and our enterprises number one around the world is our global mandate."

World Council for Corporate Governance
www.wcfcg.net
The WCFCG website gives an account of the transnational corporations that fall under its mandate. These include companies such as the Centre for Sustainability and Excellence, CSR Europe (consisting of 60 leading multinationals), International Chamber of Commerce, African Regional Youth Initiative, and Indian Oil. The site states: "The World Council for Corporate Governance was established as an independent, not for profit international network aimed to galvanize good governance practices worldwide."

Workers.TV 06/19/09—LGBT liberation and the class struggle
www.mefeedia.com/entry/06-19-09-lgbt-liberation-the-class-struggle/19908362
Shelley Ettinger lectures on patriarchy and subjugation of women within a capitalist, classist society.

Vodpod: Capitalism
http://vodpod.com/tag/capitalism
This link on Vodpod highlights several lectures, presentations or talks on capitalism from people such as Ecuadorian president Rafael Correa, Michael Porter, Naomi Klein, Nassim Nicholas Taleb, David Harvey, Alan Greenspan, Noam Chomsky, Milton Friedman, and Keith Hart.

KEY TERMS

Calvinism

liberation theology

Methodism

misogyny

patriarchy

predestination

profane

Protestant ethic

puritanism

religion

sacred

Social Gospel movement

socialism

totem

REFERENCES

Allen, R. 1975. "The Social Gospel and the Reform Tradition in Canada 1890–1928." In *Prophecy and Protest: Social Movements in Twentieth-Century Canada*. Toronto: Gage, 45–61.

Ammerman, Nancy Tatom. 1987. *Bible Believers: Fundamentalists in the Modern World*. New Brunswick, New Jersey: Rutgers University Press.

Anderson, Grace, and Juanne Clarke. 1990. *God Calls: Man Chooses: A Study of Women in Ministry*. Burlington, Ontario: Trinity Press.

Baum, Gregory. 1979. "Christianity and Socialism." *Canadian Dimension* 13 (Jan/Feb): 30–35.

Beaman, Lori G. 2001. "Molly Mormons, Mormon Feminists and Moderates: Religious Diversity and the Latter Day Saints Church." *Sociology of Religion* 62 (1): 65–86.

Bellah, R.N. 1967. *Civil Religions in America*. Daedalus 96 (1): 1–21.

Berger, Peter L. 1967. *The Sacred Canopy*. Garden City, New York: Doubleday/Anchor Books.

Betto, F. 1993 "Did Liberation Theology Collapse with the Berlin Wall?" *Religion, State and Society* 21 (1): 33–38.

Bibby, Reginald W. 1993. *Unknown Gods: The Ongoing Story of Religion in Canada*. Toronto: Stoddart.

Bibby, Reginald W., and Donald C. Posterski. 1992, 2000. *Teen Trends: A Nation in Motion*. Toronto: Stoddart.

Burman, Patrick. 1996. *Poverty's Bonds: Power and Agency in the Social Relations of Welfare*. Toronto: Thompson.

Burridge, Kenelm. 1969. *New Heaven, New Earth: A Study of Millenarian Activities*. Toronto: Copp Clark.

Chaves, Mark. 1997. *Ordaining Women: Culture and Conflict in Religious Organizations*. New York: Harvard University Press.

Chong, Kelly H. 1998. "What it Means to be Christian: The Role of Religion in the Construction of Ethnic Identity and Boundary Among Second-Generation Korean Americans." *Sociology of Religion* 59 (3): 259–286.

Clifton, J.A. 1990. "The Indian Story: A Cultural Fiction." In *The Invented Indian: Cultural Fictions and Government Policies*. New Brunswick, New Jersey: Transaction, 29–48.

Collins, R. 1982. *Sociological Insight: An Introduction to Non-Obvious Sociology*. Oxford: Oxford University Press.

Daly, M. 1973. *Beyond God the Father: Toward a Philosophy of Women's Liberation*. Boston: Beacon Press.

Dawson, Lorne L. 1998a. *Comprehending Cults: The Sociology of New Religious Movements*. Toronto: Oxford University Press.

Dawson, Lorne L. 1998b. "Anti-Modernism, Modernism, and Postmodernism: Struggling with the Cultural Significance of New Religious Movements." *Sociology of Religion* 59 (2): 131–154.

Diamond, Sara. 1998. *Not by Politics Alone: The Enduring Influence of the Christian Right*. New York; London: The Guildford Press.

Durkheim, Emile. [1915] 1976. *The Elementary Forms of Religious Life*. London: Allen & Unwin.

Ebaugh, Helen Rose Fuchs. 1993. *Women in the Vanishing Cloister: Organizational Decline in Catholic Religious Orders in the United States*. New Brunswick, New Jersey: Rutgers University Press.

Engels, Friedrich. [1884] 1978. "The Origins of the Family, Private Property, and the State." In R.C. Turker, ed. *The Marx–Engels Reader*. 2nd ed. New York: W.W. Norton, 734–759.

Everton, Sean F. 2001. "The Promise Keepers: Religious Revival or Third Wave of the Religious Right?" *Review of Religious Research* 43 (1): 51–69.

Fox, Jonathan. 1999a. "Do Religious Institutions Support Violence or the Status Quo?" *Studies in Conflict and Terrorism* 22: 119–139.

Fox, Jonathan. 1999b. "Towards a dynamic theory of ethno-religious conflict." *Nations and Nationalism* 5 (4): 431–463.

Geller, Laura, 1995. "From Equality to Transformation: The Challenge of Women's Rabbinic Leadership." In T.M. Rudavsky, ed. *Gender and Judaism: The Transformation of Tradition*. New York; London: New York University Press, 243–253.

Giddens, Anthony. 1971. *Capitalism and Modern Social Theory*. London: Cambridge University Press.

Gillespie, Marie. 2000. "Transnational Communications and Diaspora Communities." In Simon Cottle, ed. *Ethnic Minorities and the Media*. Buckingham; Philadelphia: Open University Press, 164–178.

Goldstein, Elyse. 1998. *ReVisions. Seeing Torah through a Feminist Lens*. Toronto: Key Porter Books.

Gordon, Leonard D. 1995. "Toward a Gender-Inclusive Account of Halakhah." In T.M. Rudavsky, ed. *Gender and Judaism: The Transformation of Tradition*. New York; London: New York University Press, 3–12.

Graetz, Naomi. 1995. "Rejection: A Rabbinic Response to Wife Beating." In T.M. Rudavsky, ed. *Gender and Judaism: The Transformation of Tradition*. New York; London: New York University Press, 13–23.

Haring, Hermann. 1999. "The Authority of Women and the Future of the Church." In Elisabeth Schussler Fiorenza and Hermann Haring, eds. *The Non-ordination of Women and the Politics of Power*. London: SCM Press, 117–125.

Hornborg, A. 1994. "Environmentalism, Ethnicity and Sacred Places: Reflections on Modernity, Discourse and Power." *Canadian Review of Sociology and Anthropology* 31 (3): 245–267.

Hunt, Mary E. 1999. "'We Women are Church': Roman Catholic Women Shaping Ministries and Theologies." In Elisabeth Schussler Fiorenza and Hermann Haring, eds. *The Non-ordination of Women and the Politics of Power*. London: SCM Press, 102–114.

Jong, E. 1981. *Witches*. New York: Harry N. Adams.

Kaufman, Debra Renee. 1991. *Rachel's Daughters: Newly Orthodox Jewish Women*. New Brunswick, New Jersey: Rutgers University Press.

Kolbenschlag M. 1979. *Kiss Sleeping Beauty Good-bye: Breaking the Spell of Feminine Myths and Models*. Garden City, New York: Doubleday.

Larner, C. 1984. *Witchcraft and Religion: The Politics of Popular Belief*. Oxford: Basil Blackwell.

Lecky, W. 1891. *History of England in the Eighteenth Century*. Vol. 2.

Lee, Richard Wayne. 1995. "Strained Bedfellows: Pagans, New Agers, and 'Starchy Humanists' in Unitarian Universalism." *Sociology of Religion* 56 (4): 379–396.

Luebbers, Amy. 2001. "The Remnant Faithful: A Case Study of Contemporary Apocalyptic Catholicism." *Sociology of Religion* 62 (2): 221–241.

Manning, Joanna. 1999. *Is the Pope Catholic? A Woman Confronts her Church*. Toronto: The Crossroad Publishing Company.

Marchak, Patricia. 1999. *God's Assassins: State Terrorism in Argentina in the 1970s*. Montreal: McGill–Queen's University Press.

Masire, Q.K.J. 2000. *Rwanda: The Preventable Genocide*. Organization of African Unity.

May, Melanie A. 1999. "Tracking the Ways of Women in Religious Leadership." in Elisabeth Schussler Fiorenza and Hermann Haring, eds. *The Non-ordination of Women and the Politics of Power*. London: SCM Press, 89–101.

McAteer, M. 1989. "Women in the Clergy: Numbers Keep Growing." *Toronto Star* 21 October, M29.

McLellan, Janet. 2001. "John Porter Address: Canadian Sociology and Anthropology Association." Quebec City, 28 May 2001.

McLellan, Janet. 1999. *Many Petals of the Lotus: Five Asian Buddhist Communities in Toronto*. Toronto: University of Toronto Press.

Moghissi, Haideh. 1999. *Feminism and Islamic Fundamentalism: The Limits of Postmodern Analysis*. New York: Zed Books.

Nason-Clark, Nancy. 1997. *The Battered Wife: How Christians Confront Family Violence*. Louisville, Kentucky: Westminster John Knox Press.

Nason-Clark, Nancy. 1995. "Conservative Protestants and Violence against Women: Exploring the Rhetoric and the Response." *Religion and the Social Order* 5: 109–130.

Neeman, Rina, and Nissan Rubin. 1996. "Ethnic Civil Religion: A Case Study of Immigrants from Rumania in Israel." *Sociology of Religion* 57 (2): 195–212.

Neitz, Mary Jo. 1995. "Constructing Women's Rituals: Roman Catholic Women and Limina." In Nancy Tatom Ammerman and Wade Clark Roof, eds. *Work, Family, and Religion in Contemporary Society*. New York: Routledge, 283–304.

Nesbitt, Paula D. 1997. *Feminization of the Clergy in America: Occupational and Organizational Perspectives*. New York; Oxford: Oxford University Press.

Neyer, J. 1960. "Individualism and Socialism in Durkheim." In K.H. Wolff, ed. *Essays on Sociology and Philosophy by Emile Durkheim et al*. New York: Harper and Row.

Nickson, Elizabeth. 1999. "Not 'Who am I?' but 'Whose am I?'" *Globe and Mail* (27 February 1999, D4).

Nolen, Stephanie. 1999. "Give them Jesus, but hold the theology: Religion meets popular culture." *Globe and Mail* (2 January 1999, A1).

Obama, Barack. 2008. "A More Perfect Union." Presidential campaign speech, 18 March 2008 (video and text available on multiple Internet sites).

Paper, J. 1993. "Methodological Controversies in the Study of Native American Religions." *Studies in Religion* 22 (3): 365–377.

Parkhill, Thomas C. 1997. *Weaving Ourselves into the Land: Charles Godfrey Leland, "Indians," and the Study of Native American Religions*. Albany, New York: SUNY Press.

Read, Jen'nan Ghazal, and John P. Bartkowski. 2000. "To Veil or not to Veil: A Case Study of Identity Negotiation among Muslim Women in Austin, Texas." *Gender and Society* 14 (3): 395–417.

Roof, Wade Clark, and Lyn Gesch. 1995. "Boomers and the Culture of Choice: Changing Patterns of Work, Family and Religion." In Nancy Tatom Ammerman and Wade Clark Roof, eds. *Work, Family and Religion in Contemporary Society*. New York: Routledge, 61–79.

Ruether, Rosemary Radford. 1975. *New Woman, New Earth: Sexist Ideologies and Human Liberation*. New York: Seabury.

Searl, Natalie. 1994. "The Women's Bible Study: A Thriving Evangelical Support Group." In Robert Wuthnow, ed. *I Come Away Stronger: How Small Groups are Shaping American Religion*. Grand Rapids, Michigan: William B. Eerdmans, 97–124.

Seul, Jeffrey R. 1999. "Ours is the Way of God: Religion, Identity, and Intergroup Conflict." *Journal of Peace Research* 36 (5): 553–569.

Singer, Peter. 2004. *The President of Good & Evil: Questioning the Ethics of George W. Bush*. New York: Plume.

Singleton, Andrew. 2001. "'Your Faith has Made You Well': The Role of Storytelling in the Experience of Miraculous Healing." *Review of Religious Research* 43 (2): 121–138.

Tapia, Andrea Hoplight. 2002. "Techno-Armageddon: The Millennial Christian Response to Y2K." *Review of Religious Research* 43 (3): 266–286.

Thompson, E.P. 1963. *The Making of the English Working Class*. Harmondsworth, UK: Penguin.

Tumminia, Diana. 1998. "How Prophecy Never Fails: Interpretive Reason in a Flying-Saucer Group." *Sociology of Religion* 59 (2): 157–170.

Stacey, Judith. 1987. "Sexism by a Subtler Name?" *Socialist Review* (Nov/Dec 1987): 8–28.

Waldram, James B. 1997. *The Way of the Pipe: Aboriginal Spirituality and Symbolic Healing in Canadian Prisons*. Peterborough, Ontario: Broadview Press.

Weber, Max. [1922] 1964. *The Sociology of Religion*. Boston, Massachusetts: Beacon Hill Press.

Weber, Max. [1904] 1930. *The Protestant Ethic and the Spirit of Capitalism*. New York: Charles Scribner's Sons.

Williams, Andrea S. 1996. "Catholic Conceptions of Faith: A Generational Analysis." *Sociology of Religion* 57 (3): 273–289.

Winland, D.N. 1993. "The Quest for Mennonite Peoplehood: Ethno-religious Identity and the Dilemma of Definitions." *Canadian Review of Sociology and Anthropology* 30 (1): 110–138.

Yang, Fenggang. 1998. "Chinese Conversion to Evangelical Christianity: The Importance of Social and Cultural Contexts." *Sociology of Religion* 59 (3): 237–257.

Yinger, J. Milton. 1957. *Religion, Society, and the Individual: An Introduction to the Sociology of Religion*. New York: Macmillan.

Karl Marx and the Crises of Capitalism

The April 2009 edition of *The Atlantic* features multiple portraits of social theorist Karl Marx, with the caption "He's Back" (Hitchens 2009). After three decades of inattention in mainstream economics and social theory, interest in Marxist analysis has rebounded as theorists struggle to explain the global scope of the crash of financial markets that began in late 2007 with the imploding of the US housing market. This chapter outlines Marxist thought and explores the relevance of Marx's analysis of the contradictions of capitalism for understanding the ongoing crisis.

Karl Marx (1818–1883) was a profound thinker whose work had a significant impact upon the twentieth century. His three-volume work *Capital* is a monumental study of Western industrial society. It is difficult to overstate the importance of Marx's work, and also difficult to condense his prolific writings into one short chapter. Some theorists interpret Marx as an **economic determinist** while others see him as pioneering social constructionist analysis. Some see a major break between Marx's earlier philosophical writings and his later economic analysis, while others stress an underlying continuity of thought. Interpretation is complicated by the fact that Marx died before the last volume of *Capital*, particularly his section on **class** analysis, was complete. Much of this work was pulled together by his colleagues from his notes. Marxist thought stirs up intense political feelings for or against his vision of the eventual collapse of capitalism, and his prediction that a communist world society would replace it. Such feelings tend to cloud the assessment of his work itself. It is not possible, therefore, to give a definitive summary statement of Marx's work. The overview below is only an introduction to his ideas. It is divided into three main sections: a summary of key ideas and methods in Marxist analysis of society; an outline of Marx's model of capitalism as an economic system; and the application of this model to contemporary crises in capitalism.

Historical Materialism

Historical materialism is a theory of history in which the material conditions of life are seen as ultimately determining the course of human history. For Marx, the most funda-

mental aspect of human existence is the absolute necessity for people to produce the means for their own subsistence. In order to survive, people must produce food and process it to the point where it is edible. In all but the rarest conditions of an ideal climate, people need to produce clothing and shelter and heat for warmth and for cooking. They also need to produce the tools or technology required for such processes. Even the simplest hunting and gathering economies use surprisingly complex implements. People also organize themselves in complex ways to hunt and gather, to process and preserve food, to build shelters, and so on. As the means of providing for material needs become more complex—from hunting and gathering to herding, settled agriculture, trade, and industry—the ways in which people organize themselves around these activities change in both form and complexity.

Marx reasoned that the processes by which people meet their basic subsistence needs constitute the foundation of social organization. Human production is by nature a social, cooperative activity. Any **mode of production** entails a definite pattern of **relations of production** between people. Relations of production in turn directly influence the prevailing family forms, political structures, religious ideas, and modes of thought. In Marxist terms, the economic organization of a society forms the **base**, which gives rise to the **superstructure** of social relations and prevailing values or culture of that society. For Marx, and theorists inspired by him, it makes sense to begin the analysis of economic and social life with the study of the prevailing mode of production and relations of production associated with it. All other aspects of social life can be understood as reflecting and responding to this underlying form of economic organization.

Modes of Production and Class Relations

Marx briefly traces historical changes in modes of production, and the social organization of inequality associated with them. The simplest form is **primitive communism**. The

Karl Marx (1818–1883)

National Archives/306-NT-176423

mode of production is hunting and gathering, using simple hand tools that are easily made and shared. The key means of production—the flora and fauna in the surrounding territory—are accessible to all. The resulting social relations are fundamentally egalitarian. No stratum of society is able to deny access of others to the means to provide for themselves.

The second stage is ancient society or **slavery**. This assumes a higher level of production with sufficient surplus for one class of people to be supported by the labour of others without producing anything themselves. Marx associates ancient slavery with warfare—warring communities captured people from other societies and used them for drudgery and heavy manual labour. Extensive slavery, however, is inherently limited in societies without advanced productive technology, as they cannot generate sufficient surplus to sustain a large leisured class.

The third and more significant mode of production is **feudalism**. Feudalism was the dominant mode of production in Europe throughout the ninth to the fifteenth centuries, the era generally known as "the middle ages," and remnants of it still exist in agrarian, non-industrialized societies. It is associated with settled agriculture, with land cultivated by means of draft animals, farm machinery, tools, seeds. Here, the means of production were no longer readily available to everyone. Entire communities cooperated to cultivate the land, but the sharing of resources and labour was no longer egalitarian. An important division of labour emerged in which an elite stratum of people gained the power to control the arable lands, while another stratum of people performed the manual labour of cultivating the lands. A hereditary class of **nobles** or aristocracy exercised control over the estates, commonly held in trust under a superior

military ruler or king. They extracted surplus production from **serfs**, the people who actually worked the land, in return for protecting them, maintaining law and order, and providing them with whatever was needed to cultivate the land. The serfs inherited their position as labourers. They were tied to the particular estate on which they were born, with no opportunity to leave or work land elsewhere. Only land that was too poor to bear the double burden of labourers and landlord was likely to remain in the hands of small independent **peasant** producers.

The fourth mode of production identified by Marx is **capitalism**. The term capitalism refers to an economic system based on private ownership of **capital**, or the means of production.

With the rise of industrialization, factories and industrial machines increasingly replaced land as the primary means of production, and this broke the stranglehold of the ruling elite over production. Factory owners and merchants did not owe allegiance to the ruler or king for their productive resources. The former aristocracy also became increasingly able to assert their independence from the king. The opportunity to trade wool, meat, and cereals in expanding urban markets in Europe made it lucrative for the nobility to enclose lands for sheep pastures, a production process that required little labour input. Providing for the full subsistence needs of entire communities became a liability rather than an obligation. In a long process that stretched over a century, the nobles claimed the right to fence off huge tracts of land for sheep pastures, to produce wool for sale. They enforced new laws banning former serfs from cultivating these lands, and from grazing animals or collecting firewood. In some cases they burned entire villages to force people out (Thompson 1975). Land became private property rather than a productive resource accessed by all members of the community. Some of the former serfs were able to get work as wage-labourers on big farms, tending cereal crops and sheep. The rest found themselves destitute. They had no choice but to migrate to the cities and compete with each other for whatever jobs they could get, often working under wretched conditions in the factories that were slowly opening up. Over time, industrial technology and factories have become the dominant means of production, with land becoming steadily less important. The factories and the industrial technology, like the land, are privately owned by a relatively small class of wealthy people. The mass of people who own neither land nor other capital have to sell their labour power to the owners of factories and private farms. Societies thus became increasingly organized into two great classes: the class of capitalists who own the means of production; and the class of workers who have no direct access to means of production, and must thus sell their labour power to capitalists in order to survive.

Marx envisioned a fifth and final mode of production, which he called **advanced communism**. In this vision, all important means of production in a society—farmland, factories, technology, and so on—would be communally controlled. All the productive advantages of capitalism would be combined with an egalitarian social order. The contradictions, conflicts, and limitations of earlier modes of production would be resolved.

Dialectical Method

Marx developed a method of analysis known as dialectical materialism to explore the systemic processes that underlay these sweeping historical changes in the organization of production.

He drew on the work of the German philosopher Hegel, but challenged his core assumption about the importance of ideas in history. Hegel reasoned that the evolution of human societies was driven fundamentally by processes of human thought, through which people progressively improved on the ideas of the past. The **dialectical method** is a form of reasoning that begins with prevailing ideas, explores logical contradictions or flaws in this reasoning, and proposes solutions, in successive cycles of thesis, antithesis, and synthesis. The **thesis** consists of a prevailing philosophical system or theory; its **antithesis** comprises the logical inconsistencies, internal problems, and unexplained anomalies within the system of thought; a new **synthesis** is achieved as thinkers integrate a new system of ideas that resolves the old problems. This new system in turn provides a starting point or thesis, with its own internal contradictions. The **dialectical** processes of reasoning through thesis, antithesis, and synthesis continue until perfection is reached.

Marx is said to have turned Hegel's reasoning on its head, developing a materialist rather than idealist version of dialectic. It is contradictions in the prevailing modes of production that drive historical change, Marx argued, with the prevailing ideas or systems of thought in a society merely reflecting these material conditions. In his model of **dialectical materialism**, the thesis consists of the existing organization of production; the antithesis is the internal contradictions—the gap between the productive potential of a society and flawed relations of production that limit this potential. The synthesis breaks these contradictions by establishing new ways of organizing production that unleash the full potential of emerging productive resources.

Primitive communism, the mode of production associated with simpler hunting and gathering economies, fostered egalitarian societies but only at an impoverished material standard of living. People could not develop sufficient economic surplus to sustain larger populations, or achieve sufficient leisure time to develop more advanced civilization.

Feudalism was the synthesis that resolved the internal contradictions of primitive communism, harnessing collective human energy to unleash the far greater productive potential of settled agrarian economies. But the productive potential of feudalism was hampered by its own internal contradictions. Tied labourers, who provided the physical labour needed for production, had no incentive to work harder to produce more than was necessary for their own subsistence. It was immediately obvious to them that when they worked harder to raise production, whatever surplus they produced was divided up unevenly, with the largest shares accruing to the aristocratic elites who controlled the estates. Elites in turn had little incentive to use what wealth they extracted to improve the estates. Production could expand only through pressuring serfs to work harder, or squeezing them to increase the **absolute surplus** they could produce, but this risks promoting resentment, rebellion, and sabotage. The feudal system was essentially static. Trade might improve the variety of goods available but not the overall level of production. People were tied to the land and to their inherited station in life.

Capitalism resolved the contradictions inherent in feudalism. Marx saw the transition from feudalism to capitalism as the most profoundly important change in the history of society. The privatization of means of production broke up the unity of feudal social order. The separation of economic and political spheres of activity, the emergence of a civil society of individuals, and the separation of the **state** from other areas of public activity were all interrelated aspects of the same process. Capitalism freed individual initiative from the straightjacket of feudal authority structures. Private ownership of new industrial means of production and the privatization of land promoted vastly increased levels of production. Capitalists competed with each other to develop more productive technologies to boost their production and their profits in the marketplace. Soaring productivity made possible the expansion of population and urbanization. Workers were also freed from the ties of serfdom, able to move to urban centres in search of wage-work. However miserable the conditions of factory wage-work might be, Marx still saw wage-work as an advance in human freedom over the suffocating constraints of rural serfdom (Sayer 1985, 230).

For all its advantages, however, Marx saw capitalism as inherently flawed. The antithesis of the capitalist mode of production lies in the class relations that it promotes, relations that lead to ever-increasing concentration of ownership of capital and extreme disparities of wealth and poverty. The vast productive potential of capitalism, its potential to free all humanity from drudgery and want, is doomed to be wasted, and its potential to free the human spirit crushed by extreme forms of exploitation and alienation.

Marx was convinced that ultimately the workers of the world would rebel against this flawed system and usher in a new synthesis that would combine the productive potential of capitalism with communal control over means of production—a synthesis that he called advanced communism.

We explore the social relations of capitalism in broad terms below, prior to examining Marx's model of capitalism as an economic system and its application to contemporary crises in the global economy.

Class Struggle at the Core of Capitalist Production

Capitalism, more than any other mode of production, is associated with an ever-accelerating pace of technological change and economic development. More than simply greed or desire for luxuries drives this progress. Aristocratic elites in feudal societies coveted sumptuous wealth, but they never felt the same compulsion to invest in productive technology. Unique to capitalism is the compulsion to invest the surplus in accumulating more productive resources or capital, rather than to consume it in luxuries or leisure. From where does this compulsion come?

Marxists argue that this compulsion arises from the fact that both capitalists and workers became fully dependent on markets to meet their basic survival needs, and that this dependence was the outcome of violent **class struggle**. Brenner (1977) argues that for capitalism as a mode of production to first emerge, the majority of producers had to be forcibly separated from the means to produce for themselves independently of markets. Only when producers are forced to buy or rent land in the markets, and buy labour power, do they have to be concerned with competition in the market and with maximizing profits. Brenner rejects the classical argument in economics that the expansion of trade alone would be sufficient to generate the drive to maximize profits, to specialize, and thus to promote self-sustaining economic growth associated with capitalism. Elites within feudal societies engaged in trade, selling their wool, meat, and other produce in urban markets. They squeezed surplus from tied workers to boost this trade. But they did not invest in new productive technology. They did not become "profit maximizers" in the way that capitalist producers did, because they never needed to. They could provide for all their basic needs through the feudal system of agriculture using tied workers.

Capitalists, as individual owners of small factories, were in a very different structural position. They were forced to produce goods to sell for money in markets in order to buy what they needed to survive. They also had to buy or rent all the materials needed to build their factories and machines and get necessary raw materials in the market, in order to make things to sell in the market. They also had to pay wages to buy labourers to work in their factories. They had to be able to sell their finished goods for at least enough money to cover all their production costs, or they would go bankrupt and face destitution. This meant that they had to be at least as efficient as competing capitalists, and preferably better than competitors. Those capitalists who were first to improve their productive technology would be able to dominate the market and drive out slower or weaker competitors. This is the structural root of the incessant drive to maximize profits through developing better productive technology.

Capitalists also required a mass of potential workers who were dependent on wage-work for their own survival in order to have labour power for their factories. Only when the majority of workers were forcibly separated from land, or the means to meet their own subsistence needs, were they willing to work in factories for wages. In an interdependent process, rural aristocrats privatized their fields and drove their former serfs off the lands that had sustained them for centuries. These landless people had no choice but to move to the cities and sell their labour to capitalists.

Class Struggle in Canada

Class struggles in Canada took a very different form because there were no masses of displaced serfs to provide a labour force. Indigenous peoples in Canada practiced a hunting and gathering mode of production, supplemented by horticulture and trade, including the fur trade with Europeans. They could support themselves and had little interest in becoming permanent wage-labourers. They had to be forcibly driven from the land by settlers, the buffalo exterminated, and traditional northern hunting grounds disrupted by mining, exploration, and lumber companies, before they would begin to turn to wage-labour for their livelihood.

Displaced landless people from Europe readily emigrated to Canada. During the first half of the 1800s, tens of thousands of immigrants came to Canada every year from Ireland alone, fleeing the appalling conditions of **enclosures**, economic collapse, and famine generated by economic domination from England (Pentland 1959, 459). They joined the multitudes of immigrants leaving similarly wretched conditions throughout Europe. Mass immigration from China and other parts of Asia began towards the end of the nineteenth century. Most of these immigrants were attracted to the prospect of owning land and working for themselves, rather than becoming wage-workers. Canada was especially attractive because it seemed to offer vast tracts of wilderness on which immigrants could settle and farm.

The problem for members of the business class, eager to develop capitalism in Canada, was how to staunch this outflow from the labour pool (Pentland 1959, 458–459). The government in Canada deliberately promoted land speculation to make land so expensive that immigrants would be forced to labour for many years to earn even a down payment for a farm. Policies to monopolize land for speculative purposes were implemented all across Canada, with grants of huge tracts to absentee proprietors (Teeple 1972, 46). In one day in 1767, for example, the whole of Prince Edward Island was granted to a few dozen absentee landlords. Between 1760 and 1773, Nova Scotia had a population of about 13 000, but 5.4 million acres of the best land were given in grants to individuals and companies based in Britain and the United States. Similar policies were followed in central Canada, sparking riots against land monopolies in 1794 and 1796. On the Prairies there were vast tracts of virgin land, and the Homestead Act granted 160 acres per settler. Yet even here the enormity of land speculation was eventually to stifle settlement and drive land prices far beyond the reach of the average immigrant. The Land Act of 1841 clearly expressed the objective of "creating a labour pool" by the two-pronged approach of promoting massive immigration and making land prohibitively expensive. The land speculators and the class of merchant industrialists who wanted a cheap wage-labour force to build canals and railways, and to work in factories, had close and influential ties to the people that dominated government. The wretched conditions of poverty and unemployment within the developing industrial cities of Canada from the mid-nineteenth century mirrored in many respects the conditions of early industrialization in Britain.

Globally, an estimated 1 billion people live on less than $1 per day and a further 1.5 billion live on less than $2 per day.

© Borderlands/Alamy

Alienation under Capitalism

Marx was centrally concerned with **alienation**, a concept that refers to dehumanizing social relations that he saw emerging in their purest form under capitalism. Marx saw people as essentially social beings, cooperating together in a creative productive relationship with their physical environment to transform it to meet their needs. Relations of production that stifled this cooperative, creative, and productive human essence are by definition alienating. Life within hunting and gathering societies is often harsh, but it is not alienating. People relate to the natural world and to each other in a direct and immediate way in meeting their collective subsistence needs. Under feudalism, tied labourers are exploited but not alienated in the same way as under capitalism. Under harsh feudal lords, their conditions of life might be reduced to the meanest level of survival while the leisured, ruling class lived in luxury on what the workers produced. Yet there was still a human relationship between the two great classes of those who worked the land and those who controlled it. Feudal lords acknowledged a hereditary obligation to sustain the families attached to the estates in the bad years as well as the good, and the labouring families had a hereditary right to use that land for their own needs, generation after generation.

It is only under capitalism that alienation is experienced in its fullest and harshest form, pervading every aspect of human relations. The structural cause of alienation is separation of the mass of people from the means of production. The experience of alienation has four major components: powerlessness, meaninglessness, social isolation, and self-estrangement (Blauner 1964, Ch. 1). When workers have no direct access to means to produce for their own survival needs, they are essentially powerless. To survive, they must sell their labour power as a commodity to the owners of capital, who will use it for their own productive purposes in return for a cash wage. During times of low labour demand, or high unemployment, the essential powerlessness of workers is most immediately experienced. Unwanted workers, no matter how industrious they might be, cannot use their labour power to meet their own subsistence needs because they have no access to any means of production, and they have no hereditary rights to share in what the society as a whole produces.

Workers are alienated from a meaningful relationship to their labour because whatever they produce belongs to the factory owner. The harder they work, the more their creative effort is taken from them. Factory labourers are also commonly alienated from the work task itself, which has no intrinsic meaning or sense of purpose. Under such alienating conditions, Marx suggests, people avoid work. They experience themselves as reduced to appendages of machines.

Social isolation reaches its most extreme form under capitalism because human relations are reduced to inhuman cash payment. People no longer cooperate with each other as full human beings in the production process. Capitalists are themselves as alienated as the workers, for they too are cut off from human social relations. The sole obligation that capitalists have to workers is to pay wages for labour power as and when they need it, with no further responsibility to meet the subsistence needs of people who provide that labour power, and no obligation to continue employing or supporting them when their labour power is not needed. People become estranged from their own essence as human beings when their life's work has no intrinsic meaning, when they have no control over, or relationship to, what they produce, when they feel no sense of cooperating fully with others, and when they relate to others, as others relate to them, not as full human beings but as commodities in the marketplace.

Class Struggle and Alienated Consciousness

Marx understood that the potential to transform capitalism into a new synthesis would depend on active human struggle. The impetus for this struggle, he believed, would come from the mass of working people most disadvantaged by capitalist relations of production. But for this to happen people would need to understand how capitalism works, and their own position within capitalist relations of production, to fully experience the contradictions inherent in capitalism and be able to envision the potential for change. Radical intellectuals would have an important role to play in this process.

Marx distinguished between the situation of workers as a **class-in-itself**, subject to the exploitative and alienating relations of capitalism, and the capacity of workers to become conscious of their shared class position and to act collectively in their class interests. Only then would workers form a **class-for-itself**, capable of initiating revolutionary social action.

Marx saw ideology, or a flawed understanding of the advantages of capitalist relations of production, as an idealized, empowering, and uniquely productive economic system, as a major impediment to the overthrow of the system as a whole. By ideology, Marx refers to distorted understanding that obscures how power relations work to perpetuate exploitation and inequality. In his philosophical writings, Marx argued that the prevailing ideas of any historical period will be the ideas of the ruling economic class. During feudal times in Europe, the ruling ideas projected an image of an all-powerful god who ordered human estates in their static feudal form. The image of the god as lord and master,

Marx reasoned, was a projection onto a cosmic level of feudal relations of lord, master, and serf. It worked to discipline the mass of people to accept their station in life, and to prevent revolt. As capitalism emerged as the dominant mode of production, this alienating, feudal concept of god began to lose its ruling force. A new controlling ideology emerged—that of abstract market forces.

Marx argued that this new concept of market forces, and the discipline of classical economics that emerged to describe it, reflected the ideas of the ruling capitalist class. It works to discipline the mass of workers to accept their station in life as the inevitable result of abstract, impersonal processes of competition, supply, demand, price, productivity, and the like, to which both capitalists and workers are subject. In *The German Ideology*, Marx explores the modes of reasoning, or mental tricks, that perpetuate distorted understanding of how capitalism works. The first trick is to separate prevailing ideas from the ruling class that promotes them. Classical economics represents itself as a discipline or philosophy entirely independent of capitalists. The second trick is to describe human relations in terms of abstract conceptual models. What people actually do, and how they treat each other, becomes represented by mathematical abstractions like supply–demand curves. The third trick is to treat these conceptual abstractions as actual causal forces responsible for what happens in markets. The intersection of supply-and-demand curves determines the price at which commodities exchange in the market, including the price of labour power. These "forces" appear to function in terms of laws of their own. What people do in a specific situation appears to be a response to market forces, not the cause of these processes (Marx and Engels [1846] 1970, 64; Sayer 1983; Smith 1974, 45–46).

Conceptual abstractions like market forces and economic models work to control people because the models do indeed seem to fit people's experience. Once people believe these models, they become obedient to them. Ruling elites in capitalist societies can more effectively control workers by explaining that their low wages are determined by forces of supply and demand, or that prices are dictated by commodities markets, and unemployment rates reflect productivity curves or the inevitable forces of globalization, than if they came right out and stated that elites want their big dividends and bonuses, and that special interests want to crush unions and workers' cooperatives. People accept practices like massive downsizing of business resulting in widespread unemployment as somehow inevitable, the effect of market forces beyond anyone's control.

Marx himself did not contest whether these models of classical economics were adequate for describing market forces. The problem for him is that they remain at the level of appearances without exploring the human practices that give rise to these appearances. Concepts are treated as abstract logical relations rather than historically specific social practices.

Marx dismisses these supposedly explanatory models of market forces and exchange of commodities as **commodity fetishism**. A **fetish** is an inanimate object that is worshipped for its magical powers. Commodities become fetishes in economics. Things appear to rule people instead of people producing things. Exchange appears to occur between things rather than the exchange of labour power between people. Abstract typifications are treated as having active causal agency while people become objects, their lives determined by the properties of things.

Marx argued that capitalism, more than any other social form, creates illusory appearances, because its survival depends on it. He reasoned that if it were to become obvious that all the suffering supposedly caused by abstract market forces was only a reflection of the concentration of private ownership of the means of production, and the mass of people's forced separation from it, the entire edifice would begin to totter. All Marx's later works were designed to explore how capitalism actually works, not as an abstract model but as political economy, driven by powerful vested interests.

CAPITALISM AS AN ECONOMIC SYSTEM

Marx's monumental three-volume work *Das Kapital*, translated as *Capital* (1867, 1885, 1894) explores how capitalism works as an economic system through its internal dynamics and contradictions. This model still forms the basis of contemporary political economy theory. First he sketches a simple **theory of exchange** of productive labour between people such as might occur in a barter economy. The value of goods and services that people exchange, he reasoned, would naturally come to reflect the amount of human **labour time** that goes into them. Consider the example of an economy based on hunting in which at a given time of year it takes an average hunter about one day to catch a deer but two days to catch a beaver. Fair exchange would then be two deer for one beaver. This exchange has nothing to do with the nature of the commodities themselves— the size of the animal, the amount of meat, the relative utility of deer skins over beaver pelts. It is based on the amount of human labour time it takes to catch them. If hunters could not get two deer for one beaver, they would pretty quickly stop "wasting time" catching beaver and start catching deer instead. People would start trapping beaver again only when they were sufficiently scarce, or people wanted them enough, that the labour time spent hunting a beaver would be compensated by what the beaver could be exchanged for.

Marx recognized that in advanced industrial economies the exchange of goods and services is vastly more complex, involves potentially multiple intermediate stages and vast chains of specialized workers, and is mediated through use of money. Yet he reasons nonetheless that the true exchange value or price of goods and services still fundamentally reflects human labour time.

In using labour time as the measure of **exchange value**, Marx is not suggesting that lazy people who take twice as long as others to do something will thereby be able to exchange their production for twice as much, or that people who make things quickly will get less. What counts, over the economy as a whole, is how much human labour time, on average, goes into producing goods, given the prevailing level of productive technology and skills. Marx refers to this as **socially necessary labour time**; it averages out lazy, unskilled, and unusually quick people. **Skilled labour time** includes teaching and learning in the calculation of socially necessary labour time.

Capitalist Exchange

Exchange in a capitalist system differs in important respects from the simpler example of a barter economy described above, in that the focus of the exchange is money, not the goods and services as such. Capitalists begin with money or "capital." They use money to purchase or pull together an array of productive assets, including machines, raw materials, and labour power, to produce **commodities** for exchange. A commodity, by definition, is a good or service that is produced for exchange in the market, not for immediate use by the capitalist. The capitalist's sole interest in exchanging commodities in the market is to get more money than what he started out with, or in other words to make a profit. Marx models this form of exchange as M – C – M, or money – to commodity – to more money (M-prime). Money as such has no use value. One cannot eat money or dress up in it. Its power is that it can be exchanged for anything. This power makes the desire for money very different from desire for useful commodities. There is a real limit to how much deer meat or other food or clothes we want, but no limit to how much money we want. Desire for money is, in principle, insatiable. It is this desire that drives capitalist exchange.

Corporations evolved as a particular means of raising initial money or capital, and sharing the risks involved in investing it to produce commodities. For example, a capitalist who needs a million dollars to start up an enterprise might persuade a thousand other people to loan him $1000 each, promising to pay each of them a "dividend" or a portion of the profits he hopes to make. One of the individuals who offered the initial $1000 may in turn sell her share of the enterprise, often referred to collectively as "stock," to other investors. If the enterprise is doing well and paying good dividends, these shares may be worth more money than the original investment. She might sell her $1000 worth of shares to 100 new investors for $11 each and make $1100. This would be a profit on her investment of $100, or a 10 percent return, not counting what she might already have earned in dividends. Of course, if the enterprise does not make much profit, then her shares may be worth less than the $1000 she originally invested, and she will lose money. If the enterprise totally fails, she could lose all her investment.

The critical question for capitalism is where does the extra money or profit come from? Marx argues that profit does not normally arise through dishonest or underhanded practices. Nor does it come simply from raising the price of a commodity. If all capitalists doubled the price of all commodities, the only result would be inflation, with money worth only half its former value. The only place in the system where profits can be made, Marx argues, is in the use of labour power. Human labour can produce more than its own value. A capitalist has to buy all other machines and raw materials for a fixed price in the markets, and he also has to buy labour power in the market at the going rate. Profit comes from the ability of these workers to produce commodities that have a greater money-exchange value in the market than the amount they are paid in wages, salaries, and other benefits.

This gap constitutes what Marx called **surplus value**. For example, if a worker can labour to produce a commodity with an exchange value equivalent to his daily wage in six hours, then the additional hours he works that day produces surplus value for the capitalist. Marx defines this gap between the money that workers are paid and the market value of the commodities they produce as a measure of **exploitation**. It violates the basic principle of human labour time as the measure of true exchange value. The actual level of exploitation is not easily measured. Capitalists themselves expend labour time in running their enterprise, and they must replace all the raw materials, energy, and the like, needed to make the commodities. Surplus value and exploitation arise over and above these socially necessary exchange values. The point of capitalist exchange is to maximize this surplus value.

An important qualification to this analysis of surplus value and exploitation, as we will see further below, is that profits from selling shares or stock in corporations is only loosely linked to the underlying labour power that generates surplus value. Investors use money to trade shares to make more money without directly being involved in commodity production. Much of this exchange of money for more money, or M – M, involves speculation, and is therefore

volatile. The exploitation of labour power that generates the profits used in this speculative investment is real but obscured by the fragmented and multi-layered character of ownership of capital.

Maximizing Surplus Value

In principle, Marx argues, there are three possible strategies for maximizing surplus value, or the gap between what workers are paid and the value of the commodities they produce. The first is to extend the working day. During the early stages of industrialization in Britain, workers were typically pushed to work 16-hour days, six or seven days a week, with capitalists arguing that only in the last hour did they make a profit. Ultimately, this becomes self-defeating as exhausted workers become less efficient and produce less. The second strategy is to depress real wages. This can be done by actually driving down wages, or holding wages constant while raising the price of commodities. Again there is some limit to this strategy as workers must be able to earn enough to provide for their own subsistence needs. Individual capitalists also cannot indefinitely pay less than the average market wage, because workers will leave their jobs and go to work elsewhere. The important exception is when workers have limited mobility, as in developing economies or peripheral regions where unemployment is high and workers cannot easily move from low-wage to high-wage regions.

The third strategy for raising surplus value is to develop labour-saving technology that will increase labour productivity. This is an ideal strategy in that, in principle, both workers and capitalists can gain. If a particular capitalist can introduce a new machine that enables workers to make the same commodity in half the previous time, then it is possible for the capitalist to increase wages, lower commodity prices, and still increase profits. Capitalists who are among the first to use innovative labour-saving technology thus raise their profits by beating the average labour time. This advantage, however, is likely to last for only a limited period, until competing capitalists adopt similar technology. The average labour time needed to make the commodity will drop across the economy, driving down both commodity prices and wages. The other disadvantage is that labour-saving technology reduces need for labour and so workers may be laid off. The two strategies of raising productivity and lowering wages relative to commodity prices tend to work in tandem as unemployment drives down wages, until new capitalist enterprises emerge to absorb the available labour.

Mainstream and Marxist theorists have very different analyses of the long-term implications of the dynamics driving capitalist economies. These are outlined below.

MAINSTREAM ANALYSIS: EQUILIBRIUM IN CAPITALIST MARKETS

Mainstream analysis of capitalist economic relations draws from the classical ideas of Adam Smith in his seminal work *The Wealth of Nations* (1776). Smith also argued that the exchange value of goods mostly reflects the amount of toil and trouble needed to acquire them. Expanding trade promotes wealth, he argued, as people are encouraged to become ever more specialized and thus more efficient in what they can produce for exchange, so that the value of their goods for others increases. When the demand for a certain specialized commodity exceeds the supply, people compete to acquire it and are willing to trade more of what they can offer to get it. In other words, when demand exceeds supply, the price goes up. Correspondingly, when supply exceeds demand, the price drops. Price thus works to communicate demand and supply for different goods and services. Producers, individual and corporate, gauge the kinds and amount of commodities to produce by the price they can command in the market.

Smith viewed capitalism as an inherently self-regulating system of exchange based on individual self-interest. In his opening chapter he makes the famous observation: "It is not from the benevolence of the butcher, the brewer, or the baker that we expect our dinner, but from their regard to their own interest. We address ourselves, not to their humanity, but to their self-love, and never talk to them of our own necessities, but of their advantages." Self-interest has the unintended consequence of advancing the well-being of members of the society as a whole. Smith believed that free exchange among producers in the market would result in greater overall well-being than by governments trying to artificially control markets, however well meaning such interference might be. The **"invisible hand" of the market**, he reasoned, would work best to allocate resources in society.

Market forces can nonetheless be harsh in their impact on people. Corporations are necessarily in business to make profits. They will replace employees with technology if they can thereby lower their costs and increase prices, and they will lay off workers if demand for commodities produced by such workers falls. They will do this without regard for the immediate hardships such workers will experience. Economic theory, however, reasons that in the long run imbalances in supply and demand in the market are self-correcting. Over time, investment will naturally dry up in areas of low demand and shift to areas of higher demand, with producers and investors using relative prices to make such judgments. As a current example, workers laid off in a declining sector, such as the automobile industry, will eventually be reabsorbed into emerging sectors, such as green energy and electronics, or the expanding service sector (Fernandez 2009, 109). The main issue is how long it will take for the economy to make such adjustments. Contemporary economic theory explores the role of governments in facilitating shifts in the economy by manipulating interest rates, or the cost of borrowing money, taxes, and other incentives. Governments can also facilitate adjustments in labour markets by offering unemployment insurance and retraining schemes to make labour more flexible.

The central assumption, however, is still that ultimately the free play of market forces will reach a new equilibrium. At the right price, all productive resources will be used and all commodities will clear the markets eventually. Productive investments will move out of ailing industries and into emerging areas. If governments intervene to artificially lower prices with subsidies, or artificially raise prices with tariffs or taxes, markets will work imperfectly. Labour is itself a commodity exchanged on the labour market. Specialized, skilled labour suitable for emerging markets will be able to demand a high price. Unskilled labour, or labour with obsolete skills, will be reabsorbed at a lower price. For strong believers in the free market, like Nobel Prize winner Milton Friedman, even government interference to establish a minimum wage is likely to be counterproductive in increasing unemployment levels. Labour that is relatively unskilled and unproductive will be artificially overpriced and less likely to be hired by potential employers.

MARXIST ANALYSIS: INHERENT CONTRADICTIONS IN CAPITALIST MARKETS

Marx did not see capitalist markets as tending towards equilibrium. On the contrary, he predicted that markets would lurch through ever-worsening cycles of booms and slumps, as capital becomes increasingly concentrated in fewer hands, overproduction gluts the markets, rates of profit fall, and workers experience worsening exploitation and poverty, until in the long run the entire capitalist system would collapse under the weight of its own internal contradictions. Outlined below is Marx's model of the inherent workings or "laws" of capitalism that prompted him to be so pessimistic about how the system would develop.

Law of Increasing Concentration of Capital

Capitalists compete with each other to make profits by selling commodities in the market. They maximize their market share and profits by producing commodities more efficiently and cheaply than competitors, or by bringing new and improved commodities to the market. The first capitalists to introduce new labour-saving technology can make larger profits, because they can cut the labour costs of producing the commodities and thus undersell competitors in the market. Competing capitalists must rapidly introduce similar technology to keep their production costs down, or find other ways to cheapen labour costs, or they will go bankrupt. Smaller or less efficient capitalists who cannot afford the new technology have to drop their prices in order to sell their commodities but are unable to drop their costs of production. Eventually they become uncompetitive, go bankrupt, and drop out of the market. Those capitalists who remain can buy up their competitors' machines and factories, and can expand their market share with higher-volume, lower-cost commodities. These leading capitalists can invest their increased profits into new enterprises, or into researching more productive technologies and so increase their relative dominance within the market. Over time, therefore, capitalist corporations tend to continually increase in size and decrease in numbers as they merge with, buy out, or defeat competitors.

Polarization of Classes

As dominant capitalists amass increasing proportions of productive resources and investment capital, the weaker members who form a middle class of smaller commodity producers are increasingly likely to fail and fall into the working class. Over time, a small number of very large capitalists will dominate a given sector of enterprise to form an oligopoly or even a single monopoly corporation. When this stage is reached, normally competitive relations between producers will be replaced by collusion.

Law of Falling Rate of Profit

Over time, as all capitalists remaining in the market are using new technology, the new level of productivity, or average labour time, becomes standard across the market. The price of commodities in the market will drop to reflect this new exchange value, and profits will fall. The economy will stagnate until some new technological breakthrough permits innovative capitalists, once again, to better the average productivity of labour and raise profits. A concurrent problem is that as mechanization increases, capitalists must invest significantly more money on machines relative to wages. Since profits accrue primarily from the surplus value produced by workers, the actual rate of profit across that sector of the economy starts to fall. New technology must increase productivity markedly

over older methods of production for the rate of profit to keep rising.

Increasing Immiseration of the Masses

Marxist theory uses the concept of **immiseration** as a verb to refer to the active practices within capitalism that make the lives of working masses more miserable. As **labour-saving technology** replaces workers, the rate of unemployment increases. As workers compete for a limited supply of jobs, the average price or wage-level drops. Displaced workers struggling to regain a foothold in the working class form a **reserve army of labour**, their competition for jobs serving to depress wages even further. In the long run, Marx reasoned, these processes work to force down the average wage across the market. Workers may make temporary gains in their standard of living, but these gains will always be insecure and threatened by the prospect of technological change that will make their work obsolete. Marx referred to the class of workers displaced by machines as a **lumpenproletariat** of "declassed" workers, separated from their class of origin and unable to find a place for themselves in society. This mass of ruined and impoverished people fall easy prey to reactionary or fascist ideologies and movements.

Crises of Overproduction

The central concern for capitalists is not unemployment as such, but the drop in effective demand or purchasing power in the market. Unemployed and lower-paid workers do not have the money needed to purchase commodities that flood the market. Capitalists find themselves left with surplus production that they cannot sell. They are forced to operate more and more below full productive capacity. At the same time they must make still greater efforts to develop labour-saving technology that will cut production costs so that they can sell more cheaply. Thus collectively they generate still more unemployment.

A Treadmill of Technological Innovation

Capitalists depend on significant breakthroughs in new technology and the development of new commodities to expand production. Marx saw this insatiable competitive drive to develop new productive technologies as the most positive feature of the capitalist mode of production. Capitalism works to promote innovative human potential. New technologies open up new fields of productive enterprise that in turn increase demand for labour power and promote higher wages in the short run.

Recurrent Crises of Booms and Slumps

In the long run, technological innovation cannot overcome the inherent tendencies towards falling rates of profit and retrenchment. As labour costs rise, capitalists find it more profitable to invest in yet more labour-saving technology, or to replace skilled labour with lower-cost workers, and the cycle repeats itself. The larger capitalists who command greater investment potential are in the best situation to exploit new technology, beat out competitors, and dominate the market. Remaining capitalists are driven to push down costs of production even further to undercut competitors in ever-tighter markets. In the process, they produce yet more unemployment, tighter profit ratios, more bankruptcies, and a still bigger glut of commodities that impoverished workers cannot afford to buy.

In conclusion, Marx predicted that in the long run the masses of dispossessed workers and ruined former capitalists would join in a revolution to overthrow this flawed mode of production and usher in a new synthesis. He envisioned a new socialized or communal mode of production that could harness the innovative potential of capitalism for collective well-being. Once the means of production are socialized, rather than concentrated in the hands of giant monopoly capitalists, Marx reasoned, goods and services could be produced, not as commodities to sell for profits but to meet the real needs of masses of people.

BOOMS AND SLUMPS: CRISES IN FINANCIAL CAPITALISM

The following section describes the upheaval in financial markets around the world, centred in the crash of the US housing market that began in the fall of 2007. It then explores mainstream and Marxist analyses of the crisis.

At the beginning of the first decade of the twenty-first century, North American society showed signs of general prosperity, measured particularly in rising property values. House prices seemed to be going ever upwards. House prices in the USA doubled in the decade from 1997 to 2007. In Britain they tripled (Turner 2008, 27). Generous mortgage rates offered even quite poor families an opportunity to buy into the market. Banks were offering mortgages with repayment spread over 40 years with no down payments required, and "teaser" mortgages where for the first three to five years mortgagees would have to pay only low interest rates and could even defer payments on the principal. The assumption was that by the time they would need to remortgage the property on normal interest and repayment terms, the market value of the property would have increased so that they could borrow more money. Fully 85 percent of

Americans surveyed in 2007 said they expected their home values to rise. Car companies like Chrysler, GM, and Ford were offering new cars for sale with zero down payment and no credit rating required. Credit card companies were competing with each other to offer larger credit limits. Similar patterns were evident across the European Union and beyond. In Britain, homeowners nominally owned property worth eight times their disposable (after-tax) incomes (Turner 2008, 27). It seemed that almost everyone could live now, own a new house and car, buy the latest electronic gadgets, take dream vacations, send the kids to college, and pay later when they could expect to be better off. If there were rumblings of doubt that this boom was unsustainable, few people in authority were listening.

Then by mid-2007 cracks began to appear—huge cracks. It was manifest first in the failure of the giant investment bank Bear Stearns, which acknowledged exposure to almost $400 billion in mostly worthless assets. Soon political and economic leaders were watching in horror as five more of the biggest investment banks in the world followed Bear Stearns into bankruptcy. The US federal government at first did nothing as Lehman Brothers, a firm with assets of more than $600 billion, filed the largest bankruptcy in US history in September 2008. But the government then felt forced to bail out other banks or risk a meltdown of the entire US financial system. The government also found itself compelled to take over or effectively nationalize the two giant US mortgage companies Freddie Mac and Fannie Mae, which together held or guaranteed almost half of all US mortgages. The two companies posted fourth-quarter losses of about $50 billion in 2008 from home-mortgage defaults and falling house prices. As thousands of repossessed houses began to flood the market, house prices plummeted, leaving many thousands more mortgagees owing more to the banks than their homes were worth, thus triggering yet more defaults. Investors who had bought shares in these "toxic" mortgages, expecting to make good returns, found their investments worthless. Those who had insured their investments against default placed claims against insurance companies, triggering yet more bankruptcies of giant insurance companies, including AIG, which lost a whopping $61.7 billion in 2008. As insured claims escalated, yet more banks failed as they found their assets dwarfed by debts from these claims on top of toxic mortgages.

The US Congress, which first balked in 2008 at President George Bush's request for a $700-billion taxpayer bailout of financial institutions, later agreed to President Obama's bailout package of more than $2 trillion in March 2009. To help grasp just how much money 1 trillion dollars, or $1,000,000,000,000 is, Oxford mathematics professor Marcus du Sautoy calculated that one trillion seconds would take 31,688 years to pass. One billion seconds would take 31.7 years to pass (CCPA Monitor, May 2009, 19).

Credit markets dried up as banks became so mired in bad loans that they stopped lending money. Governments tried pouring money into their banking systems and dropped interest rates to around 1 percent in an effort to free up credit and restart business enterprise, only to find banks hoarding the money against the threat of further losses, and debt-strapped businesses and homeowners unwilling to borrow money even at rock-bottom interest rates. Millions of homeowners who had been encouraged to take out loans against the supposed equity in their homes suddenly found their debt-to-asset ratio markedly worse and the value of their pension savings slashed. Companies in financial trouble laid off workers. Consumer spending dropped sharply, precipitating more retrenchment and lay-offs in other industries. The almost unthinkable happened. Giant automobile companies GM, Chrysler, and Ford together begged for a $17-billion bailout from the US government in 2008, and returned begging for another $20 billion in 2009 in a bid to avoid bankruptcy. Job losses across the entire industry, including manufacturing plants, suppliers, and dealers, are estimated in the hundreds of thousands. Automotive and manufacturing industries in the province of Ontario alone shed about 60 000 jobs in May 2009. Shares in these giant financial corporations became worthless, triggering huge losses on stock markets around the world. Individual investors, along with mutual funds, pension funds, endowment funds, and the like, all suffered major losses, averaging a third of their value. Shares in Bear Stearns alone dropped from a high of $133.20 to $2, even backed up by federal bailout money. Shares in the Fannie Mae mortgage company dropped from $50 to 75 cents. Banks and governments around the world that had invested in these once lucrative but now worthless assets saw their wealth slashed. Banks in Iceland lost investments worth close to nine times the country's annual gross domestic product (GDP), leaving the country bankrupt. The state of California, the eighth largest economy in the world, also faced bankruptcy in 2009, with a budget deficit of $26.3 billion. The state was forced to issue IOUs for $3.4 billion in July 2009 for bills it could not pay. The US economy had been running large trade deficits since the 1990s, totalling more than $800 billion by 2006. China, which by then held almost $1 trillion worth of US dollars, had invested or "parked" much of this money in the US stock market, including in housing. There is virtually no economy in the world that escaped damage from this financial meltdown in the centre of capitalism. By mid-July 2009, warning signs were emerging of a looming meltdown in commercial real estate. Commercial property values in the US have dropped even more than house prices, placing bank loans of around $2 trillion at risk of default. The next crash may well be bankrupt consumers defaulting on credit card debts.

EXPLAINING THE SLUMP: MAINSTREAM ANALYSIS

Mainstream explanations for the crisis in the financial system focus on the culture of greed and entitlement that prevails among corporate elites in US financial institutions, and the lack of effective regulation of financial transactions. The emergence of both these problems reflect belief that the self-interest of financial leaders in making profits for shareholders ought normally to be sufficient to ensure that the system works smoothly.

Mainstream analysts found ample evidence to support these arguments. Newspapers bulged with reports of executives from the big three auto companies flying into Washington on luxury corporate jets to beg for taxpayer bailouts. The executives apparently considered luxury travel a reasonable perk to top up their $25-million-plus annual salaries (ABC News, 19 Nov. 2008). AIG insurance company received a $170-billion bailout package from the US Federal Reserve, and promptly used $165 million of this taxpayer money to award bonuses to their executives, this reportedly in addition to the $121 million previously scheduled bonuses already paid out. The chairman of AIG argued that such money was necessary to attract the best and brightest staff to run the company, and hence was consistent with shareholder and taxpayer interests (*New York Times*, 14 March 2009). The same overarching culture of entitlement and excess was evident among the masses of mortgagees who had been only too ready to live beyond their means, to grab at mortgage deals they could not possibly sustain for the long term, and to maximize credit card debts.

It was primarily the absence of effective regulations governing financial transactions, however, that made it possible for elites in banking and insurance corporations to develop the complex and obscure mortgage investment schemes that led eventually to the collapse of the US housing market. Banks, mortgage lenders, real estate companies, and insurance companies all benefited from promoting "sub-prime" mortgages. These included risky mortgages with 40-year terms, zero down-payment, below-prime interest rates for three to five years, and even deferred payment on the principal loan. The catch was that much higher than normal interest rates would be charged later—making them lucrative loans. These high-risk loans were swiftly "sliced and diced" into packages with hundreds of other mortgages and sold off to investors as asset-backed securities with AAA ratings. The chance that thousands of risky loans would all default at once was deemed mathematically improbable. Packaging loans as fancy products and selling them to investors freed up money to make more loans, which created more home buyers or homeowners refinancing their mortgages, which in turn boosted house prices.

To further reassure investors, insurance companies combined with banks to offer insurance against losses through "credit default swaps." The buyer of the swap made quarterly payments to the bank in return for banks promising large payments if the assets declined in value (Hudson 2009, 95).

It is these credit-default swaps that got banks into trouble. Ever since the Great Depression, when people lost their life savings in bank failures, US banks have been required to keep separate their deposit and loan activities from selling financial securities and insurance, to avoid possible conflict of interest. However, after 25 years of lobbying Congress, US banks succeeded in 1999 in getting these restrictions lifted, arguing successfully that competing foreign banks had more access to credit and could generate more income by selling insurance. Between 2001 and 2008, the global credit derivatives market—the market for buying and selling insurance or risk associated with loans—doubled every year. The amount of money involved in sub-prime mortgages rose from $19 billion in 1995 to $56 billion by 2000 and $508 billion in the peak of 2005. Everyone involved had vested interests in pushing risky mortgages and off-loading the risks. Real estate agents working on commission had an incentive to sell more expensive houses; lenders had an incentive to maximize their interest income by approving higher mortgage limits; banks invented "structured investment vehicles" into which to sell their loans so that they did not need to keep reserves to secure them. Everyone cashed in on the fees charged to arrange these transactions. When this complex house of cards collapsed, banks that had sold insurance on the assets had to acknowledge the losses on their balance sheets (Loxley 2009, 66–67). The sliced and diced mortgage packages were so fragmented that even the banks initially had no clear idea of their level of exposure to risk.

Free or Regulated Markets: Tinkering with the Machine

After the crash, President-elect Obama, together with European political leaders, called for tighter regulations and oversight of financial transactions. Alan Greenspan, the chairman of the Federal Reserve of the USA from 1987 to 2006, and a prime supporter of deregulation of banks, acknowledged in retrospect: "I made a mistake in presuming that the self-interests of organizations, specifically banks and others, were such that they were best capable of protecting their own shareholders and their equity in the firms" (cited in Hudson 2009, 51). Proposed regulations included banning risky 40-year, no-deposit, teaser-rate mortgages, restricting what banks could sell, requiring more transparency in investment packages floated in the market, controlling credit-rating agencies so that they do not profit from the AAA ratings they bestow on such packages, and the like.

More than a year later, however, no government has taken any action, and financial institutions are lobbying hard against regulations. Government regulation of financial capital, if ever seriously implemented, would work against three decades of entrenched beliefs that free markets, in which people pursue their economic self-interests subject to minimal government interference or regulation, are the best wealth-generating option. Regulations are viewed as at best likely to be clumsy, costly, and inefficient, and at worst likely to result in major distortions dragging down economic activity (Hudson 2009, 47). Successive Republican and conservative governments in the US and Europe since the early 1980s firmly endorsed the policies of unrestricted free markets, known as "neo-liberalism." They gutted regulatory agencies by choosing partisan appointees, who were opposed to the very mandate of the agencies they headed, and by cutting funds and staff. Few were willing to reverse course.

The preferred mainstream strategy for dealing with the crisis was to patch up the immediate mess in the housing market, prop up or bail out insolvent banks sufficiently to get credit flowing again, and then trust the free market system to fix itself as millions of producers, consumers, and investors act in their own self-interests to promote commerce. Government involvement would focus on manipulating interest rates and stimulus packages to kick-start the system. Mainstream economists do not worry much about long-term deflation or falling prices, as happened during the Great Depression of the 1930s, reasoning that by pumping enough new money into the system, it will always be possible to lower the value of money relative to prevailing prices enough for prices to stabilize or begin to rise. The main fear is excess demand driving up inflation.

Theoretical models of economic activity developed by mainstream economists over the last three decades strongly support this relative hands-off approach (Hayes 2008). Economists conceptualize the economy as akin to a machine, and they have developed a series of mathematical models, measures, and indicators to assess how the machine is running. These measures provide governments with tools for tinkering with the machine. Business cycles are seen as normal fluctuations in the dynamic equilibrium of market economics. Only when these boom/bust cycles become too great, as in the housing meltdown, are governments encouraged to intervene. Two central tools for correcting excessive business cycles are monetary and fiscal (Fernandez 2009, 111). Monetary tools involve manipulating central bank interest rates. High interest rates raise the costs of borrowing money and so reduce demand and reduce inflation. Low interest rates boost borrowing and so increase demand and halt recession or falling prices. This has been the major tool used by governments to intervene in falling housing markets.

The second major tool is fiscal, used when low interest rates are insufficient to halt recession. Governments pump money into the economy to stimulate growth. Fiscal stimulus is a controversial tool because it results in governments running deficits. Governments cannot raise taxes during recessions because higher taxes tend to reduce both corporate investment and consumer spending. But government deficits mean future taxes and so meet with fierce resistance. Getting the stimulus correct is also difficult. President Bush offered $600 tax rebates to 117 million taxpayers in February 2008 as part of his $150-billion stimulus package. His expressed hope was that people would spend the windfall, and thus boost the demand curve and stimulate the economy. Critics warned that most of the money would likely be used to pay down debts, or be hoarded, and so have little noticeable effect on the economy. Critics were correct.

Stimulus or bailout packages for the automobile industry were used, but under stringent conditions designed to force the big three manufacturers back into competitive profitability. They were first required to exact concessions from unions in wages, pensions, and other benefits to bring them down to the level of Japanese car workers, and then to slash the workforce and close plants to become "leaner and meaner" before receiving state aid. The Obama government actually drove the chief executive of GM out of office for not downsizing and restructuring fast enough (Stanford 2009, 25). The great fear with providing such handouts is that they distort the markets by keeping potentially uncompetitive, obsolete companies afloat, encouraging a host of other industries to demand equivalent bailout packages, as well as worsening government deficits and thus inevitable future tax demands.

Beyond these monetary and fiscal measures, there is little more that mainstream economic advisors suggest for governments to do. The expectation is that the combination of low interest rates and targeted stimulus spending will create the conditions for a corrective upswing in normal economic activity.

EXPLAINING THE SLUMP: MARXIST ANALYSIS

Marxist analysis focuses on class conflict to explain the crisis in the financial system. This conflict has taken the form of a long-running drive by governments and corporate leaders to break the power of labour unions, dismantle the post-war welfare state, and force down wages. Back in the early 1980s, leaders like US president Ronald Reagan and British prime minister Margaret Thatcher, and their economic advisors, argued that welfareism combined with excess wages were undermining competitiveness and productivity, and thus stifling economic growth and prosperity. They

promoted free trade deals that facilitated the massive export of manufacturing jobs from North America and Europe to low-wage countries like China.

Marxist theorists argue that these policies have worked to boost corporate profits while driving down wages and effective consumer demand. Global corporations, awash in profits but facing stagnant consumer demand, have engaged for decades in wild financial speculation rather than productive investment. The result has been an ever-worsening series of asset bubbles followed by their inevitable crash. Workers in industrialized countries, struggling to maintain their living standards, have sunk into worsening debt while globally absolute poverty has increased.

Endemic Crises: A "System" Out of Control

In support of their argument, Marxist analysts point out that the current housing crisis is not an isolated aberration but part of a series of crises in the global financial system over the past two decades. The 1987 "savings and loan" crash was similar to the housing crisis of 2007. Specialized banks used low-interest, federally insured deposits in savings accounts to fund mortgages. The industry successfully lobbied Congress in 1982 to remove restrictions on interest rates and loan-to-asset ratios. Congress also cut the budgets of regulatory agencies. The banks subsequently invested heavily in speculative real estate and commercial loans. Within one year, a third of these loans were in trouble, but banks continued lending. By 1989, the industry was bankrupt and Congress had to bail out the banks to the amount of $153 billion, most of it taxpayers' money. US housing values slumped about 20 percent in 1990 and took several years to recover.

In 1997, emerging markets in South Asia that had been expanding so rapidly they were referred to as "tigers" suddenly crashed, with a massive outflow of speculative money. The value of their currencies plunged and foreign debt more than doubled, forcing countries in the region to borrow about $40 billion from the International Monetary Fund. Stringent loan conditions required governments to gut all social services, leading to mass destitution and food riots.

The Japanese economy was the envy of the world during the 1980s for its rapid growth, surging real-estate values, and booming stock market. Then the bubble burst. Property values started dropping, losing a third of their value in major cities in 1990, triggering a massive default in bank loans. As bankruptcies climbed, debt-collection agencies aggressively forced debtors to liquidate their assets to cover debts, which pushed asset prices into free fall (Turner 2008, 151–152). Once large numbers of debtors are forced to sell, prices slide, which makes remaining debts larger relative to assets, forcing still more debtors to sell off assets. Japan slid into a vicious cycle of debt deflation that lasted more than a decade. The Japanese government belatedly used the "normal" monetary and fiscal policies to stop the slide, dropping interest rates to 0 percent and pumping money into the market, but nothing worked. With so many bankrupt companies and loans in default, no one wanted to lend or borrow money. Money-market brokers picked up all the stimulus money and deposited it back in the banks. Families started hoarding money. Japanese companies, along with their Asian competitors, put all their efforts into exports—only to find markets glutted and prices falling. The recent financial crisis in the USA has made the Japanese recession worse.

Between 1998 and 2001, yet another crisis emerged on North American stock markets, known as the "dot-com" or "information-technology" bubble. Speculative or venture capital poured into exciting new Internet-based companies. Share values held by individuals nearly quadrupled (Turner 2008, 28). As share prices started rising, more speculators jumped on the bandwagon hoping for quick profits, and prices surged. Awash in money, many of these young Internet companies started selling new commodities below production costs, hoping to develop market share and brand awareness in anticipation of the big take-off. As it became obvious that markets were saturated and most of these companies would never make a profit, share prices plunged. In one day, 13 March 2000, the stock market lost almost 10 percent of its overall value. Dozens of companies, the largest being WorldCom, were found to have illegally inflated asset values to attract investors.

Governments, anxious to avoid recession in the wake of this market downturn, adopted policies of cheap money and easy credit, which fostered the next boom in the mortgage market.

The Contradictions of Capitalism: Class War in the Marketplace

Marxist analysis focuses attention on this recent historical pattern of faster and larger booms and slumps to make the point that the US sub-prime mortgage crisis was not an accident, but a symptom of fundamental flaws in the global capitalist market. Greed and lack of regulation of financial markets are certainly part of the picture, but not the root cause. Tinkering with the market through monetarism and fiscal policies—low interest rates and stimulus packages—will not work because the market is not tending towards equilibrium. From the perspective of Marxist analysis, the abstract mathematical models of the economy developed by mainstream economists constitute ideology, not science, because they obscure and distort underlying political contradictions. The underlying problem that these models do not address is class conflict, manifest in extreme concentration of wealth and inequality. This perspective is explored below, using Marx's model of the contradictions of capitalism.

Increasing Concentration of Capital   Global commerce at the beginning of the twenty-first century is dominated by giant transnational corporations. When gross corporate sales are compared with gross national product of nation states, corporations comprise half of the top 100 largest economies in the world. The nature of competitive capitalism changes significantly when a small number of large corporations dominate a sector of commerce. It is in their collective interests to compete more by cost-cutting and sales than by price wars that would threaten profit margins (Foster and Magdoff 2009, 79). Free-trade policies, combined with virtually instantaneous speed of communications around the world, have facilitated a competitive drive to move manufacturing and assembly work, and increasingly also call centres and services, from relatively high-wage industrialized societies to low-wage economies. Neo-liberal government policies instituted in the early 1980s facilitated this job transfer by removing all barriers to investment and trade abroad, without protecting workers' rights. Unfettered access to huge pools of cheap labour in countries such as China and Mexico have enabled corporations to hold down wages and benefits in the industrialized economies. Individual companies have no choice but to follow this trend or be undercut in the market. In classic Marxist terminology, there has been a huge increase in the rate of surplus value and profits to corporations at the relative expense of workers in industrialized economies.

Falling Rate of Profits   From the perspective of corporate capital, the downside of shifting jobs to low-wage economies has been stagnation in industrialized economies. Three processes are working together here: mature industrialized economies already have the basic industrial infrastructure; monopolization of sectors of the economy limits price competition and innovation; and growing inequalities in income distribution limit effective consumption demand (Foster and Magdoff 2009, 102). When a small number of corporations dominate a market they have little incentive to invest further in that market. Opportunities for productive investment with the potential to return the same or higher rates of profit decline. Automobile companies, for example, long resisted innovation in car engines as unprofitable.

Effective consumer demand in industrialized economies is also being held down by stagnant or declining aggregate wage levels. Investments poured into emerging economies to develop the factories and marketing infrastructure required to exploit the pool of low-wage workers, but once these markets became glutted, corporate shareholders found limited opportunities to productively invest their huge profits. Capitalists are primarily interested in making profits, not commodities. When they do not expect sufficient profitable returns from investing to produce commodities, they shift investments more and more into speculative financial capital. Marx represents this as a shift from M – C – M to M – M; that is, a shift from using money to make commodities to exchange for more money, to purely using money to make more money. Marxist analysts refer to this process as financialization.

Financialization
Traditionally, stocks and shares are thought of as pooled savings for investment in production. But, as noted above, shares can also be traded independently as paper claims to assets, claims that can easily be traded for money. Owners have claims not to real assets in the enterprise, but to future wealth or money. Chernomas (2009, 23) estimates that from 1950 to the early 1970s, financial assets were worth about four times the gross domestic product of the USA, but by 2007 they were worth about 10 times the GDP. Gonick (2009, 9) similarly estimates that by 2008 only 3 percent of all market transactions involved money for expanding production. The rest was for speculation in financial assets. These huge pools of easy money swirl through the markets creating asset bubbles in emerging economies as bad as those in North America (Turner 2008, 110).

People with money have turned financial markets into a giant casino in which they can play the markets 24 hours a day, betting that they can make profits on small fluctuations in value. Daily trading in world currency markets has risen from $18 billion a day in 1977 to $1.8 trillion by 2008, equivalent to the entire world's annual gross domestic product every 24 days (Foster and Magdoff 2009, 56). Investors can play the market in many ways. They can bet that a particular currency or stock will drop in value, so they borrow a large amount of it from a broker, sell it quickly, and promise to buy it back at a later date when they expect it to be cheaper. Alternatively, they can buy the right to purchase currency or stock at a fixed price in the future, betting that it will have increased in value. One can bet on the future value of almost any commodity. Futures markets in agricultural products make sense in that they stabilize future costs of needed products, but by 2005 more than 90 percent of futures markets were purely speculative. Housing markets were drawn into this casino capitalism when banks and insurance companies created mortgage-backed-securities packages and credit-default swaps for investors to trade. This betting frenzy is made more risky by the fact that most of the bets are made with borrowed or leveraged funds. Investors can potentially make huge profits if they borrow upwards of 90 percent of the money they bet, but they can also make huge losses. The estimated nominal value of bets on all derivative deals or trading in credit risks in June 2006 was estimated to be worth more than six times all the goods and services traded in the world in one year (Foster and Magdoff 2009, 58). The more that financial markets are separated from the real market in goods and services, the more unstable the markets become.

The "real" market in productive investments has become sucked into the casino frenzy as the same floods of cheap money have been used in multiple takeovers, mergers, and acquisitions, again often financed with borrowed money. In a strategy known as "Buy it. Strip it. Flip it" (Foster and Magdoff 2009, 59), investors take over a targeted firm, arrange for the firm to borrow money to pay themselves dividends, fees, and interest on the money they borrowed, and then sell off shares in the now more heavily indebted firm to pocket quick profits. These practices resemble giant, legalized Ponzi or pyramid schemes whereby investors pay themselves rewards out of future investors' money rather than real assets. Firms trying to avoid these "hostile takeovers" are pressured to adopt a strategy of loading up on debts to make themselves less inviting as targets.

Polarization of Classes
This is the core of the Marxist argument. The shift from productive economy to casino capitalism is driven by extreme inequality that is global in scope. Huge profits made by giant corporations that gain surplus value from low-wage economies flow to a tiny minority of elite shareholders. In the decade of the 1980s, Chernomas reports (2009, 21), all gains in earnings in America went only to the top 20 percent of earners. In one generation, between 1973 and 2000, the wealth of the top one-tenth of 1 percent of the population rose 343 percent, and the income of the top one-hundredth of 1 percent rose almost 600 percent, while the incomes of the bottom 90 percent fell by 7 percent. At the same time the American taxation system was altered so that the elite .01 percent who get almost all their income from dividends and capital gains are taxed at only 15 percent of income. Average wage-earners are taxed at more than double this rate. Even multi-billionaire investor Warren Buffett, the second richest man in the world, found this level of injustice hard to accept (Obama 2006, 224–226). The main determinant of membership in the capitalist class, Foster and Magdoff argue, is now ownership of financial capital rather than physical assets (Foster and Magdoff 2009, 85). The top 1 percent of people who held financial capital in the US in 2001 owned more than four times the capital of the bottom 80 percent. The richest 1 percent of Americans held $1.9 trillion in stocks, equalling the wealth of the other 99 percent of Americans put together. This inequality distorts patterns of investment and patterns of consumption.

Immiseration of the Masses Mainstream neo-liberal economics policies assume that wealth at the top will trickle down to the rest of the economy, but this has largely not happened. The United Nations Human Development Report 2005 estimates that globally one billion people live on less than $1 per day, and a further 1.5 billion people live on under $2 per day (cited in McNally 2009, 32). These people exist at life-threatening levels of poverty. McNally notes that in the spring of 2008, Western governments pledged $22 billion in emergency hunger relief, but actually gave only $2.2 billion. Meanwhile they bailed out financial institutions by $10 trillion, or 5000 times more money. Poverty in North America is less obvious than in parts of Africa, but some 36 million people in the US lack basic food security (McNally 2009). In Canada a food bank report, HungerCount 2008, estimated that each month more than 704 000 Canadians received food from a food bank. Among low-income workers, fully 14.5 percent in 2008 needed help from a food bank to feed their families.

Free-trade policies have pressured corporations to compete with each other to exploit cheap labour pools in emerging economies. Virtually all major brand-name clothing companies have moved production to places like China. They can claim not to use sweatshop labour by the legal fiat of working through subcontractors who actually run the factories. Wal-Mart has a particularly bad reputation for forcing subcontractors to compete with each other to shave pennies off rock-bottom contracts to assemble goods (see PBS Frontline/Wal-Mart). Wal-Mart is not alone.

Emerging market economies are described as "awash in money" and having "large pools of easy finance swirling through" them (Turner 2008, 110), but this is largely speculative money seeking quick profits from cheap labour pools, rather than money focused on long-term productive human development. Even small South Asian economies like Thailand, South Korea, and Indonesia have received net financial inflows in the order of $20 billion a year (Turner 2008, 112), but this has not translated into higher incomes for their populations. These countries know that they are attracting investment monies only because they offer pools of low-wage workers. If they were to raise wage levels, or raise the value of their currencies, they have good reason to fear that the taps would turn off, and the money flow elsewhere. China has a huge trade surplus with the US, and in 2007 held dollar reserves estimated to be between $800 billion and $1.5 trillion (Turner 2008, 116), but has resisted pressure to raise the value of its currency. China is already experiencing a significant outflow of investment and jobs to Vietnam and even Myanmar, where wages are lower.

Workers in industrialized societies cannot compete with these low-cost economies. They have seen their own bargaining power weaken and the value of their wages stagnate against rising prices. Real wages in the US rose steadily until the early 1970s, but then began to retrench as significant outsourcing of jobs began. By 2009, the real value of wages in America, controlling for inflation, had dropped to 1967 levels (Gonick 2009, 9). In Canada, bolstered by the Alberta oil-sands development, average wages have dropped to 1982 levels. In contrast, the average compensation to chief executive officers of the top 50 US companies in 2009 is 350 times the average worker's pay. In other words, executives earn more in one day than workers earn in a year.

Working families have managed to support their standard of living over the last decade only by having two incomes, working multiple jobs, borrowing against equity in their homes, and going heavily into credit card debt. Government policies encouraged high consumer debt in a bid to avoid recession after the crash in information-technology share prices in 2000. Increasing debt levels were disguised as long as the housing bubble lasted, but the combination of declining property values and rising unemployment have made visible these unsustainable debt levels. From this perspective, the Obama government's policy of forcing automobile companies to slash jobs, wages, and benefits to become leaner and meaner and more competitive only makes this situation worse. Effective consumer demand continued to fall throughout 2009 in a vicious cycle of further job losses.

Crises of Overproduction Crises of overproduction in North American markets became obvious in 2008 as the asset bubble in housing burst. Houses with foreclosed mortgages glutted the housing market and undermined the market for new housing. Consumers mired in debt, their assets diminished and their jobs insecure, stopped buying. The crisis spread rapidly to cars, forcing the big-three North American automobile manufacturers to cut production as thousands of unsold vehicles clogged their lots. The crises soon reverberated through related markets, hitting suppliers of components and accessories for new houses, including Canada's lumber industry, suppliers of car parts, distributors, and showrooms across the economy. As these two major industries cut production and laid off many thousands more workers, these workers and their families stopped spending money on other goods like vacations, causing cutbacks in a host of other industries. By mid-2009, close to 10 percent of the North American workforce were officially unemployed, not counting those who gave up looking for work, or who found only minimum-wage replacement jobs.

The crisis of overproduction does not reflect people surfeiting of the goods and not wanting any more. It reflects people being unable to afford to buy them. The American and Canadian governments and business elites are hoping that potentially vast consumer markets in China will resolve crises of overproduction. Wal-Mart in particular has been expanding stores across China. An elite class of multi-billionaires has emerged in China, as local entrepreneurs partner with global corporations investing in low-wage enterprises, and they provide a market for high-end luxury goods from the West. The major problem, however, is that the vast mass of potential customers have minimal effective demand. They earn near-subsistence-level wages, have insecure jobs, no unemployment insurance, no health plans, and no pensions. Hence, they hoard money rather than spend it (Hutton 2006, 167–170). Similar patterns are evident across free-trade zones in Asia and Latin America. The recession in the West cut demand for exports from China, resulting in factory closures and mass layoffs. By mid-2009 the Chinese government was reported to be pouring stimulus money into the economy, and forcing banks to lend money, in an effort to avoid mass unrest following the lay-offs. The risk is that a huge asset bubble in government-sponsored commercial real estate is being created. Japan's decade-long experience with fighting debt deflation has been that low interest rates and stimulus packages were insufficient to promote a real rise in domestic consumption. Japan's export markets were being saturated by Asian competitors even before the global recession hit.

Marxist analysis of long-term trends in Western economies suggests that the problem of overproduction is not a temporary effect of the sub-prime mortgage fiasco, but part of decades-long stagnation in the real economy—a pattern of slow growth, high unemployment and underemployment, and excess productive capacity (Foster and Magdoff 2009, 12). The authors estimate that 15 percent of North American industrial capacity was not being utilized in 1970, and this had increased to 22 percent by 2003. This is part of the pattern of falling rates of profit discussed above. By 2009, with production shutting down across the economy, the underutilization of productive potential far exceeds 2003 levels. Underutilization of labour also far exceeds official unemployment figures, as these figures hide workers underemployed in low-wage service-sector jobs below their real skill levels.

The effective level of stagnation in the "real" productive economy is obscured by non-productive investment in financialization. General Motors had been losing money on selling cars long before the 2008 crash, but made profits by offering financial services (Foster and Magdoff 2009, 54). By 2005, fully 40 percent of GM profits were from fees and interest from arranging financial transactions. Many other corporations have entered the business of offering credit cards, and large grocery chains are offering mortgages, in a bid to combat static or declining sales.

In effect, Marxists argue, the current global capitalist system of production is surviving on the basis of colossal waste—unused productive capacity and unused labour resources. The extent of the crisis of overproduction has long been masked by government spending on the mass production and consumption of military equipment—equipment destined to be blown up, or trashed as obsolete. Foster and Magdoff estimate that between 2001 and 2005, military spending comprised 28 percent of gross private investment in the US economy and fully 42 percent if residential construction is omitted from the calculation (Foster and Magdoff 2009, 44). Marxist analysts further argue that Western economies recovered from the previous Great Depression of 1929 primarily through production for the Second World War and the ensuing half century of Cold War weapons production. The New Deal to promote consumer spending helped but only to a relatively small degree (Foster and Magdoff 2009, 22; Freeman 2009, 147).

A Treadmill of Technological Innovation The prediction within the original Marxist model was that capitalists would be driven to invest in labour-saving technology in order to lower production costs in the face of declining profits and competition. The contemporary Marxist argument is that the drive to lower wage costs has been met by outsourcing work to low-wage "developing" economies, and by the quick profits to be made by speculating in financial markets. This has lowered incentives to invest significantly in alternative high-technology production.

The post-war invention of the automobile, which sparked massive additional investment in mass production factories, private networks of gasoline and service stations, and especially the government's investment in the public infrastructure of roads, also played a major role in the post-war "golden years" between 1948 and 1970 of high wages and high profits. No future technology has fully taken the place of cars. The invention of the silicon chip and computers boosted productivity and jobs, but without the same demand for government investment in infrastructure. The development of "green energy technology" seems heavily dependent on government investment, and for the short term seems unlikely to absorb the mass of workers displaced by outsourcing manufacturing and service jobs to low-wage economies.

The Future of Capitalism?

Predictions about the future of capitalism and the likelihood of swift recovery from the 2007–2009 recession/depression depends on the kinds of measures emphasized. The most likely outcome seems to be business as usual. By mid-summer of 2009, mainstream politicians and economists began to suggest, cautiously, that the recession had hit bottom and was turning around. They based this optimism on signs like rising rates of housing sales in the US, the emergence of a slim and trim General Motors from bankruptcy, and large post-bailout profits registered by the investment giant Goldman Sachs, supporting executive bonus packages averaging $700 000 each. Many mainstream economists, however, continue to fear that high unemployment combined with high debt levels might send the US economy into a downward spiral of debt deflation and declining consumer demand similar to that experienced in Japan.

Marxist political economists lament the signs of swift return to casino capitalism. This fits a recurring pattern of crash, bailout, and renewed stock-market gambling that followed previous crises (Turner 2008, 3). Few policy changes followed the savings-and-loan crash of 1989, or the crash in technology stocks in 2001. New waves of speculation and

debt soon followed, bolstered by government policies to prop up banks and stock markets. Commentators voiced fears that sudden large profits by Goldman Sachs reflect speculative investments around the government stimulus package rather than "real" growth. Financial speculation in any case does little to resolve massive job losses, continuing stagnation in real economic productivity, and yet more extreme disparities of wealth and absolute poverty on a global scale.

Above all, Marxist analysts lament the slipping away of a real opportunity to change a deeply flawed political-economic system. Nowhere in mainstream political discourse is there discussion of the radical Keynesian proposition that the fundamental goal of macroeconomics should be full employment, with speculative investment income kept to a minimum (Desai 2009, 103). Nor is there any discussion of a potential new economy oriented to promoting civilization, employment in creative arts, or the mass production and consumption of mental capacity that would not endanger the planet (Freeman 2009).

CONCLUSION

This chapter began with a Marxist theory of history that focuses on material conditions of life, tracing the links between successive modes of production and the social and class relations to which they gave rise. Marx traces how successive ruling economic elites influenced prevailing ideas, how feudal concepts of lord and master became projected onto a cosmic notion of god, and how capitalist concepts of an abstract economic system subject to mathematical laws have been projected onto global society. Marx concludes his theory of history with a search for a new materialist synthesis capable of meeting the material needs of all humanity and ending patterns of inequality and class conflict inherent in preceding modes of production.

Marx devoted his life's work to examining the capitalist mode of production, striving to make visible its internal contradictions and its alienating character. The point of such analysis, as he saw it, was not simply to understand it, but to enable people to change it—to bring about a new synthesis (Marx [1845] 1975, 3).

Mainstream contemporary analysis of capitalism views capitalism as a self-regulating system of exchange based on individual self-interest and free competition between consumers and producers in the global marketplace. From this perspective, the economy works best when government constraints are minimal. Mainstream economic models proved embarrassingly unable to predict the crash in the American financial system that precipitated the global

recession. They define it essentially as an aberration caused by excessive greed and inadequate regulations. The enormity of the financial breakdown, however, and the failure of mainstream economics to account for it, has generated renewed interest in Marxist analysis.

Marx viewed capitalism not as a system in equilibrium, but as intrinsically unstable, destined to lurch through ever-worsening cycles of booms and slumps, with increasing concentration of capital, falling rates of profits, worsening exploitation and poverty, stagnant production, and wasted human potential. From this perspective, the recession that became visible in 2007 is merely part of a sequence of similar crises in financial markets over the last two decades. Only the scale of the meltdown is unusual. Marxist analysis tracks the root of this crisis to class war in the marketplace, the decades-long neo-liberal free-trade policies that undermined strong unions and the welfare state in Western economies, and facilitated the shipping of once well-paid and unionized manufacturing jobs offshore to countries offering large pools of low-wage workers. Huge profits from these policies, combined with static or declining aggregate consumer demand in the West, have led to stagnation in the "real" or productive economy and a surge in speculative investment that bets on changing asset values. Unstable asset bubbles have been a recurring result. Meanwhile, both locally and globally the gap is worsening between the tiny minority of extremely wealthy and the growing proportions of desperately poor.

SUGGESTED READING

In his article "Gluttons at the Gate" (2009), Duncan Hood discusses the culture of "intense greed" and entitlement that has emerged among corporate executives and how, in the view of mainstream economists, this contributed to the recent crisis in financial capitalism.

Christopher Hitchens' article "He's Back: The Current Financial Crisis and the Enduring Relevance of Marx" in *The Atlantic* (April 2009, 88–95) is a light, journalistic view of how contemporary analysts are drawing on ideas from Marx to make sense of the global financial crisis that erupted in the fall of 2007.

The introduction to Graham Turner's book *The Credit Crunch* (2008) gives an overview of the US housing-market bubble that precipitated the bankruptcy of major investment US banks and insurance companies, and places this meltdown in the context of the past three decades of neo-liberal economic policies favouring relocation of jobs to low-wage countries.

The collection of essays edited by Julie Guard and Wayne Anthony, *Bankruptcies and Bailouts* (2009), offers a radical Marxist view of the financial crisis with a particular focus on Canadian experiences. Chernomas and McNally describe the extreme inequalities in income, locally and globally, which followed from the neo-liberal free-trade policies of the 1970s and the rise in household debt. Hudson discusses the systematic deregulation of banking systems from the 1980s onward that facilitated the sub-prime mortgage crisis, and the views of mainstream economic advisors who resist significant government regulation, including advisors to President Obama. Essays by Desai and Freeman sketch visions for a transformed capitalist economy more consistent with Marx's vision of a new synthesis.

Barack Obama lays out a visionary mainstream view of the economic inequalities and problems in the American economy in his chapter "Opportunity" in his book *The Audacity of Hope* (2006), written before he became US president, and before the financial crisis exploded. Obama challenges the neo-liberal policies of outsourcing jobs to low-wage countries, and tax structures that favour rich investors, but his vision falls far short of the radical Marxist view of the flawed structure of capitalism. It is a challenge to read his chapter and consider how a Marxist economist might advise him to change his economic policies.

QUESTIONS

1. How do modes of production and class relations differ between feudalism and capitalism?

2. In principle, how does Hegel's concept of "dialectical method" differ from Marx's method of "dialectical materialism"?

3. How do Marxists account for the unique compulsion to invest in capitalist economies? Why was there no similar compulsion to invest in feudal economies?

4. According to Marx, what makes the experience of alienation more pronounced under capitalism compared with feudalism? How can even wealthy capitalists be seen as experiencing alienation?

5. According to Marxist theory, how is classical economics implicated in generating alienated consciousness? What are the "three tricks" involved in ideological thinking?

6. In principle, how does capitalist exchange differ from traditional exchange in barter economies? How does the extraction of absolute surplus from serfs in feudal economies differ from the extraction of relative surplus from workers in capitalist economies?

7. What did Adam Smith see as important factors promoting economic development? How did he argue that stability and justice in economic markets would be better achieved by the free play of market forces than by well-meaning government intervention?

8. What combination of factors does Marx see as leading to recurrent crises of overproduction in capitalist economies?

9. According to mainstream economics, what key factors led to the financial crisis associated with the collapse of sub-prime mortgages in the US? What solutions do they propose for dealing with the situation?

10. In what ways do Marxist analysts see class conflict as the root of a series of recent financial crises, including the collapse of the sub-prime mortgage market? How is consumer debt involved in this process?

WEB LINKS

Stock Exchanges Worldwide
www.tdd.lt/slnews/Stock_Exchanges/Stock.Exchanges.htm
The growing interest in trading commodities and buying/selling stocks is evident from the increase in the number of stock exchanges. This site provides a list of the world's major stock exchanges within Africa, Asia, Europe, the Middle East, North America, and South America.

Canadian Council of Chief Executives
www.ceocouncil.ca
The CCCE is an umbrella organization that connects many of Canada's largest transnational corporations such as Bombardier Inc., Canadian banks and lending institutions such as Federal Express Canada, General Electric Canada, Giant Tiger Stores, IBM, and oil companies. Thomas d'Aquino, chief

executive and president, says: "We engage in an active program of public policy research, consultation, and advocacy. Building a stronger Canada economically and socially is our national mandate. Helping to make Canada and our enterprises number one around the world is our global mandate."

World Council for Corporate Governance
www.wcfcg.net

The WCFCG website gives an account of the transnational corporations that fall under its mandate. These include companies such as the Centre for Sustainability and Excellence, CSR Europe (consisting of 60 leading multi-nationals), International Chamber of Commerce, African Regional Youth Initiative, and Indian Oil. The site states: "The World Council for Corporate Governance was established as an independent, not for profit international network aimed to galvanize good governance practices worldwide."

Workers' TV 06/19/09—LGBT liberation and the class struggle
www.mefeedia.com/entry/06-19-09-lgbt-liberation-the-class-struggle/19908362

Shelley Ettinger lectures on patriarchy and subjugation of women within a capitalist, classist society.

Vodpod: Capitalism
"http://vodpod.com/tag/capitalism

This link on Vodpod highlights several lectures, presentations, and talks on capitalism from people such as Ecuadorian president Rafael Correa, Michael Porter, Naomi Klein, Nassim Nicholas Taleb, David Harvey, Alan Greenspan, Noam Chomsky, Milton Friedman, and Keith Hart.

KEY TERMS

absolute surplus

advanced communism

alienation

antithesis

base

capital

capitalism

class

class struggle

class-for-itself

class-in-itself

commodities

commodity fetishism

dialectical

dialectical materialism

dialectical method

economic determinist

enclosures

exchange value

exploitation

fetish

feudalism

historical materialism

immiseration

invisible hand of the market

labour-saving technology

labour time

lumpenproletariat

mode of production

nobles

peasant

primitive communism

relations of production

reserve army of labour

serfs

skilled labour time

slavery

socially necessary labour time

state

superstructure

surplus value

synthesis

theory of exchange

thesis

REFERENCES

Baragar, Fletcher. 2009. "Canada and the Crisis." In Julie Guard and Wayne Anthony, eds. *Bankruptcies and Bailouts*. Halifax; Winnipeg: Fernwood Publishing, 77–106.

Blauner, Robert. 1964. *Alienation and Freedom: The Factory Worker and His Industry*. Chicago: University of Chicago Press.

Brenner, Robert. 1977. "The Origins of Capitalist Development: A Critique of Neo-Smithian Marxism." *New Left Review* 104 (July/Aug.): 25–92.

Chernomas, Robert. 2009. "The Economic Crisis: Class Warfare from Reagan to Obama." In Julie Guard and Wayne Anthony, eds. *Bankruptcies and Bailouts*. Halifax; Winnipeg: Fernwood Publishing, 18–31.

Desai, Radhika. 2009. "Keynes Redux: History Catches Up." In Julie Guard and Wayne Anthony, eds. *Bankruptcies and Bailouts*. Halifax; Winnipeg: Fernwood Publishing, 123–144.

Fernandez, Lynne. 2009. "We're all Keynsians—Again." In Julie Guard and Wayne Anthony, eds. *Bankruptcies and Bailouts*. Halifax; Winnipeg: Fernwood Publishing, 107–122.

Foster, John Bellamy, and Fred Magdoff. 2009. *The Great Financial Crisis: Causes and Consequences*. New York: Monthly Review Press.

Freeman, Alan. 2009. "Investing in Civilization." In Julie Guard and Wayne Anthony, eds. *Bankruptcies and Bailouts*. Halifax; Winnipeg: Fernwood Publishing, 145–166.

Gonick, Cy. 2009. "A Great Leap Forward?" In Julie Guard and Wayne Anthony, eds. *Bankruptcies and Bailouts*. Halifax; Winnipeg: Fernwood Publishing, 8–17.

Guard, Julie, and Wayne Anthony, eds. 2009. *Bankruptcies and Bailouts*. Halifax; Winnipeg: Fernwood Publishing.

Hayes, Matthew. 2008. "Governing Business Cycles: Macroeconomic Devices and the Subsumption of the Social." Submitted to *Economy and Society*, September 2008.

Hitchens, Christopher. 2009. "He's Back: The Current Financial Crisis and the Enduring Relevance of Marx." *The Atlantic* (April 2009): 88–95.

Hood, Duncan. 2009. "Gluttons at the gate: How CEOs became obscenely overpaid, and what can be done about it." *Macleans* 122 (17): 30–33.

Hudson, Ian. 2009. "From Deregulation to Crisis." In Julie Guard and Wayne Anthony, eds. *Bankruptcies and Bailouts*. Halifax; Winnipeg: Fernwood Publishing, 46–61.

Hutton, Will. 2006. *The Writing on the Wall: China and the West in the 21st Century*. London: Little Brown.

Loxley, John. 2009. "Financial Dimensions: Origins and State Responses." In Julie Guard and Wayne Anthony, eds. *Bankruptcies and Bailouts*. Halifax; Winnipeg: Fernwood Publishing, 62–76.

Marx, Karl. 1867. Friedrich Engels, ed. *Capital*. Vol. 1: A Critical Analysis of Capitalist Production [1867]. Vol. 2: The Process of Circulation of Capital [1885]. Vol. 3: The Process of Capitalist Production as a Whole [1894]. New York: International Publishers.

Marx, Karl. [1845] 1975. "Thesis on Feuerbach." In *Karl Marx and Friedrich Engels: Collected Works*. Vol. 5. New York: International Publishers, 3–7.

Marx, Karl, and Friedrich Engels. [1846] 1970. *The German Ideology*. New York: International Publishers.

McNally, David. 2009. "Inequality, the Profit System and Global Crisis." In Julie Guard and Wayne Anthony, eds. *Bankruptcies and Bailouts*. Halifax; Winnipeg: Fernwood Publishing, 32–45.

Obama, Barack. 2006. *The Audacity of Hope: Thoughts on Reclaiming the American Dream*. New York: Vintage Books.

Pentland, H.C. 1959. "The Development of a Capitalist Labour Market in Canada." *Canadian Journal of Economics and Political Science* 25 (4): 450–461.

Sayer, D. 1985. "The Critique of Politics and Political Economy: Capitalism, Communism and the State in Marx's Writings of the Mid-1840s." *Sociological Review* 33 (2): 221–253.

Sayer, D. 1983. *Marx's Method, Ideology, Science and Critique in Capital*. Sussex, New Jersey: Harvester/Humanities Press.

Smith, Adam. [1776] 1984. *The Wealth of Nations*. London: Macmillan.

Smith, Dorothy E. 1974. "The Ideological Practice of Sociology." *Catalyst* 8 (Winter): 39–54.

Stanford, Jim. 2009. "Swinging the Axe Makes Corporate Woes Worse, Not Better." *CCPA Monitor* (May 2009), 25.

Teeple, G. 1972. "Land, Labour, and Capital in Pre-Confederation Canada." In Gary Teeple, ed. *Capitalism and the National Question in Canada*. Toronto: University of Toronto Press, 43–66.

Thompson, E.P. 1975. *Whigs and Hunters: The Origins of the Black Act*. London: Allen Lane.

Turner, Graham. 2008. *The Credit Crunch: Housing Bubbles, Globalisation and the Worldwide Economic Crisis*. London: Pluto Press.

This chapter juxtaposes the perspectives of Marxist political economy and liberal economics to explore their usefulness for understanding how the prevailing capitalist system of economic organization works within Canada. Marx analyzed nineteenth-century capitalism as a system of economic organization with immense creative potential but plagued by inherent contradictions that would fracture societies into ever more extreme divisions of wealth and poverty. He predicted that capitalist societies would ultimately collapse under the strain of these conflicts.

Contemporary political economy theory draws on Marx's work, not to make specific predictions about twenty-first-century capitalism but for insight into what Carroll (2004, 2) refers to as a distinctively capitalist way of life, or capitalist ways of organizing economic and social class relations, and their social consequences. This chapter juxtaposes political economy with the alternative liberal-bourgeois perspective, particularly in its contemporary form that is widely referred to as "neo-liberalism." Neo-liberalism rejects Marx's argument that capitalism foments inequality and class conflict. It argues instead that free market principles and competitive individualism at the core of capitalist relations hold the best hope for economic well-being of masses of people, individual freedom, and social and political democracy.

The chapter first summarizes the main tenets of Marxist political economy theory, and contrasts these with principles of liberalism and neo-liberalism. It then uses these models to explore patterns of **corporate capitalism** in Canada, the distribution of ownership and control over capital, and structural shifts that are associated with free-trade agreements between Canada and the United States and Mexico. A key issue in the debates between political economy theory and liberalism concerns class analysis, particularly the question of how capitalist economic relations affect the distribution of income across the economy. Another important issue is the relationship between political and economic institutions, focusing on how the divergent class interests of capitalists and organized labour are represented in democratic political institutions. The social constructionist perspective is useful in this debate as it helps to make visible how people actively manage economic models and concepts, and negotiate legal and political meanings, to continually bring about these economic relations. Constructionist analysis elaborates the Marxist concept of ideological hegemony to explore how the worldview of the dominant capitalist class becomes widely accepted across society and is able to drive policy initiatives, while other interests are discredited and subordinated.

Lastly, we explore the feminist perspective, which challenges both political economy and liberalism for their narrowly focused assumptions that "the main business" of the economy is to accumulate capital. Both perspectives are flawed, in that they ignore the work of women as homemakers and the "social economy" of caring for people. Feminist analysis moves issues of concern to women from the margins to the centre of discussion. It reveals the gendered character of economic power and class oppression, and places family and community well-being at the centre of economic activity. The chapter concludes with a focus on farming in Canada as a case study in the practical application of political economy theory.

 ## Marxist Theory: The Contradictions of Capitalism

A brief summary of Marx's theory of capitalism as a system of economic production is given below. Capitalism is based on the private ownership of the means of production. The term *capital* refers to the stock of productive resources required to make goods or commodities to sell, including land, factories, machines, energy, and raw materials. The class of people who own or can buy the means of production are called capitalists. Workers, those who do not own means to produce for themselves, must sell their labour power for wages with which to buy what they need to survive. Capitalists use money to buy productive resources to make goods that they hope to sell in the market for more money, or profit.

The critical question for capitalists is how to make extra money or profit. They have to buy productive resources at relatively fixed costs in the market, and they also have to buy labour power at the going rate of wages and salaries. The one aspect of production that capitalists are best able to influence is the productivity of labour—the quality and speed of work that people can produce, given the technology and working conditions that capitalists provide. The source of profits, Marx argues, is labour power, because human labour can produce more than its own value. Workers are able to produce commodities that have greater value in the market than the amount they are paid in wages, salaries, and other benefits, with more skilled workers generally creating more valuable commodities. The gap between what workers are paid and the market value of what they produce, when other fixed costs are excluded, provides a measure of the rate of exploitation of workers by capitalists.

Marx argued that the **contradictions of capitalism** stem from competitive pressure to make profits. Capitalists compete with each other to lower production costs so as to sell their commodities at a relative advantage. They strive to maximize the relative exploitation of labour through longer working hours or lower wages, and especially through labour-saving technology to raise the productivity of labour. The more successful capitalists tend to dominate markets and reap high profits as less efficient competitors are driven out of business, until remaining competitors adopt similar or better labour-saving technology and again drive down commodity prices. In the long run, Marx predicted, this pattern of increasing concentration of ownership of capital, combined with labour-saving technology, will be self-defeating. As the investment costs of machines rise relative to labour costs, the rate of profit drops. Rising unemployment and falling aggregate wages also eventually undermine the market because people cannot afford to buy the commodities, leading to crises of overproduction. Capitalism thus seems prone to recurring cycles of booms and slumps. Western capitalist economies depend on an unstable combination of global exploitation of cheap labour and cheap raw materials, insatiable drives to generate new consumer markets, vast military spending to absorb surplus production, and ideological control over prevailing political thought by the ruling capitalist class. This stability, however, is always tenuous.

These ideas are listed below as a series of predictions that guide our analysis of contemporary Canadian experience:

1. *Increasing concentration of capital.* Marx predicts that giant corporations will control the economy as smaller businesses collapse or are bought out. These corporations will constantly increase in size and decrease in number as they merge or are bought out. When one or a few companies dominate a market, they collude rather than compete.

2. *Falling rate of profit.* As more and more money is needed for investment in technology, the returns on investment decline. The economy stagnates as expected future profits to be made from investing more profits declines, especially in sectors dominated by a small number of large corporations.

3. *Polarization of classes.* Capitalists will get richer and richer with the concentration of control over markets. The middle class of small business people and **independent commodity producers** will collapse into the working class.

4. *Increasing poverty of the masses.* Unemployment continually threatens to undermine wage levels. Labour-saving technology results in more and more people competing for fewer jobs. These workers will eventually be joined by bankrupted former members of the small business class. Basic wages will stagnate or be driven down to subsistence levels. The gap between poor workers and rich capitalists will get larger.

5. *Recurrent crises of overproduction.* Due to unemployment and low wages, people lack the money to purchase the goods being produced. The ability to produce goods expands faster than markets can absorb the goods.

6. A *treadmill of technological innovation.* When capitalists cannot sell their products, they must drop their prices. They must force down their costs or increase productivity still further to undercut their competitors. Hence they are driven to develop better labour-saving technology, which will enable them to produce more goods with fewer workers.

7. *Recurrent cycles of booms and slumps.* Bankruptcies lead to unemployment and overproduction. Technological breakthroughs such as robotics and computers bring temporary affluence, but competitors catch up and the cycle repeats itself.

The advanced centres of capitalism may survive these contradictions, at least in the short run, by hyper-exploitation of cheap labour and cheap raw materials extracted from less developed countries, combined with expanding into their markets. The global conflicts generated by such inherent inequalities promote constant military spending, which in turn reduces crises of overproduction. Governments are predisposed to buy military equipment, use it up in fighting, or declare it obsolete, and buy more. In the longer term, however, the contradictions inherent in capitalism will only get worse.

THE LIBERAL-BOURGEOIS THESIS

The liberal-bourgeois thesis, which has its roots in classical economics of Adam Smith, argues that Marx had a flawed understanding of the moderating and liberating potential of competition in the economic marketplace. Competition is viewed as the key mechanism controlling both profits and wages. If profits in any one industry are too high, other entrepreneurs will rush in to compete and prices will drop; if profits are too low, entrepreneurs will pull out and invest elsewhere. Overproduction of any one commodity is similarly regulated because as sales and profits drop, entrepreneurs will shift investments to new products for which there is more demand. The mechanism of free competition similarly keeps wages fair. Workers will leave those industries in which wage-rates are too low to seek better-paying jobs, or if wage-rates are too high workers will rush into these areas until excess labour drives the rates down.

A strong advocate of this theory of competition was Milton Friedman (1978), a Nobel Prize winner in economics, and long a key advisor to the US government and to its allies in Latin America. Friedman opposed in principle any state intervention in the economy because such interference upsets the delicate balance of supply and demand in the marketplace. Minimum-wage legislation, he warned, may be morally appealing, but its effects are regressive, hurting the very workers it is designed to help. Any artificial minimum wage functions to increase unemployment as jobs that might have been viable at lower rates of pay become uneconomical. Friedman argued further that the power of huge corporations would be limited by competition if they did not receive state aid and protection. Freedom of competition in a capitalist society is, in his view, the main guarantee of democracy and individual freedom.

Liberal-bourgeois theory argues further that **advanced capitalism** has the potential to avoid or overcome most of the inequalities foreseen by Marx. The expansion of **shareholder capitalism** fosters a democratization of ownership of capital, and a separation of ownership and control through the managerial revolution. Free competition has the potential to unleash virtually unlimited innovative and productive resources to sustain higher profits for capitalists and higher standards of living for the masses of workers. The demand within competitive capitalism for continual innovation promotes a professional middle class of highly paid knowledge workers and managers that counters the tendency towards polarization of wealth. Increasing affluence generated by capitalist enterprise promises to trickle down even to the unskilled working class, sustaining a welfare state of social services and a political democracy that gives expression to competing interest groups. Developing countries similarly stand to benefit from the demand for their labour and raw materials, enabling them to develop their own competitive markets and innovative potential.

The **liberal-bourgeois thesis** thus presents a far more optimistic view of advanced capitalism, at least for the foreseeable future. It predicts that technological innovation will outpace declining rates of profit. Productivity goes up exponentially with computers and robotics. Technology itself tends to get cheaper, so that absolute profit levels stay high, and wages can rise. Shareholder capitalism will reduce the concentration of capital. The rise of the welfare state and trade unions will counter the tendency toward the increased poverty of the masses. Ultimately, the advanced capitalist societies will develop high levels of stability and consensus because the system literally "delivers the goods." People's needs will be satisfied by consumer goods, and hence class conflict will be avoided. Free enterprise will foster democratic institutions that will balance and limit the power of capitalists.

NEO-LIBERALISM

Neo-liberalism refers to an expanded and elaborated version of classical liberal-bourgeois thesis that advocates extending competitive free-market principles to all aspects of society, particularly social services traditionally provided to citizens through the government. Neo-liberalism extols the value of privatizing basic resources like water, electricity, sewage, garbage disposal, postal services, daycare, schools, universities, health services, correctional facilities, and virtually anything else that can be sold (Menashy 2007). Privatization involves converting services into businesses that charge fees, or sell services for profit. The basic reasoning of neo-liberalism is that competition to provide services for profit in the marketplace best ensures efficiency. Efficiency is defined as the provision of maximum quality of services for minimum costs. For example, if all schools had to compete for fee-paying students, the best schools that offer high quality education for competitive fees would likely attract the most students. Those schools that offer substandard services, or have inflated costs, would likely fail to attract many students and be forced to improve their standards or close. In contrast, when services are provided through government monopolies and financed through taxes, there is no competition or profit motives to ensure quality services at low costs, and no inherent pressures promoting technological innovation. Neo-liberal policies promote privatization as the solution to what they see as inherent problems of stagnation, inefficiency, and cost overruns that plague government services. Liberals further argue against high corporate taxes on the grounds that such taxes lower competitiveness of Canadian businesses and ultimately lower revenues and jobs.

In summary, while Marxist political economy theory predicts that the capitalist system will spiral downwards into chaos, neo-liberalism as economic theory and political philosophy asserts that market forces ensure an ever-expanding spiral of prosperity. Freedom to trade ensures equal opportunity for anyone with entrepreneurial spirit to offer goods and services for profit in the marketplace. The laws of supply and demand ensure fair exchange, with fair wages and profits. Individuals are rewarded on the basis of their effort and ability. Anyone who really wants to work can get a job, and by working hard can make their labour profitable and get ahead. Excessive government interference in free markets undermines prosperity. High corporate taxes stifle enterprise and harm workers by reducing job opportunities. Money in workers' pockets promotes higher consumption, higher profits, and thus more business opportunities, more jobs, more profits, and more shared wealth. Free-market capitalism spreads democracy and peace.

These vastly different predictions guide the following exploration of Canadian experience as an advanced capitalist economy. Key research questions are whether capitalist institutions are tending towards corporate concentration of capital as predicted by Marxist theory or towards a dilution of ownership in shareholder capitalism foreseen by liberalism; whether structural inequality in Canada is tending towards a polarization of immense wealth and increasing poverty, or towards a more equitable sharing of affluence and social welfare; whether state policies work primarily in the interests of corporate **monopoly** capitalism, or work to rein in the excesses of capitalism and ensure that fair market forces prevail; how competing political philosophies of Marxism and liberalism play out in the Canadian political arena; and the gendered class character of these politico-economic forces. These issues are explored below first on a broad national scale, and then specifically with respect to the primary industry of farming. The focus on farming opens up consideration of the critical issue of environmental degradation and its relation to advanced capitalism—an issue largely neglected by both Marxist theory and by classical liberalism until very recently.

CONCENTRATION OF CAPITAL IN CANADA

A central distinction between the Marxist and liberal predictions concerns the extent to which the concentration of capital in the hands of a small number of huge corporations will come to dominate and distort the market systems to the extent that the checks and balances of free competition no longer function. Patterns of ownership in the contemporary Canadian economy suggest that such a concentration of power is far advanced. Out of more than a million firms operating in Canada in 1996, a mere 25 enterprises controlled 41 percent of all business assets (Carroll 2004, 201), up from one-third in 1983 (Veltmeyer 1987, 18–23). In 1996 the largest firms with assets of $25 million or annual revenues in excess of $100 million controlled almost 80 percent of all business assets in Canada (Statistics Canada 2001, 31).

Corporate elites of presidents and chief executive officers who head these dominant enterprises, and major shareholders on their boards of directors, wield immense power through their control over how to invest vast pools of surplus capital. Beside them is a subordinate elite class of advisors—a class that Carroll terms "organic intellectuals"—corporate lawyers, management and financial consultants, engineers and scientists, and policy advisors from academe and politics (Carroll 2004, 19–21).

In the classical liberal view of capitalism, corporations grow by investing surplus capital in new productive enterprise, thus expanding the real economy to benefit everyone, at least indirectly. However, once large corporations dominate markets, and expected profits from new investments decline, corporations grow chiefly by buying out or merging with existing corporations, with the express intent of dominating markets in their spheres of operation. Much of this investment is "leveraged" or conducted with borrowed money, which makes it speculative and risky. The process involves borrowing huge sums of money to buy shares in competing companies, using the assets of the new company to pay off debts and interest, and selling shares to new investors to cover costs. So long as markets are rising it is possible to make quick profits during the acquisition process as well as from future market dominance (Foster and Magdoff 2009, 59).

Concentration takes a variety of institutional forms. **Horizontal integration** involves the consolidation of firms in the same industry, giving dominant corporations enormous power to set labour contracts and fix prices. The Bertrand Report (1981), *The State of Competition in the Canadian Petroleum Industry*, estimated that through price fixing, the then "big four"—Imperial, Texaco, Shell, and Gulf—overcharged Canadians by about $12 billion for petroleum products between 1958 and 1978. Since then Imperial has bought out Texaco. By the early 1980s, Canadian markets for tobacco, breweries, and motor vehicles were already dominated by four firms controlling 90 percent of production. In a further 20 manufacturing industries, four firms controlled 75 percent of production. The rate at which mergers occur has accelerated since the free-trade agreements of 1989 and 1994 removed barriers to cross-national investments and assured foreign-owned corporations the same property rights as national firms. The goal is increasingly not national, but global domination of markets. To give just one example, in May 2007 the Canadian newsprint giant Thomson Corporation announced a merger with Reuters of London to make the combined firm the world's largest provider of financial data and business news.

Vertical integration is another strategy followed by corporations to dominate their niche market, involving the takeover of firms that operate at different stages in the development of a product. The McCain potato company in New Brunswick consolidated its grip on potato processing in the province by incorporating seed, fertilizer, pesticide, farm machinery, storage, brokerage, wholesaling, and trucking lines into its group of companies, as well as purchasing major tracts of land.

Conglomerate mergers involve a strategy of diversifying holdings to increase stability of profits. The Thomson family empire referred to above controls an array of department stores, including Hudson's Bay, Simpsons, Zellers, and Fields, significant oil and gas interests, insurance companies, and trucking lines, as well as its central interest in the newspaper market.

Holding companies comprise corporate empires whose principal assets are shares in other companies. Prominent Canadian examples include Brookfield Asset Management (formerly Edper/Brascan) controlled by Peter and Edward Bronfman, Power Corporation controlled by Paul Desmarais, and Thomson Corporation controlled by the Thomson family.

A cursory Internet scan of these corporations gives some idea of the size of the assets they control. Brookfield (Edper/Brascan) Corporation specializes in real estate, natural resources, energy, and financial services, including Royal LePage, Noranda, and Great Lakes Power. In May 2007 the company controlled about US $70 billion in assets. Power Corporation is a group of companies specializing in financial services, including Great-West Life Insurance, London Life, Canada Life, IGM Financial, Mackenzie Financial, and Pargesa Holding. In May 2007 the company website quoted consolidated assets of $132.6 billion with additional assets under administration of $200 billion. By 2006, Thomson Corporation was the world's largest information company, active in financial services, healthcare, law, science and technology research, and tax accounting. Thomson was until recently a world leader in higher-education textbooks, until it sold Thomson Learning Assets in 2006, using the funds to buy Reuters, the world's leading news agency. In 2006 the company was valued at US $29 billion, with annual revenues of about US $6.6 billion.

It is very difficult to keep up with all the ramifications and threads of control exerted by such giant corporations because their contours can change so rapidly. Trillions of dollars flow daily at electronic speed through the Toronto stock market, itself a small market by world standards. To give just one example, Argus Corporation, founded by E.P. Taylor in 1945, was once a giant **holding company** with financial control over Canadian Breweries, Dominion Stores, Hollinger Mines, Crown Trust, Standard Broadcasting, Massey-Ferguson, and BC Forest Products. It was so powerful in the 1970s that it became the focus of a 1975 Royal Commission on Corporate Concentration. In 1978, Conrad Black bought a controlling interest in Argus from Taylor's widow, and sold off most of the assets, leaving Argus retaining control only over Hollinger Inc., itself a subsidiary of Ravelston Corporation, controlled by Black and his colleague David Radler. In 1995, Argus assets were calculated to be a mere $440 million. In 2007, Black and Radler were found guilty of siphoning millions of dollars from Hollinger Corporation for their personal fortunes. Shareholders initiated a litany of civil suits to lay claim to his assets.

Holding companies gain financial control over other companies by purchasing a majority of voting shares, or the largest single block of shares, if share ownership is widely dispersed. For example, if a company were to have assets divided equally into bonds, non-voting preferred stock, and voting common stock, the purchase of half the voting common stock, or one-sixth of the total worth of the company, would give effective legal voting control. The holding company can further convert these assets into bonds, stock, and voting stock, sell the non-voting assets, and still retain voting control over the original company or group of companies and subsidiaries (Veltmeyer 1987, 53). Primary capitalists require the services of a trusted elite class of financial, legal, and policy advisors, the "organic intellectuals," to manage these vast pools of surplus capital. Between 1995 and 2005, American corporate elites expended over US $9 trillion in a huge takeover boom (Hutton 2007a, 46). Hutton argues that these takeovers are the principle mechanism driving job losses and downsizing. When the Thomson-Reuters merger occurred in 2007, shareholders were promised to deliver $500 million in annual savings within three years, achievable mostly by merging operations and cutting staff. Business analysts in 2007 continued to describe North American markets as awash in surplus capital, and predicted a period of unprecedented mergers and acquisitions.

Corporate Concentration, Competition, and Shareholder Capital

One important implication of this concentration of capital is that patterns of competition differ markedly from the classical liberal economics model of masses of small producers offering their wares in the same market. There still is competition between giant corporations, both nationally and globally, to maximize returns on their capital investments. There is also competition among subsidiary holdings, as sub-unit managers strive to outshine each other in returning profits to their parent holding company. But consistent with Marxist analysis, competition and business opportunities at this level are far from equal. Individual clients can shift their business from one life insurance company to another, but when all available sources of life insurance are controlled by the same corporate elite, the variation will be cosmetic. Customers can shop at Zellers or Sears, rather than Hudson's Bay Company, but they cannot escape the reality that these are merely sub-departments of the same mega-store. Competition within sub-units of the same corporation does not work in the ways envisioned by the liberal bourgeois thesis. Moreover, when a few mega-corporations dominate the market in given industries, it is within their power and in their joint vested interests to mute competition so as to shore up prices and stabilize market share and profits. Such patterns of tacit cooperation are facilitated by interlocking networks of directorships among corporate elites that are explored further below. At the level of mega-corporations, competition is as likely to take the form of mergers and takeovers as heightened efficiency or undercutting prices. Small independent competitors can either be ignored or swiftly swamped with the power of the big corporations to undercut their markets—a strategy that Irving Oil is well known for in eastern Canada and Maine. The result for consumers is often conformity of prices and product lines, with limited alternatives. Customers can drive to different shopping malls, but they are likely to find little variation in stores or goods available.

The liberal thesis predicts further that increasing affluence would result in ownership of capital becoming widely dispersed among masses of small investors. Consistent with this prediction, masses of ordinary Canadians have become shareholders in corporate capital through investments in mutual funds and pension plans. Gross income from investments in Canada now compares closely with gross income from wages and salaries. But dispersal of shareholding has not translated into dispersal of control over capital. Investment companies that manage mutual funds and pensions are themselves major corporations specializing in finance capital. Their directors form an integral part of the corporate elite, managing immense pools of surplus capital. Individuals who own a few mutual-fund shares in a mega-corporation have minimal capacity to influence corporate board policies.

The distinction between "finance" and "industrial" capital has become increasingly blurred as pension and mutual-fund directors shift from passive investing to active ownership of property (Carroll 2004, 204). The Ontario

Teachers Pension Plan, for example, had assets of $106 billion in 2007. The Fund purchased Cadillac Fairview's property development company in 2000, and through this company it owns controlling interests in an array of other subsidiaries, including Toronto-Dominion Centre, Toronto Eaton Centre, Rideau Centre in Ottawa, Samsonite, Maple Leaf Sports & Entertainment, Shoppers Drug Mart, and Worldspan. In July 2007 it bid successfully to take over Bell Canada Enterprises, the telecommunications giant, for $34.8 billion, described in *The Globe and Mail* (2 July 2007, A1) as the biggest takeover in Canadian corporate history. The Ontario Municipal Employees Retirement Board similarly purchased Oxford Properties in 2001. In 2007 it had assets under management of $48 billion (*The Globe and Mail*, 7 July 2007, B5). These funds are also major shareholders of banks. Fund directors commonly sit on the boards of other corporations, where they typically favour investment strategies that maximize short-term returns to shareholders over social responsibility. The question also widely debated in business news is whether this short-term shareholder return mentality will ultimately be good for businesses or undermine long-term development. The government's Canada Pension Plan controlled assets under management of $116.6 billion in 2007, raising different business concerns about possible political interference.

In effect, Carroll suggests, pension funds have become virtually indistinguishable from other mega-corporations. Individuals who put their savings into these funds have minimal say in how the funds are managed, although some shareholders have made attempts to encourage ethical portfolios. In 2004, at the urging of Greenpeace, a group of concerned teachers urged their union to pressure the Ontario Teachers Pension Plan to adopt ethical investment practices, and in particular to stop investing in tobacco companies (Vasil 2004). Pension fund directors, however, countered that they were legally bound to invest funds in ways that maximize returns on investments. If they were to limit investment patterns as Greenpeace supporters advocated, they would risk being sued by other teachers for a shortfall in retirement pension assets. Further, even if the majority of the more than 250 000 active and retired Ontario teachers were to vote in favour of setting ethical investment limits, pension fund directors would further require that the provincial government grant them a special legal exemption from their "fiduciary duty" to seek the highest returns on investments before they could legally comply. The stakes are high. A 1 percent drop in rate of returns on $70 billion in assets could mean a loss of $700 million in the plan's value. The teachers' experiences with their pension plan fund suggest that shareholders can work together to influence the boards of institutional investors, but it requires a collectively organized social movement supported by political will.

Recession hit that political will as retirees face significant cuts to their expected retirement incomes. All these pension plans lost heavily in the 2008–09 recession. By May 2009 the Ontario Teachers Pension Plan had to pull out of the deal to buy Bell, and had to sell off most of its holdings in Bell, as the telecommunications industry was hit by the global economic recession. The Plan lost about 18 percent of its value in 2009. The Ontario Municipal Employees Plan also lost 15 percent of its $37-billion asset base. The asset base of the Canada Pension Plan dropped from $123 billion to $105 billion, a loss of 18.6 percent.

Corporate Structures: Stability and Change

A comparative study of intercorporate linkages between the top 250 Canadian firms in 1976 and 1996 (Carroll 2004) gives some insight into patterns of stability and change in the structure of corporate power in Canada. Carroll uses intercorporate linkages as a central measure of corporate integration. These linkages can be direct, as when a director or chief executive officer of one corporation sits on the board of another, or more often indirect, as when the same outside director sits on the boards of two or more other corporations. These traditional linkages remained extensive in 1996, although noticeably less thick than in 1976.

One significant change has been the growing Canadianization of corporate networks compared with the 1970s. By 1996 Canada's top 250 firms, measured by size of assets, no longer included American branch plants, as they had in the 1970s. The continental market established by the 1989 Free Trade Agreement made branch-plant production for the Canadian market largely obsolete. Also, the speed of electronic communications between sub-units of a corporation has reduced the need for on-site directors. Carroll found further that the boards of directors of foreign-based companies operating in Canada, both American and Japanese, were mostly insular, not sharing directors with other Canadian-based companies. The key players in intercorporate power networks in 1996 were almost exclusively Canadian, comprising family capitalists and institutional investors.

Significant structural reforms are also evident within the Canadian corporate boards to make the composition of boards of directors more meritocratic and democratic. By 1996 the average size of corporate boards had shrunk, with far fewer directors sitting on multiple corporate boards, fewer corporate insiders as board members, and more outsiders— people who are not themselves capitalists but who serve as expert advisors. Carroll suggests that pressures from greater global competition, and a few notable scandals and corporate failures in the early 1990s prompted these structural reforms.

The traditional old-boy networks of directors, fostered by dinners at elite private clubs, became a liability. The newer, slimmed-down boards typically included far fewer bank directors than in 1976, reflecting a decline in the centrality of banks as controllers of investment capital. With the deregulation of financial institutions, more corporations are themselves functioning as financial institutions. Institutional investors like mutual fund and pension fund directors are rivalling banks as sources of capital.

Carroll emphasizes, however, that evidence of democratization within the corporate elite does not necessarily translate into greater societal control or influence. As noted above, institutional directors are driven by a single mandate to maximize short-term returns to shareholders—they are not social reformers. Family capitalists share their corporate boards with institutional investors and top echelons of organic intellectuals as chief executive officers. But the core of capitalist power—to extract surplus, to set business strategies, and to allocate surplus capital—remain within the control of the owners of surplus capital.

The increasing influence of organic intellectuals on corporate boards reflects a **managerial revolution** on the lines foreseen by liberal economics, although not a dilution of corporate power. Former senior politicians are often sought out to serve as outside directors because of their insider knowledge of government regulations and geopolitical forces that affect business opportunities. In June 2007 former conservative prime minister Brian Mulroney joined the board of Blackstone Group Management (*Globe and Mail*, 5 June 2007, B10), a New York–based company interested in takeovers of government-regulated telecommunications industries. Compensation was reported as $100 000 a year. Mulroney continued to be a partner in the corporate law firm Ogilvy Renault, and to sit on eight other corporate boards. He only recently retired from a further five boards. Such thick interlocks across corporate boards and political parties work to sustain a corporate-political network of shared interests and worldview. They both reflect and foster an organic conscience collective that underlies competitive interests.

 # The Social Construction of Meaning: Achieving Political Will

A central interest in Carroll's network analysis of top Canadian firms was to track the capacity of the capitalist elite to act collectively. They clearly compete against each other in the marketplace for market share and profits, but they also clearly have common interests. These include maintaining the legal frameworks that manage market relations, protecting their profits or capital surplus from excessive taxation and wage demands, controlling labour unrest, limiting cyclical booms and slumps, and the like. By 1996, Canadian corporate directors were less likely to find themselves meeting fellow directors on overlapping boards, or on bank boards, or to plot strategies in exclusive club dining rooms.

The new location for intercorporate networking, Carroll suggests (2004, 157–171), has become the policy planning groups, colloquially referred to as "think tanks." Carroll identifies five major policy-planning groups in Canada in 1996—The Conference Board of Canada, the C.D. Howe Institute, the Business Council on National Issues, the Fraser Institute, and the Atlantic Institute for Market Studies. All five policy groups are closely interlinked with each other and with the Canadian corporate elite. By 1996, 262 people sat on one or more of the five boards, and the majority of policy-group directors also directed one or more leading corporations.

These Canadian policy groups are themselves linked to global policy-planning groups like the Trilateral Commission, the World Business Council for Sustainable Development, the World Economic Forum, the Bilderberg Conference, and the International Chamber of Commerce. Carroll argues that these policy groups, nationally and globally, have become the principal cultural mechanism that integrates the corporate elites and promote their interests as a class. American, European, and Canadian corporate elites meet directly in these policy groups. Canadian prime ministers and finance ministers also routinely attend conferences organized by these policy groups.

A central objective of these organizations is to influence government policies in the interests of corporate capital. They promote transnational neo-liberalism. Capitalists, however powerful they might be in the economic sphere, do not actually rule Canada. Capitalists as a class seek to exert their influence over how political leaders, legislators, media, and ultimately voters, think about issues in order to get support for, or at least acquiescence in, policies and institutions that advance the interests of corporate capitalism. When Canadian policy groups lobby the government on issues important to corporate elites, their credibility is enhanced by their apparent independence from any specific corporation. By the late 1990s, the C.D. Howe Institute was publishing 10 to 15 policy studies annually. The Business Council of Canada, comprising a select group of 150 invited chief executive officers from leading Canadian corporations, functioned as a virtual shadow cabinet, regularly sending task-force findings and recommendations on issues of

international finance, trade, investment, environment, and foreign affairs to relevant government committees. The Council also stages conferences to which media and government officials are invited. All the policy groups regularly publish books, reports, conference proceedings, and press releases with the broad objective of influencing prevailing attitudes and assumptions among the public at large towards a neo-liberal worldview.

This work is generally not done by corporate elites themselves but by their delegates—lawyers, economists, former politicians, and academics who are employed directly by the policy groups, or whose research is funded through the groups. Using 1996 data, Carroll (2004, Ch. 9) tracks thick interlocking networks linking the top 100 Canadian corporations with the top 18 Canadian universities, ranked by size, and the five bourgeois policy groups. These are two-way linkages, with universities inviting chief executive officers of corporations to sit on university boards of governors, and corporate elites inviting university presidents and senior officers to sit on corporate boards. Carroll argues that these linkages between organic intellectuals and corporate elites are critical for enabling the corporate elite as a class to realize its collective class interests—or in Marxist terms, to act as a class-for-itself in social and political arenas. To the extent that neo-liberalism as worldview becomes culturally accepted as common sense, the corporate elites can effectively achieve their will without the appearance of force. The Marxist concept of "ideological hegemony" refers to this capacity to exert power through control over prevailing ideas.

The one group conspicuously excluded from this network is organized labour, or trade union leaders. Institutionally segregated left-wing policy groups like the Canadian Centre for Policy Alternatives (CCPA), the Council of Canadians, and the National Anti-Poverty Organization offer counter-hegemonic working-class perspectives on issues. However, they carry far weaker political clout. Business-oriented policy groups are about 10 times more likely to be cited in media or in government policy initiatives than the CCPA Monitor, not least because mass media outlets are themselves corporate capitalist enterprises. The CCPA Monitor also has to make do with vastly less investment money than business-supported policy groups.

Allocative Power: Shifting the Balance of Power between Business and Government

Classical Marxist analysis holds that ideological hegemony is critical in generating the consent or acquiescence of the masses to the power of the corporate capitalist class. But in the final analysis, Marxists argue, the root of this class power rests ultimately on control over fluid surplus capital. Corporate elites have the capacity to directly determine how and where surplus capital will be invested. To the extent that workers as a class, entire communities, and political parties depend on these investments, the balance of power favours corporate elites. Neo-liberalism, as ideology and practice, works to promote the freedom of capital from social and political constraints.

Canadian corporate elites wield significant influence over Canadian politics through financial contributions to political parties. Historically, most of the leading corporations have hedged their political bets by funding both the Conservatives and the Liberals, although not always equally. Rarely have corporations funded the pro-labour New Democratic Party. In the 1988 elections, when the proposed Free Trade Agreement between Canada and the United States was the central issue, with the Conservatives under Mulroney supporting it and the Liberals under John Turner, and the NDP, opposing it, business elites made their bias clear. Corporate money poured into Conservative Party coffers (Carroll 2004, 176). Pro-free-trade forces spent an estimated $6.5 million in the last three weeks of the campaign, compared with less than one million by those opposing free trade. By 1993, the Liberal Party had markedly shifted its political agenda in favour of free trade, endorsing the more extensive North American Free Trade Agreement, bringing the Party back into favour with corporate donors. Both major parties now endorse neo-liberal economic policies.

Revisions to the Canada Elections Act pushed through by the outgoing Chrétien Liberal government in 2003 restrict the size of direct corporate donations to party election expenses, although contributions can be made by corporate "individuals" to individual candidates and ridings. These changes may limit the massive corporate intervention in elections on the scale of the 1988 federal election, but there remain many other ways that those who control surplus capital can influence policy, even when the party in power does not endorse neo-liberal ideology.

The New Democratic Party won the BC provincial elections in 1991 and 1996, but lost decisively to the Liberals in 2001, retaining only two seats. The Party came in with an elaborate social-democratic agenda that included improving the minimum wage, pay equity legislation, childcare programs, initiatives on public housing to combat homelessness, freezing utility rates and university tuition, promoting community participation in politics, environmental protection, tougher vehicle emission standards, just settlements with First Nations, and improved human rights legislation. After a decade in power, however, even party supporters concluded that it achieved

almost no durable results (Carroll and Ratner 2005). Political leaders found themselves tightly constrained by constant threats from corporate interests to withhold or pull investment capital out of the province. Every NDP policy initiative—to bring in a new labour code, to impose environmental controls on industry, to increase tax revenues to support social services—was thwarted by threats that such policies would alienate business and imperil investment opportunity in the province. At the end of the decade BC did indeed lag behind other provinces in capital accumulation.

NEGOTIATING MEANINGS: SCREENING POLICY OPTIONS

How politicians came to think about policy alternatives, the people they turned to for advice, and the interests that they tried to placate, were integrally part of processes that undermined the New Democratic agenda. Personnel within the NDP's own Ministry of Finance came to adopt the neo-liberal mantra of keeping costs down and saving taxpayers' money, to the point of cutting already meagre welfare rates. The government did manage to broker agreements with corporate business elites in private that favoured the interests of labour or other social services. But spokespersons for capital routinely criticized these same deals in public. They planned press releases that criticized the very same agreements that other company personnel had already endorsed. Commercial media also positioned themselves as the loyal business opposition bent on bringing down politicians. In effect, the NDP faced the combined power of the corporate capitalist class of British Columbia and lost.

A significant legal constraint on the power of the provincial government to take on the big resource extraction industries was the federal government's signing of the free trade agreements, the FTA in 1989 and NAFTA in 1994. The pivotal Chapter 11 of the NAFTA entrenches extensive corporate rights to control property and to manage investments to maximize profits without government interference, and guarantees these rights equally to domestic and foreign corporations. Teams of corporate lawyers acted as legal advisors to corporations in their efforts to manipulate judicial interpretations and establish legal precedents based on Chapter 11.

In 1995, the American-based Sun Belt Water Inc. filed suit against the Canadian federal government for a moratorium that the BC provincial government imposed on bulk water exports (Oliver 2005). Sun Belt sought $220 million in damages, but was more interested in long-term access to Canada's water. Corporate lawyers argued that the NDP's interest in protecting BC water resources should be interpreted under NAFTA rules as constituting the expropriation of corporate property, and thus that corporations interested in selling water should be compensated for potential loss of future revenues. Lawyers for the NDP won the first round of these legal challenges, but legal contests continued (Barlow 2005, 2007). Trilateral talks between government officials and business leaders from Canada, the United States, and Mexico on bulk water exports are still ongoing and the stakes are getting higher as American states are facing increasingly severe water shortages. Under Chapter 11, as soon as any Canadian province permits the bulk export of water for profit, all corporations across continental North America will have rights of equal treatment, and the right to compensation for any efforts to restrict export of water.

In a similar dispute in 1996, Ethyl Corporation sued the Canadian government over its ban on the importation and trans-provincial transport of a fuel additive (MMT) judged by Canada to have potentially negative environmental and human health effects. Lawyers argued that Ethyl Corporation was not getting national treatment because some production of the fuel additive was still permitted within Canada. The lawyers argued further that the scientific data pertaining to the additive was contradictory and therefore did not constitute credible scientific proof required for banning the substance. Canada was therefore imposing "unreasonable" performance requirements on the corporation, and this was tantamount to expropriation without just compensation. They asked for damages in excess of $250 million for loss of potential future profits. The Canadian government repealed the ban on transportation of the fuel additive, and paid $13 million in legal expenses to the corporation (Oliver 2005, 63–64). In a third case in 1999, the state government of California tried to phase out a different fuel additive (MTBA) based on evidence suggesting the additive was a "possible" carcinogen that had the "potential" for numerous harmful consequences, and that it was leaking into drinking water. Lawyers for Methanex Corporation of Canada sued the United States government for $970 million, arguing that scientific evidence was "contradictory" and therefore inconsistent with "credible scientific evidence" required under Chapter 11 of NAFTA. The proposed ban on the additive therefore constituted a violation of NAFTA's fair treatment clause, an instance of expropriation of corporate property, and grounds for demanding compensation for all projected future loss of profits to the company. In all these cases the efforts of politicians and environmental activists to regulate local environmental and public health issues clash directly with the efforts of corporate lawyers to prove that the legal rights of corporate citizens are being encroached upon.

NEO-LIBERAL POLICIES AND THE ROLE OF THE STATE

A key assumption of neo-liberalism that guides the relationship between corporate business and the state is that government interference in economic markets is inherently bad in that it distorts competition and creates inefficiencies. A second assumption is that the state should manage the social system in the interests of capital, and specifically that it should promote policies that maximize conditions for global competitive capital. The two free-trade deals, combined with deregulation of financial capital, have promoted the free flow of surplus capital investments across continental North America and globally.

These neo-liberal assumptions prompted pressure on the Canadian federal government in the late 1980s to privatize the two major state transportation enterprises, Air Canada and Canadian National Railway. Those in favour of government-run transportation service stressed the public-service objectives of ensuring reliable national networks that would serve smaller communities and less profitable routes. Proponents of privatization argued that the state enterprises were inherently prone to waste money by running too many unprofitable routes and paying wages above industry norms, and using taxpayers' money in unfair competition with private businesses (Gillen et al. 1988).

Other state enterprises like the post office, hospitals, nursing homes, schools, and universities are pressured to run as far as possible along the lines of a profitable commercial enterprise. Neo-liberal proponents in Canada have not taken the extreme position of advocating the privatization of education, but they do pressure the federal and provincial governments to manage the education system in ways that meet business labour-force requirements, especially the expertise in science and technology needed for competitive edge in the "knowledge economy." Governments have responded with successive task forces in higher education oriented to pressuring schools and universities to prepare students to meet corporate needs. One feature of this broader policy has been the federal government initiative to pressure universities to seek public–private partnerships for research funding, thus promoting research that directly corresponds to corporate interests.

Corporations that specialize in providing social services like daycares and nursing homes constantly lobby provincial and federal governments to open up more sections of these services to private profit, with the understanding that once such a change is made there is no going back. A key feature of the free-trade agreements is that state enterprises that preceded the signing of the agreements would not have to be privatized, but once privatized they could not be taken over again by the government without compensating all corporations conducting business in these fields for loss of potential future profits. No new state enterprises can be set up without compensation to business. Since Air Canada was privatized in 1988, no new state airline can be established without massive compensation to current and potential future private-sector airlines. The same broad ruling governs agricultural marketing boards. Boards already existing when the free-trade agreements were signed did not have to be dismantled but new ones cannot be established without compensation.

SUPPORTING GLOBAL CAPITAL

The second neo-liberal principle of fostering conditions that promote global competitive capital leads to pressures on the Canadian governments to scale down or demolish **welfare state** services. The chief argument is that the taxation levels required to pay for social services create an unfair trade disadvantage to Canadian corporations competing in the United States where corporate tax rates are lower. In 1993, Liberal Finance Minister Paul Martin faced heavy pressure from business interests to cut the federal deficit. He responded by imposing deep cuts across a wide range of social services. When the deficit was eliminated, the services were never replaced. Jim Stanford (2003), an economist with the Canadian Centre for Policy Alternatives, calculates that increases in gross domestic product worked to eliminate similar deficits in other Western countries almost as quickly without cuts to welfare, and that the cuts had more to do with neo-liberal ideology than with fiscal necessity.

With the deficit under control, neo-liberal pressures shifted focus to push for financial incentives and tax concessions to corporations. It is in this area that contradictions become most evident between the two principals of neo-liberalism—that governments should minimize interference in free-market competition, but simultaneously maximize structural supports for capital. Structural supports often entail funnelling government funds into corporate coffers. Between 1982 and 2006 the Canadian government channelled an estimated $18.4 billion to Canadian business in the form of government-authorized grants, in the last decade averaging a billion dollars a year (CCPA Monitor 13, March 2007, 2). NDP politician Stephen Lewis (1972) first coined the phrase "corporate welfare bums" to highlight this contradiction that the very business voices that pressure for welfare reductions simultaneously pressure governments to promote subsidies to themselves. Conservative Party Leader Stephen Harper promised in 2004 that his government would go after "corporate welfare bums" by cutting government subsidies, but replacing them with lower corporate taxes.

Direct subsidies risk challenges of unfair competition under NAFTA while corporate tax breaks do not. However, subsidies or "bailouts" remain extensive. When a large corporation is threatened with bankruptcy, the resulting job losses can threaten the livelihood of entire communities whose members depend on these jobs. Governments then face appeals from community leaders as well as businesses to provide subsidies. Primary resource industries in pulp and paper, fisheries, and agriculture in Canada have often been the focus of such appeals. Corporations with surplus capital to invest also routinely pressure governments for incentives, loan guarantees, tax holidays, and infrastructure supports, as conditions to invest capital in one location rather than another. By far the largest government financial supports go to corporations involved in the armaments industry, these huge subsidies explicitly exempted from NAFTA on national security grounds.

When the financial crisis hit the Canadian banking and insurance sectors, and then spread to manufacturing and staple industries, the neo-liberal principle that governments should maximize structural supports for capital quickly took precedence over keeping down the deficit, albeit with much public soul-searching. With credit markets frozen, tax revenues down, and rapidly rising unemployment hitting consumer demand for goods, business leaders pressured the federal government to follow the lead of US and European governments in bailing out the banks and pumping stimulus money into the economy. A government surplus changed into a projected $50 billion deficit.

 # Structural Inequality under Advanced Corporate Capital

Marxist and liberal economic models focus on very different features of structural inequality under conditions of advanced corporate capitalism. Marxists stress extreme disparities in wealth and poverty, while liberals stress expanding affluence and argue that wealth at the top will generally trickle down to make the poor better off. Evidence from different sectors within the Canadian economy provides support for both theoretical models.

There is ample evidence of extreme inequalities of wealth concentrated at the top of the corporate hierarchy, and poverty at the bottom. As noted above, the top 25 corporations in Canada control 41 percent of investment capital. In sharp contrast, fully two-thirds of small businesses that start up end in bankruptcy, while many others barely make minimum wage (Pinto 2007). The income gap between the top and bottom 10 percent of Canadian families has tripled over the three decades between 1976 and 2004. The average earnings of the top 10 percent of Canadian families in 2004 was 82 times that earned by the poorest 10 percent of families, compared with a gap of 31 times in 1976 (Yalnizyan 2007).

Over the past 30 years, the real value of wages in the US and Canada, controlling for inflation in the value of money, has stopped going up (Gonick 2009, 9). Corporations have taken advantage of free-trade deals and advanced communications systems to shift assembly and manufacturing jobs, and increasingly also services like call centres, to low-wage countries like China and Mexico. One result of these policies has been to weaken unions and drive down average wage levels. In the US, average wage levels in 2009 were at 1967 levels. Canada has fared better, particularly because of booming Alberta oil-sands projects, but average inflation-adjusted wage levels in Canada in 2009 were at 1982 levels. Working families have managed to sustain their standard of living only by having two incomes, and by going heavily into debt, maximizing their credit-card loans, and borrowing against rising house prices (Baragar 2009, 80–82). Over the last decade, levels of household debt have been rising at about 11 percent per year. Personal savings have dropped steadily from an average of 20 percent of after-tax income in 1982 to 2 percent by 2005.

In sharp contrast to the static or declining incomes of wage-workers, the investment incomes of the corporate rich have been rising exponentially (Hutton 2007a, 2007b). In the United States, the income of the richest one-hundredth of 1 percent of the population grew by almost 500 percent between 1972 and 2002. This happened, Hutton argues, because the social checks and balances on the incomes of corporate elites in the forms of government regulation, media scrutiny, competition rules, trade unions, or belief in the morality of social equity, have all progressively weakened. Chief executive officers virtually write their own pay deals.

A *Globe and Mail* annual report tracks the executive compensation of the top 100 highest-paid CEOs at Standard and Poor's Toronto Stock Exchange (4 June 2007, B4). Compensation comprises a mix of annual salary, annual bonus, and the cash value of other benefits, which include insurance premiums, car and housing allowances, termination or retirement payments, and "other" income such as shares, share units, trust units, long-term incentive plan payouts, gains from exercising stock options, and stock appreciation rights. At the top of the list in 2006, the two CEOs of Research in Motion Ltd. received total compensation of $54 million and $33 million. Paul Desmarais of Power Corporation came in fourth with $24 million, and the CEO of Thomson Corporation was eighteenth with $11.6 million. The CEOs of the Bank

Marxists argue that financial markets have turned into giant casinos in which investors bet they can make profits on small fluctuations in value.

Andrew Wallace/GetStock.com

of Montreal, Scotiabank, Royal Bank, and the National Bank of Canada were in the top third with average compensation of $11 million. Even these annual figures are misleading because they are cited out of context of previous years. Galen Weston of George Weston Ltd. ranked only seventy-seventh in 2006 with total compensation of $3.98 million, while in 2000 he topped the list with compensation of $32 million. James Buckee of Talisman Energy Inc. came in forty-sixth in 2006 with total compensation of $6.5 million, but in May 2007 he retired with a $1.4 million annual pension, cashed in stock options worth $24 million, and continued to hold stock options worth $52 million.

A comparable survey of the incomes of top American CEOs in 2005, listed on the AFL-CIO website, cites the average compensation of the Standard and Poor's 500 companies at $13.5 million. The CEOs of the top 100 American companies had a median compensation of $33.4 million, with the top one-third getting $50 million or more annually. Compensation is not necessarily closely tied to shareholder returns. The AFL–CIO website cites the case of IBM where share values dropped 36 percent in 2005, but the top CEO still received $4.5 million for management during difficult times.

After the stock-market crash of 2008 chief executives of major financial institutions in Canada and the US faced something of a shareholder revolt when information on the size of executive bonuses hit the media. This was especially so when it was revealed that executives of the very institutions seen as responsible for causing the crash in the stock market were in line to get multi-million-dollar bonuses paid for by government bailout money. In Canada, the federal government gave $125 billion to banks to buy insured mortgages that were in default. Shareholder groups proposed motions to require comprehensive review of executive compensation and to give shareholders a say in future compensation packages. Executives of the three big Canadian banks, Royal Bank, Scotiabank, and Bank of Montreal, reportedly volunteered to forgo bonuses of between $3–5 million for 2009 (Rita Trichur, *TheStar.com*, 3 February 2009). This means that the chief executive of Royal Bank got only about $3.8 million in 2008 compared with $10.9 million in 2007. The chief executive of the Bank of Nova Scotia voluntarily "slashed" his compensation from $9.4 million to $7.5 million, compared to the $10 million he received in 2007. Shareholders meanwhile lost about 18 percent of their investments.

Chief Executive Officer as Work Practice

CEOs are not paid these huge salaries for doing nothing. They operate at the core of the corporate capitalist system, responsible for managing strategic investments and productivity objectives to maximize profits to shareholders in highly competitive, global business environments. The CEO of newly merged corporations spearheads the work processes that accomplish what is referred to as "economies of scale." A central part of this process entails the management of complex personnel decisions required to downsize and amalgamate two formerly competing boards of directors into one integrated, cooperating board, and to oversee teams of subordinate managers as they carry out similar processes of departmental amalgamation to promote operational efficiencies at other levels of the enterprise, to eliminate duplication, handle expanded responsibilities, manage resistance that personnel changes and new organization generate, promote loyalty to the new enterprise, and the like. Most importantly, CEOs are primarily responsible for expanding a business, generating innovative technologies and operational efficiencies, promoting new product lines and new services, seeking new markets, and promoting brand loyalties that sustain market share. In Marxist terminology, they must beat the average rate of profit in the market. A CEO's own career advancement depends on achieving these objectives. Only the tough survive. The average term in office of the top CEOs of multinational corporations is about five years (Klein 2000, 255–256). Underneath this average are CEOs who stay with the same corporation for 10 to 15 years or longer. Others quit or are forced out of office in one or two years. High performers are sought out by "headhunters" or retained with the incentive of huge stock options. Underperformers are pushed out.

New CEOs are often recruited specifically to improve profitability in a company with below-average shareholder returns, and this commonly involves a ruthless cutting of underperforming sectors of the corporation. Marxist analysis focuses on the devastating impact of such practices on the mass of employees whose livelihoods depend on these jobs. Klein characterizes CEOs as "SWAT teams" employing "special weapons and tactics" to slash labour costs and push up shareholder returns. The most ruthless get the most pay. CEOs of the 30 companies with the largest layoffs got the biggest increases in their compensation packages. CEOs whose pay is directly linked to stock options are under even greater pressure to close plants, roll back wages, and cut jobs. News that a company is downsizing typically prompts a surge in stock values, driven by the widespread assumption than "economies of scale" generate profits. Larger companies are expected to outperform smaller ones because they encompass more productive potential with a smaller ratio of labour.

Public Sector Management

CEOs who work in the "public" sector of state-owned enterprises and government services have traditionally faced very different challenges, as the focus is on providing efficient services with taxpayers' money, rather than profits to shareholders. Public-sector workers in Canada generally experience more secure jobs and stronger unions than comparable private-sector workers. The trend towards commercialization of government services, however, is reducing these differences. Corporate spokespersons and analysts associated with corporate-sponsored policy groups pressure governments relentlessly to cut corporate taxes to place Canadian businesses on a more level playing field with American corporations, and to make Canada more attractive for foreign investments. They endorse a neo-liberal ideology that characterizes government services as by definition uncompetitive and therefore inefficient and wasteful. A common demand is that government services should be accountable to taxpayers just as corporations are to shareholders, or preferably that such services become privatized as profit-driven enterprises. Increasingly, private corporations specializing in management services are being hired by governments to run enterprises like hospitals and prisons, and to impose private-sector concepts of efficiency and accountability. Pressure towards public–private partnerships increases this trend. University presidents are now expected to combine the roles of academic leadership with chief executive of corporations that sell educational services in competitive markets to fee-paying students and research expertise for corporate clients seeking profitable innovations. Government ministries meanwhile demand accountability for taxpayers' contributions to higher education, with employability of graduates as a central indicator of returns on investment.

When abstract terms like "efficiency" and "accountability" are used it is important to inquire further into how the people using the terms mean them to be understood, and to recognize that how other people in different situations make sense of them may vary widely. "Efficiency" as measured by comparative speed of management of specified categories of patients through hospitals is very different from "efficiency" as measured by nursing competence in the alleviation of suffering. Similarly in the private sector, the level of "efficiency" of a corporation in generating profits over costs can vary greatly depending on which costs are included and excluded from the calculations. It can look very "efficient" to transport goods thousands of miles by truck when the costs of road maintenance, polluted air, and climate change are paid for by taxpayers or put off for future generations (Norberg-Hodge et al. 2002, 72). Calculating the "efficiencies" involved in university education also vary greatly with how primary goals of higher education are defined. Economic efficiencies are thus fundamentally and inextricably embedded in social and political interests and values—especially so when such interests and values are obscured behind conceptual abstractions like "taxpayers" and "shareholders."

The Affluent Middle Classes

Liberal and Marxist economic theories agree that competition under advanced capitalism promotes a treadmill of technological development and innovation. However, they differ in their focus on long-term consequences of such structural pressures for class relations. While liberal economics focuses on the growing affluence of a well-educated, middle-class workforce, Marxist analysis directs attention to how the corporate drive for higher profits and lower labour costs are undermining the same skilled workers that generate this affluence.

In the liberal thesis, businesses are driven to increase productivity and promote competitive advantage in global markets, and a highly educated labour force is an essential component of higher productivity. People with professional and managerial qualifications and technical skills merit the high salaries that they can command in competitive labour markets. As Western economies have become increasingly knowledge-based, the presence of an expanding affluent middle class stimulates more affluence (Hutton 2007a, 46). Educated consumers with surplus income want new sophisticated services, and thus they promote markets for new forms of economic activity. Hutton argues that knowledge-based Western and North American economies are relatively protected from cheap labour competition in

developing societies such as China. Unskilled, assembly-line manufacturing jobs have largely been subcontracted out to low-wage economies, but not the more sophisticated value-added jobs involving invention, design, financing, marketing, branding, and advertising. Western economies continue to dominate exports in the fields of new technology, brands and patents, and financial and managerial services. The export of knowledge-based services from Britain tripled in the decade between 1995 and 2005, with employment in these areas increasing from 30 to 41 percent of the labour force.

Hutton argues from this evidence that it is not true that Western economies are being undermined by competition from ultra-cheap labour in developing economies. Nor is it true that global competition is driving profits down to levels that make welfare-state services unaffordable. Ideology and lack of political will have more to do with the dismantling of the welfare state, in his view, than lack of surplus capital to fund social services. Job losses occur more as a result of cutthroat mergers and downsizing than outsourcing of jobs to China.

Here again, Hutton's analysis draws attention to the negotiated nature of the meaning of concepts in economic theory. What counts as causes from the liberal perspective counts as effects, or as altogether irrelevant, in Hutton's reworking of Marxist analysis. Corporate spokespersons can draw on the rhetoric of "economies of scale" and "global competitiveness" to legitimate mergers, acquisitions, and employee layoffs. They can also draw on the "common sense" explanation that job losses at home are caused by cheap labour in developing societies. Such explanations serve to depoliticize and deflect attention from narrowly defined economic costs and benefits that drive influential economic decision-makers. Active practices appear as abstract operation of economic systems.

OUTSOURCING THE "KNOWLEDGE ECONOMY"

The problem for the professional middle classes is that the cutthroat pressure for mergers and downsizing does not stop at the factory gates. Increasingly these pressures are engulfing the high-technology and managerial components of work. Microsoft offers a classic example of these restructuring processes. In earlier days, computer science experts working for Microsoft could look forward to secure jobs with high salaries inflated with stock options, but this market is being actively dismantled as the corporation has moved to limit full-time programmers (Klein 2000, 249–257). Microsoft still does need a central core of committed elite workers whose loyalty is bought with quarter-million-dollar salaries and stock options. But about half of all the technicians, designers, and programmers who actually work on Microsoft products are officially not Microsoft employees. They are hired through contracts with outside "payroll agencies" who function as their official employer. As outsiders, they are not eligible for insider stock options, or for pensions or other benefits. Klein describes how Microsoft laid off 63 receptionists, rehiring them through an independent agency that specializes in providing temporary workers. Those temporary workers who actually work for Microsoft for 12 months are required to be laid off for 30 days to ensure that they do not qualify for benefits as "permanent" employees. By the late 1990s, the number of "temporary workers" in Silicon Valley was three times the national average, indicating that the strategies adopted by Microsoft were pervasive.

Other skilled workers are encouraged to set themselves up as individual entrepreneurs contracting out their services directly to corporations. Some enjoy the independence, and find they can negotiate for more money when jumping between contracts than being tied to one corporation at a fixed salary. In economic boom times, entrepreneurs with sought-after skills can play the contract labour markets for high rewards. The problems come with recession, as in the late 1990s when the inflated value of technology stocks crashed. The risks of economic recession are borne mostly by contract workers. Corporations can downsize rapidly simply by not renewing contracts for a year or two until markets turn around. Suddenly, masses of highly-skilled "self-employed" contract workers can find themselves unemployed. The reality of contract work for the majority of workers, Klein suggests, is multiple temporary jobs with uneven income, no benefits or security, and little scheduling control. Universities similarly resort to limited-term contracts to hedge the risk of declines in fees as student enrolment fluctuates. The result is a cadre of permanently limited-term professors with fractured careers.

THE DECLINING WORKING CLASS

Workers who are outside the high demand sectors of the knowledge economy bear the brunt of technological innovation driving unemployment and falling real wages. The post-war era of cheap mass production is often referred to as "fordism" after Henry Ford's introduction of assembly-line technology catapulted Ford Motor Company to world leader in the production of affordable cars for mass markets. Henry Ford himself argued that it was in his company's interest to pay workers enough that they could afford to buy his cars. The very high productivity of assembly-line workers relative to other workers made this possible. Manufacturing goods for mass markets provided monotonous, low-skill jobs for masses of workers, but they were well-paying, secure jobs, with good benefits packages and with workers' rights protected by strong unions.

Over the last quarter century, however, the trend across most advanced capitalist economies has been for these "blue-collar" jobs to be replaced with low-paying, insecure and mostly part-time jobs in the retail service sector. Between 1980 and 2006, Britain experienced a 47 percent drop in manufacturing jobs, Sweden and France about 30 percent, and the United States a 25 percent drop (*Socialist Bulletin* 50 (31), May 2007, 2–3) Canada surprisingly bucked the trend with a 2 percent rise in manufacturing jobs over the same period, perhaps reflecting Canada's greater reliance on resource extraction industries than manufacturing. Manufacturing jobs comprised about 14.4 percent of all jobs in Canada in 2007, compared with 11.8 percent of jobs in the USA. But 2007 saw a major downturn in manufacturing in Canada as well, with the loss of 52 000 jobs in the first five months. The losses sparked three mass workers' protests in Ontario in May, led by the auto-workers, steel-workers, and communications, energy, and paper workers unions. Job losses across Canada rose sharply during the 2008–09 recession. A Statistics Canada Labour Force Survey for July 2009 estimated the unemployment rate to have risen from about 6 percent in 2007 to more than 8.5 percent overall in early 2009, and 9.6 percent in Ontario. These rates obscure the much higher rate of underemployed workers who lost well-paid full-time jobs and found only low-wage and part-time work.

Job losses in manufacturing before the recession are only partially accounted for by the export of jobs to low-wage developing world economies. The Socialist Bulletin notes that 85 percent of manufactured goods entering Canada still come from developed countries rather than developing ones (*Socialist Bulletin* 50 (31), May 2007, 3). The real value of goods manufactured in Canada (controlling for inflation) is about double what it was a century ago, but the number of workers needed to produce these goods has plummeted as a result of automated, labour-saving technology. Labour unions that won good contracts for workers in the post-war era of mass-production industries have lost ground. Unions' bargaining strength lies in their ability to shut down production, but this strategy cannot protect workers from corporate restructuring and plant shutdowns. The free-trade agreements make it easier for corporations to relocate jobs, leaving workers competing to attract investors. Unions are under pressure to make concessions in wages and benefits and to cut jobs in an effort to keep at least some of their members employed, while governments are pressured to provide subsidies—often with no guarantees that the plant will stay open far into the future.

Absolute numbers of jobs also do not tell the whole story of what is happening in the blue-collar workforce. An equal number of jobs may be lost in Windsor, Ontario, and created in Calgary, but hundreds of workers cannot immediately move from Windsor to Calgary, uprooting families and selling homes in a depressed area to buy new ones at three to five times higher mortgages. Job skills and qualifications suitable for one line of employment may well not fit with other available jobs. Nor can displaced workers in their late 40s and 50s easily retrain for new careers. There can thus be severe mismatches between available workers and available jobs, with high unemployment levels occurring alongside high job vacancies. Workers who lose jobs in manufacturing are more likely to sink into lower-paid, non-union jobs in retail, clerical, tourism, and similar service-sector industries than they are to rise into highly-paid knowledge economy jobs.

The general pattern across the last 25 years has been for disparities in earnings from employment to widen, with well-paying jobs gaining, while earnings in low-end jobs have been static or declining (Maxwell 2002). Comparatively, Canada is a relatively low-wage country, with 2 million workers, or almost one in four, earning below the $10-per-hour threshold that defines the **poverty line** for single adults in urban areas of the country (Rothman 2005; UNICEF 2005). Canada is second only to the USA in proportion of full-time workers earning wages below this poverty level, compared with one worker in eight in Germany, and one in 20 in Sweden. The global retail giant Wal-Mart sets the standard for minimizing retail-sector labour costs that competing corporations strive to emulate. Two-thirds of the 1.3 million Wal-Mart employees in the USA earn such low incomes that they cannot afford basic medical coverage premiums. In Canada in 2003, about one-quarter of all adult workers between the ages of 24 and 54 were paid less than $10 per hour—below the Statistics Canada poverty line for a single person. These included about one-fifth of all adult women workers and one-tenth of adult male workers (Jackson 2006). In 2003, 11.5 percent of all children in Canada lived below the poverty line, and about half of these children lived in families where at least one parent worked full time.

When the work available is low wage and part time, it is very difficult to move from welfare to work. People lose medical and dental benefits, social housing benefits, and have to pay childcare costs. Maxwell (2002) cites examples of low-income workers paying a real tax rate of 70 percent on earned income as they cross the rigid minimum-income threshold of eligibility for child tax benefits and childcare subsidies. Many low-wage workers are forced to work long hours at multiple jobs. Others supplement their income with crime. The United States federal government responded to this "welfare trap" by setting a maximum lifetime limit of five years on welfare, thus forcing the poor to take work at whatever employers are willing to pay, with no

statutory minimum. Canada, to date, has eschewed such harsh measures.

Jackson explores the debate within Marxist analysis whether the solution to the working poor is for the government to raise the minimum wage rate, or for the government to supplement low incomes with some kind of guaranteed minimum income for workers financed through taxes. The first option of a higher minimum wage risks job losses, especially for young workers as employers may find it unprofitable to hire them at the higher minimum. Option two of tax subsidies to workers risks subsidizing low-wage employers and thus pushing wage rates even lower than they would be on the free market. Neither works well for the goal of reducing poverty, because they moderate but do not resolve the underlying causes.

POVERTY AND POLICY

Liberal and Marxist economic analyses promote very different understandings of the underlying causes of poverty. The extreme neo-liberal vision of inequality promoted by the pro-business Fraser Institute policy group (Rubenstein 2003) highlights merited effort and ability as the principal explanation for huge differences in wealth and assets between the top and bottom strata of Canadians. The billionaire elite class contribute the vision and entrepreneurial skills that generate the tens of thousands of wealth-creating jobs in Canada and around the world on which the well-being of other workers depends. The richest Canadians pay the bulk of taxes that sustain the welfare state, and provide the "free goods" for the non-taxpaying poor. The selflessness and philanthropy of the rich enhances the public good for generations to come.

Such a description may well fit the Toronto icon Ed Mirvish who established Honest Ed's bargain discount store in Toronto in 1948 and turned it into an emporium with annual revenues in the millions of dollars. Over the next four decades he bought up surrounding houses and turned them into an artists' colony. In 1960, he bought the Royal Alexandra Theatre and later revived the Old Vic Theatre in London, England, and built the new Princess of Wales Theatre. He became a major patron of the theatre arts in both countries. He even established the Old Alex in Toronto, a tiny theatre for avant-garde and amateur productions. He became famous for lavish birthday parties in which he entertained tens of thousands of people in street parties, giving away pizza and pasta. Every Christmas he distributed thousands of frozen turkeys to people in need.

Rubenstein argues that business elites as a class create the surplus wealth that results in the poor being vastly better off than they would be without corporate capitalism. Large differences in wealth and assets of better-off and impoverished families primarily reflect differences in education, work ethic, and lifestyle choices that people make. While some present-oriented young people drop out of school and max out their credit cards on easy living, other young people take out student loans and develop their "human capital" qualifications, move to where the strong job markets are, get married and stay married, and defer their gratification while they build up their assets in housing, businesses, investments, and the like.

The Marxist analysis that Rubenstein parodies (Kerstetter 2002) recognizes that corporate capitalism within Canada has generated wealth-creating jobs for some sectors of the working class, especially in the new knowledge economy. But the same capitalist elite has simultaneously destroyed tens of thousands of secure, well-paying unionized manufacturing jobs that were once the mainstay of the blue-collar workforce. Tens of thousands of more new jobs created by capitalism in Canada have not been "wealth creating" but rather poverty-creating, low-wage, temporary, and part-time jobs. Higher educational qualifications increase individual chances to compete for good jobs, but do not increase the number of such jobs available to be competed for. A glut of graduates can even make it easier for employers to shift such jobs from permanent to limited-term contract jobs and so reduce the supply of quality jobs available. Marxist analysis also points to the tremendous strains on family life that come with chronic poverty, and low-wage, unstable, and part-time jobs as the principal explanation for the relationship between poverty, divorce, and single parenthood (Edin and Kefalas 2005). It is not that anti-family cultural values lead to slothful work habits and thus poverty, but rather that young men without stable work cannot afford to support a family, and young women are reluctant to marry them.

Corporate-sponsored policy groups incessantly lobby governments to cut taxes for corporations and the rich. Their argument is that high corporate taxes in Canada impede competitiveness, while lower taxes would promote business enterprise, and thus result in more jobs and more tax revenues. Marxists challenge these arguments as self-serving corporate rhetoric that pushes the welfare burden increasingly onto middle-income earners, while corporate welfare bums enjoy a major share of government subsidies and handouts. Clerical workers on limited-term contracts with Microsoft subsidize with their own lost medical and pension benefits the phenomenal wealth that billionaire Microsoft director and philanthropist Bill Gates gives to global charities. Corporate elites meanwhile limit their tax liability by moving their residence and corporate headquarters offshore, and by transfer pricing practices between subsidiaries that shift paper profits to offshore tax havens and paper losses to higher-tax locations in Canada.

In summary, Marxist analysis generally concedes the validity of liberal economics theory that advanced capitalist economies are generating new forms of wealth. The economic pie does not reduce to a simple zero-sum game, where the more A gets the less is left over for B (Hutton 2007a). As Hutton expresses it, the knowledge economy and the worldwide explosion of trade have greatly enlarged the economic resources and options available for people to make a living. The problems of global and national inequality arise from the grossly unfair rules of the game that condemn masses of people to grinding poverty in the midst of plenty. It is little comfort to Canadian workers and their families who struggle to survive on minimum-wage jobs that they are better off than the estimated half of the world, or more than 2.5 billion people globally who live on less than two dollars a day.

Feminist Political Economy

The gendered character of the capitalist economy receives limited attention from either classical liberal or Marxist political economy. Women are considered of marginal relevance to economic relations, conceptualized either as homemakers who are outside the labour market and dependents of male breadwinners, or as secondary workers whose primary responsibility is the home. Women's class location as housewives is defined through the male to whom they are most closely connected, or if employed, by their own occupational status, which is typically lower than the class location of their husband. Women are rarely located in centres of decision-making or power associated with the generation of wealth, and hence easily overlooked in economic theory.

In 1980, when economist Susan Hewlett with the Economic Policy Council in the USA tried to set up a committee to study problems of women's work, family, and childcare, with a view to making recommendations to the US president and Congress, she reportedly found no takers (Smith 1992, 11–12). Virtually no one wanted to serve on the committee because the topics were not seen as relevant for the council. The challenge of feminist political economy has been to reconceptualize the concept of economy itself, so that what women do becomes recognizable as productive economic work.

Women's Location in the Canadian Economy

The issue most widely addressed within male-stream liberal and Marxist perspectives has been women's location in the labour force compared with men. Two broad generalizations can be made. Over the last quarter century, across all Western economies, there has been a marked and persistent upward shift in women's labour-force participation overall, especially among mothers with young children. Women now constitute about half the Canadian labour force. But notwithstanding significant gains, there remains a large gap between the average incomes of women and men. Between 1965 and 2005, women's average earnings rose from about 60 percent to 73 percent of male earnings (Rothman 2005). With this rate of change, feminists point out, it would take another hundred years for women to reach parity with men. Lower average earnings reflect women's disadvantaged location within the economy relative to men—their underrepresentation at the top of the economic hierarchy and over-representation at the bottom.

Women are rare exceptions among the elite of CEOs and top professional and managerial cadres. By the late 1990s all four women who were major shareholders of the Top 250 Corporations studied by Carroll (2004, 22) achieved that status through family connections. Among them is Belinda Stronach, daughter of the founder and chief executive of auto parts manufacturer Magna International, businesswoman, and briefly federal politician and contender for the leadership of the Conservative Party of Canada. With the democratization of corporate boards, women have gained somewhat greater access to elite positions as corporate advisors or organic intellectuals but usually at the lower strata and with smaller firms. In recent years, the proportion of women in undergraduate studies in Canada equals men, although they are concentrated in different fields. Women have made inroads into the professions, including law, sciences, and engineering. But they remain heavily overrepresented in a small number of professions in education, health, and social work, professions in which they are more likely working for governments than private corporations. In law schools, more women focus on family law while more men focus on corporate law—the specialization most in demand by corporate boards.

In the professions where women numerically outnumber men, they still lag behind men in high-end senior managerial roles. Employment equity acts passed in 1986 and 1995 pressured Crown corporations and federally regulated agencies (including universities) with more than 100 employees to implement positive action plans to recruit more women into upper and middle management positions, along with visible minorities and Aboriginals, and workers with disabilities (Leck 2002). Organizations subject to these acts were required to analyze job categories in which women and other minorities are underrepresented, to review hiring policies and practices, identify barriers, and enact policies to promote more equitable representation of women rela-

tive to the available pool of qualified women. Leck reports that the number of women in middle management has risen by about 2 percent per year, although perhaps little more than would have occurred anyway with economic and demographic changes. The gap in the higher salary range of more than $40 000 a year has actually been increasing, suggesting that women have been appointed to nominally higher-level positions but not with pay increases. Women are also far more likely employed in less powerful "staff" positions requiring technical skills and supervisory responsibilities, rather than "line" management involving policy responsibilities. Hence they are blocked from further promotion into senior executive positions. In nonmanagement occupations, women are concentrated in clerical and retail work. By 2000 fully 65 percent of employed women were classified as clerical workers, down only 5 percent from a high of more than 70 percent (Leck 2002, S90).

Women frustrated by other options have turned increasingly to opening their own businesses, or self-employment. Fully 58 percent of new jobs created in Canada during the decade of the 1990s were self-employment. By 2003, one in six Canadians, comprising 2.5 million workers, were classified as self-employed, and one third of them were women. A study of self-employed women in Alberta (Hughes 2003) describes them as drawing on professional qualifications to open businesses in accounting and consulting, health services, counselling and therapies, home-based services in dressmaking, hairstyling, and small gift shops and food stores. The question much debated in the literature is whether this trend towards self-employment reflects the "pull" of independence and autonomy, individual agency and choice—the explanation favoured by the neo-liberal perspective—or "push" factors like downsizing and job loss—the favoured Marxist explanation. Statistics Canada's Survey of Work Arrangements (1997, 35–36) supports the neo-liberal perspective, suggesting that strong pull factors like desire for challenging work, a positive work environment, desire for independence and meaningful work, flexible schedule, work-family balance, and ability to work from home all contributed to a positive choice of self-employment.

Again, however, the social constructionist perspective raises questions concerning how survey questions derive their meaning. The standpoints from which respondents interpret the questions and how they intend their answers to carry meaning may be very different from the interpretations placed on them by Statistics Canada analysts and by readers of the resulting reports (Hughes 2003). Researchers working with Statistics Canada both structured their survey questions to explore the neo-liberal assumptions about the positive values associated with self-employment, and then interpreted the resulting answers in terms of these assumptions. This is an example of what the theorist Dorothy

Smith refers to as "ideological circles," where initial assumptions, methodology, and interpretive conclusions reinforce each other in a closed circle of thought. The juxtaposition of survey answers with more detailed qualitative interviews of 61 self-employed women in Alberta suggest the meanings these women intended to convey in their survey answers referred mostly to desperation to escape miserable work environments generated by job restructuring in the public and private sectors. Women who formerly worked in health services described constant threats of downsizing and layoffs, incredible stress and erosion of working conditions as government services had been decimated over the past 12 years, and burnout from growing administrative and bureaucratic demands associated with "total quality management" practices. Self-employment represented a relief from the toxic work environments generated by a decade of deficit reduction and "accountability" pressures. But for two-thirds of the women interviewed by Hughes, this relief was hedged by worry over low income from the business, fear of bankruptcy, and impossibility of saving for retirement. Among women who defined themselves as forced into self-employment by lack of other options, fully 91 percent expressed frustration with earning less than their previous employment and with low returns on their education and work experience (Hughes 2003, 445). This compares with about half of those women who more freely chose to open a business. Self-employment brought intrinsic satisfactions, but for the majority of women it did not bring income security.

It is at the bottom of the labour force that women are most heavily overrepresented. Women predominate in the low-wage, insecure, and part-time, non-union jobs in retail sales and service, and their numbers are increasing. About 22 percent of women working full time in 2005 earned less than $10 per hour, compared with 12 percent of men (Rothman 2005). Ten dollars an hour is roughly the amount needed to reach the poverty line for a single person working full time in a large urban centre. About one-quarter of all lone mothers working full time do not earn enough to raise their children above the poverty line. In 2004, 34 percent of children living below the poverty line lived in families where at least one parent worked full-time for the entire year, compared with 27 percent in 1993 (Campaign 2000: Report Card on Child and Family Poverty in Canada 2006). The proportion of part-time jobs in the Canadian labour force grew from 11 to 17 percent between 1975 and 1995, and the proportion of workers who wanted a full-time job but could not find one increased from 11 to 35 percent (Schellenberg 1995). The vast majority of these involuntary part-time workers live in families below the poverty line.

Terms like "flexible" and "part time," Klein suggests (2000, 242–243), cover a variety of actual work situations.

A "good" part-time job that working mothers may well appreciate is one with less than full-time hours but otherwise with a good hourly wage and benefits, and a regular schedule with shift lengths sufficient to compensate for the time it takes to commute to and from work. But increasingly "flexible" jobs in hotel chains and food-services corporations like Starbucks have come to mean low-wage jobs with random hours and no security or benefits. Workers are required to remain on call—available if and when management needs them, but not scheduled and not paid until called.

Explaining the Gender Gap

Classical liberal economics theory conceptualizes the gender gap in the labour market as rooted in social and cultural processes not connected with the economic system itself. Consistent with Parsonian functionalist theory in sociology, the values and orientations associated with family life are seen as clashing with those of market relations and thus as forcing some separation of spheres. Once women make the choice to become wives and mothers, the argument goes, their primary focus becomes family life, and they are thus only secondarily in the labour market. Mothers are expected to take years out of the paid labour force to raise children, or to choose part-time or less responsible work that is more easily combined with domestic responsibilities.

Shaping the "choices" women make is the pervasive assumption by employers and husbands that childcare is and ought to be primarily women's responsibility. The absence of a national, publicly funded childcare program in Canada is a further reflection of neo-liberal policies that pressure governments to privatize services.

The underlying logic is that women who are motivated to advance in their careers on a par with men must choose to avoid having children. The hard-driven, competitive corporate culture permits no "slack" to accommodate childcare or other family responsibilities. Feminine cultural values are also thought to limit women's effectiveness as workers. In principle, women can aspire to rise up the corporate ladder and break through the "glass ceiling" into corporate executive suites, but they typically lack the necessary levels of competitive, aggressive, risk-taking attitudes. Women are seen as choosing careers in teaching, nursing, and clerical work for similar reasons—that they are more compatible with time out for child-rearing and with more nurturing values than typically male professions. Women typically earn less than men because they choose less skilled, less responsible occupations. Closing the income gap would thus require women to shift careers into currently male-dominated fields, or for men to choose lower-wage service careers attractive to women.

Marxist analysis shifts the explanations for the gender gap in average earnings from private choices by individual women to structural processes within advanced capitalist economies. The unrelenting pressure within corporate capitalist economies to deskill and cheapen labour costs produces the glut of substandard jobs that vulnerable workers compete for.

Married women make up a reserve army of cheap disposable labour. They even out fluctuating demands for labour because they can be hired when there is a shortage and pushed back into unpaid domestic work at other times, without becoming welfare burdens.

Only when there is an acute shortage of educated labour, as happened in post-war Sweden, has there been concerted pressure by capitalists to persuade governments to develop publicly funded maternity and childcare leave. It is under conditions of labour shortages in the knowledge economy, when employers are anxious to retain experienced female labour, and also anxious to maintain a high birth rate, that the power relations and policy options that structure "women's choices" become visible. In Sweden, "parents," as distinct from "mothers," are guaranteed paid "parenting leave" for 18 months, which is expected to be shared by both fathers and mothers, and can be spread over a child's first eight years of life. Paid home-care services for sick and dependent people supported by taxes further "protect" corporate interests in maintaining stable female labour-force participation.

Feminist Political Economy: Patriarchal Capitalism

Feminist political economy focuses attention on patriarchal practices that sustain the hyper-exploitation of women's labour at all levels of the capitalist economy. Patriarchal assumptions are embedded in the conception of what constitutes "economy," of what counts as "work" and what services ought or ought not to be compensated with money, and in grudging accommodations made by capitalists to enable workers to balance domestic and employment responsibilities. Patriarchal assumptions also foster discrimination in hiring practices and job classifications and actively undermine policies designed to promote greater gender equity.

Challenging the "Main Business"

A feminist re-visioning of political economy articulated by Dorothy Smith (1992) challenges the flawed definition of "economy" that is implied in both the liberal and Marxist perspectives. Smith argues that Marxist political economy is itself embedded in the **ruling apparatus** of capitalism in

that it assumes the main business of the economy is the accumulation of capital. It is this starting assumption, which Marxism shares with liberal economics, that results in the view of women's service work within the paid economy as marginal, and the homemaking work performed by the vast majority of women as outside the economy altogether.

In pre-capitalist economies there is no meaningful distinction between spheres of production and reproduction. People produced what they and their children needed for their own subsistence. Capitalism rent asunder this unity between production and people's lives. Capitalism shifted the focus of production from goods that have use-value for their producers to commodities that are intended to be sold for profit. The fundamental purpose of capitalist production is not use-value but profit or surplus value. When the focus of economics shifts back from profits to use-value, then the work that women do within the paid economy and in the home appears not as marginal activity, but as central to the economic system. Within this re-visioned economic focus on use-value, it makes no sense to suggest that workers engaged in education, health, and social services are marginal workers who would be better employed in jobs that produce more shareholder profits.

Domestic Labour for Capital

A feminist reconceptualization of homemaking as work helps to make visible how it functions at the heart of the capitalist economic system. Far from being outside the economy, domestic work provides the foundation that keeps the entire capitalist system going. Pioneering feminist studies in the late 1970s and 1980s made visible the complex and demanding nature of work labelled "housework" (Luxton 1980). It encompasses all the activities involved in maintaining a home and servicing members, including the planning and preparing of meals, the financial work of consumption management, and all the complex rhythms of mother-work. Often it involves juggling several different schedules to accommodate the demands of a baby, preschoolers, school timetables, a husband's work timetable, and the woman's own work.

From the standpoint of the wider capitalist economy, domestic labour performs a variety of functions that are essential for the maintenance of labour power. Homemakers, who are mostly mothers, raise and care for children until they reach working age. Mothers are held primarily responsible for continually motivating children to regularly attend school, repairing whatever stress and damage occurs in school, so that children absorb the curricular skills and knowledge that future employers expect. In this respect mothers are centrally involved in the reproduction of the culture of corporate capitalism, eventually giving up their primary product—their children—to the corporate system. A case study of wives of Japanese corporate executives based in Toronto documents how the work of preparing their sons for success in the series of examinations required for entry into elite Japanese universities, which are the recruiting grounds for executive careers in Japanese corporations, itself became a full-time career for these corporate wives (Ueda 1995). The success of mothers in raising their children properly is itself measured by their children's success in achieving corporate careers.

Homemakers also maintain and care for workers themselves on a daily basis, performing all the backstage work required to keep workers returning, rested and ready, for another day's work. Patterns of domestic work are very closely tied to and structured by the kinds of work that husbands do. Wives of men at the top of the labour hierarchy work to sustain the pinstriped image of corporate executives and the lavish homes and stylized entertainment of business associates expected at this level. Their support work is sufficiently important that it is common practice for corporate boards to arrange to interview prospective senior executives and their partners together. Wives of low-income workers manage the very different demands of coping on inadequate incomes. They struggle to make ends meet, to buy what family members most need, and a little of what they most want, and to keep people happy in cramped and dingy living spaces. They also manage the stress of constantly motivating exploited and alienated workers to keep returning to work, because their own domestic labour depends on the money these workers bring home (Luxton 1980). These are part of the work practices that make employers of blue-collar workers favour married men as employees. In these many ways families serve as subcontracted agents of corporations, working for corporations even though they are unpaid and may never even set foot in them. Much of this unpaid domestic work is done on top of women's paid work that often makes the difference between poverty and a reasonable standard of family living.

Other research has documented the complex and extensive contributions of homemaker wives to businesses that their husbands own and operate (Hamilton 2006). This can range from being centrally involved in all aspects of the business from the start-up planning, financing, and decision-making, to keeping the books, running the home office, and typing and editing manuscripts, to being constantly on call and raising children virtually as single parents while husbands are away at work. Women commonly worked in the business without pay for years to build up the enterprise. Yet in the ways in which family members represented the business to outsiders, the image of the male as individual entrepreneur, owner-operator, and CEO of the business prevailed. Only in the details did the contribution of wives to the enterprise become evident, along with the struggles around authority.

Recession and Hyper-Exploitation

The importance of domestic work for the stability of the capitalist system becomes most apparent during periods of recession when governments are under pressure from business interests to cut spending. "Savings" in the economy are made through loading more and more work onto women in the home without paying them anything for it and actually firing many who used to do such work for pay. Armstrong (1984) notes that when governments cut back on hospital services, women take up the slack by doing the nursing at home. They spend far more time in hospitals helping to care for relatives when adequate nursing services are not available. When patients are discharged early to "save" money, women take over their convalescent care at home. When governments cut back on senior citizens' homes and residential homes for the disabled, justifying the financial cuts by arguing that these people are better off within the community, it is women who take over this chronic care nursing for free. Free, that is, to the government. It may often be at great expense to the women themselves who forfeit hours of time, and often paid jobs, to do this care work. When the state cuts back on daycare services and kindergartens, women in the home do the work. When the state cuts back on teachers, homemakers take up the slack, giving their time to supervise lunches and after-school activities, and doing the extra coaching and remedial work that teachers no longer have time to do. When youth employment opportunities are cut back, women at home take up the slack by providing homes and care for adolescents who would otherwise be independent. When wages are cut back, women make up the difference with their own labour, trying to substitute for purchases by making do, mending, sewing, knitting, managing with broken appliances. Above all, they double and treble their labour in stress management to absorb and contain the damage done to family members by such cutbacks.

All too often it is women who work in the social service sector who lose their paid jobs when the government cuts back. The government, in effect, defines their work as not in the marketplace, and thus saves all their salaries, while women continue to do the work without pay.

Viewed from the standpoint of women in the home, government restraint programs appear as the most extreme example of total exploitation. Women are driven to perform services without any pay at all and are forced to depend upon others for subsistence. Yet this enormous hidden economy of housework, worth millions of dollars in government savings annually, is invisible to traditional political economy with its focus on capital accumulation. It is treated as non-productive, as not in the economy at all, and those who do such work are seen as nonentities or dependent consumers.

Doing the "Second Shift"

There has been a revolution in the numbers of wives and mothers, including mothers of pre-school-age children, taking up full-time paid employment since the 1960s. But the revolution in numbers of husbands and fathers taking up the second shift of domestic work has been much weaker. In her pioneering research on the sharing of domestic labour in dual-career households, Arlie Hochschild (1989) discovered the most common pattern was "transitional" with wives in full-time paid employment continuing to do most or all the domestic work as well. The "modern" pattern in which husbands took equal responsibility for housework and childcare as their wives entered full-time employment was very rare. Husbands might "help" if directly asked, particularly in the most enjoyable tasks like playing with children, but still generally considered such work to be her primary responsibility.

All subsequent studies of the "second shift" concur that employed women on average work far longer hours than employed men, because they bear the major responsibilities for housework—the planning, managing, shopping, cooking, cleaning, and childcare, the nurturing, coaching, monitoring, motivating, nursing, and the general tension management of family life. This massive support work that women do frees up male workers not to do it, and thus contributes to making male workers appear as more "valuable" employees. Attributes like being "more committed to their jobs," less distracted by other worries, more available to work overtime at the office, to do rush jobs, to travel at a moment's notice, and the like, appear as merit-worthy personality attributes of individual male workers. The work that women do to produce men as more valuable employees disappears from view.

Not only are women not rewarded for the unpaid support work that they do for corporations—they are financially penalized for doing it. Even women who are not married and have no children, or who are utterly committed to their careers, appear suspect to potential employers because they potentially might later get married, or get pregnant, or take on responsibility for care of sick or elderly family members. Older women whose children are grown up avoid some of these problems—but then they are older. Male employees might take on such responsibilities as well, but statistically the risks of them doing so are lower. All these practices, and the cultural assumptions underlying them, converge to

make white married male job applicants the preferred choice for fast-track, higher-paying jobs.

Within the neo-liberal worldview, male workers appear as naturally superior. Neither corporations nor governments are seen as having any obligation to facilitate work–family balance or to provide quality childcare arrangements that are needed to equalize employment opportunities for women. Any pressure for "special arrangements" constitutes favouritism, and any efforts to counter resistance to women's advancement constitutes discrimination against men.

True gender-equity policies designed to encourage women to enter and to remain in full-time employment and in senior corporate careers and professions have been implemented only when they obviously suited corporate capitalist interests—that is, where corporate employers faced labour shortages in the skilled and knowledge economy. Sweden currently has the most advanced equity policies of any Western capitalist economy, guaranteeing state-supported maternity leave, parenting leave for mothers and fathers at close to full salary with job security protection, the option of reduced working hours during the first six years of children's lives, sick-leave for childcare, and a national childcare policy. The United States has the weakest policies, with Canada in between. Private market solutions to the domestic/childcare/paid-work balance can be very effective for workers at the high end of the income range who can afford nannies, housekeepers, and quality daycare and kindergartens. But such services are prohibitively expensive for workers with average or below-average incomes.

Employment Equity Policy and Resistance

Employment Equity Acts passed in Canada in 1986 and 1995 were intended to address systemic barriers limiting career advancement for women, and unfairness in job classification and pay scales. These Acts explicitly focused on goals for hiring women and minorities proportional to available qualified applicants, rather than quotas that might falsely imply that underqualified women had to be hired to make up the required numbers (Leck 2002). Twenty years later the proportion of women in senior managerial and professional ranks remains far below their availability in relevant labour pools. Leck concludes that the hegemonic liberal belief that all salary differentials in the "free market" reflect individual choice and merited differences, combined with neo-liberal aversion to government "interference" in the labour market, have resulted in widespread resistance to employment equity policies. Women who gained employment in the context of equity programs typically found themselves predefined as incompetent or not meriting their jobs, boycotted by other female employees, denied adequate mentoring and training programs, overlooked for subsequent promotion, and generally undermined at work to the point that their work performance suffered and they lost confidence in their own abilities—thus sustaining the self-fulfilling prophesy that employment equity undermines productivity. Fully 91 percent of 133 university students in a human resources management class viewed employment equity as discrimination against men (Leck 2002, S94). These students gave no thought to the cultural, social, and structural barriers that limit women's access to better paying jobs, presuming simply that none exist.

Another aspect of employment equity policy involves the development of objective job classification schemes designed to evaluate the skills and responsibilities associated with different job categories in the same industry or with the same employer, in order to implement legally mandated "equal pay for work of equal value." The policies are intended to push employers and workers to question whether the skills and "value-added" character of gender-typed jobs such as servicing customers or servicing machines warrant the markedly different pay scales typically assigned to them. Feminist research struggles to make visible the complex skills and responsibilities involved in positions commonly filled by women, which are defined and paid at much lower rates than positions commonly filled by men. Reimer (1991–92) describes how the work of routine clerical workers often entailed policy-related knowledge and managerial decision-making, but these skills were rendered invisible to the organization by reporting practices that attributed work completed by clerical workers to their department directors.

When employment equity challenges have succeeded, particularly in the federal civil service, they have resulted in Human Rights Tribunal decisions awarding millions of dollars in back pay to women workers (Leck 2002, S92–93). In the prevailing neo-liberal discourse, however, such settlements are not characterized as corrections to rampant discrimination against female workers. Rather, they are attacked as unwarranted government interference in the free market, and unfair penalties on taxpayers and shareholder profits. For women who have won such awards the victory is mostly Pyrrhic. A lump-sum settlement does not make up for a decade of poverty, particularly when more than half of the windfall is deducted as income tax.

Conclusion: Patriarchal Capitalism

In summary, feminist political economy exposes patriarchal processes operating at the heart of the capitalist system that work to systematically exclude and devalue women's labour. Support services that women typically provide for capital at all levels of the system are conceptualized as "outside" the economy and "free", the women who do such work are

penalized as less than fully committed workers;, and their struggles to balance unpaid and paid work conceptualized as merely personal problems. Women are not equitably employed in comparison with men. The categories of paid employment in which women are concentrated are devalued and underpaid, and policies to promote equity in hiring practices and salaries are actively resisted and disparaged.

POLITICAL ECONOMY OF FARMING IN CANADA

This section applies the theoretical debates around advanced capitalist economies to analyze restructuring processes in Canada's farming sector. Canada relies heavily on resource extraction industries like agriculture, fishing, forestry, and mining. In 2004 more than a quarter of the population of rural Canada was employed in one of these resource industries (Stedman et al. 2004, 223–224). Agriculture employed 14 percent of all Canadians, 6 percent in the Atlantic region, 11 percent in central Canada—Ontario and Quebec—28 percent in the Prairies, and 4 percent in British Columbia.

Patterns of change in the agricultural sector closely reflect the core predictions of Marxist political economy. The sector has long been described as in serious trouble with declining profits and plummeting rates of employment. The broad pattern has been one of corporate concentration in agribusiness, polarization of wealth with high agribusiness profits and declining farm incomes, increasing concentration of ownership in smaller numbers of larger farms with fewer people directly employed in farming, and falling rates of profit as farms carry high debt loads to keep up with the treadmill of technological innovation. These long-term trends are common across North America and Western Europe (Norberg-Hodge et al. 2002, 5–10). These changes have had a devastating impact on rural communities in Canada, as elsewhere.

Potato Farming in the Maritimes

Farming in New Brunswick was being transformed by labour-saving technology as far back as the 1960s. In one generation, between 1931 and 1961, farm **capitalization**, the amount of money that farmers invested in machinery, rose 450 percent while the number of workers employed in farming dropped by half and the output per worker doubled. Between 1951 and 1981, fully 80 percent of New Brunswick farms disappeared. In 1951, three million acres were being farmed by 26 000 farmers, but by 1981 only one million acres were being farmed by 4000 farmers. In Nova Scotia during roughly the same period 87 percent of farms failed, and 74 percent in PEI (Murphy 1987). By 1974 fully one-third of the Maritime population were displaced farmers (Veltmeyer 1987, 49). In subsequent decades the number of farms continued to fall. Between 1998 and 2007, New Brunswick lost another 600 farms. Across Canada the number of people employed in farming dropped by three-quarters in the last half of the twentieth century.

These figures reflect a dramatic shift in the character of farming from primarily small family subsistence farms with mixed production to a capitalist mode of commodity production for corporate food processors. The establishment of McCain's potato processing plant in Florenceville in 1957 was a major catalyst in this process. The corporation specialized in the production of frozen french fries, thus creating a concentrated market for potatoes and encouraging a shift from mixed farming to monocrop production. McCain quickly grew from a start-up operation with 30 employees to more than 6600 within 25 years. By 2007 it was a multinational frozen food corporation, with 57 plants operating in 12 countries worldwide, more than 20 000 employees, and annual revenues around $6 billion. In order to expand, the company needed to overcome the limitations of labour-intensive manual harvesting that restricted what one family could harvest to about five acres of potatoes. The introduction of mechanical harvesters in the late 1950s revolutionized potato farming. To justify the cost of a harvester, farms required a minimum of 70 acres of potatoes. Those farms that were too hilly to use the mechanical harvesters, or too small to invest in such expensive machinery, rapidly went out of business.

Over the next 25 years, McCain established a vertically integrated agribusiness processing system, controlling all elements in the production chain (Machum 2002, 141). This started with land. The McCain Corporation purchased about 15 000 acres of land in Carleton and Victoria counties (Valley Farms Ltd.) to supply its own potatoes and to gain a strong negotiating position with other farms. McCain also expanded into a series of subsidiary companies (Thomas Equipment Ltd.) that sold farm machinery—the harvesters, sprayers, tractors, and trucks that farmers needed, along with seeds (Foreston Seed Co. Ltd.), fertilizers (McCain Fertilizers Ltd.), pesticides, and storage facilities (Carleton Cold Storage Co. Ltd.). McCain also established its own trucking company (Day and Ross Ltd and M&D Transfer Ltd.) to truck its produce to markets in central Canada and beyond (McCain International Ltd.).

Subcontracting the Risks: Dependent Commodity Production

It is significant that the McCain corporation did not expand in the direction of taking over vast tracts of land to establish corporate capitalist farms. The company's experiment with its own corporate farms in the 1980s proved less profitable than reliance on independent family farms. The main variable was exploitation of labour power. Independent farm owners and their family members were willing to work very long hours without extra pay to maintain their farms, and in bad years they would work for free. In contrast, hourly wage workers and salaried managers on corporate farms would not work extra hours without overtime pay. It was thus in McCain's corporate interests not to take over the bulk of farm production, but rather to maintain family farms in a dependent relation to the corporation. The result has been that family farms of varied sizes have survived alongside corporate farms. At one end are small, low-mechanized family farms that supply all their own labour and strive to minimize debts on machinery. At the other end are highly mechanized "corporate family farms" (McLaughlin 1990), heavily invested in new technology and partially reliant on non-family labour. Corporate capitalist farms that use entirely waged labour are physically the largest in acreage but not the most numerous.

As the near-monopoly purchaser of potatoes in the province, buying from 300 to 400 individual farms, McCain exerts enormous control over individual farmers selling potatoes. A typical contract between McCain and dependent producers specified the kind of seed potato to be planted, the amounts and kinds of fertilizers and pesticides to be used, and the tonnage to be delivered to the company at the company's time and convenience. Interim storage costs and all production risks were borne by individual farmers. In a bad year, farmers would have to make up any shortfall by purchasing potatoes elsewhere to deliver to McCain. In a good year farmers might have to store potatoes at their own expense for months before the company bought them, absorbing all losses from disease or rot themselves. Banks typically refused to give loans to farmers until they had a signed contract with McCain. All debts owing to the McCain group of companies for machinery or other inputs could be deducted before the farmer would be paid.

One farmer (lecture by Darrell McLaughlin, St. Thomas University, Fredericton, 1998) describes the experience of being forced to buy potatoes from a neighbour to make up a shortfall in the amount he had contracted to sell to McCain, expecting to repay the neighbour after the sale. But he received no money for his crop. McCain wrote off the entire crop value against farm debts to other subsidiary companies, forcing the farmer to borrow money from a finance company at 18 percent interest to repay his neighbour. The farm got out from under staggering debt only by family members seeking off-farm employment—a strategy discussed further below.

In effect, small farmers became **dependent commodity producers**. As sub-contractors, these small farmers take all the risks. Technically they own their own means of production, but they are not economically independent. They are tied to agribusiness, producing raw materials for corporate food processors in a tightly integrated system in which they purchase all farm inputs from the same vertically integrated group of companies. Upstream they purchase seeds, fertilizer, chemical sprays, machinery, fuel, and labour. Downstream they sell to processors and wholesalers, or sometimes to marketing boards. Typically, farms sell little of what they produce directly to consumers, at the farm gate or through farmers' markets.

Efficiency or Exploitation?

Classical liberal economics uses concepts like "efficiency" and "economies of scale" to account for differential profitability of businesses in an industry. The market functions to regulate commodity prices by balancing supply and demand. Efficient farmers will make a fair return on their crops. Inefficient farmers whose labour productivity is too low, either because they have not invested in newer technology or their farms are too small to benefit from economies of scale, will fall below optimal productivity and should drop out of the market.

In the context of dependent commodity production, however, the concept of efficiency is ambiguous. A corporate family farm that was inherited without a mortgage and with a low debt load is in a qualitatively different business situation than a family farm with high mortgage repayments and debts on machinery. Once a farm has specialized in potatoes it is very difficult to change direction because of the high capital costs of specialized machinery. A farmer who is lucky, or who has close relations with McCain, may get to deliver potatoes early in the season without carrying the costs of storage and inevitable deterioration. In 1996 some farmers lost more than half their crop to potato blight. Blight can cause enormous damage in storage. Contracts with McCain are generally so close to optimal costs of production that any problems can result in the forced sale of potatoes at below their cost of production.

Marxist analysis of contradictions of capitalism involving falling rates of profit and polarization of wealth better fits the realities of capitalist farming than simple efficiency models. Many farms are caught in a cost-price squeeze of very high debts and falling commodity prices. Farmers are pressured to invest in expensive machinery, which requires expanded production to meet payments. Year after year the contract price for potatoes has fallen below the cost of production (Machum 2002, 145). In PEI between 1971 and 1986, potato farmers received the cost of production in only four of 15 years. During the same years potato dealers, shippers, and processors made large profits. There are stories of PEI farmers who did not have a contract with a big island processor, Humpty Dumpty, keeping potatoes in storage for a full year and eventually composting them because they could not find buyers. Processors prefer to deal with bulk orders rather than bother with small farms (Wells, 2007, 62).

Farmers survive these impossible conditions only through government subsidies (Norberg-Hodge et al. 2002, 8). Farming is heavily subsidized across North America and the European Union. Direct subsidies reached $27 billion in the USA in 2000. Overwhelmingly, governments direct their subsidies to large corporate farms, consistent with the advice of liberal economists that large enterprises practising "economies of scale" are more "efficient" and should be encouraged rather than "inefficient" smaller, undercapitalized farms. Such subsidies look like they benefit farmers, but they work to push down the price of raw materials for corporate food processors, and so maintain the economic relations that result in high profits to processors. Processors like McCain and Cargill thus appear as highly efficient while farmers appear as inefficient and living on welfare handouts. Processors also benefit from indirect subsidies that pay for research into chemical and biotech agriculture, pay the costs of removing fertilizer and pesticide residues from drinking water, and build the transportation infrastructure required for bulk transport of food over thousands of miles (Norberg-Hodge et al. 2002, 72). Again, we are reminded that "efficiency" is a slippery concept whose meaning is determined by how and what is being measured.

Farm debts in Canada have been rising sharply. In 1970 the total farm debt was $4.4 billion. By 1981 this had risen to $18.1 billion, and by 1991 it was $21.2 billion. These increases are despite the millions of dollars written off by creditors through farm foreclosures. A researcher with the left-wing Canadian Council for Policy Alternatives (Qualman 2004) estimates that when controlling for inflation, retail food prices have doubled or tripled since 1975 but actual farm incomes have been static. All the increase in prices has gone to processors. Farms have increased productivity by an average of 3.4 percent per year over this period, compared with the average productivity increase for all businesses in Canada of 1.2 percent. In other words, Qualman argues, farmers have been far more efficient than processors. Farmers have massively adopted new labour-saving and productivity-enhancing technologies, but they have not reaped the profits. Only between 5 and 10 percent of the purchase price of food in supermarkets actually goes to farmers, with more than 90 percent going to corporations that control the rest of the supply chain.

Migrant Labour—Vulnerable Labour Power

Migrant farm labour, entering Canada mostly from the Caribbean and Mexico on temporary permits to pick fruits and vegetables, are the most vulnerable and dependent subclass of workers in Canada. They come from impoverished areas with high unemployment, and need the seasonal employment to support families. But as temporary workers they are excluded from any of the benefits or protections of landed immigrants, such as unemployment insurance, welfare, or medical coverage. Nor are they covered by minimum wage legislation. Labour organizers in Canada have tried to organize them but against heavy odds.

The first ever group of 64 migrant agricultural workers became certified as a union on one farm in Canada on 27 June 2007. Problems emerged at the same moment the announcement was made on the CBC, with the individual farmer declaring that he could not pay any more to the workers than he already does, and if any new contract enforced higher wages, he would sell the farm. Many of the migrant workers themselves, speaking through translators, said they had been tricked into signing union cards without fully understanding what they were and that they did not want a union, and were fearful of losing their jobs.

The root of the problem is that each farm in Canada is legally defined as an independent employer. Labour laws require separate employee unions for separate employers. Hence the more than 18 000 migrant farm workers in Canada cannot legally form one union to set terms and conditions of their labour across thousands of individual farm owners. Each small group of workers on each individual farm has to unionize separately. Workers face the immediate risk that this one farm will respond to unionization by closing down, with the workers laid off and blacklisted from employment on any other non-union farm. The individual farm owner can also legitimately claim that he cannot afford his labour costs to be any higher than all other farms or he will be bankrupted. Yet without unions, migrant farm workers are subject to super-exploitation, legally exempted from minimum employment standards, and not eligible for unemployment insurance, social assistance, or pensions. They dare not complain about living conditions or health and safety violations, and they cannot even shift jobs within Canada for fear that they will be sent home before their contract expires and barred by immigration authorities from entering Canada the following season (Sharma 2001, 426; Basok 2002, 126).

Negotiating Corporate Order: Agribusiness and the State

The Canadian government is a major player in the farming sector. The federal government provides farm credit programs and sets interest rates on these loans. It also carries out research into seeds, although increasingly this is being given over to private seed companies, like Monsanto, which then collect royalties on the seeds. State policies in New Brunswick, as elsewhere, have been strongly slanted in favour of agribusiness. The New Brunswick government has to be mindful of the threat that a multinational corporation like McCain can easily move operations out of province or over the border into Maine if business conditions are more favourable elsewhere. Government policies towards small farmers in the province reflect classical liberal economic concepts of "efficiency" and "economies of scale." Policy statements support the rhetoric of preserving family farms but only if they function as "efficient, mechanized family farm businesses" that provide low-cost inputs to agribusiness (Machum 2002, 142). Small family farms are disparaged as inefficient, obsolete, and welfare operations. Farm bankruptcies are explained as the result of inefficient operations that are too small to make the necessary investments and scale economies to compete successfully in the market. Farm mergers and consolidation of holdings are praised.

Farmers responding to a CBC discussion on farm closures in New Brunswick (Information Morning, Fredericton, 22 May 2007) gave examples of this prevailing bias towards large investments and large farms. The New Brunswick government offers farm loans at preferred low income rates. A farmer asking for a $15 000 loan to renovate a dairy barn was denied while a neighbour who asked for $150 000 for a new barn was approved. This neighbouring farm later sold out, apparently because of excessive debt load. Other farmers explained how the absence of local produce in supermarkets was not an issue of price or quality, but quantity. Supermarkets purchase from wholesalers, not individual farms, and wholesalers demand sufficient quantity to provide all the stores that they supply. Small farms cannot meet these bulk-order demands. Hence they cannot market their produce in local supermarkets.

The Battle over Marketing Boards

Agricultural marketing boards are organizations legislated by the state to control the sale of specific products. Farmers are legally bound to sell their produce to the marketing board, which then negotiates product sales with downstream processors. By 2007, Canada had marketing boards in dairy, wheat, and "feathers" (eggs and poultry), but not in potatoes or other vegetables. Marketing boards that existed prior to the signing of the free-trade agreements are permitted to continue but no new ones can be established. The classical liberal economics view of marketing boards is that they represent a distortion or interference in the free-market determination of optimal prices through relations of supply and demand. They function as a stopgap measure to assist vulnerable and uninformed producers who are unable to compete in open markets or to negotiate fair market prices for themselves. Marxist political economy theory views marketing boards as essential regulatory tools that protect the interests of thousands of small producers against the unbridled power of corporate capitalist processors that dominate markets for agricultural goods.

The wheat marketing board in Saskatchewan is one whose existence is currently in dispute (Pugh and McLaughlin 2007). The Conservative government of Stephen Harper came out strongly in 2006 in favour of abolishing the Wheat Board's monopoly or "single-desk selling authority," arguing that it is outmoded, that farmers can use the Internet to track global wheat prices, and should be free to negotiate their own sales in global markets rather than being forced to sell to the Wheat Board. The Wheat Board could continue as a voluntary agency for farmers who choose to sell to it. From the Marxist political economy perspective, wheat markets are already grossly distorted by an **oligopoly** of five corporations that together control 80 percent of the global grain trade (Pugh and McLaughlin 2007, 9). The largest of the five, the American company Cargill, controls 60 percent of global grain trade. Along with wheat, it also handles other grains, cotton, sugar, petroleum, and financial trading. In the food sector, Cargill has a very high level of vertical integration, owning subsidiaries in food processing, futures, brokering, feed and fertilizer, grain storage elevators, and even the bank from which American farmers apply for loans (Norberg-Hodge et al. 2002, 9; Measner 2007). In 2007 this company had an estimated worth of $73 billion. The other four companies sharing the market are similarly huge transnational conglomerates handling multiple goods. Individual farmers trying to sell their wheat have limited bargaining power with these giants, unless they form a united front in the marketing board. High-volume corporate farm operators favour abolishing the Wheat Board monopoly because they anticipate negotiating lucrative deals for themselves with key buyers for top prices. Smaller farmers, however, fear that without the Wheat Board monopoly they will have no bargaining power and will be pushed to sell at a loss. In Ontario the provincial wheat board used to operate as a "single desk" selling authority for the softer Ontario wheat that is generally used in manufacturing cookies. In 2003 the Board

created an open market system, removing all limits on the amounts of grain that farmers could sell privately. The Board now handles only about one-fifth of the total crop, and returns to farmers are reported to have dropped by about 20 percent (Wells 2007, 60–61).

From Food to Biofuel

The market for grains, oilseeds, sugar, and vegetable oils is currently being transformed by a sudden and massive increase in demand for renewable fuels, or biofuels such as ethanol and biodiesel, to dilute or reduce demand for gasoline. Farmland that once grew food and livestock feed can now be mined for fuel to drive cars. About one-fifth of the corn grown in Canada in 2006, or 55 million tonnes, was diverted from food grains to ethanol plants and this is expected to more than double in the next decade (*Globe and Mail*, 6 July 2007, B3). This shift is being strongly promoted by subsidies from the United States and Canadian governments, anxious to claim that they are reducing dependence on gasoline and tackling global warming.

This shift is likely to have very uneven impacts on people at different locations in agricultural production. Vertically integrated agribusiness corporate farms supplying monocrop production to ethanol plants are likely to gain the most, with profits bolstered by the $1.5 billion biofuel subsidies over nine years promised by the Harper government in 2007 (*Globe and Mail*, 6 July 2007, B3). The same corporate lobbyists that deride marketing boards for distorting the free-market price of grain accept government subsidies to corporations for ethanol production as valuable incentive for infrastructure development to promote the new industry. Other economists, however, warn that government subsidies distort the value of ethanol, promoting a fuel that is both less efficient and more costly to produce than gasoline. At worst, the diversion of vast acreage from food to fuel production may promote global famine. The longer-term costs of mining farmland for fuel may be soil depletion on a massive scale and global food shortages. Liberal economists suggest that a beneficial side effect may be a reduction in amounts of subsidized food that Western economies dump in global markets, with a resulting gain in profits for small farmers in developing economies. The immediate effect, however, has been that workers are hit with the double blow of job losses from the recession and higher food prices.

Hog Farming

Wheat farming in Manitoba was in decline by the 1990s as the result of falling grain prices and rising freight costs. Intensive hog farming began to replace it, driven by global

Critics challenge factory farming as inhumane.

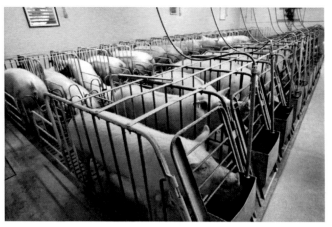

Ryan Remiorz/TCPI/The Canadian Press

demand for meat, especially from Asia. Shipping meat became more profitable than shipping grain. During the 1990s hog farming grew at a rate of 12 percent per year, surpassing wheat and canola as the leading source of provincial revenue. Corporate capitalist investment in hog farming has resulted in the familiar pattern of falling numbers of farms and increasing farm size. Between 1986 and 2000 the number of hog farms dropped by 60 percent while the average number of hogs per farm quadrupled. The largest farms with 10 000 or more hogs made up half of all farms (Novek 2003a, 570).

Corporate farms dominated the industry by 2000, comprising 40 percent of Manitoba hog farms. But as with potatoes, vertical coordination was favoured over full vertical integration. Corporations could make higher profits by contracting out actual production to individual farmers. Farmers provided the site, the labour, and most importantly the land on which the liquid waste must be spread. Hog farms produce enormous volumes of manure, and currently the only way to dispose of it is by mixing it with water and spewing the slurry over fields. Novek describes private farms as reduced to little more than latrines for the hog industry. Corporations provide all the inputs, including hogs, feed, antibiotics, veterinary services, and climate-controlled barns, and they contract to purchase the fattened-up animals for processing. Maple Leaf Foods, an offshoot of McCain's agribusiness empire, dominates the industry. In 2000 the company constructed Canada's largest packing plant, with the capacity to slaughter 90 000 hogs per week. McCain competes with USA-based Smithfield, which bought out Schneiders meat packers. The industry expected to double production in a decade. Large producers lobbied successfully to dismantle the Manitoba pork marketing board, arguing that it was blocking growth in the industry. Deregulation was heralded as a triumph by big producers and corporate

investors and bitterly opposed by small producers and environmentalists.

Similar processes of intensive livestock production are happening in the beef cattle industry in neighbouring Alberta. Young cattle are concentrated in intensive feedlots where they are force-fed high-protein foods so that they mature for slaughter in 14 months instead of three years. The artificial feeding of herbivores with animal by-products is held responsible for outbreaks of mad cow disease (bovine spongiform encephalopathy), associated with the brain-wasting Creutzfeldt-Jakob disease in humans. The discovery of a sick cow in Alberta in 2003 prompted the USA to close the border to Canadian cattle for three years, with a huge loss of revenues in the $2 billion annual export industry.

Corporate Hog Farming as Negotiated Order

In liberal economics "externalities" refer to costs of production that are not paid by the corporate producer, but suffered or paid for by surrounding communities. High-yield monocrop production requires heavy use of chemical fertilizers and pesticides, which degrade the soil and pollute rivers and lakes. Intensive livestock operations produce concentrated volumes of animal wastes that pollute air, water, and soil. The disaster in Walkerton, Ontario, in the spring of 2000, in which 2 300 people became sick and 7 died when the municipal water supply was contaminated with e-coli from cattle manure, was a particularly dramatic example of a much wider problem.

Local communities and governments typically lack both the legal mechanisms and the political will to control these externalities or to regulate corporate responsibility for these externalities. Municipalities in Manitoba lacked even the bylaws to require public hearings for new hog-farm proposals (Novek 2003a, 575). The Manitoba government also stands to gain so much revenue from hog farms that it protects investors from environmentalists rather than protecting the environment. These intensive livestock operations are a major global investment opportunity, sustaining related industries in feed mill and trucking—all important revenue sources. In 2000 a record 52 proposals were submitted for new or expanded operations worth more than $200 million, beating the record of 40 new operations two years earlier. By 2003, not a single hog barn proposal had been turned down, even in a flood-prone inter-lake area. Under Chapter 11 of NAFTA it is not even clear that governments have the power to limit the number of hog barn licences. Corporate lawyers argue that any corporation denied a licence has the right to sue government for discrimination and for potential loss of revenues.

Under this interpretation, the only effective limit on the treadmill expansion of hog farming in the region is economic. The rate of new investment will stall only when unused land becomes sufficiently scarce and therefore so expensive that it deters new investors, or when hog production outstrips demand and prices drop. In 2003 the demand for pork in China seemed insatiable. By 2009, however, economic saturation point appeared to have been reached. Manitoba hog farmers petitioned the Manitoba government for subsidies, complaining that their industry was in crisis after suffering three consecutive years of losses. Their problems included a doubling of feed-grain prices, reflecting the diversion of grain for subsidized ethanol production, and the combination of a high Canadian dollar and recession in China hitting exports. A number of badly built hog barns had also burned down, killing some 37 000 animals since January 2008. The farms were not subject to any building codes. The rejection of any government controls over the expansion of hog farming, followed by a demand for subsidies when the industry was in trouble, reflect the contradictory liberal view that governments should not interfere in free markets, but should act in the interests of global corporate business.

"Free Markets" as Legal Discourse

Novek's research (2003a, 2003b) describes how corporate hog farming became systemically "disembedded" from municipal community and provincial government controls to the extent that there were no enforceable external controls over corporate practices and no corporate responsibility for the costs or "diseconomies" associated with concentrated hog farming. A coalition of interest groups including community leaders, family farm operators, and animal welfare groups actively opposed the expansion of hog production, but with limited effect. One Manitoba resident did win a civil suit in 1975 against a neighbouring hog farm for damages from strong odours. The Manitoba government, however, responded with the Nuisance Act and the Farm Practices Protection Act to protect farmers from nuisance litigation. Government and corporate spokespersons worked up discourses to legitimate the treadmill expansion in hog farming, and to exempt it from community regulation. Chapter 11 of NAFTA requires "scientific proof" of harm as the criterion for government regulation of industries. The Manitoba government used this Chapter 11 language to exempt livestock operations from environmental regulations, by citing lack of "scientific knowledge" of harm from odours (Novek 2003b, 8). Complaints are merely subjective, not scientific, and therefore not actionable. Legislation protecting hog producers from complaints about "nuisance" uses the discourse of "right to farm" and right to carry out "normal pursuits." As critics developed the discourse of "lack of balance with nature" to challenge

the large amounts of animal waste on restricted areas, agribusiness proponents responded with the discourse of "managed scarcity synthesis" and "sustainable development" to legitimate continued growth. The government represented itself as "defender of agriculture," promoting "sustainable development" through hog farms, which provide "organic fertilizers." Provincial government coffers benefit from global investments, but rural communities mostly do not share in the profits. Small communities are decimated as small family farms are bankrupted and families move away.

Animal rights activists struggle to draw public attention to yet another cost of factory farming—the super-exploitation of animals that has become part of "normal" farming practices in these intensive livestock operations. Animals live truncated lives under miserable living conditions, crammed into cages and restricted from walking about or even turning around in the cage, so that they will fatten up more quickly for slaughter. The resulting meats are tainted with growth hormones and the antibiotics required to keep animals alive under these conditions. Lack of political will, not the inevitable results of capitalist food production, must share the blame for these conditions. Sweden has long banned the inhumane farming practices that are still permitted in Canada. In 1988 Sweden passed the Animal Protection Act that requires that technology be adapted to animals, not the reverse. The act explicitly outlaws the use of battery cages for chickens, requires that cattle be put out to graze, and that pigs are not to be tethered, have straw and litter in their stalls and boxes, and have sufficient room to move around. The problem, as Novek expresses it, is that corporate capitalist livestock production has become disembedded from social, political, and legal controls (2003a, 567). The industry is able to pursue the single-minded maximization of profits and shareholder returns on investments with no societal controls.

Bio-Engineering: Money or Life?

Yet another arena of struggle over environmental and health costs of industrial agriculture involves genetic engineering of crops and livestock. Companies aim to produce disease- and pesticide-resistant plants, so that pesticides will kill other plants but leave the target crops unharmed. They also engineer fruits and vegetables to be slow ripening, harder, easier to transport, and with longer shelf life. Livestock engineering aims to increase growth rates in cattle, sheep, pigs, and chickens, and promote disease resistance under factory farming conditions. A hormone additive for milk-producing cattle (rBST) promotes increased milk production. Five bio-technology companies currently control the markets for all transgenic seeds and 60 percent of the global pesticide market, and they gain high profits from patents in new bio-engineered life forms. Critics of biological engineering of crops highlight associated risks of allergic reactions from cross-species gene splicing, the spread of herbicide and viral resistance to wild plants with potentially serious consequences, genetic damage to wildlife, birds, and insects that feed on transgenic crops, heightened resistance to antibiotics in farm animals and people, and heightened cancer risks from growth hormones in meat and milk products. Genetic engineering of fruits and vegetables genetically engineered for easy transportation and long shelf life have resulted in food with significant loss of nutritional content (Landon and Wark 2004). Biotech industries consistently promote the benefits of genetic engineering while refusing to accept any risk liability. Governments collude in this limited liability by setting lax standards for food safety, which then shields companies from negligence claims (Norberg-Hodge et al. 2002, 63).

Governments in North America and Europe are directly involved in bioengineering, both through research funding and through regulations governing the patenting, testing, and labelling of new products. The close interconnections between the American Food and Drug Administration (FDA) and the bio-tech industry means that monitoring and controls are relatively weak (Anderson 1999, 85–104). Corporations fund the research trials that test their own inventions, and interpret the results to support favourable evaluations. Brief trials of food fed to rats have been deemed sufficient to declare food additives safe for long-term human consumption, while negative test results are downplayed. New agribusiness chemicals are tested for safety one at a time, rather than in the multiple combinations to which people may actually be exposed (Norberg-Hodge et al. 2002, 55–56). In 1998 the FDA even recommended that genetically engineered foods could be labelled organic. While this proposal failed, the companies did win legal rulings that genetically engineered foods do not have to be labelled as such. Moreover, Monsanto filed lawsuits against other organizations that tried to label their produce as not genetically modified or as not using milk from cattle treated with growth hormones. Lawyers for Monsanto also successfully threatened Fox News with reprisals if it aired a documentary on health risks to cattle and humans from the hormone to promote milk production (Norberg-Hodge et al. 2002, 105–114). Lawyers for bio-tech corporations like Monsanto draw on free-trade regulations to challenge any government interference in their right to pursue profits in the absence of scientific proof of harm. Fears about risks from genetically modified cereals, or hormones in milk, are declared to be merely subjective attitudes or superstitions. The onus of proof is on the critics to provide scientific proof of harm beyond any legally arguable

doubt in order to warrant impinging on corporate rights to do business. The particular irony in the case of hormones to promote milk production is that between 1980 and 1985 Monsanto was earning $500 million from sales of the hormone at the same time as the American government was spending about $2 billion per year to buy and destroy surplus milk to prevent prices from plummeting (Norberg-Hodge et al. 2002, 112).

Organic Farming: An Alternative to Agribusiness?

Organic farming made up only 1.5 percent of all farming in Canada in 2000, but it has been growing steadily at the rate of 15 to 20 percent per year. Statistics Canada figures for May 2007 indicated that 6.8 percent of farms across Canada were organic, and nearly one in six or 16.3 percent of farms in BC. Demand for organic produce is currently outstripping supply, making this a promising sector for new investment.

The liberal-economics argument in favour of industrial farming, involving land consolidation, specialization, mechanization, and chemical fertilizers and pesticides, is that these techniques create economies of scale which make possible the mass production of cheap food required to feed the global human population. Critics argue that calculations of the relative productivity of industrial farming over organic farming look very different when different measures are used to define productivity (Norberg-Hodge et al. 2002, 74–78). When the measure is productivity per farm worker, industrial farming wins. When the measure is productivity per unit of land, organic farms come out ahead. Organic farms employ more workers per acre because diversified crops cannot be easily mechanized, but the yields per acre are much higher. On indirect measures, like long-term sustainability of soil, protection of wildlife, quality of life of farm workers, and sustainability of rural communities, organic farming comes out way ahead.

Corporate Organic or Small-Scale? A question still debated is whether small-scale organic family farming will remain viable in Canada, or will follow the pattern of conventional agribusiness, with farms getting bigger, more capital intensive, with higher debt loads, and a focus on monocrop production for exports. The trend seems to be going this way in California, but not in New Zealand and not in Ontario. Lobbyists for agribusiness in the United States came very close in 1999 to persuading the Department of Agriculture to define organic as including "genetically modified seed, fertilized with municipal waste, and sterilized by irradiation" (Norberg-Hodge et al. 2002, 43). Much produce sold in supermarkets under the label organic comes from monocrop farms that truck produce thousands of miles. Contrasting evidence from Canada, however, suggests that organic farming has not been pervasively hijacked by agribusiness. A survey of 259 Ontario farms in 1999 concluded that they have remained unspecialized, mixed-commodity, family farms that have avoided high mechanization and debt loads (Hall and Mogyorody 2001). On average the farms grew 16 varieties of fruits and vegetables, or four-crop rotations for field crops, mixing soybeans with pasture, barley, clover, peas, wheat, and rye. These family farms survived with very little state support— although the Canadian federal government created a national organic standards accreditation system in 1999 and a research centre (Hall and Mogyorody 2001, 403).

A major factor limiting the incursion of agribusiness into organic farming is that certification of produce as organic precludes use of chemical fertilizers and pesticides. Monocrop production is so susceptible to diseases, pests, and soil depletion that it is incompatible with organic farming techniques. Conversely, mixed farming and crop rotation is incompatible with the use of specialized machinery, and so tends to remain labour intensive. Most organic farms in Ontario continued to rely on family labour, with only 5 percent of organic fruit and vegetable farms hiring migrant farm labour. About half hired some labour, but still continued to work as full-time farmers themselves.

A separate question is whether organic and conventional farmers support qualitatively different beliefs and values concerning the relationship between people and animals and the environment. The dominant worldview associated with capitalist farming includes belief in growth, progress, and profits, faith in science and technology as a basis for social decision-making, a view of nature as separate from humans, as a resource to be exploited to meet human needs, and faith in free-market economics. The alternative worldview places nurturing of the environment and sustainability above values of growth and profits, and views nature and other life forms as having intrinsic value that humans need to work with rather than subdue (Abaidoo and Dickinson 2002). A survey of Saskatchewan farmers with exclusively conventional, mixed, and exclusively organic farming techniques showed considerable overlap in worldviews but with a clear shift in preponderance of values. Conventional farmers were more likely to favour the dominant worldview while organic farmers were more likely to accept alternative views. The authors conclude that about 60 percent of organic farmers had decided to go organic primarily for profits rather than philosophical conviction. This is particularly true for the mixed farms where farmers were beginning to experiment with organic crops. Forty percent of organic farmers were fully committed to ecologically friendly and nature-centred worldviews.

The large majority of farmers from all three groups believed that markets were more important than governments in promoting improved environmental practices. Researchers were surprised that the highest proportion of respondents supporting markets—80 percent—were among organic farmers. Behind this apparent anomaly was a very different interpretive understanding of what "markets" refer to. Researchers and conventional farmers were thinking about global food processing corporations. Organic farmers were thinking about local farmers' markets and niche upscale "green markets" specializing in organic food, seeing the growth in these alternative markets as critical for the shift to organic farming. The green market caters to relatively affluent consumers who are prepared to pay more for foods that are certified free from artificial chemicals, pesticides, growth hormones, and antibiotics.

Corporate capitalist interests are seeking to gain entry into this green market, offering marginally organic foods on supermarket shelves, flown in from thousands of miles. But there remain intrinsic limits to the mass production of organic foods. For the time being, at least, organic farming provides a niche market in which small family farms can continue to survive, so long as relatively affluent consumers are willing to pay the premium for high-quality food that is produced locally and with environmentally friendly farming practices. The caveat is that as markets for organic food grow and the sector becomes more profitable, the drive to industrialize the sector also grows, with pressures to squeeze out small farmers and water down organic standards (Norberg-Hodge et al. 2002, 43; Worth 2007). Some communities are fighting back in small ways by promoting organic gardens in city lots (Werkerle 2004). Toronto food cooperatives are promoting buy-local campaigns and microenterprises that link farmers, consumers, and community kitchens. They support community gardens at public sites like libraries and in housing projects and open ground around high-rise apartments, and herb production on roof gardens. Werkerle describes it as a form of "globalization from below" in which farmers and consumers try to bypass corporate-controlled global food systems.

Feminist Perspectives: Women in Farming

Women's contribution to farming has been largely invisible and ignored by research in both classical liberal economics and Marxist political economy. Yet there would be no family farming without women's work. As Machum expresses it (2002, 133–134), when a woman marries a farmer whose primary work is a family farm operation, she also marries the farm. She has a home and an income so long as the farm succeeds, but if it fails, she loses both. Conversely, the family farm is likely to fail if the marriage fails and the woman withdraws her labour. Few women own farms in their own right, reflecting pervasive patrilineal inheritance patterns, in which farms are handed down from fathers to sons.

Women sustain the family farm through their work in farm production, their domestic and reproductive work in the farmhouse, their income-substitution work, and often additional off-farm paid employment that subsidizes the farm. On New Brunswick potato farms, farm wives are routinely involved in all aspects of potato production from driving machinery, going for parts, harvesting potatoes, managing work crews and providing their meals, and washing multiple loads of overalls for every farm worker after every truckload of potatoes is handled, to minimize the spread of diseases between farms. Farm wives were also routinely involved in the daily care of livestock. Women tell stories of having closed-circuit television links between barns and bedroom so that they could monitor lambing and calving pens. Ranchers' wives like Irene Murdoch are routinely involved in "haying, raking, swathing, moving, driving trucks and tractors and teams, quieting horses, taking cattle back and forth to the reserve, dehorning, vaccinating, branding, and doing anything else that was to be done" (Machum 2002, 136, citing Acheson et al. 1984, 26). On more highly mechanized farms women typically work in management roles, answering the telephones, keeping accounts, handling finances and payroll, and the extensive paperwork associated with government farm programs. Cash-replacement work commonly involves canning and freezing garden produce, raising chickens and selling eggs, as well as knitting, sewing, and selling crafts.

When farms are struggling financially, farm wives are the most likely farm members to seek off-farm employment (Bessant 2006; Shortall 2001; Heather et al. 2005). Off-farm jobs offer some relief from the stress of farm work, and a source of status and recognition not received on the farm. But as their income from off-farm jobs is increasingly used to pay farm debts, women are in effect working for the farm and not for themselves. The farm still remains defined as the primary family business and her work as secondary. Women work themselves to the point of physical illness in their efforts to keep their farms operational and in the process to preserve their farm family way of life and their rural communities (Heather et al. 2005, 93). But the farm is still defined as "his" and themselves as merely junior partners.

Classical liberal economics characterizes such off-farm supplementary incomes as a form of self-exploitation that serves only to subsidize unprofitable inefficient enterprises that ought to go out of business (Bessant 2006). However,

such pluriactivity appears increasingly common among family members for large as well as smaller farms. Heather et al. (2005) cite Statistics Canada data for 2001 indicating that income directly from farm operations made up merely 22.8 percent of total farm income, with 56.9 percent from off-farm employment income, and 28.3 percent from other sources, including pensions and farm subsidies. Such data indicate how severely primary producers are exploited in the agribusiness chain of food production.

Farm wives who earn off-farm incomes in their rural communities are further exploited when these secondary occupations are themselves targeted for cutbacks. Half of the 34 farm wives interviewed in rural Alberta also worked as rural nurses (Heather et al. 2005). When rural health services were regionalized and restructured in 1994, and the number of health units cut from 27 to 17, these nurses found themselves more isolated, with heavier workloads, and expected to cover more of the work formerly done by community physicians. Nursing stations were chronically understaffed, to the extent that if one nurse was out sick or took a day off, she would not be replaced, and another nurse would have to do the work of two people. The Alberta government in the mid-1990s had phenomenal revenues from oil, but chose to cut taxes rather than invest in rural health. Rural nurses absorb the extra work. Most of the wives interviewed did not identify themselves as feminists because it seemed too selfish to focus on themselves when their farms, and their entire rural communities, were at stake.

Patriarchal Rural Relations and the State Agribusiness Policy

For all the work they do in sustaining family farms, farm wives receive minimal recognition or economic return. Departments of agriculture have recognized their value to the extent of promoting farm management and agricultural training programs for farm wives (Machum 2002, 138), but with the clear assumption that their services to their farms would be "free." Patriarchal class relations in Canadian farming have long been directly sustained by Canadian state policies and legislation. Prior to 1980 farm wives had no ownership rights to the farm on death, separation, or divorce. In the infamous Irene Murdoch case, she had undeniably made a substantial contribution to the ranch for 25 years, including running the ranch by herself for five to eight months of the year while her husband left to work for the Canadian Forestry Service. Yet when they divorced, the judge determined that her work was simply what any ranch wife would do, and it did not confer any financial interest in or legal right to the ranch.

The outrage generated by this case prompted changes in legislation to improve women's rights to share marital property. The Matrimonial Property Act of 1980 formally recognized that a wife's contribution in household management and childcare, as well as financial contributions, created a right to an interest in property on marriage breakdown. In principle, wives are now entitled to half of the value of marital property on divorce. However, this rarely translates into half of the value of a farm (Keet 1990). Multiple legal exemptions, presumptions that the male farmer is the primary operator of the farm as a business, and policies to preserve viable farms continue to ensure that property-owning farm husbands retain the major share of farm property on divorce.

Most farm wives do not receive income from their farm work. The 1969 income tax guide specified that wages to a wife could not be deducted from farm income as a tax expense, although wages paid to hired hands and to children could be deducted. Wives also could not pay into the Canada Pension Plan. In 1993 the tax act was changed to permit spousal wages to be deducted from male farm incomes, but only if the wife was not a partner in the farm. Tax accountants encouraged women to take wages and to pay into the Canada Pension Plan in their own names—but to do this, she had to be legally defined as an employee, not a partner. Not surprisingly, most farm wives refuse to take this option (Machum 2002, 138–139).

Most farm organizations studied by Shortall (2001) excluded women as members, or included them only in subordinate "feminized" categories as farm-ettes (Shortall 2001). Within the organizations they typically worked on all-women committees dealing with farm family issues. Organizations like the Canadian Farm Women's Networkhave struggled to highlight issues that affect women on farms. These include the importance of legalizing their stake in the farm business, getting women involved in farming organizations and government farming bodies and marketing boards, and lobbying the Canadian Census to change farm operator categories so that women's names can appear. However they remain marginalized as merely "women's issues." The state gave funding to the Farm Women's Network for "farm women's issues" but refused to fund educational courses for women on farming issues on the grounds that these were not of specific relevance to women. The state thus reinforced gender-role segregation in the industry. The exclusion of women from farming organizations beyond gendered family committees perpetuates the limited understanding of the enormous stress and workloads that farm women carry.

CONCLUSION

In conclusion, both the liberal economics perspective and the Marxist political economy perspective contribute important insight into understanding the complexity of economic relations. The optimistic liberal view of capitalism highlights opportunities for business enterprise, wealth-generating activities, and expanding job opportunities, especially in the "knowledge economy." The Marxist perspective focuses attention on the inherent tendencies towards concentration of wealth and power in the hands of a numerically small but extremely influential capitalist elite class, and escalating class divisions between a prosperous middle class of workers employed in the knowledge economy and an expanding sector of low-income contract and service jobs that absorbs the risks and slumps of post-industrial capitalism. The different possible directions in which these relationships work in practical situations and within particular industries like farming is not inexorably determined by impersonal market forces. Rather, these directions are promoted or restricted, sustained or changed by how people come to understand and interpret what is happening, and thus how they exert their influence on laws and policies and market choices. Legal and political institutions actively collude in the dis-embedding of corporate

capitalist enterprise from community controls and thereby sustain the conditions within which narrowly defined corporate goals to maximize profits and shareholder returns trump competing interests.

It is the meticulous and mostly qualitative social-constructionist research that gives most insight into the social organization of economic relations. Such research focuses on what people do to continually bring about these systemic patterns. The work of "organic intellectuals" serves to actively sustain or undermine these systemic "market forces." These are the corporate lawyers, the physical and social scientists who conduct collaborative research with industry, the analysts who work within policy think tanks and government committees to convert theoretical assumptions into practical initiatives, and the academics and journalists who generate textbooks and mass-media representations that influence how masses of people come to think about alternatives. Feminist political-economy research that makes visible the pervasively patriarchal character of these ostensibly abstract and rational economic forces helps further to remind us that these are fundamentally social constructions. They are embedded in cultural assumptions about gender and power.

SUGGESTED READING

Duncan Hood's "Gluttons at the Gate" in *Maclean's* 122 (11 May 2009) shines a spotlight on the ever-increasing wages and benefits of Canadian and American CEOs.

Kerry Preibisch has written a number of pieces describing the exploitation of Caribbean and Mexican workers in Canada's horticultural industry. In "Interrogating Racialized Global Labour Supply: An Elaboration of the Racial/National Replacement of Foreign Agricultural Workers in Canada," Preibisch and Leigh Binford highlight and elucidate the recent trend to replace Caribbean workers with more Mexican workers (*Canadian Review of Sociology and Anthropology* 44 (1), February 2007).

Paul Wells' "Innovation isn't in Canada's DNA" in *Maclean's* 122 (3 and 10 August 2009) explains why he expects John Manley to coax Canadian businesses to become more innovative when he takes over as president of the Canadian Council of Chief Executives (formerly the Business Council on National Issues).

In *Filthy Lucre* (2009), Joseph Heath critiques the solutions that have been proposed to date for the problems that beset capitalism. He argues against what he sees as the seven fallacies of the right and the seven fallacies of the left.

In her article, "Making Change: Gender Careers and Citizenship" in *Gender Relations in Canada*, Mary Ellen Donnan discusses how women's careers in Canada are racialized and gendered. She describes the many barriers women still face in the workforce and how work is socially constructed to devalue it. Furthermore, she warns that neo-liberalization threatens to undermine any progress that has been made.

Ivy Lynn Bourgeault and Patricia Khokher's journal article "Making a Better Living from Caregiving: Comparing Strategies to Improve Wages for Care Providers" is an examination of the effectiveness of a number of strategies designed to counteract the devaluation of women's care work. Of the four strategies under review (public funding, credentialism, organization, and unionization), public funding was determined to be the most effective. However this strategy has been compromised by neo-liberalism. Their article is a good adjunct to Donnan's listed above (*Canadian Review of Sociology and Anthropology* 4, February 2006).

Suzan Ilcan argues that groups and individuals are being encouraged to take more responsibility for their own social needs. She maintains that, by privatizing social responsibilities, neo-liberal governments justify cutting and outsourcing services that have been publicly provided since the early post-war days. These services must now be provided by volunteers or purchased from private-sector providers. Furthermore, the Canadian federal public service employees that she has interviewed say that they are expected to benchmark themselves against the private sector (*Canadian Review of Sociology*, 46 (3), 2009).

Maude Barlow's book *Too Close for Comfort* (2005) gives a highly critical account of neo-liberal economic policies that fostered the North American Free Trade Agreement between Canada, the US, and Mexico. She explores the threat that these policies pose to Canada's social security systems and control over energy and water resources. She also explores how legal protections for corporations embedded in the NAFTA work to strengthen corporate resistance to efforts by Canadians to protect the environment.

The article by Carroll and Ratner, "The NDP Regime in British Columbia, 1991–2001: A Post-Mortem." (2005), gives a social constructionist account of the active practices through which major corporations in BC imposed their will on the NDP government, notwithstanding the government's commitment to socialist policies.

Joanne Leck's article "Making Employment Equity Programs Work for Women" (2002) explores the active practices that undermine efforts by professional women to achieve equality of treatment in employment, and how neo-liberal discourse works both to obscure and legitimate systemic injustice.

Karen Hughes' article "Pushed or Pulled? Women's Entry into Self-Employment and Small Business Ownership" (2003) explores both women's negative experiences of working in corporations and their struggles to go into business for themselves.

Susan Machum's study "The Farmer Takes a Wife and the Wife Takes the Farm: Marriage and Farming" (2002) discusses how deeply individual potato farmers in New Brunswick are enmeshed in the controlling network of corporate agribusiness, and also the essential contribution of farm women to sustaining family farms.

QUESTIONS

1. What are the basic tenets underlying the liberal-bourgeois thesis? How did neo-liberalism expand and elaborate these liberal principles?

2. Discuss the contradictions of capitalism as outlined by Karl Marx.

3. To whom does Carroll's concept of "organic intellectuals" refer?

4. Describe the mechanisms by which Canadian business has become concentrated in the hands of fewer and fewer corporations.

5. How does McCain exemplify vertically integrated corporate structure?

6. Discuss the debate surrounding marketing boards in Canada.

7. What role do think tanks play in Canadian business? Which of these policy-planning groups have been most influential?

8. Which groups are benefiting from our modern economic structure and which are not? In other words, has affluence "trickled down" or have the classes become polarized?

9. Why did Stephen Lewis coin the phrase "corporate welfare bums" in 1972? Is Lewis' concept applicable to the relationship between government and agribusiness today? How might it apply to the new biofuel industry?

10. What are the externalities of agribusiness associated with the burgeoning Canadian hog and cattle industries? What harm do they cause and who pays for them?

11. How are farm wives disadvantaged under Canada's property and tax laws?

WEB LINKS

Vimeo: Capitalism Hits the Fan: A Marxian View
www.vimeo.com/1962208
This is a video lecture by Dr. Rick Wolff, Department of Economics, University of Massachusetts, 7 October 2008.

Vimeo: Hippies vs. Milton Friedman: Q&A Session at Cornell University, 1978
www.vimeo.com/5143574
This lecture situates capitalism within a neo-liberal economics framework and provides an opportunity for students to debate the ideology of capitalism and economic policy.

Trilateral Commission Press Conference 1993 Annual Meeting
www.youtube.com/watch?v=xrYEvnQE1kc
A video stream from C-Span in which Trilateral Commission representatives answer questions about the notion of a world army, the conflict in Yugoslavia, and UN responsibilities.

The Sustainable Livelihoods Experience
www.wbcsd.org/web/stream/SLvideoLibrary/sl_qmm.html
This video stream discusses the role as determined by the WBCSD in developing countries around the world. The video provides great opportunity for a critical viewing of this type of message. (World Business Council for Sustainable Development, 2005.)

World Economic Forum Annual Meeting 2008
www.weforum.org/en/fp/videos/videos_AM08/index.htm
This link from the WEF provides access to 23 short interviews by business and government leaders such as Peer Schatz, CEO, Qiagen; Dr. J. Dzau, Chancellor, Health Affairs, Duke University; Sh. Mohammad bin Essa Al Khalifa, Chief Executive, Bahrain Economic Development Board; and Lee Howell, Senior Director, WEF.

The Clark Kerr Lectures: On the Role of Higher Education in Society
www.uctv.tv/series/?seriesnumber=128
UCTV brings lectures via video and podcast. Although these lectures pertain specifically to US universities, if Canada has any similarities to our neighbors to the south, these lectures and the ideology behind them are critically important. Just a few of the lectures are: "Rethinking the Student Experience in the 21st Century Public Research University"; "Federal, State, and Local Governments—University Patrons, Partners, or Protagonists"; and "Industry, Philanthropy, and Universities—The roles and Influences of the Private Sector in Higher Education."

The National Security Archive
www.gwu.edu/~nsarchiv/NSAEBB/NSAEBB65/index.html#video
This link provides access to the PBS documentary "Bill Moyers Reports: Trading Democracy" with transcript, video clips, and document files from Metalclas v. Mexico and The Loewen Group, Inc. and Raymond L. Loewen v. The United States of America."

TILMA: You, Me, and the SPP: Trading Democracy for Corporate Rule
www.youtube.com/watch?v=3Hi-z9Tfxb0
Chapter 4 of Paul Manly's documentary. Trailer can be seen at www.youtube.com/watch?v=CK3wuCS4q9k&feature=related. Full-length documentary can be ordered from http://manlymedia.com. Naomi Klein, Maude Barlow, Ken Georgetti, and Murray Dobbin are among the speakers.

Canadian Centre for Policy Alternatives (CCPA)
www.policyalternatives.ca/Reports/2008/01/ReportsStudies1814/
NAFTA Chapter 11 Investor–State Disputes to January 1, 2008. This link provides access to the press review and study released by the CCPA on NAFTA cases filed against Canada since 2006.

Marketplace
http://marketplace.publicradio.org/features/nafta/#salinas
After NAFTA: Marketplace and The Economist explore NAFTA's impact 10 years later. This link provides slideshows and podcasts for interviews and discussions concerning NAFTA. Some examples are: Former Mexican president Carlos Salinas de Gortari; Robert Reich, former Secretary of Labor, and reporter Stephen Henn reports the UPS vs. Canada case.

Warren Farrel: Wage Gap Myth
www.youtube.com/watch?v=DtjaBQMog0Q
This short video clip of a 20/20 segment indicates the backlash to the plea for equality. John Stossel and Warren Farrel attempt to prove that the wage gap is a myth. Interestingly, the website http://antimisandry.com "Anti Misandry: Curing Feminist Indoctrination" is promoted during this clip.

CNBC's The Call: Gender Wage Gap: Myth or Reality?
www.youtube.com/watch?v=Scp7s3vqTpw
Teri Lucas, Stephen Moore, and Naomi Klein respond to the reports that after university graduation the wage gap between men and women increases throughout the years. Moore states: "I don't think men have a really effective lobby in Washington either." This short clip provides a great deal of information for class discussion for students.

Bridging the Gap between Rich and Poor
www.youtube.com/watch?v=Dz3YvXw05EE

This is a 50-minute presentation brought by UCLA Anderson School of Management by Jacqueline Novogratz, Founder and CEO of Acumen Fund.

Building Bridges Radio: Canadian Auto Workers Blockade GM Headquarters Fighting Plant Closing
www.archive.org/details/BuildingBridgesRadiocanadianAutoWorkers-BlockadeGmHeadquartersAnd_293

This is a half-hour interview with Gregg Moffat, Truck Plant Chair, and "Building Bridges Radio" regarding the Canadian autoworkers blockade and General Motors plant in Ontario.

Radio New Internationalist: Labour the Point
www.archive.org/details/RadioNewInternationalistLabourthePoint

Chris Richards of *New Internationalist* magazine interviews Monina Wong from Labour Action China, Yat Paol from NGO Bismark Ramu Group in Papua new Guinea, and Pakistani sociologist Faida Shaheed regarding imported labour.

ModernMom.com
www.modernmom.com

One of the many websites dedicated to the "modern mom." The site, created by moms Lisa Rosenblatt and Brooke Burke, "provides the tools to be a well-rounded woman and empowers you to be the best mother possible." This site is an excellent example to share with students to encourage discussion of "mothering" discourse.

Big Sky Farms
www.bigsky.sk.ca/ems.html

This site is an example of what people can do when they unite with a common cause. STOP the HOGS Coalition opposes the proposal of North East Hogs/Big Sky Farms Inc. to build a mega-hog operation in their area. This site links to maps, photos, books, research, resources, and events that keep the coalition pulled together.

Patent for a Pig: The Big Business of Genetics
http://topdocumentaryfilms.com/patent-for-a-pig/

This one-hour documentary shows the impact of Monsanto's application for a patent for pig breeding in 160 countries. "If the patent is granted, pig breeding would be possible with the approval of the company." This site provides links to other documentaries such as: "We Feed the World"; "The World According to Monsanto"; and "Life Running Out of Control."

KEY TERMS

advanced capitalism

capitalization

conglomerate mergers

contradictions of capitalism

corporate capitalism

dependent commodity producers

holding company

horizontal integration

independent commodity producers

liberal-bourgeois thesis

managerial revolution

monopoly

oligopoly

poverty line

ruling apparatus

shareholder capitalism

vertical integration

welfare state

REFERENCES

Abaidoo, Samuel, and Harley Dickinson. 2002. "Alternative and Conventional Agricultural Paradigms: Evidence from Farming in Southwest Saskatchewan." *Rural Sociology* 67 (1): 114–131.

Acheson, K.J., E. Ravussin, J Wahren, and E. Jéquier. 1984. "Thermic Effect of Glucose in Man: Obligatory and Facultative Thermogenesis." The Journal of Clinical Investigation 74 (5): 1572–1580.

Anderson, Luke. 1999. *Genetic Engineering, Food, and our Environment*. Vermont: Chelsea Green Publishing.

Armstrong, Pat. 1984. *Labour Pains: Women's Work in Crisis*. Toronto: Women's Press.

Baragar, Fletcher. 2009. "Canada and the Crisis." In Julie Guard and Wayne Anthony, eds. *Bankruptcies and Bailouts*. Halifax; Winnipeg: Fernwood Publishing, 77–106.

Barlow, Maude. 2007. "Closed-door talks focusing on our water supply." *The Calgary Herald* (26 April 2007, A19).

Barlow, Maude. 2005. *Too Close for Comfort: Canada's Future Within Fortress North America*. Toronto: McClelland & Stewart.

Basok, Tanya. 2002. *Tortillas and Tomatoes: Transmigrant Mexican Harvesters in Canada*. Montreal; Kingston: McGill–Queen's University Press.

Bessant, Kenneth C. 2006. "A Farm Household Conception of Pluriactivity in Canadian Agriculture: Motivation, Diversification and Livelihood. *The Canadian Review of Sociology and Anthropology* 43 (1): 51–73.

Carroll, William K. 2004. *Corporate Power in a Globalizing World: A Study of Elite Social Organization*. Don Mills, Ontario: Oxford University Press.

Carroll, William K., and R.S. Ratner. 2005. "The NDP Regime in British Columbia, 1991–2001: A Post-Mortem." *The Canadian Review of Sociology and Anthropology* 42 (2): 167–196.

Donnan, Mary Ellen. "Making Change: Gender Careers and Citizenship." In Janet Siltanen and Andrea Doucet's *Gender Relations in Canada*. Toronto: Oxford University Press, 2008.

Edin, Kathryn, and Maria Kefalas. 2005. *Promises I Can Keep: Why Poor Mothers Put Motherhood before Marriage*. Berkeley; London: University of California Press.

Ferrie, Helke. 2004. "Make mine organic: More people are rejecting GM foods, turning to organics instead." CCPA Monitor 11 (4): 24–25.

Foster, John Bellamy, and Fred Magdoff. 2009. *The Great Financial Crisis: Causes and Consequences*. New York: Monthly Review Press.

Friedman, Milton. 1978. *Capitalism and Freedom*. Chicago: University of Chicago Press.

Gillen, David W., Tae H. Oum, and Michael W. Tretheway. 1988. "Privatization of Air Canada: Why it is Necessary in a Deregulated Environment." *Canadian Public Policy* 15 (3): 285–299.

Gonick, Cy. 2009. "A Great Leap Forward?" In Julie Guard and Wayne Anthony, eds. *Bankruptcies and Bailouts*. Halifax; Winnipeg: Fernwood Publishing, 8–17.

Hall, Alan, and Veronika Mogyorody. 2001. "Organic Farmers in Ontario: An Examination of the Conventionalization Argument." *Sociologia Ruralis* 41 (4): 399–422.

Hamilton, Eleanor. 2006. "Whose Story is it Anyway? Narrative Accounts of the Role of Women in Founding and Establishing Family Business." *International Small Business Journal* 24 (3): 253–271.

Heather, Barbara, Lynn Skillen, Jennifer Young, and Theresa Vladicka. 2005. "Women's Gendered Identities and the Restructuring of Rural Alberta." *Sociologia Ruralis* 45 (1–2): 86–97.

Hochschild, Arlie. 1989. *The Second Shift*. New York: Viking.

Hughes, Karen D. 2003. "Pushed or Pulled? Women's Entry into Self-Employment and Small Business Ownership." *Gender, Work & Organization* 10 (4): 433–445.

Hutton, Will. 2007a. "Don't blame China: It's Western business practices that widen the pay gap." CCPA Monitor (1 April 2007): 46.

Hutton, Will. 2007b. *The Writing on the Wall: Why We Must Embrace China as a Partner or Face it as an Enemy*. New York: Free Press.

Jackson, Andrew. 2006. "Are wage supplements the answer to the problems of the working poor?" CCPA Monitor 12 (June): 5–12.

Keet, Jean E. 1990. "The Law Reform Process, Matrimonial Property, and Farm Women: A Case Study of Saskatchewan, 1980–1986." *Canadian Journal of Women and Law* 4 (1): 166–189.

Kerstetter, Steve. 2002. *Rags and Riches: Wealth Inequality in Canada*. Canadian Centre for Policy Alternatives.

Klein, Naomi. 2000. *No Logo: Taking Aim at the Brand Bullies*. Toronto: Vintage Canada.

Landon, Laura, and Bruce Wark. 2004. "Measuring food from land to mouth." CCPA Monitor 11 (1): 32–34.

Leck, Joanne D. 2002. "Making Employment Equity Programs Work for Women." *Canadian Public Policy* 28 (Supplement 1): S85–S100.

Lewis, Stephen. 1972. *Louder Voices: The Corporate Welfare Bums*. Toronto: James Lewis and Samuel.

Loxley, John. 2009. "Financial Dimensions: Origins and State Responses." In Julie Guard and Wayne Anthony, eds. *Bankruptcies and Bailouts*. Halifax; Winnipeg: Fernwood Publishing, 62–76.

Luxton, Meg. 1980. *More Than a Labour of Love: Three Generations of Women's Work in the Home*. Toronto: Women's Press.

Machum, Susan T. 2002. "The Farmer Takes a Wife and the Wife Takes the Farm: Marriage and Farming." In G. MacDonald, ed. *Social Context & Social Location in the Sociology of Law*. Peterborough, Ontario: Broadview Press, 133–158.

Maxwell, Judith. 2002. "Smart Social Policy: 'Making Work Pay'." Canadian Policy Research Networks.

McLaughlin, Darrell. 2007. "Introduction: The Global Context of the Canadian Wheat Board." In Terry Pugh and Darrell McLaughlin, eds. *Our Board Our Business: Why Farmers Support the Canadian Wheat Board*. Halifax: Fernwood Publishing, 18–29.

Measner, Adrian. 2007. "The Global Grain Trade and the Canadian Wheat Board." In Terry Pugh and Darrell McLaughlin, eds. *Our Board Our Business: Why Farmers Support the Canadian Wheat Board*. Halifax: Fernwood Publishing, 30–41.

Menashy, Francine. 2007. "World Bank Education Policy: Do the Neoliberal Critiques Still Apply?" *McGill Journal of Education* 42 (1).

Murphy, Thomas. 1987. "Potato Capitalism: McCain and Industrial Farming in New Brunswick." In G. Burrill and I. McKay, eds. *People, Resources, and Power: Critical Perspectives on Underdevelopment and Primary Industries in the Atlantic Region*. Fredericton, New Brunswick: Acadiensis Press, 19–29.

Norberg-Hodge, Helena, Todd Marrifield, and Steven Gorelick. 2002. *Bringing the Food Economy Home: Local Alternatives to Global Agribusiness*. Halifax: Fernwood Publishing.

Novek, Joel. 2003a. "Intensive Livestock Operations, Disembedding, and Community Polarization in Manitoba." *Society and Natural Resources* 16: 567–581.

Novek, Joel. 2003b. "Intensive Hog Farming in Manitoba: Transnational Treadmills and Local Conflicts." *The Canadian Review of Sociology and Anthropology* 40 (1): 3–27.

Oliver, Christopher. 2005. "The Treadmill of Production under NAFTA: Multilateral Trade, Environmental Regulation, and National Sovereignty." *Organization & Environment* 18 (1): 55–71.

Pinto, Laura. 2007. "The Donald Trump illusion: Exploding the entrepreneurial myth in business education." CCPA Monitor 13 (9): 48–50.

Pugh, Terry, and Darrell McLaughlin, eds. 2007. *Our Board Our Business: Why Farmers Support the Canadian Wheat Board*. Halifax: Fernwood Publishing.

Qualman, Darrin. 2004. "Puncturing the 'farm crisis' myth: Farm crisis caused by greedy corporations, not inefficient farmers." CCPA Monitor 11 (1): 6–7.

Reed, Maureen G. 2004. "Moral Exclusion and the Hardening of Difference: Explaining Women's Protection of Industrial Forestry on Canada's West Coast." *Women's Studies International Forum* 27 (3): 223–242.

Reimer, Marilee. 1991–92. "Women's invisible skills and gender segregation in the clerical-administrative sector." *Journal of Public Sector Management* 22 (4): 29–41.

Rothman, Laurel. 2005. "Campaign 2000: Submission to the Federal Labour Standards Review Re: Part III of the Canada Labour Code." Human Resources and Skills Development Canada, 15 August 2005.

Rubenstein, Hymie. 2003. "Marxist Class Warfare Lives On." *Fraser Forum* (30–31 June).

Schellenberg, Grant. 1995. "'Involuntary' Part-time Workers." *Perception* 28 (3–4). Canada Council for Social Development.

Sharma, Nandita. 2001. "On Being Not Canadian: The Social Organization of 'Migrant Workers' in Canada." *Canadian Review of Sociology and Anthropology* 38 (4): 415–439.

Shortall, Sally. 2001. "Women in the Field: Women, Farming and Organizations." *Gender, Work and Organization* 8 (2): 164–181.

Smith, Dorothy E. 1992. "Feminist Reflections on Political Economy." In W.K. Carroll (and others) ed. *Feminism in Action: Studies in Political Economy*. Ottawa: Carleton University Press, 125–130.

Stanford, Jim. 2003. "Alternative Federal Budget 2004. Paul Martin, The Deficit, and the Debt: Taking Another Look." *Canadian Centre for Policy Alternatives* (28 November 2003): 1–16.

Statistics Canada. 2001. *Canada's International Investment Position, 2000*. Cat. No. 67-202. Ottawa: Ministry of Industry.

Stedman, Richard C., John R. Parkins, and Thomas M. Beckley. 2004. "Resource Dependence and Community Well-Being in Rural Canada. *Rural Sociology* 69 (2): 213–234.

Ueda, Yoko. 1995. "Corporate Wives: Gendered Education of Their Children." In M. Campbell and A. Manicom, eds. *Knowledge, Experience, and Ruling Relations: Studies in the Social Organization of Knowledge*. Toronto: University of Toronto Press, 122–134.

UNICEF 2005. *Child Poverty in Rich Nations Report Card No. 6.* Innocenti Research Centre.

Vasil, Adria. 2004. "What Teach is Smoking: Greenpeace Questions Ethics of Teachers' Pension Stake in Big Tobacco." *NOW Magazine Online Edition* (19–25 February 2004).

Veltmeyer, H. 1987. *Canadian Corporate Power*. Toronto: Garamond.

Wells, Stewart. 2007. "Comparing Apples and Oranges: The Canadian Wheat Board and the Ontario Wheat Producers Marketing Board." In Terry Pugh and Darrell McLaughlin, eds. *Our Board Our Business: Why Farmers Support the Canadian Wheat Board*. Halifax: Fernwood, 58–63.

Werkerle, Gerda R. 2004. "Food Justice Movements: Policy, Planning, and Networks. *Journal of Planning Education and Research* 23: 378–386.

Worth, Jess. 2007. "Overconsumption, ethical or not, is destroying the planet." CCPA Monitor 13 (9): 10–12.

Yalnizyan, Armine. 2007. "Canada's huge income gap has widened to a 30-year high." CCPA Monitor 13 (10): 1, 6–9.

Within the world community there are enormous disparities in standards of living across regions and countries. Until recently, world economies have been thought of as comprising three blocks—the First World of affluent capitalism, the **Third World** of impoverished and technologically backward regions, and the intermediate economies of socialist societies. These distinctions have become unworkable with the disintegration of the Soviet bloc and growing disparities between countries in the former Third World. The latter are now euphemistically referred to as "developing" countries.

The plethora of competing theories that try to account for economic disparities have direct practical implications for the design of national and international development programs. In this chapter we will focus first on worldwide development issues and then on the specific situation of Canada within the North American trading bloc. The complexities of economic development are daunting and we can only touch on some aspects of the theoretical debates here. Niels Bohr, winner of the Nobel Prize in Physics in 1922, is reputed to have commented that he switched from economics into physics because economics was too complicated. The subject has not become any easier since the 1920s.

 # Functionalist Theory: Modernization as Evolution

The functionalist **theory of modernization** conceptualizes societal evolution as a unilinear process of differentiation and specialization towards more complex and centralized organization. Change within the economic sphere requires simultaneous adjustments within political and administrative structures and especially within culture to maintain an integrated social system. Historically, the advancement of science and technology in developed Western societies was preceded by far-reaching changes in religious, political, and family structures.

Values such as the Protestant ethic promoted a focus on work as a religious calling and upon success within worldly activities as a sign of grace. Such values fostered the intensive commitment to work and investment of profits that characterized early capitalists in Europe.

Talcott Parsons argues that technologically backward and advanced societies have quite different cultural values. Traditional societies are typically centred on family and kinship ties, and on local loyalties, and they tend to view change as threatening to their social order. Modern societies, in contrast, emphasize individual achievement, measured in terms of objective, universal standards of performance that are applied impartially to all. Individual differences, specialization, and change are easily accommodated. Hence, a major problem that backward societies must overcome in order to emulate the advances of Western societies is **cultural lag**: the failure of other spheres of society to adapt to the economic changes that technological innovation entails.

This failure to adapt takes many forms. Localized tribal loyalties undermine a stable central government system. Administrative structures become chronically inefficient when staff are selected on the basis of nepotism rather than individual qualifications. Traditional religious values may oppose worldly success values needed for business and accumulation of capital. Above all, extended family ties may hamper individual initiative and stifle geographic and social mobility vital for taking advantage of economic opportunities. Intense family-centred values, or familism, are also associated with high birth rates. When this is combined with the transfer of modern medicines from the developed world to reduce the death rate, the result is crushing overpopulation, which leads inexorably to famine.

The Culture of Poverty

The thesis that a certain constellation of cultural values perpetuates poverty by stifling initiative for change is known as the **culture of poverty thesis**. The same explanation has been applied to account for pockets of poverty within the developed world. It is particularly associated with the early work of Oscar Lewis (1949) and Everett Rogers (1969, Ch. 2). Referring to peasants or subsistence farmers in the Third World, Rogers (1969, 19) comments that "they make the economists sigh, the politicians sweat, and the strategists swear, defeating their plans and prophesies all the world over." Their apathy and traditionalism constantly block the implementation of rural development programs.

Reluctance to innovate is associated with a syndrome of cultural traits that includes limited worldviews and low empathy, familism, mutual distrust in interpersonal relations, dependence on and hostility to government authority, fatalism, limited aspirations, lack of deferred gratification, and "perceived limited good." The trait of perceived limited good refers to the belief among peasants that the economic pie is limited and that anyone who gets ahead must be cheating others out of a share. People who do get ahead are viewed with a mixture of envy and scorn, rather than as models to emulate. Each of these cultural traits hampers modernization. These traits lead to ignorance, inability to conceive of a future different from the present, and a belief that no one outside the family can be trusted, including government development workers with newfangled schemes. Peasants display an apathetic resignation to fate because of their limited sense of control over the future. Money is not saved or invested, but is spent immediately or borrowed by other family members.

According to this functionalist thesis, the main solution to backwardness lies in continuing to transfer scientific and technological knowledge from the developed world, combined with concerted efforts to change outdated traditional values that block saving, investment, and rational organization of the economies of these countries (Chirot 1977, 3–4). This was the guiding ideology behind the American Peace Corps and Alliance for Progress, which flowered in the United States under the Kennedy administration in the early 1960s.

The 1960s were years of optimism sparked by the **green revolution**, a package of scientific developments in agriculture that promised to ameliorate famine. The package included high-yield varieties of wheat and rice, chemical fertilizers and pesticides, and large-scale irrigation projects. Together they had the potential to double or to treble yields. The other avenue for hope was the dissemination of contraceptive technology and aggressive campaigns for population control. It was hoped that, with higher agricultural yields and fewer babies to feed, the battle for adequate worldwide nutrition would be won.

These hopes were only partially fulfilled. The green revolution did raise yields, particularly among large farmers who tended to be more progressive. But the mass of small peasant farmers largely failed to adopt the new technology. The end result was an increase in the gap between rich and poor farmers. The syndrome of attitudes associated with the culture of poverty was widely cited to account for the failure of small farmers to innovate.

The goal of population control similarly met with limited success. Among the wealthier, educated classes, family size did decline, but not among the masses. During the period between 1950 and 1972, the population of Asia rose by an estimated 63 percent, Africa by 72 percent, and Latin America by 91 percent. In contrast, in North America, population increased by only 42 percent and Europe by 26 percent (Kalbach 1976, 11). A UN report estimated that the world's population reached 5.67 billion in September 1994 and is expected to reach 6 billion by 1998 (*Globe and Mail*, 14 Sept. 1994, A12).

Various explanations are offered for continuing high rates of population increase in Third World countries. Improved health care and mass immunization have reduced the infant death rate, but continuing fear of infant mortality makes people reluctant to accept sterilization before the birth and survival of large numbers of children. The medical complications and expense associated with all forms of artificial contraception limit their use, while religious and cultural factors, and especially the desire for sons, favour having many children.

The result is that increases in food production are virtually cancelled out by increases in population. In India, for example, between 1950 and 1970 agricultural yields doubled, but this barely kept ahead of the birth rate. In 1985 the worst happened. Drought in Africa precipitated famine on a devastating scale, with hundreds of thousands of people in Ethiopia, Sudan, and Chad starving to death, and millions more barely kept alive in relief camps. Famine struck these regions again in 1987–88. Only massive gifts of food from around the world stood between millions of people and starvation. The only solution, from the perspective of conventional theories, is more of the same: more technology and more cultural change.

In summary, for functionalists the causes of failure to modernize are within the structures and cultures of the backward countries themselves. Research promoted by this theoretical approach has focused particularly upon technological transfer and aid projects, internal politics and bureaucratic organization within the Third World countries, and the response of local people to small-scale development projects. The long history of frustration and limited results has offered much support for the thesis that deep-rooted structural and cultural changes must precede modernization.

The Modernization Thesis Discredited

Criticisms generated within the functionalist tradition have focused upon the limited empirical validity of some of the generalizations outlined above. It is not difficult to point to examples of traditional value orientations in developed countries and evidence of modern value orientations in Third World countries, with no appreciable impact on the level of modernization (Frank 1972). The culture of poverty thesis has been challenged on the grounds that the implied cause and effect should be reversed (Hale 1985, 55). Rather than attitudes causing economic backwardness, it is the condition of economic backwardness that causes the attitudes. Restricted information flow, exploitation, the absolute lack of access to resources needed for agricultural innovation, and the impossibility of saving money in the face of inadequate and irregular incomes are facts of everyday life for peasants in North India, especially small landowners and landless tenant farmers. Such structural factors account both for the failure to innovate and the attitudes that go with such behaviour.

Similarly, with respect to population control, there is evidence that the underlying relation between high birth rates and poverty works in reverse to the usual argument. It is poverty that drives families to have more children, especially male children, to compensate for high death rates and to ensure some means of support in old age. As real economic alternatives emerge for women to support themselves and to raise their standards of living, they choose increasingly to restrict the number of children they have. Attitudes tend to change readily in response to real opportunities for advancement. Functionalism describes the association between attitudes and behaviour, but it does not explain it.

Political Economy Theory: Underdevelopment as Capitalist Exploitation

The strongest challenge to the functionalist theory of modernization has come from the perspective of political economy. Ironically, the main point of this criticism is that functionalist theory has failed to live up to its own insistence that parts should be understood in relation to the total system. The development of any one region or nation can be fully understood only by how it functions in relation to the total system. Political economy theory shifts the focus from the internal structures of poor countries to the functioning of the world economic system in which they are embedded.

Functionalist theory suggests that economic backwardness in the Third World reflects a culture of poverty.

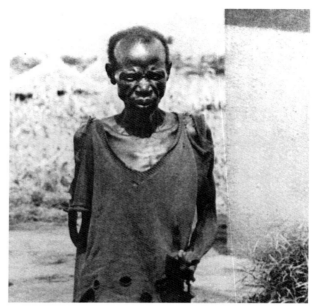

Photo courtesy of CARE Canada

The central argument, which we explore below, is that the wealth of some countries and regions and the poverty of others are, and always have been, systematically related. Frank (1972, 3) rejects outright the notion that somehow Third World societies have not yet developed, or that they lack the required cultural or other prerequisites to copy Western development. The Third World, he argues, is not simply **undeveloped**, continuing to exist in some unchanged, traditional pattern. These societies are **underdeveloped**. Their resources have been, and still are being, plundered, and their internal economies are undermined by processes of a world capitalist economic system.

Historically, most now impoverished Third World societies were subject to the destructive impact of **mercantilism**, **colonialism**, and **imperialism**. The economies of many regions of Africa were devastated by the slave trade, while the indigenous societies of Latin America were crushed by European conquerors plundering the regions in search of precious metals. The economies of conquered regions were directed primarily in the interests of the imperial powers, which focused upon the extraction of resources to fuel imperial development, while simultaneously retarding and distorting the internal development of the regions themselves. Even now, in many parts of Africa, the main roads go from centres to the ports, rather than to other African centres (Hoogvelt 1976). African interregional telephone lines still link up through Britain.

Imperial governments fundamentally transformed indigenous social structures and often divided up territories with no respect for traditional tribal lines. "Divide and rule" tactics often involved favouring selected local elites or encouraging the immigration of ethnic minorities into the colonies, to act as a buffer group between the colonial power and the local people. East Indians, for example, were used in this way in many of the British colonies in Africa. Such people acted as business middlemen, local administrators, and tax collectors for the colonial era. The legacy of tribal conflicts and class disparities along ethnic lines still plagues the new nation-states.

Most colonized countries have now gained political independence, but this has not brought effective economic independence. Their economies are still dominated by forces of the world capitalist economic system over which they have little control. This externalized control through economic pressures is referred to as **neo-imperialism**.

International Capitalism: The Practices of Dependent Development

A major contribution of Gundar Frank's analysis of underdevelopment has been to focus attention on critical mechanisms through which the centres of advanced capitalism are able to exploit dependent economies. These include control over capital, control over patterns of investment, domination of market relations, decisive bargaining power in the labour market, and political clout, including the use of force as a last resort. We will examine these five mechanisms in turn.

Control over Capital   There has been a net outflow of capital from poorer regions such as Latin America to wealthier regions such as the United States for most of this century. This is despite foreign aid payments, which appear to go from rich to poor nations. This outflow takes many forms, one of the most visible of which is debt repayment. Debts have reached crisis proportions in many Latin American and African countries. Interest payments due on loans are so great that they comprise more than one-third of total national income earned from exports in some of the poorest countries of Africa. The situation is so bad that newspaper articles in June 1988, during an economic summit for leading industrialized nations, speculated on how many babies starve to death for each dollar of interest repaid. These are babies who might not have died if debt repayments could have been spent on clean drinking water or minimal health care in desperately poor countries. The debt repayment problem is made worse by currency devaluations forced on debtor nations by the International Monetary Fund.

The outflow of money from poor to rich nations also occurs in less obvious forms. Cheap exports and overpriced imports, often directly controlled by multinational corporations, generate large profits and dividends that flow back to the corporate home base, together with payments for royalties and financial services of all kinds. Multinational empires often also have close ties to banks and hence have preferential access to large investment loans over struggling smaller companies within the host societies. Multinationals are, in any case, relatively independent of banks because they can use profits from one sector of their activities to finance new investments elsewhere. Their commanding control over access to finance capital gives them effective control over investment policy.

Control over Patterns of Investment   Access to capital gives multinational corporate empires almost total control over decisions about where and how to invest. Such decisions are routinely made in the interests of the corporations themselves and focus on export-oriented production rather than on provision of basic public resources such as roads, railways, and electrical power lines and generators that are needed to promote local industry. Export-oriented production also takes away money and other resources that might have been invested in production geared to the needs of the host societies. Corporations have the power to create boom and bust economic cycles, as they can choose to shift centres of production from one region, or from one country, to another, depending on where the greatest profits might be made. Host societies can do virtually nothing about such decisions. Corporate interests have helped to create a new international division of labour, with many countries specializing in production of one or two goods each.

Market Relations   Corporate empires have the capacity to exert decisive control over market relations between poor countries and the world economic system. In the first place, an estimated 30 percent of all world trade is no longer in the marketplace but occurs directly between affiliates of multinational corporations (Martin 1982, 95). Martin concludes that the "open market" is a convenient fiction when applied to international trade. **Transfer pricing** refers to the price that a parent company sets in selling supplies to its own branch plants or the price at which the parent company purchases goods produced or assembled by the branch plants. In this internal corporate economy, concepts such as costs and benefits or profits do not have fixed values. They are the outcome of accounting practices. Prices can be manipulated to maximize the outflow of profits to corporate headquarters. Underpriced imports may give a competitive edge to an affiliate over local companies. Alternatively, imports may be overpriced to reduce paper profits and local taxes. Either tactic increases the hidden outflow of money from poor to rich. Martin (1982, 109) estimates that such transfer pricing may account for 82.6 percent of capital returns to headquarters.

Vertically integrated companies also directly control the marketing of products. Six multinationals, for example, control 60 percent of the world production of bauxite and 80 percent of aluminum production (Martin 1982, 100). Sometimes a single corporation controls the export of all bauxite produced in one country to its own plants at home. All the bauxite from the Dominican Republic is sent to Alcoa plants in the United States, while all Haiti's bauxite goes to one Reynolds plant in Texas. The economy of an entire country may be dependent upon the export of one or two specialized products that are under the control of one multinational corporation. The country is thus totally vulnerable to the fluctuations in the market price for these products and to the whim of the corporate directors deciding where and how they will market the products.

Labour Market Relations

In the worldwide labour market, the workers in poor countries provide a vast pool of cheap labour. They have little bargaining power and few rights or benefits. Giant companies can potentially shift production to wherever labour is cheapest, and this gives them a powerful bargaining tool for playing off one country against another. In 1976, for example, General Electric was negotiating worldwide to build an assembly plant for televisions (Martin 1982, 93). Hourly wages in Taiwan were 37 cents and in South Korea 52 cents. General Electric was negotiating with Indonesia offering 17 cents per hour. Anti-union legislation may also be a part of the bargaining demands of the corporation. Corporations can force or persuade states to enact legislation to ban strikes, picketing, and other union activities as the price for locating a plant in their region.

Political Force

Should business interests or investments be at risk, large corporations exert substantial political clout. Within the host country itself, the presence of an indigenous capitalist class that benefits directly from foreign capital investments helps to stifle unified opposition. The ultimate backup for this international system is the military might of the metropolis country. In the early 1970s, when the democratically elected socialist government of Salvador Allende proposed to nationalize the American-owned copper mines of Kennecott and Anaconda in Chile, the corporations were able to mobilize the support of the American government and the Central Intelligence Agency (CIA) to overthrow the regime (Martin 1982, 120–121). International banks, including Canadian banks, cooperated by cutting all credit to Chile. Other international corporations operating in Chile drained their local **subsidiaries** of money and denied supplies of needed resources such as mechanical spare parts, hence bringing the Chilean economy to a halt. International Telephone and Telegraph (ITT) had substantial holdings

in Chile and feared nationalization. Corporate directors conspired directly to bring about the downfall of the government through specific forms of armed and funded intervention organized through the American CIA.

In conclusion, it is important to recognize that dependency theory does not reflect the inexorable working of an invisible hand, with people as mere pawns. It is the result of strategies intended to have specific and foreseen effects. Multinational corporations are oriented towards making profits and increasing their own capital to satisfy large shareholders. Their policies are not designed to raise living standards for the mass of people in the Third World, and it should not be surprising that this is not their major effect.

Dependent Capitalist Development

There is continuing debate within the political economy perspective on how these processes of economic domination work, and whether it is more useful to focus on international trade relations, as Frank does, or modes of production, as traditional Marxist theory does. In practice, as Brenner's analysis shows, the two processes are intimately related.

Brenner (1977) argues that a precondition for capitalism is the separation of the mass of people from the means of producing their own needs. It is this dependence on markets for survival that drives people with capital to invest in new technology to raise productivity and that also drives those without capital to sell their labour power for wages.

The proletarianization of labour has been largely achieved in most Third World countries. The slums and shanty towns around almost all big cities are flooded with impoverished rural people desperate to sell their labour power at almost any price (Foster-Clark 1978), but the corollaries of compulsive investment and rising productivity have not followed.

Foster-Clark argues that this is really **dependent capitalism**—imported from outside in a form already fully developed. Impoverished developing countries, struggling to compete in world capitalist markets, face all the contradictions of capitalism full blown: the crises of falling rates of profit, the extreme concentration of capital in huge corporate empires, overproduction, unemployment, and misery as masses of unemployed people the world over compete to sell their labour to investors at the lowest possible wages.

Third World countries are in the worst possible position to try to compete with monopoly capitalists. Companies such as Exxon and General Motors command more wealth than the entire economies of most Third World countries (see Table 1). Poor countries, trying to develop their economies, are no match for these giants. The best they can hope for is to compete among themselves to attract what investment they can get, with the carrots of

Table 1 Largest 100 Countries and Companies, 1985*

Rank 1985	Rank 1976	Name	GNP/Sales (billion $ US)	Rank 1985	Rank 1976	Name	GNP/Sales (billion $ US)
1	1	USA	3634.6	42	40	*Texaco*	46.3
2	2	USSR	N/A	43	54	Thailand	41.9
3	3	Japan	1255.0	44	47	*Chevron*	41.7
4	4	West Germany	613.2	45	30	Yugoslavia	38.9
5	5	France	489.4	46	66	*American Tel & Tel*	34.9
6	6	UK	425.4	47	59	Colombia	34.4
7	7	Italy	348.4	48	49	Philippines	32.8
8	8	Canada	334.1	49	76	Hong Kong	30.6
9	9	China	281.3	50	61	Libya	30.5
10	10	Brazil	187.3	51	71	Egypt	30.1
11	13	Australia	182.2	52	44	Greece	29.5
12	20	Mexico	171.3	53	87	*E.I. du Pont*	29.5
13	15	India	162.3	54	72	Malaysia	29.3
14	11	Spain	160.9	55	74	United Arab Emirates	28.8
15	18	Iran	157.6	56	58	*General Electric*	28.3
16	14	Netherlands	132.6	57	64	Pakistan	27.7
17	27	Saudi Arabia	109.4	58	67	*Standard Oil (Indiana)*	26.8
18	24	*General Motors*	96.4	59	—	*IRI*	26.8
19	17	Sweden	91.9	60	95	*Toyota*	26.0
20	21	Switzerland	91.1	61	73	*ENI*	24.5
21	23	*Exxon*	86.7	62	65	New Zealand	23.3
22	42	Korea, Rep of	83.2	63	77	Israel	22.4
23	31	*Royal Dutch/Shell*	81.7	64	86	*Atlantic Richfield*	22.0
24	32	Indonesia	80.6	65	62	Kuwait	21.7
25	19	Belgium	77.6	66	57	*Unilever*	21.6
26	28	Argentina	76.2	67	60	*Chrysler*	21.3
27	12	Poland	75.4	68	117	*Matsushita*	20.8
28	16	German Democratic Republic	N/A	69	104	*Hitachi*	20.5
29	36	Nigeria	73.5	70	—	*Remex*	20.4
30	33	South Africa	73.4	71	—	*Shell Oil*	20.3
31	22	Czechoslovakia	N/A	72	98	*Elf-Aquitane*	20.1
32	25	Austria	64.5	73	69	Chile	19.8
33	41	*Mobil*	56.0	74	75	*Franàaise des Petro*	19.3
34	34	Norway	54.7	75	55	Portugal	19.1
35	29	Denmark	54.6	76	63	Peru	18.8
36	38	*Ford Motor*	52.8	77	84	*US Steel*	18.4
37	39	Finland	51.2	78	89	Ireland	18.3
38	51	Algeria	50.7	79	106	*Nissan Motor*	18.2
39	53	*IBM*	50.1	80	114	Singapore	18.2
40	26	Turkey	47.5	81	68	*Phillips*	18.1
41	35	Venezuela	47.5	82	91	*Siemens*	17.8

83	85	*Volkswagenwerk*	17.8	92	120	*Occidental Petroleum*	14.5
84	82	*Daimler-Benz*	17.8	93	79	*Hoechst*	14.5
85	97	*Nestlé*	17.2	94	—	*Fiat*	14.5
86	102	*Petrobas*	16.1	95	—	*Samsung*	14.2
87	130	*United Technologies*	15.8	96	112	*Mitsubishi*	14.1
88	118	*Phillips Petroleum*	15.7	97	—	*Hyundai*	14.0
89	88	*Bayer*	15.6	98	—	*General Motors (Canada)*	13.9
90	108	*Tenneco*	15.4	99	—	*Imperial Chemical*	13.9
91	80	*BASF*	15.1	100	123	*Sun*	13.8

Source: Veltmeyer (1987, 78–79). From World Bank (1987); *Fortune*, 4 Aug. 1986.
* Countries are ranked by gross national product (GNP) and companies by sales. Countries are shown in roman type, companies in italic. Deficiencies in the data sources kept this table from being truly complete. The World Bank does not list a few countries, such as Taiwan. Others, such as Romania, Hungary, and Bulgaria, were in the 1976 list (they would have ranked 37, 43, and 45 respectively in this table) but were missing for lack of data in 1985; consequently, they are omitted from this table, where they would likely have ranked somewhere in the 50s. Similarly, some very large companies, such as National Iran Oil and Renault, were omitted from the *Fortune* list; others ranked in the top 100 in 1985 but not 1976, or vice versa.

cheap labour, cheap raw materials, minimal taxation, and anything else the giant corporations want. This is not the stuff of which balanced and self-sustaining economic growth is made.

In terms of the **dependency theory** model developed by Frank, such poor countries form **hinterlands** for the **metropolis** or centre of capitalism. Hinterlands are the underdeveloped areas that supply cheap labour and cheap raw material or semi-processed goods to the developed centres. Metropolises are the centres of capitalism, which dominate surrounding regions, extracting their economic surplus. Capital accumulation at the centre siphons off capital from the periphery. Frank conceptualizes the world capitalist system as hierarchically organized, with each smaller metropolis forming a hinterland for yet larger centres, with the ultimate metropolis in New York or Tokyo.

Frank's model is valuable in countering the notion that the causes of poverty lie within the poorer regions themselves. But it has been widely criticized for invoking a crude functional determinism that cannot account for variation in rates of development. Newly industrializing countries are not all characterized by supercheap labour and state repression (Sayer and Walker 1992, 242). There are also many other countries that have supercheap labour but that show no signs of capitalist development. The dynamics of international division of labour are more complex than Frank's model can accommodate. The view of the world as divided into exporters of primary products who are poor and exporters of manufactured goods who are rich is simply not accurate (Gidengil 1989, 95). The mechanisms that tie Third World labour and production into these arrangements are not explicated, nor is the relative importance of cheap labour pools in resolving the crises of capitalism, compared with other factors (Wood 1989, 123–124).

Key terms such as *metropole* and *hinterland* are also vague, particularly when smaller metropoles are seen as constituting hinterlands for bigger ones. In this era of corporate monopoly capitalism, corporate empires rather than hierarchies of nation-states constitute the metropolises. The biggest 23 corporations in the world have their headquarters in the United States, but Canada is also home base to a number of multinationals, as are Japan and many European countries. As we will see, being home base to a multinational corporation does not guarantee wealth or economic development. Many poorer regions of Canada and the United States also find their productive potential siphoned off by corporate empires.

Restructuring Dependent Development

Gidengil (1989) suggests that dependency is best understood not as an explanation for underdevelopment, but as a form of relationship that constrains possibilities for development. Dependent regions or countries are those that lack an autonomous capacity for change and growth. Their development potential is tied to decisions made beyond their borders, and over which they have little or no control. They are integrated into the world economy in a subordinate position and this is reflected in internal structures. Typically, foreign capitalists form alliances with local power blocs of indigenous capitalists and large landowners, with the local state as mediator (Gulalp 1990, 152–153). Local decision-making and development initiatives are tightly constrained by such alliances.

Gulalp suggests that underdeveloped capitalist countries such as those in Latin America are most likely to have political democracy within early stages of economic development (1990, 158). Elected governments can maintain popularity among voters by promoting local manufacturing industries to replace foreign imports, subsidizing such enterprises and protecting them from cheap foreign imports by high tariff barriers, and also by instituting state welfare policies. But these democracies are vulnerable to "crises of accumulation." The states cannot generate sufficient revenues to sustain these programs because of very low levels of productivity and profits in local industries. Local manufacturers lack the capital to invest in advanced labour-saving technology, and hence produce goods that are of poorer quality and higher unit costs than foreign manufacturers. They also pay lower wages and provide only a limited tax base. The result is a low standard of living relative to other countries, which fosters popular unrest. Indigenous capitalists also have vested interests in forming self-seeking alliances with foreign capitalists that undermine protectionist policies. Military regimes are the likely outcome of such internal conflicts. Since they do not need popular electoral support, they are better able to quell resistance from local people, dismantle the welfare state, abandon protectionist policies, and permit foreign capitalists to exploit local resources and cheap labour. This takeover of the domestic economy by foreign capital is often supported by financial agencies such as the International Monetary Fund. Military regimes may in turn give way to civilian governments in which the local capitalists who are most closely tied in with international business interests come to dominate policy.

These are deeply destructive processes of class struggle that do not fit any simplified model of bourgeoisie versus proletariat. The collapse of internal administrative structures associated with them cannot be resolved by adjustments to backward cultural values. The struggles vary widely across developing societies in different regions. In the Middle East and the Far East, the resources that can be exploited locally, their location in the international system, and the constellation of alliances between local and international capital, vary greatly from the Latin American situation and give rise to different patterns of class struggle. What they have in common are the constraints set by a global economy dominated by centres of advanced capitalism.

Restructuring Advanced Capitalism

Advanced capitalist economies do not form a unified bloc with common policies. They, too, are caught up in the contradictions of capitalism, the endemic crises of accumulation reflected in falling rates of profit, overproduction, and unemployment. Competing factions within the capitalist class struggle to maintain **competitive advantage** in global markets. Alliances with developing countries are an important aspect of these strategies, but they cannot be reduced simply to the drive to deskill and cheapen labour in the hope of undercutting competitors' prices.

There are two major types of competitive strategies: one involves trying to minimize inputs and labour costs in given markets; the other tries to promote innovative product development that gives rise to new consumer markets (Sayer and Walker 1992, Ch. 2). The first strategy is associated with "Fordism" or the mass production of standardized products. Complex assembly work is fragmented into highly repetitive tasks that can be learned easily and performed quickly. A competitive edge depends on minimizing per unit costs of production and on mass consumer markets. The second strategy is associated with "flexible specialization" geared to smaller-batch production for specialized markets. This requires close working relationships between parent plants and suppliers, and among scientists, design engineers, and skilled shop-floor workers who can shift rapidly in a variety of activities. A competitive edge depends on a continual stream of innovative and quality products that attract consumers.

Standardized assembly work is most easily transferred into Third World countries. Abundant supplies of supercheap labour, low taxes, and lax environmental and working standards promise to minimize production costs. These conditions are not conducive to flexible product innovation, however. The standardized product may be cheap but still lose market share to higher quality alternatives, even at higher unit prices. Sayer and Walker suggest that highly integrated groups of interdependent firms in Japan are well adapted to production based on flexible specialization. Foreign competitors cannot easily copy their innovations. There is little incentive for firms within these Japanese groups of companies to subcontract work to centres of cheap labour.

Patterns of international division of labour reflect these complexities. Regional inequality is endemic to advanced capitalism in that high-technology production flourishes where potential users of innovative products are also concentrated. Innovation in the field of computers, for example, is intimately associated with customers' demands and often involves close consultation with them in both production and marketing. The producers of such products are not scattered across different regions. "Silicon Valleys" tend to be highly localized, although the assembly of standardized components may be dispersed.

Sayer and Walker conclude that an adequate understanding of international development must give much greater attention to the complexities of social division of labour rather than class struggle (1992, 268–270). They suggest that the failure of Marxist theory to come to terms with division of labour undermines our understanding of the mechanisms of capitalism. It also undermines the ability of socialist theory to help socialist economies replace these mechanisms with superior forms of organization. Sayer and Walker suggest that socialist economies in Eastern Europe collapsed in large part because they could not manage the division of labour involved in economic production. In capitalist societies, the relationship between demand for goods and their supply by industry is managed through prices in the market. High demand for limited goods causes their prices to rise, and thus encourages individual manufacturers to shift production from low-demand goods to high-demand goods where they can expect to make greater profits. In centrally planned socialist economies, there is no price mechanism. Planners must guess how much of each kind of produce people in a society will need or want and direct production accordingly. The decisions involved are so impossibly complex that the result is chronic inefficiency, gluts and shortages, and decisions are made on the basis of political influence rather than rational economic factors.

Restructuring Socialist Economies

The disintegration of socialist economies in Eastern Europe, beginning with the demolition of the Berlin wall in 1989, was widely hailed as the triumph of capitalism and democracy over totalitarianism. Masses of people demonstrated in the streets demanding that Western-style political democracy replace the one-party communist system. They also pressured for a free market system to replace discredited centrally planned economies. Hundreds of thousands of East Germans flocked to West Berlin to gaze in awe at the consumer goods in the stores. Polish leader Lech Walesa begged American and Western European businesses to invest in Poland. Economists and business people in the Soviet Union, Czechoslovakia, and Hungary swiftly joined the clamour for foreign investment. People in these countries see the correlation between Western capitalism and high standards of living. Correlation readily becomes interpreted as causation, and capitalism is seen as a potential cure for lower living standards in the Eastern bloc. The hope is that by opening their economies to Western investors and free market principles they, too, will encourage investment, high labour productivity, and the accumulation of wealth.

The euphoria surrounding the dismantling of communist parties and the introduction of *perestroika* and *glasnost*, restructuring and freedom, is now largely spent, amid an increasingly grim reality of economic and political chaos. The class struggles emerging within Soviet society reflect deep contradictions that offer no easy transition to advanced capitalism.

The old system of centralized planning generated an elite of party officials and top-level administrators who wielded enormous power and enjoyed high salaries and other perks. At the same time, the mismatch between supply and demand within the public sector spawned a powerful mafia of black marketeers, hoarders, and speculators (Kotovsky 1992, 169). Members of these two groups have the capital to take greatest advantage of newly opened markets and are reputed to be rapidly enriching themselves. But this enrichment has been chiefly through speculative trading ventures rather than production.

Since 1987 in the Soviet Union, factory and farm managers have had direct access to overseas markets. One result has been a boom in the export of consumer goods for sale abroad at lower than world prices. The corollary has been the destruction of linkages between enterprises within the domestic economy and the disappearance of goods in which the society was formerly self-sufficient. In 1991, some 2500 cooperatives were established to compete with the public sector, but Kotovsky (1992, 169) estimates that only 20 percent of them went into production. The rest went into pure commerce, speculating in buying and selling commodities. Such non-productive investments are generating a small class of nouveau riche, while the mass of people are experiencing a frightening collapse in their standards of living and soaring crime rates.

It is too early to judge the long-term outcome of these new economic policies. But processes that generated economic growth in Western capitalist countries in the past will not necessarily work the same way in the context of contemporary international capitalism. People in the Eastern bloc are facing the same contradictions of global capitalism as the struggling economies of the Third World.

Foreign Aid: Philanthropy or Commercial Interests?

Carty (1982) begins his discussion of the Canadian International Development Agency (CIDA) with a quotation that defines foreign aid as money you take from poor people in a rich country and give to rich people in a poor country. Over the 30-year period between 1951 and 1981, CIDA contributed approximately $11 billion to finance thousands of projects in over 90 countries. In addition, it shipped millions of tons of food and other supplies for emergency relief. But, Carty (1982, 150) concludes, the Third World is as impoverished, exploited, and oppressed now as it was three decades earlier.

There are several reasons why Canada gives foreign aid: it reflects a philanthropic concern to reduce human suffering; political interests in gaining allies and international influence; and commercial interests in boosting export markets for Canadian goods. Carty argues that commercial interests, backed by a very powerful lobby, have taken precedence. He calculates that fully 60 percent of the total CIDA aid budget was spent within Canada on Canadian goods, commodities, and services, creating over 100 000 jobs in Canada. Much aid is unabashedly oriented towards export promotion. The goal is to hook recipients on Canadian inputs in the form of replacement parts, repairs, and services. Development projects also build the infrastructure of roads, railways, and power supplies required by foreign investors (Carty 1982, 168).

While projects that are potentially beneficial for Canadian exports receive massive financial support, other projects that might help to raise the standard of living of people in poor countries are starved of funds. Commitments for health, welfare, clean water supplies, and education, which might more directly benefit recipient countries, dropped off steadily between 1976 and 1978 in the absence of powerful backers.

The real costs to Canada of CIDA aid may be almost zero once one deducts: debt forgiveness on past loans; the transfer of surplus wheat, milk, and rapeseed that we could neither eat nor sell commercially; all the bilateral aid tied to the purchase of Canadian goods and services; loan repayments made to nongovernmental organizations based in Canada, which then spend the funds in Canada; and the projected unemployment benefits the Canadian government might have had to pay if these Canadian beneficiaries were not employed (Carty 1982, 171).

Canada's food aid program, while valuable for strictly emergency relief, has been challenged as actually promoting and perpetuating the emergencies it tries to alleviate. In 1976, some 600 000 tons of international food aid was shipped to Bangladesh, yet scarcely 10 percent of it may have reached the destitute. The rest provided cheap, subsidized food for the influential middle classes. Meanwhile it encouraged government complacency about the food crisis and undermined the local markets for the crops of small producers. Many were forced into bankruptcy.

New strategies developed since 1976 are designed in principle to promote "integrated rural development," with more aid going to the less privileged sectors of sharecroppers and small peasant farmers. But Carty suggests that little has changed in practice. World Bank credit still goes principally to medium and larger farmers for commercial enterprises.

Peasants with medium-sized holdings are often selected as target populations because they have enough land to be integrated into "modernized and monetarized" agricultural systems as good credit risks. On the plus side, productivity increases, but at the cost of transforming peasant producers into commercial agriculturalists. They become part of the **agribusiness** system as consumers of agricultural inputs and as producers of crops suitable for further processing.

Carty concludes that what the Third World really needs is not foreign aid, but a restructuring of international economic relations. Between 1970 and 1979, CIDA disbursed some $2.4 billion in aid, but in this same period the 10 recipient countries experienced a trade deficit with Canada of about $2.4 billion. This trade imbalance wiped out even the nominal value of the aid.

Agribusiness and Famine   It is with respect to food production that the interests of multinational corporations engaged in agriculture diverge most obviously from the interests of the mass of people in Third World countries. Policies to maximize profits have been directly implicated in the causes of famine. Lappé (1971, 16) aptly sums up this relationship when she states simply that "land that grows money can't grow food."

The problem of using land to grow money began during the colonial era when Western powers took over vast tracts of land in subject countries for plantations. Beckford (1973, 120–122) cites a long list of countries in Asia, the Caribbean, and Latin America that are primarily plantation economies, with the bulk of their agricultural resources devoted to foreign-owned plantations producing crops for sale to overseas markets.

The size of such operations is enormous and is steadily growing as corporations buy more land or push neighbouring farmers out of business. The United Fruit Company in Latin America demanded 5000 acres of the best arable land before it would start a plantation. The company did not use this much land but wanted to hold it in reserve in case they might want to expand in the future. United Fruit controlled 100 percent of the export of bananas from Guatemala in 1966 and 70 percent of banana exports from Costa Rica and Panama (Barnet and Muller 1974). In many instances, the area of land taken over is so vast that it provides the only source of employment for people living in substantial parts of the countries concerned.

Plantation crops include tobacco, rubber, tea, coffee, cocoa, cotton and fibres, sugar, and more recently marijuana, for the North American market. All such crops are grown for export only. They cannot be eaten by local people as staple foods. Even crops such as sugar cane are now being grown in Brazil, not for food, but to produce alcohol as a substitute for gasoline. Many Third World countries depend on these cash crops for their survival. Coffee alone provides the economic livelihood for 40 developing countries.

Feder (1976) describes in some detail how this process of takeover and control occurs. Corporations control production, processing, transport, storage, and financing. They either employ local people directly or extend credits and inputs on a contract basis with prearranged terms of sale advantageous to the corporation. A corporation that grew strawberries in Mexico, for example, enjoyed cheap land rentals and cheap wages. When the soil became depleted from overproduction, the company moved to a new location. Impoverished ex-employees remained behind. Most of the benefits of exports do not go to local people, or to labourers on plantations, but to big companies, which remit profits abroad.

The most serious ramification is that local farmers who produce the bulk of subsistence food crops are pushed out onto marginal land where yields are low. Food production falls. Farmers try to compensate by pushing into what was once forest or grazing land. Deforestation and progressive depletion of poor soils result. Food prices rise faster than the prices of export crops, so that foreign exchange earnings are not sufficient to pay for the food imports needed.

Droughts, famine, and environmental bankruptcy are not unpredictable acts of God. They are caused by human mismanagement, overcultivation, deforestation, and overgrazing, which have ruined the soil's ability to absorb water. The topsoil blows off, and droughts and flash floods result.

These processes seem to have triggered the massive famine in Ethiopia. Even at the height of its famine, though, Ethiopia continued to export coffee and meat, largely because it needed the foreign exchange to pay debts. This export production is supported by the Food and Agriculture Organization of the United Nations and by the World Bank.

"Land that grows money can't grow food." Droughts and famine are caused by human mismanagement, overcultivation, deforestation, and overgrazing.

Karen Kasmauski/Corbis

 # Patriarchy: The Underdevelopment of Women

Women, the main producers of subsistence food crops throughout the world, have fared the worst from policies that promote cash crops over local food crops. In the international system of stratification, women are at the bottom. They work the hardest, produce the most, but own and earn the least.

The functionalist model of modern society proposed by Parsons explicitly excludes women from economic development. Women are defined as specialized homemakers who are or should be financially dependent upon their husbands. They are conceptualized in functionalist development theory as homebound, family-oriented wives and mothers, concerned with socialization and religious training of children, and hence naturally conservative. They are enjoined to behave in accordance with traditional cultural norms, to stress emotions, diffuse and particularistic family ties, and ascriptive values, while men take care of the instrumental roles (Hale 1985, 53).

But the evidence belies this conceptualization of women's lives in the Third World. Women's unpaid labour is estimated to produce one-third of the world's annual economic product. Their work accounts for more than half the food produced in the Third World and as much as 80 percent of food produced in Africa (Sivard 1985, 5). Yet women are largely excluded from agricultural development projects sponsored as part of the green revolution. Only men are defined as farmers; women are farm wives. Projects for women may include some information on high-yielding seeds, but rarely are women taught the business side of farming. Even progressive land reform policies, intended to give ownership rights to those who work the land rather than to absentee landlords, have served to weaken rather than strengthen women's rights to land. Their traditional land-use rights are ignored, and land is vested in male household heads (Sen 1985, 27). Western individualistic values are imposed on others. In the Kano River project in Nigeria, communally owned lands were registered only in the name of the "senior owner," almost always a man. Women, along with junior men, lost all their rights (Sen 1985, 35).

Women are systematically disadvantaged with respect to all five of the mechanisms noted by Frank as perpetuating neo-imperialism. Firstly, women have the least access of any Third World group to credit and other financial resources. Because they do not own land legally, they have no collateral (Hale 1985, 58–61). Secondly, investments in agricultural technology are directed towards cash crops, which produce the money to repay loans rather than towards food that will be eaten locally. Women desperately need appropriate technology to reduce the four to six hours a day needed to search for cooking fuel and to fetch water, but this has a low priority in World Bank objectives. Thirdly, in the markets, women at best scratch out a living in petty trade, which requires minimal capital investment. Fourthly, women also come last in the labour market. Women who work as field labourers in India, for example, are typically paid half the wage rates of men. As jobs such as weeding and threshing are mechanized, men tend to take them over, leaving even fewer jobs for women. In the growth industries for exports, women tend to be concentrated in the most poorly paid sweatshop work where they have no bargaining power (Sen 1985, 28–29). Lastly, any concerted efforts to raise the status of women tend to be resisted with patriarchal force. Sen (1985, 20) particularly stresses the extent to which fears of sexual aggression manipulate and threaten women's lives, especially in the labour market. Male chauvinism and religious fundamentalism serve to reinforce these processes that keep women in subordinated positions.

Development policies have resulted in the position of women in the Third World being systematically underdeveloped. In many regions, their situation frequently deteriorates from one of independent control over subsistence production to that of unpaid labourers begging for money for food from men who control the expanding cash economy (Rogers 1980, Ch. 6; Hale 1981, 152).

Feminists demand fundamental changes in the vision of development. Their goal is to make development more people-centred instead of cash-centred. Sen emphasizes that gender subordination, which is integral to Parsons' model of a modern social system, must be eradicated before people-centred development can take place. Such development must begin with women because their work is central to survival (Sen 1985, 13–16). Women have to be empowered before such changes can take place.

Development Efforts as Social Construction

The macro-level analyses of development policies and programs described above present a picture of frustrated goals and limited achievements. They point to the structures that hamper social change, but generally offer little insight into the active agency of the people involved. The social constructionist approach to development focuses attention on the everyday practices that collectively produce these outcomes, and also the organized practices by which theories are constructed, research undertaken, and results written up

and disseminated, so that what passes as factual knowledge about development gets produced.

Feminist work in development has long struggled to redress systematic biases in data collection that contribute to ignorance of the situation of women in the Third World on the part of people charged with designing projects to help them. At the level of powerful international agencies such as UNESCO, women were conspicuous only by their absence until well into the 1970s (United Nations 1980). The data available from professional and government agencies as a basis for planning were oriented primarily to male relevancies and particularly the relevancies of market economies (UNESCO 1981). Data on workforce participation, for example, systematically hid the enormous contribution of women in the unpaid subsistence sector. When work is measured in terms of contractual paid labour, women's work is defined so as not to exist. Similarly, when knowledge is measured by years of formal schooling, village women appear to be utterly ignorant. Myths of women as ignorant and idle dependants of men thus become the dominant perspectives in terms of which programs for women are designed. Decades of feminist work have only begun to undermine these statistical images.

After two decades of struggle, women's offices and programs now exist in most of the major international development agencies such as the United Nations, UNESCO, United States Agency for International Development (USAID), The World Bank, Ford Foundation, Canadian International Development Agency (CIDA), and the like. This network of organizations is a major location in which knowledge about women in the Third World is produced (Mueller 1986). But this knowledge is generated by and for development agencies. It is focused around aid projects, and what is relevant for the aid bureaucracies to know in the technical management of these projects. The documents required for project organization consist of detailed time schedules, budgets, and quantified standards to judge efficiency. All the messy problems of the complex, disorderly, real-world conditions in underdeveloped countries become translated into mechanical problems for which there are managerial solutions. These documents provide the basis for project evaluation, supplemented occasionally by brief site visits. They are the products of professionals' and academics' work, and they feed into objective, rational decision-making and management work at the headquarters of the international development agencies. These project procedures direct attention away from the local settings in which field workers and residents struggle directly with the overwhelming problems of poverty and underdevelopment. These local people are effectively excluded and silenced.

Mueller (1986) argues that these processes are an important part of the mechanisms that subject Third World countries to relations of ruling by First World agencies. Having more women employed in the development agencies does nothing to resolve this subjection. These women become part of a professional network of knowledge production that sustains a discourse about development in which the Third World comes to be seen only in a relation of dependence to the First World, subject to management and control by the First World agencies. The discourse has succeeded in creating a type of underdevelopment that is politically and economically manageable (Escobar 1984–85, 388). In the view of some radical critics, the projects sustained by such discourse have not only failed to solve problems of underdevelopment, but actively create more impoverishment and underdevelopment (Mueller 1986, 38).

When we shift the focus from international agencies to the local settings in which development projects take place, another network of practices becomes visible that excludes and silences the people most directly involved, while systematically undermining and disorganizing the work that they do. A study of development projects designed to improve the living standards of women and children in rural North India made visible some of these failure-producing practices (Hale 1987a, 1987b). The concept of *grassroots* participation in the implementation of projects is widely supported by development agencies as a response to the criticism that too much control is exerted by external agents. But at village level this is commonly translated into practices that give elite males control and veto power over projects intended for women. Project organizers in the North Indian villages sought the permission of district and village-level councils and village headmen, institutions from which women are systematically excluded. When elite males on the councils disapproved of the projects, they could and did block their implementation. Subsequently, when the programs did begin operations, it was these same male elites who acted as grassroots overseers, who haggled over which women should host clubs and classes in the village, and who were responsible for verifying that supplies were received and distributed as intended. These men had little personal interest in ensuring that free food and medicines reached children in the poorest areas of the village and put great pressure on women workers to divert the supplies elsewhere. Women, as would-be recipients of the services, had no control at all.

Notions of sisterhood, drawn from early feminist scholarship, supported a view of women as relatively undifferentiated, and led to practices that failed to take account of stratification in implementing the schemes. The organization of clubs and classes in the homes of elite women, closely linked with the dominant male faction, effectively ensured that few, if any, women from the poorest households would attend. Village women hired to implement nutrition pro-grams for children were supposed to carry out regular visits to homes in the poorest areas of the villages to check on the health of children. High-status teachers found this task so onerous and distasteful that few ever did it. Helpers who were hired to work with these teachers, however, commonly came from the same lower-class backgrounds as those families most in need of home visiting. They might willingly have done this work, but no attempt was ever made by program organizers to employ them in this manner. As illiterate women, they were defined in advance as too ignorant to be given such responsibilities. In effect, the organizational practices denied lower-class women the competence and authority to speak, even when they were present.

Organizational practices systematically silenced women involved in adult education, both as students and as teachers, serving to perpetuate stereotyped conceptions of the situation and needs of women, and also made possible the subsequent explanations for the limited impact of the schemes in terms of personal inadequacies of the women themselves. The official view that the problems facing village women were those of ignorance, idleness, and apathy had its counterpart in the view of the teaching role as simply providing information, without needing further skills. Village women with a grade 8 education were hired as nursery-school and adult-literacy teachers. They were given minimal teacher training, on the assumption that anyone who could read could show others and that women were used to looking after children. The practical problems of the teaching situation were never considered, and when the teachers failed to cope, they were seen as lazy and incompetent.

Women employees within the bureaucracy of the development programs found themselves silenced by systematic practices of subordination and exclusion. Their superiors rarely consulted them on how the projects were running, and when the women offered advice they were not usually heeded. In effect, they were not accorded the authority to speak, or to be listened to. Their views on their own problems, and possible solutions to them, were not made visible within the organization. The only explanations considered were those imposed on them from superiors who had no first-hand experience of village work.

When the focus shifts from operations in the villages to the work-life experiences of women employees in the development bureaucracy, what becomes visible are the organized practices that gave rise to the women's apparent incompetence to do their jobs, particularly the failure of women supervisors to exercise authority. Field research uncovered widespread evidence of neglect of duties by women workers and some blatant corruption, virtually all of which went unpunished. When women supervisors were asked specifically how they had tried to deal with such problems, they gave repeated examples of how their disciplinary actions had been countermanded by senior male bureaucrats. Orders to cut the pay of negligent workers, or to dismiss subordinates caught stealing food supplies were routinely cancelled by more senior males, allegedly in return for bribes or sexual favours. The resulting breakdown in authority relations was treated as fact by onlookers, imposed back upon the situation as an explanation for the failure of various aspects of the project, and then used as justification for arguments that women should be excluded from authority positions because they were inadequate to handle the responsibilities. What was most disturbing was that the women themselves lacked the means to reflect upon, formulate, and articulate their own experiences. They internalized the dominant interpretations of apathy and incompetence, not only as a description of the helplessness that they felt, but as an explanation for it. When questioned on the problems which their programs were encountering, the women blamed themselves and fellow workers as uneducated housewives lacking the competence to do their jobs. None of them offered interpretations in terms of the patriarchal authority relations that were continually disorganizing their work. The systematically constructed chaos in which these women worked remained unarticulated, even by themselves. The official project evaluation that was sent to headquarters identified the central cause of failure as the decision to hire village women who were previously housewives and who lacked higher education. The managerial solution proposed was to close down the project locally, and start again on a much smaller scale elsewhere with a staff of educated women brought in from outside. Local residents were left to work around the remnants of the failed project.

On a very small scale, the powerlessness of these women in their work mirrors the powerlessness of Third World peoples generally in their relations with foreign development agencies and foreign corporations that control the decisions that influence their lives. The particular experiences of these women in this one project cannot be generalized to other contexts. What is important here is the form of analysis that seeks to translate factual evidence and explanatory theories back into the activities of the people who produce them.

CANADIAN DEVELOPMENT IN A WORLD CAPITALIST SYSTEM

By most measures Canada ranks as a wealthy, advanced capitalist economy. It has a high average standard of living, and is home base to a number of multinational corporate empires. But these broad generalizations disguise pockets of severe poverty and regional disparities. Canada is also struggling with its own problems of dependent development in a North American context.

Historically, the development of the Canadian economy has been very closely tied to imperial Europe and later to the United States. Until the mid-nineteenth century, Canada enjoyed privileged trading status with Britain, especially for grain; but with the repeal of the Corn Laws, Canadian merchants turned increasingly to the United States as a trading partner. A limited Reciprocity Treaty was signed between Canada and the United States in 1854, promoting free trade between the two countries, but it was abrogated by the US in 1866 in retaliation against the Canadian government for its seeming support of the Confederacy during the American Civil War. The Canadian Confederation was formed in 1867, and, about a decade later, John A. Macdonald's **National Policy** was instituted. This policy established high tariffs against American goods entering Canada. Its primary goal was to pressure American businessmen to invest in Canada and to establish subsidiaries here, in order to avoid tariff barriers. This policy encouraged the development of a **branch-plant economy**. In almost every year since 1900, Canada has absorbed one-third of all investment capital exported from the United States (Veltmeyer 1987, 77). Canada now has the largest branch-plant economy in the world. By 1987, 49 percent of the top 500 corporations in Canada were foreign-controlled, mostly by Americans, and they earned 50 percent of all manufacturing profits (Hurtig 1991, 55).

The Canadian economy reaped many benefits from these investments but at the price of **dependent development**. Like many newly developing countries, Canada's internal economic structures are constrained by international relationships of dependence that limit autonomous capacity for change and growth (Gidengil 1989). Critical decisions affecting development in Canada are made by centres of corporate enterprise located in the United States, and the benefits of such growth flow disproportionately south of our borders. Trade between Canada and the United States is dominated by multinational corporations. Veltmeyer (1987, 86) estimates that, in 1983, between 75 and 80 percent of all imports and exports involved parent-subsidiary transfers by foreign corporations. In such transactions, transfer-pricing arrangements normally apply, to Canada's net disadvantage.

The distorting effects of this dependent development are revealed in the types of commodities exported and imported. Canada is near the bottom of the industrially advanced capitalist countries on measures involving manufactured exports. Typically, for a branch-plant economy, Canada largely exports raw materials and semi-processed goods and imports manufactured goods. Canada also lags far behind other industrialized countries in the proportion of gross national product spent on research and development. Such research is highly centralized in corporate headquarters located outside Canada.

This is the economic context in which the recent free trade deals were negotiated. The bilateral Canada–United States Free Trade Agreement (CUSFTA) was signed in January 1989 and the trilateral North American Free Trade Agreement (NAFTA) among Canada, the United States, and Mexico was signed in 1993. The negotiations leading up to the 1989 agreement were intense and bitter. The Canadian election in November 1988 was fought almost entirely around this issue, with the Conservative Party, led by Brian Mulroney, strongly in favour and the Liberals and New Democrats strongly against the deal. The money spent by the government, the Conservative Party, and big business to support the deal has been estimated at $56 million over two years, about 10 times what was spent by those campaigning against the deal (Fillmore 1989, 14). Pro-free trade forces spent $3.5 million during the last three weeks of the campaign alone. The re-election of the Mulroney government made the signing a fait accompli. The subsequent trilateral deal was negotiated with relatively little public debate or opposition.

Opponents of the 1989 deal feared that Canada's already shaky control over internal economic structures and resources would be further diluted. If high tariffs under the National Policy encouraged the establishment of American branch plants in Canada, then the dismantling of these tariffs under free trade posed the risk that branch plants would be closed down, and their operations relocated to the parent company, with potentially enormous job losses in Canada. At the same time, the deal made American direct investment in Canada's resource-extraction industries easier, and guaranteed access to all Canada's energy resources on equivalent terms with Canadians. Advantages that Canada might have gained from conserving these resources, or from boosting export prices relative to prices charged to national businesses and consumers would be lost. Control over our primarily natural resources would thus be weakened.

A closely related fear was that Canadian businesses would be unable to compete in North American markets without some protective tariffs. The contradictions of advanced capitalism that led to the increasing concentration and polarization of wealth seemed likely to increase, to the net detriment of Canada. Giant corporations, already dominating American markets, have the capacity to service the entire Canadian market with existing productive capacity, and at per unit costs lower than smaller Canadian competitors could achieve. Under such **imperfect competition** conditions, the logic of free-market competition does not hold.

Canadian businesses start out with many competitive disadvantages relative to American businesses. Fair competition requires a "level playing field" in the sense of approximately equal operating conditions, but between Canadian and American economies, the field is far from level. Canada has a harsher climate, and higher energy and transportation costs, which have particularly severe consequences for agricultural production. Canada also has a higher standard of social services, particularly unemployment insurance, Medicare, and family allowances; it has higher minimum wage rates than apply in the southern United States; and it has a commitment to provincial equalization payments—all of which translate into higher corporate and individual taxes. Higher taxes mean higher production costs and consequently higher prices for equivalent commodities. If these conditions continued unchanged, Canadian businesses might be bankrupted by the unfair competition, or driven south of the border, again with severe loss of jobs in Canada. Before this happened, the Canadian government would likely face intense pressure to cut social services to harmonize with the lower standards in the United States.

Opponents of the deal were also deeply concerned with the implications of free trade in services, particularly financial services such as banking and insurance, management and consulting firms, and those engaged in information technology, education, and the like. The Free Trade Agreement provided for the right of national treatment to be extended to all firms competing for contracts, explicitly including contracts to supply services on behalf of federal and provincial governments. Canadian cultural industries were exempted from these conditions, but opponents argued that Canadian social institutions would be inexorably Americanized in any case, by the loss of control over services and the downgrading of social security. Canadian nationhood itself seemed in jeopardy.

This severely negative view of free trade propounded by the Left did not prevail, but neither were these fears dispelled. Those who poured their funds into supporting the deal emphasized the advantages and new opportunities that it might bring. But they also argued that under prevailing conditions of economic dependency, Canada had little choice; rejecting the deal in the hope that the status quo would continue was not a viable alternative.

On the positive side, classical economics theory holds that expansion of trade promotes division of labour, specialization, and rising productivity, which in principle makes possible higher wages and lower consumer prices. Conversely, tariffs distort trade and protect inefficient production (Wonnacott 1987). Much trade between Canada and the United States was already free from tariffs in 1989, but there remained important barriers in industries such as textiles, clothing, footwear, and furniture, and multiple non-tariff barriers such as quotas, prohibitions on certain imports, and preferential government purchasing of locally produced goods and services. The removal of such protectionist measures promised to force Canadian industry to become more efficient.

Economists, such as Paul Wonnacott (1987) of the Institute for International Economics, further argued that free access to the huge American market would increase the potential for **economies of scale** in Canadian manufacturing. Any industry has large overheads and fixed costs—a factory, machinery, skilled workers, an energy supply, production, storage, and transportation facilities, and the like—needed even for low levels of production. In principle, maximum efficiency is achieved when production is increased to the point where all factors of production are fully utilized. But this presupposes sufficiently large markets so that all products can be sold. The small and widely dispersed Canadian market is too confining to promote efficient mass production.

Economies of scale are best realized with specialized production and concentration on long production runs with limited items. Wonnacott uses the example of the Canadian furniture industry to suggest that it would be more efficient to produce huge quantities of one specialized item for a North American consumer market of 250 million people than a variety of products for a national market of 25 million. In principle, profits rise and prices fall, to everyone's benefit. What was required, he argued, was an adjustment period that was provided for by the slow reduction in tariffs over a 10-year period after the deal came into effect.

Wonnacott's thesis itself presupposes "Fordism," a model of standardized mass production with competitiveness based on price cutting and the corollary of deskilled, cheap labour. It also presupposes that small Canadian firms can find a market niche—offering a product that giant manufacturers are not already geared to produce at maximum efficiency. Competitiveness based on rapid product innovation and customized production for higher-income markets depends on different principles of production. Such flexible production is potentially less vulnerable to shifts in consumer demand, but it presupposes the capacity for ongoing research and development, versatile work teams, and integrated groups of companies. Canada's heritage of a branch-plant economy has generated internal business structures with limited capacity to adapt to this alternative organization of production.

Any system of production, however, requires access to markets, and Canada is particularly dependent on the American market. Wonnacott notes that several attempts to develop trade with Europe have not succeeded. Prime Minister Pierre Trudeau tried this policy during the 1970s, but the share of exports to Europe actually declined from 19 percent in 1970 to 15 percent in 1980 and to 7 percent in 1985. A strong argument in favour of accepting the Free Trade Agreement was that it would protect Canada from the risk of being shut out of United States markets by their growing **protectionism**, at the same time that protectionism was rising in Europe. The slow pace of international negotiations on a General Agreement on Tariffs and Trade (GATT) made the bilateral agreement with the United States all the more attractive (Rocher 1991). Surveys conducted after the deal was signed suggest that capitalists who supported the deal were not antinationalist, but rather saw Canada's sovereignty as dependent on economic growth and continentalism as their best hope for accomplishing this.

The free trade negotiations took place in a wider context of global changes in the structure of capital and trading blocs that left business and labour feeling vulnerable on both sides of the border. The Canadian labour movement felt threatened by the potential job losses that might accompany the deal, but avoiding the deal in favour of the status quo promised little protection from global trends that were undermining security of jobs and markets. New world competitors were forcing the pace of technological innovation and trade specialization in any case, regardless of what happened with the Canada–United States deal. Oligopolies that once ensured stable investments and market control were losing this control by the mid-1970s as the customized production of innovative products for higher-income markets became a critical competitive strategy (Warskett 1990, 123–125). Even a giant corporation like International Business Machines (IBM) of America could not hold on to its markets (Sayer and Walker 1992, 241–242). The company cut many thousands of skilled jobs in its restructuring program. The freedom of capitalists to shift both financial and physical investments anywhere in the world further undermines job security in Canada and the United States. Low-wage jobs can always be undercut by still lower wages elsewhere. The real target, Warskett suggests, was never really the Free Trade Agreement as such. It was, and still is, the struggle to control global capital.

Capital, the State, and the Free Trade Agreements

The North American Free Trade Agreement, encompassing Canada, the United States, and Mexico, and ongoing negotiations with more than thirty other countries in Latin America, exemplifies both the central and the marginal character of the state in bourgeois society (Sayer 1985, 39–40). It makes visible in a peculiarly overt and written form the practices by which states maintain the forms of society whose productive activities are governed by market forces. Leading politicians from the three states, together with their professional support staff of bureaucrats, lawyers, and economists, were centrally involved in structuring the highly complex deal—a deal that encompassed over 1000 pages of regulations plus 4300 pages of enabling legislation, and amended 27 major Acts of the Canadian Parliament. Yet the terms of the Agreement are intentionally designed to minimize the power of any of the three governments to intervene in the free play of markets.

Analysts argue that the principles written into the NAFTA are not primarily about either trade or tariffs. They are about the commercialization of society (Calvert and Kuehn 1993; *Peace Research* 1993; *Canadian Forum*, special issue Jan. 1993; Weston et al. 1992). The Agreement institutes a new legal, regulatory, and investment framework for international business. It limits the ability of governments to regulate the economy while shifting a wider range of public sector activities into the private marketplace. It establishes the right of corporations located in any of the three countries to "national treatment" with respect to any business operations, including investments and bidding on contracts. Stringent rules protect corporate interests by providing for extensive compensation to firms for any loss of market opportunity that might accrue from any violation of the Agreement by future governments (Santer 1993).

These regulations extend far beyond what is generally thought of as business activities, to commercialize all forms of social services. The chapter on "Mandate of Services" includes sweeping coverage of all possible aspects of provision of services—production, distribution, marketing delivery, transportation connected with the service, and insurance (Calvert and Kuehn 1993, 16). All these aspects are intended to be open to profit-making enterprises. The services considered include education, daycare, insurance, pensions, hospitals and health care—in fact, any conceivable social service that is not specifically designated as an "existing service" provided by government at the time the Agreement was signed. The Agreement has a built-in "ratchet effect" (Calvert and Kuehn 1993, 30) permitting movement only in the one direction of increasing commercialization. Provision of any new services is automatically in the open commercial market, and rights of "national treatment" apply. The Agreement also commits governments to a continual review of exempted or nonconforming services, so that nothing is permanently exempt.

The climate of corporate and business interests is further protected by a greatly expanded definition of "intellectual property." Protection of patents on new products is extended, notably a 20-year protection on new drugs, and a 50-year protection on computer programs, now recognized as "literary works" (Dillon 1993). Intellectual property laws also cover interactive computer and audiovisual learning devices, out-of-country cable and satellite transmission of educational programs, courses, and learning aids that have been given patent protection, biotechnology, and multiple other "products" (Dillon 1993, 41). Knowledge itself is now defined as private property. Stringent regulations to control

unauthorized use of such property include right of seizure, forfeiture, and destruction of infringed goods.

These principles of government protection for international commerce are now being actively extended across Latin America in fast-paced negotiations (*Peace Research* 1993). The Colombian government agreed to the Intellectual Property Law in 1992 as a preliminary to starting free trade negotiations with the United States. It is also pushing ahead with policies of domestic economic liberalization, the *apertura* model, that United States trade officials emphasized as preconditions for extending the NAFTA. This liberalization includes repayment of foreign debts on schedule and accomplishing the goals set by the World Bank, such as stabilizing currency and reducing inflation, no matter what the domestic social costs.

Countries throughout Latin America are struggling to meet these preconditions. The United States government is encouraging the formation of regional trade blocs, such as the Andean Pact, both to make negotiations easier and to spread some of the burden for enforcing these policies from United States international financial institutions such as the International Monetary Fund.

If the NAFTA is extended across Latin America as planned, it will achieve a number of objectives important to United States business interests. Chief among them is that it will ensure access to Latin American markets on terms favourable to the multinational corporations and subject to United States trade laws. It locks signatory states into binding international agreements designed to make economic restructuring permanent. The commercialization of society that is integral to the NAFTA is effectively binding on future governments. Cameron notes that legally the United States can more easily get out of the agreements than can Canada or Mexico. The American Congress ratified the deals through fast-track legislation that can be overridden by a subsequent law passed by Congress. To have the status of an international treaty, standing above domestic legislation, the deals would have had to be ratified by two-thirds of the American Senate (D. Cameron 1993).

The context of negotiations, and part of the explanation for the urgency with which they are being pursued by the United States government is the United States' own declining political and business influence in the global economy. It is being challenged, if not overshadowed, by the resurgence of Japan and the European Economic Community. The NAFTA provides special protection for American business by tying Canada and Mexico into a trading bloc that discriminates against external trading partners (D. Cameron 1993; M. Cameron 1993). The NAFTA's chapter on rules of origin sets the proportion or quantity of a product that must originate in North America before it can qualify for preferential, duty-free entry to the trading bloc. Fuzzy terms like *substantial transformation* and *regional value content* of components have been used to justify **countervailing duties** against Honda cars assembled in Canada but destined for United States markets. Japan has served notice that it intends to challenge the NAFTA rules of origin in the next round of negotiations under the General Agreements on Tariffs and Trade.

The United States economy is increasingly vulnerable to the mobility of capital and competition from low-wage countries, including Mexico and other Latin American countries potentially joining NAFTA. In an effort to protect its interests, the United States government pushed for workers' rights to be officially on the agenda for the next round of GATT talks. This proposal met with concerted opposition from representatives of developing countries, who saw it as a ploy for discriminating against products made in the Third World. What developing countries fear is that industrialized countries will insist on high standards of labour rights, environment protection, and human rights that poor countries are unable to attain, and then use this failure as grounds for trade barriers. Beneath the high-sounding moralisms is a ploy to exclude Third World goods from First World markets—in effect, protectionism for business interests in industrialized countries.

The Uruguay Round of trade talks was signed at Marrakesh on 15 April 1994, after seven years of talks involving 125 countries. Before being implemented, it has been ratified by the legislatures of those countries where it is a requirement, including Canada (*Globe and Mail*, 16 April 1994, B3). Commentators estimate that most of the benefits of this round of talks will flow to industrialized nations. But they project that developing countries will wield much greater influence in the next round of talks, scheduled to begin as soon as the Uruguay Round is ratified.

The Effects of the Free Trade Agreements on Canada

It is impossible to separate the effects of the Canada–United States Free Trade Agreement from the simultaneous effects of the severe recession that hit most of the advanced capitalist countries of Europe and North America in the early 1990s. Few of the positive hopes of liberalized trade, expanding markets, economies of scale, and rising productivity, envisioned by the supporters of free trade, have been realized. Many of the dire warnings of opponents of the deal, especially massive job losses, declining investments, and severe cutbacks in Canadian social programs, have come to pass. There is little dispute over the evidence that Canadians generally are worse off in the mid-1990s than they were in the mid-1980s. The only question is the extent to which the free trade deal can be blamed for this decline, or whether the recession might have been worse if compounded with American protectionism. By April

Corporate agribusiness food-processing techniques have resulted in cruel and inhumane treatment of animals.

1994, the combined federal–provincial debt had reached $661 billion, or 93 percent of the gross domestic product, a ratio of debt to size of economy widely seen as unsustainable.

Staunch nationalists like Mel Hurtig (1991) and Maude Barlow (1990) directly implicate the Free Trade Agreement in the severity of the recession in Canada. Hurtig cites detailed evidence to support his claim that a systematic deindustrialization of Canada has occurred since 1989. Canada lost some 264 000 manufacturing jobs in the first two years of the Agreement and stood dead last among the top 13 industrial powers in industrial production performance. Since 1987, the average monthly rate of job creation dropped every year from 40 600 in 1987, to 26 300 in 1988, to 13 200 in 1989, to minus 7400 in 1990 (Hurtig 1991, 17). Another estimate puts job losses in Ontario alone at 500 000 in three years following the signing of the CUSFTA (Spratt 1992, 8). Profits to Canadian businesses dropped steadily, and business bankruptcies rose. Barlow documents the progressive privatization and deregulation of services such as transportation, telecommunications, and utilities, with the consequences typically being increased foreign ownership, takeovers, bankruptcies, and commercial oligopolies (1990, 33–48).

Foreign investment totalled $88 billion between 30 June 1985 and 30 June 1990, but 92 percent of this investment took the form of foreign takeovers of Canadian businesses, producing no increase in productive capacity or jobs. Moreover, much of this takeover money was from profits generated in Canada. One result of this rash of takeovers is that between 1989 and 1991 corporate debt rose about twice as fast as government debt, with interest costs as a percentage of pretax profits rising from 22 percent to 45 percent (Hurtig 1991, 164). Also typical of dependent economies, the flow of money out of Canada in the form of dividends exceeded money coming into Canada in direct investments by a factor of 10 to one (Hurtig 1991, 64–65).

Foreign-owned companies created fewer and poorer jobs and less diversified exports than Canadian-owned companies. For every billion dollars in profits between 1978 and 1984, Canadian companies created 5765 jobs and American-owned companies in Canada created 17 jobs (Hurtig 1991, 75). Profits from foreign-owned corporations pour out of Canada, much of them in the form of untaxed transfer pricing. Hurtig cites the case of Canada Safeway, which reported interest expenses of $52.5 million in 1990, mostly the result of assuming a $484-million debt for the parent company in California.

Barlow similarly documents the number of plant closures, particularly in such sectors as textiles, clothing, furniture, and auto parts, which experienced drops of between 25 to 30 percent in manufacturing capacity during 1989–90. These industries typically employ low-technology, assembly-line manufacturing processes that can readily be moved to *maquiladoras*, component assembly plants in Mexico, offering labour at $6 per day.

The food-processing industry in Canada is also hard hit by the double problem of high-priced supply-managed farm produce and higher base wages in Canada, and the prospect of cheap American imports. Companies such as Campbell Soup, Gerber baby foods, St. Lawrence Starch, Rowntree, Hostess, Hershey, and Kraft are all closing plants in Canada or turning them into warehouses while production shifts south of the border (Barlow 1990, 60). The supply management programs established in dairy, eggs, chicken, and turkey production in Canada are under siege and seem unlikely to long withstand the competition from cheaper American goods now that tariff protection has gone. Even the legitimacy of supply management is being openly questioned (Skogstad 1993). The end of supply management, however, would probably mean the end of independent family farms. In Canada in 1988, the production of eggs, poultry, and dairy products was spread among some 2500 family farms. In the United States about a dozen integrated companies, located almost exclusively in the low-wage southern states, controlled most of the American chicken industry. They can produce chickens at 25 percent below Canadian farm prices, but at high social and humanitarian costs. In these "chicken cities" birds live out their eight-week lives under wretched conditions, crammed into battery cages that are cleaned out at best once a year. Birds have to be heavily drugged with antibiotics to survive under such conditions. In 1994, corporate agribusiness bragged openly about extending this superrationalization of chicken production to the production of pork. Pigs, whose level of intelligence far exceeds that of dogs, are confined in cages too small for them even to turn around. Conveyor belts carry them from birth to slaughterhouse.

Social Programs   Cutbacks in social programs became increasingly extensive in the early 1990s, much as predicted by opponents to the free trade deals. Again, no one seems to question that the process itself is happening, only whether it would have occurred regardless of the deals, in response to recession and changing views of the appropriate role of government in capitalist society. Four major programs affected are unemployment insurance (UI), family allowances, old age pensions, and Medicare. Unemployment insurance was particularly targeted by the Americans as a potentially unfair government subsidy to business, especially to seasonal businesses such as fishing. Shortly after the deal was signed, the Canadian government withdrew its contributions, making it strictly employer–employee funded. New barriers to qualifying for the insurance were introduced, the duration of benefits were reduced, and amounts cut. In April 1994, a federal government task force proposed dropping the employer premiums on the grounds that "a payroll tax is a tax on jobs." UI would become a pure insurance scheme paid for entirely by employees, and with benefits cut to a maximum of 26 weeks. The explicit goal of the task force was for Canada to have the lowest payroll taxes of any industrialized country (*Globe and Mail*, 8 April 1994, A1–2).

With the goal of cutting the cost of social programs as part of tax and deficit reduction, old age pensions were de-indexed, and a claw-back provision added to eliminate higher-income pensioners from benefits. Universal family allowances were similarly eliminated in early 1993, and replaced with an income-related scheme that is not fully indexed against inflation.

Medicare, a system of universal public medical insurance, first established in 1966, is still the jewel in the Canadian system of social programs. Ironically in this case, by the 1990s American business interests began to lobby the United States government to implement a similar scheme, on the grounds that the extremely high cost of private insurance premiums for employee health benefits were rendering them uncompetitive with Canadian businesses. In Canada, however, the future of Medicare is threatened by escalating costs. Efforts to cut costs have resulted in layoffs, privatization, and contracting out of services. Fuller (1993) sees these changes as directly reflecting the NAFTA philosophy of commercialization of services. The potential for profits from health care are high, given that the health industry constitutes about 10 percent of the gross domestic product.

The Canadian health-care system has three main sectors: the public sector of provincial health insurance, hospitals, laboratories, rehabilitation and outpatient care; the quasi-public non-profit facilities dependent on public funding; and the private sector of clinics, extended care, home care, diagnostic laboratories, and outpatient treatment. Fuller (1993, 16) estimates that the private sector has been growing rapidly as the public sector is being cut back. In 1990, the federal government froze its cash grants to the provinces for two years and fixed the rate of future growth in payments to the gross national product (GNP) minus 3 percent, to begin in 1992. In 1991, Bill C-20 further escalated the reduction in cash transfers. Private health insurance is expanding to cover gaps in services as governments cut back. Private drug plans are particularly important. Blue Cross covers prescription drugs, eyeglasses and contact lenses, dental care, semi-private hospital rooms, private physiotherapy, ambulance service, and out-of-country medical treatment. Medicare still covers basic health needs.

The Canada Health Act of 1984 entrenched the principles of universality, equal access, comprehensive services, portability across provinces, and public, non-profit administration of health insurance. In May 1994, the federal government moved to punish British Columbia for extra billing by cutting transfer payments until they stopped the practice. Alberta was also targeted for allowing a two-tier system of private clinics that charge extra fees for early access to certain tests and surgical procedures. The federal government has also taken to emphasizing lower health-care costs in Canada relative to the United States as a competitive business advantage for Canada. However, the clout of the federal government to protect Medicare is being steadily reduced as the value of transfer payments recedes relative to tax transfers. Also, the ratchet effect built into the NAFTA means that as more specialized services are privatized or contracted out, they cannot be reabsorbed into Medicare without compensating all businesses that might lose potential markets.

The Commercialization of Service

Under the NAFTA rules, management consulting firms are increasingly moving into the fields of health and education. They operate in terms of definitions of *efficiency* that focus principally on minimizing operating costs in order to maximize profits. This focus is what makes the contracting out of service management so attractive to cash-strapped governments. But the practices that produce financial efficiency frequently come with important social costs that are not factored into business accounting. Terms such as *efficiency* and *rationalization* cannot be defined apart from the values that determine how they are operationalized in specific contexts. Practices that are efficient in relation to one set of objectives may be totally inefficient for different goals.

Cohen (1988) describes the management practice of computerizing patient-illness classifications in order to calculate the type and amount of nursing care needed in hospitals. One effect of maximizing the "efficient" use of

nursing services is to reduce full-time regular nursing staff to a minimum, where the majority of nurses are on call, their work scheduled in part-time and irregular shifts. Efficiency for the hospital is bought at the cost of severely deteriorating conditions of work for the nurses. Quality of patient care deteriorates as nurses have no discretion to give individuals the extra attention they feel they need. The value of time spent talking to and reassuring worried patients is not readily included in computerized measures of care needed. A poll conducted for the Ontario Nurses Association in 1988 indicated that around 15 percent of Ontario nurses were planning to leave the profession because of excessive patient loads and demoralizing working conditions (*Globe and Mail*, 15 April 1988, A4).

Similar processes are occurring with respect to child-care services in Canada. Profit-oriented companies are big business in the United States, and the free trade deals guarantee them **right of national treatment**—that is, the right for businesses located outside the country to be treated in exactly the same manner as local businesses in bidding on any federal and provincial contracts to provide services. The Conservative government's decision in 1988 to direct childcare funding to mothers, rather than to establish government-run childcare centres, plays directly to a profit-oriented system. No government daycare system can be set up in Canada in the future without compensating all these service firms for loss of potential markets.

Alternatives to the Free Trade Agenda

A major problem in the debates surrounding free trade is that both supporters and opponents tend to be oriented to the same model of economic development, with the main question being whether nationalist or continentalist policies are likely to work best. Largely missing from the public debate are core questions concerning what visions of development we have and whether the continental market-driven form of economic organization can fulfill those visions.

In the middle of the free trade negotiations, in April 1987, the Brundtland Report, entitled *Our Common Future*, was published under the auspices of the United Nations World Commission on Environment and Development. Its core message is that the model of development assumed in the free trade agenda is endangering global survival. Development that is driven by corporate concentration and investment decisions geared to maximizing short-term financial returns is not ecologically sustainable. It is generating environmental damage of staggering magnitude in the Third World and in industrially developed nations.

Current emphasis on cash crops for quick profits encourages mining the soil to maximize immediate outputs rather than conserving it as a future resource. The control of vast acres of land in Third World countries by agribusiness results in the majority of local producers being pushed onto marginal land that cannot sustain intensive production. As the output of subsistence food crops falls, desperate farmers exploit still more marginal lands in a vicious cycle. Rainforests are hacked down for timber and agricultural settlement, but shallow forest soils tend to erode quickly. Watersheds deteriorate, and floods and droughts have a steadily worsening impact. The Brundtland Report estimated that tropical forests were being reduced at the rate of 7 to 10 million hectares annually, while the world's deserts were expanding annually at the rate of 6 million hectares. As habitats are altered, plant, animal, and insect species are decimated.

A preliminary report of the *Project on Environmental Change and Acute Conflict* at the University of Toronto (*Globe and Mail*, 10 May 1994, A19) warns that aggregate data showing worldwide improvements in levels of literacy, health, food production, and population control obscure critical regional variations. The project's director, Homer-Dixon, agrees with optimists that human ingenuity may be able to overcome resource scarcity through new technology and reformed social institutions. But poor countries most affected by scarcity are least able to promote such ingenuity. Scarcity generates severe political stress in the form of intense rivalries among interest groups and elite factions, and rising social dissatisfaction. Homer-Dixon attributes the vicious ethnic animosity that broke out in Rwanda in 1994 to severe land scarcity, soil depletion, and food production that is declining rapidly relative to the increasing population. He might have added that Rwanda has a plantation economy, deriving most of its earnings from the sale of coffee (Beckford 1973, 120–122).

Canada is a technologically advanced society with a high level of ingenuity, but this has not protected us from severe ecological problems, generated by superexploitation of natural resources. Vast stretches of the Prairies are being mined to produce monocrop cereals year after year with the aid of chemical fertilizers and pesticides. The result is soil reduced to the texture of dust. Soil erosion in Canada alone is costing farmers in the region of $1 billion a year. Overirrigation is causing the waterlogging, salinization, and alkalization of soils. In Newfoundland, the precipitous decline in fish stocks off the North Atlantic coast forced the total shutdown of the industry in 1993.

Industrial Pollution

Energy consumption has risen exponentially in the industrialized world over the last quarter century, particularly the consumption of wood, oil, gas, coal, and nuclear power. The burning of fossil fuels creates problems of atmospheric pollution, global warming, acidification, and industrial air pollution. Air pollution is damaging vegetation, corroding buildings and vehicles, and killing lakes and fish. Chlorofluorocarbons used in aerosol sprays, refrigeration, and the manufacture of some plastics, especially styrofoam, are known to damage the earth's ozone layer. Waste disposal companies in developed countries often bypass stringent pollution control legislation at home by pressuring impoverished African countries to take hazardous wastes.

The extension of the Free Trade Agreement into Latin America sets up pressures to harmonize environmental standards downwards. The NAFTA permits governments to enforce "generally agreed international environmental or conservation rules or standards," but requires that such measures be "the least trade-restrictive necessary for securing the protection required" (Swenarchuk 1993, 13). Any standards that might be considered disguised restrictions on trade, or that are not fully supported by available scientific evidence, are ruled out. The *maquiladoras* located in northern Mexico are described as producing an environmental cesspool, routinely dumping toxic chemicals into rivers, and operating under conditions harmful to the health of employees (Barlow 1990, 67). It is not in the competitive self-interest of other corporations to protect the environment if their comparative costs of production rise as a consequence. At the same time, the principle of government non-intervention in the market that is enshrined in the Free Trade Deal curbs the power of individual governments to impose controls.

The economics of this form of development change abruptly, however, once the "polluter pays" principle is introduced into the equation. This kind of industrial development is not only ecologically unsustainable, but it is also prohibitively expensive when the costs of pollution are calculated into economic models. The firms producing the acidic smog in their coal furnaces would have to pay for all the damage to lakes, rivers, vehicles, buildings, and human health in the areas reached by the polluted air and acid rain. Under this altered accounting, the economics of conservation and pollution control are many times more cost-efficient than they appear to be now.

Brundtland also notes the staggering costs of urban sprawl created by the concentration of industries in central areas. Urban sprawl, which occurs both in developing and developed economies, results in pollution, housing crises, rising crime rates, and so on. If the industries that locate in urban areas are charged for the full social and environmental costs of urban sprawl, the economics of relocation in smaller centres will look much more appealing. This is particularly true for high service firms where computerized communications systems make geographic decentralization cheap and efficient.

The Brundtland Report's basic conclusion is that we have to call a halt to the kind of economic development that is endangering the survival of the planet. That does not mean we have to stop development. This is not a viable option in a world where the most basic needs of masses of people are not being met. It does mean that the form that such development takes must be altered so as to be ecologically sustainable on a long-term worldwide basis.

Mainstream economics, North American style, still has a long way to go to deal with the problems raised in the report. In practice, environmental costs, such as social welfare costs, are generally left out of business equations. They form *hidden diseconomies* or real costs that, if actually paid by the companies responsible for the pollution, would greatly reduce their profits, and might well turn these apparent profits into deficits. But such costs are not counted by corporations because normally it is not the corporations that pay them. The people and other creatures whose lives are damaged or destroyed by the pollution pay the price.

With this shift in focus, the question of unfair subsidies appears in a very different light from the perspective of the free trade debate. When North American companies are permitted to operate without practising energy conservation and without pollution control devices, they are being very heavily subsidized by taxpayers who pay for road repairs and acid rain damage. The economics of using trucks rather than railways reverses when these hidden subsidies are taken away. Further, companies locating in metropolitan centres are being heavily subsidized when the costs of urban sprawl are paid by taxpayers. If and when all these hidden subsidies are removed, the economic advantages of relocating in peripheral areas, such as Cape Breton or the interior of British Columbia, might be very considerable.

Traditional economists such as Paul Wonnacott argue that government subsidies promote inefficient production. The blind spot of such economists lies in the extremely narrow definition of **subsidy** utilized in the equations. The implicit, and sometimes explicit, assumption of mainstream economics in leaving the hidden diseconomies out of their equations is that industry could not pay such costs without destroying all profitability. Hence, they are best ignored.

From the perspective of political economy theory, the contradictions inherent in advanced capitalism generate these problems, and cannot resolve them. Trainer (1985, 217) suggests that if the system were even to try to practise conservation and to cut back on wasteful production, "there would be economic chaos. Factories would close, businesses would go bankrupt, people would be thrown out of work and there would be extensive social and political disruption." Trainer's message is that nothing short of radical social revolution will solve the problems we face.

Trainer's blanket indictment of capitalism expresses an extreme position. But there is wider support for the conclusion that market forces alone cannot resolve the social and environmental problems that capitalism generates. It is necessary to rethink the ideological underpinnings of the North American Free Trade Agreement that marginalizes the role of the state. There are few models for conceptualizing a form of capitalism that is subject to political control.

Sweden came closer than other Western European countries in the state management of capitalism in the 1980s. The government enacted stringent policies to control industrial emissions, and it successfully carried out a 10-year program to reverse acidification of lakes (Melander 1988). Pollution control itself became a billion-dollar business. The pulp and paper industry operates in Sweden under very different rules of forest management than in Canada. The same Swedish-based multinational that practises the worst forms of clear-cutting and resource exploitation in Nova Scotia practises sustainable harvesting and reforestation in Sweden (McMahon 1987, 100–103). The difference lies not in company ideology or commitment to profitability, but the political controls within which capitalism operates.

In July 1988, Sweden passed an Animal Protection Act that governs the conditions of factory farming. To understand how important this is, think back to the description earlier in this chapter of chicken farms in Canada and the southern United States. This kind of inhumane farming is now outlawed in Sweden. Violations of the law are punishable by fines or imprisonment of up to one year. The law includes nine provisions:

1. All cattle are to be entitled to be put out to graze.
2. Poultry are to be let out of cramped battery cages.
3. Sows are no longer to be tethered. They are to have sufficient room to move. Separate bedding, feeding, and voiding places are to be provided.
4. Cows and pigs are to have access to straw and litter in stalls and boxes.
5. Technology must be adapted to the animals, not the reverse. As a result, it must be possible to test new technology from the animal safety and protection viewpoint before it is put into practice.
6. All slaughtering must be done as humanely as possible.
7. The government is empowered to forbid the use of genetic engineering and growth hormones, which may mutate domestic animals.
8. Permission is necessary for pelt and fur farms.
9. Doping animals for competition and events is prohibited.

The Act explicitly outlawed the use of battery cages for chickens. A background statement on the Act notes that animal protection and the prevention of cruelty to animals are central ethical issues and an essential part of Swedish cultural heritage.

The Swedish government's actions to curb the excesses of capitalism in these examples is a reminder that there is no inexorable system of market forces existing over and above people, to which societies must submit. There is nothing inevitable about "chicken cities" in the southern states, or factory farming, or the destruction of Nova Scotia forests. These things happen because so many political leaders, and the people who vote for them, have come to accept the ideology that such things are inevitable, or that economies will collapse if we even try to change things to become more socially or ecologically responsible.

It is also clear that Canada cannot follow Sweden's example without either abrogating terms of the CUSFTA and NAFTA by imposing tariffs on cheap factory-farm imports from the United States, or by negotiating with our trading partners to adopt similarly high standards of animal husbandry and environmental protection.

The major questions for free trade look very different from this perspective. Will free trade provide a route for moving towards the principles of sustainable development or towards worsening environmental stress? Will market relations become more open to social and political controls? How might the free trade agreements be used to promote continental pollution control and ecologically sustainable agricultural and industrial practices? How can such issues be incorporated into public political debate in Canada and the United States on our common future?

There are no easy answers to these questions, but the quality of life for future generations of Canadians and Americans will depend very heavily on how they are addressed. These questions force us to rethink not only how to achieve development, but also why and in what direction. Is the expansionist, profit-driven notion of development that currently dominates economic and political thinking actually what we collectively need? Or does it offer only the illusion of progress, while covering up a deteriorating quality of life for most of the inhabitants of the planet? We need to look beneath the veneer of economic and technological rationality that drives our society and explore the additional cultural, emotional, and moral dimensions of rational action. Without this wider vision, much of what we call development may be fundamentally irrational.

SUGGESTED READING

George M. Foster, *Traditional Societies and Technological Change* (1973), gives a sympathetic and perceptive account of problems of development from the perspective of functionalist theory. Foster gives extensive evidence of cultural, social, and psychological barriers to change in traditional societies. He suggests that anthropological analysis of traditional social systems is a valuable aid to promoting technological change.

Everett M. Rogers, *Modernization Among Peasants: The Impact of Communication* (1969), elaborates the concept of the culture of poverty in traditional societies. He advocates a top-down model of development through which the better educated and innovative people are first encouraged to adopt new technology, in the hope that subsequently the more backward peasants will copy these role models.

A classic work in Marxist theory of underdevelopment is André Gundar Frank's "Sociology of Development and the Underdevelopment of Sociology" (1972). Frank documents how the economy of Latin America is being systematically plundered by wealthy nations, especially the United States, which take out far more money than they ever put in through loans and investments. An excellent source of information on how Canadian capitalists plunder poor countries is the collection of articles edited by Robert Clarke and Richard Swift, *Ties that Bind: Canada and the Third World* (1982).

A comprehensive study of women and development is Barbara Rogers, *The Domestication of Women: Discrimination in Developing Societies* (1980). Rogers documents how women's interests are damaged by development programs that ignore their needs and give priority to men.

The issue of regional disparities and underdevelopment in Canada is explored in Henry Veltmeyer's "The Capitalist Underdevelopment of Atlantic Canada" (1979). Veltmeyer argues that the relative poverty in Atlantic Canada has been created by corporate capitalist policies designed to extract profits from peripheral areas and to centralized production.

Arguments against free trade are explored in two comprehensive collections of short articles. Duncan Cameron, ed., *The Free Trade Deal* (1988), and E. Finn, ed., *The Facts: The Facts on Free Trade—Canada Don't Trade It Away* (1988). The many articles and commentaries included in these collections explore wide-ranging issues around economic disparities and possible social and cultural costs of free trade. Mel Hurtig's powerfully argued polemic *The Betrayal of Canada* (1991) documents the economic crises facing Canada two years after signing the first Free Trade Agreement.

John Calvert and Larry Kuehn provide a comprehensive and very readable analysis of the principles of commercialization of society and government non-intervention that are embedded in the North American Free Trade Agreement in *Pandora's Box, Corporate Power, Free Trade and Canadian Education* (1993).

G.H. Brundtland, *Our Common Future* (1987), documents the extensive destruction of the environment wrought by intensive farming techniques and resource extraction for industry. Brundtland argues persuasively that this form of development is not sustainable in the long term.

QUESTIONS

1. What cultural traits are associated with reluctance to innovate, according to the functionalist perspective on development?

2. What factors have reduced the impact of technological advances in agriculture in Third World countries?

3. How are international market relations implicated in the continuing relative poverty of Third World countries?

4. What are the major problems facing Third World economies in Foster-Clark's analysis of "dependent capitalism"?

5. In Gulalp's view, why are political democracies likely to be unstable and short-lived in Third World countries?

6. How does flexible specialization differ from Fordism as a strategy for achieving competitive advantage?

7. How is agribusiness implicated in famine in Third World countries?

8. In Mueller's view, how is the work of professionals in development agencies implicated in the failure to address the problems faced by people, and particularly women, in Third World countries?

9. How is the North American Free Trade Agreement implicated in the "commercialization" of society?

10. What is the core message of the 1987 Brundtland Report on economic development?

KEY TERMS

agribusiness

branch-plant economy

colonialism

competitive advantage

countervailing duties

cultural lag

culture of poverty thesis

dependency theory

dependent capitalism

dependent development

economies of scale

green revolution

hinterland

imperfect competition

imperialism

mercantilism

metropolis

National Policy

neo-imperialism

protectionism

right of national treatment

subsidiary

subsidy

theory of modernization

Third World

transfer pricing

underdeveloped society

undeveloped society

REFERENCES

Barlow, M. 1990; 1991. *Parcel of Rogues: How Free Trade is Failing Canada.* Toronto: Key Porter.

Barnet, R., and R. Muller. 1974. *Global Reach.* New York: Simon & Schuster.

Beckford, G.L. 1973. "The Economics of Agricultural Resource Use and Development in Plantation Economies." In *Underdevelopment and Development: The Third World Today.* Ed. H. Bernstein. Harmondsworth, UK: Penguin, 115–151.

Brenner, R. 1977. "The Origins of Capitalist Development: A Critique of Neo-Smithian Marxism." *New Left Review* 104 (July/Aug.): 25–92.

Calvert, J., with L. Kuehn. 1993. *Pandora's Box, Corporate Power, Free Trade and Canadian Education.* Our Schools/Our Selves Education Foundation. Monograph series no. 13 (July/Aug.).

Cameron, D. 1993. "One America." *Canadian Forum* (Jan.): 9–10.

Cameron, M. 1993. "Developing a Bloc Mentality." *Canadian Forum* (Jan.): 15–16.

Carty, R. 1982. "Giving for Gain: Foreign Aid and CIDA." In *Ties that Bind: Canada and the Third World.* Ed. R. Clarke and R. Swift. Toronto: Between the Lines.

Chirot, D. 1977. *Social Change in the Twentieth Century.* New York: Harcourt Brace Jovanovich.

Cohen, M.G. 1988. "U.S. Firms Eager to Run Our Institutions— For Profit: Americanizing Services." In *The Facts: The Facts on Free Trade—Canada: Don't Trade It Away.* Ed. E. Finn. Canadian Union of Public Employees 10 (2).

Dillon, J. 1993. "Intellectual Property." *Canadian Forum* (Jan.): 11–12.

Escobar, A. 1984–85. "Discourse and Power in Development: Michel Foucault and the Relevance of His Work to the Third World." *Alternatives* 10: 377–400.

Feder, E. 1976. "How Agribusiness Operates in Underdeveloped Agricultures." *Development and Change* 7 (4): 413–443.

Fillmore, N. 1989. "The Big Oink: How Business Won the Free Trade Battle." *This Magazine* 22 (8): 13–20.

Foster-Clark, A. 1978. "The Modes of Production Controversy." *New Left Review* 107 (Jan.–Feb.): 47–77.

Frank, A.G. 1972. "Sociology of Development and the Underdevelopment of Sociology." In *Dependence and Underdevelopment: Latin America's Political Economy.* Ed. J.D. Cockcroft, A.G. Frank, and D.L. Johnson. New York: Doubleday, 321–397.

Fuller, C. 1993. "A Matter of Life and Death: NAFTA and Medicare." *Canadian Forum* (Oct.): 14–19.

Gidengil, E. 1989. "Diversity Within Unity: On Analyzing Regional Dependency." *Studies in Political Economy* 29 (Summer): 91–122.

Gulalp, H. 1990. "The State and Democracy in Underdeveloped Capitalist Formations." *Studies in Political Economy* 32 (Summer): 145–166.

Hale, S.M. 1987a. "The Documentary Construction of Female Mismanagement." *Canadian Review of Sociology and Anthropology* 24 (4): 489–513.

Hale, S.M. 1987b. *The Elusive Promise: The Struggle of Women Development Workers in Rural North India.* Montreal: Centre for Developing-Area Studies, McGill University.

Hale, S.M. 1985. "Integrating Women in Developmental Models and Theories." *Atlantis* 11 (1): 45–63.

Hale, S.M. 1981. Review of B. Rogers, *The Domestication of Women: Discrimination in Developing Societies.*London: Tavistock. In *Atlantis* 7 (1): 151–152.

Hoogvelt, A.M. 1976. *The Sociology of Developing Societies.* London: Macmillan.

Hurtig, M. 1991. *The Betrayal of Canada.* Toronto: Stoddart.

Kalbach, W. 1976. "Canada: A Demographic Analysis." In *Introduction to Canadian Society.* Ed. G.N. Ramu and S. Johnson. Toronto: Macmillan.

Kotovsky, G. 1992. "The Former Soviet Union in the Era of Primitive Accumulation and Kleptocratic Rule." *Studies in Political Economy* 38 (Summer): 167–174.

Lappé, F.M. 1971. *Diet for a Small Planet.* New York: Ballantine.

Lewis, O. 1949. *Life in a Mexican Village: Tepoztlan Restudied.* Urbana, Illinois: University of Illinois Press.

Martin, D. 1982. "Facing the Octopus: The Transnational Corporation." In *Ties that Bind: Canada and the Third World.* Ed. R. Swift and R. Clark. Toronto: Between the Lines, 87–148.

McMahon, S. 1987. "The New Forest in Nova Scotia." In *People, Resources, and Power: Critical Perspectives on Underdevelopment and Primary Industries in the Atlantic Region.* Ed. G. Burrill and I. McKay. Fredericton, New Brunswick: Acadiensis Press, 99–105.

Melander, T. 1988. *Saving Lakes.* Trans. C. Thorn. Gothenburg, Sweden: Informator AB.

Mueller, A. 1986. "The Bureaucratization of Feminist Knowledge: The Case of Women in Development." *Resources for Feminist Research* 15 (1): 36–38.

Peace Research (no specific author). 1993. "The Implications of Free Trade and the NAFTA for Latin America." (Abridged version of "Free Trade: Manifest Destiny Without Gunboats," *Free or Fair Trade* 1 (2)). *Peace Research* 25 (1): 77–84.

Rocher, F. 1991. "Canadian Business, Free Trade and the Rhetoric of Economic Continentalism." *Studies in Political Economy* 35 (Summer): 135–154.

Rogers, B. 1980. *The Domestication of Women: Discrimination in Developing Societies.* London: Tavistock.

Rogers, Everett. M. 1969. *Modernization among Peasants: The Impact of Communication.* New York: Holt, Rinehart and Winston.

Santer, M. 1993. "A Tool to Dismantle the Public Sector." *Canadian Forum* (Jan.): 15–16.

Sayer, A., and R. Walker. 1992. *The New Social Economy: Reworking the Division of Labour.* Cambridge, Massachusetts: Blackwell.

Sayer, D. 1985. "The Critique of Politics and Political Economy: Capitalism, Communism and the State in Marx's Writings of the Mid-1840s." *Sociological Review* 33 (2): 221–253.

Sen, G. 1985. *Development, Crises, and Alternative Visions: Third World Women's Perspectives.* New Delhi: Development Alternatives with Women for a New Era (DAWN).

Sivard, R.L. 1985. *Women: A World Survey.*Washington: World Priorities.

Skogstad, G. 1993. "Policy Under Siege: Supply Management in Agricultural Marketing." *Canadian Public Administration* 36 (1): 1–23.

Spratt, S. 1992. "The Selfishness of 'Free' Trade." *Perception* 16 (4): 8.

Swenarchuk, M. 1993. "NAFTA and the Environment." *Canadian Forum* (Jan.): 13–14.

Trainer, E. F. 1985. *Abandon Affluence!* London: Zed Books.

UNESCO. 1981. *Women and Development: Indicators of Their Changing Roles.* UNESCO Socio-Economic Studies, No. 3. Paris: UNESCO.

United Nations. 1980. *Report of the World Conference of the United Nations Decade for Women: Equality, Development and Peace.* Copenhagen, 14–30 July. New York: United Nations.

Veltmeyer, H. 1987. *Canadian Corporate Power.* Toronto: Garamond.

Warskett, G. 1990. "Capital's Strength and Labour's Weakness under Free Trade." *Studies in Political Economy* 33 (Autumn): 113–134.

Weston, A., A. Piazze-McMahon, and E. Dosman. 1992. *Free Trade with a Human Face? The Social Dimensions of CUSFTA and the Proposed NAFTA.* Ottawa: The North–South Institute.

Wonnacott, P. 1987. *The United States and Canada: The Quest for Free Trade. An Examination of Selected Issues.* Policy Analyses in International Economics, vol. 16. Washington, DC: Institute for International Economics.

Wood, P.J. 1989. "Marxism and the Maritimes: On the Determinants of Regional Capitalist Development." *Studies in Political Economy* 29 (Summer): 123–153.

The Sociology of War and Terrorism

INTRODUCTION

War has been a pervasive feature of recorded human history. Sorokin (1937, cited in Ikenberry 2001) documented 967 wars between 500 BC and AD 1925, an average of one war every two to three years, not counting the two world wars of 1914–18 and 1939–45. The end of the Second World War ushered in a period of Cold War lasting more than 40 years between the two superpowers—the United States and the Soviet Union. Each superpower developed, stockpiled, and repeatedly threatened to use nuclear weapons capable of total global destruction. Regional wars involving the United States in Korea, Vietnam, across Latin America, North Africa, the Middle East, and Afghanistan carried the ever-present threat of boiling over into superpower confrontation.

The threat of global nuclear war receded with the internal breakup of the Soviet Union in 1989. The decade of the '90s was characterized from the American perspective as one of peace and prosperity (Ikenberry 2001), an era of "Pax Americana," in which the US commanded the status of unrivalled military superpower in a uni-polar world. Yet there were multiple regional wars during this period. In 1992 alone, Ikenberry counts 34 regional wars, including in Iran, Iraq, Somalia, Rwanda, Liberia, Turkey, Chechnya, Algeria, Angola, East Timor, Indonesia, the Balkans, and between Israel and the Palestinians. The United States was involved in the brief Gulf War against Iraq in 1991, following Iraq's invasion of Kuwait, and also in the conflict in the Balkans in the mid-1990s, following the breakup of Yugoslavia, along with its allies in the North Atlantic Treaty Organization (NATO).

Pax Americana was abruptly shaken on September 11, 2001, by a terrorist attack on American soil (often referred to simply as 9/11—or "nine eleven"). A group of 19 men of Middle Eastern origin living in the United States hijacked four commercial passenger jet airliners, crashed two of them into the twin towers of the World Trade Centre in New York, and a third into the Pentagon near Washington, killing almost 3000 Americans. The fourth hijacked aircraft crashed into a field in Pennsylvania. The terrorists were associated with the loose network of Islamic extremists, then based in Afghanistan, known as al Qaeda, an abstract noun meaning "network" or "base" (Dyer 2004, 94).

The event prompted US president George W. Bush to declare a new Global War on Terror, an open-ended and borderless war. In a document entitled *The National Security Strategy of the United States*, submitted to Congress in September 2002, Bush declared the policy that the Unites States has the right to use its military might in "preventive war" against its perceived enemies, to act pre-emptively to exact regime change, and to remove the capacity of other nations to develop weapons of mass destruction, without prior approval of international law under the United Nations (Dyer 2004, 14; Carroll 2006, 485). In October 2001, the Bush administration launched a war against the Taliban government in Afghanistan, holding them responsible for sheltering the al Qaeda leader Osama bin Laden and his terrorist training centres. Canada became heavily involved in the post-invasion conflict. In March 2003, the Bush administration declared war against Iraq to destroy the regime of Saddam Hussein, characterizing it as a terrorist rogue state harbouring weapons of mass destruction. The subsequent resistance and civil wars in both countries is ongoing and threatens to destabilize the entire Middle East. Al-Qaeda has since claimed responsibility for two further successful acts of terrorism in Western societies—the train bombing in Madrid, Spain, on 11 March 2004, killing 190 people, and the transit bombing in London, England, on 7 July 2005, killing 52 people. Suicide bombings and other terrorist acts have become commonplace events across the Middle East, and in the war zones of Iraq, Afghanistan, Israel, and Palestine. Civil wars characterized by extreme ethnic violence erupted in the Balkans between Serbs, Croats, and Albanians, and in Rwanda and Burundi between Tutsi and Hutu. Guerrilla wars and insurgencies, often fuelled by tribal-based war lords with well-armed militias, continue to tear apart many African states, including Zaire or the Congo, Liberia, Uganda, Sudan, Somalia, and many former Soviet republics. This list is far from exhaustive.

The challenge of this chapter is to use the theoretical tools of different sociological perspectives to explore the social structures and processes that promote and sustain global and civil wars, and in contrast, the processes that may promote and sustain peace.

✸ Functionalist Perspectives on War

Classical functionalist theory has analyzed nation states as total social systems. Within these systems, the institution of the military functions to manage conflicts with external social systems.

Contemporary functionalist analysis has gradually shifted focus to conceptualize the entire world order as increasingly a single social system within which nation states and regions function as subsystems (Hardt and Negri 2000; Giddens 2000, 1998). This shift in perspective draws attention to the role of supra-national institutions, and especially institutions organized on a global scale, in managing relationships and conflicts within a single world system.

The analysis of a single world system is vastly more complex than the focus on subsystem units, but the underlying theoretical assumptions remain essentially the same. All social systems require institutions to manage material economic needs and to regulate deviance, and they function most smoothly when members share a common culture of dominant beliefs and values. In a single world system the functions once performed by military institutions should become obsolete, with social order managed systemically through institutions of law and policing. Functionalist theories of global society draw extensively on the Durkheimian thesis of morality and cohesion within societies, and the transition from mechanical to organic forms of organization, developed in his thesis *The Division of Labour in Society* ([1893] 1964). Durkheim argued that the expansion of communication over vast areas, the increase in population size and mobility, and interdependence through division of labour, inevitably combine to undermine mechanical solidarity based on cultural sameness of small, isolated societies. Cohesion in the modern world lies less in homogeneous cultures than in organic functional interdependence of heterogeneous parts, or nation states, in increasingly global economic relations. Mutual interdependence creates the conditions needed for stronger bonds between nations and a more cohesive world system than was possible between fragmented, self-sufficient, homogeneous states. But the overarching multinational or world system still needs institutions that regulate just division of labour among interdependent parts, and an integrating cultural system of shared values and beliefs that must be cosmopolitan—grounded in respect for cultural diversity and for universal human rights.

From this functionalist perspective, the roots of war lie primarily in the fragmented, insular character of nation states that maintain militaristic relations with societies that are viewed as "external" to their own, and that fail to embrace cosmopolitan values that can override divisive nationalist, ethnic, and religious cultural identities in an increasingly intermixed multi-ethnic and multi-religious world society. This cultural lag both reflects and exacerbates the uneven and restricted development of organic economic interdependence at a global level, coupled with weak international regulative institutions. The hope for world peace lies in the promotion of cosmopolitan values, fostered through increasing economic interdependence, and policed through global and regional institutions founded on integrative democratic principles.

The following analysis begins with an historical overview of the structure and function of military institutions and militaristic culture within nation states, and the efforts after the Second World War to shift away from militarism and towards globally interdependent institutions, integrated through cosmopolitan values and policing.

Military Institutions: The Functions and Culture of War

All complex societies have military institutions, armed forces that serve two primary functions—attack and defence. Military force, or the threat of such force, provides a means by which more powerful societies can impose their will on less powerful neighbours, to resolve conflicts, to expand territory and resources, and to further societal interests beyond established system borders. Military institutions simultaneously provide societies with means to defend their territory, resources, and people against such external attacks.

Military institutions are unique in complex societies in that they legitimate killing under orders. Members of armed forces are required to work in tightly integrated teams that can be ordered to kill targeted people defined by military leaders as "enemies." These enemies may be clearly recognizable members of opposing military teams, but also commonly include entire communities of people, civilian as well as military. Members of the military must be able to endure combat conditions when opposing military teams are targeting them. Force, in the context of the military, has little to do with natural aggression. Soldiers who have killed many people during wartime are not feared or regarded as murderers when they return home (Giddens 1991, 460). Rather they are honoured and publicly decorated for valour.

Recruits to military service require extensive role training or socialization to work as a team, to obey orders, to dehumanize the enemy to the point that they can torture and kill them as ordered, while maintaining a normal family life in off-duty hours (Henslin and Nelson 1996, 435). Combative and violent team sports among boys is one mechanism widely used by societies to encourage the predispositions of physical strength and endurance, pain tolerance, teamwork, and tactical planning favoured in military recruits (Connell 1983, 18; Kidd 1987, 259; Levin 1993, 39). But more than sports is required to turn recruits into combat-ready soldiers. An anecdotal description of a boot camp (Michalowski 1982) reveals how instructors have been known to whip raw recruits into soldiers. Recruits are stripped of their individuality, paraded in uniforms, exercised until they vomit, and taunted by drill sergeants who scream homophobic insults and punish the entire group of recruits when one cannot keep up the pace, until the group finally turns on and beats up the weakest member. Intense emotional solidarity that emerges between soldiers under combat conditions is a critical ingredient preparing soldiers for armed combat. Individuals who cannot bring themselves to fire their weapons at the "enemy" will do so to protect their comrades in arms.

The honour, respect, and ceremony accorded to military service by nation states serves to validate the role of soldier. Those who have shown valour in combat are publicly decorated with medals. Those who die receive state funerals. Ceremonies and memorials to mark past wars continually remind current soldiers and potential recruits that military service is distinctive, highly valued work, invested with pride and nationalist fervour. It is not just a job. It is service to the nation. Nonetheless, the high incidence of post-traumatic stress disorder (PTSD) among soldiers returning from combat reveals that desensitization to theatres of violence is not easily achieved. Wars are always fought at high personal cost to soldiers, and a society's rulers are constrained not to engage in them lightly.

The Game or Art of War

The utility of using military force, or war, to further political ends is tempered by the dysfunctional consequences, the extremely high costs of waging war, and the risks of losing. In the art of war, as the Prussian general and strategist Carl von Clausewitz describes it (1993), violence can rapidly escalate if both societies are bent on forcing the enemy to submit. Logically the maximum use of force is restrained by the practical reality that no state can deploy all its forces at once, and no war is ever final. Any state that is considering war has to judge the importance of what it hopes to gain, against the military strength of intended opponents, and the cost of large-scale destruction and deaths that result from war. The special challenge in the contemporary war

against non-state terrorists is that, because they are not directly answerable to civilian populations, they may be less constrained by such rational calculations of benefits and costs (Ignatieff 1997, 125–128).

This brings us back to the other primary function of military forces—defence. So long as there are aggressive or potentially aggressive neighbouring societies with military forces, one's own society needs military forces of sufficient strength to dissuade potential aggressors from mounting an attack, or to resist such attacks. Without a sufficiently strong military a society faces the permanent threat of being run over by external societies, one's territories or hunting grounds annexed, one's people enslaved or driven off, and resources appropriated. Over historical time across most parts of the world, boundaries between societies and social groupings have shifted many times. Empires have waxed and waned. Subordinated societies and groupings have jockeyed for position and fought for independence. Changes in power relations between societies have been established through battle. The distinction between defence and attack becomes blurred as territorial incursions can be variously interpreted as protecting what one owns or regaining what one has lost.

The appearance of the relative strength of the military forces of one's own society compared with those of neighbouring societies matters greatly in the game of war, because appearance powerfully influences the calculations that military leaders of other societies can be expected to make of the costs of attack and likelihood of success. Deception, intelligence, and threats are thus inherent features of military activity (Ritter 2007, 33). Ideally, one's own military strength should be, or should appear to be, at least equal and preferably better than the military of one's neighbours. This is the root of the insatiable arms race between nations. Any technological advance in military tactics and technologies by one society gives temporary advantage in attack or defence, but prompts catch-up advances in neighbouring societies. The game never ends.

Global Warfare: The Emergence of the Military-Industrial Complex

Military institutions that emerged during the two world wars, especially the Second World War of 1939–1945, differed in fundamental ways from earlier modes of military organization. These changes were in response to enormous increases in the scope of conflict, exponential advances in the technological power of weapons, and the massive destruction of civilian populations and infrastructure, far beyond military forces themselves. This section focuses on the structure and culture of the Pentagon—the bureaucratic command centre of the American military, the largest military establishment that has ever existed in the world. The American government currently spends more on its armed forces than the rest of the world combined.

The American armed forces expanded from one quarter of a million to 8.3 million men between 1940 and 1943, an expansion far exceeding the availability of qualified officers (Carroll 2006, 28). The military adjusted by shifting from reliance on the leadership qualities of officers to centralized bureaucratic organization. Impersonal bureaucratic decision-making, with centralized decisions driven by technological capacity, was capable of far greater destructiveness than individual leaders. The result, Carroll argues, was the emergence of a monster—an unchecked behemoth that retiring American president Dwight Eisenhower later referred to in his farewell address in January 1961 as the "military-industrial complex."

Institutions develop cultures—overarching systems of shared meanings, beliefs, values, and associated behavioural norms that come to prevail among members of the institution, which are transmitted to new members through socialization. Carroll's study of Pentagon military policy during the Second World War describes an institutional culture of unlimited violence. Pentagon staff endorsed violence not simply to defeat an enemy, but as a means to demoralize and terrorize enemy populations into unconditional surrender. The incendiary bombing of the German cities of Hamburg and Dresden set aside all pretense of focusing on military targets. The goal was to destroy the cities and everyone in them in their entirety (Carroll 2006, 80).

As Germany surrendered, Pentagon strategists turned their attention to Japan. On 10 March 1945, 300 bombers dropped 1665 tons of napalm on Tokyo, killing between 80 000 and 100 000 people (Carroll 2006, 94–96). It was followed by bombing raids on another 66 Japanese cities, which killed more than 900 000 civilians. These numbers far surpassed the total of Japanese combat dead. Almost all the victims were women, children, and elderly people, because the men were away in the army. Carroll gives these details to support his argument that the firebombing had already set the cultural precedent for the use of the atomic bomb as soon as it was ready in August 1945. The slaughter culminated with dropping the first atomic bomb over Hiroshima on 6 August 1945, which left 120 000 to 150 000 dead, and three days later a second bomb over Nagasaki, which left 70 000 to 80 000 dead.

This slaughter happened more than a month after the Japanese government had clearly indicated it was ready to surrender. The men who planned and orchestrated the use of the atom bombs knew they were not essential to end the war. Japan was already seeking terms of surrender. The primary function of the bombing appears to have been political—to signal to the world, and especially to the emergent super-

The Japanese government was seeking terms of surrender before the atom bomb was dropped on Hiroshima.

Bettmann/Corbis

power, the Soviet Union, the absolute military supremacy of America. LeMay and others who served in bomber command acknowledged later that, had they lost the war, they would have been charged with war crimes (Carroll 2006, 97). By the end of the Second World War, Carroll argues, the culture of war had redefined the nature of the enterprise from victory over the enemy to the enemy's elimination. The goal of war was unlimited destruction, the military had the technological means to achieve it, and it could be orchestrated with impersonal, bureaucratic efficiency.

The Rise of Supra-National Institutions to Manage Conflict

Following the horrors of two world wars, political leaders endorsed a series of supra-national institutions and rules to manage military conflict and to promote and regulate interdependent economies, reinforced by codes of cosmopolitan values.

Throughout most of the history of complex societies and nation states, there have been no effective institutions or rules to govern inter-society relations. Waging war on one's neighbours broke no formal laws. In the space between societies, might was right, and the spoils of war went to the victor (Dyer 2004, 200). The invention and demonstrated use of nuclear weapons, however, profoundly changed the calculable costs of war. Superpower nations and their allies now controlled the means to annihilate life on earth if they should ever use their growing stockpiles of nuclear weapons. National leaders came together at the end of the Second World War in 1945 to establish the United Nations Organization (the UN) with the single central goal of avoiding another world war. All signatories to the United Nations Charter agreed that henceforth it would be illegal for any sovereign state to wage a war across an international boundary. Violators could be subject to sanction by the United Nations as a whole, and any territory gained would not be internationally recognized. National boundaries were considered fixed by 1945, regardless of how they may have been changed by earlier conflict. The UN was given no power to intervene in military conflicts within national boundaries, with the one important exception of preventing genocide, defined as acts committed with intent to destroy, in whole or in part, an ethnic, racial, or religious group. No distinction was drawn among signatories between democracies and dictatorships. The five superpowers at the time—US, the Soviet Union, China, Britain, and France—were given vetoes over UN resolutions, both to induce them to sign, and because the UN lacked the power to enforce sanctions over them, short of another global confrontation. The United Nations started out as a shaky and limited international institution for the governance of war, but memory of the carnage of the Second World War helped to shore it up as all the signatories had vested interests in making it work. Subsequent Geneva Conventions spelled out rules for warfare, to distinguish between combatants and non-combatants, to avoid deliberately targeting civilians, to respect basic rights for prisoners of war, to provide medical treatment for victims, and the like (Ignatieff 1997, 109–163). Dyer argues that while wars did not end with the founding of the United Nations, the system of international rules did make a difference (2004, 205–215). Superpowers at least paid lip service to the rules in regional conflicts within their spheres of influence, and the rules gave them an honourable means to back away from lethal confrontations with each other.

Over time, other political and economic institutions emerged alongside the UN to manage international relations. The institutions of the World Bank (WB), the International Monetary Fund (IMF), and the General Agreement on Tariffs and Trade (GATT) were intended to aid Europe's economic recovery from the devastation of war. The GATT began in 1947 with 23 countries but eventually expanded into 75 countries before it became reconstituted as the World Trade Organization (WTO) in 1995.

In Europe the post-war Council of Europe, established in 1949, gradually evolved into the European Economic Community and eventually a full European Union (EU), with the first elections held for a European Parliament in 1979. The European Union is widely heralded as a political and economic model for global governance (Giddens 1998, 141). It encompasses and binds together sovereign states that were ranged against each other barely 35 years earlier in a war that resulted in the deaths of an estimated 70 million people. With the collapse of the Soviet Union in 1989, the European Union embraced East Germany, and gradually expanded to include Eastern bloc nations.

As national and regional economies have grown more interconnected, there has been a massive growth of cooperative organizations at regional levels. Multiple supra-national free-trade agreements have emerged in response to rapidly expanding global trade, and the demands of transnational business corporations for regulations to protect property rights and contracts. These organizations are not directly concerned with avoiding wars. But to the extent that they involve member states in interdependent networks of economic relations, they decrease the probability of military conflicts among them. The vision is essentially the Durkheimian one of organic solidarity through economic and political interdependence displacing the more fragmented solidarity of ethnic homogeneity. World trade, global electronic economic ties, and instantaneous communications and information flow all help to pull people upward from local to global relations. Strong states in the past prepared for war, Giddens argues, but strong states drawn into an interdependent global economy and into supra-national institutions have to accept limits to their sovereignty (Giddens 1998, 130). They are less likely to go to war with each other both because they have other mechanisms for resolving conflicts and because they have too much to lose from the breakdown of cooperative activities.

Cosmopolitan cultural values constitute the last critical pillar in the vision of a new world order. Global economic relations both require and promote the spread of democratic institutions that in turn reduce the propensity for war. Democracies, Giddens asserts with optimism, "do not go to war with each other" (1998, 149). Moreover, as globalization draws diverse peoples into supra-national economic and political relations, traditional cultures are weakened. Traditions do not necessarily disappear, Giddens argues (2000), but they are not lived in traditional ways. Faced with diversity, people necessarily must reflect on their traditions, and justify them to themselves and others in comparison with other ways of doing things. Traditions become "detraditionalized" as matters of choice. Cosmopolitan values of tolerance and dialogue that embrace cultural diversity provide the foundations needed for peace in an interdependent world.

The State of Near-Global-War: Cold War Militarism in a Bipolar World

The great divide between communism and capitalism shattered the fragile post-war vision of global organic interdependence. For more than 40 years between the end of the Second World War in 1945 and the collapse of the Soviet Union in 1989, world politics was separated into two superpower constellations—the Soviet Union with its Chinese allies and satellite states, and the United States with its

Western allies. The superpower constellations remained economically isolated from each other, providing no basis for a sense of interdependence to develop. No overarching trade agreements emerged. Extreme differences in foundational economic, religious, and cultural values hampered meaningful communication. Strong military institutions and militaristic cultures generated a climate of mutual fear. The fact that each side knew, or believed they knew, that the other had the technological means and the will to annihilate their society intensified distrust and fear to levels of mutual paranoia. All other conflicts around the world eventually got dragged into these two constellations.

Differences in foundational political and economic structures and related cultural values were viewed as profound. The Soviet Union was committed to communism, valuing centralized state-run economic relations and one-party political structures. It was avowedly secular and promoted community consensus over individual freedom of thought and speech. The United States was committed to free-market capitalist economic relations and multi-party liberal democracy. It too was politically secular but strongly endorsed Christian and increasingly fundamentalist Christian religious culture in opposition to godless communism.

Militarism flourished in this polarized world. All efforts at diplomacy were undermined by a paranoid culture of distrust that developed within military and political institutions in both the United States and the Soviet Union, in which nothing said by "the enemy" could ever be accepted on face value. In the perceived abse nce of any shared system of cultural values, global social control was premised on force of military supremacy. As the Soviets developed their own atomic bomb, the Americans countered with a hydrogen bomb, about one thousand times more powerful than the bomb dropped on Hiroshima. Soviet rulers felt they had no option but to copy, and so the nuclear arms race was on.

The Culture of Militarism and Fear

The culture of paranoia that prevailed within the Pentagon over the next three decades defeated virtually every effort to rein in the nuclear arms race. Every proposal to reduce the nuclear threat only served to increase it. The argument that the deterrent effect of "massive retaliation" was probably unworkable, in the event of an attack with nuclear weapons, convinced Pentagon strategists that a first-strike preparation was essential. Instant preparedness was combined with continual surveillance of Soviet military activities, and a plan to bomb them at any sign of movement, with or without orders from the United States president (Giddens 2000, 216). Intelligence evidence that the Soviets were far behind the Americans in nuclear capability by 1961 prompted Pentagon strategists to calculate that

a Soviet first strike was more likely, because the Soviets had to know they would not be able to retaliate from an American first strike (Giddens 2000, 270). The 1971 agreement to cap the number of missile launchers promoted the development of multi-warhead missiles (Giddens 2000, 347). The policy of promoting anti-ballistic missiles that might in principle intercept and neutralize nuclear weapons promoted the development of more, not fewer, ballistic weapons. American strategists reasoned that Soviet strategists would think that since anti-ballistic missiles (ABMs) were unlikely to withstand a full-blown Soviet first strike, the real American motive behind developing anti-ballistic missiles was probably to catch the Soviet's remaining retaliatory forces after America had hit Soviet targets with a first strike (Giddens 2000, 322). Hence, in this paranoid and convoluted Cold War reasoning, the US's development of defensive anti-ballistic weapons would give the Soviets an incentive to pre-empt it with a first strike of its own. Defence and offence thus reversed polarities. The nuclear arms race overpowered every effort to curb it.

The only nuclear weapons policy that won the support of military strategists in the Pentagon was "mutual assured destruction" or MAD (Giddens 2000, 213). The way to peace was to prepare for all-out war, with a nuclear arsenal so immense and so widely dispersed across American military bases around the globe that Soviet attackers could be certain that American retaliation would annihilate them, no matter how successful a Soviet first strike against America might be.

Anti-Communism in American Culture

The culture of paranoia fanned outwards from the Pentagon to all branches of American government, manifest in intense anti-communist suspicion and witch hunts that became known as McCarthyism. Throughout the 1950s Senator Joseph McCarthy and his supporters headed committees and private-industry panels that accused and aggressively interrogated thousands of Americans on suspicion of being communists or communist sympathizers. More than a hundred people were jailed and thousands were fired from their jobs and blacklisted on flimsy evidence, often supplied by secret informants.

Anti-communist sentiments were further fanned by the fundamentalist Protestant Christianity of evangelist Billy Graham. Graham and his supporters vilified communism in pulpits and through evangelical television programs across the US as a political system that was against God, Christ, the Bible, and everything religious. Violence against the Soviet Union was heralded as a sacred act willed by God (Carroll 2006, 184). When such religious messages were heard against the backdrop of pervasive fear of nuclear war and possible annihilation, they deeply impacted on American mass culture. Any criticism of the excesses of capitalism was readily interpreted as evidence of communist sympathies. Priests within the Catholic Church who supported liberation theology, the interpretation of Christ's message of love and equality as a call for social justice for the poor, were targeted as communist sympathizers and silenced by the Pope.

Under the Nuclear Umbrella: From Cold War to Conventional War

Miraculously during this Cold War period, the button reputed to be in the American president's office in the White House that might have signalled the start of a nuclear war, or the equivalent button in the Soviet leader's office, was never pushed. But the United States became involved in brutal regional wars fought with conventional weapons under the umbrella justification of saving the free world from the spread of communism. Conflicts the world over became sucked into the vortex of American–Soviet distrust, viewed as either directly instigated by Soviet expansionist policies, or as providing opportunities that communists would exploit.

Wars in the Far East   The United States became involved in two long, drawn-out wars in the Far East—the Korean War from 1950 to 1953 and the Vietnam War between 1965 and 1973—both legitimated by the avowed goal of preventing communist forces sweeping south from China to potentially dominate all of Southeast Asia. In total, more bombs were dropped on Vietnam than by the Allies in the Second World War, and some 30 000 American troops died. But defeating guerrillas proved far more difficult than the Pentagon anticipated. The guerrillas had much popular support, they knew the territory, and they could not be easily routed from the jungles through bombing raids. Open warfare eventually subsided with the Paris Peace Accord of 1973. Across America, the anti-war movement grew to fever pitch, and the US Congress challenged Pentagon power by voting to cut off all funding for military aid to South Vietnam. Saigon, the capital of South Vietnam, fell to insurgents, and communists came to power in Cambodia and Laos. Carroll records the sense of frustration and rage among Pentagon leaders to this double blow of defeat in Southeast Asia and Congressional interference, vowing that never again would the American military be so disgraced, nor military command of nuclear weapons be compromised (Carroll 2006, 360). Key personnel among Pentagon staff—Rumsfeld, Cheney, Perle, Wolfowitz, Armitage, Powell, and Rice—would be chief military advisors when George W. Bush assumed the presidency some 28 years later.

Civil Wars across Latin America   While the Americans were propping up the regime in South Vietnam against pro-communist insurgents, they were also being drawn into conflicts spreading across Latin America. Here also, American involvement was fuelled by fears that Soviet communist influence would spread into America's southern underbelly.

The most direct Soviet–American confrontation occurred in Cuba. President Kennedy became convinced that the Soviets were developing a nuclear missiles site in Cuba, only 90 miles away from the American border. In October 1962 Kennedy ordered a blockade of international waters around Cuba to prevent passage of Soviet ships that might carry weapons. The Soviets denounced the blockade as illegal under United Nations law, and an act of war. The outbreak of nuclear war appeared imminent, but as the world held its breath, both sides retreated from the brink. In secret negotiations, the Soviet president Khrushchev agreed to remove missiles from Cuba provided Kennedy agreed to remove American nuclear weapons from sites in Turkey—only 16 minutes away from Moscow (Carroll 2006, 265). Hawks in the Pentagon made it clear that they considered Kennedy's retreat an act of appeasement.

Intense fear of the spread of communism within the United States government and among military advisors provided justification for repeated intervention in the internal affairs of countries across Central and South America throughout the entire Cold War period. The two major strategies were to undermine left-leaning governments or social movements that might possibly provide avenues for Soviet influence, and conversely to support anti-communist regimes. Contrary to Giddens' optimism, the American government did go to war against many democracies in Latin America. American forces trained and equipped brutal military dictatorships in Chile, Nicaragua, El Salvador, Guatemala, and Honduras. Dictatorships were seen as preferable to democratically elected governments that were soft on communism.

Wars in the Middle East   Conflicts in the Middle East, and particularly the Arab–Israeli wars, provided yet another theatre in which Cold War politics were played out. The League of Nations, the international body formed at the end of the First World War, divided up the territories of the former Ottoman Empire among the victors. It granted France a mandate over Syria and Lebanon, and Britain a mandate over Iraq and Palestine. It was thus the British who oversaw the breakup of Palestine to create the state of Israel in 1947. Initially, an alliance between Israel and the Soviets seemed likely, reflecting the communal and socialist leanings of early Jewish settlers, strong trade unionism, and the migration of waves of Soviet Jews to Israel (Kimmerling 2001, 202–207). The Soviets also sent military and financial aid to Egypt, Syria, and Iraq to strengthen their influence in the region, thus prompting the Americans to step up their military aid to Egypt.

During this period when the US military was mired in Vietnam, Israel began to function as a proxy military base for the US in the Middle East. In the six-day war of 1967, Israel used its decisive technical superiority in the air to crush its Arab neighbours Egypt, Jordan, and Syria. Israel achieved a fourfold increase in territory, colonizing Egypt's Sinai Peninsula, the West Bank of Jordan, including East Jerusalem, the Gaza Strip, and Syria's Golan Heights. From 1967 onward Israel became America's most important military ally and base in the Middle East, receiving military and economic aid worth about $3 billion annually, to a total of more than $140 billion in 2004 dollars (Mearsheimer and Walt 2006, 1–2). Israel's role is to sustain a balance of power in the region in favour of the US, and to help push Arab states into the American rather than Soviet sphere of influence (Abu-Manneh 2007). The US in turn has used its veto power in the United Nations more than 30 times to block all resolutions condemning Israel's domination of the Occupied Territories, and its refusal to give up territory illegally obtained through war.

Iran and Iraq   The Soviets and the British occupied Iran during the Second World War and used it as a conduit to send military supplies to the Soviets. As the war ended, the Americans signed agreements with Iran to supply military aid and training, in an effort to drive out Soviet influence. During the 1950s the British and Americans conspired to overthrow the democratically elected, socialist-leaning government of Mohammed Mossadegh, and then propped up the autocratic and militaristic rule of Shah Pahlavi. Their influence over Iran suffered a major and unexpected setback in 1978, however, when a popular Islamist uprising overthrew the unpopular Pahlavi regime.

Neighbouring Iraq, meanwhile, took advantage of the upheavals caused by the Islamic Revolution to invade Iran, hoping to win back oil-rich border areas. The leader of the Iraqi Ba'ath Party, Saddam Hussein, expected to be able to play off the Soviets and the Americans against each other to his own advantage. The two superpowers, however, supplied arms and aid to both Iraq and Iran, thus helping to keep them both tied up in a drawn-out eight-year war with each other that cost an estimated one million lives. The Soviets aided Iraq to retain it as a client state, but also aided Iran in the hope of reducing Iran's interference in conflict in Afghanistan. The Americans aided Iraq to safeguard oil supplies and contain the anti-Western regime in Iran. At the same time, however, US President Ronald Reagan made secret deals to sell weapons to Iran, using profits from the deals to fund anti-communist rebels in Nicaragua.

The War in Afghanistan   The last major superpower confrontation of the Cold War era focused on Afghanistan. The dual goals of American intervention, according to President Carter's National Security Advisor Zbigniew Brzezinski (interview in *Le Nouvel Observateur*, Paris, 15–21 January 1998), were to undermine yet another pro-communist regime and also to goad the Soviets into a potentially ruinous and unwinnable war, much as Vietnam had been for the Americans. Afghanistan was already in a state of near civil war. In 1978, the Soviet-backed People's Democratic Party of Afghanistan had taken power in a military coup. It pursued policies of aggressive land reform and brutal repression of opposing factions that promoted mounting unrest among factions of large landowners, many of whom were also Muslim clerics (Ahmed 2005, 7). The American CIA seized the opportunity to recruit warlords as mercenary rebel groups and to provide training and weapons to Islamic fundamentalist groups massing in the border areas with Pakistan. When the Soviets invaded Afghanistan in 1979 to shore up their ally, the UN condemned the move as an illegal invasion of a sovereign state. This legitimated a vast flow of military and financial aid to the Afghan resistance from the US, Saudi Arabia, Britain, and China through Pakistan. Osama bin Laden, a devout Sunni Muslim and son of a billionaire Saudi family, was actively recruited and approved by the American government to organize the US-funded training camps in Pakistan, and to recruit Islamist fighters. The decade-long war in Afghanistan worked as Brzezinski had hoped, with the Soviets suffering enormous losses before Soviet president Gorbachev abandoned the campaign and withdrew troops in 1989.

The End of the Cold War

When Mikhail Gorbachev came to power in Moscow in March 1985, he inherited a Soviet economy wrecked by the combination of 40 years of a nuclear arms race, the Afghan quagmire, and a rigid, state-run economic system. Gorbachev wanted change. He pulled out of Afghanistan, instituted political and economic reforms at home, and began negotiations with the Americans to end the ruinous nuclear arms race (Carroll 2006, 404–412). His policies of openness (*glasnost*) and restructuring (*perestroika*) led to the non-violent independence of the 15 Soviet republics by December 1991. Economic restructuring opened the way for a market economy and cooperative enterprise with foreign partners. An agreement to reduce nuclear warheads, followed by the breakup of the Soviet Union in 1991, officially brought the Cold War era to an end. Somehow these two superpowers had managed to avoid engaging each other directly in nuclear war, but an estimated 21 million people lost their lives between 1945 and 1987 in the superpower proxy wars across the world (Carroll 2006, 413).

Vision of a New World Order

From the perspective of American functionalist sociology, the breakup of the Soviet Union heralded the failure of communism or "Marxism" as a political system and the triumph of the Western model of democratic free-market capitalism. It opened the possibility of establishing a single unified world social system, held together by global communications, interdependence through a global system of trade and business enterprise, managed by global financial institutions, and integrated through a cosmopolitan cultural system of liberal democratic free-market values. China retained its communist political system, but has increasingly embraced capitalist economics, promoting private enterprise and Western investment capital alongside state-owned factories. Developing societies across the globe are being drawn into the global capitalist economic system. Transnational corporations form the connective fabric for the interdependent world system. They produce the commodities that sell in global markets and, more importantly, they produce the subjectivities, the homogenizing consumer free-market cultural values that integrate the global system.

Hardt and Negri use the term *Empire* (2000), with a capital E, to emphasize that this emergent form of Empire has no boundaries, no barbarian outsiders, or competing empire with which to go to war. They argue that within a single world system the role of military institutions, designed to fight external enemies, is logically redundant. Policing, rather than military, is required to resolve conflicts within the system. Coordinated world reaction to Saddam Hussein's invasion of Kuwait in August 1990 is seen by Hardt and Negri as an expression of a new kind of war—war reduced to the status of police action, carried out by the world system to enforce law and order (Hardt and Negri 2000, 12). Between 1980 and 1988 Saddam Hussein had been able to play off Soviet and American military backers to prop up his eight-year war against Iran. But in August 1990, when he invaded the neighbouring sovereign state of Kuwait without provocation, something crucial in the world system had changed. Initially he faced economic sanctions authorized by the United Nations Security Council. When he refused to withdraw, he was hit by a UN-authorized coalition force of 35 nations, led by America. There was no external superpower to exploit the conflict. Military-police action launched in January 1991 lasted barely a month, and was decisive in driving Saddam's forces back behind their Iraqi borders.

Pax Americana or Unending War?

The decade of the 1990s began with the hope of a "peace dividend." The era of overt conflict between two superpowers and imminent threat of nuclear war was over. The vision of an integrated world society free from the scourge of major wars seemed within reach. But the peace dividend proved short-lived.

Michael Ignatieff (1997, 72–86), while touring war-ravaged regions in 1995 with wearied and resigned UN Secretary-General Boutros Boutros-Ghali and directors of the International Red Cross, describes repeated scenes of violence characterized by such barbarism and chaos as seeming barely even to resemble von Clausewitz's notion of "rational war." Sites of mass slaughter included Srebrenica in Yugoslavia, Rwanda, Burundi, Angola, Mozambique, El Salvador, Haiti, Namibia, Uganda, Cambodia, and the list goes on. In Afghanistan, as the Soviet occupying power withdrew, the country plunged immediately back into civil war. Rival warlords, with their tribal backers, and their private militias awash in sophisticated Soviet and American weapons, turned to fighting each other for political power, land, and command of the drug trade. Ethnic-tribal conflicts were complicated by the Taliban fighters, Islamic fundamentalists drawn to Afghanistan to fight the infidel Soviets, who saw their chance to establish a pure Islamic state.

All across Africa, retreating European colonizers left in their wake a slew of failed states, lacking the basic infrastructures needed to maintain a monopoly of violence in the hands of the state. Arbitrary colonial boundaries commonly bore no relation to former ethnic and tribal divisions. Most emergent states functioned at best as marginal, vulnerable, and exploited players on the fringes of world markets. Civil wars commonly broke out along ethnic-tribal divisions for control over land, resources, drugs, diamonds, government offices and largesse, and the relatively vast sums of external military and financial aid flowing through government and non-government organizations. The worst of such conflicts exploded in Rwanda in April 1994 with the genocidal slaughter of an estimated 800 000 Tutsi, or about three-quarters of Rwanda's Tutsi population, along with moderate Hutu supporters. This slaughter was perpetrated by members of the majority Hutu ethnic group, as UN peacekeepers stood aside and world leaders debated whether the crimes fitted the definition of genocide that might warrant United Nations intervention in a sovereign state.

Newly emergent states on the southern boundaries of the former Soviet Union—Uzbekistan, Tajikistan, Turkmenistan, and Azerbaijan—similarly struggled with weak infrastructure, corrupt governments, and insurrection involving old Soviet and new Islamic factions (Ignatieff

1997, 126). Yugoslavia, on the eastern border of the old Soviet Union, was the most Westernized of the republics, described as a relatively open, multi-ethnic state. But it too started to break apart after the death of Tito in 1980. Ethnic-religious divisions between Serbs, Croats, Albanians, and Kosovars, with long histories of conflict between Orthodox, Catholic, and Muslim, exploded into violent struggles for regional autonomy and independent statehood.

Cultural Divisions in Failed States: The Retreat from Modernity

Functionalist explanations for civil wars and violence that centre around ethnic and religious divisions focus on the problems inherent in the transition from mechanical to organic solidarity—that is, the transition from small, homogeneous, and self-sufficient communities held together by their sense of sameness to larger heterogeneous societies held together by interdependence and cosmopolitan values that respect individual differences and human rights. The transition to integrative cosmopolitan values at a global level is a comparatively recent phenomenon with many societies experiencing different degrees of cultural lag. The "liberal experiment" in the West in which respect for the individual and for human rights trumps narrower ethnic, racial, and nationalistic group identities is far from fully achieved (Ignatieff 1997, 68).

Relative exclusion from global economies, and the revolution of rising explanations, provides a partial explanation for civil unrest. "Failed states," such as those discussed above, are generally in no condition to ensure their citizens equal participation in global economic interdependence, except at the lowest, most exploited level. Autocratic dictatorships, such as those that characterize many Arab states, also generate widespread frustration among their populations who feel themselves excluded from the opportunities for better lives that mass communications make visible.

Economic frustrations, however, do not account for the surge in violence along specifically ethnic and religious lines. Such violence reflects a retreat into narrowly defined homogeneous group loyalties.

The classic argument proposed by Samuel Huntington (1996) is that ancient fault lines of ethnicity and culture always lie beneath the veneer of cosmopolitanism. In times of stress, people naturally cleave to traditional, repressive cultural nationalism. Others argue that the roots of intense ethnic loyalties displayed by people in the context of civil wars have recent rather than ancient or primordial origins. In modern, complex societies people have multiple potential identities, with the ethnic or religious backgrounds of their forebears often of relatively minor significance. Primordial

cultural fault lines did not always run through the back gardens of villages in Yugoslavia where former neighbours now find themselves divided into hostile "Serb" or "Croat" militias, Ignatieff argues (1997, 44–46). The Yugoslav state collapsed first. Then people began to fear for their safety, and only then did they turn to ethnic nationalism for protection. Under such conditions of fear and an increasingly fragile sense of self-identity, minor differences assume mammoth importance. The underlying assumption, however, remains that ethnicity constitutes a primary group identification for people, and one to which they naturally cling or to which they naturally return in times of fear (Corey 2004). This retreat into ethnicity is thought to be especially likely when ethnicity is tied to distinct religious traditions.

A further variant of this argument that links ethnic nationalism and fear is that processes of modernization expose people living in traditional closed societies to tremendous stresses (Giddens 2000, 61–67). The anxiety generated by globalization can result in paralyzing fear that motivates people to cling to and exaggerate beleaguered tradition. For Giddens, fear of globalization is the root of ethnic xenophobia and religious fundamentalism.

Religious Fundamentalism and the "War on Terror"

In functionalist analysis, the primary explanation for the appeal of religious fundamentalism is pervasive cultural anxiety for people facing the upheavals associated with processes of modernization and globalization. A core feature of fundamentalism is anti-modernism. Western liberalism is seen as spreading negative values of individualism, selfishness, and hedonism that threaten to undermine the moral integrity of society. Religious fundamentalism offers emotional security based on a return to the moral certainty of religiously defined rules of behaviour.

Christian fundamentalists in America spoke out strongly in support of the Cold War struggles against Soviet Communism as the anti-Christian evil empire. They called on America to fulfill her destiny in the world as a nation founded in Puritanism, called by God to promote Good and oppose Evil. These biblical messages can be found throughout George W. Bush's speeches to the nation after 9/11 (Singer 2004). Islamic fundamentalism offers a similar call for devout Muslims to return to the moral security of Islamic law, and to fight against the evils of modernist hedonistic culture associated with the West.

In Afghanistan, during the era of Soviet occupation, a revolutionary group known as the Taliban (Arabic for "religious student") emerged as a political force with backing from the US, Pakistan, and Saudi Arabia. The Taliban succeeded first in ousting the Soviet invaders, and eventually in subduing the civil war between rival warlords. They established a government based on extremely rigid and conservative Wahhabi Sunni interpretations of Islamic law combined with conservative Pashtun tribal codes. Veterans from these revolutionaries, including Osama bin Laden, provide the inspiration and leadership for a loose association of Islamic militants, collectively referred to as al Qaeda, who share the goal of trying to rid the Muslim world of the corrupting influence of the West.

The War on Terror President George W. Bush cited the devastating September 11, 2001, terrorist attacks on targets inside America as the pivotal moment for the start of a new kind of war—a "Global War on Terror" declared against terrorists and against all states that harbour terrorists, anywhere in the world. He characterized the war as a battle between good and evil, between those who uphold the values of individual human rights, political and economic freedom, against reactionary enemies who hate the liberties they see in Western societies. In his address to Congress on 17 September 2002, Bush outlined strategies for fighting this new war, including the principle that America has the right, in the name of self-defence, to act pre-emptively against emerging potential threats anywhere in the world, before they are fully formed. The rules of war agreed to in the United Nations Charter of 1948 would no longer limit American military action.

The first state targeted in the War on Terror was the Taliban government in Afghanistan, after it refused to immediately hand over Osama bin Laden, the man that the American government believed planned the 9/11 attacks. The campaign began with the aerial bombing of Afghanistan on 7 October 2001, followed by American, British, and Canadian ground forces in the spring of 2002. The second state targeted was the government of Saddam Hussein in Iraq, in March 2003. The Americans saw Saddam Hussein as a rogue ruler who had used chemical weapons against minority ethnic Kurds in his own country, and who was developing and holding weapons of mass destruction with the intent of using them to threaten American security. As of 2008 both campaigns continue, with no clear victory in sight. Combined American and allied military superiority easily achieved the first objectives of toppling the offending regimes, but stabilizing the new pro-Western regimes, and calming the waves of insurrection and terrorism that followed, proved far more difficult.

Pax Americana as New Imperial Order: The Culture of Militarism

With the declaration of a global war on terror and the rapid military response to 9/11, the Bush administration confirmed two central messages. First, the Empire had a new enemy, not in the form of a rival superpower state, but a loosely coordinated, anarchic network of terrorists, with tentacles reaching into all nations of the world, including the US. Secondly, the American military, either unilaterally or with allies, intended to tackle this new enemy with all the institutions of war. The command post of the new open-ended and global war was not to be the United Nations, but the Pentagon.

The culture of militarism involves a combination of social structures and values that romanticize soldiers, and emphasize military supremacy and military might as a central feature of national pride and sense of national security, even in peacetime. Militarism as a system of values is reflected in civilian politics in priority given to funding the military over other social services, in respect and deference shown to military advisors, and in the high value placed on military experience, especially in senior ranks as credentials for civilian political office. Militarism in US popular culture is reflected in major increases in marketing and sales of military toys, games, videos, and clothing (Giroux 2009). Militarism is also reflected in heightened emphasis on fear, force, and punishment as social controls in civilian life.

In the decade of relative peace between the breakup of the Soviet Union in 1991 that ended the Cold War and President Bush's declaration of the Global War on Terror in 2001, the scope and power of America's military-industrial complex did not contract—rather it kept on expanding. The culture of militarism had long been entrenched among senior staff at the Pentagon, the institutional heart of this complex. Within this cultural system, the state of war is seen as normal, with unchallenged military might accepted as the essential foundation of national security.

Throughout the post-Cold War decade, Pentagon advisors continually pushed the policy message that America had to keep expanding its military capability in critical areas across the globe—Europe, Northeast Asia, the Middle East, Southwest Asia, backed up by ever-increasing military budgets. As early as 1992, after the first Gulf War with Iraq, these advisors counselled that the US should invade Iraq and finish the job. They repeated this message in 1998, three years before the 9/11 attacks (Dyer 2004, 128; Alterman 2004). When the US was attacked on September 11, 2001, Pentagon advanced planning immediately went into action. The 9/11 attacks proved so opportune for expanding the powers of the Pentagon and the military-industrial complex generally that it prompted widespread support for conspiracy theories suggesting that, even if the Pentagon and the CIA did not directly cause 9/11 events, they did nothing to prevent them from occurring, despite extensive forewarning (Ahmed 2005).

The open-ended Global War on Terror has justified massive further increases in military spending and a further concentration of power in the Pentagon (Carroll 2006, 495–496). The CIA's covert operations were put under the control of Secretary of Defense Donald Rumsfeld for the purpose of "preparing the battlefield all around the world." What followed was the militarization of the entire US society, in the sense that national security would come to trump all other issues. Other countries quickly adopted the Bush concept of "preventive war" against terrorists and any states that harbour terrorists to justify military operations of their own, including Russia against Chechnya, and Israel against its neighbours. Any and all insurgency could readily be cast under the rubric of "terrorism."

Within Israel, Kimmerling argues (2001, 208–237) the culture of militarism has penetrated so deeply into society that the military is civilianized and civilians militarized. Multiple ethnic cleavages have coalesced around conflict as a crucial part of collective identity, expressed through pervasive acceptance of the necessity of institutional violence and permanent preparation for war. Military service is the supreme duty of all citizens. The major premise assumed by militarism is that Israel's security depends on making her neighbours understand that the Jewish state is indestructible, its military might vastly superior, and its willingness to use violence unquestionable. The war against Lebanon from July to September 2006, even though massively one-sided in its destruction, created great angst among Israelis precisely because it was not sufficiently decisive as to crush opponents into submission. The militaristic cultures in Israel and in the US are closely intertwined, and sustained over many years by powerful networks of Jewish American organizations committed to sustaining America's military support for Israel. This network, termed the "Israel Lobby" (Mearsheimer and Walt 2006), includes key figures in the Pentagon, Congress, and the State Department, prominent policy think tanks, and Christian evangelicals wedded to the notion that Israel's rebirth fulfills biblical prophecy.

Lessons for Peace in Functionalist Analysis

The insights that functionalist analysis offer for promoting peace on a world scale focus primarily on issues of policing world society, containment of rogue states, intervention to strengthen and repair civic institutions in failed states, and also intervention to defuse the violence associated with anti-modernist retreat into ethnic nationalism. The analysis also calls for moral leadership in the difficult transition from narrow nationalistic and ethnic identities to broader values of respect for cosmopolitan diversity, human rights, and justice on which interdependent economic systems can be established.

Analysts draw on the theory of "failed states" to advocate moral intervention by stable (Western) states to help more fragile states to create or rebuild their civic institutions, and especially to establish professional armies and police that can monopolize the use of force within their territory, and better police their borders against international terrorists (Ignatieff 2004, 1997, 72–108).

Functionalist analysis of the roots of ethnic conflict in failed states and economic upheavals of modernization and globalization also provides a rationale for "just wars" to intervene in explosions of violence that sometimes escalate into genocide or ethnic cleansing. A global sense of shame and guilt still shrouds the failure of the UN to intervene in the massacre in Rwanda that left 800 000 dead in 1994, and the continuing failure to intervene in the ongoing horrors of ethnic cleansing, rape, and slaughter in Sudan. In comparison, NATO interventions in Bosnia and Kosovo in the 1990s, however inadequate in themselves, appear as relative success stories in that protagonists were pushed to the bargaining table, and violence did not escalate (Ignatieff 1997, 100).

At best, moral intervention in war zones, and intervention to assist less modernized regions to make the transition into global interdependence, both express and reinforce commitment to cosmopolitan values of human rights that comprise the integrative cultural core of the Durkheimian vision of global organic solidarity. At worst, such intervention by a Western militaristic superpower and its allies into the internal affairs of other countries constitutes a new form of global imperialism, the white man's burden to dominate and control other civilizations, justified by thinly veiled assertions of Western cultural superiority. Analysis of militarism in North American popular culture has prompted calls for cultural studies to expose and challenge the values of violence and force at the level of toys and video games, and to challenge also the complicity of schools in promoting values of fear, force, and surveillance, and acting as recruitment stations for the military (Giroux 2009).

Theorists who challenge the immense power and influence of the military-industrial complex within American society cast America itself in the role of rogue state, and American military institutions as primary threats to world peace (Chomsky 2006). They argue that peace is better served not by threat of military deterrence, but by strengthening alternative and more truly global institutions like the United Nations, international law and treaties safeguarding human rights, and the International Criminal Court, to police rogue states and terrorist activities. These are the very institutions that the Bush Administration weakened by exempting the US, as lone superpower, from their provisions (Ignatieff 2005).

The Political Economy of War

The political economy perspective shares with functionalism the view that military institutions are a normal feature of social systems, and especially of nation states. Wars serve as a mechanism to forcibly impose one society's interests against others, and as defence from outside attack. In contrast to functionalism, however, political economy theory traces the roots of war not in the clash of cultures or cultural lag in the transition to modernism, but in underlying struggles around access to means of production and available material resources. Wars are analyzed not as functioning in the interests of social systems as a whole, but as serving the class interests of economic elites.

Wars have been a feature of societies with all known modes of production—primitive communism, slavery, feudalism, capitalism, and Soviet-style state communism. In classical Marxist analysis, however, capitalism is singled out as the system most inherently prone to war, as one means to manage inherent contradictions within capitalist economic systems. Wars provide a mechanism through which regionally powerful economic elites can expand access to productive resources and markets in other regions to their own competitive advantage. Militaristic cultures tend to emerge and be sustained in contexts where military institutions are tightly tied to powerful economic interests.

Imperialism and World Wars

Classical Marxist analysis readily accounts for the First and Second World Wars in 1914–18 and 1939–45 as rooted in imperialist rivalry between advanced European states for cheap or rare raw materials and markets (Mandel 1986). European powers annexed massive territories in Asia, Africa, and the Americas, exploiting their resources and populations, and associated markets and trade routes to promote their manufacturing industries. The logic of imperialism, Mandel argues, was to secure cheap supplies of oil, rubber, copper, nickel, tin, manganese, and the like. To this end, sea lanes had to be kept open, export markets expanded, and foreign competitors crushed. As unconquered space for overseas expansion diminished, intra-European conflicts grew beyond the point where they could be contained by conventional diplomacy or localized wars in the colonies. The rulers of Germany, along with their Austro-Hungarian and Ottoman allies, turned to war as a means to wrest control over the colonies and dependent territories of Britain and France. The First World War ended with Germany being crushed and allied empires carved up among the victors.

During the inter-war period, capitalist economies experienced massive economic failure known as The Great Depression, marked by a precipitous downward spiral of unemployment, overproduction, and falling profits. Civil wars in Russia and China had resulted in communist rule, raising fears among economic elites in Western Europe that they might themselves face revolt among workers to overthrow the capitalist system. All leading capitalist nations were driven to seek new world markets to boost their economies. Japan declared war on China, with the goal of expanding its economic domination across Asia, and thus threatening British and American interests. Simmering rage within Germany over ruinous war reparations found expression in fascism and re-militarization. War broke out again as Germany sought to reassert domination over Central Europe, invading Austria, Czechoslovakia, and Poland, and then France. The Soviets were drawn in to challenge German expansionism across their spheres of influence in central and Eastern Europe. The two spheres of war in Asia and Europe were tied together through strings of imperialist interests that stretched around the globe.

By the end of the Second World War the European empires were largely broken up, having proven too unwieldy and too expensive to maintain. Israel is arguably the last example of a European colonial-settler state, its policies driven more by interests in territorial acquisition than capitalist profits (Abu-Manneh 2007, 3). Most colonies gained independence from direct political control by Western powers, but freedom from Western economic dominance was to prove more difficult.

Ethnic Wars in Post-Imperial States

Political economy theory traces the roots of ethnic conflicts in post-colonial states directly to divide-and-rule policies implemented by colonial rulers. The legacy of the colonizers was racialized or ethnicized class war. The 53 states that gained independence in Africa after the Second World War were characterized by great diversity of indigenous ethnic groups, languages, and religions, which bore little relation to the boundaries that colonial rulers had carved up. But ethnic diversity in itself does not account for the multiple civil wars across Africa. Most of these tribal and sub-tribal groups lived in close proximity for centuries without constantly being at war with each other. Colonialism changed these dynamics. Colonial rulers exploited ethnic divisions and promoted cultural values of racialization and violence. Foreign domination and economic exploitation inevitably generate resentment, resistance, and sometimes violent uprisings among subjugated people. One tactic that colonial rulers used to deflect this anger was to develop buffer groups of favoured middle-level administrators, who were often chosen for ethnic distinctions from the majority population. Buffer-group members owed their privileges and therefore their loyalties to the colonial powers, and looked to them for protection. When colonizers left, the bitter divisions and inequalities remained.

The explosion of violence in Rwanda in April 1994 during which an estimated 800 000 people were slaughtered in 100 days was a legacy of this imperial class structure (Masire 2000, Ch. 2). In Rwanda, German and Belgian rulers cemented and rigidified what were previously relatively fluid ethnic differences between Tutsi and Hutu. Colonizers favoured Tutsi for school places and civil service jobs in the colonial administration. By 1959, Tutsi, who were 15 percent of the population, held three-quarters of the school places, 95 percent of civil service jobs, 43 of 45 posts as chiefs, and 578 of 589 sub-chief posts. This privileged class position that Tutsi enjoyed came crashing down in 1959 when the Belgian colonizers imposed "democratic" elections that brought the Hutu majority to power. Years of resentment against Tutsi elites were unleashed, promoted by unstable Hutu-backed regimes, threatened by the power of Tutsi intelligentsia. Tensions reached the boiling point in the early 1990s as falling world prices for tea and coffee undermined the fragile Rwandan economy (Verwimp 2003), and the Habyarimana government tried to deflect blame for economic disaster onto Tutsi.

Many political actors share immediate responsibility for the genocide in Rwanda. Political economy theory makes visible the continuing imprint of colonial rule—the long history of violence, and racialized, tribalized class divisions that colonial rulers fostered all across Africa. Direct colonial rule has ended but neo-imperialism continues with Western corporations extracting minerals, diamonds, oil, and other raw materials from Africa, and in the process exacerbating and funding civil wars.

The Cold War: Capitalism versus Communism and Socialism

The presence of a thriving communist state in Eastern Europe always posed the ideological threat that it might foster revolt among workers within capitalism. Its very existence might encourage workers within capitalist economies to develop class consciousness of their own exploited position and thus bring about Marx's prediction that they would rebel and smash their capitalist chains. In this sense both functionalist and political economy perspectives see foundational conflict of cultural values between communist and capitalist systems as underlying four decades of Cold War hostility. Political economy theory, however, focuses attention on the more tangible and immediate economic threat that communist states posed to corporate capitalist

interests. Advanced capitalist countries had engaged in two horrendously destructive world wars driven by competing interests to dominate resources and markets across the globe. In the post-war world, Soviet and Chinese communist empires meant that huge regions stretching from Eastern Europe across Central and Northeast Asia were closed to capitalist expansion. Western corporations could no longer trade freely in these markets nor extract cheap resources. It became imperative to Western business interests to prevent communist states from expanding any further, at the same time as they had ideological interests in disrupting and discrediting the communist alternative in the eyes of the Western working class. The escalation of the nuclear arms race and incessant proxy wars that characterized the Cold War years were designed as much to weaken Soviet and Chinese economies as to defend Western societies from any immediate threat of military invasion.

The emergence of inward-looking, democratic socialist governments in the Southern Cone of Latin America during the 1950s and '60s raised the spectre of even more restricted business markets and blocked access to productive resources (Klein 2007, 56–83). Governments in countries including Chile, Argentina, Uruguay, and Guatemala began to develop protectionist policies of import restrictions and high tariffs on foreign goods, combined with nationalization of important productive resources like oil, arable land, and mines. Iran during the Mossadegh administration and Indonesia under Sukarno developed similar policies. These policies blocked North American and European multinational corporations from expanding into the regions and thus directly threatened profits. Ideologically also, democratic socialism posed an even greater threat to capitalism than totalitarian communism in the Soviet Union because it was much harder to vilify (Klein 2007, 542). Klein argues that American military intervention and support for terrorist organizations in these states during the Cold War years was driven by the capitalist imperative to force open these economies to foreign investors, more than fear of Soviet power in America's underbelly.

The civil wars that subsequently erupted in these countries, marked by workers' resistance to policy changes, and massively violent state terrorism to crush that resistance, attest to how important it was to capitalist interests to stamp out socialism, and how severely working-class interests were eroded by the economic policy shifts that followed. Klein gives a few figures to illustrate the brutality of these civil wars. In Chile in 1973, when General Pinochet replaced Allende, roving death squads arrested and tortured some 80 000 "subversives" and more than 3000 disappeared or were executed. Torture and terror were the preferred weapons of social control. Altogether, the US-supported military juntas that replaced democratic socialism with free-market capitalism in the Southern Cone of Latin America are held responsible for the murder of tens of thousands of people and the torture of hundreds of thousands more (Klein 2007, 120). In Indonesia the death tolls were even higher.

Post Cold-War Wars and the Politics of Oil

By the beginning of the 1990s, the collapse of the Soviet Union, together with major policy shifts in China to open the economy to private ownership and consumerism, opened vast new regions for Western corporate business. What also opened up to Western oil companies was the prospect of access to known and projected new oil fields around the Caspian Sea. Oil is the most important of all the productive resources underpinning Western capitalist economies, and by the 1990s the double-edged threat of declining resources and increasing demand was already recognized. Two-thirds of the already developed oil supplies are located in the states surrounding the Persian Gulf, the largest of these being Iran, Iraq, and Saudi Arabia.

With the breakup of the Soviet Union, the oil-rich Central Asian provinces became newly independent countries—Azerbaijan, Uzbekistan, Turkmenistan, and Kazakhstan—and their governments were open to more lucrative markets and investment partners, rather than continuing to send all their oil exclusively to Russia. The US government lost no time in negotiating to establish military garrisons in these former Soviet republics (Carroll 2006, 446).

The US also actively intervened in the civil wars in Afghanistan in the hope of backing a ruling group that would stabilize the warring factions and be amenable to an American-owned pipeline (Ahmed 2005, Ch. 1). US support for the Taliban government started to come apart only when it became obvious not only that the regime's brutality and religious extremism was destabilizing the country, but also that the regime would not conclude a reasonable deal on the pipeline proposal. Taliban leaders were warned either to cooperate on the pipeline or risk being bombed. By July 2001, two months before the 9/11 attacks, US bases in neighbouring Tajikistan were preparing to attack the Taliban government by mid-October, before winter snow. After 9/11, this pre-planned attack went ahead within two weeks, with internal assistance from the Northern Alliance. By December 2001 a new pro-American, Afghanistan Transitional Administration was installed. Hamid Karzai was appointed as Chair and warlords from the Northern Alliance given government posts. Karzai had been a top advisor to the California-based oil company UNOCAL in negotiations with the Taliban. Plans for the pipeline, however, had to be shelved because, seven years after the regime change, US, Canadian, and NATO forces combined have still been unable to stabilize the governance or to quell the Taliban resistance.

Yugoslavia

The US was embroiled in two other theatres of war during the same period—Yugoslavia and Iraq. In both cases, political economy analysis traces critical economic interests that underlay, and arguably determined, US and allied involvement in the conflict—the drive to secure stable, low-cost sources of oil, and the drive to open up corporate investment opportunities and markets.

NATO military engagement in Yugoslavia is typically framed in functionalist analysis and in mass media accounts as humanitarian intervention to manage ethnic violence between the majority Orthodox Serb population and minority Catholic Croatians, Muslim Bosnians, and Albanian Kosovars. Political economy analysis frames this engagement very differently. Ethnic conflict is seen as the result of destructive IMF policies designed to force open the formerly closed socialist economy to Western investment, combined with military intervention by NATO that promoted ethnic conflict to gain political and economic influence in the region. A policy paper developed by the Reagan administration in 1984, entitled "US Policy Toward Yugoslavia" (Hudson 2003, 57), spelled out the objective of overthrowing communist governments and parties and integrating Eastern European countries into capitalist world markets. A major barrier to this integration was Serbian leader Slobodan Milosevic, who remained committed to a decentralized, worker-managed socialism. Hence, he had to be removed.

Throughout the Cold War years, Yugoslavia had benefited from favoured status and aid from the West as an important buffer state between Western capitalist economies and Soviet Communism, but with the collapse of the Soviet Union in 1989, that advantage was gone. Yugoslavia came under heavy pressure to open up her formerly protected markets and to sell off her hundreds of state-owned enterprises to Western corporate buyers. At the time the Yugoslav economy was in trouble. Soviet markets were imploding, and with Western markets in recession, tens of thousands of migrant workers returned to Yugoslavia, thus worsening unemployment and cutting off foreign currency payment remittances. Yugoslavia borrowed heavily from the IMF, and was then crushed by variable interest rates that rose to 18.7 percent by 1981. The IMF made "structural adjustment" a condition of carrying the loans—privatization, deregulation, and cuts to government services. In the economic chaos and unemployment that resulted, the country began to fragment (Chossudovsky, 1998, 243–263). The richer republics of Slovenia and Croatia were already more tied into European Union markets, and they resented having to subsidize poorer republics. They pushed for independence and integration into the European Union.

The Croatian nationalist leader, Tudjman, declared unilateral independence, defined on ethnic lines as "Croatia for the Croats." Ethnic Serbs, who formed about 13 percent of the population of Croatia, voted to form an autonomous region of Serbian Krajina and remain within the wider Yugoslavia. Violence exploded as Germany and the EU immediately recognized Croatian independence. NATO military forces responded to Tudjman's call to protect his new national boundaries from the Serb-dominated Yugoslav Army. In the ethnic cleansing that followed, some 300 000 Serbs were driven from their ancestral homes in Croatia into what remained of Yugoslavia. The next republic to break away and then to fragment was Bosnia. The US supported the Bosnian ruling Muslim faction as legitimate rulers of a new independent state, while Serbs inside Bosnia fought to retain an independent Serbian republic that would still be attached to the shrinking remains of Yugoslavia. Three years of civil war finally ended when intensified bombing by NATO forces drove the Serbs to accept the Dayton Accord in November 1995.

The terms of this agreement, Hudson argues, revealed the economic interests driving the US and its NATO allies (2003, 121–122). Bosnia would become a protectorate of the United Nations, with legislative and executive power resting with the UN High Representative. The Bosnian economy would be run by the IMF. The Accord determined that the first governor of the Central Bank of Bosnia would be an IMF outsider, and all democratization and reconstruction would be controlled by foreign nominees of the IMF, the United Nations legislature, and the Organization for Security and Cooperation in Europe. The Accord in effect instituted a full colonial administration in Bosnia, ensuring that the new state economy would be wide open for business, with rapid privatization of all socialist enterprises, and with foreign investment and imports under favourable terms dictated by the IMF.

The third stage of the Yugoslav wars was fought in Kosovo, an autonomous region within the borders of Serbia with an 85 percent ethnic Albanian population. Again, Hudson argues, the US used its influence to break up Yugoslavia, at the price of another war, rather than to back the more peaceful option that might have held the federation together. When the war eventually ended under pressure from Russia, Kosovo became a UN protectorate with 40 000 troops stationed in the region. Kosovo, like Bosnia, was open for business, with the European Union controlling reconstruction and economic development in accord with IMF guidelines. Kosovo declared unilateral independence

from Serbia on 17 February 2008. A cursory search of the Internet for "Kosovo oil pipeline" reveals a host of websites suggesting that negotiations for a trans-Balkan oil pipeline through Kosovo were actively under way. The American military base of Camp Bondsteel in Kosovo will provide security.

In summary, political economy analysis of the wars that broke up Yugoslavia places the economic interests of NATO leaders and self-serving local politicians at the root of supposedly "ethnic" conflicts, not primordial cultural attachments. In each phase of the civil wars, Hudson argues, NATO leaders backed breakaway ethnic minority factions, providing money and weapons, and the lure of rapid recognition and integration into EU markets, to promote their own economic interests in crushing the socialist economic model favoured by Serbian leader Milosevic.

Politics of Oil and Markets in the Middle East

Politics in the Middle East are unavoidably about oil, given the reality that two-thirds of the world's known oil supplies are in the region, and the further reality that resources are declining and world demand escalating. The three major oil producers are Saudi Arabia, Iran, and Iraq, and US relations with all three regimes have become problematic.

America's closest ties remain with the ruling royal family of Saudi Arabia, in a mutually beneficial relationship stretching back for more than three decades. The US gets a steady, reliable supply of cheap oil and approval for two military bases in Saudi Arabia, while the House of Saud gets multiple billions of dollars in oil revenues, a steady supply of weapons to shore up its unpopular autocratic rule, and secured multi-billion-dollar investments in American equities (Unger 2004, 4; Shanks 2001, 8). The Saudi ruling regime benefits from having Arab frustrations focused on Israel as the enemy rather than fomenting revolution at home (Abu-Manneh 2007, 13). Saudi rulers have grown immensely rich from this arrangement, but little of this wealth has filtered down to the masses. From the perspective of most of its citizens, Saudi Arabia is a failed state, characterized by poverty, unemployment, arrested development, and extreme religious repression. Economic and political backwardness in the midst of such staggering oil wealth made Saudi Arabia a prime breeding ground for terrorists. Opposition to American military bases in Saudi Arabia was cited by al Qaeda terrorist leader, Osama bin Laden, as a major reason for plotting the terrorist attack. Fifteen of the 19 hijackers involved in 9/11 attacks were from Saudi Arabia.

Historically, the US had close ties with the autocratic regime of Shah Pahlavi in Iran, but this came to an abrupt and unforeseen end in 1978 when Islamic fundamentalists ousted the Shah. Students loyal to the theocratic regime stormed the US embassy in November 1979, and held 52 staff hostage for more than a year, as "enemy spies," until US president Ronald Reagan won their release by secretly trading weapons. In 2002, President George Bush listed Iran, along with Iraq and North Korea, as part of an "axis of evil" threatening the Western world with weapons of mass destruction.

A long history of US and British involvement in Iraq preceded the decision by President George W. Bush and British Prime Minister Tony Blair to launch a military invasion of Iraq on 20 March 2003, to topple the Iraqi ruling dictator Saddam Hussein. Britain gained control over Iraq after the collapse of the Ottoman Empire during the First World War, and maintained military bases there after Iraq was granted nominal independence in 1932. The huge oil fields discovered in Iraq in 1927 makes this a strategically critical region.

The British and the Americans, along with other Gulf States, supported Iraqi military dictator Saddam Hussein during his eight-year war against Iran from 1980 to 1988. They helped to supply him with chemical and other weapons of mass destruction that they subsequently accused him of possessing. It was during this period that Saddam carried out dozens of attacks against rebellious Iraqi Kurds, using bombs that released chemical poisons. The worst attack on the town of Halabja in March 1988 killed 5000 civilians. The Americans and British ignored these crimes so long as Saddam was useful to their larger purpose of containing Iran. They, and other Gulf States like Saudi Arabia, had good reason to fear that if Saddam lost the war with Iran, then radical Iranian Islam might sweep across southern Iraq and into Kuwait (Jenkins 2003, 172). In the politics of oil and big business a military dictatorship is easier to manage than an Islamic fundamentalist theocracy. During the Cold War era, the US could not risk Saddam Hussein siding with Soviets, although it was well known that he was playing off both superpowers for weapons and favours.

The US-led Invasion of Iraq

The overt reasons that US president George W. Bush and his British ally Tony Blair gave for invading Iraq on 20 March 2003 were to overthrow a rogue regime that was hiding weapons of mass destruction, supporting global terrorism, and guilty of committing acts of terrorism using chemical warfare on its own citizens. Political economy theory, however, focuses attention on deeper economic goals—to gain control over Iraqi oilfields and to transform the Iraqi economy in the process into a model free-market capitalist system open to Western business. Control over oilfields, in itself, was probably not decisive, Dyer argues, in that Middle

East states are as eager to sell oil as the West is to buy it. The prospect of rapidly escalating demand for oil from developing economies, and especially from China, however, creates a powerful incentive for the US government to maintain military control over oil supplies and shipping routes (Dyer 2007, 56–58). Permanent military bases in the Gulf region ensure that, in a crisis, the US could cut off China's oil imports while safeguarding its own supplies. From this perspective, the US government supports militarism in Israel primarily to weaken Arab states. "Regional stability," Dyer argues, means stable American access to oil, not strong Arab states nor peace for Israel. A "moderate" Arab state is one subordinate to America, while an independent Arab state is "extremist." The militarists may be correct in that exploitation of resources belonging to others inevitably involves force.

The Politics of Expanding Capitalist Markets

The centrality to the invasion of the second goal of transforming the Iraqi economy became evident in the speed and intensity with which American capitalist interests were pushed forward. On 1 May 2003, only 42 days after the invasion, President Bush announced an end to major combat operations in Iraq, beneath a banner declaring "Mission Accomplished." A mere eight days later, plans were announced for the "establishment of a US-Middle East free trade area within a decade" (Klein 2007, 396). The vision was for a "free," as in free-market and free-enterprise, Iraq with a booming capitalist economy that other states in the Middle East would envy and strive to emulate. It was also to be a highly profitable investment zone for Western corporations. Klein argues that the Bush administration had no exit strategy from the invasion and occupation of Iraq because the US never had any intention of leaving.

US presidential envoy Paul Bremer took up his appointment as head of the Coalition Provincial Authority in Iraq on 11 May 2003. He immediately decreed a series of new investment laws designed to open Iraq's economy to foreign corporate ownership under very favourable terms. Iraq's more than 200 state-owned enterprises were put up for sale, with the new laws permitting foreign investors to own 100 percent of Iraqi assets, and to take 100 percent of profits out of the country, with no requirement of reinvestment, and no tax on profits. Corporate taxes inside Iraq were dropped from 45 percent to a flat rate of 15 percent. Members of the Iraqi business class had virtually no hope of buying their national companies, because they had minimal access to investment funds in comparison with US-based multinational corporations. Moreover, the new laws prohibited Iraq's Central Bank from offering financing to state-owned enterprises. Bremer further ensured that these investment laws were enshrined in the new Iraqi Constitution before elections were held, so that any incoming parliament could not change the rules (Klein 2007, 410–425). Bremer held back on privatizing the biggest prize—Iraq's state-owned oil company, only because he was warned by Iraqi advisors that for an occupying force to take a subjugated state's primary resources before a national government was in place would constitute "an act of war" under the UN Charter. This would have to wait until elections could be held and the Iraqi transitional government installed in 2005.

As events transpired in Iraq the entire vision of a model capitalist economy has had to be delayed, as insurrection and violence continued to tear the country apart five years after the 2003 invasion. Klein argues that rage among middle- and working-class Iraqis at the wanton destruction of the civil service and rampant sell-off of Iraqi assets to foreign companies played a central role in the post-war eruption of hostility towards American occupiers. Peace plans were proposed by Iraqi political leaders at various stages of the war and occupation, but they were rejected out of hand by the Anglo-American coalition because they affirmed the legitimacy of Iraqi resistance groups and allowed no permanent coalition military bases in Iraq, no special deals for American or British access to cheap oil, and no radical restructuring of the Iraqi economy to facilitate foreign investment (Holland and Jarrar 2008; Dyer 2007, 30).

The Military-Industrial Complex: Wars for Profit

Classic Marxist analysis has always argued that wars function to ease contradictions of capitalism. Wars solve crises of unemployment as surplus workers join the armed forces and are killed off. Crises of overproduction are resolved as weapons are bought to be blown up, or become obsolete, and so promote new purchases. Thus, while masses of people suffer horrendously from wars, capitalists in corporations involved in weapons production and arms sales can make vast profits, and workers in these industries rely on them to make a living. An estimated 21 000 new millionaires emerged in the US from war profiteering during the First World War (Buchheit 2008, 22).

There is ample evidence in Western societies of vast sums of money dedicated directly and indirectly to war. In 2006 the Stockholm International Peace Research Institute estimated the value of global military expenditure as about US$1 trillion. The US alone spent an estimated $528 billion on weapons, or about 4 percent of its Gross Domestic Product (GDP). America's military budget is now estimated to exceed those of all other countries of the world combined, not even counting the funds spent on the war in Iraq. Britain ranked second in military expenditures at $59.2 billion, and Canada fourth at $14.6 billion, or 1.1 percent of GDP.

Demonstrating that wars generate profits does not prove that profits cause wars. Decisions about going to war or making peace are not normally made by companies that profit from war contracts, nor are decisions about peace normally made by companies whose profits are hurt by wars. A deeper level of analysis is needed to explore the institutional connections and leverage that corporations have on the politics of war.

Structural changes in the Pentagon to contract out to private corporations many of the core functions of military activity, including strategic planning, have begun to change on a fundamental level the relationship between government and profits. This is so much so, Klein argues (2007, 377), that it is no longer possible to draw a clear line between government and corporation. Corporations do not lobby for access to government—they are the government. Journalistic accounts of the meteoric rise in profits of two major defence contractors, The Carlyle Group (Briody 2003) and Halliburton (Briody 2004), document the revolving-door connections between government and business positions. These corporations have routinely hired senior civil servants into senior executive positions, including ex-presidents, former secretaries of defence, former chairmen of critical government commissions, because of their strategic contacts with governments. These senior corporate executives are later often hired back into top government positions, for the most part keeping close personal and financial connections to the corporations.

It is in this context of tightly interlinked personnel networks that the culture of militarism is most likely to prevail—a context in which the same people making military decisions are directly tied to powerful economic interests of business corporations servicing the military.

Under Defence Secretary Rumsfeld's direction between 2001 and 2006, private corporations were hired on contracts to carry out virtually every function of the armed forces. These contracts were not just to supply gear and weapons, but to build entire cities for American soldiers in the Balkans and in Iraq. By 2008 there were an estimated 47 000 primary corporations with Department of Defence contracts and 100 000 sub-contractors (Turse 2008). Dozens of senior civil servants resigned from the Department of Homeland Security to form private corporations to bid on government contracts, tapping into a vast new market in what Klein calls "disaster capitalism." Klein estimates that in the first Gulf War in 1991 there was one contractor for every one hundred US soldiers. By the beginning of the second war in Iraq in 2003 this had risen to one in 10, and by the following year to one contractor for every four soldiers (Klein 2007, 458). Senior government officers associated with these corporations made multi-million-dollar personal fortunes from these contracts and from the surging value of stock options that they controlled.

The same companies that made fortunes on Pentagon contracts to carry out the war later made fortunes on contracts for Iraqi reconstruction projects—companies including Bechtel, Halliburton, Parsons, KPMG, and Blackwater (Buchheit 2008, 24). None of the contracts were opened to competition; no Iraqi firms were able to bid on them; no Iraqi workers were employed; no Iraqi state-owned enterprises were given any share in reconstruction work. Multinational corporations based in the US preferred to bring in their own $900-a-day mercenaries (Buchheit 2008, 452).

The result of this uncontrolled and unsupervised spending spree was a spectacular failure to reconstruct even basic services in Iraq. By 2006, three years after the invasion, Iraqi cities still had only limited electricity, and two-thirds of the population did not have clean water or sewage. Oil production was down to two-thirds of its pre-war levels (Dyer 2007, 18). The Coalition Provisional Authority readily blamed this spectacular failure to achieve minimal reconstruction objectives on mounting insurgency in Iraq. They did not acknowledge how much this insurgency was inflamed by the mounting rage among impoverished Iraqi businesses and working classes at being shut out of reconstruction work.

Back in America, widespread fear of terrorist attacks, fanned by endless government warnings, prompted a boom in high-technology, homeland-security industries, including all forms of surveillance, information gathering and information data mining, bomb-detection devices, and the like. Israel is another country whose economy has benefited greatly from pervasive insecurity associated with the global war on terror. The truism that violence and instability are bad for business profits no longer holds in the new era of "disaster capitalism," in which major corporations depend for profits on delivering military supports, security, surveillance, anti-terrorism technologies, and reconstructions from all kinds of man-made and natural disasters (Klein 2007, Ch. 21). The more pervasive the levels of insecurity, the greater their profit potential. The inherently endless and unwinnable "War on Terrorism" has become good for business. Israel, which has experienced years of Palestinian terrorism, has become home to numerous high-technology firms that sell their anti-terrorism expertise across the globe. One result of the rapidly expanding homeland-security economy, Klein suggests, is that Israeli leaders are losing their incentive to find a peaceful settlement with the Palestinians.

Ethnic Violence and Civil War in Iraq

Political economy theory traces the roots of the so-called "sectarian" or ethnic violence within and between Sunni, Shiite, and Kurdish groups in Iraq, not in primordial ethnic/religious hatreds or in cultural lag, or fear of modernization, but in responses to foreign occupation, and the economic devastation that followed the 2003 invasion. Sunni and Shia people had lived in mixed neighbourhoods in Baghdad and other large Iraqi cities without major sectarian conflict before the invasion. During the decades of Ba'ath Party rule, Iraq had become an increasingly secular society with relatively high standards of living and formal education. The combined effects of the 1980–88 war with Iran and a decade of UN sanctions following the Gulf War in 1991 had already seriously undermined the Iraqi economy. Conditions became vastly worse after the 2003 invasion. Millions of unemployed Iraqis, facing long-term destitution, had few incentives to cooperate with their occupiers. Rather, they had strong incentives to join local militias led by political extremists.

From the functionalist perspective, which prevailed in how the occupying powers and Western media discussed Iraq, sectarian divisions were blamed for the fighting, which then explained why the laissez-faire, free-market model economy could not take off. In the political economy variant of the "failed state" explanation, however, cause and effect are reversed. The insurrection and civil war in Iraq is explained as a reaction to the destruction of Iraq's economy. Had Americans moved swiftly after deposing Saddam Hussein either to leave the country and let the Iraqis decide their own governance, or to support the centralized "socialist" economy in Iraq, remove sanctions, reopen Iraq's factories, provide funding for Iraqis to organize their own rebuilding of infrastructure, replace damaged schools and health clinics, left the existing civil service and professional occupations intact, and, above all, protected the national oil economy, the outcomes of the invasion of Iraq could have been very different. Without the 60 percent unemployment that ravaged post-war Iraq, the recruitment of thousands of Iraqis into privatized sectarian militias and terrorist gangs might not have happened. However, the speed with which the Americans began building up to five long-term military bases in Iraq, and American special envoy Bremer enacted legislation to dismiss some half-million government employees, and to privatize and sell off Iraqi enterprises, suggests that the Americans originally had no intention of leaving quickly, and every intention of dismantling and privatizing Iraq's state enterprises and social services for foreign corporate investment. Wiping Iraq's economy clean, Klein argues, was the central objective of the war itself, as it had been for American policy in Latin America. Only the fierceness of Iraqi resistance had been underestimated.

Lessons for Peace in Political Economy Analysis

The central insight of political economy analysis is that promotion of world peace requires challenging the economic underpinnings of war. An important place to begin this challenge is with the international institutions set up to manage global economic interdependence after the Second World War—the International Monetary Fund and the World Bank. IMF policies that promote privatization, deregulation, and cuts to government social spending are held responsible for impoverishing masses of people in pursuit of free-market investment opportunities for corporations. In this sense the protests against World Trade Organization meetings in Seattle in November 1999 and Hong Kong in December 2005 are directly linked to the anti-war protest movement.

In her optimistic conclusion to her analysis of global disaster capitalism, Klein suggests that this backlash against IMF policies has begun (2007, 523–561). A number of countries in Latin America, including Venezuela, Argentina, Bolivia, and Uruguay, have reverted from military dictatorships to democracies. People have voted in leaders that support re-nationalization of key industries, socialist economic programs to promote land reform and greater income equality, and that eschew IMF loans and policies. The IMF's lending portfolio worldwide has dropped from $81 billion in 2005 to $11 billion in 2008, and the ratio of IMF loans to Latin America has dropped from 80 percent in 2005 to 1 percent (Klein 2007, 550). Neighbouring countries are experimenting with forms of trade bartering to avoid IMF loans.

Prospects for peace in the world will also require drastic reorganization of Western economies to reduce global competition for oil. So long as Western governments are desperate to secure and expand access to cheap oil in a context of declining supplies and increasing demand, these governments, Canada included, are predisposed to support the military intervention in the Middle East. Promotion of alternative energy sources and energy conservation are thus directly linked to the anti-war movement.

Efforts to develop a UN international treaty to control the arms trade, spearheaded by Britain since 2005, hold out the possibility of limiting the escalation of profits from the trade that underpins the military-industrial complex and the culture of militarism that it spawns.

 # War as a Social Construction

"Truth is so precious that she should always be attended by a bodyguard of lies."

—Winston Churchill (cited in Rutherford 2004, 60)

Interpretive perspectives study the language of war, the meaning-making practices through which governments and members of a society come to understand engagement in large-scale political violence as reasonable, justifiable, and even "normal" activity, that they will sustain for long periods of time (Jackson 2005, 1–7). Wars are always exceptional. They involve sanctioned engagement in kinds of behaviour that are universally considered criminally deviant in normal times—the deliberate killing of people seen as "enemies" and the destruction of their property on a very large scale. Wars consume enormous economic resources and entail the virtual certainty of large-scale loss of lives of people in one's own society. Wars require consent of masses of people—their active involvement and their acquiescence. Without such consent, it is very difficult for those in power to sustain war for any length of time, especially in democracies. Consent has to be continually renewed; it is always contested and never completely achieved.

Hence, wars have to be made to look meaningful to vast numbers of people across widely differing social positions. Techniques of persuasion, both the public language through which wars are described and accounted for, and the practices that embed these dominant meanings in policy, are fundamental to the conduct of war.

Symbolic interaction explores the subjective meanings or definitions of the situation that guide how people in diverse situations and experiences come to understand war. In this approach the aim of sociological analysis is not to determine the "correct" definition, but to enable people with very different views on war to move beyond stereotyped views of "enemies" and opponents, to better understand how people in different locations meaningfully come to see the same events in different ways. Labelling theory and drama highlight techniques of persuasion and how they work to influence prevailing definitions of what is happening. Ethnomethodological analysis shifts the line of questioning to explore how people work their way through the torrent of information from multiple sources about ongoing war as it pours into their daily lives. The strategies that people use to selectively pay attention, and to cut the torrent into sets of meaningful "events," mediate the potential impact of media messages. Not all messages are equally powerful, nor are they equally effective with different audiences. Analysis of the discourse or ways of talking about war favoured by professionals and people in positions of authority clarify how public opinion is moulded into consensus around governing agendas for war. Discourse analysis pays close attention not just to what is found in official pronouncements, but what is omitted and how nuances of meaning are slanted to promote preferred views of war and to discredit others. Institutional ethnography explores how dominant meanings become enacted into policy and embedded in the routine everyday practices of people working in, and clients of, multiple institutional settings that are drawn into the ruling relations of waging war. The activities of vast numbers of people in disparate settings, who normally never see or know each other, are coordinated through policy statements, or texts, that encompass bodies of rules and regulations. The ruling practices standardize the meanings or definitions of situations that guide how people in multiple settings recognize and respond to events, and so accomplish what it means to be a nation at war.

Interpretive perspectives raise profoundly difficult questions about how wars happen. Why is opposition to war so limited that war can be accurately described as "a pervasive feature of recorded human history"? How do governments in democratic societies persuade people to support going to war? How do so many people acquiesce to political violence on a massive scale, with all the associated practices of suspending civil liberties, diverting vast sums of money from other government functions and social services, and risking violent retaliation against their own communities? How are hundreds of thousands of young men and women persuaded to join military units, take up weapons, and go off to fight against strangers in foreign lands? How are others persuaded that acting as suicide bombers, to kill themselves while killing enemy "others," is how they are willing to die? How do so many people come to accept as normal, and reasonable, that their governments will invest taxes, and their scientists invest careers, in developing more and more destructive weapons, even when not waging war? How do politicians and party members come to accept that it is reasonable to cooperate with often unsavoury foreign governments, to set up military prisons, to use torture as a means to extract information, and the like? How do people who have lived together as neighbours, often for generations, come to redefine each other as enemies, and as legitimate targets for militarized aggression in civil wars? These questions are explored below with reference to two very different kinds of war: the civil war in Yugoslavia between 1990 and 1999, and the "war on terror" associated with the invasion of Iraq in 2003.

Yugoslavia 1990–1999: Orchestrating Civil War

The civil wars in Yugoslavia resulted in the breakup of what had been widely regarded as a relatively open, progressive, and stable socialist society into a collection of ethnically defined mini-states. This breakup involved violent ethnic cleansing at a level that justified outside intervention to force warring factions apart. This intervention was the first major military engagement by the US and NATO following the collapse of the Soviet Union and the end of the Cold War era. It was the first test of Pax Americana—of how international bodies like the United Nations, and military alliances like NATO, would police deviance in the post Cold-War Empire.

From the standpoint of Yugoslavia the core question is how Yugoslav people, who had lived together as "Yugoslavs" without military conflict for more than 40 years since the Second World War, came to think of themselves as distinctively Slovene, Serb, Croat, Bosnian Muslim, or Kosovar Albanian, and as enemies to each other. Interpretive theories explore the active practices of political leaders that constructed and fostered such identity shifts, and how these constructions became internalized by people living in Yugoslavia. From the standpoint of outsiders, the focus is on active practices through which specific groups in the conflict came to be defined as "victims" and "aggressors," and thus who was defined as warranting military support and who deserved to be bombed.

Leadership and Political Propaganda

In 1990 the political system in Yugoslavia switched suddenly from a centralized one-party communist state without organized opposition parties to post-communist "democratic elections." Aspiring political leaders within constituent republics of Yugoslavia were able to frame the widespread desire for greater freedom from the centralized state apparatus within the familiar political discourse of ethnic nationalist interests, and to do so without any well-organized political opposition (Denitch 1994). The kind of leaders who came to the fore were those most skilled at manipulating an ethnic nationalist message for political power—Tudjman in Croatia, Izetbegovic in Bosnia, and Milosevic in Serbia. Milosevic was distinct in that he attracted both Serbian nationalist and centrist socialist votes. As the most numerous and the most widely dispersed of the officially recognized "nationalities" within Yugoslavia, Serbs had the most interest in keeping a centralized federation.

These newly elected leaders who came to power on ethnic nationalist platforms had vested political interests in bolstering those sentiments among their electorates in order to strengthen their own power base. Each of them engaged in mass propaganda to promote ethnic-based identities and fears, perhaps because each of them judged the initial support for those messages to be weak. The techniques they used included a selective revisiting of history to exaggerate politically useful events, pervasive discourses of historical and contemporary victimhood, embellished with concepts of "genocide" and even "holocaust" analogous to the Jewish experience, and control over mass media to promote their message and stifle criticism (MacDonald 2002). These political myths were performative in the sense that they were systematically developed to serve as a basis for generating and justifying policy (MacDonald 2002, 54). They were used to legitimate claims to territory, to justify retaliatory or self-defensive violence, and to appeal to outsiders to intervene militarily on the side of their group.

The Serb leader, Slobodan Milosevic, organized a mass rally to commemorate the 600th anniversary of the historical defeat of the "Serb nation" by Ottoman Turks in the Battle of Kosovo in 1389, framing it as analogous to the fall of Jerusalem for the Jews (MacDonald 2002, 71). The myth also served to strengthen the claim that Kosovo was part of Serbia. Milosevic also promoted a collective sense of historic Serb victimhood by frequent and exaggerated reference to war crimes against the Serbs perpetrated by the Croat Ustasa party that collaborated with Nazi Germany during the Second World War. Serbia's own history of wartime violence was sanitized and justified as righteous freedom fighting, defending themselves from genocide, and saving Yugoslavia from fascism.

The Croat political leader, Franjo Tudjman, and his supporters promoted a similar discourse of ancient and contemporary victimhood, casting the expansionist goals of a "Greater Serbia" as principal villain. He stifled criticism of his propaganda by purging any media editors, managers, and journalists who challenged him, including all journalists with mixed Serb/Croat parentage (MacDonald 2002, 102–103). When he further purged Serbs from the police force, universities, and most government bureaucracies, he faced no backlash in the mass media.

The sense of distinctive national identities and historic grievances that Ignatieff terms "the narcissism of minor difference" (1997, 34) were actively orchestrated by political leaders to strengthen their basis of electoral support and political clout. Myths of suffering dug up from half a century earlier served as resources in the conflicts of the 1990s, whipping up the sense that conflict was inevitable. Yet the European Union that these same leaders courted and hoped to join had brought together bitter enemies from the World War. Ethnic conflict was not inevitable. It had to be constructed.

Classical functionalist analysis assumes the salience of ethnic identity as primordial signifier of personal identity, rooted in family. This assumption, however, cannot be easily applied to Yugoslavia. Census data for the 1990s recorded intermarriage between Serbs and Croats as 20 percent of the population, with far higher proportions in larger cities like Sarajevo and Dubrovnik (Denitch 1994, 6). Substantial numbers of urban dwellers did not identify themselves as Muslim, Serb, or Croat in the census, but simply as "Yugoslav." When extended family members of the one-fifth of intermarried couples—their parents, siblings, uncles, aunts, and cousins—are counted, close to half the population of pre-war multi-ethnic Bosnia likely had both Serbs and Croats among their close relatives. The civil wars tore families apart. The civil wars that destroyed Yugoslavia were not driven by pressure from below, Denitch argues, but precipitated by policy decisions and mass propaganda of the leaders of various republics, reinforced by external support.

Policies of Ethnic Separatism

Franjo Tudjman began to push the objective of political independence for Croatia as soon as he came to power in 1990, under the inflammatory motto of "Croatia for the Croats." When Serbs, who formed 13 percent of the population, voted to remain with the Yugoslav federation, Tudjman denounced them as rebels. The leaders of Germany and the European Union enormously boosted the legitimacy of Tudjman's actions when they accorded international recognition to Croatia as an independent state just a few months later, in December 1991 and January 1992.

In Bosnia, the Muslim leader Izetbegovic followed Croatia's lead in declaring unilateral independence from Yugoslavia in October 1991. Bosnia was far more ethnically mixed than Croatia, with about 40 percent Muslim, 34 percent Serb, and 18 percent Croat. Political leaders from the three ethnic divisions were close to signing an agreement in March 1992 that would have seen Bosnia remain within a modified Yugoslav federation (Hudson 2003, 109), but American diplomats persuaded the Muslim leader, Izetbegovic, to hold out for an independent Bosnia.

Political leaders in the European Union favoured quick recognition of Bosnian independence, with international protection, even though the American Central Intelligence Agency (CIA) itself warned that civil war would break out if this independence claim were recognized, as 70 percent of the citizens would be deemed ethnic minorities (Hudson 2003, 102).

The swift international recognition accorded to these independence declarations by leaders of ethnic sub-groups, Denitch argues (1994, 81), played a decisive role in promoting the legitimacy of their regimes. The discourse of "right to self-determination," when applied to ethnic subgroups in mixed populations, promoted the brutal ethnic cleansing policies that followed. Once acts of brutality begin to happen, they promote a cycle of revenge, which turns nationalist claims that ethnically mixed populations can not live together into self-fulfilling prophecies. Provoking brutality can thus be useful strategy to mobilize support.

The Politics of Revenge and Fear

Major transformations in sense of self-identity and frames of thinking are involved in turning what were once mostly ordinary young men into committed members of paramilitary groups capable of massacring their former neighbours. They have to internalize an extreme version of ethnic nationalism and sense of victimhood, and also come to frame their actions towards members of presumed hostile ethnic groups in terms of notions of collective guilt for past injustices and justifiable revenge (Oberschall 2000; Enloe 2006, Ch. 7). Socialization through intensive peer pressure to show solidarity and ethnic loyalty in the all-male militarized microculture of a militia is part of the process through which such values are learned.

Enloe investigates the history of one ethnic-Serb man living in Sarajevo in Bosnia, who was convicted in 1992 of murder and mass rape of Bosnian Muslim women. Just two years earlier he was an unskilled worker in a textile factory, with no previous history of violence and no involvement in nationalist politics. His sister was married to a Bosnian Muslim man. Boris Herak ran away from Sarajevo when the city came under siege, and was "taken in" by a Serb militia group who offered shelter and protection. It was through older men in this group, Enloe argues, that he learned to think about his own life as an impoverished factory worker as linked to a larger history of how Muslim Ottoman imperialists had oppressed his ancestors, and how their Muslim descendants were now oppressing and threatening people like him in Bosnia (Enloe 2006, 105).

Among Yugoslav people generally, the way they thought about militia activity in their communities was also shifting. In normal times, groups of young men threatening people with guns can expect harsh reaction and punishment, but in the political climate of increasing insecurity and fear people reacted differently. In northwest Bosnia in April 1992, about the same time that the European Union officially recognized the Bosnian Muslim leader's claim to independence, Serb paramilitaries were able to invade and take over the government of the city of Prijedor and the nearby town of Kozarak, without organized opposition from moderate Serbs (Oberschall 2000). They executed a hit-list of Muslim leaders, looted and burned their houses, and fired non-Serbs from their jobs.

The core question that Oberschall explores is why moderate Serb citizens permitted Serb paramilitaries to commit such atrocities in their communities. Classic explanations of state breakdown or persecution as a minority did not apply in Prijedor. It had been a peaceful city until the paramilitaries came. Serbs and Muslims were each about 40 percent of the population. Serbs were not an oppressed minority in the town. They held important positions in communications, medical, and social services, and were well represented in local government. There was no anarchy, no state breakdown, and there had been no spontaneous violence between Serbs and non-Serbs. Yet town residents expressed a pervasive sense of impending crisis, deriving this sense not from immediate experience but from the propaganda that they heard from Serb, Croat, and Muslim political leaders. The messages they cited included reports that Serbs in Kosovo were experiencing "genocidal" terror, and that Muslims were planning to take over Yugoslavia, cut Europe in half with a line from Bosnia to Kosovo and Albania to Turkey, and replace the population with Muslims. Serb refugees in the town who had fled their village claimed that Muslims had a hit-list of names drawn up and that they intended to kill Serb men and enslave Serb women in harems. They believed this because "they had heard it on the radio" and "had heard that Serbs had uncovered this plan." Yet in their actual experience, they acknowledged that their Muslim village neighbours had always been good and decent people, who had never harmed them.

In normal times, such narratives would have been dismissed as absurd, but in the crisis frame generated by mass propaganda, villagers found such stories plausible. Seen through this crisis frame, the actions of Serb paramilitaries seemed reasonable. Ordinary people felt they could not avoid taking sides in the ethnic polarization. As one Serb taxi driver in Prijedor expressed it: "No one wanted the war, but if I don't fight, someone from my side will kill me, and if my Muslim friends don't fight, other Muslims will kill them" (Oberschall 2000).

Propaganda for External Support

Political leaders inside Yugoslavia all lobbied for international support for their causes of separation from, or preservation of, the Yugoslav federation. International recognition for independence claims was a critical stage in gaining influence and legitimacy in their home states. As the civil wars progressed, international support in the form of money, weapons, and ultimately direct military intervention by the United States and other NATO members to bomb opposing forces was decisive to the outcome of the wars. All this international support went to the breakaway ethnic nationalist leaders, Tudjman in Croatia and Izetbegovic in Bosnia. No Western power sided with the Serb leader, Slobodan Milosevic, even though he was elected president of Serbia from 1989 to 1997 and elected president of the Federal Republic of Yugoslavia from 1997 to his electoral defeat in 2000. Traditionally Russia had been Serbia's closest ally, but Russia was undergoing drastic internal upheaval with the collapse of communism and brutal transition to a free-market economy. It offered no military assistance to Yugoslavia-Serbia, although it did intervene to help broker peace deals.

Western political discourse and media representation largely described the conflict breaking Yugoslavia apart as caused by aggressive Serbian expansionism. Western involvement, and particularly the two episodes when NATO bombed Serb forces, was justified as "humanitarian intervention" to save Muslims in Bosnia and Kosovo from violent ethnic cleansing. The Serb leader was variously represented as an extreme nationalist, a warlord and "the Serb butcher" (Johnstone 2002, 17). Serbs were likened to Nazis and Milosevic himself to Hitler. Whenever in doubt, the Western media attributed all atrocities to Serbs (Johnstone 2002, 65).

Rather than debating the factual accuracy of these representations, interpretive theory focuses attention on active practices by political leaders that worked to construct and circulate these international characterizations of the conflict.

Managing Global Media

The Croatian government hired the American-based public relations firm Ruder Finn Global Public Affairsto manage communications with influential politicians outside Croatia. The firm signed a contract "to promote a strong leadership role for the United States in the Balkans" (Johnstone 2002, 69). Advisors from Ruder Finn established a crisis communication centre to manage contacts with the US, British, and French media. They coached ministers in how to write press releases and letters for foreign media, how to manage press conferences, and how to handle personal contacts with foreign politicians, including with US congressmen that the company sponsored to visit Croatia to see selected examples of wartime destruction. By the summer of 1992, Serb, Muslim, and Croat forces had all set up prison camps for activists who threatened their respective territorial control. Ruder Finn focused attention exclusively on the Serb camps. The agency circulated to foreign media an iconic image of "a thin man behind barbed wire" with the caption "Ethnic cleansing means camps, rapes, murders, executions, and mass deportations of non-Serb populations . . . a murderous ideology" (Johnstone 2002).

Press releases sent out by Ruder Finn were riddled with factual lies, Johnstone maintains, but foreign media, predisposed to believe the worst about the Serbs, never checked the sources. The iconic "thin man" photograph was one such construction: the man was not in a camp, and the barbed wire surrounded the photographer, not the man (Johnstone 2002, 73). An account of one girl who was sexually assaulted by three Serb prison guards was embellished for foreign press as "maybe tens of thousands of assaults against Muslim and Croat women in Serb prison camps in northern Bosnia" (Johnstone 2002, 79). The State Commission for War Crimes in Sarajevo also claimed 20 000 well-documented cases of rape intended to force Muslim women to conceive Serb children. No documentation and no babies ever materialized, Johnstone claims (2002, 81). The International Red Cross later concluded that while there were abuses on all sides, there was no evidence of systematic rapes. The propaganda worked, however, to establish in foreign media and political discourse the belief that Serbs were guilty of human rights atrocities on a massive scale. In May 1999 the US State Department issued a report entitled "Erasing History: Ethnic Cleansing in Kosovo" in which it was alleged that 90 percent of Kosovo Albanians had been driven from their homes. The claim was later proven wildly inaccurate (Johnstone 2002, 89), but it provided justification for bombing Serb positions in Kosovo. The vast majority of Kosovars who fled their homes actually did so to escape the NATO bombing.

Techniques to vilify Serbs in Western political discourse and media representations, and thus bolster Western military intervention in the conflicts, included "black propaganda"—staging attacks on members of one's own community in order to blame the violence on enemies, and repeated provocation of the enemy to incite retaliation that would discredit them. During the four-year siege of the city of Sarajevo in Bosnia, Serbs were held responsible for three explosions in 1992, 1994, and 1995, which killed civilians, including people standing in a breadline and in a marketplace. Later, French and British investigators concluded that the attacks had been orchestrated by Muslims (Johnstone 2002, 66–67; Hudson 2003, 116). This was possibly done by Islamic fundamentalist fighters recruited from Iran, who culturally had little in common with the secular pork-eating and wine-drinking Muslims in Bosnia.

Another atrocity that was questionably blamed on Serbs was the massacre of 45 Kosovar Albanians in the village of Racak in Kosovo on 15 January 1999, a massacre that helped to legitimate NATO bombing of Serb positions in Kosovo. The Serb account, which was later supported by forensic investigation, was that members of the US-backed Kosovo Liberation Army (the KLA) provoked Serb soldiers to pursue them into the village by killing five Serb police and two Albanians. The KLA later trucked in corpses and invited foreign "verifiers" to witness the apparent mass execution (Johnstone 2002, 243; Hudson 2003, 167).

The worst mass killing in the Yugoslav conflicts occurred in the town of Srebrenica, the site of a UN "safe haven" for Bosnian Muslim civilians, where between 3000 to 8000 Bosnian Muslim men were massacred by Serb militias in July 1995. The Srpska Serb government acknowledged the atrocity and issued an official apology in June 2005, but contested the circumstances leading up to the violence and the numbers killed (Hudson 2003, 117; Johnstone 2002, 110). The Serb version of events was that the haven was being used to launch military strikes against Serb communities in the surrounding area. Serb militias blockaded the town and eventually stormed it with tanks, only to find it virtually undefended. Muslim fighters had withdrawn and remaining UN peacekeepers were too few in number to protect the civilians. In the violence that followed, Serb militiamen separated Bosnian Muslim men from women and children, and summarily executed many of them.

An American-sponsored International Criminal Tribunal set up in The Hague indicted Bosnian Serb leader Radovan Karadzic for war crimes on 24 July 1995 for the Srebrenica massacre, defining it as "genocide" (Johnstone 2002, Ch. 2). The failure to adequately defend or to demilitarize Srebrenica, Johnstone argues, was part of a political game. US diplomats were pressing Bosnian Muslims to simplify the division of territory by letting the Serbs keep the area around Srebrenica in return for leaving western Bosnia, a shift that resulted in a drop in overall territory held by Bosnian Serbs from 70 percent to 40 percent. What the outside world learned at the time, however, was only that Serbs were guilty of genocide. Western media represented the conflict as one in which rebel Serbs had "seized 70 percent of Bosnian territory," and the Bosnians were fighting for control over "occupied territories" (Hudson 2003, 113). What this representation obscured was that Serbs had lived in the area for more than three centuries, and there were only about 500 000 fewer Serbs in Bosnia than Muslims.

In summary, these multiple practices of information management resulted in extensive mass media coverage of the Yugoslav conflict in Europe and North America, but that coverage was selective and pervasively framed to support "humanitarian intervention" to counter the violent ethnic cleansing associated with Serbian expansionism. What people knew, or thought they knew, and specifically *how* they knew it, resulted in widespread public support for the US–NATO military engagement. There were always alternative representations, particularly in socialist publications and websites that analyzed the engagement as Western imperialism bent on destroying the socialist-oriented

Serbian-Yugoslav party (see the World Socialist website). However, these alternative frames never achieved credibility in Western mass media.

The prevailing image of the wars in Yugoslavia remains that of ethnic conflicts run wild, with Western military intervention as valuable assistance to prevent worse bloodshed. Social constructionist analysis reveals how pervasively and successfully political leaders within Yugoslavia, and their backers in the NATO alliance, worked to provoke these conflicts and to manipulate them for political and economic gain. Denitch sums up this view bluntly: "Yugoslavia did not die a natural death—it was murdered" (Denitch 1994, 69).

The War on Terror

On 20 September 2001, nine days after the terrorist attacks on the World Trade Centre and the Pentagon, American President George W. Bush declared a "War on Terror." The war he envisioned was defined very differently from conventional war in that the enemy was not a foreign government with a conventional army and a clearly defined territory. Rather, it was "a collection of loosely affiliated terrorist organizations known as al Qaeda," that numbered in the thousands and were spread across more than 60 countries.

By the following September 2002, the war on terror was elaborated in the *National Security Strategy of the United States* into what is often termed the "Bush Doctrine" of pre-emptive war. The United States claimed the right to use its military might against its perceived enemies to exact regime change to prevent such countries from developing highly destructive weapons, and to take such military action without constraint of international law or UN approval. This doctrine was put into practice six months later in March 2003 in the invasion of Iraq to remove the regime of Saddam Hussein. Two other countries, Iran and North Korea, were also named as part of the "axis of evil," and hence potential targets for pre-emptive war.

The United Nations Charter of 1948, born out of the horror of two world wars, defined invasion of a sovereign state as a violation of international law, and a war crime subject to international punishment. Preventive war—that is, military action to defend one's own country against imminent attack from another—is legitimate under international law, but pre-emptive war in the absence of imminent threat is not. Terrorism is a method rather than a defined enemy that can be clearly targeted. The wars launched against Afghanistan and Iraq required careful justification aimed at winning support or acquiescence of diverse constituencies. Interpretive theories explore how the American government and its supporters sought to generate and sustain a frame for thinking about these wars as inherently reasonable,

Nine days after terrorists attacked the World Trade Center, President Bush declared a global War on Terror.

Tamara Beckwith/Rex Features

good, and just military action. In official political discourse the 9/11 terrorist attacks provided that legitimation.

Discursive Practices in the "War On Terror"
On 11 September 2001, 19 hijackers of Middle Eastern origin living in America took over four American civilian airliners. Two airliners were deliberately crashed into the twin towers of the World Trade Centre in New York, a third crashed into the Pentagon buildings near Washington, and a fourth crashed into a field in Pennsylvania. A total of 2974 people were killed. Of the 19 hijackers, 15 were from Saudi Arabia, two from the United Arab Emirates, and one each from Egypt and Lebanon. In brief, these facts constitute the "event" that is referred to as 9/11.

News coverage in America pervasively invoked descriptions of shock and horror at the unprovoked murder of innocent people, tragedy for the thousands of families who lost loved ones, and heroism of those who took part in rescue operations. Official reactions across the world condemned the attacks. However, this response was not universal. In

Palestinian territories there were reports of jubilation in the streets, with an estimated three thousand demonstrators in Nablus waving flags and handing out sweets as victory signs. Affluent Egyptians in Cairo cheered more quietly, suggesting that maybe the hijackers got it right, and America got what it truly deserved (Bricmont 2007, 24–25).

These strikingly different reactions reflect vastly different frames of reference in thinking about the events. Palestinian demonstrators characterized the 9/11 attacks as "revenge" for America's unwavering support for Israel's militaristic and expansionist policies. Videotaped messages from Osama bin Laden, a leading organizer of Islamic resistance fighters against Soviet occupation of Afghanistan, characterized the 9/11 attacks as reasoned response to decades of American military interventions in Muslim countries, and specifically to rage at the presence of American military bases in the holy lands of Saudi Arabia.

To be effective in representing 9/11 as a justification for war, American political discourse needed to counter such hostile interpretations and to promote the alternative frame of American victimization and right to defensive revenge. Major political speeches, like President Bush's address to the nation on 20 September, are carefully crafted in advance by cabinet advisors and professional speech writers (Jackson 2005, 26). Texts are "released" for mass media publication, in this case by the Office of the Press Secretary. All President Bush's major speeches are readily available on the Internet (search for Bush Congress speech September 2001). These speeches are intended to be defining moments, to shape how audiences think about current events. They are also intentionally performative—designed to function as a base for future policy that may well be sketched out in the same speech, or follow-up speeches. Discourse analysis explores how such speeches work to create and sustain prevailing definitions of the situation, and to counter potentially damaging alternative frames (Jackson 2005, Ch. 2).

Bush's 20 September 2001 address opens with reference to the global outpouring of grief, sympathy, and support for America triggered by the horror of the 9/11 attacks, and then defines the event as "an act of war against our country . . . the first act of war on American soil in 136 years . . . except for one Sunday in 1941." This definition functions to justify war as reasonable retaliation. The oblique reference to "one Sunday in 1941" places 9/11 in the same interpretive frame as the Japanese attack on Pearl Harbor that justified America's entry into the Second World War.

The speech then unequivocally names the perpetrators of this act of war as "al Qaeda" defined as an Islamic extremist network of global reach led by Osama bin Laden, and further that this network influences and supports the Taliban regime that is brutalizing the people of Afghanistan. The speech then sets out the first policy: it warns the Taliban to surrender to

America immediately, and without negotiation or discussion, all al Qaeda leaders and every person in the support structure, to dismantle all terrorist training camps, release all foreign nationals in prison, and give full access for American inspectors to all training camps, or face immediate war.

The speech then shifts attention to the broader frame of "all terrorist groups of global reach." Without direct reference to the oppositional interpretations of 9/11 that was visible in the celebrations in Palestine, the speech works to address them through the frame of "Americans are asking, why do they hate us?" The answer: "They hate our freedoms . . ." The motives attributed to terrorists invoke classic themes of good or evil, civilization or barbarism, democracy and freedom or fascism, Nazism and totalitarianism, prosperous and pluralist global modernity or feudal tribalism. It is not just America but the entire modern world that terrorism targets, and in response to this evil, America's messianic role in the world is to fight for democracy and freedom.

Discourse analysis focuses attention not just on the points included in a political speech but also on relevant issues that are obscured or omitted. This speech is noticeably silent on the charges raised by bin Laden concerning the long and dark history of American political and military support for unpopular dictators in Middle Eastern countries, or military bases in Saudi Arabia. The speech also omits mention that 15 of the 19 hijackers were from Saudi Arabia. The target of America's revenge is to be the Taliban regime, not the House of Saud. Attention is focused on destruction of the World Trade Centre—symbol of global economic integration, economic freedom, and modernization. But the speech omits reference to the third aircraft hitting the Pentagon—symbol of America's global military supremacy. Among all the motives that President Bush attributed to the hijackers in his speech, there is no mention of the actual motives that bin Laden himself articulated. Al Qaeda's influence on and support for the Taliban is mentioned, but not the historic role that the American government itself played in promoting al Qaeda and the Taliban in Afghanistan. The impression Bush gives in his speech is that 9/11 had no history. It happened and America responds from that event forwards in time. The question: Why do they hate us? has been answered without reference to anything America might have done in the past. Nor does Bush elaborate any methods other than war for dealing with terrorism, or any possible relevance or role for the United Nations.

Propaganda as Performance: Making the Case for Wars

The Bush administration used its conception of 9/11 as "an act of war" by al Qaeda terrorists based in Afghanistan, and sheltered by the Taliban, to legitimate and justify America's invasion of Afghanistan. Aerial bombing of the Afghan cities of Kabul and Kandahar commenced on 7 October 2001. The link between 9/11 and the Afghan war, however, was tenuous in two respects. America did not have clear evidence that the Taliban regime was directly involved in or had foreknowledge of 9/11. Further, the bombing began even as the Taliban were trying to negotiate through Pakistan some way to hand over Osama bin Laden or to have him tried in an Islamic court (Jackson 2005, 141, citing Mahajan 2002, 30). These qualifications were not public knowledge when the war started. What the American public knew, or thought they knew, was that the Taliban aided and supported the terrorists who plotted and masterminded the devastating attack on America, and further that the regime was so fanatical and cruel, even to its own citizens, that all negotiation was impossible, and its destruction essential.

The link between 9/11 and the invasion of Iraq was more indirect and required more convoluted arguments. The carefully crafted 90-minute speech presented by US Secretary of State Colin Powell to the UN Security Council on 6 February 2003 was designed to make this case [for transcript, search for Colin Powell UN on the Internet]. Powell drew on an array of satellite intelligence photographs, taped conversations, and eyewitness accounts to argue that Saddam Hussein's government was hiding weapons of mass destruction from UN inspectors in mobile truck factories and dual-use facilities, that he was in direct contact with al Qaeda terrorists, and was negotiating to purchase materials needed to develop nuclear weapons.

Representatives of European and other member states in the UN Security Council, with the exception of Britain, were generally not persuaded that Powell had made the case for a UN-sanctioned invasion of Iraq. Most were not convinced by murky surveillance evidence. More importantly, they reasoned that whatever threat the Hussein regime might pose, it would be better dealt with by the continuation of UN sanctions and inspections than by military invasion (Rutherford 2004, 39). Fear of American militarism and growing religious fervour with which the Bush administration promoted America's role as world police force was more widespread than fear of Saddam Hussein's regime.

The American Public-Opinion Machine: Making the Case at Home

The administration's efforts to convince audiences to support the proposed invasion of Iraq met with far greater success among the American public. In its effort to "win hearts and minds" the State Department hired public relations consultants to continually monitor public concerns and responses to the most recent policy statements and messages (Rutherford 2004, 31–49). Public opinion polls were raised to the status of high-technology science. Polls were used to gauge the mood and concerns of different constituents, as a guide to formulating public statements, and then people were polled again to see how well the messages were working to win support for the government's war policies, to guide the next wave of propaganda. Used in these ways, polls do not simply measure existing public opinion, they also help to create that opinion. Pollsters are able to phrase questions and interpret results to create public impressions of "what the public thinks," which in turn influences how individuals evaluate their own thinking, and their willingness to go along with mainstream views.

The administration drew on a wide variety of motives to promote support for the war in Iraq from widely varied publics. The most important initial motive was to represent the Iraqi governing regime as a known terrorist threat, one that was developing and concealing weapons of mass destruction and giving support to members of the al Qaeda terrorist network. Public opinion polls showed widespread feelings of anger, belligerence, and insecurity among American people following the 9/11 attacks. No one could know whether America might soon be targeted again. People widely regarded swift and decisive retaliation for the carnage of 9/11 as essential to deter terrorists from future attacks. Debates about motives, historical grievances against America, or other excuses terrorists or their supporters might cite, were considered beside the point—nothing could justify the 9/11 carnage. Political messages about terrorist threats from Iraq fed directly into these feelings. In multiple public speeches, President Bush, along with senior government members, elided references to Iraq, al Qaeda, and 9/11 to create a subjective impression that they were linked, even though they could not give direct proof of such links. These messages were so successful that months after the war began, the majority of Americans polled believed that Saddam Hussein's regime was responsible for 9/11, and that the US army had actually discovered weapons of mass destruction in Iraq (Rutherford, 2004, 33; Hunt and Rygiel 2006, 8).

Opinion polls before the war indicated that most Americans were in favour of military action to oppose Saddam Hussein's regime, but with the qualification that they preferred a war supported by the United Nations, rather than Americans going in alone. These polls influenced the Bush administration to try to push the UN Security Council through Powell's speech. When this failed to win desired UN support, the Bush administration shifted its message at home to derogating the UN as an ineffectual bunch of clowns who shared America's assessment of the Iraqi regime but lacked the resolve to take action. In place of "UN support" the war rhetoric referred consistently to "coalition forces" and "the coalition of the willing" to convey the impression of extensive international participation with American forces.

Opinion polls revealed that the proposed invasion of Iraq was invoking widespread fears that it might result in another Vietnam-style quagmire with huge loss of civilian and American military lives. Official spokespersons responded with messages emphasizing that the Iraq war would be waged with precision weapons that would strike only military targets. Hence minimal ground troops would be involved in the assault, and minimal "collateral damage" of civilian dead expected. Opinion polls further revealed stronger public support for "humanitarian intervention," like the bombing of Kosovo to prevent Serbian genocide against hapless Albanian Muslims, than a war in which America was clearly the aggressor. Propaganda messages drew on these feelings with extensive reference to "coalition forces" as liberators, freeing oppressed Afghan and Iraqi people from brutal dictatorships. Images of atrocities inflicted on Afghan women and girls by barbaric Taliban forces received widespread coverage on American television, along with messages about how Saddam Hussein had murdered his own Kurdish citizens with mustard gas, and how he lived in sumptuous wealth while Iraqi citizens were dying of starvation under UN sanctions because Saddam would not give up his weapons of mass destruction. The "Israel Lobby" also worked feverishly to promote the case for war to achieve regime change in Iraq, seeing Saddam Hussein as a major threat to Israel. The US and Israel, they argued, were vulnerable to the same terrorist threats and thus had common interests in war (Mearsheimer and Walt 2006). Frequent invocation of God's blessing, and calling from God to rid the world of "evildoers" in President Bush's addresses to the nation, reinforced the message of humanitarian intervention, with America playing a messianic role in spreading freedom and democracy to the people of the Middle East and beyond.

In summary, the Bush administration's message for war worked on multiple levels to win support from constituencies with widely differing opinions and concerns. It built up a sense of exceptional grievance and victimhood associated with the 9/11 attacks, and catastrophic threat from rogue terrorist states that required forceful defensive action, patriotism, and pride in American military forces, science-fiction images of smart bombs and precision weapons, and humanitarian leadership to temper barbaric forces with freedom, democracy, and prosperity. It was a very strong message. Absent from the message was any direct reference to economic interests in controlling Iraqi oil or opening up the Iraqi economy for Western corporate ownership. For critics of capitalist rhetoric, "freedom" referenced free markets, open to Western commerce and investment, while "democracy" referred to a pro-Western, pro-business government free from socialist/communist/fundamentalist leanings. But these alternative meanings were not spelled out in official speeches.

The Power of Propaganda: Stifling the Anti-War Movement

The success of propaganda can be measured by the extent to which opponents adopt the language and assumptions of the dominant message, even while attempting to criticize it (Bricmont 2007). By this measure the Bush administration was very successful inside America. Republicans and Democrats in Congress overwhelmingly voted in favour of giving Bush the powers to wage war. The anti-war movement within America attracted only limited public support. The movement's messages, Bricmont argues, became trapped in the mainstream discourse by "guilt weapons" (Bricmont 2007, Ch. 6). If you are opposing the war then *you* are supporting the enemy—evil regimes like the Taliban and Saddam Hussein. If you don't support Saddam Hussein then *you* admit he is a ruthless dictator and murderer who ought to be deposed. If you don't support the war then what are *you* going to do to protect Afghan women from the Taliban, or to prevent Saddam from gassing Kurds again? How are *you* going to defend America from another 9/11 attack? How would *you* have prevented Hitler from murdering millions of Jews? And so on. Answers to such challenges require complex and nuanced responses with extensive information to which few people have access, and few audiences give time to listen.

People did voice more opposition to the war in Iraq than Afghanistan, mostly from the Marxist perspective, with slogans like: "It's the crude, dude" and "No blood for oil." These messages failed to gain legitimacy or momentum, in part because they were never picked up or responded to in official discourse. Anti-war protest marches were restricted and controlled by tightly defined permits and heavy police presence. Marches and rallies that did take place were consistently downplayed or ignored in the mass media (Nitsch 2008). Opinion polls in mid-March 2003 indicated that, while 47 percent of respondents had some misgivings about going to war without UN approval, most were already convinced that war was inevitable. Ninety percent of those polled had not participated in any anti-war demonstration and knew no one who had, and two-thirds had negative views of anti-war protesters (Rutherford 2004, 46).

The variety of motives invoked in support of war proved particularly powerful in undermining opposition. When any one or more of the motives were discredited, others filled the gap. Absence of evidence of weapons of mass destruction in Iraq, and absence of any proof of Iraqi involvement in 9/11, did not discredit the entire invasion because Saddam was still a known tyrant who had murdered his own citizens, who would stop at nothing to boost his own power, and without whom the ultimate goal of a free and democratic Iraq could emerge, and so on. Deposing him was still "the lesser evil" to doing nothing and leaving him in place (Ignatieff 2004,

163). Once the invasion began, invocation to patriotism, to "support the troops," and not to undermine their efforts by implied opposition, further stifled dissent.

Selling War Once the invasion of Iraq began, official propaganda about the conduct of the war kicked into high gear. The challenge for the Pentagon and the Bush administration was how to prevent the horror of the real wartime carnage from undermining public support. Pentagon elites shared the conviction that the Vietnam War was lost because hostile public opinion pressured Congress to cut funds. They were determined not to let this happen again, but were also aware that a total information blackout would be impossible in an era of global mass communications and free-wielding Internet. Information would have to be very carefully managed.

The Pentagon hired the global public relations firm of Hill and Knowlton to manage information about the war. This was the same firm that managed information for the Pentagon on the 1991 Gulf War and was responsible for the rumour that Iraqi soldiers had emptied Kuwaiti babies out of hospital incubators, leaving them to die on the floor (Rutherford 2004, 61). All government information on the war was coordinated through the new centralized Office of Global Communications. The office mandated the use of "coalition forces" to refer to the American-British forces, the phrase "war of liberation" to refer to the invasion, and "death squads" to refer to Iraqi resisters.

The Pentagon managed information on the conduct and progress of the war through a combination of official briefings and embedded reporters. Pentagon spokespersons instituted daily press conferences in time for breakfast television shows. They were thus able to give the official spin on events directly to the public without reporters being able to influence or "mediate" it. The US command headquarters at Doha, Qatar, gave daily "before" and "after" pictures designed to showcase precision bombing of selected targets. The Pentagon spent $250 000 to build a set in Qatar as a suitable backdrop for these media performances.

The Pentagon managed immediate reporting of the war through the new practice of embedding some 600 hand-picked journalists with the American armed forces (Rutherford 2004, 71). These journalists presented compelling details of troop experiences and activities, but overwhelmingly showed the war from the perspective of American troops. Embedded reporters sounded like soldiers, typically using "we" to refer to military activities (Gallagher 2008, 123). Non-stop 24-hour coverage of the war, especially by CNN, created the illusion for viewers of being in the field with the soldiers, watching the assault on Baghdad occurring in real time. But while viewers, like the soldiers, saw and heard the flash and thud of bombs smashing into distant targets, they did not see the carnage occurring in the city streets.

Also, by agreement with the government, the US media did not show images of American dead or American prisoners of war. It was possible to see such images for those who knew where to look on the Internet through the Arab television station Al Jazeera, broadcasting from Qatar, with correspondents stationed in Baghdad. However, such sources could be readily denounced as enemy propaganda. Images of soldiers dropping food and medicines over Afghan and Iraqi cities, rescuing aid workers, and handing out candy to children, boosted the image of humanitarian war.

Public relations experts at the Pentagon manufactured news events to support the war effort to the degree that fact blurred into pure fiction (Gallagher 2008). In April 2003, American commandos filmed themselves carrying out a daring mission to rescue an injured US soldier, Private Jessica Lynch, who had been captured by Iraqi forces. Video footage was played over and over on American television showing the rescue team rushing Lynch from the Iraqi hospital to a waiting army helicopter as the team fought off sniper fire from nearby buildings. The attached story cited "anonymous government sources" describing how Private Lynch had fought fiercely against her captors, shooting several enemy soldiers and emptying her weapon before being stabbed and finally taken prisoner, and raped by her captors (Gallagher 2008, 126).

It later turned out that Private Lynch actually rolled her vehicle in an accident and was knocked out. She never did fire her weapon or shoot anyone or get stabbed, and was not raped. Moreover there were no Iraqi soldiers at the hospital and no sniper fire during the "rescue." Hospital staff had actually tried to return Lynch to American lines more than once but American forces forced them to turn back. Fox News drew huge audiences when it kept showing the rescue video. However, when ABC News attempted objective reporting of the fabricated event, they apparently received hundreds of complaints from viewers that they were "undercutting the military." American audiences seemed to prefer the simulation to the reality. ABC staff actually invited viewers to imagine how Lynch might have been raped, even though she had no memory of it.

More revealing of American fabrication of their young white woman soldier as hometown hero is the evidence that an African American woman soldier, Shoshana Johnson, was captured in the same episode as Lynch, held prisoner for 22 days, and shot in both legs, but no video was taken of her ordeal and she never became a media hero—while Lynch was offered a million-dollar film contract (Brittain 2006, 82–83). Brittain notes further that Private Lori Poestewa, a member of Lynch's military convoy, was the first Native American woman to die while on combat duty, but her death received little attention. Gallagher concludes that the Bush administration deliberately hired simulation experts to continually manufacture

hyper-real spectacles that bore little connection to real life (Gallagher 2008, 120).

Media outlets drew pervasively on familiar cultural themes of adventure movies to frame the torrent of disconnected images of war that swamped the 24/7 coverage (Rutherford 2004, 132–141). These themes include tragedy, adventure, science-fiction, action, human interest, mystery, comedy, and farce. Both audiences and journalists risked being drawn in to the movie-style theatre of the show, with the emotional detachment that they use to watch Hollywood movies.

Media Acquiescence Why were the mass media apparently so complicit in support of the war? Chomsky's characterization of America as a "propaganda state" needs qualification in that the American journalists do not function as captive mouthpieces of the state, as did writers under Goebbels' control in Nazi Germany (Rutherford 2004, 184–188). What needs to be explained is why there was such broad consensus in mainstream American mass media in support of the war in Iraq, in spite of strong legal protection for freedom of speech and freedom of the press (Shah 2008). A powerful set of influences pushed media towards support for "the semantic politics of terror" (Cottle 2006, 20). These included direct and self-imposed censorship of journalists, military control over embedded journalists, a sense of deference towards political and military elites, the dramatic appeal of real-time coverage of war, the importance of appearing sufficiently patriotic to maintain audience ratings, and deeper corporate profit motives.

Important structural features predispose mass media to present primarily the official administration viewpoint. US mass media are mostly privately-owned commercial enterprises that depend on advertising revenues and subscriptions. They cannot risk seriously upsetting big corporate advertisers, or losing mass audience ratings by taking stands that may appear unpatriotic. Global multinational corporate owners like Disney, AOL-Time Warner (owners of CNN), Viacom, General Electric (owners of NBC), and Robert Murdoch's News Corp, which owns FOX (Shah 2008, 47), share the mindset of global free markets. General Electric is itself a military contractor. American government advisors met with heads of media corporations in November 2001 to discuss patriotism and war coverage. The attorney general, John Ashcroft, warned critics of restrictions on free speech that their tactics would aid terrorists and erode national unity (Jackson 2005, 170). These major media outlets cooperated by refusing to sell airtime to peace coalition MoveOn.org trying to advertise anti-war messages (Rutherford 2004, 45).

Mundane practical considerations for doing the job of daily news production pressures journalists to rely heavily on official sources for information, because they are quick, cheap, readily available, and credible sources. There are also real limits to what anyone, including journalists, can ultimately learn about the shadowy world of global terrorism (Jenkins 2003, 138). Conspiracy theories abound but most of them are bogus. Journalists who cite unqualified sources risk harming their reputation for serious reporting.

Journalists depend on the good will of federal law enforcement and intelligence agencies to get credible information, and so cannot question the credibility of these sources too closely. Journalists generally know that officials will use them from time to time to plant questionable information leaks and slanted coverage, but consider it worth the price. CNN journalists once used Arab and Palestinian personnel in 2002 to cover the Israeli invasion of the West Bank. They obtained strikingly different views of events, but it cost them dearly. They were cut out of interviews and briefings with senior Israeli sources, excluded from scenes of Israeli military actions, got no breaking news, and risked being replaced on the regional satellite system with the more pro-Israeli Fox Network (Jenkins 2003, 143–144). CNN reportedly made amends by offering a series of large interviews with families of Israeli terror victims, and they promised to be vigilant in future against "pro-Arab bias." A CNN executive aid also reported getting 6000 email messages in a single day from the American "Israel Lobby" complaining about a story that Lobbyists saw as critical of Israel (Mearsheimer and Walt 2006, 13).

Speeches from government sources are often broadcast live, excluding critical comments (Jackson 2005, 167). Networks also relied heavily on the expertise of military analysts, usually retired senior officers, for commentary on the progress of the war in Iraq, and these analysts in turn relied on their insider information from Pentagon elites to retain their status as informed spokespersons for the networks. Only some years later did internal Pentagon documents, obtained through the Freedom of Information Act, reveal just how tightly these analysts were being manipulated to reproduce Pentagon briefings as "their own ideas," and monitored to ensure conformity (Barstow 2008). What the networks also did not know, or did not care to ask questions about, was that most of these military analysts had conflicting interests in that they were working as lobbyists for corporations seeking lucrative military contracts.

These patterns of close working relationships between media, government officials, the Pentagon, and the military-industrial complex help to explain how the official government-Pentagon account of the invasion of Iraq came to prevail in mainstream media coverage. However, the consensus was never total and never secure. In liberal democracies, Cottle argues, there is a strong expectation among audiences that journalists will provide balanced information rather than propaganda, and professionalism among journalists themselves reinforces this expectation. Independent journalism and oppositional accounts did challenge the pro-war message.

Cottle estimates that about 74 percent of media coverage fit the simplistic frames of reporting disconnected events without in-depth analysis, or relaying statements from people in authority. Exposé or investigative journalism comprised only a small 0.3 percent of all news coverage. This means that out of over three hundred hours of television coverage, there was about one hour of critical investigative work. The major reason is that such work is so expensive and time-consuming. The kind of research that goes into a book like Naomi Klein's *Shock Doctrine* takes a tremendous research commitment.

Intermediate levels of coverage that used more complex frames of contest and contention—presenting either two opposing views, or an array of voices—made up about 19 percent of media coverage. Here the major limitation on American media coverage of the war was the consensus that developed between Republican and Democratic parties in Congress to support the war (Bricmont 2007, 156). Rival party members may have focused on different motives—military might, economic advantage, protecting Israel's interests, or humanitarian intervention, but their consensus around going to war meant that journalists had limited contest or contention to work with. Only by 2008, when Democratic presidential candidate Barack Obama, and to a lesser extent Hillary Clinton, began campaigning on the platform of the Iraq war as a big mistake, could journalists get easy access to oppositional frames. In contrast, in Canada, where political support for Canada's military involvement in Afghanistan was divided, journalists could present contested views of the war. In 2008 the CBC presented a series on Canada's failing mission in Afghanistan, and the *Globe and Mail* prepared a series on the Taliban's view of the war, revealing that most were fighting to get foreign troops out and an Islamic government in, with no interest in global jihad, al Qaeda leaders, or terrorism.

Media coverage alone is insufficient to explain the limited anti-war sentiment among the American public. Uniformity in American mainstream media coverage reflected uniformity of thinking not only within Congress, but across multiple levels of opinion leaders, within churches, schools, universities, professional associations, and pressure groups (Jackson 2005, 20). Social actors at all these levels contributed to spreading the message of fear of terrorism, as they had contributed to fear of communism during the Cold War era. This wider climate of fear and insecurity helped to discredit critical alternative accounts of war that were available.

Institutionalization of Fear and Insecurity

The power of discourse lies in the extent to which it becomes translated into practical policy initiatives that build the dominant interpretations into the everyday working activities of major social institutions. The Bush administration began the process of building the discourse of "war on terror" into domestic institutions with the announcement in the 20 September 2001 speech of a new Department of Homeland Security. On 26 October 2001, Bush signed the USA PATRIOT Act into law. This massive 342-page Act covered 350 subject areas, 40 federal agencies, and carried 21 legal amendments (Jackson 2005, 14). The acronym USA PATRIOT stands for "Uniting and Strengthening of America to Provide Appropriate Tools Required to Intercept and Obstruct Terrorism." Provisions of the act gave officials extraordinary surveillance powers to execute nationwide search warrants, to tap emails, electronic address books and computers, to view bank records, and to conduct roving wiretaps on phones anywhere. People who use the Internet to search "suspicious" websites like Al Jazeera were warned they could be watched. Officials were also authorized to detain immigrants without charge for two weeks on suspicion of supporting terrorism, and to deport immigrants who raise money for organizations deemed to be possibly supporting terrorist activity. The secretary of state gained the power to designate any group, foreign or domestic, as "terrorist," and these powers were not subject to review. The new Department of Homeland Security incorporated the immigration and naturalization service, the Coast Guard, Customs, the Federal Emergency Management Agency, and others. The government allocated well over $100 billion to homeland security alone in the first two years.

Homeland security—or in effect the institutionalization of fear of terrorism—operates across multiple bureaucracies to coordinate the activities of vast numbers of workers at all levels of bureaucracy (Jackson 2005, 16–22). At the top policy level is guiding language of core principles and assumptions that form the basis of policy. These principles were reiterated in the more than 6000 public speeches by officials in the first two years after 9/11. At the second level are the mass of new laws, policy documents, and strategy statements that define the work of policy administrators. At the third and largest level are the internal operations manuals, rules, and standard operating procedures, woven together by interdepartmental memos, emails, and the like, which direct the routine everyday work practices of people doing their jobs in hundreds of agencies and institutions involved in counterterrorism. These millions of pages of text routinize and control how ordinary people go about ordinary activities of using government services, identifying themselves, using public transportation, mailing parcels, going cross-border shopping, visiting relatives abroad, and the like. The PATRIOT Act was re-authorized with a few amendments in July 2005, and again signed into law on 9 March 2006.

These institutional practices have become so deeply embedded into routine everyday work of so many organizations, jobs, and activities that they will be extremely difficult to reverse, even by a new administration opposed to the PATRIOT Act. The practices reinforce a culture of fear and insecurity that drives masses of people not only to acquiesce in their loss of civil liberties, but also to actively demand that search and surveillance procedures be improved to allay their fears of terrorism.

Such extreme versions of homeland security laws and practices have not been instituted in Canada, so that reminders to be fearful are not part of everyday life in Canada. Canadians have also so far escaped a serious terrorist attack. But many heed the warning of US Ambassador Paul Cellucci that they need to contribute to American homeland security systems if Canada expects to depend on the US for protection from terrorism. The combination of security certificates, greatly heightened security checks at all airports, demands for passports to cross the once-undefended borders between Canada and the US, and a series of highly publicized terrorism charges against Muslims living in Canada, work to sustain a sense that what is "normal" has changed (Sharma 2006). In Canada anti-terrorism regulations work through the seemingly innocuous bureaucratic label of the Department of Citizenship and Immigration. They target "non-whites" and "those perceived to be Muslims" as national security threats.

Lessons for Peace from the Social Constructionist Perspective

The strength of symbolic interactionist research is its potential to make understandable and meaningful to multiple participants in military conflict how others define the situation of war, and how they think and experience their lives. Resistance to the politics of ethnic separatism requires the ability to "take the standpoint of the other." Ideally, journalistic coverage of war needs to move outside the limits of embedded journalism to carry coverage from the standpoint of opponents, to interview Serbs as well as Croatians, Bosnians and Kosovars, to talk with the Taliban, as correspondents with the *Globe and Mail* did in 2008, to incorporate stories carried by Arabic media like Al Jazeera. The provision of such alternative journalism itself requires that Western governments and military advisors do not sanction it, and that members of mass audiences continually and vocally demand, expect, and reward such coverage. Such commitment to free speech in mass media is not readily achieved in times of war.

The Internet has the potential to develop as a critical tool for peace in that it can bring to Western audiences the direct experiences, thoughts, and amateur cell-phone videos of people living in Iraqi suburbs, in Palestinian refugee camps, and in women's groups in Afghanistan. This in turn requires that the Internet remains relatively free from direct surveillance and manipulation by military and political elites, and that people learn how to use Internet sources effectively. To overcome information management in the context of war, it is not sufficient merely to believe one source rather than another, or to assume that something that looks like an amateur video is more authentic or "true" than an account by an embedded journalist. People need the media-literacy skills to be able to draw from alternative sources an awareness of the gaps and omissions in mainstream political discourse, in order to ask critical questions that resist being swept up in propaganda. Teachers in schools and universities have a potentially critical role to play in helping young people to develop these skills. So do journalists and talk-show hosts. They may not be able to control the public speeches and media events that political and military leaders and analysts project in prepackaged form into mass media. However, they do have some leeway to analyze speeches, to show audiences how they are designed to have the impact they do, what is included, and especially what is excluded from such presentations. Again, this presupposes that mass audiences will support these kinds of active journalism rather than challenging it as unpatriotic or as not supporting the troops.

The effectiveness of opinion polls to work as war propaganda can be challenged in two ways. The professionals who design and carry out such polls need to be held accountable for how they design questions and impose interpretations on answers. As audience members we need to develop the ability to go behind the questions to think about the biases built into them, and to challenge claims about what the public are told are public opinions that seem to come from nowhere. Public opinion polls are believable only when we know what the questions are and the context in which people answer them.

Anti-war movements need to challenge official definitions of the situation that support a call to war. They also need to avoid being drawn into the "guilt weapons" that suggest that opposition to war implies support for negative behaviour attributed to "the enemy." The central message of opposition to war is support for alternative, less destructive means to achieve positive results, and criticism of the hypocrisy of claims that war will solve humanitarian problems. Support for international law and the institution of the United Nations are an important part of the alternative—not because these institutions are perfect, but because they offer the lesser evil to war.

In the context of civil wars and their aftermath, peace initiatives require efforts to re-establish and sustain a sense of "normal times" in place of crisis and fear. People who have lived through periods of fear, crisis, disruption, and extreme violence associated with civil wars need time and support to begin to reconcile what has happened and to trust in the stability of normal times. The work of truth and reconciliation commissions is often an important part of these processes. So also are the efforts of peace activists like the Quakers and the Mennonite Central Committee, and workers in non-government aid organizations who try to create safe contexts in which members of formerly enemy communities can try to work together.

Peace activism within Western societies also needs to continually challenge the bureaucratic institutions and laws that work to normalize fear and ethnicize and racialize suspicion. In America this means challenging the excesses of the PATRIOT Act, and in Canada challenging security certificates and the intensified immigration and border controls, and demands for ever-stronger surveillance systems that build on fear of those labelled as "other." Ordinary people can begin to resist the cultural foundations of war at the level of routine, everyday institutional bureaucratic practices that work to promote fear, insecurity, and racialized and ethnicized suspicions. Smith identifies this potential for action as "making change from below" (2007). Making positive change from below involves forming alliances across groups with similar values and interests, encouraging individuals to become political subjects who can act and connect into political objectives that start at the local level and move outwards. Anti-war actions can include practices like using the Internet to gain a voice and transform consciousness, speaking out at the level of schools, churches, community organizations, and university classrooms where voices can be heard, insisting as parents that our children are taught history and civic studies differently so that they can see the connections between imperialism, exploitation, global business practices, immense inequalities between societies in the north and the south, and the ubiquity of war. We can insist also that our children are taught critical literacy so that they can think in questioning ways about information available through official sources, mass media, and the Internet, so that as a society we become less dependent on official propaganda for information. We can also act locally to change ruling relations at the level of how government works, through involvement in campaigns to push local governments to practice ethical purchasing, and to join coalitions of progressive electors to undermine escalating military spending (Smith 2007, 22–23).

▣ Feminist Perspectives on War

War is gendered. Overwhelmingly it is men who are centrally featured in all images of war. Military combat units have been and continue to be virtually exclusively comprised of men in all organized armed forces across the globe. Women in military service predominate in traditional support roles as clerks, administrators, and nurses. Men also comprise the overwhelming majority of gun-wielding militia members and rock-throwing rioters in scenes of civil wars. Men are the fighters and the protectors while women are the protected—the ones who wait at home for their men—their fathers, brothers, husbands, and sons to return from battle. Images of women in war zones centre around grieving mothers struggling to maintain their domestic roles in war-shattered families and refugee camps, outsiders to the active work of fighting wars.

Gender-role differences in war are so pronounced that they are commonly assumed to be biologically determined. Men on average are physically much stronger than women, predisposed to greater aggression by far higher levels of testosterone, not hampered by limitations of pregnancy and breast-feeding, and hence naturally the hunters, and by extrapolation the fighters who expand and defend their communities' resources. Women who are hampered by pregnancy, who give birth and nurture infants, and provide care for the young, the sick, and the elderly are naturally more passive, more inclined to seek peace, and to remain close to the home.

Feminist analysis unpacks these gendered images to explore the active practices through which men are foregrounded, pressured, and twisted into fighting roles, while women are backgrounded, excluded, and twisted into griever roles. In tracing how women are located in relation to war, feminist analysis simultaneously illuminates how the locations of men are constructed. Words like "natural," "tradition," and "always," as in phrases like "generals are naturally men" or "women are naturally homemakers," Enloe argues, are excuses for not thinking analytically about how gendered patterns are constructed and maintained (2006, 2).

Women are involved in war in multiple ways. Military leaders require support from women in order to wage war. Wartime propaganda routinely calls on women to bear and raise their sons for war, and to "give" their sons to the war effort rather than protecting them by helping them to avoid army service (Peterson 1998). Women are enjoined to strengthen the community by bearing as many children as possible, and to mark the community ethnically by their exaggerated commitment to traditional patterns of behaviour (Nikolic-Ristanovic 1998). While images of bravery and

death in war focus on male soldiers, women increasingly suffer disproportionately from modern warfare, aerial bombardment that kills enemy civilians more than enemy fighters (York 1998, 23). Women are particularly targeted for sexual violence as a means to humiliate and destabilize "enemy" communities (Chenoy 1998).

Women have also become actively involved in fighting wars. During the First World War, the British government recruited women to support the war effort by working in munitions factories where they risked death from dangerous fumes, explosions, and accidents (Woollacott 1998). The government awarded some women the Order of the British Empire for their bravery and sacrifice during explosions in these factories. Women have fought in many nationalist liberation struggles against colonial rule across Africa, Asia and Latin America (Mulinari 1998; York 1998, 22; Carter 1998). The American military recruited women in relatively large numbers for the 1991 Gulf War and then used this to brag that American women in army fatigues were more liberated than women who still wore burqas (Klein 1998, 148; Jeffreys 2007, 24).

Feminist analysis calls into question both the naturalness of male aggression and female passivity. Since not all men at all times are violent or militaristic, gendered analysis needs to explore why, and under what conditions, do some men join regular armies, other men join irregular militias, while yet other men become draft-dodgers or publicly oppose war. To the extent that women are not present in military combat units or in higher echelons of war planning, we need to explore what the mechanisms are that keep women on the margins of military organization. Since some women do support and participate in armed conflict we need to explore further which women under which circumstances volunteer for military service, encourage their sons to be soldiers, or shield them from the draft (Enloe 1998, 50–53). The overdrawn image of women as nurturers and caretakers both limits the roles seen as appropriate for women and feeds into the stereotype of men as naturally militaristic (York 1998, 21).

Manufacturing Military Masculinity

A central line of argument within feminist discourse is that the military depends on aggressive masculinity, and further that the military needs to produce this aggressive masculinity. It is not simply innate in new recruits (Jeffreys 2007, 18; Enloe 1983). Most men do not want to fire guns at other men, and most soldiers do not aim their guns directly at "enemy" soldiers, even when under orders to do so (Grossman 1966, cited in van de Pitte 2008, 187). Superior officers in Nazi police units in Poland that were responsible for several mass killings of Jews during the Second World War did not assume that men under them would be willing or ready to kill Jews (Browning 1992). The officers slowly conditioned the recruits to cope with the psychological stress of killing by a series of assignments involving increasing levels of violence over several months, along with anti-Semitic propaganda and messages promoting pride in German nationality and masculinity as police officers. The immediate superior of men in the special units responsible for the massacres also gave his men a non-killing option. The effect of this option was that men who chose the non-shooting option excused themselves in front of fellow officers as "too weak" to kill. They thus promoted and affirmed the valued machismo of those who were manly enough to kill (Enloe 1998, 57; Grossman 1966, 185).

Feminist theory further argues that pornography and prostitution function both as means to enhance aggressive masculinity and as outlets for and expressions of that aggression. Military commanders frequently promote pornography and prostitution, and even condone sexual assaults by soldiers as tools to enhance aggressive masculinity and boost morale and camaraderie among soldiers required for an effective fighting force (Ruddick 1998; Enloe 2006, 119). The pattern of aggressive masculinity considered appropriate for the military is typically defined in ways that exaggerate male/female differences and represent men as rightly superior to and dominant over women. Boot-camp songs are full of violent sexual fantasies about readiness to rape women, sodomize the dead, and the like (Ruddick 1998, 217). Drill sergeants commonly whip new recruits into shape with insults that they are performing like women or pussies (Jeffreys 2007, 18).

Prostitution is endemic around military bases and widely supported by military planners as a sexual outlet for soldiers needed to sustain their fighting effectiveness. Hosts of people, including bar and brothel owners, local police and mayors, national and foreign finance ministry and defence officials, public health officials, and civilian pimps are all involved in creating and maintaining prostitution around military bases (Turpin 1998, 6). The sex trade in civilian life is routinely associated with heightened levels of violence against women, violence that is tacitly condoned by lax law enforcement and minimal penalties. Militarized prostitution around overseas bases is particularly prone both to violence and to impunity for perpetrators (Kirk and Okazawa-Rey 1998, 311). Soldiers who return from battle conditions are often angry, fearful, and deeply stressed, and they unleash it in violent sexuality on the bodies of women working in the bars and brothels. In an environment where women are "served up like fast food, laced with racism" (Enloe 2006, 120), the gap between prostitution and rape is narrow.

Rape as Organized Military Practice

Military training manuals and histories of military engagements generally do not include discussion of rape or sexual violence as a weapon of war. But there is nonetheless widespread evidence that both organized armies and informal militias have systematically used rape as a tactic to dominate, crush, and demoralize enemy communities (Copelon 1998).

In the context of civil wars, rape has been conceptualized as a particularly brutal form of message between men (Nikolic-Ristanovic 1998). Amnesty International and Human Rights Watch both reported that rape was a central tactic used by Hutu militias during the 100 days of genocidal violence against Tutsi in Rwanda. Estimates run as high as a half-million women sexually violated, often in public gang rapes. During the civil wars in Guatemala and El Salvador, military elites orchestrated torture and rape as tactics to crush rebellion. New recruits were pressured to collaborate in the abuse of civilians and prisoners as part of their training to submit to military command (Matthews 1998). Men signal dominance over other men by raping "their" women. Impregnating the enemy's women becomes a weapon in ethnic cleansing. It functions to destroy families and destabilize communities. Women are doubly violated, both by the rape itself and by the process of giving birth to children who bear the mark of their rapist and their ethnic enemies. There are few services to help these women deal with the psychological trauma involved.

Sexual assault of prisoners in the American-controlled military prison of Abu Ghraib in Iraq was noteworthy less for the violence than the fact that the sexual humiliation and degradation targeted male prisoners (Zine 2006, 33; Jeffreys 2007, 22–23). The torture in Abu Ghraib involved "turning men into women . . . or dogs"—forcing naked Iraqi male prisoners to crawl over broken glass wearing only

Sexual humiliation and degradation in Abu Ghraib prison targeted male prisoners.

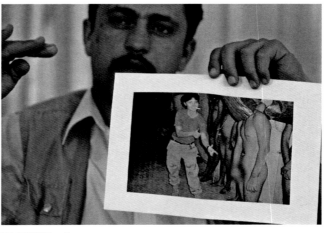

REUTERS/Oleg Popov

sanitary towels, ordering prostitutes to stand over a prisoner and menstruate on him, a female guard making a male prisoner crawl with a leash tied around his neck, threatening naked prisoners with attack dogs, and the like. Jeffreys notes that hard-core civilian pornography is full of scenes like these, and they work to transform the victim into a compliant slave to feed the sexual fantasies of the voyeurs (2007, 22). American military men were likely familiar with such pornography.

A complex question for feminist analysis is how armies and militias condition large numbers of ordinary men to commit the kind of atrocities that occur during wars. One answer is that they reflect in exaggerated form the patriarchal values and misogyny already present in civilian culture, and expressed in hard-core pornography that is pervasive in Western societies (Ruddick 1998, 222; Reardon 1998; Jeffreys 2007, 19; Kelly 2000, 55). Patriarchal family structures promote hierarchy, competition, aggression, and violence. War is the natural progression of these values. The direct nature of the links between violence in personal and political lives is evidenced by marked increases in rates of domestic violence during times of war (Lentin 1998, 338).

Others argue that while cultural misogyny may be a precondition it is not sufficient to account for atrocities of massive scale and viciousness. The story of Boris Herak, a Serb who was convicted by Bosnian authorities of raping 16 Bosnian Muslim women and murdering some of them during the civil war in Yugoslavia between 1991 and 1993, gives some insight into the active practices of Serbian militia forces in working up new recruits to commit such sexual violence (Enloe 1998, 2006, Ch. 7). Enloe argues there is no evidence that Herak was either particularly racist or violent towards women before he "fell in" with a Serbian militia group after he ran away from the siege of Sarajevo. It was among these militiamen that he learned to label himself as a "Serb" and a "man" whose life chances had been ruined by the Muslim imperial ancestors of his Bosnian neighbours. It was also among the militiamen that he learned to avenge himself specifically against Muslim women. Boris claimed in a prison interview with a journalist that his militia captain had ordered the men to go to a restaurant in town to rape girls there, so as to raise their fighting morale (Enloe 1998, 58–59). Enloe concludes that the rapes orchestrated by Serbs in prison camps in Bosnia should have come as no surprise to anyone. Rape is a commonplace tactic of war. Only the official silence about it is surprising.

The association between military organization and aggressive masculinity carries over into United Nations peacekeeping forces. The same readiness to fight and to kill is not required in peacekeeping forces, but similar patterns of exploitation and violence towards women are still evident, perhaps reflecting the fact that UN forces draw directly from soldiers in member states. In conflict zones of Cambodia and Mozambique, UN peacekeepers became actively engaged in organizing the local sex trade (Jeffrey 2007, 19; Kelly 2000, 58). Nordstrom argues further that there exists a thriving international industry to sell girls from war zones into child prostitution. The industry operates with virtual impunity under the noses of UN peacekeepers in places like war-torn Mozambique (Nordstrom 1998). The UN High Commissioner for Refugees (UNHCR) has further documented sexual attacks on women and girls in refugee camps by UN peacekeepers as "a major problem" (Turpin 1998, 6), but one for which there are few if any repercussions for the perpetrators.

A common feature of these accounts is the level of impunity that soldiers and militia members seem to have even in instances of well-documented mass rape. The Geneva Conventions of 1949 and 1977 explicitly prohibit rape, enforced prostitution, and indecent assault, and recommend special protection for female prisoners. However, these crimes are treated separately from crimes of violence and are not explicitly listed among the "grave breaches" of "wilful killing, torture, or inhumane treatment" and "wilfully causing great suffering or serious injury" that all nations are enjoined to investigate and prosecute (Copelon 1998, 66).

Women in Military Organizations Women currently constitute a small but growing proportion of people employed in military services. Israel remains the only country that includes women in conscription. Among NATO forces involved in the 1991 Gulf War, women comprised 11 percent of American forces, 9 percent of Canadian, 5 percent of British, and 2.5 percent of French troops (D'Amico 1998). By 2008, women comprised about 15 percent of the American and 10 percent of the Canadian armed forces.

In almost all these cases, however, the positions open to women within the military are restricted. They are excluded from the infantry and direct combat roles in American and Canadian armed forces, and across all NATO forces. Very few women rise to ranks that involve command. Israeli women are called to do military service, but only before they become pregnant, or until they marry, and they are not eligible for combat roles (Klein 1998).

Feminist activists are divided on the question of whether to push for equal participation and unrestricted access to military roles for women. Liberal feminist analysis makes the case that the inclusion of greater numbers of women in military organizations is both an equity issue and a means to change military culture. In many societies military service offers well-paying career roles and forms

Women currently constitute a small but growing proportion of people employed in military services.

Bob Daemmrich/Photo Edit

an important step to subsequent civilian careers and political influence (Jeffreys 2007, 16). Women's inequality in the armed forces is bound up with inequality as citizens. If women wish to claim equal citizenship with men, they should have an equal obligation to fight for their country. Pregnancy and childcare complicate women's military involvement but are not insurmountable. Women's increased participation in the military arguably might boost morale more effectively than pornographic videos, and potentially change military culture away from gratuitous violence towards values more in tune with humanitarian intervention. In increasingly high-technology warfare, physical strength and hyper-masculinity is arguably becoming less important as a requirement even for combat roles.

The major counterargument to the liberal-feminist position is that aggressive masculinity remains such a central defining value of military culture that women will never be accepted as equal members of the military, especially if they start to push their way beyond accepted ancillary roles.

Military men are prone to use a variety of forms of harassment to preserve their gendered masculine turf, including "sabotage, foot-dragging, feigning ignorance, constant scrutiny, gossip and rumours, and indirect threats" (Jeffreys 2007, 18, citing Miller 1997). There are serious contradictions between respect for women as colleagues and use of women in brothels. Women in the military face double jeopardy from enemy fire, and from sexual violence from male colleagues. Women who do experience harassment in the military are easily silenced (D'Amico 1998, 124). If they try to speak out they risk an array of potential countercharges—of initiating the sexual interaction, of being a troublemaker, of deliberately scheming to ruin the reputation and career of a "fine officer," or of being a lesbian and unsuitable for military service. The chances are high that no action will be taken against the supposed offending male officers. If women quit the forces to escape the harassment, they risk prosecution for insubordination or desertion.

The US feminist organization, the Miles Foundation, is a private, non-profit organization set up in Washington, DC, to provide services to victims of sexual violence associated with the military and to strive to improve US armed forces response to violence against women (Jeffreys 2007, 20). They received 129 complaints of rape in their first 18 months up to April 2004. The US Department of Defense subsequently carried out its own investigation and found more than a thousand cases of reported "sexual misconduct" in the military in 2003 and 900 in 2002. Another survey carried out by the Veteran Affairs Medical Centre in Iowa City in 2003 found that 30 percent of female veterans reported rape or rape attempts during military service. Three-quarters of the 506 women, aged between 20 and 83, reported some sort of sexual harassment during their service. A camp safety officer is reported as warning women not to go anywhere on base unescorted or alone at any time, even to use the latrine, because of the risk of rape (Jeffreys 2007).

Rape as Discursive Practice   Feminist research has widely documented the climate of aggressive masculinity in the armed forces, and the prevalence of sexual assaults, especially in the context of war. The questions remain whether these patterns reflect a uniquely aggressive military culture hostile to women, an exaggerated form of more widespread patriarchal culture, or perhaps an overstatement of trends that may not be markedly different from civilian contexts. Measurement of the incidence and prevalence of sexual assaults in wider society remains difficult and contentious. A study of women's experience of rape and attempted rape in a large and representative sample of 6159 students at 32 American college campuses (Koss 1988; discussed in Gilbert 1993) reported that 27 percent of female students had been victims of rape and a further 15 percent of attempted rape. These rates are comparable to those recorded by the Miles Foundation noted above. These figures can be interpreted simultaneously as a stinging indictment of the level of aggressive male sexuality on college campuses, and as a challenge to extreme arguments by feminists like D'Amico (1998, 124) and Carter (1998, 109) that sexual violence within the military is so high as to preclude the possibility of women's empowerment within military service.

The figures also raise questions about how concepts like rape and attempted rape are conceptualized and measured by researchers and by their respondents. The distinction between sexual assault as a crime of violence, and overly pressured and unwanted sexual encounters often in the context of heavy drinking, are not easily drawn, either by investigators or participants.

Accusations of rape in the context of war carry complex political messages. They give voice to the victims of the brutality of enemy forces, and the exploitation of vulnerable women in refugee camps. They also function as ammunition in wartime propaganda to discredit the "enemy" and legitimate attacks against them. Serbs are described as using women prisoners to create pornographic videos that portrayed Croats as responsible for the sexual violence (Rejali 1998, 27). The public relations firm Ruder Finn that was working with Croat leaders published stories in 1999 that indicted the Serb military as orchestrating the rape of between 3000 and 30 000 Bosnian Muslim women in their "ethnic cleansing" campaign, along with the rape of "tens of thousands" of prisoners. These reports helped to legitimate NATO bombing of Serb military positions. Subsequent investigations found little evidence to support these claims (Johnstone 2002, 69).

Feminist researchers who stand by their research evidence documenting sexual aggression against women in the military argue that the real incidence of sexual assaults are far higher than those reported. Only a small proportion of all women who have been sexually assaulted are willing to speak out because to do so might jeopardize their military careers. They would likely not be believed, their reports would be trivialized, and minimal if any corrective action would be taken against the perpetrators (Enloe 2006, 69–82). Muslim women who were victimized by Serb aggression are even more reluctant to speak out about the atrocities because they face shame in their own communities, and even risk honour killing for the shame that their sexual violation supposedly brings to their families (Jeffreys 2007, 18). If only between 5 and 10 percent of all victims of rape are willing to speak about it, then actual rates may be 10 to 20 times higher than those publicly counted.

The problem with such claims, however, is that they function as "incorrigible propositions" (McKendy 1997). They cannot be proven either true or false. They function to legitimate hostility and potential revenge against those labelled as perpetrators. To question the discourse around sexual assaults, however, risks feeding into a counter political discourse of denial that discredits victims. Given how difficult it is to obtain clear information about incidence and prevalence of sexual assaults in the military, and especially during times of war, there is no easy conclusion to heated exchanges of charges and denials. It may be simultaneously true that both the extent of aggressive masculinity and sexual bullying in the military is widespread, and that the majority of members of the military, female and male, do not experience or participate in such behaviour. The more critical research question is how military organizations are set up to deal with specific instances of aggressive sexuality, and whether perpetrators or victims can expect to be supported by institutional practices or condemned.

When pictures of the torture of Iraqi prisoners by American guards at Abu Ghraib prison in Baghdad hit the Internet, and then the mass media in 2004, the dominant representation of the scandal was in terms of individual "bad apples," not representative of US prison guards as a whole. Private Lynndie England, shown jeering at a heap of naked male prisoners, and dragging one around by a leash, was characterized as depraved, unmarried, pregnant, and having an affair with a male guard known to have beaten his former wife (Jeffreys 2007, 22). Jeffreys' own account focuses on the male guard—"a sadist who would sew up prisoners' wounds with a needle and thread after beating them, and take pictures of his work." Lynndie England, she suggests, was another of his victims, a young woman of junior rank, sexually involved with him, and used by him to stage his sadistic pornographic video, because her presence deepened the humiliation of exposed Iraqi men. What both accounts omit, however, is the actions of US Secretary of Defence Donald Rumsfeld, who endorsed as official policy the use of torture and "exceptional rendition" to extract information from prisoners.

Policies at the very top of the American military hierarchy that endorsed torture as a strategy in the war on terror functioned to create or to actively organize a military organization that would not investigate torture. Individuals at the bottom of the military hierarchy could be scapegoated as "bad apples." However, it was the structured bureaucratic impunity from sanction or prosecution within the military that encouraged them to engage in the behaviour they did, and to videotape the behaviour to amuse and impress colleagues, which further led the female director of Abu Ghraib prison to permit, or to turn a blind eye to, such behaviour under her watch. These policy directives and the structural practices that follow from them, more than the psychology of individuals, best account for particular instances that come to light. Likewise, the official policy of incendiary bombing of civilian populations as military strategy for demoralizing the enemy during the Second World War produces, as features of military bureaucratic organization, the immunity for individual soldiers who commit atrocities against "enemy combatants." Ambiguity within UN conventions and war tribunals on whether to investigate and prosecute mass rape by soldiers and UN peacekeepers as war crimes continues to provide tacit support for atrocities against women.

Manufacturing Militarism among Women

The participation and support of women is important in multiple ways for the conduct of war: as fighters and military support workers; as mothers, wives, and lovers of male fighters; as caregivers and comforters; and as political agents who accept the legitimacy of war. Political and military leaders cannot assume that women will support militarism. That support has to be worked up and continually sustained. Without this, women may refuse to volunteer for military work, counsel men in their lives to reject military careers or dodge the draft, refuse sexual partnerships with militaristic men, take their children and run away, vote against militarist political leaders, organize and promote peace activist social movements, and undermine the war effort by challenging its legitimacy, exposing its violence and morally degrading practices, perhaps even forwarding tactical information to the opposing side, and the like.

Feminist analysis explores the active practices through which political and military elites have tried to orchestrate women's support for war, and women's participation in and resistance to these pressures. Enloe warns that women, like men, have diverse reactions to war, reflecting different social locations and experiences. Critical questions concern which women under which circumstances are more or less likely to volunteer for military service, to participate in nationalist struggles, to encourage their sons to join the military or to shield them, to join peace activist movements, or to disparage them.

The extent of nationalist propaganda oriented specifically to mothers is a measure of how political leaders assess the importance of support from this sector of the population for the war effort. In the early 1990s women's organizations from across regional and ethnic lines in Yugoslavia spoke out forcefully against the senselessness of civil conflict (Nikolic-Ristanovic 1998, 234). Nationalist

leaders countered with propaganda aimed at shifting women's self-identity as "mothers" to that of "citizens" of an emerging nation state. They glorified women as the biological reproducers of the nation, using this rhetoric to justify restricting access to contraceptives and to abortions. Nationalist propaganda was ultimately successful in dividing the women's protest movement and labelling anti-war protestors as traitors.

Political elites, from contexts as diverse as the US during the Second World War and the Nicaraguan government fighting Contra rebels, have designed propaganda messages to appeal to women as "mothers of soldiering sons" to direct their spirit of sacrifice for their children to the nation as a whole (Bayard de Volo 1998). Organizations like the Gold Star Mothers Club in America, and the Mothers of Heroes and Martyrs in Nicaragua, promoted the values of nationalism and patriotism through honouring the ultimate maternal sacrifice of mothers who lose their child in service of their nation at war. The Canadian equivalent is the Silver Cross Mothers, one of whom is chosen every year by the Canadian Legion to lay a wreath at the National War Memorial in Ottawa on behalf of all mothers who have lost a child in service to Canada. The common theme in these organizations is that of martyrdom for the greater cause. The mobilization of grieving mothers, symbolically and literally, delivers a powerful pro-war message and undercuts the potential for grief to undermine national commitment to war. The discourse of motherhood is tied to that of militarism and nationalism through the notion of "acceptable and meaningful death," rather than useless suffering (Scheper-Hughes 1998). Military propaganda enjoins mothers to find consolation in thinking of their children as martyrs who died purposefully and well. Such thinking, Scheper-Hughes argues, is as important to the military as to mothers. To challenge the rightness of war is to admit the possibility that young sons and comrades have died meaningless, violent deaths.

A long-time peace activist mother in Israel explores how powerfully having a son serving as a conscript in the Israeli army impacts upon women's anti-war activism (Mazali 1998). Sons in the military, she argues, socialize parents into acceptance of the military, regardless of their parents' personal convictions. Activist mothers silence themselves to support their sons, fearing that open dissent would jeopardize their sons' rank, placements, and promotions within the military. Even parents with long-term commitment to peace activism display deep-rooted complicity with military duty. It is far easier for parents to view military service as an unavoidable fact of Israeli life than to contemplate as their personal responsibility the duty to educate and acculturate their children to dodge the draft, with all the consequences such action would hold for citizenship within Israel. A single-parent mother signed consent forms for her only son to join a combat unit, even when she could have refused. It never really crossed her mind that she should stop him. Another peace-activist mother spoke of her shame at how she responded when her son suggested he might try for a military computer unit. She blurted out "So your friend Uri will bust his guts and you'll be sitting at a computer"—implying that her son would be shirking his duty (Mazali 1998, 282).

Once a son enters the military, the work of supporting him frequently comes to dominate family life. Parents put off other travel to be able to visit him or have him come home whenever possible, keep the phone free in case he calls, pander to his wishes and free him from domestic responsibilities during his home visits, and refrain from any criticism of military activities he participates in, even when this might involve operations in the occupied territories that they would have fiercely criticized at other times. Parents of recruits who were killed in a military training accident reacted with rage and public condemnation of the commanding officer for incompetence, yet they still refrained from questioning the premise that military service itself was necessary. Parents are socialized to know what can be said and what must remain silent.

In these multiple ways parents accept, support, and reinforce the sense of moral rightness of military service, even when they are morally opposed to Israel's military assaults on the occupied territories and Lebanon. Support for their sons translates into support for the army. One mother apologized for her uneasy silence by saying that she felt she had no right to impose her "personal entanglement" with peace activism onto her son, thus reducing such activism to the level of merely personal psychology. The Israeli military relies on this silencing of parental dissent in order to sustain the draft and the political culture of militarism.

Embedded Feminism: Selling War as Humanitarian Intervention

Feminist analysis of political discourse generated by Western governments to describe wars in Afghanistan and Iraq explores what they see as part of a strategy to co-opt and subordinate feminist politics to sustain popular support for the wars (Hunt and Rygiel 2006). Wars initially justified ousting dangerous regimes that harboured terrorists and controlled weapons of mass destruction, and continue to be justified as humanitarian intervention to liberate local people from oppressive regimes by fostering democracy, human rights, and especially by fostering women's liberation. The Taliban's appalling record of oppression against women in Afghanistan, flogging women for appearing in public without male escorts, or with body parts showing, women barred from jobs, and girls barred from school, is frequently grist for prime-time television programs. In contrast to these stories of Muslim and Arab victimization of women, American, British, and Canadian soldiers appear as liberators, striving to make it safe for women to appear again in the streets, to participate in new small businesses to weave carpets or make cloth bags for sale, and to send their girls to school.

In a new image of military masculinity, male soldiers appear as caring and generous towards people they have liberated, cradling a child whose parents have been killed in Iraqi crossfire, giving toys, books, and clothes to Iraqi children, setting up a charity to pay school fees for another child whose father has died (Scott 2006). Soldiers help Afghan children to regain something of their childhood lost under the oppressive Taliban regime that barred television, videos, music, and even flying kites. Liberated children are shown buying DVD players and other toys. US television hosts stories of the millions of dollars raised for America's Fund for Afghan Children established in October 2001 for American children to contribute money for Afghan children. US popular culture represents war as stories of protection and rescue in which American soldiers are heroes. Stories of American "moms" going to war focus on their stamina and their feminism—sleeping in barracks with family photos under their pillows. Commentaries by children waiting for their soldier parents to come home help to depoliticize the war—the brutality and horror of war disappearing behind stories of courageous moms and dads. The video that American commandos filmed of themselves carrying out a daring rescue of an injured American soldier, Private Jessica Lynch, captured by Iraq forces, fed into this new masculine image of soldiering men protecting vulnerable women.

Feminist Challenges to Embedded Feminism

The feminist critique of this representation of humanitarian warfare on behalf of women's liberation is that it seriously distorts the realities of war, both by what it includes and what it leaves out. First, there is little evidence to indicate that the Bush administration was seriously committed to women's liberation. Feminist critics in America claim the administration systematically undermined women's organizations, cut strategic funding for women's issues, repealed legislation favouring employment equity and childcare leave, cut funding for reproductive choice at home and abroad, and the like, yet claims status as promoting women's liberation through war (Eisenstein 2006). The messianic campaign to go to war on behalf of Muslim and Arab women does not ring true.

The depiction of war as humanitarian intervention can be read as a contemporary variation of century-old myths of Western imperialism spreading superior civilization to the barbaric East, with white women rescuing their barbaric sisters and in the process pushing for higher status and emancipation at home (Hunt 2006, 54). These myths obscured the domination and exploitation of colonial societies that greatly harmed the situation of women and men in these societies, without doing much to liberate Western women either. Women's organizations within Afghanistan, like the Revolutionary Afghanistan Women's Association (RAWA), report that the situation of women in Afghanistan has deteriorated rather than improved since the invasion and occupation by Western forces. The violence unleashed by the war destroyed thousands of lives, left millions of civilians vulnerable to land mines and roadside bombs, and harmed the economy and livelihoods of women and their families. Warlords associated with the US-backed Northern Alliance who now occupy positions of power in the Kabul government, are as conservative and misogynist as the Taliban. They continue to engage in widespread sexual violence, forced marriage, and domestic violence.

Feminist organizations within Afghanistan have been silenced by violent opposition from conservative men who discredit all feminism as instruments of Western cultural imperialism that threaten Muslim culture and tradition. Muslim feminists find themselves fighting Western Islamophobia that represents all Muslim women as oppressed victims on one hand, and a deeply entrenched patriarchal interpretation of Islam at home (Zine 2006). Faith-based Muslim women struggling to liberalize interpretations of Islam feel themselves undermined by secular feminists who reject Islamic texts and symbols such as headscarves as intrinsically oppressive to women.

Western feminist organizations find themselves deeply divided on the issue of whether to support or oppose the war. Some women saw the rhetoric of humanitarian warfare as an opportunity to push for human rights and concern for women's equality in American foreign policy (Hunt 2006, 57). The same rhetoric, however, represented women who did not support war as failing their Afghan sisters, and as traitors to America. It has worked to undermine anti-war activism within the women's movement, which was perhaps its original intent.

Women in Peace Movements

Women have been at the forefront of anti-war movements across the globe. The close connection that feminist theory draws between cultural values of patriarchy and aggressive masculinity and war carries the implication that opposition to war needs to begin with opposition to hierarchy and violence in everyday life. The goal is not simply to end a particular war in a never-ending sequence of wars, but to change society from the level of family life outwards to endorse more feminine values. Women used their moral authority as mothers in Argentina to challenge the violence of military rule during the "dirty war" of 1976–1983. The "mater dolorosa" or grieving mothers walked in the main square in Buenos Aires on Thursday afternoons, carrying pictures of their "disappeared" children—victims of the kidnapping and killings that the military junta would not admit to having committed. During times when virtually all forms of dissent risked brutal reprisals, the actions of these mothers carried a powerful symbolic message of protest against which the junta could not easily retaliate.

The ironic experience of peace activist organizations is that it is easier to attract membership and support during peacetime, but that during periods of active war their organizations are decimated and relatively silenced. The conflicted feelings that silence mothers with sons in the Israeli military engulf the entire peace movement during periods of active conflict (Mazali 1998, 272). Members themselves advocated that they should hold no protests during Israel's invasion of Lebanon in 1982, for fear that they might undermine the determination and morale of troops and so put them in greater danger. The effect was that they could protest the war only when it was over, and their boys were out of danger. Peace activists seeking accommodation with Palestinians experienced a backlash of feelings against them during the height of the first intifada or Palestinian uprising between the late 1980s and early 1990s. Passersby jeered at them as "whores of Arafat" and "sexually frustrated women" (Lentin 1998, 339).

A history of the New York branch of the Women's International League for Peace and Freedom between 1914 and 1955, during the two world wars and beyond (Alonson 1998), documents how deeply political, racial, and class conflicts divided peace activists themselves. White and African American members split on whether the movement should endorse the US Senate Anti-Lynching bill in 1939. Members also split over the question of whether the US should remain neutral in wars raging in Europe. The National Board favoured neutrality but the New York branch argued that neutrality meant helping the stronger side in the Spanish civil war—the military-business ruling class over the workers party, or fascists over the communists. Jewish members argued that neutrality against Hitler's Germany was morally wrong in the face of the persecution of Jews. The New York branch wanted a boycott of German goods, but the National Headquarters did not. Membership in the peace movement dropped to very small numbers during the Second World War, and fear of communism hampered efforts to revive the movement during the post-war McCarthy era. Peace activists were widely regarded with such suspicion that it was hard even to find a meeting place. By the early 1950s members turned their suspicions onto themselves, visiting prospective members' homes to assure themselves they were not communists before permitting them to join.

Lessons for Peace in the Feminist Perspective

The central lesson of feminist analysis is that the personal is always political. War and peace activism cannot be dissociated from struggles against domestic violence, inequality, sexism, and racism in societies as a whole. Feminist analysis raises awareness that political and military elites depend upon support from women to sustain the practices of war, even when women are not part of the military organizations and not included in centres of power where decisions about war are made. This awareness implies that withdrawal of such support will make a critical difference in undermining the capacity of governments to wage war. It matters how parents raise their children to express masculinity and femininity in their daily lives, the kinds of toys, videos, and other games that they encourage. How masculinity and femininity are constituted and rewarded in interpersonal relations between adults also impact directly on propensity for war, and especially for violence that accompanies civil wars.

To the extent that practices around prostitution and pornography in military organizations and militias promote the aggressive masculinity that drives the will to violence and protracted war, challenging these practices can encourage peacemaking. This does not mean trying to ban the sex trade around military bases, but rather regulating the sex trade in feminist ways. Empowering women in the sex trade in both military and civilian contexts to control the conditions in which they choose to sell sexual services will alter the character of masculinity and femininity as they are fostered in these contexts. Critical to such empowerment is the enforcement of regulations that criminalize and punish violence between customers and providers of sex. Regulations that ensure that soldiers and peacekeepers know they will be held fully legally responsible by their own governments for any children that they might father through these relationships may further motivate men to take the precautions that will protect the health of themselves and others. Such changes have the potential to

foster ways of seeing relationships within the sex trade as normal human and humane relations rather than depersonalized expressions of aggressive masculinity. Pornography oriented to erotica also fosters different expressions of masculinity than pornography in its violent, aggressive, hard-core forms.

Rape as a tactic of war to demoralize enemy communities needs to be addressed at a global level by efforts to pressure the United Nations to clearly list rape as a "grave breach" of human rights that all member nations are enjoined to investigate and prosecute. Unequivocal designation of rape by members of armed forces against women in war zones as a war crime would go some way towards ensuring that violations will be prosecuted at the level of commanders who permit such practices and soldiers who perform such acts, and that these rules apply to victorious armies as well as those defeated. Sexual violence against prisoners of war, refugees, and "illegal combatants" need to be defined as war crimes, subject to universal prosecution at the level of United Nations courts. Changing international law will not be sufficient to change practices, but would provide greater leverage for political actors to challenge such violence and to demand accountability.

Feminist research reveals how strongly the experience of having sons serving in the military compromises how women as mothers feel they can express their peace activism. It draws attention to the need for national and international coalitions among peace activists so that there are others to speak out on behalf of those silenced. Activism is essential at times and in countries not at war on behalf of those living in countries at war, where activism is muted. People who are not directly impacted by having relatives in the military have especially important roles to play. Experience of women in peace movements who have found their organizations muted by racial and ethnic divisions suggests further that, to be effective, peace activism needs to work in collaboration with organizations that promote interracial and interethnic relations. Broad coalitions that encompass diverse identities have a better chance to avoid being drowned out and subordinated to patriotic nationalism during wartime.

Lastly, recognition of how negatively Western quasi-colonial claims to cultural superiority impact on the lives of Muslim and Arab women helps to expose the emptiness of claims to promote war as a form of humanitarian intervention to improve targeted societies. The future of women in Muslim and Arab societies, like everywhere else, is better served by promoting global justice in economic and educational relations, and working in cooperation with women's organizations within countries, rather than through waging war.

CONCLUSION

Wars entail immensely complex practices of organized violence across societal boundaries, and they impact upon and draw in diverse groups of people, often with very different interests and purposes. Wars are ongoing processes that are continually generated, negotiated, sustained, and undermined over time. The effort to draw on different sociological perspectives helps to reduce the risk of imposing one-dimensional explanations onto multidimensional social processes.

The functionalist perspective explores the culture of militarism as a system of values that romanticizes soldiers and military supremacy and gives priority to military spending over other social services, even in peacetime. It also draws attention to the structure and culture of military institutions like the Pentagon as they sustain and promote militaristic responses to global conflict. Cultural explanations for war trace the influence of militarism, failed states, tribalism, and conservative retreat from globalization. The political economy of war explores the influence of the politics of oil and the drive to forcefully expand capitalist market economies on the historical and contemporary politics of war. These politics exacerbate and manipulate cultural conflicts for economic gain.

Social constructionist analysis profoundly disturbs our sense that we "know" how and why wars happen. This perspective centres attention on the politics of knowledge of war, the active practices that militarize religious and ethnic identities, moralize political and economic conflicts, and impose dominant explanations, motives, and understandings onto the conduct of war.

Feminist analysis challenges us to think beyond gender stereotypes to explore the active practices that contribute to the manufacture of militaristic masculinity and femininity, and that draw sexual violence into the discourses and conduct of war.

SUGGESTED READING

James Carroll's book *House of War: The Pentagon and the Disastrous Rise of American Power* (2006) gives an insider's view of the culture of militarism and paranoia that pervaded the Pentagon, through the Second World War and the Cold War to the invasion of Iraq in 2003. Chapter 5 describes how close we came to nuclear war with the Soviet Union in the 1960s.

Robin Corey's "Liberalism at Bay, Conservatism at Play: Fear in the Contemporary Imagination" 2004 discusses the debate between Samuel Huntington and Michael Ignatieff over how ethnic and cultural differences can explode into civil war between former neighbours. Anthony Oberschall's "The Manipulation of Ethnicity: From Ethnic Cooperation to Violence and War in Yugoslavia (2000) gives a deeper insight into active practices through which military and political leaders in Yugoslavia manipulated, whipped up, and exploited ethnic divisions to serve their nationalistic interests.

Naomi Klein's journalist book *The Shock Doctrine: The Rise of Disaster Capitalism* (2007) is a powerful, far-reaching analysis of how corporate greed foments war through an insatiable drive to control strategic resources like oil, and to expand capitalist free markets across the globe. Michel Chossudovsky's chapter "Dismantling Former Yugoslavia: Recolonising Bosnia-Herzegovina," in his book *The Globalization of Poverty: Impacts of IMF and World Bank Reforms* (1998), is a stinging indictment of how Western corporations used IMF policies to undermine the formerly socialist economy of Yugoslavia and break up the Federation.

From the interpretive perspective, Paul Rutherford's *Weapons of Mass Persuasion: Marketing the War Against Iraq* (2004) details the multiple ways in which political elites in the Bush administration, and the mass media, conspired to manipulate information and win mass consent to war against Iraq in 2003. David Barstow's article "Behind TV Analysts: Pentagon's Hidden Hand" (*The New York Times*, 20 April 2008) documents how Pentagon elites manipulated media analysts cum corporate lobbyists to promote the Pentagon line on war.

From a feminist perspective Sheila Jeffreys' article "Double Jeopardy: Women, the US Military and the War in Iraq" (2007) discusses how American women have experienced violence within the American military, and also how they participated in violence against Iraqi prisoners in the infamous Abu Ghraib prison in Baghdad.

Cynthia Enloe has written extensively on how aggressive masculinity and militarized femininity are socially organized in the practices of war. Her chapter "All the Men Are in the Militias, All the Women Are Victims: The Politics of Masculinity and Femininity in Nationalist Wars" (2006) analyzes how a Serb man was socialized in the Serbian militia during the Yugoslav war to rape and murder "enemy" Muslim women.

QUESTIONS

1. How does functionalist theory see processes of development and modernization implicated in war?

2. In what ways do Huntington and Ignatieff differ in their understanding of how cultural differences or the "clash of civilizations" are implicated in war?

3. How do lessons for peace that come out of functionalist theory differ from lessons drawn from political economy theory?

4. Outline the core features of a "culture of militarism" in North American society.

5. Explain the many institutional processes that link desire for profits and decisions about war in the military-industrial complex.

6. How were public opinion polls carried out in the US implicated in winning support for the 2003 invasion of Iraq?

7. List core processes that help to explain why mass media in the US came to pervasively support the US invasion of Iraq.

8. Explain the idea that a climate of fear conducive to war has become institutionalized in American society.

9. Explain the feminist argument that there is nothing "natural" about aggressive military masculinity—it has to be socially constructed.

10. How is militarism among women implicated in war, even when women are not directly involved in active combat roles?

WEB LINKS

MSN.com
http://video.msn.com/video.aspx?mkt=en-us&vid=b3de1e96-57c4-42d6-9e4e-7605a82e2934

This link provides several news streams on the "bumbling bureaucracy of FEMA" during the Katrina disaster: 1) "Symbol of a bumbling bureaucracy"; 2) FEMA eviction notices; 3) New FEMA director and so on. This site should be used as an example of how media has framed "fault" during and after this disaster.

PBS Frontline—The Storm
http://www.pbs.org/wgbh/pages/frontline/storm/view/

This PBS documentary explores the "chain of decisions" during and after the Katrina disaster. "In examining the Katrina story, FRONTLINE looks at the rocky history of the Federal Emergency Management Agency, FEMA, and how in the wake of 9/11, FEMA was downgraded from a Cabinet-level agency to a sub-department in the new Department of Homeland Security (DHS)."

PBS Frontline—On Our Watch
http://www.pbs.org/wgbh/pages/frontline/darfur/

Nowhere is the failure of government decision-making and bureaucracy more evident and visible than on the continent of Africa. "In On Our Watch, FRONTLINE asks why the United Nations and its members once again failed to stop the slaughter" in Darfur. This site provides links to the video, interviews, analysis, timeline, and the opportunity to join in a discussion for this documentary. This site also links to the documentaries "Ghosts of Rwanda" and "Sudan."

REFERENCES

Abu-Manneh, Bashir. 2007. "Israel in the U.S. Empire." *Monthly Review* (March 2007): 1–25.

Ahmed, Nafeez Mosaddeq. 2005. *The War on Truth: 9/11, Disinformation, and the Anatomy of Terrorism.* Northampton, Massachusetts: Olive Branch Press.

Alonson, Harriet Hyman. 1998. "Dissension in the Ranks: The New York Branch of WILPF vs. the National Board, 1914–1955." In Lois Ann Lorentzen and Jennifer Turpin, eds. *The Women & War Reader.* New York; London: New York University Press, 296–302.

Alterman, Eric. 2004. "Fear: What is it Good For?" *Social Research* 71 (4): 997–1014.

Barstow, David. 2008. "Behind TV Analysts: Pentagon's Hidden Hand." *The New York Times* (20 April 2008).

Bayard de Volo, Lorraine. 1998. "Drafting Motherhood: Maternal Imagery and Organizations in the United States and Nicaragua." In Lois Ann Lorentzen and Jennifer Turpin, eds. *The Women & War Reader.* New York; London: New York University Press, 240–253.

Bricmont, Jean. 2007. *Humanitarian Imperialism: Using Human Rights to Sell War.* Delhi: Monthly Review Press.

Briody, Dan. 2004. *The Haliburton Agenda: The Politics of Oil and Money.* Hoboken, New Jersey: John Wiley and Sons.

Briody, Dan. 2003. *The Iron Triangle: Inside the Secret World of the Carlyle Group.* Hoboken, New Jersey: John Wiley and Sons.

Brittain, Melisa. 2006. "Benevolent Invaders, Heroic Victims and Depraved Villains: White Femininity in Media Coverage of the Invasion of Iraq." In Krista Hunt and Kim Rygiel, eds. *(En)Gendering the War on Terror: War Stories and Camouflaged Politics.* London; Burlington, Vermont: Ashgate Publishing, 73–96.

Browning, Christopher. 1992. *Ordinary Men: Reserve Police Battalion 101 and the Final Solution in Poland.* New York: Harper Collins.

Buchheit, Paul, ed. 2008. *American Wars: Illusions and Realities.* Atlanta: Clarity Press.

Buchheit, Paul. 2008. "Illusion: We Fight for Peace and Democracy." In Paul Buchheit, ed. *American Wars: Illusions and Realities.* Atlanta: Clarity Press, 16–26.

Carroll, James. 2006. *House of War: The Pentagon and the Disastrous Rise of American Power.* Boston; New York: Houghton Mifflin.

Carter, April. 1998. "Should Women Be Soldiers or Pacifists?" In Lois Ann Lorentzen and Jennifer Turpin, eds. *The Women & War Reader*. New York; London: New York University Press, 33–40.

Chenoy, Anuradha M. 1998. "Militarization, Conflict, and Women in South Asia." In Lois Ann Lorentzen and Jennifer Turpin, eds. *The Women & War Reader*. New York; London: New York University Press, 101–110.

Chomsky, Noam. 2006. *Failed States: The Abuse of Power and the Assault on Democracy*. New York: Metropolitan Books.

Chossudovsky, Michel. 1998. *The Globalization of Poverty: Impacts of IMF and World Bank Reforms*. Halifax: Fernwood, 243–263.

Clausewitz, Carl von. 1993. M. Howard and P. Paret, trans. and eds. *On War*. New York: Knopf.

Connell, R.W. 1983. *Which Way is Up?* Sydney: Allen and Unwin.

Copelon, Rhonda. 1998. "Surfacing Gender: Reconceptualizing Crimes Against Women in Time of War." in Lois Ann Lorentzen and Jennifer Turpin, eds. *The Women & War Reader*. New York; London: New York University Press, 63–79.

Corey, Robin. 2004. "Liberalism at Bay, Conservatism at Play: Fear in the Contemporary Imagination." *Social Research* 71 (4): 927–962.

Cottle, Simon. 2006. "Mediatizing the Global War on Terror: Television's Public Eye." In Anandam P. Kavoori and Todd Fraley, eds. *Media, Terrorism, and Theory: A Reader*. Lanham, Maryland: Rowman & Littlefield, 19–48.

D'Amico, Francine. 1998. "Feminist Perspectives on Women Warriors." In Lois Ann Lorentzen and Jennifer Turpin, eds. *The Women & War Reader*. New York; London: New York University Press, 119–125.

Denitch, Bogdan. 1994. *Ethnic Nationalism: The Tragic Death of Yugoslavia*. Minneapolis; London: University of Minnesota Press.

Durkheim, Emile. [1893] 1964. *The Division of Labour in Society*. New York: Free Press.

Dyer, Gwynne. 2007. *The Mess They Made: The Middle East After Iraq*. Toronto: McClelland & Stewart.

Dyer, Gwynne. 2004. *Future: Tense: The Coming World Order*. Toronto: McClelland & Stewart.

Eisenstein, Zillah. 2006. "Is 'W' for Women?" In Krista Hunt and Kim Rygiel, eds. *(En)Gendering the War on Terror: War Stories and Camouflaged Politics*. London; Burlington, Vermont: Ashgate Publishing, 191–199.

Enloe, Cynthia. 2006. *The Curious Feminist: Searching for Women in a New Age of Empire*. Berkeley; Los Angeles; London: University of California Press.

Enloe, Cynthia. 1998. "All the Men are in the Militias, All the Women are Victims: The Politics of Masculinity and Femininity in Nationalist Wars." In Lois Ann Lorentzen and Jennifer Turpin, eds. *The Women & War Reader*. New York; London: New York University Press, 50–61.

Enloe, Cynthia. 1983. *Does Khaki Become You*. London: Pluto Press.

Gallagher, Stephen. 2008. "Jessica Lynch, Simulacrum." *Peace Review: A Journal of Social Justice* 19: 119–128.

Giddens, Anthony. 2000. *Runaway World: How Globalization is Reshaping Our Lives*. New York: Routledge.

Giddens, Anthony. 1998. *The Third Way: The Renewal of Social Democracy*. Cambridge, UK: Polity Press.

Giddens, Anthony. 1991. *Introduction to Sociology*. London; New York: W.W. Norton.

Gilbert, Neil. 1993. "Examining the Facts: Advocacy Research Overstates the Incidence of Date and Acquaintance Rape." In Richard J. Gelles and Donileen R. Loseke, eds. *Current Controversies on Family Violence*. Newbury Park, California: Sage, 120–132.

Giroux, Henry A. 2009. "Public Pedagogy, Media Power and the Biopolitics of Militarization." In Jeffery Klaehn, ed. *The Political-Economy of Media and Power*. Peter Lang (forthcoming 2009).

Grossman, Lt. Col. David. 1966. *On Killing: The Psychological Cost of Learning to Kill in War and Society*. Boston: Little Brown.

Hardt, Michael, and Antonio Negri. 2000. *Empire*. London; Cambridge, Massachusetts: Harvard University Press.

Henslin, James, and Nelson, Adie. 1996. "War: A Means to Implement Political Objectives." *Sociology: A Canadian Edition*. Toronto: Allyn and Bacon Canada.

Holland, Joshua, and Raed Jarrar. 2008. "Illusion: We Stay in Iraq to Prevent further bloodshed among Iraqis." In Paul Buchheit, ed. *American Wars: Illusions and Realities*. Atlanta: Clarity Press, 43–45.

Hudson, Kate. 2003. *Breaking The South Slav Dream: The Rise and Fall of Yugoslavia*. London: Pluto Press.

Hunt, Krista. 2006. "'Embedded Feminism' and the War on Terror." In Krista Hunt and Kim Rygiel, eds. *(En)Gendering the War on Terror: War Stories and Camouflaged Politics*. London; Burlington, Vermont: Ashgate Publishing, 51–71.

Hunt, Krista, and Kim Rygiel. 2006. "(En)Gendering the War on Terror: War Stories and Camouflaged Politics." In Krista Hunt and Kim Rygiel, eds. *(En)Gendering the War on Terror: War Stories and Camouflaged Politics*. London; Burlington, Vermont: Ashgate Publishing, 1–24.

Huntington, Samuel A. 1996. *The Clash of Civilizations and the Remaking of World Order*. New York: Simon and Schuster.

Ignatieff, Michael. 2005. "Introduction: American Exceptionalism and Human Rights." In Michael Ignatieff, ed. *American Exceptionalism and Human Rights*. Princeton, New Jersey: Princeton University Press, 1–26.

Ignatieff, Michael. 2004. *The Lesser Evil*. Toronto: Pearson

Ignatieff, Michael. 1997. *The Warrior's Honour: Ethnic War and the Modern Conscience*. New York: Henry Holt.

Ikenberry, John. 2001. "American Grand Strategy in the Age of Terror." *Survival: International Institute for Strategic Studies* 43 (4): 19–31.

Jackson, Richard. 2005. *Writing the War on Terrorism: Language, Politics and Counter-Terrorism*. Manchester; New York: Manchester University Press.

Jeffreys, Sheila. 2007. "Double Jeopardy: Women, the U.S. Military and the War in Iraq." *Women's Studies International Forum* 30: 16–25.

Jenkins, Philip. 2003. *Images of Terror: What we Can and Can't Know About Terrorism*. New York: Aldine de Gruyter.

Johnstone, Diana. 2002. *Fool's Crusade: Yugoslavia, NATO and Western Delusions*. New York: Monthly Review Press.

Kelly, Liz. 2000. "Wars Against Women: Sexual Violence, Sexual Politics, and the Militarized State." In Susie Jacobs, Ruth Jacobson, and Jennifer Marchbank, eds. *States of Conflict: Gender, Violence and Resistance*. London: Zed Books, 45–65.

Kidd, Bruce. 1987. "Sports and Masculinity." In M. Kaufman, ed. *Beyond Patriarchy: Essays by Men on Pleasure, Power and Change*. Toronto: Oxford University Press, 250–265.

Kimmerling, Baruch. 2001. *The Invention and Decline of Israeliness: State, Society, and the Military*. Berkeley: University of California Press.

Kirk, Gwyn, and Margo Okazawa-Rey. 1998. "Making Connections: Building an East Asia–U.S. Women's Network against U.S. Militarism." In Lois Ann Lorentzen and Jennifer Turpin, eds. *The Women & War Reader*. New York; London: New York University Press, 308–322.

Klein, Naomi. 2007. *The Shock Doctrine: The Rise of Disaster Capitalism*. Toronto: Knopf Canada (Random House).

Klein, Uta. 1998. "War and Gender: What Do We Learn From Israel?" In Lois Ann Lorentzen and Jennifer Turpin, eds. *The Women & War Reader*. New York; London: New York University Press, 148–154.

Koss, Mary P. 1988. "Hidden Rape: Sexual Aggression and Victimization in a National Sample of Students in Higher Education." In A.W. Burgess, ed. *Rape and Sexual Assault II*. New York: Garland, 1–25.

Lentin, Ronit. 1998. "Israeli and Palestinian Women Working for Peace." In Lois Ann Lorentzen and Jennifer Turpin, eds. *The Women & War Reader*. New York; London: New York University Press, 337–342.

Levin, Jack. 1993. *Sociological Snapshots: Seeing Social Structure and Change in Everyday Life*. Thousand Oaks, California: Pine Forge Press.

Lorentzen, Lois Ann and Jennifer Turpin, eds. 1998. *The Women & War Reader*. New York; London: New York University Press.

MacDonald, David Bruce. 2002. *Balkan Holocausts? Serbian and Croatian Victim-centred Propaganda and the War in Yugoslavia*. Manchester; New York: Manchester University Press.

Mahajan, R. 2002. *The New Crusade: America's War on Terrorism*. New York: Monthly Review Press.

Mandel, Ernest. 1986. *The Meaning of the Second World War*. London: Verso.

Masire, Q.K.J. 2000. *Rwanda: The Preventable Genocide*. Report to the Secretary General of the United Nations, May 2000.

Matthews, Irene. 1998. "Torture as Text." In Lois Ann Lorentzen and Jennifer Turpin, eds. *The Women & War Reader*. New York; London: New York University Press, 184–191.

Mazali, Rela. 1998. "Parenting Troops: The Summons to Acquiescence." In Lois Ann Lorentzen and Jennifer Turpin, eds. *The Women & War Reader*. New York; London: New York University Press, 272–286.

McKendy, John P. 1997. "The Class Politics of Domestic Violence." *Journal of Sociology and Social Welfare* 24 (1): 135–155.

Mearsheimer, John, and Stephen Walt. 2006. "The Israel Lobby." London Review of Books (23 March 2006).

Michalowski, Helen. 1982. "The Army Will Make a 'Man' Out of You." *Reweaving the Web of Life: Feminism and Nonviolence*. Philadelphia: New Society, 326–335.

Miller, Laura. 1997. "Not Just Weapons of the Weak: Gender Harassment as a Form of Protest for Army Men." *Social Psychology Quarterly* 60 (1): 32–52.

Mulinari, Diana. 1998. "Broken Dreams in Nicaragua." In Lois Ann Lorentzen and Jennifer Turpin, eds. *The Women & War Reader*. New York; London: New York University Press, 157–163.

Nikolic-Ristanovic, Vesna. 1998. "War, Nationalism, and Mothers in the Former Yugoslavia." In Lois Ann Lorentzen and Jennifer Turpin, eds. *The Women & War Reader*. New York; London: New York University Press, 234–239.

Nitsch, Judi. 2008. "Illusion: We Fight to Defend our Personal Freedoms." In Paul Buchheit, ed. *American Wars: Illusions and Realities*. Atlanta: Clarity Press, 27–44.

Nordstrom, Carolyn. 1998. "Girls Behind the (Front) Lines." In Lois Ann Lorentzen and Jennifer Turpin, eds. *The Women & War Reader*. New York; London: New York University Press, 80–89.

Oberschall, Anthony. 2000. "The Manipulation of Ethnicity: From Ethnic Cooperation to Violence and War in Yugoslavia." *Ethnic and Racial Studies* 23 (6): 982–1001.

Peterson, V. Spike. 1998. "Gendered Nationalism: Reproducing 'Us' versus 'Them'." In Lois Ann Lorentzen and Jennifer Turpin, eds. *The Women & War Reader*. New York; London: New York University Press, 41–49.

Reardon, Betty A. 1998. "Women or Weapons?" In Lois Ann Lorentzen and Jennifer Turpin, eds. *The Women & War Reader*. New York; London: New York University Press, 289–295.

Rejali, Darius M. 1998. "After Feminist Analyses of Bosnian Violence." In Lois Ann Lorentzen and Jennifer Turpin, eds. *The Women & War Reader*. New York; London: New York University Press, 26–32.

Ritter, Scott. 2007. *Waging Peace: The Art of War for the Antiwar Movement*. New York: Nation Books.

Ruddick, Sara. 1998 "Woman of Peace: A Feminist Construction." In Lois Ann Lorentzen and Jennifer Turpin, eds. *The Women & War Reader*. New York; London: New York University Press, 213–226.

Rutherford, Paul. 2004. *Weapons of Mass Persuasion: Marketing the War Against Iraq*. Toronto: University of Toronto Press.

Rygiel, Kim 2006. "Protecting and Proving Identity: The Biopolitics of Waging War through Citizenship in the Post-9/11 Era." In Krista Hunt and Kim Rygiel, eds. *(En)Gendering the War on Terror: War Stories and Camouflaged Politics*. Burlington: Ashgate Publishing, 145–167.

Scheper-Hughes, Nancy. 1998. "Maternal Thinking and the Politics of War." In Lois Ann Lorentzen and Jennifer Turpin, eds. *The Women & War Reader*. New York; London: New York University Press, 227–233.

Scott, Catherine V. 2006. "Rescue in the Age of Empire: Children, Masculinity, and the War on Terror." In Krista Hunt and Kim Rygiel, eds. *(En)Gendering the War on Terror: War Stories and Camouflaged Politics*. London; Burlington, Vermont: Ashgate Publishing, 97–117.

Shah, Anup. 2008. "Illusion: The Mainstream Media Gives U.S. Balanced Reporting." In Paul Buchheit, ed. *American Wars: Illusions and Realities*. Atlanta: Clarity Press, 47–54.

Shanks, George. 2001. "Limitation of War and the Pursuit of Justice." *Social Justice* 28 (3): 5–27.

Sharma, Nandita. 2006. "White Nationalism, Illegality and Imperialism: Border Controls as Ideology." In Krista Hunt and Kim Rygiel, eds. *(En)Gendering the War on Terror: War Stories and Camouflaged Politics*. London; Burlington, Vermont: Ashgate Publishing, 121–143.

Singer, Peter. 2004. *The President of Good and Evil: Questioning the Ethics of George W. Bush*. New York: Plume, Penguin.

Smith, Dorothy E. 2007. "Making Change from Below." *Socialist Studies* 3 (2): 7–30.

Svirsky, Gila. 1998. "The Impact of Women in Black in Israel." In Lois Ann Lorentzen and Jennifer Turpin, eds. *The Women & War Reader*. New York; London: New York University Press, 329–336.

Turpin, Jennifer. 1998. "Many Faces: Women Confronting War." in Lois Ann Lorentzen and Jennifer Turpin, eds. *The Women & War Reader*. New York; London: New York University Press, 3–18.

Turse, Nick. 2008. *The Complex: How the Military Invades Our Everyday Lives*. New York: Metropolitan Books.

Unger, Craig. 2004. *House of Bush, House of Saud: The Secret Relationship Between the World's Two Most Powerful Dynasties*. New York: Scribner.

Van de Pitte, Margaret. 2008. "What is Wrong with a Military Career?" *Peace Review: A Journal of Social Justice* 19 (2): 183–189.

Verwimp, Philip. 2003. "The Political Economy of Coffee, Dictatorship, and Genocide." *European Journal of Political Economy* 19 (2): 161–181.

Woollacott, Angela. 1998. "Women Munitions Makers, War, and Citizenship." In Lois Ann Lorentzen and Jennifer Turpin, eds. *The Women & War Reader*. New York; London: New York University Press, 126–139.

York, Jodi. 1998. "The Truth about Women and Peace." In Lois Ann Lorentzen and Jennifer Turpin, eds. *The Women & War Reader*. New York; London: New York University Press, 19–32.

Zine, Jasmine. 2006. "Between Orientalism and Fundamentalism: Muslim Women and Feminist Engagement." In Krista Hunt and Kim Rygiel, eds. *(En)Gendering the War on Terror: War Stories and Camouflaged Politics*. London; Burlington, Vermont: Ashgate Publishing, 27–49.

Max Weber and Rationality in Western Culture

Max Weber (1864–1920) is a monumental figure in the history of the social sciences. He was a historian, sociologist, and philosopher who left an indelible mark on the philosophy of history and on social science methodology. The scope of his scholarship is enormous. He wrote major books on comparative religions of Europe, India, and China, on the economy and political structures of democracy in Western Europe, on music and musical forms, the rationality of law, and the structure and function of complex bureaucratic organization.

Background

Weber was born almost 50 years after Marx. Much of his work was a reaction to Marx or, more particularly, to the oversimplified versions of Marxist thought that focused on economic determinism in social life. The two men wrote within very different cultural settings. Marx and his colleague Engels carried out much of their research and writing in Britain during the early period of industrialization. By this time, the feudal estates had been broken up into grazing pastures. The peasants who formerly farmed these lands had been driven off. Masses of landless and desperately poor people flooded the cities seeking wage-work as their only means of survival. They lived under appalling conditions in city slums and worked in the coal mines and expanding textile mills that fuelled the industrial revolution. The emerging merchant-capitalist class effectively challenged the political power and privileges of the declining aristocracy.

Weber lived in Germany during the period when the country was emerging from a collection of divided states into a unified and modern country under Otto von Bismarck. Germany's development was based upon centralized administration and the armaments industry rather than on private capitalism. It promoted a different view of the state and different theories of power and administration than those in Marx's work (Lee and Newby 1983, 169). Weber observed the outbreak of World War I and the concurrent collapse of the international socialist movement

Max Weber (1864–1920)

Library of Congress

into nationalist blocs: the European proletariat supported their nation states rather than the international working-class movement. Weber lived to see the Bolshevik Revolution in Russia in 1917, the collapse of the Spartacist Revolution in Berlin in 1919, and the rise of the Weimar Republic in Germany after the war.

In his personal life, Weber experienced long periods of severe depression. These are reflected in his profound pessimism concerning the future direction of Western civilization. He was intensely aware of the gap between the intended goals and ideals and the often unintended consequences of the means required to attain those goals. Weber himself long defended the ideal of a strong and unified Germany, only to feel contempt for the Kaiser and the policies that led Germany into World War I and eventual military defeat. In his work he argued strongly against any simplified theories of social change, emphasizing instead the complex probabilistic character of all theories of human action. Human action is the outcome of free will, he argued, and such freedom can never be described through fixed relations of cause and effect.

Weber's Scholarship

Weber struggled to synthesize the very different intellectual traditions that were prevalent in Europe at the time. Among them was **idealism** with its Hegelian emphasis on ideas and values as the distinctive moving force of human history. This was in contrast to Marxist theories of **historical materialism**, which contended that class conflict was the driving force of history and the primary determinant of human fate. The idealists emphasized human freedom and uniqueness, which could never be reduced to deterministic rules. Countering them were the **positivists** who sought to apply the methods of the natural sciences to the study of human behaviour, seeking predictive or deterministic laws of action. Functionalist analysis adopts almost exclusively a positivist approach to sociological research, as does the classical political economy perspective.

Weber tried to reconcile the commitment to notions of individual freedom and religious values with the apparently contradictory commitment to a scientific study of human behaviour and to an emphasis on economic materialism in history. He tried also to reconcile the obvious commitment of all researchers to political goals and values with the demand for objectivity in social science research. Lastly, he tried to reconcile the objectives of democracy, with its commitment to representative government based upon participation of an informed population, and the mechanism of bureaucracy, which seemed essential to democracy and yet at the same time was its greatest threat. It is the mark of Weber's brilliance that he was largely able to achieve these syntheses in his work.

WEBER'S METHODOLOGICAL CONTRIBUTION
Methodology in Social Science

Weber's study of methodology in the social sciences provides the foundations for contemporary ethnomethodology and interpretive sociology. Weber sought to synthesize the objective, empirical methods of the natural sciences with the intuitive aspects of the humanities.

Positivism attempts to analyze the social system in terms of causes and effects in the same way that biological systems are analyzed. Weber argues that this is impossible. Because people think about what they do, it is inappropriate

to apply such lawlike, or **nomothetic**, generalizations to human behaviour. People have purposes; their behaviour is meaningful to them. In biology we do not ask chemicals or microbes why they do things. We just account for what happens by reference to the laws of science. But with people, we do have to ask why. Our actions are determined not only by objective conditions and forces, but also by the subjective meanings that we attach to our actions—in other words, by our own responses for doing something.

Weber also wanted to avoid the opposite trap of idealism—the view that all human behaviour entails unique spiritual events that can only be grasped by intuition or empathy. For idealists, the only explanation possible seems to be **ideographic**—unique, subjective, intuitive. The "science" in social science seems to be impossible.

We seem to be forced to choose between the view that human action is predictable, which implies determinism, or the view that people have free will and hence that their actions are not determined by outside forces, and so are not predictable. Weber denies the validity of this apparent dilemma. He argues that meaningful behaviour, or behaviour guided by free will, is not unique and unpredictable or without any pattern or order. Unpredictable or random behaviour would not be meaningful; it would be mindless. Weber resolves the conflict between free will and determinism by arguing that there is no real contradiction between them. Action that is meaningful is, by its very nature, not haphazard, random, or patternless. The scientific study of meaningful behaviour is possible precisely because it is meaningful and therefore organized and predictable. It requires a different kind of explanation from that of the natural sciences, but it is nonetheless amenable to scientific study.

Weber defines sociology as "the science which attempts the interpretive understanding of social action in order thereby to arrive at a causal explanation of its cause and effects" (Ashley and Orenstein 1985, 213). For Weber, then, sociological analysis must do two things. First, it must explore the meaning of actions for the people involved. Second, it has to show how this meaning provides a causal explanation for the behaviour. **Social action** is, by definition, any human conduct that is meaningfully oriented to the past, present, or future expected behaviour of others. People relate to each other in meaningful ways, and it is these shared meanings that define our expectations of others and ourselves.

The Study of Meaning   Weber draws heavily upon the work of his friend and colleague, Georg Simmel (1949; 1950), who first developed the concept of *verstehen*, or understanding, as crucial to sociological analysis. Sociologists have to become involved in the process of understanding because the actions that they are trying to explain are actions to which people themselves attach meanings. People do what they do because it is meaningful to them. We can hardly ignore what these meanings are when we try to explain what they do. This does not mean that pure intuition is sufficient for analysis. We still need objective evidence. We need to develop techniques for interpreting meaning so that others can repeat the study and check the results.

The question is how do we do this. How can we develop an objective, verifiable, repeatable study of meaningful action? We need to remember that meaningful action is not random, but purposive and therefore organized by the people involved.

Verstehen involves putting ourselves in the position of the people we are studying and trying to reconstruct the interpretations that they might give to their own action (Ashley and Orenstein 1985, 212). We feel we have explained the unusual behaviour of people in general, when we come to the point where we can say with some assurance that if we had similar life experiences and value orientations, and had found ourselves in similar circumstances, we could understand how we ourselves might have behaved in a similar way. This is a tall order, but we can do it precisely because we are studying fellow human beings. This is an advantage that sociologists have over physical scientists. The latter study objects from the outside, but in social science we study people as subjects engaged in meaningful behaviour, and we can approach an interpretive understanding of that behaviour from the inside.

Direct understanding or reconstruction of action is sometimes possible. It is relatively easy to arrive at a rational understanding of logical relations, such as at the reasoning involved in concluding that $2 + 2 = 4$, or in concluding that certain facial expressions are a manifestation of anger (Giddens 1971, 148). At other times, in order to make behaviour intelligible, we need to understand people's underlying motives. It is relatively straightforward to understand rational means-end selection, as when people have a clearly stated objective with straightforward means to achieve it. In other contexts, the understanding of motives may require much deeper searching. Weber is well aware that human motives are complex. Similar actions may be done for a variety of underlying motives, while similar motives may be related to different forms of actual behaviour (Giddens 1971, 149). People can also waver between conflicting motives.

Given the complexity of human motivation, Weber argues that explanations in sociology must take the form of **probabilities** rather than the absolute predictions characteristic of the natural sciences. We have achieved an adequate explanation when the motive that we understand to be behind the behaviour in question would reasonably, or with some measure of probability, give rise to the kind of behaviour observed.

Such causal relationships or predictions are inevitably subject to qualifications and exceptions. They reflect the particular historical situation in which people find themselves. For example, Weber argued that the Protestant religion was an important causal influence on the rise of capitalism in Europe. Capitalism also flourished in Japan but clearly not because of Protestantism, although there may have been a similar pattern of values in Japanese culture that triggered capitalistic behaviour (Ashley and Orenstein 1985, 214). Weber's model of typical characteristics of Calvinist values, in contrast to typical Catholic values, makes possible broad generalizations about the relationship between religious ethics and business practices in Europe of that period. In the very different climate of the 1990s there may be no such relationship.

Marx, too, recognized the historical character of explanations when he criticized the economists of his time for treating concepts such as supply, demand, commodities, labour power, and so on, as universal categories without realizing that they only exist within and because of the very particular and historically situated pattern of organization of economic relations of capitalism.

Human Agency Weber's demand for adequacy at the level of meaning led him to challenge functionalist approaches to the study of human society. Functionalism, he argued, is useful in providing a place from which to begin analysis. But the simple analogy between biological systems and social systems soon breaks down. Sociologists need to go beyond functional uniformities to arrive at an interpretive understanding that takes account of the meanings that an action had for the people involved (Giddens 1971, 150).

It is easy for sociologists to be lured into explanations that refer to the social system as a whole, but one must never forget that the conceptual entity *society* is nothing more than the multiple interactions of individuals in a particular setting. Only individual people are agents who actually carry out subjectively understandable action. In functionalist and much Marxist writing, this collection called society tends to take on a **reified** identity of its own. The word is only a convenient descriptive summary. But it is converted into a thing and then is used in explanations as if it were an acting unit with its own consciousness: society does such and such, or society has certain needs, and so on. This is similar to the complaint that Marx raised against the political economy of his day and its tendency to refer to market forces as doing things to people, while losing sight of the fact that people, and only people, do things.

This is not to say that a sociologist should never use concepts that refer to collectives such as states or industrial corporations, but, Weber insists, we must remember that these collectivities are solely the result of organized actions of individual people. People may organize collectively to do something, and we may refer to this collective organization as, for example, a corporation, but corporations as such do nothing.

Weber's second demand, for adequacy at the level of causality, led him to reject the opposite extreme of **psychological reductionism** (Giddens 1971, 151). Psychology is certainly relevant to sociological understanding, as are several other disciplines. But we cannot understand how people are organized collectively or analyze these emergent institutions by examining only the psychological makeup of individuals. Psychology is likely to draw heavily upon sociology in understanding the sociocultural influences that mould individuals.

Weber draws a careful distinction between the related disciplines of sociology and history. For Weber, history is concerned with the causal analysis of particular culturally significant events and personalities. Sociology, on the other hand, deals with the observation and explanation of general patterns of behaviour. History may well draw upon such general explanations to account for unique events. Weber saw himself primarily as a historian, but in his major work, *Economy and Society* ([1922] 1968), he was more concerned with uniformities of socioeconomic organization, in effect, with sociology.

Causal Pluralism   Weber's concern with adequacy at the level of causality also led him to insist on a strategy of **causal pluralism**; that is, on searching for multiple causes for social phenomena. He rejected as misguided and inadequate the efforts of some theorists, and particularly the approach of oversimplified Marxism, which attempt to explain social phenomena in terms of single factors such as economic determinism. Marx criticized Hegel for trying to analyze ideas without any regard for the social conditions in which they emerged. Weber agreed with Marx's criticism, but he also attacked the opposite fallacy committed by many of Marx's disciples who tried to analyze economic forces without regard for the subjectively meaningful response of individuals to their economic circumstances.

For Weber, sociological explanations have to encompass both objective conditions and subjective forces, for it is through subjective understanding and analysis that these objective conditions come to influence human actions as they do. Ideas and values cannot therefore be dismissed as mere by-products of class position, which can be ignored in explanations. Likewise, the economy is not an entity to which people adjust. It is the outcome of people's subjectively meaningful collective behaviour.

Ideal-Type Constructs   Weber advocated **ideal-type** constructs as a method of inquiry that would be adequate at

the level of meaning or interpretive understanding of actions and would at the same time make possible objective and replicable analysis. Ideal-type constructs are theories that accentuate typical characteristics or elements of action. They are not intended to be literal or accurate descriptions of reality, but rather hypothetical models that can be compared with real situations.

Weber argues that this is not so much a new method as a clarification of what social scientists typically do when they try to isolate key elements in a situation. Tönnies developed the model of *gemeinschaft* meaning "community" and *gesellschaft* meaning "association" to accentuate the distinctive characteristics of pre-industrial and urban societies. Durkheim developed the models of mechanical and organic solidarity to accentuate typical forms of social cohesion in undifferentiated and specialized societies. Weber himself developed a series of ideal types of social action that he used as frameworks for exploring distinctive patterns of meaning and action among people in industrial capitalist societies. His ideal-type model of bureaucracy will be described at length later in this chapter.

Objectivity in Social Science   Weber demanded that the study of meaningful action be based upon objectively verifiable and repeatable research. This led to his deep concern with the place of values in research and how objectivity might be possible. Values necessarily enter research as aspects of the subject matter. They also enter as features of the researchers' orientation to the study. Researchers reveal their values by selecting from the infinity of possible subjects those that appear to them to be important or of interest. Nonetheless, Weber insists, the methodology and the outcome of research must be objective; that is, it must be independent of the values of the researcher.

Central to his concern with objectivity is Weber's insistence that science itself cannot pass judgment on values. It is impossible to establish values or ideals scientifically or to decide on a scientific basis what ought to be done. All that science can do is evaluate the adequacy of alternative practical means available for the attainment of given ends, the probable costs of selecting one means over another, and the additional or unforeseen consequences that may arise from particular means.

Weber frequently analyzed the struggle for revolutionary socialism in these terms (Lee and Newby 1983, 200). He argued that the very goal of freedom that is part of the ideal of socialism is threatened by the use of force as a means to achieve socialism and by the political repression inevitably associated with the use of force. He also predicted that the consequences of trying to establish a socialist economy within a largely hostile capitalist world would result in multiple difficulties that would undermine the practice of socialism.

Thirdly, and most importantly, he predicted that whatever means were used to bring about socialism, the ideals of socialism would be compromised by the organizational means needed to coordinate such a society, namely the bureaucratic state. Through his analysis, Weber could show the probable costs and long-term negative consequences of the struggle for socialism but, as he acknowledged himself, such analysis could never answer the ultimate question of whether the struggle would be worthwhile.

In Canada, the free-trade debate provides another example of the limitations of scientific analysis. Social science analysis can add to the debate by showing the probable consequences for various sectors of Canadian and American societies of measures incorporated within the agreement: threatened job losses in some sectors versus the promise of job gains in others; the probable impact upon Canada's cultural industries and social services; and so on. But what such analysis can never determine is whether the end justifies the means, or whether questions of culture or sovereignty should outweigh questions of economic gain, or whether losses to some people count more or less than gains to others. Science cannot answer these questions, which are based on values. At its best, science can only show what the probable costs will be of various means or actions that may be taken towards the attainment of desired goals.

Weber's powerful essays on "Politics as a Vocation" and "Science as a Vocation" address these ethical dilemmas. Weber distinguishes between two fundamental ethics: the **ethic of ultimate ends** and the **ethic of responsibility** (Gerth and Mills 1946, 120). Neither ethic is in and of itself morally superior to the other. The ethic of ultimate ends is essentially religious. Those who pursue such an ethic are so totally committed to their objective that any means are acceptable if they will further this objective. Such people are not swayed by the consequences, however negative, of their means. When members of the Sons of Freedom sect of the Doukhobors in British Columbia practise arson, for example, they do so in the fervent belief that they are called by God to cleanse the world by fire of idolatry and evil. The immediate negative consequences for themselves or others may be of concern to them, but they do not affect their decision whether or not to commit such an act. The ultimate ethic of purification in the service of God has higher value.

Alternatively, those who accept the ethic of responsibility must take account of the consequences of their actions or means chosen to further their goals. They must calculate at each step the probable consequences of and possible hardships and suffering caused by efforts to obtain their goal. This is particularly true in the face of the recognition that the decisive means for politics is violence. Political authority in any state implies a monopoly of the legitimate use of force. Science cannot answer the question

whether, or to what extent, the end justifies the means. Those who imprison Doukhobor women for the crime of arson, and who consider paroling or pardoning them, must weigh the multiple consequences of these actions. They must take responsibility for the probable deaths of the imprisoned women on hunger strike and for the probable property damage in the further acts of arson that may result if the women are freed, and so on.

The recognition that science cannot pass judgment on questions of values led Weber to insist that professors should not teach political positions, any more than religious convictions, to students in the classroom (Gerth and Mills 1946, 145–147). Professors have the same opportunities as other people to air their views in the political arena. They should not use the lecture room for this. Weber was reacting against the practices of the German professors of his day who routinely used their lecterns as pulpits to impose a particular political view of the German state onto students.

Scientific objectivity has nothing to do with ethical neutrality or fence-sitting, or taking some middle road. It has to do with commitment to the examination of facts, facts that are often inconvenient for our own or others' opinions. The ultimate questions of values and commitment lie beyond science, in the realms of faith and revelation.

WEBER'S SUBSTANTIVE CONTRIBUTION
Types of Action Orientation

Weber's model of types of action orientation outlines four basic kinds of meaningful actions or typical orientations that individuals may adopt in relations with one another.

The simplest orientation, **traditional-rational** behaviour, comprises action based on habit. It involves the least amount of conscious thought. Neither the purpose of the actions nor the alternatives are consciously considered. Traditional-rational actions are done because they always have been done that way.

A second orientation, **affective-rational**, is based on emotions. Actions are expressions of emotions, of passions, and they have an immediacy that involves neither calculated weighing of means or consequences nor commitment to values.

A third kind of orientation is **value-rational**. Here the primary focus is upon an overriding ideal, as in religion. Deeply committed people do not ask the consequences of their actions. They do what they believe is right, regardless of the outcome for themselves or others. This is the value orientation that underlies the ethic of ultimate ends.

The fourth and most important basis for authority is **purposive-rational** action. This involves the rational

Table 1 Action Orientation and Legitimate Authority

Types of Action	Types of Legitimate Authority
Traditional-rational (customs)	Hereditary rulers: kings, queens, tribal patriarchs
Affective-rational (emotions)	Charisma of people with extraordinary gifts or supernatural powers: Jesus, Gandhi, Hitler
Value-rational (beliefs)	Religious dogma: Bible, Koran, Talmud, authority of church elders
Purposive-rational (practical effects)	Rational-legal regulations: bureaucratic rules, formal office, civil law

selection, among alternative means, of action that is the most effective for a given end. It includes rational consideration of consequences in relation to other goals. This kind of rationality is easiest to understand and to analyze and is the basic assumption of theory in economics.

It is important to recognize that all four types of orientation are rational. Action in relation to religious values and emotions are equally rational and equally predictable, as are actions based on custom or habit, once the basic orientation itself is known.

This fourfold model of typical action orientations serves to guide research into the meaning of action from the perspective of the participants' own views of that action. The resulting causal explanation suggests the probability of responses of a certain kind, given the action orientation.

Model of Authority   Weber uses this **typology** as a basis for his subsequent model of legitimacy of political authority (see Table 1). He draws an important distinction between power that is based on authority and power based on brute force. Authority is legitimate in that the subordinates themselves accept that those in authority have a right to rule, and therefore to expect compliance, even if one might not always agree with particular policies. Weber defines authority in practice as the probability that a given order will be obeyed by a specific group of people. He argues that there are three bases of authority: traditional; charismatic; and rational-legal.

The simplest and historically the most prevalent basis for authority is **tradition**. Orders are accepted as legitimate when they come from traditional incumbents of hereditary positions. The authority of an elder and patriarch and the divine right of kings rest on such legitimation. Persons exercising power enjoy authority by virtue of their inherited status. Such authority is likely to have force only in relatively stable and unchanging societies.

Authority wielded by **charismatic** figures is very different. Here legitimation is based on the emotional response of followers to a leader who appears to have extraordinary gifts

or supernatural virtue and powers. Great figures in history such as Jesus, Hitler, Gandhi, and Joan of Arc have had such charismatic authority and moved thousands and even millions of people to follow them. E.P. Thompson (1963, 421) described the charismatic power of prophets such as Joanna Southcott whose aura of spiritualism and extraordinary revelation drew a large cult following in England at the turn of the eighteenth century. Charisma means that people are so drawn by the dynamism of the particular person that they are willing to follow that individual without questioning the specifics of policies or direction. The inclusion of Hitler in the list of charismatic figures should be a warning that charisma is a force that can move people for evil as well as for good, or for fleeting goals as well as for critical social

Martin Luther King, Jr., and Malcolm X were charismatic leaders whose radical visions of the future challenged established American ways.

Library of Congress

movements. It is a powerful force for change, but tells nothing about the direction that such change might take.

Weber saw charisma as the most dynamic and free expression of individual creativity, but also the most transitory of all forms of authority. The rise of charismatic figures is associated particularly with periods of trouble and emergency when people are already predisposed to respond to calls for change. A charismatic leader is always a **radical** in challenging established practices and going beyond the rules of everyday life towards new visions.

The problem with authority based on charisma is that it is inherently unstable, lasting only so long as the leader survives and continues to manifest the extraordinary qualities that initially drew the followers. The inevitable death of the leader gives rise to the problem of succession since no successor can hope to command the same charisma. Weber suggests that succession can only take two basic forms. Either it can relapse into hereditary rule based on traditional authority or it can be formalized by elections and rules of organization that shift towards rational-legal authority.

Rational-legal authority is the most important basis for legitimation of power in Weber's model. He saw it as a precondition for the emergence of a modern state and the fundamental legitimation for bureaucratic administration. Rational-legal authority is based on acceptance of the utility of the rules themselves. Orders are obeyed without concern for the personality of the authority figure who set such rules, because the rules themselves are perceived as rational and purposeful.

The Sociology of Power

In his study of political power, Weber sought to elaborate the insights of Marx on the economic basis of class and class struggle. Weber advocated a wider focus on other bases of group identity and organized political action, and hence on alternative bases of power, including the power vested in state administration. These relations, Weber argued, are too complex to be reducible to the single dimension of ownership of the means of production within a society. He developed an alternative model of power that incorporates three distinct, although closely related, dimensions: class; status; and party.

Class Weber shared with Marx the assumption that ownership or non-ownership of the means of production was a major determinant of class position. But he shifts the focus from one of relationships among people in the production process to relative life chances in the labour market. He defined **class** as the chance to use property, goods, and services for exchange in a competitive market. The most advantaged group in a capitalist economy is made up of the owners of land, factories, and financial capital, while the least advantaged class comprises people with no property and no skills. In between them are the middle classes. They comprise those who have some property—the petite bourgeoisie—and those like the intelligentsia, who have some skills. Weber recognized that the proletariat or working class is split by skill differentials. Those with privileged education or professions have very different life chances in the marketplace and very different access to political power than do blue-collar workers who own no property. Such divisions, he predicted, would limit the emergence of class consciousness, since these different life chances would give rise to different values and perspectives upon the world.

Status Weber agreed with Marxist theorists that economic relations of class are central determinants of individual life chances. But he also insisted that actual life chances are too complex to be reducible to economics alone. **Status** also plays a critical role. Status, for Weber, refers to social prestige and honour and is reflected, above all, in styles of life (Gerth and Mills 1946, 186–194). Attributes ascribed by birth, such as nobility, race, ethnicity, sex, and religious affiliation, may be more immediately influential than objective class position in the development of group identity. The nouveau riche, people who make money in business or in a lottery, may well have the financial attributes of the upper class, such as expensive homes and possessions, but they may not have the status to gain acceptance from other members of the upper class. They may well be shunned by families with old wealth and breeding. With the passage of time, the offspring of the nouveau riche may gain acceptance within high-status circles.

Political action is likely to reflect status group as class. Historical conflict between Catholics and Protestants in Northern Ireland, for example, cannot be reduced to class conflict. Similarly, in Canada, the struggle for a distinctive identity among the Québécois, Native peoples, Doukhobors, and many other ethnic minorities cannot be reduced to relative economic advantage alone. Weber recognized that status is frequently a basis for exclusion or relative disadvantage in the market and that this may well foment group conflict and hostility. He insisted, however, that religious and ethnic identities exert an independent causal influence on group identity, styles of life, and life chances.

The relation between class and status in Weber's sociology is one of mutual influence. Shared class position within the economy may foster distinctive values and orientations towards life that can draw people together. In his study of comparative religions, Weber draws many parallels between economic experience and religious values. Disprivileged people, for example, are oriented towards otherworldly religions that promise salvation and just compensation for suffering on earth. Nobles are attracted to the view of a god of passion, wrath, and cunning who can be bribed with booty from war. Bureaucrats favour a comprehensive, sober religion such as Confucianism in China, which is expressed in terms of disciplined order and abstract values. Merchants are generally skeptical or indifferent to otherworldly religions that preach salvation, preferring worldly and nonprophetic theology. Shared religious orientation can in turn serve to reinforce separate group identities and loyalties, which may then be reflected in politics. For Marx, the economy has primacy, but for Weber, status is a related but distinct and powerful force in the political arena.

Party   The concept of **party** for Weber refers to actively organized relations in the political arena. Parties are oriented towards communal action designed to influence policy in favour of specified goals (Gerth and Mills 1946, 194–195). They may represent interests determined through class or through status, or through a combination of the two. Occasionally they represent neither. They differ widely in terms of both the means used to attain power and the kind of community interests that they represent. Above all, the structure and operation of parties reflect the structures of ruling, whether based on hereditary rule, democratic processes, or military coercion or other forms of violence.

A Culture of Rationality

Weber's study of the rise of rationality in Western European culture, and its formal expression in capitalism and bureaucratic forms of state administration, stands as a major contribution to contemporary sociology. Weber returned again and again in his work to the theme of purposive-rational action and rational-legal authority as embodying the central features of modern industrial society.

Weber saw purposive rationality as the distinguishing characteristic of Western civilization. Other types of action orientation—towards tradition, emotions, or values—are identified by Weber as rational in the sense that they can be understood as organized and meaningful behaviour. But they are qualitatively very different forms of action from the distinctly calculated, goal-oriented strategies that constitute purposive-rational action. The differences are so striking that there is some debate whether the term *rational* should properly be applied only to purposive-rational behaviour. Weber clearly considered the latter to be a superior form of rationality, involving calculated orientation towards the efficient use of available means for attaining clearly thought-out goals. Its predominance in Western culture accounts in large part for the spectacular progress of Western civilization. Weber found this calculated form of rationality to pervade all aspects of Western culture—religion, law,

business, administration, politics, art, music, architecture, education, and formal organization, the ultimate expression of which is bureaucracy.

Weber highlighted worldly rationalism in many aspects of Western culture. Western music, for example, pioneered the development of chord patterns and arithmetical relations. Moreover, the formal writing and timing of music for orchestras developed only in the West. Western art moved towards an emphasis on realism and perspective; architecture was dominated by engineering principles, focusing on straight lines and prefabricated buildings rather than intricate designs. Science promoted emphasis on mastering the world.

Rationality also characterized the development of mass education. Weber suggests that this was intimately tied to the demand for trained experts for newly developing rational-legal administration. The education system was oriented to special examinations by means of which incumbents of official positions could be selected on the basis of merit rather than personal considerations. There was also a demand for regular curricula with standardized content.

Rationality found formal expression at all levels of social organization. It was a central principle in the development of Western legal systems as traditional practices and arbitrary local regulations were replaced by a universal, impersonal legal system. Such a system spread over national and international markets and was essential for the development of capitalism. To do business with people across many different regions and societies, capitalists needed the assurance of a unified and calculable system of laws and regulations governing contracts.

The development of rationality in business was visible in several other areas. Rational bookkeeping was critical since it permitted the calculation of profits and losses in terms of money. Capitalism required wage-labourers who were not tied to hereditary obligations to nobles, but who were free to sell their labour power in the market. It also required the absence of restrictions on economic exchange in the market. Capitalism benefited from the development of technology constructed on rational principles, free from religious or cultural sanctions. Weber suggests that Hinduism may have retarded the development of technology in India by vesting it with religious significance and linking it with hereditary caste occupations. In contrast, the more rational religion of Protestantism was important in promoting the development of capitalism in Western Europe.

In *The Protestant Ethic and the Spirit of Capitalism* ([1904] 1930), Weber argued that there was an affinity between the worldly ethic of Calvinism and the rise of capitalism. Protestant doctrine held that it was morally proper and a sign of God's grace to amass wealth. At the same time, Calvinism discouraged spending money on idle consumption or to aid the poor, whose destitution was a sign of damnation. No other ethic, Weber suggests, could have been more exactly suited to the needs of capitalism. Calvinism provided the rational and emotional motivation for the calculated accumulation and reinvestment of profit.

Weber did not claim that Protestantism caused capitalism, although critics have accused him of this. Rather, he saw the affinity between the two—a mutually supportive relation in which the religious ethic encourages behaviour conducive to business rationality while, at the same time, the experience of capitalism generates a propensity to accept a supportive religious ethic.

Above all, the development of capitalism required rational-legal administration. Bureaucracy, which embodies this principle to its fullest extent, was, for Weber, the most rational form of large-scale organization. An office within a bureaucracy is impersonal, separated from the private life and attachments of the incumbents, and obligations are due not to the individual, but to the office itself.

Bureaucracy

Weber's ideal-type model of **bureaucracy** is the most famous and the most influential of all his typologies of social action. There are seven elements to this model (see Table 2).

Table 2 Weber's Model of Bureaucracy

1. Permanent offices guarantee continuous organization of functions, which are bounded by written rules.

2. The rules set out specialized tasks, with appropriate authority and sanctions, so that everyone knows precisely who has responsibility for what.

3. These specialized functions are organized in terms of the principle of hierarchy and levels of graded authority. Lower offices operate under the control and supervision of higher offices.

4. The principle of trained competence ensures that the incumbents of these offices have thorough and expert training, appropriate for their level within the hierarchy.

5. The resources of the organization are strictly separated from those of the individuals who occupy the different offices. This was a critical change from past practice when tax collectors, for example, were required to pay a certain amount from what they collected to the state and live on the surplus.

6. Administrative actions, decisions, and rules are recorded in writing. The combination of written documents and continuous organization of official functions constitutes the office.

7. These rules guarantee impersonality in the operations of the office, allowing neither favours nor patronage.

The Official   Weber elaborated a further model of the position of the official (Gerth and Mills 1946, 198–204). He stressed that the office is a **vocation**, with performance a duty not exploited for personal gain. Prescribed training and examinations are prerequisites for such employment. These promote the rationality in education noted above. Officers have specified obligations and fixed salaries. They are selected on the basis of their technical qualifications and not favouritism, nepotism, or ascribed characteristics. They are appointed rather than elected. Election, suggests Weber, would compromise the strictness of hierarchical subordination because incumbents would owe loyalties to those who elected them. As appointed officials, they are directly subordinate to the superior who appoints them. Work is a lifetime career, with a fixed salary and the right to a pension. This further serves to reduce susceptibility to bribery or to the temptation to use the office for personal profit. Independence from personal considerations in the discharge of official duties is legally guaranteed by tenure. The result of this form of organization is impartial performance of duties with maximum calculability and reliability.

It should be emphasized that Weber was constructing an ideal-type model of bureaucracy and bureaucratic officials. He was not claiming that any existing bureaucracy would exactly fit all these characteristics. The model is intended to function as a theoretical tool for practical research. It abstracts typical features and their typical interrelations. The extent to which any specific organization conforms to or deviates from this model is a matter for empirical research.

Advantages of Bureaucracy   Bureaucracies have major advantages over other forms of organization, such as honorific administration by courtiers, relatives of the ruler, or amateurs. Bureaucratic organizations have decisive technical superiority. They can operate with precision, speed, and with unambiguous and predictable performance based on rules. They ensure continuity, unity, and strict subordination, which reduces friction between officials. Personal and material costs of administration are reduced to a minimum.

Once fully established, bureaucracy is virtually indestructible. It is *the* means of carrying out community action. It can be made to work for anyone who can control it, because discipline and compliance are built into the structure. The system itself is able to ensure that the staff within the organization cannot squirm out of their responsibilities, for the specialized duties of each office are clearly spelled out. The consequences of bureaucratic power depend on the direction in which it is used. It is at the disposal of varied political and economic interests. As a technical means of organized action, it is vastly superior in effectiveness to any mass action that is not so organized.

Weber argued that bureaucracy was essential to many developments in the modern world. Capitalism needed the precise rules of bureaucracy to organize trade over long periods of time and in foreign countries. A centralized administration was critical for the development of a unified German state. In addition, bureaucracy is indispensable for democracy. As Weber expresses it, the fate of the masses depends on the steady, correct functioning of state administration. It is essential for the equality of treatment implied in democracy. All clients must be treated the same and be subject to the same uniform rules. Such equality presupposes impartial, regulated organization that operates without hatred or passion, without favouritism or prejudice. Weber argued that it is impossible to get rid of bureaucracies, for only such a system provides protection from undependable and amateur administration, favouritism, and corruption.

The Iron Cage

The negative side of bureaucracy lies in its power to compress all human diversity into conformity with its regulations. Bureaucracy threatens to become, in Weber's words, an **iron cage**, imprisoning the human spirit. For Weber, the bureaucratic mode of organization represents the purest expression of purposive-rational action. He never doubted its technical efficiency or its indispensability for rational capitalist enterprise and state administration. Yet he was deeply pessimistic regarding the negative impact of bureaucracy on the quality of modern life. No sphere of social action more completely exemplifies Weber's warning that the means needed to achieve valued ends may have negative consequences that undermine or destroy the very ends themselves. Weber feared that bureaucratic organization threatened the most cherished political goals of the twentieth century: democracy and socialism.

Weber believed that bureaucracy, based on principles of technical expertise and professional secrecy of office, and swollen to millions of functionaries, would come to exercise virtually unassailable power. Democracy, with its goal of social levelling and equality of treatment, could not function without bureaucratic organization, yet this form of administration has the inherent effect of promoting and sustaining a closed group of officials, with the authority of officialdom, raised over public opinion. People would find themselves disempowered against the bureaucratic experts.

Not only ordinary people, but also their elected representatives would be affected. Efficient bureaucracy rests on technical superiority of knowledge. Inevitably, officials would welcome a poorly informed and hence powerless parliament. There are built-in incentives for officials to fight every attempt of parliament to gain knowledge of bureaucratic affairs. Elected ministers depend on bureaucrats for information on which to base policies.

The loyalty of officials lies not with the general public or the electorate, but with the bureaucracy itself. Their vocation is to serve their official duties. In Canada, as in other Western democracies, it is a criminal offence for civil servants within the state administration to divulge internal policy documents to the public. One official in the Department of Indian Affairs who leaked information about proposed cutbacks to Native funding was summarily dismissed.

Socialism, no less than multi-party democracy, is threatened by bureaucratic administration. Socialism may abolish the power of the bourgeoisie through the socialization of the means of economic production, but it cannot abolish the power of the new class of officials. In all probability, Weber thought, officialdom might come to exert even more of a stranglehold on society under socialism because the countervailing forces of entrepreneurs and free enterprise under capitalism would be absent.

Weber argues that it would be illogical to try to control bureaucratic power by making the inner workings of officials subject to the scrutiny of laypeople. This would undermine the efficiency, speed, calculability, and impersonality of the bureaucratic machine itself, and thus undercut the very qualities that make for superior administration.

Weber saw that the inevitable consequence of the smoothly running bureaucratic machine would be the dehumanization of all who come into contact with it. The rigidly defined regulations and responsibilities of an office provide for calculated efficiency but, as a consequence, the individuality of people who must relate to it, either as employees or clients, cannot be admitted. Bureaucracies are oriented towards *formal* rationality—the purposively rational performance of standardized and routine functions. They are opposed in principle to the *substantive* rationality of individual circumstances. A system designed to treat everyone equally inevitably lacks the flexibility to treat individual cases as unique. Those who do not fit the patterns for which the rules are established cannot receive the specialized services they may need. For them the formally rational system becomes substantively irrational.

Those who work as employees within the bureaucracy are even more rigidly subject to its regulations. They operate as cogs in the machine. The major requirement for their position is unquestioning and strict adherence to written regulations within their narrowly defined areas of jurisdiction. Their individuality has no place within such a system, for it would disrupt the calculated order.

Weber believed that the iron cage spread beyond bureaucracy itself, for this mode of organization is only the extreme expression of the purposive-rational orientation that dominates all aspects of Western civilization itself.

Science brings with it the demythification of the universe. As Weber expresses it, "the fate of our times is characterized by rationalization and intellectualization, and above all, by the 'disenchantment of the world'" (Gerth and Mills 1946, 155).

For Weber there is no escape. "To the person who cannot bear the fate of times like a man," Weber offers only the retreat into silence and into the old religions. Weber feels that it is understandable that people should turn to religion in the hope of finding a refuge from scientific rationality and an alternative account of the meaning of life. Those who embrace religious doctrine are unable to face reality as it appears in the light of rational, scientific study. They may find comfort in the church, but only at the price of closing their minds to scientific knowledge, an intellectual sacrifice that Weber finds unacceptable. Such a retreat must inevitably fail to satisfy people because they are compelled to recognize their concomitant loss of intellectual integrity. As Weber sees it, "the arms of the old churches are opened widely and compassionately for [us]," but this emotional escape is only for those who cannot "meet the demands of the day." The iron cage of rationality is the fate of our time.

The Limitations of Weber's Thought

It is not easy to criticize Weber's thought on intellectual grounds, for it seems that all the usual criticisms are synthesized or neutralized by Weber himself. The approach of functionalism, which locates people as socialized members of an overarching system, is subsumed and transcended in Weber's work. The classical structuralist Marxist thesis, which seeks to understand human alienation in the exploitative relations of capitalism, is also incorporated. Marxism offers no ultimate escape from the experience of alienation and dehumanization, for socialism is also an iron cage, albeit of a different sort. Exploitation under capitalism is only replaced by a deeper dehumanization under centralized bureaucratic control. The interpretive focus on individuals as makers of their own social world is, or seems to be, incorporated as well through Weber's emphasis on meaningful understanding. This understanding is subsumed in his ideal-type model of action orientation.

Weber is his own best critic. He acknowledges that the logical conclusions to his own arguments point to a world that he finds unbearable, dehumanized. For long periods of his life he was profoundly depressed and unable to work. This depression can only be partially accounted for in terms of his personal life and psychological makeup. In part it stemmed from the intellectual hell created by his own ideas.

Rational Action Re-examined: The Feminist Challenge

How can we challenge Weber's theory so that we are not condemned to the same disenchantment and despair? A basic problem in Weber's work seems to lie in its starting assumption, in the conceptualization of rationality itself. Weber divides rationality into four distinct types of orientation: traditional, affective, value, and purposive rationality. He claims that Western civilization is characterized by the triumph of the last form as reflected in science, in capitalism, in a worldly success ethic in religion, in rational-legal authority, and ultimately in bureaucratic organizations.

The question Weber does not raise is: How can a civilization, or a mode of organization, be rational if the result is the destruction of the human spirit itself? Weber is deeply aware that the rational choice of means may destroy the intended ends but he does not question the rationality of purposive action dissociated, as it is, from cultural traditions and emotional or spiritual foundations. He sees such separation as necessary for the modern world, whatever its emotional costs.

When Weber separates types of rationality, he is following a long intellectual tradition in Western thought. This tradition commonly draws a distinction between rational and emotional behaviour. Men tend to be thought of as more rational and intellectual while women are conceived of as more emotional and natural or physical. The masculine principle is thus rational. It is perhaps for this reason that Weber slips into the easy characterization of those who retreat into religion as people "who cannot bear the fate of the times like a *man*." The assumption seems to be that, in the modern world, retreat into emotions and religious values is inappropriate for men although perhaps acceptable and even normal for women.

Feminist theory, more clearly than other theoretical approaches in sociology, has challenged the separation of rational and emotional, of masculine and feminine, as an injustice to the nature of both women and men. Despite the enormous scope of his scholarship, and the depth of his insight, Weber nowhere explicitly considers the position of women or their role in the development of Western civilization. He does not seem to question their absence from intellectual debate. In his personal life, it is clear that his mother was a central figure in his own intellectual development and that his wife Marianne was the person who held him together during his years of depression and made it possible for him eventually to begin work again. Yet the role of women remains invisible in his intellectual work on the nature of man and civilization. How can this happen?

The feminist critique points to the major flaw in his starting assumptions of action orientation. He separates types of rationality so that purposive-rational-legal action—the masculine principle—is separated from the emotional and value-oriented dimensions—the feminine principle. Weber's characterization of Western civilization is, implicitly, a profoundly sexist characterization, although he did not perceive it as such.

The malaise in Weber's work is in essence the malaise of Western civilization itself. Weber sees only too clearly the nature of this disorder: the disenchantment inherent in a civilization that elevates purposive-rational action to the highest form. But he is unable to transcend this view. In Marcuse's terms (1964), he remains trapped in **one-dimensional thought**, unable to conceive of viable alternatives that do not entail intellectual retreat.

It is the breakdown of the unity of cultural, emotional, and spiritual elements of purposive action that makes possible the colossal destruction wrought in the name of rational modernization in the pursuit of profit. The decision of a capitalist to exploit other people and the environment, to further the goal of short-term profit, is one that has emotional and moral components, whether these are recognized or not. It is also a decision embedded in a habitual or traditional mode of action in Western culture. Weber's artificial division into types of orientation, with only one dimension given recognition, does not hold up. The alternative view, which is reflected in feminist theory, albeit often in confused and half-understood ways, is that no individual, no action, no organization, no civilization can be truly rational if it does not integrate the "masculine" and the "feminine," such that tradition, emotion, and spirituality are integrated into purposive action.

The practical critiques of Weber's thesis on rationality usually have not gone this far, but they reflect the recognition that purposive-rational action, separated from other considerations, is often irrational, particularly in its practical embodiment in bureaucratic modes of organization. Weber's thesis that bureaucracy is the most efficient mode of organization has been challenged precisely because bureaucracy reduces employees to trained robots and clients to standardized cases where their real circumstances cannot be taken into account.

The Marxist critique within organization theory rejects the notion of rationality as the root of bureaucratic structures. It raises the possibility that the very notion of rationality itself is a form of ideological hegemony to legitimate the exploitation of the mass of employees by those who direct the organization. Rationality is an ideology of the most invidious kind because it seems so neutral, so objective, that even to challenge it seems unreasonable.

Theorists who have been most influenced by Weber's own methodological concern with interpretive understanding of human action have challenged his thesis as an unjustifiable reification of a system. From the perspective of the social construction of reality, and of ethnomethodology, Weber's model functions as ideology, or as a convenient way of accounting for what people seem to be doing, but not as a causal explanation for behaviour. The model of bureaucracy pays too little attention to the understanding that individuals themselves have of their relationships with one another. Nor does it pay enough attention to what people actually do, as distinct from what they are supposed to be doing according to the formal plan. The formal model is not a literal description of reality, but rather an accounting procedure, a way in which people have learned to talk about what they do to make sense of it.

CONCLUSION

The legacy of Weber in contemporary sociology is enormous. His concern with promoting a social science methodology that would have interpretive understanding as its central objective is only just coming to fruition with the development of ethnomethodology.

Weber's substantive and theoretical contribution to sociology was profoundly shaped by his lifelong dialogue with the ghost of Marx. Weber tried to build upon and go beyond the basic conception of the nature of capitalism and class in Marxist theory while rejecting the oversimplified versions of Marxist thought that reduce human behaviour to economic determinism. Weber insisted that emotional life, values, meaning, or culture must be taken into account as critical aspects of all human behaviour, including economic activities. His famous study of The Protestant Ethic and the Spirit of Capitalism explores the religious and moral basis of the drive to accumulate wealth, which helped to foster the development of capitalism in Europe. His other historical and comparative studies of religions and sects in Europe, India, and China focus upon the interrelationship between life experiences, based on class position and mode of production, and forms of religious thought.

Weber shared with Marx an emphasis on the economic base of life chances in relation to modes of production, but he broadened this focus to explore the diversity of class experience. Weber recognized that in a complex, industrial society skills in themselves constitute a form of means of production. Those who have skills to sell in the marketplace are in a profoundly different class position from propertyless, unskilled labourers. Weber emphasized the importance of status in the formation of social groups. Status is based on ascriptive criteria of ethnicity, race, sex, age, and the like. For Marx, these were merely secondary reflections of economic class position, but for Weber they appeared as important determinants of life chances in their own right. The fact that these variables work at the level of meaning and emotion, rather than material need, makes them no less important as dimensions of human experience. Weber shared with Durkheim an awareness of the importance of social cohesion, which cannot be reduced to dimensions of class.

Weber's distinctive contribution to sociology lies in his analysis of rationality in Western culture and its particular expression in the rise of bureaucratic modes of formal organization in business and government. Weber's model of bureaucracy has profoundly influenced the development of organization theory in sociology. Much of the work in the field is either an elaboration or test of his insights, or a critical counterproposal to them. In contemporary postindustrial society, characterized by the corporate concentration of capital, multinational corporations the size of nation states, and centralized state administrations, these bureaucratic organizations are not merely facts of life, but dominant features of human experience.

SUGGESTED READING

A very readable selection of writings by Max Weber is provided by Stanislav Andreski, ed. *Max Weber on Capitalism, Bureaucracy and Religion: A Selection of Texts* (1983). Andreski provides a brief introduction to Weber's writings, followed by selected excerpts from writings on the uniqueness of Western capitalism, cultural factors that impeded the development of capitalism in the ancient world and in Asia, and the rise of Protestantism and rationalism in the West.

Another useful source is the collection of Weber's writings edited by W.G. Runciman, *Weber: Selections in Translation* (1978). See particularly Part 1, "The Foundations of Social Theory," with selections on social organization, classes, status groups, and parties, and Chapter 18, "The Development of Bureaucracy and Its Relation to Law."

The selection by H.H. Gerth and C. Wright Mills, *From Max Weber: Essays in Sociology* (1946), is generally very heavy reading, but it provides an excellent introduction to Weber's theory of bureaucracy in Part 8, especially the first two selections, "The Characteristics of Bureaucracy" and "The Position of the Official."

QUESTIONS

1. How does Weber reconcile the idea that human action is based on free will with the idea that it is predictable?
2. Why does Weber believe that explanations in sociology must take the form of probabilities rather than clear predictions?
3. What is the role of ideal-type constructs in sociological research?
4. How does Weber modify Marx's definition of *class*?
5. Distinguish between the ethic of responsibility and the ethic of ultimate ends.
6. How does rational-legal authority differ from traditional authority?
7. Why does Weber insist that bureaucratic officials should be appointed rather than elected to office?
8. How does Weber account for the historical association between the rise of capitalism and Protestantism?
9. Why did Weber claim that bureaucracy was fundamentally incompatible with democracy?
10. What is the basis of the feminist critique of Weber's notion of purposive-rational action?

KEY TERMS

affective-rational action

bureaucracy

causal pluralism

charismatic authority

class

ethic of responsibility

ethic of ultimate ends

historical materialism

idealism

ideal-type model

ideographic

iron cage

nomothetic

one-dimensional thought

party

positivists

probability

psychological reductionism

purposive-rational action
radical
rational-legal authority
reification
social action
status

traditional authority
traditional-rational action
typology
value-rational action
verstehen
vocation

REFERENCES

Ashley, D., and M. Orenstein. 1985. *Sociological Theory: Classical Statements*. Boston: Allyn & Bacon.

Gerth, H.H., and C.W. Mills. 1946. From *Max Weber: Essays in Sociology*. New York: Oxford University Press.

Giddens, A. 1971. *Capitalism and Modern Social Theory*. London: Cambridge University Press.

Lee, D., and H. Newby. 1983. *The Problem of Sociology*. London: Hutchinson.

Marcuse, H. 1964. *One-Dimensional Man*. Boston: Beacon Press.

Simmel, G. 1950. "The Metropolis and Mental Life." In *The Sociology of George Simmel*. Glencoe, Illinois: Free Press, 409–424.

Simmel, G. 1949. "The Sociology of Sociability." *American Journal of Sociology* (Nov.): 254–261.

Thompson, E.P. 1963. *The Making of the English Working Class*. Harmondsworth, UK: Penguin.

Weber, M. [1922] 1968. G. Roth and G. Wittich, trans. *Economy and Society: An Outline of Interpretive Sociology*. New York: Bedminister Press.

Weber, M. [1904] 1930. *The Protestant Ethic and the Spirit of Capitalism*. London: Unwin University Books.

Functionalist theory, particularly as elaborated by Talcott Parsons (1902–1979), was generally accepted in North America as the orthodox approach to the study of society during the 1950s and 1960s, and was claimed by some to be virtually equivalent to sociology as a whole. It remains the mainstream theoretical approach in the United States. The study of society as a functioning system, comprising interdependent institutions that each perform specialized functions for the social whole, still dominates the format of most introductory texts in sociology. Only in the last decade or so has more critical political economy theory begun to achieve equivalent stature in Canada.

The core ideas of functionalism are contained in the analogy that Herbert Spencer drew between social systems and biological organisms. Biological organisms are first and foremost bounded systems; that is, they are distinct entities or bodies that maintain themselves in a state of relative equilibrium or balance. They have built-in self-regulating mechanisms that keep the body in a relatively stable state, continually compensating for environmental changes. The human body, for example, maintains the same basic temperature and has a very narrow range of tolerance for fluctuations in this temperature. If too hot, we automatically begin to sweat, and the resulting evaporation cools us. If too cold, we begin to shiver, our body hair becomes more erect, and body temperature rises. Similarly, a complex enzyme system triggered by insulin keeps the blood sugar level in balance, continually compensating for extra sugar absorbed from food and sugar used up in exercise. Biological sciences explore these balancing mechanisms while medical sciences seek to intervene during extreme situations of illness or injury when the natural equilibrium breaks down.

In order to maintain themselves in a state of equilibrium or health, organisms have basic needs that must be met. We all know that green plants need some minimal access to light, water, and water-soluble minerals in order to survive. The human body, at a minimum, needs food, water, shelter, and a tolerable temperature range for survival. A host of higher-order needs must be met for our bodies to function at full capacity. All organisms are made up of specialized parts that have specific functions for the body as a whole. If any one part is missing or malfunctioning, it has repercussions for the rest. A central concern of biological sciences is to explore these specialized functions and how the various parts work together. Bodies can be conceptualized as made up of numerous subsystems, such as the digestive system, the nervous system, the blood circulatory system, and so on, which are themselves comprised of multiple subparts. All must work together in coordinated ways for the organism to function in a healthy way. Most of us are not conscious of these subsystems working, except when something abnormal happens. Then we turn to the medical and biological sciences for explanations.

Talcott Parsons (1902–1979)

Courtesy of Harvard University Archives

The Analogy between Biological and Social Systems

Functionalism as a social science seeks to analyze societies in ways analogous to the biological study of organisms. The society itself is conceptualized as a bounded, self-maintaining system, comprising numerous specialized parts that must function together in coordinated ways. These multiple parts and subparts of societies, such as families, religion, education, and political and economic structures, are analyzed in terms of their functions or contributions to the operation of the whole system. Each of these parts can in turn be analyzed as a system, with system prerequisites and regulating mechanisms.

Certain operating assumptions in the biological sciences have also been taken over in functional analysis in sociology. The first basic assumption is that organisms are best analyzed as **functional unities** rather than as disconnected bits. While it may be very valuable for individual researchers to focus on specialized parts, it is important never to lose sight of the fact that these parts operate only within the environment of the body as a whole.

A second working assumption is **universal functionalism**. Any characteristic of an organism is assumed to have some necessary function that it performs for the body as a whole. Scientists may not yet know what the function of a particular tiny element of a cell or an enzyme might be, but that quest itself becomes a meaningful focus for future research.

The third working assumption, which is closely related to the second, is **functional indispensability**. Each and every element of an organism is assumed to have its own unique and specialized function that the organism would miss if that part were absent or damaged. The argument goes that if organisms did have vestigial or accidental parts that served no useful function, such parts would in all likelihood atrophy and disappear over time. The persistence of certain characteristics is itself an important indication that they serve some useful function.

In functionalist theory in sociology, these same basic assumptions of functional unity, universal functionalism, and functional indispensability guide research questions. A society is analyzed as essentially a social system that cannot be reduced to fragmented groups of people. In this sense, the whole is greater than the sum of the parts. Recurrent characteristics of societies are assumed to perform necessary functions, and an adequate explanation for their persistence consists of discovering and explicating what these functions are. They may be obvious or *manifest functions*, which are widely acknowledged by society's members, or *latent functions*, which may not be consciously recognized by many people but which nonetheless meet important social needs. For functionalists, the value of sociological research lies in disclosing these latent functions, hence increasing our understanding of why certain elements of our society have the characteristics they do.

Durkheim and Erikson's analyses of the latent function of crime in the maintenance of group boundaries and distinctive identities are good examples of the functionalist approach. Coser's (1956) insightful analysis of the social functions of conflict is another example. He shows that, like pain in an organism, conflict gives advance warning of strains within the social system and encourages adaptations or innovations that reduce the conflict and so increase levels of comfort and well-being in society. Two-party or multiparty political systems are especially functional for airing conflicts early and dealing with them in constructive and integrative ways rather than allowing them to build up to an explosive point. The universal characteristic of stratification in societies has also drawn particular attention from functionalist theorists. Their basic explanation is that some system of inequality of rewards meets the essential function of motivating the more able and committed people in a society to strive for the more difficult and socially important jobs. In each of these examples, functional analysis shifts the focus of inquiry from the origins of certain patterns in society to why they persist. The operating assumption for research is that social structures continue because they serve some immediate useful purpose for the society.

The term *useful* itself deserves further consideration since it raises the question, useful for what? Functionalist theorists answer this question essentially the same way biologists do. Different features of society are functional when they help in some way, either manifest or latent, to maintain a stable and integrated social whole, that is, to maintain the state of dynamic equilibrium.

Functionalism promised to provide a truly scientific approach to the study of society. It enabled sociology in a sense to come of age and to join the other natural sciences such as biology, adopting analogous research strategies in the study of social systems. Sociology promised in principle to achieve a unification of all the sciences. The practical value of sociology is that it promised to provide the basic research knowledge required for promoting a harmonious and integrated social order. In a world torn apart by wars and facing the upheavals of the scientific-technological revolution of the twentieth century, such a science was urgently sought and readily accepted.

PARSONS' MODEL OF A SOCIAL SYSTEM

Variants of the functionalist approach had long proven their usefulness in anthropology for the study of small, relatively isolated tribal societies. But it was Talcott Parsons who unquestionably deserves credit for systematizing and elaborating functionalism for application to advanced industrial societies. Parsons is credited, more than any other social theorist, with developing the scientific credibility of sociology. Through his efforts, sociologists began to play an advisory role to governments (Buxton 1985, Ch. 7).

Early in his career, Parsons undertook the intellectually enormous task of trying to synthesize major theories of society into a comprehensive framework around the notion of a system of social action. In his book *The Structure of Social Action* ([1937] 1968), he insisted that such a unifying system had to begin with a **voluntaristic theory** of action. People in society are not like cells in a body, preprogrammed to behave in fixed ways. People make free choices. With rare exceptions, people feel that they do what they do voluntarily, and yet the outcome of these individual actions and choices is a stable social system. How is this possible?

In his second major study, *The Social System* (1951), Parsons formulated a basic model of society, its major parts, and how they are integrated in patterned ways. The model begins with individual actors as the basic building blocks. The critical problem that Parsons grapples with is order. How is order possible in a social system made up of individuals who are capable of making free choices? How can choices be, at the same time, free and yet predictable in an orderly way? The answer, for Parsons, lies in Durkheim's conception of the *conscience collective*: order is produced by moral or normative consensus. Parsons himself criticizes Durkheim for downplaying the central importance or normative consensus in industrial society and for failing to explain the basis of compliance to norms, except through fear of sanctions.

For Parsons, the basis of compliance, and hence the key to the problem of how order is sustained, lies in the internalization of norms. Actors cooperate because they internalize proper courses of action as well as the related values that make them feel shame or loss of self-respect if they fail to live up to these moral values. Knowledge that others share these values and will also react negatively to noncompliance further confirms people in their desire to conform (Heritage 1984, Ch. 2). From this perspective, norms are internalized as **need dispositions**. This means that people tend to want to act in conformity with norms and feel dissatisfied if they cannot do so. Norms can be treated as causes of action. Individual actors make choices in the context of particular situations with given means, with ends in view, and with underlying values. These voluntary choices take the form of patterned and predictable behaviour because of the internalization of shared norms at the fundamental level of individual personalities. Ostensibly subjective individual choices become amenable to objective or external scientific analysis in terms of the patterns of values that constrain and determine conduct.

Values can be said to be institutionalized as part of the normative order of society when they are widely internalized. They are institutionalized when the vast majority of society's members choose to conform, feel guilt or shame if they do not conform, expect such conformity of each other, and react negatively with criticisms or punishment when these expectations are not met. The innermost circle of control is the internalized desire to conform and internalized guilt, bolstered by approval or disapproval of our friends and close associates. Eventually, economic sanctions come into play as we risk not being hired, losing our jobs, or losing out on benefits when others disapprove of us. Force comes into play only as a last resort.

Roles and the Social System

Shared values alone are insufficient to produce a stable social system of functionally interrelated parts. More detailed sets of behavioural prescriptions are required. These give precise directions for how to behave in different situations and are provided by the **institutionalization** of typical roles. In the Parsonian model, society comprises a system of roles. Roles are typical ways of behaving in predefined situations and exist independently of any individual in a particular situation. We learn how to behave in such roles, which are predefined for us in varying degrees of detail.

Parsons' voluntaristic theory of action begins with the study of actors and behaviour in typical situations, rather than with the study of total individuals. The social context sets the actor's role.

The process by which we learn the behavioural expectations of different roles and the underlying values that motivate conformity to them is termed *socialization*. Socialization is a lifelong process in which we learn by modelling ourselves on others. As children, we learn first by watching our parents as role models. We later expand our horizons to others whom we want to emulate. As with core societal values, we come to internalize these behavioural expectations and want to conform to them as part of a basic need to belong and to be approved of. As adults we learn a great variety of different roles, but the process is essentially the same. What society expects of us we come to expect of ourselves. In a sense we become our roles; they become part of us and how we identify ourselves. Hence we feel a sense of duty to fulfill our roles and pangs of guilt if we fail to live up to them.

Individuals perform a series of roles over a lifetime. They also perform a number of distinct and partially connected roles at any one time. Imagine, for a moment, that you are a parent, a classroom teacher, a town councillor, the director of a fundraising committee, and a member of a local homeowners' association. In some situations, you may find yourself wearing several hats at once. This might occur if there happens to be a petition from the homeowners' association to the town council about where to locate a proposed school playing field for which you are a fundraiser. All of these roles have to be integrated. According to Parsons, the personality comprises the system that integrates the various roles that one person plays.

Role Theory

A branch of functional analysis loosely referred to as **role theory** (Biddle and Thomas 1966) concerns itself with our interactive behaviour. The study of **role sets** analyzes overlapping roles and reciprocal expectations for behaviour in specific situations. The terminology here can be confusing. Sometimes the role set consists of the variety of roles played by one person. More commonly, role sets refer to the variety of roles played by different people that interact or impinge upon each other in a given situation. In either case, the theoretical issues raised are similar.

Different roles are associated with different behavioural expectations that may not always be compatible. A familiar example is that of a school. Overlapping roles include those of students, teachers, parents, head teachers and other administrators, school boards, and support staff such as secretaries, cooks, and caretakers. Sometimes one person may play several of these roles at once, as in the case of a school secretary who is also the parent of a student at the school, or a teacher who may also be a parent and a member of the school board. More commonly, these roles will be played by different people. Each of these positions comprises a set of typical behaviour expectations, and the incumbents of each role have expectations concerning each of the overlapping roles. **Role strain** occurs when incumbents of related roles have differing sets of expectations. For example, parents and teachers may differ in their conception of the teaching role and appropriate classroom behaviour. These potential strains are usually minimized by **role segregation**, a separation in time and space that partially insulates any one role from the others. Parents generally enter classrooms and meet with teachers only at specified and delimited times. School board personnel similarly set policies but do not participate in the day-to-day running of the classroom, unless serious breaches of role expectations occur.

A different kind of role strain occurs within individual actors trying to balance the demands of simultaneous roles that they play in different situations. The role sets of career person and parent, for example, entail different and competing expectations. Again, this potential strain is reduced by segregation of roles in time and space. At certain times of the day and in certain places, the role demands of the job take precedence; at other times, those of parenting are more important. Problems occur only when the role segregation

breaks down, as when children are sick and require parenting during the workday or when a parent is trying to work at home. Such strains may be reduced by a subset of rules permitting time off work for extraordinary parenting problems, or by the careful segregation of one room in the house for the office. A wealth of detailed case studies in the role theory tradition has documented the reciprocal expectations and rules concerning contingencies of behaviour that permit such complex sets of roles to function smoothly.

Parsons thus bases his model on internalized moral consensus, which guides choices, and internalized expectations for behaviour in typical situations. Both of these are learned through socialization. He then turns his attention to the construction of an elaborate model of the total action system.

The Social System in a General Scheme of Action

Parsons (1978, 18) defines social action as consisting of "the structures and processes by which human beings form meaningful intentions and, more or less successfully, implement them in concrete situations." He conceptualizes this action system as comprising four primary subsystems that are hierarchically organized in relation to each other: the cultural system, the social system, the personality system, and the behavioural organism. Together they form what Parsons terms the **"cybernetic hierarchy"**; that is, a hierarchy of systems of control and communication in human action. Each of these four subsystems of action are referred to as systems in their own right or as subsystems with reference to the total action system.

The **cultural system** is the broadest of all the subsystems of action. It forms the top of the hierarchy of control. It comprises the system of beliefs, rituals, values, and symbols—including language as a symbol system—through which people confront ultimate questions about reality, the meaning of good and evil, of suffering and death. Culture is thus fundamentally religious. A cultural system is normally broader than any one society. Many societies, for example, share a common Christian culture. In areas containing many societies, distinct cultural systems, such as Muslim and Christian, for example, may intermingle. In his abstract model, Parsons does not consider the possibility that a stable society may encompass more than one cultural system.

The **social system** operates at the second level in the **hierarchy** of control. It institutionalizes overarching cultural values into structures and processes that collectively organize action. Norms translate cultural values into specific regulations that define the status, rights, and obligations of members. Through such structures, the social system manages the potential for conflict and disorganization between elements in the action system and so maintains social order. The critical function of the social system is to integrate the cultural system with the personality systems of members and the physical requirements of the behavioural organism. The cultural system functions reciprocally to legitimate these societal-level institutions.

A **society** is a particular type of social system, characterized by what Parsons (1978, 22, 29) terms "territorial integrity and self-sufficiency." A society is a large-scale social system that controls behaviour within a given territory, has relatively clear membership status, and is capable of meeting all the life needs of members at all stages of life. In terms of such a definition, Canada can be considered both a society and a social system. A monastery of celibate monks is a social system but not a society because it has to recruit members from outside. The distinction between society and social system is ambiguous in practice. It is unclear whether communities such as a province or a Hutterite colony, for example, constitute a society or merely a social system. The argument tends to focus on relative territorial control, relative self-sufficiency, or relative clarity of membership status. To the extent that Canada is not economically self-sufficient, even its status as a society could be questioned. In practice, these terms are often used interchangeably, although social system is reserved for settings that are obviously not self-sufficient.

The third system in Parsons' scheme of social action is the **personality system**. Individual personalities are in some sense unique, but they are also constrained and patterned by the social and cultural systems in which they develop. Personality is the learned component of the behaving individual, with socialization as the critical process in the formation of personality. The social system integrates the personality system and the cultural system through the organized processes of learning, developing, and maintaining adequate motivation for participating in socially valued and controlled patterns of action (Parsons 1978, 25). Individual value commitments are formed by the shared cultural system while individual motivations are harnessed primarily by internalized loyalties and obligations to the family system. The fundamental function of the personality system within the action system is orientation towards the attainment of goals. The personality system serves the social system through the performance of roles in collectively organized actions.

The fourth subsystem in social action is the behavioural organism. The **behavioural organism** provides the energy for all the higher-level systems and also grounds the action system in the physical environment. The social system integrates the behavioural organism into the action system through organizing the processes that meet the basic requirements of food and shelter and the allocation of resources among producers and consumers.

System Prerequisites The action system as a whole and each of its subsystems are conceptualized by Parsons as meeting a set of four **prerequisites** on which the balance of each system depends. These prerequisites are **latency** or **pattern maintenance**, **integration**, **goal attainment**, and **adaptation**. With respect to the total action system, the cultural subsystem meets the function of latency or pattern maintenance, serving as a reference system of values and meanings in terms of which the other elements in the system are patterned. The social system meets the function of integration, organizing, and coordinating the elements in the system. The personality system meets the function of goal attainment, providing the fundamental motivating drive for action. The behavioural organism meets the function of adaptation, relating the action system to the physical environment that constrains action. These four functions—goal attainment, adaptation, integration, and latency—are often referred to as Parsons' **GAIL model** (see Figure 1).

Each subsystem of the action system has to meet the same set of four **system prerequisites**. Within the social system, for example, the function of goal attainment is performed by political structures, including pressure groups, political parties, and governing bodies such as parliament. It is through such structures that priorities and future directions of the society are sorted out. Economic structures perform the function of adaptation, both developing and distributing resources through such agencies as farms, factories, and the marketplace. The function of integration is provided by law and administration. They serve to coordinate activities, regulate contracts, and generally pull the parts of the social system together. Latency or pattern maintenance is performed by such institutions as schools, churches, and families, which socialize the younger generation, motivate conformity, and support people emotionally.

Within each subsystem there are yet smaller subsystems that have to meet the same prerequisites through various internal structures. The subsystem of a school, for example, needs a governing body to determine goals, including priorities for teaching and budget estimates. Schools also require adaptive mechanisms to get needed funds for salaries,

Figure 1 Parsons' GAIL model

Goal Attainment	**Adaptation**
• set priorities	• get resources
• mobilize members	• distribute where needed
Latency	**Integration**
• manage tensions	• co-ordinate activities
• motivate performance	• keep people informed

supplies, equipment, and maintenance. This may be primarily from government allocations, private school fees, parental contributions, or fundraising drives. Schools also need internal administrative structures to coordinate activities. Lastly, schools need staff who are committed to the work of latency, instilling in both teachers and students a continuing commitment to the school's educational values and the preservation of school discipline.

Family systems can similarly be analyzed in terms of how these four basic needs are met. All families need to have some mechanisms or some person responsible for making key decisions on such matters as major financial investments, where to live, and so on. Someone in every family must also perform the basic breadwinner role, earning the resources on which family members depend for their survival. Someone must coordinate activities and ensure that supplies are bought, meals prepared, clothes cleaned, and so on, to be ready as needed by different family members. Families also need to manage the inevitable tensions between the sexes and generations if the family is to continue to hold together as a functioning unit.

Parsons' overarching model is a series of systems with subsystems that have sub-subsystems, and so on. They can be visualized as a series of boxes within the larger box of the action system. The social system box contains important institutional subsystem boxes, each of which has to fulfill the same basic GAIL functions (see Figure 2).

This model looks very impressive in the abstract, but critics complain that the distinctions are very fuzzy in practice. It is far from clear which box specific items fall into. Is the economy purely involved in the adaptation function, or is it also a part of the goal attainment or pattern maintenance functions? Is family primarily oriented to pattern maintenance, or more properly also part of the integration, goal attainment, and adaptation functions? There are no easy answers to these questions. Parsons' theoretical writings tend to be at a high level of abstraction where such questions are not raised. Parsons' major contribution to theory lies, perhaps, in his overall vision of social life in terms of interacting systems, rather than in the convoluted abstract models that he builds.

Pattern Variables The last major dimension of Parsons' overall conception of action systems is his systematization of typical dilemmas of choice in any given role. In any specific behaviour by an individual there is potentially

Figure 2 Structure of General Action Systems

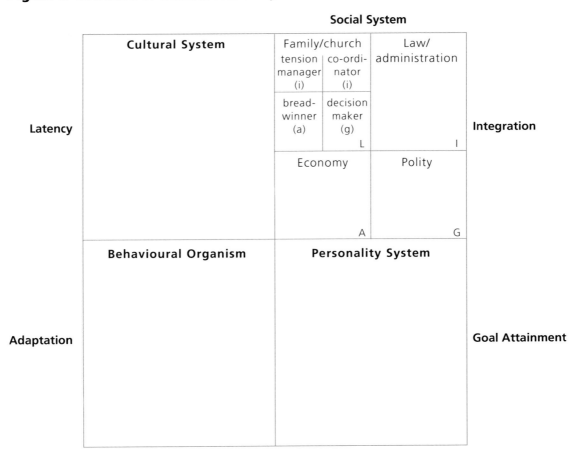

Table 1 The Pattern Variables

Traditional or Family Set	Modern or Occupational Set
Affectivity • show emotional involvement	Affective neutrality • remain emotionally neutral
Particularism • judge relative to age, experience, effort, enthusiasm	Universalism • judge relative to objective standards of excellence
Ascription • give special consideration to relatives, friends	Achievement • consider only specific qualifications
Diffuseness • co-operate, help, and support in as many ways as possible	Specificity • strictly limit involvement
Self • give priority to personal interests over what others want	Collectivity • give priority to group interests over personal preferences

a vast array of orientations towards action that might be adopted. Parsons argues that these can be organized into four options, each associated with one of two opposing sets: traditional or modern. These patterned sets of dichotomous options are what he terms **pattern variables**. The traditional or family set comprises the orientations of affectivity, particularism, ascription, and diffuse obligations, while the modern or occupational set comprises affective neutrality, universalism, achieved characteristics, and specific obligations. Parsons conceptualizes any role relationship as analyzable in terms of these two sets of action orientations. Table 1 shows the two sets of pattern variables.

The first variable is **affectivity** or **affective neutrality**. This concerns the amount of emotion that should properly be displayed in a role. Relations between family and friends are expected to involve some emotional warmth, while relations with clients in a business or professional situation are expected to be formal or affectively neutral. People may rightfully get upset if such expectations are not met in either context.

The second variable concerns whether **particularistic** or **universalistic standards** of evaluation for role performance are appropriate. Particularism refers to special treatment based on the relationship of the person or the group to oneself. Friends are not measured against objective standards. But in the business world, or when hiring a lawyer or going to a medical doctor, objective universalistic standards are appropriate. Professionals are judged relative to the universally defined standards of their profession and not by whether or not one likes the individual personally.

A third variable concerns appropriate criteria for assessing an actor, whether by **ascriptive characteristics** or **achieved characteristics**. Ascription refers to "who one is," and those characteristics that we are born with, such as family of origin, sex, appearance, and racial or ethnic background. Achievements are those characteristics that we

earn by learning special skills or gaining credentials. The first set of characteristics is more important for family or social contacts, the second for business contacts.

A fourth pattern variable concerns the nature of obligations involved in an interaction, whether **diffuse** or **specific**. Obligations towards family and friends tend to be diffuse; friends and relatives call upon each other for a variety of services and support. Business and professional relations are confined to the precise task at hand; neither party to the relationship has any right to ask for or to expect anything more.

A last dimension of role relations is self versus collectivity. This concerns whether the action in question is oriented primarily towards individual interest or towards group goals and interests. Parsons himself accorded this variable less importance in his general model because it was less clearly a dichotomous choice. Individual and group interests frequently overlap, and aspects of both may be involved in any specific role interaction. One does not always have to choose between them.

Parent–child and professional–client relationships are presented by Parsons as polar opposite types of action orientation. Ideally, the relationship of a parent to a child is emotionally affective; evaluations are particularistic with full considerations given to the special situation and abilities of the particular child; assessments are based on ascriptive criteria; role obligations are diffuse. Totally opposite expectations prevail in a professional–client relationship such as that between doctors and their patients. Both doctors and their patients are required to maintain a stand of affective neutrality towards each other. One's judgment of a doctor is appropriate in terms of universalistic criteria of the profession and the doctor's professional qualifications and abilities, and not whether the doctor is male or female, an old family friend, or a newcomer. Finally, obligations are confined to the specific issue of providing medical advice.

A fundamental assumption made by Parsons is that the basic pattern variables and their associated action orientations within families and within the world of industry and business are diametrically opposed. Hence, conflict between them is virtually inevitable whenever the two spheres overlap. This potential conflict is avoided in advanced industrial societies by the specialization and segregation of family roles from work roles. This segregation involves not only time and space but also, characteristically, personnel. Men take primary responsibility for work roles while women take responsibility for the diffuse, emotionally charged role of nurturing children. Parsons is not saying that it is impossible for a person to combine the two roles, but that it is difficult and that social norms prescribe in advance which role—family or work—will take primacy when conflicts arise. The segregation of male and female roles found in nearly all societies is thus seen as meeting a basic functional need. Parsons argues that biological differences between men and women, associated with childbirth, breast-feeding, and different average muscular strength, naturally predispose men to specialize in work roles outside the home and women to specialize in childcare and homemaking.

A wealth of research in the role-theory tradition has analyzed typical patterns of role relations in various situations in terms of Parsons' pattern variables and has examined reactions to violations of these expectations. Parsons himself (1961) did an interesting analysis of the role of elementary schoolteacher, usually filled by a woman. Parsons argues that a female teacher helps to prepare young children for the transition from the pattern variables appropriate for

relations between themselves and their mother at home, to the impersonal pattern variables of the work world. Such a teacher shows affectivity or emotional warmth towards the children and responds to their ascriptive characteristics, and yet at the same time introduces them to universalistic standards of performance and to more limited, specific role obligations than they are used to with their parents.

Modernization   Parsons maintains that entire societies can be analyzed in terms of how they meet the basic GAIL prerequisites and the prevailing orientations towards pattern variables. For Parsons, modernization involves a progressive differentiation of structures by which each of the four prerequisites are met. In traditional societies, the kin group is primarily responsible for meeting all of these needs. The **patriarch** or family head tends to set the major goals for the rest of the members. The adaptation function—the economy—is embedded in kin and family groups. The family and the patriarch are primarily responsible for societal integration, with power relations organized along age–sex lines. Family socialization is likewise of primary importance in teaching the values and skills that assure the maintenance of established patterns of behaviour from one generation to another.

In modern societies, however, the role of the family has receded to only a partial responsibility for the fourth function. Societal goals are set by specialized role incumbents such as politicians and bureaucrats. Economic activities have moved outside the family circle into factories and corporations. Patriarchs have lost much of their former authority, and societal integration is maintained by specialized legal systems and the civil service. The fundamental teaching roles involved in pattern maintenance have also moved outside the family into the realms of schools, churches, and law enforcement agencies. Families now specialize in early childhood socialization and tension management through emotional support of members.

Parsons argues further that traditional and modern societies differ in fundamental ways in types of action orientation. Traditional societies, based on kinship, are oriented primarily towards affective, particularistic, ascriptive, and diffuse role relationships. A very different set of pattern variables prevails in advanced industrial societies, characterized as they are by differentiation and specialization of roles. Universalistic standards and evaluation of contacts on the basis of achievement are functional requirements in technologically complex roles. Specialized roles necessarily carry only specific obligations, which in turn promote affectively neutral relationships.

Nowhere are these patterns more apparent than in the realm of public administration. Traditional societies, suggests Parsons, often adopt the formal structures of bureaucracy

Challenging the functionalist view of family roles, this father provides day care for other children so he can stay at home with his son.

Elly Godfroy/Alamy

from advanced industrial societies but not the cultural patterns. The result is nepotism, graft, and inefficiency as personnel selection is made on the basis of family connections and other ascriptive criteria rather than on the basis of skills, and the new role incumbents are then expected to favour friends and family in dispensing patronage from their office. Efficient bureaucracy is functionally necessary for advanced industrial activities. This efficiency requires that appointments be made on the basis of expertise and that operations be impartial. The logical implications of the Parsonian model are thus that the modernization process requires both structural and cultural changes in traditional societies, to promote differentiation and specialization of formal structures and to give primacy to a different set of pattern variables.

It is clear that Parsons developed an extremely elaborate model of the structure of social action. For more than two decades this model has dominated sociological research. It has been so influential that alternative perspectives still tend to identify their own position in opposition to it.

PROBLEMS WITH FUNCTIONALIST THEORY

Serious criticisms have been raised against functionalism, both as a general theoretical approach and with respect to specific elements of Parsons' model. These theoretical issues are addressed here, with particular reference to the alternative approaches of political economy and ethnomethodology.

When sociologists try to explain the existence of certain structures or patterns in society by reference to the functions that these structures perform for the social whole, they are implicitly suggesting that the structures exist because they are necessary. Families perform the basic function of socializing children, thus we have families; stratification performs the function of motivating talented people to strive for important jobs, thus we have stratification. This is, of course, an oversimplification of the argument but it helps to reveal the problem, which Merton (1967) calls the *fallacy of functional indispensability*.

Merton points out that there may very well be, and in fact usually are, functional alternatives to these structures. Societies do need some way to socialize children, but there are potentially other ways of doing this than in families. For example, small agricultural communes in Israel experimented successfully with raising children in group homes without having families as we know them (Spiro 1958). Societies do have to motivate people somehow to take difficult jobs, but perhaps there are other motivations besides money. Merton suggests that we can reasonably expect to find some structures or patterns in society to meet important needs. But identifying these structures is not the same as explaining why we have the specific types of structures—

the kind of families or the kind of social stratification—that we find in our society.

Hempel (1970, 127) makes the same point but carries it further. Society may need something, but this does not necessarily mean that it will get it. Durkheim argues, for example, that in order to have social cohesion we need social justice and full employment so that everyone feels they are valued members of the community. But we are a very long way from satisfying either need.

Another problem with functionalist arguments is the difficulty in defining what is necessary for society to function. In biology, it is a fairly straightforward matter to define health and sickness and hence to claim that certain states are necessary for the healthy functioning of the organism. But it is much more difficult to define what a healthy or sick society looks like. One might argue that Canada is sick because we do not have full employment, but there are a great many people in the business community who would not share this opinion. With such uncertainty as to what constitutes a need, the functionalist argument that structures exist because they are necessary becomes untenable.

Hempel points to yet another snag in the argument—the time ordering seems to be wrong. Something exists now because of some effect it will have in the future. Consider the statement, "birds have wings in order to fly." This is a functionalist argument. It seems to imply that birds got together one day, decided flying would be nice, and so started developing wings! The fact that birds have wings enables them to fly, but that does not explain how wings developed. If wanting to fly were sufficient cause for having wings, we would all have them. Functionalism describes the *effects* of certain structures, but it does not go very far towards explaining how or why these structures exist. Biologists delve deep into the structure of genes and genetic inheritance to explain the processes and mechanisms by which complex structures like wings are perpetuated in bird species. This goes a long way beyond explaining wings by showing how they function. Hempel concludes that functionalism is a useful descriptive approach, but it does not explain much about social structures.

It is important not to overstate this criticism. Describing the effects or functions that particular structures have is itself a difficult and useful achievement, particularly when these effects are latent or not recognized by many people. This restricted version of functionalism is valuable, provided we recognize its limitations. Functionalists who are largely content with this level of analysis have produced many insightful studies.

One such study is Merton's (1967, 125–135) analysis of the latent functions of political rackets run by party bosses in America. He asks why political rackets run by party bosses persist. Patronage, bribery, graft, and the protection of criminals clearly violate established moral codes. They persist, Merton argues, because they satisfy subgroups' needs that cannot be met by culturally approved social structures. First, the party boss consolidates what is often widely dispersed power to the point where he can actually get things done. Second, he can get around bureaucratic red tape to ensure provision of social services for people otherwise lost in the technicalities. Third, the boss can provide privileges to big business, by acting to control and regulate unbridled competition, without being subject to public scrutiny and control. He is especially important in providing aid to businesses that provide illicit services and hence that are not protected by regular government controls. Fourth, the party patronage controlled by the boss provides avenues for upward social mobility for ambitious individuals who lack legitimate avenues to attain success. Hence, political rackets cannot be understood merely as self-aggrandizement for power-hungry individuals who could be cleaned out of the system. Political rackets constitute the organized provision of services to subgroups that are otherwise excluded from or handicapped in the race to get ahead. These are important latent functions that the socially approved political structures cannot adequately meet. Hence, the political rackets persist.

Serious criticisms remain, however, even when the claims for functional analysis are confined to the level of descriptive insights. Merton draws attention to two related problems, which he terms the *fallacy of functional unity* and the *fallacy of universalism*. In biology, the assumption of functional unity holds that every element within a biological organism is functional or useful for the good of the entire organism. The assumption of universalism holds that each and every element found within an organism must perform some necessary function. Merton argues that, however reasonable such assumptions sound in the context of a biological organism, they constitute fallacies when applied to elements within social systems.

The general argument that structures exist because they are functional for the social system assumes that the system operates as a unitary whole. Merton argues that given structures may be beneficial or functional for certain groups in society but not necessarily for others. A high rate of unemployment, for example, is functional for reducing wage demands and so enhancing the competitive advantage of business, but it is not functional for the groups of people who are unemployed or for their family members. Neither is it functional for other small businesses that depend on selling goods to families of unemployed people. At best, one might be able to talk about a net balance of functional advantage. But Merton pushes the criticism further to insist that functionalism should routinely take account of **dysfunctions**; that is, the possibility that some structures have

a net balance of negative consequences for a society or for large numbers of its members.

Traditional functionalism begins from the premise that recurrent characteristics in a society, like elements within a biological organism, can be explained by reference to the functions that they perform for the maintenance of the system as a whole. But carried to its logical extreme, this position can lead to what look like absurd claims. One can argue that suicide is functional for relieving tensions; wife battering is functional for enhancing male dominance; war is functional for generating high profits and high employment.

These claims themselves are not false. Suicide, war, unemployment, and crime do have advantages for certain people. The problem lies in the assumption that they benefit the society as a whole. The key question for critics of functionalism is, functional for whom? The corollary, of course, is, dysfunctional for whom? When the issues raised by functionalism are reformulated in this way, important dimensions of power and conflict of interest are introduced into the analysis.

A recurrent criticism of functional analysis, and particularly of Parsons' model of a social system, has been that it does not deal adequately with power. Parsons tends to assume that power generally takes the form of authority, which is used in the interests of system adjustment. Not surprisingly, this formulation has been hard to sustain.

Marxist critics argue that corporate bosses wield enormous power over the economy and over political decisions. The mass of workers may view the exercise of such power as arbitrary and illegitimate, but they are unable to oppose it effectively. The result of confrontations between bosses and workers may be disorder and alienation rather than orderly system adjustment. The power exercised by men over women in families has similarly been challenged by feminists as illegitimate. The exercise of patriarchal powers may lead to family breakdown and divorce rather than to stable marriage.

Functionalism started out with great promise as a unifying scientific approach towards sociological analysis, but it seems not to have lived up to expectations. The major contributions of this perspective lie in two broad areas. First, it recognizes the fundamental interdependence of different parts of society. It increases sensitivity to the fact that change in any one part of society affects all other interrelated structures as well. Second, and perhaps more importantly, functionalism has encouraged a wealth of descriptive research that has documented latent or hitherto unsuspected effects of recurrent patterns of behaviour.

The elaborate typologies of system needs and pattern variables worked out by Parsons have, on the whole, not proven particularly useful. System needs are notoriously difficult to establish. Attempts to classify structures as performing one need or another are often not successful. Additionally, each pattern variable is better understood as a continuum rather than a dichotomy and also as varying widely with circumstances rather than as a fixed orientation for given roles.

In summary, the problems associated with traditional functionalist analysis are serious. The system of explanation for the persistence of structures in terms of their functions for the social system is logically flawed. It does not deal adequately with dysfunctions or negative aspects of social structures, nor does it provide an adequate basis for the analysis of power, conflict, and disunity in society. It has thus gained the disrepute of being reactionary and conservative, providing ideological justification for the status quo.

CRITICAL REFORMULATIONS OF FUNCTIONALIST THEORY

In this section we explore the efforts of theorists, particularly in the Marxist and ethnomethodological traditions, to reformulate functionalism into a potentially more adequate and descriptively useful approach.

A revised model of functionalist analysis proposed by Stinchcombe (1968, 80–100) first addresses the question of the flawed explanatory logic of traditional functionalism. Hempel and others may argue that functionalism cannot go beyond descriptive statements, but the fact remains that most functionalist analysis still aims to do more than describe functions. The tendency is always there to argue that certain structures may exist because they serve certain functions. In other words, some theorists use the functions, or effect, as explanations for the existence of the structures.

Stinchcombe suggests that these logical problems can be resolved if two important changes are made in traditional functionalist analysis. The first change is the explicit recognition and incorporation of intent into the explanation. It makes sense to argue that existing structures are caused by their future consequences if you explain that certain individuals or groups of people intentionally select and reinforce certain structures because they find the effects of such structures beneficial. The second change is that such an explanation needs to examine the mechanisms by which such structures are selectively reinforced and preserved over time. Stinchcombe calls such processes **feedback mechanisms**. In the biological sciences, the exploration of the precise mechanisms and feedback loops by which an equilibrium is achieved is a central part of any explanation of the functions that parts perform for the whole. But to date, functional analysis in sociology has tended to assume equilibrium, without demonstrating the mechanisms through which such effects are sustained. In short, for Stinchcombe, adequate functional explanations should show that structures exist and are perpetuated over time because they are deliberately reinforced by individuals or groups who find their effects beneficial and who have access to mechanisms that are effective in such reinforcement.

Stinchcombe only hints at what some of these mechanisms might be. Some structures may persist simply because no one has any particular interest in stopping them, and because they work sufficiently well that no one has much incentive to seek alternatives. It simply costs too much time and effort to change things. Other structures may be less generally appreciated by all members of the society and hence have to be defended by more overt means. These means might include: control over the socialization of young people to ensure that they are instilled with the proper values; access to mass media, which influence how people think and what they know about; and influence over the selection of successors to policy-making situations in society and control of the rules under which successors work.

Marxist Functionalism

Stinchcombe's reformulation of functional analysis directly incorporates notions of power and the unequal ability of different individuals and groups in society to reinforce those social structures that they find beneficial. Stinchcombe (1968, 94) in fact defines the power of a class in terms of its relative effectiveness as a cause of social structures. In this respect, he explicitly relates his ideas to Marxist analysis and to the Marxist assertion that the dominant culture of a society is the culture of the dominant class. The reason why elites are able to perpetuate their values and mode of organization of society is that they have privileged access to and control over all the key mechanisms that reinforce structures. Elites are in a particularly advantageous position to influence the mechanisms that produce the semblance of moral consensus central to the Parsonian model of the social system. Not only do they control and direct most mass media outlets, they also pay professional people to defend and disseminate appropriate values. Members of the elite are also in the best position to select their own successors and to ensure that their values are perpetuated in the future operation of important organizations in society.

The notion of **Marxist functionalism** proposed by Stinchcombe retains the more insightful aspects of functionalist theory. In particular, he retains both the concept of society as comprising an interrelated system of parts and the mode of analysis that describes and explains the persistence of structures by reference to their consequences. He also emphasizes purposive action as the foundation of his model. The crucial change from the Parsonian model is that Stinchcombe introduces the concepts of class and unequal power. He replaces the notion of society-wide normative consensus with the view that dominant ideas are those perpetuated by the actions of the members of an elite class.

Richard Quinney's analysis of law functioning to protect the interests of the capitalist class is a prime example of Marxist functionalism. Society is conceptualized as a system of interdependent parts, but it is explicitly a capitalist system. The parts function to protect the elite class and to control and suppress class conflict, which might disrupt this system.

The risk in Quinney's approach is that he repeats earlier logical flaws in functional analysis, namely the fallacies of universal functionalism, functional unity, and functional indispensability. Everything exists because it is functional for the capitalist system—unemployment is functional for profits, welfare is functional for controlling potential revolt—and the description of some effect provides an explanation for the persistence of such structures. Stinchcombe's reformulation of the logic of functionalism still applies here. An adequate explanation still requires detailed analyses of the feedback mechanisms: who controls them, how they operate, how potential opposition or change is prevented. The capitalist system persists not because of its own inner momentum, but because people with powerful vested interests take actions to reinforce it on an ongoing basis.

A closely related criticism of functionalism stems more directly from the analytical work of Marx himself than from subsequent political economy theory. When Marx challenged the ideas of the classical economists of his time, he asked a difficult question: What kind of actual social relations must be experienced in order for this kind of economic model to be formulated? Ideas, in other words, do not arise from nowhere. They arise from people's attempts to make sense of their own limited experience. When this same kind of question is asked of Parsons' work, it challenges the claim that his model of a social system is abstract, scientific, and universally applicable. Critics would argue that concepts such as GAIL functions and pattern variables originate within, and refer to the historically specific circumstances of, capitalism. They make sense only in relation to the impersonal capitalist system of commodity production for money.

This criticism can be made clearer if we examine Parsons' analysis of, first, the differences between family and occupational subsystems and, second, the medical profession. Prior to capitalism, there was no clear break between family and work roles for most people. They commonly merged together in household enterprises. Under feudalism, landowners had clearly established personal obligations to provide for the peasant families that were attached to their estates. It was only with the advent of the capitalist wage-labour system that owners of the means of production freed themselves from hereditary obligations towards workers. It

was capitalism that segregated production from the home and reduced personal relations to inhuman cash payment in the labour market. It is precisely such a system that is captured in Parsons' concepts of affective neutrality and impersonal and specific role obligations. These concepts cannot be applied universally to all economic systems.

Similarly, there is nothing inevitable about the nature of medicine that would give rise to Parsons' characterization of the doctor–patient relationship as involving affectively neutral, universalistic, achievement-oriented, and specific role obligations. For centuries the opposite was the case. Healing was practised by women whose skills were passed on for generations. The art of healing was integrated into total caring for the person. It was a neighbourly service where the healer knew her patients and their families. She knew about the disappointments, anxieties, and the overwork that could mimic illness or induce it (Ehrenreich and English 1979, Ch. 2). Healing was a diverse and creative process that involved many little kindnesses and encouragements and an understanding of the patients' fears and strengths. But under capitalism, the "art of healing" became the "science of medicine," practised by men as a commodity to be sold at a high price. Male practitioners went to tremendous lengths to protect their commodity, undermining the natural healing of women by burning them as witches and by outlawing midwifery and the practice of medicine by those without credentials. Since women were systematically barred from medical schools until late in the nineteenth century, they were effectively prevented from practising medicine. This set of historically specific practices produced the image of doctors described by Parsons.

Parsons' model and the analyses that flow from it are thus faulted for justifying, under the guise of scientific objectivity, a particularly inhuman form of social relations. By treating such relations as universal, abstract truths about society, Parsons glosses over the historically specific and particular social organization that gives rise to the relationships that he encapsulates in his model.

Some have argued that the Parsonian model is, and was intended to be, an important tool in the legitimation and hence perpetuation of the capitalist nation state (Buxton 1985). Professional social science functions as a powerful mechanism for social control. Parsons defines professionals as a disinterested or affectively neutral class of experts, operating in terms of universalistic standards of science, committed to the specific objectives of research rather than diffuse political obligations, and dedicated to collective societal well-being rather than self-interest. Hence they command authority as impartial advisers to government. Functionalist theorists have advised the business and political elites how to neutralize destabilizing features of change and so bolster the system. Functionalism also provides a means not to see the underlying realities of class, power, and exploitation within the capitalist system. Buxton goes so far as to suggest that Parsons himself might have been aware of the ideological character of his theory, or certainly that many of his followers who adopted and promoted functionalism in social analysis saw it as a means to reduce class tensions.

Psychoanalysis and Socialization

The basic assumption of the functionalist equilibrium model is the internalization of social norms. Individuals, it is argued, come to accept the norms and values of society as their own, and hence they voluntarily regulate themselves in conformity with expectations. The major problem with this perspective is that it does not explain deviance. People appear to conform because they are preprogrammed to act only in conformist ways, much like ants in an anthill.

Dennis Wrong (1961) argues that such reasoning is blatantly naive. In reality, people can never be socialized to this extent. Human nature is far too complex for that. Wrong draws on psychoanalytic theories to suggest that socialization at best achieves only a veneer of conformity over individual self-will, and this conscious self-will is itself only a veneer over much deeper unconscious or semiconscious passions and desires that forever threaten to overwhelm orderly, conformist behaviour.

In psychoanalytic terminology, the **id** comprises the vast reservoir of life forces—sexual passions, drives, and energy—of which the individual is at best only partially aware. The conscious self or **ego** seeks to express and to realize these fundamental drives and passions. They are only superficially held in check by the **superego** of learned social norms and values. This model is illustrated in Figure 3. Intensive and rigid socialization, such as the kind that puritanical religious sects seek to impose, may succeed in repressing socially unacceptable sexual drives and passions.

Figure 3 Model of the human mind in psychoanalytic theory

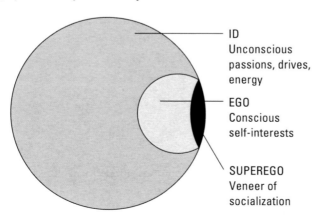

ID
Unconscious passions, drives, energy

EGO
Conscious self-interests

SUPEREGO
Veneer of socialization

Socialization may even succeed in pushing them out of the conscious mind altogether, but it can never eliminate them totally. A permanent tension is set up within the individual psyche between repressed drives, guilt, and social conditioning, with the latter continually at risk of being overwhelmed by deep emotional forces. When people are viewed from this perspective, the functionalist vision of societal equilibrium achieved by internalization of norms appears fragile indeed.

The Ethnomethodological Critique

The approach of ethnomethodology—particularly the work of Garfinkel, who was a student of Parsons—offers a different kind of challenge to the functionalist notion of a voluntaristic theory of action. Heritage (1984) draws attention to the illusory character of this supposedly voluntary choice. In practice, actors seem to be left with no choice at all because the script is already written. Parsons characterizes people as role-players with internalized norms and fixed expectations. These role-players are assumed to share their interpretation of the situation and their knowledge of appropriate rules for behaviour. In effect, says Garfinkel, they are "judgmental dopes" (Heritage 1984, 108). They appear to make no judgments of their own. Like mindless robots, they simply follow rules programmed into them.

The alternative perspective of ethnomethodology allows for a much greater fluidity in behaviour. For a start, in real situations we assume that other people are making responsible and meaningful choices in their actions, such that each of us can and do hold ourselves and other people accountable for behaviour. Furthermore, real situations are not predefined. A constant problem in deciding how we should behave or respond to the behaviour of others is in determining what is going on in the first place. Our actions and those of other people define the situation, not the other way around.

Boughey (1978, 171) gives an example of this in his description of cards night at a church. Six rambunctious men were laughing and joking as they played poker. After a particularly raucous outburst, a woman from a nearby table admonished them, "Shshsh! You're in church, you know!" One poker player waved her off with the response, "Naah! But this is cards!" In effect, all the participants in this scene were **defining the situation**. We might conclude that, since the players were so raucous, they must have given priority to the role of "card-playing" rather than to that of "being in church." Conversely, if the men had quieted down after the admonishment, we might conclude that, after a temporary lapse, they followed the behavioural prescriptions appropriate for the role of being in church. The important point is that a functionalist could only tell after the fact what was going on by the kind of behaviour displayed. Boughey and the ethnomethodologists are interested in how people actively choose and create the situation for themselves by choosing how they are going to behave.

Heritage (1984, Ch. 5) gives an example of a situation in which one person meets another and greets her. The norm states that greetings should be reciprocated. If the other person does indeed return the greeting, then everything appears normal. But if she is silent, then the situation is not normal, and a chain of guesses as to what else is going on is immediately set off: maybe she didn't hear; she was deep in thought; she deliberately snubbed me; she wasn't who I thought she was; she doesn't remember me; my new hairpiece sure fooled her. There is no passive actor responding in learned ways to a predefined situation. Rather, there is a person actively involved in creating what is happening and what will happen next.

Ethnomethodologists carry out infinitely detailed and careful research in order to explore how people actively make sense of and create the social world and reproduce it as intelligible for each other. What is significant here is the important criticism that this approach raises against traditional functionalist analysis. The basic functionalist assumption of internalized norms and expectations of behaviour is shown to be insufficient as an explanation for social order.

CONCLUSION

What remains of functionalist analysis when these criticisms are taken into account? The model of society as a system rather than a collection of disconnected parts remains a central assumption of sociological analysis. Functionalism draws attention to the mutual influence of interdependent elements of society. It also focuses attention on voluntary or purposive action and the importance of typical roles and expectations in guiding behaviour. Functionalism has prompted much valuable descriptive research into the effects of given structures or patterns of behaviour on society.

The weaknesses of functionalism lie in its rigidity, the tendency to assume that existing structures are necessary, because functional, without considering alternatives and especially without considering dysfunctions or damaging effects that given structures may have for less powerful sectors of society. Functionalism typically fails to recognize the essential fluidity and creativity in people's relations with each other. At the system level, functionalism can be faulted for failure to deal adequately with issues of power, conflict, and exploitation in society, except in terms of institutionalized pressure groups. This has marked functionalism as a conservative ideology in the eyes of more critical theorists.

SUGGESTED READING

The most convenient and accessible selection of Parsons' writing is contained in Peter Hamilton's collection, *Readings from Talcott Parsons* (1985). A broadly descriptive article in the collection is "Age and Sex in the Social Structure of the United States." It would be instructive to compare the division of sex roles within different age groups in the 1950s, as outlined by Parsons, with that of the present. In the article "Illness and the Role of the Physician: A Sociological Perspective," illness, particularly mental illness, is treated as a type of deviant behaviour in terms of the sick person's failure to fulfill expectations connected with his or her roles in society. Sickness itself is viewed as a social role in relation to a set of distinctive norms defining appropriate behaviour, such as exclusion from certain normal obligations. The therapist is seen as not just applying technical knowledge to problem cases, but as restoring equilibrium to the social system.

Another broadly descriptive article by Parsons is "The School Class as a Social System: Some of its Functions in American Society" (1961). This article examines the ways in which aspects of the structure of primary and secondary school classes function to adapt young people to adult roles. The students' transformation from family members to members of the wider society is analyzed in terms of Parsons' pattern variables.

A brief but demanding exposition of Parsons' scheme of the components of society can be found in his book *Societies: Evolutionary and Comparative Perspectives* (1966).

QUESTIONS

1. Distinguish between *manifest* and *latent* functions.

2. How do *need dispositions* influence behaviour, according to Parsons?

3. What four subsystems are involved in Parsons' notion of the *cybernetic hierarchy*?

4. What are the different societal functions of the adaptation system and the latency system in Parsons' GAIL model?

5. What are the pattern variables typically associated with the family subsystem?

6. In Parsons' model, what constellation of pattern variables are typically associated with traditional, preindustrial societies?

7. What critical argument does Merton use to challenge the *fallacy of functional indispensability* that underlies much work in functionalist theory?

8. What two important modifications are proposed by Stinchcombe to resolve problems with the functionalist argument that institutions exist because they are functional for society?

9. How does feminist work on women as healers challenge the Parsonian model of pattern variables as historically specific rather than universal?

10. In what respect does Garfinkel's critique of Parsons' model of social action imply that all people are "judgmental dopes"?

KEY TERMS

achieved characteristics

adaptation

affectivity/affective neutrality

ascriptive characteristics/ascription

behavioural organism

cultural system

cybernetic hierarchy

defining the situation

diffuse obligations

dysfunctions

ego

feedback mechanisms

functional indispensability

functional unity

GAIL model

goal attainment

hierarchy

id

institutionalization

integration

latency

Marxist functionalism

need dispositions

particularism/particularistic standards

patriarch

pattern maintenance

pattern variables

personality system

prerequisites

role segregation

role set

role strain

role theory

social system

society

specific obligations

superego

system prerequisites

universal functionalism

universalism/Universalistic standards

voluntaristic theory

REFERENCES

Berger, P.L. 1963. *Invitation to Sociology: A Humanistic Perspective*. New York: Anchor Books.

Biddle, B.J., and E.J. Thomas, eds. 1966. *Role Theory: Concepts and Research*. New York: John Wiley and Sons.

Boughey, H. 1978. *The Insights of Sociology: An Introduction*. Boston: Allyn & Bacon.

Buxton, W. 1985. *Talcott Parsons and the Capitalist Nation State: Political Sociology as a Strategic Vocation*. Toronto: University of Toronto Press.

Coser, L.A. 1956. *The Functions of Social Conflict*. Glencoe, Illinois: Free Press.

Ehrenreich, B., and D. English. 1979. *For Her Own Good: 150 Years of Experts' Advice to Women*. Garden City, New York: Anchor Books.

Hempel, C.G. 1970. "The Logic of Functional Analysis." In B.A. Brody, ed. *Readings in the Philosophy of Science*. Englewood Cliffs, New Jersey: Prentice-Hall.

Heritage, J. 1984. *Garfinkel and Ethnomethodology*. Oxford: Polity Press in association with Basil Blackwell.

Merton, R.K. 1967. *On Theoretical Sociology: Five Essays, Old and New*. New York: Free Press.

Parsons, T. 1978. "The Concept of Society: The Components and Their Interrelations." In A. Wells, ed. *Contemporary Sociological Theories*. Santa Monica, California: Goodyear, 18–31.

Parsons, T. 1961. "The School Class as a Social System: Some of its Functions in American Society." In A.H. Halsey, J. Floud, and C.A. Anderson, eds. *Education, Economy and Society*. New York: Free Press.

Parsons, T. 1951. *The Social System*. New York: Free Press.

Parsons, T. [1949] 1964. *Essays in Sociological Theory*. New York: Free Press.

Parsons, T. [1937] 1968. *The Structure of Social Action*. New York: Macmillan.

Quinney, R. 1975. "Crime Control in Capitalist Society: A Critical Philosophy of Legal Order." In I. Taylor, P. Walton, and J. Young, eds. *Critical Criminology*. London: Routledge & Kegan Paul.

Spiro, M.E. 1958. *Children of the Kibbutz*. Cambridge, Massachusetts: Harvard University Press.

Stinchcombe, A.I. 1968. *Constructing Social Theories*. New York: Harcourt Brace and World.

Wrong, D. 1961. "The Oversocialized Conception of Man in Modern Sociology." *American Sociological Review* 26 (April): 183–193.

The Family: The Site of Love, Exploitation, and Oppression

Functionalist theory views society as an integrated and self-maintaining system, analogous to a living organism. Like an organism, it is composed of numerous organs or institutions that are structured to meet the specialized needs or prerequisites of the social system as a whole. The system normally exists in a state of dynamic equilibrium. Built-in mechanisms balance change in one part of the system with complementary changes in other parts, so that the order of the whole is maintained despite major changes in structure. Within subsystems of action, or institutions, are individual roles, which comprise typical patterns of action. The entire system is held together by the mechanisms of **normative consensus** and shared role expectations. These values and expectations for behaviour are internalized by members of society through the complex process of socialization.

The family is an institution that plays a vital part within this functionalist model of society. Functionalists argue that the family is extremely important, indeed indispensable, for the survival of society. For many theorists, society itself can be conceptualized as made up of families linked together. The family is a universal institution; no known society has existed without it. The central integrative process of socialization—the internalization of behaviour patterns and values—occurs primarily within the family. Institutions such as school and church also play a part in the socialization process, but this is generally only after the newborn infant has developed into a socially functioning child. The few documented cases of feral children, or those who have survived in the wild or in extreme isolation without family contact, indicate that these children's behaviour is less than human. Even after they have been intensively trained in clinics, these children have not been able to learn to talk or to think in terms of the symbolic meaning systems that distinguish humans from other animals. Functionalists suggest that, without families, there would be no humanity and hence no society. Functionalists accord no other social institution such central importance. For this reason, the study of sociology of the family offers the strongest test of the contributions and the limitations of the functionalist perspective.

Functionalist Theories of the Family

Any institution can be studied from two related perspectives: the contribution of that institution to the functioning of society as a whole; or the institution's internal functioning as a subsystem in its own right, with its own set of prerequisites for maintaining a dynamic equilibrium.

The four main functions that the family unit performs for society are: reproduction of society's members; socialization of new members, especially newborn and young children; regulation of sexual relations; and economic cooperation to sustain adults and their offspring. The family constitutes the basic emotional or expressive social unit, providing nurturing, protection, and affection for members, controlling their behaviour, and channelling fundamental sexual and reproductive drives into socially acceptable forms. Although reproduction and sexual relations can and do take place outside of families, they are only socially legitimated within families. Reiss suggests that this is because the family context best ensures the nurturance of the newborn, with kinship groups on both the father's and the mother's side acknowledging a relationship with, and some responsibility for, the child (Reiss 1976, Ch. 2).

The family occurs in a great variety of forms in different societies. There are **extended families**, in which several generations of kin live in the same dwelling usually under the authority of the most senior male or the most senior female in a matriarchal society, and **nuclear families** consisting of isolated couples with their dependent children. Legitimate sexual relations include **monogamy** (one man with one woman) or forms of **polygamy** (more than one spouse). The more common form of polygamy is **polygyny** (one man having two or more wives), but some societies practise **polyandry** (one woman having more than one husband). Whatever the particular arrangement favoured in a given society, functionalists argue that there is an essential core that is universal. This core was defined by George Murdock (1949, 2):

> The family is a social group characterized by common residence, economic cooperation, and reproduction. It includes adults of both sexes, at least two of whom maintain a socially approved sexual relationship, and one or more children, own or adopted, of the sexually cohabiting adults.

Not all members of a society conform to this pattern of living at any one time, but most people spend a significant part of their lives in a family situation. In Canada, most people marry and have children, and most of these children will do the same when they are adults. Kinship ties remain extremely important to people throughout life, even for those individuals who do not form families of their own.

The nuclear family core of two sexually cohabiting adults of the opposite sex, together with their dependent children, is seen by functionalists as having an essential biological foundation (Goode 1982, 15–32). This thesis incorporates the core ideas of **sociobiology**, a branch of sociology closely associated with functionalism, which studies the biological bases of social behaviour. Functionalists argue that the vital institution of family is rooted in sexual drives and the imperative of reproduction, and in the sociological imperative of transforming the biological organism of a newborn baby into a human or social being. Unlike many animals, the argument goes, human babies are born with relatively few instincts. They rely upon a complex brain to learn, through symbols and abstractions, the essentials of survival in society. This necessitates a long period of social dependency that lasts well into adolescence and beyond in industrial society. Because of this, there is a relatively long period during which the nurturing mother depends upon care and support of other adults, usually the husband/father, to meet her economic needs while she is engaged in childcare.

Many biological drives predispose humans for male-female pair bonding. Goode suggests that, despite the fact that there is some homosexuality, people are preprogrammed for heterosexuality. The constancy of the human sex drive, far more intense than is needed for reproduction itself, promotes long-term, stable relations between men and women. The biologically based impulse of jealousy reinforces this pair bonding through the urge to regard one's mate as one's exclusive sexual property. Another very general biological drive is territoriality, the natural desire to settle in one location and defend it from others. This is combined with a biologically determined reproductive strategy of having few offspring and caring intensively for them, rather than producing many offspring at once and leaving them to fend for themselves. All these traits create strong impulses in humans to form families.

Functionalists argue that sexual differences promote heterosexual bonding. Only women undergo menstruation, pregnancy, and lactation, and hence they are biologically predisposed to perform the task of caring for children. Breast-feeding intensifies the bond between mother and child. Women are relatively weak during pregnancy and just after birth; hence natural choice as well as efficiency dictate that they will stay close to home and children. Males, on the other hand, have greater strength and aggressiveness, which gave them the edge in early hunting societies and hence provided a biological basis for early male dominance. Lionel Tiger (1977) argues that "man the hunter" was preprogrammed for aggression and dominance over females and also for strong male bonding in hunting packs. This predisposition for male bonding gives man an advantage in politics and in business. Tiger argues that women are preprogrammed to be submissive and to be oriented towards their children rather than to form bonds with other women. These biological predispositions favour the sex-role division of labour within families, with women concentrating on nurturing roles within the home while men concentrate on the role of economic provider.

Functionalists posit that sociological factors stemming from the nature of work in industrial societies strongly reinforce this biologically based tendency towards sex-role division of labour within families. Parsons argues that family and industry are based on diametrically opposed patterns of action orientation and hence must be separated if both are to function effectively. Family life is based on emotional ties between members; membership is dependent on ascriptive characteristics and not qualifications; individuals are judged by particularistic values as unique family members; and there are diffuse obligations to meet each others' needs in multiple ways. Industry necessarily operates in terms of totally different patterns. Relations among people in industry are emotionally neutral; membership is ideally determined by achievements; judgments are based upon universalistic criteria of standards of performance; and obligations are specific to the particular transaction. The specialization of sex roles, with women concentrating upon the internal affairs of the family while men concentrate upon occupational roles, best serves to minimize confusion of values across the two spheres.

In functionalist analysis, the family constitutes a social system with its own internal needs that must be met if the family is to maintain its equilibrium. Individual families, like society as a whole, must meet the four basic prerequisites of goal attainment, adaptation, integration, and latency or pattern maintenance. Parsons and Bales (1956, Ch. 1) analyze how families function internally to divide up roles along sex-specific lines. Bales maintains that small groups typically develop two kinds of leaders: an **instrumental leader** who gets tasks done; and an **expressive leader** who supports and encourages group members and smooths over tensions. Parsons proposes that, within families, one adult, typically the male, performs instrumental tasks, while the female performs the expressive roles. In terms of system prerequisites, instrumental roles include goal attainment and adaptation. The man typically represents the family to the external social system, making the key decisions that set family goals and earning the resources needed for the family to adapt to its surroundings and survive. Expressive roles are oriented towards the internal needs of the family, meeting the prerequisites of integration and latency by supporting and nurturing people, smoothing over tensions, and teaching the family values and patterns of behaviour to the children. Parsons argues that these functional imperatives reinforce, if they do not totally mandate, sex-role division of labour within families.

Spencer (1976, Ch. 11) speculates on what might happen if a particular husband and wife decided to change this pattern. In order to challenge male control over goals and adaptation decisions, she argues, a couple must first acknowledge their present functions. Western societies generally mandate a certain pattern of sex-role specialization, such that the male is obliged to support and defend his wife and children. Thus society penalizes the male if both partners want to stay home. If men and women want equal work opportunities, both must take equal responsibility for support of the family. If the wife were to become the chief breadwinner, Spencer argues, then she would have to have authority within the household. If her job required her to move, then the rest of the family would have to move with good grace. If she pays the bills, she would have to decide the family budget. If she is to be fit and awake for her job, then her dependants would have to protect her health, her mood, her rest, and so on, by obeying her requests. Spencer notes that these are the prerogatives now enjoyed by men and resented by women. She concludes that traditional roles are designed to protect children and are functionally necessary, at least to some degree.

Functionalists also argue that the typical nuclear family pattern, consisting of a married couple with their children, is mandated by the requirements of industrial society. Industrialization is founded on free labour markets and a flexible, mobile workforce. Workers and their families must be willing to move as and where the breadwinner's work demands. The nuclear group is much more mobile than the extended family group, which is commonly tied to landed property.

In summary, functionalism appears to offer a comprehensive theory that accounts for all the essential features of family as we know it in industrialized society. The heterosexual pair bonding at the core of any family system stems from biological imperatives—not merely the sex drive, but the need for long-term nurturing of newborn infants and children. The sex-role division of labour within families and the segregation of women's domestic nurturing work from male instrumental roles in the workforce are rooted both in biological predispositions and in the very distinctive values and behaviour orientations of family life and occupational roles in industrial society. The authority of males in the home in terms of the allocation of money also reflects the imperatives of the breadwinner role that men normally hold. The demands for a mobile workforce account for the predominantly isolated nuclear family residence pattern. The explanation seems complete. It suggests that efforts to change family life or sex roles in any significant way are impractical.

CRITIQUE OF FUNCTIONALIST THEORY

The functionalist theory of the family has come under considerable attack, however, primarily for elevating a historically specific form of family into a universal principle. The theory ignores the wide diversity of family forms. Such diversity renders a rigidly defined notion of the family, such as that proposed by Murdock (1949), useless. Functionalist views of the family have been challenged, especially by Marxist and feminist theorists, as an ideology that seeks to justify the status quo while ignoring the ways in which family life is constrained by interests associated with capitalism and patriarchy. These are interests that benefit in multiple ways from exploiting the cheap labour of women in the home. Functionalism supports that exploitation by legitimating it as if it were unavoidable and universal. The traditional functionalist model of the family has been criticized particularly for a false universalism that implies that all the functions associated with family life are necessarily met by a single institution in which all functional elements are combined. In Eichler's view, such theorizing is flawed by four major biases: monolithic; conservative; sexist; and microstructural (Eichler 1988, Chs. 1–4). In this section we briefly examine each of these biases in turn.

Monolithic Bias   The **monolithic bias** is inherent in Murdock's definition of the family, which functionalists tend to treat as a given. A host of alternative family forms that have existed in other societies, and that are emerging in contemporary industrial societies such as Canada, are simply ignored or treated as problematic deviations. Anthropologists have long been familiar with examples of cultural patterns in other societies that violate some or all elements of Murdock's supposedly universal family form.

The Nayars of South India had, until the beginning of the twentieth century, a family form that incorporated none of the attributes considered essential by functionalists. Family life was not organized around sexually cohabiting pairs. There was no economic cooperation between women and their sexual partners, and the children of such liaisons had no socially recognized relationship with their biological fathers. They might not even know who their father was. Nayar families were organized around the female line. The joint family comprised the mother, her siblings, and her own and her sisters' children. A brief ceremony took place before girls reached puberty that linked each girl with a man from her own social rank. The ritual functioned only to establish female adult sexual status. From then on, women were free to have sexual relations with whomever they chose. Children lived in their mother's joint family home. Men did not live with their sexual partners; they continued to live in their own mother's household. All property belonging to the joint family was inherited through the mother's line. The mother's eldest brother commonly managed the property, but he did not own it and could not dispose of it. His principal relationship with children was as uncle to his sisters' offspring (Liddle and Joshi 1986, 28, 51–52).

Other studies suggest that in Jamaica, and in poor black communities in the United States, nuclear families are also not the norm. The stable relationship is between a woman and her children, while she has only temporary and sequential relations with male partners (Reiss 1976, 14–15).

Functionalists have responded to these challenges to the universality of the family by proposing various redefinitions around the mother-child dyad or, more commonly, by dismissing variations as rare aberrations that prove the general rule (Reiss 1976, Ch. 2). The Nayar culture can be viewed as an anthropological anomaly that developed in the exceptional circumstances of extensive migration of males in search of work as soldiers. The fact that this type of family broke down in the early twentieth century during British rule in India indicates that it was not a viable form. Critics doubt whether such a system could work in any larger society. The female-headed households among poor blacks do not represent a cultural ideal so much as the collapse of normal family life in the face of the abject poverty and chronic unemployment of black males. The ideal remains permanent marriage and stable fatherhood.

But charges of monolithic bias cannot be avoided simply by dismissing these family forms as aberrations. Eichler challenges the monolithic bias squarely within the North American society that functionalist theory is designed to explain. She argues that the image of family as the monogamous nuclear group comprising husband, wife, and their biological children applies to only a minority of structures that participants themselves regard as family. The argument that most individuals may have lived in a nuclear family at some time in their lives does not alter the fact that the majority of people in Canada are not now living in such families. Functionalists arbitrarily exclude from their definition of family a multitude of other arrangements: common-law couples (see Table 1); commuting couples where spouses have careers in different places and meet only on weekends or holidays; couples who do not have children; couples whose children live elsewhere; **reconstituted families** where one or both spouses may have children living elsewhere; single-parent families; homosexual couples; and so on.

Eichler suggests that if functionalists insist on having one definition to cover all forms of family, it would have to look something like the following: A family is a social group that may or may not include adults of both sexes, may or may not have children born in wedlock, or originating in the marriage, may or may not be living in a common residence, may or may not be sexually cohabiting, and may or may not include love, attraction, economic support, and so on (Eichler 1988, 4).

Eichler proposes that the attempt to define the family should be abandoned in favour of an alternative approach that empirically researches the dimensions of family life. The important dimensions that Eichler (1988, 6) singles out are procreation, socialization of children, sexual relations, residence patterns, economic cooperation, and emotional support. Functionalists assume that members of a family will be high on all dimensions. A husband and wife will have children together, socialize them, have sexual relations with each other, live together, cooperate economically, and give each other emotional support. This global assumption is false. Eichler addresses each dimension in turn, suggesting how it needs to be reconceptualized in terms of a range of behaviour options that vary widely, depending on circumstances.

The dimension of *procreation*, for example, has been radically affected by the number of couples choosing to remain childless and by the high rate of divorce and remarriage. Eichler (1988, 243) cites evidence that, in Canada in 1985, one in three marriages ended in divorce. Statistics Canada data indicate that between 15 and 20 percent of brides or grooms in 1985 were previously married. We can estimate that between one-quarter and one-third of all Canadian children grow up in reconstituted families where one of the adults with whom they live is not their biological parent.

The dimension of *socialization* is likewise a variable. A child may be socialized by both biological parents together, or by one parent alone, or one parent with one step-parent, or one parent and step-parent in one house and another parent and step-parent in a second house, or some other combination of possible arrangements. It also cannot be assumed that simply because a parent lives in the same house

Table 1 Number of Persons Living in Common-law Unions, by Age Group and Sex, Canada, 1981, 1986, and 1991

Age Group	1981		1986		1991	
	Men	Women	Men	Women	Men	Women
Total	356 610	356 610	486 945	486 945	725 945	725 945
15–19	8 340	32 450	4 655	21 535	6 570	26 135
20–24	83 080	109 625	81 630	123 500	89 195	138 485
25–29	88 120	77 675	122 670	116 085	163 840	169 060
30–34	61 160	47 865	90 335	76 730	140 410	130 900
35–39	38 715	29 325	65 010	52 670	101 305	91 980
40–44	24 230	18 715	42 395	33 950	76 735	65 490
45–49	17 630	13 275	26 525	21 110	53 570	42 130
50–54	13 315	10 290	19 215	14 430	34 155	24 310
55–59	9 080	7 450	13 710	10 410	24 020	14 680
60–64	5 740	4 770	9 245	7 625	16 330	9 710
65+	7 200	5 170	11 555	8 895	19 815	13 065

Source: Reproduced by authority of the Ministry of Industry, 1994. Adapted from Statistics Canada (1994a), *Age, Sex, Marital Status, and Common-law Status*, Cat. 92-325E.

as a child that that parent is involved in socialization. It is quite possible and probably common for one parent to do most of the socialization work while the other does very little. Similarly, we cannot assume that when parents are divorced, the absentee parent is necessarily not involved in socialization. It may well be that divorced fathers give more time and attention to children than do fathers in two-parent households who take it for granted that the mother will do all the child-rearing work. Even the assumption that socialization gets done by parents can be questioned in a society in which very large numbers of young children spend most of their waking time in childcare centres, or with nannies, and in the company of television.

The notion that *sexual relations* take place only between married or cohabiting partners can readily be challenged. Lifelong chastity in marriage may be the exception rather than the rule. This, in turn, has important implications for procreation. It cannot simply be assumed that all children are the biological offspring of the mother's spouse.

Residence patterns also vary widely. In divorced and reconstituted families, children may have two separate family homes and commute between them. It is possible, although rare in our society, for children to have one residence while the parents rotate. Many two-career families have two or even three separate homes, one near the husband's and/or the wife's work and another family home elsewhere. Many more couples may live in one place during the winter and another during the summer.

Economic cooperation cannot be treated as given within a family. Functionalists conceive of the husband-breadwinner providing economic resources for the homemaking wife and their children, but many other arrangements are common. A sole breadwinner may pool all income for joint family use, or may keep some or most of the money for private use and give only a housekeeping allowance to the spouse. In extreme cases, the non-employed spouse may get no money at all—the breadwinner keeps everything and makes all decisions about what to buy. Two-income families have another set of possible arrangements; this is compounded when there are adult, income-earning children living at home.

The last dimension of family interaction, *emotional relations*, may vary all the way from close, loving, and mutually supportive ties to shallow and detached relations with little emotional involvement. In extreme though by no means uncommon situations, emotional relations may be characterized by abuse, violence, and hatred.

Traditional functionalist theory is not adequate to explore the dimensions of family life because the theoretical structure itself is too rigid. The monolithic bias is so pervasive that most sociology of the family textbooks, even in the 1980s, ignore the huge number of reconstituted families and all other forms of living arrangements not organized around heterosexually cohabiting pairs (see Figure 1). All other family forms are predefined as "problem families" regardless of how participants feel about them. We know little or nothing about the internal economies of families, because functionalism does not go beyond treating families

Figure 1 Percentage Distribution of Census Families, by Family Structure, 1971 and 1986

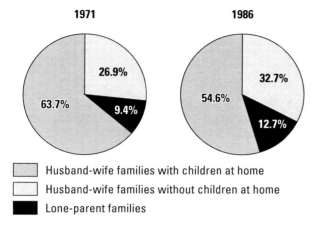

1971   1986

26.9%   32.7%

63.7% 9.4%   54.6% 12.7%

▨ Husband-wife families with children at home
☐ Husband-wife families without children at home
■ Lone-parent families

Source: Statistics Canada, 1971 and 1986 Censuses of Canada.

as economic units. Most textbooks ignore the issue of family violence entirely or at best treat it as an aberration. This is notwithstanding the evidence of extensive wife battering and the physical and sexual abuse of children. Eichler suggests that, far from being an aberration, emotional stress and violence may be normal occurrences in families. The situation of enforced intimacy between people of different sexes, different careers, different incomes, and markedly different ages would normally be seen as conducive to high stress in any context other then families. Why would we expect families to be immune?

Conservative Bias   Other biases compound the distortions arising from a monolithic focus. Eichler criticizes traditional sociology of the family literature for its **conservative bias**, reflected in a pervasive failure to focus upon changes that are transforming family life. Demographic variables are high on the list of critical changes. People in Canada are having fewer children than in the past and are living much longer. Declining fertility rates mean that most women experience pregnancy only twice in their lives. A full-time mothering role is no longer a lifetime expectation. Over half the adult women in Canada are employed outside the home. Even for the stereotypical family, the period of "Mom, Dad, and the kids" may cover only a limited stage in the family life cycle. Couples who have one or two children in their early twenties can look forward to twenty to thirty years of working lives after their children have left home. They can also realistically expect 10 or more years of life after retirement.

Changes in longevity have been dramatic and are having a profound impact on family life. Eichler (1988, 42) notes that in 1931, the average life expectancy for a male at birth was 60.0 years, but this had risen to 70.2 years by 1986. The rise in life expectancy for women was even larger: from

62.1 years in 1932 to 78.3 years in 1986. Thus, women, on average, outlive men by more than eight years, and they also tend to marry men who are older than themselves.

The combined effect of women's longer life expectancy and men's older age of marriage leads to very different experiences for women and men (Eichler 1988, 42–43). Figures for 1986 show that 74 percent of men aged 65 and older were married, compared with 42 percent of women aged 65 and older who were married, and 46 percent widowed. Roughly 12 percent of both groups were single, separated, or divorced (see Figure 2). These differences mean that the majority of men can expect to be cared for in their old age by their younger wives, while women of the same age can rarely expect to be cared for by their husbands. It would take a dramatic change in marriage patterns to redress this imbalance, but there is no evidence that this is happening.

Eichler points out that the pattern of long widowhood for women is particularly problematic because of the uneven distribution of earnings and pensions between women and men. Women who have worked as homemakers all their lives have no individual pension entitlements when their husbands die, other than the universal old age pensions paid

Figure 2 Marital Status of Elderly Men and Women, Canada, 1986

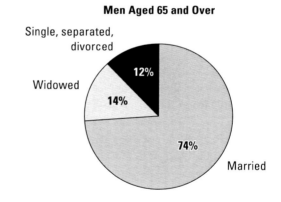

Men Aged 65 and Over

Single, separated, divorced

Widowed

12%

14%

74%

Married

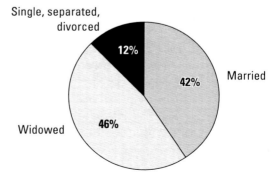

Women Aged 65 and Over

Single, separated, divorced

12%

42%   Married

Widowed   46%

Source: Statistics Canada, 1986 Census of Canada.

by the government. Women generally spend more years outside the paid labour force than men to care for children. Even when they do work full time, they earn significantly less money than men. Low earnings translate into low pensions. Poverty rates rise steeply for women in the older age groups, where most are widowed. The 1992 poverty rates are shown in Figure 3.

The rise in average life expectancies also means that a greater proportion of people are living into their 80s and 90s. What this means is that people who are themselves elderly and retired commonly have parents who require care. These responsibilities fall particularly heavily upon women, since it tends to be women rather than men who do the caring work within families. Many women around 65 years of age may find themselves caring for their own very elderly mother, and perhaps their father and in-laws, as well as for their older, retired husband. This is a great deal of work to do at an age when the woman herself might have expected to be able to retire from the obligations of looking after other people.

All of these are very dramatic changes from family life in Canada only a few generations earlier, yet they receive little attention in functionalist theory.

Sexist Bias The **sexist bias** in family sociology is reflected in the pervasive stereotyping of female and male roles around images of the pregnant woman and man the hunter. Such images are largely irrelevant in an era when few women have more than two pregnancies, and the vast majority of men neither hunt nor have jobs that require hard physical labour. This stereotyping perpetuates the myth that women are only marginally involved in the workforce and that men are marginally involved in home-life and child-rearing. Still worse, functionalist theory elevates such myths to the level of functional imperatives, conveying the impression that alternative lifestyles threaten the equilibrium of family and occupational subsystems, and hence threaten society itself.

Microstructural Bias Lastly, the **microstructural bias** in functionalist theory is reflected in a primary focus on the internal workings of individual family units. Most sociology of the family textbooks give little consideration to the impact of the wider political economy and the nature of government policies as they affect family life. Functionalists tend to discuss family problems as if they arose from inadequacies in the role of performance of individual members, rather than from external pressures on people. The microstructural bias is inherent in each of the other biases described above. We cannot understand what is happening to families apart from studying the political economy in relation to which people organize their personal lives.

Figure 3 Poverty Rates, 1992

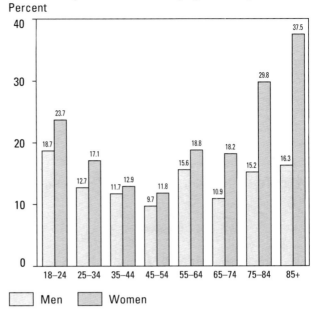

Poverty Rates for Persons by Age and Sex, 1992

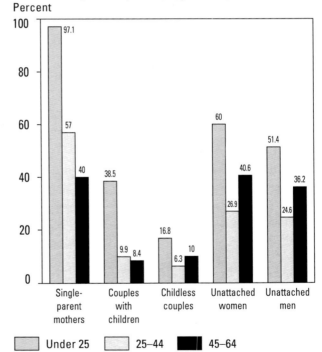

Poverty Rates by Family Type and Age of Head, 1992

Source: National Council of Welfare (1994, 32).

 # Marxist Theories of the Family

The Marxist approach to sociology of the family challenges the microstructural bias of traditional functionalist theory. Marxists argue that both the organization of economic production in the wider society and the way people earn their living critically influence the organization of family life. The family form that functionalists assert as universal represents only one historically specific form, prevalent only at a certain stage in the development of capitalism and only for members of a certain social class. Marxist feminists accept this broad analysis of the relationship between modes of production and family forms but give special attention to the impact of the economy on women's roles within the family. They challenge Parsons' notion of a separation between the **private realm** of family life and the **public realm** of industry. They claim that the demands of capitalism intrude into the most intimate personal relations of family life. Homemakers work for the corporations as much as employees do. The only difference is that the homemakers' work is not acknowledged and is not paid for.

The Marxist Theory of Patriarchy

The Marxist perspective draws its initial inspiration from an early essay by Engels ([1884] 1978), a long-time colleague of Marx. Engels speculates that the earliest form of family was probably communal, based on relatively free sexual relations and organized around matriarchal households, reflecting the known biological relation between mother and child. The family form among the Nayars, described earlier, closely resembles the model that Engels had in mind.

Engels argues that this original matriarchal family form was probably undermined by two factors: the knowledge of paternity and male control over private property. Awareness of the male role in conception represented a profound leap of knowledge, Engels suggests, with important implications for power within the family, especially when combined with control over property. As the means of subsistence changed from hunting and gathering to more settled herding and agriculture, men gained control over land and domestic herds and thus over the economic surplus. As men gained wealth, they wanted to control inheritance through the male line. This necessitated control over women's sexuality and over their offspring. Monogamy and patriarchy emerged together, Engels suggests. Monogamy was strictly required for women; men could still enjoy relative sexual freedom. This inequality gave rise to prostitution. Engels comments that "the overthrow of mother right was the world historic defeat of the female sex. The man seized the reins of the house also, the woman was degraded, enthralled, the slave of man's lust, a mere instrument for breeding children" (Engels [1884] 1978, 736).

Engels suggests that inegalitarian family forms would disappear only under two possible situations. The first was where people were so poor that men would have no property to inherit or pass on. The second was under a system of communal ownership of the means of production and equal employment of women in a socialist society. This would remove forever the basis of male power over women.

Engels' essay, and particularly his theory of the transition from matriarchy to patriarchy, is speculative, based on little anthropological evidence. But his argument concerning the importance of control over property as a determinant of male dominance in the household is widely accepted.

Capitalism and Family Forms in Canada

In a series of essays, Dorothy Smith (1977, 1979, 1983) traces changing forms of property ownership associated with the development of capitalism in Canada. She examines how these changes transformed relations between women and men in the home. During the early homesteading period, she argues, a husband and wife shared all property. They depended on each other and worked together to produce everything they needed to survive. There was no separation between domestic and productive work. Men cleared and plowed land for crops while women maintained gardens, kept chickens, pigs, and cows, helped in the harvest, and preserved the food. Women owned not only what they produced, but also whatever money they could make by selling surplus vegetables, eggs, and butter in the market. Thus, a basic economic and social equality existed between wife and husband.

This equality changed in a subtle but significant way with the transition from subsistence homesteading to cash production. Land speculation led to escalating prices, and settlers required heavy mortgages to buy land and equipment. This meant that they were no longer merely producing food for the subsistence needs of their families. Their survival depended on producing cash crops like wheat from which to earn the money to pay bank loans. Laws of property, debt, and credit endowed only the husband with full economic status in a marriage. Land was held as collateral for loans and mortgages made to him. The result, suggests Smith, was drudgery and tyranny for farm wives, who were totally subordinated to their husbands. They laboured on the homesteads, but all their labour went to pay off bank loans. When the mortgage was finally paid off, the farm belonged legally only to the husband. Women owned nothing. All the results of their labour were appropriated by their husbands.

The powerlessness of farm wives was underlined by the Supreme Court of Canada decision in 1975 concerning Irene Murdoch. She had worked on the family farm for 25 years with her husband but, after their divorce, the court decreed that she had no legal right to any of the farm property. Women who worked with their husbands in other kinds of small business enterprises found themselves in essentially the same situation. They had no assurance of a share in the assets of a business to which they had contributed.

It took a national outcry from women's organizations after the Murdoch decision to change the law to give women a share in marital property and family business.

As capitalism had advanced, the petite bourgeoisie—people who earn their living by means of family farms and family-run businesses—had declined. In the current era of corporate monopoly capitalism, the vast majority of Canadian families depend upon employment in large corporations and state bureaucracies. This dependence on wages and salaries from work done outside the home and beyond the control of family members has critical implications for the working lives of those adults who still remain within the home. Typically, men were the first to leave the home to work for wages. Women continued to do domestic work and to care for children, but they were cut off from the productive enterprise. Production was no longer centred on the home but took place in factories to which they did not have access. Marxists argue that this historically specific change in the development of capitalism produced the separate role of housewife and the model of the private family segregated from the occupational world. This is the same model that Parsons treats as a universal principle.

Marxist feminist theorists argue that women's work in the home remains crucial to the productive enterprise. The ties that bind homemakers to the corporations are less immediately visible than those binding employees but, nonetheless, almost all aspects of their working days are dictated by corporate demands. Women's labour within the home is appropriated by corporations in multiple ways, but this relation tends to be covered up by the misleading notion of the homemaker's work as a private service to her breadwinner husband. Smith argues that this "private service" by homemakers for their husbands and children may ultimately be responsible for holding together the entire system of capitalist relations of production. Smith rejects the simplistic version of Marxist theory that claims that class structure determines family structure. She insists that we must examine what people do in their everyday lives to produce the relations that we subsequently come to see as the class structure. Women's work in the home is an integral part of the processes through which class relations are produced and maintained on a daily basis. It is these work processes that we briefly explore below.

The Social Construction of Class Relations in the Home

Whether or not women work outside the home, they maintain the responsibility for homework. This responsibility and the ways in which women's homework is appropriated by capitalism vary with the social class or occupation of employed family members, which may include the women themselves. A working-class wife has to put a home together, often under conditions of poverty and inadequate housing. Her labour is vital in the struggle for some measure of comfort on a limited income. Her efforts make it possible for people to survive on incomes that may barely meet subsistence needs. Her fundamental work for the corporation is to keep her husband working under these conditions. Corporations know well that married men make more stable workers than single men because of their responsibility to support their families. It is less easy for married men to leave if they do not like the working conditions. The working-class wife supports the capitalist system against her husband because she depends so heavily upon his wages to provide for herself and her children. She cannot let him quit. An unemployed man may commonly be punished by his wife, through nagging, criticism, and humiliation, to pressure him back into the workforce.

Luxton (1980, Ch. 3) describes with stark realism the harsh lives of women married to miners in the single-industry town of Flin Flon in northern Manitoba. The working lives of these housewives remain totally tied to the rhythms of their husbands' work. A housewife must get up long before the mine whistle goes, to get her husband up, fed, and ready for work, and she must be there to greet him with his dinner when he returns. When he is working shifts, she must alter her entire schedule to meet his needs and yet still maintain the school schedules of their children. She must keep the children quiet and out of the way when he is sleeping, do her housework only when it will not disturb him, provide meals when he wants them, and in effect manage the family so that he turns up regularly for work. In a sense, she is as much an employee of the mine as he is, but she does not get paid.

The appropriation of the labour of middle-class women by capitalism takes a different form. In material terms, their lives may be more comfortable and their homemaking responsibilities easier to meet than those of working-class housewives because they do not have to struggle against poverty. But the wives of men who hold managerial and executive positions within corporations may have less personal autonomy as they find themselves more trapped by the demands of the corporation. Smith (1977) argues that, while a working-class man has a job within a corporation, a man in a more senior rank plays a role for the corporation. He must meet the image of a corporation man, and it is his wife's duty to maintain this image and to mould their children to fit it. The family home becomes something of a subcontracted agency of the corporation. The housewife works to produce the image that the corporation wants. The image that is on display is largely set by the media and disseminated in glossy magazines and television advertising; the housewife herself has little control over it. It is subtly but rigidly enforced within the corporate hierarchy. An executive whose personal and family appearance does not conform to the corporate mould tends to be viewed with suspicion and overlooked for promotion.

Middle-class women routinely support the careers of their husbands by relieving them of household and child-care responsibilities.

The corporate man is then free to display his undivided loyalty to the corporation by spending long hours of over-time at the office on evenings and weekends and travelling on business whenever requested. In the highly competitive corporate world, such behaviour is often essential for mobility up the corporate hierarchy. The support work that wives do often begins very early in men's corporate careers. A wife may work to support her husband through college. Subsequently, she may help his career by entertaining his business associates and doing unpaid secretarial work. The wife of a professor often helps with the research, sorting, and editing involved in writing, although the resulting work bears only his name. Corporations thus appropriate the labour time of the wives of their executives and professional staff through the support services that wives are routinely expected to provide for their husbands. The competence of wives, especially wives of executives, to perform these support roles can be so important that some corporations have insisted on interviewing not only the male applicants for senior positions, but their wives as well (Kanter 1977).

A middle-class homemaker further serves the corporation through absorbing the tensions generated by the career demands made on her husband. In this there is a Catch-22; when she supports and repairs him and sends him back refreshed, she is in fact supporting the external system that oppresses him. But, like her working-class counterpart, she has little choice. To be a good homemaker, she must make her husband's success visible. She cannot afford to let him fail.

Corporations also appropriate the mothering work of middle-class women. Middle-class status is inherited not through property, but through careers, and mothering work is essential to this process. The academic streaming of children begins very early in the education process, and a mother who wants her children to succeed in future corporate careers must groom them even in infancy so that they will perform well from the first days of kindergarten. Her children's failure in school will be seen as evidence that she does not love them enough.

In times of economic recession, women's unpaid labour in the home absorbs the resulting social problems. As unemployment rises, women are disproportionately affected, laid off more frequently, and pushed into part-time work. They bear the increased burden of the emotional stress felt by workers who risk being unemployed or who may be squeezed out in corporate mergers. Women in the home must absorb the extra work no longer being done by professionals when social services are cut back for the elderly, the handicapped, and the sick (Armstrong 1984, Ch. 7).

In these multiple ways, homemakers work for the corporate capitalist system—work for which they receive no pay and rarely any acknowledgment. The enormity of their exploitation is hidden under the myth of private family life. Until the women's movement began to have some impact, all the work that women did in the home was not even identified as work. It was considered merely "a labour of love" (Luxton 1980).

Research in the Marxist feminist tradition has documented the processes through which relations of political economy intrude into the most intimate relations of love and marriage. Luxton's study of Flin Flon shows how courtship and marriage are affected by the economy of this single-industry mining town, in which there are few well-paying jobs for women. Marriage is the only viable option for adult women in the town. This reality pervades the dating game and sexual activities. Boys have the chance to earn good money working in the mine while girls do not. Girls therefore trade sexual favours for a good time and economic rewards. Boys pay for the date and expect, sooner rather than later, that the girl will "come across." This same dependency continues after marriage and is made all the more evident if pregnancy has forced a quick wedding. Both the woman and the man feel trapped by her dependence on his wages.

Luxton (1980, Ch. 6) suggests that this economic reality is at the root of much domestic violence. She describes the explosive tensions that revolve around the fact that he earns the money and she spends it. Men who come home drained and exhausted from a day's work at the mine often feel they have a right to control the household because they are responsible for its subsistence. Many of the women whom Luxton interviewed described how they took the brunt of their husband's resentment against his job. One woman summed it up this way: "He puts up with shit every day at work and he only works because he has to support me and the kids. Weren't for us he'd be off trapping on his own—no boss" (Luxton 1980, 70). Women blame themselves, feeling guilty for having induced male hostility and aggression by being a burden. Women absorb the tensions. In extreme cases they absorb violence and beatings. More commonly, they deny themselves even basic needs because they cannot escape the sense of guilt that they are spending "his" money on themselves. This is the reality that is glossed over in the abstract functionalist category of "tension management."

Such dependent relationships may only be marginally improved for most women who take up employment outside the home. Having their own income allows women some independence, but the reality is that few women can hope to earn enough to support themselves and their children above the poverty line. With the exception of a minority of professional women, a male wage is still essential to support an average middle-class family lifestyle.

In summary, Marxist feminists argue that family relations and domestic work are embedded in the political economy of corporate capitalism. Homemakers are agents of tension management and pattern maintenance for corporations, but their work is not acknowledged and not paid for. They remain outside the corporations and so cannot influence any of the decisions that direct their lives. Smith (1977) sees this as the root of depression and mental illness among women. Women are oppressed in a nameless way by a system from which they appear to be entirely separated and yet which comes to rule the most intimate aspects of their lives. This thesis avoids the monolithic and conservative biases evident in functionalist theory by analyzing family structures in their historical and class contexts. Family forms in Canada changed markedly with transformations in capitalism from early homesteading, through cash cropping and small business, to the current form of monopoly capitalism. The thesis also incorporates an analysis of the processes through which people socially construct the realities of family life in the situation in which they find themselves.

The Radical Feminist Critique: Capitalism or Patriarchy?

The **radical feminist** perspective shares with Marxism an appreciation of the impact of capitalism on family life, but challenges the narrow, deterministic focus on political economy as the cause of family structures. These theorists argue that this tunnel vision of traditional Marxists gives inadequate attention to relations of patriarchy or gender hierarchy that cannot be subsumed under capitalism. In particular, they challenge the more deterministic version of Marxist theory, sometimes referred to as Marxist structuralism, that explains family structures by reference to their functions for the capitalist system.

Marxists would argue, for example, that the privatization of women in the home occurs because it is functional for capitalism (Armstrong and Armstrong 1985). Capitalism is based on free wage-labour that requires the separation of a public, commodity-production unit from a private subsistence unit in which free labourers are reproduced and maintained. Hence the subordination of women appears to be a necessary condition for the capitalist system. Structuralist Marxists also describe the position of women as a reserve

army of labour, which can be stored cheaply within the home, as necessary for the capitalist system. The implications of this thesis are that the **privatization** of women was not evident in the pre-capitalist era. It arose with capitalism and will decline with the transition to socialism.

Radical feminists argue that the evidence does not support this thesis. In pre-capitalist Europe, the economy may have centred on domestic production in which women were involved, but this did not ensure gender equality, either in family practice or in religious and social ideologies. In many parts of contemporary Asia, in both Hindu and Muslim cultures, the traditions of **purdah**, which include an emphasis on the extreme subjugation and segregation of women within the home, still persist. The origins of the purdah system long predate the emergence of capitalism. If anything, this extreme privatization of women has begun to break down under capitalism, as more women gain access to education and professional employment outside the home.

The Marxist thesis shows how capitalism accommodates and uses existing inequalities between women and men in the household, but this is not sufficient to explain why such inequalities developed in the first place or why they persist (Miles 1985). We still need to explain why capitalism developed in such a way as to bolster men's power over women. We need to explain why the sexual division of labour appears as it does. Why is it, almost invariably, women and not men who are engaged in unpaid domestic labour? Marx tends to treat this as the biological nature of things, but it is by no means biologically determined that women must do the domestic work beyond the actual physical acts of giving birth and breast-feeding. Why is it mostly women who bear the double burden of domestic work and a paid job? Why do husbands continue to do so little domestic work in comparison with their wives, even when wives are employed full time? Why is it that the issue of whether a wife should be employed takes on the connotations of a threat to male power and status? Reference to the needs of capitalism does not seem to explain this. Marxist theory would actually predict the opposite response—that men would generally welcome any reduction in the economic burden of a dependent wife.

The prevalence of domestic violence is also not adequately explained within the Marxist thesis. Economic dependence helps to explain the vulnerability of women to male power, but it does not explain why so many wives are battered in the first place (Miles 1985, 47). Nor does economic dependence account for other forms of male violence against women and children, such as rape, incest, and sexual harassment. It cannot explain practices such as burning widows alive on the funeral pyres of their husband, footbinding, genital mutilation, and **dowry murders**, which are prevalent in some non-Western societies.

Radical feminists assert that Marxist theory describes but does not explain male supremacy inside and outside the home. The exploitation of workers under capitalism and the oppression of women by men are not equivalent concepts (Eisenstein 1979, 22). Relations of patriarchy have to be addressed directly. In trying to subsume issues of patriarchy under the blanket explanation of capitalism, Marxist theory functions as an ideology. It can serve to legitimate male domination over women by displacing responsibility onto the economy.

This misuse of Marxist theory was powerfully illustrated at a meeting of the Canadian Asian Studies Association in response to a paper describing women's oppression in Pakistan under President Zia's "Islamization" program (Rafiq 1988; Hale 1988). Part of the paper referred to Islamic law concerning rape. A woman who claims she has been raped requires no less than four male witnesses, all of impeccable character, before she can press charges in court. Otherwise, her case will be dismissed, and she herself can be sentenced to public flogging for having engaged in unlawful sex. Men in the audience reinterpreted this paper in terms of the capitalist mode of production, debating how it was in the interests of the capitalist class to keep women at home as cheap labour. In this determinist, structuralist version of Marxism, the men who commit the violence disappear; it is the system that appears to do things. A woman's experience of being raped, with those who violate her not only immune to punishment, but able to have her flogged for even mentioning what they had done to her, was excluded from the debate. It became trivialized as a form of false consciousness, while the concerns of men with their own class oppression took precedence. Radical feminist theory addresses this failure to analyze the oppression of women by placing the issue of patriarchy at the centre of sociology of the family.

The Roots of Male Power

O'Brien (1981) challenges the original thesis proposed by Engels that links male power and control over property. Engels argues that, with the development of settled agriculture and herding, men controlled the means of production and hence the wealth of society. Men sought control over women in order to ensure that their property would be inherited by their own biological children. Thus, the institution of monogamy for women became important. O'Brien suggests that this thesis has too many unquestioned assumptions. Why did men gain control over property in the first place? Why did it have to be inherited through the male line? Why did it have to be inherited individually rather than by the community as a whole? Among the **matrilineal** Nayar in South India, land and animals were communally owned by the mother's joint family and inherited by her

children. Men did not have the right to own or to dispose of such property. Why and how did men come to wrest control from the original matriarchal communal families?

O'Brien proposes that the basic causal relationship between control over property and control over women's sexuality should be reversed. Men, she suggests, seek to control property in order to control women's sexual and reproductive powers, not the other way around. The material base of the gender hierarchy is the means of reproduction of children rather than production of material goods. When a women has sexual freedom, a man has no way of knowing which, if any, of her children he fathered. Paternity is reduced to an abstract idea. O'Brien argues that male alienation from birth, and thus from human continuity through children, is profound. This alienation can only be partially overcome by the institution of monogamy, through which a man asserts an exclusive right of sexual access to a particular woman.

Male power over women is not automatic, but is the result of continual struggle, in which final victory is impossible. Men can struggle to control women, but it is women who control reproduction. Male control over a woman's reproductive powers, and hence male appropriation of her children as his own, is always uncertain. It depends upon absolute faith in her chastity or upon the strictest possible control over her, including her seclusion from other men. It depends also on trust in other men. But such trust is tenuous, especially in the context of war, competition, and hierarchical divisions among men. Male dominance over other men in war is often expressed through sexual violation of the women "belonging" to the enemy.

O'Brien situates the origin of the private family, and the split between the private realm of women and the public realm of men, in this male struggle for exclusive sexual access to women, rather than in the development of capitalism. The economic dependence of women on men and the inability of women to support themselves and their children apart from a man are essential mechanisms for male control over women. The inheritance of property from father to son is also of paramount importance in the social assertion of the principle of paternity over biological maternity. Male control over property and inheritance thus remains central in O'Brien's thesis, but for different reasons than Engels proposes.

The major difference between the two formulations becomes evident in predicting the behaviour of males who own no property. Engels predicts that when men have no property to control or to transmit to children, they will have no interest in controlling women. O'Brien predicts that such men will still try to control women's sexual and reproductive powers through any other means at their disposal, including sexual violence.

The history of the mother-centred Nayar households gives insight into the nature of the struggle for control over family property and women's reproductive powers. The Nayar family organization did not disappear as an inevitable result of developments in agriculture industrialization. It was deliberately and systematically undermined by the British Imperial government in India.

The British passed a series of laws between 1868 and 1933 that broke up the matrilineal households and imposed a monogamous, male-headed marriage system. The first law held that a man had to provide for his wife and children, a law that had no meaning in the Nayar situation. The next law declared that the wife and children had the right of maintenance by the husband. Again this had little effect because the Nayar did not register marriages. Then followed various Nayar Regulation Laws that decreed that the brief ceremony that took place when a girl reached puberty constituted a legal marriage that could only be dissolved through a legal divorce. The man gained the right to inherit the property of his wife rather than sharing in the communal property of his mother's household. Further laws declared that all property held in common in the matrilineal household could be broken up and inherited, and that a man's heirs were no longer his sister's children but his wife's children. The laws were part of a long struggle for supremacy between men and women within the Nayar communities, and they are still bitterly resented and resisted by the Nayar women. Males gained the advantage under the British, both through the laws and through access to an English education, which enabled men but not women to obtain administrative posts in the British colonial service. Men thereby gained personal income and economic independence from the communal household, and they were granted the legal right to dispose of this private property as they wished (Liddle and Joshi 1986, 28–29).

In Canada, male power over women and property was similarly imposed through patriarchal laws. It was not the inevitable outcome of capitalist farming that dispossessed women homesteaders, but specific laws that required a man to have single, unencumbered title to real estate for it to stand as collateral for mortgages and loans. It was only after the Irene Murdoch case in 1975 that these laws were revised to permit and subsequently to require joint ownership by husband and wife of family property used as collateral. Native women were dispossessed by the British North America Act, which decreed that any Native woman who married a non-Native forfeited all her rights to Native status and to band property. It was 1984 before this law was changed, and then only after it had been challenged before the World Court.

Given that ownership of property is such an important mechanism in male control over the sexual and reproductive powers of women, it follows that women's paid employment outside the home threatens that control. Radical feminist theory argues that men fear the expansion of income-earning opportunities for their wives, even though this relieves them of the economic burden of a dependent family. The theory predicts that men will strive to minimize the level of economic independence and also that they will strive to reassert control through other mechanisms including domestic violence and medical and legal control over reproduction.

Limits to Economic Freedom for Women   Liddle and Joshi (1986, Part 4) argue that class hierarchy in the labour force is built upon and reinforces gender hierarchy. Women are employed but predominantly within low-paid job ghettos. Their incomes supplement their husbands' earnings but do not supersede them. Few women earn sufficient money to provide for themselves and their children at an average standard of living. They still depend on a male wage earner.

The unequal division of domestic labour within the home is cited by Liddle and Joshi as a primary mechanism ensuring the continued economic and familial dominance of men. Even when women are employed in full-time jobs outside the home, they commonly bear almost the entire responsibility for domestic work. Men, by and large, refuse to do this work, or at best contribute only in the least onerous areas. Men appropriate women's labour in the home to restore their own energies. They return to work relaxed and refreshed, while women return to work exhausted from doing three jobs: domestic work; childcare; and the work for which they are paid. Then women are penalized in the labour market for having less strength and energy and making slower career progress than men.

Childcare outside the home is limited and expensive, so that only women who earn above-average incomes can afford it. The majority of women are faced with the choice of taking long periods of time out of the paid labour force to care for young children or of working themselves to exhaustion trying to do everything. Women who take such time out, or who begin to develop a career only in their late 30s or early 40s, present no competition to men who are far advanced in their positions.

This inequality in the labour force stemming from women's responsibility for domestic work becomes apparent whenever marriages break down. Wives are legally entitled to an equitable share in family property, but husbands take their income-earning capacity with them. All too often, women find themselves left with half a house, but without the income to maintain it.

This artificial separation between the realms of public and private, the world of men and the world of women and

Few women earn enough money to support themselves and their children.

children, creates its own dynamic that tends to reinforce male efforts to control and possess women. The public realm is associated with rational and technical concerns of production, and the private family with meeting emotional needs. Men come to depend on women in the home to meet their ongoing need for nurturing or mothering, in addition to their need for women to procreate and to nurture their children. This may be especially so in societies where men are discouraged from being nurturing themselves and where they spend their working lives in a public realm, which is characterized by competitive, fragmented, impersonal, and emotionally neutral or non-affective relationships. Long after children have been born and raised, men may still seek to possess women in order to ensure that their own nurturing needs are met. This need for personal nurturing may be so overwhelming for some men that they become jealous of their own children and the attention they are given by the nurturer-mother.

Domestic Violence The threat and the reality of domestic violence, in all its forms, is another powerful mechanism for asserting male control over women and children. Until recently, wife beating had both religious and legal approval. The Roman Catholic law of chastisement enjoined a husband to beat his wife for her moral betterment. This injunction was carried over to British common law and Canadian and American law and only began to be challenged towards the end of the nineteenth century. Fathers were also endowed with the religious prescription and legal right to discipline their children using physical force.

In addition to physical battering, children are also victims of sexual abuse. Estimates of such abuse vary widely depending on the measurements used (Badgley 1984, 114). The rate most commonly cited is that one in five girls and one in 10 boys have experienced unwanted sexual attention. Guessing rates by pitting the findings of different sources against each other is a largely futile exercise. But the fact that physical and sexual abuse of children occurs in a significant number of families is not in dispute. Why does such behaviour occur?

The Marxist thesis attributes the violence primarily to the frustration experienced by men who are employed or are trapped in low-paid, alienating jobs. Radical feminists dispute this explanation as inadequate to account for the extent of wife battery and incest. An American study (Shupe, Stacey, and Hazlewood 1987, 21–22) cites evidence that the social background of wife batterers in selected counselling sessions and police records mirrored the population at large with respect to age, education, race, ethnicity, religion, and occupation. The one exception was that the percentage of unemployed men among the batterers was double the national average. Unemployed men seem more likely to batter, perhaps because they have lost the economic basis of their control over their wives, but this does not alter the evidence that men from all strata of the population—including doctors, lawyers, politicians, ministers, and police officers—beat their wives. Similarly, many of the men who commit incest are "pillars of the community" in other respects.

Various psychological explanations have been put forward to account for wife battering. They include the common argument that it is a symptom of other emotional problems that can stem from trauma from abuse as a child, learned behaviour from watching an abusive father, lack of communication skills with the spouse, low self-esteem, lack of emotional controls, and the need to express repressed anger and frustration (Adams 1988). Radical feminists argue that such explanations only offer excuses for the batterer to continue the behaviour. They also do not account for why the batterer's behaviour is directed at his wife. Batterers rarely assault anyone other than their wives. They do not habitually lose emotional control or lack of communication skills in other contexts.

Radical feminists argue that one has to examine the practical gains that accrue to the batterer from his violence;

that is, fear and submission in his victim and compliance with his wishes (Adams 1988; Ptacek 1988). Wife battering is essentially a controlling behaviour designed to create and maintain an imbalance of power in the household. Battery and sexual abuse of children are the extreme expressions of male assertion of property rights over women and children. Less extreme forms of such controlling behaviour include verbal and non-verbal intimidation and psychological abuse, pressure tactics like withholding financial support, accusations or threats of infidelity, and ultimatums and deadlines that force a woman to comply with her husband's wishes (Adams 1988, 191–194). Such persistent humiliation can be pushed to the point where competent, professional women have their self-esteem destroyed (Forward and Torres 1987, 15–85).

Not all expressions of violence are by husbands against wives. Some wives abuse their husbands, but it is currently impossible even to guess at the rate. It would appear that much of the violence directed by wives towards husbands is defensive or retaliatory. The relatively small number of unprovoked attacks on men by female partners seems often to involve jealous ex-wives and ex-girlfriends. Firestone (1971, Ch. 6) suggests that many women are so intensely socialized to see their own self-worth in terms of being a sexual partner for a male that when their relationship breaks down and the male begins to see another woman, their sense of self-worth and identity are shattered. Occasionally these feelings may turn to rage and hatred. Such responses, however, are not equivalent in form or intent to the systematic, repeated brutality that constitutes wife battering. While it may be true that much abuse experienced by husbands goes unreported, the same is true of abused wives. We do know that the overwhelming majority of people who are injured in domestic violence are female. There is a vast body of evidence of systematic, severe, intimidating force used by men against women, while there is no such evidence for women against husbands (Dobash and Dobash 1988, 60–62).

The problems of wife battering and sexual abuse of children are very deep-rooted in our society. They reflect both the identification of masculine sexuality with aggression and the pervasive socialization of males to be aggressive. They also reflect the patriarchal structures of family life that accord authority, power, and control to the father figure. Such power carries with it the inherent risk of corruption. Thirdly, they highlight the emotional shallowness of relations among men, which leaves the family as the only source of human warmth and sensuality. But this source is itself constrained and distorted by the emphasis on exclusivity, possession, authority, and control. Wives and children bear the emotional brunt of these distorted relations.

Custody Battles: Shared Parenting or Patriarchal Control?   Divorce is a fact of life in Canadian society (see Table 2), but its frequency does not lessen the traumatic effect on the parties involved. Divorce invariably means a significant drop in the income of single-parent families headed by women. Divorced fathers who do not want to pay child support face no effective pressure to do so. The default rate on court-ordered support payments has been estimated to be between 80 and 90 percent (Crean 1989, 20). While the court generally awards custody of children to mothers, about half the fathers who contest custody win their case, often in the face of evidence of minimal previous involvement in nurturing, and despite evidence of physical or sexual abuse (Chesler 1991). Sexual abuse of children is difficult to prove, and mothers who raise the issue not only risk having their credibility challenged in court, but jeopardize their own custody claims by being labelled as an unfriendly parent who is trying to block rightful access by the father.

Table 2 Number of Divorces, Canada, 1950–91			
Year	Number of Divorces	Year	Number of Divorces
1950	5 386	1971	29 685
1951	5 270	1972	32 389
1952	5 650	1973	36 704
1953	6 160	1974	45 019
1954	5 923	1975	50 611
1955	6 053	1976	54 207
1956	6 002	1977	55 370
1957	6 688	1978	57 155
1958	6 279	1979	59 474
1959	6 543	1980	62 019
1960	6 980	1981	67 671
1961	6 563	1982	70 436
1962	6 768	1983	68 567
1963	7 686	1984	65 172
1964	8 623	1985	61 980
1965	8 974	1986	78 160
1966	10 239	1987	90 872
1967	11 165	1988	79 872
1968	11 343	1989	81 009
1969	26 093	1990	78 488
1970	29 775	1991	77 031

Source: Reproduced by authority of the Minister of Industry, 1994. Adapted from Statistics Canada (1994h), *Marriage and Conjugal Life in Canada*, Cat. 91-534E, table 18, p. 47.

Custody battles over children and the demand for mandatory joint legal custody following divorce are forming a new arena of struggle between principles of feminism and patriarchy. Of particular concern to feminists are the threatening implications of seemingly progressive legislation aimed at ensuring the rights of divorced fathers in relation to their children. Mandatory joint custody legislation was passed in 36 American states between 1980 and 1988.

Across Canada, joint custody is an option but not a presumption. The Ontario Divorce Act of 1985 closely parallels the Ontario Children's Law Reform Act, which states that the courts may award custody or access to one or more persons, but without any policy legislation favouring joint or sole custody. In each case "the best interests of the child" are paramount. A private member's bill introduced in the Ontario legislature in January 1988 sought to commit the province to mandatory joint custody, but the bill was not passed. Opponents emphasized the distinction between shared parenting and joint legal custody.

Medical and Legal Control over Reproduction

The struggle for control over women's reproductive power continues in the public arenas of medicine and law. In Canada, the medical profession has almost entirely succeeded in wresting technical control over childbirth from women (Burtch 1988). Formerly, O'Brien suggests (1981, 10), childbirth was an affirmation of sisterhood, a rite shared by the mother-to-be, the midwife, and other women friends who attended the birth in the community. However, as a government-financed health-care system developed, and as the traditional healing arts were professionalized and institutionalized, midwives were shut out. It became normal for childbirth to take place in an antiseptic hospital delivery room under the control of predominantly male obstetricians. Until very recently, it was normal for the mother to be drugged into semiconsciousness, her feet tied up in stirrups, while the baby was pulled out with forceps. While some accuse feminists of romanticizing simpler childbirths, feminists insist that the issue is male supremacy or, specifically, the supremacy of male doctors over mothers and midwives. Available evidence indicates that the mortality rate for home births with a midwife is as low or lower than physician-attended births in hospitals. Yet medical control remained absolute. Midwifery did not die out in Canada but it had no legal status. Women who attended home births could face criminal charges, especially if the newborn died. By law, a doctor had to be in attendance at a birth. As recently as April 1989, a Montreal doctor was suspended for six months for letting a midwife deliver the baby of one of his patients, without him being in the room.

Only in the 1990s did this control over birth by the medical profession begin to weaken, partly in response to pressure from the women's movement, and partly to cut medical costs. The province of Ontario led the way in 1986 with a decision to establish midwifery as a self-regulated profession. Five years later, the Midwifery Act was proclaimed, permitting midwives to work in maternity wards. On 1 January 1994, midwives were granted the right to admit women to hospital, deliver babies, and send them home, without consulting a doctor (*Globe and Mail*, 14 May 1994). In 1994, Quebec passed legislation approving midwifery in eight free-standing birthing centres, but they met fierce opposition from doctors because they are not based in hospitals. By 1994, only one centre was still operating.

Recent developments in reproductive technology, including test-tube babies, embryo transplants, surrogate motherhood, and assisted insemination, further this process of control over birth by predominantly male scientists. This medico-scientific takeover of birth is being combined with increasing legislative controls over the lives of pregnant women. Court-ordered stays in hospital and Caesarean sections against the mother's will have already occurred in Canada (*Globe and Mail*, 1 August 1986, D1–2). A Vancouver lawyer hired to fight one such case commented that one should not underestimate the male fixation on having the perfect son and heir, or what a man might do if a woman pregnant with his child was perceived to be disobeying orders that related to having that perfect baby. The desperation of some men to find a **surrogate mother** for artificial insemination with their sperm, and the amount they are prepared to pay for this service (around $15 000 US plus expenses), underline how important biological reproduction is to many men.

The Canadian Royal Commission on New Reproductive Technologies, which issued its formal report in December of 1993, came out strongly against the commercialization of

Midwives can now deliver babies in Ontario, allowing women to take back some medical control over childbirth.

any aspect of human reproduction, including the sale of sperm or fetal tissue. The report also stressed the importance of a pregnant woman's autonomy and right to bodily integrity. It opposed any judicial intervention in pregnancy, favouring voluntary care and assistance to pregnant women instead (Canadian Royal Commission on New Reproductive Technologies 1993, 24). However, the Commission also favoured the establishment of a federal regulatory and licensing body for reproductive technology, and proposed strict limits on the availability of treatment that is still considered experimental. It recommended that in-vitro fertilization technology for preconception arrangements, for postmenopausal women, and for profit should be banned. Commercial fertilization clinics would also be banned. If such recommendations are adopted, women's choices would remain tightly controlled by professional decision-makers, and all other commercial avenues for treatment blocked within Canada.

The Abortion Debate: Pro-life or Pro-patriarchy?

The abortion issue is at the centre of the political struggle surrounding reproductive rights in Canada and the United States. In January 1988, the Supreme Court of Canada struck down Canada's existing abortion law as unconstitutional because it was being applied in an arbitrary and discriminatory manner. There were huge geographic disparities in accessibility, and women experienced long and sometimes dangerous delays in having abortions approved. The Supreme Court decision added fuel to the political struggle between the opposing forces.

New legislation on abortion proposed by the Mulroney government in 1989 marginally passed a House of Commons vote but was defeated in the Senate on 31 January 1991. Since then Canada has had no legislation governing abortions. The Medical Services Act of Nova Scotia, which prohibited the performance of abortions outside of hospitals, was also struck down in October of 1990. The Morgentaler abortion clinic in Halifax was thus declared lawful. In the summer of 1994, Morgentaler challenged a similar law in New Brunswick by opening a free-standing abortion clinic in Fredericton. Another clinic is planned for Prince Edward Island, the only province in which no abortions are available, even in hospitals. The struggle continues around whether medicare will cover the cost of abortions performed in clinics.

The issue of a woman's right to an abortion never seems to be settled once and for all. Physicians who are known to perform abortions continue to have their careers and their lives threatened by anti-abortion activists. On the surface, the anti-abortion lobby speaks to a humanistic concern for the sanctity of human life and a reluctance to kill that potential life for motives of convenience. But opponents of the lobby fear that the "pro-life" label obscures a political agenda that is fiercely anti-feminist (Eichler 1985; Dubinsky 1985). In principle, Eichler argues, the pro-life stand should be consistent with supporting every effort to minimize unwanted pregnancies and to maximize all forms of social support that would encourage pregnant women to keep their babies. But in practice, the lobby groups fighting hardest to have abortion declared illegal are publicly against most of the policies intended to help women with children.

The anti-abortion movement in the United States campaigned strenuously to bring about the defeat of the Equal Rights Amendment, which would have prohibited discrimination on the basis of sex (Eisenstein 1984). They actively opposed welfare payments to mothers, public daycare programs, and **affirmative action** policies to promote employment for women. A similar lobby group in Canada, REAL Women (Realistic Equal Active for Life), is anti-abortion and is also against welfare and against enshrining equality provisions for women in the Charter of Rights and Freedoms. The REAL Women platform opposes abortion under all circumstances; opposes the contraceptive pill as suppressing maternal instincts; opposes sex education in schools as inciting immorality; opposes welfare and public daycare as undermining family responsibilities; opposes affirmative action for women in employment because this creates competition with male breadwinners; opposes feminist counsellors in homes for battered women because they advocate the breakup of the family; opposes the National Action Committee on the Status of Women as anti-family and anti-housewife; and favours the right of a woman to be a full-time homemaker and the obligation of her husband to support her.

This agenda is a clear example of the politics of the "New Right." At the root of the New Right political agenda is a concern with the preservation of the traditional patriarchal family form, centred on the private family home. Women perform the expressive roles of full-time homemaker, mother, and nurturer of the family members, while men are responsible for public instrumental roles as providers. Policies to promote women's employment, state welfare, and public daycare are all seen as threatening such families by relieving men of their primary provider role. To the extent that women's domestic work and men's family responsibilities ensure a cheaply maintained, rested, committed, and stable workforce, such policies also threaten capitalist interests. The New Right fears that contraception and abortion rights trivialize the mother role, reduce male commitment or obligation to support mothers and children, and hence undercut the social foundations of a stable family and workforce.

The clash between New Right politics and feminism essentially revolves around the different views of the ideal family. Conservatives frequently claim that feminism leads to the breakdown of the family. The family that conservatives have in mind is the traditional patriarchal form that ensures male authority and female domesticity and dependence. The feminist movement advocates a very different form based on a consensual and egalitarian union that maximizes freedom of choice in the division of roles and responsibilities between spouses.

The National Action Committee on the Status of Women (NAC) is an umbrella organization that represents a broad range of feminist concerns. Its policy platform challenges the economic exploitation of women in the home and in the labour force, and challenges the mechanisms of male oppression of women through economic dependence, the domestic burden, family violence, and medico-legal controls over women's reproductive freedom. Specific policies favoured by NAC include affirmative action in employment, universal and affordable childcare, transition houses for battered women, income support for women and children to escape the dependency that makes women vulnerable to domestic violence, and protection of women's reproductive choice through safer and more effective contraception, maximum support services for pregnant women, and abortion as a backup. In this context, abortion rights symbolize the inviolable right of women to control their own reproductive power.

The vision of family at the root of the feminist political agenda is a consensual union between equal partners, free from relations of dependency and without any forced sex-role division of labour between private and public, expressive and instrumental tasks. This vision of family equality presupposes a transformation in the position of women in the labour force and in the ways in which work time is organized. The feminist platform shares with the nascent men's liberation movement a belief that the alienation of men from children can be overcome not through possession of women and children, but through participation as equals in the nurturing process. If men as parents are to assume equal responsibilities with women for domestic and childcare work, then the ways in which men as workers are exploited by capitalism will also have to be transformed.

The abortion debate has become a focal point for struggle around these two very different conceptions of family. Both sides claim to be defending the true interests of women and children. Eisenstein (1984, Ch. 7) suggests that the New Right political agenda appeals to many women because it addresses their real material conditions in a patriarchal and capitalist society. The reality is that the mass of women with children are dependent on male breadwinners for their survival. The women's movement, combined with developments in capitalism, has widened opportunities for women beyond traditional domestic roles, but this opportunity is largely illusory. Women predominate in low-paid job ghettos. Rising divorce rates mean that many women must struggle in abject poverty as single parents. The superwoman image of professionals who manage to combine careers with domestic and childcare responsibilities has limited appeal for women who already feel overburdened. Feminism threatens their security without being able to bring about the radical social and economic change needed to provide women with real alternatives.

The Limitations of Radical Feminism

The weakness of radical feminist analysis of family life stems from its overly narrow focus. The perspective has drawn attention to widespread and serious problems of violence and abuse within families, which have been overlooked or downplayed by other approaches. But radical feminist research also tends to overstate the case for patriarchy to the extent that the abnormal becomes the norm. Some sources speculate, for example, that as many as one girl in two and one boy in three are victims of incest, an estimate that encompasses virtually every family in Canada. When concepts are pushed to this extreme, it becomes impossible to make distinctions between different experiences of family life. Radical feminism runs the risk of generating its own form of monolithic bias.

We know that, however pervasive the hidden problems might be, not all people experience family life as abusive. Most people do get married, and most of those who get divorced subsequently remarry. The majority of women and men thus appear to find marriage worth the struggle, or at least feel that it is more rewarding than living alone.

There is evidence of widespread changes in family roles. Husbands and fathers are increasingly getting involved in domestic work and in the nurturing of children, albeit generally not at the same level of responsibility as women. The combination of shorter working hours, free weekends, and changing conceptions of fatherhood means that children and fathers are more closely involved with each other than in the past. The real suffering of many fathers who are separated from their children by divorce cannot be subsumed under the blanket explanations of desire for revenge and legal control over their ex-wives.

The problem for radical feminist theory is to account for these different experiences. The pioneering work of feminist research into family violence means that we can no longer discount the 10 to 20 percent of families characterized by wife battery and other forms of abuse. But neither can we discount the majority of families where couples manage to establish mutually supportive relations and where children can look to both fathers and mothers for nurturance and emotional support. We need more research into the processes that account for this variation.

We are still far from understanding the factors that encourage egalitarian marriages and shared parenting as opposed to patriarchy and rigid role differentiation. Such analysis will need to take into account the context of political economy and the processes that exploit people and help to perpetuate role differentiation and yet simultaneously provide opportunities for women to be financially independent. The analysis will also need to take into account the emotional stress generated by patriarchal family forms and the evidence that men who abuse wives and children were commonly abused themselves when young. Abuse may generate the emotional insecurity that finds expression in the drive for domination and possession in marriage. From this perspective, patriarchy appears less as the expression of male power than of chronic insecurity, powerlessness, and fear. This remains speculation. Feminist theory has opened up the debate by focusing attention on issues that have been ignored by mainstream theories. But the research needed to explain the conflicting patterns of egalitarian and patriarchal families, and nurturing and abusive family relations, is still in its infancy.

CONCLUSION

Family life may be the most difficult area of sociology to study. It is so familiar and so emotionally charged that it is hard for us to distance ourselves from it. Sociological analysis has moved a long way from the original functionalist view that sex-role divisions within the nuclear family were natural, rational, and efficient adaptations to industrial society. But functionalist formulations still dominate most sociological textbooks. Monolithic, conservative, sexist, and microstructural biases in functionalist analysis of the family are being eliminated only with difficulty. Research in the Marxist tradition shows how different family forms are embedded in economic relations that exploit both women and men and set constraints on their lives. Feminist theory reveals other aspects of the family as the central arena for the struggle between competing principles of gender equality and patriarchy. The processes that influence the outcome of these struggles are still far from understood.

SUGGESTED READING

An excellent source of statistical information on families in Canada is Margrit Eichler's *Families in Canada Today: Recent Changes and their Policy Consequences*, 2nd ed. (1988). Eichler takes a very critical approach to traditional sociology of the family and provides quantities of data to back her argument that family life in Canada is diverse and rapidly changing.

For the functionalist perspective, a particularly useful source is the short text by William J. Goode, *The Family*, 2nd ed. (1982). He presents an easily readable account of the functions that families perform for the society as a whole.

For the Marxist feminist approach, an excellent book is Meg Luxton's *More than a Labour of Love* (1980).

Luxton presents an in-depth description of the lives of three generations of women in a small mining town in northern Manitoba. She conveys through the words of the women themselves how deeply their family lives are influenced by the economic reality of their dependence on male wages.

For a radical feminist perspective, an excellent source book is the collection of articles edited by Yllö and Bograd, *Feminist Perspectives on Wife Abuse* (1988). Articles here by Dobash and Dobash, by Adams, and by Saunders give insight into the experience of wife battery and the problems of doing research and analysis in this area.

QUESTIONS

1. List four critical functions of family according to functionalist theory.

2. a) List two respects in which Nayar family form deviates from the functionalist view of universal family form.

   b) How does functionalist theory typically discount this deviation?

   c) How does feminist theory challenge the functionalist account of the collapse of Nayar family form?

3. What procedure or methodology does Eichler recommend to avoid "monolithic" bias in research on family life?

4. Regarding conservative bias, what two critical factors are commonly cited as radically altering family structure?

5. What functionalist bias is particularly addressed by Marxist theory of family?

6. What single factor is seen by Engels as accounting for monogamy for women?

7. According to Engels, what two conditions are necessary to eliminate inequality within families?

8. In Smith's historical survey, why did women's farm labour change from equality to drudgery and tyranny under the capitalist mode of production?

9. List three ways in which the labour of middle-class home-makers can be seen as appropriated by corporations.

10. How is mothering-work implicated in ideological hegemony with respect to capitalism?

WEB LINKS

ONF/NFB The World Changes: Our Stories Live On
http://nfb.ca/film/other_side_of_the_ledger/
George Manuel, president of the National Indian Brotherhood, narrates this National Film Board of Canada documentary "The Other Side of the Ledger: An Indian View of the Hudson's Bay Company" to tell the story of the "Indian and Eskimo perspective" of the Hudson's Bay Company. In 1670, Charles the Second gave the Hudson's Bay Company 100 million square miles of land and absolute monopoly on trade and hunting. This land was owned by the Indian and the Eskimo. This documentary shows the 300th anniversary celebration of the Hudson's Bay Company in 1970.

Hidden From History: The Canadian Holocaust—The Untold Story of the Genocide of Aboriginal Peoples
http://hiddenfromhistory.org
This site links to archived radio broadcasts from 2002 to 2007, and includes topics such as: "Contanita, Mohawk citizen"; "Political and non-political torture and abuse"; "10 Guineas for a Micmac scalp in Nova Scotia"; "Holocaust Denial in Canada"; "Theft of our water by multinationals and the wider genocide it represents"; and "Hypocrisy and murder: is it synonymous with organized Christianity?" Residential survivors tell of witnessing murder, torture, electro-shock experiments, involuntary sterilization, and drug-testing experiments on the children of residential schools. This site also links to the documentary "Unrepentant: Kevin Annett and Canada's Genocide" and videos such as "US Government Sterilization Program Against Native Women in the 1970s."

The Laurier Institution and UBC Continuing Studies Podcasts
www.cstudies.ubc.ca/podcasts/details.html
This site links to several podcasts from UBC Continuing Studies. "Multiculturalism and Canada's World", presented by Canada's World, The Laurier Institution, and UBC, is a one-hour podcast by Michael Adams. Adams has written a controversial book *Unlikely Utopia: The Surprising Triumph of Canadian Pluralism* whereby he claims that Canada may be the "experiment that worked" when it comes to attitudes and policies towards diversity and multiculturalism. His lecture is just as controversial and interesting.

Google Videos
http://video.google.ca/videoplay?docid=-2345327208638990338&q
and
http://video.google.ca/videoplay?docid=-844462559392032348&ei=TLI7SortN
These are the first and second links of a three-part series. Although Part 3 is not posted, the first two provide an interesting lecture by Professor Ross Perigoe on the role *The Gazette* played in the racial profiling of a Montreal Muslim community. His claim is that journalists often do not know the harm they are doing when they write what they do; and uses 9/11 as the catalyst date of reference. Using critical discourse analysis, Perigoe explores "who spoke in the next twenty days": leaders—President George W. Bush; white victims—a white story; Muslims themselves—East and West; and journalists.

UCTV—University of California Television
"http://www.uctv.tv/search-details.aspx?showID=14211"
"The Travels of a T-shirt in the Global Economy: The Markets, Power, and Politics of World Trade." In this 50-minute video, professor Pietra Rivoli explores the extensive power of market racism by following the path of a T-shirt "from a Texas cotton field to a Chinese factory to a clothing market in Africa."

YouTube: Chinese Head Tax Apology
http://www.youtube.com/watch?v=hDAjMbeRgBg
This short public-relations video shows Stephen Harper's apology to the Canadian Chinese and recognizes the appointments of Chinese Canadians to high-profile government posts such as former Governor General Adrienne Clarkson, Senator Vivienne Poy, and Lieutenant-Governor of British Columbia Dr. David Lam. The short video should be discussed and analyzed in sociology and political science classes within the context of past and current policies and realities of Chinese Canadian people.

KEY TERMS

affirmative action

conservative bias

dowry murders

expressive leader

extended families

instrumental leader

matrilineal

microstructural bias

monogamy

monolithic bias

normative consensus

nuclear families

polyandry

polygamy

polygyny

private realm

privatization

public realm

purdah

radical feminist

reconstituted families

sexist bias

sociobiology

surrogate mother

REFERENCES

Adams, D. 1988. "Treatment Models of Men Who Batter: A Profeminist Analysis." In K. Yllö and M. Bograd, eds. *Feminist Perspectives on Wife Abuse*. Beverly Hills: Sage, 176–199.

Armstrong, P. 1984. *Labour Pains: Women's Work in Crisis*. Toronto: Women's Press.

Armstrong, P., and H. Armstrong. 1985. "Beyond Sexless Class and Classless Sex: Towards Feminist Marxism." In P. Armstrong, H. Armstrong, P. Connelly, A. Miles, and M. Luxton, eds. *Feminist Marxism or Marxist Feminism: A Debate*. Toronto: Garamond, 1–38.

Badgley, R.F., chair. 1984. *Sexual Offences Against Children*. Vol. 1. Ottawa: Canadian Government Publishing Centre.

Burtch, B.E. 1988. "Midwifery and the State: The New Midwifery in Canada." In A.T. McLaren, ed. *Gender and Society: Creating a Canadian Women's Sociology*. Toronto: Copp Clark Pitman, 349–371.

Chesler, P. 1991. *Mothers on Trial: The Battle for Children and Custody*. New York: Harcourt Brace.

Crean, S. 1989. "In the Name of the Fathers: Joint Custody and the Anti-Feminist Backlash." *This Magazine* 22 (7): 19–25.

Dobash, R.E., and R.P. Dobash. 1988. "Research as Social Action: The Struggle for Battered Women." In K. Yllö and M. Bograd, eds. *Feminist Perspectives on Wife Abuse*. Beverly Hills: Sage, 51–74.

Dubinsky, K. 1985. "Lament for a 'Patriarchy Lost'? Anti-Feminism, Anti-Abortion, and REAL Women in Canada." *Feminist Perspectives Series*. No. 1. Ottawa: Canadian Research Institute for the Advancement of Women.

Eichler, M. 1988. *Families in Canada Today: Recent Changes and Their Policy Consequences*. 2nd ed. Toronto: Gage.

Eichler, M. 1985. "The Pro-Family Movement: Are They For or Against Families?" *Feminist Perspectives Series*. Ottawa: Canadian Research Institute for the Advancement of Women.

Eisenstein, Z.R. 1984. *Feminism and Sexual Equality: Crisis in Liberal America*. New York: Monthly Review Press.

Eisenstein, Z.R. 1979. "Developing a Theory of Capitalist Patriarchy and Socialist Feminism." In Z.R. Eisenstein, ed. *Capitalist Patriarchy and the Case for Socialist Feminism*. New York: Monthly Review Press, 5–40.

Engels, F. [1884] 1978. "The Origins of the Family, Private Property, and the State." In R.C. Tucker, ed. *The Marx-Engels Reader*. 2nd ed. New York: W.W. Norton, 734–759.

Firestone, S. 1971. *The Dialectic of Sex*. London: The Women's Press.

Forward, S., and J. Torres. 1987. *Men Who Hate Women and the Women Who Love Them*. New York: Bantam.

Goode, W.J. 1982. *The Family*. 2nd ed. Englewood Cliffs, New Jersey: Prentice-Hall.

Hale, S.M. 1988. "Using the Oppressor's Language in the Study of Women and Development." *Women and Language* 11 (2): 38–43.

Kanter, R.M. 1977. *Men and Women of the Corporation*. New York: Basic Books.

Liddle, J., and R. Joshi. 1986. *Daughters of Independence: Gender, Caste and Class in India*. New Delhi: Zed Books.

Luxton, M. 1980. *More than a Labour of Love: Three Generations of Women's Work in the Home*. Toronto: Women's Press.

Miles, A. 1985. "Economism and Feminism: Hidden in the Household—A Comment on the Domestic Labour Debate." In P. Armstrong, H. Armstrong, P. Connelly, A. Miles, and M. Luxton, eds. *Feminist Marxism or Marxist Feminism*. Toronto: Garamond.

Murdock, G.P. 1949. *Social Structure*. New York: Free Press.

O'Brien, M. 1981. *The Politics of Reproduction*. London: Routledge & Kegan Paul.

Parsons, T., and R.F. Bales, eds. 1956. *Family, Socialization, and Interaction Process*. London: Routledge & Kegan Paul.

Ptacek, J. 1988. "Why Do Men Batter Their Wives?" In K. Yllö and M. Bograd, eds. *Feminist Perspectives on Wife Abuse*. Beverly Hills: Sage, 133–157.

Rafiq, F. 1988. "Women in Islam with Reference to Pakistan." Paper presented at Canadian Asian Studies Association meeting, Windsor, 9 June.

Reiss, I. 1976. *Family Systems in America*. 2nd ed. Hinsdale, Illinois: Dryden Press.

Shupe, A., W.A. Stacey, and L.R. Hazlewood. 1987. *Violent Men, Violent Couples*. Toronto: Lexington Books.

Smith, D.E. 1983. "Women, Class and Family." In R. Miliband and J. Saville, eds. *The Socialist Register*. London: Merlin.

Smith, D.E. 1979. "Women's Inequality and the Family." Department of Sociology, Ontario Institute for Studies in Education. Mimeographed.

Smith, D.E. 1977. "Women, the Family, and Corporate Capitalism." In M. Stephenson. *Women in Canada*. Don Mills, Ontario: General, 32–48.

Spencer, M. 1976. *Foundations of Modern Sociology*. Englewood Cliffs, New Jersey: Prentice-Hall.

Tiger, L. 1977. "The Possible Biological Origins of Sexual Discrimination." In D. Brothwell, ed. *Biosocial Man*. London: Eugenics Society, 23–40.

Stratification: Meritocracy as Ideology

Inequality is a pervasive feature of social life. It may be manifest in disparities in access to money and other material resources, in the power to manipulate events in one's own interest, in the prestige enjoyed in relations with others, and in the overall quality of life. The extent of these disparities varies widely across societies. In an industrially advanced economy such as Canada's, very few people are so poor or disadvantaged that their physical survival is threatened by starvation or lack of rudimentary shelter and sanitation. Yet, as we have seen in earlier chapters, Canada does have a visible and growing underclass of homeless and destitute people who rely on food banks and hostels for a meagre survival. At the other extreme, Canada has a class of super-rich, comprising mostly members of the corporate elite, some of whom rank among the richest people in the world.

Various forms of inequality commonly go together, suggesting that there are important causal relationships between them. Powerful people are often rich, command high prestige, and enjoy pleasurable, even luxurious, lifestyles. The poor are often powerless, scorned, and live in misery. Yet there is no inevitable association between these elements. Winning a lottery, for example, may bring wealth and leisure but not necessarily influence or prestige. A large income may not improve the quality of life if it is earned at the expense of chronic anxiety in the high-pressure corporate rat race. In terms of influence, even poor people can exercise power, especially if they are politically united.

Societies vary greatly in the degree of opportunity for **mobility**; that is, the likelihood that people born poor may eventually become wealthy and influential or that people born rich may fall in status. Canadians tend to think of their society as relatively open, offering opportunities for mobility through individual effort and achievement. But we know that social position is very commonly inherited. Children tend to attain a similar social position to that of their parents or to move slightly upwards or downwards. Members of certain groups are disproportionately better or worse off than others. Children from white Anglo-Saxon Protestant (WASP) backgrounds have very different life

Children of First Nations peoples have very different life chances than do children from WASP backgrounds.

©2009 Clark James Mishler/AlaskaStock.com

chances on average than children of First Nations parents or black parents. Why is this so?

The explanations for inequality offered by different sociological theories reveal core assumptions concerning the nature of social order. Traditional functionalism stresses individual merit. It posits that inequality reflects rewards for individual contributions to the functioning of society. Marxists stress the importance of control over critical means of production for accumulating wealth in industrial society. Variations in income among the mass of working people reflect the relative utility of different workers for the owners of capital. Interpretive theory looks within the grand schemes of functioning social systems, capitalism, and patriarchy to explore what people do in their everyday relations to produce the patterns of inequality that we subsequently perceive as merit, class, or gender hierarchies. Feminist theory focuses on disparities in wealth, power, prestige, and leisure between women and men, arguing that men, on average, are advantaged in all of these respects. These disparities reflect patriarchy, or the power of men over women, which is distinct from, although associated with, capitalism. These theoretical perspectives, and their relative strengths and limitations, are examined below.

Functionalist Theory: Stratification as Meritocracy

The traditional functionalist theory of **stratification** begins from the basic observation that no society is classless. There must be a universal necessity for such stratification. It must perform some function for the social system as a whole, a function so important that no society can do without it.

Davis and Moore (1945) provide one of the clearest functionalist explanations for why stratification occurs. Their central concern is with inequality of positions in society, not the characteristics of the individuals in those positions. The basic theoretical question is why roles themselves differ in prestige and rewards. They find the answer in the functional requirement of placing and motivating individuals in any social structure. A social system must distribute members into social positions and must instill in members the desire to perform the attached duties once in the position. This is a continuous challenge because people are constantly being born, aging, retiring, and dying. Competitive systems such as our own stress motives to achieve the positions; non-competitive systems, such as socialist societies, stress motives to perform the duties. Both systems, however, require motivation.

Roles differ enormously in the demands they place on people. If all roles were equally important, and everyone were able to do all of them, then placement would be no problem. However, some jobs are more agreeable, some serve more important social functions, some require more talent and training, and some require that duties be performed more diligently. Therefore, say Davis and Moore, a differential reward system is necessary. These differential inducements form part of the social order and produce stratification. Rewards may include sustenance and comfort provided by economic incentives, self-respect and ego development provided by prestige and power, or recreation and diversion made possible by more leisure time. These rewards are built into positions and constitute the rights that are related to the duties of the roles. Inequality is thus necessary, inevitable, and justifiable.

Two primary factors determine the relative rank of different positions: their importance for the society and the scarcity of personnel for the positions. Important jobs need sufficient rewards to ensure competent performance, but if such jobs are easily filled, great rewards will not be needed. Garbage collector and janitor, for example, are important jobs, but they are relatively easy to fill and so are not highly rewarded. On the other hand, important jobs that require both talent and long training must be well rewarded. No one would go through the training and do the work of a modern medical doctor, the argument goes, unless the position carried great material reward and prestige.

Variations among societies in the income received by the highest- and lowest-paid members are primarily explained by the degree of specialization of roles. Highly industrialized societies such as Canada have an immense variety of specialized occupations, each of them associated with small gradations in income and prestige. Simpler, less industrialized societies have a more limited range of occupations, which tend to require less specialized training. There are fewer gradations of income and prestige. The nature of functional emphasis—whether sacred or secular—also affects rewards. Industrialized societies place greater emphasis on science and technology than on religion, and so scientists and technicians get higher pay. In other societies where science is relatively undeveloped, religious leaders may have far greater influence, prestige, and material rewards than do scientists.

In summary, functionalists argue that stratification is justified on the basis of merit. The critical moral issue for functionalist theory is not equality of rewards, but rather equality of opportunity to compete for them. The true battle is over merit versus inherited advantage.

Critique of Functionalism

Equal Opportunity   Much of the research generated by the functionalist thesis of stratification has focused on questions of social mobility and differential opportunities for access to positions that carry the highest rewards. Research in the sociology of education has cast doubts on the notion that rewards are based on merit. Tumin (1973) challenges the argument that only a limited amount of talent is available within a population to be trained in appropriate skills for important jobs. He maintains that stratification itself limits the talent pool. We can never know what talents are available among children born to impoverished and disprivileged homes when poverty so pervasively affects their relationship with the school system. Rich children have all the advantages and hence do better in school, get the credentials for better jobs, and in turn give advantages to their own children.

Unequal distribution of motivation to succeed, so important to functionalist theory, is itself a direct product of stratification. Poverty breeds hopelessness. Imagination, curiosity, and aspiration are systematically blunted when children experience powerlessness and humiliation first-hand. It is hard to develop one's full potential under such conditions. The result is low credentials, poorly rewarded jobs, and another generation of children who are stunted and trapped in the poverty cycle.

The argument that conversion of talent into skills requires sacrifices during the training period, and hence merits rewards, again treats the effects of stratification as its cause. Poor families cannot afford to buy books and school supplies or to pay for dance or music lessons, and so on, without cutting back on food money. Poor families cannot afford to keep children in school after the minimum school-leaving age or to send them to university without great sacrifices. The expenses involved are not sacrifices for wealthy parents in the professions. Pay differentials between the unskilled work available at school-leaving age and the professional careers available to university graduates more than compensate students who defer the gratification of an early job. Tumin estimates that any loss of income is usually regained within seven to 10 years of employment. After this, the lifetime earnings of graduates greatly surpass those of untrained people (see Table 1).

Unequal Importance
The second pillar of the functionalist thesis on stratification is that the most important jobs in society must be the most rewarded, particularly when they require special skills. But, Tumin asks, how is importance to be measured? A typical answer is that importance is calculated in terms of a position's indispensability for society, but it is not difficult to find exceptions to this rule. Farming, for example, is important for survival in any society, and it requires skills that take a lifetime to learn, but it is not well rewarded. In terms of industry, during wartime it proved easier to dispense with supervisors than to spare factory workers, but this relative indispensability is not translated into wages.

The real problem is conceptual. Relative importance is a value judgment that is inextricably tied to relative financial rewards. In other words, the argument is circular. Those jobs that are better paid tend to be regarded as more important, regardless of their actual contribution to society or the actual skill levels required for the work.

Women and Stratification
This kind of circularity is especially evident in relation to work habitually done by women. As a sex, women have lower social status than men, so that work identified as "women's work" tends to have low status. The skills and responsibilities involved in such work tend to be downplayed or ignored. Then the lower average earnings of women in the labour force are justified on the grounds that women are concentrated in low-status work. The circle is completed when women themselves internalize such evaluations of what they do, and the low pay associated with it, as justifying the lower status of women generally.

The most extreme example of these processes occurs in relation to homemaking. This is a critical, multidimensional job that, like farming, takes a lifetime to learn. But it goes unpaid and commands such low status that people habitually apologize for doing it. Up until recently, homemaking was not even defined as work.

Within the paid labour market generally, skills associated with women's work are undervalued and underpaid. Nursing, for example, is a high-stress, extremely important job that requires a great deal of responsibility. The survival and recovery time of patients often depend more upon the quality of nursing care than on intermittent doctors' visits. The job demands long hours, shift work, and advanced technical skills that require a university degree and years of practical experience. But one would never know this judging from the salary and status that nurses command.

On some university campuses, the starting salary for secretarial staff (virtually all women) is several dollars per hour below that for people who mow lawns (virtually all men). It would be very difficult to argue that lawn mowing is either more important or more highly skilled than the work that secretaries do. The skills of advanced clerical workers are commonly ignored by bureaucratic classification systems that characterize such work as routine delegated tasks.

Women and men might do virtually identical work, but the work done by women tends to be called by a different name and to command lower status and salaries than the work associated with men. Positions like seamstress versus tailor, or cook versus chef, readily come to mind. In Muslim countries, where the work of buying household supplies is habitually done by men, it is seen as requiring important decision-making authority. When the same work is habitually done by

Table 1 Average Income of Full-year, Full-time Workers by Level of Education and Sex, 1991

Education	Men	Women
Grade 0 to 8	$27 116	$18 138
Some secondary education	32 348	20 709
High-school graduation	33 583	23 265
Some post-secondary	35 845	24 891
Post-secondary diploma	37 887	26 951
University degree	56 522	40 537

Source: Reproduced by authority of the Minister of Industry, 1994. Statistics Canada (1994d), *Earnings of Men and Women*, Cat. 13-217, pp. 36–37.

women, as in our society, it tends to be thought of as a mundane routine.

Relative Scarcity of Personnel

The functionalist thesis claims that relative scarcity of personnel raises rewards. Jobs that are easily filled need not be paid well. Women who compete with each other for limited jobs in the traditional women's occupations know this well. Tumin (1973), however, points out that scarcity is often artificially constructed in order to protect incomes. For example, predominantly male unions have historically tried to bar women and immigrants from access to unionized jobs, arguing that these groups would lower wages. Women were once barred from entry into universities and hence from any profession that required a university degree. Professions have commonly been in a position to restrict access through their control over accreditation.

First-year admissions into medical schools in Canada were sharply reduced in the early 1980s and again in 1993 to an overall cut of 14 percent (Ryten 1994). Also, in 1993 for the first time, the number of women enrolled in first-year medicine exceeded the number of men, reflecting a 29 percent drop in the number of men admitted since the early 1980s. These limitations on enrolments have the approval both of provincial governments and physicians' lobby groups, but for different reasons. Provincial governments hope to reduce the "oversupply" of doctors suggested by some reports on medical personnel and thereby to save money on medicare payments. Physicians, on the other hand, lobbied successfully for cuts in enrolments and for restrictions on the licensing of immigrant doctors in order to limit the number of physicians and thus ensure their continued high salaries. Medical associations can then pressure

Historically, male unions took an active role to ensure that women were confined to low-paying, subordinate positions.

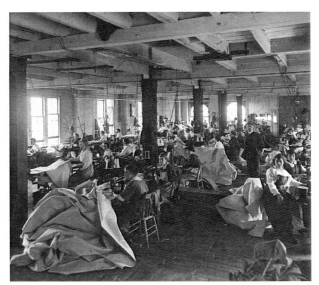

National Archives of Canada/PA-42949

for a fee schedule increase on the grounds of doctors' stressful work and the long hours they put in. Women doctors are more willing to trade high incomes for shorter working hours in group practices, but the male-dominated profession seems unlikely to encourage this.

Another common practice in limiting access to positions is to raise the qualifications needed to get into a job, thus putting up hurdles to stifle competition from below. Jobs in business and management, for example, which even a decade ago only required high-school graduation, now increasingly require university degrees. This effectively blocks competition from those who have learned their skills from work experience but do not have paper credentials.

Motivation

The last pillar of the functionalist argument is that differential rewards, and hence stratification, are necessary in order to motivate people to fill the more demanding positions. These rewards include money or material goods, leisure, respect, and prestige. Tumin's challenge to this thesis is that there are other kinds of motivators that could achieve the same results. An important one is work satisfaction. Positions that require training are usually the most interesting and the least routine. Tumin questions whether such positions need high pay to attract candidates and to ensure competent job performance. Other motives for job performance include the sense of a job well done, prestige from a social duty performed well, or increased leisure hours if the work is particularly demanding or difficult. Women commonly flock to jobs that give them the same time off and holidays as the schools so that they can cope with the extra work and responsibility of having children at home and not have to face the major expense of daycare.

Another question is whether money is, in fact, entirely effective as an **extrinsic reward**. In capitalist society, money is emphasized but people attracted by high salaries are just as likely to peddle their services elsewhere to the highest bidder. High salaries do not command loyalty. Senior executives, on average, remain only about four years with any one firm. There is an old joke about people in politics: they are the best politicians that money can buy. The question is whether people who can be bought with money actually do make good politicians or good anything else.

In summary, Tumin's critique points to the fallacies of unity, indispensability, and universal functionalism. Disparities in material rewards may be demonstrably valuable for certain sectors of society, but they can simultaneously be damaging for others. Large differences in income may be useful for motivating people, but they are not indispensable. People can and frequently do commit themselves to doing important work out of a sense of responsibility for others, or for the pleasure and excitement of the work, without demanding high incomes in return. Many persisting differences in prestige, wealth, and power do not serve useful functions for society at all. Functional importance of different positions is a value judgment. Stratification itself limits talent and restricts educational opportunities while other techniques restrict access and cause scarcity to drive up incomes. Training for skilled jobs either is not, or need not be, a sacrifice. People can be motivated to fill positions on the basis of intrinsic job satisfaction and the prestige of the office, without gross inequalities in standards of living.

Marxist Theory: Inequality as Class Exploitation

Marxists agree with traditional functionalists that stratification does perform very important societal functions, but they argue that these functions specifically help to perpetuate capitalism as an economic system. The central Marxist argument is that stratification functions to preserve a system of expropriation of wage labour from the mass of people. Profits from this expropriation accrue to an elite minority of owners of capital. Stratification is at the same time profoundly functional for capitalists and dysfunctional for the interests of the majority of people who must sell their labour. This perspective rejects the **meritocracy thesis** as an ideological distortion that, rather than questioning the structure of the system within which people are forced to compete, blames the individuals who do not get to the top of the reward system.

The Structure of Unequal Opportunities

Marxist analysis begins from the premise that because of the structured inequality of positions in society there is no possibility of equality of opportunity for the masses. A simplified model of a social system illustrates the problem (Himelfarb and Richardson 1979, 174). Assume a perfectly closed society in which there are 1000 positions, 10 percent of which are elite and the remaining 90 percent ordinary. Then assume that each of these 1000 role incumbents has one child. What will happen to these children as they come to take over from their parents? In a society based absolutely upon inherited advantage, the 100 elite children will take over from the 100 elite parents, with no elite positions left for anyone else. The 900 children of people in the ordinary jobs will remain at the same level.

What will happen in the opposite case, where there is no inherited advantage and everyone has an equal chance to get an elite job? Only 10 percent of all positions, or 100 jobs, are elite. With perfect equality, 10 percent of elite children, or 10 children, will get elite positions and the rest will have ordinary jobs. Ten percent, or 90 of the 900 ordinary children will get remaining elite positions, with the other 810, or 90 percent, remaining where they are. It is clear that, when there are few really good or elite positions to be had, it makes little practical difference to the masses whether they are filled by inherited advantage or absolute equality. Most people will not get such positions in either case.

Any real change in opportunity for ordinary people will require a change in the structure of positions so that there are many more good jobs to be had. After World War II there were huge increases in the United States in middle-class technical, managerial, and white-collar jobs, as well as pink-collar jobs for women. This expansion is the root of the American Dream, the myth that anyone can achieve upward mobility if they have enough drive and talent. After the war, children whose parents had struggled through the Great Depression found that there were many more well-paying jobs to be had. Children from elite homes enjoyed their usual advantage, but there were still many good positions opening up for others. Subsequently the picture changed. With recession came widespread unemployment and cutbacks in the economy. Fewer jobs meant that more children would not get positions equal to those of their parents, no matter how hard they tried. The structure of the job market and the distribution of wealth have to change in order to turn this around.

How does capitalism as a system function to give rise to the structure of the job market? This structure is largely treated as a given within traditional functionalist theory, so that the only question of interest is why existing jobs are rewarded differently. But for Marxists, the changing pattern of the job market itself requires explanation. Bowles and Gintis (1976, 10) insist that capitalist production is not simply a technical process, but is also a social process in which the central problem for employers is to maintain a set of social relations and organizational forms that will enable them to exploit wage-labourers to extract a profit. The objective of the system is to get the most production for the least wages; that is, to get workers to produce commodities of greater market value than the wages that they receive. Extremes of wealth and poverty are necessarily built into how this system works, and individual differences in abilities or effort count for little.

The problem for capitalism as a system is how to prevent revolt. Marxists ask how it is possible to maintain an inegalitarian system in relative equilibrium. What are the mechanisms that minimize the risk of workers forming coalitions to drive up wages or to wrest direct control over the means of production for themselves? The stability of the capitalist system is by no means assured. It has to be actively worked at.

Credentialism as Ideology

An important component assuring the stability of capitalism is force. Capitalists have the power to hire and fire people, and they can also call upon coercive laws to keep labour in line and to weaken unions. But naked force is itself inherently unstable in that it generates hostility and revolt. What is essential to the long-term stability of the system is that workers themselves come to accept the inequalities as just, or at least as inevitable, and therefore become resigned to them, even if they do not actively support them. The system of stratification or differential prestige ranking among workers serves this function, particularly when it is bolstered by the meritocratic ideology of traditional functionalism.

The stratification system, suggest Bowles and Gintis (1976, 81–85), is a direct reflection of capitalist policies of **divide and rule**. Its function is to fragment workers. In its cruder form, ascriptive criteria of race, ethnicity, and sex are manipulated to justify differential rewards. In the United States, older white males, particularly WASPs, are favoured for supervisory positions while immigrants, blacks, and women are given low-paid subordinate jobs. Those in superior positions are encouraged to see themselves as coming from better stock, while subordinates internalize their relative inferiority. The risk of coalitions to form a united front against capitalist employers is thus minimized.

Now that such ascriptive criteria are becoming increasingly discredited as a basis for legitimating inequalities, **credentialism** has come to take their place. This is precisely the meritocratic thesis of functionalism. Marxists agree that motivating people to strive for higher credentials does indeed perform an important function for capitalist society, but it is that of justifying inequality. People with different credentials readily come to see themselves as meriting different rewards. This effectively fragments wage-labourers and lessens the possibility of revolt. Those with relatively low credentials come to see themselves as meriting only limited rewards. Bowles and Gintis (1976, 81) argue forcefully that this is not merely a side effect of stratification but is its primary and intended purpose. Capitalists, they argue, will accede to higher wages for certain groups only when this increases social distance between groups of workers and strengthens capitalist control. Capitalists need to cement the loyalty of supervisors to the organization rather than to workers. Hence managers receive higher pay and privileges, regardless of relative scarcity of personnel.

It is important to recognize that Marxism reverses the cause-and-effect relation between credentials and rewards accepted by traditional functionalists. Functionalists, as we saw above, argue that certain jobs need people with higher skills and credentials. Since these people are in relatively scarce supply, the function of higher pay is to attract them to these difficult and important jobs. Marxists argue the reverse. Capitalism requires that workers be fragmented and stratified in order to minimize the risk of coalitions to challenge the controlling position of the capitalist class. Therefore, largely irrelevant criteria, such as race, ethnicity, sex, and credentials, are used as excuses to reward people differently and so divide them from each other. The function of focusing on credentials is to divide and rule workers by artificially stratifying them.

This is such a turnaround from how we are accustomed to think about credentials and rewards that it deserves further scrutiny. Bowles and Gintis categorically deny that schooling and credentials are actually needed for most jobs that currently demand them. True, there has been an explosion in public education in North America in recent decades, with ever-greater proportions of young people completing high school and seeking post-secondary education. True, on average, there is a **linear relation** between years of formal schooling and economic rewards: the more schooling, the more pay. But this is not due to any essential requirement that better-paid jobs be filled by people with higher abilities. If such were the case, one would expect a very high correlation between measured intelligence and economic success. We do not find this. When measured intelligence and academic ability are controlled, the relation between years of schooling and pay remains virtually unaltered. It seems to be the piece of paper that counts, not the ability level (Bowles and Gintis 1976, 107).

The history of the Ontario Public School system offers a classic illustration of the triumph of credentialism over work experience (Cassin 1992). At the time when individual schools were consolidated into school districts, women predominated as both rural and primary school teachers. Most of them had graduated from high school and had two years of Normal School training. After consolidation, a new credential structure deemed that university studies in specific subjects were more important than experience for salary and promotion. Teachers with the most experience, predominantly women, were placed at the bottom of the teaching hierarchy. During times of retrenchment in the 1930s and 1970s, teachers with secondary school certification in specific subject areas, mostly men, were granted access to teaching positions in primary schools even though they had no experience or training in primary-level teaching. They coped in large measure because women teachers on the job taught them everything they knew. Conversely, primary school teachers were barred from applying for positions in secondary schools, no matter how experienced they were, if they lacked the formal subject-area credentials.

The Deskilling of Work

Further support for the argument that the function of the growing emphasis on credentials is to fragment workers rather than to meet essential job requirements is that there is little evidence of any major increase in the complexity of jobs in advanced capitalist societies. If anything, the process seems to be working in reverse. Once-skilled jobs are being systematically **deskilled**; that is, they are broken down into simple component operations that can be easily learned. This process has been going on for a long time, dating back at least to the era of **Taylorism**, or **scientific management**, in the last decades of the nineteenth century (Braverman 1974, Ch. 4). The expressed goal of Taylor's time-and-motion studies was to break the power that skilled craftsmen wielded through their control over knowledge of the work process. Work was minutely analyzed and broken down into component parts, each of which could be assigned to a different worker. Only the boss retained knowledge of the whole process. Taylorism served two functions for capitalism. It fragmented workers and cheapened labour costs. Employers thus deliberately created the mass of repetitive and unskilled jobs that traditional functionalists point to as deserving only low pay and low prestige.

Braverman argues that this deskilling process has continued unabated, with more and more skilled and even professional occupations being degraded into fragmented, repetitive tasks. Workers are continually being replaced by machines, their skills rendered obsolete. Assembly lines and automation have replaced proud crafts. The impetus for deskilling work was not that average workers were unable to learn the jobs. The problem for capitalists has been that skilled workers are harder to control. They can use their knowledge and skills as bargaining chips to get concessions. They also tend to think of themselves as more deserving of rewards. In effect, they threaten profits. People doing simple, fragmented tasks have minimal bargaining power and come cheaper.

INCO in Sudbury successfully broke the skills and power of mine workers by introducing new technology to automate work. Highly skilled people, who commanded high salaries and prestige among other workers, found their jobs disappearing (Clement 1981, Ch. 10). Children of men who once had skilled jobs at the mine can no longer expect to get similar positions in Sudbury, no matter how motivated and well-educated they might be.

This deskilling, fragmenting, and routinizing of work is not an inevitable consequence of modern technology. It is the result of the kinds of technology that owners of capital opt to promote and how they use it. Teams of skilled workers can put together entire cars themselves as readily and efficiently as can be done on assembly lines. The president of Volvo in Sweden experimented with precisely such teamwork during a period of relatively full employment when he found he could not keep workers in fragmented assembly-line jobs (Gyllenhammer 1977). The function of job fragmentation is not to ensure greater technical efficiency but to break down workers' power, cheapen their labour, and so raise profits.

There is a serious problem for the capitalist system, however, with reducing all jobs to unskilled, repetitive, minimum-wage work—how to prevent coalitions of workers from forming to overthrow the system. The answer in the steel industry was to introduce artificial job ladders. In effect, the owners created a system of stratification to fragment the workers. Petty differences were exploited, linked to credentials such as years of experience and apprenticeship certificates, and used to justify small differences in prestige and piece-rate payments. Workers competed with each other to get the better jobs, and the unions cemented these different pay scales in formal contracts. This was exactly what management wanted. If such petty differences in the job ladder can be linked to race and ethnic differences, so much the better.

Skilled Labour under Capitalism

Braverman's thesis on the systematic deskilling of work has recently come under criticism from other Marxist theorists for oversimplifying labour-market processes in advanced capitalism (Morgan and Sayer 1988; Sayer and Walker 1992). The strategy of deskilling, and thus cheapening and controlling the workforce, may enhance profits in long-established mass production industries, but it may spell economic disaster in high-technology industries where rapid product innovation is occurring. Morgan and Sayer argue that in such industries competitive advantage and profit maximization depend not on producing a standard product more cheaply than competitors, but on high quality and product innovation. Traditional firms that opt for a cheap, deskilled labour force that is tightly controlled will not be able to keep up in the race for product innovation and so will likely face bankruptcy. Rapid innovation requires a workforce that is highly educated in science and advanced technology, and a management team capable of directing rapid and complex organizational changes. Highly skilled, innovative workers cannot be controlled by the tactics of Taylorism (Morgan and Sayer 1988, 26).

From this viewpoint it makes sense for capitalists to fund applied university research and graduate programs, especially in the sciences, engineering, and business management. More is at stake than empty credentialism, or a desire to divide and rule the workforce. Business interests have promoted a series of public and private reports over the last decade debating whether North American high-school and college students are adequately prepared in mathematics and sciences (Darrah 1994, 64). A central concern is that Japanese capitalists may be outperforming Americans in high-technology industries because of better-educated workers.

Sayer and Walker's (1992) comparative study of the structure of American and Japanese corporations suggests that very different patterns of workforce stratification have been developed in the two countries. Major Japanese corporations have reduced or eliminated the hierarchical job ladders and the proliferation of small distinctions in tasks and pay scales described by Bowles and Gintis. These have been replaced with three broad classifications incorporating a variety of jobs. Individual workers are encouraged to learn wide-ranging skills so that they can switch easily between jobs and so maximize flexibility in production. Hence, these corporations place a high premium on worker loyalty, and they foster it with guarantees of job security and salaries linked to length of service rather than location on a job ladder. These firms also promote contact, information exchange, and cooperation among production workers on the shop floors, engineers, and managers. The intent of such management styles is to maximize the speed and the quality of product innovation, with production workers better able to understand new product designs, and engineers better able to recognize and correct production flaws. This kind of production system is not compatible with the strategy of shipping components to cheap labour assembly plants in the Third World.

The core argument in Sayer and Walker's analysis is that more than one possible structure of labour relations is compatible with advanced capitalism. The seemingly inexorable process of deskilling and cheapening labour described by Braverman is not inevitable. It is a historically specific pattern associated with a certain period of American capitalism and a certain kind of production. It is profitable mainly in association with a highly standardized product and long, mass production runs.

One consequence of a mix of mass production and high-technology industries is that processes of deskilling jobs and upgrading skills may occur simultaneously in different sectors of an economy, resulting in very uneven patterns of high unemployment generally, combined with shortages of skilled labour. Declining real incomes may be the lot of the mass of workers who compete for deskilled jobs while an elite of university graduates in the sciences, engineering, and applied management may be in high demand and able to command high salaries.

Summary

Political economy theory sets out to debunk the **technocratic-meritocratic thesis** of stratification as an ideological smokescreen that legitimates and therefore helps to perpetuate inequality and exploitation. It challenges functionalist theory for ignoring the processes through which capitalism structures the job market, deskills many jobs, fragments workers, and breaks their bargaining power, and then justifies low pay on the grounds that they are doing unskilled work. Advanced capitalism, organized around multinational corporations, produces an extremely unequal structure of job opportunities beyond the control of individual workers. Explanations for stratification that focus on individual efforts and abilities obscure these larger structural processes that constrain individual life chances.

Traditional structural Marxist theory, exemplified in the work of Bowles and Gintis, and Braverman, has been challenged in recent Marxist work for an oversimplified economic determinism. It is giving way to a more dynamic class analysis that explores the diversity of ways in which labour can be managed and exploited for profits in advanced capitalism. But the core argument remains that social inequality is a product of profit-driven corporate interests. Only such effort and ability as directly feeds these profits are likely to be rewarded.

The Social Construction of Stratification

In both functionalist and political economy perspectives on stratification, such key concepts as *jobs*, *duties*, *responsibilities*, *skills*, and *credentials* are taken for granted as common-sense aspects of work. Social constructionist theory challenges each of these concepts and the pattern of reasoning that underlies them. These concepts are embedded in the professional discourse that has emerged around employment equity policies, and the ongoing political debates concerning whether North American workers are adequately prepared for work that is being transformed by technological and organizational innovations.

Central to this discourse is the notion of jobs. Jobs are conceptualized as separate from the persons hired to do them and the quality of individual performances. A job constitutes an identifiable set of duties or tasks, associated with a defined bundle of skills required to get the tasks done. Individual jobs make different contributions to the overall organization or enterprise of which they are a part. Jobs, the value of their contribution, and associated pay scales, are analyzed as structural features of organizations. Within this discourse, workers are decomposed into job incumbents with typical profiles or bundles of skills. Skilled workers appear to move freely between workplaces, carrying their skills like baggage.

This way of thinking about jobs fits readily into the functionalist theory of meritocracy discussed above. The vision of equity in employment that emerges within this discourse focuses on the routine application of standard procedures. Tasks and skills are identified, and pay scales set, prior to anyone being hired. The aura of neutrality and objectivity is further assured by hiring external consultants to design an employment equity policy for a specific organization. Independent management teams are assumed to be unbiased because they do not directly profit from the implementation of the schemes they design. So long as hiring practices also follow objective procedures, matching workers' skill bundles to task-requirement bundles, equity on the basis of merit seems assured. The problem for employers is to attract appropriately qualified individuals, while educational institutions are enjoined to equip students with the skills called for in a given workforce.

Social constructionist analysis suggests that the appearance of neutrality and objectivity is illusory. Employment equity policies are an aspect of management oriented principally to the justification of pay differentials. Systemic, or structured, inequality in the treatment of employees is embedded within them. Workers appear to be and indeed *are* treated the same in ways that are authorized, sanctioned, and accepted practices of organization, and yet have the consequence of inequality (Cassin 1991, 4).

The central argument is that while the discourse of jobs appears to reflect common-sense understanding of work, it fundamentally misrepresents the nature of work. The distinction between work as what people do, and jobs as disembodied sets of tasks, obscures what people actually have to do to accomplish completed tasks and the knowledge that goes into such accomplishment.

The assumption that jobs can be decomposed into bundles of separate skills that can be listed does not correspond to how people experience the simultaneity of their work. In practice, workers are commonly required to juggle many tasks simultaneously, and amid constant interruptions. In the computer assembly plants studied by Darrah (1994), workers were expected to work on several units at once, depending on the availability of parts, and to repair several units at different stages in diagnostic cycles, as well as responding to other workplace demands. Individually, simple tasks required complex memory work under such conditions, but memory work was not part of the job description. Secretarial work is also routinely carried on in the context of continual interruptions from a wide range of disparate sources, including supervisors, bosses, a host of people flowing in and out of the office exchanging information, asking questions, wanting services, raising complaints, and telephones ringing, which all need to be attended to in the same limited space of time available to do the word processing, filing, and other paperwork expected. Listing tasks individually and measuring the skill required to do each one in turn gives a seriously inadequate picture of the complexity of the work being accomplished.

The notion that specific skills can be clearly identified as required for specific tasks obscures the difficulty involved in making such connections, and the potentially disparate ways in which similar work may be accomplished by different people. In his study of computer assembly workers, Darrah (1994) found little consensus as to which individual tasks or which skills were central to getting the work done, beyond the most basic level of some manual dexterity. Production managers based their hiring requirements on standard job descriptions that they borrowed from other local firms. This explained why system repair technicians were called upon to display knowledge of electronic principles such as Ohm's Law. Once on the job, both technicians and managers concurred that such knowledge was irrelevant. Management stressed literacy skills as essential for workers to communicate clearly between shifts, but in practice few of them had such skills. Communications did sometimes get scrambled, but the plant kept running, so presumably literacy was not as essential a skill as managers implied. Troubleshooting was identified as a single skill by engineers, supervisors, and machine operators alike, but in practice operators dealt with trouble in a wide variety of ways, using memory, reasoning, cooperation, and random guesswork. There was no single skill that could be labelled *problem solving*.

Workers further described many other aspects of their work that they found essential to getting the work done, but that did not appear in any specified skills list. These included developing strategies for dealing with aging and frequently recalcitrant machinery, strategies for conveying acceptable impressions of work commitment in front of management, and ways of training new supervisors to provide appropriate support before they were transferred out of the plant. All the supervisors saw was their work in training the operators.

The Community of Practice

An important asset in problem solving and in getting the routine work done proved to be support networks among workers. Darrah found that computer assembly workers compensated for gaps in their own abilities by pooling their heterogeneous skills to help each other. The main challenge facing a newly hired operator was to develop a network of helpers who would assist when inevitable problems arose. The conceptualization of jobs as performed by individual workers with bundles of skills makes this "community of practice" invisible (Darrah 1994, 82; Lave and Wenger

1991). The shift in focus from job to work group raises the possibility that overall plant performance may depend less on attracting individually skilled workers than developing a cooperative work environment, in which workers can routinely help and learn from each other.

The focus on workplace also facilitates a shift in emphasis for skills that workers bring with them to opportunities for learning on the job. It was in this regard that Darrah found blatant contradictions between the management's overt demand for skilled workers and systemic, organizational barriers to skill development. Management claimed to want educated workers who could "see the big picture" and understand the overall system of production. Yet workers complained repeatedly of being blocked in their efforts to learn more. Supervisors routinely prohibited any documentation that would allow workers to learn more and possibly advance their careers. Repair technicians were barred from having schematic drawings of the computers they repaired on the grounds that it was their job merely to replace faulty circuit boards. It was someone else's job to repair the boards. In one instance, production workers were granted a tour of the firm's customer service department in an adjacent building. They found that much of the work overlapped, particularly with respect to faulty products that customers had returned. Both departments reported the exchange of ideas valuable, but the production manager banned further excursions because he feared workers might use them to transfer to another department. These routine practices of information control reflected in structure and intent the deskilling practices referred to by Braverman (1974). Only the rhetoric of senior management had changed. Supervisors still boasted of controlling workers through ignorance.

Job Description as Ideological Practice

The gaps between jobs as task bundles described in job evaluation schemes and work as experienced by people cannot be bridged merely by adding elements to the bundle. The process of description itself is flawed. Descriptions appear to arise directly out of job design as objective statements, but these descriptive practices are themselves embedded in a managerial discourse that takes for granted distinctions between mental and manual labour, or between design and execution of tasks, and that also assumes the gendered character of work. Cassin (1991, 31–32) compares the following typical description of clerical work with what an equivalent description of managerial work would look like. Firstly, with respect to clerical work:

> Typically, employees are engaged in preparing, transcribing, systematizing and maintaining records, reports and communications by manual processes, or by operating various machinery and equipment; conducting analytical and investigative duties; determining the nature of enquiries and dealing with callers and customers in a service capacity/performing a variety of related admin support tasks under guidance and direction of Supervisory/Mgt personnel.

An equivalent description of management work might be as follows:

> Typically (mgt) employees are engaged in talking on telephones, attending formal and informal meetings (32), chairing formal and informal meetings, touring company facilities, presiding over honorary occasions, representing the company in a variety of capacities, reading, answering, and writing reports, correspondence and other documentation, responding to requests of various kinds from subordinates, colleagues, customers, superiors.

As Cassin remarks, the first description appears reasonable while the latter appears ludicrous. We are used to managerial work being described by terms such as plan, organize, coordinate, control, and decide. These terms describe mental processes, not physical descriptions of what managers can be seen to be doing. Clerical work could also be described in terms of mental processes—the planning, organizing, coordinating, and decision-making work involved. But all this managerial work is obscured by descriptions framed in terms of manual performance of tasks. Clerical descriptions focus on essentially "empty" functions that give no indication of the knowledge involved in doing any of the work, the contexts in which such work gets done, or the organizational relevance of this work. It is such omission that accomplishes the view of clerical work as contributing only limited value to organizations and thus warranting limited pay. Conversely, the inclusion of organizational context and relevance is what creates the basis for designating managerial work.

Cassin's central point is that clerical work is inherently managerial and administrative work. The routine designations "managerial," "administrative," and "clerical" work and occupations are by and large distinctions *within the same domain of work* (1991, 30). Job evaluation schemes are premised on the assumption that jobs are to be defined by their differences, rather than by their sameness to each other. But this premise obscures the essentially collaborative and overlapping character of work. The "sealing off" of clerical work from managerial work also contributes to the construction of a domain of gender-segregated jobs—women's work—before there are any incumbents in the positions.

The close cooperation between clerical and managerial work, and the fine line dividing them is reflected in the work of the *Conditional Sales and Rental Clerk Position* in a

Consumer's Gas Company (Cassin 1991, 58–59). The woman holding this position was responsible for determining the creditworthiness of customers and authorizing sales up to a value of $1500. Considerable judgment, knowledge of credit practices and sales contracts, and interactional abilities were involved in this work. The clerk prepared a report on creditworthiness, formed a judgment, and then sought approval from her supervisor. She represented the company to the customers—finding out what they wanted, offering explanations, and dealing with people variously angry, frightened, threatened, and abusive. Her work was a very significant contribution to the company. Indeed, sales could not take place without her. Yet none of this was visible in her job description, which focused on the routine completion of paperwork. The fine line separating clerical from managerial designation was drawn at the point where the supervisor approved or questioned the final judgment. Seen from this viewpoint, the separation of mental from manual labour did not result in the deskilling of clerical *work*, but a downgrading of the job.

Similar research by Reimer (1987) documents how clerical staff routinely organize the work of their superiors, collecting materials, setting priorities, arranging agendas, dealing with correspondence, and the like. Complex judgments are involved in this work, which presuppose comprehensive knowledge of an organization. Yet their work was conceptualized by both themselves and others as comprising routine, delegated tasks, variously referred to as answering mail, typing or word processing, filing, and finding things. Even the advanced computerized technology and software packages that secretaries now manage are more likely to be described as "making their work easier" than as enhancing it (Cassin 1991, 58).

Invisibility of Skills as Social Construction

The invisibility of managerial forms of work performed by subordinates does not arise from accidental oversight, and cannot be corrected merely by pointing it out. Institutionalized invisibility is accomplished through organized sets of relationships that also accomplish relations of class and gender. Documents are central to these processes of recording, recognizing, and attributing work within formal organizations. They provide a way of tracking how the division between mental and manual, and design and execution is organizationally sustained.

The work of nursing is a stereotypically female occupation which, although it is recognized as a profession, is accorded relatively low status within the medical hierarchy of hospitals, and significantly lower pay than other medical personnel. Nurses routinely perform aspects of managerial,

administrative, educational, and diagnostic work as part of patient care, yet only a small part of such work is documented (Gregor 1994). The dividing line in the hospital hierarchy was graphically recorded in the hospital studied by Gregor in a pamphlet called "Your Medical Team." This pamphlet, which was given to each new patient as part of the process of admission, described the qualifications and responsibilities of medical personnel a patient might encounter. It included attending physician, resident physician, intern, clinical clerk, and head nurse. The qualifications, ranking, work organization, and responsibilities of nurses below the level of head nurse were not mentioned. In effect, the people most directly involved in the daily care of patients did not appear as members of the medical team.

Institutional recognition of the educative work performed by nurses was accorded specifically to pre-operative education provided to patients in the surgical ward. Nurses were required to document that such work had been done by entering it into their patients' charts on a form entitled "Pre-op Patient Education Check List." Its content was also documented in a teaching manual "Before and After Surgery" to be used by nurses in instructing patients.

The educative work actually done by nurses extended far beyond this required minimum, but it received no official recognition, and even the nurses themselves generally failed to name it. Gregor records talk between nurses and patients in which nurses explained aspects of diagnosis and treatment, informed patients about various tests, clarified the meaning of symptoms, advised patients how to aid recovery, and explained aspects of hospital administration. Patient care could hardly have proceeded without such talk, but all that nurses were doing officially was "administering medication" or "checking the intravenous." The omission has potentially far-reaching implications in a period when hospital administration is being contracted out to management consulting firms. The computerized calculation of nursing staff ratios and time needed for patient care routinely incorporates only the officially sanctioned tasks listed in job descriptions.

The invisibility of educative work performed by nurses was further obscured by the fact that much of it contravened the recognized medical hierarchy. Nurses routinely advised less experienced health-care workers and physicians on appropriate pieces of equipment, how various kinds of medical work processes could be initiated through use of requisition forms, where to find such forms, and how to fill them in. Nurses also became involved in aspects of the diagnosis and treatment of patients. This often took the form of a "problems list" by which nurses informed hospital physicians about medical work that needed their attention. Such lists were prepared daily, usually by night nurses, and modified during the day as old problems were solved and new ones identified. Examples included "patient vomited

500cc. leave I.V. in?" or "re-order senecot—no bowel movement." The critical difference between the problems list and the pre-operative, education check list described above was that it was not officially sanctioned. The lists were written on plain paper and never found their way into hospital records. In other instances, nurses were observed contacting a physician to explain a patient's problem, then suggesting the appropriate drug treatment and the normal dosage. The resulting prescription, however, carried only the physician's name. The collaborative character of the work process is actively hidden from view. As with the example of the clerical worker discussed above, the knowledge and judgment used by the subordinate worker was rendered invisible. Only the superior was officially recognized as making the decision, while the subordinate appeared merely to carry out orders. The suppression of the active involvement of subordinates in forming decisions is part of the set of practices that sustains the organizational hierarchy.

The organization of work within the hospital limited the opportunities for nurses to learn more about diagnoses and treatment plans in ways that paralleled the experience of computer assembly workers described above. Physicians routinely scheduled their rounds at the same time of day as nurses changed their work shifts. Even when physicians did come during the day, it was also not their practice to invite nurses to come with them when they went to see a patient. Such organizational practices, Gregor suggests, had the function, and perhaps also the direct intent, of maintaining the status of the physician as authoritative knower in matters of patient care.

Maintaining the Fictions

The view of work as hierarchically ordered sets of task bundles that merit differential rewards does not come naturally. It has to be worked at. The incorporation of workers' representatives on committees charged with designing job evaluation systems constitutes an important mechanism in gaining commitment to the schemes and in training workers to think in the appropriate conceptual framework (Cassin 1992, 68–73). Participants in these committees learn the job evaluation system, learn about jobs from this perspective, and learn to make and to defend judgments and decisions made within the constraints of job evaluation. Cassin suggests that an intensive orientation process is required to "break in" new members to a thinking process that belies common-sense experience of work.

Job descriptions define who is authorized to know certain aspects of work, and these relations of hierarchy are continually reproduced and reinforced through displays of superordination and subordination. Gregor describes how nurses maintained the fiction of "doctor's orders" in relations with patients when they were quite capable of giving

advice directly, and in fact even when they had initiated the doctor's order in question. In one of many examples, a patient asked a nurse how long she should wait before taking the bandages off her leg. The nurse responded with: "You will have to ask your doctor" followed by questions such as: "When will he come to see you next?" and "When is your next appointment?" After it became clear that the doctor had visited the patient, omitted any mention of removing bandages, and would not be seeing the patient for another six weeks, the nurse said it would be okay to soak the bandages off after 10 days. How much nurses told patients depended primarily on the personality of the attending physician and what he would allow, not on what the nurses knew. Experienced nurses quickly warned incoming nurses what to expect in this regard.

The costs of this socially constructed hierarchy on those in subordinate positions are high. The most obvious cost is financial. The fine line separating managerial from managed can mark large differences in income. More subtle, but equally destructive, are the costs in terms of social well-being and mental health. Blue-collar workers located at the bottom of the job-status hierarchy are much more likely to experience feelings of powerlessness and self-depreciation that closely mirror the symptoms of reactive depression (Archibald 1978, 177–180).

Summary

Social constructionist theory complements in many respects the political economy analysis of stratification in the workforce. Both critique the artificiality of job ladders and the lost potential for cooperation and pooling of knowledge that such distinctions tend to create. But constructionist analysis focuses attention on the routine practices through which **doing hierarchy** comes to be accepted and legitimated in common-sense reasoning as merited. In challenging the discourse of jobs and job evaluation, it also calls into question the extent to which distinctions between mental and manual labour, and design and execution of tasks, can be sustained in everyday experience of work.

Feminist Theory and Stratification

Women are subordinated to men in Canadian society on just about every measure of social status—the average incomes they earn, ownership of property, control over capital, participation in politics, and representation in managerial, administrative, and decision-making bodies. Women's contributions to society in general, and to the world of work in particular, are not accorded the same value or recogni-

Figure 1 Labour Force Participation Rates for Women and Men over 15 Years of Age, Canada 1911–93*

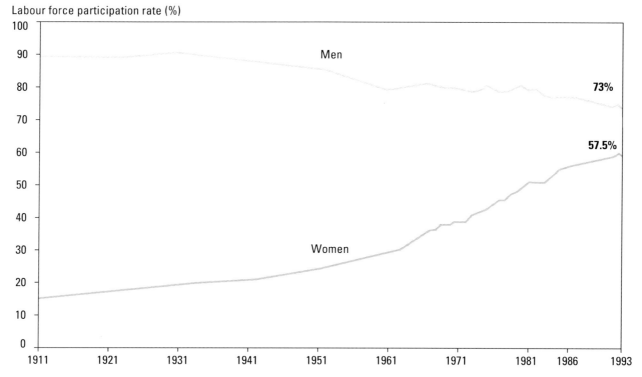

*Figures for 1941 include persons on Active Service on 2 June 1941.

Source: Eichler (1988a, 95). Adapted from Statistics Canada, 1961 Census of Canada, Vol. III (Part 1) Labour Force, table 1, for 1911–61; for 1966–79: Cat. 71-201 Historical Labour Force Statistics, pp. 151, 153, 158; for 1981–84: Historical Labour Force Statistics, 1984, Cat. 71-201, p. 220, D767895, p. 225, D768005; for 1985–86, Cat. 71-001; for 1986–93, Cat. 71-201.

tion as those associated with men. Feminist theory addresses this systemic gender inequity and the generalized inadequacy of mainstream theories to account for it.

Statistics on the gender composition of different occupations in Canada present extensive evidence of the lower status of women generally in the workforce. The proportion of adult women in the labour force more than doubled between 1941 and 1981, and it continues to rise (see Figure 1). But women are heavily overrepresented in the reserve army of part-time, seasonal, and cheap labour.

In labour-market theory, the market is generally understood as being divided into two sectors. Jobs in the primary sector are characterized by relatively good wages and working conditions, and opportunities for promotion, whereas jobs in the secondary sector are short-term, low-paid, and dead end. White males hold the majority of jobs in the primary sector, while females form the large majority of workers in the secondary sector, along with many men from visible minorities (Armstrong and Armstrong 1990, 62).

Women are concentrated in a small number of occupations—clerical, service, sales, health, and teaching—with

three-quarters of employed women in the first three of these categories. When women enter professions they are overrepresented in low-status and low-paid categories. They are far more likely to be the dental hygienists, librarians, therapists, or dieticians than the dentists, doctors, lawyers, engineers, or university professors (see Table 2). These patterns are changing, but very slowly.

An important impetus for change has been the implementation of the equality rights section of the Canadian Charter of Rights and Freedoms in 1985, the federal Employment Equity Act passed in 1986, and particularly the section of the Act concerned with the Federal Contractors Program. The Act requires that all federally regulated companies (banks, transport, and communications companies) set up **employment equity** programs and file annual public reports on the demographic composition of their workforce, including data on salaries and promotions for women and minorities.

The first reports filed in 1988 revealed major inequities in pay scales for women and men, and restricted employment opportunities for disabled people and visible minorities. Women

Table 2 Female Workers in Selected Professional and Technical Occupations, 1971 and 1981

Occupation	Female % of Occupation		% of all Female Workers	
	1971	1981	1971	1981
Dental hygienists, assistants, and technicians	76.6	81.1	0.3	0.4
Social workers	53.4	62.6	0.2	0.4
Librarians and archivists	76.4	80.2	0.2	0.3
Physiotherapists, occupational, and other therapists	81.6	84.6	0.2	0.2
University teachers	16.7	24.6	0.1	0.2
Physicians and surgeons	10.1	17.1	0.1	0.1
Pharmacists	23.1	41.3	0.1	0.1
Psychologists	47.2	52.0	0.1	0.1
Dieticians and nutritionists	95.3	94.0	0.1	0.1
Lawyers and notaries	4.8	15.1	—*	0.1
Industrial engineers	3.3	12.2	—	0.1
Dentists	4.7	7.9	—	—
Total	29.0	39.4	1.5	2.1

Source: Armstrong and Armstrong (1984). Adapted from *1971 Census*, vol. 3.2, table 8; and from *1981 Census, Labour Force–Occupational Trends* (Cat. 92-920), table 1.

—* means less than 0.1 percent.

were concentrated in the majority of jobs paying less than $25 000 while men predominated in jobs that paid more than $35 000. Women were rarely represented in the very high-paying jobs. Roughly 10 percent of the 13 800 male employees with Air Canada, for example, earned more than $70 000. Only four out of the 6300 women working for the corporation earned that much (*Globe and Mail*, 22 October 1988).

The Act has come under heavy criticism from advocacy groups for not incorporating penalties for failure to practise employment equity. The Act leaves it up to individual members of disadvantaged groups to challenge these companies in court, using human rights legislation. But such action requires considerable time, money, and effort, and legal expertise, as well as proof that failure to hire or to promote a particular individual was due to discrimination and not to some other factor.

The section dealing with federal contractors does have some teeth, in that every company that has 100 or more employees, and that wants to bid on a federal government contract of more than $200 000, must prove its commitment to gender and minority equity in terms of hiring, training, salary, and promotions. No equity plan, no federal contract (Kates 1988). These companies are under pressure to promote women and minorities into managerial positions, and also to keep them. Before the Act, Kates suggests, a request for maternity leave was an instant ticket to a dead career, but companies are now more prepared to offer flexible policies in order to retain women in senior positions.

Employment equity policies and associated job evaluation schemes have had some success in redressing overt discrimination in hiring practices, and in winning pay increases for categories of women workers found to be paid significantly less than men in closely comparable jobs. But the impact of such cases on the overall pattern of income differentials between women and men in the workforce is small. As we have seen above in the social constructionist critique of job evaluation schemes, systemic discrimination remains largely invisible. Job descriptions are gendered at basic common-sense levels of practical reasoning. Hiring and promotion procedures that follow strict rules of gender neutrality and objectivity still have gendered outcomes. Compensation for work done appears to be gender-neutral, based entirely on objective job characteristics, yet the pervasive outcome is that work primarily done by women is accorded less worth than work primarily done by men (Cassin 1991, 1–2).

The initial concentration of women and men in different entry-level job categories has cumulative implications for progression and career advancement. In order to appear qualified for promotion into managerial positions, junior personnel need to display knowledge and experience in policy areas, as well as decision-making capabilities. But as we have seen above, clerical, sales, and service jobs are normally described in ways that obscure such experience. Personnel managers use job descriptions to structure performance appraisals, orienting questions around recognized task-related competences. Resulting evaluation procedures and interviews

Pay equity programs have had some success, but systemic discrimination is largely invisible.

This woman's work is as valuable as a man's.

That's why Pay Equity is the law.

Get the facts!
Call the hotline:
Toll free in Ontario
1-800-387-8813

THE
PAY EQUITY
COMMISSION
=

Pay Equity Commission, Ontario

may give no scope for workers to display the managerial knowledge they might have. Jobs in which women are concentrated generally offer little scope for discretion, advancement, authority, or higher salaries. Clerical positions qualify women to compete for other clerical positions, but not for administrative or management positions, even at the entry level. Affirmative action programs designed to get more women into management appear to offer privileged and unfair competition to women. The structural barriers that make affirmative action necessary remain invisible.

◉ Feminist Challenge to Traditional Theory

Functionalist perspectives on stratification and effort, and socially learned differences in occupational choices by individual women and men, serve to legitimate rather than challenge gendered inequality. Job evaluation schemes to date largely mirror functionalist assumptions. Traditional political economy theory, although much more critical of

stratification, has mostly ignored its gendered character. The working class is generally conceptualized as an undifferentiated whole in labour-market theory, with marginal attention to women (Brittan and Maynard 1984, 56). Inequality between workers is broadly accounted for in terms of the interests of the capitalist class in fragmenting working-class solidarity so that some segments can be exploited for cheap labour while others control them.

This thesis, however, does not explain why women are so consistently singled out for super-exploitation at the bottom of the job and wage heap (Armstrong and Armstrong 1990, 66). Nor does it explain why male workers have for so long seen it as legitimate that fellow workers should be in subordinate, lower paid, and often insecure and temporary work because they happen to be female (Beechey 1977). It is hard to blame capitalism for the pattern of women's economic subordination that long predates it. Capitalists can and do take advantage of this subordination, exploiting women as a pool of cheaper labour, controlling male workers by the threat that they can be replaced by cheaper women, and buying the compliance of men to the wage-labour hierarchy by appearing to favour them with differential rewards (Hartmann 1979). Such arguments, however, fall far short of claiming that capitalism causes gender inequality.

Historically, capitalism was associated with improvements in the relative social status of women by providing some opportunity for women to earn an income independently of men. Capitalists also stand to benefit from the increasing numbers of married women entering the labour force, in ways that go beyond exploitation of cheap labour. Wage-earning women expand the market for consumer goods of all kinds and open up market opportunities in the service sector to supplement domestic labour with daycare, take-out food, and domestic cleaning services.

A different order of explanation seems to be needed to explain the subordination of women in the labour force which goes beyond the structuralist argument that the pattern persists because it is in the interests of capital. Such an argument functions as ideological justification for patriarchy in that it obscures more fundamental relations of male power and oppression of women (Brittan and Maynard 1984, 52–55; Cockburn 1981, 54; Hartmann 1979). Hartmann focuses attention directly on how male workers individually, and collectively through unions, have acted to exclude women from well-paid jobs, preserving them as male strongholds. She traces what she sees as "centuries of patriarchal social relationships" in which men pushed women into subordinate economic roles. In Canada, women always worked alongside men in developing homesteads and family farms, yet patriarchal laws dispossessed them, vesting ownership rights in men. Men commonly kept that control even after death by willing the farms to their sons. During the early development of factories, men resisted factory labour, preferring their greater independence in agricultural work. Women and children were available as "more docile and malleable" labour, itself reflecting their long-term subordination to men in agriculture. As industrialization progressed, men dominated the skilled trades while women filled less important positions as casual labourers and assistants.

The potential problem with this arrangement was that the cheap labour of women might undercut men's jobs and wages, especially in a tight job market. Male-dominated unions took active steps to control this threat. Hartmann documents systematic actions by male unions to exclude women from membership, and to prevent them from entering apprenticeships and gaining the skills required for equal status jobs. Fear of job competition does not account for this pattern, since the same men who excluded women and girls from learning trades offered such training to boys. In principle, both male and female workers could have joined together in unions to demand equal pay for women and men, and thus eliminate the threat of cheaper female labour. But this rarely happened. More commonly, male unionists used their organizational force to eliminate women from factories. In one example, male spinners even plotted to set fire to a factory in which girls were working at wages below those of male unionists.

Such overt discrimination against women in the workforce has been virtually eliminated in Canada. Women and men who do the same work within the same organization are guaranteed equal pay. Women have been joining unions in steadily increasing numbers. The Canadian Labour Congress fully endorsed equality rights for women in employment, and unions have become active in pushing labour benefits for women workers, including improved maternity benefits. But there remains much overt and covert resistance to the acceptance of women as colleagues in traditionally male occupations. Companies that have actively instituted policies to hire more women managers to comply with the Employment Equity Act and qualify for government contracts have also had to address the sexist attitudes of some male managers. In one report of an interview with a woman applicant for a management position with the Canadian Imperial Bank of Commerce, a male manager displayed such attitudes when he asked her if she was married or had any marital plans, and then commented later that she was not all that attractive. The senior manager at the bank commented: "John's good, but he's got a problem with women. It will cost him" (Kates 1988).

In practice, however, it is women in management who more often bear the costs of male resistance to their presence on the team. This resistance undermines women's effectiveness as managers, which then becomes attributed to the women themselves as evidence of their relative incompetence compared with men. The veiled hostility of male managers, especially younger ones who feel they are competing directly with women for promotion, may take such forms as withholding important information, sidelining women managers at meetings, creating behind-the-scenes barriers to co-operation, deliberately sabotaging projects, or transferring a bad worker to the woman's department to foul things up. Sexist comments betray male discomfort at having to work with women, even when this is denied. Token women managers are subjected to constant scrutiny, which rates them lower than male colleagues regardless of their actual job records and blocks appointments and promotions that would give them authority over men.

The difficulties that many women managers experience in gaining informal acceptance among male members of management teams carry implications that go far beyond personal enjoyment of work. Darrah's (1994) research, described above, indicates the importance of newly hired workers developing a network of helpers who can assist when problems arise. It is this community of practice that makes it routinely possible for workers to compensate for individual weaknesses and enhance their overall competence. When women managers are not part of the informal social networks among male managers at the pub, the golf course, and elsewhere, they lose critically important opportunities for gaining insider knowledge of what is happening, how to present themselves and their work, how to discuss its policy relevance and not merely its technical adequacy, and so on. All these factors directly impact on their apparent potential for promotion (Cassin 1979; Kates 1988). On top of all this, women may find themselves pressured to underplay their abilities in front of male colleagues who feel threatened by competent women. Displays of subservience and deference to male views and male authority may be essential to gain a minimum of co-operation from such colleagues, and to avoid open harassment (Liddle and Joshi 1986, 178–180). Such compromises help to sustain the myth of women's relative incompetence, which further reduces the probability of their receiving recognition and promotion.

Domestic Division of Labour and Social Inequality

The most severe impediments to gender equality within the workplace may lie outside the workplace itself, in the very uneven distribution of domestic responsibilities between women and men. Most research in Canada and elsewhere concurs that even when married women are employed full-time, they still do the bulk of domestic work and childcare. The class hierarchy presupposes the gender hierarchy in the sense that the organization of work and working hours assumes that workers are generally not involved in domestic labour or childcare. Such work is presumed to be done by someone else. The class privileges of professional women similarly depend upon the gender subordination of other women who will perform domestic service work and childcare so cheaply that they absorb only a portion of the money that professional women themselves earn (Liddle and Joshi 1986, 150–151).

The greatest impediment to women's success in corporate careers remains the very long, 65-hour workweeks commonly expected of young executives on the fast track (Kates 1988). Men have traditionally been able to put in such long hours primarily because their wives have absorbed the bulk of their domestic responsibilities. But few women have spouses or other adults at home who can take up most of the domestic and mothering work. Men have a career advantage in this regard, but at a high price. Men who value home life and parenting lose out in their careers relative to traditional men in a corporate culture where being at the office during evenings and weekends, and willingness to uproot and to travel on corporate business, are taken as measures of career commitment.

Few women feel able or willing to pay such a high price for a career. An article in the *Globe and Mail* business magazine entitled "Thanks, But No Thanks" (Maynard and Brouse 1988) describes the lives of women who graduated with masters of business administration degrees from the University of Western Ontario. They got good, although not top, jobs as corporate business executives and were "keenly watched and courted [as] the standard bearers in women's drive for equality at work." They found themselves burned out and under extreme stress in the face of inhuman demands to give 110 percent to clients and 120 percent to children, to work from 7:30 a.m. to 6:30 p.m. and on weekends, and to travel for the company. Added to this was the desperate struggle to find and keep adequate daycare and the guilt that their children were victims of their relentless career demands. It was as if the companies were deliberately pushing women beyond human limits to prove they could not be equal to men and should give up and go home. According to the article, many of them did just that, or they started their own businesses. A few companies have moved some way towards reducing such strain, particularly under the pressure to make public their adherence to employment equity. But this has stopped at the level of maternity leave provisions and some flexibility in working hours. In August 1994, the Canadian Bar Association approved motions stating that time off for family responsibilities should not normally delay a lawyer's eligibility for partnership in a firm or affect the right to equitable pay (*Globe and Mail*, 22 August 1994, B1). They also endorsed a motion that law firms should apply flexible treatment to men and women with children. They backed off, however, from making it a "legal duty" that firms accommodate such lawyers and from endorsing equal pay for women working shorter hours because of children. The lawyers prided themselves as "definitely leading all the other professions" on the issue.

Equality Rights as Ideology

The equality rights provisions in the Charter or in employment equity policies do nothing to redress such experiences. The principle of equality based on *sameness* in the treatment of women and men in the workplace ignores the additional demands of home and childcare that are socially defined as women's responsibility. The strain of trying to do too much is readily attributed back to individual women as their personal inadequacy. It has prompted some feminist advocates like Betty Friedan (1981) to eschew earlier arguments that housewives were not living up to their potential, and to advocate motherhood as a valid career option.

Eisenstein (1984) rejects such "feminist revisionism" in favour of a conceptual shift in the meaning of equality. Feminism, she argues, shows up fundamental contradictions in the liberal philosophy of equal opportunity and merited hierarchy. The ideology of equal opportunity covers up an unequal system that privileges men by their ascribed sexual status. Affirmative action policies that try in very minor and insignificant ways to redress this systemic privileging of men are attacked within liberalism as discrimination against men. The feminist movement threatens the foundations of liberal individualism by making visible women's situation as members of a sexual class. Women as child-bearers and child-rearers face major systemic disadvantages that cannot be alleviated by abstract notions of equal opportunity.

True gender equality, Eisenstein argues, will be achieved only when child-bearing and child-rearing become socially inconsequential; that is, when they do not restrict women's choices, and do not result in women being segregated in the institution of private, domesticated motherhood, or forced into economic dependence on men, or into secondary wage-earner status. Such equality implies far-reaching social and political changes that are not envisioned in current equality rights provisions within the Canadian Charter.

What would such a world look like? It might include, among other policies: reproductive freedom; new visions of childcare and health care; statutory parenting leave that would acknowledge both the special needs of childbirth and the equal parenting responsibilities of mothers and fathers; flexible working hours; a fundamental rethinking of the notions of worker or employee to include the presumption of domestic and childcare responsibilities as intrinsic to the experience of work; economic independence for mothers that presupposes profound changes in the conceptualization of private family and social responsibility. These suggestions are only a beginning—the theory of true gender equality and what it would entail for society has scarcely begun to be developed. The absence, or gross inadequacy, of such policies in most industrial societies, attests to how patriarchal these societies are.

CONCLUSION

This exploration of stratification in capitalist society has taken us a long way from traditional functionalist analysis with its certainty of differential skill and requirements and merited differences in prestige and rewards. As the concepts used in analyses change, so also does the nature of the reality being talked about. Where traditional functionalists talk of "stratification," for example, Marxists talk of "class." *Class* essentially refers to power based on relationship to the means of production; stratification is essentially a prestige ranking. For traditional functionalists, stratification is based on innate individual differences in abilities and motivation, but seen from the political economy perspective it refers primarily to the relative utility of different positions for the capitalist system at any one time (Boughey 1978, 130). Good jobs can quickly crumble into nothing once they cease to be useful to corporate employers. Members of the prestigious upper middle class of corporate executives found this out to their cost during the 1980s and 1990s. Cutbacks in middle management positions have left many unemployed.

The dimension of power or powerlessness is central to the Marxist analysis, not the differences in income or lifestyle that occupy traditional functionalists. It certainly helps to have scarce skills that are high in demand, but it does not alter the fact that shifting labour-market demands, or new technologies, or just an overabundance of other people with similar skills can rapidly wipe out any advantage. Distinctions between professional, middle class, working class, and lower class begin to look unimportant under such conditions. What they have in common is insecurity and dependency on the labour market.

Marxist theorists acknowledge the need for skills and professional training, and the need to attract particularly able, qualified, and dependable people to certain jobs. However, they use different criteria to answer the moral question of what differential rewards should be. Personal need and labour time, rather than importance and scarcity, are the key variables. The well-known Marxist motto is: "To each according to need and from each according to ability." True justice requires equality in power, prestige, and property. People deserve equal power to influence government in their own society, equal dignity as human beings, and equal access to a good standard of living (Boughey 1978, 130). People do not automatically warrant a higher standard of living just because they happen to be born brighter, or with wealthy parents, or because they lucked into an elite job. In theory, people could be rewarded for the labour time they give to their jobs. The time taken to develop skills can be calculated into the amount. So can the extra time involved in doing quality work. Those who support more dependants should take home proportionately more money. These are the principles that underlie current state salary policies in China.

Social constructionist theory introduces a qualitatively different dimension into this analysis of stratification. It focuses attention on the practices through which people work up and accept notions of jobs and skills as common-sense features of work. Like Marxism, it draws attention to the often arbitrary character of hierarchical divisions between jobs. It explores how such divisions are accomplished, particularly in the professional discourse of management experts in the field of job evaluation. It explores also how people adopt such accounts as "the way things are" and act accordingly.

Feminist theory, often in close association with social constructionism, makes visible how these practices are gendered. It explores, moreover, how a gender hierarchy, built on inegalitarian division of domestic labour, is presupposed in the organization of labour relations. Reform of institutionalized patriarchy requires fundamental changes in the organization of society, changes that go far beyond a shift in attitudes or procedures to establish formal equity in the evaluation of male and female job applicants.

SUGGESTED READING

An excellent source of statistical information on inequality in Canada is Henry Veltmeyer, *Canadian Class Structure* (1986). Veltmeyer takes a strong, structuralist Marxist approach to inequality, showing how capitalism works to create a class of super-rich at the top of the Canadian hierarchy and a class of poor and sometimes destitute people at the bottom.

For a clear presentation of functionalist theory of stratification, the article by Davis and Moore, "Some Principles of Stratification" (1945), is excellent. It is an older publication, but the main argument is very clear, without being hedged or qualified to avoid criticism. The rebuttal by Melvin Tumin, "Critical Analysis of 'Some Principles of Stratification'" (1953), is also very straightforward.

For the Marxist approach, an excellent book is Harry Braverman's *Labour and Monopoly Capital* (1974). This descriptive and readable book presents a strong argument for the importance to capitalism of deskilling workers.

For the ethnomethodological perspective, any of the studies by Erving Goffman are valuable. They are all very readable descriptions of how everyday life is managed in ordinary interactions. One short book by Goffman is *Interaction Ritual* (1967).

Charles Darrah's article "Skill Requirements at Work" (1994) provides an insightful social constructionist analysis of work that challenges the adequacy of common-sense notions of skill, and also draws attention to the importance of interpersonal networks in generating and transmitting crucial work-related knowledge. The article also discusses how the deskilling practices of management seriously hamper the efforts of workers to learn more about their work.

It should have become apparent throughout this debate that education is related in critical, although contradictory, ways to stratification. Schools and colleges, with their technological-meritocratic principles, have become central arenas within which relations of stratification are worked out. It is to the analysis of the education system that we now turn.

From the perspective of radical feminism, Heidi Hartmann's "Capitalist Patriarchy and Job Segregation by Sex" (1979) presents a groundbreaking study of how male unions systematically limited the job opportunities open to women. A journalistic article by Rona Maynard and Cynthia Brouse, "Thanks, But No Thanks" (1988), documents the high stress experienced by women in corporate executive careers.

QUESTIONS

1. What do Davis and Moore see as the functional prerequisites that generate stratification in all known societies?

2. How can Tumin argue that, in a sense, equality and opportunity are inherently in conflict?

3. How does Tumin critique the argument that differential financial rewards are essential to motivate people to do important and difficult jobs?

4. What structural changes lie behind the American Dream that anyone can achieve upward mobility through talent and effort?

5. How does Marxist theory challenge the relationship between credentials and financial rewards?

6. In Braverman's classical Marxist theory, what is the functional importance of job ladders in industry? How might such structures be dysfunctional for competitive advantage in high-technology industries?

7. How does the notion of work as a *community of practice* undermine the notion that specific jobs require specific skills?

8. How do the job descriptions of clerical and managerial work function as ideological practices that distort understanding of what people are actually doing?

9. How can the incorporation of workers' representatives in job evaluation committees serve to further distort rather than enhance understanding of what workers actually do?

10. How is domestic division of labour directly implicated in gender inequality in paid work?

KEY TERMS

credentialism

deskilling

divide and rule

doing hierarchy

employment equity

extrinsic rewards

linear relation

meritocracy thesis

mobility

scientific management

stratification

Taylorism

technocratic-meritocratic thesis

REFERENCES

Archibald, W.P. 1978. *Social Psychology as Political Economy*. Toronto: McGraw-Hill Ryerson.

Armstrong, P., and H. Armstrong. 1990. *Theorizing Women's Work*. Toronto: Garamond.

Beechey, V. 1977. "Some Notes on Female Wage Labour in Capitalist Production." *Capital and Class* 3 (Autumn).

Boughey, H. 1978. *The Insights of Sociology: An Introduction*. Boston: Allyn & Bacon.

Bowles, S., and H. Gintis. 1976. *Schooling in Capitalist America.* New York: Basic Books.

Braverman, H. 1974. *Labor and Monopoly Capital: The Degradation of Work in the Twentieth Century.* New York: Monthly Review Press.

Brittan, A., and M. Maynard. 1984. *Sexism, Racism and Oppression.* Oxford: Basil Blackwell.

Cassin, A.M. 1992. Expert testimony before Supreme Court of Ontario on behalf of the Federation of Women Teachers' Association of Ontario in the case between Margaret Tomen, Applicant, and Ontario Public School Teachers' Federation and Ontario Teachers' Federation, Respondents.

Cassin, A.M. 1991. "Women, Work, Jobs and Value: The Routine Production of Inequality—A Report with Special Reference to Consumers Gas." Expert testimony before Ontario Pay Equity Tribunal. March.

Cassin, A.M. 1979. "Advancement Opportunities in the British Columbia Public Service." British Columbia Economic Analysis and Research Bureau, Ministry of Industry and Small Business Development.

Clement, W. 1981. *Hardrock Mining: Industrial Relations and Technological Change at INCO.* Toronto: McClelland & Stewart.

Cockburn, C. 1981. "The Material of Male Power." *Feminist Review* 9 (Autumn): 41–59.

Darrah, C. 1994. "Skill Requirements at Work: Rhetoric versus Reality." *Work and Occupations* 21 (1): 64–84.

Davis, K., and W.E. Moore. 1945. "Some Principles of Stratification." *American Sociological Review* 10 (2): 242–249.

Eisenstein, Z.R. 1984. *Feminism and Sexual Equality: Crisis in Liberal America.* New York: Monthly Review Press.

Friedan, B. 1981. *The Second Stage.* Fort Worth, Texas: Summit.

Gregor, F.M. 1994. "The Social Organization of Nurses' Educative Work." Ph.D. thesis, Dalhousie University, Halifax, Nova Scotia.

Gyllenhammer, P. 1977. *People at Work.* Reading, Massachusetts: Addison-Wesley.

Hartmann, H. 1979. "Capitalist Patriarchy and Job Segregation by Sex." In Z. Eisenstein, ed. *Capitalist Patriarchy and the Case for Socialist Feminism.* New York: Monthly Review Press, 206–247.

Himelfarb, A., and C.J. Richardson. 1992. *Sociology for Canadians: A Reader.* Toronto: McGraw-Hill Ryerson.

Himelfarb, A., and C.J. Richardson. 1979. *People, Power and Process: Sociology for Canadians.* Toronto: McGraw-Hill Ryerson.

Kates, J. 1988. "The Quiet Revolution." *Report on Business Magazine* (July): 58–64.

Lave, J., and E. Wenger. 1991. *Situated Learning: Legitimate Peripheral Participation.* New York: Cambridge University Press.

Liddle, J., and R. Joshi. 1986. *Daughters of Independence: Gender, Caste and Class in India.* New Delhi: Zed Books.

Maynard, R., with C. Brouse. 1988. "Thanks, But No Thanks." *Report on Business Magazine* (Feb.): 26–34.

Morgan, K., and A. Sayer. 1988. *Microcircuits of Capital: "Sunrise" Industry and Uneven Development.* Cambridge, UK: Polity Press.

Reimer, M.A. 1987. "The Social Organization of the Labour Process: A Case Study of the Documentary Management of Clerical Labour in the Public Service." Ph.D. thesis, Ontario Institute for Studies in Education.

Ryten, E. 1994. "Getting into Medical School in the Nineties: Who's In? Who's Out?" *ACMC Forum* 26 (4): 13–26.

Sayer, A., and R. Walker. 1992. *The New Social Economy: Reworking the Division of Labour.* Cambridge, Massachusetts: Blackwell.

Tumin, M. 1973. *Patterns of Sociology.* Boston: Little Brown.

Compulsory public schooling for children is a central feature of all industrialized societies. In Canada, the beginnings of a public school system can be traced back to the early 1840s in Ontario (MacDonald 1988, 102–103). In 1846, a general board of education was set up to examine the state of education in the province and to make recommendations for developing a common school system. In 1850, an Act was passed to regulate the classification of teachers and to establish boards of public instruction for each county to certify teachers and to select textbooks. In 1871, free, compulsory education was established. Children between the ages of seven and 12 had to attend school four months per year. In 1919, the school-leaving age was raised to 16. Secondary school fees were abolished two years later. Other provinces slowly followed Ontario's lead.

In contemporary Canada, schooling is compulsory between the ages of six and 16, although many children are enrolled in formal educational institutions at an earlier age and remain in school past the legal school-leaving age. Statistics Canada data indicate that the numbers of children enrolled in pre-elementary education increased by 9 percent between 1977 and 1984, and a further 9 percent by 1991 to a total of 466 123 children in 1991. During the same period the proportions of people aged 15 to 19 still in full-time education rose from 64.5 percent to 77.4 percent. Many people continue their formal education in a postsecondary institution. Full-time postsecondary enrolment grew by 33 percent between 1981–82 and 1991–92 to a total of nearly 900 000, with 62 percent of these at university.

Why has compulsory and advanced education achieved such importance in industrial societies like Canada? What forms does education take? What are the explanations for inequalities among different social groups in access to and achievement in education? These are some of the central questions we examine in this chapter.

Theories of education are very closely linked to the theories of stratification. In industrial society, careers have become more important than inherited wealth in determining the standard of living of the majority of people. These careers, in turn, depend on access to education. As in the previous chapter, we present the traditional functionalist perspective first, followed by the Marxist structuralist critique. Both of these approaches are challenged by contemporary efforts to reformulate theories of education in less deterministic ways. Such challenges give central attention to the social construction of schooling in daily interaction in classrooms and to feminist efforts to radically transform the curriculum and teaching methods.

Functionalism: The Liberal Theory of Education

Next to the family, education ranks as the most important institution within the traditional functionalist model of the social system. Education is responsible for developing moral or normative consensus, which is at the centre of social integration and pattern maintenance. It is also critical for giving young people the skills that will enable them to adapt to rapidly changing economic conditions.

The Ideal of Liberal Education

The nineteenth-century philosopher and reformer John Dewey advocated a free and universal school system as vitally important for democracy and for developing industrial society. He believed that schools have a central role to play in the psychic and moral development of the individual. By helping to develop the cognitive and psychomotor skills of students, schools also offer each individual the chance to compete openly for privileges in society (Bowles and Gintis 1976, 20–23). Dewey saw universal education as a powerful mechanism for reducing extremes of wealth and poverty and for fostering equality. In his view, universal schooling was not only desirable in itself, but it was also an efficient way to train a skilled labour force. It would be, therefore, eminently compatible with capitalism.

This vision of the education system as democratic, just, and efficient stands at the heart of the functionalist view of stratification in industrial society. Functionalism focuses primarily on the objectives of socializing young people in the skills and moral commitment necessary for them to take over adult roles within the social system. The goal is to ensure the continuity of the system itself. Functionalists define equality of opportunity primarily in terms of meritocracy. The desired outcome of schooling, therefore, is that the more able and motivated students are allocated to the more difficult and important social roles.

The Functions of Schools

Parsons' essay, "The School Class as a Social System" (1961), provides a statement of the basic assumptions underlying the functionalist theory of education. In this essay, Parsons argues that families are not adequate to prepare children for adult roles in advanced industrial societies, primarily because the values and commitments appropriate for kinship roles conflict with those of the workplace. A primary function of schools is to help children to make the transition from the value orientations of family life to the affectively neutral, universalistic, and achievement-oriented values of the work world.

Parsons suggests that it is significant that close to nine out of 10 elementary school teachers are women. The nurturing orientation that these teachers provide gives young children some continuity with the mother role and absorbs the strain of achievement and differential ranking. Children can relate to their female teacher and try to please her as they do their mothers. They have the same teacher for a whole year in all subjects. At the same time, the teacher is not a mother but is in an occupation. Each year children have a new teacher. This reinforces particularistic role identification. They also learn that the teacher judges them according to their achievements. Parsons further suggests that it is significant that traditionally a high proportion of American school teachers are unmarried. They thus avoid the contradictory demands of maternal and occupational roles for women.

Senior classes are differentiated into specialized subject areas, each taught by a different teacher. The majority of these teachers are men. Specialization by male teachers reduces attachment to any one teacher and promotes and reinforces the masculine image of affective neutrality and specificity. Hence children learn the pattern variables appropriate for adult sex roles.

At the same time, schools socialize children in required commitments and capabilities for adult roles. *Commitment* comprises two broad aspects: societal values and performance of specific roles. The two components of *capabilities* are skills to perform the task and role responsibility; that is, the ability to live up to the expectations of others. The school is thus crucial for the allocation of young people into future roles on the basis of achievement. At the elementary level, where cognitive skills appear relatively simple, the moral component of responsible citizenship takes precedence. Students are graded both for achievement and for "responsible good behaviour" such as respectfulness and cooperativeness in class. Parsons sees these as fundamental moral skills, important for future leadership and initiative. Stratification on the basis of cognitive skills is translated into college preparatory streaming at grade 9. Parsons admits that the ascriptive characteristics of class of origin influence this streaming, but he concludes that the main force is still achievement.

Parsons' essay is a masterpiece in displaying the working assumptions of the functionalist approach. The first assumption is *functional indispensability*. Parsons conveys the impression that all aspects of American schools in the 1950s had important functions within the education system and could not be easily replaced. He further accepts the basic assumption of *functional unity*. Any established patterns are regarded as good for the educational system, for society as a whole, and for individual members. There is no question in his model that practices such as the early streaming of children on the basis of behaviour rather than cognitive abilities might not be functional for all sectors of society. The third basic assumption, *universal functionalism*, is evident in Parsons' effort to find a valuable purpose for every detail that he notices. Nothing is dismissed as an irrelevant or useless habit left over from earlier times or from other life situations.

The main problem with this approach is that almost any change in the status quo is problematic. We are left with the impression that any change in the school system, such as using male teachers in elementary grades or married women specialists in later grades, or having mixed playground activities for girls and boys together, would be psychologically disturbing for the students. Contemporary functionalist theories have largely discarded Parsons' assumptions concerning the importance of such details as spinsterhood for elementary teachers, but in other respects his essay still expresses the core ideas of functionalism.

The main functions of the school system, as highlighted by Parsons, can be summarized as follows:

1. to teach the values of achievement, universalistic standards of judgment, and emotional neutrality appropriate for specialized occupational roles;

2. to train in specific skills and knowledge appropriate for occupational roles;

3. to ensure the appropriate selection and allocation of young adults to occupational roles in accordance with merit, as measured by universal standards of achievement;

4. to legitimate inequalities in material rewards in democratic society through principles of merit established in the school grading system;

5. to develop stable social relations with age peers outside the family;

6. to inculcate appropriate sex-role identification.

The functionalist approach to the sociology of education has largely accepted this list of functions defining the roles that schooling plays in society, particularly in preparing children for the job market. The main focus of the debate has been on the extent to which schools are able to meet the moral goals set out by Dewey: to provide equality of opportunity to all children for personal and intellectual development and academic attainment across different social classes, races, and ethnic groups. More recently, the importance of sexual equality has also been recognized. The growing consensus is that, notwithstanding concerted efforts at educational reform, schools are failing miserably with respect to the goal of equality.

Equality and Educational Opportunity

The concept of *equality* in education has been understood in several contradictory ways. During the early era of the common school system, emphasis was placed on **equality of condition** or sameness. A common curriculum was planned for all children as a standardized, age-graded program of studies without reference to individual differences in interests or abilities. Later the interpretation of equality shifted to emphasize **equality of opportunity** for all children to develop their individual potential. A variety of curricula were planned to reflect the different needs, capacities, and interests of students, and their different occupational futures. Differential treatment is justified on the basis of merit. Specialized and advanced education would be open to all children who qualify on the basis of effort and ability.

The acknowledged difficulty with offering differentiated programs is that they can become a source of inequality of opportunity. Children risk becoming trapped in educational streams that limit their future options. A third approach shifted the focus to *equality of outcome*. A range of educational opportunites, resources, and different teaching methods were designed to meet the special needs of individual children, with the goal that all students would succeed in school to the best of their innate abilites.

Each of these approaches tries to grapple with the evidence of persistent and marked differences in the formal educational attainment of students from different backgrounds. These cannot be accounted for solely by variations in intellectual ability. Porter, Porter, and Blishen (1982) conducted an extensive survey of 2571 Ontario students in grades 8, 10, and 12 to explore the relationship between the backgrounds of students and their aspirations to attend university. The researchers found a direct and strong relation between the father's occupational status and the student's aspiration to graduate from grade 13 and to enter university (see Figure 1). The higher the occupational status of the father, the more likely the student was to want to complete grade 13. Seventy-six percent of students whose fathers were in the higher professional category intended to go on to university, compared with 46 percent of students whose fathers had unskilled jobs. This gap could only be partially accounted for by the different ability levels of students. The researchers found that social class background was a more powerful indicator of aspiration to graduate from university than was measured mental ability (Porter, Porter, and Blishen 1982, 61).

Among the high-ability boys, 77 percent of those with upper-middle-class backgrounds aspired to graduate from university. The corresponding figure for lower-class boys was 47 percent. At the other extreme, among the low-ability boys, 46 percent of those with upper-class backgrounds aspired to university. By contrast, only 22 percent of low-ability boys

Figure 1 Percent Wanting to Graduate from University, by Socioeconomic Status, Mental Ability, and Sex, Grade 12

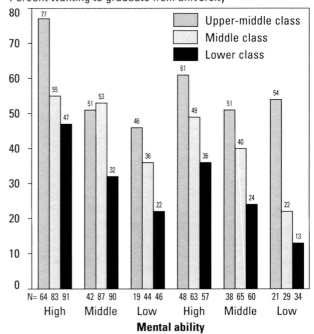

Source: Porter, Porter, and Blishen (1982, 61).

with lower-class backgrounds wanted to graduate from university. Thus, there is a 24 to 30 percentage-point difference in proportions of boys aspiring to university that can be accounted for by the effect of social class background. Grade 12 girls show similar differences in aspirations by social class. Among girls with high mental ability, 61 percent of the upper-middle-class girls aspired to university compared with only 36 percent of lower-class girls, a difference of 25 percentage points.

When grade 12 boys and girls are compared, boys have higher aspirations than girls across most categories of social class and mental ability. The exceptions occur among middle-ability and low-ability students within the upper-middle class where girls equal or exceed boys in aspirations.

These findings concerning the link between social class and aspirations for higher education closely mirror the results of research conducted in the 1950s in the United States by Tumin (1973, 46–54). This similarity suggests that the intervening 20 years of educational reforms had little effect on class bias in educational attainment. However, the differences between the sexes in the Ontario data are significantly less than in Tumin's data. Tumin found that, in every category of class and mental ability, boys had consistently higher educational aspirations than girls. The rise in aspirations among upper-middle-class girls in the Ontario data is striking.

A follow-up study of the Ontario grade 12 students confirmed the predicted relation between social class background and actual attendance at university, particularly among the high-ability students. In this group, 74 percent of the upper-middle-class students went to university compared with 62 percent of the middle-class and 59 percent of the lower-class students. Low-ability students showed similar differences in their rate of attendance by social class. Among the medium-ability group, however, there was an insignificant difference in attendance rates among the three classes.

In summary, the data suggest that the occupational class status of the father has a significant effect on the likelihood of children aspiring to and attending university. The influence of social class exceeds that of mental ability, especially for boys. Students whose fathers are professionals are particularly likely to intend to go to university, even when their mental ability is low. Girls generally lag behind boys in their aspirations to attend university, although the differences seem to be decreasing, particularly within upper-middle-class families.

Functionalist Explanations for Class and Gender Bias in Educational Attainment

Functionalists view education as a system that provides for the appropriate allocation of young people into occupational roles on the basis of ability. How, then, do they explain the large numbers of high-ability students choosing not to attend university? Porter, Porter, and Blishen (1982, 25–29) draw upon the classical functionalist ideas of socialization and self-concept to explore the class and sex differences that are associated with the wasted talent. As we have seen in earlier chapters, socialization is the process through which children learn appropriate social roles and rules of behaviour for the groups in which they find themselves. These rules reflect those of the wider social settings of neighbourhood, social class, and religious group within which families are located. Through interacting with others, children learn to conform to the behaviour that others expect and learn to expect approval and esteem from others for such conformity. Of great importance to children is the approval of significant others. These people first consist of immediate family members and later the children's peers and teachers. Porter, Porter, and Blishen predict that the roots of ambition lie in the early socialization process when the influence of parents is likely to be paramount.

Self-Concept Self-concept, the image that we hold of ourselves, is closely related to socialization. Children develop a sense of who they are through coming to see themselves as they appear to others. Boys and girls growing up in different social classes come to develop different conceptions of themselves and their abilities. These self-concepts may not accurately reflect innate mental abilities, but they powerfully influence what children believe they can do, and therefore what they are willing to try.

Porter, Porter, and Blishen devised a series of questions to measure students' self-concepts and to determine who acted as their significant others. Their data suggest that parents seem to be more significant than either teachers or peers in influencing educational aspirations for the majority of children. In every social class, and for both sexes, a greater proportion of students aspired to university when parental influence was high, than when it was low. The high or low influence of peers made relatively little difference. Teachers appeared to have even less influence than peers on future educational plans.

The researchers found large differences between social classes in the amount of direct assistance that parents gave children with schoolwork. At the grade 10 level, they found a difference of 27 percentage points between upper-middle and lower-class boys, and 13 percentage points between upper-middle and lower-class girls in this regard. By grade 12 these differences rose to 34 and 41 percentage points respectively.

Self-concept of ability seems to be powerfully linked to parental influence and to school performance but minimally linked to measures of mental ability or to teacher's influence (Porter, Porter, and Blishen 1982, 125–129). Self-concept seems to account for the generally lower educational aspirations of girls relative to boys. The researchers found that girls had a lower self-concept of their own ability than boys for every measure used. Their striking finding was that girls achieved consistently better grade point averages in school than boys for every level of mental ability, and yet they had consistently lower self-concepts of their abilities than boys for every category of ability and performance. Girls, it seems, may be held back by their own low conceptions of themselves.

The researchers link the low self-concept of girls to a combination of socialization and realistic appraisal of the roles they see females perform, both of which are inconsistent with academic success and achievement. Girls, they suggest, are socialized to be overly dependent on the opinions of others and to be submissive. They are more likely to accede to the demands of female teachers and to perform well in school. But because they are not encouraged to be independent, they do not develop confidence in their ability to cope with their environment, and they receive less encouragement from parents to continue their education. They are taught to realize their ambitions through marriage and to passively accept the social status of their husbands.

Boys, on the other hand, are socialized to be independent and autonomous from their mothers, so they resist female teachers in early grades. But, as they near school-leaving age, they are under pressure to qualify for university, as this is linked to future male occupations. They encounter more male teachers in high school and new subjects associated with males in our culture. Thus, boys perform less well than girls throughout school but have higher self-concepts and are significantly more likely to go on to higher education.

If this analysis of the differential socialization and lower self-concepts of girls relative to boys accurately accounts for the 1971 data, it would appear that dramatic changes have occurred in gender socialization in one generation. In 1971, when Porter, Porter, and Blishen did their study, females comprised only 37.7 percent of full-time undergraduate enrolment. But by 1987–88, 50.3 percent of all full-time undergraduates were women, rising to over 53 percent by 1991–92 (see Figure 2). The proportions in graduate programs remained stable between 1981 and 1991 with roughly three women to every four men enrolled. These figures suggest that the pattern found by Porter, Porter, and Blishen—that girls generally lack sufficient self-confidence in their abilities to develop high educational aspirations—no longer holds in the 1990s. We need new studies of family socialization to understand what changes have taken place and whether girls are attending university

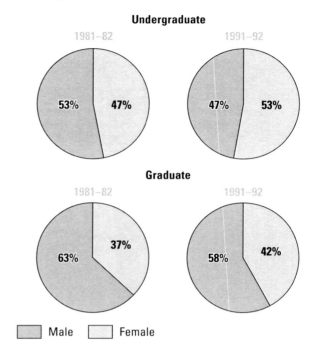

Figure 2 Full-time University Enrolment, by Level and Sex, Canada, 1981–82 and 1991–92

Source: Reproduced by authority of the Minister of Industry, 1994. Statistics Canada (1994e), *Education in Canada: A Statistical Review*, Cat. 81-229, p. 51.

in numbers equal to boys because of, or in spite of, prevailing patterns of socialization.

The more general findings of Porter, Porter, and Blishen concerning differential educational aspirations and attainment by social class have not been challenged by any more recent data. The researchers conclude that different patterns of family socialization by social class constitute the primary cause of wasted talents in the education system. Parents are of central importance as significant others for children and are therefore significant in promoting or reducing educational aspirations. Upper-middle-class parents are more likely to take an interest in, and to help with, their children's schooling and to emphasize success in education as a factor in their approval and esteem. They promote higher aspirations in their children (see Figure 3).

Schools may try to develop teaching methods to counter the negative influence of lower-class backgrounds on students, but the real solution seems to lie in changing the norms and values of lower- and lower-middle-class parents. Schools provide an avenue for upward social mobility, particularly in Canada. It is up to the students themselves to choose to take advantage of the opportunities provided.

Figure 3 Program by Socioeconomic Status, Grade 12

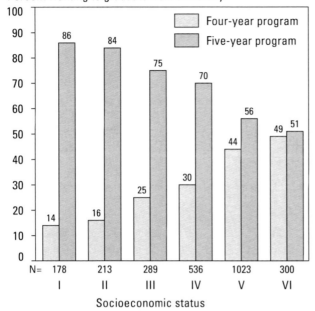

Percent wanting to graduate from university

Source: Porter, Porter, and Blishen (1982, 193).

The Political Economy of Education: Schooling in Capitalist Society

The Marxist structuralist perspective is rooted in very different conceptions of stratification in capitalist society and of the associated role of education. It focuses primarily on the structure of the school system rather than on the aspirations of individual students. Differences in aspirations are regarded as the effects rather than the causes of inequality in education. Functionalists blame lower-class students for not wanting to take advantage of opportunities for higher education and social mobility. Marxists argue that the school system is structured in such a way as to virtually ensure their failure. In focusing on individual aspirations rather than underlying structures, functionalist theory acts as an ideology; that is, a means not to see what is really going on in the school system.

In this section we draw heavily on the work of Samuel Bowles and Herbert Gintis to illustrate the broad outlines of the Marxist structuralist perspective on education. Their study, *Schooling in Capitalist America* (1976), is widely cited as a seminal work that inspired a decade of Marxist-oriented research in education.

In a summary statement of their theory, Bowles and Gintis (1988) point to the contradictions between democracy and capitalism. Political democracy is based on rights invested in the person. The central problems for democracy concern how to maximize participation in decision-making, shield minorities against majority prejudice, and protect majorities against undue influence of an unrepresentative minority. The economic system is based on the principle of rights invested in property. The central problems are how to minimize participation of the majority (the workers), protect a specific minority (capitalists and managers) against the will of the majority, and subject the majority to the will of an unrepresentative minority.

Schools are caught in the middle. They are part of the democratic state system, but they are responsible for educating young people to fit into the economic system. Bowles and Gintis (1976, 54) argue that most of the problems in the school system stem from this contradiction between a democratic political system and a totalitarian economic system. The liberal conception of education, first put forward by Dewey, emphasizes three fundamental goals: (1) developing the full potential of individual students with respect to cognitive, physical, emotional, critical, and aesthetic powers; (2) promoting equality through common public schools that would overcome disadvantaged social backgrounds; and (3) ensuring social continuity through preparing young people for integration into adult social roles. Bowles and Gintis argue that these three goals are fundamentally incompatible. Schools cannot promote full personal development and social equality while integrating students into alienating and hierarchically ordered roles within the economy.

The problems are compounded by the compulsion within advanced capitalist economies to develop labour-saving technology that will either displace workers altogether or deskill them in order to cheapen their wage-labour and so raise profits. Bowles and Gintis accept the main theme of Braverman's *Labor and Monopoly Capital* (1974), which predicts that the vast majority of skilled craftworkers, clerical staff, and even professionals will be systematically deskilled and fragmented by technological advances. The resulting class structure will be characterized by a mass of low-skilled workers, controlled by a small class of supervisors and managers, with a very small elite class of highly skilled professionals and executives who run the huge corporations in the interests of the owners of capital. A principal function of schooling in relation to such a system is to prepare the mass of children to fit into a largely deskilled, fragmented, and hierarchical class system. Their natural abilities and desire for autonomy need to be suppressed rather than enhanced to make them comply.

Seen from this perspective, both the evidence of an apparent waste of talented lower-class children who drop out of school, and the lack of fit between mental ability and postsecondary education, take on new meanings (see Table 1). Schools perpetuate class inequality because this is precisely what they are intended to do. Lower-class children are channelled into dead-end vocational streams, drop out of school early, and thus provide a ready supply of workers to fill the mass of unskilled jobs. Middle-class children, regardless of ability, stay in the education system long enough to get credentials that qualify them for better-paid positions. Bowles and Gintis argue that the main function of such credentials is to make distinctions between workers, and particularly to legitimate the higher pay and status of supervisors relative to workers. Very few of the people who achieve higher credentials actually find they need what they learned to do their jobs.

Bowles and Gintis (1976, 97–100) cite many examples to back up their argument that the relation between credentials and rewards is largely arbitrary. People who earn credentials, but who lack other attributes of superior status, tend not to get high economic rewards. For example, the economic returns on schooling—average increments in salary for each additional year of formal education—are twice as high for white males as for blacks and women in the United States. White males of upper-class background experience returns on education 66 percent higher than white males of lower-class background. Even when years of experience on the job are identical, white males are likely to have higher earnings than blacks and women.

Body image is also important. Bowles and Gintis cite the results of one study that suggested that height was a more important determinant of earnings than either grade point average or a cum laude degree. Another survey of 15 000 executives found that those who were overweight were paid significantly less, the penalty being as much as $1000 a pound. People are much less likely to challenge the prestige, authority, and higher earnings of distinguished-looking older white males, regardless of their actual abilities, than they would if younger, overweight, black women were promoted to supervisory positions.

From the perspective of traditional functionalism, such patterns are irrational—inexplicable holdovers of ascriptive criteria in what should be the impersonal and achievement-oriented bureaucratic world of business. But from the Marxist structuralist perspective these patterns serve to reinforce the status consciousness that fragments workers.

Structural Correspondence Theory

Structural correspondence theory argues that there is a close correspondence between how relationships are structured within schools and within the workforce. Schools reproduce the social relations required for production. Bowles and Gintis (1976, Ch. 6) trace historical parallels between significant changes in the American capitalist economy and developments in the school system. The origin of the common schools in the mid-1830s in the United States coincided with the expansion of the factory system and the widespread labour unrest associated with it. What the factory owners desperately needed was not a skilled labour force, but a disciplined one. Common schools enforced military discipline and values of order, neatness, politeness, and punctuality that served to transform an ill-disciplined immigrant and farming populations into a docile and disciplined factory workforce.

The subsequent progressive education movement, and greatly increased enrolment in public schools, coincided in the United States with the expansion of corporate capitalism between about 1890 and 1930 (Bowles and Gintis 1976, Ch. 7). Corporate bosses needed a mass of middle-ranking

Table 1 Labour Force Participation and Unemployment Rate by Education and Sex, May 1994*

Level of Education	Unemployment Rate	
	Male	Female
0–8 years	16.4	16.3
Some secondary education	16.8	15.0
High-school graduate	9.9	9.8
Some post-secondary	12.7	13.2
Post-secondary diploma	9.2	8.6
University degree	5.5	5.7
Total	11.0	10.2

Level of Education	Participation Rate	
	Male	Female
0–8 years	41.7	19.3
Some secondary education	64.3	42.5
High-school graduate	81.6	63.9
Some post-secondary	80.9	70.6
Post-secondary diploma	84.8	70.9
University degree	86.3	80.5
Total	74.0	57.6

*The table shows relatively small differences in unemployment rates between males and females with comparable levels of education, although there are large differences in official participation rates. The participation rate measures the proportions of people who are employed or actively seeking work at the time of the survey.

Source: Reproduced by authority of the Minister of Industry, 1994. Adapted from Statistics Canada (1994b), *Canada Year Book 1992*, table 5, p. B-16.

Common schools enforced military discipline and moral education well suited for training a docile and disciplined factory work force.

Ontario Archives

employees who could be trusted to work without direct supervision in clerical, sales, bookkeeping, and junior supervisory roles. These employees also had to be divided socially from the lower-level workers whom they supervised. More than obedience and punctuality was required. These employees had to internalize an identification with the employer and the corporation. It was this kind of stratified workforce that the mass high schools produced. Schools expanded greatly in size and became bureaucratic, hierarchical, and competitive, ousting the once uniform curriculum of the common schools.

Social relations within vocational and college-track classes came to conform to different norms, consistent with the kinds of jobs for which children were being prepared. Vocational streams emphasized close supervision and obedience to rules, whereas college-track classes encouraged a more open atmosphere emphasizing internalization of norms, independent activities, and limited supervision. Near the top of the educational hierarchy, four-year colleges came to emphasize creative and critical thinking congruent with careers at senior levels of corporate hierarchies.

A classic in this research is the study by Jean Anyon (1980) into how social studies and language arts were taught in five elementary schools located in different communities in the eastern United States. The research describes marked variation in patterns of classroom interaction by the social class background of those attending school. Instruction in the elite school for the children of executives emphasized the development of analytical reasoning and leadership skills. Lessons were creative. Students made presentations to the class and criticized each other's work. In the middle-class school, lessons were very different. Language arts, for example, was reduced to grammar. Teachers checked for right answers rather than for critical

understanding of the questions. In lower-class schools, children seemed to be taught primarily to follow rules set out by the teacher for completing the exercise. Their work was evaluated not by whether the answers were right, but whether the rules had been followed.

These differences reflect and reinforce the family backgrounds from which the different streams of children are drawn. Working-class parents favour stricter educational methods, directly reflecting their own knowledge that submission to authority is essential to getting and holding a steady job. Their children form the majority of pupils in vocational education streams. Professional and self-employed parents prefer a more open atmosphere with greater emphasis on motivational controls rewarding students for achievements rather than for obedience and good behaviour. Such an atmosphere is more consistent with their position in the labour force. Their children are mostly destined for college-track classes.

A third phase in the development of the education system, marked by the expansion of higher education in the 1960s, coincided with the effective domination of the capitalist economy by corporate and state sectors (Bowles and Gintis 1976, Ch. 8). Self-employed entrepreneurs were relegated to increasingly peripheral roles. White-collar and professional employment expanded but became more fragmented and compartmentalized. The expansion of community colleges and diploma courses came in response to this shifting job market, producing what Bowles and Gintis refer to as skilled, subprofessional, white-collar workers. This category includes lower-level supervisors, secretaries, and paraprofessionals in dentistry, law, teaching, and medicine.

Liberal functionalists would largely agree with such an analysis, but Marxist structuralist theory goes further to draw attention to the changing social relations of higher education. Bowles and Gintis ask why the stress on free inquiry and liberal arts in higher education gave way to an emphasis on vocationalized and compartmentalized packages of credits. Why did the student politicization of the 1960s occur? Why has there been an overexpansion of graduates? The main answer they give is that free inquiry was appropriate for the entrepreneurial class, but not for corporate employees, except at the highest levels. Student radicals were drawn mostly from members of the declining entrepreneurial class who resented the loss of autonomy over their working lives. Mass higher education produced a surplus army of people with bachelors degrees and subprofessional qualifications, and this served to break their bargaining power in the labour market. Corporations thus gained access to a highly skilled workforce, while salaries and other concessions could be held to a minimum. Corporate profits were protected. The training of elites has now shifted further up into graduate and postgraduate education. Free inquiry tends to be stressed only at this heady level.

The pressure on universities to serve industry has now become more overt. It takes the form of cutbacks in public funding to force these institutions into greater direct cooperation with corporations. The result is that university autonomy is undermined, funding in less marketable liberal arts and humanities programs is threatened, and, even in the favoured science and engineering faculties, pure research is subordinated to short-term profit motives. Bowles and Gintis suggest that community colleges have already largely succumbed to pressure to produce the labour force that corporations want. They offer the veneer of higher education for lower-class students but, in reality, they may be little more than "high schools with ashtrays," channelling students into dead-end vocational programs (Bowles and Gintis 1976, 211).

Educational Reform: The Losing Battle?

Proposals for educational reform are compromised by the corporate context in which they are evaluated and implemented. Alternative, non-bureaucratic forms of schooling designed to promote the creative potential of children have operated in many pilot projects. They tend to be very successful in their own terms, and are described with great enthusiasm by teachers and students, but rarely do they expand beyond isolated schools for small numbers of privileged students. Bowles and Gintis blame reformers, not for their objectives, but for their narrow focus on schools while failing to target the wider economy that schools mirror.

The educational reformer Ivan Illich has long railed against the stultifying character of the North American public school system, which incarcerates students in classrooms, cuts them off from the real world, and teaches them to distrust their own knowledge and experience and to rely on experts (Illich 1971). "Knowledge" is treated as a packaged commodity that becomes the private property of those who attain credentials, while those who lack such paper credentials are predefined as incompetent. Illich proposes an alternative system of education in which students would recover responsibility for their own teaching and learning through watching people at work and learning alongside them. For Bowles and Gintis (1976, 255–262), the main problem with this vision of a deschooled society is that it treats the socialization agency of the school as the basic explanatory variable. But dismantling schools will not cure the effects of capitalism that cause schools to function as they do. Individuals cannot be held personally responsible for their own deschooling when schooling is obligatory for 10 years and is the major means of access to a livelihood.

Schooling for Contemporary Capitalism

Critics of the structural **correspondence theory** suggest that Bowles and Gintis oversimplified the relationship between schools and capitalism. The rise of common schools in Upper Canada preceded the expansion of factories by some 25 years, discrediting the argument that their original purpose was to train workers for industrial capitalism (MacDonald 1988; Curtis 1987). The Ontario School Act of 1943 followed soon after the rebellions in Upper Canada in 1837–38 and seems to have been centrally concerned with promoting values of patriotism and citizenship in children. This was not incompatible with training a disciplined factory workforce, but it did require a balancing of interests between democracy and capitalism.

The assertion that vocational schools were intended to prepare children for failure and entry into unskilled, dead-end jobs is also overstated. Automation and the systematic deskilling of the workforce have played an important role in increasing profits to capitalists in mass-production industries. But the thesis that all capitalists want deskilled, cheap labour ignores the importance of rapid product innovation and a highly flexible, adaptive labour force in competitive global capitalism. The expansion of higher education since the 1960s, and the funds that capitalists have donated to certain university faculties, cannot be totally dismissed as credentialism. Authoritarian classrooms and standardized curriculum packages are not functional for the production of creative, innovative workers.

The signing of the North American Free Trade Agreement (NAFTA) in 1993 promises to usher in a new era of structural correspondence between the Canadian education system and global capitalism, characterized by the commercialization of society (Calvert and Kuehn 1993). Many aspects of education reflect a shift from a publicly funded social service to a private, profit-oriented system. Under NAFTA rules, once any aspect of the provision of educational services is opened to private contract, it cannot subsequently return to government control without all relevant United States firms being compensated for loss of market opportunity. Profit-making postsecondary training firms are expanding rapidly in Canada while funding for community colleges is being cut. Business colleges now routinely offer courses in keyboarding, computing skills, bookkeeping, and accounting. Any effort by governments to return such courses to the publicly funded community college system could be challenged under NAFTA regulations as unfair practices limiting markets for private firms.

The difference between public-service and private-profit educational institutions is, in any case, narrowing. In the language of administrators and new university presidents, education is increasingly being described as a product that managers market. Students are consumers and corporations are stakeholders. University administrators are corporate managers with objectives to run universities like a business, selling a product for which they must attract revenue or close down. Corporations are encouraged to rent university facilities for research in return for copyrights and patents. By 1993, 15 universities and an estimated 800 researchers were linked with over 170 companies in joint research projects. Universities compete with each other to attract funding deals with corporations, as government revenues are frozen or reduced.

Provision of food services in schools is already being privatized with giant corporations like Burger King and McDonald's running school cafeterias. United States companies are also guaranteed **right of national treatment** in the publishing and distribution of textbooks. Intellectual property rights have been established over a wide range of educational materials including cable and satellite transmission of proprietary educational programs, courses, and learning aids that have patent protection. Educational television is fast becoming big business with companies providing equipment to schools in return for showing programs that carry commercials. The company Youth News Network incorporates a computer chip into its equipment to monitor how often a show is viewed, for how long, and at what volume, to be sure teachers don't "cheat" and spend time teaching instead of watching the show (Calvert and Kuehn 1993, 101).

The corporate agenda impacts on educational programs in multiple ways. Business groups are able to exert increasing pressure on high-school and university curriculum planning, arguing that Canada's global competitiveness depends on schools training children in business-oriented skills. In community colleges in particular, overt constraints are placed on teaching in the interest of serving business. Muller (1989) documents how any new programs introduced in community colleges in British Columbia are constrained to conform to local business interests. Standardized forms and procedures govern how new programs are to be presented to the provincial government. These forms require the signatures of relevant employers in the locality of the college—who might be expected to hire students graduating from such programs—to indicate that they have been consulted and have given their approval. Community college management standardizes the curriculum so it is no longer the prerogative of individual instructors. It is even possible for a student to take an instructor to court for breach of contract if the published course curriculum does not appear to have been strictly followed. Student services staff are explicitly directed to guide students toward training for which there are immediate jobs in the local market

(Muller 1990). Instructors are also required by college management to keep up with any and all technological innovations, such as computer-designed instruction, that industry wants. Muller concludes that community college management, in effect, works for local industry, while being financed by the state.

Publishing companies exercise significant control over the context of the texts that are made available to teachers (Apple 1986, Ch. 4). Acquisitions editors and decision makers in these companies are mostly males with a background in marketing. They focus principally on what they think will sell. The goal is to produce texts with standard content that will be used for years in multiple schools. Apple stresses the urgent need for detailed research into the routine daily work processes and the politics of publishing companies that produce textbooks.

Teachers are increasingly under pressure to use curriculum packages, with heavy emphasis on the preparation of worksheets and the standardized testing and evaluation of students. One effect of such packaged teaching, Apple suggests, is to deskill teachers, reducing them to technicians rather than professionals who control their own activities (Apple 1986, Ch. 2). Apple fears that the growing emphasis upon teaching computer literacy in schools will exacerbate the trend toward standardization and depersonalization of classrooms. Computer manufacturers foist machines onto schools, even offering a free machine for every classroom, in the hope that parents will be motivated to buy school-compatible models for their children to practise on at home. Computers come with standard software packages for classroom instruction. Rarely do these programs incorporate the richness of the professional experience of teachers. Nor do they include the "soft" curriculum of liberal arts. Humanities, ethnic studies, culture, history, politics are all likely to lose out to the mathematical and technical subjects that are readily adaptable to computers. Teachers may find themselves reduced to technicians running programs.

The influx of computers also seems likely to exacerbate class differences between schools. Rich schools can afford multiple machines for personal instruction, and wealthy parents are able to buy computers for home use. Poorly endowed schools and poorer students are not able to have these advantages. Apple argues, too, that elite children are more likely to learn the intellectually stimulating aspects of programming, while lower-class children are trained to use computers for drill and practice sessions.

Cutbacks in government funding for schools influence the social relations of schooling for teachers no less than for the children from poor families. Dorothy Smith and the Wollestonecraft Research Group (1979) document how cutbacks in school funding affect the everyday work of teachers and produce the classroom rigidities for which teachers are subsequently held responsible. When there is not enough science equipment for all pupils to conduct their own experiments, teachers have to demonstrate the experiments while pupils watch passively. Larger classrooms mean that small-group work and seminars become less and less possible. Children who receive less hands-on experience and less attention get bored and distracted, discipline problems increase, and authoritarianism increases. Teachers do not have time to go through batches of essays or independent projects, so they assign fewer of them and rely more on uniform examinations. Teachers give more and more of their personal time to make up the shortfall in staffing until they burn out and leave the profession or become resigned to lower standards and autocratic methods. The schooling patterns criticized by Bowles and Gintis then take shape. The manifest function of budget cutbacks is to save taxpayers' money. The effect is increasingly authoritarian and rigid classrooms. The contrasts between the creative teaching in schools for elite children and the uninspired, autocratic styles of teaching in lower-class schools may well have more to do with teachers trying to cope with large classes and minimal teaching aids in lower-class schools than with any deliberate intention by such teachers to reproduce relations of class.

Standardized teaching practices are also becoming the norm in undergraduate university programs, although overt controls are less in evidence. Increasing enrolments in the face of limited budgets mean huge lecture halls, oppressive one-way teaching techniques, programmed assignments, and a reduction in individual projects. Students in lower-level sociology and psychology courses are more likely to be tested by multiple-choice examinations, marked by computers, which require rigid conformity to preprogrammed textbook answers. Fighting such trends requires tremendous effort on the part of professors who have to mark several hundred individual essays. Creative undergraduate research becomes progressively less possible as classes of 100 or more students descend on libraries that can only afford one copy of each book and that have cut journal subscriptions to save money and space. These are the ways in which the social reality of undergraduate education for middle-level corporate conformity is socially constructed.

Schooling for Oppressive Social Relations

A central argument within the Marxist theory of education is that the school system within capitalist societies is designed to mould children to accept and submit to hierarchical and inegalitarian class relations within capitalist societies. Schools for children at the bottom of the social hierarchy exhibit these oppressive characteristics the most clearly. Bowles and Gintis claim that within American pub-

lic schools, relations between administrators and teachers, teachers and teachers, teachers and students, students and students, and also between students and their work, all replicate the hierarchical and fragmented division of labour within corporations (Bowles and Gintis 1976, 131). The content of the curriculum may be designed to teach the values of democratic citizenship, equality, freedom of speech, and so on. But the hierarchical relations within schools teach a very different lesson of submission to a rigid, rule-bound, and autocratic system. The usual liberal argument condoning such patterns is that students are children. They have not reached the stage of adult maturity when democratic rights of free choice would be appropriate.

Schools resemble factories in multiple ways. The architecture of the buildings, with separate rooms, offices, and recreation areas, arranged differently for staff, teachers, secretaries, and students, reproduces in concrete form the division of labour of the school. The seating arrangement in classrooms, with students in rows facing the front area controlled by the teacher, reinforces the hierarchy in which the teacher has authority and the students submit. The lessons of authority and submission are reported in the routines and rituals of the classroom that require students to speak only when spoken to and to leave and enter classrooms only when bells sound. Through such practices, children become inured to the discipline of the workplace. They develop the types of personal demeanor and self-image that fit them for future occupational roles in factories and bureaucracies. They learn to accept vertical lines of authority. They learn to accept the curriculum package offered. They learn to be motivated primarily through the extrinsic rewards of the grading system rather than the intrinsic pleasures of learning. Students are also fragmented through the insidious emphasis on competition and continual ranking and evaluation (Bowles and Gintis 1988, 2–3; 1976, 131).

The educational reformer Paolo Freire similarly decries the destructive impact of education on lower-class children, based on his observation of education in the slums of Brazil and ghetto schools in America (1970). He describes what he refers to as a banking concept of education. Students in classrooms are treated as objects rather than as acting subjects. They are containers to be filled by the teacher. The more meekly the receptacles permit themselves to be filled, the better students they are. In this system the teacher teaches and the students are taught; the teacher knows everything and the students know nothing; the teacher thinks and the students are thought about; the teacher talks and students listen; the teacher chooses and enforces the choice and the students comply. In the process, schools perpetuate oppression by reinforcing subordination, passivity, and apathy among students. Teachers are created by and in turn reproduce the **culture of domination**. Students learn to respond with fatalism and docility towards authority and to direct their anger against comrades, rather than against their dominators. Their overwhelming aspiration is to take the place of the dominator and to boss others in their turn.

Education for Native Peoples

These descriptions of oppressive schooling may seem far removed from the everyday experience of Canadian university students who are used to the college-preparatory track of Canadian high schools. But for members of socially disadvantaged groups in ghetto classrooms in Canada, the parallels can be only too glaring. The following section, which focuses on an aspect of Canadian Native school experience, tries to bring this reality closer to home.

The traditional education of Native children took place through total involvement in community life. Children learned through sharing the lives of adults, through watching, listening, and learning by participation in the domestic, economic, political, and ceremonial life of the community. Formal schooling for Native children in Canada was first provided by missionaries and later by government schools. Attendance at these schools became compulsory. Children from isolated bands were taken away from their communities and placed in residential schools. The explicit goal of residential schools was **assimilation**, or moulding Native children into whites. Native parents had no voice in what was taught. The language of instruction was English or French, and children were commonly punished for using their own language in

The hidden curriculum of the culture of domination was evident in both residential and reserve schools for Native children.

Calgary Herald Print Collection, Glenbow Archives, Calgary

school. This overtly imperialistic form of schooling was later replaced by smaller schools located within the band communities, particularly for the elementary grades. This shift toward educating Native students within their home communities was an important change, but much of the hidden curriculum of cultural domination remained intact. The description that follows is drawn from two anthropological studies of schools located within two Kwakiutl Native villages situated along the northwest coast of British Columbia (Wolcott 1967; Rohner 1967). It is supplemented by an overview of formal education in an American Native community (Wax, Wax, and Dumont 1964).

The hidden curriculum was manifest in the explicit assumption of many white educators in Native schools that only what the schools taught was worth knowing. Wax, Wax, and Dumont (1964, 67) refer to this attitude as the **vacuum ideology**. Teachers emphasized what they saw as the meager experience of Native children outside school and catalogued their multiple deficiencies relative to white children. The Native children's home experiences, the stories they heard from their parents, the skills of hunting, fishing, and trapping that they learned from parents were simply ignored because they fell outside the school curriculum. Teachers generally knew nothing of Native culture, values, or language, and had no respect for them either.

Teachers commonly lamented the overwhelming passivity of Native children, but this may well have been a symptom of the dehumanizing character of the schools and the breakdown in communication between teachers and pupils (Wax, Wax, and Dumont 1964, 98–99; Wolcott 1967, 92). The older the children grew, the shyer they seemed to become, so that by the eighth grade they were mute to all interrogation. Upper elementary grades were characterized by silent classrooms, the silence providing a shield behind which an unprepared, unwilling student could retreat. The teachers became ridiculous, futile figures, and they responded by condescension and dislike toward Native students. Students would arrive late for school and would drift home at midday, start some task, and not return. They refused any active participation in classroom work. They expected boredom and even asked for highly repetitive work like copying. They had learned to equate the classroom with endless repetition, and they reacted against any variation in routines attempted by a new teacher. Their typical response was, "We didn't come to school for this, we came to do our schoolwork" (Wolcott 1967, 100).

This overt passivity within the classroom was combined with covert, horizontal violence against each other, which Freire observed among the oppressed people in Brazil (Wolcott 1967, 93). Younger children complained of being mercilessly teased, tortured, and bullied by classmates, behind the teacher's back. Some children absented themselves for days in fear. The only advice their mothers could give was to keep out of the way of the bigger children and not provoke them.

The school curriculum seemed irrelevant to the lives of adolescents on the reserves. Not only did it do nothing to prepare them for future jobs in their village, but it also actually conflicted with their informal education gained through participating in adult activities. Pupils resented attending school when they could otherwise be doing vital things like helping their fathers with fishing and clam digging.

The quality of academic performance in these reservation schools, measured in terms of universalistic grade standards, was abysmal (Wolcott 1967, 111; Rohner 1967, 110). The teachers, trained to respond to universalistic standards, found it almost impossible to adjust. When they administered normal intelligence tests, the Native students performed at near idiocy level. It was a hard shock for teachers, despite their knowledge that such tests are culturally biased. Teacher attitudes generally were highly unfavourable toward Native people. The village school studied by Rohner (1967, 105) had a turnover of eight teachers in 14 years. Four of the eight had generated great hostility within the village. One had become so afraid of villagers that he had nailed up all the windows of his home and had refused to let his children play in the village. Another was so hated by the Native peoples that the superintendent had to remove him. Parents were equally intimidated by the teachers and were reduced to silence whenever they attended parent-teacher meetings. They asked only that the school open every day, start on time, and keep the pupils busy. Discipline problems were to be resolved by the teacher (Wolcott 1967, 86).

Given these kinds of school experiences, it would be miraculous if more than a small minority of Native pupils made it through to high-school graduation. Marxist structuralists would argue that they were being educated for failure. The oppressive school system defined all aspects of Native culture and traditional knowledge as irrelevant. It judged the students by white cultural standards and found them so ignorant that they were ranked as borderline mental defectives. Pupils learned to expect nothing but boredom and endless repetition in school, an expectation that exactly fits the menial, low-paying jobs that Native adults commonly attain in white capitalist society.

Since these studies were conducted there have been concerted efforts to address these problems. Many Native communities, in cooperation with the federal government, have begun to take control over their own education, and many universities in Canada and the United States have introduced Native Studies programs into their arts curriculum. The strategies seem to be working, evidenced in significantly higher numbers of Native students pursuing some form of postsecondary education in recent years. Enrolment of

Table 2 Enrolment in University and Post-secondary Institutions for the Registered Indian Population, Canada, 1960–61 to 1992–93

School Year	University Enrolment	Post-secondary Enrolment[1]
1960–61	60	n/a
1965–66	131	n/a
1970–71	432	n/a
1975–76	2071	n/a
1980–81	4455	n/a
1985–86	5800	11 170
1986–87	n/a	13 196
1987–88	n/a	14 242
1988–89	n/a	15 572[2]
1989–90	n/a	18 535
1990–91	n/a	21 300
1991–92	n/a	21 442
1992–93	n/a	21 566

Notes:

[1] Includes Bill C-31 population. Total number of registered Indians funded by DIAND enrolled in post-secondary institutions also includes the number enrolled at university.

[2] Since 1988–89, numbers include students in the University and College Entry Program (UCEP).

Source: Indian and Northern Affairs Canada (1993), table 16, p. 41.

Native students in all postsecondary institutions nearly doubled between 1985–86 and 1992–93 from 11 170 to 21 566 students (see Table 2). Enrolment in university increased from a mere 60 Native students in 1960–61 to 5800 in 1985–86. The proportions, however, still remain well below those for Canadians as a whole (see Figure 4).

Status Natives are eligible for financial assistance to attend university under the Postsecondary Student Assistance Program, but this funding was capped in 1989. This freeze on funding coincided with a significant increase in the numbers of Native students eligible under the program. The implementation of Bill C-31 granted recognition of aboriginal status to women who had formerly lost it by marrying men who were not status Natives. These women and their children now also qualify for financial assistance as defined within treaties. Band councils now have to make difficult decisions about how to allocate limited funds among a larger group of competing claimants.

Schooling and Poverty

Poverty exacerbates the problems of racism, language, and cultural divisions against which Native peoples struggle. Children in poverty, who comprised an estimated 18.2 percent

Figure 4 Post-secondary Participation Rate: A Comparison

Full-time Post-secondary Enrolment Rates Registered Indians Compared to All Canadians

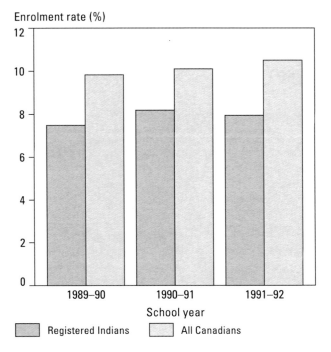

Enrolment rate (%)

Legend: Registered Indians | All Canadians

Source: Indian and Northern Affairs Canada (1993), chart 17, p. 42.

of all children in Canada in 1992, face problems of ill health, malnutrition, and daily humiliation as a routine part of their educational experience (National Council of Welfare 1994). A study by the National Council of Welfare (1975) documents that poor children are more likely than others to be born premature and underweight, to contract childhood diseases, and to miss one to three months of school in a year because of illness.

The social effect of poverty on children, and their isolation from others in the classroom, may be less visible than inadequate clothing and ill health, but they are equally damaging to the children's educational aspirations and sense of well-being. Poor children face the humiliation of not being able to bring in money for special school events or excursions. They cannot afford to buy art supplies, sports equipment or uniforms, or instruments for the school band, and so they cannot join in many of the extracurricular activities open to other children. The list of barriers goes on and on (Gabriel 1986). Humiliation fosters withdrawal, defeat, and resentment. It drains them of the motivation to give their best efforts. Poor children lack money for school books and basic supplies, which makes it hard for them to keep up with homework. Cutbacks in school budgets often mean that teachers cannot provide books for all students

and cannot permit them to take books home because they must be stored away and used in other classes. Poor children are also more likely to live in inadequate and overcrowded homes where they may have no quiet place to study. Teachers used to be able to supervise quiet study periods after school hours, but with budget and staff cutbacks, such "frills" are eliminated.

Poor children in senior classes may lack the time and energy for schoolwork because they take long hours of employment at minimum wage. If school counsellors suggest they would be better off quitting school to join the army or take a typing job, they are likely to agree. Realistically they see little possibility of mobility into professional occupations when all the people around them only have low-paying semiskilled jobs. **Headstart programs** for children in deprived areas may end up only making things worse because they raise unrealistic expectations, resulting in bitter disappointment for adolescents faced with limited opportunities.

The Limitations of Political Economy Theory

The major criticism of classical political economy theory of education concerns its reductionist and deterministic formulation. Ironically, an approach that began as a radical critique of traditional functionalism depends in practice on the same logic. The structure of parts are explained by their functions for the social system as a whole. The difference is that, in Marxist theory, the system is specifically capitalist. The explanation invokes rigid historical **reductionism**. All changes in the school system since its inception in the 1840s are explained as responses to the needs of capitalism (Aronowitz and Giroux 1985, 71, 117; Cole 1988, 7–37; Moore 1988, 58–61; Apple 1988, 124).

A significant problem with this form of explanation is that it presupposes a passive view of humanity. Human agency plays little part in the analysis. Teachers and students are reduced to mere pawns of the capitalist system (Aronowitz and Giroux 1985, 71). According to Marxist structuralists, schools legitimate inequality and limit personal development to aid in the process whereby youths are resigned to their fate (Bowles and Gintis 1976, 266; Cole 1988, 35). From the perspective of social constructionist theory, Aronowitz and Giroux endorse the Marxist critique of capitalism, but challenge the oversimplified version that tries to reduce all explanations of human behaviour to position in the class structure. They argue (1985, Ch. 2) that it is essential to recognize the role of teachers as professionals who are actively involved in the creation of what constitutes education. Teachers are not mere technicians who deliver standard curriculum packages and who function to preserve a hierarchical social order. For the best of them the opposite is closer to the truth, as teachers struggle to break the hold of inherited disadvantages, and push their students to develop enquiring minds and go on to academic careers. Historically, teachers have been active in professional associations that have fought for better working conditions, and for a greater say in what and how teachers teach and who evaluates them, and for control at the level of classroom practice (Apple 1986, 75). Students, too, are active in shaping the social relations of classrooms. The classic study by Willis (1981) documents how "the lads" in working-class schools in Britain actively resisted the efforts of teachers, imposing their own antischool values on the classroom that mirrored the factory-floor culture of working-class men. When Bowles and Gintis blame schools for reproducing class relations of capitalism, they may be attacking the wrong target, blaming schools for reproducing a culture that teachers are vainly trying to break.

Critics point out that, despite the Marxist commitment of Bowles and Gintis, the outcome of their theory is politically reactionary. It supports the status quo in that it leaves no space for individual or collective action to change the situation. The only viable option seems to be resignation or radical pessimism (Aronowitz and Giroux 1985, 79; Cole 1988, 35). More significantly, this ostensibly Marxist argument has been appropriated by spokespeople for the right wing in the United States. Conservatives are in full agreement with the view of Bowles and Gintis that schools are an adjunct to the labour market. They complain only that schools do not do this preparatory work well enough. The left wing seems to have no alternative to offer and to be constrained to silence (Aronowitz and Giroux 1985, 5–6). Aronowitz and Giroux (1985, 128) suggest that, despite their diametrically opposing political values, the philosophies of Marxist structuralism and capitalism share an uncritical acceptance of **scientism**: a reliance on simple cause and effect explanatory models that tend to reduce people to objects at the mercy of structural economic forces.

In this critique, we have referred to Marxist structuralism rather than Marxist theory in general, because there are important developments within contemporary Marxist theory that retain a radical critical perspective while rejecting the deterministic aspects of structuralism. This perspective shifts the focus of research from macro-studies of capitalism to the everyday interaction within the classroom of teachers and students.

How is it that capitalists are somehow able to dictate how people should relate to each other within classrooms? How do administrators, teachers, and students make sense of what is happening? How do they respond to such pressures? Why do they put up with them? When and how do they resist? These kinds of questions prompt a very different kind of research from that prevailing in either functionalist or

Marxist structuralist approaches. Rather than mass surveys or sweeping historical overviews, **cultural Marxism** and the **social construction of reality** perspectives favour research into the intimate details of interpersonal relations within classrooms. It is these relations that we explore below.

The Social Construction of Schooling*

Proponents of the social construction of reality do not view classrooms as the effects of social structures. Classrooms are the location within which the **social structures** of class, gender, or race are produced. The causal processes involved are the meaningful interactions between people in intimate everyday activities. Many studies of classrooms are beginning to piece together the mechanisms that produce what Bowles and Gintis identify as the social relations of capitalism.

The Social Construction of "Academic Ability" and "Merit"

Research in both the functionalist and political economy traditions has demonstrated how children are streamed on the basis of apparent capabilities and commitments, beginning in kindergarten or first grade; how pervasively such streaming carries over into senior classes when children are directed into vocational and academic programs; and the close correlation between such streaming and the social class backgrounds of the children. But we still have little understanding of how this happens. We need to get beyond the circular reasoning that capitalist society needs to reproduce and to justify class divisions. Social constructionist research explores the practices that accomplish what teachers come to recognize as "bright middle-class children" and also the common-sense reasoning through which the behaviour of young children becomes coded into categories such as "academically gifted" or "not very bright."

Observations and analysis of conversations between mothers and children in Toronto play-schools (Noble 1982; 1990) reveal the complex interactional practices through which these mothers produced the school readiness of their children. This mothering work involved training children in how to think in terms of abstract concepts and how to interact with other children and adult authority figures in ways that would fit them into the organization of school

---

*The draft of this section on social constructionist approaches to education was prepared by Dr. Peter Weeks as an extension of his work on the microsociology of everyday life for this text.

classrooms. Mothers continually prompted children into elaborating their sentences, introducing proper nouns and adjectives that were largely redundant in the immediate context. For example, one child displayed a small cut and explained, "I hit it here." Mother adds, "You hit your knee on the step."

Mothers also routinely took advantage of children's topics and activities to build mini-lesson structures into their interaction. A child playing with beads shows one to her mother and says, "Look what I got." Mother replies, "You've got beads. What colour are they?" More than a simple conversation is involved in such exchanges. The mother already knows the answer to the question and the child knows that the mother knows. The child is being encouraged and taught to display knowledge for adult evaluation (Noble 1982, 21).

Another mother playing alongside her child with a farm animals puzzle continually named and talked about each animal in turn, and also continually stressed the abstract category frame, "These are all <u>animals</u>, animals that live on the farm. Now let's put all the <u>animals</u> back in their place." When all the pieces were in place the mother asked, "How are all of these the same?" If the child failed to get the right answer, the mother might have prompted, "They are all _____." Another day the exercise will be run through again. Mothers showed by their intonational stress, and the energy directed to making it fun, just how favoured such games are.

Conversations with kindergarten teachers revealed how important such mother-child interactions can be in the subsequent evaluation of children as precocious and "ready for academic work" or "not very bright." Children in kindergarten were encouraged to engage in "free play," but not all play was regarded equally. Children who chose "mere play," like slides and sand box, were seen by teachers as not ready to go on to academic work. Children who "spontaneously" chose the ostensibly more mentally demanding matching and categorizing equipment were seen as ready to move ahead (Noble 1982, 12).

Children whose mothers had convincingly presented puzzle-matching games as fun have a distinct advantage. It was important for teacher evaluations that children respond to the instructional "question-answer-evaluation" sequence. When a teacher asks a child, "That's a nice truck. How many wheels does it have?" the child who does not respond appears as "not very bright" or "not very verbal" compared with the child who immediately responds with the number. The interpretive framework used by the teacher takes for granted that the child has been test-broken into this instructional sequence, but this presupposes years of prior exposure to such question-answer "games" and the interactional awareness that they *must* respond.

In another kindergarten classroom, the teacher displayed a picture of rain coming out of a cloud and asked, "What other word do you think of when you think of the word *rain*?" (Noble 1982, 29). Children offered a range of experiential associations like "raincoat," "umbrella," and "boots," but they were all passed over until the answer "weather" was offered. Children who have been sensitized in advance to their mothers preferring category words like "These are all animals" have a distinct advantage. Similarly, children who fill their sentences with proper nouns and adjectives appear brighter and more verbally advanced than children who do not bother to state the obvious.

A requirement of the organization of kindergarten classrooms is that children know they must drop their own activities and attend to the relevances of the teacher, and with appropriate posture and facial displays. Noble gives the example of children dropping whatever else they are doing to sit in a circle when the teacher announces that it is circle time for reading (1982, 16–18). Years of prior work, of subordinating bodies so that instruction can take place, are required for children to appear to do this "naturally" and so to appear bright and interested in what the teacher is doing. Parents may carry out this intensive one-on-one work over years, first positioning infants in front of objects they want the infant to focus on, screening other objects from view, and even pinning down limbs to enforce appropriate looking and listening. If this bodily learning is not already in place when a child enters school, it is difficult for a teacher to remedy it, even in very small groups. Noble describes scenes of kindergarten teachers struggling to restrain children in circles so that storytime could begin, and forcibly holding one child's head so he would pay attention to instructions.

Noble suggests that mothers with conventional middle-class backgrounds are far more likely to be familiar with such child development work than parents with lower-class backgrounds, and to have more time and resources with which to accomplish it. This observation, however, begs the further questions of how mothers acquire these child-developing competences and the conditions under which motherwork gets done.

Intelligence as Interactional Competence

Differences in levels of **interactional competence** among kindergarten children are directly reflected in supposedly formal or objective tests of intelligence. Noble (1990) gives three examples of test questions in the Wechsler Preschool and Primary Scale of Intelligence (WPPSI) (see Table 3). An answer is assigned a score of 0 if unacceptable; 1 for a response that is appropriate but vague, experiential, or

Table 3 Test Questions in the Wechsler Preschool and Primary Scale of Intelligence (WPPSI)

Example 1: Vocabulary Section

What is a knife?

Something to cut with . . . a weapon	2 points
Something to kill with	1 point
I have one . . . I play with it	0 points

Evidently, the 0 option is hopelessly experiential and does not treat *knife* as a general category. 1 is too restricted in terms of range of uses to count for the full 2 points.

Example 2: Similarities Section

Why shouldn't you play with matches?

So people won't get hurt . . . so your house won't burn down	2 points
You get burned . . . you can hurt yourself	1 point
You'll get a spanking	0 points

Though all these answers involve reasoning processes, some count more than others. While the 2-point answer is generalized in taking account of persons and property, the 0 option represents a refusal to take an adult view of morality.

Example 3: Comprehension Section

Why should children who are sick stay home?

So the class won't get the germs	2 points
So you don't get sicker	1 point
Their mommies get mad if they go out	0 points

To get the 2 points, the child again must take a generalized perspective, considering the interests of the organization (the school) rather than merely one's own.

Source: Adapted from Noble (1990, 54).

idiosyncratic; and 2 for a "better" answer that is more general, precise, and categorical.

According to Noble, what counts as intelligence includes:

1. being rule-governed, i.e., oriented to standard and conventional forms rather than personal and idiosyncratic ones;

2. being able to take a generalized position, external to yourself, and think in terms of the needs and interests of organizational entities beyond yourself;

3. being able to orient only to information given and solve questions asked only within the frame provided (Noble 1990, 55).

A child must know that general, categorical, and precise answers are preferred by adult testers over personal, experiential answers, in order to appear intelligent.

A similar study explores children's common-sense reasoning by asking them how they decided on their answers to a reading test (MacKay 1974a, 183–84). One stimulus sentence was about an animal that had been out in the rain. The "correct answer" was a picture of a room with dotted wallpaper walls and a floor imprinted with a trail of animal tracks. One child misperceived the picture to be the outside of a house, with the dotted wallpaper being

snow flakes. She consequently chose the "wrong" answer and scored zero. But her explanation clearly demonstrates interpretive skills in coming up with reasonable accounts of the world.

These interpretive studies reveal "brightness" as an interactional accomplishment rather than a measure of "real" intellectual capabilities. Teachers usually describe students in terms of cognitive attributes such as "bright" or "highly verbal" or else "nonverbal" or "not having a clue." But while these appear to be common-sense to teachers, Noble asserts that these are "ideological formulations" (1990, 45). In effect they are "class-defining practices."

Streaming as Practical Accomplishment

Teachers exercise a monopoly of professional competence to determine the academic ability and appropriate educational stream of children in school. How these allocative decisions are made influences the future career opportunities of children. Interpretive approaches to education have tried to make visible the common-sense reasoning practices through which teachers accomplish streaming as visibly and accountably appropriate.

Studies that use a **labelling theory** approach show how teachers' practices in categorizing children as they enter kindergarten can shape the children's entire school careers. Labelling theory was first developed in relation to studies of deviance. It explores the thesis that deviance is not inherent in any particular action, but in the judgments of witnesses. Those judgments determine how the person committing a "deviant" act comes to be treated thereafter.

Rist (1977) outlines a four-step process by which initial evaluations affect future options beginning with (1) the various evaluative mechanisms, both formal and informal, (2) how students react to them, (3) outcomes for personal interaction, particularly between teachers and students, and (4) the consequences of having a certain evaluative tag for the options available to students in the school (Rist 1977, 293). Rist argues that through such processes, failure in school becomes a self-fulfilling prophesy as teacher expectations are operationalized in the classroom to produce what the teacher had initially assumed.

Rist carried out a longitudinal study of an inner-city American urban ghetto school following the progress of children in kindergarten through to second grade. Within eight days of beginning kindergarten the teacher permanently assigned each child to a seat at one of the three tables for the remainder of the school year, based on her perception of their academic promise. Her judgments were based on immediate experience of interacting with the children in class for the first few days, together with knowledge of their older siblings, and information from admission forms and school social workers indicating which children were welfare recipients. The children assigned to Table 1, nearest the teacher, were generally more talkative to the teacher and more familiar with standard American English, and they participated well as group members.

One can speculate that children who had been coached in their prekindergarten years to use elaborate sentences with proper nouns and adjectives, who are cued in to the compulsory instructional form of question-answer-evaluation sequences, who know that abstract, category terms are preferred over personal associations in question-answer games, who choose matching and categorizing toys over the sandbox, and who have learned to subordinate their bodies and facial expressions to adult relevances, are far more likely to end up at Table 1. It was also clear in Rist's study that the children assigned to Table 1 were neat and clean in appearance and of higher average socioeconomic backgrounds than the children assigned to Table 3.

Once assigned to Table 1, these children were designated as "fast learners" and received more teaching time and attention while the "slow learners" at Table 3 were taught less frequently, subjected to more control, and received less support from the teacher. The gap in completion of academic material between the two groups widened during the course of the school year. Objective measures of past performance seemed to confirm the appropriateness of initial labelling on the eighth day of kindergarten. Two years later, the children from Table 1 in kindergarten were almost all together in Table 1 of grade 2, labelled as the "Tigers" or the winners, and they were still receiving more teaching time than other groups.

Another study of teachers' labelling practices (Becker 1977) confirms the high correlation between assessments of ability and socioeconomic backgrounds. He records a typical teacher's assessment of "slum" children:

> They don't have the right kind of study habits. They can't seem to apply themselves as well. Of course, it's not their fault; they aren't brought up right. After all, the parents in a neighbourhood like that really aren't interested. . . . But as I say, those children don't learn very quickly. A great many of them don't seem to be really interested in getting an education. . . . It's hard to get anything done with children like that.

Children from upper-class neighbourhoods seemed to respond much more readily than slum children to ideas and suggestions from teachers and concentrated more on lessons. To get attention in a chemistry class in the slum area school, teachers felt they had to do flashy demonstrations with lots of noise and smoke.

Maintaining the Home-School Relation

Each of these studies, by Noble, Rist, and Becker, repeats the same observation that the behaviour of children in kindergarten is closely correlated with socioeconomic status. The children who fit most readily into the social organization of schools are "middle-class" children. But we still have limited understanding of how differences in parenting practices by social class are accomplished. We need more research into the organization of peoples' lives and the meanings that people bring to the situations they find themselves in—to the grinding effects of poverty and the disorganizing practices that continually threaten to disrupt what poor people manage to put together. The teacher's comment that parents in poor neighbourhoods "really aren't interested" in the lives of their children is a summary term for ignorance rather than an explanation of differences in parenting work.

Intensive parenting work is also involved in accomplishing the appearance of being an "interested" parent (Noble 1982, 39–67). "Support" for school is not merely a matter of positive attitudes; it involves real resources of time, energy, and skills. Parents require tacit knowledge of

Literacy support groups attempt to redress the imbalance of different parenting practices.

A child's *mind* is an *open* book.

As a parent, it is your responsibility to fill the pages of a child's mind with wonder and joy. Reading together is a delightful way of accomp-lishing this and a means of ensuring that your child's future remains an open book.

Prepare a young mind for tomorrow. Open a book today.

Distribution of this message was made possible by the Canadian Advertising Foundation.

ABC Canada Literacy Commission

what kind of support work and what kind of communication is appropriate. Managing parent-teacher interactions requires skills in picking up cues from teachers, knowing acceptable ways of asking questions about a child's progress or about what goes on in the classroom, and ways of expressing concern that will be interpreted by teachers as cooperative, responsible, and emotionally stable rather than hostile, unreasonable, or overprotective. These are class-related skills. Middle-class mothers are likely to have far more experience of interacting as equals with people in professional careers than do working-class mothers.

The teaching profession generally claims expertise in the specific field of cognitive development with parents responsible for auxiliary work. Noble describes parent-teacher meetings as often providing a forum for teachers and principals to disseminate professional views on child-management to parents, with parents being held accountable for the socioemotional development. Parents can establish their presence as "interested" by asking about their child's "adjustment problems" in the classroom, and otherwise deferring to the teacher's professional expertise. Teachers, in turn, may be influenced to notice and to give more attention to a particular child in order to have some-thing to talk to an "interested" parent about. But the parent-teacher relationship must be handled carefully if it is to result in protecting and improving children's chances at school.

Many working-class parents do not know how to play the parent-teacher game, do not feel at ease in contact with the school, and do not know how to raise topics with teachers. They withdraw under the weight of accumulated small intimidations and join the ranks of parents who appear "not interested" in their children. Parents who openly confront teachers and challenge their expertise may be regarded as "trouble-makers" with "personal problems," and they may well generate retaliation against their children in the classroom. Parents need to know how streaming works operationally. Objections to disadvantageous streaming decisions are more likely to be successful when parents do not attack test scores or teachers directly, but use the jargon of testing to focus on discrepancies.

In summary, the relationships between teachers as professionals and both children and parents from middle-class backgrounds work more smoothly than relationships with working-class families. Noble's work tries to make visible the interactional and discourse skills that accomplish this relation. Becker interprets his data as teacher reactions to cultural variations associated with social-class backgrounds, but much more than mere prejudice is involved.

Kindergarten teachers in Noble's study had to depend on children's willingness to sit quietly in a circle in order to read stories to them. On bad days, virtually one-on-one bodily monitoring was needed, with an adult blocking get-aways and physically separating children from their toys before circle time could begin (Noble 1982, 16). A wide range of interactional competences, bodily subordination, and attending to adult relevances have to be assumed before lessons can happen.

Lessons as Social Accomplishments

Lessons do not happen naturally by themselves, either for students or for teachers. A branch of ethnomethodology known as **conversation analysis** researches detailed features of student-teacher interaction in lessons, using the technique of audio- and video-recordings. The questions explored include: the organization of turn-taking (McHoul 1978); teacher strategies to maximize participation of the class as a cohort (Payne and Hustler 1980); the detection and handling of deviance (Hester 1991); the overall organization of lessons from beginning to end (MacKay 1974a; Mehan 1979); and collaboration in students' writing stories employing computers (Heap 1986).

Weeks's study of primary-school oral reading lessons (1985) makes visible the error-correction sequences by which teachers alert a student that there is a problem and present an opportunity for the student to come up with the correct word. Complex interpretive practices or working assumptions are involved in both teacher and student getting the correction completed. The teacher may only hint at a problem with a brief "hm hm." The student has to have sufficient interpretive skills to pick up on the hint, figure out what the problem is, which word is wrong, and what to do about it. After a two-second pause the student enunciates another word, in a rising tone that indicates uncertainty or waiting for confirmation. The teacher's second "hm hm," with a different tone from before, means something quite different from the first utterance—a positive evaluation of the student's answer. Following this, the student resumes reading aloud from the text.

Highly complex but tacit interactional competences are assumed between teacher and student, and other members of the reading group, to get through this self-correction instructional sequence. Other correction techniques involve the teacher giving explicit directions like "Watch for the period!"—but even then the student has to know what to do with it. It is clearly not enough just to watch for a period; the reader has to manage proper intonation and to make a break at the right place. Students who are not attuned to such cues will not be able to follow the lesson.

Other studies explore the turn-taking organization of classrooms, and how teachers maintain authority by such practices as controlling the turn-taking, selecting specific students for next turns, who then have to return the "floor" to the teacher rather than hold on to it or select other students to speak (McHoul 1978). Teachers may organize lessons by posing a question that students lack the resources to answer at the beginning, but that they come to answer in the end through processes of hinting and filling in (Hammersley 1990). Teachers also commonly use "undirected questions" addressed to the class-as-a-whole, such as "Who knows the distance between Toronto and Montreal?" Such seemingly open invitations to respond are accompanied by the practice of students raising hands to bid for a turn, with the teacher as arbiter among competing bids.

It is through such practices that teachers organize the collectivity of students as a **cohort**—as one collective party to the talk with the teacher acting as the other party (Payne and Hustler 1980, 56). Students are thus led to take the teacher as their single focus of attention, with any one student being a potential target for the teacher's next question. Such practices also discourage students from talking to each other, except for prompting each other with candidate answers. Students who have not mastered the proper posture and facial expressions for conveying attention to the teacher are likely to be targeted.

Other research suggests that teachers tend to use positive evaluations like "That's right," "Okay," or "Well done" quite frequently, while avoiding negative ones by such tactics as offering cues to correct answers, and asking other members of the class if they agree or have other suggestions (McHoul 1990). This can be seen as another way of accomplishing "cohorting" by opening opportunities for wider student participation, and using each answer as an occasion for further instruction (Weeks 1994). When such tacit cohorting work and turn-taking practices fail to elicit appropriate responses from students, as in the slum schools described by Becker (1977), or the Native schools described in the previous section, teaching may be experienced as very difficult, if not impossible.

The Limitations of Social Constructionism

Interpretive perspectives open up the "black box" of schooling to show the complex interaction between background factors like social class and the routine practices of the school. We begin to see the practices that constitute what is traditionally understood as cultural deprivation, and how the social structural characteristics of inequality are accomplished through intimate everyday interaction in classrooms.

The potential strength of this approach can also become its weakness. Explanations that focus on the intimate behaviour of individuals in classrooms risk losing sight of the structural contexts in which such interactions are embedded. Individual mothers, teachers, and students appear as blameworthy for failing to prepare students adequately for school, or for failing to adapt classroom instruction to compensate for different behavioural profiles. It remains important to recognize how structures of capitalism—the commercialization of education and the impact of corporate agendas on curriculum budget cutbacks, intensification of teachers' work, standardized curriculum and evaluation packages imposed on teachers, and the like—constrain teaching and learning in critical ways. The special contribution of the interpretive perspective is that it provides ways of seeing how these seemingly external structural factors work, through the activities of people at the level of everyday interaction.

Feminist Theory in Education

Until the beginning of the twentieth century women in Canada were largely excluded from all forms of higher education, and most had little formal schooling beyond learning to read and write. By the 1990s, the pattern was dramatically different. Women and men are equally likely

Figure 5 Percentage Distribution of Full-time Fall Enrolment in Post-secondary Career Programs by Sex and Program Field, Canada, 1990–91

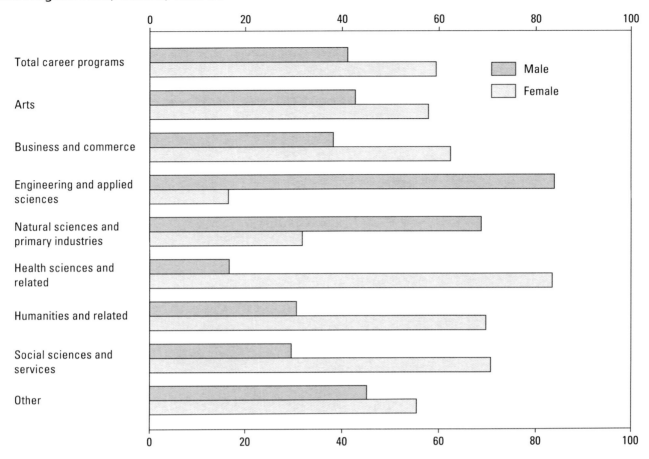

Source: Statistics Canada, Cat. 81-222, p. 17.

to graduate from high school and enter undergraduate programs; however, they remain concentrated in different fields of study. Women are overrepresented in arts, nursing, and domestic science programs, and significantly underrepresented in mathematics, physical sciences, computer science, and technology (see Figure 5 and Table 4).

Feminist research in education has focused attention on the different experiences of girls and boys in the school system. Much of this research has adopted the theoretical perspectives and methodology of social constructionism, recording detailed observation of classroom interaction to explore the practices through which gender differentiation is accomplished. Richer's (1979) study of an Ontario kindergarten class displays multiple ways in which the teacher emphasized gender distinctions. Gender was repeatedly used to organize classroom activites. Boys and girls were asked to line up separately before moving from one activity to another, to go to the library, the gymnasium, or the dining room, and to get ready to go home. Boys and girls hung their outdoor clothing in sep-

arate areas. Commonly they were pitted against each other by such comments as "Who can do this the fastest, boys or girls?" In coordination exercises commands were routinely given separately to boys and girls: "Boys, put your fingers on your nose; girls, put your hands in your laps; boys, touch your toes," etc. When any of the children responded to an activity intended for the other sex, the teacher commonly drew attention to it with a comment like "Are you a girl? I thought all along you were a boy" (Richer 1979, 201).

Observations of classroom interaction suggest that teachers may respond differently to girls and boys, and in ways that encourage boys to dominate classroom space while subtly devaluing the girls. Sadker and Sadker (1987, 144) found that teachers in the classes they observed tended to accept answers shouted out by boys who did not raise their hands and wait to be given a turn. When girls behaved similarly they were more likely to be reprimanded. Observations of elementary grades suggest that girls tend to be quieter and more obedient whereas boys are more likely to bounce

Table 4 Full-time Undergraduate Enrolment, by Field of Study and Sex, Canada 1983–84 and 1991–92

Field of Study	1983–84 Percent Male	Percent Female	Total	1991–92 Percent Male	Percent Female	Total
Agricultural and biological sciences						
Agriculture	62.9	37.1	4 713	54.5	45.5	3 511
Biology	50.2	49.8	9 639	44.9	55.1	17 200
Household science	3.6	96.4	3 513	9.2	90.8	3 651
Veterinary medicine	45.9	54.1	1 053	35.7	64.3	1 187
Zoology	54.4	45.6	781	43.2	56.8	1 017
Education						
Education	25.6	74.4	27 431	25.3	74.7	37 777
Physical education	47.7	52.3	12 260	51.5	48.5	15 428
Engineering and applied sciences						
Architecture	70.0	30.0	2 220	64.0	36.0	2 344
Engineering	90.2	9.8	37 724	84.0	16.0	39 897
Forestry	88.4	11.6	1 335	80.9	19.1	1 325
Fine arts	39.7	60.3	13 872	38.3	61.7	16 459
Health professions						
Dental studies and research	73.8	26.2	1 982	59.7	40.3	1 749
Medical studies and research	58.2	41.8	8 411	54.8	45.2	8 389
Nursing	3.2	96.8	6 634	6.6	93.4	7 428
Pharmacy	32.8	67.2	2 696	38.5	61.5	3 183
Rehabilitation medicine	10.6	89.4	2 510	16.0	84.0	3 796
Humanities						
History	58.6	41.4	4 745	54.4	45.6	11 844
Languages	28.0	72.0	12 757	26.7	73.3	18 352
Other	51.7	48.2	9 858	46.9	53.1	13 401
Mathematics and physical sciences						
Chemistry	67.7	32.3	3 052	60.8	39.2	3 938
Geology	79.3	20.7	3 249	72.4	27.6	1 201
Mathematics	64.6	35.4	8 262	60.9	39.1	9 063
Computer science	72.7	27.3	12 250	79.8	20.2	9 039
Physics	88.2	11.8	2 407	83.0	17.0	2 753
Social sciences						
Business and commerce	58.8	41.2	48 835	54.1	45.9	57 382
Economics	68.8	31.2	10 009	67.8	32.2	12 278
Geography	64.1	35.9	4 466	60.0	40.0	7 680
Law	55.8	44.2	9 892	48.8	51.2	11 284
Political science	63.1	36.9	6 712	56.0	44.0	12 933
Psychology	27.4	72.6	13 187	23.9	76.1	23 184
Social work	18.3	81.7	4 227	16.9	83.1	5 587
Sociology	34.0	66.0	6 157	29.2	70.8	13 404
Grand Total*	52.6	47.4	397 351	49.8	56.2	485 418

Source: Reproduced by authority of the Minister of Industry, 1994. Adapted from Statistics Canada (1994e), *Education in Canada: A Statistical Review*, Cat. 81-229, table 13, pp. 84–87.

*Individual totals will not add up to grand total because certain smaller fields, labelled "other," are omitted from this table.

around, ask questions, and be aggressive. One of the consequences seems to be that teachers generally find girls easier to deal with, so concentrate more attention on boys. Boys are likely to receive more disapproval, scolding, and other forms of negative attention than do girls, but they are also likely to receive more attention and praise (Huston 1983, 439; Basow 1986, 126). Teachers also admitted to finding boys more fun to teach (Schneider and Coutts 1979; Russell 1987, 240). Russell's observations of grade 12 classes revealed that teachers were one-and-one-half to five times more likely to direct questions to boys than to girls. Girls dominated verbal interaction with the teacher in only 7 percent of the classes, while boys dominated in about 63 percent. In only about 30 percent of classes did teachers seem to select girls and boys equally in turn-taking interaction.

Observational studies also suggest that teachers tend to hold different expectations about the academic abilities of girls and boys. When girls outperformed boys in early grades, teachers explained their "overachievement" as a result of their docility and conscientiousness, subtly devaluing their work (Russell 1987, 241). Conversely, when girls fell behind boys in high-school mathematics and science courses, teachers were inclined to treat this as "natural" and consistent with their lower expectations for girls in these subjects. Girls were more likely to be advised to drop such subjects than coached to improve their performance (Shapiro 1990, 57). High-school counsellors routinely encouraged high-achieving girls into "women's work" such as social work, teaching, and secretarial positions rather than into better-paid male-dominated business and professional positions (Russell 1987). Years of exposure to such classroom practices may accomplish what Porter, Porter, and Blishen (1982, 125–129) describe as the lower self-esteem of girls and lower self-assessment of their abilities than boys, even when they outperformed boys on school tests.

An explosion of feminist studies of classroom practices and school textbooks since the 1970s, combined with political lobbying, has produced significant changes in the Canadian school system (Mackie 1991, 162–165). Much effort has gone into changing the content of textbooks and school curricula to include nonsexist materials and present women in a wider variety of nonsex-typed activities (Gaskell and McLaren 1987, 8). Efforts are also being made by universities to encourage more girls in high school to consider careers in science and engineering (Armour 1988).

The question is whether such remedial actions will be sufficient to overcome wider social pressures beyond the schools. Richer (1988) carried out a comparative study of cohorts of students in an Ottawa elementary school before and after a seven-year consciousness-raising program in the school. The school established a "positive action committee"

that provided films and reading materials for teachers on issues of gender and organized several seminars on teaching practices. In 1979, and again in 1986, children in grades 1 through 6 were asked to draw a picture of themselves engaged in their favourite activity. Comparison of the pictures showed virtually no drop in sex stereotyping. In 1986, fully 97 percent of boys' drawings and 87 percent of girls' drawings depicted sex-segregated activities. Richer concludes that influences outside the school have a greater impact on children than classroom teachers.

More detailed studies of classroom interaction are beginning to uncover ways in which students actively resist efforts by teachers to challenge gender and class stereotypes. Girls from a lower-class district in England collectively sabotaged lessons by tacitly and even blatantly withdrawing their attention (McRobbie 1978). When asked what they did during math lessons, they gave such answers as "carve boys' names on my desk," "comb my hair under the lid of the desk," "put makeup on, or look in my mirror." McRobbie suggests that while parents and teachers do try to encourage girls to study more to get a good job, the girls' own immediate experience of the types of jobs open to women like them does little to induce them to focus on schoolwork. They know that their chance for a decent home and money to support their children depends primarily upon the superior wages of a man. Hence, from as young as thirteen and fourteen years, their preoccupation is with boyfriends and going steady. Success in the classroom consists of asserting their "femaleness" and spending vast amounts of time discussing boyfriends in loud voices that disrupt the class.

This is irrational behaviour from the perspective of the teachers who, at least initially in their careers, are committed to trying to break this pattern and open new options for the girls. But it is fully rational from the perspective of the working-class girls themselves in the face of their expectations for their own future. Actually, it may be the teachers who are being unrealistic and irrational in assuming that they can somehow change the life chances for more than a minority of these girls. It is little wonder that many teachers become more realistic with experience and opt for a more class-biased curriculum to which the girls will respond. In a sense schools fail the girls, but in another sense girls fail the schools. The process of class and gender formation is thus mutually constructed within the everyday struggles of the classroom.

Feminism in the Universities

As noted above, women are entering Canadian universities in greater numbers than ever before, equalling the numbers of men at undergraduate level. Feminist research, however, suggests that women students generally experience university campuses as very much "male turf," with resentment, petty harassment, and depreciation of women commonplace.

A study by Hall and Sandler (1984) suggests that female students generally, and especially those who enrol in the traditional male bastions of physical sciences and engineering, face a "chilly campus climate" that is not conducive to learning. Women students tend to receive less attention and less feedback than male students from the predominantly male faculty. They are more likely to experience disparaging comments about their work or their commitment to studies, or comments that focus on their appearance rather than their performance. They are likely to be counselled into lower career goals than men. As graduates, they are less likely to be included as co-researchers with faculty in academic publications. Women who interrupt their studies, or attend part-time while raising children, are not taken seriously. A commentary written by a female geology student some 10 years after this article was published suggests that little has changed (*Globe and Mail*, 13 July 1994). The student recounts being the butt of a series of more and more threatening practical "jokes" in the geology labs, combined with a constant barrage of insulting remarks about women in general. Repeated sexual comments and innuendoes from one of her chemistry professors were directed at female students in the class.

Males dominate classroom and seminar discussions. Male styles of communication are highly assertive, combined with physical gestures that express ease, dominance, and control. They are more likely to interrupt other speakers and to control the topic of conversation. In laboratory classes, female students routinely complain that men take control over the equipment, relegating female students to note-takers. Females tend to be more personal in their communications, offering more self-disclosure rather than impersonal and abstract styles of speech. This style is disparaged as less intelligent. Women are more reticent in taking over conversations and tend to encourage other speakers. They often feel that they are imposing on advisers rather than that they have a right to ask questions.

Athletic activities by women get less support and attention than do male sports teams. Women are demeaned when campus organizations screen pornographic movies as fund-raisers and when student newspapers publish sexist articles and advertisements. Women who live in residences often face petty harassment from men in the guise of fun. In 1989, a rash of such actions and verbal assaults directed at female students, and feminists in particular, made headlines in Canadian newspapers. At Queen's University some male students mocked a campaign against date rape on campus by displaying posters bearing slogans such as "No Means Tie Her Up" and "No Means Kick Her in the Teeth" (*Globe and Mail*, 11 Nov. 1989, D1–2; 17 Nov. 1989). Engineering students' newspapers at Queen's and the University of Alberta, in particular, have been criticized for sexist content "that portrays women in a thoroughly demeaning and abusive manner" (*Globe and Mail*, 13 Dec. 1989, A5).

On 6 December 1989, a man armed with a semi-automatic rifle entered the engineering building at the University of Montreal. He massacred 14 women engineering students before turning the gun on himself. In a three-page suicide note found on his body, the man expressed his hatred of feminists, claiming that they had ruined his life. In the days that followed, seven male students at the University of Toronto set off firecrackers outside the women's residence, spreading panic. Following this experience, administrations on many campuses took steps to institute or strengthen policies against sexual harassment, to curtail the sexist content of engineering newspapers, and to set up programs to support and promote women in sciences and engineering. We have yet to see how effective these initiatives will be.

Feminist Pedagogy

Feminists also criticize traditional methods of teaching within universities as perpetuating a masculine orientation to learning that alienates women students. They echo the work of Paolo Freire in challenging oppressive and hierarchical approaches to knowledge as truths handed down from authority figures. Emphasis in lectures and seminars on competition, confrontation, and winning debates in a public forum, intimidate and silence many women, along with other students outside the dominant white middle-class male group, who lack a sense of social mastery, or lack the will to put others down. Belenky et al. (1985) suggest that women generally respond better to "connected teaching" that emphasizes creative reflection on personal experience, and that confirms not merely that women can learn, but that they already know something through personal experience.

The problem they highlight is that hierarchical methods of teaching are so closely associated with authority and professional competence that lecturers who are committed to involving students as equals in the classroom, and who affirm the value of knowledge based on personal experience, risk appearing weak and incompetent to their students (Bezucha 1985; Friedman 1985). Female professors can find themselves simultaneously challenged and resented by students, whichever approach they take. Students who accept authority, high standards, discipline, and toughness from male professors, often deeply resent the same demands from female professors. It violates their sense that females should not be in authority positions over them. Feminist pedagogy also clashes with the hierarchical structure of universities, and the necessity of grading students on classroom performance.

Feminist Theory and Resistance

The introduction of women's courses into the curriculum of Canadian universities in the 1970s met with strong opposition, bordering on rage (Smith 1992, 208). The women professors who were trying to develop the courses were subject to personal insults and their professional competence was called into question. Traditions of rational debate did not seem to extend to consideration of women's studies. By the mid-1990s, most Canadian universities have established some courses spread across the arts curriculum, but women's studies programs still tend to be seen as frills, given second-rate status and limited funds. Students aspiring to professional and corporate careers are discouraged from taking such courses. A common strategy for sidelining feminist courses, Bezucha suggests (1985, 90), is for established professors to support hiring a few women to teach designated women's studies courses, and then to use this to justify not including anything on women in the content of their own courses. Ignorance of feminist theory and research is studiously maintained. This studied ignorance is not emptiness or mere absence of knowledge. It is an active refusal to learn (Aronowitz and Giroux 1985, 159).

Students who are exposed to feminist theory develop their own forms of resistance, as their established frameworks of meaning are challenged. One response is to deny the validity of any evidence that goes against the dominant view of reality. Culley describes the common reactions of students, both female and male, when exposed for the first time to readily available statistics on education, employment categories, and income levels of women compared to men:

> Who published those statistics?" (U.S. Department of Labor.) "When was that?" (Any time before yesterday is pre-history.) "Those figures must be based on women who work part time." Or, "A lot of women choose not to work, you know, are they in there?" Then soon after, "You can't get anywhere hating men, you can't blame them." And quietly to themselves or to each other, "I heard she's divorced, she's probably a lesbian or something" (1985, 212).

Culley suggests that it is important for teachers to let students express these defensive efforts to distance, discount, and deny. Only then can these responses be examined and questioned. Other professors who teach feminist theory describe instances of outright hostility from some students who actively try to disrupt classes by joking, chatting loudly, jeering, and attacking the credibility and professional competence of the professor (Bezucha 1985, 214; McIntyre 1986).

For all the difficulties encountered, feminist theory and research has made a significant impact across the arts curriculum. Traditional approaches may still be dominant but they have lost their taken-for-granted character. As radical pedagogy, feminism is potentially an agent of change through both the process and the content of teaching. Charlotte Bunch (1983) describes how she left university teaching to work full-time in the women's movement but later returned to university because she had become convinced that the development of feminist theory is essential to political action. Theory is not just a body of facts and opinions. It involves the development of explanations that can guide actions.

Bunch proposes a four-part model of theory. The first part is *description*. Changing people's perceptions of the world through new descriptions of reality is usually a prerequisite for changing that reality. In the 1960s, few people would have thought of American women as oppressed, but now the injustices and oppression experienced by women are widely recognized. Feminist work, which described that oppression in a number of different ways, played a critical role in making it visible. The second element of theory is *analysis*. Analysis involves trying to understand why the reality described in feminist work exists and what perpetuates it. The third element is *vision*. The work of envisioning what should exist involves examining our basic assumptions about human nature and relationships. The fourth element of theory is *strategy*. Theoretical understanding of how social relations work is essential to planning ways of changing those relations. Teaching feminist theory thus involves teaching the basic skills of critical literacy—how to read, analyze, and think about ideas—and challenging students to develop their own ideas and to analyze the assumptions behind their actions.

CONCLUSION

Compulsory schooling has a profound effect on children's lives and upon their life chances after leaving school. This much is beyond dispute. It also seems clear that children with different class, gender, and ethnic characteristics experience schooling and higher education in very different ways, and end up with markedly unequal levels of educa-

tional attainment and formal credentials. Different perspectives in sociology struggle with the questions of how and why schooling affects children in these ways.

Functionalist and political economy perspectives agree that schools perform the function of selecting and allocating children for adult roles within the economy, but they focus on very different factors in their analysis of how this selection process works. Functionalists suggest that, by and large, schools do provide equal opportunities for all children to reach their full academic potential and to strive for social mobility. They locate the causes of unequal attainment by class and by sex primarily in socialization processes that occur within families, largely outside the influence of schools. Political economy theory, in contrast, locates the causes of low aspirations and unequal attainment in capitalism. This perspective takes for granted the argument that capitalists seek to standardize and deskill work in the interests of cheapening labour and increasing profits. Scope for creativity seems confined to the elite who direct the huge corporations. This political economy is held responsible for structuring schools in the corporate image.

The social constructionist perspective begins from the assumption that people, in their everyday interactions, create the social world and give it the patterns and the meanings that we come to see as the structures of capitalism. Research into intimate interaction within classrooms explores how students react to and against the pressures of school, in terms of how they themselves foresee the utility or irrelevance of education for their future lives. Teachers also struggle to retain some autonomy in their working lives, amid pressures to adopt packaged curricula, textbooks, and technical devices pushed by corporate interests, often acting in concert with school boards and college management.

The central debate within this perspective concerns how far it is possible for people to retain autonomy of thought and action in the face of the established ways of thinking within the prevailing culture. Teachers are criticized by radicals, and increasingly also by members of the business class, for not developing the capacity for creative and innovative thinking in their students. Yet, they themselves work in contexts that seem increasingly designed to minimize their own capacity for creative teaching. Feminist pedagogy is one form of teaching that takes seriously the possibility of challenging and changing established social relations by developing the power of critical reflection in students. The question for the future is whether this power will be neutralized and accommodated in the service of greater profits, or whether people will use it to push for more fundamental change.

SUGGESTED READING

An excellent study of education from the functionalist perspective is by John Porter, Marion Porter, and Bernard Blishen, *Stations and Callings: Making It Through the School System* (1982). Chapter 1 of this book discusses the theory of equality and educational opportunity, exploring the different interpretations that can be placed on the notion of equal opportunity. Chapter 3 outlines in a clear and precise form the basic ideas of socialization and self-concept in functionalist and symbolic interaction theory. The authors then incorporate these concepts into an elaborate explanatory model that guides their research into educational aspirations. The text includes many easily understandable statistical graphs and tables.

The main text that presents the structuralist Marxist perspective is by Samuel Bowles and Herbert Gintis, *Schooling in Capitalist America* (1976). A briefer introduction to the ideas debated at length in the text is provided in a collection of articles edited by Mike Cole, *Bowles and Gintis Revisited: Correspondence and Contradiction in Educational Theory* (1988). In the prologue and Chapters 12 and 13, they address some of the criticisms raised against structuralist Marxist theory. Chapters 1 and 3 provide a brief but useful overview of criticisms of the work of Bowles and Gintis.

A good introduction to the social construction of reality approach, and one that complements the work of Bowles and Gintis, is by Jean Anyon, "Social Class and the Hidden Curriculum of Work" (1980). She describes in detail the very different teaching techniques that she observed in elementary school classes in working-class, middle-class, and elite school districts. A classic study in the rejection of school values by working-class children is P. Willis, *Learning to Labour: How Working Class Kids Get Working Class Jobs* (1981). Willis shows how boys have absorbed the shopfloor culture of their working-class fathers, including sexist and racist values, and utilize them to support their rejection of school. A similar study by Angela McRobbie, "Working-class Girls and the Culture of Femininity" (1978) describes how these girls reject the school culture in favour of their paramount concern with sexuality and attracting boyfriends.

Michael Apple's work, *Teachers and Texts: A Political Economy of Class and Gender Relations in Education* (1986), explores the contemporary work of teachers. Apple documents the pressures that threaten to reduce the role of teachers from autonomous professionals to deskilled technicians, constrained to use standardized curriculum packages.

A good overview of the feminist approach to education is provided by a collection of articles edited by Jane Gaskell and Arlene Tigar McLaren, *Women and Education: A Canadian Perspective* (1987). Among other useful updates, the collection includes a reprint of the classic article by Dorothy Smith, "An Analysis of Ideological Structures and How Women Are Excluded: Considerations for Academic Women" (1975).

QUESTIONS

1. What does Parsons see as the functional importance of women teachers in primary education?

2. Distinguish between *equality of condition*, *equality of opportunity*, and *equality of outcome*.

3. In what sense can the goals of liberal education—the development of individual potential, equality, and social continuity—be seen as internally contradictory?

4. How does structural correspondence theory account for the shift in higher education from broad liberal arts to packages of credits?

5. What principles does the educational reformer Ivan Illich advocate in his vision of a deschooled society, and why is this vision rejected as unrealistic by the Marxist theorists Bowles and Gintis?

6. How is the North American Free Trade Deal implicated in the structural correspondence between schooling and global capitalism?

7. What problems are highlighted by the notion of *a vacuum ideology* in reference to the policies of white educators towards Native peoples?

8. In what respects is intelligence an interactional accomplishment rather than a measure of intellectual capabilities?

9. What practices are involved in parents accomplishing themselves as "interested" in their children's education from the perspective of teachers?

10. What teaching practices are implicated in promoting the passivity of girls relative to boys in typical classroom interaction?

KEY TERMS

assimilation

background understandings

cohort

conversation analysis

correspondence theory

cultural Marxism

culture of domination

equality of condition

equality of opportunity

headstart program

institutions

interactional competence

labelling theory

meritocracy thesis

psychological reductionism

reductionism

right of national treatment

scientism

social construction of reality/social constructionism

social structures

structural correspondence theory

vacuum ideology

REFERENCES

Anyon, J. 1980. "Social Class and the Hidden Curriculum of Work." *Journal of Education* 162 (Winter): 67–92.

Apple, M. 1986. *Teachers and Texts: A Political Economy of Class and Gender Relations in Education*. London: Routledge & Kegan Paul.

Apple, M. 1988. "Facing the Complexity of Power: For a Parallelist Position in Critical Educational Studies." In *Bowles and Gintis Revisited: Correspondence and Contradiction*. Ed. M. Cole. London: Falmer Press, 112–130.

Armour, M.A. 1988. "The WISEST Approach." *New Trial* 43 (Autumn): 21–23.

Aronowitz, S., and H.A. Giroux. 1985. *Education Under Siege: The Conservative, Liberal, and Radical Debate Over Schooling*. Hadley, MA: Bergin and Garvey.

Basow, S.A. 1986. *Gender Stereotypes: Traditions and Alternatives*. 2nd ed. Monterey, CA: Brooks/Cole.

Becker, H.S. 1977. "Social Class Variations in the Teacher-Pupil Relationship." In *School and Society*. Ed. B.R. Cosin et al. 2nd ed. London: Routledge & Kegan Paul.

Belenky, M.F., B.M. Clinchy, N.R. Goldberger, and J.M. Tarule. 1985. *Women's Ways of Knowing*. New York: Basic Books.

Bezucha, R.J. 1985. "Feminist Pedagogy as a Subversive Activity." In *Gendered Subjects: The Dynamics of Feminist Teaching*. Ed. M. Culley and C. Portuges. London: Routledge & Kegan Paul.

Bowles, S., and H. Gintis. 1976. *Schooling in Capitalist America*. New York: Basic Books.

Bowles, S., and H. Gintis. 1988. "Prologue: The Correspondence Principle." In *Bowles and Gintis Revisited: Correspondence and Contradiction*. Ed. M. Cole. London: Falmer Press, 1–4.

Braverman, H. 1974. *Labor and Monopoly Capital: The Degradation of Work in the Twentieth Century*. New York: Monthly Review Press.

Bunch, C. 1983. "Not by Degrees: Feminist Theory and Education." In *Learning Our Way: Essays in Feminist Education*. Ed. C. Bunch and S. Pollack. Trumansburg, NY: Crossing Press, 248–260.

Calvert, J., with L. Kuehn. 1993. *Pandora's Box, Corporate Power, Free Trade and Canadian Education*. Our Schools/Our Selves Education Foundation. Monograph series no. 13 (July/Aug.).

Cole, M. ed. 1988. *Bowles and Gintis Revisited: Correspondence and Contradiction.* London: Falmer Press.

Culley, M. 1985. "Anger and Authority in the Introductory Women's Studies Classroom." In *Gendered Subjects: The Dynamics of Feminist Teaching.* Ed. M. Culley and C. Portuges. London: Routledge & Kegan Paul, 209–218.

Curtis, B. 1987. "Preconditions of the Canadian State: Educational Reform and the Construction of a Public in Upper Canada, 1837–1846." In *The Benevolent State: The Growth of Welfare in Canada.* Ed. A. Moscovitch and J. Albert. Toronto: Garamond.

Freire, P. 1970. *Pedagogy of the Oppressed.* New York: Seabury.

Friedman, S.S. 1985. "Authority in the Feminist Classroom: A Contradiction in Terms?" In *Gendered Subjects: The Dynamics of Feminist Teaching.* Ed. M. Culley and C. Portuges. Boston: Routledge & Kegan Paul, 203–209.

Gabriel, J. 1986. "School and Stratification." Honours thesis, St. Thomas University.

Gaskell, J., and A.T. McLaren, eds. 1987. *Women and Education: A Canadian Perspective.* Calgary: Detselig.

Hammersley, M. 1990. *Classroom Ethnography: Empirical and Methodological Essays.* Toronto: OISE Press.

Heap, J.L. 1986. "Classroom Talk: A Criticism of McHoul." Paper, Department of Sociology, Ontario Institute for Studies in Education.

Hester, S. 1991. "The Social Facts of Deviance in Schools: A Study of Mundane Reason." *British Journal of Sociology* 42 (Sept.): 443–463.

Huston, A.C. 1983. "Sex Typing." In *Handbook of Child Psychology.* Ed. P.H. Mussen. Vol. 4. Ed. E.M. Hetherington. New York: John Wiley & Sons, 387–467.

Illich, I. 1971. *Deschooling Society.* New York: Harper & Row.

MacDonald, P. 1988. "Historical School Reform and the Correspondence Principle." In *Bowles and Gintis Revisited: Correspondence and Contradiction.* Ed. M. Cole. London: Falmer Press, 86–111.

MacKay, R.W. 1974a. "Conceptions of Children and Models of Socialization." In *Ethnomethodology: Selected Readings.* Ed. R. Turner. Harmondsworth, Eng.: Penguin, 180–193.

Mackie, M. 1991. *Gender Relations in Canada: Further Explorations.* Toronto: Butterworths.

McHoul, A.W. 1978. "The Organization of Turns at Formal Talk in the Classroom." *Language and Society* 7: 183–213.

McHoul, A.W. 1990. "The Organization of Repair in Classroom Talk." *Language and Society* 19: 349–77.

McIntyre, S. 1986. "Gender Bias Within the Law School." Memo to all members of the Faculty Board. Queen's University, 28 July.

McRobbie, A. 1978. "Working-Class Girls and the Culture of Femininity." In *Women Take Issue: Aspects of Women's Subordination.* London: Hutchinson, 96–108.

Mehan, H. 1979. *Learning Lessons: Social Organization in the Classroom.* Cambridge, MA: Harvard University Press.

Moore, R. 1988. "The Correspondence Principle and the Marxist Sociology of Education." In *Bowles and Gintis: Correspondence and Contradiction.* Ed. M. Cole. London: Falmer Press, 51–85.

Muller, J. 1989. "Ruling Through Texts: Developing a Social Service Training Program for a Community College." *Community Development Journal* 24 (Oct.): 273–282.

Muller, J. 1990. "Co-ordinating the Re-organization of Ruling Relations: Management's Use of Human Resource Development for the New Brunswick Community Colleges." In *Political Economy of Community Colleges: Training Workers for Capital.* Ed. J. Muller. Toronto: Garamond.

National Council of Welfare. 1975. *Poor Kids. A Report by the National Council of Welfare on Children in Poverty in Canada.* Ottawa: National Council of Welfare.

National Council of Welfare. 1994. *Poverty Profile 1992.* Ottawa: National Council of Welfare.

Noble, J. 1982. "Fitting the Child to the Classroom: What Mothers Do." Paper prepared for Project 3648. Department of Sociology in Education, Ontario Institute for Studies in Education, Toronto.

Noble, J. 1990. "Social Class and the Under-Fives: Making the 'Differences' Visible." *Our Schools/Our Selves* 2 (April): 42–61.

Parsons, T. 1961. "The School Class as a Social System: Some of its Functions in American Society." In *Education, Economy and Society.* Ed. A.H. Halsey, J. Floud, and C.A. Anderson. New York: Free Press.

Payne, G.C.F., and D.E. Hustler. 1980. "Teaching the Class: The Practical Management of a Cohort." *The British Journal of Sociology of Education* 1 (1) 49–66.

Porter, J., M. Porter, and B.R. Blishen. 1982. *Stations and Callings: Making it Through the School System.* Toronto: Methuen.

Richer, S. 1979. "Sex-Role Socialization and Early Schooling." *Canadian Review of Sociology and Anthropology* 16: 195–205.

Richer, S. 1988. "Schooling and the Gendered Subject: An Exercise in Planned Social Change." *Canadian Review of Sociology and Anthropology* 25: 98–107.

Rist, R.C. 1977. "On Understanding the Process of Schooling: The Contributions of Labelling Theory." In *Power and Ideology in Education.* Ed. J. Karabel and A.H. Halsey. New York: Oxford University Press, 292–305.

Rohner, R.P. 1967. *The People of Gilford: A Contemporary Kwakiutl Village.* Ottawa: National Museums of Canada.

Russell, S. 1987. "The Hidden Curriculum of School: Reproducing Gender and Class Hierarchies." In *Feminism and Political Economy: Women's Work, Women's Struggles.* Ed. H.J. Maroney and M. Luxton. Toronto: Methuen, 229–246.

Sadker, M., and D. Sadker. 1987. "Sexism in the Schoolroom of the '80s." In *Gender Roles: Doing What Comes Naturally.* Ed. E.D. Salamon and B.W. Robinson. Toronto: Methuen, 143–147.

Schneider, F.W., and L.M. Coutts. 1979. "Teacher Orientations Towards Masculine and Feminine: Role of Sex of Teacher and Sex Composition of School." *Canadian Journal of Behavioral Science* 11: 99–111.

Shapiro, L. 1990. "Guns and Dolls." *Newsweek*, 28 May: 56–62.

Smith, D.E. 1992. "Whistling Women: Reflections on Rage and Rationality." In *Fragile Truths: 25 Years of Sociology in Canada.* Ed. W.K. Carroll (and others). Ottawa: Carleton University Press, 207–226.

Smith, D.E., and the Wollestonecraft Research Group. 1979. "Educational Cutbacks and the Workload of Elementary Teachers." *Women in the Educational Workforce*. Status of Women Tabloid. Canadian Teachers' Federation. Sept.

Tumin, M. 1973. *Patterns of Sociology*. Boston: Little Brown.

Wax, M.L., R.H. Wax, and R.V. Dumont Jr. 1964. "Formal Education in an American Indian Community." *Social Problems* 11 (Spring) Supplement: 1–126.

Weeks, P.A.D. 1994. "The Quest for Reasonableness and Reasoning in a Mathematics Lesson." Paper, Department of Sociology, University of Manchester.

Wolcott, H.F. 1967. *A Kwakiutl Village and School*. Toronto: Holt, Rinehart & Winston.

Sociology of Race and Ethnic Relations

The analysis of racial and ethnic relations in society presents a major challenge to theories of social order, both functionalist and Marxist. The presence of diverse ethnic and racial groups within a society complicates traditional functionalist assumptions about social cohesion. The persistence of what Porter (1965) calls a **vertical mosaic**, with marked inequalities between different racial and ethnic groups on measures of class, status, and power, challenges our understanding of social hierarchy. In Canada, people of white Anglo-Saxon Protestant (WASP) origin are overrepresented at the top of the economic hierarchy while Aboriginal people are overrepresented at the bottom. Various other European and non-white people range in between. Ethnic inequalities are also gendered—experienced very differently by women and men. Yet as soon as we try to pin down concepts like ethnicity and race they become elusive, their constantly shifting and contested meanings inseparable from the social practices of "ethnicization" and "racialization" that continually bring them into being. Traditional assumptions about the coincidence of racial and ethnic identity with geographic location and nation states are increasingly challenged by the realities of globalizing economic networks. These networks are associated with transnational flows of finance and personnel, cosmopolitan professional and managerial elites, and increasingly fluid labour migration. Instantaneous global communication networks have the potential to link migrants simultaneously to places of residence, places of origin, and to fragmented communities across the diaspora. The tools of sociological analysis are challenged to remain relevant in these new realities.

 # Traditional Functionalism: Consensus or Conflict?

The concept of shared culture is centrally important in functionalist theory of social order. Moral consensus is seen as internalized during early childhood socialization within the family, and reinforced through religion and education. Components of culture include language, history, religion, symbol systems, values, behavioural norms, expectations, and attitudes—in effect, the totality of what Durkheim refers to as the *conscience collective* of a community of people.

Functionalist theory views our sense of belonging to a cultural community or ethnic group as fundamental to our sense of personal identity. When asked who we are, we typically refer to some ethnic group as "our people" or "our community." Ethnic identity is understood in classical functionalist theory as "primordial," deeply rooted in ties of kinship, blood, common territory, shared language, and religious traditions, which all invoke strong emotions (Shils 1957, 142; Horowitz 1985, 57; Geertz 1973, 259). It is extremely difficult to break ties with the ethnic group of one's birth, especially since it implies renouncing obligations to people closest to us. Children of ethnically mixed parentage are expected to experience some sense of marginality or partial belonging to two exclusive groups, unless mixed-blood people become an ethnic grouping in themselves, like the Métis of western Canada. In short, the definition of an "ethnic group" in functionalist theory closely parallels that of a society as a whole, with a common culture functioning as the central institution maintaining social cohesion.

The concept of **race**, as distinct from **ethnicity**, refers to shared visible and inherited physical characteristics that are socially noticed, with skin colour as the most important. In principle, racial diversity should not give rise to the same societal problems as ethnic diversity, since race does not constitute any threat to cultural consensus. In practice, however, race tends to be confounded with ethnicity. Members of any given ethnic group tend to see themselves as racially homogeneous, and thus to regard people of visibly different racial stock as outsiders. Distinct racial characteristics commonly function as markers of ethnic difference.

The emphasis within functionalist theory on internalization of shared culture suggests that some level of ethnocentrism is normal. **Ethnocentrism** refers to an exaggerated view of the superior qualities and rightness of the culture of one's own group. **Stereotypes** refer to simplified versions or mental cartoons that we form of other ethnic groups by overgeneralizing or exaggerating their distinctive characteristics. **Prejudice** is the logical mirror image of ethnocentrism. It involves pre-judging, usually in negative terms, the characteristics that we assume are shared by members of other ethnic groups. **Racism** applies such prejudices towards groups that we perceive to be different on the basis of inescapable genetic characteristics. In functionalist theory, these ethnocentric, stereotyped, prejudiced, and racist attitudes are understood as themselves part of the culturally learned attitudes that we internalize through socialization. Socialization also provides us with shared notions of the relative status of our own and other groups within the society.

Implications for Political Organization

Functionalist theory associates shared culture with social cohesion and order. This implies that an ethnically homogeneous society is more likely to be stable and secure, while ethnically and racially mixed societies, such as Canada, are more prone to instability, divisions, and conflict (Walling 2000). Theoretically, ethnic minorities may not have internalized the expected values or behaviours common to the majority group, so that interaction may be strained and social controls weak. Where desire for approval and acceptance is weak, force plays a greater role in maintaining order, which in turn implies domination by one cultural group. The safest meeting ground for different ethnic groups is likely to be the impersonal marketplace. Classical theorists suggest that harmony between distinct ethnic groups is most likely when they have both economic and legal autonomy, so that each group controls its own members' lives (Kuper 1969, 14–16; Van den Berghe 1969, 75–78).

Given the disruptive potential of ethnic differences, classical theory proposes four viable options or models for maintaining social order: **domination, separation,** or **assimilation** of ethnic minorities. The fourth option, *multiculturalism,* is proposed as viable for social harmony under the particular conditions of modern secular, rational societies.

The first two options are seen as mechanisms to help states to manage or contain ethnic conflicts, but not ultimately to resolve them. In the long run, Walling suggests, either domination or separation work to escalate insecurities. Ethnic minorities that experience exclusion and repression are more likely to identify intensely with their own subgroup and to struggle for some measure of political autonomy, which in turn threatens the integrity of the state and casts doubt on their political loyalties. Globally, such struggles have often erupted into civil wars, or politics of ethnic cleansing, as states try to drive politically dangerous minorities out of the state's territorial boundaries, or as self-identified ethnic minorities struggle for autonomous statehood.

Walling cites a chilling history of ethnic cleansings from before the Middle Ages right through to the present. Historically, Canadian governments have employed policies of ethnic cleansing, to deport Acadians from the Maritimes in 1755, and to expel Canadians of Japanese origin from British Columbia in 1942. In Europe during the inter-war period, 1919–1938, policies intended to better fit ethnicity to national boundaries in the interests of increasing state security resulted in forced population movements of some 21 million refugees in Europe alone. More recently, in 1992, the federation of Yugoslavia split apart amid brutal policies of ethnic cleansing. Violence against ethnic minorities was condemned by outsiders as crimes against humanity, but excused by many insiders as no more than overzealous acts of nation-building. Similar justifications were proposed for the Iraqi government's brutal suppression of ethnic Kurds.

Classical theory proposed assimilation as the ideal solution for the problems of ethnic diversity. It resolves the cultural threats to social cohesion and eliminates the need for control. The concept of assimilation refers to the process by which minority ethnic groups gradually adopt the lifestyles, language, values, and customs of the dominant group. Structural integration is expected to follow as minorities enter the social organization of the dominant group. Gordon (1964) suggests that groups tend to lose language and culture first, but to hold on to religion and practice inter-ethnic group marriage. The final stage is such total amalgamation that ethnic background is forgotten.

Classically, assimilation is seen as being accomplished over three generations. New immigrants or first-generation settlers struggle to speak the host language, and are likely to retain strong emotional ties to home-country and ethnic subgroup. Women who remain in the home may adjust more slowly than men exposed to the public sphere of work. Their children, or the second generation, are typically socialized into aspects of both cultures. Numerous ethnographic studies suggest these children experience culture conflict, feeling torn between cultural values and religion learned at home and new cultural values learned in school and neighbourhood. Family values, focused around sexuality, marriage, and religion, are likely to change more slowly than secular values. By the third generation, however, the children of children born or raised in the new country are typically fully assimilated. This is the theory of the "melting pot." Waves of migrants come, settle, and then gradually intermarry as they move out into and merge with the surrounding ethnic mainstream population.

The problem with this vision of assimilation is that it runs counter to functionalist emphasis on presumed strength of primordial ethnic attachments. It seems more likely to happen among small numbers of voluntary migrants immersed in a new culture, but less likely among peoples experiencing forced or non-voluntary migration, or within larger ethnic minority groups, and groups with significant cultural differences from the host society. Resistance to assimilation by migrants is often compounded by resistance from the host society promoted by prevailing attitudes of ethnocentrism and racism. Where host societies feel threatened by the potentially divided loyalties of ethnic minorities, states have resorted to tactics for forced assimilation. These have typically taken the form of breaking up minority communities, banning minority ceremonial and religious practices, restricting use of minority languages, and intensive re-education of minority children (Walling 2000). Sometimes such strategies work to disperse minorities, but more often, Walling suggests, they exacerbate problems of resentment, ethnic closure, and resistance that promote struggles for greater self-determination.

The fourth option of *multiculturalism* represents a significant shift within functionalist theory from seeing culture as all-embracing to viewing it as a more partial and private component of societal integration. It draws implicitly on Durkheim's model of organic solidarity in advanced industrial societies characterized by specialization and differentiation. Sameness based on shared culture becomes less important for social cohesion than interdependence and mutual obligations among individuals with specialized activities. This shift from mechanical to organic solidarity supports the view that cultural diversity can be successfully accommodated provided that a foundation of core societal values are maintained—namely the values of mutual respect for diversity and for individual human rights.

The model of multiculturalism implies a set of assumptions—that people live in society as members of culturally defined communities, that different communities can exist equitably within one society, and that individuals can participate actively in the society as a whole while maintaining their identity and membership within a minority cultural community. As subsystems within a wider societal system, ethnic communities can serve many positive functions for members. These include providing material and emotional supports, aiding the adjustment of immigrants and refugees, overcoming isolation, reinforcing a sense of belonging, articulating group interests, and promoting economic and political involvement in society (Kelly 2003, 38). In Durkheim's terms, such ethnic communities function to reduce anomie, providing an intermediate level of belonging between individuals and modern nation states. Ethnic community attachments are seen as functioning globally as well as within individual societies, to give comfort and security in an era of rapid and disruptive change and accelerated

rates of migration (Giddens 2000, 62–63; Richmond 2002, 708; Richmond 1988, 7–8). Giddens argues that in modern secular societies, ethnic traditions are necessarily no longer lived in traditional ways. They are maintained for rational, reflective reasons—because they are comforting, and not out of blind, unquestioning adherence. Hence, they are more flexible, open to continual adjustment or reinvention to fit changing circumstances. People can maintain their membership within distinctive ethnic, cultural, and racial communities while at the same time interacting as equals with members of other diverse cultural communities within wider social and political institutions (Kelly 2003; Kim 2004). Differences are privatized—celebrated and protected as a source of family values and emotional belonging, but at the same time depoliticized or separated from the public realm of secular, democratic political institutions and free-market economics. The challenge for modern societies is to manage diversity so as to preserve national unity, or in effect to make societies safe for diversity and safe from diversity (Fleras and Elliott 2003, 286). This is seen as best achieved by institutionalizing the two principles of difference and equality.

A brief overview of Canadian social and political history shows how all four of these different models of minority group relations have prevailed at different times, and with different ethnic groups.

Domination The first model, where one ethnic group exercises institutional domination over another, characterizes the experience of Native peoples in Canada. Over more than two centuries of violent conflict, white settler society achieved decisive domination over Aboriginal tribal communities. As the fur trade declined and white settlers pushed westward onto the Prairies, Aboriginal peoples were driven off their lands onto small reserves. Threats of war and starvation forced treaties onto captured populations (Lawrence 2004, 30). The Indian Act of 1869 established the legal, political, and economic dominance of the federal government over almost every aspect of reservation life. Successive modifications to the Indian Act subordinated Aboriginal peoples as wards of state, treated much like minors. Elected band councils, with limited powers, replaced former indigenous governments and confederacies (Lawrence 2004, 33). The Minister of Indian Affairs had the authority to attend all band council meetings, to veto any bylaws that the bands might pass, to control their finances, to approve all expenditures, and to dictate land sales. Similar practices of conquest and domination of Aboriginal peoples occurred in what is now the United States, and in European colonies in Australia, New Zealand, and beyond. The Canadian system for governing reservations was adopted as a model by the white South

African government for managing black residents in segregated "homelands."

Institutional Separation

First Nations   Contemporary relations between Aboriginal peoples and the Canadian federal government are slowly moving away from domination towards the model of institutional separation and partial self-government, albeit under far from equal status. For Aboriginal peoples the meaning of reserves has shifted from "colonial tool" to territorial foundation for Aboriginal identity and self-government. Aboriginals increasingly insist on their tiny band communities being recognized and referred to as "First Nations" and their negotiations with the federal government, however unequal they might be, as nation-to-nation negotiations.

Progress towards the devolution of powers to First Nations has been painfully slow, reflected in interminable litigation and occasional violent confrontations. One of the worst was the Oka crisis in Quebec in 1990, during which the Mohawk Warriors of Kanesatake blocked the Mercier Bridge into Montreal in an armed standoff that lasted 78 days. The struggle was focused around blocking a proposal to build a golf course on traditional Aboriginal land. Nonetheless, the principles of conditional autonomy, self-government and self-determination for First Nations peoples are slowly being worked out. Models of self-determination vary with the size and resources of different bands, but there are roughly between 60 and 80 recognized Nations within a thousand or so Aboriginal communities. Two of the most significant accomplishments in self-determination to date have been the establishment of the territory of Nunavut in 1999 and the Nisga'a agreement of 2000 in BC, a settlement described as "the first treaty since 1859" (Fleras and Elliott 2003, 168).

The debates, however, continue. Is the Nisga'a treaty a step backward towards race-based apartheid under another name, or a step forward towards autonomous nationhood within the Canadian federation? A further problem with the model of autonomous First Nations is that relatively few of the more than one thousand reserve communities in Canada are large enough for this to be viable. First Nations also exclude the majority of people who claim Aboriginal identity but who have lost their status or band membership, or moved to urban areas. We discuss these issues further below.

Quebec   The model of institutional separation also characterizes the relations between the predominantly Francophone province of Quebec and the rest of predominantly Anglophone Canada. The British North America Act of 1867 established Canada as a bilingual federal system to accommodate the French in Quebec. The British colonial government could subdue but not dominate Quebec as it had the Aboriginal people, nor could it hope to assimilate French Catholics into English Protestants. Institutional separation appeared to be the only viable option in the British government's desire to unify the North against the rebellious American states.

From the beginning, however, this arrangement has been unstable. The relationship has been variously referred to as "two solitudes" or as "two scorpions in a bottle" (Fleras and Elliott 2003, 211). Canada seems to be in constant danger of either separating into two autonomous nations or reverting to the first option of quasi-colonial domination.

John Porter (1979, 106) writes enthusiastically of the special relationship of "binationalism of French and English Canada as the founding principle of Confederation." This relationship only makes sense, he suggests, because of very specific historical conditions. The fact that 80 percent of French Canadians live in Quebec gives them a homeland that was conquered. This helps to make sense of, and to give impetus to, the notions of separation and eventual formation of a French state. In practice, the ideal of "separate but equal" status implied in the separation model has never been a reality. The French ethnic group, even within Quebec, has until very recently formed a class with deprived status. French elites within the church and the state in Quebec collaborated with the federal government in return for protected status, but the mass of unilingual Francophones occupied the low ranks in the class structure. Professional and business elites in Quebec have been predominantly English Canadians or Americans, and the language of business has clearly been English. The few Québécois who attained professional occupational status had to function in English.

The Royal Commission on Bilingualism and Biculturalism, established in 1963, concluded that either Canada would break up or that there would have to be a new set of conditions for Quebec's future existence (Porter 1979, 107). In 1969 the Official Languages Act moved towards providing special status for Quebec in Canada. It formalized bilingualism in the federal civil service, together with concessions, especially in social welfare legislation. But strife continued. During the 1960s a small group calling itself the Quebec Liberation Front (FLQ) used propaganda and terrorism against federalist targets to promote the goal of an independent socialist Quebec. This culminated in 1970 in the "October Crisis" when FLQ cells kidnapped two political leaders. One of them was murdered. The federal government, with Quebec's approval, invoked the War Measures Act to quell the "apprehended insurrection." The FLQ had largely fizzled by 1971, but separatist struggles have continued to the present.

The Parti Québécois first came to power in 1976, dedicated to achieving independent nationhood for Quebec by political means. In 1977, Quebec passed the French Language Charter (known as Bill 101) declaring Quebec officially a monolingual province, with French as the pre-ferred language of work, education, commerce, and service delivery. The Quebec government argued that the move was essential to preserve the French language and with it French culture from being swallowed up by English North America. The 1980 referendum on sovereignty association was only narrowly voted down. Subsequent efforts by the Canadian federal government to gain Quebec's support for constitu-tional reform in the proposed Meech Lake Accord in 1987 and the subsequent Charlottetown Accord in 1992 both failed. In September 1994, the Parti Québécois was again elected. In 1995 it held another referendum on sovereignty, which failed by a margin of less than 1 percent. Quebec's his-tory gives much supporting evidence for the functionalist thesis that ethnic pluralism in separate communities living side by side is inherently unstable and destined to be associ-ated with continual conflict and stress.

Integration through Assimilation

From the classi-cal functionalist perspective, assimilation is by far the best option for achieving societal cohesion. It involves a process over time by which members of ethnic minorities absorb the cultural patterns and values of the dominant ethnic group until eventually they merge with the majority. Successive Canadian governments have tried to force the assimilation of Aboriginal peoples by a variety of means that together amount to a pattern that Aboriginal people see as cultural genocide. Aboriginal religious traditions and practices were widely outlawed. Missions were established with the goal of converting these supposedly heathen peoples to Christianity. From the 1880s onward, generations of Aboriginal children were forcibly removed from their communities and sent great distances away to be taught in residential Christian schools, where children were routinely punished for speaking Native languages (Davies and Guppy 1998, 131). The last of these schools were closed in the 1970s.

The Federal White Paper on Aboriginals introduced in 1969 by then Minister of Indian Affairs, Jean Chrétien, pro-posed a strategy that combined assimilation with legal ex-tinction, under which the special status of Aboriginal peoples would be terminated, and their land and assets divided on a per-capita basis to individuals. Aboriginal leaders rejected the legal proposals outright as "callous expediency" and the vision of assimilation as "cultural genocide" (Fleras and Elliott 2003, 183). Ensuing struggles converged in 1982 with the constitutional recognition of Aboriginal status and treaty rights under the Canadian Charter of Rights and Freedoms. Belatedly, the devastation caused to Aboriginal communities by the destruction of their families and cultures is slowly being recognized by the Canadian government. By 2006 the federal government approved a $4 billion out-of-court settle-ment package to compensate an estimated 80 000 people

Justice Murray Sinclair, Manitoba's first Aboriginal judge, was appointed Chair of the Indian Residential Schools Truth and Reconciliation Commission on 15 July 2009.

THE CANADIAN PRESS/Sean Kilpatrick

eligible for redress from incarceration in the 80 or so Canadian residential schools. The settlement recognized both the physical and sexual abuses that some of the children suf-fered, and acknowledged the pervasive loss of their cultures. On 11 June 2008, Prime Minister Stephen Harper rose in the House of Commons to offer a formal apology for the residen-tial school system, referring to it as a "sad chapter" in Canadian history. In his speech, which was broadcast nation-wide, Harper stated unequivocally: "Today we recognize that this policy of assimilation was wrong, has caused great harm, and has no place in our country." The Liberal opposition leader, Stéphane Dion continued: "Today's apology is about a past that should have been completely different," he said. "But it must be also about the future. It must be about collective reconciliation and fundamental change." NDP Leader Jack Layton added: "It is the moment to finally say we are sorry and it is the moment where we start to begin a shared future on equal footing through mutual respect and truth."

Schools for Aboriginal children in some of the larger reserves now teach heritage languages and traditions, actively assisted by Native Studies programs in some Canadian universities. For most people of Aboriginal descent, however, these changes come far too late. Their loss of traditional cultures is virtually complete, although integration as equals in non-Native society remains elusive.

Immigration and Potential for Assimilation

Immigration policies in Canada have historically been guided by assumptions about the perceived ease with which different kinds of migrants might be assimilated into white settler society. People from England were always preferred, although not without concerns that lower-class girls might be "unsuitable" (Arat-Koc 1999, 129–132). The colony of

Quebec similarly preferred migrants from France. Nineteenth-century Canadian politicians were dubious that non-French, non-British Europeans could be successfully assimilated into Canadian culture. Such people were recruited mostly to open up the prairies, in small settlements isolated from white settler society. There was outright skepticism that culturally and racially more distinct Asian and African people could ever fit in with white culture (Li 2003). Regulations such as a head tax and continuous journey rules were implemented to block the immigration of people from China, Japan, and India, even while European immigrants were being courted with incentive plans. Even when male migrants from Asia were accepted as labourers, women from these countries were banned, on the grounds that they and their children would not be assimilable (Thobani 2000, 36).

Racist attitudes that prevailed within the host society contributed significantly to the marginalization and segregation of Aboriginal peoples and immigrants considered "less assimilable." Second-generation Canadians of Japanese and other Asian origins were educated in Canadian schools, spoke fluent English, and often converted to Christianity, yet still found themselves discriminated against as outsiders. Such attitudes both facilitated and justified policies that fit the definition of ethnic cleansing. During the Second World War, 20 881 Canadians of Japanese origin were expelled from coastal areas of British Columbia in 1942 and interned in work camps and ghost towns in the interior. After the war they were offered the option of deportation to Japan or indentured labour in prairie farms. All their property—homes, farms, fishing boats, and businesses—were confiscated and sold by the Canadian government to pay relocation costs (Adachi 1978; Sunahara 1981). National security concerns that Japanese in Canada might aid Japan during the war were cited as the official excuse for the expulsion, although no Japanese Canadians were ever charged for disloyalty to Canada. The charge that racist attitudes were centrally involved in these policies is supported by evidence that German Canadians in the Maritime provinces were not subjected to any such wartime controls.

Multiculturalism: Integration without Assimilation

The presence of Francophone Quebec within Canada was an important impetus for the shift from the politics of assimilation to multiculturalism. By the mid-twentieth century it was obvious that Francophone Québécois were fiercely resistant to assimilation into the dominant English Canadian culture. It was also an era of increasing migration of non-European and non-white peoples into Canada, as the supply of potential immigrants from Europe declined. The Immigration Act of 1967 abolished formal preference on the basis of race or ethnicity, instituting instead a points system that highlighted skills and capacity to contribute to the Canadian economy. Critics have noted that immigration practices are still biased in favour of people from Europe through the geographic location of offices, points for proficiency in English or French, and leeway given to immigration officers in selection criteria (Simmons 1998). Nonetheless, by the 1990s immigrants from various parts of Asia comprised about half of all newcomers, one-fifth from the Caribbean or Africa and one-fifth from Europe (Abu-Laban and Gabriel 2002, 14–15). Statistics Canada census data for 2001 indicated that 13 percent of the Canadian population identified themselves as visible minorities (the category defined as non-Aboriginal and non-white). Almost all of them lived in metropolitan centres, with three-quarters in the three cities of Toronto, Vancouver, and Montreal.

Multiculturalism, within a bilingual framework, was first proclaimed by the Trudeau government in 1971 and entrenched as a fundamental principle of the Canadian Constitution in Section 27 of the Charter of Rights and Freedoms in 1982. The Charter also includes a very broad statement prohibiting discrimination. This is embedded in a particularly expansive definition of rights to equality *before* the law and *under* the law, and equal *protection* and equal *benefit* of the law. These four qualifying definitions of rights have been interpreted by the Supreme Court of Canada as intended to protect minorities not only from deliberate or intended discrimination but also from rules that have the effect of disadvantaging minorities. A classic example of such a rule concerned height restrictions on eligibility for employment as police officers, which was found to have a discriminatory effect on Canadians from Asian origins, who are physically smaller on average than Europeans. Another was the rule that men entering Canadian Legion premises remove head coverings, which discriminated against Sikhs who wear turbans for religious observance. The ruling has also been interpreted as requiring employers to make "reasonable accommodations" for cultural differences, such as scheduling hours of employment to permit Fridays or Saturdays to be holidays for religious observances and not exclusively Sundays.

The principles of multiculturalism have been further emphasized in subsequent policy amendments to the Multiculturalism Act in 1988 and 1997. In a recent statement, under the Department of Canadian Heritage, multiculturalism is defined in terms of the three goals of identity, civic participation, and social justice (Abu-Laban and Gabriel 2002, 113–114). The primary goal of identity entails "fostering a society that recognizes, respects, and reflects a diversity of cultures such that people of all backgrounds feel a sense of belonging and attachment to Canada," and further that the state will develop among "Canada's diverse people, active citizens with both the opportunity and capacity to participate in shaping the future of their communities and their culture," and guarantees of "fair and equitable treatment that respects the dignity of and accommodates people of all origins."

The organization and leadership structures within ethnic communities in Canada vary widely in response to such factors as recency of large-scale migration, numbers and level of concentration in certain cities and regions, internal regional, language, and religious differences, and the like. A common pattern has been for leaders to be drawn initially from religious institutions, and gradually to be replaced by younger generations of educated and professional people (Jedwab 2001). These leaders often represent their community's interests in relations with the state.

Within Canada at the federal level, multicultural policies have involved state funding for ethnocultural groups to maintain their cultures and foster cultural interchange and language training. Critics such as Trinidad-born novelist Neil Bissoondath (1994, 219) and Peter Li (1994) argue that such programs have marginalized minority artists as producing low-status folkloric art rather than high-status art that wins acclaim in galleries and museums. Judy Young (2001), however, argues in response that government grants under multicultural policies have functioned successfully to promote cultural and racial diversity in Canadian literature. She cites a host of minority Canadian writers whose books have received national and international recognition as Canadian literature, in part through the assistance of the program.

Multicultural policies within schools are largely the responsibility of provinces in Canada, and they reflect the regional diversity in migrant settlement. The 1996 Census showed that fully 42 percent of Toronto residents were immigrants, 35 percent of Vancouver, and 18 percent of Montreal (Abu-Laban and Gabriel 2002, 14–15). Relatively few immigrants settle in the Atlantic region. Migrants from Asia and the Pacific Rim are concentrated in British Columbia while migrants from the Caribbean and Africa are more numerous in Ontario.

Multicultural education required major changes in standard approaches to education that were designed to assimilate children into the mainstream dominant anglo-cultural norm. The avowed goal of multiculturalism is to be child-centred and inclusive, representing diversity as necessary, normal, and beneficial for Canadian society (Fleras and Elliott 2003, 324–334). Early approaches that focused on exposing children to a variety of cultures were widely challenged for portraying overly static and romanticized views of cultures that risked trivializing or stereotyping differences. Emphasis has slowly shifted from descriptions of different cultures to a focus on relationships between cultural groups and problems of hierarchy and inequality. School curriculum has slowly shifted towards

giving more time to exploring issues of racism, dispossession, and imperialism, especially with respect to relations between white settler society and Aboriginal people. Efforts are being made to address institutional features that act as barriers to successful inclusion and equal achievement of minority students, including the culture of the school, the hidden curriculum of white normative values in curriculum materials, and teacher attitudes and practices. This has gradually evolved into more explicitly anti-racist education designed to empower visible minorities.

The process of educational reform for multiculturalism has not been easy. Strong differences of opinion exist on how far "reasonable accommodation" to cultural diversity can be made before it detracts from the wider goal of enhancing inclusive Canadian citizenship. One contentious issue has involved accommodation to religious prescriptions that conflict with the secular orientation of Canadian education and gender equality. Fundamentalist Christian and Muslim parents have objected to Canadian schools being too inclusive of diversity in teachings on such matters as homosexuality, and not inclusive enough in teaching such matters as creationism, or accommodating religious prescriptions around modesty of dress, appropriate separation of boys and girls, separate prayer rooms, prohibitions on depicting human figures, and the like. By 2002 there were 18 separate Islamic schools in Toronto with more than 2000 students enrolled, and about 725 separate schools across Ontario, the vast majority Christian fundamentalist (Fleras and Elliott 2003, 338). The debate continues as to whether such separate schools reflect "multiculturalism in action" or the failure of multicultural policies. Similar debates surrounded the proposal to legalize Islamic Sharia tribunals in Ontario to settle family disputes. The proposal

Multiculturalism, within a bilingual framework, is entrenched as a fundamental principle in the Canadian Charter of Rights and Freedoms.

CP PHOTO/Jonathan Hayward

was eventually abandoned as incompatible with Canadian Charter principles of equality rights for husbands and wives.

Challenges to Multiculturalism   Culturally based attitudes and values that promote ethnocentrism and racism represent a continual threat to the goal of harmonious multicultural diversity. As noted above, functionalist theory sees primordial ethnic attachments as inherently conducive to beliefs about the superiority of one's own culture and the inferiority of others. Such views readily spill over into racism. The long cultural history of Eurocentrism and racism in white settler society is not easily overcome. Lawrence (1982) describes the roots of common-sense racism in British culture, embedded in notions of "white" as the colour of purity, and "black" as dirty or soiled, and of white people generally as having a natural superiority of upbringing and breeding compared with more childlike dark-skinned people they encountered in the colonies. Discrimination and prejudice have been common experiences for visible minorities living in Canada, both from politicians who favour racist immigration policies and in everyday treatment from neighbours (Reitz and Breton 1998; Chen 2004; Li 2003).

Three decades of official multiculturalism have not been sufficient to silence entirely the neo-conservative view that cultural differences threaten Canadian unity, and that "newcomers" from "non-traditional sources" may have irreconcilable values that threaten Canada's democracy. The view that mainstream Canadian cultural values need to change in order to better accommodate culturally diverse immigrants is rarely endorsed. As Li expresses it, racialized new immigrants are represented as multicultural objects, rather than subjects whose values, aspirations, and wishes need to be taken into account (2003, 10).

The picture, however, is mixed. Neo-conservative attitudes such as those Li describes may be widespread but they are not universal. In surveys, some two-thirds of Canadians indicate that they do *not* see multiculturalism as threatening Canadian unity (Jedwab 2001), and three-quarters did not agree with the racist notion that Canada may be accepting "too many" visible minority immigrants (Galabuzi 2006, 72). In Chen's historical study of people from China living in Peterborough, Ontario, prior to multicultural policies, widespread racism did not preclude the development of long-term friendships and respect between Chinese and white neighbours (2004, 86–87). Chen's description, however, implies strongly that the wholesale adoption of white Canadian culture with respect to dress, language, and even religion, was a precondition for improved relations. The message is one of assimilation rather than multicultural tolerance.

The "War on Terror" and Limits to Multiculturalism

Heightened fear of international terrorism in the aftermath of the 11 September 2001 attack in the USA, and subsequently in Madrid and London, constitutes a significant challenge to the ideal of multiculturalism. Canada, along with the USA and other Western countries, has enacted far-reaching security legislation to protect the state against terrorism. A critical difference between security and regular policing is that the focus is on watching and controlling people who might pose potential risk of committing acts of violence in the future, rather than on apprehending criminals (Hörnqvist 2005). In the pervasive climate of fear and suspicion, Muslim communities as a whole, and especially immigrant communities from Middle Eastern states, are finding themselves under suspicion as potential "aliens within." The immense diversity of Islamic cultures across the world is obscured in popular discourse as the adjective "Islamic" is readily linked in media shorthand and popular talk with fundamentalism, extremism, and terrorism.

In many of the member states within the European Union the shift from policies of multiculturalism towards assimilation or monoculturalism has become overt within regulations governing immigration (Fekete 2005). This shift is reflected in compulsory language and civics tests for citizenship applicants under threat of deportation, loss of residency rights, and social security payments. Immigration regulations governing "family reunification" have been modified to require that family members over the age of 12 must prove they have accepted European values and norms as a precondition for immigration. Citizenship rights, even for the second- and third-generation children of immigrants have been subordinated to anti-terrorist legislation. In September 2004 the government of France moved to ban the wearing of hijab, or headscarves, in schools. German states likewise banned Muslim teachers from wearing hijab. In effect, Fekete argues, the war on terror has become inseparable from debates on the limits of cultural diversity in Western societies.

In Canada, official commitment to multiculturalism remains strong. Immediately after the 11 September 2001 attacks, all levels of government within Canada stressed the importance of not stigmatizing members of Canadian Muslim communities. Many municipalities adopted measures aimed at strengthening bonds with Muslim community leaders (Helly 2004, 41–44). Helly criticizes Canadian officials, however, for remaining largely silent since this initial outreach, failing to be proactive in dealing with waves of anti-Muslim "hate crimes" that erupted during the months following the terrorist attacks. The Canadian Islamic Congress published figures indicating a 1600 percent increase in hate crimes against Muslim individuals or places of worship between September 2001 and September 2002, an increase in real numbers from 11 to 173 attacks (Helly 2004, 26).

The picture, however, is mixed. As Helly notes, on the positive side, there were no calls by any Canadian political leaders for restrictions on the immigration of Muslims to Canada, or for internal controls. On the contrary, there has been widespread acknowledgement that there may be no viable option to multiculturalism given the reality of cultural diversity in Canada. A survey of Canadian Muslims in 2002 records a mix of prejudicial and supportive behaviour towards Muslims by white neighbours. Sixty percent of respondents are reported as saying that they had experienced bias or discrimination since the terrorist attacks. One-third agreed that their lives had changed for the worse, they felt disliked by fellow Canadians, and were concerned for their own safety and that of their families. On the other hand, 61 percent of these same respondents agreed that "they had experienced kindness or support from friends or colleagues of other faiths" (Helly 2004, 42). Also, since 2002, the spate of hate crimes declined, due in part to the efforts of networks of local organizations to defuse conflicts (Helly 2004, 28). Canada's commitment to multiculturalism has been credited for the absence of race riots like those in France in 2005.

In conclusion, the functionalist perspective focuses analysis on the continuing strength of primordial cultural and ethnic attachments. The general assumption that follows from traditional functionalist theory is that ethnically and racially mixed societies, such as Canada, are inherently unstable and prone to divisions and conflicts. The structural enforcement of multiculturalism in political and legal institutions, and its reinforcement in schools as secondary agents of socialization, functions to moderate but not to eliminate this potential for conflict. Consistent with this theoretical approach is the evidence that, since the end of the Cold War in the 1990s, the vast majority of conflicts across the world have involved civil wars, or ethnic conflicts within multicultural states.

 # The Political Economy Perspective: Racist Capitalism

The political economy perspective focuses attention on how economies are organized—the structure of labour markets and struggles for material resources. These economic conditions are highlighted as the root cause of tensions between different racial and ethnic groups, rather than the clash of cultures. Prevailing attitudes, including ethnocentrism, prejudice, and racism, reflect societal organization of economic relations, and specifically class locations within capitalist economies, rather than supposedly primordial cultural attachments. Marxist analysis views culturally learned attitudes and practices not as irrelevant to the understanding of inter-group conflicts, but as responses to economic interests. Inequalities in access to economic rewards and opportunities, rather than multicultural intolerance, are highlighted as central concerns for political action. The classical or strong version of this theoretical approach, sometimes called "structural Marxism," subsumes or reduces the understanding of race relations to class analysis, suggesting that ultimately only class interests and class conflicts explain group relations. The more nuanced contemporary political economy perspective explores how class interests influence and modify the mobilization of racial and ethnic group identification in some contexts to promote hostilities and separation, and in other contexts to promote a coming together around shared interests. The increasingly global character of economic organization is heralded by theorists such as Hardt and Negri (2000, 43–44) as potentially generating cosmopolitan linkages between workers around the globe struggling together for economic justice, which may eventually overshadow fragmented allegiances to ethnic groups.

Colonialism: The Origin of "Race" and "Racism"

The concept of "race," with attendant notions of innate biological differences between types of people, has its roots in European imperialism and colonialism. Word usage shifted from the earlier reference to the distinction between blue-blooded aristocracy and commoners to that between "white men" and the "black," "yellow," and "red" peoples of Africa, Asia, and the Americas (Solomos and Back 1994). Europeans, with their advanced military technology and gunboat diplomacy, found it appealing to think of themselves as innately superior to the peoples they conquered, and as destined to take on "the white man's burden" of governing and civilizing the more "primitive races" they encountered. Such thoughts assuaged the sense of guilt associated with the brutality of conquest and subsequent plunder of resources that fuelled industrialization in Europe. Different European powers carved up continents with scant regard for the tribal, ethnic, and cultural identities of subordinated people, and they routinely promoted a subordinated elite class of local administrators to act as buffer groups between themselves and the masses, attributing an intermediate racialized status to them.

The social impact of these practices has had a very long reach into twentieth-century post-colonial nation building. Political economy theory argues that the violence that has so often wracked post-colonial states is more usefully understood as class conflict than as ethnic cleansing. Intensified commitment to cultural values and practices disparaged under colonial rule provided emerging leaders with a tool for mobilizing people to assert themselves against European domination and arrogance. Resentment against racialized buffer groups who buttressed and mimicked colonial rulers readily exploded into violence as Europeans withdrew. In the ensuing power vacuum, local leaders and international corporate power brokers have conspired to manipulate ethnic subgroup loyalties in their bid to assert control over natural resources such as oil, minerals, diamonds, and lands suitable for agribusiness interests.

Drohan (2003) uses this kind of analysis to account for a range of violent conflicts still raging across Africa. Across South Africa, Zimbabwe, the Congo, Mozambique, Angola, Nigeria, Sierra Leone, Sudan, Uganda and Rwanda, similar violent histories can be told. The worst yet has been the genocidal violence in Rwanda. Historically, Belgian colonial rulers delegated extensive power and privileges to a minority of Tutsi tribesmen that served them as a buffer group. The Belgians also racialized the Tutsi as supposedly more European in features than the majority Hutu. Then they left them to their fate as newly democratic elections brought the majority Hutu government to power with independence in the 1950s. As successive Hutu governments faltered amid severe recession in the monocrop coffee economy, they deflected growing unrest into attacks against prominent Tutsi, accusing them of treasonous plots to destabilize the government (Masire 2000; Verwimp 2003). Tensions exploded in April 1994 after the Hutu president was killed in a plane crash. An estimated 800 000 people, mostly Tutsi and moderate Hutu, were murdered over a period of three months. The Belgian government and the United Nations were warned repeatedly that such a massacre was imminent, but failed to take any preventive action. While it is clear that political leaders were able to mobilize ethnic subgroup hostilities and loyalties in this conflict, it is also clear that a clash of cultures was irrelevant. Peoples categorized as Tutsi and Hutu are indistinguishable from each other in terms of physical features, language, religion, or other cultural practices.

Across Latin America similar histories have unfolded of post-colonial civil wars between ethnic-class factions, often fuelled and financed by transnational corporate interests intent on quick profits from resource extraction. Indigenous peoples, whose villages and homelands have come in the way of mining interests, have been indiscriminately eliminated. Again, these struggles have had little to do with clash of cultures, unless by cultural values one means the clash of corporate capitalist shareholder values pitted against those of subsistence farmers seeking a different kind of living from the land.

Post-Colonial "Race and Ethnic Relations"

By the end of the Second World War, most of the former colonies had achieved political independence from European rulers. Expanding post-war capitalist manufacturing economies in Europe, along with the white settler societies of North America, were experiencing significant labour shortages. These changing political-economic realities fostered profound changes in the character of global migration and encounters between peoples from different continents. In the past these encounters had been mostly confined to a relatively small class of European elites directly involved in the colonial service, and personnel in the armed forces and trading companies. White Americans and black Africans encountered each other mostly through the infamous slave trade, which brought captured Africans to work as slaves in Southern American plantations. But from the 1950s onwards, people from Africa, Asia, and Latin America began to migrate to Europe and North America in ever-increasing numbers. They were both pushed by poverty and wars at home, and pulled by the hope of greater economic opportunities. The general population of urban centres in Europe came into close contact with people from "the colonies" for the first time. As the character of encounters changed, the concept of race and "race relations" shifted from focus on biological differences to preoccupation with culture contact and assimilation. (Solomos and Back 1994). Sociological studies of race relations in Britain from the 1960s to the 1980s focused principally on descriptive ethnographies of ethnic communities, and boundary relations between ethnic groups.

The period of recession and economic restructuring during the 1980s resulted in high levels of structural unemployment that hit the immigrant workers and their families especially hard. Corporations increasingly opted to relocate unskilled mass production work to Asia to exploit vast supplies of ultra-cheap labour. Marxist analysis of the crises of capitalism, plagued with cyclical booms and slumps, was increasingly applied to the study of race and ethnic relations. The central argument was that the quality of these relations would directly reflect the severity of competition for jobs, and for related material resources like affordable housing and social services (Rex and Moore 1967; Brittan and Maynard 1984, 35–36). Desperate migrant workers were willing to accept low-waged jobs, while local workers resented the competition and the threat their cheaper labour represented for wage levels generally. At the same time, evidence of unemployed migrants drawing income assistance fosters more resentment and challenges that they are unfairly abusing social services intended for locals. Marxist ideology might foster the hope that workers would unite in a common struggle against exploitative capitalism. But the experience of Europe in the 1980s and 1990s found that the more common outcome was escalating conflict, as capitalist employers exploited the situation to pit subgroups of workers against each other, both to lower average wages and to deflect resentment against the slumps in the labour market.

The contemporary era of globalized capital and communications has promoted new and accelerated forms of labour migration. An elite cosmopolitan class of professionals and managers and experts in information technology move around freely across the globe in the service of transnational corporations. Also highly mobile are skilled workers in resource extraction industries, especially oil workers, along with skilled scientists, health-care workers, and teachers. Competing at the bottom of international labour markets are seasonal farm workers and domestic service workers. Richmond (2002) estimates that by the beginning of the 21st century there were 120 million people working outside their country of birth, excluding "permanent" emigrants. Political upheavals on a global scale are also producing reactive migration of refugees from conflict, famine, and environmental degradation. Andersson (2005) recounts the desperate struggles of undocumented transmigrants from across Latin America trying to get into the United States to find work.

The result, Richmond concludes, is that almost all countries now have multiracial and multilingual populations that cut across class levels. The experiences of cosmopolitan elites who embrace hybrid cultures as creative and emancipating are very different from those of destitute refugees, or unskilled migrant workers, and different again from disempowered local workers competing for increasingly precarious, temporary, contract and casual work (Galabuzi 2006, 10). Complicating the picture further is evidence of population decline and demographic imbalance across Western Europe and in Canada as the post-war "baby boomers" near retirement and birth rates decline. Political and economic leaders in these countries increasingly extol higher immigration as necessary to provide the mass of service workers and taxpayers to support rapidly aging populations. Optimistic scenarios view these changes as potentially heralding a more integrated universal world system (Hardt and Negri 2000), while others foresee intensified nationalism and ethnocentrism as threatened populations fight to maintain their privileges or to carve out niches for themselves in competitive, exploitative, and unstable labour markets. The cosmopolitan discourse and postnational loyalties of high-flying economic elites do not resonate easily with the experiences of the mass of non-mobile, middle- and low-waged workers looking to the state to protect basic services (Yegenoglu 2005).

The next section explores in more depth how these historical shifts in economy and migration have impacted on race and ethnic relations in Canada.

Canada: Racialized Class Formation in White Settler Society

Processes of class formation in Canada have been inherently racialized from the earliest years of European incursion into the lands that are now Canada. Fur trading companies like Hudson's Bay were designed to profit European governments. They were never intended to enrich indigenous peoples. Natives supplied most of the furs, bartering them for European technology, clothes, and trinkets, but they were not permitted to enter the forts as paid employees (Bourgeault 1983). White women were also banned from the forts, so that the companies would not have to meet the costs of supporting families. Mixed-blood children born of liaisons between European men and Native women were disowned in European law as the responsibility only of their Native mothers. In the eastern territories, Mohawk traders were better able to exploit the arrival of Europeans by positioning themselves as autonomous middle-men traders between warring factions of English, French, and Dutch merchants (Alfred 1995, Ch. 2). But this economic base largely evaporated with peace settlements after the War of 1812. With the steep decline in the fur trade by the mid-1800s, European merchant capitalists had little need for indigenous people. European settlers, intent on exploiting the "empty wilderness" for ranching and agriculture, drove them out of their way, confining them to reservations on lands mostly unsuitable for European-style settlement. The vast herds of buffalo, along with deer, moose, and caribou that had sustained countless generations of indigenous peoples, were equally in the way of European settlers and their numbers rapidly decimated.

Economically, it may have been inevitable that indigenous hunting and gathering economies would decline with the influx of settlers (Stanley 1964, 3–5). But it was not inevitable that indigenous peoples would be forcibly excluded from alternative ranching and agricultural economies. It was not inevitable that European settlers would be allocated 160 acres of farmland per family while Native families received only 10 acres or less, and that of poor quality. The Indian Act of 1896 that established these reserves also gave extraordinary powers to the Minister of Indian Affairs to manage these reserves, and to expropriate lands for railways, mining, hydroelectricity, and other development interests in later years. The National Indian Brotherhood of Canada estimates that as much as half of all allocated reserve lands were lost through such expropriations between 1900 and 1930 alone (Kellough 1980, 348). Laws developed by and for white settler governments in the interests of capitalist development of resources made such appropriations easy, but made claims for compensation by indigenous inhabitants impossibly difficult to pursue, since the laws required claimants to hold clearly defined, individual property rights recognized under European law (Martin 2002; Gill 2002; Blomley 2004).

The visibly racialized class structure of the emerging white settler society of Canada was actively managed by immigration laws designed to mesh different cohorts of migrants with labour-force requirements. Immigrants from England and France were actively recruited to meet capitalist labour needs in expanding urban centres. Capitalists facing a shortage of wage-labour for their factories pushed successive governments to promote land speculation designed to stem the leakage of labourers into independent farm ownership (Pentland 1959, 458–459; Teeple 1972, 46). Land prices in eastern Canada were raised to such high levels that migrants were forced to work for many years as wage labourers in factories before they could think of becoming independent farmers. The Manitoba government under Clifford Sifton in the 1890s also aggressively recruited "stalwart peasants in sheep-skin coats" (Troper and Weinfeld 1999, 3) from other parts of Europe specifically on the understanding that they were willing to open up isolated tracts of wilderness for commercial farming. Under pressure from business and railway interests in the 1870s and 1880s, the Canadian government instituted laws to permit Chinese and other Asian males to enter western Canada primarily as cheap labour for heavy and dangerous work such as blasting track for the Canadian Pacific Railway. Companies advanced ticket money for the journey to Canada in return for signed bonds to work for periods of five to 10 years. Immigrant labourers were not permitted to bring wives or children. Companies held all Chinese workers' earnings and were obliged to provide only the bare essentials for their workers. An estimated 600 Chinese labourers died during railway construction from accidents and appalling living conditions (Bolaria and Li 1988). Once the railway was completed they were exploited as cheap labour in mining, fishing, and sawmills, as the supply of manual labour from Europe declined. They commonly worked for wages that were between one-half to one-quarter of wage rates paid to white workers. By the 1900s white workers who feared this ultra-cheap competitive labour began to agitate fiercely for restrictions on Asian immigration. White workers conceptualized Asians not as fellow workers who deserved protection from exploitation, but as aliens who should be driven out. Politicians campaigned for restrictive legislation that first imposed a head tax on all Chinese and Japanese immigrants, and then virtually blocked all immigration from Asia until after the Second World War. Across Canada, Asian workers faced discrimination from employers that pushed them into the lowest-paid jobs in ethnic businesses such as laundries and restaurants (Chen 2004; Li 2003).

Slavery existed in Canada, but without the demand of plantation economies it never became widespread. Yet pervasive racist discrimination still pushed black migrants into the lowest-paid marginal jobs. Blacks who entered Canada as Empire Loyalists after the American revolution of 1783 were promised land along with the white Loyalists, but the promises were never kept. Either they received no land at all or were given barren plots on the fringes of townships. Compelled to work at wage-rates of a quarter of those of white workers, they were both despised and feared by white workers as competition in the labour market.

Within this sad history, race and class are inextricably tied together. Business elites supported racist immigration policies that ensured a supply of exceptionally cheap and compliant labour. Indentured Chinese immigrant workers, controlled by highly restrictive contracts and in virtual debt bondage to employers who paid their passage, had few resources to challenge appalling working conditions. Racially segregated employment patterns minimized the likelihood of migrants from Europe joining forces with migrants from Asia to struggle for shared interests. Black workers, similarly isolated in segregated settlements and risking deportation to slave-owning states to the south, likewise had few social resources to mobilize for collective action. At the same time, the visible presence of large numbers of super-exploited, non-white workers tamed the potential for collective strike action by somewhat better-paid white workers. Strikes for better working conditions did happen. The Winnipeg General Strike of 1919 is one of the largest and best known, when an estimated 30 000 workers left their jobs. However, this strike was quickly broken by a combination of police brutality, the discrediting of leaders as communist aliens from Eastern Europe, and a hastily passed law permitting the government to deport British-born immigrants.

Canada's Labour Force in the Twenty-First Century: A Multicultural Vertical Mosaic

As noted above the Immigration Act of 1967 officially abolished any formal reference to race or ethnic background of immigrants, favouring instead a system of preferential ranking based on a combination of points for education, proficiency in English or French, and employment skills that matched shortages in the Canadian labour market. The Charter of Rights of 1982 explicitly forbids discrimination on the basis of race or ethnic origin, and the Employment Equity Act of 1995 goes beyond passive non-discrimination to pressure federal government agencies and companies doing business with the government to actively recruit and promote qualified visible minorities, along with Aboriginals, disabled workers, and women, to achieve a workforce proportional to the size of these groups in the Canadian labour force as a whole. Business and political elites widely endorsed these policies on three major grounds. Canada can no longer afford to display overt racism against China or Japan now that they are major trading partners with Canada. Also, a multiracial and multiethnic labour force gives Canadian businesses an advantage in language and cultural competence needed to promote international trade. Thirdly, the Canadian economy needs immigrants to compensate for a shrinking and rapidly aging population. Migration from formerly favoured European and North American societies has fallen to very low levels. In total, 3.7 million immigrants came to Canada over the 25 years between 1968 and 1992. Almost half of them fitted the category of "visible minorities," with 35.7 percent from Asia and 12.2 percent from Africa and the Caribbean (Galabuzi 2006, 2).

The central question Galabuzi explores is how these visible or racialized migrants and racialized Canadians generally have been integrated into the Canadian economy, measured by such variables as the kind of jobs they get, unemployment rates, and employment incomes when job skills and education are taken into account. He notes first that global economic restructuring has resulted in an expanding proportion of jobs in Canada that fit the pattern of "precarious work"—temporary, part-time, contract, and casual work with low pay, no benefits, no job security, and poor working conditions. Racialized persons are concentrated in such jobs in higher proportions than their numbers in the labour force (Galabuzi 2006, Ch. 1). In 1995, only one-third of Canadian-born racialized earners were employed in full-time, full-year jobs compared with half of other Canadian-born earners (Galabuzi 2006, 105). Visible minorities have higher levels of unemployment, at 12.6 percent, compared with 6.7 percent for the general population in 2001 (Galabuzi 2006, 16). They are more likely to be living below the poverty line at 35.6 percent, compared with 17.6 percent of the general population, not including Aboriginals (Galabuzi 2006, 17), and their average incomes are 25 percent lower (Galabuzi 2006, 91). As a measure of the problem of racism in Canada, Galabuzi cites evidence that African Canadian university graduates in Toronto have the same rate of unemployment as white high-school dropouts (2006, 204).

Conventional explanations in terms of lower education or poorer quality of "human capital" for visible minorities are not supported by the evidence that visible minorities, selectively approved for immigration according to the points system since 1968, have higher average levels of education than the general population. By 1990, 40.7 percent of immigrants had university degrees and a further 20.2 percent had trade and college education, compared with Canadian averages of 22.2 percent and 31.7 percent respec-

tively (Galabuzi 2006, 111–113). Recent immigrants, half of whom are visible minorities, are highly educated and have advanced job skills. Yet they are not able to translate these educational advantages into professional careers. Even after 10 or more years of residence in Canada, visible minority immigrants are not catching up. When controlling for length of stay, the average income of racialized immigrants is lower than for non-racialized immigrants.

Galabuzi argues that this evidence of racialized inequality in the Canadian economy reflects extensive barriers to accreditation of immigrant qualifications that have not been resolved in the almost 40 years since the points system was introduced. This resistance, he argues, itself reflects racist assumptions about human worth. Migrants from Asia, Africa, and Latin America with advanced degrees and professional practice in fields such as medicine, dentistry, nursing, veterinary science, law, social work, teaching, engineering, and trades, such as plumbing, accounting, and mechanics, are being enticed into Canada (Galabuzi 2006, 52). Yet when they get here they find that Canadian licencing bodies will not accept their qualifications as adequate to practice in Canada. Individuals are told that they must virtually repeat their training in Canada before they can sit licencing examinations. Such demands are made without any provision to help immigrants meet the costs of such retraining and with limited places made available for them. Even doctors who have passed all their licencing examinations still find they cannot get essential residency positions because the number of such positions available is closely tied to numbers of Canadian medical-school admissions. Employers of non-professional labour cite different reasons, like risks associated with language and cultural barriers, for reluctance to hire immigrants before they have extensive Canadian employment experience. Immigrants are caught in the impossible situation of being required to have prior Canadian employment experience in their field before employers will hire them to work in Canada. Structural adjustment programs like intensive job-related language training and job shadowing, which might fast-track immigrants into careers commensurate with their qualifications are not offered.

Charter rights, multiculturalism, and employment equity policies all notwithstanding, there is still a racialized vertical mosaic in the Canadian economy. Critics of the government policies charge that they sound good in principle but have no teeth. The federal Employment Equity Policy has no mechanisms to enforce compliance and no sanctions for failure. Trudeau's Multiculturalism Policy stressed cultural equality for minorities, not economic or political equality (Ng 1995). As Bannerji scathingly expresses it, visible minorities demanded the end of racist capitalism—and instead got "multiculturalism" (2000, 89). Business elites promote voluntary "diversity management" as good for business (Wrench 2005), but in practice they focus on the "soft option" of sensitivity training for managers, rather than the "hard option" of structural equality in hiring and promotion practices.

Ideological Hegemony: Preserving Privilege

A central prediction in Marxist analysis is that the prevailing cultural values of a society, continually reinforced by economic and political elites, will be those that support and justify the position of the economically privileged class. Such values predictably serve to mystify or obscure the exploitative features of capitalist economic organization in favour of rationalizations or ideologies that protect privilege as merited achievements. Commonly accepted explanations for the evidence of a racialized class structure in Canada, as in other Western capitalist societies, conform to this predicted pattern.

Structural barriers to the integration of visible minorities as equals in Canadian economy are all but ignored in prevailing explanations, in favour of a focus on presumed failings in the visible minorities themselves. Employers and licencing bodies assume from the start that foreign qualifications and experience are likely to be inferior to Canadian qualifications unless conclusively proven otherwise. Evidence that Canadian markets are full of cars and electronics manufactured in Asia is not taken as proof of the competence of Asian-trained scientists and mechanics who made them. Experimental research with matched white and visible-minority job applicants have demonstrated that employers routinely screen out minority applicants without even interviewing them, on the presumption that they would not have the abilities of white applicants (Galabuzi 2006, 153). Evidence of excessively high unemployment among visible minorities in the 1990s was translated in government policies as evidencing the need to apply an even more rigorous points system to potential immigrants to ensure "higher quality applicants, and to cut back on sponsored or family class immigration as imposing too much of a drain on social services." Canadian political parties became preoccupied with concerns about "illegal" immigrants and "bogus refugees" who "abuse" social services and should be apprehended and deported (Kirkham 1998, 248–253). When poverty and frustration among visible minority immigrants finds expression in criminal activities, this has readily become translated in political and media debates as further evidence of the presumed low quality of visible minorities themselves, and as culturally predisposed to criminal lifestyles.

Studies of the attitudes of white workers towards visible minorities commonly reflect a parallel set of assumptions that protect the interests of white workers against the potential claims of visible minorities to more of the economic pie. Such attitudes include the assumption that white workers generally are superior to visible minority workers; that the disadvantaged status of visible minorities, if true, is most likely their own fault; that the economy cannot absorb more immigrants without jeopardizing the hard-earned and tenuous economic stability of middle-class workers and their families; and that employment equity or affirmative action policies constitute unwarranted discrimination against white workers. Rubin's (1994) study of struggling working-class white families in America suggests that people commonly believe in equal opportunity and white superiority at the same time. In their common-sense reasoning, whites ought to get the better jobs because they are better workers, and hence if black or other minority-group workers are hired ahead of themselves it is due to discriminatory affirmative action rather than merit. Members of Italian and Greek minorities who had themselves faced discrimination as immigrants to America readily endorsed prejudices against other minorities, especially black Americans, as inferior workers to themselves (Noivo 1998). Homeowners feared that the value of their properties would decline if visible minorities, and especially black Americans, started to buy houses in their neighbourhood (Massey 2005). When federal laws made it illegal to discriminate openly against black buyers, real estate agents and mortgage lenders used more subtle means. Typically, they would withhold information about available properties in white neighbourhoods, and require black homebuyers to make higher down payments and meet more stringent repayment schedules to qualify for mortgages (Massey 2005).

Relatively privileged families in a middle-class town in England actively resisted efforts to settle refugees in their community, even on a temporary basis. They signed petitions and organized demonstrations against a plan to use a local hotel as a refugee shelter on the grounds that the Saltdean economy could not cope with the influx (Grillo 2005). They argued that it was difficult enough for local people to care for their own elderly and needy people, without the added burden of caring for refugees who might also be a crime risk. Cutbacks to social services in the wake of recession made these arguments plausible. Shopkeepers in a London neighbourhood vented their resentment at Muslim immigrants for undermining the neighbourhood community (Wells and Watson 2005). With their businesses already threatened by large supermarkets, these shopkeepers felt further sidelined and unable to compete for business from these alien newcomers with their preference for halal meat and ethnic goods.

In all these studies, white respondents pervasively denied that they were racists, insisting that their views were factually realistic and legitimate. Any suggestion that affirmative action policies might be necessary or valid to ensure equal treatment for visible minorities was fiercely resisted. Affirmative action was variously characterized by whites as blatant discrimination against whites, as itself racist, as a violation of fundamental principles of equality, as giving underqualified visible minorities an undeserved easy ride, and actually making the situation worse for visible minorities who got jobs, scholarships, or other benefits, by confirming that they were not good enough to succeed without such discriminatory favours (Kleiner 1998; Augoustinos et al. 2005; Donnelly et al. 2005). Even those who conceded that Aboriginals face more obstacles than whites contended that whites also have disadvantages but overcome them with determination and effort. White respondents referred to principles of equality, individual merit, and achievement to discredit affirmative action and employment equity. They discussed racism but only to deny its relevance. They did not see or did not comment on the central requirement of these policies that minority applicants be appropriately qualified. Totally obscured in the common-sense understanding that white respondents displayed was any awareness of white privilege, the pervasive favouring of white applicants, the pervasive discrediting of foreign credentials and experiences as obviously inferior to Canadian credentials, the continuing colonialism that denies Aborigi-nal forms of title to lands and resources, and the pervasive structural barriers that generations of racialized poverty place in the way of all but the strongest individuals to compete on the basis of standards solely defined by white educators and employers. When Rubin asked her black American respondents for their thoughts on affirmative action, their views were surprisingly similar to those of white respondents. They too insisted that merit should count, and advocated a true meritocracy in which blacks would be hired equally with white workers. What they saw differently was that black workers faced so much discrimination and so many barriers to equal opportunity that without affirmative action few of them would ever be hired.

From the political economy perspective, these common-sense forms of thinking, and the ethnocentrism and racism they displace, do not have their roots in primordial ethnic attachments or in childhood socialization. They have their roots in the class relations of capitalism. They serve to protect white privilege, justify racialized inequalities as reflections only of individual merit or lack of merit, and obscure the structural workings of global corporate capitalism, which continually throw up displaced and dispossessed refugees and asylum seekers on Europe's shores (Sivanandan 2001). White resentment against structural unemployment gets deflected into blaming people even more vulnerable than themselves for increasing competition for precarious jobs. Resentment at the gutting of social programs in the name of deficit reduction gets similarly deflected onto "illegal aliens" or "bogus refugees" or "asylum seekers" who supposedly clog up the system and abuse taxpayers' money. Collectively these attitudes function as part of the ideological hegemony that shores up the capitalist system.

 # The Social Constructionist Perspective: Racialization and Ethnicization as Social Accomplishments

The social constructionist perspective focuses attention on processes of ethnicization and racialization—that is, the processes through which people come to identify themselves and others or to feel themselves labelled by others as members of some particular ethnic or racial grouping.

Ethnic and racial identities are seen as negotiable features of social relationships rather than fixed, with the boundaries of exclusion and inclusion changing with specific historical and social situations and experiences. The salience given to ethnic or racial labelling relative to multiple other potential social relationships, like age-grouping, occupation, religion, political affiliation, gender, and sexual orientation, is also historically and socially specific. To the extent that people think of ethnic or racial identities as fixed by birth, or as centrally defining features of themselves or others, this sense of rigidity and centrality of boundary definitions itself has to be explained by reference to social processes that fix and enforce such identities. These boundary-defining processes work simultaneously at the level of shared group understandings of the kinds of people who are included in or excluded from membership categories, and individual choice of private and publicly claimed membership. These processes fundamentally involve relations of power—the power to define oneself and others and to have those definitions recognized and acted upon, and conversely the power to exclude and to have those exclusions count.

Defining the "Other": State Policy and Identity Formation

The British imperial government and later the federal state of Canada passed a series of laws and amendments to laws, including the Indian Act, various Immigration Acts and the Multiculturalism Act, which functioned to create boundaries of inclusion and exclusion around minority status.

The indigenous inhabitants of what is now Canada have struggled for centuries to define their individual and collective identities within the dominating frame of colonial legislation. During the fur-trade era, the children born of liaisons between men from Europe and indigenous women were considered "Indians." Their mothers and her kin were held responsible for these children, and explicitly not their white fathers. The intent was that mixed-blood offspring would have no legitimate claim to the wealth generated by the trading forts (Bourgeault 1983). Later, as white settlers came in ever increasing numbers, settler governments pressured indigenous peoples to sign treaties restricting them to reserved lands, in return for various rights. The interests of successive colonial governments was now in minimizing the numbers of people who would be legally recognized as "status Indians" with treaty entitlements to live on reserved land and to have access to education, medical, and other benefits.

The first federal Indian Act of 1867 explicitly recognized *only* the descendants of Native males as legally status Indians, thereby excluding vast numbers of mixed-blood children of Native women and white fathers from any legal claim to Native ancestry. They became Canadians of Aboriginal descent, but not socially recognized as either Natives or whites. Over time, the Indian Act, with its legalized discourse of classification and regulation, worked to create among regulated peoples and their descendants, the subjective identities of status Indian and non-status or excluded people (Lawrence 2004). The Act gave white bureaucrats, hired as Indian agents, extensive powers to define the boundaries of legal residence on these reserves, and the right to evict "squatters" and "trespassers." In one extreme case, a treaty signed in 1877 created the Pahpahstayo Reserve on 40 acres, which are now part of South Edmonton, but a mere nine years later, all the residents were declared to be merely mixed-bloods and no longer status Indians entitled to a reserve. They were forcibly removed and the reserve ceased to exist (Lawrence 2004, 43).

The Gradual Enfranchisement Act of 1869 functioned to further restrict the numbers of status Indians by enticing and forcing individual men, along with their wives and descendants, to give up their status in return for parcels of land, jobs with the military, the right to vote, and the like (Lawrence 2004, 32–33). Successive government policies and practices, often of questionable legality, worked to further obscure and obliterate the Aboriginal status of thousands of people. Native children, rounded up and sent to residential schools, were stripped of their ancestral languages and cultures. School officials routinely changed the names of individuals or their families on residential school admission forms. Indian agents removed the names of orphans sent to these schools from their band lists. Census takers refused to

Residential schools stripped Native children of their ancestral languages and cultures in an effort to assimilate them into European Canadian culture.

Glenbow Archives NA-5719-4

categorize individuals as "Natives" on government forms, categorizing them as "French" or "black." Native wives were listed as "French" on marriage registries. During the 1960s, as residential schools declined, federal social workers gained authority to remove children from difficult family situations on reservations for off-reserve adoption. Many thousands of children lost their status as Natives, and their connections to family as tribe, through the bureaucratic erasure of their origins (Lawrence 2004, 37).

The struggles of Aboriginal peoples to define their own identities still continue within Canadian courts, on terms set by white settler governments. Recent and still ongoing land-claims cases in Canada and the USA commonly revolve around legal definitions of Aboriginal status. In a case involving the Gitksan and Wet'suwet'en peoples of Northern British Columbia (Lawrence 2004, 4), the Supreme Court of Canada determined that the claimants must not only prove that they have had unbroken governance of the land and land use for 12 000 years, they must also prove that they are essentially the same people as their ancestors were, in effect that they have retained intact and unchanged their bloodlines and primordial Native cultural traditions. Evidence of cultural change or "assimilation" is thus being defined legally as evidence of loss of Aboriginal status. In 1986 the Indian Act was revised yet again to grant limited status to Native women who had lost their status on marriage to non-status men, with the condition that Native band councils gained the right to decide whether these new "status Indians" would gain band-membership status. Some bands have opted to use blood quantum of between 25 and 100 percent as the working definition of band membership, copying the racist criteria imposed by Canadian courts in land-claims disputes (Lawrence 2004, 68; Alfred 1995).

Alfred argues that the rigid culture-based boundaries and ostensibly racist definitions of membership adopted by Kahnawake Mohawk near Montreal do not reflect ancestral values, which were actually far more fluid. Rather, they reflect the struggle of the Mohawk to define themselves in the context of ongoing Euro-Canadian efforts to destroy Aboriginal status and culture.

Multiculturalism as Policy: Creating Ethnics

The Canadian Multiculturalism Act, first proclaimed by the Trudeau government in 1971, is represented as recognizing and giving official status and protection to a wide variety of culturally distinct communities. These diverse communities became established in Canada as the new Immigration Act of 1967 facilitated the migration of non-white people from around the world. Social constructionist analysis, however, challenges this representation of pre-existing ethnic communities that arrive in Canada, exploring instead how the Act works to create and perpetuate the subject communities that it defines. Trudeau's policy speech in 1971 can be read as actively defining for members of parliament, and for Canadians generally, how to read the situation of worldwide migration into Canada as one of "multiple cultures," and the policy issue as one of protecting "multiple cultures" (Ng 1995). The situation could have been read very differently, and arguably more accurately, as one of global economic migrants who experience a vertical mosaic of unequal access to the Canadian economy. From this alternative perspective, salient policy issues would focus on the need for flexible recognition of foreign qualifications and work experiences, expanded bridging training and job shadowing, and the need for anti-racist training and legislation governing employers and unions, all designed to promote greater equality in labour-force absorption. Instead, the central focus of Trudeau's policy is on "cultures." He proposed four policy initiatives designed to provide assistance to ethnic minority communities in their desire to contribute to Canada, to overcome cultural barriers to participation, to promote creative cultural encounters in the interests of Canadian national unity, and to provide basic language training in English or French. These initiatives were defined as the responsibility of the Citizenship Branch of the Department of the Secretary of State, with no responsibilities delegated to the Department of Employment and Immigration.

It has been widely argued that the true policy concern underlying the Multiculturalism Act was not to deal with ethnic minorities at all, but to manage heightened tensions between Francophone Quebec and the rest of Canada, especially following the FLQ kidnapping crisis in October of 1970. The Act established official bilingualism to appease Quebec while characterizing Canada-outside-Quebec as multicultural in contrast to Quebec's supposedly narrow homogeneity (Ng 1995; Fleras and Elliott 2003, Ch. 8; Bannerji 2000, Ch. 3). Whether in the interest of placating Quebec or other minorities, the focus of bureaucratic attention was centred squarely on the management of culturally distinct ethnic minority communities in Canada.

Policy initiatives developed through multiculturalism envision encouraging leaders within various ethnic communities to consult with the state on matters of interest to their communities, to develop liaisons with local members of parliament, and to apply for funds to promote cultural festivals and heritage language retention, as well as funds for training in Canada's two official languages. A central argument put forward by Ng and Bannerji is that these initiatives, and the forms they take, work to create or bring about the appearance of ethnic communities that the Act presupposes. In effect, government policies themselves form part of the boundary-defining processes that constitute ethnic difference.

Promoting "Ethnic" Leaders Ethnic communities are expected to have ethnic leaders who represent their communities in national politics. A plethora of formal consultations have emerged at all levels of government in Canada, including for immigration hearings, social services, equity programs, policing, government departments, crown corporations, hospitals, and school boards, supported by a plethora of lectures and conferences sponsored by ethnic associations and universities across Canada (Amit-Talai 1996). Self-identified ethnic leaders have come forward to fill these political roles as spokespersons, consultants, and advisors to the government. For every "crisis" in ethnic relations that becomes identified, some new committee gets struck to consult with ethnic communities. The result, suggests Amit-Talai, is the emergence of an "official ethnic minority circuit" from which the same names get put forward repeatedly for each new committee. Many such people make full-time careers out of the circuit, as equity officers, race-relations advisors, intercultural training consultants, committee appointees, and staff in ethnic minority and civil rights associations. While the political goal of extensive consultation with ethnic communities may sound impressive, it may be limited in practice to repeated conversations with the same small clique of individuals.

The elusive question is who do these individual "leaders" represent, or for whom do they speak. A survey of studies of leadership in ethnic groups suggests that disunity is the norm rather than the exception (Jedwab 2001). Categories like "Muslim" or "South Asian," for example, encompass a multiplicity of ethnic subgroups that cannot be represented by one spokesperson. Any one identifiable subgroup also commonly encompasses multiple factions along lines of gender, class, political orientation, traditional to secular outlook, and the like. But self-styled ethnic community leaders are under pressure to gloss over divisions and conflicting priorities. They need to project a sense of ethnic unity and consensus to non-members to bolster their own claims to be representatives of the "community" with the government. In reality, Amit-Talai suggests, many of these minority circuit players may be marginal members of the ethnic communities they claim to represent, and be viewed with suspicion by insiders.

Interrogating Ethnic "Community"

The concept of ethnic community contains a double irony in that while ethnic communities as lived experience at a local or neighbourhood level have often been ignored, the notion of "ethnic community" as conceptual abstraction has become entrenched in the discourse and politics of multiculturalism.

City planners have routinely shown scant regard for community ties at the local level of small neighbourhoods, especially when they get in the way of building roads, or facilitating urban slum clearance for value-added commercial development. The black settlement of Africville in Halifax was bulldozed in 1964 to make way for a park, with no regard for the extended family ties and support networks that had sustained the settlement for more than a century (Clairmont and Magill [1974] 1999; Nelson 2002). The 400 black residents of Africville did feel a strong sense of community and attachment, albeit to an impoverished area of substandard housing. Forty years after the city forcibly removed the residents and bulldozed their homes, the 400 former residents, along with their descendants, were still organizing annual reunions at the site.

The concept of "ethnic communities" that pervades the political discourse of multiculturalism has little or nothing to do with lived experience of extended kin and support networks that people may develop with their friends and neighbours. It refers to an abstract categorization of people along lines of race and ethnicity, lines that are presumed to tie people together. Trudeau's speech on multiculturalism asserts as common-sense knowledge that people migrating to Canada come as members of ethnic communities, or form such communities once they arrive. Yet no such assumptions about community membership are made about Canadians who are considered mainstream, like immigrants from England. In classical sociological theory the notion of "community" implies a sense of nostalgia for a more backward lifestyle while "individuals" in modern urban industrialized societies form loose-knit associations around varieties of specialized interests. Critics question this common-sense assumption that mainstream Canadians form "associations" while "ethnic" Canadians form "communities" (Alleyne 2002). Migrants typically arrive as individuals, or as members of nuclear families, Bannerji suggests (2000, 159). They may well look to close kin for help with getting settled, but whether they confine their primary interaction to ethnic enclaves depends more on a sense of external rejection from the host society than yearning for homogeneity.

Studies of migrants who came from the same geographic and ethnic backgrounds have commonly not supported the notion that they form close-knit folk societies, with shared cultural boundaries and mutual interests, envisioned in the discourse of ethnic community. Refugees from the war in Bosnia had mostly lived in multi-religious and multi-ethnic cities and many were intermarried with Serbs and Croats (Kelly 2003). A Refugee Action Committee formed in Britain struggled to create a sense of community among the refugees, with the idea that this would be helpful for their adjustment to Britain. But in Kelly's view, such organizing produced at best a tenuous, contingent community, dependent on a few leaders who expected to benefit from assistance offered to "refugee communities" from the host state. Otherwise the Bosnian association was internally faction-ridden, with few volunteer workers and no sense of group obligation. The so-called Iranian community in London, England, appeared similarly tenuous (Sreberny 2000). There is no "Iranian community" in London, Sreberny concludes, only a few local drop-in centres.

Negotiating Ethnic/Racial Communities

If we abandon the notion that ethnic or racial communities occur naturally, then the evidence that people do sometimes mobilize around ethnic/racial markers needs to be explained. How and why, and under what kinds of circumstances, do people sometimes come to think of themselves as members of ethnic communities? Conditions within the host society, as much as conditions intrinsic to minorities themselves, are implicated in ethnic identity formation. A study of the emergence of Hindu self-identity among university students in Britain suggests that it developed primarily as a response to multicultural politics, and the sense of being marginalized and not fully accepted as "British" despite being born and raised in England. They described how they had begun to use the label "Hindu" in response to incessant questioning from fellow British students about who they were. Their chosen label "British" only prompted further questioning about where they were really, originally from. They also had to respond to constant questioning about whether they were like "this crap Asian program on black families" shown in television documentaries and films. Hindu won out as the only positive label that seemed available. Alternative geographic-origin labels like India or East Africa did not fit either as they had never seen these places. They were also "not Pakistanis," "not Muslims," and "not blacks." The label "Hindu," Raj suggests, worked as an ethnic resource, an active response to the experience of being marked as racially and culturally different, and to increasing pressure from multicultural politics to assert some fixed religious-ethnic identity. The label Hindu was mostly without religious content, as these students had not been socialized into Hindu practices, and knew little about them. Once at university, the student Hindu Association gradually drew them in with explanatory talks on Hindu philosophy and prominent Hindu politicians as guest lectures.

The emergence of "black" as actively negotiated and hotly contested political label in contemporary Britain reflects similar struggles to label a sense of shared issues (Sudbury 2001). Sudbury rejects the theoretical frame of "ethnic resource mobilization" on the grounds that most of the women attracted to the Organization of Women of African and Asian Descent (OWAAD) in 1978 did not come with ready-made identities to collective action, and they shared no common ethnic resource of language, religion, geographic origins, or other elements of culture. The emerging OWAAD political identity focuses on shared experiences of racism and marginalization as non-whites in Britain. The irony is that an important impetus for diverse people to come together under the umbrella label of "black" has been to challenge pervasive stereotypes that represent all non-whites as the same. Activist black writers studied by Reynolds (2002) struggled against reductionist multicultural awareness that promotes "black literature" only when it fits the stereotype of black experience as centred on poverty, discrimination and/or abuse, and the writers' journeys of self-exploration and self-discovery. Accounts that do not fit this genre tend to be rejected by publishers as not fitting what audiences would expect black authors to be writing about.

What these ethnicized and racialized people have most in common is not shared culture, but shared experience of "othering," marking them as outsiders, as visible minorities, or as multicultured, different from the whiteness and Europeanness that is taken for granted as mainstream culture. Highlighted in Bannerji's accounts of the lives of non-white immigrants in Canada are experiences that few "invisible" or mainstream Canadians ever need to notice, but that few visibles can afford to ignore (2000, Ch. 3). They include all-pervasive state regulations governing the lives of immigrants, the interrogation and suspicion they face when meeting requirements for visas and permits to enter, to travel, to study, or to bring family members. They include also a heightened awareness of public expressions of racism that those who are not targeted can more easily ignore—the anti-immigration stance of the Western Guard, the Heritage Front, the Reform Party, the neo-Nazi rock band Rahowa—its name an acronym for Racial Holy War (Bannerji 2000, 110). There are also the stories of rejected migrants hiding for months in church basements in fear of deportation back to countries from which they have fled, of black men shot by nervous and trigger-happy police, of skinhead attacks on Jewish property, of the frozen bodies of Aboriginal youth dumped by police miles outside of Prairie cities. Such stories intensify the sense of fear and exclusion felt by those who are othered in Canadian society. Visible minorities know themselves to be the primary targets of the heightened surveillance that comes with fear of terrorism. The ubiquitous closed-circuit television (CCTV) surveillance creates lines in public spaces "that blacks cannot cross and whites cannot see" (Fiske 2000, 53). Aboriginal and visible minority people are tracked and followed, stopped and searched, questioned and excluded, with the aid of technologies that are experienced by invisibles as unobtrusive, benign, and helpful.

Contemporary global concerns around the "war on terror," with associated involvement of the USA, Canada, and Britain in wars in Iraq and Afghanistan, and threats against Iran, also impact on the sense of identity migrants from these countries may feel with their homeland or kin still in these regions. So also does nightly news coverage of conflicts and natural disasters around the globe. It seems likely that people from Iran who showed little sense of a sustained "Iranian community" in London, when studied by Sreberny in the late '90s, may have responded differently in 2009 when Iran was being regularly portrayed in the media as under threat of sanctions or war for starting up its nuclear energy program, or on the verge of another violent revolution.

In the era since the 11 September 2001 terrorist attacks in New York and Washington, Muslims living in the West have had to negotiate their sense of identity in the context of heavily stereotyped media coverage. They encompass a staggering diversity of socio-cultural backgrounds from Far East, Middle East, and Palestine, different regions of Africa, the former Soviet Union, Eastern Europe, and the Balkans, as well as Western Europe and North America, and they follow vastly differing religious practices, ranging from fundamentalist to reformist and secular. All this diversity tends to be homogenized into simplistic stereotypes of "the Islamic mind" in Western mass media. People who have very little in common find themselves lumped together as if they formed a single "Islamic community."

Constructing the Vertical Mosaic: Insights from Institutional Ethnography

As described above, Statistics Canada data reveal a vertical mosaic of patterned inequalities in the Canadian labour force along racial and ethnic lines stretching back over many years (Porter 1965; Galabuzi 2006). Continuing reluctance by professional licencing bodies and employers to recognize foreign qualifications and work experiences account for some of the barriers facing professionals who migrate to Canada. But job qualifications alone are not sufficient to ensure equal employment opportunities for racialized and ethnicized people. The studies explored below give insights into the discriminatory effects of routine organizational practices through which decisions about hiring, retaining, and promoting people are made. These practices are often subtle and largely unacknowledged by those responsible for them or by those who benefit from the competitive advantages they sustain. They work at all levels of the class system.

An ethnographic study of a counselling agency designed to assist immigrant women with finding employment in Toronto describes in detail how bureaucratic accounting practices required by government regulators worked to ghettoize immigrant women in sweatshop, garment-factory jobs from which counsellors had been trying to help them escape (Ng 1988). Ng describes how counsellors, desperate to retain the funding on which their own salaries depended, were driven to prioritize what government regulators counted, namely the number of jobs filled. A steady supply of job openings was a crucial requirement for meeting hiring quotas, and the bulk of these job openings were supplied by garment-factory bosses. Counsellors listed these job openings and bullied clients into taking them, even when they knew that working conditions were substandard, wages offered to immigrant "trainees" and piece-rate workers were below the statutory minimum, and employers practised blatantly racist hiring restrictions. In effect, Ng concludes, once the counselling agency got government funding, it ceased to serve immigrant women. It became an agency of the state managing cheap immigrant labour on behalf of garment-factory bosses.

A personal narrative account by an Asian American sociology professor provides another point of entry for exploring discriminatory hiring practices, in her case with respect to professional university appointments at the elite end of the labour market (Glenn 1997, 94–99).

Officially, such appointments are governed by rigorous peer evaluation processes involving the presentation of scholarly publications, research talks, teaching evaluations, interviews, and collegial decision-making. Yet these procedures were routinely subverted when visible minority candidates were being considered. White male academics, disinterested in scholarship on gender, race, or ethnicity, commonly did not bother to read the research papers presented by minority applicants, or dismissed their scholarly significance. They valued avoiding conflict with colleagues more than fighting injustices against the excluded. Hence, it only took one or two prejudiced individuals in a large faculty to block minority appointments. Another common strategy which subverted appointments that were explicitly intended to attract visible minority applicants was to leave the position vacant on the excuse that no minority applicant was good enough, or that only one famous minority scholar would do, and that person was unavailable, or that the position warranted a salary far below what qualified applicants were already earning. That many such applicants did eventually have successful careers at other universities, including Glenn herself who became a full professor of sociology at the prestigious University of California, Berkeley, is evidence that prejudice rather than poor qualifications played the central role in such exclusion. The result, suggests Glenn, is that visible minority professors remain underrepresented as a token presence at American universities and ghettoized in departments of Chicano, Native American, or African American studies. Mainline departments remain "white male bastions," ignoring scholarship that focuses on issues of race, ethnicity, and gender.

Since 1995, Canadian universities have been required by the Federal Employment Equity Act to work towards fair representation of visible minorities and Aboriginal peoples, along with women and people with disabilities. But these official policies offer little protection from the kinds of covert discriminatory practices described by Glenn, because they become visible only as evidence of underqualified applicants. The proportions of tenured professors and professors in senior ranks in Canadian universities from the four employment-equity categories still fall well below the proportions available in the talent pool of graduates with doctorates from Canadian universities.

The potential talent pool of visible minority applicants is itself artificially restricted by familiar factors of poverty, restricted role models, low self-esteem, low encouragement, and other barriers that visible-minority students typically experience at earlier stages in their education. An ethnographic study of Chinese students in a Canadian school (Jackson 1987) reveals how even well-meaning advice from sympathetic teachers and counsellors contributed to Chinese students opting for unchallenging vocational courses over courses that might qualify them for university entrance. The sense of alienation and marginalization that many Aboriginal students experience in Canadian universities likewise contributes to their dropping out in large numbers.

Accomplishing Whiteness: The Invisible Norm

In classical sociology, as well as in everyday talk, terms like "ethnic" and "multicultural" have been used to refer mostly to non-European, non-white people. Contemporary research in identity politics is shifting the focus of attention increasingly towards the invisible majority in Western societies—to those whose bodies escape attention. Warren's research (2003) gives detailed ethnographic attention to how students enrolled in theatre classes in New York routinely perform race. He finds invisible normative whiteness pervasively constructed through literature and discourse that assumes the reader is white unless otherwise designated. To be white is to be human, to be human is to be white (Warren 2003, 22). White bodies in films become noticeable as white only in contrast to black bodies. The unacknowledged, unnamed body is presumed white until signalled otherwise. It is precisely this incessant repetition of colour-blind normative whiteness in student performances, Warren suggests, that constitutes white identity and gives whiteness such cultural power.

The power of normative whiteness to erase awareness of white privilege is reflected in studies of social-work practice with mixed clientele. White social workers in a London borough with mostly black clientele largely rejected the idea that the professional skills or approach needed to work successfully with black families would be any different from white families (Stubbs 1985). They strongly opposed the appointment of black social workers as inherently racist and even discriminatory in that it would subject black families to underqualified workers. If black social workers were to be hired, they argued, they should be trained and supervised by "regular" social workers to ensure that they performed their work in the same way. "Good black social workers," in effect, were white social workers. They did not see that they were not serving black families well, and did not understand how racism impacted on their client's lives. Only when there were sufficient black social workers to form a caucus were black social workers able to challenge the routine practice of removing children from black neighbourhoods to white foster families, and to propose collective politically radical action as potentially more constructive social work practice with families in racialized and impoverished black neighbourhoods than typical individual counselling.

Predominantly white social workers in an agency for abused women in the southern USA expressed similar conviction that if they provided similar services for all their clients in a colour-blind way, then the outcomes would be similarly effective for abused women from white and black families (Donnelly et al. 2005). They could readily suggest reasons why relatively few black women used their services—black women identified with abusive male partners as injured by racism, viewed it as a form of race treason to turn them into white male authorities, or to seek refuge in a shelter run by white women in a white neighbourhood. They failed to conceptualize these systemic differences as warranting different kinds of outreach and services for black women than the counselling they offered white women, counselling that typically favoured leaving abusive male partners and laying criminal charges. In effect, their colour-blind commitment to providing one normative standard service for all masked systemic privileging of white clients, a privileging that they had no interest in changing.

The charge that colour-blind normative whiteness in service provision is inherently racist in the context of critical systemic differences along racial and ethnic lines typically promotes reactions of rage and incomprehension in white service providers. When black minority workers in a shelter for battered women in Toronto raised such accusations, predominantly white staff were so enraged and hurt that the centre closed down (Henry et al. 1995, 162–165). The conflict erupted over the policy favoured by professional white social workers of allocating more funding for counselling, a policy that "underqualified" black staff challenged as individualizing and depoliticizing the racism that was undermining the family lives of black clients.

Feminist commitment to democratic, egalitarian, and consensus decision-making seems to have exacerbated the marginalization felt by women of colour in these organizations, because they felt under constant pressure to go along with what the majority white workers advocated (Scott 2005). Informal friendship networks closely reflected lines of class and race, with the more highly qualified and numerically dominant white workers able to exert their influence over others. Minority women of colour found they either had to argue constantly and appear racist and uncooperative in the process, or give up in silence, or leave.

Affirmative Action: Equity or Reverse Racism?

Charges and countercharges of racism reflect sharply differing understandings of processes of racialization and ethnicization. Those who support affirmative action policies and who challenge colour-blind normative whiteness point to evidence of systemic inequality. From this perspective, some form of affirmative action for visible minorities seems necessary to counter preferential treatment and opportunities that majority white authority figures afford to normative white applicants and colleagues. Aboriginal people see their access to welfare, health, and educational benefits not as "affirmative action" at all, but as hard-won treaty rights, cruelly extracted in return for colonial domination that drove their ancestors from the land and destroyed their traditional livelihoods. From the perspective of colour-blind normative whiteness, however, all forms of affirmative action and employment equity policies appear as racist practices. Any form of "special treatment" for Aboriginals or other visible minorities discriminates against merit-worthy individuals who happen to be white, many of whom themselves struggle against disadvantaged social and economic status.

A study of how white American college students talk with each other about black students details how they routinely collaborated in sustaining pseudo-arguments that discredited affirmative action policies (Kleiner 1998). By pseudo-arguments, Kleiner means one-sided arguments that are never challenged, and simulated straw-man arguments raised only to be discounted. Students repeatedly concurred in claiming that university entrance scholarships go overwhelmingly to undeserving black students who squander the money without ever having to work for it, who get a free ride in college, who have their college grades inflated, and when they graduate, manipulate affirmative action policies to get jobs for which they are not qualified. Most admitted that slavery and discrimination were bad in the past, but countered that blacks have already been compensated enough, yet they keep harping back on past wrongs and blaming whites who had nothing to do with them. Collaboratively, such talk functions to discredit black claims, while defending the correctness of white students' beliefs against insinuations of racism, and asserting their own comparative victimization by policies that favour minorities against themselves. The arguments are pseudo, Kleiner suggests, in that they are never tested against evidence. Objectively, how hard was it/is it for the descendants of slaves to pull themselves into the American mainstream? What are the statistics on socio-economic status of black families with children in contemporary America? How hard have most black students had to work to qualify for college entrance? How hard do average black students work in comparison with average white students to pass college courses? How often, if ever, do faculty actually inflate the grades of visible minorities? How often, if ever, do patently incompetent black graduates actually get and hold down good jobs that they are incompetent to perform? Statistically, how do black graduates compare with white graduates in career paths? They also do not ask the reverse-onus questions: How were blacks and other visible minorities being treated in the past that warranted the implementation of affirmative action policies? How com-

monly were merit-worthy black students denied the opportunity to attend university or to win scholarships because assessors scoffed at grades and references from low-status ghetto schools? How commonly were merit-worthy black graduates shut out from good career openings because assessors felt more secure hiring white graduates? What evidence is there that racial discrimination still routinely occurs in America? By never raising such questions and never researching for evidence that might answer them, students collaborate in protecting each other from charges that they themselves hold racist attitudes, and they collaborate in mutually reinforcing their own sense of resentment.

A study of talk by white students in Australia about affirmative action for Aboriginal students displays a similar pattern of pseudo-argument (Augoustinos et al. 2005). Students collectively defended the principles of individual merit and equal treatment as paramount, claiming that everyone can succeed if they try hard enough. If Aboriginals do not succeed as well as whites, they tell themselves, it is because they have not learned the same values of individual hard work. Policies to assist Aboriginal students to attend university only make the situation worse by giving them an easy ride. Aboriginal students get university places and jobs that they do not have to work for and do not deserve. This in turn undermines their self-esteem by confirming their inferiority and inability to compete as equals with whites. Again, such assertions are not questioned, nor tested with evidence. Statistically, what is the relationship between individual effort, qualifications, and financial rewards in the labour force when race and ethnicity are taken into account? How systemically unequal are the family situations and school experiences of Aboriginal and white children? How hard is it for Aboriginal students to qualify for university entrance compared with white students? How hard do they work to graduate? What are the long-term, intergenerational effects of promoting university education for Aboriginal people?

These authors trace in the discourse of these students the core elements of contemporary racism. The blatant and hostile racism of the past, which focused on biological superiority and inferiority of groups, has been widely discredited and is rarely openly expressed. What replaces it is a more subtle racism that attributes systemic inequalities to the intensity with which different cultural groups embrace values like self-reliance, discipline, hard work, achievement, initiative, and innovation. Inequalities, both global and local, thus appear as merited. In the ideology of contemporary racism, discrimination and disadvantages occurred only in the past. The current tactics and demands by visible minorities are thus undeserved and unfair, and serve to victimize the majority white people (Augoustinos et al. 2005, 316–317).

The special irony in this common-sense reasoning is that even as it denies the systemic validity of group differences, it encourages a racialized and ethnicized self-identification as "white" people whose very "invisibility" leaves them vulnerable to being ignored as others make claims on the system. A discourse of "unfairness" permeates complaints voiced by British locals in the suburb of Saltdean to government plans to house asylum seekers in a local hotel (Grillo 2005). Small shopkeepers in a London neighbourhood voiced a similar discourse of feeling abandoned by politicians who direct economic resources to "asylum seekers," while if you are English, white English or black English, you get left out (Wells and Watson 2005, 270), and if you say anything, you will be called racists. Is their talk "racist"? Yes and no, Grillo concludes. It is a multi-layered discourse full of coded references. It incorporates old racist fears of stigmatized, racialized "others" who threaten house values, and new racism's questioning of cultural compatibility. It also incorporates a litany of negative pre-judgments and fears about asylum seekers as likely to be cheating or lying to get into the country, abusing the welfare system, and possibly involved in criminal gangs or terrorist activities. Common-sense discourse offers few reasons for cheerfully welcoming asylum seekers or immigrants as new neighbours, although it concedes that individuals may be merit-worthy and deserving of compassion.

To understand how the local discourse of Saltdean protestors came to have these characteristics, one needs to look beyond the context of local talk between neighbours to explore the larger national talk on which it drew (Grillo 2005, 245). In a spiralling process of claims, counterclaims, rejoinders, and rebuttals, local people routinely echoed statements attributed to politicians that were repeated in television talk shows, and then picked up in letters to the editors of local newspapers, and repeated again when local people were asked by reporters to give comments. It is to this larger national talk that we now turn.

Constructing Public Opinion

Public opinion surveys have been widely criticized for how easily they can be manipulated by the way questions are worded and answers interpreted to fit the biases of those designing the surveys. But the question of how opinion surveys produce "meaning" is more complex than clearing away distortions to get more accurate representations. The opinions people hold are themselves a reflection of what people know about a topic, or more precisely what people *think* they know and *how* they know it (Lewis 2001, 15). To understand how people come to know about racialized and ethnicized people we need to explore further the discourse of people in positions to manage the flow of information,

including politicians, professional writers, and opinion leaders, how they are represented in mass media, and how audiences are attuned to respond to media reports (Cottle 2000, 1–30; Van Dijk 2000, 33–49; Van Dijk 1993).

Van Dijk argues that it makes sense to focus on the discourse of political and intellectual elites because they are particularly influential in producing common-sense understandings. These are the people whose opinions are sought and reproduced in the media, and who are most often asked to comment on claims made by others. It also makes sense to focus on respectable moderate parties rather than extreme fascist or white supremacist parties because the latter are more readily discredited. Further, he argues, we need to go beyond mere content analysis to focus on nuances in the text—*how* people say things, the metaphors and euphemisms they use, the disclaimers and qualifications they insert, that carry the emotional tones that audiences pick up. When political elites make disclaimers like "we have nothing against foreigners but . . ." or "it is sad for refugees but . . ." the "but" carries a powerful implicit message that the speaker is not racist, but realist, and that hearers should be suspicious and wary (Van Dijk 2000, 41). When political leaders and their media coverage define the topics as "illegal immigrants, reception problems, social problems, resentment, deviance, illegal immigration, bogus refugees, floods of immigrants, crime-ridden minorities," and the like, they feed into the new racism. The message being repeated here is that everything about immigration is negative.

The extensive public consultations on immigration initiated by the Canadian federal government in 1994 slanted questions in ways that encouraged exclusionary, negative and problem-oriented responses. Canadians were asked how immigration should be managed to increase the benefits to the Canadian economy and reduce the costs, including costs specifically associated with excessive demands on social services and how to better detect and reduce abuses. Canadians were further invited to comment on how cultural diversity affects the social and cultural life of Canada, how much importance should be given to family reunification and whether there are special groups, institutions, and programs that need to be protected (Thobani 2000). Rather than trying to answer these questions, Thobani challenges the prejudiced assumptions behind them and the negative frame they gave to the consultations. Canada is a nation of immigrants, yet the consultations presumed that only non-immigrant Canadians would be consulted about the "others." The questions further presumed a homogeneous "social and cultural life" that might need to be protected from the diversity that immigrants cause, and that outside of economic benefits, immigrants and the family members they try to bring with them produce costs and abuses that need to be better managed. It is not surprising, Thobani argues, that responses to the consultations fitted this frame, supporting subsequent policy changes to demand higher skills and job-readiness, to restrict family migration, and to make immigrants pay higher fees for processing and settlement. The consultation process might have had very different outcomes had all Canadians—native-born and foreign-born—been consulted, and had questions been focused around themes like how Canada could better assist immigrants to be economically successful, to bring family members more quickly, to have better access to social services they need, and to contribute their vibrant cultures more fully to the Canadian mosaic.

Academic writing, and particularly the content and tone of writing about race and ethnic relations included in introductory sociology texts, also warrants close scrutiny for how they frame students' understanding of issues, since students will make up the next generation of professionals (Van Dijk 1993, 164–177). Van Dijk criticises the texts he reviewed for pervasive use of the passive descriptive tense—as in phrases such as "blacks were conquered and enslaved" because they elide the core question of exactly who was responsible for doing what to whom, and with what long-term consequences. Standard definitions of "racism" and "prejudice" that focus on irrational individual beliefs and attitudes about the biological superiority or inferiority of certain "races" absolve people who use cultural explanations. Professors who assess white applicants as superior because they do research on more significant topics and publish in more prestigious journals are not challenged to think of themselves as racist or prejudiced. A definition of discrimination as disqualifying members of one group from opportunities open to others can be used to discredit affirmative action. Attacks on Aboriginal treaty rights can be represented as anti-racist activism. Such weak conceptualization, Van Dijk argues, obscures the systemic power and dominance relations between groups that fundamentally characterizes racism, and the systemic protection of privileges that perpetuate racialized and ethnicized inequality. Essentialized representations of cultural homogeneity both for "Canada" and ethnic minority "communities" are also commonplace. A detailed analysis of the portrayal of Aboriginal peoples in a survey of 77 Canadian introductory sociology textbooks faults them for stereotyped images, historical inaccuracies, factual errors, and the prioritizing of outsider-anthropological accounts over Aboriginal voices (Steckley 2003). In so doing, Steckley concludes, sociological textbooks mostly perpetuate "relations of ruling" rather than working to expose and undermine these relations.

Mass Media and Public Opinion

Mass media, including television, newspapers, magazines, and movies, exert a powerful influence of public opinion

through the kinds of information that are covered or ignored, and the ways in which minority issues are framed. News and current affairs programs on television and in newspapers are particularly influential in that they are seen as presenting factual information. It is through mass media that Canadians learn much of what they feel they know about minorities, and also how minorities learn about themselves and each other, and develop a sense of their place as Canadians within the wider society.

Media are not monolithic. The framing of issues around minorities differs significantly across sources like the CBC or the Fox network, *The Globe and Mail* or a tabloid paper, in part because their producers know they are appealing to very different audiences. Journalists also draw on different explanatory theories to frame their current events stories, like the recent arrest of people suspected of planning a terrorist attack in Toronto—whether the psychology of angry disaffected youth, impressionistic kids egged on by a dangerous fanatic that moderate Muslims have been warning authorities about, the culture of Islamic extremism, the global war on terror and how Canada is next on Osama bin Laden's hit list, recent history of Canadian military involvement in Afghanistan, or the need to protect thousands of innocent and peaceful Canadian Muslims from attacks by fanatics of a different stripe.

The problem for media producers in the era of "infotainment" is that news and current affairs programming are required to be entertaining as well as informative, in order to provide a steady audience for advertisers. Hence they tend to be geared to providing excitement through dwelling on the bizarre and the bloody. Information is encapsulated into two-minute sound bites and slanted to appeal to the presumed interests of mainstream audiences (read normative white invisible Anglo-Canadian), with the result that visible minorities tend to get noticed mostly when there is trouble. The normal humdrum everyday lives of the vast majority of people is not newsworthy.

The increased hiring of visible minority journalists in recent years has had mixed results. As low-status newcomers it is difficult for them to influence entrenched patterns in media production (Wilson 2000). Those who refuse to conform mostly leave the profession.

The 500-channel universe of specialty television offers some scope for programming designed for minority audiences. They significantly influence how individuals negotiate their sense of themselves as members of minority "communities," being drawn together as audiences watching the same programs. Aboriginal television channels, for example, encourage the retention of indigenous languages, and promote information exchange and networking. The dramatization of Hindu sacred texts by the state television of India, serialized over a four-year period between 1988–92, was projected to Hindu audiences around the globe (Gillespie 2000). The series reached regular weekly audiences of an estimated 100 million people in India alone. It is credited by some analysts as powerfully contributing to the promotion of Hindu nationalism and anti-Muslim sentiments in India (Singh 1995; Rajagopal 2000). Controversy over a site of worship at Ayodhya, the mythical site of the birthplace of the Hindu god Rama, boiled over in January 1992 into communal violence during which hundreds died. The series was also watched by possibly another 20 million outside India. Audience members interviewed in England spoke of how powerfully the series impacted upon them, creating a sense of intimate connection with kin back in India. They also spoke of their disdain for a British version of the Mahabharata epic that, in their view, misrepresented the spiritual message of morality and honour as a simplified soap-opera story of a feisty Draupadi who calls on divine intervention to get back at her obnoxious relatives.

Studies of audiences' reactions reveals that there is a complex and nuanced relationship between text and reception. One cannot simply read audience reactions directly from a content analysis of text. Nor is there a simple deterministic relationship between ethnic background of audience member and how a text will be interpreted. Meanings are negotiated by people who draw on existing interpretive frames and background understandings, including their sense of the credibility of sources, and conversations with others who watched the same programs to make sense of what they saw (Hooks 1992). Studies of audiences are further plagued by methodological problems around what constitutes a representative sample audience, with the risk of creating artificial groups of strangers who collectively produce situated responses in research settings to programs that they might not otherwise watch (Ross 2000).

Within these limitations, there is much evidence that different audiences interpret the same evidence in sharply different ways that reflect racialized and ethnicized background understandings of events. Black and white Americans, both audience members and jurors, came to opposite conclusions concerning the probable innocence or guilt of O.J. Simpson, a famous black American football player accused of the murder of his white wife and her friend in 1994 (Fiske 2000; Cottle 2000, 13–14). Black females were more likely to see Simpson as innocent than were white males. Their situated local knowledge as powerless people made it seem credible that police would tamper with evidence to get a conviction. They were also more likely to follow the trial in the tabloid press, and to watch Oprah Winfrey-style talk shows, both media sources that habitually

challenge official versions of events. Similarly, black audiences watching the amateur video of Rodney King being beaten by police in Los Angeles in 1992 (Gabriel 2000, 73) were more likely to see a defenceless black man on the ground being kicked by police, while whites were more likely to see in the same video a picture of a violent black male being appropriately subdued after being sexually abusive towards a white female police officer. A rare equivalent skepticism was triggered in Canada in 2006 when two white Canadian women were implicated by Mexican police in the murder of a couple on holiday in Cancun. Canadian media widely endorsed the argument that the Mexican police might plant incriminating evidence in the women's room in order to shift the spotlight from local people to protect their lucrative tourist trade.

Conclusion: Manipulating Public Opinion

How readily can public opinion be manipulated to whip up racialized and ethnicized hostilities, or conversely to quieten them and promote multicultural tolerance? On the one hand there is evidence that the pronouncements of political leaders, academic elites, and mass media are influential in formulating public opinion. Historically, xenophobia was whipped up in Canada in 1942 against Japanese Canadians in the context of heightened wartime fear. By 1946 when the war was over and fears subsided, the propaganda lost force. The climate of public opinion changed, and widespread protests against the injustice prevented the government from deporting more Japanese, and pushed for their re-enfranchisement (Sunahara 1981). At present there is some fear that public opinion in Canada might be whipped up against Muslims in the context of heightened fear of terrorism, but it seems unlikely. Political and professional elites are officially committed to multiculturalism and to the protection of Muslim rights. Media framing of issues around the "war on terror" and conflicts in Afghanistan, Iraq, and Palestine is diverse and frequently critical of international politics, and there is no generalized climate of fear in Canada.

In the USA, however, the dynamics governing public opinion are significantly different. There was a heightened climate of fear both abroad and within the country in the years after the 11 September 2001 terrorist attack, with the Bush administration repeatedly issuing yellow and orange alerts prompting citizens and security forces to be hyper-alert. With America actively at war in Iraq and Afghanistan, and committed to the defence of Israel, there was strong pressure on political and academic leaders to be unanimous in their support for the war on terror in the abstract, and for the troops on the ground. American scholars

Barack Obama being sworn in as president of the United States of America.

Ralf-Finn Hestoft/Corbis

of Middle Eastern Studies report an active stifling of any real debate, reminiscent of the anti-communist frenzy of the Cold War era (Bourne 2004; Beinin 2004). American mass media, with a few exceptions, policed themselves in a form of literal or figurative embeddedness with the American military at war.

By 2008, when Barack Obama was campaigning hard to become president, the climate had changed. Immediate fears of terrorist attack had subsided, and criticism of American soldiers dying in a misguided war in Iraq became mainstream. Obama promoted a different political discourse around the concept of "a more perfect union" (campaign speech, 18 March 2008) in which all Americans could take pride, working together to move beyond the racism and divisions of the past. Once he became president in 2009, Obama could draw on his mixed heritage, which includes Muslim relatives in Kenya, to reach out to Muslims globally to project a new image of America as embracing racial and ethnic diversity.

In summary, from the social constructionist perspective there is no fixed reality that can be objectively described, no unbridgeable differences between pre-existing ethnic or racial groups to be documented. Rather, there are systemic practices engaged in by people in various positions of authority and influence, as well as ordinary people in their everyday interactions, through which we negotiate, sustain, or undermine our experiences and interpretations of the world as racialized and ethnicized.

 # Feminist Perspectives: Gendered, Racialized, Ethnicized Relations

Western feminist theory was rocked in the 1980s by charges that feminist concepts and perspectives were racist (Carby 1982, 1999). Critics raised three closely related issues. Feminist thought and activism, they argued, focuses almost exclusively on struggles central to the interests of white middle-class Western women. This theorizing, however, is represented as applying universally to all women, while the voices of women of colour who try to articulate very different concerns are either ignored or openly discounted. The sharpest criticism was that white middle-class Western women are themselves complicit in the oppression of racialized women. This section explores the roots of this critique, and changes in contemporary feminist theorizing.

Patriarchy in European Colonial Rule

European women were largely banned from Canada during the early fur-trade years. European men who were employed to develop and run the forts on behalf of trading companies presumed they could get sexual access to indigenous women who hung around the forts while men were working traplines. Sometimes these liaisons grew into long-term family relationships, but they were not accorded recognition by the churches or in law as marriages. Men owed no legal responsibilities to the women or their children. Eventually, as European wives became available, men routinely dissolved these informal "country marriages" with Aboriginal women.

The historical situation of European women in the colonial settlement of Canada reflects the strongly patriarchal structures of nineteenth-century British society. Prior to reforms to marriage laws beginning in the 1880s in Britain, wives were legally subsumed under their husband's legal status. Any property or inheritance she might bring to the marriage became the legal property of her husband. He also had sole legal custody of the children (Smart 1984). Any woman who left her marriage, for whatever reason, had no right to maintenance, or even to see her children again. Women's subordination in marriage was widely defended as both sanctioned by the Bible and as functional for the preservation of stable family life. The Jesuit priest Paul Lejeune, who tried to civilize and Christianize the Innu of Labrador, wrote of his astonishment and strong disapproval of the easy egalitarianism that he saw between Innu women and men. One of his goals for the Innu was to institute the ideal of patriarchal family relations, including the proper subordination of wives to husbands, and the corporal disciplining of children (Bear-Nicholas 1994).

Political and religious elites of the time opined that the proper role for white middle-class women coming to Canada in increasing numbers by the nineteenth century was to promote civilized domestic life for the settlers (Henderson 2003). In effect, Henderson argues, the leaders of white settler society saw "well-governed" women as the pillars of white rule, or "race-making" in the colonies. Concepts of proper gender roles and normative sexuality were inherently part of the self-definition of white settler nationalism from the beginning. In the discourse of British colonial rulers, a self-disciplined society could claim rightful status as a self-governing colony, while societies considered less civilized, and incapable of self-discipline, should continue to be ruled as dominions. The merging of gender, sexuality, and nationalism evident in British colonial rule is reflected also in the subaltern nationalisms that emerged with independence struggles among colonized people, including Aboriginal people in Canada, as we will see further below. Women's bodies, their dress and decorum, functioned as powerful sites for symbolic representation of cultural reproduction (Kim-Puri 2005; Henderson 2003).

Henderson argues further that we cannot simply accept what middle-class colonial women wrote at the time as authentic statements of how women themselves might have thought, because their status as moral educators or social reformers was the only acceptable public role available to them. Women argued that they should be given the right to vote because of their natural civilizing influence. Back in Britain, women argued for the right to become volunteer police officers on the grounds that they could better police their sexually fallen lower-class sisters than could men. In Canada, women set up immigration societies to monitor and control the working-class girls brought to Canada as suitable wives for white male settlers, and suitable "mothers of the nation" (Arat-Koc 1999, 129–132). Not all white women qualified as civilized. There was much debate at the time as to whether "Irish" qualified as "white." Their colonized status often trumped their skin colour. There are horrifying stories of destitute women from Ireland who worked, or rather slaved, in bars and brothels in Britain and the colonies. Men are described as routinely urging these women to drink to insensibility, and then gang-raping them on bar tables (Razack 1998, 343). White middle-class women who ran the immigration societies took it upon themselves to supervise and police the women they recruited from Britain for domestic service in Canada, requiring them to sign contracts to work in assigned domestic-service placements for one year. Women deemed "unsuitable" by reason of sexual or other misconduct were reported to the authorities for deportation (Arat-Koc 1999).

Within patriarchal role definitions thought appropriate for women at the time, women were classed into two broad categories—virginal daughters who would become respectable domesticated wives and mothers, or in effect the property of white males. Otherwise they were classed as whores—women who were presumed to be sexually available outside marriage to service white male sexual appetites. Overwhelmingly it was non-white or "racialized" women—black, Asian, Aboriginal, and occasionally subaltern whites like the Irish—who were objectified as sexual targets (Razack 1998). It was their hyper-availability as sex objects, Razack argues, that served to define and support the hyper-respectability of white middle-class women. Aboriginal women were routinely labelled as prostitutes if found off their reserves, and they could be fined or thrown in prison for up to six months on suspicion of vagrancy (Lawrence 2004, 52). Indian agents also routinely withheld welfare rations to impoverished families on reserves as a bargaining chip for sexual favours. Enslaved black women and household servants were similarly vulnerable to the presumption of sexual availability.

The Indian Act: Constructing Patriarchal Aboriginal Status

The Indian Act, and its many revisions since it was first enacted in Canada in 1869, was inherently and intentionally patriarchal (Lawrence 2004). Legal status as Indian, with recognition for treaty rights and obligations, was only inherited through the male line. White women who married status-Indian men were defined as status Indians, and their offspring were similarly deemed full-blood status Indians. However, under Section 12(1)(b) of the Indian Act, status-Indian women who married a non-status male were deemed no longer Indian. They and their children lost all rights to live in their former communities, to inherit any property, or to be buried on the reserves. Illegitimate children of status-Indian mothers were likewise excluded, unless their father was known to be status Indian. Many thousands of Indian women who had formed liaisons with white men were cut out and often left destitute.

The Indian Act also imposed exogamy on Native women—requiring them to move to their husband's community on marriage (Lawrence 2004, 51). This requirement systematically broke up the matrilineal clan system of land control among the Iroquois Confederacy. Formerly, while men organized the hunting, clan land available for hunting was inherited through women. The Indian Act abolished this. The legislation further divided reserves into individual lots inheritable only through the male line (Lawrence 2004). Wives were forced to live on their husband's reserve, but denied the right to inherit land on his reserve. Women thus lost all their former political roles in the governance of their own societies.

Bill C-31 and the Aftermath

Blatant discrimination against Native women embedded in the Indian Act was first legally challenged in 1971 by Jeanette Lavell and Yvonne Bedard, two Native women who had lost status through marriage (Lawrence 2004, 56–63). Lavell challenged the deletion of her name from her band list, while Bedard challenged her eviction from a house willed to her by her mother. Both argued that this treatment violated the Canadian Human Rights Act as discrimination on the basis of race and sex. In 1973 the Supreme Court of Canada ruled against them. The Court determined that since the impugned clauses of the Indian Act applied only to women, and not to all Natives, it did not constitute discrimination on the basis specifically of "race." Further, since Native women who lost status acquired the same status as all other non-Native Canadian women, the clause was not "sexist." The Court further determined that the Human Rights Act in any case could not overrule the Indian Act.

Maliseet women of Tobique eventually successfully challenged the discriminatory rule in the Indian Act that deemed women could not own property on the reserve, a rule that resulted in women and children being homeless when marriages broke down. The Tobique women joined with Sandra Lovelace in an appeal to the United Nations Human Rights Committee on the grounds that loss of status on marriage under Section 12(1)(b) of the Indian Act constituted a violation of minority rights "to enjoy their culture, practice their religion, and use their language in community with others from the group." The UN Court ruled in their favour and put pressure on the Canadian government to change the Act. In expectation of these changes, the Canadian government created an interim policy that allowed First Nations bands to request suspension of Sections 12(1)(b) and 12(1)a(iv). The latter clause, known as the "double mother" clause, removed status from men as well as women whose mother *and* paternal grandmother were non-status. Lawrence records that 53 percent of all bands requested suspension of the double mother clause—which directly affected men living on reserves. But only 19 percent chose to suspend the clause challenged by Lovelace that affected Native women who married non-status men and so lived outside the reserves (Lawrence 2004, 61).

Gender discrimination under Section 12(1)(b) of the Indian Act was finally amended in 1985 to conform with Section 15(1) of the Canadian Charter of Rights and Freedoms. Native women would no longer lose their status and rights on their reserves on marriage to non-status men.

This seeming victory, however, was won for Native women at high cost. The National Indian Brotherhood fought against the amendment on the grounds that it violated their rights as First Nations to determine their own citizenship. Further, it was argued, women have a stronger responsibility as "mothers of the nation" to choose to marry within their communities and should not expect redress if they choose to marry out. Moreover, bands needed protection from white husbands. The outcome was a compromise in which some women regained their formal Native status but male-dominated band councils gained the right to determine whether or not these women would be accorded band status, or the right to reside on the reserve.

Inheritance rights still discriminate against women. Women reinstated in 1985 only received partial status. They can pass their status on to their immediate children, but their grandchildren, males as well as females, cannot inherit Indian status. Status-Indian males confer status on both their children and grandchildren regardless of who they marry, although non-status wives cannot now gain status. Women who marry non-status men retain their status and confer status onto their children. However, their grandchildren permanently lose their status on marriage unless their spouse has status. Illegitimate children of status-Indian mothers are also non-status, unless the father has status. In effect, within two generations from 1985 only descendants of status-Indian males will continue to have status. The "bleeding off" of native band members is likely to be greater since the amendments than before.

This 1985 Act was almost immediately challenged again under the Equality Rights provision of the Charter. Sharon McIvor, a woman who regained status for herself and her son, challenged the discriminatory provision that bars her son's children from holding Indian status. After a legal challenge that took 22 years to conclude, the BC Court of Appeal ruled unanimously in April 2009 that the 1985 Act violates the Charter. In June 2009 the federal government agreed that it would not challenge the ruling, and that the Indian Act would be changed. Some Aboriginal leaders are advocating that the entire Indian Act should be scrapped as long-outdated colonial legislation.

Post-Colonial Gendered Ethnicity

Visible-minority immigrants entering Canada under the new Immigration Act of 1967 have mostly come from regions of the world that were formerly subject to European colonial rule. The politics of resistance and cultural nationalism that developed in these regions were profoundly influenced by the experience of foreign domination and the inferiorizing cultural discourse of foreign rulers. British imperial rulers spread the same gendered cultural standards of white middle-class domestic respectability for their women in Africa and Asia as they did in Canada, with similar undercurrents of racialized denigration of "other" women as exotic and sexually available. In formal political discourse and practices, behaviour that mimicked the European version of masculinity and domestic femininity were praised, while other practices were scorned as alien and culturally inferior.

Wherever they encountered matriarchal economic and political systems, they undermined them. British rulers systematically broke up the matriarchal system of landholding among the Nayar of Malabar in Kerala, South India, in ways that parallel closely their destruction of female-centred forms of communal governance among the Iroquois. Traditionally, Nayar people held land communally within extended families, passing it down from mother to daughters (Liddle and Joshi 1986, 28–29). Men had access to land as brothers and sons but did not own or transfer land through marriage. British colonial rulers, however, insisted that communal lands be broken up and inherited only through the father's line to sons. They further insisted that men be made legally responsible for their "wives" and children. They enforced this by the practice of employing exclusively men in the civil service bureaucracy, with this individual male-wage economy gradually replacing the former communal landholding economy. In political dealings, similarly, British rulers would only appoint and negotiate with men. In Africa, for example, British rulers banned the practice they found common in Nigeria, of having women on local councils, insisting that such positions only be held by men.

At the same time that the British undermined matriarchal organization, they characterized non-Western forms of patriarchal organization as primitive and inferior. In India, British rulers expressed moral outrage at the practice among Hindus of *sati*—the burning of widows on the funeral pyre of their husband—female infanticide, child marriage, plural wives, arranged marriages, and extended family systems. They scorned dress codes favoured among wealthier women of wearing veils and Muslim women wearing full-length covering or burqa. Ironically, British courts worsened the situation for lower-class Indian women by interpreting practices followed mostly by Hindu elites as uniformly applicable to all women (Liddle and Joshi 1986, 26). They also denigrated the greater tolerance in some Islamic societies for gay and lesbian relations.

As pressure for self-rule intensified in India, British rulers used "the women's issue" as a justification for foreign rule. They characterized the treatment of Hindu women as primitive and savage, and as evidence that Indians were not fit to rule themselves (Liddle and Joshi 1986, 31). This strategy worked to divide the nationalist movement in India and to shackle the indigenous women's movement. On one hand British rulers seemed to be supporting femi-nist causes, but on the other, these same causes became discredited as foreign cultural domination, and the women who advocated them discredited as supporting colonial rule.

In the oppositional cultural discourse of independence struggles, women's bodies, their dress and decorum, became powerful signifiers of nationalist aspirations. Traditions that marked off Hindu and Muslim cultures from Western culture became intensified and often associated with militarized surveillance of women (Kim-Puri 2005). During the early years of post-colonial rule, it was common for pro-Western elites trained in colonial bureaucracies to mimic European rule. Representing themselves as modernizers and secularists, post-colonial rulers in Algeria, Egypt, Iran, and Turkey repeatedly attempted to force Muslim women to remove the veil. In the backlash against their often corrupt, inept, and Western-oriented rule, these modernizing elites were widely rejected as imposing cultural colonization. The practice of women wearing the veil became emblematic of Islamization and resistance to Western capitalist-dominated pressures for globalization (Franks 2000). Muslim women who did appear unveiled in public found themselves vulnerable to sexual harassment, especially those women not wealthy enough to travel in private cars. Nationalist leaders tried to purge their cultural narratives of references to what they saw as Western secular and libertine culture. The result was often that traditional religious practices and associated gender-role prescriptions became more rigidly enforced than in the past (Eid 2003).

Western militaristic discourse surrounding the "war on terrorism" and "Islamic fundamentalism" has added to this thick stew of gendered, religious nationalism. The characterization of the treatment of Afghan women under Taliban rule as "barbaric" became part of the legitimation for war in 2002, along with the Taliban providing a safe haven for al Qaeda terrorists (Thobani 2003). In Western discourse, the military invasion of Afghanistan is represented as liberating for Afghan women. Within Afghanistan itself, however, it casts supporters of indigenous women's resistance movements as traitors.

Gendered Ethnic Politics within Canada

Immigrants to Canada commonly bring memories of independence struggles with them. They are also inevitably exposed to ongoing nationalist struggles through global mass media and communication with relatives back in their home countries. In addition, the lived experience of being racialized and ethnicized as visible-minority refugees and immigrants within Canada resembles in some respects the experience of colonization (Bannerji 2000, 157–158). Multicultural politics encourages a sense of self-identification as members of distinct ethnic communities—an identification that is continually promoted by leaders whose own political influence is enhanced by claims to represent or speak on behalf of identifiable ethnic communities. These communities, Bannerji suggests, function like "mini-cultural nationalities," subject once more to white rule. People tend to react to their sense of being subordinated outsiders by a defensive reinvention of tradition that can become even more rigid than in the countries they have left behind.

This reinvention of tradition profoundly impacts on the lives of migrant women. Failure to conform can be read in multiple negative ways. It can be read as echoing the disrespect for their own ethnic group, and as a challenge to the status of men who are already feeling humiliated by their subordinated overall status in white society. It can further be read as a threat to the image of a unified ethnic community that male political elites use to wield influence in wider Canadian multicultural politics. For these and similar reasons women may personally internalize a desire to conform to traditional expectations as well as feeling socially pressured to do so. Family honour or shame is closely linked to women's decorum in traditional culture, to her remaining within the home or appropriately chaperoned by male relatives outside the home, acceptance of marriage to a partner who is approved of and chosen by her elders, and especially with respect to sexual chastity. Those who flaunt such expectations are likely to be judged harshly and avoided, or subject to more severe physical punishment (Bhardwaj 2001). In the context of strong community sanctions for non-compliance, what women themselves say about traditional dress codes and other gendered expectations reflects a complex mix of inner conviction and outward conformity.

Muslim women who wear traditional Islamic clothing such as the headscarf (hijab) or full-body covering (burqa or chador) within predominantly Islamic societies often speak of a sense of privacy and protection that such clothing affords them. They can gaze upon men without being themselves subject to male gaze, and they can go about in public with relative anonymity. Wearing the same clothing in Western societies, however, can provoke very different reactions from others (Franks 2000). Women commonly feel themselves the object of gazing by foreigners who range from just curious to hostile. They are also commonly labelled as primitive and backward, or as pitiable, subordinated women. Rather than feeling safe outside their homes, such reactions may discourage them from going out or trying to mix with other women. Franks tells the story of a white-skinned British Muslim woman, the daughter of an Egyptian father and English mother, who opted to wear hijab against her parents' wishes. Her parents feared, rightly, that she would be stared at. She wanted to show solidarity with and be recognizably Muslim to Bosnian refugees coming to England to escape the civil war in Yugoslavia. Blending in, by not following either Islamic dress codes or religious observances, she reasoned, had not prevented Bosnian Muslims from being attacked and murdered by Christian Serbs and Croats, so hiding her own Muslim identity would probably not protect her either. When she herself started wearing hijab in England, her middle-class English associates studiously avoided her, seeing her as making a spectacle of herself, and even as a traitor to her own white race.

Violence in the Lives of Racialized Women

Life for women who observe traditional Muslim lifestyles within South Asian enclave communities in Western societies can be experienced as extremely restricted, especially for those who do not speak the host society language (Bhardwaj 2001; Bannerji 2000, Ch. 5). Bhardwaj notes that among Asian females in the age range of 15 to 35, the rate of suicide, suicide attempts, and other forms of self-harm are two to three times higher than among white and African and Caribbean female counterparts. Reflected in this misery is pervasive domestic violence and abuse against women, which is tacitly supported by the community leaders as a means to maintain traditional controls. Women themselves are constrained to silence, afraid of backlash against them if they speak out against abusive male kin, and fearful of how they will be heard by outsiders. Women have almost nowhere to turn. They cannot confide in physicians or social workers from their own Asian communities because these professionals often see themselves as self-appointed guardians of the culture and may report women who seek help with depression back to their families. Injured women who seek hospital treatment may also find that the only people available to translate for them are maintenance and cleaning staff who likely will report back to family members.

Patriarchal attitudes and practices are certainly deep-rooted in South Asian cultures, existing long before migration to Canada. But Bannerji suggests that while these practices are loosening up in India, in response to the women's movement and economic changes, they seem to be growing more rigid in South Asian ethnic enclaves in Canada (Bannerji 2000, Ch. 5). Patriarchal immigration laws are doubly implicated in this rigidity, in that they both heighten the power of male household heads and simultaneously silence women and close off avenues for support and help. Under contemporary immigration laws, primary independent-class economic migrants are overwhelmingly men. Their wives, regardless of levels of education or work experience, are admitted as legally dependent family-class migrants. Their male sponsors are required to support them financially for 10 years. Sponsored wives are ineligible for social assistance, or for assisted language or job training. If they leave their marriage, for whatever reasons, or their male sponsors refuse to support them, they are liable to be deported back to their country of origin. Women who are victimized in abusive marriages have few options or hope for redress.

Aboriginal women in Canada also endure significantly higher rates of domestic violence than do non-Aboriginal women (Monture-Angus 1999). Monture-Angus describes violence as an everyday fact of life for Aboriginal women of all ages. A hard legacy of colonialism, family breakdown following residential school experiences, destroyed economies, and anger and frustration at limited future options all contribute to this violence. But so too does the patriarchal Indian Act that establishes men as the carriers of Aboriginal status and property rights within reserves. Wives and children are especially vulnerable in situations of family breakdown since the husband has the presumptive right to live in the family home. In the past, women who lost status by marrying a non-status man lost all rights to return to live on their former reserve if their marriage should fail. Now they retain their status, but band membership and access to band housing and resources are tenuous. The non-status wives of status-Indian males also have increased vulnerability since their right to live on reserves depends upon the marriage continuing. All these rules mean that Aboriginal women and children are more vulnerable when marriages fail than are non-Aboriginal Canadian women.

Racial and Ethnic Divisions within Western Feminist Movements

The mainstream white feminist movement in Canada, as in Europe, was forged in the struggle to break out of the patriarchal nineteenth-century mould of women's proper place as domestic guardians of moral decorum, legally subordinated to husbands. Women of colour who joined with Canadian feminist movements in greater numbers from the 1980s onward found themselves generally welcomed, but their voices and concerns subordinated and ignored wherever they differed from the mainstream feminist agenda. These differences have proven profound. What white feminists identified as universal features of feminist struggle, women of colour increasingly challenged as the limited concerns of specifically middle-class and white women (Carby 1982, 1999; Afshar and Maynard 2000). They challenged white women further to face up to their own complicity in the oppression of Asian, black, and Aboriginal women.

The white feminist focus on family as the site of oppression does not resonate with the experiences of black feminists. Historically, slavery was the primary site of oppression for black women, with family life fundamental for survival. Slaves had to fight to sustain any semblance of family life against slave-owners who would sell men and women separately for their own profit and convenience. Racialized economic inequality continues to undermine black family life, as such a high proportion of young black men lack the financial means to support families. Black feminists struggle for greater recognition and respect for female-centred kinship systems that do not conform to standard North American family forms. White feminist struggles to break from normative definitions of delicate feminine decorum and domesticity also do not resonate with black women and working-class women generally, who were always expected to perform heavy physical labour. The centrality of the right to paid employment and independent income in white feminist liberation similarly means little to black women who have commonly shouldered the burden of financially supporting their children, only to have their women-headed families decried by sociologists as pathological. Greater opportunity for black men to earn decent incomes is equally as important for black women's liberation as employment for themselves. Black women also mediate the contradictions experienced by white women between family and work demands through the domestic and childcare work that black women perform for white middle-class families.

The treatment that black women's experience as domestic workers and nannies in white households is a central focus of Carby's characterization of white women as themselves oppressors of other women. In this arena, Carby argues, white women placed their class interests before sisterhood with subordinated and often racialized "other" women. Canadian immigration law created the special category of "live-in caregiver program," to fill the demand from middle-class women desperate to find quality childcare and domestic help to enable them to be employed outside the home. Third World women, mostly from the Philippines and the Caribbean, are given temporary, two-year work permits to reside in Canada provided they work as live-in domestic servants (Arat-Koc 1989, 2001). These workers are tied to their employer's household as workplace and home, commonly called upon to work hours far in excess of other jobs, and to perform multiple tasks that are not contractually limited. Their income is not subject to minimum hourly wage regulations because they are "live-in" and not legally permitted to unionize. The Canadian government deducts taxes from their earnings for employment insurance and the Canada Pension Plan, even though they are explicitly not eligible for these benefits. Should they leave their place of employment for whatever reason, they are reclassified as "visitors" and given only two weeks to find another live-in domestic-worker position or be deported (Arat-Koc 2001, 364).

Changes to the legislation in 1991 now permit temporary care workers to apply for landed-immigrant status after two years. However, there is no guarantee of approval. Domestic work is explicitly not counted as a work-skill under the points system. Hence, in order to qualify, women must demonstrate that they have undertaken educational upgrading while in Canada, at their own expense, to have a chance of being considered. While black women solve the childcare crisis for wealthy, and usually white, Canadian families, their own children are necessarily left behind with kin in their countries of origin.

Sexual Liberation

Racialized women's struggles for greater control over their sexual lives, and for freedom from sexual oppression, also reflect very different lived experience. While nineteenth-century middle-class white women struggled for greater freedom of sexual expression against the stultifying asexual norms of bourgeois family life, their lower-class servants, and especially racialized Aboriginal and black women, struggled to defend themselves from the pervasive assumptions that they were sexually available outside marriage—to their employers, and to any man who offered money. Historically, Razack argues (1998), the elevated sexual status of middle-class white women was protected at the cost of degraded sexual status of enslaved and colonized women. White men who fiercely guarded the chastity and virginity of women of their own kin, expected easy sexual access to racialized "other" women. Even forced sex with these "other" women was not considered in law to be rape, unless the encounter was particularly brutal.

Contemporary global patterns of sex trafficking in women and children for the sex trade reflects similarly racialized patterns of Third World women servicing affluent Western male customers, both in European brothels and around military bases and sex-tourist destinations (Farr 2005). They are drawn mostly from Southeast Asia, South Asia, Latin America and the Caribbean, and Africa. Since the fall of the Soviet Union in 1991, women have come increasingly from Soviet republics. Many of these trafficked women are abducted, sold into debt bondage by impoverished families, or lured by the promise of better-paying jobs in the West and then trapped in a vicious circle of debt bondage, violence, and threat (Farr 2005, 25–45). Others are driven into prostitution by destitution, with illegal migrants being especially vulnerable.

Liberal feminist activists have challenged societal and state prudery that stigmatizes sex-trade workers, and have advocated legalizing the trade to empower workers and facilitate better regulation of the terms and conditions of work (Shaver 1994). But racialized women have counter-challenged

this liberalizing approach as inherently racist (Razack 1998, 2000). The characterization of sex-trade work as an arena for women's choice does not fit with the lived experience of racialized poor women in Western societies. For racialized women who live in inner-city slum areas, the status of "prostitute" is not a choice but a presumption. Within the sex-trade world, Razack argues, there are recognizably three kinds of women. White women on suburban streets who are rarely sexualized, black and Aboriginal women on the same streets who are routinely sexualized and propositioned by taxi drivers, and racialized women in inner-city slums who are presumed to be prostitutes. Liberal feminist discourse in the sex trade appears racist because it ignores the reality that *only* white women can talk like this, because only white women have a choice in whether they wish to be seen as sexually available. White women from the suburbs can choose to "go slumming," to enter prostitution zones like the Stroll in Regina, and to experiment with the sex trade. To them it feels exotic and liberatory to make men pay money for sex, especially for women working in the high end of the sex trade as escorts, strippers, dancers, or performers in peep shows. For urban poor Aboriginal women who routinely inhabit "the Stroll" there is no choice. Moving out to the suburbs is not an option.

The liberal feminist discourse is also racist in that it ignores the routine and racialized character of the violence that is enacted on women's bodies by the white men who visit the Stroll looking for sex. Razack describes these encounters as the contemporary site of enactment of colonial white male identity. Colonizing white males defined themselves as entitled to dominate space, entitled to the land they took over, and entitled to use violence to push other bodies from that space. They continue to define themselves as colonizing white males through their enactment of entitlement to buy and use the bodies of racialized others (Razack 2000). Razack describes in graphic detail the discourse and practices of the two white males eventually convicted of murdering Pamela George on Easter weekend in 1995. Razack describes the two university undergraduates repeatedly bragging to their friends that they "want to go find a hooker and beat and rape her" (Razack 2000, 113). They felt entitled to brag about such behaviour to their fellow male campus athletes, and to trust in their tacit acceptance, approval, and even admiration for such acts, and their expectation that such information would not be used against them. Lawyers defending them at trial spoke of what the boys had done as "darn stupid things," but nonetheless commonplace behaviour in the locality—drinking heavily, picking up a prostitute, hitting her, and leaving her in the country to walk back by herself. What Razack sees in the trial is how little the victim mattered. Her death was an inconvenience that got the boys into trouble.

Colour-blind discourse was studiously maintained throughout the trial, with references made only to "the Hungarians" and "the prostitute." The racist and colonial subtext of two dominant white men who raped and beat up a Native woman was carefully silenced. Silenced also is the colonial history that accounts for so many women of Aboriginal descent in the inner-city slum zone, and for the violence that is normalized as part of contractual sex. For Razack, how little Pamela George mattered to her murderers or to the justice system is the measure of ongoing colonialism.

Summary

The critique of feminist theory by women of colour requires a more complex and nuanced response than colour-blind "inclusion" or the politics of "add women of colour and stir." A more racially and ethnically sensitive feminism needs to be more historically situated and comparative. White feminists need to give up the myth that their story is the sole legitimate herstory, and become more aware of themselves historically and in the present as oppressors of subordinated "other" women (Carby 1999). Institutional ethnographies of feminist organizations show that a philosophy of collaborative egalitarianism is not sufficient in itself to achieve egalitarian racial and ethnic integration in contexts of unequal social power (Scott 2005). Scott calls for more active and intentional listening to the voices and concerns of women who are differently situated, together with active practices that empower subordinated women to get their concerns acted upon at the centre of the feminist political agenda.

CONCLUSION

Functionalist theory, which begins with the assumptions that distinct ethnic groups exist, and that ethnic group identity is a centrally important feature of individual self-definition, still dominates social thought and government policies. The role of shared culture in fostering social cohesion leads to the expectation that relationships at the boundaries of different ethnic groups are likely to be difficult. Ethnic conflicts as such require no further explanation. The achievement of stable multiculturalism in a complex society like Canada is what needs analysis and explanation. It is found in the separation between more private realms of family and church from the public realm of commerce and politics.

Political economy theory also largely accepts the assumption that distinct ethnic groups exist, but analyzes conflict between them as rooted primarily in competition over economic resources and exploitative labour-market relations rather than cultural differences as such. The long and violent history of European colonial expansion and ongoing global corporate capitalist drive to extract resources and profits are the processes that drive international migration from poor developing countries to rich corporate capitalist centres. These same processes promote systemic inequality and labour-market competition, which fuel ongoing conflict between the host society and immigrants. Racism as a doctrine of superiority and inferiority based on genetic differences is itself rooted in colonialism. The racialized vertical mosaic in Canada is deep-rooted in the history of white settler society.

Social constructionist analysis questions common-sense views of ethnic and racial groups, challenging us to conceptualize as ongoing processes of ethnicization and racialization. Identities are negotiable features of social relations. The salience of race or ethnicity in any given situation is something that needs to be explained. State policies are powerfully implicated in identity formation, evident in the long and conflicted history of the Indian Act and policies that promote culture over labour-market integration as the primary focus for Aboriginal and immigrant populations in relations with white European Canadian host society. White normative discourse routinely obscures practices of white privilege and systemic discrimination as merited entitlement, while colour-blind discourses visualize the redress of systemic disadvantage as racism.

Feminist analysis has made visible the patriarchal character of colonial policies, and how the politics of resistance and cultural nationalism have impacted on women as colonial subjects and as immigrants. Such analysis has also exposed the patriarchal assumptions built into immigration policies and multicultural politics that privilege male household heads over female "dependents." Feminist perspectives have struggled to incorporate the lived experiences of women of colour, learning that this process requires more than colour-blind inclusion on the same terms as white middle-class women, and more than inclusion in egalitarian consensus decision-making alongside white majority professional staff. It has required a re-evaluation of core ideas within feminist theory itself to recognize the valid but ethnic-class-specific character of some aspects of white middle-class feminist struggle. It has further required acknowledging the extent to which white middle-class women themselves have been complicit in the exploitation of impoverished sisters.

SUGGESTED READING

Beaman, Lori, and Peter Byer, eds. 2008. *Religion and Diversity in Canada.* Leiden; Boston: Brill. This book contains many discussions on multiculturalism, particularly as it applies to religious diversity. The following three chapters are suggested reading:

Cowan, Douglas E., "Fearing Planes, Trains, and Automobiles: Sociophobics and the Disincentive to Religious Diversity," 67–73. Cowan argues that Canada has a history of fearing diversity. He cites the refusal of landing rights to a boatload of Sikhs, our reaction to Jehovah's Witnesses, and the uproar over polygamy in Bountiful, BC, as examples of fear-based behaviour.

Lefebvre, Solange, "Between Law and Public Opinion: The Case of Quebec," 175–198. Lefebvre examines the concept of "reasonable accommodation" at the centre of discussions before the Bouchard-Taylor Commission in Quebec. The commission was set up in response to reactions to a Sikh schoolboy's kirpan, the building of a succah on a condo balcony, and to the Muslim student request for space for daily prayer. Lefebvre questions how "reasonable" will be defined and who will define it. She also asks why it is a matter of "accommodation."

Beaman, Lori, "A Cross-National Comparison: Canada, France and the United States," 199–216. Beaman outlines the different approaches to multiculturalism in the three countries. She argues that the notions of reasonable accommodation and tolerance entrench the sense of "other" lesser minorities thereby perpetuating Christian hegemony. Canada, she argues, must decide whether to follow the accommodation approach to multiculturalism or take the course of real equality.

Barack Obama's speech on race entitled "A More Perfect Union" was given in Philadelphia on 18 March 2008 in the wake of the controversial remarks made by Obama's one-time pastor, Rev. Wright. Transcripts of the speech are available on multiple websites, including: www.nytimes.com/interactive/2008/03/18/us/politics.

A look at how one Saskatchewan law firm stands to profit from compensation to survivors of residential schools can be found in Jonathon Gatehouse's "Residential schools cash draws closer." *Maclean's* 120, 16 April 2007, 24.

Jean Lock Kunz and Stuart Sykes' *From Mosaic to Harmony: Multicultural Canada in the 21st Century* (2007) is a policy research initiative of the Government of Canada. The paper charts the evolution of multiculturalism in Canada from its inception as government policy in 1971 to today. It traces how the focus, problems, and solutions of multiculturalism changed from decade to decade. It then summarizes the results of regional round tables identifying the current aim, focus, and problems of multiculturalism at the beginning of the twenty-first century.

Tania Das Gupta's "Immigrant Women's Activism: The Past Thirty-Five Years," in Genevieve Fuji Johnson and Randy Enomoto, eds. *Race, Racialization and Antiracism in Canada and Beyond*, describes the resistance of immigrant women and women of colour to middle-class white feminist theory. She describes how they developed their own community groups to provide English language training, job training, health care, shelters, etc. She traces their gradual participation in feminist groups like National Action Committee on the Status of Women (NAC) and the eventual election of a black woman, Sunera Thobani, as president of NAC. Das Gupta describes how many of these groups were shut down when the government slashed their funding in the name of deficit reduction.

Derek McGhee's *The End of Multiculturalism? Terrorism, Integration and Human Rights* (2008) notes that multiculturalism is perceived as a failure by many in Britain. It is seen by many as the cause of acts of terrorism and as producing "home-grown terrorists." He argues that human rights are being eroded by security concerns. Government, he argues, has responded by introducing new anti-terrorism legislation that facilitates sending suspects elsewhere to be "tortured by proxy." Attitudes, he says, are shifting away from rights and towards a "civic accommodation" model. He cites Tony Blair as arguing that Britons should see sharing values as their patriotic duty.

QUESTIONS

1. Outline the four options that have been proposed, from time to time, to maintain social order in the face of ethnic diversity.

2. How were ethnic differences privatized by Canada's multicultural policy?

3. How has the war on terrorism tested the limits of multiculturalism, particularly with regard to Muslims in North America and Europe? How do you account for the fact that multiculturalism has been more successful in Canada than elsewhere, despite these challenges?

4. What evidence is there to support the political economy contention that tension between race and ethnic groups is not a matter of cultural differences, but rather a matter of economic conditions and class conflict?

5. Why did business and political elites endorse the protection of visible minorities in the Charter of Rights and Freedoms (1982) and the Employment Equity Act (1985)?

6. How did Galabuzi define "precarious work"? How did he utilize that concept to demonstrate the racialized face of

Canada's workforce today? What evidence did he present to refute the commonly held notion that the workforce reflects the education, skills, and experience of its participants?

7. From the social construction perspective, Canada's laws create boundaries of inclusion and exclusion that socially construct ethnicity. How has Canadian law and policy restricted the number of Natives to qualify as status Indians? Why did the Government of Canada want to exclude as many as possible from that category?

8. How does the concept of "colour–blind normative whiteness" disguise white privilege and, thereby, render many social services useless to minority groups?

9. Discuss the common-sense racism evidenced in the reverse racism talk of American and Australian university students.

10. How have women of colour critiqued feminist theory? What role have white women played in the oppression of women of colour?

11. Maliseet women mounted a successful court challenge to the Indian Act on the grounds of discrimination. How has the reaction to that legal victory meant that band membership would be limited in the future?

KEY TERMS

assimilation

domination

ethnicity

ethnocentrism

prejudice

race

racism

separation

stereotypes

vertical mosaic

REFERENCES

Abu-Laban, Yasmeen, and Christine Gabriel. 2002. *Selling Diversity: Immigration, Multiculturalism, Employment Equity, and Globalization*. Peterborough, Ontario: Broadview Press.

Adachi, Ken. 1978. *The Enemy That Never Was: A History of the Japanese Canadians*. Toronto: McClelland & Stewart.

Afshar, Haleh, and Mary Maynard. 2000. "Gender and ethnicity at the millennium: from margin to centre." *Ethnic and Racial Studies* 23 (5): 805–819.

Ahmadi, Nader. 2003. "Migration challenges views on sexuality." *Ethnic and Racial Studies* 26 (4): 684–706.

Alfred, Gerald R. 1995. *Heeding the Voices of our Ancestors: Kahnawake Mohawk Politics and the Rise of Native Nationalism*. Toronto; New York; Oxford: Oxford University Press.

Alleyne, Brian. 2002. "An idea of community and its discontents: Towards a more reflexive sense of belonging in multicultural Britain." *Ethnic and Racial Studies* 25 (4): 607–627.

Amit-Talai, Vered. 1996. "The Minority Circuit: Identity Politics and the Professionalization of Ethnic Activism." In Vered Amit-Talai and Caroline Knowles, eds. *Resituating Identities: The Politics of Race, Ethnicity, and Culture*. Peterborough, Ontario: Broadview Press, 89–114.

Amit-Talai, Vered, and Caroline Knowles, eds. 1996. *Resituating Identities: The Politics of Race, Ethnicity, and Culture*. Peterborough, Ontario: Broadview Press.

Andersson, Ruben. 2005. "The New Frontiers of America." *Race and Class* 46 (3): 28–38.

Arat-Koc, Sedef. 2001. "The Politics of Family and Immigration in the Subordination of Domestic Workers in Canada." In Bonnie J. Fox, ed. *Family Patterns, Gender Relations*. Oxford; New York: Oxford University Press, 352–376.

Arat-Koc, Sedef. 1999. "'Good Enough to Work but not Good Enough to Stay': Foreign Domestic Workers and the Law." In E. Comack, ed. *Locating Law: Race/Class/Gender Connections*. Halifax: Fernwood, 125–159.

Arat-Koc, Sedef. 1989. "In the Privacy of Our Own Home: Foreign Domestic Workers as Solution to the Crisis in the Domestic Sphere in Canada." *Studies in Political Economy* 28 (Spring): 33–56.

Augoustinos, Martha, Keith Tuffin, and Danielle Every. 2005. "New racism, meritocracy and individualism: Constraining affirmative action in education." *Discourse and Society* 16 (3): 315–339.

Bannerji, Himani. 2000. *The Dark Side of the Nation*. Toronto: Canadian Scholars' Press.

Bannerji, Himani. 1995. *Thinking Through. Essays on Feminism, Marxism, and Anti-Racism*. Toronto: Women's Press.

Bear-Nicholas, Andrea. 1994. "Colonialism and the Struggle for Liberation: The Experience of Maliseet Women." *University of New Brunswick Law Journal* 43: 223–239.

Beinin, Joel. 2004. "The New American McCarthyism: Policing Thought about the Middle East." *Race and Class* 46 (1): 101–115.

Bhardwaj, Anita. 2001. "Growing up Young, Asian, and Female in Britain: A Report on Self-harm and Suicide." *Feminist Review* 68 (Summer): 52–67.

Bissoondath, Neil. 1994. *Selling Illusions: The Cult of Multiculturalism in Canada*. Toronto: Penguin Books.

Blomley, Nicholas. 2004. *Unsettling the City: Urban Land and the Politics of Property*. New York; London: Routledge.

Bolaria, B.S., and P. Li. 1988. *Racial Oppression in Canada*. 2nd ed. Toronto: Garamond.

Bourgeault, R. 1983. "The Indian, the Metis and the Fur Trade: Class, Sexism and Racism in Transition from 'Communism' to Capitaism." *Studies in Political Economy* 12: 45–79.

Bourne, Jenny. 2004. "Reviews: Anti-Semitism or Anti-criticism?" *Race and Class* 46 (1): 126–140.

Boyd, Monica. 1999. "Canadian, eh? Ethnic Origin Shifts in the Canadian Census." *Canadian Ethnic Studies* 31 (3): 1–19.

Brittan, A., and M. Maynard. 1984. *Sexism, Racism and Oppression*. Oxford: Basil Blackwell.

Brown, Jessica Autumn, and Myra Marx Ferree. 2005. "Close Your Eyes and Think of England: Pronatalism in the British Print Media." *Gender and Society* 19 (1): 5–24.

Bruno-Jofré, Rosa, and Dick Henley. 2000. "Public Schooling in English Canada: Addressing Difference in the Context of Globalization." *Canadian Ethnic Studies* 32 (1): 38–54.

Carby, Hazel V. 1999. *Cultures in Babylon: Black Britain and African America*. London; New York: Verso.

Carby, Hazel V. 1982. "White Woman Listen! Black Feminism and the Boundaries of Sisterhood." In *The Empire Strikes Back: Race and Racism in 70s Britain*. Centre for Contemporary Cultural Studies, London: Hutchinson, 212–235.

Chen, Zhongping. 2004. "Chinese Minority and Everyday Racism in Canadian Towns and Small Cities: An Ethnic Study of the Case of Peterborough, Ontario, 1892–1951." *Canadian Ethnic Studies* 36 (1): 71–92.

Chua, Peter, Kum-Kum Bhavnani, and John Foran. 2000. "Women, culture, development: A new paradigm for development studies?" *Ethnic and Racial Studies* 23 (5): 820–841.

Clairmont, D.H., and D.W. Magill. [1974] 1999. *Africville: The Life and Death of a Canadian Black Community*. Toronto: McClelland & Stewart.

Cottle, Simon, ed. 2000. *Ethnic Minorities and the Media*. Buckingham; Philadelphia: Open University Press.

Davies, Scott, and Neil Guppy. 1998. "Race and Canadian Education." In Vic Satzewich, ed. *Racism and Social Inequality in Canada: Concepts, Controversies & Strategies of Resistance*. Toronto: Thompson Educational Publishing, 131–156.

Donnelly, Denise A., Kimberley J. Cook, Debra Van Ausdale, and Lara Foley. 2005. "White Privilege, Color Blindness, and Services to Battered Women." *Violence against Women* 11 (1): 6–37.

Drohan, Madelaine. 2003. *Making a Killing: How and Why Corporations Use Armed Force to do Business*. Toronto: Random House.

Eid, Paul. 2003. "The Interplay between Ethnicity, Religion, and Gender among Second-Generation Christian and Muslim Arabs in Montreal." *Canadian Ethnic Studies* 35 (2): 30–55.

Essed, Philomena. 2000. "Dilemmas in leadership: Women of colour in the academy." *Ethnic and Racial Studies* 23 (5): 888–904.

Farr, Kathryn. 2005. Sex Trafficking: The Global Market in Women and Children.

Fekete, Liz. 2005. "Anti-Muslim Racism and the European Security State." *Race and Class* 46 (1): 3–29.

Fiske, S.T. 2000. "Stereotyping, prejudice, and discrimination at the seam between the centuries: Evolution, culture,mind, and brain." *European Journal of Social Psychology* 30: 299–322.

Fleras, Augie, and Jean Leonard Elliott. 2003. *Unequal Relations: An Introduction to Race and Ethnic Dynamics in Canada*. 4th ed. Toronto: Prentice Hall.

Franks, Myfanwy. 2000. "Crossing the borders of whiteness? White Muslim women who wear the hijab in Britain today." *Ethnic and Racial Studies* 23 (5): 917–929.

Gabriel, John. 2000. "Dreaming of a White . . . " In Simon Cottle, ed. *Ethnic Minorities and the Media: Changing Cultural Boundaries*. Buckingham; Philadelphia: Open University Press, 68–82.

Gagnon, Julie E., Francine Dansereau, and Annick Germain. 2004. "'Ethnic' Dilemmas?: Religion, Diversity and Multicultural Planning in Montreal." *Canadian Ethnic Studies* 36 (2): 51–70.

Galabuzi, Grace-Edward. 2006. *Canada's Creeping Economic Apartheid: The Social Exclusion of Racialized Groups in the New Century*. Toronto: Canadian Scholars Press.

Geertz, C. 1973. *The Interpretation of Cultures*. New York: International Universities Press.

Giddens, Anthony. 2000. *Runaway World: How Globalization is Reshaping Our Lives*. New York: Routledge.

Gill, Sheila D. 2002. "The Unspeakability of Racism: Mapping Law's Complicity in Manitoba's Racialized Spaces." In S. Razack, ed. *Race, Space, and the Law: Unmapping a White Settler Society*. Toronto: Between the Lines, 157–184.

Gillespie, Marie. 2000. "Transnational Communications and Diaspora Communities." In Simon Cottle, ed. *Ethnic Minorities and the Media*. Buckingham; Philadelphia: Open University Press, 164–178.

Gordon, M.M. 1964. *Assimilation in American Life*. New York: Oxford University Press.

Grillo, Ralph. 2005. "'Saltdean can't cope': Protests against asylum-seekers in an English seaside suburb." *Ethnic and Racial Studies* 28 (2): 235–260.

Haggerty, Kevin D., and Amber Gazso. 2005. "Seeing Beyond the Ruins: Surveillance as a Response to Terrorist Threats." *Canadian Journal of Sociology* 39 (2): 169–187.

Hardt, Michael, and Antonio Negri. 2000. *Empire*. London; Cambridge, Massachusetts: Harvard University Press.

Hartman, Andrew. 2004. "The Rise and Fall of Whiteness Studies." *Race and Class* 46 (2): 22–38.

Helly, Denise. 2004. "Are Muslims Discriminated Against in Canada Since September 2001?" *Canadian Ethnic Studies* 36 (1): 24–47.

Henderson, Jennifer. 2003. *Settler Feminism and Race Making in Canada*. Toronto: University of Toronto Press.

Henry, Frances, Carol Tator, Winston Mattis, and Tim Rees. 1995. *The Colour of Democracy: Racism in Canadian Society*. Toronto: Harcourt Brace.

hooks bell. 1992. *Black Looks: Race and Representation*. New York: Routledge.

Hörnqvist, Magnus. 2005. "The Birth of Public Order Policy." *Race and Class* 46 (1): 30–52.

Horowitz, D.L. 1985. *Ethnic Groups in Conflict*. Berkeley: University of California Press.

Iganski, Paul, and Barry Kosmin, eds. 2003. *A New Antisemitism? Debating Judeophobia in 21st-century Britain*. London: Profile Books.

Jackson, Nancy S. 1987. "Ethnicity And Vocational Choice." In Jon Young, ed. *Breaking the Mosaic: Ethnic Identities in Canadian Schooling*. Toronto: Garamond, 165–189.

Jedwab, Jack. 2001. "Leadership, Governance, and the Politics of Identity in Canada." *Canadian Ethnic Studies* 33 (3): 4–37.

Kellough, G. 1980. "From Colonialism to Economic Imperialism: The Experience of the Canadian Indian." In J. Harp and J.R. Hofley, eds. *Structured Inequality in Canada*. Scarborough, Ontario: Prentice-Hall, 343–377.

Kelly, Lynnette. 2003. "Bosnian Refugees in Britain: Questioning Community." *Sociology* 37 (1): 35–49.

Kim, Claire Jean. 2004. "Imagining race and nation in multiculturalist America." *Ethnic and Racial Studies* 27 (6): 987–1005.

Kim-Puri, H.J. 2005. "Conceptualizing Gender-Sexuality-State-Nation: An Introduction." *Gender and Society* 19 (2): 137–159.

Kirkham, Della. 1998. "The Reform Party of Canada: A Discourse on Race, Ethnicity and Equality." In Vic Satzewich, ed. *Racism and Social Inequality in Canada: Concepts, Controversies & Strategies of Resistance*. Toronto: Thompson Educational Publishing, 243–268.

Kleiner, Brian. 1998. "The Modern Racist Ideology and its Reproduction in 'Pseudo-Argument'." Discourse & Society 9 (2): 187–215.

Kundnani, Arun. 2004. "Wired for war: military technology and the politics of fear." *Race and Class* 46 (1): 116–125.

Kuper, L. 1969. "Plural Societies: Perspectives and Problems." In L. Kuper and M.G. Smith, eds. *Pluralism in Africa*. Berkeley: University of California Press, 7–26.

Lawrence, Bonita. 2004. *"Real" Indians and Others: Mixed-Blood Urban Native Peoples and Indigenous Nationhood*. Lincoln; London: University of Nebraska Press.

Lawrence, Errol. 1982. "Just Plain Common Sense: The 'Roots' of Racism." In *The Empire Strikes Back: Race and Racism in 70s Britain*. Centre for Contemporary Cultural Studies, University of Birmingham: Routledge.

Lewis, Justin. 2001. *Constructing Public Opinion: How Political Elites Do What They Like and Why We Seem To Go Along With It*. New York: Columbia University Press.

Li, Peter. 2003. "The Place of Immigrants: The Politics of Difference in Territorial and Social Space. *Canadian Ethnic Studies* 35 (2): 1–13.

Li, Peter 1994. "A World Apart: The Multicultural World of Visible Minorities and the Art World of Canada." *Canadian Review of Sociology and Anthropology* 31 (4): 365–391.

Liddle, Joanna, and Rama Joshi. 1986. *Daughters of Independence: Gender, Caste, and Class in India*. London: Zed Books.

Martin, Melinda. 2002. "The Crown Owns All the Land? The Mi'gmaq of Listuguj Resist." In G. MacDonald, ed. *Social Context & Social Location in the Sociology of Law*. Peterborough, Ontario: Broadview Press, 229–246.

Masire, Q.K.J. 2000. *Rwanda: The Preventable Genocide*. Report to the Secretary General of the United Nations, May 2000.

Massey, Douglas S. 2005. "Racial Discrimination in Housing: A Moving Target." *Social Problems* 52 (2): 148–151.

McAndrew, Marie. 2003. "School Spaces and the Construction of Ethnic Relations: Conceptual and Policy Debates." *Canadian Ethnic Studies* 35 (2): 14–29.

Monture-Angus, Patricia. 1999. "Standing Against Canadian Law: Naming Omissions of Race, Culture, and Gender." In Elizabeth Comack, ed. *Locating Law: Race/Class/Gender Connections*. Halifax: Fernwood, 76–97.

Nakano Glenn, Evelyn. 1997. "Looking Back in Anger? Remembering My Sociological Career." In B. Lazlett and B. Thorne, eds. *Feminist Sociology: Life Histories of a Movement*. New Brunswick, New Jersey: Rutgers University Press, 73–102.

Nelson, Jennifer J. 2002. "The Space of Africville: Creating, Regulating, and Remembering the Urban 'Slum'." In S. Razack, ed. *Race, Space, and the Law: Unmapping a White Settler Society*. Toronto: Between the Lines, 211–232.

Ng, Roxana. 1995. "Multiculturalism as Ideology: A Textual Analysis." In Marie Campbell and Ann Manicom, eds. *Knowledge, Experience, and Ruling Relations: Studies in the Social Organization of Knowledge*. Toronto: University of Toronto Press, 35–48.

Ng, Roxana. 1988. *The Politics of Community Services: Immigrant Women, Class, and State*. Toronto: Garamond.

Noivo, Edite. 1998. "Neither 'Ethnic Heroes' nor 'Racial Villains': Inter-Minority Group Racism." In Vic Satzewich, ed. *Racism and Social Inequality in Canada: Concepts, Controversies & Strategies of Resistance*. Toronto: Thompson Educational Publishing, 223–242.

Obama, Barack. 2008. "A More Perfect Union." Campaign Speech, 18 March 2008. Available as video and transcript on many Internet sites, including www.msnbc.com.

Pentland, H.C. 1959. "The Development of a Capitalist Labour Market in Canada." *Canadian Journal of Economics and Political Science* 25 (4): 450–461.

Porter, J. 1979. "Ethnic Pluralism in Canadian Perspective." In *The Measure of Canadian Society: Education, Equality and Opportunity*. Toronto: Gage, 103–137.

Porter, J. 1965. *The Vertical Mosaic: An Analysis of Social Class and Power in Canada*. Toronto: University of Toronto Press.

Radhakrishnan, Smitha. 2005. "'Time to Show Our True Colours': The Gendered Politics of "Indianness" in Post-Apartheid South Africa." *Gender and Society* 19 (2): 262–281.

Raj, Dhooleka Sarhadi. 2000. "'Who the hell do you think you are?': Promoting religious identity among young Hindus in Britain." *Ethnic and Racial Studies* 23 (3): 535–558.

Rajagopal, A. 2000. *Politics after Television: Religious Nationalism and the Retailing of Hindutva 1987–1993*. Cambridge: Cambridge University Press.

Razack, Sherene H. 2002. *Race, Space, and the Law: Unmapping a White Settler Society*. Toronto: Between The Lines.

Razack, Sherene H. 2000. "Gendered Racial Violence and Spatialized Justice: The Murder of Pamela George." *Canadian Journal of Law and Society* 15 (2): 91–130.

Razack, Sherene. 1998. "Race, Space, and Prostitution: The Making of the Bourgeois Subject." *Canadian Journal of Women and the Law* 10: 238–276.

Reitz, Jeffrey G., and Raymond Breton. 1998. "Prejudice and Discrimination in Canada and the United States: A Comparison." In Vic Satzewich, ed. *Racism and Social Inequality in Canada.* Toronto: Thompson.

Rex, J., and R. Moore. 1967. *Race, Community, and Conflict.* Oxford: Oxford University Press.

Reynolds, Tracey. 2002. "Re-thinking a black feminist standpoint." *Ethnic and Racial Studies* 25 (4): 591–606.

Reynolds, Tracey. 2001. "Black mothering, paid work and identity." *Ethnic and Racial Studies* 24 (6): 1046–1064.

Richmond, Anthony H. 2002. "Globalization: implications for immigrants and refugees." *Ethnic and Racial Studies* 25 (5): 707–727.

Richmond, Anthony H. 1988. *Immigration and Ethnic Conflict.* London: Macmillan.

Ross, Karen. 2000. "In Whose Image? TV Criticism and Black Minority Viewers." In Simon Cottle, ed. *Ethnic Minorities and the Media: Changing Cultural Boundaries.* Buckingham; Philadelphia: Open University Press, 133–148.

Rubin, Lilian. 1994. *Families on the Fault Line: America's Working Class Speaks About the Family, the Economy, Race and Ethnicity.* New York: Harper Collins.

Scott, Ellen K. 2005. "Beyond Tokenism: The Making of Racially Diverse Feminist Organizations." *Social Problems* 52 (2): 232–254.

Shaver, Frances M. 1994. The Regulation of Prostitution: Avoiding the Morality Traps." *Canadian Journal of Law and Society* 9: 123–145.

Shils, E. 1957. "Primordial, Personal, Sacred and Civil Ties." *British Journal of Sociology* 8 (2): 130–145.

Simmons, Alan. 1998. "Racism and Immigration Policy." In Vic Satzewich, ed. *Racism and Social Inequality in Canada.* Toronto: Thompson.

Singh, S. 1995. "The Epic on Tube: Plumbing the Depths of History—A Paradigm for Viewing the TV Serialization of the Mahabharata." *Quarterly Review of Film and Video* 16 (1): 77–99.

Sivanandan, A. 2001. "Poverty is the New Black." In *The Three Faces of British Racism,* special issue of *Race and Class* 43 (2).

Smart, Carol. 1984. *The Ties That Bind: Law, Marriage and the Reproduction of Patriarchal Relations.* London: Routledge & Kegan Paul.

Solomos, J., and L. Back. 1994. "Conceptualising Racism: Social Theory, Politics and Research." *Sociology* 28 (1): 143–161.

Sreberny, Annabelle. 2000. "Media and Diasporic Consciousness: An Exploration among Iranians in London." In S. Cottle, ed. *Ethnic Minorities and the Media.* Buckingham; Philadelphia: Open University Press, 179–196.

Stanley, G.F.C. 1964. *Louis Riel: Patriot or Rebel?* Canadian Historical Association Booklet no. 2. Ottawa: Canadian Historical Association.

Staub, Ervin, Laurie Anne Pearlman, and Vachel Miller. 2003. "Healing the Roots of Genocide in Rwanda." *Peace Review* 15 (3): 287–294.

Steckley, John. 2003. *Aboriginal Voices and the Politics of Representation.* Toronto: Canadian Scholars Press.

Stockden, Eric W. 2000. "Pluralism, Corporatism, and Educating Citizens." *Canadian Ethnic Studies* 32 (1): 54–71.

Stubbs, Paul. 1985. "The employment of black social workers: from 'ethnic sensitivity' to anti-racism?" *Critical Social Policy* 12 (Spring): 6–27.

Sudbury, Julia. 2001. "(Re)constructing multiracial blackness: Women's activism, difference and collective identity in Britain." *Ethnic and Racial Studies* 24 (1): 29–49.

Sunahara, Ann. 1981. *The Politics of Racism: The Uprooting of Japanese Canadians During the Second World War.* Toronto: Latimer.

Teeple, G. 1972. "Land, Labour, and Capital in Pre-Confederation Canada." In G. Teeple, ed. *Capitalism and the National Question in Canada.* Toronto: University of Toronto Press, 43–66.

Thobani, Sunera. 2003. "War and the politics of truth-making in Canada." *Qualitative Studies in Education* 16 (3): 399–414.

Thobani, Sunera. 2000. "Closing ranks: racism and sexism in Canada's immigration policy." *Race and Class* 42 (1): 35–55.

Troper, Harold, and Morton Weinfeld. 1999. *Ethnicity, Politics, and Public Policy: Case Studies in Canadian Diversity.* Toronto: University of Toronto Press.

Van den Berghe, P.L. 1969. "Pluralism and the Polity: A Theoretical Exploration." In L. Kuper and M.G. Smith, eds. *Pluralism in Africa.* Berkeley: University of California Press.

Van Dijk, Teun A. 2000. "New(s) Racism: A Discourse Analytical Approach." In Simon Cottle, ed. *Ethnic Minorities and the Media.* Buckingham; Philadelphia: Open University Press, 33–49.

Van Dijk, Teun A. 1993. *Elite Discourse and Racism.* London: Sage.

Verwimp, Philip. 2003. "The Political Economy of Coffee, Dictatorship, and Genocide." *European Journal of Political Economy* 19 (2): 161–181.

Walby, Kevin. 2005. "How Closed-Circuit Television Surveillance Organizes the Social: An Institutional Ethnography." *Canadian Journal of Sociology* 30 (2): 189–214.

Walling, Carrie Booth. 2000. "The History and Politics of Ethnic Cleansing." *International Journal of Human Rights* 4 (3): 47–67.

Warren, John T. 2003. *Performing Purity: Whiteness, Pedagogy, and the Reconstitution of Power.* New York: Peter Laing.

Wells, Karen, and Sophie Watson. 2005. "A Politics of Resentment: Shopkeepers in a London Neighbourhood." *Ethnic and Racial Studies* 28 (2): 261–277.

Wilson II, Clint C. 2000. "The Paradox of African American Journalists." In Simon Cottle, ed. *Ethnic Minorities and the Media: Changing Cultural Boundaries.* Buckingham; Philadelphia: Open University Press, 85–99.

Wrench, John. 2005. "Diversity management can be bad for you." *Race & Class* 46 (3): 73–84.

Yegenoglu, Meyda. 2005. "Cosmopolitanism and Nationalism in a Globalized World." *Ethnic and Racial Studies* 28 (1): 103–131.

Young, Jon, and Robert J. Graham. 2000. "School and Curriculum Reform: Manitoba Frameworks & Multicultural Teacher Education." *Canadian Ethnic Studies* 32 (1): 142–155.

Young, Judy. 2001. "No longer 'Apart'? Multiculturalism Policy and Canadian Literature." *Canadian Ethnic Studies* 33 (2): 88–97.

Weber's analytical model of bureaucracy has been taken up in diverse ways by different theoretical perspectives in sociology. Traditional structural-functionalist analysis has focused primarily upon questions of function and efficiency in meeting the objective goals of organizations.

Marxist structuralism refocuses the question around deeper issues of power and the apparatus of ruling embedded in the interlocking bureaucratic structures of contemporary society. This approach challenges in fundamental ways the claims to scientific objectivity and neutrality in traditional functionalist models of efficient administration. It explores the central significance of bureaucratic structures as determinants of the hierarchical divisions that we come to recognize as class and also the gendered inequalities produced through the job ghettos and limited roles made available to women within them.

Different approaches within the broad framework of interpretive theory question the taken-for-granted assumption that bureaucratic structures exist as entities that do things or have effects. They explore alternative views of bureaucracy as socially constructed through the authoritative procedures of officials and through the accounting practices by which people make sense of what they do. Interpretive theory has its roots in Weber's methodological insistence on grounding sociological analysis in the study of meaning, and his rejection of holistic concepts that tend to lose sight of the fact that only people are active agents. Bureaucratic organizations are, after all, nothing more than collections of people trying, more or less competently, to get things done. These organizations cannot exist independently of the meaningful understanding of the people involved.

The complex work of Michel Foucault is used in this chapter to draw together the Marxist structuralist and interpretive perspectives. Foucault believes that our social world comes to be known to us, and to have the form it does, through **discourse** about it; that is, through how we talk about it. However, it is also our lived experience of the social world that creates our knowledge and our mode of talking about it. For Foucault, this circle is virtually closed, as the way we talk or think structures our experience, which structures the knowledge expressed when we talk. As we have seen many times in earlier chapters, people commonly draw on prevailing theories about human behaviour to organize how they talk about their own experiences, which then appears to provide further ethnographic confirmation for the theory itself.

In the last section of this chapter we explore the discourse of radical feminism, a way of thinking that begins from the standpoint of people whose central experience of nurturing children in families is very different from the bureaucratic mode of public life. As women increasingly merge private and public realms in their own lived experience, their emerging knowledge makes possible a radically new discourse. It suggests ways of thinking in which the nature of rationality itself, and with it the entire bureaucratic edifice, is called into question.

 ## Traditional Functionalism: Bureaucracy as Efficient

Parsons' early essay "Suggestions for a Sociological Approach to the Theory of Organizations" (1956) aptly summarizes the traditional structural-functionalist perspective. Organizations exist as definite structures designed for attaining specific goals. For Parsons, the question of what constitutes a bureaucracy poses few problems. Organizations are, by definition, formal structures set up for specific purposes, with actions coordinated to these ends. Efficiency is measured by success in achieving these ends. The structure of organizations consists of the roles of participants and the values that define and legitimate their functions. Mechanisms for implementing goals consist of the *board*, or top level, which makes policy decisions, and the *line* administration, which makes allocative decisions for optimal use of resources in pursuit of goals. *Personnel management* is responsible for coordination and integration of subunits, and for ensuring appropriate motivation through coercion, incentives, and therapy. Lastly, the *workers* themselves are responsible for production. The organization, which interacts with its external environment, is viewed as a single unit with a single goal.

Testing the Model

Empirical research in the functionalist tradition has commonly taken Weber's model of bureaucratic structures as a framework for analyzing how particular organizations function. Many of these studies indicate that the model is not always a good predictor of organizational efficiency, and that it needs to be modified to state precisely the conditions under which bureaucracy will or will not work efficiently.

A study by Blau (1955) casts doubt on the Weberian model through evidence that bureaucratic procedures actually cause inefficient behaviour. Blau studied four sections of a state employment agency in the United States. The work involved screening and counselling job applicants, referring them to appropriate job vacancies, and notifying the state unemployment insurance agency of people refusing jobs without good cause. Measures of job performance included number of interviews per month, number of clients referred to jobs, number of placements, and number of notifications to the unemployment insurance office of fraud.

Blau found that the bureaucratic procedures designed to ensure strict performance accountability directly undermined efficiency. Employees geared their work to what counted. They concentrated on shallow, high-speed interviews, and multiple referrals. Handicapped clients or those needing counselling were discarded because they lowered performance ratings. They also cheated on each other, hiding job vacancies to boost their own placement records, and they falsified statistics to inflate placements.

The degree of inefficiency created by those practices only came to light by comparison with one section of the agency where the employees were all army veterans whose jobs were guaranteed. They could afford to ignore performance ratings. They cooperated in their work and shared knowledge of all job openings. They also spent more time counselling applicants because they genuinely cared that these people, many of whom were themselves veterans, find suitable jobs. The result was that this section actually filled more job openings and placed more people than did the other sections. The bureaucratic rules that controlled the work of employees in other sections of the agency actually created inefficiency because they hampered cooperation.

Blau has not been alone in finding that bureaucratic modes of organization cause inefficiency. Merton (1957)

drew attention to the "cogs in the machine mentality" of many career bureaucrats who have learned not to think or to act for themselves but to rigidly follow prescribed rules. Such responses may be functional in routine work but are totally dysfunctional in situations requiring innovation.

Burns and Stalker (1961) highlight the same point in their study of 20 Scottish electronics firms. These firms were struggling to diversify their products in a postwar market where their traditional government defence contracts for radar equipment were declining. Most of these firms were organized in ideal-typical bureaucratic forms, with fragmented, carefully designated jobs in production, sales, and design, coordinated through a rigidly defined hierarchy of responsibilities. This formal organization proved disastrous for innovation. Everything new was, by definition, outside the jurisdiction of predefined offices. Hence more and more decisions were passed up to the top of the hierarchy while those below refused to do anything until they received direct orders. The inevitable result was that the manager was swamped and subordinates paralyzed. The typical bureaucratic response was to set up a new role to handle the new problem, but that person's job depended upon the continuation of the problem! This is a typical case of **goal displacement** found in many studies of bureaucracies, where maintaining one's own department takes priority over the total enterprise. The subgoal tends to become that of enhancing the prestige and resources of one's own section at the expense of others.

The few firms in Burns and Stalker's study that did manage to innovate successfully scrapped the hierarchy and the predefined, fragmented jobs in favour of cooperative teamwork and collective responsibilities.

A study by Dalton (1959, 342–351) documents the perennial conflicts between technical staff and administrators in bureaucracies. Technical staff were supposed to suggest improvements in functioning, but any such proposals were bitterly resented by administrators, who felt that their own expertise and authority were being challenged. The result was resistance, bordering on sabotage of new ideas.

These are all relatively old studies and are quite well known. They point to serious inefficiencies in typical bureaucratic modes of organization and suggest that more flexible, cooperative, and less hierarchical systems work better, at least for tasks that are not totally routinized. Yet bureaucracy is more pervasive than ever. Burns and Stalker found that, in many of the electronic firms, the employees themselves actively resisted attempts to break down the bureaucratic system. They seemed to prefer fixed tasks that left no doubt exactly what the workers were responsible for and what they were not responsible for. They preferred to be left alone to get on with their jobs without any further commitment.

The theoretical question these studies raise is why there should be such resistance to more cooperative, less hierarchical modes of organization. The Weberian argument that bureaucracy is more efficient is not an adequate explanation.

Political Economy Theory: Bureaucracy, Power, and Control

Political economy theory, which is rooted in classical Marxist analysis of the structures of capitalism, challenges traditional functionalism by asking what segment of society finds bureaucracy functional and efficient. It questions the image of organizations or societies as unified systems with goal consensus and explores instead the dimensions of inequality, class, and power within organizations.

Proponents of political economy theory have pointed out that, historically, factories did not emerge as the result of new technology or concerns with efficient mass production (Marglin 1974–75). The factories actually preceded the technology. They emerged as the result of the interest of owners of the raw materials in exerting greater control over workers. The older putting-out system, where workers took raw materials to their homes and brought back finished goods, was not conducive to close control over the pace of work. Factories were created so that workers would be under the constant surveillance and direct control of the bosses. It was very inefficient for the workers, however, because they could no longer integrate child care and other domestic work with production.

It can be argued that all the characteristics of bureaucracy listed by Weber are required, not for efficiency of production, but for surveillance and control over unwilling workers. They reflect and gloss over antagonistic class interests. Gouldner (1952) addresses several questions concerning Weber's model. What kinds of obligations and responsibilities are established in Weber's model? What aspects of behaviour are rendered predictable and calculated? What aspects of organizations are left conspicuously unpredictable? Gouldner answers that the rules defining workers' obligations are the most predictable, while rules defining workers' rights, or management obligations, are the least predictable. Workers have had to form unions to force the establishment of rules concerning seniority, job security, grievance procedures, sick leave, holidays, and the like. Rules defining conformity are the most rigid at the bottom of the organizational hierarchy, where workers are subjected to clocking in and out. Rules are least rigid at the top. Senior managers have much more leeway to arrive late or to take breaks when they want to. The level of impersonality also varies. It is strongest between ranks, defining how sub-ordinates and superiors are to interact, but least rigid among formal equals, especially at the top of the rank. Gouldner concludes that Weber's model does not represent an abstract model of efficiency at all, but rather the narrow perspectives of management experts.

In his major empirical study of bureaucratization in a gypsum factory, Gouldner (1954) traces the actual stages in the development of rigid rules. Initially, the factory was anything but bureaucratic. It was located in a small rural community where workers and supervisors grew up together. The organization was easygoing, with minimal attention to rules so long as the work got done. Job switching was permitted and, when vacancies arose, promotion of local people was favoured over importing outside experts, even if the locals were less qualified.

All this changed when head office personnel appointed a new boss from outside the factory who was under pressure to improve the organization. Workers resented him. They wanted a local boss and feared the loss of their old privileges. The new boss found himself forced to impose bureaucratic rules to break the resistance of the workers. He could not use the old cooperative relations to motivate workers because he himself was resented by them as an outsider. Hence he relied upon formal rules to back his authority. He displaced their hostility onto superior officers by arguing that the rules came from senior management. Rules were clear and could be rigidly applied to everyone. They permitted spot-checking or supervision at a distance and so lessened the outright expressions of hostility generated by close supervision. Relations between workers and management worsened to the point of a wildcat strike. Ironically, the resolution of the workers' grievances resulted in still more bureaucratization as work roles and responsibilities were even more rigidly defined and delimited. It was clear what workers did and did not have to do, and supervision could become still more impersonal (Gouldner 1965). Gouldner concludes that the main function of bureaucratic rules in the gypsum mine was not to raise efficiency of production, but to impose discipline on reluctant workers. Rules were a symptom of class hostility between workers and bosses.

A historical study into the origins of job structures in the United States steel industry traces the process of job fragmentation and deskilling of workers (Stone 1974). It was not technical advances, but the class struggle between workers and owners of the Carnegie steel mill, that generated these changes. Before 1892, steel was made by teams of skilled workers with unskilled helpers, using the company's equipment and raw materials. Skilled workers were in complete charge of the labour process. They divided the tasks among themselves, set the pace of the work, and determined pay differentials, with overall pay based on the price of steel. By the 1890s, however, demand for steel was rising, and the owners wanted to raise production and their own profits. A new manager used armed men to close down the plant, lock out the workers, and break their union. New machines were installed, which doubled or trebled productivity while wages went up only marginally. Work was reorganized so highly skilled craftsmen were reduced to semiskilled labourers.

Finally, to break the unified resistance of workers, the owners instituted artificial job ladders. Very minor differences in skill levels were written into distinct job classifications with different pay levels. Workers thus found themselves competing against each other and currying favour with supervisors to get small promotions. Subsequent union contracts cemented these artificial divisions between workers by negotiating bonuses, pay scales, and seniority clauses in line with the new job classifications. The way the work is organized in the steel industry is both produced by the class struggle and used as a weapon in that struggle.

These critical studies change in significant ways the conception of rationality and efficiency on which Weber based his legitimation of bureaucracy. Bureaucratic organizations have been shown in several different contexts to be much less efficient than nonhierarchical, cooperative models, especially when flexibility or innovation is needed. Yet bureaucracy persists. These authors suggest that it persists primarily because it is the most efficient method of controlling reluctant workers while deflecting hostility and opposition. Deskilled, fragmented workers are easily controlled and exploited by managers who monopolize skilled knowledge for themselves. Workers themselves may come to prefer it as a way of minimizing their own commitment to the organization. Bureaucracy is clearly not a neutral mode of organization. It is intimately associated with inequality and power.

Bureaucracy and Oligarchy

Weber did not question the ultimate functional efficiency of bureaucracy for meeting the goals of whoever was in control, and for this he can be justly faulted. What he did see with stunning clarity was the almost unassailable power that bureaucracy confers upon the elites who control it. Weber likewise did not see job fragmentation as related to a deliberate deskilling process. He was, however, very much aware of the political consequences of the resulting concentration of knowledge and technical expertise in the hands of a bureaucratic elite, and the disempowerment of both functionaries within the bureaucratic machine and the mass of people outside it.

It was the sophisticated German bureaucratic apparatus, for example, that was key to the success of the Nazis in accomplishing the "final solution" to the "Jewish problem" (Berger 1993). The extermination of Jews was translated into mundane tasks that numberless functionaries performed without leaving their desks. It became a matter of bureaucratic competence, efficiency, and problem-solving abilities. The railroad bureaucrat, for example, was able to fulfill his functional role by treating the transportation of Jews to death camps as equivalent to transporting any other passengers to any destination. He was responsible only for assuring that their fares were correctly paid.

Weber's recognition of the inherent tendencies toward **oligarchy** within bureaucratic organizations, and the threat that these pose to democracy, has powerfully influenced the development of theory in political sociology. Robert Michels ([1911] 1949) drew extensively upon Weber's work to develop the concept of the **iron law of oligarchy** to explain the processes of concentration of power in ostensibly democratic political parties and trade unions. He shared Weber's conviction that organization is essential for the expression of collective will. A disorganized mass of people can rarely accomplish anything. They are easily subject to suggestion by skilled orators and are easily swayed by the emotions of the moment. Sober and disciplined decision making is virtually impossible in mass meetings. Some form of delegation of responsibilities is thus essential, but then the problem of hierarchy begins to emerge.

In principle, the person who is elected as leader within a democratic organization is the servant of the masses and can be deprived of office at any moment. Perhaps the ideal is rotating office bearers. But leadership responsibilities and roles are complex. They require technical knowledge and experience that can only be learned over time. People with legal or technical training have a distinct advantage in such roles. As they develop expertise, however, a gulf inevitably widens between them and the masses who elected them to office. The mass of the people lacks information to make clear decisions, and mass involvement wastes time and limits flexibility of action.

Exactly as Weber recognized, secrecy constitutes a critical source of power. As the gap in knowledge grows between leaders and the masses, more committee meetings are held in secret, and the rank and file get only summary reports. Government bureaucrats welcome a poorly informed parliament because they gain greater freedom of action and freedom from surveillance. Michels recognized that unions could become more oligarchic than political parties because the leaders control the funds and can determine legal strikes. During negotiations they can also claim to know the market better than do members.

In principle, election to office should make incumbents accountable to the electorate and therefore promote democracy. In practice, as Weber pointed out, elections undermine the values of efficiency, impartiality, and expertise in the operation of bureaucracies. A glaring example of this occurred in Philadelphia, where more than 50 municipal judges, who are elected to office, were accused of accepting bribes. They were reported to have perpetuated racketeering by having a virtual price list for turning a blind eye to crimes. The chancellor of the Philadelphia Bar Association concluded that such racketeering is almost unavoidable in a system where elected judges receive salaries of $80 000 but where their campaigns cost up to $100 000. It was difficult to prove that bribes were anything more than legitimate campaign contributions. Moreover, there seemed to be a great deal of public tolerance for this behaviour. "While it is unclear whether voters are cynical or merely ignorant," every judge who was suspended for accepting bribes was easily re-elected to office (*Globe and Mail*, 31 Dec. 1987, A1–2).

Within political parties and unions, where leaders are elected, the mass of membership tends to become indifferent toward the organization. While a small inner circle allows for speed of action, it means that most members are left out. Long-tenured leaders tend to develop an aura of indispensability; the masses feel incompetent to handle their own affairs.

The main threat to the power of a leader is not the masses, but a takeover bid from a new dominant figure. It is difficult to succeed in such a bid because the established elite has the advantage of material resources, time, and support staff. Often elite figures have a full-time, paid staff to develop propaganda; they control the main supply of information; and their high position leads others to emulate them. They may try to co-opt potential new leaders by giving them high-level posts and then demanding loyalty, or try to discredit them and label their followers disloyal. The mere threat of abdication, combined with the threat that the party will lose the next election or the union will lose in negotiations, may be sufficient to get the masses to toe the line. The trump card is to convince the masses that they are incompetent to run affairs without a leader. Hence, Michels concludes, a radical change of leaders can occur, but it is relatively rare and often unstable.

The short-lived leadership change within the United Steelworkers Union of America, Ontario office, in 1985, seems a classic case of oligarchy at work. A newspaper report (*Globe and Mail*, 9 Nov. 1985) suggests that the union establishment was shocked in 1981 by the election to office of a rank and file member on a platform of union reform. Union staff traditionally had a strong influence on union politics, but the newcomer, a tough militant who led a long strike at INCO in Sudbury two years earlier, broke this pattern. His problem was that, once in office, he was unable to accomplish much reform. He was unable to challenge the political machine of his rivals. He lacked the administrative expertise to crack the entrenched bureaucracy. Four years later, his dreams were broken as he was beaten in the elections by an establishment candidate. The union executive reportedly hired a public relations firm to run their campaign. Slick campaign literature was designed for the executive's candidate, and behind them there was the might of the president's office at Steelworkers headquarters in Pittsburgh.

Michels concludes that the ideal of rule by the masses never occurs and cannot occur. The reality is a circulation of dominant elites. It is perhaps in the face of this level of powerlessness that people come to accept bribery as an effective, if illegitimate, means of exerting influence over officials.

Bureaucracy and Communism

Michels criticizes Marxist theory for failing to take account of administration in theories of power. Socialism, he argues, is not merely a problem of economics, but also of administration. Large amounts of capital require bureaucracy to organize them, and with this comes hierarchy of control and technical expertise. Hence, the iron law of oligarchy re-emerges. The masses, he argues, will always submit to the minority.

Mosca ([1939] 1960) echoes similar sentiments, arguing that there will always be elites who can monopolize power and advantages through control of political party structures or any large-scale bureaucratic administration. The elite has the advantages of publicity, information control, education, specialized training, and qualifications. Elites also have the advantage of a lifetime of experience that they are able to hand down from one generation to another. Pressure from discontented masses does influence leaders, but whenever established leaders are disposed, another elite minority will have to be elected in their place.

In the final months of 1989 and into the 1990s, the peoples of many countries in Eastern Europe were struggling with this problem of how to oust entrenched Communist Party elites and bureaucrats. Mass demonstrations, protests, and strikes precipitated the resignations of established Communist Party elites. But the difficult task that remained was to select new people to fill the resulting power vacuum. Before free elections could be held, parties had to be organized and candidates found. Periodic elections provide a mechanism for the circulation of elites but do not eliminate the need for them. Nor do elections resolve the problem of rigid bureaucratic structures.

The stranglehold of bureaucracy on life in Soviet society was generally recognized even by the strongest supporters of communism. Marx's assumption that a classless society would in principle protect citizens from the ravages of a bureaucratic state clearly was not sustained in practice.

Barry Smart (1983) argues that two events in Europe in 1968—the popular uprisings among students and workers in France in May of that year and the "Prague Spring"—

irrevocably shattered the dreams of European socialists. The protest movements in France formed independently of the trade unions and the French Communist Party, the conventional political institutions of opposition. The generally conservative and unsympathetic response of the Communist Party to these demonstrations revealed the barrenness of the institutionalized and hierarchical forms of political protest. In theory, the Communist Party should have been at the forefront of the uprising, championing the rights and interests of the workers. In practice, the party proved to be out of touch and even hostile to a workers' movement that it did not control. Later that year, the Soviet Union invaded Czechoslovakia to crush the spontaneous social protest movements known as the Prague Spring. Smart argues that this invasion nullified any claim by the government of the Soviet Union to social, economic, political, or moral superiority over capitalist systems.

The massacre of demonstrators in Tiananmen Square in Beijing in June 1989 similarly undermined the legitimacy of Communist Party rule in China. For some three weeks prior to the massacre, several thousand people, led by Beijing University students, camped in the square to pressure for greater democratization in the country. They were denounced as counterrevolutionaries by Communist Party leaders, and the army was ordered to drive them out of the square. Foreign reporters estimate that hundreds of people were shot or crushed by army tanks. The oligarchic structure of the Communist Party was revealed in the power wielded by a handful of old men. It also became evident how effectively the bureaucracy could control information so as to present a version of events that minimized the massacre, exonerated the army and the party, and silenced criticism. China is generally acknowledged as a state relatively impervious to international pressure; to this can be added the fact that Western countries, led by the United States, seem reluctant to alienate so significant a trading partner by tying trade to human rights.

The critical challenge for Marxist theory is to account for the prevalence of Stalinist dictators in communist societies in which theorists had predicted a gradual withering away of state powers. The conventional Marxist response to such repression has been to return to classical texts in an effort to substitute new interpretations of doctrine. In Smart's view, none has yet been able to resolve the crisis of Marxism: the continuing incompatibility between theoretical expectations and patterns of development in Western capitalist societies and the realities in existing communist states. Indeed, in the late 1980s, challenges to communist rule throughout Eastern Europe were so sudden and so sweeping that some commentators were led to proclaim the end of history—the universal triumph of liberal-capitalist democracy (Fukuyama 1989). Ongoing struggles among ultraright nationalists, free-market advocates, and old-guard communists in former republics of the old Soviet Union make such a pronouncement seem premature.

These grandiose claims, however, have a hollow ring. In principle, the basic ideology of capitalism, which stresses free enterprise, individualism, and hostility to big government and state interference, should have worked against the development of a bureaucratic state in Western societies. But it has not. The iron cage of bureaucracy is not so easily escaped. Weber argued that bureaucratic forms of organization are an essential and unavoidable feature of centralized and industrialized societies, regardless of whether they are organized along capitalist or communist lines. Bureaucratic elites wield power by virtue of knowledge and technical superiority. This power base, Weber argues, is far stronger than the raw power of ownership or control over the means of production because it is founded on the legitimating principle of rationality itself. As Weber saw it, purposive-rational organization is inherently bureaucratic and leads inevitably to oligarchy and dehumanization. Neither communist nor democratic procedures would be sufficient to overcome this. New approaches within interpretive theory have begun the work of pushing beyond both functionalist and classical Marxist theories, toward a critical analysis of bureaucracy and how relations of power are rationalized.

BUREAUCRATIC SOCIETY

This section draws heavily on the work of Kathy Ferguson (1984) who bases her analysis of **bureaucratic society** on the work of Foucault. In Ferguson's view, bureaucracy, as an all-pervasive mode of social organization, actually creates the kind of social system that structural-functionalist theory describes: a self-maintaining system that reduces people to sets of fragmented roles. In Ferguson's theory, bureaucracy and society become synonymous. The institutionalized sets of roles that bureaucracy makes available to us, together with bureaucratic descriptions of and justifications for these roles or job classifications, structure our social world and shape how we think about it.

Bureaucracy has become so all-pervasive as to leave people with virtually no options. To remove oneself from bureaucracy is to lose almost all important social connections, while to embrace one's role is to lose the dimensions of oneself that do not coincide with organizational roles. The cost of conformity is resignation, while the cost of resistance is disintegration. Whatever course of action one takes is already determined by the organizational environment (Ferguson 1984, 91–92).

For Ferguson (1984, xii), the central issue is bureaucracy itself, a mode of organization that hurts, twists, and damages people and limits human possibility. Bureaucracy represents "the scientific organization of inequality" through which people are dominated and oppressed. At the same time, it legitimates such practices in the name of rationality and efficiency. Conflict-ridden class relations are disguised in the language of administration.

Bureaucracy can be seen as a self-maintaining social system. Whatever the ostensible services that a bureaucracy might have been set up to accomplish, they tend to become secondary to the interests of members in keeping the machinery running. The central concern of bureaucrats tends to be the maintenance of a stable environment with predictable behaviour from functionaries within the organization and from clients and customers outside it.

Ferguson's analysis, however, goes far beyond a description of the system. She takes up the challenge that social constructionism must necessarily examine the mechanisms through which the system is maintained. The primary function of bureaucracy is control, which is maintained in the face of continuing resistance and pressures toward nonconformity. Such maintenance requires the constant renewal of mechanisms that keep the structures intact. These mechanisms include isolating individuals, depersonalizing relations, and distorting communications. The constant appeal to efficiency conceals the control function that hierarchy performs within bureaucracies. Individuals are isolated in their fragmented and delimited roles. Their potential individual contribution is so limited that they are rendered expendable and therefore powerless. The absorption or co-optation of a few key individuals into management creates the illusion of upward mobility and hence promotes loyalty, while supervision, roles, and the hoarding of knowledge control the mass of people.

People interact with others only as role occupants. We come to see each other from the perspective of the organization and the roles we play in it rather than as whole persons. Likewise, in the wider society, people are commonly referred to as if they only existed in terms of standard bureaucratic categories. We come to think of "taxpayers" pitted against "workers" or "citizens" versus "welfare recipients." It is hard to keep sight of the reality that these are not distinct people but common dimensions of experience. The conception of people in terms of fragmented and competing roles tends to perpetuate our dependency on the very organizations that cause this fragmentation.

Bureaucratic language further depersonalizes people and reinforces this role fragmentation. The **language of technics** replaces the language of human action: dialogue, debate, and judgment are replaced by feedback, input, and output. Class conflicts are depersonalized when firing people is described as "reductions in force" or "downsizing" (Ferguson 1984, 15–16). Opposition is pacified by the ideological construction of rational administration as neutral,

efficient, and effective. Interpretive theory seeks to deconstruct such bureaucratic language by exploring how such discourses produce their meanings.

The language of technics, for example, was pervasive in the Nazi bureaucratization of the solution to the "Jewish problem" (Berger 1993). Much effort was devoted to constructing a legal definition of the target population that was amenable to precise bureaucratic categorization, requiring precise reactions from functionaries.

The three practices of authorization, routinization, and dehumanization worked to minimize opposition. Authorization norms allow role occupants to avoid taking responsibility for the consequences of their actions. Routinization eliminates the need to make decisions, especially when moral questions arise. Dehumanization constitutes victims as nonpersons reducible to statistical categories. Berger concludes that the "final solution" to the "Jewish problem" was socially constructed through bureaucratic processes that were in themselves quite ordinary or banal.

Resistance

Opposition may be silenced, muted, or distorted by the conceptions of administrative neutrality and efficiency but, in Foucault's view, it can never be totally destroyed. If people really could be reduced to their roles, to their organizational identities, then the mechanisms of bureaucratic control would no longer be necessary. The intensity of control is itself a measure of the pervasiveness of resistance. In practice, people are never reduced to total conformity. The exercise of power generates the very resistance to which it responds. Foucault argues that power relations presuppose resistance.

No matter how efficient bureaucracies may be in promoting conformity and passivity, uncertainties remain. Control is never total. People within the organization may ignore information they receive or distort information that they pass on, and so produce **intelligence failures**. People who direct the organizations fail to achieve intended results because they base their commands on inaccurate and incomplete information. The goals of individual members will never coincide completely with organizational goals. These discrepancies give rise to continual pressures toward resistance.

Bureaucratization is thus not an accomplished entity, but a process, a struggle between control and resistance. Mechanisms of control must be constantly reproduced to overcome the opposition that control itself generates. Yet at the same time, bureaucracies must disguise these efforts to deal with conflict in order to maintain the image of administrative neutrality and efficiency upon which their legitimacy and control depends (Ferguson 1984, 17–21). The result is more and more centralization, more standardization of rules and regulations, and ever-increasing ratios of supervisors or managers to actual workers. Ferguson estimated there was one supervisor for every three to four workers in the United States in 1984. By the mid-1990s this picture has changed dramatically as computerized monitoring has taken over the work of supervision. Electronic surveillance is many times more detailed and intrusive than human supervision could be.

Society as a whole can be conceptualized as a dense network of interlocking organizations that together form a **technical civilization** penetrating all aspects of social life. Each organization acts as a potential resource for other organizations in an overall collaborative network. Foucault (1980, 106) refers to this as a "closely linked grid of disciplinary coercions" that enforce inequality, normalcy, and control. Unions collaborate with corporations to control workers through contracts. Drug companies make deals with the federal government to change patent laws and with medical associations to promote their products. Clusters of organizations act as suppliers, subsidiaries, distributors, and research organizations for each other. Corporations, together with relevant state agencies, provide banking, legal, managerial, advertising, and public relations services for each other. They come together as loose, flexible, very stable networks of interlocking institutions, their minor conflicts contained within a climate of cooperation (Ferguson 1984, 38–42). Increasingly, all such organizations come to resemble each other and utilize shared knowledge of techniques of management. Prisons come to resemble factories, schools, barracks, and hospitals, which in turn come to resemble prisons (Foucault 1977, 229).

Normalization

Foucault emphasizes that this bureaucratic, technical civilization cannot be understood in such purely negative terms as repression or constraint. When we think of power in terms of sovereignty, or as imposed by elites from the top down, then we focus on laws, but disciplinary power is not imposed from above. It is exercised through ordinary, everyday activities, and it actually produces how we think of normal reality. It is characterized by **therapeutic intervention** in everything. Professionals who engage in such intervention justify it in terms of efficiency and technical expertise in the production of **normalized**, productive people. In Foucault's scheme, social work, police, and military become fused. Individual and collective life is controlled through the disciplines of the social sciences and related techniques of administrative law, policy analysis, social work, public administration, and rational planning.

The most intimate aspects of personal life and social relations are subject to the cult of rationality within this therapeutic civilization. Hochschild (1983, 171–177) refers to **emotional labour** in her description of how flight attendants are trained to manage feelings and facial and body expressions to produce the required response in the customer. The flight attendant learns the techniques of emotional management with the aid of instruction manuals. The goal is not genuine communication but eliciting appropriate responses from customers, which will raise profits for the airline.

Corporate executives pay up to $75 an hour to take courses from behavioural psychologists in how to use a well-modulated voice (*Globe and Mail*, 24 Dec. 1987, B1–2). "The goal is to develop a 'voice image' that conveys confidence, trust, warmth, and believability to improve the way others respond." The objective is to "help business clients talk their way to success," measured in terms of being persuasive enough to close deals. In Ferguson's terms, people learn to substitute technique for connectedness, to attach emotions to functions and not to any person. As soon as a new technique is available, experts apply it to whatever is at hand. Bureaucracy is the organized expression of this **managerial mentality**.

This **cult of rationality** in emotion management is never totally successful in reducing all emotions to the plastic responses required. The exercise of such techniques itself generates resistance and withdrawal. Hence, such control requires constant policing and constant repetition, reflected in such practices as annual retraining courses for flight attendants.

THE BUREAUCRATIC CONSTRUCTION OF CLASS

Weber's analysis of class in capitalist society modified Marx's thesis by shifting the ground of class and class relations from the question of ownership of means of production to life chances within the marketplace. The move from market capitalism to corporate capitalism has changed the basis of class relations. Ownership of the means of production is no longer a central issue for the vast majority of people. Control over the means of production has become increasingly concentrated in fewer and fewer hands within giant corporate empires and holding companies. Careers within corporate bureaucracies are now the central determinant of class position of the majority of people, with career entry tightly tied to credentials. Location within the bureaucratic hierarchy and the conditions that determine who gets the positions are now the key factors in the social construction of class.

Ferguson identifies the layers produced by rigid and fractionalized job hierarchies within this organizational class system. Directors and executives make policy; the new working class of highly skilled, technical, managerial, and professional workers administer the implementation of these policies; the industrial and clerical working class with lower educational requirements have highly routinized, fragmented work; the bottom level of marginal workers have casual jobs within the secondary labour market. Casual workers are the people who move back and forth between the roles of workers and clients of unemployment and welfare agencies.

The class system within industrial societies has its origin within such corporate bureaucratic entities. The arrangement of jobs within bureaucracies is very deliberate and is justified in terms of efficiency but perpetuated by the need for control. In this respect at least, the lives of the mass of people in advanced capitalist societies may differ little from the experience of life within state socialist societies.

People who occupy different rungs of the bureaucratic class order have substantially different work situations when measured in terms of income, health and safety, trust, and freedom from close supervision. But they share the same system that de-individualizes them and objectifies their activities and relations (Ferguson 1984, 88). The power that bureaucracy exercises over people is so hard to see because that power becomes so totally part of the activities themselves. It is what people do. If power were always oppressive and negative, it would not be so powerful. It is accepted because it seems productive (Foucault 1980, 119).

Subordination within the bureaucratic hierarchy produces character traits displayed by subordinate, dependent, and powerless people, traits that Ferguson suggests closely resemble the stereotype of femininity. Subordinates must be constantly concerned with impression-management because their well-being depends upon pleasing superiors. Conformity is central to their survival within bureaucracies and is produced by close surveillance. Their career mobility depends upon pleasing superiors and moulding one's behaviour to fit what superiors want. Career manuals warn aspiring junior managers not to make suggestions that challenge the organization's established ways of doing things. Successful innovations by those who fail to conform to expected bureaucratic patterns of behaviour will be resented rather than welcomed, as they threaten the established order.

The higher up the organizational hierarchy, the more important impression-management and conformity is. As Kanter (1977) has pointed out, social similarity becomes a critical measure of trustworthiness among managers where close surveillance is difficult. As a result, people from cultural backgrounds other than the norm, or people who look different, such as blacks and women, find it extremely hard to break into management ranks, no matter what their competence. They do not fit; they cannot be trusted to conform.

Resistance from within bureaucratic organizations is limited and individualistic. Union radicals and activists at all levels tend to attack individual abuses by particular superiors, or aim at particular policy reforms, rather than attacking the system as a whole. They leave the bureaucratic order intact (Ferguson 1984, 120).

Clients, who seek assistance from social service agencies, occupy the lowest rung on the organizational class structure. Often they are omitted from analyses of organizational hierarchies, and yet they are important in the larger class structure of which an organization is part. "There are growing numbers of organizations whose purpose is to process, regulate, license, certify, hide or otherwise control people," and clients are the prime targets (Ferguson 1984, 123). Customers, who purchase goods and services from bureaucracies, have relatively more independence of action than clients, but neither group has much influence over the organizations on which it depends. Professionals who work in advertising, marketing, and sales are concerned with controlling the behaviour and attitudes of customers, much as employees in welfare bureaucracies are concerned with controlling poor people. Ferguson (1984, 123) suggests that the ghettos of the urban poor are becoming increasingly like total institutions, subject to administrative controls that define, monitor, categorize, produce, and supervise the inhabitants' behaviour.

The poor, as clients of service bureaucracies, must learn to conform to the required image: they must learn to please, to present the appropriate responses, to give recognition to administrative authority, to flatter, and to legitimate the bureaucracy and its rules (Ferguson 1984, 144–146). Ferguson describes the immense strain that this places on poor people. They must learn to treat themselves as categories, to read clues, to control themselves, to anticipate demands, to calculate acceptable responses, and to offer them as signs of deservedness. Even to become clients they must first become cases and pass examinations to demonstrate their eligibility and deservedness. If successful, they are rewarded by becoming the obedient subjects of bureaucratic management. The traits of dependence and passivity help to perpetuate their situation by lowering their self-esteem and ability to assert themselves or to organize collectively. A very few individuals can challenge this by tactics of confrontation but, as Ferguson suggests, such strategies work only because they are rare. It is easier for the administration to give in to the few individual agitators than to fight them, but any organized resistance is likely to be short-lived and easily controlled. Welfare bureaucracies provide financial support to client organizations that then must conform to continue receiving support.

The roles available to clients are very limited, and even the ordinary activities of life tend to be redefined in managerial terms. Patients, for example, do not hold dances, they have "dance therapy"; they do not play volleyball or cards, they have "recreation therapy" (Ferguson 1984, 137). The most intimate aspects of their personal lives are known to the bureaucracy, while they themselves are not seen as entitled to claim any special knowledge about their situation of poverty, crime, illness, or despair.

Neither Ferguson nor Foucault intend to attack the personal intentions or integrity of caseworkers within bureaucratic agencies. The cause of the problems does not lie in the attitudes, intentions, or personal lack of humanity of these caseworkers, but within the structure of the bureaucracy itself. Both clients and caseworkers are trapped within the same agency and the same fragmented roles. Caseworkers are institutionally constrained regardless of what they think of their clients.

Ferguson describes caseworkers with very different attitudes: some are advocates who care deeply about client rights, some are mediators, and some are narrowly bureaucratic. But these differences in attitudes do not translate into differences in behaviour (Ferguson 1984, 139–140). Their fragmented job responsibilities and the necessity of translating everything in terms of bureaucratic forms and paperwork homogenizes their behaviour. In the end, the differences in attitudes disappear as there is no room for their expression. Work becomes paperwork, with clients ultimately experienced as nuisances in the pressure to complete the forms and get the work done.

In Foucault's terms, power produces the subjectivities. What he means by this is that the very nature of bureaucratic activities produces the attitudes and behaviour of the people—both clients and caseworkers—that in turn perpetuate these bureaucratic activities.

THE BUREAUCRATIC CONSTRUCTION OF GENDER

Bureaucratic practices produce and reproduce **gender-class**, the situation of women in relation to men in society, as part of the social construction of class society. Ferguson (1984, 3–4) suggests that feminism and bureaucracy arose together in Western society. The shift from market to corporate capitalism and the rise of large-scale bureaucracies increased the need for supervision and record keeping, and created opportunities for middle-class women to move from work in the home to paid work in bureaucracies.

Kanter (1977, 3) describes corporations as "people producers." Huge multinationals virtually run the world economy and control most of the jobs. Within such corporations, women perform clerical services while men manage. Women are in organizations but practically never run them. Management theories frequently justify this practice with stereotypes of men as rational and therefore suited for decision-making positions. Conversely, women are viewed as emotional and thus better suited to work as people handlers in personnel departments and reception areas (Kanter 1977, 25).

In her study of women in the British Columbia civil service, Cassin (1979) explores some of the reasons why affirmative action programs to increase the number of female managers are unlikely to be successful. Men in junior roles in the organizational hierarchy tend to interact far more with male managers and so learn how to present themselves and how to discuss their work in terms of its management or policy implications. When they apply for promotion, they know how to present the right image, and they are well known to those who appoint them. Women, in contrast, tend to be outside this old boys' network. This separation is compounded when they have children and have to restrict their after-hours socializing and overtime work. Women are not taught how to present themselves, and they tend to describe their work in terms of professional and technical competence rather than policy implications. They thus generally sound less like managers in promotion interviews and have less experience and a more limited informal knowledge of organizational policies and practices than do men at junior levels.

Kanter describes at length the patriarchal and patrimonial structure of bureaucratic organizations. By **patrimony**, she means the process by which career ranks and other perks are passed down from male mentors in senior management to junior ranking males with whom they have a fatherly relationship. Management teams are constituted through what Kanter (1977, Ch. 3) refers to as processes of virtual "homosexual reproduction" within the old boys' networks. The women who are the secretaries of such men are regarded and treated much as wives. Their primary role is to provide multiple personal services and total loyalty to the

Women managers are still generally excluded from the "old boys network" that sustains a patrimonial system of promotion.

boss. They may be promoted along with him, but rarely if ever without him or over him.

The real wives of these male managers are also part of the corporate image, formally outside the organization, paid nothing, and discouraged from visiting the office, but with all aspects of their lives dictated by the corporate image required for their husbands to succeed. As Kanter (1977, 107) puts it, men symbolically bring two people to their jobs, while women are seen to bring less than one, because they are expected to maintain all home commitments.

Women managers are still generally excluded from the "old boys' network" that sustains a patrimonial system of promotion. The very few women who are promoted up the organizational hierarchy function as tokens, their effectiveness undermined by their systematic exclusion from the old boys' networks that sustain men. They are talked about, passed over, and compared in multiple ways that weaken their effectiveness. Extensive literature on women in management gives advice on how women can function more like men in order to succeed. This literature blames failure on such weaknesses as emotionalism, fear of success, lack of experience of team sports, and inability to delegate responsibilities or to discipline subordinates effectively (Fenn 1980; Hennig and Jardim 1981; Larwood and Wood 1977). But, as Kanter points out, it is difficult to play on a team if other team members do not want you on it.

Contemporary studies of women in bureaucracies continue to focus largely on how to break this dual labour market through effective programs or training schemes that will facilitate the promotion of women into senior managerial positions in more than token numbers. A plethora of instruction books give advice to women on how to use and to copy male mentors to develop bureaucratic skills to get ahead. Ferguson rejects this approach as seriously misguided. What she fears most, as we will discuss further, is the co-optation of the women's movement into bureaucratic society. Bureaucracy is a means to human oppression and not to liberation. Ferguson hopes for more radical change than this.

THE DECONSTRUCTION OF BUREAUCRATIC DISCOURSE

There is a serious problem with the deeply depressing picture of bureaucratic society presented above. People appear as cogs in a machine, fractionalized elements within the iron cage. The worst of Weber's nightmare vision of bureaucracy and rationality appears to have come true. Weber himself, however, insisted that only people do things, and that their actions can only be fully understood in terms of the meanings that people themselves bring to what they do.

Concepts like *bureaucracies* are abstractions that refer to groups of people who are collectively organized to do something. Bureaucracies as such do nothing. References to bureaucracy and bureaucratic structures may be seen as a way of accounting for what people are doing rather than literal descriptions of what is actually happening.

We have already seen discrepancies in analyses of bureaucratic organizations. Structural functionalists argue that bureaucratic modes of organizing people exist because they are efficient. Political economy theory challenges this by arguing that such organizational practices arose primarily to control people and may actually be very inefficient. Other research is beginning to debunk the argument that bureaucratic modes of organizing people work by deskilling people at the bottom of the hierarchy and concentrating knowledge and hence power at the top. Studies that have looked in depth at what people actually are doing at the bottom show otherwise.

In a study of advanced clerical workers, Reimer (1987) found discrepancies between job descriptions and performance. The job description of clerical workers within the organization chart defines their work as "routine delegated duties" involving limited educational skills or responsibilities. In practice, however, much of the work done by clerical staff requires independent thought, initiative, considerable skills, and comprehensive knowledge of the operations of the organization in which they work. Often, completed tasks are automatically attributed to the manager who delegated the task. The actual skills involved in the routine aspects of clerical work habitually go unnoticed to the extent that even the people doing the work tend to describe what they do in unskilled terms such as "filing" and "sorting." The same work of collecting information done by someone in a more senior rank would be called "researching."

Cassin's (1980) study of women workers in the British Columbia civil service makes similar observations. She points out that many of the clerical staff were actively engaged in managerial work but often without recognizing it themselves. The task of opening and sorting the mail, for example, may sound unskilled, but in practice it requires considerable knowledge and experience. The secretary has to know what must receive immediate attention and what can wait. If a letter contains an inquiry, the secretary needs to know where to find the information to provide the answer and must make it available for the boss. In effect, as secretaries sort mail, they are actually structuring their bosses' jobs, making key prioritizing decisions before the boss even gets involved. If they make mistakes, like putting on the back burner what should have received prompt attention, the ramifications could be serious.

Officially, these managerial skills are nonexistent because the job description does not mention them. Yet at an informal level, these hidden skills are acknowledged. This is revealed in the sometimes bitter observations of secretaries that they taught their boss everything he knows, only to see him promoted while they remain behind to run the office and train another neophyte.

Such practices may be little different when the boss is female. They are built into the very pattern of bureaucratic relations. Subordinates are required to take the role of their superior, to internalize it, and to apply it as a guide for their behaviour. One secretary describes how she continually covers up errors made by her incompetent boss, knowing that this supervisor would blame her for things that go wrong while taking all credit for things that go right (Ferguson 1984, 108).

The Documentary Construction of Reality

How does the actual lived experience of people get so distorted that they come to believe the distortions themselves? Smith (1974) terms this the **documentary construction of reality**. It is a convenient fiction in job classification that one evaluates jobs and not people, the roles and not the role incumbents. Then anything that does not fit the organization chart—as when both worker and supervisor insist that a junior clerical worker is performing managerial work—can be put down to "person and performance," which is not evaluated because it is defined as not relevant.

What job classification workers do, then, is evaluate the organization chart itself. The reality of what people are actually doing does not enter the picture. So the fiction goes on. A few exceptions can be forced through, under various excuses, but the prevailing fiction, that official job descriptions represent what people do, remains unchallenged.

What can we learn from this? That injustices abound in the hierarchically ordered scale of prestige and differential pay? Yes, certainly. That sexism is rampant, in that it is frequently women whose acknowledged skills are appropriated by their male bosses? This is true as well, but there is more. From the perspective of interpretive theory, what is really important is that we begin to see that the notion of a structured hierarchy of skills and responsibilities itself is only a useful fiction that justifies and mystifies class and power. The organization chart provides an accounting procedure, not a description of what people actually do.

Yet it is precisely these organization charts, these official bureaucratic job descriptions, that provide the descriptive data base from which other people draw their analyses of class structure. Like coroners categorizing deaths, job classifiers in bureaucracies label what they assume people do, or ought to be doing. They thus produce the labour-force statistics on the percentage of professional, manage-

rial, paraprofessional, clerical, and semi- or unskilled workers. Statistics Canada records these convenient fictions in neat tables, which sociologists then use to produce their accounts of the occupational class structure of Canadian society. If the managerial work of people in nonmanagerial job categories actually gained recognition, along with the non-managerial work that some people in supposedly managerial job categories do, the actual class structure of Canadian society might look very different. The gender-class structure would certainly look vastly different. How different we do not know. Our knowledge of what people do comes to us so totally worked up by bureaucratic accounting procedures, guided by the fiction of organization charts, that what is actually going on is almost impossible to know. We would have to start from scratch.

The issue of unrecognized work goes far beyond the challenge to formal organization charts. As we have seen in earlier chapters, we have good reasons for asking how much teaching housewives do, or how much nursing and social work they do, or how much diagnostic and doctoring work nurses do, how many articles or even doctoral theses are put together by spouses. If we question far enough, our taken-for-granted reality—that housewives do housework and managers manage—may come to seem entirely fictional. The work of exploring behind the social construction of reality has scarcely begun.

BUREAUCRATIZATION AS SOCIAL CONSTRUCTION

Foucault views power, not as a commodity or possession in the hands of the state or an elite class, but rather as a process that pervades all levels and all aspects of social life. Networks of disciplinary power are so pervasive as to be virtually synonymous with society itself (Smart 1983, 112). For Foucault, "the increasing organization of everything is the central issue of our time" (Dreyfus and Rabinow 1982, xxii).

To understand power in this sense, it becomes necessary to study the mechanisms, techniques, and procedures at the actual point of application. Rather than viewing power as descending from the top down, Foucault conceptualizes it as ascending from the most intimate personal events of life—the everyday methods of observation, recording, calculation, regulation, and training through which individuals are disciplined and normalized in society. The elites within the ruling class may use such mechanisms for their own purposes, but the mechanisms themselves do not originate within the bourgeoisie and neither do they disappear with the overthrow of the ruling elite. The **apparatus of ruling** remains to re-emerge intact after the political revolution (Smart 1983, 82–87).

The possibility of a **disciplinary society**, a form of power based not on punishment but on intimate knowledge and regulation of individuals, emerged with the development of the human sciences such as psychology and sociology. Rational-technical knowledge and administrative procedures merged in bureaucracies as a tremendously powerful mechanism to control people.

This form of power is potentially far more effective than repression or prohibition because it rouses less resistance, costs less, and is directly tied in with the actual services of educational, military, industrial, and medical organizations through which such power is exercised. To challenge it seems like challenging reason itself. Education, for example, is concerned with developing knowledge that can be used to control people. Students of education learn how to manage classrooms so that children conform to what is expected of them. Such power is legitimated in ways that brute force could never be. It appears as productive and positive: it produces well-behaved, conformist, normalized people who are productive members of society.

Bureaucratic Discourse: Language and Power

One last question remains. How do organizations come to exercise such power over us? They even have the power to create our sense of what is real, including our sense that the organizations themselves are factually real entities. There seems to be a circular process going on. The activities of people whom we refer to as officials in organizations help to create our taken-for-granted factual knowledge about our society, but it is also precisely our taken-for-granted belief in organizations that gives them the power to do so.

Control over the mind is much more powerful than control over the body. Once the way we think is controlled, to the point that we cannot think of any alternative to the present ways of doing things, then we control ourselves. Hence, when Foucault looks for the basis of power in society, he does not look at structures or institutions but rather at knowledge, at how people learn to think. When he refers to knowledge as power, and discourse as political activity, he is referring to how thought controls people.

Education is central to this process. Ferguson suggests that education has come to control and discipline students less through marks than through the definition of knowledge itself, which is tightly tied to careers. In North American universities, a broad focus on liberal arts is losing ground to professional and technical training, such as social work, criminal justice, public and business administration, and so on. These are highly specialized training programs with little focus on the big picture and little critical content. The very activity of learning and the subject matter being absorbed moulds students into their future bureaucratic roles. Such knowledge, like the role itself, is fragmented and discontinuous. Narrowly specialized expertise with appropriate credentials provides a perfect justification for narrowly specialized and hierarchical bureaucratic roles. Ferguson (1984, 45) refers to this as the "lifeboat mentality." All that concerns students is obtaining credentials in order to find a secure organizational niche. Once they find such a niche, they will not need to be controlled from the outside. They will control themselves from the inside, their subjective consciousness meshing with the organizational definitions of their situation.

Foucault connects the two meanings of **discipline**: orderly conduct and a branch of knowledge. From this point of view, social science theories that analyze bureaucratic organizations as efficient and rational systems are political ideologies. In other words, they are part of the domination. When we believe these theories we act accordingly. The discipline of public administration, for example, assumes from the start that organizations are concrete entities, that they are efficient and rational, and that people can be regarded as role incumbents and managed to maximize efficiency. These theories reproduce the viewpoint of managers and give it scientific credibility. At the same time, they reflect how deeply this managerial mentality is rooted in how we think. Structural Marxist theory helps only a little. It draws attention to conflicting class interests in organizations, but we still end up thinking that organizations are efficient, rational systems for capitalists to make profits, and that people are role incumbents.

Interpretive theory tries to argue that organizations do not exist as entities at all. They exist only in thought as ways of accounting for what people are doing. People are not role incumbents except insofar as they learn to think about themselves in such terms. But language is enormously powerful. As soon as you read the word *organization*, you are likely to start thinking about some entity because that is what the word means to us. I might try to talk about "organizational ways of acting," but you will likely translate this straight back into the familiar words *organization* or *bureaucracy* and wonder why I cannot write plain English instead of jargonese.

It is only a very short step from learning to think in terms of organization language to being controlled by it. Smith (1979a) describes this way of talking as "using the oppressor's language." Think about the situation where a union organization's explanation for why women do not come to meetings is female apathy. In terms of the union's language, a union is a democratic organization set up for the benefit of its members. It is based on voluntary attendance. When we start with this definition, the notion of apathy seems an acceptable explanation for members not bothering to turn up. But when we stop thinking in terms of the organization's language, and start looking at what people are actually doing, the concept of apathy disappears. We see that meetings are organized at times and in places that make it very hard for women to attend. Women are responsible for caring for children, for getting dinner, and for doing housework after work. This fact actually frees men to go to union meetings. We also begin to see that when women do attend meetings, they are shouted down and ignored and their concerns are not treated as very important. What we see is something that looks much more like patriarchy than apathy, but the language of democratic union organization cannot express this.

It is not organizations as such that control us, but language, knowledge, and the discipline of social science itself. For Foucault it is a closed circle. Language creates our experience; our experience creates the language in which we come to talk about that experience; how we come to talk about it structures our experience, and so on (Ferguson 1984, xiii). The prevailing forms of power and knowledge create the subjective self-consciousness of individuals themselves, including the professionals who create the power and knowledge. There seems to be no way out of this **bureaucratic discourse**.

Bureaucracies and the Social Construction of Knowledge

Interpretive theory explores how our ways of thinking about everyday reality are put together, and particularly how the work of people within complex organizations structures what we come to think of as factual knowledge. Zimmerman's (1974) work is a classic study of what people in one organization do to produce facts, and how what they produce becomes factual knowledge for people in other organizations. Zimmerman studied workers in an unemployment insurance agency who have to determine whether certain individuals are or are not eligible for benefits. An important criterion is that the potential recipient must have actually looked for work during the previous month. But how can this be established? The applicant's word is not trustworthy, nor is the word of family members or friends. The one kind of evidence that insurance workers took as uncontrovertible fact was a piece of paper supplied by another formal organization stating that so-and-so applied for such-and-such a post. While they challenged every personal source of proof, they refused even to consider the possibility that the informant from the other organization might make up the document or statement as a personal favour. The fiction of impersonal role incumbents could not be challenged without the entire fiction of a factual reality coming apart.

Once someone in an organization has declared a person eligible for services like unemployment insurance, that becomes fact for anyone else in any other organization where such information might be relevant. The same goes for proof of birth date. It must be supplied by a piece of paper from a formal organization. People who need any kind of government service soon learn that they must carry such pieces of paper around to every appointment. As Zimmerman puts it, pieces of paper produced by people in organizations become "fact for all practical purposes" for people in other organizations. Statements made by people are suspect, but statements made by impersonal role incumbents are treated as impersonal, unbiased facts.

Tuchman carries this exploration further in her study *Making News* (1978), where she shows that anything said by officials is treated as factual for the practical purposes of newspaper reporters. Information from such sources is reproduced as straight facts while anything said by people who are not officials is presented as conjectures that may or may not be true. It is very difficult for readers to penetrate to the source of these "factual" statements because they are not presented in a way that encourages questioning.

Smith (1979a) has analyzed how different accounts of a street riot appear when given by the police rather than by the people in the street. The accounts of bystanders tend to be written in very personal and local ways: "I was standing here and saw and heard this and I thought that. . . ." The account attributed to the police, however, tends to be quite different. The distinct observations and thoughts or conclusions of different individuals in different places, who happened to be working as police, all get merged into one official police account, which is impersonal, abstract, and not tied to any one person's observations or location. Again, what people say is just personal opinion, whereas what role incumbents say is fact.

 # Feminist Discourse and the Possibility of Resistance

For Foucault, the circle of social control through language and experience is never complete. People can never be totally reduced to the sum of their roles. Hence there is always resistance. The exercise of power generates its own resistance. But this resistance is muted and partial. It tends to be expressed by powerless people who live on the periphery of the bureaucratic order. Foucault himself focused upon the criminal and the insane, the misfits for whom clinics and prisons are invented. These are the people most able to see the gap between their experience and how it is described by officials. But their protest is subdued. It lacks legitimacy; it is not sanctioned. We tend not to consider such people worth listening to.

Ferguson, however, suggests there is another voice of protest and resistance that is less easily dismissed: the voice of feminism. She argues that the different voice of women has the potential to break this closed circle of experience and discourse because women are marginal to these bureaucratic structures and yet at the same time are educated, resourceful, and increasingly visible.

Women have the potential to provide a radical alternative because the traditional standpoint of women has been outside bureaucratic organizations. Women have been more centrally concerned with reproduction and with nurturing children, which provides them with a radically different experience of human relations. Women, as caregivers, nurturers, and providers for the needs of others, are necessarily oriented toward co-operative and non-hierarchical relations. Bureaucratic organizations of hierarchically ordered, narrowly specified roles and responsibilities are anathema to women's primary experience of life as mothers, daughters, and wives. Boys, suggests Ferguson (1984, 160), learn to separate themselves from mothering to identify with the more aloof, separate, and specialized roles of fathers as breadwinners, while daughters never fully make this separation.

As women are emerging from the private life of the home to join public life as employees in ever-increasing numbers, they bring with them the potential for a radically alternative view of collective organization more in keeping with their experience. Ferguson and others (i.e., Gilligan 1982) suggest that radical feminist discourse focuses upon nurturing, concern, and connectedness with others. It incorporates a different definition of rationality in which emotion is viewed as something that people do. Emotion is not the opposite of reason. It is central to reason itself as a way of experiencing the world. An emotionless person is fundamentally irrational. Emotion is a potential avenue to "the reasonable view" (Ferguson 1984, 200). Feminism also calls for a restructuring of the relations between private and public life so that they cease to be defined as opposites and can be integrated. However, this is unlikely to happen without radically changing the character of family or workplace or both. As Parsons' work implies, family-oriented values cannot enter the workplace without changing the bureaucratic model of neutral, universalistic, and specific pattern variables appropriate for fragmented, hierarchical roles.

Ferguson points to an alternative mode of organization in such feminist projects as bookstores, health collectives, newsletters, shelters, crisis centres, and the like, which are able to minimize ties with bureaucratic organizations. There are occasional glimpses of what might be possible as professional women in law and medicine pool their practices and organize flexible working hours and client-sharing in order to integrate work and family care. Feminist projects, in principle, are committed to internally decentralized and

Professional women bring alternative, antibureaucratic concepts to the workplace.

antibureaucratic organization; they rely on personal, face-to-face relations rather than formal rules; and they encourage egalitarian rather than hierarchical relations. They see skills and information as resources to be shared rather than hoarded (Ferguson 1984, 189–190). Should such modes of organization seem fanciful or inefficient, we should remember that bureaucracies have also been shown to be very inefficient, especially in contexts that require innovation. Bureaucratic structures are oriented more to control and exploitation of a reluctant work force than to efficiency in achieving other goals.

An example of feminist principles of organization in action is the Icelandic Woman's Alliance or Kvennalistinn. The alliance took shape in the early 1980s as the conviction grew among Icelandic women that it would take a women's party to get women's issues to the centre of the political agenda. The party won enough seats in the April 1987 elections to hold the balance of power in Iceland's parliament. The party's organizational structure is explicitly in accord with feminist principles described above. There is no formal leader. Leadership functions are rotated among members. An active mentorship policy ensures that large numbers of women are trained to act as representatives for the party in meetings and campaign debates. No office holder may serve longer than six to eight years. The Alliance operates by consensus, not by majority vote. Members have to work at issues together until some compromise can be found to include all of them. This ensures that individuals cannot dominate or control issues within the party. The party actually refused to join a ruling coalition in 1987 when it became clear that it would have been forced to abandon key principles and so weaken its position as an alternative voice.

Socialist Feminism

Measured against such alternative visions, the discourse of the radical left often fails. The goal of socialist revolution, when defined in economic class terms, only promises to repeat the problems in a different form. Smith and Malnarich (1983) hint at the limitations of traditional Marxist thought when they ask, Where are the women in socialist and communist political organizations? Unions have historically regarded women as competitors rather than partners. In contemporary leftist organizations, women comprise about half the membership but are excluded from almost all leadership positions. They are not included in theoretical work. They are absent from political education and propaganda structures and from journal and newspaper editorial boards, and they are rarely involved in political analysis.

Why is this so? Smith and Malnarich reject the organization language that offers apathy as the explanation. They point to the triple workload of women militants. Like men in the movement, women often combine wagework with political work, but they also do housework: the caring and nurturing work; the production and reproduction of people; the financial, material, and emotional maintenance of the family. Smith and Malnarich suggest that militant men are mostly too busy to help out at home, and they almost never share responsibilities fully. Smith and Malnarich root the problem in socialist ideology itself, which defines family and personal life as a private, nonpolitical matter and ignores the interconnection between production and reproduction. In effect, socialists are reproducing capitalist relations in their own organization. They define the working class as those who sell their labour, thus excluding women and children and perpetuating the fragmentation within the working class itself.

The implication of this study is that traditional Marxism needs to merge with feminism before it can hope to offer an alternative that will not turn out to be more of the same with new masters. This, of course, raises the question of the type of feminism with which Marxism should be aligned.

Liberal Feminism: The Risk of Co-optation

In Ferguson's view, the central threat to feminism is the risk of co-optation. She suggests that earlier waves of feminism were defused by the expanding bureaucratic society. The first wave radically challenged the **cult of domesticity**, which rationalized the exclusion of women from the public world. Women argued that their domestic skills and experience provided ideal training for careers in politics, teaching, social services, and other spheres of life. This radicalism, however, became muted into **liberalism** and **consumerism**. The collective movement among women was abandoned in favour of defining female independence in terms of personal fulfilment (Ferguson 1984, 49–51, 179–182). Meanwhile, the demands placed on private life to satisfy all human needs steadily increased as public, bureaucratized life became more emotionally barren.

The second wave of feminism pressured for equality in terms of legal rights. Ferguson suggests that late capitalism's answer to this challenge has been more bureaucracy and the cult of rationality. Feminism raises a radical critique against bureaucracy as an inhuman form of organization, but this critique risks being reduced to a concern with eliminating barriers to women's equal representation in executive positions. This focus on individualism and equality rights for women is important in changing the predominantly male character of bureaucracies, but it promises little real change in the structures that create oppression. The problem is how to be heard in a bureaucratic society when bureaucracy itself appears as the problem.

Ferguson challenges the legal equality approach to feminism on two counts. First, she rejects the belief in individual upward mobility as "the illusion of the epoch" (Ferguson 1984, 183–192). The message of all the how-to books for women is fundamentally the same: conformity. Women are taught to see their careers in totally bureaucratic images, that is, in terms of hierarchy and fast-track mobility rather than in terms of the intrinsic meaning or value of actions. People are seen as competitors for scarce resources, and co-operation is defined in largely instrumental terms. The price of individual mobility is thus absolute capitulation to the bureaucratic system, with no prospect for change.

The second illusion for Ferguson is the focus on abstract legal rights. On the one hand, this is essential to guarantee access of women to institutions and to legal protection. But on the other hand, it can lead to acceptance of the bureaucratic game. Women are absorbed into the structures rather than fighting against them. The gender-class job ghettos may begin to crack, but the bureaucratic class hierarchy itself remains largely intact. Feminist critiques can slip into concerns for integration on equal terms with men in a system that fundamentally "hurts, twists, and damages people and human possibilities" (Ferguson 1984, xii).

There are signs of this in Canada as women's issues become translated in terms of career equality with men and bureaucratized, institutionalized child care by experts. In 1987 when the federal government announced small increases in financial support for day-care, a strong feminist voice argued that this money should be channelled into training day-care workers and setting up accredited centres. Beneath this important concern for standards and for places is the unspoken assumption that quality care can and should be measured in terms of formal credentials and government-licensed institutions. The natural expertise of mothers who have raised their own children and who earn money by caring for the children of others is discounted in favour of institutionalized credentials. The people who will teach the new credentials come from the disciplines—early childhood education, child psychology, social work—that were so feared by Foucault and Ferguson. The real need for child care might be translated into total bureaucratic control, with children required to be placed in day-care from very early ages, as they are now required to attend school, unless their parents are trained child-care specialists. There is the risk that careers for women and bureaucratized day-care for children will silence the last bastion of authentic alternative discourse in this world where "the increasing organization of everything is the central issue of our time" (Foucault in Dreyfus and Rabinow 1982, xxii).

This bureaucratic interference in the lives of people now has the potential to precede birth. In 1993, a Royal Commission in Canada examined the implications of issues involved in new reproductive technologies. Scientists now have the technology to screen "test tube baby" embryos genetically before they are implanted in their mothers' wombs. Those whose genes indicate that they will develop inherited abnormalities, such as hemophilia, are discarded. One doctor involved in the development of this technology argues that, in the future, couples who choose not to avail themselves of this screening procedure, and who give birth to disabled children, should be held criminally negligent (Pappert 1989).

Some critics suggest that resistance to the bureaucratic co-optation of feminism itself implies a return to the cult of domesticity and women being limited to the private sphere. It is clear, however, that neither of these options is acceptable. What we need is a more fundamental reintegration of private and public spheres so as to obliterate the artificial barriers between family and productive work, between women and men, between childhood and adulthood. The objective is not to bureaucratize families so as to minimize their interference with traditional careers, but to humanize other spheres of life.

Much of the work to date in women's studies has focused on making visible women's domestic work. Smith (1987b) urges us to look beyond this traditional focus to recognize that what women are doing is far, far more important than mere domestic work. In this deeply fragmented, irrational culture, what women are doing is nothing less than holding the entire system together.

Men's Liberation

There remains one more potential voice of radical resistance to our bureaucratized world: the voice of **men's liberation**. It is a voice as yet far more deeply subjugated than feminism. In a world so obviously patriarchal, with men in general so obviously occupying superior positions over women in all spheres of life, it is hard even to conceive that men might need liberation. Many men fail to see what else they could want, except perhaps to have their cake and eat it; that is, to retain their dominance within all formal institutions while having richer private lives as well. But the need for men's liberation cannot be so easily dismissed.

The evidence of wife battering and child abuse and the mounting complaints by women that men typically fail to take any responsibility for emotional relationships, plus the evidence of increasing violence on the streets, can be viewed in two not incompatible ways. Women can be seen as victims of patriarchal power, vented increasingly against those women who do not follow traditional roles. Alternatively, such trends can be seen as evidence of the overwhelmingly destructive nature of the bureaucratized world in which most men make their lives. They indicate how severely men are being hurt, twisted, blunted, and dehumanized.

Men's liberation seeks to redefine what it means to be male and to challenge the separation of men from those aspects of life that involve nurturing, caregiving, and reproduction of life itself. It strives for a radical change of structures that now reward competition, aggression, manipulation, and mastery over the material world, and the absence of emotion, at the expense of what it means to be human.

From this perspective, radical feminism and men's liberation have the same goal: the radical demolition of the bureaucratized, hierarchical, specialized, rule-bound, conformist society. Weber's formal rationality has become what he feared it would: an emotional wasteland, an iron cage. The radical critique reveals the fundamental irrationality of Western civilization. This critique demands the unity of cultural, emotional, and spiritual elements of purposive action and rejects their segregation into private and public, or feminine and masculine, spheres of life. A social order based on fragmentation does not and cannot provide a meaningful life for the majority of people.

CONCLUSION

Weber's vision of bureaucracy as an iron cage that imprisons people remains centrally relevant to contemporary industrial society, both communist and capitalist. Bureaucratic organization seems so pervasive that trying to avoid its influence would be tantamount to withdrawing from society itself. Sociological analysis is still far from grasping the full complexity of the processes involved in such organization.

Bureaucratic society has not emerged entirely as Weber conceptualized. Functionalist theory is based on Weber's ideal-type model of bureaucracy as a system of regulations that ensures the efficient co-ordination of specialized activities for given ends. This model has been discredited by evidence that the rigid formal structures associated with bureaucracy undermine co-operation and stifle initiative and innovation. Yet functionalist analysis cannot be easily dismissed. It may be the most popular perspective in sociology precisely because it comes closest to expressing how people feel about themselves in bureaucratic society. The functionalist model of society, which sees individual role incumbents as socialized to conform to expected norms of behaviour, articulates for people their everyday experience of fragmented and ordered lives that bureaucratic processes generate.

The Marxist structuralist tradition places capitalist relations of production at the centre of analysis. The most important contribution of this perspective has been to demonstrate that bureaucratic modes of organization have more to do with capitalist control over a reluctant work force than with efficiency of performance. This strength, however, may also be its limitation. The focus on capitalism has been criticized as too rigid to explore the complexity of bureaucratic power relations that do not stem from ownership of the means of production in the classic sense.

Emerging forms of analysis in the interpretive tradition push this criticism still further. Relations of power and con-trol remain central to the analysis of bureaucratic society, but they are conceptualized in a radically different way from that of Marxist theory. Power is seen as flowing not from the elite down, but from the bottom up. Power is realized in the everyday activities of people at work, in the details of how records are kept and forms are filled in, in how language is structured, and in the forms of talk through which we make sense of what people do. Interpretive theory challenges the myth of the machine, the external bureaucratic structure that engulfs people. Yet at the same time, the theory manifests the awesome power of language and bureaucratic thought, through which rationality itself becomes a trap.

The social sciences form part of the relations of power to the extent that their theories legitimate and perpetuate forms of language and thought that trap people. Theories provide accounts of what people do in terms of external structures that are rational and efficient or powerful and inevitable. To challenge such accounts seems to challenge reason. The possibility of resistance lies in new forms of discourse and radically different conceptions of power and human potential. Contemporary sociology is perhaps both part of the problem and part of the solution. It contributes to the iron cage of bureaucratic rationality. At the same time, it offers the capacity to analyze and to question and thus the possibility of resistance and change.

SUGGESTED READING

A dated but very straightforward statement of the functionalist view of bureaucracy is the article by Talcott Parsons, "Suggestions for a Sociological Approach to the Theory of Organizations" (1956). Parsons presents a short, clear model of how such organizations should work.

An old but brief and clear critique of Weber's model of bureaucracy from the perspective of structuralist Marxism is by Alvin Gouldner, "On Weber's Analysis of Bureaucratic Rules" (1952). Gouldner shows how the meticulous statement of regulations and duties that characterize the ideal-type bureaucracy applies only to the obligations that workers owe to an organization. The rules specifying the duties and responsibilities of the organization toward the worker are rarely spelled out so clearly. Unions had to fight for these in separate contracts.

Stephen Marglin's article, "What Bosses Do" (1974–75), argues that the rise of factories, where workers were brought together under the supervision of a boss, long preceded the invention of heavy machinery that made collective factory work necessary. He argues that the purpose of factories was to control workers, not to make efficient use of new technology.

The book by Kathy Ferguson, *The Feminist Case Against Bureaucracy* (1984), is an excellent feminist study of Foucault's view of bureaucratic society. This book is very heavy reading and not easy to understand. It is perhaps best used as a reference work for additional information on certain sections of her analysis that are referred to in this chapter.

A more readable and entertaining look at life within a bureaucracy is Rosabeth Moss Kanter's *Men and Women of the Corporation* (1977). Kanter delights in showing up the status games that go on in relations between male bosses and their female secretaries and among male managers vying for prestigious office space. Kanter also provides a very perceptive view of how bureaucracy carries over into the private family lives of employees.

For a view of how bureaucracies help to create what passes as knowledge, see Gail Tuchman, *Making News: A Study of the Social Construction of Reality* (1978). Tuchman describes how reporters rely very heavily upon official spokespersons from bureaucracies to provide much of what they report as factual information.

QUESTIONS

1. How does Blau's study of a state employment agency suggest that precise measures of job performance can inhibit efficiency?

2. What practices are involved in *goal displacement* in organizations?

3. How does the Marxist historian, Marglin, challenge the notion that factories were organized to utilize the technology of steam engines?

4. What does the Marxist Gouldner see as the true function of bureaucratic rules and regulations within capitalist organizations?

5. Why does Michels claim that election to formal office is insufficient to undermine *the iron law of oligarchy* in political parties?

6. What is Foucault referring to with the notion of *technical civilization*?

7. How is bureaucracy implicated in the social construction of gender differences?

8. How are organization charts implicated in analysis of the class structure of a society?

9. What are the two meanings that Foucault associates with the term *discipline* and how does he link them in his study of power relations?

10. In Ferguson's view, how might women be in a privileged position to see beyond the apparent rationality of bureaucratic organization?

KEY TERMS

apparatus of ruling

bureaucratic discourse

bureaucratic language

bureaucratic society

consumerism

cult of domesticity

cult of rationality

disciplinary society

discipline

discourse

documentary construction of reality

emotional labour

gender-class

goal displacement

intelligence failures

iron law of oligarchy

language of technics

liberalism

managerial mentality

men's liberation

normalized

oligarchy

patrimony

technical civilization

therapeutic intervention

REFERENCES

Berger, R.J. 1993. "The 'Banality of Evil' Reframed: The Social Construction of the 'Final Solution' to the 'Jewish Problem.'" *The Sociological Quarterly* 34 (4): 597–618.

Blau, P.M. 1955. *The Dynamics of Bureaucracy*. Chicago: University of Chicago Press.

Burns, T., and G.N. Stalker. 1961. *The Management of Innovation*. London: Tavistock.

Cassin, A.M. 1979. *Advancement Opportunities in the British Columbia Public Service*. British Columbia Economic Analysis and Research Bureau. Ministry of Industry and Small Business Development.

Cassin, A.M. 1980. "The Routine Production of Inequality: Implications for Affirmative Action." Paper, Ontario Institute for Studies in Education.

Dalton, M. 1959. *Men Who Manage*. New York: Wiley.

Dreyfus, H.L., and P. Rabinow. 1982. *Michel Foucault: Beyond Structuralism and the Hermeneutics*. Chicago: University of Chicago Press.

Fenn, M. 1980. *In the Spotlight: Women Executives in a Changing Environment*. Englewood Cliffs, NJ: Prentice-Hall.

Ferguson, K.E. 1984. *The Feminist Case Against Bureaucracy*. Philadelphia: Temple University Press.

Foucault, M. 1977. *Discipline and Punishment: The Birth of the Prison*. London: Allen Lane.

Foucault, M. 1980. *Power/Knowledge: Selected Interviews and Other Writings 1972–1977*. Ed. C. Gordon. New York: Pantheon.

Fukuyama, F. 1989. "The End of History?" *The National Interest* (Summer).

Gilligan, C. 1982. *In a Different Voice*. Cambridge, MA: Harvard University Press.

Gouldner, A.W. 1952. "On Weber's Analysis of Bureaucratic Rules." In *Reader in Bureaucracy*. Ed. R.K. Merton, A.P. Gray, B. Hockey, and H.C. Selvin. New York: Free Press, 48–51.

Gouldner, A.W. 1954. *Patterns of Industrial Bureaucracy*. New York: Free Press.

Gouldner, A.W. 1965. *Wildcat Strikes*. New York: Free Press.

Hennig, M., and A. Jardim. 1981. *The Managerial Woman*. New York: Anchor Books.

Hochschild, A. 1983. *The Managed Heart*. Berkeley, CA: University of California Press.

Kanter, R.M. 1977. *Men and Women of the Corporation*. New York: Basic Books.

Larwood, L., and M.M. Wood. 1977. *Women in Management*. Lexington, MA: Lexington Books.

Marglin, S.A. 1974–75. "What Bosses Do." *Review of Radical Political Economy* 6: 60–112; 7: 20–37.

Merton, R.K. 1957. "Bureaucratic Structure and Personality." In *Social Theory and Social Structure*. Ed. R.K. Merton. Glencoe, IL: Free Press, 249–260.

Michels, R. [1911] 1949. *Political Parties*. Glencoe, IL: Free Press.

Mosca, G. [1939] 1960. *The Ruling Class*. New York: McGraw-Hill.

Pappert, A. 1989. "Social Debate Rages Over Unlimited Scope of Test Tube Babies." Part 1 of series The Reproductive Revolution. *Toronto Star*, 7–12 Oct.

Parsons, T. 1956. "Suggestions for a Sociological Approach to the Theory of Organizations." *Administrative Science Quarterly* (June): 63–69.

Reimer, M.A. 1987. "The Social Organization of the Labour Process: A Case Study of the Documentary Management of Clerical Labour in the Public Service." Ph.d. thesis, Ontario Institute for Studies in Education.

Smart, B. 1983. *Foucault: Marxism and Critique*. London: Routledge & Kegan Paul.

Smith, D.E. 1974. "The Social Construction of Documentary Reality." *Sociological Inquiry* 44 (4): 257–268.

Smith, D.E. 1979. "Using the Oppressor's Language." *Resources for Feminist Research*. Special publication no. 5 (Spring).

Smith, D.E. 1987. "Feminist Reflections on Political Economy." Paper presented at the Learned Societies. Hamilton, ON.

Smith, D.E., and G. Malnarich. 1983. "Where Are the Women? A Critique of Socialist and Communist Political Organization." Paper presented at the Conference on Marxism: The Next Two Decades. University of Manitoba.

Stone, K. 1974. "The Origins of Job Structures in the Steel Industry." *Review of Radical Political Economics* 6 (2) (Summer): 113–173.

Tuchman, G. 1978. *Making News: A Study in the Social Construction of Reality*. New York: Free Press.

Zimmerman, D.H. 1974. "Fact as a Practical Accomplishment." In *Ethnomethodology: Selected Readings*. Ed. R. Turner. Harmondsworth, Eng.: Penguin.

FUNCTIONALIST THEORY: MEDIA IN THE SOCIAL SYSTEM

The functionalist perspective identifies mass communication as a critically important set of **institutions** for maintaining societal integration. Mass media—newspapers, magazines, radio, television, movies, and more recently the Internet—express and transmit culture. **Culture**, in functionalist theory, comprises the collectively shared **system** of beliefs, **values**, and rituals that form the glue that holds **social systems** together. Technologically, mass communication provides the essential means to link people from the local level of villages and neighbourhoods to larger towns and cities, the nation state, and increasingly to the international forum. Media provide meeting grounds, performing at a national level the **functions** met locally by village public squares and town hall meetings. Individual Canadians participate in a national culture through sharing common experiences and civic rituals as they tune in simultaneously with millions of others to watch evening news broadcasts, sports events, and other entertainment. These virtual experiences in turn form shared topics for conversation between friends, neighbours, and colleagues, and fellow bloggers on websites of mutual interest. In addition, media serve the economy by bringing buyers and sellers together through advertising.

Collectively, the media make possible the existence of modern democratic nation states such as Canada. They are the principal means by which citizens can learn about their own **society** and thus gain some sense of themselves as members of this larger whole. Mass media provide the basic information, and the discussion and debate required for effective citizen-participation in government. Most Canadian citizens will never attend debates in the House of Commons or meet the prime minister. We recognize political leaders and learn about issues and policies primarily through mass-mediated "news" that reaches us through newspapers, radio, and television broadcasts, and online news sites. Ideally, media also function as watchdogs, seeking out the insider knowledge needed to oversee and critique government activities (Baker and Dessart 1998, 134–135; Taras 1999, 3). Contemporary radio and television often mimic town hall meetings in regular phone-in programs on current affairs. Newspapers also have pages of letters to the editor. Most such media also have online editions that invite visitors to comment on articles.

There is a close systemic interrelationship between the institutions of mass media and the institutions of government (Nesbitt-Larking 2001, 138–141). The Canadian government is first and foremost a *proprietor* of Canadian media, owning the Canadian Broadcasting Corporation, the National Film Board, and the National Arts Centre. The government controls both appointment of personnel and budgets. Secondly the government is a *regulator*, licensing private broadcasters and determining required levels of Canadian content. The state is further a *catalyst* or facilitator of media businesses, offering financial incentives and cheap postal rates for Canadian papers and magazines, and purchasing advertising space. The state as **actor** supplies material for news; and as *masseur* manages news releases, times press statements, and offers interpretations or "spins" on local, national, and international news events. As *ideologue* and as *conspirator* the state influences in many ways the **dominant values** and perspectives that frame how mass media represent Canadian issues to audiences.

The routine daily work of journalists strengthens institutional connections between media and government. Much news coverage is planned well in advance by following the agendas of political leaders, committees, event planners, and the like. Police records are checked each morning for data on the previous night's crime news. Official spokespersons, or "authorized knowers," from established bureaucratic institutions provide trusted sources of facts that make up the daily news. Journalists also rely heavily on politicians from leading parties for coverage of official business of government and as sources of expert opinion and commentary. Through these institutional linkages, journalists associated with print, radio, and television help to familiarize citizens with the routine work of governance, and to legitimize, and sometimes challenge, current policies and perspectives.

Media in Canada or "Canadian" Media?

Canada's unique geography and relatively short history as a nation arguably gives mass media a special importance in national integration. Canada has a relatively small population dispersed over an immense geographic area spanning five time zones, and with three-quarters of its population living within 150 kilometres of the 9000-kilometre-long American border. Historically, waterways and the building of the Canadian Pacific Railway (Innis 1930), and later the Trans-Canada Highway, provided critical east–west communication links, later followed by air travel. Each shift in technology, McLuhan argues, accelerated the human function of movement, making possible new kinds of cities and new patterns of human association and action (1964, 7).

New technologies of radio and satellite television transformed our sense of hearing and vision, altering the scale and scope of human interaction and making possible instantaneous global communication. Different forms of communication arguably promote different response patterns (Postman 1993, 16). The medium of print promotes logic, sequence, history, exposition, objectivity, detachment, and discipline, favouring individual autonomy and competition. Television emphasizes imagery, narrative, presentness, simultaneity, intimacy, immediate gratification, and quick emotional response. Television is also a one-way system of communication, controlled from the centre, making it a useful tool for totalitarian regimes (Negroponte 1995, 32–33). The Internet, in contrast, is an open system, linking individuals directly with each other through global networks, potentially transforming our sense of community, relationships, and the possibilities for citizen-led democracy.

The establishment of specifically Canadian systems of mass communication capable of integrating Canada as a nation state has always been difficult, due to cultural diversity within Canada, and close proximity to, and integration with, American systems of communication. Culturally, Canada has always been divided into two settler colonies of French and English, along with multiple First Nations societies, and an increasingly heterogenous mix of immigrant populations. The further challenge is that mass media carry American culture into Canada (Taras 1999, 1). Radio and television held special promise as technologies that could integrate Canada's scattered population, but they simultaneously increased Canadian exposure to American culture.

The first public radio licence was issued in Canada in 1919, but within a decade broadcasters were complaining that American frequencies were interfering with their transmissions and Canadians were choosing to tune in to American stations (Peers 1988, 283). These concerns prompted sweeping government regulations that treated radio as a national public service rather than a profit-making industry. The 1932 act that created the Canadian Radio Broadcasting Commission (CRBC) empowered the federal government to regulate broadcasting, to grant licences, to lease or construct stations, and to originate and transmit programs. The CRBC was the forerunner of the Canadian Broadcasting Corporation (CBC) established in 1936. A mixed system of public and private ownership was developed in which the government carried the infrastructure costs of building transmission stations, especially those broadcasting to small and remote populations, while private affiliates agreed to carry public programming and to fill in the hours on the public system. The government also established the National Film Board in 1939, providing subsidies to private producers based in Canada.

The federal government gave the CBC a special mandate to try to integrate French- and English-speaking Canadians into one nation. It first experimented with a mix of programs in two languages, and then formed the separate French-language network, La Société Radio Canada (SRC), in 1941. French Canada was insulated from American broadcasting by language differences but simultaneously insulated from English Canada, raising fear that the two systems might further insulate "the two solitudes." Under the Trudeau government in 1968 a new act specified that there was to be a single system "effectively owned or controlled by Canadians so as to safeguard, enrich, and strengthen the cultural, political, social, and economic fabric of Canada (Nesbitt-Larking 2001, 71). As a condition of receiving a licence to broadcast on Canadian airwaves, private broadcasters were required to provide 55 percent Canadian content, with 40 percent of this scheduled during the prime-time 6 pm to midnight time slot (Vipond 2000, 157).

Private broadcasters always chafed under the restrictions, arguing both that the publicly funded CBC was unfair competition and that the Canadian content requirements threatened profits. The logistics of regulating Canadian content also proved difficult. The vision may have been hours of Canadian drama, music, and public affairs, but the practice was more likely to be hours of cheap game and quiz shows. Private broadcasters minimized the expense of producing or buying Canadian when they could fill their broadcasting hours with much cheaper American reruns. National Film Board documentaries were mostly aired on

CBC stations. Films made in Canada, even with government subsidies, have commonly been tailored to appeal to more lucrative American markets, and are likely to contain minimal specifically Canadian content.

The rationale for licensing channels when bandwidths were limited was undermined in the 1990s as digital technology and co-axial cable ushered in the 500-channel universe. Regulators responded by requiring that all packages for pay TV must include two Canadian channels for each American channel. The new problem, however, with the plethora of niche channels specializing in topics like cooking, travel, hobbies, and sports, is that even Canadian channels carry minimal Canadian content. Critics lament that the reality is hyper-**fragmentation** rather than the nostalgic image of millions of citizens tuning in to the same Canadian cultural experiences (Taras 1999, Ch. 4).

Holding Canada Together: The Challenge of Two Solitudes

The Canadian government continues to control CBC radio and television networks and their French-language equivalent, the SRC. Their mandates, under the Broadcasting Act of 1991, are "to contribute to shared national consciousness and identity" and give expression to regional and linguistic differences, reflect the multicultural and multiracial makeup of Canada, and offer a range of programming that "informs, enlightens, and entertains" (Taras 1999, 127). As part of this mandate, the CBC and SRC networks are expected to give major coverage to Canadian public events and rituals like the opening of parliament, the federal budget, elections, Canada Day celebrations, Remembrance Day ceremonies from the cenotaph in Ottawa, and the like. Taras estimates that some 70 percent of CBC television comprises news and current affairs. Coverage of other rituals such as *Hockey Night in Canada*, national and international sporting events with Canadian athletes, and Canadian music, film, and other artistic events fill out the programming. During the constitutional crises of the 1990s both French and English networks covered hours of debate around the Meech Lake Accord of 1990, the Charlottetown Accord of 1992, and the Quebec Referendum on sovereignty in 1995. However, coverage for the two different publics differed so much that each accused the other of bias. The further problem is that long-term commitment to covering political debates risks losing audiences. Given a choice between watching parliamentary debates and question periods or tuning into multiple private stations showing American reruns, comedies, sports, game shows, and crime thrillers, potential audiences tend to prefer the private options. Vipond estimates that by 2000 less than 10 percent of English-speaking audiences were watching CBC television and 20 percent of French-speaking audiences were watching SRC in Quebec.

As ratings fall, the private broadcasters strengthen their argument that Canadian consumers should not have to contribute tax funds to a public service that most rarely watch, and further, that the CBC's quest for advertising dollars constitutes unfair competition since its services are already subsidized. Severe budget cuts to the CBC and the National Film Board during the 1990s resulted in less regional programming and still further drops in ratings. In the multi-channel universe it seems that the CBC's mandate to promote Canadian cultural nationalism is falling mostly on the ears and eyes of a relatively small section of mostly better-educated middle-class audiences. Private, commercial radio and television carry most of the mass media transmissions. Their priorities are profits rather than national integration.

Canadian Newspapers   The history of newspapers in Canada reflects Canada's colonial past. Early colonists looked to Europe for news. The French government actually banned printing presses in Quebec, fearing loss of control over newspapers (Vipond 2000, 7). Political parties in English Canada started to issue their own highly partisan weekly papers as they began to contest the terms of British rule. As immigration, urbanization, and public schooling created a large literate population, independent business proprietors began to publish papers. By 1857 there were 291 papers in circulation in Canada, with almost every town having at least one (Nesbitt-Larking 2001, 40). The content was about two-thirds advertising, and one-third chatty human-interest stories, serialized novels, science columns, sports, women's pages, and comics (Vipond 2000, 14–15).

Publishing was highly politicized in these early days, with "criticizing a member of the ruling **class**," justified or not, being a crime subject to imprisonment (Vipond 2000). Nesbitt recounts the story of one proprietor, Joseph Howe, charged in Nova Scotia in 1835 with "wickedly, maliciously and seditiously contriving, devising and intending to stir up and excite discontent and dissatisfaction among her majesty's subjects" for accusing magistrates and police of stealing money from the people. This was considered libellous, even though the accusations were proven. Jurors challenged the law, however, by refusing to convict Howe despite instruction from the judge.

Newspapers expanded in size and circulation as the century progressed, changing from small four-page weeklies to multi-page dailies with mass circulation among urban literate populations. Ownership became concentrated in the hands of smaller numbers of wealthier business tycoons. In 1913 there were 138 Canadian daily papers, each with its own publisher, but by 1970 there were 116 papers with only 40 publishers. Mergers continued apace.

Fears that the concentration of newspaper ownership in Canada was threatening democracy were being voiced as far back as the mid-1970s. Small numbers of media tycoons were in a position to act as **gatekeepers** of information to the masses, able to filter what they considered newsworthy, and to slant coverage of policy issues. Structurally they tend to be politically conservative, supporting the status quo, pitched to appeal to the average reader, and careful not to displease large business advertisers. Profit-driven media corporations have incentive to cut costs by cutting staff and space devoted to news, and especially by cutting the number of expensive journalists. Owners of multiple papers can spread the same lead stories across different papers, and use syndicates to fill inside pages. It is much cheaper for corporate media to buy stories from global agencies like Associated Press, Reuters, and Agence France-Presse than to fund foreign bureaus to cover the stories themselves.

Fears of excessive concentration of newspaper ownership came to a head in 1980 when the Thompson and Hollinger chains colluded to close rival newspapers in Ottawa and Winnipeg. Also, by this time the Irving family owned all five English-language papers in New Brunswick. The 1981 Kent Commission on newspaper ownership recommended the radical breakup of newspaper holdings, with no owner permitted to hold more than 5 percent of Canada's total newspaper circulation, or more than five papers, or more than one within a radius of 500 kilometres (Vivian and Maurin 2009, 37). However, no action was ever taken on these recommendations. The Thompson and Hollinger chains merged under the ownership of Conrad Black, and then Black's holdings in turn were bought out by CanWest Global in 2000. Federal laws protecting Canadian cultural industries from the North American Free Trade deal have so far prevented Canadian newspapers from being swallowed up by American media giants, but they did not prevent concentration within Canada.

By 2001 there were 104 daily papers in circulation in Canada, with 90 percent of them owned by five newspaper tycoons. The largest chain, CanWest Global Corp, owned by Israel Asper, controlled 50, or almost half of all daily papers. Other big Canadian media corporations include CTVGlobemedia, Quebecor, Corus Entertainment, and Rogers (Vivian and Maurin 2009, 14). Each of them comprised multimedia conglomerates owning newspapers, specialty television channels, and music and video stores. Ownership patterns shift constantly as corporations seek new acquisitions in some areas and sell off less profitable subsidiaries.

A survey of 3012 Canadians in 2004 suggested that television was edging out newspapers as the preferred source of news (Vivian and Maurin 2009, 158), with 67 percent of respondents favouring television, 42 percent papers, and 33 percent the Internet. Preferences overlap, with many people accessing more than one source. Newspapers still seemed to dwarf other news sources for overall content and coverage of news, with about 31 million daily papers sold in Canada each week in 2007 (Vivian and Maurin 2009, 38). Respondents saw newspapers as carrying more news in more depth than television.

Optimism about the long-term future of newspapers, however, was badly shaken by 2009 as a recession hit advertising revenues hard at the same time as subscriptions fell. Newspapers everywhere are experiencing fierce competition from online news sites that are essentially free for people who already have access to high-speed Internet, and that can bypass corporate news media gatekeepers. The once dominant CanWest Global, weighed down by debt from its purchase of the movie distributor Alliance Atlantis in 2008, had to seek bankruptcy protection in 2009.

The Internet as Mass Communication Medium

The Internet as a medium for mass communication has expanded exponentially over the past decade. As recently as the mid-1990s, most home computers would take five minutes to download one colour picture and were incapable of handling videos. By 2009 most home computers could load and play colour videos with the same speed and quality as digital television. High-speed Internet and web technology allows millions of individual computer users to communicate with each other by means of emails, listservs, news groups, bulletin boards, Internet relay chat rooms, and instant messaging, and also to talk face-to-face using web cameras. The complexity of the web overcomes the limitations of monologue, detachment, and rigid sequencing that McLuhan identified with print medium. Electronic writing can link laterally with other sites and with earlier comments, and invites interactive conversation. People are using Internet technology to create entirely new online communities focused around specialized interests and not bounded by geography or nationality. In multiuser virtual environments like Lambdamoo and Second Life, participants use computer code to create virtual selves, or avatars, that can visually interact with other avatars in complex online environments (Thurlow et al. 2004). Workers and professionals can attend seminars, and students can attend lectures in virtual classrooms and interact with instructors and with each other through their avatars.

These virtual environments have been heralded as creating the first truly free society, allowing people to invent self-regulating communities in which individuals can freely choose whether to participate (Lessig 2006, 2). Participants are free to explore and play with diverse identities and virtual selves freed from physical characteristics and disabilities. There can be no physical violence. Interaction is based entirely on typewritten speech that is constitutionally protected from government interference.

Research that explores the cultures of Internet communications and virtual reality environments challenge some of these claims, revealing that cyberspace is not dissociated from the regular social world. Networking sites like Facebook, MySpace, and Twitter are sites in which reputations are gained and lost, romantic attachments generated and broken, individuals bullied and shamed or flamed (Solove 2007). Unlike the local gossip in the village square or around the office water cooler, shaming on the Internet can rapidly become global in scope and have an unrelenting permanence in cyberspace. Personal information broadcast into cyberspace is widely exploited for commerce, fraud, and crime. Avatars existing only in virtual environments can disguise the personal characteristics of **race**, age, sex, orientation, and the like of their creators. But that does not protect their creators from the hurt of disparaging racist, ageist, sexist, and homophobic communications. Avatars can be vandalized and attacked, leaving their creators feeling vulnerable and hurt. The relative anonymity of virtual sites allows such communications to become more virulent. Special-interest Internet groups also tend to become more extreme in their views and reactions when they are sheltered from criticism.

Democracy and News on the Web The Internet has developed as the new frontier for disseminating news, becoming the medium of choice among youth already familiar with digital social networks and discussion groups. As a medium, the web is profoundly altering the nature of news and news gathering. It provides an accessible public means for individuals to create, post, search for, and comment on news in ways that challenge the gatekeeping power of establishment media. Leading broadcasters in television, radio, and newspaper have themselves been pressured into developing online versions.

Online sites are unmatched in their speed and flexibility in covering breaking news and local stories, with individuals capable of posting updates in a matter of minutes, with no limits on size or content, and with the newest materials appearing at the top of a piece of reporting. Preference for online news over regular sources decisively shifted in the USA, Allen argues (2006, 13), when masses of people were frantically trying to get news about the Oklahoma City bombing in April 1995, and when passenger jets crashed into the World Trade Center on September 11, 2001. Mainstream media were simply not fast enough or comprehensive enough to get all the information out. When long-distance phone lines into Oklahoma became

jammed with callers, online news groups opened up their sites for people to exchange messages. During the 9/11 crisis tens of millions of people logged onto all the major online news sites searching for news, with CNN.com alone averaging 9 million hits per hour (Allen 2006, 53).

Citizen-journalism came of age in the USA during these crises. Bystanders with access to cell-phone cameras were posting pictures to the web within minutes of the terrorist attacks, and giving eyewitness accounts. Others created links to these multiple pictures and comments, forming webs of information that were being constantly updated. As CNN journalists were trying to interview authority figures about what was happening, people caught up in the events and bystanders in the street were creating and posting their own accounts. They conveyed a sense of immediacy and authenticity that accounts by mainstream journalists and announcers in television studios could not replicate. This sense of embeddedness in the scene was especially stunning in coverage of the London transit bombing on July 7, 2005. Many trains were trapped in the underground system with journalists unable to get to them. Passengers on the trains were able to upload cell-phone videos directly onto YouTube or online news sites, along with first-hand accounts (Allen 2006, 143–167). Citizen-journalists posted similar insider accounts of Hurricane Katrina in August 2005. Amateurs on the scenes of such events are now able to publish their "bottom-up" personal experiences and comments directly on the web without needing to wait for some outside journalist to come and interview them. Allen contrasts the immediacy of citizen-journalists talking with victims of the 2004 tsunami in Indonesia with the artificiality of typical "helicopter journalism" provided by foreign correspondents from news agencies flying in from outside to cover the scene with help from taxi drivers (Allen 2006, 5).

Weblogs, or blogs, have become an integral part of citizen-led journalism. Blogs are a form of online diary in which people post descriptions of events, along with opinions and commentary. By mid-2000, people were posting new blogs at the rate of 75 000 a day, or almost one per second (Allen 2006, 172). Given the enormous amount of information now posted online, bloggers who are interested in news perform a valuable service by surfing the web for interesting news items and providing links to them, along with their own takes on the significance of events. Others can log into their sites to check out the news. Time-strapped journalists often check blog sites themselves to catch up on the latest issues.

News-bloggers tend to be driven by passion for their topic rather than profit, and the content of their blogs are often politicized and partisan, reminiscent of early partisan newspapers. At their best, they fill the political role of citizen-watchdogs, sniffing out rumours and scandals without the editorial constraints of corporate media. Bloggers can post anonymous tips and leave it to fellow bloggers to check out their validity—a practice that would not be tolerated from professional journalists. American blogger Matt Drudge is credited with first breaking the stories of improper sexual conduct by former US president Bill Clinton (Allen 2006, 38–43). The Drudge Report catapulted to fame, with White House staff themselves reportedly logging into his site 2 600 times in the first 12 hours after Drudge posted the allegations, and the site received up to 300 000 general hits a day as the story unfolded. Drudge's fiercely anti–Democratic Party site became so popular that AOL started paying him $3000 a month in royalties.

A host of bloggers began to regularly link their sites in a network of commentary dedicated to challenging what they perceived to be the liberal bias of mainstream media (Allen 2006, 87). During the 2004 elections, bloggers fiercely defended incumbent US president George W. Bush from the charge first printed in the *Boston Globe* that Bush had shirked his National Guard duties. Bloggers whipped up a host of experts to discredit copies of Bush's service memo as faked, pushing veteran CBS reporter Dan Rather to resign when he could not defend his criticism of Bush against the onslaught (Allen 2006, 93). Bloggers also picked up on an obscure posting by an ABC journalist who noted racist remarks by Congress House Leader Trent Lott that ABC News itself refused to cover. Bloggers shamed Lott by creating links to his history of similarly racist remarks, eventually forcing him to resign his position.

The more left-wing dissident news site Indymedia.org grew out of the confrontation between police and protestors at the world trade meetings in Seattle in 1999 (Allen 2006, 123–124). Activists used the web to organize protests and to counter the mainstream media's exclusive focus on fights. Indymedia's rallying cry became "Don't hate the media. Be the media." Operating on a shoestring budget with borrowed equipment, Indymedia reporters were able to interview bystanders and highlight instances of police brutality that mainstream media had been ignoring. It became such a clearinghouse for alternative news that even professional journalists came to draw upon it. By the time the US invaded Iraq in 2003, Internet news sites, both for and against the war, were highly organized, able to handle live video and audio reports and multimedia shows (Allen 2006, Ch. 6), and even included a freelance journalist who persuaded readers of his blog to finance his extended stay in Iraq to cover the war on the ground.

By 2006 co-operative independent media sites had grown up in 145 different city centres in 45 countries across six continents (Allen 2006, 125). They operate mostly as open sites without editorial control in which individuals can post their own accounts of events. The sites are sup-

ported by small financial contributions from users. One such site, OhMyNews in South Korea, promotes the concept of every citizen as a reporter, or netizen, offering small cash payments for stories that cover priority issues. With an average of over 200 stories sent in and two million hits a day, Korean politicians cannot afford to ignore the site.

Independent low-cost news sites continue to emerge in Canada and the US, often developed by one or two lead writers and inspired by the desire to challenge mainstream conformity. The three-year-old BC news-site thetyee.ca won two prestigious Canadian awards for excellence in journalism in 2009. The site was founded in 2003 by a veteran journalist from the *Vancouver Sun* chafing against the editorial conservatism and conformity (Fiona Morrow, *Globe and Mail*, 22 August 2009).

Governing the Internet: Order and Law in Cyberspace

Like the vision of a virtual world free from corporate or government control, the vision of a universe of free citizen-journalists communicating with the masses needs qualification. The promises of unfettered communication and democracy have been tempered from two directions—the need that web-users themselves feel for governments to impose order onto the virtual reality, and the interests of different governments in clamping down on dissidence.

The need for order in cyberspace reflects the classic Hobbesian struggle between freedom and protection. Net users became willing to give up some of their freedom in return for a social contract to control abusers (Lessig 2006, 2–3). Participants in the virtual reality space of Second Life welcomed the move by the site's organizers to eliminate a deviant avatar coded to sexually abuse other avatars. Participants who have spent months creating complex avatars and environments, or who increasingly spend big money to hire computer programmers to write code for them, want protection from computer hackers intent on stealing or vandalizing their programs.

In the real world of business and commerce the stakes are higher. EBay, an online auction initially operated on the basis of trust and reputation and an informal system to settle disputes, soon became overwhelmed by fraud and hackers (Goldsmith and Wu 2006, Ch. 8). Threatened with a class-action suit in 2000 by defrauded buyers, eBay began to hire its own law enforcement officers. By 2004 its staff of 800 full-time security officers was still not sufficient to handle the fraud. For eBay to continue, it required government law enforcers. Businesses operating in the borderless Internet found themselves vulnerable to borderless crime. A skilled hacker living in Russia found ways to break into US business websites and blackmail them for bribes under threat of having their files ruined. It took a complex FBI sting operation to lure the man out of Russia so that American authorities could get a hold of him (Goldsmith and Wu 2006, 163–164). Such experiences are paving the way for international agreements to manage cybercrime.

The web itself may be borderless, but governments have developed ways to control its operations within national borders. They have increasingly moved to exert their control over activities on the Internet, not through managing the web as such, but through targeting intermediaries, including Internet service providers (ISPs), web search engines like Yahoo and Google, and companies issuing the credit cards used to pay for illegal commerce and international gambling. In one early example, the government of France took action against the Internet search engine Yahoo to force it to block a website selling Nazi memorabilia, a practice illegal in France (Goldsmith and Wu 2006, 1–9). Yahoo at first claimed that such sales were not illegal at their point of origin in the US and that it could not block French buyers from finding the memorabilia on the Internet. Yahoo backed down when it had to admit that it could and did control the distribution of advertising for French-only audiences, and the French government threatened to seize Yahoo assets, including its Internet servers in France.

Limits to Free Speech

The freedom that the Internet offers users to voice opinions and be heard simultaneously carries multiple threats of misuse. At an individual level these threats include vulnerability to shaming, invasion of privacy, and libel, and at a government level, the threat of dissident organization. Precedent-setting court decisions in Canada in 2009 have now determined that Google is legally required to disclose the identity of bloggers charged with posting insulting or defamatory messages against others. These rulings follow a history of similar ones in the US. While it is easy to blog anonymously, it is also easy for ISPs to trace blogs to individual computers and identities, and courts can require disclosure. Law, however, remains an expensive and blunt instrument for individuals to protect themselves with against such attacks.

Open news sites are also vulnerable to vandalism and fraud. Wikimedia sets high standards for citing sources and has volunteers checking for overt bias in postings. But Wikimedia felt forced to shut down its experimental site inviting readers to join the debate on the war in Iraq because it was inundated with disparaging and unsubstantiated claims (Goldsmith and Wu 2006, 139). In August 2009, Wikipedia announced new editorial controls over English-language articles about living people, requiring that any changes be approved by volunteer editors before they are made visible (New York Times News Service, 25 August 2009). Independent news-site bloggers are not subject to the

professional standards of verification, and this has resulted in a risky mixture of facts and scoops along with fabrications and lies. The Drudge Report that carried the scoop about Clinton's improprieties later carried a fabricated story insinuating that Democratic presidential hopeful John Kerry had had an extramarital affair with a woman whom he later pressured to flee the country (Stuart 2006, 41). Victims have turned to the law to fight back. Drudge was served with a $3-million lawsuit for falsely citing a Clinton aide as guilty of spousal abuse, and the lawsuit also named AOL as a party to the suit because AOL carried the blog and was paying royalties to Drudge at the time (Stuart 2006, 41).

Managing Dissidents

The hope that the Internet would spread information, free speech, and thus democracy across the world has faded. Governments use technological controls to censor and block information carried on the web, to identify and punish individuals and sites producing subversive postings, and to flood chat groups and websites with pro-government information and opinions. Yahoo, the browser that once promoted free speech to sell Nazi memorabilia, now provides the government of China with technology to block web users in China from accessing sites that carry information the government wants blocked. The technology works at the level of servers, diverting any postings identified as carrying potentially subversive content that contains keywords like "multi-party democracy," "Taiwan," or "Falun Gong" (Goldsmith and Wu 2006, 10; Zittrain 2008, 105). A group from the organization Journalists Without Borders tried to penetrate this shield, without success. However, a Chinese journalist who sent an email to a pro-democracy website in the US was promptly identified and sentenced to 10 years in prison. The same control technology works in both directions, allowing the government to continually monitor chat-room conversations. The government also pays people to influence opinions in chat rooms. Small numbers of individuals can circumvent the filters by writing specialized computer codes and by inventing secret languages, but they cannot communicate with the general population (Zittrain 2008, 103).

Western powers have at times used similar technological controls to monitor and influence information on the web. During the 2009 debates surrounding universal health coverage in the USA, corporate interests favouring private insurance swamped emails and chat rooms with messages promoting fear and rejection of the proposals. After the 9/11 terrorist attacks, US federal legislation officially authorized electronic eavesdropping as an anti-terrorist tool. The increased use of appliances that are tethered to a central source for routine updates simplifies centralized surveillance and control. The FBI is able to eavesdrop on conversations in any vehicle with OnStar navigation systems.

Law enforcement agencies can reprogram the microphone in mobile phones so they can listen to conversations even when the phone is not in use (Zittrain 2008, 110). They can also use the automatic update feature on any personal computer linked to the web to turn on the computer's microphone and video camera, and to search any documents stored on the machine. These techniques can also be used to search for unauthorized copies of copyrighted material, child pornography, and anything else deemed contrary to the public interest. Only laws protecting individual privacy from unwarranted government intrusion limit more widespread use of such technologies.

Websites frequented by users critical of the government are routinely monitored. Indymedia servers were briefly seized in Britain in October 2004, disabling 21 of its sites worldwide. This seizure was allegedly instigated by pressure from the FBI on behalf of the Swiss and Italian governments (Allen 2006, 128). The British government also seized Indymedia servers in June 2005 on the grounds that an anonymous blog was inciting readers to damage British rail property. Governments also use the web to co-opt citizens to help with surveillance of suspicious activities. The US government has routed signals from surveillance cameras along the US–Mexico border onto websites, inviting people to alert the police if they see suspicious activities (Zittrain 2008, 209). Millions of people check the sites and email the police when they see what might be illegal immigrants or drug smugglers crossing the border.

In summary, the wild-west days of the Internet have been tamed. The Internet has revolutionized mass communication, but these new technologies are being integrated into the mainstream normative order and the social, legal, and political systems that sustain it.

Political Economy: Corporate Mass Media

Mass media, with the exception of publicly funded broadcasters, are business corporations. Internet sites were initially independent of corporate backers but the more successful, frequently visited sites are steadily being drawn into the business circuit through advertising dollars and outright purchase of the sites. Media business corporations are primarily oriented to making money. They sell news, information, and entertainment as a means to generate profits directly and as a means to attract customers whose attention they sell to advertisers. Advertising agencies are themselves giant business corporations that sell their ability to attract customers to their clients' goods and services.

They use mass media as competitive spaces into which advertisements can be inserted. These economic realities profoundly influence the nature of mass media content. All forms of media selectively promote content that maximizes profit through fee-paying consumers or advertising revenues. Corporate media promote and transmit the values of free-enterprise, corporate capitalist business culture. The distinctive values of particular national cultures are merely superimposed over this increasingly global cultural consensus.

The Structure of Corporate Media Business

Whether you hear about current events and issues on the radio, watch programs about them on television, or read about them in magazines, the format and coverage is likely to be very similar. You can read the latest popular book, watch the movie version—either by renting or buying the DVD version or waiting for it to appear in the television movie series—and buy toy versions of the latest cartoon characters. You can hear the new tunes on the radio, watch them acted out in music videos on all-day television channels, and download them individually or in albums from the Internet.

The basic sameness in infotainment and entertainment fare reflects in large part the overlapping ownership and control of the different media by a small number of **multinational business corporations**. These media corporations compete for shares of mass audiences and mass advertising dollars, and for dominance over niche audiences and advertisers. When a small number of corporations dominate a particular industry like info-entertainment, straight competition hurts profits. It becomes more profitable to collude, to subdivide markets into niche interests, or more commonly to merge operations in order to acquire or eliminate former competitors and thus consolidate markets. Extended processes of financial mergers and acquisitions have resulted in a small number of multimedia, multi-billion dollar, multi-national corporations like News Corporation, AOL Time Warner, Disney, Sony, and Viacom, whose holdings typically cross movie studios, radio stations, television channels, newspapers, magazine and book publishing houses, sound recording studios, and Internet sites (Taras 1999, 71–77; Allen 1999, 51–56).

Wikipedia, the co-operative online encyclopedia, carries reasonably accurate and updated profiles of the holdings of these major corporations.

News Corporation, founded and controlled by Rupert Murdoch, is currently one of the world's largest media conglomerates, with annual revenues in 2009 of US$32.996 billion. Founded in Adelaide, Australia, it

Rupert Murdoch controls News Corporation, the world's largest media conglomerate in 2009 with revenues of about US$33 billion.

moved its headquarters to New York in 2004 to attract more American investors. Murdoch became a naturalized US citizen to be permitted under American law to own American television. A website listing News Corp holdings in 2009 includes the Hollywood blockbuster movie studio Twentieth Century Fox and 16 other studios making films for television, specialized and general market programs, including religious programs, comics, and children's programming. In addition News Corp controls multiple satellite television stations, including Sky News in the UK, and broadcasting. The corporation also owns or controls over 80 cable television channels spread worldwide. In the field of newsprint, the corporation lists 26 Australian papers and British papers that include the tabloids the *Sun* and *News of the World*, the prestigious *Times* and *Times Literary Supplement* and the *Sunday Times*. In the US, it owns the leading financial newspaper, the *Wall Street Journal*, and similar financial papers in Europe and Asia, and the Marketwatch website, as well as a series of local and regional papers, and 28 magazines. The corporation also has major holdings in publishing, owning HarperCollins Publishers, a major publisher of trade and academic texts

with bases in Australia, Britain, and the USA. It also owns the music production studio MySpace Records and an array of Internet sites, including the social networking site MySpace. Miscellaneous holdings include an array of sports teams, upscale sports bars and restaurants, and advertising companies. Such multimedia holdings make it possible for the corporation to publish a book, sell it through its own agencies, serialize the story in its magazines, develop a movie version, distribute the movie through its own cinema chain, export the video or DVD through its global holdings, advertise it on its own television stations, and tie in characters to vacation theme parks.

Sony Corporation is a similar global giant, with annual revenues of over US$79 billion in 2008. Based in Japan, Sony owns Columbia Pictures; Cineplex, Odeon, and Loews theatres; Sony PlayStations; satellite television channels; music studios; and electronics industries producing televisions, discs, computers, and cellphones. The corporation AOL Time Warner was formed from the amalgamation of Turner Broadcasting, Warner Communications, and America Online. It listed an annual revenue of US$47 billion in 2008. It has similar holdings in movie studios, film libraries, cable channels (including the influential 24-hour-a-day Cable Network News), magazines (including *Time*, *People*, *Fortune*, *Life*, *Entertainment Weekly*, and *Sports Illustrated*), comics, the sports franchises Atlanta Braves and Atlanta Hawks, theme parks, and a baseball stadium (Vivian and Maurin 2009, 17; Allen 1999, 51–56).

These huge corporate empires merge into one another, often forming partnership ventures. Their massive holdings are not stable over time because they are constantly being traded (Vivian and Maurin 2009, 17). Parent companies are driven by profits. They may strip subsidiaries of assets and sell them off to raise cash, particularly during periods of economic recession when companies find themselves too heavily leveraged or lacking liquidity—technical terms for carrying too much debt and lacking immediate cash to meet ongoing costs like salaries and interest payments on debts. Employees can never be sure that their jobs are secure, particularly because it is common practice for parent companies to borrow money to buy a **subsidiary**, strip it of assets or use it to borrow money to cover costs of its purchase, and then sell it—a practice known as "Buy it. Strip it. Flip it" (Foster and Magdoff 2009, 59). The other common practice, for which Murdoch is famous, is to practice **economies of scale** by combining operations and laying off or downsizing staff in the new company.

Canada's info-entertainment industry has not been swallowed up by these global giants because of federal laws regulating ownership of cultural industries, although that does not prevent Canadian citizens from buying satellite dishes to pick up American stations, and watching CNN and Fox News rather than the CBC. Major Canadian media conglomerates in 2008 included CanWest Global, CTVglobemedia, Quebecor, and Corus (Vivian and Maurin 2009, 14).

CanWest Global owned the Global Television Network, 11 daily papers (including *The National Post*), a series of conventional and digital specialty channels, and Alliance Atlantis, which produces and distributes film and television programs. Following its seeking bankruptcy protection in 2009, the company is likely to be broken up and assets sold to pay debtors. CTVglobemedia owns CTV Newsnet and Report on Business Television, the CHUM Radio Network, a range of specialty channels including MuchMusic, Bravo, and BookTV, and the major national paper the *Globe and Mail*. Quebecor owns Vidéotron, the largest cable television network and Internet provider in Quebec; *Le Journal de Montréal*; Sun Media Corp, which owns 20 major papers, including the *Toronto Sun* and the *Ottawa Sun*; Osprey media group, which owns 21 newspapers; and TVA Group, which owns dozens of broadcasting properties. Quebecor is well known for the practice of cross-promotion, using its newspaper and magazine holdings to advertise and promote its television programs. Corus, a spinoff from Shaw Communications, specializes in radio stations in Western Canada, country music television, and children's television and book publishing.

Internet as Corporate Mass Media

News sites on the Internet were initially developed by people anxious to get around the imposed conformity of corporate media gatekeepers. Those on the right side of the political spectrum sought to challenge what they saw as the liberal bias of mainstream journalism and promote commentary that strongly supports a free-enterprise, free-market, and small-government focus. Those on the left sought to challenge what they saw as the business-as-usual bias and promote commentary that highlights the exploitative and destructive character of corporate business practices. Over time the character of the Internet shifted from **radical** fringe towards mainstream, able to attract mass audiences as technology improved to permit Internet users to progress from text to pictures, soundtrack, and now full-colour, real-time video streaming. The number of Internet users has expanded from thousands to billions, doubling every three months, to an 800 percent annual increase in 1996 (Vivian and Maurin 2009, 139). It spurred the dot-com mania of 1999–2000, when investors poured close to $1 trillion into all expanding fibre-optic cable, and a host of Internet start-up companies and Internet service providers. When the investment bubble burst in 2001, major investment banks became part owners of the Internet.

In the process of this rapid expansion, the content of the Internet shifted towards the mainstream. Internet news sites have become business sites. Almost all mainstream newspapers, magazines, radio, television, and sound recording media have website versions. The radical fringe sites of right and left still exist on the Internet, but they have been pushed to the margins. Web-browsers like Google and Yahoo that prioritize sites by numbers of viewers rarely pick them up.

Individual bloggers can post their comments free once they have high-speed Internet access, but to become a big player, like Matt Drudge with his Drudge Report, they need to raise sufficient revenue to turn their blogging into a full-time job. Established websites require revenues to sustain computers, servers, maintenance staff, and writers. Some alternative sites, like Z Magazine, manage to raise funds through subscriptions from loyal readers, but this is difficult to sustain when most people are accustomed to surfing the web for free. For most sites, the primary source of revenues and business profits is advertising. The value of a website is determined primarily by the amount of advertising it attracts, which is a function of number of hits, or people, visiting the site.

Internet sites now trade on the stock exchange and share values give a measure of the extent to which these sites are now businesses. In the summer of 2009 a Russian investor purchased a 2-percent interest in the social networking site Facebook for $200,000, making its total value about $4 billion—somewhat less than in 2007 when the giant software company Microsoft bought a 1.6 percent share in Facebook for $240 million (Matt Hartley, *Globe and Mail*, 27 May 2009). Microsoft also teamed up with General Electric's media company NBC in 1996 to form the Internet site msnbc.com. It offers interactive multimedia news, commentary, and interviews. Facebook generated between $200 million to $400 million in 2008, although these are small earnings when compared with Google's revenue for 2008 of $21.75 billion. Google works on a click-through payment system. Advertisers measure audiences by the number of visits or clicks on websites. Advertisers pay Google to place advertisements on thousands of sites, including narrow-interest blog sites. Google pays the site a fee for every blog visitor who clicks on the sponsored advertising link. Advertising on the Internet increased over 5000 percent in a decade (1997–2006) (Vivian and Maurin 2009, 139). Big sites like that of the *New York Times* pay Google a licence fee for readers to use its technology to search the *Times* site. Google can then place relevant ads on the *Times* site and pays a click-through fee to the *Times* when a reader clicks that ad. For example, if the *Times* has a story on Jamaica, Google can place ads for travel to Jamaica on the site. Of the estimated $10 billion that advertisers spent on online messages in 2004, Google received $1.9 billion (Vivian and Maurin 2009, 193–95).

Advertising agencies are themselves huge business corporations. Some are global agencies: Omnicom had revenue in the $13 billion range in 2008, and Interpublic and WPP London had revenues of $6.5 to $7.5 billion. Smaller Canadian advertising agencies, like Cossette Communications Group (Quebec), MDC Partners (Toronto), and Maritz Canada (Mississauga), post revenues in the $200 to $500 million range. They sell their specialized ability to package fast-paced information about their clients' goods and services and place them in locations that maximize the number of relevant viewers. Advertisers favour mainstream sites for their product placements because few businesses want to link their goods and services to sites that are hostile to corporate business interests. Niche sites are supported only when they attract a sufficiently large portion of subgroup audiences. Two Canadian digital channels, Edge TV and Women's Television sports channel, hoped to appeal to large niche audiences, but were cancelled in 2003 when they failed to attract sufficient viewers in order to attract advertising revenues (Vivian and Maurin 2009, 13).

The Internet and Journalism   As mass readers have shifted from newsprint to Internet, so have advertising dollars. This has resulted in serious revenue shortfall for major newspapers. *New York Times* columnist Frank Rich opined, in his 9 May 2009 article "American Press on Suicide Watch," that major papers like the *Los Angeles Times*, the *Philadelphia Inquirer* and the *Boston Globe* are at risk of closing, and other papers are slashing staff. Journalists have been hit already by corporate consolidation and downsizing as parent corporations try to save money by copying stories across different papers and purchasing news and fillers from syndicates like Associated Press, and using lower-paid staff to rewrite the pieces for specific papers. The concern that Rich voices is that news blogs on the Internet are not substitutes for professional journalism, and they do not pay salaries for journalists. Blogs like the Drudge Report are sometimes able to lead with scoops or leaks because they are not subject to the same rules and ethics of verifiability expected of professional journalists, and hence they can cite speculative tidbits from anonymous sources. For the most part, however, blogs offer only commentary and opinion on items of news first published in mainstream media. Blogs cannot replace the in-depth investigative reporting produced by professional journalists with technical expertise and insider contacts. Blogs use the work of professional journalists without directly paying for it. The fear is that as masses of people turn to the Internet rather than the press for news, the number of professional journalists will decline and the quality of news will deteriorate. The *New York Times* attached a survey to the Internet article by Rich asking viewers whether they would be willing to pay a subscription for online news, or possibly micropayments for each piece, much like purchasing individual songs from iTunes for 99¢. In the future, bloggers who cite writings by journalists may have to pay for the privilege.

Corporate Media Political Power: Money and Times

Corporate mass media influence society in ways that are both overt and subtle through their control over money, access to mass audiences, the content of information that reaches mass audiences, and the prevailing cultural values and worldviews that are embedded in the selection and framing of that information.

Corporate media, like other large corporations, potentially wield political power through the financial contributions they can make to political parties and individual campaigns. Unique to corporate media, however, is the control they wield over when and how political leaders are able to communicate with mass audiences. Those who manage the media influence who gets air time, who gets praised or savaged in television talk shows, editorials, and newspaper columns, and who gets offered book contracts (Taras 1999, 78). This control gives media moguls unique power as political lobbyists. No one messes with the big broadcasters in the USA, Taras suggests, because politicians need media coverage. Rupert Murdoch, owner of Fox News Channel, is well known for his partisan support of the Republican Party. Likewise in Canada, the Asper family, owners of CanWest Global, gave strong support to the Conservative Party and the pro-Israel lobby. Conrad Black, former owner of Hollinger International, similarly made no secret of his intention to use the medium of Hollinger's newspapers to promote conservatism in Canadian politics.

Overt political influence by media is tempered in Canada by the presence of CBC radio and television, which also reduces the political power of corporate media in Canada relative to the USA. Part of the mandate of the CBC is to provide equitable time for representatives of all recognized political parties and to cover party political broadcasts during elections. The power to influence elections by partisan editorials, talk shows, and the like is also tempered by the fact that such tactics are sufficiently obvious that they elicit rebuke and cynicism from audiences.

Corporate Media Political Culture   The subtle framing of news and content through business-oriented culture attracts less attention than the overt clout of money and media coverage. Yet it is arguably more significant in molding public opinion precisely because it is less visible. Readers and viewers absorb it without consciously thinking about it. The neo-liberal worldview has prevailed over the last three decades in North American and in Western economies generally, and corporate mass media have played a significant role in sustaining it. Neo-liberalism promotes core values of competitive individualism, individual responsibility for one's own well-being, the benefits of competition in all fields of activity, the value of merited achievements, the greater efficiencies to be gained from reliance on private business enterprise providing services for profit, limited reliance on government, and minimal rates of taxation on private wealth. Private wealth alone is seen as the driving force behind progress. Governments are valued for maintaining law and order, stabilizing markets, promoting trade, and ensuring the free flow of money, and they are otherwise chastised for spending, or rather wasting, money.

These values underlie the corporate mass media culture, which has variations of American or Canadian culture superimposed over it. Different sub-sectors of mass media lean towards liberal or conservative—or Democrat or Republican—views, but the core values of capitalist culture remain constant. These values are rarely flagged or raised as issues for debate. They are simply assumed, treated as common sense and implicit in how editors and journalists select or overlook items for inclusion as news and how they frame issues and tell stories. The neo-liberal worldview forms what Marxist theorist Antonio Gramsci refers to as **ideological hegemony** (1971; Nesbitt-Larking 2001, 86–88). It is the seen-but-not-noticed component of mass culture. It works to obscure exploitative class relations inherent in **capitalism** and to manufacture mass consent to corporate business practices.

Owners of mass media outlets typically deny that they exercise direct influence over media content. And for the most part, they do not need to keep an eye on their media because they appoint senior editors who share their worldview. André Prefontaine, a managing editor who worked for Power Corporation, then for Hollinger under Conrad Black, and later for Quebecor, denied ever experiencing corporate bosses picking up the telephone to tell him what was to be written (Winter 1997, 88). Prefontaine's strongly conservative, neo-liberal views made such close monitoring unnecessary. However, journalists like James Winter who try to write articles with a critical Marxist orientation, critical of exploitative business practices, opposed to free trade policies that do not protect workers' rights, supportive of union strike actions, or sympathetic to demonstrators opposing bank practices, soon find their articles severely edited or rejected (Winter 1997, 92–100). Techniques for stifling journalistic dissent include changing headlines and opening paragraphs to alter the frame or spin of the story,

watering down the content, suggesting different sources and contacts to comment on issues, downgrading the story to interior pages and shorter column space, or dropping the story entirely. Eventually the journalist could even be dismissed. Concern with how advertisers might respond to specific stories significantly influences their likelihood of being covered. A seemingly benign article about how to sell one's own house prompted real estate agencies to shift their advertising contract from the *Kingston Whig-Standard* to its rival tabloid the *Kingston This Weekend* in the early 1990s (Winter 1997, 103). The *Windsor Star* pulled an article critical of Chrysler Corporation paying large bonuses to its chief executives while granting workers only a 1.5-percent increase (Winter 1997). The newspaper would not risk losing its lucrative advertising revenues from Chrysler. A decade later such stories flooded left-wing blogs and even made headlines in mainstream media in 2009 when near-bankrupt corporations used bail-out money to pay large bonuses to executives. But they were quickly tempered by alternative stories emphasizing how struggling executives were pulling their companies out of bankruptcy and back into profitability—notwithstanding a few individual bad apples.

Analysis of the content of Canadian newspapers throughout the 1990s by research teams of faculty teaching communication studies documents a systemic pattern of under-reporting or censoring of potential national news stories critical of corporations (Winter 1997, Ch. 6). Such stories include the weakening of Clean Water regulations in the USA and the threat this poses to Canada, creeping **privatization** of the Canadian health care system, how high interest rates rather than social spending drive inflation, how neo-liberal debt-reduction strategies in New Zealand resulted in a doubling of the national debt, chronic unemployment and higher suicide rates, human rights violations associated with the Oka crisis in Canada in 1990 when Mohawk people tried to block the town of Oka's plan to build a golf course and parking lot on land claimed by the Mohawk, human rights violations in Mexico following the NAFTA agreement, and Canada's role as a global supplier of armaments and weapons. Systematically over-represented were what Winter calls "junk-food-news" about the sexual peccadillos of royalty and politicians, spectacular murder trials, and other crimes that (mis)present the world's problems in terms of individual psychology.

Within the neo-liberal framework, corrupt business practices can be exposed. Elite journalists continue to unmask the powerful and ask probing questions about politicians and government figures, but rarely are powerful elites in the chief executive offices of private corporations subject to the same public scrutiny. This selective genre of "attack journalism," Taras suggests, may give the appearance of

Mother Jones magazine struggles to provide an alternative voice critical of capitalism, with limited access to corporate funding.

CSI WATERGATE: NIXON TAPE GAP SOLVED?
OBAMA VS. ISRAEL LOBBY • MEET THE GOP'S NEW PIT BULL • PINK BRAIN SYNDROME

Mother Jones
SMART, FEARLESS JOURNALISM
MotherJones.com
September + October 2009 | $5.95

THE SPIN
PURE
FANCIED BY CELEBS*
EVERY DROP IS GREEN
UNTOUCHED BY MAN
LIVING WATER

FIJI
NATURAL ARTESIAN WATER
500mL (1.05PT)

THE FACTS
TWICE THE PLASTIC
PUTS LIPSTICK ON A JUNTA
DIESEL POWERED
HIDES IN TAX HAVENS
LOCALS DRINK DIRTY WATER

strident social criticism while functioning to support the neo-liberal **ideology** that private enterprise and not incompetent governments should run the economy (1999, 53–59). Cynicism towards government can undermine democracy by suggesting that voting is pointless because nobody can be trusted.

Domhoff enjoins activists on the political left to stop blaming the media for their own failure to communicate a positive alternative to the corporate capitalist system (2003, Ch. 2). Barker rejoins (2009) that it is almost impossible for leaders on the political left to consistently present a progressive political alternative to capitalism in mainstream media. The media's pervasive representation of critics of **corporate capitalism** as violent demonstrators led by irresponsible leaders undermines the credibility of alternative politics. The few critical messages that do penetrate the media gatekeepers are those that conform more closely to a vision of free-market solutions to social problems such as environmental degradation, or corporate self-regulation of excesses of sweatshop **exploitation** of labour, or charitable foundations. In this process of co-opting critical messages, any more radical critique of capitalism is

effectively silenced. Alternative publications like *Mother Jones*, the *Nation* and the *Progressive* struggle to survive financially because they cannot attract corporate advertising dollars. Hence they cannot afford the massive mailings and campaigns needed to build up their circulations (Barker 2009, citing Parenti 1986). The British Labour newspaper the *Daily Herald* was forced to close in 1964, despite a circulation of over 1.2 million readers, because subscriptions could not make up for a drop in corporate advertising dollars.

Spokespersons for global corporate media empires also typically downplay the charge that their empires promote cultural **imperialism**. Overtly, there is much evidence that media empires adjust to niche markets and to local interests, adopting local languages and giving freedom to local editors and producers to design their own programs. But at the more subtle level the hegemonic influence of corporate culture continues. Latin American and Asian subsidiaries produce their own programming in their own languages, but the style and content often closely copy mainstream western media with talk shows that air individual private lives for public entertainment, situation comedies, and music videos; and dubbed American reruns serve as cheap filler (Vivian and Maurin 2009, 297).

Culture on the Web

The Internet has revolutionized the production and distribution of creative art. A small band, working from a garage production unit can make music and distribute it on its own label, bypassing the five major recording labels that hitherto controlled 85 percent of all music production. Music files are shared over the Internet, allowing individuals to create their own music libraries of mixed songs and soundtracks freed from the constraint of buying high-priced albums. New technology for sound and video file sharing and editing ushered in a new form of art made from cutting and recombining clips from existing videos to create new visions and meanings. Ordinary people can now participate and collaborate in the creation of music and film in ways never before possible.

Stifling Internet Culture: Closing Down the Commons
Corporations with business interests in producing and distributing music and film have rushed to protect their turf, hiring lobbyists and lawyers to close down these threats to their monopolies and profits. They used copyright laws to criminalize the file sharing of music and launched lawsuits against 12 000 individuals for using the Kazaa application to copy music. A fine for stealing a CD from a store might routinely be under $1000, but corporations sought punitive damages in the hundreds of thousands

of dollars to try to strangle the new technology (Lessig 2004, 177–182, 200). In a recent case a US federal judge ordered a single mother to pay $1.92 million or $80 000 per song in statutory damages to a record company (*Globe and Mail*, 20 June 2009). While the company knows it cannot actually get this much money from the individual, it can use the court order to strip the guilty person of every asset she has. A truce of sorts was reached when Apple Inc. established iTunes, which legally permits people to download individual songs for 99¢ each. It saves having to buy an entire album to get one song, and avoids the risk of viruses spread through file sharing. The struggle continues, however, for individuals to be allowed to copy music they have actually purchased onto mobile players (Lessig 2004, 189, 203).

The Recording Industry Association of America (RIAA) pushed to further strangle Internet file sharing by launching a $98 billion lawsuit in 2002 against a student who wrote code for a search engine with the capacity to copy files (Lessig 2004, 51). The student argued that he had done nothing illegal in merely writing code, but he would have needed at least $250 000 to fight the case, money he would have no way to ever recover. When the student caved, the RIAA responded by demanding the student's entire summer earnings of $12 000 just to drop the case against him. The same RIAA successfully lobbied Congress to impose rules that force Internet radio to pay a copyright fee to a recording artist for every song of the artist's that is transmitted, a fee that terrestrial radio does not have to pay (Lessig 2004, 196). The RIAA also campaigned in 2003 to force Internet service providers to identify individual Internet users who may have violated copyright law, without notifying the customer, leaving individual families liable for $2 million in damages if only a single copied CD is found on their computer.

Corporate lawyers have also successfully lobbied Congress over many years to repeatedly extend copyright law to cover every form of creative work for an increasing numbers of years. A law that originally covered only registered published work for 14 years, with one renewal if the author were alive, was extended 11 times in 40 years to cover everything, registered or not, for the life of the author plus 95 years, and this includes any derivative or take-off (Lessig 2004, 116–138). The result, Lessig argues, is that a vast array of creative work, especially films that have a short lifespan, will disintegrate into dust before anyone can copy even pieces of them for creative recombining. Even when works have not been registered and no one even knows who or where the authors are, they cannot be copied even in the tiniest part for risk of a crippling lawsuit. Walt Disney made fortunes copying characters from silent films and from *Grimm's Fairy Tales* but no one in the future can make a take-off of any recognizable

Disney character without paying crippling copyright fees. A film producer who wanted to create a retrospective video about the acting career of Clint Eastwood spent a year tracking down and paying every bit actor in every film clip used (Lessig 2004, 100). Legally he may not have been in violation of the "fair use" clause that permits quotations for critical review, but he could not afford to risk a possible lawsuit for copyright infringement. The capacity that Internet technology makes available for individuals to cut and paste music and films into new pastiches, or to bring old films to new audiences, is effectively being crushed by copyright law. In Lessig's view, the free culture of the Internet is being replaced by a permission culture where creativity requires the prior paid approval of power-holders or creators from the past (2004, xiv).

Corporate lawyers are using the Digital Millennium Copyright Act to ban writing any code that might be used to circumvent existing computer code, even if it is not being used for that purpose (Lessig, 157). Showing people how to write code to make Sony's dog icon dance to jazz is illegal because it infringes on Sony's code. Computer code is itself copyrighted creative work and this itself is giving rise to multiple litigations claiming infringement of earlier code.

Closing the Loopholes: Code as Law   Law is an effective but expensive and blunt instrument to control creative work in Internet commons. Increasingly corporations are using code to control and limit how consumers can use their work. Printed books can be freely lent and borrowed, read multiple times, and bought and sold through used bookstores. The use of electronic books, however, can be restricted through computer code that prevents them from being copied or exchanged through file sharing, prevents any page or quote from being printed, and even prevents a book from being electronically read aloud. Downloaded music and films digitally recorded from television can be coded so that while it is possible to copy or share them electronically the resulting copies can only be played three times or kept for three days before they self-destruct (Zittrain 2008, 107). In effect, code becomes law.

Corporations are also promoting the marketing of tethered devices that can be accessed through the Internet but with the digital code and programming controlled by the vendor. Initially Internet technology was open, in the sense that anyone with sufficient expertise could look at the code and write new software to permit a host of new technologies, including file sharing and Internet telephone service. Networks connected personal computers directly, without going through corporate vendors. Telephone corporation AT&T lost a court challenge that would have blocked unauthorized foreign attachments from using the telephone lines (Zittrain 2008, 11–18, 81). Newer technologies like mobile phones, video game consoles, video recorders, iPods, iPhones, and Blackberries, however, are tethered to their vendor and programmed not to accept any new software without the vendor's prior approval. The technologies are also programmed to periodically check with the vendor for updates. The vendor can send new code, including code for surveillance, directly to the appliance. Consumers are also being encouraged to use tethered services such as word processing and photograph storage that give the vendor power to disable access at any time and to code the information in ways that restrict the transfer of information to different service providers (Zittrain 2008, 124). The potential power of centralized control was demonstrated in 2006 when the maker of the digital video recorder TiVo successfully sued the satellite television distributor EchoStar for infringing upon TiVo patents, and the judge ordered EchoStar to disable all storage to and playback from subscribers' machines (Zittrain 2008, 103). While this order was eventually stayed, it made clear that customers could have lost all their recorded programs through a command from the vendor. The combination of copyright laws and tethered code are working to restrict the creative cultural potential of the Internet. Freedom to take digital gadgets apart and experiment with new possibilities for code and new combinations of cultural work are increasingly being restricted to corporate players.

Conclusion

Political economy theory concurs in part with functionalist theory in highlighting the integrative function of mass media in enhancing and transmitting shared cultural consensus, but it characterizes this culture as promoting a narrow corporate agenda that dulls people's critical awareness and questioning of capitalist economic systems. Mind-numbing "wallpaper" television (Bausinger, cited in Nesbitt-Larking 2001, 280) and radio broadcasts pump out endless streams of popular music, crime thrillers, situation comedies, game shows like *Who Wants To Be A Millionaire*, and pseudo-reality TV like *Survivor, Big Brother,* and *Real Housewives* and travel, cooking, and sports shows, to fill the gaps between advertising. The central preoccupation of all private broadcasting is to lure advertising revenues, and this in turn requires strategies to keep audiences mindlessly tuning in with a steady diet of light entertainment. Serious material like news tends to be framed in the same fast, action-packed entertainment formats of thrillers, sports, and soap operas, none of which promotes critical reflection. The Internet offers access to significantly different, alternative, and oppositional news sources, but these are at risk of being swamped by the volume of online versions of corporate media outlets. Corporate interests are also succeeding in narrowing the scope of the Internet as a creative commons.

Social Construction: Mass Media and Negotiated Meaning

Theorizing Media

The social constructionist perspective focuses research attention on processes through which mass media construct and communicate meanings, and how these meanings are continually appropriated or ignored, challenged, resisted, changed, and reconstituted by their audiences. From this perspective, mass media do not describe events but rather define what counts as the reality of events. Descriptions appear to be objective or factual to the extent that they conform to accepted ways of presenting information, and prevailing assumptions about which sources are believable. Culture is understood not as a relatively fixed set of beliefs and values but as social practices that generate shared meanings (Barker 1999, 9). Communication involves social practices of encoding and decoding meanings, with audiences involved as active constructors of meanings in their own right. Social constructionist research explores the active practices by which people produce, disseminate, receive, and interpret communications to produce shared meanings.

Producing News Media content that identifies itself as "news" makes a special claim to represent reality and objectivity and carries a special power to define for audiences what they feel they know about what is happening at local, national, and international levels. Social constructionist research explores awkward questions like "How do journalists produce something that is socially recognizable as news, rather than fiction or entertainment?"; "How do they recognize what counts as 'news'" from the infinity of all possible happenings?"; "How do they find out sufficient information to produce reports, and then package their reports to appear as acceptably factual and objective to count as 'news' rather than opinion or even fiction?"; and "How do they do this routinely, every day of the year?" Nesbitt-Larking cites the story of a Californian student radio station that announced one evening at 6:00 p.m., "Good evening. Here is the six o'clock news. Nothing happened today" (2001, 175). Did nothing happen—or nothing newsworthy? Or did student reporters not have the time to find something newsworthy to report on?

Early research explored the tacit rules that journalists typically used to distinguish newsworthy, "reportable" events from mere happenings (Tuchman 1978; Hall 1981, 234; Allen 1999, 62–63). Such events include dramatic conflicts or misfortunes that can be easily interpreted and related to the lives of the expected audience, and prescheduled events than can be fitted into available local, national, or international news slots.

Journalists cannot simply wait for newsworthy events to happen. They need strategies to generate such events on a daily basis, including knowing where to look and who to ask. Most journalists have specialized topic areas, such as consumer affairs, business, finance, education, the environment, health, art, the "women's page," travel, and the like. Topic areas have related "beats and bureaus" that journalists can check daily for happenings that can be rendered newsworthy. Daily records make for attractive news sources. These include daily police patrol reports that list crimes, accidents, and other calls; hospital admissions; court schedules; scheduled political activities; and question periods in the House of Commons and provincial legislatures. Scheduled events make it easier for journalists to arrange their workloads. Scheduled public appearances by celebrities to public arenas are likely to get **worked up** as news, even if nothing happens. Newsgathering organizations like Reuters and Associated Press guarantee a steady flow of predigested newsworthy materials that can be quickly worked up to suit local audiences and interests. Such services provide cheap stock filler for many news holes. The result is that happenings that are recorded by organizations are most likely to become defined as "news."

Journalists have to generate reports or broadcasts every day to fit inflexible schedules. Fixed formats for deciding what matters and what details are worthy of notice help to generate fast reports (Allen 1999, 63–64). So does the standard news format of headline plus summary of key points, followed by softer description and commentary that can be chopped to fit the size of the news hole. To get the work done quickly, it also helps to write in forms that will be readily accepted by editors and not get sent back for revisions. Successful journalists—those who secure long-term employment—are likely to be those who conform to views that editors see as reasonable. These routine work practices by journalists function to reinforce the power of institutional spokespersons to define what constitutes news for practical purposes. Journalists retain some autonomy to present alternative viewpoints and interpretations, but they work within the constraints of not undermining their future access to institutional sources of information.

Managing Mainstream Journalism Politicians, celebrities, and opinion leaders go to great lengths to try to control their media exposure. Media management strategies have become an industry in their own right with public relations, or PR, experts hired to manage public images and plan relations with media. Journalists, meanwhile, have developed strategies of their own to manage the manipulators. Nesbitt-Larking (2001, 156–158) describes some of this "interplay of influence" between the Canadian government and the media during the 1970s and '80s. The Liberal Party tactics to manage the media included issuing major announcements at the last minute so that journalists would have no time to develop commentaries, reporting "bad" news on Friday afternoons, releasing prepared statements direct to audiences without permitting editing or commentary, and rewarding supportive journalists with special access and "scoops" while punishing others. The party staged press conferences with the use of spin doctors to give the best possible spin on policies and actions, and with venues, seating, camera angles, and the like chosen to project the best image. Reporters countered these tactics with elaborate public commentary on the manipulation tactics themselves and by cultivating contacts with independent sources of information, including opposition party members, lobbyists, interest groups, and academics. Photojournalists with high-power zoom lenses were on the lookout for gaffes such as a prominent male politician patting a female politician on her buttocks, and Prime Minister Jean Chrétien grabbing a protestor around the neck (Nesbitt-Larking 2001, 158). Conservative Prime Minister Stephen Harper accused the national media of liberal bias, deliberately opposing and attacking his government. He responded by shunning the media, often refusing to meet with journalists or to answer their questions. He preferred to send out fixed press releases and to talk directly only with less oppositional local media.

Live interviews of celebrities, politicians, and experts on radio or television provide important forums for elites to get their views across to potential audiences of millions, but they can also be risky and unpredictable. Officials may try to find out the exact nature of questions before granting interviews with reporters, but they can never totally control how live programs will go or the images that will come across to potential audiences of millions of people behind the microphones and cameras. Media-savvy US President Barack Obama found this out when he joked on *The Tonight Show* with Jay Leno (19 March 2009) that his poor bowling skills were "like the Special Olympics or something." He apologized profusely for the implied insult to athletes with disabilities.

Journalists or anchors who work as media interviewers are often celebrities or public figures in their own right. Their primary concern is to entertain and hold the attention of audiences, and the search for new information from interviewees is secondary. Allen (1999, 97–98) describes how television interviewers work at personalizing interviews by "ventriloquizing" the voices of ordinary people, to create the image of themselves as asking the kinds of questions to which "ordinary viewers" would want answers. Politicians and celebrities routinely respond by keeping their remarks to highly scripted statements. They have to be constantly on guard against unexpected lines of questioning, or making some loose comment that can be aired repeatedly, and exaggerated out of context to discredit them (Taras 1999, 55–56). Constant media attention creates the feeling of living in a fishbowl. Princess Diana spoke of being hounded wherever she went by "paparazzi," or hordes of photographers armed with zoom lenses that can take pictures from kilometres away. She and her boyfriend died in a high-speed car crash in Paris in August 1997 as photographers raced after them.

Media interviews are part of this fishbowl. Pressure to present news as infotainment or information-as-entertainment geared to audience ratings for advertisers creates incentives to dramatize interviews and to highlight conflicts and **deviance** and a sense of crisis. In the genre of "attack journalism," politicians and other public figures can find themselves pilloried by a media out to sensationalize events. Former Canadian Prime Minister Kim Campbell, defeated in 1993, complained that the press were out to destroy people, dwelling on the negative "to the point of gratuitous cruelty" (Taras 1999, 56). Outside of the mainstream media the Internet can be used to spread gossip about celebrities, which can in turn become the topic of probing interview questions. Reporters across America drew on the Drudge Report in 1998 to publicize gossip about US President Clinton's affair with a White House intern. Such coverage came close to bringing about his impeachment from office.

Elite control over the content of news is further eroded by dissent and disagreement in their ranks. Journalists provide important conduits for disgruntled and subordinated voices to exert influence. A classic tactic is to leak privileged information anonymously to sympathetic journalists, who can then cite it as "from unnamed inside sources." Part of the routine work of competent journalists is to foster trusted relationships with a variety of insiders to encourage such leaks. Official sources compete among themselves to discredit other views and lay claim to possessing the primary definition of the issue at hand. It may well not be clear whether there is a primary definer of the reality of any given issue at any specific time, and those holding a commanding perspective may not hold on to that hegemony for long (Schlesinger and Tumber 1994, 17–21; Deacon and Golding 1994, 202; Allen 1999, 72). Sometimes the fall from power can be dramatic. In a special double issue (30 December 2002–6 January 2003), *Time* magazine's cover story was "The Whistleblowers" featuring interviews with three women: Cynthia Cooper of Worldcom, Coleen Rowley of the FBI, and Sherron Watkins of Enron. Each woman had gone public during 2002 about corporate

wrongdoing at the top. Stephen Harper dealt with the risk of informants by ordering his government caucus members to confine media relations to scripted, preauthorized remarks controlled from the centre.

Getting Heard in Mainstream Media   Interest groups and social movements routinely strategize to gain media attention for their concerns by cultivating sympathetic contacts, seeking coalitions, anticipating strategies others will use, and continually monitoring the impact of their efforts and adjusting accordingly (Schlesinger and Tumber 1994, 39). The more successful strategies are those that fit best with the routine pressures that journalists face to get materials together and reports ready in very restricted time frames, and for limited news holes. These include having copy-ready materials that journalists can slot directly into their own reports, handing out advance copies of talks or speeches, and scheduling press conferences at convenient hours with handouts covering pertinent information (Allen 1999, 75–77).

When all else fails oppositional groups can resort to "disruptive access" (Allen 1999, 81): making news by creating surprise, shock, and trouble, balancing the need for media attention against the risk of being publicly discredited as a threat to law and order. The environmental protection organization Greenpeace pulled off several stunts in the 1990s that won extensive media coverage, but also generated backlash for disrupting legitimate business (Allen 1999, 73). Clow's study (1993) of media coverage of the anti-nuclear movement in the 1980s documents how its message was largely discredited, dismissed, and swamped by the vastly greater coverage given to nuclear-industry spokespersons and scientists claiming that nuclear energy was safe, pollution-free, and low cost.

Internet Culture: The Creative Commons

The Internet has revolutionized how people communicate, how we search for information, and potentially how we can participate in the creation and transmission of news. Anyone with access to the Internet can post a blog with information and commentary that they want to make public. The challenge in getting information into the public arena is not in posting it on the Internet, but in attracting the attention of viewers to one blog among the myriad of others. The era when one salacious or innovative blog could be expected to gain some attention has passed. Increasingly, individual bloggers are participating in collectives that combine entries around similar themes and interests in the hope of developing a reputation as a site for others to check. Commonly these collectives strive to offer alternative views or opposition to mainstream media. Indymedia, or Independent Media News, first developed in 1999 as a site for protesters at the World Trade Organization meetings in Seattle, Washington, to voice their concerns and their experiences with riot police, in opposition to the mainstream media that represented them as troublemakers or rabble. Indymedia grew in two years into 83 sites in 31 different countries and by 2006 numbered 150 sites. These are open sites to which anyone can post entries, with content monitored by volunteer collectives. The sites encourage entries about social movements and protests that oppose the neo-liberal pro-business agenda. The Huffington Post is another site that began as an amalgamation of three blogs in 2005 and has grown into a major online newspaper with regular contributions from journalists, politicians, celebrities, and a collection of some 3000 bloggers. The Post boasted in 2008 that it had raised $15 million from investors to expand its investigative journalism.

These independent websites are able to operate very differently from establishment media, bringing attention to issues and content that the establishment would not cover. During the American invasion of Iraq in 2003, independent journalists and citizen-reporters were able to post stories and pictures of events inside Iraq that would have been off-limits to embedded reporters allowed to travel with the troops. These included the now infamous pictures and accounts of torture at Abu Ghraib prison.

Increasingly, mainstream news outlets have altered how they attract news to compete with independent blog sites. Journalists often check the larger blog sites for possible scoops that they can use in their own reports. Matt Drudge noted that when journalists from CNN and other mainstream news channels cited "anonymous sources" they were often citing him, especially when he broke the scandal about President Clinton's sexual affairs. Mainstream broadcasters have also opened online sites of their own, encouraging audiences to use their site to post blogs with information, commentary, and responses to questions and programs. Mainstream news has thus become more interactive as a result, with editorial opinion-leaders less able to control debates. The challenge now is fast becoming how to organize mass blogging to influence the impression of which way the tide of public opinion is flowing on key issues.

The challenge for participatory journalism is how to ensure reasonable accuracy and reliability of postings from thousands of independent bloggers and how to weed out the deliberately false, misleading, libellous defamatory, cruel, or simply crank postings. Collaborative sites mostly rely on built-in fact-checking by volunteer reader-editors who check and take down any new postings that do not pass collective **norms** of acceptable journalism for the site. Readers can also immediately challenge the fairness and veracity of postings with counter postings of their own.

Mainstream journalists frequently deride such informal fact-checking as naive. Professors warn students not to use Wikipedia, the collaborative online encyclopedia, as a trustworthy source of information because anybody could write anything on the site or change entries at will. In practice, however, the built-in fact-checking mechanism of having thousands of volunteer editors primed to look at new and altered entries has proven surprisingly good at weeding out fraudulent entries that do not clearly cite sources of information. In one experiment a student made up a quote that he attributed to the French composer Maurice Jarre, which he added to a Wikipedia page hours after Jarre's death in March 2009. Members of Wikipedia's group of 1500 volunteer "administrators" spotted the bogus quotation by the absence of attribution and removed it three times within minutes or a few hours of it being posted (Seattle-Post-Intelligencer www.seattlepi.com/business/1700ap_eu_ireland_wikipedia_hoaxer.html). However, this was not before dozens of mainstream journalists for newspaper websites in Britain, Australia, and India had picked up the bogus quote from Wikipedia and inserted it into their obituaries. A month later none of the mainstream newspapers had noticed the error. Only one, the UK *Guardian*, posted a public correction when informed of the hoax. Others quietly removed the quotation from their websites, but some continued citing it even after being told it was bogus.

Managing the Message: Constructing Texts

The form as well as the content of mass media texts and broadcasts affects how they convey meaning. **Content analysis** is a conventional approach to studying text by counting key words and references to provide an objective measure of coverage. In a study of foreign news coverage on Canadian television, for example, countries and topics were counted to determine that the US and western Europe got maximum coverage, with less developed countries covered only during some major disaster like an earthquake, hostage-taking, or military coup (Hackett 1989; Nesbitt-Larking 2001, 254–255).

Discourse analysis poses deeper questions about how texts work to convey meaning through how they highlight, downplay, or omit issues and how they convey implicit explanations and moral lessons through descriptive terms. The same facts about violent confrontations, for example, can be packaged through the **discourse** of freedom fighters, defence of civilization, and independence from despotic rule, or of terrorism by marauding factions seeking to destabilize governments and throw nations into chaos. Prevailing neo-liberal values of free markets, individualism, and **consumerism** are conveyed through such rhetorical forms. Key signs of the pet interests and biases of those who control the media include lengthy and unusual special features, news stories that stress odd angles, and big stories not covered or briefly dismissed (Nesbitt-Larking 2001, 175). Extensive work by Teun van Dijk exposes the inherent **racism** in much media coverage of crime stories and issues of immigration and poverty (1993).

Semiotics explores the use of icons, signs, and symbols to encode meanings in texts. Stylistic devices to signal that content is to be considered news, rather than fiction or opinion, include stating headlines and opening sentences in unqualified fact form, as in "X happened," and citing statements by accredited sources without quotation marks. A subtle shift in a sentence structure to state "She said that X happened," or to add qualifiers like "apparently," or "seemingly," clues hearers to the possibility that the happening of X might be a matter of opinion, or subject to dispute (Smith 1990a; 1990b; Williams 1997, 29). A powerful way to signal that what follows is intended to be understood as fact is to schedule messages in the space or time slot conventionally set aside for "news." Framing devices used to signal seriousness and distinction from other entertainment include opening graphics and sounds to signal interruption in the flow of entertainment; an emphasis on being "live" to create a sense of urgency and immediacy, ticking clocks to signal up-to-the-minute information, world maps to signal bringing the world to "us", hard polished surfaces of news desks and file folders of notes to shuffle to signal professional detachment, formal speech, and a steady gaze into the camera lens (Allen 1999, 99–100). Back in 1939, Orson Welles unintentionally generated mass panic when he used the conventions of a radio news broadcast to announce that there had been an invasion from Mars (Nesbitt-Larking 2001, 283). A number of follow-up news broadcasts were required to convince nervous audiences that it really was "just fiction."

Photographs and video camera angles similarly employ icons to convey meanings: flags and uniforms convey nationalism, and the angle of a subject's head and eyes signal authority or guilt (Barthes 1967, 89–90). Advertisers use cultural icons and signs that trigger instant recognition by audiences to get their message across in a few seconds—white lab coats for scientists, aprons for mothers, athletes for health, and so on. Politicians and celebrities routinely hire advertising specialists who manipulate images to support the self-impressions they wish to make and follow up with public opinion polls to test the efficacy of the image.

The Undecidability of Text

The central problem with all **textual analysis**, as with political images, is the inherent undecidability of meanings.

Sophisticated analysis may reveal implicit neo-liberal biases, racism, and the like in a text, but there is no guarantee that diverse audiences will interpret the texts the way **deconstruction** exposes it or the way the authors intended. Meanings are temporal and fluid. Once people recognize that certain forms of dress, camera angles, and props (like flags) are being used to create impressions, they risk being interpreted as unconvincing gimmicks. Even when the content of a text appears to be transparently obvious, it can be interpreted differently by people with different frames of reference. Nesbitt-Larking (2001, 235–236) gives the example of the grainy home video of Rodney King being arrested by Los Angeles police. Millions of viewers became convinced that the video captured the spectacle of police beating defenceless Rodney King, yet jurors interpreted the same footage as police acting in self-defence against a threatening suspect (Nesbitt-Larking 2001, 236–237). Similarly, the police and the prosecuting lawyer argued for markedly different interpretations of the bystander video of the Polish immigrant Robert Dziekanski being Tazered by police in Vancouver International Airport on 14 November 2007.

Diverse audiences, like discourse analysts, are actively involved in constructing meanings as they listen to news, watch television, and read newspapers. It is easy to show that mass media audiences are barraged with advertising and urged to consume, to the point that newspapers have been characterized as in the business of "selling audiences to advertisers" rather than selling newspapers to readers. But the image of audiences as dupes of advertisers oversimplifies the interpretive processes through which diverse audiences, in diverse social settings, respond to media texts. Advertising is not always persuasive. Audiences can ignore the message, tune out, turn off the set, switch channels, or construct their own deconstruction of texts. Advertisements that rely on **stereotypes** of women, or racial or ethnic groups, to get a quick message across risk public challenge from savvy media watchers such as the feminist network Media Watch. Audience reactions cannot be read directly from text.

Audiences and Interpretations: The Dynamics of Decoding
Early studies of audience reactions built on class analysis, tracing links between how people respond to media and their lived experiences as workers and families of workers in differing socio-economic positions. Research by Hall (1980, 138) and colleagues at the Centre for Contemporary Cultural Studies (CCCS) at Birmingham University in England suggests that audiences have three main options for decoding news: preferred, negotiated, and oppositional responses.

The preferred or hegemonic response is to accept descriptions of events in news as commonsense. An example would be to accept the representation of union demands for higher wages as inflationary and therefore putting productivity and future jobs at risk. A negotiated response is one that goes along with the general description but feels uncomfortable with it, or sees discrepancies that qualify the interpretation. Workers, for example, might accept the general case that wage demands fuel inflation, but they see the demands of particular workers as reasonable catch-up and so not threatening inflation. An oppositional interpretation rejects the dominant description as false. Workers may see inflation as resulting from corporate greed or government mismanagement, with wage demands as irrelevant. In a multi-channel media universe, people are able to make some choices between media. People who are uncomfortable with mainstream news may stop watching news broadcasts altogether or search for oppositional Internet news sites instead.

Political-economy analysis of tabloid papers like the *Sun* and the *Mirror* in Britain suggests that they are geared to savvy working-class audiences who pride themselves on seeing through the arrogance and pretensions of elites (Allen 1999, 112). While the respectable press projects an aura of top-down authority and believability, the tabloids project an aura of bottom-up common sense and incredulity. Headlines like "Sex Change Woman Makes Self Pregnant! . . . Scientists confirm 'first of a kind' case" or "Elvis is Alive" use the discourse of **science** to poke fun at those who would believe authoritative claims too readily. Tabloids also delight in offering exposés of the improprieties of the mighty.

Research on audience responses show that they cannot be understood simply as a function of class position. Studies in which regular tabloid readers were asked to describe what they see in the papers and why they like reading them have yielded surprising results. Bird found that tabloid readers in Britain were mostly white, female, and middle-aged or older (1992, 113). They described reading tabloids as fun, exciting, interesting or gossipy, and providing a break from the constant flow of bad news in the mainstream press. They expected not balanced reporting but a sense of shared jokes and voyeuristic glimpses into movie stars' romances and government waste, with a sufficient sense of realism to make them titillating (Bird 1992, 204–205).

The downside of tabloids from the perspective of promoting social criticism or empowering readers to struggle for social change is that they depoliticize issues. They tend to explain events primarily in terms of nefarious personal motives, without the in-depth structural criticism of capitalism that might promote resistance rather than resignation (Nesbitt-Larking 2001, 99; Fiske 1992, 57; Allen 1999, 113–114). Their facade of displaying "what people like our readers really think," also works to legitimate much negative thinking, characterized as misogynist, racist, and homophobic (Allen 1999, 116–117; Bird 1992, 204–205; Dahlgren and Sparks 1991, Dahlgren and Sparks 1992; Engel 1996; Franklin 1997; Stephenson and Bromley 1998). Studies of audience responses to characters in television series like Alf Garnet in *Till Death Us Do Part* and Archie Bunker in *All in the Family* reveal that the ironic intentions of the writers may well be lost on audiences (Nesbitt-Larking 2001, 289; Dr Fleur and Ball-Rokeach 1989). The writers' intentions in each case was to discredit **prejudice**, racism, and **sexism** by association with bad-mouthed, bullying characters. But audiences often identified sympathetically with the characters as "blokes like us." Writers of *The Cosby Show* hoped that the portrayal of an attractive and successful African-American family would foster respect and acceptance, but audience members often commented that the show supported their view that black people could make it like everyone else and those who failed had only themselves to blame (Nesbitt-Larking 2001, 290).

These audience studies, in turn, have been faulted methodologically for a flawed conception of attitudes as fixed characteristics that individuals hold, rather than fluid expressions of meaning that are negotiated in situations (Nesbitt-Larking 2001, 293). An old study by LaPiere (1934) demonstrated that what people say they would do is not what they actually do when faced with real situations. Proprietors of hotels and guest houses in America in the 1930s commonly reported in mailed **questionnaires** that they would not give service to Chinese and other non-whites, yet a few months earlier they had each done so. People make choices, form opinions, and negotiate meanings as part of ongoing social situations. Paper-and-pencil responses to anonymous questionnaires are totally different social exchanges from serving someone who walks up to the counter. Likewise, how one responds to characters like Alf Garnet or Archie Bunker in a focus group with strangers in a research laboratory may be very different from watching such shows with friends in a pub or with one's partner and children at home. Questionnaires and focus groups are artificial audiences created by researchers. They cannot reproduce the social relations of family, friends, and colleagues within which people routinely watch television and talk about issues in the media.

Studies of active practices that people use to negotiate shared meanings of news and other programs try to locate their studies as closely as possible in the everyday worlds in which people live and, where possible, to record their conversations. Two early studies in England in the 1980s explored how people use television in their everyday lives (Hobson 1980; Morley 1986). These studies describe many homes where the six o'clock news is on but most of the family are not giving it much attention. Children do not like watching news, alternately describing it as boring, too serious, or too upsetting. Mother is busy getting the evening meal, and the children fed. Father may be the only one relaxing after work, giving some attention to news. Similar scenes occur at nine o'clock. When the familiar music and icons appear to signal news time, they also signal that the entertainment is over and children start getting ready for bed. Newscasters may be trying to be as lively and entertaining as possible but most of the family audiences are giving little attention, unless some particularly gory scenes are being displayed or some issue of immediate local relevance is being aired. One survey that asked people what they could remember from a newscast they had just watched reports most could only recall one or two items out of 20. In the family world of multiple tasks and limited attention spans, the big advantage sports games have is that a roar goes up when big action happens and people can turn to look in time for the instant replays. The time when homemakers are most likely to actually pay attention to the television is during the peace and quiet of the mid-afternoon when the soaps are on. Men are likely to discuss bits of news and sports with their colleagues at work, while homemakers discuss the soaps. As these conversations bring pleasure, people are triggered to give more attention to the programs their friends talk about so they can contribute more to subsequent conversations.

It is through these conversations, as much as through the crafting of signs, symbols, expert commentaries or "talking heads" within the text of the programs that people come to negotiate their opinions on issues and what media messages mean. Barker conceptualizes media as resources on which people draw for their personal identity projects (1999, Ch. 5). When people chat together about characters in soaps or stories in the news, they are simultaneously testing out the boundaries of permissible behaviour among their friends—how they would feel if their child were having a homosexual relationship, their daughter were pregnant or dating some foreign boy, or doing drugs, or whatever. They also negotiate explanations for "deviant" behaviours—why would this character have done that? Could they imagine themselves or people they know doing that? In such conversations people are not passive dupes, repeating textual messages from the media, but active participants in the meaning-construction process, negotiating on an ongoing basis how to think about issues and which programs, channels, newspapers, and magazines are worth paying attention to.

In conclusion, the meaning of texts is undecidable or indeterminate from the texts themselves, but not thereby random or meaningless. Their meaning emerges through the ongoing social relations within which people engage with texts. To ask what a text means is therefore to engage with the exploration of complex social relations.

 # Feminist Theory: Gendered Representation

Feminist media studies explore mass media as arenas of struggle around the politics of how to represent **gender** and feminism. The feminist movement is dedicated to making visible and ultimately changing the patriarchal features of culture and social organization. Mass media are centrally involved in creating, transmitting, and sustaining culture, and they are also potentially important as allies in the struggle for social change. As members of organizations that produce mass media and as audiences of media content, women and men negotiate gendered identities and social practices, and also negotiate how to understand and respond to feminism as a social movement. Feminist research explores issues of **employment equity** within media institutions and barriers that limit access by women to positions of influence. It also studies how media represent cultural expectations and assumptions around **gender roles** in society, especially how the media represent feminism as a social movement committed to changing these roles. Marxist-feminist research explores how profit-driven media corporations and advertising agencies exploit gender and sexuality in the interests of capitalist consumer culture. More radical feminist research draws attention to how media represent issues around sexual exploitation and violence. Contemporary research into how audiences interpret and respond to mass media content challenges the assumption that there is a direct or simple relationship between the images media project and how women and men in different social situations engage them. Media content provides resources that people draw upon as they construct and negotiate a sense of themselves as gendered. Feminist analyses of media contribute to such ongoing gender-identity projects.

Women in Media Organizations

Feminist analysis of employment equity in mass media organizations explores two main issues—the relative positions and ranking of women and men, and the extent to which women's increasing presence in these organizations is influencing cultural messages by mainstream journalism around issues important to women. The anticipation in much feminist work has been that increased access by women to employment in institutions that produce mass media—newspapers, magazines, radio, television, and film—would influence media coverage of issues important to women and thus help to change prevailing cultural beliefs and values. The general impression from this research is that change has been slow and not always positive.

Women are visible in significantly increased numbers in media institutions. Since the mid-1980s, women's organizations like Media Watch and the actors' union ACTRA have been monitoring both sexism and the under-representation of women in media, and put pressure on media organizations to employ more women. By the 1990s fully two-thirds of journalism school graduates in the USA were women. The Canadian Broadcasting Corporation has the highest proportion of women on staff, reflecting the federal government's endorsement of **affirmative action** policies. By 1998, 46 percent of CBC journalists were women, compared with only 11 percent in 1976 (Nesbitt-Larking 2001, 185). Private broadcasters have changed more slowly.

While the number of women employed in media is increasing, their **status** and influence collectively remain low. The general **consensus** is that women are *in* mass media but they do not run them. By the late 1990s, none of the top 25 media outlets in the USA had women at the helm, and few had women in senior management positions. Only 10 percent of upper-level executive positions in Hollywood feature film studios were held by women (Rhode 1997, 10). Rhode cites surveys indicating that male reporters prepared two-thirds of front-page newspaper stories and 85 percent of television reports. A similar survey concluded that by 1998 only one-third of women employed in journalism in the USA were correspondents and they covered 28 percent of news (Vavrus 2002, 169). Job opportunities for journalists in newspapers generally have declined as newspaper chains have centralized their editorials and columnists and have come to rely more on wire services rather than local reporters (Nesbitt-Larking 2001, 351). As more junior staff, women are more directly affected by downsizing than men. Overall, women are over-represented among the part-time, insecure, and freelance staff (firm numbers are difficult to get). Such jobs are also more readily combined with childcare and domestic responsibilities.

Women tend to dominate niches within media enterprises, rather than be evenly distributed. Van Zoonen describes both horizontal and vertical gender segregation in European media, with women concentrated in the less prestigious and less influential roles (1994, 50–62). More women began to be employed in radio as radio became displaced by television. Also more women are employed in local than in higher-status national positions. Women prevail in programs that focus on domestic issues such as children's television and education, consumer and human interest features, and entertainment, while men dominate in political programs, covering foreign and current affairs

and economics. In what seems like a reversal of this pattern, women have formed the majority of news readers in Dutch national television since the 1980s. However, this trend seems to be directly related to changes in editorial policy to identify the news more with human interest stories, events, and personalities. The image they wanted in news anchors was that of a "mum who tucks you in after an emotional day" (Van Zoonen 1994, 60).

Women on the Internet

Historically, patterns of access to the Internet have been highly gendered as well as classed. By the late 1990s women were estimated to comprise only about 15 percent of Internet users, with poor and ethnic minority women being particularly excluded (Millar 1998, 19). Early self-described cyber-feminists like Susan Myborgh (1997) and Sadie Plant (1997) foresaw the Internet as providing women with extraordinary opportunities to become involved politically. They argued that the medium is a potential social leveller that can obscure differences like gender, race, class, and age. Speed rather than brawn is what counts on the Internet, and women's supposedly greater language and communication skills should be an asset in cyber-communications. Cyber-feminist online groups like Geekgrrl, Cybergrrl, and Nerdgrrl set out to support and promote a subversive image of women's empowerment through the net (cited in Millar 1998, 60).

Millar herself, however, was less optimistic, concerned that the hype around the transformative potential of the Internet mimics too closely the mainstream message that the net will give women new opportunities to perform traditional office jobs at home, where they can combine childcare with jobs like transmitting pizza orders (Millar 1998, 21). For a minority of professional women, the Internet can indeed be transformative, allowing them to explore, research, write, communicate, and entertain themselves while in the comfort and security of their homes; but for most women, Millar predicted, the promise of new lifestyles would be limited (Millar 1998, 11). The vision of the Internet as a social leveler is only slowly and partially being realized.

Accessing the Internet   In North America, women working as secretaries were often the first to use computers in business offices, as the technology was adapted to the stereotypically female work role of typing and word processing. But as the power and capacity of computers expanded, men dominated their use (Spender 1995, 166–168; Millar 1998, 49). The proportion of women in computer science programs dropped from 28 percent in 1978 to 13 percent by 1985. UK data showed a similar drop in the proportion of girls studying advanced computer science in school from 22 percent in 1978 to 11 percent in 1993 (Cresser et al. 2001, 462).

In homes and schools boys rather than girls were encouraged to think of computers as the primary toy for them. Girls found themselves pushed aside as boys elbowed their way into first place at the keyboard controls. Early computer games were mainly of the "drop dead variety" (Spender 1995, 180–186) that appealed mostly to boys. Girls who liked relationship games found little to interest them either in the games designed for boys or the Barbie doll games for girls. The result, Spender suggests, was that from an early age girls were pervasively turned off by computers while boys gained the confidence to manipulate the machines. This translates into male-dominated university-level computer science labs with the few women who enter them feeling like interlopers in a men's locker room (Spender 1995, 182; Cresser et al. 2001, 462). Male domination in computer programming in turn translates into far more Internet content being designed by men and slanted towards male interests, including violent video games and pervasive pornography. The utopian vision of the high-technology world represented in computer magazines like *Wired* pictures a world dominated by men (Millar 1998, 90).

Current studies that measure frequency of access by women and men to the Internet suggest that the gender gap in access has closed—with variations depending on whether they use computers mostly at work or at home (Dholakia 2006)—but gender differences in usage remain significant. Among employed women and men in the USA, the gap in competence with information technology has closed, reflecting major advances in the use of computers for office work (Hiroshi and Zavodny 2005). Actual measures of web-navigating abilities suggest there is not much difference across gender, but women still tend to assess their own skills as lower than what men assess theirs (Jackson et al. 2001). This higher sense of anxiety and perceived incompetence in using computers carries over into more restricted and less creative uses of the Internet. A study of first-year students at the University of Illinois in Chicago in 2007 showed that male and female students accessed the Internet about equally, but males were significantly more likely to share creative work—music and videos and photography— on the web. Females were more likely to express creativity in poetry and fiction, but when the level of creativity was controlled, they were less likely to share their creativity online. Only when the researchers also controlled for perceived skill in using the Internet were female students equally likely to share their creative work (Hargittai and Walejko 2008).

Using the Internet Studies of how women and men in North America use the Internet suggest that pre-

existing gender stereotypes are being reproduced in cyberspace. When women and men search the web, they tend to look for different information, packaged in different ways. A comparative study of two general-interest online websites that attract the highest numbers of female and male viewers, iVillage.com and AskMen.com shows that their content closely mirrors that of print magazines (Royal 2008). IVillage focused on parenting and pregnancy, health and fitness, beauty and relationships, home and money, while AskMen focused on business, dating, sports, and gambling. Articles about the Internet featured in iVillage discussed strategies for protecting children from harmful content and the latest filtering software. Educational resources on the Internet were discussed in terms of uses for homeschooling children, women studying while caring for children at home, and home-based work. None of the articles about the Internet on the AskMen site discussed issues of children, family, or educational uses of the Internet. Articles about technology assumed greater knowledge of Internet terminology, and discussed issues in more depth. Articles on both sites covered dating, but the site for women focused on issues of safety, while articles on the men's site focused on picking up cues while dating. The authors conclude that Internet content continues to divide users across gender lines.

Small differences in how women and men use the Internet continue to reflect traditional gender-role stereotypes with women as more expressive and men as more instrumental in orientation. Women use both the telephone and electronic mail more to sustain a larger network of connections with family and friends. The contents of women's emails are more likely to be expressive, sharing thoughts and feelings in ways designed to promote companionship and social support. Men use email less frequently and focus more on tasks and information exchange (Hiroshi and Zavodny 2005; Jackson et al. 2001; Wasserman and Richmond-Abbott 2005; Boneva et al. 2001).

These seemingly traditional forms of letter writing between women on the web are becoming transformed through the networking capacity of the web into more public forms of writing. Women are publishing diaries, "e-zines," or weblogs that combine sharing personal experiences and political views and critiques of patriarchal features of mainstream society (Cresser et al. 2001). E-zines give ordinary women opportunities to express their own voices in public in ways that mainstream media do not allow. Links to webpages of friends and bloggers with similar interests helps to create networks of female authors. These links to real-life institutional emails and to webpages of friends and family members promoted a sense of authenticity in the content. E-zine authors also actively encouraged other women to experience on-line authorship by sharing knowledge and tips about building a site, and linking their sites to web authoring sites and materials. Many of these women authors, however, spoke of feeling intimidated by pervasive sexism and **misogyny** on the web. Their openness and activism in publishing personal diaries associated with their real names and email addresses made them vulnerable to offensive and hostile emails from men attacking and ridiculing the feminist content in e-zines (Cresser et al. 2001, 461–462). Those who openly expressed their desire for women-only sites were vilified as sexist. Another problem that these web authors acknowledged was that access to web publishing was limited to a small percentage of better-off women in Western societies. A quick survey of private home pages of Croatian users revealed 30 women authors compared to 537 men. Of these 30, one third had been closed down and most others were described as little more than classified ads (Cresser et al. 2001, 468). The implication is that even when women do have physical access to computers and the Internet, they do not feel safe or comfortable expressing themselves openly over the Internet. The traditionally conservative and patriarchal Croatian society is not conducive to freedom on the net for women.

Feminist Organizing on the Web

The early cyber-feminist vision of the transformative potential of the Internet as social leveler and as a medium especially suited to women's communication skills has proven stubbornly difficult to achieve. An outreach effort in Champaign County, Illinois, to empower low-income residents—mostly single-parent African-American women—by distributing computers, found that recipients did use them to search for information online, but rather strictly monitored and limited the computers' use by children or people outside the family for fear the computers might be damaged (Mehra et al. 2004). The article makes no mention of recipients using their computers for email or networking, probably because few of their friends had access. It is easier for poor people to acquire a computer than to pay the monthly fees for high-speed Internet. A similar outreach program designed to empower African-American women promoted access and training sessions in Internet uses, and created a SisterNet website with content relevant for their lives, including scenarios for coping with depression, diabetes, and other common diseases. The organizers found, however, that they still needed to rely primarily on printed versions of website content that they could distribute offline through social spaces frequented by black women, like hair salons and churches.

Barriers to the inclusion and empowerment of marginalized communities on the web are formidable, but not insurmountable. Determined feminist organizers have found ways to make the web work for them. As early as 1997, two local African-American women in Philadelphia used the Internet to organize a major political event to highlight and protest devastating social problems affecting the black community (Everett 2004). They networked through the more than 16 million women who used computers at work for processing payroll, word processing, and managing inventory, sales, and reservations to spread information about their proposed Million Women March and rally. Women who learned about the proposals on their office computers printed out materials from the website to distribute to other women who did not have access to computers. The organizers were thus able to effectively bypass the mass media that would not publicize or endorse their events. Everett describes the event in October 1997 as amazingly successful, mobilizing about 1.5 million people, mostly black women for a march on the political centre of Philadelphia. During the same year, feminist activists used the Internet to organize the First CyberSpace International in Germany. They challenged both the **postfeminist liberalism** of mainstream media and the pervasive use of cyberspace as "toys for the boys" with the motto "the personal computer is the political computer" (Everett 2004).

A survey of 50 feminist organizations in North America (Vogt and Chen 2001) reveals that the Internet has become a central tool for the women's movement. It provides a quick and cheap means to lobby decision-makers on feminist issues, to keep drawing attention to important issues, and to mobilize supporters. Websites are useful for attracting new members to the core groups and also for cross-coalition alliances. In some cases, as with Gender Watchers, the website itself functions as the institutional core of the organization, linking members through databases, networks, listservs, and emails. The non-hierarchical and decentralized character of the Internet is particularly appreciated by feminist organizers. The hundreds of websites, with news services, listservs, and bulletins on special interests help both to reduce the mass of information to manageable amounts and to focus efforts on specific and local goals and issues, rather than the mass demonstrations of earlier years. The main concern that women voiced with dependence on the Internet is that poor and less advantaged women have restricted access, especially those in developing countries. Nonetheless, the plethora of feminist websites has helped to overcome some of the middle-class-white-Western bias of early feminist organizing, and to provide a mechanism for including voices and issues from the margins. The Internet also facilitates linking local and global networks on special issues. On his first day in office, January 22, 2001, US President George Bush imposed the "Global Gag Rule" prohibiting any agency receiving funds from the US Agency for

International Development from using its own funds to provide medical counselling or referrals for abortion services. Feminist news services such as Feminist Majority, Gender Watchers, and Women's World News were able to broadcast global responses to this gag rule in a matter of hours.

In summary, women's experiences of the Internet have been mixed. The dominant image is of women's relative exclusion from centres of power that control Internet content, their lower sense of competence in use of computers, a sense of cyberspace as sexist and patriarchal, and a pervasive sense that it perpetuates gender stereotypes. But cyberspace is nonetheless a space that women are appropriating for networking, publishing, and feminist activism. A Google search for feminism on the Internet reveals a growing network of sites that link local activists to global organizations. A number of important sites are listed at the end of the chapter.

Women in Journalism: Conformity or Change?

The hope that more women in journalism might result in more feminist media content has not been widely realized. Women who consider entering the profession of journalism are pressured from the beginning of their training to their entry into careers to conform to the prevailing male ethos of news work. Schools of journalism in the USA rarely offer courses that include a women's studies or feminist perspective on issues. For the most part a postfeminist liberal view prevails. Postfeminist liberalism identifies individual attitudes and career expectations rather than structural or organizational factors as the main explanation for the history of male dominance in journalism. It is women rather than organizations that need to change. Schools of journalism offer few courses specifically on women in journalism and list them as marginal electives rather than required courses. Such courses also tend to focus on topics like how to find female spokespersons on non-traditional issues rather than controversial issues like feminism and patriarchal culture (Van Zoonen 1994, 57). Instructors tend to dismiss or ridicule the idea that there might be an explicitly feminist way to engage in journalism. Studies of male and female students in journalism suggest that they share very similar attitudes, priorities, and preferences, and have similarly stereotyped views of audiences (Tuchman 1996, 13–14). Female journalism students, for example, described themselves as very interested in news yet described most other women as interested only in the human interest and family topics that traditionally fill "women's pages."

When women enter the profession they face strong pressures to conform to the **role models** of professional male colleagues if they are to win respect as part of a team of co-workers (Allen 1999, 130–135). Women working as talk-show hosts were as likely as men to entice sexist comments from celebrities in their pre-interview preparatory work and to avoid any expression of feminism or other radical comments in order to stay in line with the views of stations airing their programs. Women working for newspapers quickly learn to produce the kinds of stories and features that editors prefer. Those with more radical commitments are likely to find their career advancement blocked.

A few women had entered the high-tech world of *Wired* magazine by the late 1990s. The president of *Wired* was a woman, as were 15 percent of the authors (Millar 1998, 85). Their contributions to the magazine, however, were mostly ghettoized in articles that focused on sex, dating and the life stories of a few exceptional women in the computer world. Articles about such women typically represented them as non-threatening to the male turf. The technology theorist Donna Haraway, for example, was presented as "soft-spoken fiftyish, with an infectious laugh and a house full of dogs and cats . . . like a favorite aunt" (Millar 1998, 100). Such articles were vastly outnumbered by articles representing cyberspace as filled with sexually promiscuous women surfing the net in search of hyper-macho men (Millar 1998, 104).

This pervasive resistance to change helps to explain why women leave the profession in higher numbers than men. Despite half or more of journalism school graduates being women, women remain under-represented in news coverage and bylines, women's issues are still not considered newsworthy, they are not routinely sought out as valued sources of information or opinion, are still commonly referenced through their relationship to some man, and are described in ways that draw attention to clothing and appearance (Media Watch 1991).

Openly feminist writers face an uphill struggle getting their work accepted seriously in mainstream media outlets. An obscure study cited by Van Zoonen (1994, 43–45) documents the complex practical struggles by the creators of the strongly feminist script *Cagney and Lacey* to get their work produced. The plotline of *Cagney and Lacey* involves two female police officers who uncover a brothel headed by a "godmother," with male prostitutes and female customers. When first proposed as a film script in 1974, no film studio would produce it, declaring it not feminine, soft, or sexy enough. In 1980 the television network Columbia Broadcasting System (CBS) agreed to produce a scaled-down television movie version, but on the condition that "two sexy young actresses" of the network's choice play the parts. A massive letter-writing campaign and lobbying effort by the editors of Ms magazine encouraged CBS to try out a weekly series based on the characters, but this was cancelled after two episodes.

The network argued that the Cagney character, a single, independent, tough urban cop, was too unfeminine and too "lesbian" to attract viewers and advertisers—this despite excellent audience ratings for the first movie. The study records the struggles by the creators of the series at multiple levels of the network **hierarchy** to get even this grudging support. Network executives became directly involved in script development. A planned episode about abortion was downgraded to a false pregnancy scare, omitting any discussion of options open to a pregnant single woman. The central lesson for feminist writers, Van Zoonen warns (1994, 46), is that for scripts to be accepted, they must be censored to match the comfort level of media networks.

With the advent of cable television and the multichannel digital media universe, some of these pressures have been reduced. Women have developed their own specialty television channels and they have long been producing feature films with feminist content in Studio D, a feminist wing of the Canadian National Film Board. The downside, however, is that specialty channels tend to reach audiences only among the already converted, and it is difficult to attract sufficient advertising dollars to fund expensive productions.

Representations of Women in Mainstream Media

Early surveys of how women are portrayed in mainstream media, particularly in advertising, reveal the typical media woman as "the wife, mother, and housekeeper for men," as a sex object to sell products to men, and otherwise portrayed as spending her time and money on cosmetics, jewellery, and clothes in an effort to be beautiful for men (Van Zoonen 1994, 66; Janus 1996, 7). Women prevail in the home, where they cook, launder, and clean, while men give orders and advice and eat meals. If portrayed as employed at all, women are shown in a handful of stereotyped jobs. The list of adjectives associated with male characters on children's television are aggressive, constructive, knowledgeable, active, independent, brave, strong, dominant, loyal, impatient. The qualities listed for female characters are deferent, silly, weak, overemotional, dependent on males, affectionate, romantic, and passive (Janus 1996). Magazines aimed at teenagers push images of heterosexual femininity, leisure, and consumption (McRobbie 1991).

Representations of female roles on the Internet remain overwhelmingly traditional. Cyber-games marketed for girls and women favour designing fashion for blond Barbie doll models. Female roles in games marketed for boys and men are predominantly violent warriors or aggressive femme

fatales—seductive, sexual, and potentially dangerous women waiting to be tamed (Millar 1998, 100–108).

Marxist-feminist reading of these media images argues that relations of patriarchal capitalism, rather than sexist cultural values, provide the stronger explanation for how women are represented in capitalist mass media (Janus 1996, 8; Tuchman 1996, 12). Media may simply reflect the reality of women's limited and subordinate occupational roles and their primary responsibility for domestic work. Comic images of women as flighty and scatterbrained may reflect the realities of frazzled and fragmented working lives of homemakers with young children (Perkins 1996, 22). The relevant comparison is not between women and men in media, but women's actual distribution in the labour-force and how they appear in media. By implication, as more women become business executives in real life, business newspapers are more likely to represent them in such roles.

An alternative Marxist argument is that the pervasive association of women with mass media images of home, family, leisure, pleasure, tourism, and luxury cars works as an emotional safety valve for the masses of working men in boring, dehumanizing, and alienating jobs. Media images of women provide a diversion from the realities of exploitative, profit-driven, corporate capitalism, much as images of exotic oriental women and unspoiled beaches in tourist brochures mask the realities of neo-colonialism (Williams 1996). Capitalist consumer culture is about escapism, not realism, as are the tabloid pin-up girls, the "women's weepies," and popular romance fiction.

Advertising Feminist research highlights how advertising mimics soft-core pornography in representing women as sexual objects for men, with images focusing on legs, lips, and silky skin to sell cosmetics and fashion. Caribbean women in exotic and provocative clothing adorn tourism advertisements, and women dressed as geisha girls offer tea in advertisements for Japanese Air Lines. Advertisements that associate ultra-slim models with food and diet products are ubiquitous in magazines aimed at female readers. Ads in the high-technology magazine *Wired* commonly use images of a Greek goddess or celestial muse, or blond, white cyber-Barbies in traditional roles of teacher, mother, or librarian, inspiring young people to consume computer technologies.

Tabloid newspapers flaunt their models of bikini-clad and topless women, represented as sexy and fun, a tonic against gloomy news and feminists or "women-libbers" who threaten the fun of ordinary decent folk (Allen 1999, 144–145). British tabloid the *Sun*, with its famous full-page topless female models on page 3, has a daily circulation of 3.8 million copies, dwarfing the circulation of the more serious *Times* at 0.8 million and the Guardian at 0.4 million (Allen 1999, 112).

Allen qualifies the implication that the tabloid press is inherently more sexist than the "quality," or mainstream, press, suggesting that in the latter, sexism may be more insidious because it is less obvious or explicit (1999, 147; Bird 1992, 76–77). Allen cites such practices as male-centred naming of women in the news—as wife, girlfriend, or mistress of some male; using gendered descriptive terms like a woman's age, physical appearance, and marital status (e.g., "the 34-year-old blond mother of three") to refer to women, but not to men; and using the pronoun "he" for people in general, or "man-on-the-street" for public opinion. All of these practices tend to trivialize news about women and encourage readers to adopt the preferred masculine orientation to the news stories. A host of discursive practices **typify** the reader of news and public affairs as male and readers of soft "human-interest" stories and domestic issues like health, fashion, and beauty as female.

Media Coverage of Women's Issues

Representations of Feminism
The meanings associated with feminism and the women's movement are politically charged and hotly contested, with activists and anti-feminists both struggling to foreground certain meanings while obscuring others. Media representations have far-reaching implications for levels of political support. Media privilege what Vavrus (2002, Ch. 1) terms a *postfeminist* individualist and white-middle-class elitist meaning of feminism while obscuring the continuing disadvantaged position of women as a **gender-class** within society, and rejecting the central feminist concern with collective political action for structural change. The prevailing media view is that feminism is dead, or at least outdated because the playing field is now level. Successful individual women are highlighted and valorized, which implies that women who do not succeed have only themselves to blame. It is not antithetical to feminism in the sense of being pro-**patriarchy** or advocating male dominance over women, but it denounces feminism as excessive or irrelevant. This individualist mindset incorporates certain goals of second-wave feminism—the right of women to work in jobs with good salaries formerly reserved for men and the notion of free choice in parenting. However, the structural conditions that make such choices far from free or available for most women are not part of the picture. Women who suffer economically, and especially women on welfare, are marginalized as inadequate, personal failures.

The more overtly anti-feminist edge to this media representation of feminism blames the women's movement and feminism for promoting unrealistic expectations among women that result in widespread dissatisfaction and stress. News stories highlight harried women exhausted from juggling paid work and parenting, with the favoured solution being for women to cut back on career aspirations and public responsibilities in favour of domestic concerns, at least until children reach college age (Rhode 1997, 13; Crittenden 1996). Feminists are criticized for elevating careers over family and thus betraying both women and children and going against women's essential nature as mothers.

Feminism is also held blameworthy for promoting a strident "political correctness" that makes relations between women and men more difficult, complicating normal flirting relations in the office with the spectre of sexual harassment charges. Ideally, postfeminist liberals argue, liberated women should expect to handle such interpersonal disagreements themselves. Feminists are characterized as exaggerating problems, representing women as victims, and undermining liberating sexual relations (McClusky 1997, 57). Caricatures of feminists in *Time* magazine during the 1970s and 1980s depicted them as "bra-burning, strident, humourless, extremists, hairy-legged, and probably lesbians" (Rhode 1997, 14). Van Zoonen recounts efforts by the Dutch media to find "feminists" who would denounce Madonna's CD and book *Erotica* as pornographic, with the intention that feminists would be denounced in turn for their narrow-mindedness towards popular culture (1994, 1). When no self-defining feminist could be found to present such views, the program was cancelled. Given such mass media representation of feminism, there is little wonder that a survey conducted by Crittenden on USA college campuses found few women willing to apply the label to themselves (Vavrus 2002, 173). *Wired* magazine similarly denounced any feminist writers who questioned the ubiquity of pornography on the Internet as firebrand feminists who threaten the freedom of the Internet with the thought police (Millar 1998, 132).

Obscured or distorted by this hegemonic media representation of feminism are defining objectives of the second-wave feminist movement. These include fighting for specific cultural, occupational, economic, and other structural changes needed at a societal level to address the struggle women experience in balancing workplace and domestic responsibilities in ways other than privatization of women in the home, and which recognize and redress the systemic causes of the stunning levels of poverty in single-parent, female-headed households. Defined in these terms, the playing field upon which women and men supposedly compete for careers appears far from level. Also obscured in postfeminist liberalism is the women's movement's struggle to redress the continuing systemic under-representation of women in positions of political and economic decision-making and influence in social institutions, including institutions of mass media. Also obscured are the efforts within the feminist movement to encompass the ethnic and racialized character of gendered disadvantages, to recognize the multi-faceted oppression experienced by First Nations women and other women of colour, including their greatly disproportionate vulnerability to sexual violence. Women who have been active in these collective struggles for social justice find little of themselves in the depoliticized mainstream media representations of feminism. A cartoon in *Wired* magazine depicted a hippy-style woman happily working at her computer at 4:00 a.m. She wears a T-shirt emblazoned with the motto "Take back the Night." The feminist movement's political movement to empower women to take the night back from sexual predators that make it dangerous for women to walk the streets alone at night is dumbed down to an invitation to women to play on their computers at night.

Media Representation of Violence against Women

The feminist movements of the 1960s and 1970s fought to expose the prevalence of violence against women. Contemporary feminist media research focuses on continuing struggles around the politics of representation of domestic violence, date rape, and sexual assault, in both news coverage and drama. The feminist perspective argues that much of this violence is grounded in pervasive cultural values that sexualize women's bodies as available for male pleasure, especially when these bodies are non-white. Media coverage frequently feeds into these cultural values by normalizing images of red-blooded men while sanctioning "loose" female behaviour. Internet games often feature violent sexuality as fun, pitting the player against highly sexualized bad girls, wearing studded leather breast supports and chains, waiting to be overcome by skilled cyber-warriors (Millar 1998, 104–105). One game, Night Trap, invites players to join with vampires attacking nearly nude girls (Millar 1998, 133).

Media representations of teenage sexual behaviour and date-rape scenarios typically present boys as naturally sexually active and assertive, and girls as naturally more reticent about sex. Girls who "go too far" by initiating sex tend to be presented as deviant and asking for trouble (Higgins and Tolman 1997). These authors cite an article in *Newsweek* (Yoffe 1991) about parents who were shocked when girls phoned their teenaged sons, bought them gifts, and chatted over the phone about their sexual desires. Adjectives used in the article to describe the girls include: "obsessed," "confused," "emotionally disturbed," "bizarre," "abused," "troubled," and their behaviour as "bewildering" and "frightening." Yet what the girls are doing, suggest Higgins and Tolman, is no more than what would be considered natural for boys. Date rape is typically represented as miscommunication rather than crime, with girls being blamed for

not communicating effectively or for giving off mixed messages through provocative behaviour. American media gave extensive coverage to a study suggesting that date-rape advisers on campuses exaggerate the issue and spread unwarranted fears among female students (Higgins and Tolman 1997). Ironically, media promote these fears by sensationalizing the statistically rare crimes of lone women who are raped by strangers in public places, while downplaying the more typical cases of women raped by male acquaintances (Daly and Chasteen 1997). The implicit message is that women need male protection and should not go out alone.

News-media coverage of sexual assault crimes commonly reinforce the "Madonna or whore" myth—either the woman is an innocent virgin and hence the man a depraved monster, or the woman is of loose morals and she drove the man to lust (Allen 1999, 150). The explanation of "individual madmen" prevailed in media representation of Marc Lepine, who murdered 14 women at École Polytechnique in Montreal in 1989, largely discounting feminist theories that his behaviour was an extreme expression of a more pervasive anti-feminist cultural backlash in society. More generally, media coverage warns women that they are vulnerable and should naturally take precautions, or else they should expect what happens. Such coverage, Allen suggests, may even incite violence against women by normalizing it. Women who are involved in prostitution, or who frequent areas of cities where prostitution commonly occurs, are largely represented as asking for whatever violence they suffer.

News coverage of sexual assault varies greatly with the ethnic-racial-class characteristics of the individuals involved, both in terms of the likelihood of the assault being noted, and in terms of associated explanations. Media attention is most likely when the victim is a white, middle-class woman and the alleged assailant black, and explanations are structured in terms of generic race and class characteristics (Russo 1997, 250). In contrast, when the assailant is white and middle class, personalized explanations, in terms of individual life stories, are foregrounded. Crimes against women of colour, who are proportionally the most vulnerable to violence, are least likely to get media attention. New York tabloid newspapers highlighted a rash of rapes and murders committed against white middle-class women in 1993, while a similar number of rapes against women of colour were virtually ignored (Russo 1997, 270). The story of an African-American woman gang-raped and murdered by a group of young men in her neighbourhood was barely mentioned, while neighbourhood alerts were widely circulated in the media after an attack on a woman in a white neighbourhood (Russo 1997, 255). Non-white women who are working as prostitutes are doubly **stigmatized** and get little sympathy from either police or media.

In Canada, three middle-class white high school boys who raped and murdered a Native woman working as a prostitute were largely exonerated in press coverage. The explanation of red-blooded boys celebrating their high school graduation prevailed (Razack 1998). This standard representation began to change significantly only with publicity around the trial of Robert William Pickton, who, after body parts of some 26 different women were unearthed on his pig farm, was convicted in 2007 of murdering six women.

Anti-Feminist Media Backlash The greater use of sexual harassment regulations by women to challenge behaviour they find offensive has generated significant responses of anger and fear, which find ready expression in media. American mass media coverage of the US Senate's consideration of African-American Judge Clarence Thomas's nomination for the US Supreme Court in 1991 overwhelmingly supported him against charges that he should be disqualified because of a history of sexually harassing

Mainstream media widely asserted that Sonia Sotomayor displayed racist and feminist bias for suggesting that her background as an impoverished Latino woman would be an asset in the US Supreme Court.

behaviour. Anita Hill, herself an African-American and a law professor formerly employed under Clarence Thomas, recounted numerous incidents of behaviour she labelled sexual harassment, including explicit sexual comments and overtures. A media frenzy resulted, with most of the mainstream press joining Senate committee members in vilifying Hill, characterizing her as a vindictive, over-sexed temptress, and a calculating, frustrated spinster whose amorous designs on her superior had been rebuffed, and who was seizing an opportunity to bring a big man down. Thomas, allegedly with coaching from Bush aides, discredited the charges by characterizing them as "the high-tech lynching of a black male" (Vavrus 2002, Ch. 2).

Media commentary generated an air of crisis and panic around the charges, suggesting that democracy itself would be threatened if this private and personal matter were permitted to sway the Senate's decision. The institutional integrity of the United States political system would be threatened if a frustrated spinster could impugn the reputation of a top official. Furthermore, all black professionals would be threatened if Thomas were symbolically lynched in this manner. All men in positions of authority would be at risk if any girl with a petty grudge could use harassment claims to bring a man down. Media coverage reduced sexual harassment from a public issue of rampant sexism in Washington institutions to a private disagreement between Hill and Thomas that should not be relevant to public office.

Media coverage of Senate hearings for the nomination of Latino lawyer Sonia Sotomayor for appointment to the US Supreme Court in 2009 took more seriously the argument that despite her impeccable qualifications she might be unsuitable for the position because of racist and feminist bias. Sotomayor had commented in 2001 that her background as a Latino and a woman who had grown up in poverty would help her to bring more nuanced judgment to the Supreme Court than white males who lacked that richness of experience.

Campus Media The politics of representing harassment have been played out in American college campus media, generating similar, if less explosive, backlash against feminism (McCluskey 1997). After one campus fraternity house was closed following multiple complaints of residents harassing female students, local media gave extensive coverage of counter complaints that the closure violated fraternity rights to freedom of association. McCluskey lists a series of **double standards** evident in media commentaries on victim narratives by college women and men. One anecdote of a woman being raped on campus was balanced by two anecdotes of men falsely accused. Feminists were criticized for whipping up a false sense of women as victims, while men were defended for whipping up fears that men would become victims of false accusations. Campus media challenged the weak methodology of surveys that tried to count the number of women claiming to have been raped but did not challenge the weak evidence provided by men that false accusations are widespread. Articles shamed privileged college women as whiners for complaining when the real victims are downtrodden poor women who have no chance of attending college, yet the articles failed to mention that the men doing the criticizing were themselves elite white college men. Another article criticized women as weak for seeking legal redress for harassment that they ought to be able to deal with themselves, yet it went on to support legal redress for men who felt victimized by feminist displays of date-rape posters and to support soldiers who expressed fear of possibly having to share communal showers with gay men. McClusky concludes that victims' stories are acts of power as well as **powerlessness**. Harassment was formerly only a problem for women. Men paid attention to harassment only as they began to realize that their careers might be damaged by harassment charges.

Radio and television talk-shows in the US have provided another venue for public expression of strident anti-feminist backlash sentiments (Williams 1997). Surveys suggest that the majority of listeners and participants in anti-feminist shows hosted by Rush Limbaugh and Howard Stern are white males. The prevailing sentiments expressed are that white males have been reduced to an oppressed minority within America, with no power and no opportunities. Blame for this situation is placed on a combination of feminism, black power, and immigration, all bolstered through discriminatory affirmative action programs.

In summary, the picture that emerges of mainstream media representations of feminism, particularly in the USA, is that at best it projects a postfeminist liberal interpretation of the feminist movement as having outlived its usefulness, and at worst it portrays feminism as a subversive movement that is undermining liberal values of equality and freedom.

Finding Feminist Voices: Mass Media for Women

A critique from within feminist cultural studies challenges not the findings as such but the limited frames within which mainstream media are viewed and the resulting overly unified image that emerges (Van Zoonen 1994, Ch. 5). While women as feature writers, journalists, and editors are under-represented in mass media at large, they are over-represented in certain mass media genres aimed more directly at women, particularly daytime television with games, talk shows, and soap operas; women's magazines; and romantic fiction or "women's weepies" (Van Zoonen 1994,

66). What researchers have found therein is a complex mixture of traditional "feminine" fare with features on diet, fashion, cosmetics, cooking, and the like, illustrated with ultra-slim models, but also a strong representation of alternative feminist discourse around a range of topics of central concern to women. Hanigsberg (1997) surveyed a wide selection of popular American women's magazines focusing on beauty and fashion, including *Allure*, *Elle*, *Essence*, *Glamour*, *Self*, and *Vogue*, with circulation figures in the millions. She concludes that feminism is alive and well, even ubiquitous in these magazines, although not often explicitly labelled as such. Alongside the fluff and beauty and "how to get a man and keep him" advice, are serious articles with strong feminist content on women's health, the female condom, girls and education, violence against women, sexism in the justice system, new birth control methods being stalled by right-wing pro-life forces, the kind of treatment women receive in courts when they are victims of spousal abuse or rape, new rape laws, gender bias in prisons, and a host of other issues prominent in feminist politics. Hanigsberg also credits *Essence* with consistent coverage of women and race issues, and excellent critical coverage of the Hill-Thomas hearings.

Soap operas on daytime television are another genre commonly dismissed as fluff, but a number of these have dramatized issues like date rape, sexual assault by an acquaintance, and domestic violence and have incorporated strongly feminist analysis. The serialized multiple plot lines that unfold over months, rather than a couple hours of a regular movie, permit exploration of long-term trauma to victims who suffer flashbacks, emotional stress, and damaged future relationships. Brooks (1997), an African-American lawyer and law professor, praises the level of legal realism found in these soaps, the detailed explanation of limits to probing of victims' past sexual practices under rape-shield legislation, and presentation of feminist legal reasoning, often articulated through the character of a female defence lawyer. Brooks notes that her female law students typically rated soap operas as legally realistic while male students lambasted them as ridiculous. The difference in readings, she suggests, is that daytime soaps focus on aspects of law that matter to women—laws that offer little protection from sexual violence and that can deprive mothers of custody of their children. Her female students could relate to these issues far more readily than her male students. The soap opera genre also regularly explores changes in contemporary family forms: employed mothers, single parents, interracial dating, and custody battles—again incorporating much feminist analysis (Karpin 1997). Advice columns in magazines and mainstream newspapers also mix culturally traditional messages about being a good wife, mother, and daughter-in-law with strongly feminist-inspired advice on how to get out of abusive domestic relationships, complete with information on how to contact women's help centres and transition houses, and warnings to keep escape plans secret because abusers are control freaks who can act in dangerously irrational ways.

Docudramas, or made-for-television movies that dramatize stories from the news, provide another avenue for feminist dramatic productions. They are far cheaper to produce than blockbuster Hollywood feature films, and can still reach wide audiences. The docudrama *The Burning Bed* was watched by an estimated 75 million viewers (Rapping 1997). It dramatized the story of Francine Hughes, a battered wife who set her husband's bed on fire after 17 years of abuse. She was acquitted of murder on grounds of temporary insanity.

The fact that most of these feminist writings and productions are not labelled "feminist," and that they appear in traditionally feminine contexts like glamour magazines and soap operas may enable them to reach mass audiences among women who do not think of themselves as feminists.

Postmodern Feminism: Dethroning the Text

Postmodern feminist research does not generally dispute the descriptive findings of content analysis, but it does challenge any simple extrapolation from content to effect on audiences. Images that advertisers intend to arouse feelings of pleasure and leisure in the service of consumption may backfire on feminist audiences who read such images as sexual exploitation. They may also be read as fun and critics dismissed as prudish. Surveys suggest that many tabloid newspaper readers are white, female, and middle-aged or older, who see the daily pin-up girls as affirming values of family life, fun, and pleasure (Bird 1992, 113; Allen 1999, 114). Romance novels, with their stories of tough masculine heroes who crumble under the love of heroines, can be read as political tracts that exploit the dissatisfactions of housewives, offering them pseudo-distractions to disguise their low status and limited leisure in patriarchal societies (Radway 1984). The problem with such readings is that they set feminists apart from and above other readers, suggesting that women ought not to enjoy tabloids, romance novels, or glamour magazines, or that if they do they suffer from **false consciousness** (Van Zoonen 1994, 113). Van Zoonen's point is that several readings are simultaneously possible. She gives the example of two films starring Madonna: *Gentlemen Prefer Blondes* and *Desperately Seeking Susan*. Both can be read simply as soft-core pornography, selling women's bodies to men for male pleasure. But they can also be enjoyed by women for their focus on friendship and sexual desire among women (Van Zoonen 1994, 95–96). Madonna allows oppositional scope for women to enjoy their own bodies and to return male gaze. In short,

these nuanced and oppositional readings of texts demonstrate that neither media nor culture is a closed system. Audience responses cannot simply be predicted from media content or from cultural norms. A deeper study is needed of the active practices through which people in different social situations decode available texts.

Postmodern Feminism and Audience Studies

The postmodern feminist perspective focuses on how people generate, sustain, and change their sense of themselves as gendered persons. In this view, people are not socialized by mass media into conformity to certain predefined gender patterns. Rather, people draw selectively on media content as resources for thinking about themselves. Research explores how people engage with media representations, including how they make choices on what to read or what to watch on television, and how they relate it to their own lives.

Audiences, like producers, are actively involved in the social construction of meaning. People in different life situations choose and respond to productions differently, seeing different elements as compelling or irrelevant, and finding different representations realistic or ridiculous. Initial readings are also seen as tentative, open to revision as people talk over first impressions with others.

Early audience studies of the 1980s, which focused mostly on housewives, suggest that both men and women make highly stereotyped choices (Hobson 1980; Morley 1986). Women said they preferred to watch the afternoon soap operas and programs about the "women's world," and actively avoided watching programs about the "men's world" of news, current affairs, scientific, and documentary programs, dismissing them as boring and depressing. In the micropolitics of households, men typically controlled the channel changer and chose the programs. The initial interpretations of these data offered by Hobson and Morley was of pervasive conformity to **gender-role socialization** that sets women's place in the home. Van Zoonen, however, reads a more complex self-representation into the women's response. By insisting that they only watch programs about their "women's world" and rejecting those about the "men's world," these homemakers are making powerful statements about themselves as homemaker-women and as feminine women, in front of interviewer and husband. Through their program preferences they construct and project a particular kind of gendered identity. Also, watching soap operas provides resources for particular kinds of conversations that women share regularly with other women, and that may from time to time have profoundly feminist content and implications. Women actively debate issues of **morality**, ethics, and sexuality built into the plot lines, negotiating among themselves the permissibility of certain sexual identities, such as being a lesbian or being sexually adventurous (Barker 1999, 128–140). They also explore reasons or explanations for such behaviour, including the mitigating circumstances and social pressures that influence choices of individual characters. Barker concludes that the young women in the study are actively creating meaning, and also actively engaged in fashioning themselves as moral and ethical people. A study of young women from South Asian and Caribbean immigrant families in London, England, reveals a similar fascination with soap opera characters and plots (Ross 2000). In their lengthy discussions and arguments over the realism and permissibility of behaviour dramatized by immigrant character parts, they too negotiated their sense of themselves in relation to complex diasporic cultural identities.

In conclusion, feminist media studies are difficult to summarize because they are so diverse. The prevailing image of mass media is that they are gendered cultural organizations, embedded in capitalist, profit-driven enterprises that are dependent on advertising for the bulk of their revenues. As such, mass media reflect a hegemonic postfeminist liberal ideology that largely dismisses the feminist movement as outdated, or even threatening to mainstream liberal values. Yet in contradictory ways, mass media remain critically important as conduits for disseminating feminist awareness.

CONCLUSION

The functionalist perspective focuses attention on how mass media express and transmit the shared cultural values and stock of social and political information that function to integrate modern nation states and to make democratic participation possible. Canadian studies explore the special mandate of the CBC to integrate English and French Canada and to safeguard Canadian ownership of mass media in an effort to mitigate the impact of pervasive American broadcasting on Canadian cultural identity, especially in the multimedia and multi-channel universe. The increasing importance of the Internet as a potentially borderless source of news and entertainment has changed in fundamental ways the power of governments and media corporations to manage information. Citizen journalists and commentators can use the Internet to get around traditional media gatekeepers. Amateur artists have the means to publicize, market, and share creative culture independently from corporate entertainment giants. Corporate elites in turn are pressuring governments to bring new forms of law, order, and control to cyberspace.

Political economy theory focuses attention more directly on mass media as multimedia entertainment and infotainment business corporations, primarily interested in generating profits through selling audiences to advertisers. The culture that mass media transmit is overwhelmingly that of corporate business elites, saturated with the ideology of neo-liberalism. Internet sites have increasingly taken on the character of corporate businesses, trading on the stock exchange and centrally focusing on attracting advertising. Business corporations in the entertainment industry are imposing their own forms of control over Internet content through copyright laws and increasingly through digital codes that tether electronic devices to their vendors. Alternative left-wing publications and Internet sites that challenge hegemonic corporate business thinking do exist, but they are financially strangled by their inability to attract corporate advertising dollars.

Social constructionist theory shifts the focus away from the structural **determinism** implicit in both functionalist and political economy analysis of the media to highlight the active practices of people inside and outside media corporations. Through these practices, meanings are variously taken up, ignored, challenged, resisted, and changed. Research in this tradition explores how journalists generate and frame what becomes constituted as "news" and how these news-making processes are negotiated through ongoing interaction between journalists, politicians, and celebrities in the media fishbowl. Collaborative Internet news sites have revolutionized the processes through which news gets produced. The existence of these sites is in turn pushing mainstream media to be more interactive with their audiences. **Interpretive theory** reminds us further that audiences, no less than producers of mass media content, are involved in determining the meaning of content. Audiences do not simply absorb content. They actively negotiate it.

Feminist theory explores the gendered character of mainstream mass media and the Internet and the politics of the representation of gender and feminism. Women increasingly work in mainstream media but rarely seem able or willing to significantly influence its content. Women have lagged behind men in access to the Internet, and much of what they find there mirrors traditional stereotypes of women's domestic roles and interests. Feminist networking forms a small but significant component of otherwise conservative or overtly sexist Internet content. Feminism as a social movement has been largely incorporated into mainstream media as postfeminist liberalism, an ideological standpoint that takes as given women's equality rights, while ignoring or deriding more politicized, activist forms of feminism. Radical feminist voices can be found in specialized Internet websites and magazines by those who know where to look. Audience studies suggest that radical feminist thought can also be found in unexpected places like afternoon television soap operas and embedded in magazines designed for homemakers, where they dramatize critical issues of domestic abuse, sexual violence, divorce, and women living in poverty unable to care adequately for their children. The insights of interpretive theory holds equally for feminist theory—that the meanings associated with mass media content cannot simply be determined from the text. Rather, they are fluid and continually negotiated in the contexts of women's everyday lives.

SUGGESTED READINGS

Stuart Allen's book *Online News* (2006) gives an excellent overview of the rise of Internet journalism and its impact on how news is represented. Chapter 7, "Participatory Journalism," looks in detail at collaborative online news sites like IndyMedia, OhmyNews, and Wikinews, and their struggle to combine openness with quality and accuracy of coverage. The chapter explores also how these online sites have promoted greater interaction between mainstream journalists and audiences.

Michael Barker's article "Blame the Media" (2009) offers a critical political-economy analysis of power relations that make it almost impossible for leaders on the political left to consistently present a progressive political alternative to capitalism in mainstream media.

Melanie Millar's book *Cracking the Gender Code: Who Rules the Wired World?* (1998) is a somewhat dated but insightful look at the patriarchal character of cyberspace. Chapter 3, "The 'Wired' Machine," gives a detailed exposé of the hyper-masculine content of a magazine designed for people interested in computers.

The article "Feminisms and the Internet" by Vogt and Chen (2001) explores how feminist organizations have found ways to harness the power of the Internet to promote women's organizations, both locally and globally.

QUESTIONS

1. In what ways are mass media considered essential for modern democratic nation states like Canada? How have these roles changed with the advent of the Internet?

2. What special roles does the Canadian Broadcasting Corporation play in relation to Canadian media? Explain the distinction between media in Canada and Canadian media.

3. How have governments worked to impose order and control over the Internet?

4. Explain the mechanisms through which corporate interests structure media content, even when corporate elites do not exercise direct influence.

5. How are Internet sites increasingly being drawn into business corporations? Explain ways in which business interests stifle culture on the Internet.

6. Explain the active practices through which journalists generate newsworthy events.

7. Explain the active practices through which citizen-journalists create and manage news on the Internet. How does the work of mainstream and Internet journalism differ?

8. Explain the concept of the "undecidability of text." How are studies of audiences insightful but also limited as means to understand how people in their everyday lives interpret media content?

9. What key factors seem to explain why the increase in the numbers of women working in journalism has not significantly influenced mass media content?

10. In what ways has the Internet been used to promote coverage of issues important to women? In what ways is the Internet limited as a tool for promoting issues important to women?

WEB LINKS

CBC Digital Archives: Marshall McLuhan, The Man and His Message

http://archives.cbc.ca/arts_entertainment/media/topics/342/

This CBC site provides an archived library of 10 television clips and eight radio clips of interviews with McLuhan. These clips range from 1 minute, 33 seconds to 18 minutes. Just a few of the clips and pods are "Gzowski Interviews McLuhan," "McLuhan for the Masses," "Oracle of the Electric Age," and "McLuhan and Mailer Go Head to Head."

Vodpod Marshall McLuhan on the TODAY Show

http://vodpod.com/watch/51681-marshall-mcluhan-on-the-today-show

This link brings us what McLuhan has to say about using television as a medium for a political debate. He considers the "characters who scripted the show." This is a brief but interesting analysis by McLuhan of the "misuse of the television medium" and a "scripted" debate by those "experts" "who have no idea what the TV medium is made out of."

National Film Board
www.nfb.ca

The Canadian government-owned National Film Board of Canada brings a diverse offering of Canadian documentaries, animations, alternative dramas, trailers, playlists, upcoming online releases, and "hundreds of films, anytime, anywhere, for free." The NFB collection includes over 13 000 Canadian productions. The NFB has over 409 French films and 695 English.

National Arts Centre
www.nac-cna.ca

The Canadian government-owned National Arts Centre provides coverage of upcoming events and opportunities to purchase tickets. The site brings short YouTube clips of upcoming events such as orchestra (e.g. *The Radiance of Mozart*), English theatre (*The Drowsy Chaperone*), French theatre (*Littoral*), and dance (Margie Gillis, *Thread*). This site gives sociology students the opportunity to explore Canadian arts and culture as defined by the Canadian government.

Canadian Broadcasting Corporation
www.cbc.ca

The Canadian government-owned CBC provides information under the subheadings of news, sports, entertainment, radio, TV, and religion. This site links to regional news, kids' games, CBC books, music, CBC documentaries, CBC digital archives, and arts and entertainment stories. Archived stories include "Leonard Cohen in Three Acts," "Changing Climate, Changing Trees," "Brian Steward: Beyond Images," "The Principal and the Anthem," and "Immigration/Diversity: Imagine Adoption's Troubling Legacy."

YouTomb
http://youtomb.mit.edu/youtube/IS5fkO9uE3A

This site's claim is that it is a "research project of MIT Free Culture whose purpose is to investigate what kind of videos are subject to takedown notices due to allegations of copyright infringement with particular emphasis on those for which the takedown may be mistaken." *The Boys of St. Vincent* was removed from YouTube. The notice "This video has been removed due to terms of use violation" has been posted.

Torrentz
www.torrentz.com/f025794500264e96056d24e9c6d0597cfa2b43fd

Torrentz is a site that provides movie downloads. Torrentz download locations for *The Boys of St. Vincent,* for example, are: FastDownload.com, Binverse.com, Vertor.com, thepiratebay.org, torrenthound.com, and monova.org.

Manufacturing Consent: Noam Chomsky and the Media
http://video.google.com/videoplay?docid=-5631882395226827730

This Canadian documentary running 167 minutes explores the media and its dissemination of propaganda.

Office of the Commissioner of Lobbying of Canada
Lobbyist Registry Tutorials
http://29040.vws.magma.ca/help-aide.php?page=cer-4&lang=eng
*Create a new in-house corporate registration: Step 4, corporate lobbyists.*This is an audiovisual step-by-step guide for people/companies that want to contribute to/lobby political parties and public office holders.

Online Video Guide (OVG)
www.ovguide.com/ http://tv-links.cc/movie/wag-the-dog.htm

This site allows the user to download full-length movies and TV shows, radio broadcasts; games; NASA news and stories; Korean, Taiwanese, and Japanese dramas; cartoons; and the official Comedy Central site—complete TV episodes, a forum, and a blog. Searching *Wag the Dog* brings the user to a page where the movie can be downloaded free from many different sources. *Wag the Dog* is a movie about a US president, a Hollywood producer, and a Washington spin doctor.

All in the Family—Archie Bunker Meets Sammy Davis
www.youtube.com/watch?v=O_UBgkFHm8o

This short video clip brilliantly shows the embedded discourse of racism and prejudice—and "tolerance."

MBW MoviesbyWomen.com
http://moviesbywomen.com

Movies by Women is a site dedicated to recognizing the works of women directors. "The mission of the group was to attain equality for women in film and television, and all media now known or hereafter devised, worldwide, in perpetuity." The databank provides a list of female-directed movies including *28 Days, Abduction: The Megumi Yokota Story, Bend it Like Beckham, Daughters of the Sun, Fast Times at Ridgemont High, God Sleeps in Rwanda,* and *Nuyorican Dream.*

Portrayal of Women in Indian TV Serials
www.youtube.com/watch?v=v6N7g90zC80

Dr. Abhilashi Kumari, Dr. Anita Dighe, and Sabina Kidwai discuss how the portrayal of and attitude towards Indian women have changed since the 1980s and the influx of "soaps and serials". "Programs watched by so many women cannot be ignored."

Tennessee Guerilla Women
http://guerillawomentn.blogspot.com/2008/05/
media-misogyny-tsunami-of-feminist.html
"Media Misogyny: A Tsunami of a Feminist Backlash Brewing."This link highlights the media's representation of women and the backlash against feminism. Also, "Sexism Sells, but We're Not Buying It" is a short but important look at the male view of women in power . . . or not.

WMC The Women's Media Center
www.womensmediacenter.com/sexism_sells.html

This site, led by "Emmy-winning journalist, writer, and producer Carol Jenkins, works with the media to ensure that women's stories are told and women's voices are heard." WMC uses social networks such as Facebook and Twitter to send out their messages. U.S. News and World Report, The Huffington Post, and Yahoo.com as well as the blog Majority Post are sources linking to WMC. *Progressive Women's Voice* trains women for media work, while *SheSource.org* is a database of over 500 women experts in "all fields." The library holds 366 documents, including "My Subversive Barbie," "The OHIP Card—The Benefits are Priceless," "Supa: A Report from Kenya by Mana Lumumba-Kasongo," and "Girls Need to See Women Rise to Political Power."

KEY TERMS

actor

affirmative action

capitalism

class

consensus

consumerism

content analysis

corporate capitalism

culture

deconstruction

determinism

deviance

discourse

discourse analysis

dominant values

double standards

economies of scale

employment equity

exploitation

false consciousness

feminist theory

fragmentation

functions

gatekeepers

gender

gender roles

gender-class

gender-role socialization

hierarchy

ideological hegemony

ideology

imperialism

institutions

integration

interpretive theory

misogyny

morality

multinational business corporations

norms

patriarchy

political economy theory

postfeminist liberalism

powerlessness

prejudice

privatization

questionnaires

race

radical

role models

science

semiotics

sexism

social systems

society

status

stereotypes

stigmatized

subsidiary

system

textual analysis

typify

values

worked up

REFERENCES

Allan, Stuart. 2006. *Online News*. Maidenhead, England: Open University Press.

Allan, Stuart. 1999. *News Culture*. Buckingham: Open University Press.

Baker, William, and George Dessart. 1998. *Down the Tube: An Inside Account of the Failure of American Television*. New York: Basic Books.

Barker, Chris. 1999. *Television, Globalization and Cultural Identities*. Buckingham and Philadelphia: Open University Press.

Barker, Michael. 2009. "Blame the Media." *Swans Commentary*, March 23. http://www.swans.com/library/art15/barker16.html.

Barthes, R. 1967. *Elements of Semiology*. London: Cape.

Bird, S.E. 1992. *For Enquiring Minds: A Cultural Study of Supermarket Tabloids*. Knoxville: University of Tennessee Press.

Boneva, Bonka, Robert Kraut, and David Frohlich. 2001. "Using E-Mail for Personal Relationships." *American Behavioral Scientist* 45: 530–549.

Brooks, Dianne L. 1997. "Rape on Soaps: The Legal Angle." In Martha A. Fineman and Martha T. McCluskey, eds. *Feminism, Media, and the Law*. New York and Oxford: Oxford University Press, 104–119.

Clow, Michael. 1993. *Stifling Debate: Canadian Newspapers and Nuclear Power*. With Susan Machum. Halifax: Fernwood.

Cresser, Frances, Lesley Gunn, and Helen Balme. 2001. "Women's Experiences of On-line E-Zine Publication." *Media, Culture and Society* 23: 457–473.

Crittenden, Danielle. 1996. "The Mother of All Problems." *Saturday Night* (April), 44–54.

Dahlgren, Peter, and Colin Sparks, eds. 1991. *Journalism and Popular Culture*. London: Sage.

Dahlgren, Peter, and Colin Sparks, eds. 1992. *Communication and Citizenship*. London: Routledge.

Daly, Kathleen, and Amy L. Chasteen. 1997. "Crime News, Crime Fear, and Women's Everyday Lives." In Martha A. Fineman and Martha T. McCluskey, eds. *Feminism, Media, and the Law*. New York and Oxford: Oxford University Press, 235–248.

Deacon, David, and Peter Golding. 1994. *Taxation and Representation: The Media, Political Communication and the Poll Tax*. London: John Libbey.

Dholakia, Ruby Roy. 2006. "Gender and IT in the Household: Evolving Patterns of Internet Use in the United States." *The Information Society* 23: 231–240.

Domhoff, G. William. 2003. *Changing the Powers that Be: How the Left Can Stop Losing and Win*. Lanham, MD: Rowman & Littlefield.

Engel, Matthew. 1996. *Tickle the Public: One Hundred Years of the Popular Press*. London: Victor Gollancz.

Everett, Anna. 2004. "On Cyberfeminism and Cyberwomanism: High-Tech Mediations of Feminism's Discontents." *Signs* 30: 1278–1286.

Fiske, John. 1992. "Popularity and the Politics of Information." In Peter Dahlgren and Colin Sparks, eds. *Journalism and Popular Culture*. London: Sage.

Foster, John Bellamy, and Fred Magdoff. 2009. *The Great Financial Crisis: Causes and Consequences*. New York: Monthly Review Press.

Franklin, Bob. 1997. *Newszak and News Media*. London: Arnold.

Goldsmith, Jack, and Tim Wu. 2006. *Who Controls the Internet? Illusions of a Borderless World*. Oxford and New York: Oxford University Press.

Gramsci, Antonio. 1971. *Selections from Prison Notebooks*. Ed. and trans. Q. Hoare and G. Nowell-Smith. New York: International Publishers.

Hall, Stuart. 1980. "Encoding/Decoding." In Stuart Hall, Dorothy Hobson, Andrew Lowe, and Paul Willis, eds. *Culture, Media, Language*. London: Hutchinson.

Hanigsberg, Julia E. 1997. "Glamour Law: Feminism through the Looking Glass of Popular Women's Magazines." In Martha A. Fineman and Martha T. McCluskey, eds. *Feminism, Media, and the Law*. New York and Oxford: Oxford University Press, 72–83.

Hiroshi, Ono, and Madeline Zavodny. 2005. "Gender Differences in Information Technology Usage: A U.S.–Japan Comparison." *Sociological Perspectives* 48 (1): 105–135.

Higgins, Tracy E., and Deborah L. Tolman. 1997. "Law, Cultural Media[tion], and Desire in the Lives of Adolescent Girls." In Martha A. Fineman and Martha T. McCluskey, eds. *Feminism, Media, and the Law*. New York and Oxford: Oxford University Press, 177–192.

Hobson, Dorothy. 1980. "Housewives and the Mass Media." In Stuart Hall, Dorothy Hobson, Andrew Lowe, and Paul Willis, eds. *Culture, Media, Language*. London: Hutchinson.

Innis, Harold. [1930] 1967. *The Fur Trade in Canada*. Toronto: University of Toronto Press.

Jackson, Linda A., Kelly S. Ervin, Philip D. Gardner and Neal Schmitt. 2001. "Gender and the Internet: Women Communicating and Men Searching." *Sex Roles* 44 (5–6): 363–379.

Janus, Noreen Z. 1996. "Research on Sex Roles in the Mass Media: Toward a Critical Approach." In Helen Baehr and Ann Gray, eds. *Turning It On: A Reader in Women and Media*. London: Arnold; New York: St. Martin's Press, 4–10.

Karpin, Isabel. 1997. "Pop Justice: TV, Motherhood, and the Law." In Martha A. Fineman and Martha T. McCluskey, eds. *Feminism, Media, and the Law*. New York and Oxford: Oxford University Press, 120–135.

LaPiere, R.T. 1934. "Attitudes vs. Actions" *Social Forces* 13: 230–237.

Lessig, Lawrence. 2006. *Code: Version 2.0*. New York: Basic Books.

Lessig, Lawrence. 2004. *Free Culture: The Nature and Future of Creativity*. New York: Penguin Books.

McCluskey, Martha T. 1997. "Fear of Feminism: Media Stories of Feminist Victims and Victims of Feminism on College Campuses." In Martha A. Fineman and Martha T. McCluskey, eds. *Feminism, Media, and the Law*. New York and Oxford: Oxford University Press, 57–71.

McLuhan, Marshall. 1964. *Understanding Media: The Extensions of Man*. New York, Toronto, and London: McGraw-Hill.

McRobbie, Angela. 1991. *Feminism and Youth Culture*. Houndmills, England: MacMillan Education.

Mehra, Bharat, Cecelia Merkel, and Ann Petereson Bishop. 2004. "The Internet for Empowerment of Minority and Marginalized Users." *New Media and Society* 6: 781–802.

Millar, Melanie Stewart. 1998. *Cracking the Gender Code: Who Rules the Wired World?* Toronto: Second Story Press.

Morley, David. 1986. *Family Television: Cultural Power and Domestic Leisure*. London: Comedia.

Negroponte, Nicholas. 1995. *Being Digital*. New York: Alfred A. Knopf.

Nesbitt-Larking, Paul. 2001. *Politics, Society, and the Media: Canadian Perspectives*. Toronto: Broadview Press.

Parenti, Michael. 1986. *Inventing Reality: The Politics of News Media*. New York: St. Martin's Press.

Perkins, T.E. 1996. "Rethinking Stereotypes." In Helen Baehr and Ann Gray, eds. *Turning It On: A Reader in Women and Media*. London: Arnold; New York: St. Martin's Press, 21–23.

Plant, Sadie. 1997. *Zeros + Ones: Digital Women + The New Technostructure*. New York: Doubleday.

Postman, Neil. 1993. *Technology: The Surrender of Culture to Technology*. New York: Vintage Books.

Rapping, Elayne. 1997. "The Movie of the Week: Law, Narrativity, and Gender on Prime Time." In Martha A. Fineman and Martha T. McCluskey, eds. *Feminism, Media, and the Law*. New York and Oxford: Oxford University Press, 91–103.

Razack, Sherene. 1998. "Race, Space, and Prostitution: The Making of the Bourgeois Subject." *Canadian Journal of Women and Law* 10: 338–376.

Rhode, Deborah L. 1997. "Media Images/Feminist Issues." In Martha A. Fineman and Martha T. McCluskey, eds. *Feminism, Media, and the Law*. New York and Oxford: Oxford University Press, 8–21.

Royal, Cindy. 2008. "Framing the Internet: A Comparison of Gendered Spaces." *Social Science Computer Review* 26 (2): 152–169.

Ross, Karen. 2000. "In Whose Image? TV Criticism and Black Minority Viewers." In Simon Cottle, ed. *Ethnic Minorities and the Media*. Buckingham and Philadelphia: Open University Press, 133–147.

Russo, Ann. 1997. "Lesbians, Prostitutes, and Murder: Media Constructs Violence Constructs Power." In Martha A. Fineman and Martha T. McCluskey, eds. *Feminism, Media, and the Law*. New York and Oxford: Oxford University Press, 249–266.

Schlesinger, Philip, and Howard Tumber. 1994. *Reporting Crime: The Media Politics of Criminal Justice*. Oxford: Clarendon.

Smith, D.E. 1990a. *The Conceptual Practices of Power: A Feminist Sociology of Knowledge*. Toronto: University of Toronto Press.

Smith, D.E. 1990b. *Texts, Facts and Femininity: Exploring the Relations of Ruling*. London: Routledge & Kegan Paul.

Solove, Daniel J. 2007. *The Future of Reputation: Gossip, Rumor, and Privacy on the Internet*. New Haven and London: Yale University Press.

Spender, Dale. 1995. *Nattering on the Net: Women, Power, and Cyberspace*. Peterborough: Broadview Press.

Stephenson, Hugh, and Michael Bromley, eds. 1998. *Sex, Lies and Democracy: The Press and the Public*. London: Longman.

Taras, David. 1999. *Power and Betrayal in the Canadian Media*. Peterborough: Broadview Press.

Thurlow, Crispin, Laura Lengel, and Alice Tomic. 2004. *Computer Mediated Communication: Social Interaction and the Internet*. London, Thousand Oaks, and New Delhi: Sage.

Tuchman, Gaye. 1978. "Women's Depiction by the Mass Media." In Helen Baehr and Ann Gray, eds. *Turning It On: A Reader in Women and Media*. London: Arnold; New York: St. Martin's Press, 11–5.

Tuchman, Gaye. 1996. *Making News: A Study in the Social Construction of Reality*. New York: Free Press.

Van Zoonen, Liesbet. 1994. *Feminist Media Studies*. The Media, Culture & Society Series. London, Thousand Oaks, and New Delhi: Sage.

Van Dijk, Teun A. 1993. *Elite Discourse and Racism*. Sage Series on Race and Ethnic Relations, vol. 6. Newbury Park, London, and New Delhi: Sage.

Vavrus, Mary Douglas. 2002. *Postfeminist News: Political Women in Media Culture*. SUNY Series in Communication Studies. New York: State University of New York Press.

Vipond, Mary. 2000. *The Mass Media in Canada*. 3rd ed. Toronto: James Lorimer.

Vivian, John, and Peter J. Maurin. 2009. *The Media of Mass Communication*. 5th ed. Toronto: Pearson.

Vogt, Christina, and Peiying Chen. 2001. "Feminisms and the Internet." *Peace Review* 13: 371–374.

Williams, Patricia J. 1997. "Hate Radio: Why We Need to Tune In to Limbaugh and Stern." In Martha A. Fineman and Martha T. McCluskey, eds. *Feminism, Media, and the Law*. New York and Oxford: Oxford University Press, 22–26.

Winter, James. 1997. *Democracy's Oxygen: How Corporations Control the News*. Montreal, New York, and London: Black Rose Books.

Zittrain, Jonathan. 2008. *The Future of the Internet and How To Stop It*. New Haven and London: Yale University Press.

Glossary

There are many terms in sociology that do not have standard meanings. They are used differently depending on the theoretical perspective of the writer. The definitions suggested below provide a guide to the meaning of terms as they are used in this text. They are not definitive in the sense of specifying how such terms are utilized in all sociological writing. Many theoretical concepts require extensive explanation to capture their full meaning. The best way to understand terms in sociology is to see how they are used in context. There is little value in trying to memorize definitions.

Absolute surplus For Marx, the amount of surplus production available when workers are driven to work as hard as possible and given the lowest possible standard of living.

Abstract labour time Marx uses this term to refer to the average amount of time it takes to produce a given commodity in a society with a given level of technology and knowledge.

Accounting/Accountability In ethnomethodology, these terms refer to the ways in which people use their common-sense knowledge and background understandings to make sense to themselves and to one another of what is going on.

Acculturation The process through which newcomers learn and adopt the prevailing attitudes and values of the group or society that they are entering.

Achieved characteristics Characteristics that one earns by learning skills or gaining credentials.

Actor In functionalism, the conception of a person as a role player within a system of roles.

Adaptation Parsons uses this term to refer to securing needed resources for an activity and distributing them among the people involved.

Adjacency pairs This term is used in conversation analysis to refer to aspects of the structure of typical, orderly conversations. One expects that a certain kind of comment by a participant in a conversation will immediately be followed by a corresponding comment from another participant (i.e., that a question will be followed by an answer).

Advanced capitalism For Marxist theorists, an economic order in which national and international markets are dominated by huge corporations rather than characterized by competition among entrepreneurs.

Advanced communism An economic system where all the important means of production in a society—land, factories, technology—are communally owned. Everyone shares access to them and everyone labours collectively according to their ability to meet the collective needs of the community.

Affective-rational action A term used by Weber to refer to action oriented to emotions.

Affectivity/Affective neutrality Parsons uses these terms to refer to the amount of emotion that should properly be displayed in a given role.

Affirmative action Action taken as part of a policy designed to increase the representation of members of specified groups deemed to be disadvantaged or underrepresented in certain positions relative to their numbers within the population as a whole.

Agency The capacity of individual people to act in consciously chosen ways to influence social structures.

Agribusiness The network of international corporations that controls production, processing, transport, storage, and financing of agriculture.

Alienation Marx uses this term to refer to the dehumanizing character of social relations, particularly under capitalism. The term is used more generally to describe a syndrome or combination of characteristics including powerlessness, meaninglessness, isolation, and self-estrangement.

Altruism Regard for others as a principle of action. Also, a readiness to put the interests of other members of society or those of society as a whole over personal interests.

Altruistic suicide The form of suicide committed by people who are so intensely integrated into their social group or community that they are willing to sacrifice themselves for the good of that community.

Anomic division of labour For Durkheim, a forced specialization that is experienced as unjust or as not regulated by reference to a clear and meaningful system of values.

Anomic suicide The form of suicide committed by people who have lost any clear sense of values that regulate and give meaning to their lives.

Anomie In general this refers to a breakdown in moral order. Durkheim uses the term to refer to the experience of a relative absence or confusion of values and a corresponding lack of meaningful regulations or a clear position and objectives in life.

Anomie theory of crime A theory developed by Merton, which attributes variations in propensity for criminal behaviour to the discrepancy between culturally valued goals and access to socially approved means to achieve them.

Anti-Semitism Prejudice against Jews.

Antithesis See Dialectic; Dialectical materialism.

Apparatus of ruling A term developed by Smith to refer to the organized activities that form part of the overall mechanisms for control in a society, including the activities of individual people who work in government offices and the forms and regulations that guide their behaviour.

Ascriptive characteristics/Ascription Refers to the characteristics with which we are born, such as age, sex, height, and racial or ethnic background.

Assimilation The process through which individuals or groups of people lose their distinctive ethnic or minority group patterns of behaviour and values and adopt the values and behavioural expectations of the dominant group.

Autocracy Rule from above, without democratic participation.

Automation Mechanical or electronic control of a process.

Average labour time For Marx, the typical amount of time it takes a worker to produce a particular commodity with the technology that prevails in a given society.

Background understandings In ethnomethodology, the knowledge that competent participants in an activity or conversation can be expected to have, which allows the activity or conversation to be understandable to them without any further explanation.

Base A term used by Marx to refer to the social relations of production.

Behavioural organism For Parsons, the human biological organism, which provides the fundamental energy and drive for activity and which also links the social system with the physical environment.

Berdache A term used in anthropology to refer to people whose social identity is neither male nor female, but encompasses aspects of both.

Biological theory of race The theory that people with different skin colours evolved from distinct subspecies of humans and that they have innately different levels of intelligence and other attributes.

Bourgeoisie Those who own capital, or the means of production, and who hire wage-labourers to produce commodities for sale in order to make profits; capitalists.

Branch-plant economy A society in which a significant proportion of all business enterprises are branch plants; that is, subsidiaries of multinational corporations with headquarters in another country.

Breaching experiments A methodological approach in ethnomethodology that involves disturbing what the researcher thinks might be an unquestioned or taken-for-granted rule of normal behaviour in order to test the extent to which that normal behaviour is subsequently disturbed.

Bureaucracy Generally, a formal organization characterized by a hierarchical chain of command and precisely delimited roles and responsibilities governed by written rules. For Foucault and Ferguson, bureaucracy constitutes the scientific organization of inequality through which people are dominated and oppressed. See Disciplinary society; Iron cage.

Bureaucratic discourse Foucault uses the term to refer to a form of talk that translates all human concerns and human interaction into narrow technical language relevant for organizational purposes and for predefined classifications that relate to the specialized work of officials.

Bureaucratic language Description of human interaction in terms of technical jargon referring to regulations defining responsibilities of role incumbents in organizations, often for the purpose of obfuscation.

Bureaucratic society For Foucault, a society in which bureaucracy is the all-pervasive mode of social organization. See Disciplinary society.

Business-class immigrant A category within the Immigration Act that refers to people who have capital to invest in Canadian industries and businesses and can provide guarantees that they will create employment opportunities in Canada.

Calvinism Weber uses the term to refer to the religious doctrine of John Calvin, which advocates a sober, frugal lifestyle and a disciplined obligation to work as a means to serve God. It emphasizes the doctrine of predestination: that salvation is attainable by God's grace alone and that the identity of those who will be saved is known by God from the beginning of life.

Capital The stock with which a company or person enters into business. The means of production. The accumulated wealth that is used in producing commodities.

Capitalism A system of production in which capital, or the means of production, is privately owned by a small, elite class of people. The mass of people have no direct access to means of producing for their own needs. They depend on selling their capacity to labour to those who own the means of production.

Capitalists Owners of capital or the means of production who hire wage-labourers to produce commodities for sale. The bourgeoisie.

Capitalization The expansion in the amount of wealth invested in a business in order for it to remain competitive. Undercapitalized enterprises are those with insufficient investment in technology to remain competitive in the market.

Causal pluralism For Weber, a research strategy that involves searching for multiple causes for social phenomena.

Causality A relationship of cause and effect that is assumed to exist between two or more variables.

Census/Census data Data obtained through comprehensive surveys of the entire population of a country, carried out with government funding and commonly with the force of law to compel people to answer the questions.

Charismatic authority For Weber, authority legitimated by the extraordinary gifts or supernatural powers that the leader appears to have.

Chicago School (The) A theoretical and methodological approach to urban sociology associated with the University of Chicago during the late 1920s and 1930s. An approach that emphasized the three variables of size, density, and cultural heterogeneity as critical determinants of the character of social life.

Circles of social control The mechanisms by which conformity is produced, including guilt, desire for approval, economic sanctions, and force.

Class Generally, the location in a hierarchically stratified work force, commonly divided into a set of ranked categories, on the basis of relative income and level of education or skill required. Alternatively, the location within a bureaucratic organization as defined by job classification schemes. Marx defined class as location in relation to the means of production, mostly as owners and nonowners, with some intermediate classes. Weber expanded Marx's definition to refer to differential life chances and the chance to use property, goods, and services for exchange in a competitive market.

Class-for-itself In Marxist theory, the collectivity of members of a class who recognize their shared class position and come together to act in their class interests.

Class-in-itself Marx uses the term as a theoretical concept referring to all people who share the same relationship to the means of production (i.e., capitalists as the class of all owners).

Class reductionism The thesis that inequalities associated with gender, ethnicity, or race can be explained by class interests.

Class struggle The conflict between those who own the means of production and those who do not. For Marx this is a dynamic process of struggle by which working people most disadvantaged by the existing relations of production struggle to change those relations.

Cohort Persons banded together for the purposes of analysis, particularly on the basis of being born during the same period of time.

Colonialism The process of establishing settlements in a conquered territory with the administration of such settlements fully or partially subject to control by the conquering state.

Commodity Anything produced for exchange and not for use by the producer.

Commodity fetishism The tendency to attribute causal agency to commodities exchanged in the marketplace, as if the commodities determined relations between people.

Common-sense understandings Assumptions about how and why things work the way they do, based on immediate, personal experience.

Communism See Advanced communism; Primitive communism.

Community A body of people living in the same locality. Alternatively, a sense of identity and belonging shared among people living in the same locality. Also, the set of social relations found in a particular bounded area.

Competitive advantage Special conditions prevailing in certain areas that enable businesses to produce certain kinds of commodities more cheaply than they can be produced elsewhere.

Conflict theory The study of society, or specific elements of society, conceptualized as made up of parts held together by hierarchical relations of power and dependency. Conflict is seen as endemic.

Conformist A category in Merton's anomie theory of crime. One who accepts socially valued goals and socially approved means to achieve them.

Conglomerate mergers The consolidation of diverse industries within one corporation.

Conscience collective For Durkheim, the totality of beliefs and sentiments common to the average citizens of the same society. The French term is translated into English in two ways. *Collective conscience* refers to the collective sense of what is morally right and wrong. *Collective consciousness* refers to a sense of belonging and commitment to a collectivity or community of people.

Consensus In cultural Marxism, a kind of one-dimensional or group thinking manipulated by mass media and the professions to ensure that the values and behaviour expectations of the ruling class will prevail. See Ideological hegemony.

Conservative bias Generally, being disposed to maintain existing social institutions and to oppose efforts to change or reform them.

Conspicuous consumption A term referring to buying and displaying expensive items in order to demonstrate wealth and so enhance one's social status.

Consumerism The high value placed on the ownership or purchase of goods as a means of attaining personal happiness and as a measure of personal success and well-being.

Content analysis A methodological approach that involves the organized counting of content of written materials in relation to predefined categories that are determined by the theoretical hypothesis.

Contradictions of capitalism For Marx, the thesis that the capitalist system of production necessarily works in such a way that it generates problems that become steadily more disruptive for production as the system evolves. Eventually, capitalism is destined to collapse under its own internal problems.

Conversation analysis A theoretical approach within the broad perspective of ethnomethodology that explores the typical ways in which talk is structured by participants.

Corporate capitalism An economic system in which huge business enterprises are able to dominate the market and substantially influence or determine the supply and price of many commodities.

Correlation A statistical term referring to the degree to which change in one variable is associated with change in another variable.

Correspondence theory This theory, developed by Bowles and Gintis, posits that the pattern of social relations established in one institution (i.e., schools) parallels in critical respects the pattern of social relations established in another institution (i.e., industry).

Counterculture A system of norms and values held by members of a subgroup or class within a society that contradicts or opposes a significant number of the norms and values that prevail within the society as a whole.

Countervailing duties Import taxes that one country imposes on certain commodities from another country to compensate for subsidies that the exporting country has given to producers of the commodities.

Credentialism In Marxist theory, the thesis that formal qualifications are emphasized by capitalists to create artificial division and competition among workers rather than because such qualifications are essential for performance of particular jobs.

Critical literacy The capacity to reflect upon and to question the content of what one reads.

Critical theory Any sociological theory or research that challenges the legitimacy of the established social order and that seeks to understand the workings of that society as a basis for action to change it.

Cult of domesticity A set of attitudes and values that justifies the segregation of women in the private realm of the home.

Cult of rationality Justification of everything by reference to the supposedly objective principles of scientific and technical efficiency.

Cultural feminism Explores culturally patterned ways of talking and thinking about women that often denigrate the female and the feminine.

Cultural lag The failure or excessive slowness of prevailing values and norms in a society to adapt to economic changes associated with technological innovation.

Cultural Marxism Closely associated with the social construction of reality perspective, this is a variant of Marxist theory that emphasizes ideological hegemony rather than the determining force of capitalist structures in explaining social relations in capitalist societies.

Cultural system In functionalism, the system of beliefs, rituals, values, and symbols, including language as a symbol system, through which people confront ultimate questions about reality, the meaning of good and evil, suffering, and death.

Culturalism See Cultural Marxism.

Culture The set of shared ideas about what constitutes ideal behaviour within a given society.

Culture of domination A system of values and behavioural expectations that condones or legitimates subordination of the mass of people to autocratic rule.

Culture of poverty thesis The thesis that poverty is caused or perpetuated by the attitudes and values of poor people, which inhibit them from taking action to ameliorate their situation.

Cybernetic hierarchy For Parsons, a hierarchy of systems of control and communication in human action.

Deconstruction The detailed study of text to reveal how an author conveys meaning to readers.

Deconstructionism The detailed investigation of how texts are organized or internally constructed so as to achieve their meaning.

Deferred gratification Forgoing immediate pleasures or rewards in order to work toward greater future rewards.

Defining the situation In symbolic interaction and ethnomethodology, the process of negotiating the meaning of what seems to be going on. .

Demography/Demographic The study of vital statistics of a population, including such information as population size, births, marriages, deaths, migration, and so on.

Dependency theory A theory that the poverty evident in the Third World and in poorer regions of developed economies is generated and perpetuated through systematic exploitation by developed capitalist economies.

Dependent capitalism The experience of capitalist development in Third World countries caught in an already highly advanced corporate capitalist world system.

Dependent commodity producers A class of workers who own their own means of production of certain commodities but who are controlled by the corporate monopoly processors and distributors who dominate the market for what they produce. See also Petite bourgeoisie.

Dependent development The restricted pattern of development within a region or country where the economy is controlled externally by capitalist metropolises that develop the locality only as a resource hinterland. See Dependency theory.

Dependent variable The variable that is assumed to depend on or be caused by other variables included in research.

Deskilling The process of breaking down a complex operation or activity into simple component operations that can be easily learned.

Determinism Any thesis that sees human activity as caused or controlled by forces independent of human choice or will. See Economic determinism.

Deviance Behaviour that does not conform to behavioural expectations prevailing in a given group or community.

Deviant subculture See Subcultural theory of deviance.

Dialectic Recurrent cycles of thesis, antithesis, and synthesis. Thesis refers to the original idea, philosophy, or system of thought. Antithesis represents the logical inconsistencies, problems, and anomalies within the thesis. The synthesis is a new system of ideas, thoughts, or philosophy that resolves these contradictions.

Dialectical materialism The application of dialectical reasoning to the organization of production. Thesis represents the existing organization of production. The antithesis refers to the tensions or problems that impede or shackle the full productive potential of this organization. The synthesis is a new form of organization of production that overcomes these problems and unleashes the full productive potential of the available means of production.

Dialectical method The application of dialectical thinking to a given problem, clarifying the original situation, explicating the contradictions inherent in it, and seeking a synthesis or new approach that will resolve these contradictions.

Differential association theory A theory that attributes variation in propensity for criminal behaviour to relative closeness of involvement with others whose subcultural values condone criminal behaviour.

Differential opportunity theory A theory that attributes variation in propensity for criminal behaviour to the relative availability of legitimate or illegitimate means to achieve valued goals. See Innovator.

Differentiation Generally, the process of becoming less alike as the result of performing more specialized social roles. Spencer used this term to refer to the breakdown of simple, unspecialized structures into many separate parts.

Diffuse obligations The perceived right of others, such as close family members, to expect a variety of services and support.

Disciplinary society The term is used by Foucault to refer to social order maintained through power based on intimate knowledge and regulation of individuals rather than on punitive sanctions.

Discipline Foucault uses this term to refer both to orderly conduct and to a branch of knowledge.

Discourse For Foucault, how we come to talk about our social world, which determines how it comes to be known to us and to have the form that it does.

Discourse analysis A research methodology that explores how professionals frame issues, and the relations of power embedded within these frames.

Distributive justice The quality of fairness in the distribution of rewards or resources among participants in a situation or activity.

Divide and rule The policy of encouraging schisms within a mass of subordinate people to reduce the likelihood of concerted action by subordinates, making them easier to control.

Documentary construction of reality For Smith, a theoretical approach that focusses on how the seemingly neutral language of bureaucratic forms and categories actively structures social relations and what comes to be seen as factual information.

Documentary method of interpretation In ethnomethodology, the active search for patterns in the vague flux of everyday interaction, as a fundamental element of practical, everyday reasoning. This search is based on the premise that there is always an underlying pattern to everyday activity or conversation. Surface appearances are treated as evidence of, or as documenting, this presumed underlying pattern.

Dogmatism An assertion of opinion that is authoritarian.

Doing hierarchy In ethnomethodology, the actual practices of people in ongoing social interaction that produce and reproduce the experience of some individuals as inferior or superior to others.

Domestic labour debate A body of theory concerned with where and how homemakers fit into the capitalist economic system.

Dominant culture The set of values and behavioural expectations that prevails in a given society and that legitimates and supports the activities that directly benefit the dominant class. In capitalist society, the dominant culture is that which legitimates the activities of the capitalist class in the pursuit of profit.

Dominant values The values of the powerful class that tend to prevail within a society.

Domination In ethnic relations, the state of one ethnic group exerting regularized and institutionalized rule over other ethnic groups.

Double standard Standards that are viewed as positive when attributed to one gender but negative when attributed to the other.

Dowry murder A new bride murdered by her husband or his family because the amount of goods or money that the woman brought to the marriage is deemed inadequate. Dowry murder allows the husband to remarry to collect additional dowry.

Dramaturgical model Goffman's theoretical approach that studies how people creatively act out particular social roles in a manner analogous to how actors in a play creatively interpret their script.

Dynamic equilibrium In functionalist theory, the maintenance of balance and order between elements of a society by systematically adjusting for change in one element by complementary changes in other related elements.

Dysfunctions Effects or consequences of any given structure or pattern of behaviour that are damaging for some other element or for people in the wider social system.

Ecological fallacy A logically false or misleading argument that attempts to draw inferences about individuals from aggregate data.

Economic determinism A form of theorizing that reifies the abstract concept of an economic system, such that the system of production is held to cause or to determine all major aspects of social life, without reference to human agency.

Economies of scale A principle of economics that asserts that as the size of a business enterprise increases, the cost of producing any one unit of output decreases.

Ego In psychoanalytic theory, the conscious self that seeks to express and to realize fundamental drives and passions.

Egoism For Durkheim, a value system that places self-interest at the centre. Also, systematic selfishness, reflecting the absence of a sense of social bonds and commitment to other people.

Egoistic suicide The form of suicide committed by individuals who have lost any sense of social bonds linking them to other people.

Embourgeoisement thesis The thesis that, under capitalism, working-class people will become or are becoming steadily wealthier to the point that their lifestyles closely resemble those of professional middle-class people.

Emotional labour The work of managing facial expressions and manipulating the emotional responses of clients as part of one's job.

Empiricism A commitment to and quest for knowledge based on observation and experiment.

Employment equity Legislation and policies designed to ensure that women and men employed in jobs of equivalent levels of skill, responsibility, difficulty, etc., receive equivalent levels of pay.

Enclosure Feudal landlords' practice of fencing off huge tracts of arable land for sheep pastures thereby depriving serfs of access to land for subsistence crops.

Enumeration In survey research, the process of counting the total membership of a particular set of people from which a sample is to be drawn.

Equality of condition A policy that stresses sameness. In education, it means that a standardized age-graded curriculum be available for all students regardless of individual ability or interests.

Equality of opportunity A policy that, in principle, gives all individuals an equivalent chance to compete for social positions that carry relatively higher rewards. See Meritocracy thesis.

Equilibrium In functionalism, the maintenance of balance and order between elements of a society over long periods of time.

Ethic of responsibility For Weber, moral principles that take account of the probable consequences of actions.

Ethic of ultimate ends A term used by Weber to refer to morality based on obedience to religious doctrine or to what is perceived as the will of God, or some absolute value, regardless of the consequences.

Ethnic/Ethnicity Identity as a member of a distinctive cultural group associated with a particular country or region of origin. Social constructionists argue that ethnicity is used as an ideology that blames differences and inequalities caused by discriminatory treatment of certain people on intrinsic personal characteristics of the victims.

Ethnocentrism A belief that one's culture or way of life is superior to others. An exaggerated view of the quality and correctness of the culture of one's own groups. A self-centred view of social life lacking respect for the different perspectives or values of other people.

Ethnomethodology A theoretical approach that focusses on micro-interactions and explores the methods or practical reasoning that individuals use to make sense of what is going on around them. Ethnomethodologists argue that the process of formulating an account of what is happening produces reality for the practical purposes of participants.

Evolution A theory positing that societies developed from simple undifferentiated societies into highly complex industrial societies in a way analogous to evolution in the natural world where single-cell organisms evolved into complex advanced organisms.

Exchange value For Marx, the amount of human labour time that goes into the production of a commodity. The value of one commodity relative to another is measured by the labour time needed to make the commodities.

Experiment A methodological approach that, ideally, holds constant everything that might influence the phenomenon of interest and then allows one variable to change in a controlled manner. Any subsequent change observed in the phenomenon of interest is then attributed to the influence of the manipulated variable.

Exploitation A measure of the gap between the money that workers are paid and the market value of commodities they produce, once other production costs are deducted.

Expressive leader One who is primarily responsible for relieving tensions and smoothing social relations in a group.

Extended family A family in which several generations of kin live in the same home.

Extrinsic rewards Payment or other benefits received for doing some activity. The opposite of intrinsic rewards.

Fact Datum. That which is known as the result of empirical investigation conducted according to objective scientific methods of observation and experiment. Also, that which is attested to be correct by an appropriate official within a formal organization. See also Social facts.

False consciousness The condition of some members of the working class who fail to understand their true or objective long-term class interests to the extent that they are predisposed to support a system of production that exploits them.

Familism Particularly close attachment to kin, and high value placed on family membership, combined with generally shallow relations with nonkin.

Family-class immigrant See Sponsored immigrant.

Family wage The policy of paying male workers sufficient wages to support their wives and children.

Fatalistic suicide The form of suicide committed by people who feel their lives are entirely regimented by group norms.

Feedback mechanisms The processes through which given structures or patterns of behaviour are selectively reinforced and perpetuated over time.

Feminist movement Collective protest and political action to ameliorate the subordinate situation of women in society.

Feminist theory A perspective that takes as its starting point the situation and experiences of women in questioning the adequacy of any analysis of human behaviour. See also Marxist feminism; Radical feminism.

Fetish An inanimate object worshipped for its supposed magical powers. See Commodity fetishism.

Feudalism/Feudal system An economic system in which land is the primary means of production. Land is owned by a hereditary elite of nobles or lords and is worked by a hereditary class of labourers or serfs who are tied to the land.

Folk society An ideal-type model of isolated rural society.

Fragmentation The subdivision of tasks or responsibilities among workers such that each worker performs highly repetitive and monotonous actions devoid of any intrinsic interest or sense of importance.

Frankfurt School (The) See Critical theory.

Function For functionalists, the basic needs or conditions that must be met by a social system in order to maintain itself in a state of equilibrium. Also, the particular contribution of parts of a social system to the maintenance of the whole system.

Functional indispensability For Parsons, the assumption, borrowed from biology, that every element found within a social system is indispensable for the functioning of that system. Hence, no element can be removed or changed without some negative effect for the system as a whole.

Functional unity For Parsons, the assumption, borrowed from biology, that every element found within a social system has effects or consequences that are good for the entire system.

Functionalism/Structural functionalism The study of society as a functioning system comprising interdependent institutions or patterned relations that are stable over time, and that perform specialized functions for the whole. The central focus is on how order is maintained between elements of society. Any given pattern of relations or structures within society is explained by reference to the effects or functions that such patterns have for the wider whole.

GAIL model See System prerequisites.

Gatekeepers People who are in a strategic position to transmit or screen out information, especially in the media.

Gemeinschaft A theoretical model of a society as a community of people united by relations of kinship, a strong sense of community identification, and shared values and norms. A community.

Gender Culturally learned differences in behaviour of males and females.

Gender-class Socially constructed location of women and men relative to the organization of the activities of production and reproduction. See also Sexual class, which is often used synonymously with gender-class.

Gender-ethnic-class Location within the occupational hierarchy based on the combination of gender, ethnic background, and marketable job skills.

Gender-role socialization The process by which children are taught and internalize behaviour deemed appropriate for their particular sex.

Gender roles Markedly distinct and nonoverlapping roles for typical activities for women and men.

Generalized other A group or class of people whose overall responses to us play an integral part in the development of our own sense of self-identity. Similarly, a class or team of people whose reactions we try to anticipate.

Gentrification The process of change by which large numbers of middle-class newcomers buy up residential properties in formerly working-class zones, and renovate them into upscale housing. These houses then become too expensive for working-class families to buy.

Gesellschaft A theoretical model of an association of people related only by transitory and superficial contacts that are formal, contractual, and specified in character. An association.

Goal attainment For Parsons, establishing priorities among competing goals and mobilizing members involved in a given activity to attain them.

Goal displacement The tendency for groups or organizations set up to achieve some specific objective to shift priorities from this original objective to a concern with maintaining the group or organization itself.

Green revolution A package of scientific developments in agriculture that promises to increase yields.

Headstart program A policy of providing enriched learning experiences for young children from economically and culturally deprived families to help them keep up with the achievements of more advantaged children.

Hegemony Relations of ruling through which the consent of subordinate classes to capitalism is achieved, particularly through control over how people think.

Heterosexism The institutionalized organization of social relations that assumes that all women will be tied to men, usually in relations of sexual and economic interdependence.

Hidden curriculum That which is taught by the form of teaching rather than by the explicit content of lessons.

Hidden diseconomies The costs or negative consequences of economic activities that are not counted in corporate cost-benefit analyses, because members of the wider society, rather than the enterprise engaging in the activities, suffer from, and pay for, these consequences.

Hierarchy Graded or ranked positions within a society or organization.

Hinterland Underdeveloped areas that supply cheap labour and cheap raw materials or semiprocessed goods to developed centres.

Historical materialism For Marx, the thesis that the processes by which people meet their basic subsistence needs constitute the foundation of social organization. Hence, the analysis of social life should begin with the study of prevailing modes of production and the relations that these generate between people.

Historical sociology The study of how human actions generate social structures over time.

Holding company A company that holds sufficient shares in multiple other companies to control their executive boards.

Horizontal integration A corporation that owns or controls all or most stages in the production of a specific commodity, including production and supply of all raw materials, manufacturing, distribution, and retail sales.

Human relations school of management A style of management that gives priority to generating a friendly and relaxed social atmosphere in the workplace, on the assumption that contented workers are more productive. The term can be used pejoratively to refer to management styles that manipulate a friendly social atmosphere among subordinates to divert attention from the deeper reality of exploitation.

Humanism For Durkheim, a form of religion or spirituality in which the central value is devotion to humanity rather than to a divinity.

Hypothesis A prediction made on the basis of a theory.

I and Me Terms used by Mead to refer to two aspects of the individual. The I is the impulsive, spontaneous aspects of self. The Me is learned identity, incorporating the common attitudes and meanings of the group to which one belongs.

Id In psychoanalytic theory, the vast reservoir of unconscious and semiconscious drives and passions, especially sexual drives, that underlie and energize our conscious activities.

Idealism A philosophy that emphasizes ideas and values as the distinctive moving force of human history. The view that all human behaviour entails unique spiritual events that can only be grasped by intuition, not by objective scientific method.

Ideal-type model A theoretical model that is designed to highlight the typical characteristics of the kind of social organization being studied.

Ideographic Explanations based on unique, subjective, intuitive accounts.

Ideological hegemony The capacity of the dominant class to rule through control over prevailing ideas or culture. It ensures that the mass of people accept as legitimate the activities that directly benefit the dominant class.

Ideology Systems of values that justify certain kinds of action or ways of life, sometimes to the detriment of other people. Belief systems that strongly influence the way we see social reality. They tend to sensitize us in certain ways and blind us in others. Dorothy Smith uses the term to describe a method of inquiry about society that results in a systematic means not to see and not to know what is actually happening.

Immiseration A verb that refers to active practices within capitalism that make the lives of working masses more miserable.

Imperfect competition In economic theory this refers to a situation in which a few giant producers or purchasers of a commodity are able to dominate the market and to act in collusion rather than in competition.

Imperialism The practice of one state extending its sovereignty over another by force, usually for the purpose of economic exploitation.

Imperialism of rationality A form of control over, or manipulation of, people. It is exercised by presenting certain kinds of behaviour as consistent with reason or scientific knowledge, such that any disagreement or resistance seems irrational.

Inclusive language Nonsexist language. Gender-neutral language that does not use masculine nouns and pronouns generally to include feminine forms.

Independent commodity producers A class of workers who own their own means of production of certain commodities, generally referring to people engaged in farming, fishing, and the like. See also Petite bourgeoisie.

Independent immigrant A category under the Immigration Act that refers to people whose entry into Canada is subject to economic requirements and criteria measured by a point system.

Independent variable A factor included in research as a possible cause of some phenomenon of interest. It is treated as known or given for the purpose of the research and not as itself requiring explanation.

Indexicality In ethnomethodology, the context-dependent character of the meaning of words or actions. The thesis that words or gestures always stand for or indicate a broader background and that this background understanding is essential for words to have meanings.

Indicator An observable feature that is used in research to measure a particular concept.

Industrial Revolution The period of transition associated with the eighteenth century in Europe when the primary means of production changed from land to machines located in factories.

Industrialization Mechanization. The transition from dependence on human and animal energy to fossil fuels. Usually associated with a shift in primary means of production from land to machines located in factories.

Inner city A general term referring to the central residential areas within large cities, usually characterized by high density housing.

Innovator A component of Merton's anomie theory of crime. One who accepts socially valued goals but adopts socially disapproved means to achieve them.

Institutional ethnography A theoretical and methodological approach that studies the active processes through which people construct their social reality through their everyday working activities in a local setting (ethnography). It then links these local dynamics to the wider institutional context that shapes them.

Institutionalization The establishment of certain patterns of behaviour as typical and expected to the point that they are generally taken for granted as appropriate by most members of a society.

Institutions Typical ways of structuring social relations around specific functions or needs of a society.

Instrumental leader One who is concerned with and who directs task performance in a group.

Integration Generally, to combine parts into a whole or to combine individuals into cohesive collectives. Spencer uses this term to refer to the evolutionary process of developing a central co-ordinating agency, such as state administration, to regulate relations between specialized elements of society. Parsons uses the term to refer to co-ordinating the behaviour of different members or role incumbents in a particular activity and maintaining orderly interrelations between role players.

Intelligence failure Loss of effective control in organizations resulting from distorted or inadequate information.

Interactional competence See Background understandings.

Interlocking directorships A situation where one person serves on the board of directors of two or more companies.

Internalization The process of learning group values and behavioural expectations and wanting to conform to them from an inner sense that they are morally right.

Interpretive theory A paradigm that focusses on micro-interactions and how people present themselves to each other and come to understand the surface and underlying meanings of their interaction. The perspective includes symbolic interaction and the dramaturgical model. Ethnomethodology is sometimes included with the interpretive perspective although it is distinct from traditional symbolic interaction. See Verstehen.

Intersubjectivity The capacity of knowing what another person actually intended.

Interviewer bias The interviewer's preconceived opinions or personal characteristics that influence the interaction with the respondent and influence in a measurable way the information being sought.

Invisible hand of the market The thesis that the competition between the mass of sellers, trying to get the best price for their commodities, and the mass of buyers, trying to buy commodities at the cheapest price, will produce the best outcome in the long run without external planning.

Iron cage Weber's vision of bureaucracy as an all-powerful system of organization that would regulate all aspects of individual life.

Iron law of oligarchy The process whereby power within any organization comes to be wielded by a tiny elite minority. A process hypothesized to occur regardless of democratic principles or procedures.

Isolation Absence of a sense of social bonds or belonging with other people. Particularly loss of a sense of loyalty or commitment to one's workplace. See Alienation.

Kin universe The average number of kin with whom an individual remains in regular contact.

Labelling theory An approach that focusses on how stereotypes or fixed mental images are applied to certain kinds of people, particularly by officials in positions of power, and the effects that this application has on the self-concepts and future behaviour of the people so labelled.

Labour-saving technology Machines designed to perform work previously done by people.

Labour theory of value For Marx, the theory that the average labour time that goes into the production of a commodity, with a given level of technology, determines the exchange value of that commodity.

Laissez-faire system An economic system that operates without any government control or regulation. Advocacy of such a system.

Latency See Pattern maintenance.

Latent functions Those effects or consequences of any given structure or pattern of behaviour that are important for maintaining social order but that are not directly recognized by people involved in the behaviour.

Leveraged buy-outs The practice of borrowing money to buy a controlling interest in a firm in the hope that assets so gained will generate sufficient profits to pay off the debt.

Liberalism Generally, a belief in the values of free enterprise and equality of opportunity for individuals to compete for social and economic rewards on the basis of merit. Used in a positive sense, it refers to a willingness to help individuals to overcome disadvantages or to open up opportunities for disadvantaged individuals. Critics use the term to refer to people who advocate piecemeal reform of the social system rather than radical or major changes to social structures. Critics also use the term to describe the tendency to blame inequality on personal merit or personal failings without acknowledging the structural constraints that disadvantage many groups.

Liberal-bourgeois thesis A theory that emphasizes the positive aspects of capitalism as an economic system. It is considered by Marxists to constitute the ideology of the bourgeoisie. Also, a thesis that associates capitalism with free enterprise and competitive markets that potentially provide opportunities for all people to improve their standard of living. See Liberalism.

Liberal feminism Feminist theory that focusses on establishing equal treatment for women and men as individuals in law, employment, and other public roles.

Liberation theology A religious doctrine that holds that the call to achieve social justice is central to the Christian message. See Social Gospel movement.

Linear relation An apparent relationship between two variables such that any change in the value of one variable is associated with an equivalent change in another variable.

Looking-glass self For Cooley, the way in which people reflect on how they appear to other people who are important to them, how their appearance is being judged by such people, and the effect of such reflection in feelings of pride or shame.

Lumpenproletariat In Marxist theory, unemployed workers who form a reserve army of cheap labour power to be used by capitalists as they require additional labour power.

Macro-micro debate The debate between sociological theorists about how to understand the link between the details of momentary experience and large-scale, long-term social processes.

Macrosociology The analysis of large-scale and long-term social processes, often treated as self-sufficient entities such as state, class, culture, and so on.

Macrovariable A variable that cannot be reduced to micro-elements.

Managerial mentality The thesis that organizations are rational and efficient entities and that people can be regarded as role incumbents and managed to maximize efficiency of co-operative activities. Generally, the endorsement of the viewpoint of managers.

Managerial revolution The thesis that ownership of corporations has become separated from control over them. The belief that managers rather than capitalists run corporations.

Manifest functions The consequences of any given structure or pattern of behaviour that are openly recognized and intended by the people involved in the behaviour.

Marginal workers A class of workers who are frequently unemployed or who can find work only in a succession of temporary and low-paid jobs.

Marxist feminism Feminist theory that focusses on the role of economy and private property in the subordination of women to men.

Marxist functionalism The modification of functionalist analysis to incorporate notions of power and unequal ability of different individuals and groups to selectively reinforce those social structures that they find beneficial.

Marxist structuralism The theory that utilizes the model of the capitalist system and its internal contradictions as an explanatory framework to account for specific characteristics of contemporary capitalist society.

Maternal deprivation theory The theory that young children require extensive physical and social contact with their mothers in order to become psychologically well adjusted and hence that all evidence for adult maladjustment, particularly delinquent behaviour, can be explained by inadequate maternal attention.

Matriarchy Social organization in which the mother is the head of the family.

Matrilineal Ancestry and inheritance through the mother's line.

Me See I and Me.

Meaninglessness Absence of a sense of involvement in a worthwhile activity. The term refers particularly to fragmented work where one individual's contribution is so small as to seem worthless. See Alienation.

Mechanical solidarity Durkheim used this term to describe a form of cohesion that is based fundamentally on sameness.

Members' competences See Background understandings.

Men's liberation A social and political movement concerned with challenging stereotypes of masculinity and the associated sex roles that confine men to the public occupational realm.

Mercantilism Trade, particularly referring to the historical period when European countries effectively dominated world trade and amassed great wealth at the expense of less developed countries.

Meritocracy Inequality in social rewards based on individual differences in ability and effort.

Meritocracy thesis In functionalist theory, the thesis that hierarchy and social inequality are accounted for by the need to motivate the more talented and competent individuals to occupy the more important and difficult roles in society.

Metaphysical stage A stage in Comte's model of the evolution of societies. Societies in the metaphysical stage are characterized by a prevailing belief in a single deity. Phenomena are explained by reference to abstract forces or ultimate reality rather than to a multiplicity of spirits.

Methodism A puritanical religious doctrine that stresses spiritual egalitarianism, grace through penitence, strictness in religious practice and moral behaviour, and submission to authority.

Methodological holism The principle that social experiences must be explained in terms of forces that operate at the level of the social system as a whole.

Methodological individualism The theory that social experiences can be reduced to the characteristics of individual people. See Psychological reductionism.

Metropolis The centre of capitalism, which dominates surrounding regions, extracting their economic resources.

Microhistory The study of how personal interaction is shaped over time.

Microsociology The detailed analysis of what people do, say, and think in the actual flow of momentary experience.

Microstructural bias A tendency to concentrate on the internal workings of organizations rather than to examine the effects of wider political and economic forces on them.

Microtranslation strategy The attempt to show how large-scale social structures can be understood as patterns of repetitive micro-interactions.

Military-industrial complex The thesis that there is a close affinity between the interests of the elites within the military and industry.

Military-industrial-political complex The thesis that there is a close affinity between the personnel and the interests of elites within the military and industry and senior ranks of the civil service and government ministries.

Minimal responses Responses intended to display continuing interest in a conversation, such as "uh hmm," "uh huh," and "yeah."

Misogyny Generalized hostility towards women.

Missing what, the The practical reasoning and background understandings that participants rely on to produce collective behaviour like jazz performance or a conversation, that other researchers treat as basic data.

Mobility Geographic mobility refers to movement from one locality to another. Social mobility refers to a change in relative status, either up or down the social class hierarchy.

Mode of production Marx uses this term to refer to the prevailing way in which a society transforms the material environment to meet subsistence needs.

Monogamy Having only one mate. Marriage between one man and one woman.

Monolithic bias The assertion that a particular phenomenon is uniform throughout, allowing no variation.

Monopoly Exclusive possession of the trade in some commodity by one individual or one corporation.

Morality Durkheim uses the term to refer to the expression of the relationship between individuals and society.

Multinational corporations Business enterprises that operate in one or more countries in addition to the country housing the corporate headquarters.

Multivariate analysis An aspect of survey research in which statistical techniques are used to see how sets of variables interact in combination.

National Policy The policy instituted by John A. Macdonald in 1878 to establish high tariffs against US goods entering Canada in order to encourage industrialization in Canada. The effect was that US businesses invested in branch plants within Canada.

Natural attitude This term is used in ethnomethodology to refer to people's tendency to assume that social interaction is meaningful, without their reflecting on how such meaning comes to be perceived and sustained.

Natural laws Statement of a causal relationship between physical phenomena, held to be universally true under given conditions.

Need dispositions Parsons uses this term to refer to the way people tend to act in conformity with norms and feel dissatisfied when they cannot do so. Individual choices take the form of patterned behaviour because of the internalization of shared norms.

Neo-imperialism The practice of one country exerting effective control over the economy of another country and exploiting its resources even though it has formal independence.

Noble Under the feudal system, one who controls the estate on which serfs work.

Nomothetic Lawlike generalizations. Deterministic cause and effect relations.

Normalization Foucault uses this term to refer to a manipulated conformity managed by rational social science principles and legitimated by reference to models of healthy psychological and social adjustment. See Therapeutic intervention.

Normative consensus In functionalist theory, this refers to a social group's shared acceptance of a set of values and behavioural expectations as legitimate and appropriate. The establishment of normative consensus is considered critical in the maintenance of a stable social order to which members willingly conform.

Norms Typical expectations for behaviour in given situations that are seen as legitimate and appropriate.

Nuclear family A family unit comprising two sexually cohabiting adults of the opposite sex together with their dependent children.

Objectivity The attempt to present and to deal with facts, uncoloured by the feelings, opinions, and viewpoints of the person presenting them. Objective evidence is that which is accepted as factual and independent of the subjective opinions or theories of any observer.

Oligarchy Rule by a few people at the top without democratic participation.

Oligopoly Concentrated possession of the trade in some commodity by a few individuals or a few corporations.

One-dimensional thought The inability to conceive of viable alternative ways of organizing social relations. Acceptance of the status quo and of the prevailing ways of thinking as the only credible option.

Order theory Closely related to systems theory, a perspective in which the central focus is on how a stable balance is maintained between elements of a social system.

Organic solidarity Durkheim uses this term to refer to a form of cohesion based upon specialization and interdependence.

Other For Mead, those people whose responses to us play an integral part in the development of our own sense of self-identity.

Out-group A group of people considered sufficiently different as to be outside one's own cultural group.

Outsiders Nonconformists. People whose lifestyles or characteristics visibly violate at least some of the norms that define membership within a given community. See Symbolic brackets.

Overlaps and interruptions Sections of conversation when one person begins to talk while another party to the conversation is still talking.

Paradigm A broad theoretical perspective that may encompass several more specific but related stories. A pattern.

Participant observation A methodological approach in which the researcher shares as fully as possible in the everyday activities of the people being studied in order to understand their lives through personal experience.

Participatory management A form of management in which workers are permitted some involvement in making decisions, usually as a way of winning their support for the implementation of such decisions.

Particularism/Particularistic standards For Parsons, evaluation based on the particular abilities, interests, and efforts of an individual.

Party Weber uses the term to refer to organized relations within the political arena, designed to influence policy in favour of a tribe or family.

Patriarch Father and ruler of a tribe or family.

Patriarchy A social system based on male dominance and female subordination.

Patrimony Property inherited from one's father. Also used to refer to a system of senior male mentors conferring rank or privileges onto specifically chosen junior males.

Pattern maintenance Parsons uses the term to refer to the mechanisms to manage tensions and ensure that individual role players in an activity have the skills and motivation needed to perform their given role(s) appropriately. Latency.

Pattern variables For Parsons, a patterned set of dichotomous options that systematize typical dilemmas of choice in any given role.

Pay equity Equal pay for equal work means that women and men who do identical work should receive identical pay. Equal pay for work of equal value means that workers in different jobs should receive the same pay when their work involves the same level of skill, responsibility, or difficulty.

Peasant A person who works the land to produce food and other materials for immediate consumption rather than for sale or exchange. In discussions of feudalism, the term is often synonymous with serf. Generally, one who works the land.

Personal troubles Mills uses the term to refer to the private matters that lie within an individual's character and immediate relationships.

Personality system Parsons uses the term to refer to the learned component of individual behaviour. Socialization is a critical process in its formation.

Petite bourgeoisie Marx uses the term to describe the class of people who own their own means of production and work for themselves but who hire little or no additional wage-labour.

Phenomenology A theory of the methods or grounds of knowledge based on the premise that all knowledge constitutes interpretations of basic sense experience. The study of how sensory information becomes interpreted as meaningful.

Piece-rate payment A system of payment based on the number of items or units of work completed, rather than on the length of time worked.

Plutocracy A ruling class of wealthy persons. Rule by the wealthy.

Polarization of classes Marx's thesis that, under capitalism, wealth will become progressively more concentrated in the hands of a tiny elite class of capitalists as the mass of people become steadily more impoverished.

Political economy theory A theoretical perspective in which the central explanatory framework for analyzing society is the Marxist model of capitalism. The dynamics of the capitalist economy are seen as the fundamental determinants of political structures and action.

Polyandry One woman having more than one husband at the same time. Wife sharing.

Polygamy Having more than one spouse at the same time.

Polygyny One man having more than one wife at the same time. Husband sharing.

Positive society The third stage of Comte's model of the evolution of societies. Positive society is characterized by a commitment to scientific rationality. Scientists rather than priests are the intellectual and spiritual leaders, and explanations take the form of regular lawlike connections between phenomena based on observation and experiment.

Positivism/Positivist A scientific approach to the study of society that seeks to emulate the methodology of the physical sciences. Emphasis is placed on quantitative, objective data rather than on subjective or impressionistic research. Conclusions are based upon observation and experiments that are assumed to provide factual, objective evidence, independent of the theories or opinions of any observer. Also, the search for deterministic or lawlike relations of cause and effect governing human behaviour. The philosophical assumption that observation and experimentation constitute the only valid human knowledge. In ethnomethodology the term refers to an ideology that accords the subjective interpretations of sense experience by other people.

Postfeminist liberalism A view that works to depoliticize feminism by attributing all power differentials and under-representation of women in positions of status and influence to individual weaknesses rather than to patriarchal societal structures.

Postmodernism A complex term that refers to architectural styles that incorporate a pastiche or merging of multiple styles in one building. In sociological theory, a perspective that rejects the search for grand theories or unifying explanations for society, conceptualizing social reality as heterogeneous, fluid, and contingent.

Poverty line A level of income below which people are defined as poor. Commonly calculated on the basis of the proportion of total income required to meet basic subsistence needs of food, shelter, and clothing in a particular society.

Powerlessness Lack of control over factors directly affecting one's life, particularly lack of control over one's work and fear of unemployment. See Alienation.

Practical reasoning In ethnomethodology, the methods by which ordinary people, in their everyday practical affairs, mutually create and sustain their common-sense notions of what is going on.

Precontractual basis of contract Durkheim uses the term to refer to a collective commitment to shared values that are a moral precondition for orderly contractual relations. It refers, in particular, to a commitment to respect for individual differences and human rights.

Predestination See Calvinism.

Prejudice Prejudging, usually in negative terms, the characteristics that are assumed to be shared by members of another group. Preconceived opinion or bias against or in favour of a person or thing. Commonly used to refer to negative opinions of people regarded as outside one's one cultural group.

Prerequisites Those needs or functions that must be met within any social system for that system to maintain a state of balance or equilibrium.

Prescriptive norms Shared behavioural expectations concerning what one should do or how one ought to behave in a given situation.

Presentation of self The image that we try to create for ourselves in the eyes of other people whose opinion we value.

Primitive communism An economic system characterized by a simple hunting and gathering technology where the means of production—the local plants and animals—are accessible to all, and no one has ownership rights to the terrain or to its resources

Private realm In functionalism, the aspects of society perceived as oriented toward personal life, particularly family and leisure activities.

Privatization In the domestic labour debate, this refers to the process of separating domestic work, and the people—mostly women—who perform it, from other productive activities.

Probability The recognition that social phenomena have multiple causes and involve elements of free choice that cannot be predicted with certainty but can be explored with respect to the likelihood of their occurrence.

Procedural norms Rules that govern how a particular activity, such as contract negotiations, should proceed.

Profane Durkheim uses this term to describe that which does not belong to the sacred. Mundane, ordinary.

Proletariat Wage-labourers who survive by selling their labour power. Those who do not own any means to produce for themselves.

Proscriptive norms Shared behavioural expectations concerning what one should not do or what is unacceptable behaviour in a given situation.

Protectionism The situation where duties are applied to imported goods to raise their sale price relative to the price of equivalent local goods, usually to compensate for higher local production costs.

Protestant ethic Weber uses this term to refer to the moral value accorded to work as a spiritual duty and a sign of God's grace. This value system emphasizes accumulation of wealth as a sign of grace; poverty, laziness, and idle luxury are seen as signs of moral depravity and damnation.

Psychoanalysis A body of theory that focuses on infantile sexual drives and their repression within the nuclear family as the foundations of adult personality.

Psychological reductionism The attempt to explain collective social processes by reference only to the psychological processes within the individuals involved.

Psychologism See Psychological reductionism.

Public issues Mills uses this term to refer to the broad social forces that affect the life experiences of many people in similar circumstances.

Public realm In functionalism, aspects of society, particularly economic and political institutions, that are perceived to be oriented toward the society as a whole.

Purdah A cultural tradition among East Indians that emphasizes the seclusion of women in the home, as part of a pattern of restrictions on their behaviour. Literally, a curtain, especially one serving to screen women from the sight of strangers.

Puritanism A doctrine that emphasizes extreme strictness in moral behaviour such that frivolity, idleness, and luxury, and sex other than for procreation are condemned.

Purposive-rational action Weber uses this term to describe action based on calculation of the most effective means to achieve a particular desired outcome, balanced against probable costs.

Qualitative methods Methods that are not based on quantitative procedures. These methods are used to explore small settings in depth with the goal of gaining insight that may form the basis for generalizations.

Quantitative methods A methodological approach that counts instances of specified aspects of human behaviour in order to derive broad generalizations about patterns of experience.

Questionnaires A formulated series of questions used in survey research.

Race A concept that refers to people's visible and inherited physical differences that are socially noticed. It is commonly associated with differences in skin colour.

Racism Prejudicial attitudes toward groups perceived to be different on the basis of inescapable genetic characteristics. Feelings of antagonism, commonly associated with hostile and discriminatory behaviour toward people of a different race or visibly distinct descent group.

Radical One who advocates fundamental change that goes to the root of the existing social order as distinct from one advocating piecemeal changes.

Radical feminism Feminist theory that focuses on control over sexuality and relations of reproduction.

Radical microsociology The study of everyday life in second-by-second detail, using such techniques as audio and video recordings to permit the detailed analysis of conversations and nonverbal interaction.

Rationalization Cost-benefit analysis generally, with both costs and benefits defined primarily in narrow and technical terms rather than incorporating all social and emotional costs and benefits. Also, concentrating production in one or a few large enterprises with the objective of minimizing unit production costs. An aspect of the strategy of maximizing economies of scale.

Rational-legal authority Weber uses the term to describe authority legitimated by reference to the practical utility of the rules themselves.

Reality disjunctures Occasions when people hold different interpretations of the facts of a situation and challenge those held by others.

Rebel A category in Merton's anomie theory of crime. One who replaces socially valued goals with alternative goals and who adopts alternative means to achieve these new goals.

Recipe knowledge Awareness of typical patterns of actions, learned through socialization, that provide a basis for interpreting the meaning of particular actions.

Reconstituted family A family produced by combining some members of two previously separate families, usually produced by the second marriage or one or both spouses who bring children from a previous marriage or partnership.

Reductionism The tendency to explain complex phenomena by reference to a single cause. The attempt to explain complex social processes by reference only to some lower level of analysis (i.e., to explain social phenomena by individual psychology). See Psychological reductionism.

Reflexive/Reflexivity In ethnomethodology, the assumption that there is a mutually determining relationship between appearances and underlying patterns. What one notices about an object or event is contingent upon what one assumes it to be. Similarly, what one assumes it to be is contingent upon the details that one notices.

Refugee status Status that can be accorded those fleeing to a foreign country to escape persecution.

Regulation Durkheim uses the term to refer to values and rules that restrain individual self-interest for the good of the social whole.

Reification The tendency to impute causal force or motives to abstract concepts such as society or markets instead of to the activities of people.

Relations of production Refers to how people organize to produce goods.

Relations of reproduction Refers to how people organize to produce children and raise them to maturity.

Relative deprivation The subjective experience of poverty or loss in comparison with other people rather than in terms of an absolute measure of penury.

Relative surplus Marx uses this term to refer to the amount of surplus production available after payment of wages, when the productivity of workers is increased through labour-saving technology.

Religion Durkheim describes religion as a unified system of beliefs and practices, relative to sacred things, which unite into a single moral community—a church—all adherents.

Repressive law Durkheim uses the term to refer to law that is essentially religious in character and that is concerned with punishing offenders who have transgressed the shared values of the community.

Reserve army of labour Marx uses the term to refer to those people who can be drawn into the labour market when needed by

capitalists but let go, often to return to unpaid domestic work, when no longer needed.

Restitutive law Durkheim uses this term to refer to law that is concerned with the regulation of contracts and the re-establishment of reciprocal obligations between members of a society.

Retreatist A category in Merton's anomie theory of crime. One who rejects or gives up on socially approved goals and who fails to conform to behavioural expectations.

Right of national treatment Part of the free trade agreement between the US and Canadian governments. Any enterprise based in one country but doing business in the other would be subject to the same regulations as those that apply to local enterprise.

Ritualist A category in Merton's anomie theory of crime. One who rejects or gives up socially valued goals but conforms to behavioural expectations.

Role A typical pattern of behaviour in a predefined situation or status. In ethnomethodology, interpreting behaviour after the fact so as to render it meaningful or accountable, rather than random.

Role conflict Conflict resulting from incompatible role demands.

Role distancing Goffman uses the term to refer to a way of performing a social role so as to convey to onlookers the impression that this is not an activity to which one is wholeheartedly committed.

Role model A person whom others strive to emulate in the performance of a particular role.

Role segregation A separation of roles in time and space, which partly insulates one role from others.

Role set The set of all roles with which a person interacts in the process of playing a specific role. Alternatively, the set of all the different roles that any one person plays simultaneously.

Role strain The conflicting expectations and demands that the person playing a specific role experiences from other people in the wider set of related roles. Also, the conflicting expectations and demands that people experience when playing several different roles simultaneously.

Role-taking Mead uses the term to describe the way in which children develop an image of themselves through trying to see themselves as they appear to others.

Role theory In functionalism, the theory concerned with the patterns of interaction established in the performance of typical activities or functions in society.

Ruling apparatus The totality of processes through which the work of governing a society occurs, including the work of employees in local offices and the forms and documents around which their work is organized.

Sacred For Durkheim, that which is set apart by a community of people as the expression or symbol of highest spiritual value. Often, but not necessarily, that which is consecrated to a deity.

Sample A separated part of a population or type of situation being studied, which is used in research to illustrate the qualities of the population from which the part is drawn.

Science A search for knowledge that tries to test tentative assumptions or explanations through the systematic search for evidence.

Scientific management A principle of management of manual work based on the fragmentation of tasks into their smallest component actions, each of which can be precisely regulated through time and motion studies to achieve the maximum possible speed of performance. Sometimes referred to as Taylorism, after Frederick Taylor, the engineer who first developed the system.

Scientism A reliance on simple cause-and-effect explanatory models that imply that external forces rather than human agency determine human experience.

Secondary analysis Analysis that uses data collected in previous research for some other purpose.

Secondary deviance Used in labelling theory to refer to deviance caused or prompted by the sense of being considered a deviant person by other people.

Self The image of oneself comprising both spontaneous feelings and learned attributes.

Self-estrangement Absence of a sense of personal involvement or pride in what one does and hence a detachment from it. See Alienation.

Semiotics The study of how people convey meaning through both language and a host of other non-linguistic signs and gestures.

Semiproletarianization The situation of people who were formerly self-sufficient producers but who have to take part-time wagework to survive.

Separation In the context of ethnic relations, this term refers to two or more distinct ethnic groups living within the same nation-state but maintaining separate political, economic, and cultural institutions and having minimal interaction.

Serf A tied labourer on a feudal estate. A person whose service is attached to the land and transferred with it.

Sets of roles See Role set.

Sex Biological differences in reproductive capacities of males and females.

Sex roles Activities that are defined within a particular culture as the typical responsibility only of women or only of men.

Sexism/Sexist bias Stereotyped and usually derogatory attitudes or discriminatory behaviour toward people of one sex, commonly but not necessarily toward people of the opposite sex.

Sexual class Location of women and men relative to the organization of the activities of reproduction involving conception, pregnancy, childbirth, nurturing, consuming, domestic labour, and wage earning.

Shareholder capitalism The thesis that ownership of capital is becoming democratized through large numbers of people owning shares.

Shoptalk The shorthand jargon that can be used in conversations between people who share specialized background understandings.

Significant others People whose relationship to us and whose opinions of us are important.

Signified The mental concept to which a signifier refers; e.g., a picture of a suitcase with an arrow (signifier) refers to the baggage claim area in an airport (signified).

Signifier The physical form of a sign. In language, the sound or the word.

Skilled labour time A concept developed by Marx to refer to the time it takes for a skilled person to produce a commodity. It includes the average time taken to learn the skill, including the teacher's time.

Slavery Economic organization in which some persons are the legal property of another or others and are bound to labour for them.

Small groups laboratories Rooms that, in order to facilitate experiments, are designed to permit a researcher to control a wide variety of factors that might influence interaction within a small group of people.

Social action In functionalism, the structures and processes by which people form meaningful intentions and, more or less successfully, implement them in concrete situations. Weber used the term to refer to any human conduct that is meaningfully oriented to the past, present, or future expected behaviour of others.

Social construction of reality/Social constructionism A theoretical perspective, loosely associated with Marxist theory, that explores how the immediate practical activities of people in their everyday working lives produce the patterns that we subsequently come to recognize as social structures.

Social facts Durkheim uses this term to refer to social phenomena that are experienced as external to the individual and as constraints on the individual's behaviour.

Social Gospel movement A movement that stresses the doctrine of collective social responsibility and the links between Christianity and socialism. Concepts of sin and salvation are interpreted in social rather than individual terms.

Social order In ethnomethodology, the active processes of creating and sustaining notions of underlying patterns in the otherwise undefined flux of experience. It is accomplished through practical, everyday reasoning.

Social structures A broad macrosociological term, referring to large-scale and long-term patterns of organization in a society. Roughly equivalent to social institutions. In ethnomethodology, the outcome of practical reasoning processes engaged in by sociologists and others, to account for what seems to be going on. See Institutions.

Social system In functionalism, the structures and processes that collectively organize action and manage the potential for conflict and disorganization to maintain order over time.

Socialism A political and economic theory that advocates collective responsibility for the well-being of members of a society.

Socialist feminism Feminist theory that focuses on the linkages between the economy and domestic division of labour.

Socialization The lifelong process through which we learn the values and expected patterns of behaviour appropriate for particular social groups and specific roles. This learning process is particularly intense in infancy but continues throughout life as we change roles and group membership.

Socially necessary labour time See Abstract labour time.

Society Generally, the multiple interactions of individuals in a particular setting. A set of forces exerted by people over one another and over themselves. In functionalism, the term refers to a relatively self-sufficient, functioning social system comprising interdependent parts—polity, economy, family, administration, and so on—that each perform specialized functions for the whole. Parsons uses the term to refer to a large-scale social system that controls behaviour within a given territory, has relatively clear membership status, and is capable of meeting all the life needs of members from birth to death.

Sociobiology The study of the biological bases of social behaviour.

Sociological imagination The capacity to understand the relationships between elements of society and their impact on individual lives. The ability to use information in a critical way to achieve an understanding of what is going on in the world and what may be happening within one's own life experience.

Sociology The scientific study of society. The study of relations of social life. Mills uses the term to refer to the study of the major parts or structures of society (polity, economy, church, family, and so on), how these are interrelated, how they came to be as they appear, how they are changing, and the qualities or characteristics of the people involved. Weber uses this term to refer to the science that attempts the interpretive understanding of social action to arrive at an explanation of its cause and effects.

Solidarity Durkheim uses the term to refer to the emotional experience of cohesion and bonding between individuals so that they feel integrated into a social whole.

Specific obligations The perceived right of others to expect only a narrow range of services confined to the precise task at hand, such as in a business contract.

Sponsored immigrant A category within the Immigration Act that refers to people who are permitted to enter Canada as the dependents of a resident of Canada who agrees to take financial responsibility for them.

Standardized questionnaires Survey questionnaires with a predefined set of fixed answers from which the respondent can choose.

State Within the social construction of reality approach, the term is used to refer to the whole spectrum of government, including the behaviour of people at all levels of the civil service and related bureaucracies, agencies, departments, and offices.

Status Generally, the position that one occupies in a society. Weber uses the term to refer to social prestige and honour accruing to a person or office.

Status degradation ceremonies A term used by Garfinkel to refer to rites or actions that publicly signal a drop in social status of a person from a normal member of a group or community to a deviant or stigmatized person.

Stereotypes Simplified versions of other groups of people. Such mental cartoons are formed by generalizing too much or exaggerating people's characteristics on the basis of too little information.

Stigma/Stigmatization Disgrace attaching to some act or characteristic.

Stratification The hierarchical organization of people in occupations that are differentially rewarded in terms of income, prestige, and authority. A general ranking or pattern of inequality in a society, commonly measured in terms of occupation, income, and education.

Structural correspondence theory See Correspondence theory.

Structural functionalism See Functionalism.

Structuralism See Marxist structuralism.

Structure See Social structures.

Structuring The process in time through which actions at any one time set constraints upon subsequent actions.

Subcontracted agency An organization that is used by another to supply goods or to perform work. The term is used figuratively to refer to domestic workers who provide a variety of goods and services for the benefit of corporations, even though not regulated by a specific contract.

Subcultural theory of deviance Growing out of Merton's anomie theory of crime, this theory posits that deviance and crime reflect the values of the subculture of which the deviant is a member.

Subculture A distinctive subset of values and behavioural expectations shared by a particular subgroup within a society.

Subjectivism Any approach that explains human activity solely by reference to individual motivation without considering broader structural forces and constraints.

Subsidiary A company controlled by another company that owns a majority of its shares.

Subsidy Money contributed to an enterprise by the state.

Subsistence Provision of the necessities of life but with little surplus for luxuries or profit.

Subsistence wage The minimum wage required to cover the cost of sustaining workers and reproducing the next generation, given prevailing standards of living and education required by such workers.

Substantive norms Rules that govern what activities should be done (i.e., the responsibilities of participants in a contract).

Suburbs Residential areas in outlying districts of cities, usually characterized by relatively low-density housing.

Superego In psychoanalysis, the veneer of learned values and behavioural expectations that control drives and passions.

Superstructure For Marx, all aspects of culture, ideas, religion, legal, and political institutions, and so on, that are seen as determined by the prevailing mode of production in that society.

Supply-curve demand The relationship between supply of a commodity in the market and the demand for it, mediated by the price.

Surplus value For Marx, the difference between the value of the wages paid and the value of the commodities produced by the worker.

Surrogate mother A woman who becomes pregnant in order to produce a child for someone else.

Survey research A methodological approach that utilizes questionnaires or structured interviews in which a series of questions are asked of a sample of people. Answers are then analyzed with the aid of computers to provide broad comparative information.

Survival of the fittest The thesis that those biological organisms and societies that survive and prosper are the fittest or best adapted to their environment.

Symbolic brackets Erikson uses the term to refer to the culturally defined limits of acceptable behaviour that distinguish members of a community from nonmembers.

Symbolic interaction A theoretical approach within the interpretive perspective. It focuses on micro-interactions and how people use gestures and language to convey typical meanings in interaction with others who share a common cultural background.

Symbols Observable events such as sounds and images that refer to objects or concepts other than themselves.

Synthesis See Dialectic; Dialectical materialism.

System A complex whole. A set of connected parts.

System prerequisites For Parsons, the basic requirements of pattern maintenance, integration, goal attainment, and adaptation found in any ongoing social system and subsystem.

Systems theory The study of society as a whole or of specific elements of society as functionally interrelated elements, analogous to a biological organism or an organ within such an organism. The central focus is on how a stable balance is maintained between elements.

Taboo Sacred ban or prohibition.

Taylorism See Scientific management.

Technical civilization A vision of society as comprising a dense network of interlocking bureaucratic organizations penetrating all aspects of social life. See Bureaucratic society; Disciplinary society.

Technics/Language of technics The use of computer terminology to refer to human interaction (i.e., feedback, input, output instead of dialogue, debate, judgment).

Technocratic-meritocratic thesis The theory that hierarchy and social inequality in industrial societies reflect differential competence of individuals with respect to science and technology. See Meritocracy thesis.

Text See Textual analysis.

Textual analysis A methodological approach that involves the detailed study of particular pieces of writing to reveal how meaning is constructed by the text.

Theological stage A stage in Comte's model of the evolution of societies. In the theological stage, societies are dominated by primitive religious thought, and explanations for phenomena are expressed primarily in terms of supernatural forces.

Theory of exchange In Marxist analysis, the theory that the exchange value of a commodity is determined by the amount of labour that goes into a commodity. Under capitalism, the basis of exchange is money, rather than another commodity.

Theory of modernization A theory originating in Spencer's model of societal evolution. It sees societies evolving toward increased differentiation and specialization in political, cultural, economic, and social areas.

Therapeutic intervention For Foucault, the process of manipulating conformity and consensus in society through technical means developed in the social sciences and justified by reference to efficiency and healthy psychological and social adjustment.

Thesis See Dialectic; Dialectical materialism.

Third World The impoverished and technologically backward regions of Latin America, Africa, and Asia.

Totem Any natural object, especially a local animal or plant, that is recognized as the symbol or emblem of a clan or sometimes of an individual.

Traditional authority For Weber, authority legitimated by custom, such as that of hereditary rulers.

Traditional-rational action Weber uses the term to refer to action that is based on habit.

Transcripts Written reproductions of conversation in which all hearable details of talk are included, such as intonation, pauses, the stretching of vowels, and the overlapping of turns.

Transfer pricing The prices charged when goods and services are exchanged between a parent corporation and one of its subsidiaries or between two subsidiaries of the same parent corporation.

Transsexual A person who has undergone a more or less permanent sex change.

Turn-taking How participants in a conversation organize the transfer of talking from one person to another.

Typify/Typifications Sets of shared assumptions concerning what is normal behaviour for people in related roles or social positions. See Background understandings.

Typology A theoretical model defining different categories or elements of a phenomenon.

Underdeveloped society A society in which critical economic resources have been and still are being plundered and the internal economy undermined by processes within the world capitalist economic system.

Undeveloped society A society in which the economy continues to function in an unchanged, traditional pattern without benefit of technological advance.

Universal functionalism Parsons uses the term to refer to the assumption, borrowed from biology, that every element found within a social system must perform some function for the whole society.

Universalism/Universalistic standards For Parsons, evaluation based on objective criteria that apply equally to any person performing a given activity.

Unobtrusive measures Measures that avoid the possibility of influencing the phenomenon being measured.

Utterances In ethnomethodology, sounds made by a person before they have been interpreted as having any meaning.

Vacuum ideology An attitude that children from minority cultures learn virtually nothing worth knowing outside of school.

Value-rational action Weber's term for action based on beliefs.

Values The beliefs shared among members of a group or society concerning qualities thought to be desirable or esteemed.

Variable Any phenomenon that has more than one value.

Verstehen The interpretation of behaviour as involving meaningful intentions. A methodological approach that involves trying to reconstruct the interpretations that the people being studied might give to their own actions.

Vertical integration Enterprises that operate at different stages in the production of a particular commodity and are consolidated into one corporation.

Vertical mosaic A pattern of stratification in which members of different racial and ethnic groups are arranged vertically with respect to each other in terms of class position.

Victimless crimes Transactional crimes where the persons involved participate willingly in exchanging goods and services and do not see themselves as either criminals or victims. Crimes against morality where there are no clear victims.

Vocation For Weber, performance of the responsibilities of an office as a duty, not for personal gain.

Voluntarism An explanation for action that refers to the rational and free choice of the actor.

Voluntaristic theory For Parsons, a theory of social action that explains social order by reference to mutual agreement or consensus between actors.

Welfare state A state that provides a range of social services for workers, including such benefits as health care, unemployment insurance, welfare payments, pensions, and the like. Such services ameliorate the effects of cyclical ups and downs in the economy as well as helping workers survive personal crises.

White-collar crime Violations of the law committed by professional and business people.

Worked up An expression used by Smith to describe the state of raw sense data having been categorized and organized in terms of an interpretive framework in the process of communicating it.

Index

Cicourel, A.V., 63
Cineplex, 568
circles of social control, 17, 17f
citizen-journalism, 564–565
city life. See urban communities
civil inattention, 84
civil war, 14, 363–364, 373–389
Clairmont, D.H., 155, 156–157, 519
Clark, A., 221
Clark, L.M.G., 129, 217, 223
Clark, S.D., 20, 142, 143, 144, 152
Clarke, J., 258, 260
class and class relations
    and aspirations for higher
        education, 476
    bureaucracy, 547–549
    class-for-itself, 274
    class-in-itself, 274
    class struggle. See class struggle
    computers, and class differences in
        schools, 482
    drug wars, 206–207
    education and, 490–491
    exploitation, and stratification, 457–460
    gender, influence of, 114–116
    gender-class, 549, 587
    gender relations, influence on, 116–117
    Marxist perspective, 23, 40
    Marx's class analysis, 269
    middle classes, affluent, 304
    mode of production, 269–271
    polarization of classes, 278, 284, 292
    propertied class, and law, 201–202
    property laws and class struggle, 205
    publishing, 562
    puritanism and the working class,
        246–247
    and race, 513
    racialized class formation in white
        settler society, 512–513
    religion, and class conflict, 247–249
    schools and class inequality, 479
    social construction of class relations in
        the home, 440–442
    sociology of power, 408
    Weber's definition, 408
    working class. See working class
class-for-itself, 274
class-in-itself, 274
class struggle
    and alienated consciousness, 274–275
    in Canada, 272–273
    class war in the marketplace, 283–287
    at core of capitalist production, 272
    dependence on markets, 272
    dependent development, 336
    history of, 23
classical liberal economics. See
    liberal-bourgeois theory
classless society, 544
Clausewitz, C.von., 357

Clayman, S.E., 96
Clegg, S., 201
Clement, W., 459
clergy, women as, 259
clerical work, 462–463
clients of bureaucracies, 548–549
Clifton, J.A., 250
Clinton, Bill, 566, 576, 577
Clow, M., 36, 577
Cloward, R.A., 196
CNN, 564, 569
co-operative independent media sites, 565
co-optation, 555–556
Cockburn, A., 207
Cockburn, C., 467
code, digital, 573–574
codes of ethics, 65, 66
Cohen, A., 207
Cohen, A.K., 41, 42, 196
Cohen, A.P., 149
Cohen, J.N., 61, 72
Cohen, M.G., 348
cohesion, Durkheim's theory of, 169–172
cohort, 142, 492
Cold War
    anti-communism in American
        culture, 360
    capitalism vs. communism and
        socialism, 368
    from Cold War to conventional war,
        361–362
    culture of militarism and fear, 360
    end of the Cold War, 362–363
    functionalism, 359–363
    generally, 3
    militarism, 359–360
    political economy theory, 368
Cole, M., 486
Collins, R., 76, 240
colonial rule, 27–184, 527–528
colonialism, 153–154, 331–332, 367–511
colonization, 201–202
Columbia Broadcasting System
    (CBS), 585
Columbia Pictures, 568
Comack, E., 193, 201, 204, 207, 216,
    221, 222
Comarow, M., 71
commercial interests, 337–339
commercialization of service, 348
commodities, 25, 275, 277–278
commodity fetishism, 275
common-law unions, 436t
common-sense understandings, 5, 6
communism
    advanced communism, 271
    anti-communism in American
        culture, 360
    and bureaucracy, 544–545
    vs. capitalism, 368
    in Eastern Europe, 544

France, student uprising in, 545
    Prague Spring, 545
    primitive communism, 269, 271
    socialist economies, restructuring, 337
    Stalinist dictators, 545
    Tiananmen Square massacre, 545
community
    see also loss of community thesis; rural
        communities; urban communities
    accomplishing "community," 151–153
    and association, 136–137
    boundaries as social relations, 152
    demolishing community, 153
    and economy, 139
    ethnic communities, 519, 520
    feminist perspective, 158–161
    gemeinschaft, 136–137
    gendered community space, 158–161
    gendered inequality in community
        life, 160
    gesellschaft, 136–137
    humane form of, 136
    interpretive perspectives, 149–158
    as life-world, 150–151
    limits of community, 148–149
    Marxist theory, 139
    organization of community economy,
        159–160
    patriarchy in ethnic folk communities,
        160–161
    physical infrastructure of place, 150–151
    political economy analysis, 143–144
    rethinking the concept, 149–158
    settler cities, 153–154
    social constructionist perspectives,
        151–153
    social dislocation, 153
    subsistence level of living, 143
    symbolic interactionism, 150–151
    symbolic meaning, 149
community controls, 198–200
community of practice, 461–462
community policing programs, 199, 215
compensation claims, 202
competing interests, 27
competition patterns, 295–297
competitive advantage, 336
competitive strategies, 336
competitive struggle, 168
compliance, 418
Comte, Auguste, 167–168
concentration of capital in Canada,
    294–297
concentric zone theory, 137
confession, 124
confidentiality of informants, 65
conflict
    class conflict, and religion, 247–249
    colonization of the inner city, 202–204
    family breakdown, and social
        disorder, 19

ethnic minorities (*continued*)
    political elites, 160
    as subculture, 17
    suicide rates, 186–187
ethnic relations. *See* race and ethnic
    relations
ethnic separatism, 376
ethnicity, 502
ethnicization, 516–520
ethnocentrism, 7, 502–503
ethnomethodology
    accountability, 86
    background understandings, 85, 88
    breaching experiments, 34
    conversation analysis, 34–35, 68–69,
        93–97
    derivation of term, 32, 86
    described, 32–35, 85–91
    documentary method of interpretation,
        89–91
    feminist studies, contributions to, 91–93
    focus of, 50
    functionalism, critique of, 428–429
    indexicality, 87–89
    members' competences, 89
    "the missing what," 97
    plausible deniability, 99
    practical reasoning, 86
    reality disjuncture, 91
    sex, determination of, 119
    social construction of gender, 91–93
    and social structures, 86–87
    studies of work, 97–101
    utterances, 87
European Economic Community, 359
European Union, 21
Everett, A., 584
Everton, S.F., 261
everyday life. *See* microsociology
evolution, 168
evolutionary explanations, 106–108
excessive integration, 173
excessive regulation, 173
exchange value, 275
exclusion, 148–149, 157–158
executive compensation, 297,
    302–303
exogamy, 45
expanding capitalist markets, and war,
    371–372
experiments
    breaching experiments, 34–87
    critique of an experiment, 59
    dependent variable, 58
    described, 58–60
    ethical issues, 60–61
    hypothesis, 59
    independent variable, 58
    limitations of social experiments, 60
    measurement of variables, 59
    replication, 59

small groups laboratories, 60
    vs. survey research, 62
    variable, 58
expert commentaries, 580
exploitation, 276, 315–316, 572
exploitative sexuality, struggle against,
    129–130
expressive leader, 434
extended families, 432
extrinsic reward, 456

F

Facebook, 31, 564, 569
facts
    elusive nature of, 7
    as indicators, 173
    and interpretive framing, 36
    material evidence, 36
    as ongoing accomplishments, 86
    vs. opinions, 36
    reality disjuncture, 91
    social facts, 170
    symbolic interactionism, 30
failed states, 364
Fairclough, N., 24, 28, 68, 72
Faith, K., 198, 212, 213
faith communities, 21
Falardeau, J.C., 141
fallacy of functional indispensability, 424
fallacy of functional unity, 425
fallacy of universalism, 425, 427
false consciousness, 591
Faludi, S., 44, 130
Falun Gong, 566
familism, 140
family
    breakdown of, and deviant behaviour, 197
    breakdown of, and social disorder, 19
    capitalism, and family forms in Canada,
        439–440
    common-law unions, 436t
    conservative bias, 437–438
    critique of functionalist theory, 434–438
    dimensions of family life, 435
    economic cooperation, 436
    emotional relations, 436
    extended families, 432
    familism, 140
    family socialization, problems in,
        111–112
    family structure, 437f
    fear message, 212
    function of, 14, 48
    functionalist theories, 432–434
    home-school relation, 490–491
    inconsistent values, 48
    inegalitarian family forms, 439
    institution of the family, 14, 48
    Marxist theories, 438–440
    microstructural bias, 438
    monogamy, 432

monolithic bias, 434–437
    nuclear families, 432
    patriarchy, Marxist theory of, 439
    policing families, 213
    polyandry, 432
    polygamy, 432
    polygyny, 432
    as primary agent of socialization, 178
    private realm, 439
    procreation, 435
    radical feminist critique, 442–450
    reconstituted families, 67, 435
    residence patterns, 436
    role in functionalist model of
        society, 432
    role of the family, 423
    sexist bias, 438
    sexual relations and, 436
    social construction of class relations in
        the home, 440–442
    socialization, 436
family law
    abuse and violence, 221
    custody as unequal equality rights,
        220–221
    gender equality, and the Charter,
        219–220
    history of, 218–219
    Indian Act of 1876, 220
    maintenance awards, 219–220
    marital property laws, 219–220
family systems, 421, 422
family wages, 115
famine, 338–339
farming
    agribusiness and famine, 338–339
    agribusiness and the state, 316
    agribusiness practices, 178
    bio-engineering, 319–320
    biofuels, 317
    corporate farming, 178
    corporate order, negotiation of, 316
    dependent commodity production,
        314–315
    efficiency *vs.* exploitation, 315
    farm wives, 321–323, 439
    feminist perspectives, 321–323, 439
    free markets as legal discourse, 319
    hog farming, 317–319
    marketing boards, 316–317
    migrant labour, 316
    organic farming, 320–321
    potato farming in the Maritimes,
        313–314
    rural communities, and corporate
        farming, 178
    vulnerable labour power, 316
Farr, K., 533
fatalistic suicide, 173, 174–175
faulty-parenting thesis, 211
FBI, 567, 576

fear
    of crime, 211–213
    culture of militarism and fear, 360
    institutionalization of fear and
        insecurity, 386
    interpretation of evidence of fear of
        crime, 215
    politics of fear, 377
    and terrorism, 214–215
    theorizing crime and fear, 213–215
Fedec, K., 225, 226, 227, 228
Feder, E., 339
Federal Contractors Program, 465, 466
feedback mechanisms, 426
Fekete, L., 509
femininity, 117, 122–123
feminism. *See* feminist perspective
feminist code of ethics, 65
Feminist Majority, 584
feminist networking sites, 46
feminist perspective
    see also gender; women and girls
    abstract legal rights, 555
    as agent of change, 497
    anti-feminist media backlash, 589
    "backlash" position, 44
    black feminists, 532–533
    bureaucracy, and possibility of
        resistance, 553–556
    bureaucratic co-optation, 555–556
    Canadian legal history, review of, 126
    central assumptions, 38–39
    child prostitution, 227–228
    child sexual abuse, policing, 224–225
    class, and women, 40
    clergy, women as, 259
    and community, 158–161
    conformity, 555
    contemporary religious institutions,
        women in, 257–259
    core assumptions, 50
    corporate capitalism, 307–313
    cult of domesticity, 555
    cultural feminism, 43, 51
    culture, 45–46
    cyber-feminist online groups, 582
    depoliticized feminism, 263–264
    disillusionment with Marxist
        sociology, 40
    diversity in feminist thought, 42–43,
        51, 125
    domestic division of labour and social
        inequality, 468–469
    domestic labour for capital, 310–312
    domestic violence, and religion,
        263–264
    domestic violence, policing, 221–222
    economic development, 340–342
    education, 492–497
    embedded feminism in war, 394–395
    emergence of, 38

employment equity policy, and
    resistance, 312–313
equality rights as ideology, 469
and ethnomethodology, 91–93
exploitation of women during
    recession, 311
family, 442–450
family law, 218–228
farming in Canada, 321–323
feminist organizing on the Internet,
    583–584
feminist pedagogy, 496
feminist sociology, three main stages, 51
feminist theory, 40
first wave of feminism, 555
focus of, 50–51
four-part model of theory, 497
fundamental notions of gender,
    challenges to, 42
gender bias in mainstream social
    science, 41–42
gender gap in labour market, 309–310
gender identity, 44–46, 50
gender processes, 50–51
gender relations, 125–131
gendered character of oppression, 41
gendered community space, 158–161
gendered ethnic politics in Canada,
    530–531
gendered inequality in community
    life, 160
gendered production of knowledge, 51
gendered representation, 580–592
gendering, 38–39, 43
hearing women's religious voices,
    261–262
implicit functionalism underlying, 131
institutionalized misogyny in
    religion, 257
kinship in urban folk communities, 159
law, 218–228
lessons for peace, 396
liberal feminism, 43, 126–127, 555–556
limitations of, 131
"main business," feminist challenge to, 310
and mainstream sociology, 39–40
Marxist feminism, 43, 51, 127–128,
    581, 586
on the media, 580–592
media representations of feminism,
    586–587
men's liberation, 130
militarism among women, manufacturing,
    393–394
military masculinity, manufacture of,
    388–389
military organizations, women in, 390–391
and new schools of thought, 42
Oedipus complex, 45
organization of community economy,
    159–160

organizations, principles of, 554
paradigms, 40
patriarchal Aboriginal status, 528
patriarchal capitalism, 310, 313
patriarchal profamilism, 261, 263
patriarchy and religion, 256, 257
patriarchy in ethnic folk communities,
    160–161
patriarchy in European colonial rule,
    527–528
patriarchy thesis, 126
peace movements, 395–396
and political correctness, 587
politics of feminism, 44
pornography, 228
post-colonial gendered ethnicity,
    529–530
vs. postfeminist liberalism, 44
postmodern feminism, 591–592
race and ethnic relations, 527–534
racial and ethnic divisions within
    Western feminist movements, 532–533
racialized women and violence, 531–532
racist feminist discourse, 533–534
radical feminism, 43, 51, 129–130,
    442–450, 556
rape as organized military practice,
    389–393
rational action, challenge to, 412–413
relations of patriarchy, 39, 40–41
relations of reproduction, 50, 128
religion, 256–264
religious institutions, feminization of,
    259–261
representation, 45–46
reproduction, relations of, 38
resistance to feminist theory, 497
rural life as gendered accomplishment,
    158–159
schools of feminist thought, 43–47
second shift, 312
second wave of feminism, 555, 587
selling war as humanitarian
    intervention, 394–395
sex trade, policing the, 225–227
sexual assault, policing, 222–224
sexual liberation, 533–534
social construction of gender, 91–93
socialist feminism, 43, 51, 128–129, 555
stratification, 464–470
suburbia, 159
suicide, 184–187
teachers' responses and expectations,
    493–495
theorizing sexual diversity, 44
traditional stratification theory,
    challenge to, 467–470
underdevelopment of women, 339–340
universities, feminism in, 495–496
vision of God as male, 257
war, 387–397

feminist political economy, 307–313
feminist psychoanalysis, 109
feminist theory, 40
Fenn, M., 112, 550
Ferguson, K.E., 545, 546, 547, 548, 549–550, 551, 552, 553, 554, 555, 556
Fernandez, L., 277, 281
Ferrada-Noli, M., 178
fetish, 275
feudalism, 270, 271
Feyerabend, P.K., 8
file-sharing technology, 29, 574
Fillmore, N., 343
financial crises, 279–281
financial markets, 284
financialization, 284
Findlay, B., 122
Fine, G.A., 112, 122
Fineman, M., 220
Firestone, S., 446
first impressions, 82
First Nations communities
    see also Aboriginal peoples
    anomie, 144
    cooperative networks, 27
    cultural differences, and criminal justice system, 18
    distinct society, 14
    powerlessness, 205
    religion. See Aboriginal spirituality
    research ethics protocols, 71
    suicide. See Aboriginal suicide rates
    systemic dysfunction, 14
    treaty rights, 21, 204–205
first wave of feminism, 555
First World, 329
First World agencies, 531
First World War, 367, 388
fiscal tools, 282, 283
Fishman, P., 94–95
Fiske, J., 579
Fiske, S.T., 520, 526
flawed performance, 32
Fleras, A., 504, 505, 506, 508, 518
Fleur, 580
folk society model
    challenging the folk society model, 140–141
    described, 139–140
    familism, 140
    myth of Quebec motherhood, 141–142, 141f
    Quebec folk society, 140–142
food production. See farming
force, 17
forced division of labour, 172
Fordism, 336, 344
Fortune, 568
Forward, S., 446
Foster, J., 148, 215, 283, 284

Foster, J.B., 283, 284, 286, 294, 569
Foster-Clark, A., 333
Foucault, M., 36, 44, 124, 125, 210, 213, 540, 545, 546, 547, 548, 549, 551, 552, 553, 556
Fox, J., 243–244
Fox News, 569, 570
fractionalized work, 172
fragmentation, 20–21, 172, 556, 562
framing devices, 578
France, 544–545, 566
Frank, A.G., 331
Frank, B., 44, 120, 121–123, 131
Franklin, B., 580
Franklin, S., 45
Franks, M., 530, 531
fraud, 566
free markets, 281–282, 319
free speech, 566
free trade alternatives, 348–349
free trade deals, 283, 285, 343, 344, 347, 349
    see also Canadian development; North American Free Trade Agreement
Freedom of Information Act, 385
Freeman, A., 286, 287
Freeman, D., 66
Freire, P., 483
French-Canadian folk society, 140–142
French Revolution, 169
Freud, Sigmund, 45, 108–109, 210
Friedman, B., 469, 496
Friedman, M., 293
Friedman, Milton, 293
front regions, 82
Fukuyama, F., 545
Fuller, C., 347–348
function, 168, 560
functional indispensability, 417, 474
functional unities, 417, 474
functionalism
    Aboriginal suicide rates, 178
    actor, 16
    assumptions, 13
    basic assumption, 428
    belonging and personal identity, 502
    biological and social systems, analogy between, 417
    biological root of gender relations, 107
    breakdown of social order, 48
    bureaucracy as efficient, 540–542
    The Chicago School, 137–142
    civil war, 363–364
    classic example of functionalist analysis, 15
    Cold War, 359–363
    conflict, and religion, 243–244
    conservative bias, 437–438
    core processes, 48
    crime rates and weakening civil order, 195

critical reformulations, 426–429
criticisms of, 424–426, 434–438, 454–457
cultural divisions in failed states, 364
cultural integration in multicultural societies, 20–21
culture, 15, 17–19, 48, 560
dynamic equilibrium, 48
dysfunctions, 48, 425
early Canadian law and societal values, 192–193
economic development, 329–331
equal opportunity, 454–455
ethnomethodological critique, 428–429
fallacy of functional indispensability, 424
fallacy of functional unity, 425
fallacy of universalism, 425, 427
family, 432–434, 438
feedback mechanisms, 426
feminist challenge to traditional stratification theory, 467–470
focus of, 48
foundations of social order, 16
functional indispensability, 417, 474
functional unities, 417, 474
game or art of war, 357
gender roles, 109–113
global warfare, 357–358
globalization and national culture, 21–22
individual rights vs. social cohesion, 193–194
latent functions, 417, 424–425
law, 192–195
liberal theory of education, 473–477
manifest functions, 417
manifest vs. latent functions, 15, 48
Marxist functionalism, 426–427
mass communication, 560–567
media in the social system, 560–567
microstructural bias, 438
military-industrial complex, 357–358
military institutions, 356–357
modernity, retreat from, 364
modernization as evolution, 329–331
monolithic bias, 434–437
moral order, 194–195
motivation, 456–457
national cultures in global society, 20
new world order, vision of, 363
Parson's social system model, 417–424
Pax Americana as new imperial order, 365–366
peace, lessons for, 366
political organization, 503–509
poverty, and crime, 205
power and, 425
psychoanalysis and socialization, 428
race and ethnic relations, 502–510
reifying society, 78, 85

relative scarcity of personnel, 456
religion, 239–244
religious individualism, 241–242
religious revivalism, 242–243
research focus, 48
role, 15–16, 48, 76–77
role conflict, 16
role set, 16
role strain, 16
secularization thesis, 239–241
sexist bias, 438
social order, 192–195
social systems and individual members, 15–19
socialization, 15, 16–17, 48
society, 432
society as a functioning system, 13–15
Stinchcombe's revised model, 426
stratification, 454–457
suicide, 177–179
systemic conflict and dysfunction, 19
systemic dysfunctions, 14
unequal importance, 455
universal functionalism, 417, 474
variations in functions, 48
war, 356–366
women and stratification, 455
working assumptions, 417
functionalist theory of gender roles. *See* socialization theory
fundamentalism
anti-communism in American culture, 360
black community, 247
domestic violence, 263
fundamentalist women's discourse, 263
politicizing religious beliefs, 255
prophecies, failure of, 254
religious fundamentalism, and "war on terror," 364–365
religious identities, sustaining, 253
religious revivalism, 242–243
roots of, 242
sacred meaning, negotiation of, 252
suffering, and symbolic healing, 253
Fyvel, T.R., 42

G

Gabriel, J., 486, 507, 508, 526
GAIL model, 420, 423
Galabuzi, G-E., 509, 514, 515, 521
Gallagher, S., 383, 384
game of war, 357
Gane, M., 175
gang subculture, 196–197
Gans, H., 147
Garfinkel, H., 33, 34, 86, 87–88, 87*n*–88*n*, 89, 90, 91, 92, 93, 96, 97, 98, 120
Garigue, P., 141, 147
Garroutte, E.M., 177
Gaskell, J., 117, 495
gatekeepers, 563

gathering, 82
gay liberation, 125
gay men
    see also homosexual
    discrimination in employment, 118
    as distinct social category, 116
Geekgrrl, 582
Geertz, C., 502
Geller, L., 258, 261
Gelles, R.J., 222
gemeinschaft, 136–137
gender
    see also feminist perspective; women and girls
    and bureaucracy, 549–550
    challenges to fundamental notions of gender, 42
    class, influence on, 114–116
    and conversation, 94–95
    defined, 106–107
    differences, and biological theories, 108
    division of labour, 117, 118
    feminist perspective, 38
    foundations of gender, 106–109
    gender-class, 549
    Marxist perspective, 38
    and occupations, 465, 465*t*–466*t*
    representation of, 580–592
    as social construction, 121
    social construction of, 91–93
    subordinates, and female boss, 551
    and suicide, 184–187
    use of term, 119
gender bias in mainstream social science, 41–42
gender-class, 549, 587
gender equity, 51
gender-equity policies, 312
gender gap in labour market, 309–310
gender identity, 44–46, 50
gender processes, 50–51
gender relations
    biological explanations, 106–108
    biology *vs.* social learning, 106–109
    class, influence of, 116–117
    contraception, effect of, 106
    femininity, accomplishing, 122–123
    feminist theories, 125–131
    functionalist theory of gender roles, 109–113
    liberal feminism, 126–127
    Marxist feminism, 127–128
    masculinity, accomplishing, 121–122
    men's liberation, 130
    political economy of gender relations, 113–118
    power and resistance, 125
    psychoanalysis, 108–109
    radical feminism, 129–130
    sex and gender as social constructions, 118–125

socialist feminism, 128–129
socialization theory, 109–113
study of, 106
terminology, 119
gender-role socialization, 109, 591–592
gender roles
    behavioural traits within a culture, 110–111
    defined, 106–107
    functionalist theory of gender roles, 109–113
    and the media, 581
    power differentials, 113
    primary socialization, 110
    socialization theory, 109–113
    variations among cultures, 109–110
gender socialization, and crime, 197–198
Gender Watchers, 584
gendered ethnic politics in Canada, 530–531
gendered inequality in community life, 160
gendered law, 218–228
gendered policing of gender-neutral laws, 226
gendered representation, 580–592
gendering, 38–39, 43
general action systems
    adaptation, 420
    cybernetic hierarchy, 419–420
    described, 419–420
    GAIL model, 420
    goal attainment, 420
    integration, 420
    latency maintenance, 420
    pattern maintenance, 420
    pattern variables, 421–423, 422*f*
    structure of, 421*f*
    system prerequisites, 420–421
General Agreement on Tariffs and Trade (GATT), 344, 359
General Electric, 569
General Motors, 26
genetically modified foods, 23–24, 319–320
genocide, 363, 366, 368, 379
Gentlemen Prefer Blondes, 591
gentrification, 147, 151, 154–155
geographic changes, 25
George, Dudley, 154
Gérin, L., 141
Germany, 584
Gerth, H.H., 406, 408, 409, 410, 412
Gesch, L., 241
gesellschaft, 136–137
Giddens, A., 15, 19, 21, 27, 34, 80, 199, 238, 356, 359, 360, 364, 404, 405, 504
Gidengil, E., 335, 342
Gilbert, N., 391
Gill, S.D., 197, 202, 512

Gillen, D.W., 300
Gillespie, M., 255–256, 262, 526
Gilligan, C., 554
Gintis, H., 457, 458, 473, 478, 479, 480, 481, 483, 486
Girdner, L.K., 221
girls. *See* women and girls
Giroux, H.A., 365, 366, 486, 487, 497
Glamour, 590
glasnost, 362
Glenn, 521
global capitalism, 23–25
global corporate culture, 28–29
global financial markets, 24
"Global Gag Rule," 584
Global Television Network, 569
global "war on drugs," 207
global warfare, 357–358
globalization
    global corporate culture, 28–29
    multinational corporations, 25–26, 35
    and national culture, 21–22
    neo-conservative argument, 21–22
    neo-liberal argument, 21–22
Globe and Mail, 569
goal attainment, 420
goal displacement, 541
Goffman, E., 1, 31–32, 80, 81–85, 96, 97, 101, 102
Goldberg, S., 107, 108
Golding, P., 576
Goldsmith, J., 566
Goldstein, E., 257, 258, 260
Gonick, C., 284, 285, 302
Goode, W.J., 107, 433
Google, 29, 566, 570, 584
Gorbachev, Mikhail, 362
Gordon, J., 221
Gordon, L.D., 260
Gordon, M.M., 503
Gouldner, A.W., 542
government enterprises, 300–301
government institutions, and mass communication, 560
Grace, E.K.P., 225
Graetz, N., 263
Graham, Billy, 360
Graham, M., 177
Gramsci, Antonio, 27, 571
grassroots participation, 341
Gray, S., 116
Graycar, R., 220, 221
Great Depression, 3, 367
Green, L., 178
green revolution, 330–334
Greenberg, D.F., 197
Greenglass, E., 110, 111
Gregor, F., 70
Gregor, F.M., 463
Grillo, R., 515, 524
Grossman, D., 388, 389

Grosz, E., 45
Guardian, 577, 586
Guidon, H., 140
guilt, 17
Gulalp, H., 335–336
gun-free zones, 200
Guppy, N., 506
Gyllenhammer, P., 459

H

hackers, 565–566
Hackett, 578
Hackett, R., 68
Halbwachs, M., 176
Hale, S.M., 8, 110, 112, 331, 339, 340, 341, 443
Hall, A., 321
Hall, E.T., 138
Hall, R.M., 496
Hall, S., 575
Hamilton, E., 311
Hamitic hypothesis, 248
Hammersley, M., 492
Hanigsberg, J.E., 590
happiness
    indicators of, 173
    and integration, 173
    and regulation, 173
Haraway, Donna, 585
Hardt, M., 25, 29, 356, 363, 510, 512
Hargittai, 582
Haring, H., 259
Harlow, H.F., 107
harmful business practices, 209–210
Harper, D., 148
Harper, Stephen, 32, 301, 576
Hartley, M., 569
Hartmann, H., 467
Hartmann, H.I., 118, 127
Hayes, M., 281
Hazlewood, L.R., 445
headstart programs, 486
Heap, J.L., 95, 491
Heather, B., 322
Hebdige, D., 41, 42
hegemony, ideological, 515–516
helicopter journalism, 564
Helly, D., 509–510
Hempel, C.G., 424
Henderson, J., 528
Hennig, M., 111, 112, 550
Henripin, J., 141n
Henry, F., 149, 522
Henslin, J., 357
Heritage, J., 89, 93, 94, 96, 97, 418, 428, 429
Hermer, J., 214
Hester, S., 91, 491
heterogeneity, 138
heterosexism, 115, 122, 433
Hewlett, Susan, 307

hidden curriculum, 484
hidden diseconomies, 350
hierarchy
    cybernetic, 419–420
    network, 585
Higgins, T.E., 588
high unemployment, 26
Hill, Anita, 589
Hiller, H.H., 65, 72
Himelfarb, A., 457
Hinch, R., 129
Hindu communities
    arranged marriage and submission, 263
    nationalism, 255
    purdah, 442
    religious conflict, 243
    religious television programming, 255–256
    women, and feminist themes, 262
hinterlands, 335
Hiroshi, O., 582, 583
Hirschi, T., 196
historical materialism, 269, 403
The History of Sexuality (Foucault), 124
Hitchens, C., 269
Hobson, D., 580, 591–592
Hochschild, A., 117, 185, 312, 547
Hodge, G., 143
Hoffman, L.W., 110
hog farming, 317–319
holding companies, 295
Holland, J., 372
Hollinger media chain, 563, 571
Holtrust, N., 221
home births, 447
home-school relation, 490–491
homeless persons, 155, 203
homemaking, 117, 118, 310–312, 441, 455
homicides, 221
homosexual
    see also gay men; lesbians
    adoption of label, 125
    forced therapy, 124–125
    introduction of term, 124
    legal punishments, 124
    rise of gay culture, 125
Hoogvelt, A.M., 331
Hooks, B., 526
horizontal integration, 294
Hörnqvist, M., 509
Horowitz, D.L., 20, 502
Horwitz, A.V., 180
Howell, S., 149, 153
Hudson, I., 281
Hudson, K., 369, 376, 378, 379
Hughes, Francine, 590
Hughes, K.D., 308
Hughes, P., 222, 227
human agency, 12, 404–405, 486
Human Rights Act, 33
human rights legislation, 194, 217

Human Rights Watch, 389
humanism, 171
humanitarian intervention, selling war as, 394–395
humanitarian needs, 14–15
Hunt, K., 382, 394, 395
Hunt, M.E., 258, 260
hunting-and-gathering economies, 23
Huntington, S.A., 364
Hurricane Katrina, 564
Hurtig, M., 342, 346, 347
Hussein, Saddam, 30, 363
Hustler, D.E., 492
Huston, A.C., 495
Hutchby, I., 96, 97
Hutton, W., 286, 295, 302, 304
hybridization, 21
hypothesis, 59

I

Icelandic Woman's Alliance, 554
id, 428
ideal-type constructs, 405
ideal-type model, 139
idealism, 403
idealization, 81
identity
    gender identities, 44
    gender identity, 46
    identity formation, 516–517
    as social construction, 37–38
identity politics, 37
ideographic, 403
ideological hegemony, 27, 298, 515–516, 571
ideological ideas, 28
ideological practices, 5
ideology
    as biased form of method of inquiry, 5
    credentialism, 458
    criminology as ideology, 211
    defined, 5, 28
    equality rights as ideology, 469
    ethnic folk community as political ideology, 158
    limitations and intolerance, 6
    Marxist perspective, 274
    of others, 5–6
    as socially generated ideas, 5
    sociological analysis of, 5
    storytelling as ideological work, 254
    vacuum ideology, 484
Ignatieff, M., 357, 359, 363, 364, 366, 376, 383
Ignatieff, Michael, 32
Ikenberry, J., 355
Illich, I., 481
imagined communities, 152–153
immigrants. See immigration
immigration
    see also ethnic communities; race and ethnic relations

acculturation, 62
assimilation, 506–507
discriminatory hiring practices, 521–522
East York, and subtle practices of exclusion, 157–158
gendered ethnic politics in Canada, 530–531
identity as hyphenated Canadians, 256
immigration laws, 193
immigration laws in Canada, 192–193
labour migration, 511–512
public consultations, 524
racism, 507
religious communities, 256
suicide rates, 186–187
war on terror, and sense of identity, 520
Immigration Act, 518, 529
immigration laws, 193
immiseration, 278, 284–285
impartiality, 6
imperfect competition, 343
imperialism, 331–332, 367, 572
impression management, 81, 85, 548
imprisonment, 198–199
improvisation, 85
in-depth interviews, 69
In Times Like These (McClung), 40
incest, 45
INCO, 544
income, average, 455t
income gap, 24
inconsistent role expectations and values, 48
independent commodity producers, 292
independent media sites, 565
independent variable, 58
index of social deprivation, 179
indexical talk, 34
indexicality, 35, 87–89
Indian Act, 220, 517, 528–529
indicators, 173
indigeneous peoples. See Aboriginal peoples
individual life chances, 3
individual rights, 193–194
individualism
    moral individualism, 171
    radical individualism, 241–242
    religious individualism, 241–242
industrial pollution, 349–351
Industrial Revolution, 167
industrialization, 114, 136, 270, 548
Indymedia.org, 565, 567, 577
inefficiency, 541
inequality. See stratification
information revolution, 1
information-technology bubble, 283
informed consent, 65
inherent contradictions in capitalist markets, 277–279
inner city, 147–148, 154–155, 202–204

Innis, H., 561
innovators, 195, 196
insecurity, institutionalization of, 386
The Insights of Sociology (Boughey), 8
institutional ethnography, 35–37, 44, 50, 69–72, 218, 521–527
institutional separation. See separation
institutional talk, 95, 96
institutionalization, 418
institutionalized misogyny, 257
institutions
    examples of, 48
    family as, 14
    mass communication, 560
    military institutions, 356–357
    multi-functional nature of, 14
    political institutions, 14
    roles, 48
    study of, 13
    superstructure, 22
    supra-national institutions, 358–359
instrumental leader, 433
integration, 168, 170, 173, 420, 506–509, 561
intellectual products, 29
intellectual property, 345
intelligence as interactional competence, 488–489
intelligence failures, 546
interaction biases, 66
interaction order, 84–85
interaction process, 80
interactional competence, 95, 488–489
intercorporate networking, 298
interest groups, 576–577
interlocking organizations, 547
internalization, 48
international agencies, 531
international capitalism, 332–335
International Criminal Tribunal, 379
international development. See economic development
international division of labour, 336
International Monetary Fund, 21, 24, 282, 359
international "war on drugs," 207
Internet
    accessing the Internet, 582
    advertising, 570
    avatars, 564
    bloggers, 564–565, 566, 569, 577
    blogs, 570, 583
    and China, 566
    citizen-journalism, 564–565
    closing the loopholes, 573–574
    co-operative independent media sites, 565
    code as law, 573–574
    control of creative work, 573–574
    and corporate mass media, 569–570
    Creative Commons, 577

men and boys (*continued*)
    military masculinity, manufacture of, 388–389
    roots of male power, 443–444
    suicide, 174
    using the Internet, 583
    and women's movement, 130
Menashy, F., 293
Meng, L., 186
Mennonites, 251
men's liberation, 130–556
mercantilism, 331
mergers, 562, 567, 568–569
merit, 487–488
meritocracy
    doing hierarchy, 464
    stratification as, 454–457
meritocracy thesis, 457
Merkel, U.D.O., 15
Merton, R.K., 15, 85, 195, 195*t*, 424–425, 541
Merton's typology of modes of adaptation, 195, 195*t*
Messner, M., 111
Mestemacher, R., 226
metaphysical stage, 167
Methodism, 246–247
methodologies
    see also research
    census data, 66–67
    conversation analysis, 68–69
    documentary analysis, 68
    ecological fallacy, 175
    experiments, 58–61
    institutional ethnography, 69–72
    interviews, 64–65
    official records, 66–67
    participant observation, 65–66
    qualitative methods, 58, 70–71
    quantitative methods, 58
    research techniques working together, 69–70
    statistical analysis, 67
    survey research, 61–63
    textual analysis, 68
    and theoretical perspectives, 58
    unobtrusive measures, 66–69
    Weber's contribution, 403–406
metropolis, 335
Michalowski, H., 357
Michels, R., 543, 544
Michelson, W., 138, 159
micropayments, 570
microsociology
    critical role of, 82
    defined, 76
    described, 76–78
    dramaturgical model, 81–85
    ethnomethodology, 85–101
    labelling theory, 80–81
    macro-micro debate, 102

    microtranslation strategy, 76
    radical microsociology, 76
    social structures and, 76
    symbolic interactionism, 78–80
Microsoft, 569
microstructural bias, 438
microtranslation strategy, 76
middle classes, affluent, 304
Middle East
    and politics of oil, 370–371
    US-led invasion of Iraq, 371
    wars in, 361–362
Middleton, N., 178, 179
Midnight Sun, 120
midwifery, 447
Midwifery Act, 447
migrant farm labour, 316
migrant farm workers, 24
migrant workers, 511–512
Miles, A., 442
militarism
    among women, manufacturing, 393–394
    Cold War militarism, 359–360
    culture of militarism, 360, 365–366
    as system of values, 365
military-industrial complex, 357–358, 372–373
military institutions, 356–357
military masculinity, manufacture of, 388–389
Millar, M.S., 582, 585, 586, 588
millennialism, 242
Miller, L., 391
Miller, W.B., 196
Mills, C. Wright, 1–5, 406, 408, 409, 410, 412
Miner, H., 140, 148
minimal responses, 94
The Mirror, 579
Mirvish, Ed, 306
misogyny, 257, 583
"the missing what," 97
Mitchell, J., 45
mobile phones, eavesdropping on, 567
mobility, 453
mode of production, 23, 269, 271
modernity, retreat from, 364
modernization, 423–424
modernization as evolution, 329–331
Moghissi, H., 257, 259, 261, 263, 264
Mogyorody, V., 321
monetary tools, 281, 283
monogamy, 432
monolithic bias, 434–437
monopoly, 294
Monture-Angus, P., 204, 205, 211, 220, 222, 532
Moon, R., 214
Moore, D., 144
Moore, R., 486, 511
Moore, W.E., 454

moral conservative movement, 128
moral individualism, 171
moral order, and law, 194–195
morality
    altruism, 170
    Durkheim's theory of, 169–172
    and law, 170–172
    laws, 193
    mechanical solidarity, 170, 171
    moral order, and law, 194–195
    organic solidarity, 170, 171
    origins and nature of, 169–170
    postmodern feminism and audience studies, 592
    regulation system, 170
    scientific study of morality, 170
    social facts, 170
    solidarity, 170
    Victorian morality, 193
Morgan, E., 107–108
Morgan, K., 459
Morley, D., 580, 591–592
Morris, A., 198
Morris, R., 206
Morrow, F., 565
Mosca, G., 544
Moser, J., 214
Mother Jones, 572
motivation
    critique of, 456–457
    extrinsic reward, 456
    unequal distribution of, 455
motive talk, 32
Ms magazine, 585
msnbc.com, 569
MuchMusic, 569
Mueller, A., 4, 340–341
Muise, G.M., 144, 160, 161
Mulinari, D., 388
Muller, J., 482
multicultural societies
    cultural integration in, 20–21
    language, 20–21
    official policy, 21
multiculturalism
    within bilingual framework, 507
    challenges to, 508–509
    education, 508
    ethnic communities, 519, 520
    ethnic leaders, promotion of, 518–519
    ethnics, creation of, 518–520
    as integration without assimilation, 507–509
    labour force in twenty-first century, 513–514
    limits to, 509–510
    model of, 504
    multicultural policies, 508
    as policy, 518–520
    principles of, 507–508
    race and ethnic relations, 503

shift to, 507
and war on terror, 509–510
Multiculturalism Act, 507–518
multinational business corporations,
 25–26, 35–37, 549, 567
multivariate analysis, 62
Murdoch, Robert, 567, 568, 570
Murdoch decision, 439–440
Murdock, G.P., 433, 434
Murphy, T., 313
Muslim communities
 see also Islam
 Bosnian Muslims, 244
 in Canada, 510
 Hindu/Muslim conflicts, and the
  media, 255
 immigrant religious communities, 256
 purdah, 442
 sense of identity, 520
 women, and traditional Islamic
  clothing, 531
 women and rape, 263
mutual assured destruction (MAD), 360
Muzychka, M., 65
Myborgh, S., 582
MySpace, 31, 564, 568
MySpace Records, 568
myth of equality, 11
myth of Quebec motherhood,
 141–142, 141f

N

Naffine, N., 204
Nakano Glenn, E., 38, 40
Napoleonic Wars, 169
narrowly specialized expertise, 552
Nason-Clark, N., 263
Nathan, R., 65
Nation, 572
National Action Committee on the Status
 of Women, 449
National Arts Centre, 560
national cultures
 functionalist perspective, 20
 future of, 21
 and globalization, 21–22
National Film Board, 155, 560, 561,
 562, 585
National Policy, 342
National Post, 569
nationalism, 243, 578
nations, as subsystem units, 21
Native peoples. *See* Aboriginal peoples;
 First Nations communities
natural attitude, 34
natural laws, 168
natural will, 136
the Nayar of South India, 434–435,
 443, 444
Nazi bureaucratization, 543, 546
Nazi ideology, 5

Nazi memorabilia, sale of, 566
NBC, 569
Neal, M., 176
near-global-war, 359–360
need dispositions, 418
need for approval, 17
Neeman, R., 240
negotiated consensus, 80
Negri, A., 25, 29, 356, 363, 510, 512
Negroponte, N., 561
Neilson, L.C., 221
Neitz, M.J., 260
Nelson, A., 357
Nelson, J.J., 155, 156, 204–519
neo-conservative argument, 21–22
neo-imperialism, 332
neo-liberalism, 21–22, 283, 285, 293–294,
 300–301, 306, 312, 571, 572, 578
 see also capitalism; corporate capitalism
  in Canada; liberal-bourgeois theory
Nerdgrrl, 582
Nesbitt, P.D., 259, 260
Nesbitt-Larking, P., 20, 27, 560, 561, 562,
 571, 574, 575, 578, 580, 581
netizen, 565
Neuringer, C., 184
new reproductive technologies, 447–448,
 556
New Right, 128, 448
New York Times, 570
Newby, H., 402, 405
news. *See* mass communication; media
news, and the Internet, 564–565
News Corporation, 568
News of the World, 568
news production, 574–575
newspapers
 Canadian newspapers, 562–563
 corporate media political culture,
  571–572
 Internet and journalism, 570
 underreporting or censorship, 572
Newsweek, 588
Neyer, J., 239
Ng, R., 69–515, 518, 521
Nicholson, J., 7
Niebrugge-Brantley, J., 42
Nikolic-Ristanovic, V., 389, 393
Nip, J.Y.M., 150
Nitsch, J., 383
Noble, J., 487, 488, 489, 491
nobles, 270
Noivo, E., 515
Nolen, S., 241
nomothetic, 403
nonpersonal treatment, 84
Norberg-Hodge, H., 304, 313, 315, 317,
 320, 321
Nordstrom, C., 390
normalization, 547
normalized, 547

normative consensus, 432
normative paradigm, 76
normative whiteness, 522
norms
 collaborative sites, 577
 first-come, first-served, 85
 invisible norm, 522
 male and female behaviour, 113
 need dispositions, 418
 situational proprieties, 83
 and social constructionist perspectives, 29
North, Oliver, 99–100
North American Free Trade Agreement,
 21, 299–300, 301, 343, 344–345,
 481, 563
Norway, 153
Novek, J., 318, 319
Novogrodsky, M., 117
nuclear families, 432
Nuernberger, K., 69
nursing, 463–464
nurturing, function of, 15

O

Oakley, A., 64
Obama, Barack, 247, 284, 527, 576
Oberschall, A., 377
objectivity, 6, 405–406
objects of involvement, 83
O'Brien, M., 46, 129, 443, 447
occasion, 82–83
Occupational Health and Safety
 Act, 209
Odeon, 568
Oedipus complex, 45
the official, 410
official records, 66–67
Ohlin, L.E., 196
OhMyNews, 565
oil, politics of
 and Middle East markets, 370–371
 post Cold-War wars, 369
Oka crisis, 572
Okazawa-Rey, M., 389
Oklahoma City bombing, 564
old boys' network, 549–550
oligarchy, 543–544
oligopoly, 317
Oliver, C., 300
Olwig, K.F., 152
Omnicom, 570
one-dimensional thought, 413
O'Neill, P., 70
online communities, 563
OnStar, 567
Ontario School Act, 481
Opie, A., 69
opinion, 36
oppressive social relations, 483
Orbach, S., 122
Orenstein, M., 403, 404

organic farming, 320–321
organic solidarity, 170, 171
organization charts, 551
organization language, 552–553
organization theory, 413
organized crime, 206
organized labour. *See* unions
Osprey media group, 569
others, 16
Otsu, A., 178
Ottawa Sun, 569
Our Common Future, 348
Outsiders (Becker), 80
outsourcing the knowledge economy,
    304–305
overlaps, 94
overproduction, crises of, 278, 285–286, 292

P

Pachner, J., 9
paparazzi, 576
Paper, J., 250, 251
Pappert, A., 556
paradigms, 40
paradox of wealth and poverty, 25–26
Parenti, M., 572
Park, R.E., 137
Parkhill, T., 250
Parnaby, P., 196
Parsons, Talcott, 77, 78, 329, 339,
    416, 418, 419, 420, 423, 433,
    474, 540, 554
    see also functionalism; Parson's social
    system model
Parson's social system model
    compliance, basis of, 418
    criticisms, 425–427
    cybernetic hierarchy, 419–420
    GAIL model, 420, 423
    general action systems, 419–424
    generally, 417–418
    modernization, 423–424
    need dispositions, 418
    pattern variables, 421–423, 422f
    role theory, 419
    roles and the social system, 418–419
    system prerequisites, 420–421
    values, institutionalized, 418
    voluntaristic theory, 418
part-time jobs, 309
Parti Québécois, 505–506
participant observation
    described, 65–66
    ethical issues, 66
    informed consent, 66
    replication, lack of potential for, 66
    systematic controls, lack of, 66
particularistic standards, 422
party, 409
patriarch, 423
    media coverage of women's issues, 587

patriarchal capitalism, 310, 313
patriarchal profamilism, 261, 263
patriarchy
    abortion debate, 448–449
    custody, 446–447
    and economic development, 339–340
    in ethnic folk communities, 160–161
    European colonial rule, 527–528
    inevitability argument, 108
    invisibility of relations of patriarchy, 41
    Marxist theory, 439
    patriarchal Aboriginal status, 528
    patriarchal profamilism, 261, 263
    patriarchy thesis, 126
    and postfeminist liberalism, 44
    relations of patriarchy, 39, 40–41
    religion and, 256, 257
    underdevelopment of women, 339–340
    and world religions, 257
patrimony, 549
PATRIOT Act, 386
pattern maintenance, 420
pattern variables, 421–423, 422f
Payne, G.C.F., 492
peace
    feminist perspective, 396
    functionalism, 366
    political economy analysis, 374
    social constructionist perspective,
        386–387
    women in peace movements, 395–396
Peace, K.A., 196
peace dividend, 363
peace movements, 395–396
peasants, 201, 270
Pecora, V.P., 72, 212, 215
Pence, 222
Pentland, H.C., 272, 273, 513
People, 568
perception
    barriers to, 91
    reality disjuncture, 91
    reflexive nature of, 89, 89f
perestroika, 362
performances, 81–82
Perkins, T.E., 586
personal choice, 12
personal troubles, 4–5
personality system, 420
personnel management, 540
perspective by incongruity, 81
perspectives in sociology. *See* sociological
    perspectives
Peterson, V.S., 388
phallus, as symbol of power, 45
pharmaceutical drugs, 207–208
Philadelphia, 544–584
Philadelphia Bar Association, 544
Philadelphia Inquirer, 570
philanthropy, 337–339
Phillips, M., 147

photojournalists, 575
physical infrastructure of place, 150–151
physician/patient. *See* professional/client
    interaction
Pickering, W.S.F., 175
Pickton, Robert William, 588
Piddington, R., 147
Pinto, L., 301
Plant, S., 581, 582
plausible deniability, 99–101
polarization of classes, 278, 284, 292
policing
    child sexual abuse, 224–225
    community policing programs, 199, 215
    domestic violence, 221–222
    families, 213–214
    gendered policing of gender-neutral
        laws, 226
    generally, 198–200
    sex trade, 225–227
    sexual assault, 222–224
    social constructionist perspective,
        215–216
policy options, 299–300
policy-planning groups, 298
The Polish Peasant in Europe and America
    (Thomas and Znaniecki), 68
political economy theory
    see also Marxist perspective
    Aboriginal peoples, education for,
        484–485, 485t, 485f
    advanced capitalism, restructuring,
        336–337
    anomie, 144
    "authentic" religious identities,
        negotiation of, 251
    bureaucracy, 542–545
    bureaucracy and communism, 544–545
    bureaucracy and oligarchy, 543–544
    Calvinism, 245–246
    in Canada. *See* corporate capitalism in
        Canada
    Canada's labour force in twenty-first
        century, 513–514
    capitalism. *See* capitalism
    capitalist class, distinctive religion of,
        245–246
    central argument, 113
    civil war in Iraq, 373
    class, 23
    class conflict, and religion, 247–249
    class influence on gender relations,
        116–117
    class situation, influence of gender on,
        114–116
    class struggles, 23
    Cold War, 368
    colonialism, 510–511
    colonization, legalization of, 201–202
    colonization of the inner city, 202–204
    vs. conflict theory, 22

privacy laws, 567
private realm, 439
privatization, 300, 442, 571
privilege, preservation of, 515–516
pro-life, 448–449
probabilities, 404
problem solving, 461
procreation, 435
production
    crisis of overproduction, 49
    feudal mode of production, 23
    function of, 15
    mass production, 23, 336
    mode of production, 23, 269, 271
    relations of production, 41
    workers' responsibility for, 541
profane, *vs.* sacred, 238
professional/client interaction, 77–78,
    95, 422
profit, wars for, 372–373
Progressive, 572
progressive education movement, 479–480
*Project on Environmental Change and Acute
    Conflict*, 349
The Promise Keepers, 261
propaganda, and the elite, 544
propaganda during war
    and anti-war movement, 382, 383–385
    "black propaganda," 378
    for external support, 377–378
    and leadership, 375–376
    media acquiescence, 384–385
    as performance, 381
    power of propaganda, 383–385
    selling war, 383–384
propertied class, 201–202
property laws and class struggle, 205
prophecies, failure of, 254
prostitution, 130, 225–227, 389
protectionism, 344
protectionist measures, 343
Protestant ethic, 246
*The Protestant Ethic and the Spirit of
    Capitalism* (Weber), 409
Protestantism
    see also religion
    Calvinism, 245–246
    Christian Right, 249
    colonial rulers, 248
    conflict, 243
    domestic violence, 263
    fundamentalism, 240, 242, 261
    see also fundamentalism
    millennialism, 242
    The Promise Keepers, 261
    Protestant ethic, 246
    Unitarian Universalism, 241
    women, ordination of, 257–258
Pryor, E.T., 66
Psathas, G., 32
pseudo-argument, 523

psychoanalysis, 45, 108–109, 428
psychological reductionism, 405
Ptacek, J., 446
public administration, 423–424
public housing projects, 148–149
public issues, 4–5
public opinion
    construction of, 524–525
    manipulation of, 526–527
    and mass media, 525–526
    pollsters, 63
public realm, 439
public relations, 32
public sector management, 303–304
Pugh, T., 317
punishment, 198–199, 210
purdah, 442
puritanism, 245, 246–247
purposive-rational orientation,
    406–407, 545

Q

Qadeer, M.A., 143
qualitative methods, 58, 70–71
Qualman, D., 315
quantitative methods, 58
Quebec
    distinct society, 14
    family ties and urban residence, 147
    fertility data, re-evaluation of,
        141–142, 141f
    folk society, 140
    institutional separation, 505–506
    midwifery, 447
    multiculturalism, shift to, 507
    myth of Quebec motherhood,
        141–142, 141f
    Parti Québécois, 505–506
    Quiet Revolution, and suicide rates, 177
    referendum, 14, 562
    settlement pattern, 141
Quebecor, 563, 569, 571
queer theory, 44
questionnaires, 61–62, 580
    see also survey research
queues, 86
quietism, 244
Quinney, R., 201

R

Rabinow, P., 551, 556
race, 502, 510–511
race and ethnic relations
    academic writing, 525
    affirmative action, 522–524
    assimilation, 503, 504, 506–507
    attitudes of white workers, 515–516
    Canada's labour force in twenty-first
        century, 513–514
    colonialism, 510–511
    defining the "other," 516–518

domination, 503, 504
ethnicization as social accomplishment,
    516–520
feminist perspectives, 527–534
functionalism, 502–510
gendered ethnic politics in Canada,
    530–531
identity formation, 516–517
ideological hegemony, 515–516
institutional ethnography, 521–527
invisible norm, 522
multiculturalism, 503, 504, 507–510,
    518–520
patriarchal Aboriginal status, 528
patriarchy in European colonial rule,
    527–528
political economy perspective, 510–516
political organization, implications for,
    503–509
post-colonial, 511–512
post-colonial gendered ethnicity,
    529–530
preservation of privilege, 515–516
pseudo-argument, 523
public opinion, and mass media,
    525–526
public opinion, constructing, 524–525
public opinion, manipulation of,
    526–527
racialization as social accomplishment,
    516–520
racialized class formation in white set-
    tler society, 512–513
racialized inequality, 514
racialized women and violence, 531–532
racist capitalism, 510–516
reverse racism, 522–524
separation, 503, 505–506
sexual liberation, 533–534
social constructionist perspective,
    516–520
vertical mosaic, 521–527
Western feminist movements, 532–533
whiteness, accomplishing, 522
racial communities, 519, 520
racialization, 516–520
racialized class formation in white settler
    society, 512–513
racialized inequality, 514
racism, 503, 507, 510–511, 578, 580
racist capitalism, 510–516
racketeering, 544
Radbord, J.L., 221
radical, 569
radical feminism
    abortion, 448–449
    custody battles, 446–447
    described, 43, 51, 129–130, 442
    domestic violence, 445–446
    family, 442–450
    limitations, 449–450

limits to economic freedom for women, 444–445

vs. Marxist perspective, 442–443

and men's liberation, 556

reproduction, medical and legal control over, 447–448

roots of male power, 443–444

radical individualism, 241–242

radical leaders, 408

radical microsociology, 76

Radler, David, 208

Rafiq, F., 443

Rajagopal, A., 526

Ramp, W., 150, 210

Rance, S., 207

random sample, 61

Rankin, J., 51

Ransom, D., 206, 207

rape

see also sexual assault

as discursive practice, 391–393

in marriage, 129

and Muslim communities, 263

as organized military practice, 389–393

seduction scenario, 223

trials, 223

Rapping, E., 590

Rapport, N., 142

Rather, Dan, 565

rational-legal authority, 408

rational war, 363

rationality

culture of rationality, 409–410

as emotional wasteland, 556

feminist challenge, 412–413

formal rationality, 411

organization theory, 413

substantive rationality, 411

rationalization, 348

Ratner, R.S., 299

Razack, S., 588

Razack, S.H., 160, 202, 219, 227, 528, 533

Reagan, Ronald, 99–100

"real" factors, 7

REAL Women, 448

reality-defining contests, 36

reality disjuncture, 91

Reardon, B.A., 390

reasoned procedure, 7

rebels, 195, 196

recession, 26, 311–511

recipe knowledge, 34

reconstituted families, 67, 435

Recording Industry Association of America, 573

Redfield, R., 137, 139, 140, 142, 148

reductionism, 486

reflexive process, 89, 89f

regional inequality, 336

regions, 82

regulated markets, 281–282

regulation, 170, 173, 560

regulation of Internet, 565–567

regulation system, 168

reified identity, 404

reifying society, 78, 85

Reiman, J., 200, 201, 206, 214

Reimer, M., 4

Reimer, M.A., 463, 550

Reiss, I., 435

Reitz, J.G., 509

Rejali, D.M., 392

relations of patriarchy, 39, 40–41

relations of production, 41, 269

relations of reproduction, 38, 50, 128

relations of ruling, 35, 50, 70, 211, 218

relative scarcity of personnel, 456

religion

see also specific religions

Aboriginal spirituality. *See* Aboriginal spirituality

"authentic" religious identities, negotiation of, 251

Calvinism, 245–246

capitalist class, distinctive religion of, 245–246

central doctrines, 238

Christian Right in the U.S., 249

and class conflict, 247–249

colonial rulers, interests of, 247–248

community memory, 239

and conflict, 243–244, 247–249

cults, 243, 254

culture, and religious beliefs, 239

depoliticized feminism, 263–264

domestic violence against women, 263–264

Durkheim's fundamental definition, 238

establishment churches and the radical fringe, 247–249

ethnic diversity, challenge of, 240–243

feminist perspectives, 256–264

feminization of religious institutions, 259–261

functionalist theory, 239–244

fundamentalism. *See* fundamentalism

as gendered politics, 256–264

gendered religious nationalism, 530

Hamitic hypothesis, 248

hearing women's voices, 261–262

immigrant religious communities, 256

institutionalized misogyny, 257

liberation theology, 247–249

mass media and transnational religious politics, 255–256

Methodism, 246–247

minority religious communities, 243–244

patriarchal profamilism, 261, 263

and patriarchy, 256, 257

political economy perspective, 244–249

politicizing religious beliefs, 254–255

as practical accomplishment, 250–251

predestination, 245

prophecies, failure of, 254

Protestant ethic, 246

puritanism, 245, 246–247

radical individualism, 241–242

religious convictions, 171

religious diversity, challenge of, 240–243

religious identities, sustaining, 252–253

religious individualism, 241–242

religious revivalism, 242–243

religious television programs, 255–256

sacred meanings, negotiation of, 251–252

sacred *vs.* profane, 238

secularization thesis, 239–241

social cohesion, 243

social constructionist perspective, 249–256

Social Gospel movement, 247

spiritual healing, 253–254

storytelling as ideological work, 254

symbolic healing, 253–254

symbolic meanings, 251–252

symbolic repair work, 254

vision of God as male, 257

Weber's contribution, 245–249

women as clergy, 259

women in contemporary religious institutions, 257–259

religious fundamentalism. *See* fundamentalism

religious individualism, 241–242

religious revivalism, 242–243

renewable fuels, 317

replication, 59

Report on Business Television, 569

representation, 45–46

repression, 547

repressive law, 170

repressive religious law, 171, 172

reproduction

general understanding of, 45

medical and legal control over, 447–448

new reproductive technologies, 447–448

relations of, 38, 50

relations of reproduction, 128

reproductive technologies, 447–448

research

see also methodologies

breaching experiments, 34

ethnocentrism and, 7

functionalism, 48

general principles, 7

in institutional ethnography, 35

interaction biases, 66

systematic and public accumulation of experience and observations, 7

systematic doubt, 7

reserve army of labour, 278

residence patterns, 436

residential schools, 154, 205, 484
resistance, 125, 497, 546–547
restitutive law, 171, 201
restorative justice, 206
restorative justice programs, 199
retreatists, 195, 196
retrospective interpretation, 90
Reuter, P., 206
Reuters, 575
revenge, politics of, 377
reverse racism, 522–524
Rex, J., 511
Reynolds, T., 520
Rheingold, H., 110
Rhode, D.L., 581, 587
Rich, Frank, 570
Richardson, C.J., 219, 457
Richer, S., 493, 495
Richmond, A.H., 62, 89, 504, 512
Richmond-Abbott, 583
Riecken, T., 198, 221
right of national treatment, 348, 482
Rioux, M., 140
Rist, R.C., 490
Ritter, S., 357
ritual practices, 17
ritualists, 195
Roberti, J., 226
Roberts, R., 179
Rocher, F., 344
Rogers, 563
Rogers, B., 340
Rogers, E.M., 330
Rohner, R.P., 484, 485
role
    concept of role, 15–16
    differences in demands, 454
    of family, 423
    in formal organizations, 16
    and functionalism, 15–16, 48, 76–77
    gender roles, 106
    institutionalization, 418
    in institutions, 48
    internalization, 48
    over lifetime, 418
    performance, 19
    sex roles, 106
    and social system, 418–419
    specialization of roles, 454
    work roles, 77
role conflict, 16
role distance, 85
role expectations, 16, 17, 48
role models, 16, 585
role occupants, 546
role segregation, 419
role set, 16
role sets, 419
role strain, 16, 419
role theory, 16–419, 423
romantic fiction, 590

Roof, W.C., 241
Roots, R.I., 200
Roscoe, W., 120
Rosenhan, D.L., 90
Rosnes, M., 221
Ross, K., 526, 592
Rossow, I., 177
Rothenberg, P.S., 43
Rothman, L., 306, 308
routinization, 546
Rowley, Coleen, 576
Rowley, S.W., 129, 222, 224
Royal, C., 583
Royal Commission on Bilingualism and
    Biculturalism, 505
Rubenstein, H., 306
Rubin, L., 515
Rubin, N., 240
Ruddick, S., 389, 390
Ruether, R.R., 256
rule by the masses, 544
ruling apparatus, 310
rural communities
    see also community
    The Chicago School, 137–139
    contemporary, 142–143
    folk society model, 139–142
    rural life as gendered accomplishment,
        158–159
    suicide, 177–178
rural-urban debate. See loss of
    community thesis
Russell, P.A., 200, 215
Russell, S., 495
Russo, A., 588
Rutherford, P., 374, 381, 382, 383, 384
Rwanda, 247–248, 363, 366, 368, 511
Rygiel, K., 382, 394
Ryten, E., 456

S

Sacco, V., 196, 212
Sacks, H., 94, 96
Sacouman, R.J., 144
sacred
    meaning of sacred realm, 238
    vs. profane, 238
    sacred meanings, negotiation of,
        251–252
Sadker, D., 493
Sadker, M., 493
Safe Streets Act, 216
Said, E., 31
Sakinofsky, I., 177, 179
same-sex conversations, 94
Sampath, 182
sample, 61–62
Sandberg, K., 220
Sandler, B.R., 496
Saner, H., 206
Santer, M., 345

Saussure, F. de, 18
Sayer, A., 335, 336, 344, 459, 460
Sayer, D., 271, 274, 344
scale formation, 121
scales, 63
Schegloff, E., 94, 95
Schellenberg, G., 309
Scheper-Hughes, N., 393
Schissel, B., 67, 211, 213, 214
Schissel, W., 197, 222
Schlesinger, P., 576
Schneider, F.W., 495
"The School Class as a Social System"
    (Parsons), 474
Schooling in Capitalist America (Bowles and
    Gintis), 478
schools and schooling
    see also education
    bullying, and suicide, 177
    and class inequality, 479
    computers, and class differences, 482
    contemporary capitalism, 481–483
    crime prevention, 199
    democratic political system vs.
        totalitarian economic system, 478
    function of, 14–15, 474–475
    funding cutbacks, 482–483
    headstart programs, 486
    home-school relation, maintenance of,
        490–491
    marginalization, and suicide, 177
    oppressive social relations, 483
    and poverty, 485–486
    residential schools, 154, 205, 484
    secondary socialization, 110
    shift to, as site of education, 15
    socioeconomic status, 490–491
Schutt, R.K., 59, 60
Schutz, A., 34, 87, 98
science
    see also social science
    defined, 6
    discourse of, 579
    empiricism, 167
    impartiality, 6
    and judgment, 406
    objectivity, 6, 8, 405–406
    and personal choice, 12
    and social facts, 170
"Science as a Vocation" (Weber), 406
scientific management, 459
scientific objectivity, 6–8
scientism, 487
Scott, C.V., 394
Scott, E.K., 522, 534
Scott, K., 58
Scott, V., 130, 131
search engines, 566
Searl, N., 253
Second Life, 563
second shift, 312

second wave of feminism, 555
Second World War, 3, 367
secondary deviance, 200
secondary socialization, 110
secret deviants, 81
secularization thesis, 239–241
Seidman, S., 44
self, 31
Self, 590
self-concept, 476–477
self-defence, 222
self-employment, 308
self-fulfilling prophesies, 31
self selection, 59
self *vs.* collectivity, 422
semiotics, 578
semiproletarianization, 144
Sen, G., 339, 340
sensationalism, 576
sense-making practices, 35–37
separation
    First Nations, 505
    Quebec, 505–506
    race and ethnic relations, 503
September 11, 2001 terrorist attack,
        355, 564
    see also terrorism
Serbia. *See* Yugoslavia
serfs, 270
service, commercialization of, 348
settler cities, 153–154
Seul, J.R., 239, 244
sex
    berdache, 120
    classification by sex, 119
    defined, 106
    enforcing two sexes, 120–121
    as social construction, 119–120
    three or more sexes, 120
    use of term, 119
sex dichotomy, 106
sex drive, 433
sex roles, 106
sex trade, 130, 225–227, 533
sex trafficking, 533
sexism, 11, 580, 583
sexist bias, 438
sexual abuse, 177, 224–225
sexual assault
    see also rape
    allegations, 217
    doctrine of recent complaint, 224
    media coverage, 588
    past sexual history of complainant, 224
    policing, 222–224
sexual diversity, 44
sexual double standards, 225–226
sexual harassment, 118, 580
sexual liberation, 533–534
sexual orientation, 118
    see also gay men; homosexual; lesbians

sexual politics, 106
sexual relations, 436
sexuality
    as biological fact of life, 123
    exploitative sexuality, struggle against,
        129–130
    masturbation by children, 124
    within medical discourse, 124
    as social construction, 123–125
Shaffir, W., 149
Shah, A., 384
shaming, 566
Shanks, G., 370
shared parenting, 446–447
shared symbols, 78–79
shareholder capital, 295–297
shareholder capitalism, 293
Sharma, N., 316, 386
Sharrock, W.W., 13
Shaver, F.M., 225, 226, 533
Shaw Communications, 569
Sherman, L.W., 59, 61
Shils, E., 502
Shock Doctrine (Klein), 385
Shortall, S., 322, 323
Shulman, N., 146, 157
Shupe, A., 445
side involvement, 83
Siegel, L.J., 206, 207, 209, 213
Siemiatycki, M., 157, 158
sign activity, 81
signified, 18
signifier, 18
Silver, J., 149
Silverman, D., 64
Simich, L., 157
Simmel, G., 137, 403–404
Simmons, A., 507
Sinclair, C.M., 178
Singer, P., 249, 364
Singh, S., 526
Singleton, A., 254
situation, 82
situational improprieties, 83
situational proprieties, 83
Sivanandan, A., 516
Sivard, R.L., 339
skid row, 148
skilled labour time, 275
skilled labour under capitalism, 459–460
Sklair, L., 28
Skogstad, G., 347
slavery, ancient, 270
slumps, 49, 279, 280, 281, 282–287, 292
small groups laboratories, 60
small-town life. *See* loss of community thesis
Smart, B., 545, 551
Smart, C., 126, 129, 131, 211, 216, 218,
        219, 221, 223, 225, 228, 527
Smith, Adam, 277, 387
Smith, D., 194, 482

Smith, D.E., 5, 39, 40, 41, 42, 46, 67, 68,
        70, 72, 91, 122, 123, 181, 184, 216,
        274, 307, 310, 387, 439, 440, 442,
        497, 551, 552, 553, 555, 556, 578
Smith, G., 58, 65, 122
Smith, G.W., 44
Smith, L.T., 71
Snider, L., 209
social action, 403, 419–424
social changes, 3–4
social class. *See* class and class relations
social cohesion, 193–194, 243
social construction of bureaucracy,
        551–553
social construction of gender, 91–93
social construction of knowledge, 553
social construction of mass media,
        574–580
social construction of reality, 90, 487
social constructionist perspective
    Aboriginal suicide rates, 182–183
    academic ability, 487–488
    American public-opinion machine,
        381–382
    anti-war movement, stifling, 382,
        383–385
    class relations in the home, 440–442
    community boundaries as social
        relations, 152
    community of practice, 461–462
    corporate capitalism, 297–299
    criminal justice system, 210–217
    criminology as ideology, 211
    cultural communities beyond spatial
        location, 152–153
    cultural meanings and identities, 37
    culture and identity as social
        constructions, 37–38
    defining the "other," 516–518
    described, 29–30
    economic development, 340–342
    education, 487–492
    enforcing two sexes, 120–121
    ethnic separatism, 376
    ethnicization as social accomplishment,
        516–520
    ethnomethodology, 32–35, 50, 85–101
    faulty-parenting thesis, 211
    fear, politics of, 377
    fear of crime, 211–213
    femininity, accomplishing, 122–123
    focus of, 49–50
    global media management, and war,
        378–379
    home-school relation, maintenance of,
        490–491
    identity formation, 516–517
    immigrant religious communities, 256
    institutional ethnography, 35–37, 50
    institutionalization of fear and
        insecurity, 386

Sudbury, J., 520
Sudnow, D., 97, 98
suicide
    see also suicide rates
    and alienation, in Aboriginal
        communities, 179–180
    altruistic suicide, 173, 174–175
    anomic suicide, 173, 174
    attempts, 184–185
    in China, 186
    covering up suicide, 181
    Durkheim's study, 173–176
    egoistic suicide, 173
    fatalistic suicide, 173, 174–175
    feminist perspective, 184–187
    functionalist perspectives, 177–179
    as gendered practice, 184–187
    the Inuit, 183–184
    label, implications of, 181
    methodological challenges to
        Durkheim's study, 175
    Muslim women in South Asian enclave
        communities, 531
    political economy perspective,
        179–180
    rural and urban differences, 177–178
    social order, and suicide rates, 173–175
    theoretical challenges to Durkheim's
        analysis, 176
Suicide (Durkheim), 176
suicide rates
    see also suicide
    Aboriginal communities. *See* Aboriginal
        suicide rates
    and capitalism, 179
    cross-cultural comparisons, 186
    provincial variations, 179
    as social constructions, 180–184
    as social facts, 173
    and social order, 173–175
    Statistics Canada, 176–177
The Sun, 568, 579, 586
Sun Media Corp, 569
Sunahara, A., 507, 526
Sunday Times, 568
superego, 428
superstructure, 22, 269
supra-national institutions, 358–359
surplus value, 276
surrogate mother, 447
survey research
    biased assumptions, built-in, 63
    context-dependent answers, 63
    distortions, 63
    enumeration, 62
    vs. experiments, 62
    false answer categories, 63
    invalid combinations, 63
    limitations of, 62–63
    multivariate analysis, 62
    quality of questions asked, 63

questionnaires, 61–62
random sample, 61
sample, 61–62
scales, 63
and sociology, 61
variety of techniques, 62
sustaining system, 168
Sutherland, E.H., 196
Suttles, G.D., 148
Sweden, 310, 350–351
Swenarchuk, M., 349
Swift, J., 24
Swift, K., 213
Swift, K.J., 5
Switzerland, 567
symbol, 79
The Symbolic Construction of Community
    (Cohen), 149
symbolic healing, 253–254
symbolic interactionism
    community as life-world, 150–151
    described, 30–32, 50
    facts, 30
    microsociology, 78–80
symbolic meanings, 251–252
symbolic repair work, 254
Synnott, A., 114
system, 560
systematic doubt, 7
systemic conflict and dysfunction, 19
systems theory, 58

T

tabloid papers, 579–580, 586
talk. *See* conversation analysis
talk at work, 95
talking heads, 580
Tapia, A.H., 254
Taras, D., 560, 561, 562, 567,
    570–571, 576
Taylorism, 459
teachers' responses and expectations,
    493–495
technical civilization, 547
technical skills, 14
technocratic-meritocratic thesis, 460
technology
    and capitalism, 25, 272, 278, 286, 292
    and conversation, 96–97
    file-sharing technology, 29
    labour-saving technology, 278
    privacy, 82
    reproductive technologies, 447–448
    surplus value, raising, 276
"teen image," 29
teenage sexual behaviour, media
    representations of, 588
Teeple, G., 273, 513
television. *See* media
terra nullis doctrine, 202
terra populi doctrine, 202

terrorism
    see also war on terror
    and Charter principles, 194
    culture of militarism, 365–366
    and fear, 214–215
    institutionalization of fear and insecu-
        rity, 386
    Islamic societies, characterization of, 31
    September 11, 2001 terrorist attack, 355
Tester, F.J., 176, 178, 182, 183
tethered devices, 574
texts, 35, 68
textual analysis, 68, 578–580
    see also discourse analysis
Thatcher, Margaret, 199
theological stage, 167
theoretical thinking. *See* sociological
    perspectives
theorizing sexual diversity, 44
theory of exchange, 275
theory of modernization, 329–331
therapeutic intervention, 547
thesis, 271
thetyee.ca, 565
Third World
    see also economic development
    agribusiness and famine, 338–339
    assembly work, 336
    colonialism, 331–332
    control over capital, 332
    control over investment patterns, 332
    cultural lag, 329
    culture of poverty thesis, 329–330
    dependent capitalist development,
        333–335
    dependent development, practices of,
        332–334
    foreign aid, 337–339
    growing disparities within, 329
    imperialism, 331–332
    labour market relations, 333
    market relations, 332–333
    mercantilism, 331
    neo-imperialism, 332
    political force, 333
    population increases, 330
    structural disadvantages, 28
    systematic biases in data collection, 340
    underdevelopment of women, 339–340
    women, powerlessness of, 340–342
Thobani, S., 507, 524, 530
Thomas, Clarence, 580–589
Thomas, E.J., 15, 419
Thomas, W.I., 68, 80
Thompson, E.P., 201–202, 246, 270, 407
Thompson media chain, 563
Thorne, B., 39, 51
Thrasher, F.M., 196
Thurlow, C., 150, 563–564
Tiananmen Square massacre, 545
Tiger, L., 107, 433